"In this impressive systematic theology, Robert Letham sets before us the ripe fruit of a long career of devoted scholarship. He does so with clarity, confidence, and thoughtful judgment. The result is an elixir drawn from Scripture into which he has carefully stirred ingredients from Patristic orthodoxy, medieval theology, and Reformation and post-Reformation confessionalism. These are judiciously mixed by a theologian conscious that he is writing for the twenty-first century. *Systematic Theology* is Letham's personal bequest to the church of Jesus Christ. A magnum opus indeed—which students, ministers, and scholars will find to be a real stimulation to their theological taste buds!"

Sinclair B. Ferguson, Chancellor's Professor of Systematic Theology, Reformed Theological Seminary

"This is a first-class volume, impressively erudite, yet eminently readable. Scrupulously biblical, but at the same time recognizing the value of Christian tradition, it draws extensively, but judiciously, on the insights of the early church fathers, the Reformed confessions, and federal theology, while remaining in constant dialogue with the world of contemporary theological scholarship. The overall organization reflects Letham's independence of judgment, and the end product is not only a Reformed systematic theology of enduring value but also an encyclopedic reference work for both historical and systematic theology. Unsurpassed in its field."

Donald Macleod, Professor Emeritus of Systematic Theology, Edinburgh Theological Seminary

"Robert Letham has blessed us with a systematic theology that is sure to stimulate reflection, discussion, and deeper understanding of both the Holy Scriptures and the church's interpretations of them to formulate its theology over the last two millennia. One does not need to agree with every detail of Letham's magnum opus to realize that here is a treasure house of Christian wisdom on the whole counsel of God that will inform your mind and move your heart and affections to serve your Savior and Lord more single-mindedly and zealously than ever before."

Joel R. Beeke, President and Professor of Systematic Theology and Homiletics, Puritan Reformed Theological Seminary

"Robert Letham writes systematic theology as it should be written. His work is marked by a careful dialogue between the Bible and the great creedal and confessional traditions of the church, always aided and abetted by a panoply of great theologians from the past and the present. This work is marked by clarity of thought and ecumenicity of spirit. Here we have the full fruits of a lifetime of thinking theologically."

Carl R. Trueman, Professor of Biblical and Religious Studies, Grove City College

"Robert Letham's *Systematic Theology* is located within the great tradition of Christian theology, drawing upon Patristic, medieval, Reformational, and contemporary sources. Letham keeps his focus where it belongs—upon the unfathomable richness of the triune God in his being and works. He expounds difficult topics in simple, concise prose, yet without being simplistic. Where Letham occasionally offers fresh formulations of doctrinal topics, he invariably does so in a way that is respectful toward more traditional treatments. Theologians, students of theology, and church members alike will find Letham's work a wonderful gift to the church."

> **Cornelis P. Venema,** President and Professor of Doctrinal Studies, Mid-America Reformed Seminary

"A systematic theology written from a classical Reformed perspective that takes a fresh approach and aims to reach an audience not schooled in the technical terminology of the discipline—it is a tall order, but Robert Letham has triumphed with a text that is both readable and reliable. Not only pastors and students but also ordinary churchgoers will grow in their faith as they study a book with such depth and clarity of vision. A masterpiece."

> **Gerald Bray,** Research Professor of Divinity, History, and Doctrine, Beeson Divinity School

"Robert Letham has produced a substantial Reformed systematic theology which is not so much *multum in parvo* as *multum in magno*. He starts with the doctrine of God and the Holy Trinity rather than with the necessity and sufficiency of special revelation. In this sense it may be said that he stresses the catholicity of Reformed doctrine and does justice to the place of natural theology in it, reflecting his own Trinitarian expertise. Letham's style is not only clear but also fair-minded, giving space to alternative views. Letham is good at the big doctrinal pictures and sensitive to the need to drill down at particular points. He judges between central and peripheral issues. He is to be warmly congratulated on this new book."

> **Paul Helm,** Professor of Theology and Religious Studies Emeritus, King's College, London

"Robert Letham writes as no novitiate but as one who has given his life to understanding and explaining the Christian faith, addressing not only theologians and pastors but also the intelligent man and woman in the pew. I appreciate his contextualized treatment of topics, particularly his appropriation of historical figures often absent in confessionally Reformed approaches to theology. One may differ with him here or there, but I appreciate what he brings to many difficult matters, offering correctives to certain tendencies that even good Reformed thinkers might indulge. It is good to have one so thoroughly conversant with the history of the church, as well as the Bible, to write a systematic theology that resonates for our times as does this one. I heartily commend this new work to all. *Tolle lege!*"

> **Alan D. Strange,** Professor of Church History, Mid-America Reformed Seminary

"Robert Letham's *Systematic Theology* is the fruit of demanding exegetical work wrapped in a deep appreciation for all the great theology that God has provided for his people through ecumenical creeds and doctrinal standards. It is meant to be faithful to the past and grandly succeeds in that intention. While Letham clearly embeds his theology in properly understood church tradition, he is not afraid to address current theological trends. The text is exceptionally well written, easily comprehended, massively researched, and a drink of cool water for those thirsting for more of God and his Word."

Richard C. Gamble, Professor of Systematic Theology, Reformed Presbyterian Theological Seminary

"*Systematic Theology* tells the story of the gospel and brings it to bear on Christian faith and life. This fresh approach is catholic in its scope and distinctly Reformed in its teaching. It is refreshingly nonpolemic, taking the best of the entire Christian tradition with great charity and deep discernment. The fact that I do not agree with everything in the book is part of what makes studying a systematic theology like this so humbling. We are pilgrims on the path to glory, walking in communion with the triune God and longing to see Christ as he is. Letham's work persuasively and winsomely helps us along this path."

Ryan M. McGraw, Morton H. Smith Professor of Systematic Theology, Greenville Presbyterian Theological Seminary

"I enthusiastically welcome the publication of this volume by Robert Letham. Keenly informed by the richness of his own Reformed tradition, *Systematic Theology* engages the best of Christian thought—Patristic, medieval, Reformation, modern, and contemporary—on a deep and fruitful level. There is nothing parochial about this book; reading it will be a joyous education for students and pastors. It deserves a wide audience among Reformed Christians and beyond."

William B. Evans, Younts Professor of Bible and Religion, Erskine College

"Robert Letham writes with a teacher's knack for illustration, a preacher's liveliness and warmth, and a scholar's breadth—all of these in exemplary service to what certain Reformers called 'prophecy': the powerful conveyance of the Word of God that enlivens and purifies the saints' worship. Extended throughout these chapters is the doctrine of union with Christ. Letham's Protestant account of *theōsis* near the end of the volume, articulated as a perfecting of this union, not only culminates his book-long engagement with Eastern Orthodox authors and traditions but also goes a long way in addressing the need felt by many young evangelicals for thicker connection to early-church formulations and writings. Avoiding easy answers at every turn, Letham's contagious enthusiasm for the simple genius of the Christian tradition will inspire readers to live, believe, and preach Scripture more earnestly and fully."

Andrew Keuer, Professor of Theology and Ethics, Greek Bible College

Systematic

THEOLOGY

Robert Letham

WHEATON, ILLINOIS

Systematic Theology

Copyright © 2019 by Robert Letham

Published by Crossway
    1300 Crescent Street
    Wheaton, Illinois 60187

Cover design: Jordan Singer

First printing 2019

Printed in the United States of America

Hardcover ISBN: 978-1-4335-4130-8
ePub ISBN: 978-1-4335-4133-9
PDF ISBN: 978-1-4335-4131-5
Mobipocket ISBN: 978-1-4335-4132-2

Library of Congress Cataloging-in-Publication Data
Names: Letham, Robert, author.
Title: Systematic theology / Robert Letham.
Description: Wheaton: Crossway, 2019. | Includes bibliographical references and index.
Identifiers: LCCN 2018061095 (print) | LCCN 2019021796 (ebook) | ISBN 9781433541315 (pdf) | ISBN 9781433541322 (mobi) | ISBN 9781433541339 (epub) | ISBN 9781433541308 (hc)
Subjects: LCSH: Theology, Doctrinal. | Reformed Church—Doctrines.
Classification: LCC BV75.3 (ebook) | LCC BV75.3 .L48 2019 (print) | DDC 230/.42—dc23
LC record available at https://lccn.loc.gov/2018061095

Crossway is a publishing ministry of Good News Publishers.

SH   29 28 27 26 25 24 23 22 21 20 19
15 14 13 12 11 10 9 8 7 6 5 4 3 2 1

For Joan

Contents

PART 2   THE WORD OF GOD

PART 7   THE SPIRIT OF GOD AND THE PEOPLE OF GOD

Acknowledgments

In compiling this tome I am indebted to many people. Since this is the largest book I have written—and it is unlikely that I shall ever write a longer one—I would like to express my thanks to all who have helped me along the way, some of whom are no longer here to read this. Thinking back to earlier days, I reflect with gratitude on the encouragement I received from my parents, †Andrew and †Dorothy Letham, as well as †Erroll Hulse and Peter Lewis, the exegetical rigor of †Philip Edgcumbe Hughes, the clear teaching of Robert B. Strimple, the total immersion in Reformed theology of Norman Shepherd, and the gracious support of my doctoral supervisor, †James B. Torrance. A legion of scholars and theologians, though long dead and from other times and places, nevertheless still speaks with a clear and compelling voice; you may detect some of them in the index of names. As part of the one holy, catholic, apostolic church they are fellow pilgrims. Without them, I could not have written this or any other comparable book; without their insights and contributions it is hard to envisage where the church would be.

I want to thank friends and colleagues who have read various chapters and made helpful and constructive comments, including Paul Helm, Paul Wells, Keith Mathison, James Dolezal, Alan Strange, Tony Lane, Kevin Giles, Tom Holland, Ron Di Giacomo, Peter Lewis, and Todd Matocha. In particular, Jonathan Humphreys read the entire manuscript and made some invaluable comments on clarity and intelligibility. None of these can be charged with any inadequacies, which are entirely my responsibility. This is a much better book for their contributions.

I am greatly appreciative of the encouragement I have received from Justin Taylor at Crossway ever since we discussed in 2012 the possibility of writing a systematic theology. I would like to thank an anonymous reader for his or her comments, most of which I have incorporated. Thom Notaro has made invaluable editorial suggestions, and the entire team at Crossway deserves high praise.

My colleagues, past and present, at Union School of Theology have contributed to making it a pleasant place to work, teach, think, and write. In particular, Donald Mitchell, our brilliant librarian, greatly helped when I was in hot pursuit of an obscure abbreviation. A range of students there, at Westminster Theological Seminary in both Philadelphia and London, at Reformed Theological Seminary in Washington, DC, and at London School of Theology (as it now is) have posed incisive questions through the years.

Finally, but first in all other ways, I am profoundly thankful to my wife, Joan, for her love, encouragement, and continual support in over forty years, and for our children, Elizabeth, Caroline, and Adam, together with our grandchildren.

Above all, I give thanks to the Father, the Son, and the Holy Spirit, the indivisible Trinity, the living God, who in Christ has turned us from death in sin to share his life and so to become partakers of the divine nature. To him alone be glory, now and ever, and unto the ages of the ages.

Robert Letham
Easter 2018

Permissions

I wish to thank the following for permission to include sections, in edited, revised, or compressed form, drawn from content previously published (see details at the appropriate places in the text):

- Inter-Varsity Press, for material in chapters 16, 17, and 19 here, drawn from *The Message of the Person of Christ* (2013); in chapter 19, from *The Work of Christ* (1993).
- P&R Publishing, for material in chapters 2, 3, and 9, drawn from *The Holy Trinity: In Scripture, History, Theology, and Worship* (2004); in chapters 6 and 13, from *The Westminster Assembly: Reading Its Theology in Historical Context* (2009); in chapters 21 and 26, from *Union with Christ: In Scripture, History, and Theology* (2011); and in chapter 26, from *The Lord's Supper: Eternal Word in Broken Bread* (2001).
- Christian Focus Publications, for material in chapter 17, drawn from *Through Western Eyes: Eastern Orthodoxy: A Reformed Perspective* (2007); in chapter 24, from *A Christian's Pocket Guide to Baptism* (2012).
- J. Mark Beach, editor of the *Mid-America Journal of Theology*, for abbreviated material in chapter 15, drawn from my article "'Not a Covenant of Works in Disguise' (Herman Bavinck): The Place of the Mosaic Covenant in Redemptive History," *MAJT* 24 (2013): 143–77.

Scripture quotations are from the ESV® Bible (The Holy Bible, English Standard Version®), copyright © 2001 by Crossway, a publishing ministry of Good News Publishers. Used by permission. All rights reserved. All emphases in Scripture quotations have been added by me.

Departures from the ESV marked "my trans." are my own rendering, based on Nestlé-Aland, *Novum Testamentum Graece*, 28th ed. (Stuttgart:

Deutsche Bibelgesellschaft, 2012); or *Biblia Hebraica Stuttgartensia*, ed. K. Elliger and W. Rudolph (Stuttgart: Deutsche Bibelstiftung, 1967/1977); or *Septuaginta: Id est Vetus Testamentum Graece iuxta LXX interpretes*, 8th ed., ed. Alfred Rahlfs, 2 vols. (Stuttgart: Württembergische Bibelanstatt, 1935, 1965).

English translations of the Apocrypha are from *The Oxford Annotated Apocrypha: The Apocrypha of the Old Testament: Revised Standard Version*, ed. Bruce M. Metzger (New York: Oxford University Press, 1965).

Abbreviations

†	deceased
ANF	*The Ante-Nicene Fathers*, ed. A. Roberts and J. Donaldson, rev. A. C. Coxe (repr., Grand Rapids, MI: Eerdmans, 1969–1973).
AugStud	*Augustinian Studies*
BAG	Walter Bauer, William F. Arndt, and F. Wilbur Gingrich, *A Greek-English Lexicon of the New Testament and Other Early Christian Literature* (Chicago: University of Chicago Press, 1957).
BQ	*Baptist Quarterly*
BSac	*Bibliotheca Sacra*
CCC	*Catechism of the Catholic Church* (London: Geoffrey Chapman, 1994).
CCSL	Corpus Christianorum: Series Latina (Turnhout: Brepols, 1953–).
CD	Karl Barth, *Church Dogmatics*, trans. Geoffrey W. Bromiley, 14 vols. (Edinburgh: T&T Clark, 1956–1977).
CH	*Church History*
CTJ	*Calvin Theological Journal*
CTQ	*Concordia Theological Quarterly*
CO	John Calvin, *Opera quae supersunt omnia*, ed. Guilielmus Baum et al., 59 vols., Corpus Reformatorum (Brunswick, 1863–1900).
CO2	*Ioannis Calvini opera omnia* (Genève: Droz, 1992–).
CSEL	*Corpus Scriptorum ecclesiasticorum Latinorum* (Vienna, 1866–).

DJG	*Dictionary of Jesus and the Gospels*, ed. Joel B. Green (Downers Grove, IL: InterVarsity Press, 1992).
DLNT	*Dictionary of the Later New Testament and Its Development*, ed. Ralph P. Martin and Peter H. Davids (Downers Grove, IL: InterVarsity Press, 1997).
DPL	*Dictionary of Paul and His Letters*, ed. Gerald F. Hawthorne (Downers Grove, IL: InterVarsity Press, 1993).
DRev	*Downside Review*
DS	Heinrich Denzinger, *Enchiridion symbolorum definitionum et declarationum de rebus fidei et morum*, ed. Peter Hünermann, 38th ed. (Frieburg: Herder, 1998).
EECh	*Encyclopedia of the Early Church*, ed. Angelo Di Berardino, trans. Adrian Walford, 2 vols. (New York: Oxford University Press, 1992).
EQ	*Evangelical Quarterly*
GCS	*Die Griechischen Christlichen schriftsteller der ersten drei jahrhunderte* (Berlin, 1897–).
HTR	*Harvard Theological Review*
IJST	*International Journal of Systematic Theology*
Institutes	John Calvin, *Institutes of the Christian Religion*, ed. John T. McNeill, trans. Ford Lewis Battles (Philadelphia: Westminster Press, 1960).
JBL	*Journal of Biblical Literature*
JETS	*Journal of the Evangelical Theological Society*
JRT	*Journal of Reformed Theology*
JTS	*Journal of Theological Studies*
LG	*Lumen Gentium*
LN	Johannes P. Louw and Eugene A. Nida, *Greek-English Lexicon of the New Testament Based on Semantic Domains* (New York: United Bible Societies, 1988).
LS	Henry George Liddell and Robert Scott, eds., *A Greek-English Lexicon*, rev. Henry Stuart Jones, 9th ed. (Oxford: Clarendon, 1940).

LW	*Luther's Works*, ed. Jaroslav Pelikan, American edition, 55 vols. (St. Louis: Concordia; Philadelphia: Fortress, 1955–1974).
LXX	Septuagint
MAJT	*Mid-America Journal of Theology*
MTheol	*Modern Theology*
NDT	*New Dictionary of Theology*, ed. Sinclair B. Ferguson, David F. Wright, and J. I. Packer (Leicester: Inter-Varsity Press, 1988).
NEB	New English Bible
NH	*New Horizons in the Orthodox Presbyterian Church*
NIV	New International Version
NPNF[1]	*Nicene and Post-Nicene Fathers of the Christian Church*, first series, ed. Philip Schaff (repr., Grand Rapids, MI: Eerdmans, 1978–1979).
NPNF[2]	*Nicene and Post-Nicene Fathers of the Christian Church*, second series, ed. Philip Schaff (repr., Grand Rapids, MI: Eerdmans, 1979).
NTS	*New Testament Studies*
OS	*Joannis Calvini opera selecta*, ed. Peter Barth and Wilhelm Niesel, 5 vols. (Munich: Kaiser, 1926–1952).
PG	Jacques-Paul Migne et al., eds., *Patrologiae cursus completes: Series Graeca*, 162 vols. (Paris, 1857–1866).
PL	Jacques-Paul Migne et al., eds., *Patrologiae cursus completes: Series Latina*, 217 vols. (Paris, 1844–1864).
PRRD	Richard A. Muller, *Post-Reformation Reformed Dogmatics: The Rise and Development of Reformed Orthodoxy, ca. 1520 to ca. 1725*, 2nd ed., 4 vols. Grand Rapids, MI: Baker, 2003.
PrEccl	*Pro Ecclesia*
RTPM	*Recherches de Théologie et Philosophie Médiévales*
RD	Herman Bavinck, *Reformed Dogmatics*, ed. John Bolt, trans. John Vriend, 4 vols. (Grand Rapids, MI: Baker Academic, 2003–2008).

RSV	Revised Standard Version
RÉAug	*Review des Études Augustiniennes*
SBET	*Scottish Bulletin of Evangelical Theology*
SCG	Thomas Aquinas, *Summa contra Gentiles*
SCJ	*The Sixteenth Century Journal*
SJT	*Scottish Journal of Theology*
ST	Thomas Aquinas, *Summa theologia*
SwJT	*Southwestern Journal of Theology*
SVTQ	*St Vladimir's Theological Quarterly*
StPatr	*Studia Patristica*
Them	*Themelios*
TynBul	*Tyndale Bulletin*
TDNT	G. Kittel and G. Friedrich, eds., *Theological Dictionary of the New Testament*, trans. Geoffrey W. Bromiley, 10 vols. (Grand Rapids, MI: Eerdmans, 1964–1976).
UR	*Unitatis Redintegratio*
VE	*Vox Evangelica*
WCF	Westminster Confession of Faith
WLC	Westminster Larger Catechism
WSC	Westminster Shorter Catechism
WTJ	*Westminster Theological Journal*

Introduction

There is more than one way to write a systematic theology. Most begin with a lengthy section called "prolegomena," which, as one colleague remarks, few bother to read. Much of what goes into such a chapter is addressed in this introduction.

What follows is intended to be *Christian* theology. I am an ordained minister in the Reformed tradition. In this I intend to be catholic, building on the ecumenical consensus of the early centuries of the church. The Reformed have classically seen themselves as part of the one holy, catholic, and apostolic church for which Christ gave his life to redeem. I recognize the tensions that exist here.[1] I find Thomas Oden's claim to unoriginality inspiring, in his hope that nothing of his own might intrude on his representation of the great tradition of the church.[2] I cannot say I have achieved this.

This book also is written from a confessional position. I am committed to the Reformed faith as it is expressed in the Westminster Assembly's Confession of Faith and Catechisms and other kindred documents. The Westminster divines were thoroughly versed in the history and theology of the church, citing the fathers and medieval theologians freely, respecting adversaries like the Roman Catholic Bellarmine, and citing him on occasion as an authority.[3]

This raises the question of the relationship between Scripture and tradition, discussed more fully in chapter 7. Tradition, viewed as the past teaching of the church in its confessions, creeds, and representative

---

1. See Robert Letham, "Catholicity Global and Historical: Constantinople, Westminster, and the Church in the Twenty-First Century," *WTJ* 72 (2010): 43–57.
2. Thomas C. Oden, *The Word of Life*, vol. 2 of *Systematic Theology* (New York: Harper & Row, 1989), xvi.
3. Robert Letham, *The Westminster Assembly: Reading Its Theology in Historical Context* (Phillipsburg, NJ: P&R, 2009), 94–95.

theologians, effectively represents the sum total of the accumulated biblical exegesis of the Christian church. It is not on a par with Scripture— some of it may even mislead us—but we neglect it at our peril and use it to our great advantage. I make no attempt in what follows to reinvent the exegetical wheel. I engage in close biblical exegesis where it is necessary to consider a matter more thoroughly.

This is where the common misunderstanding of the post-Reformation slogan *sola Scriptura* can be confusing. When the slogan was devised, it was never intended to exclude the tradition of the church. Instead, it asserted that the Bible is the supreme authority. Adherence to the idea that the Bible is the only source to be followed was the mistake of the anti-Nicenes in the fourth century, the Socinians of the sixteenth and seventeenth centuries, the Jehovah's Witnesses in the nineteenth century, and many other sects and heretics. Effectively, it says that my understanding of the Bible is superior to the accumulated wisdom of every generation of Christians that has ever lived. Enough said.

So I agree with Oliver Crisp concerning the respective weight to be given to various authorities:

1. Scripture is the *norma normans*,[4] the *principium theologiae*. It is the final arbiter in matters theological. . . . the first-order authority in all matters of Christian doctrine.
2. Catholic creeds, as defined by an ecumenical council of the Church, constitute a first tier of *norma normata*,[5] which have second-order authority. . . . Such norms derive their authority from Scripture to which they bear witness.
3. Confessional and conciliar statements of particular ecclesiastical bodies are a second tier of *norma normata*, which have third-order in matters touching Christian doctrine. They also derive their authority from Scripture to the extent that they faithfully reflect the teaching of Scripture.
4. The particular doctrines espoused by theologians including those individuals accorded the title Doctor of the Church which are not reiterations of matters that are *de fide*, or entailed by something *de fide*, constitute *theologoumena*, or theological opinions, which

---

4. A norming, adjusting, or measuring standard by which other measuring tools are to be measured.
5. A standard or measure that is itself subject to, and defined by, a greater standard.

are not binding upon the Church, but which may be offered up for legitimate discussion within the Church.[6]

From this, I value a retrieval and restatement of the historic doctrines of the church. Experience shows that every few years new and exciting proposals arise, capture scholarly attention, and carry the day to the virtual exclusion of any competing claims. Yet, in ten or twenty years these intriguing new perspectives are discarded, overtaken by newer and even more exciting proposals. I am not being flippant—I have great interest in new research and appreciation for new insights it may bring—but this common phenomenon does give one pause to wonder just how long the latest predilections will last.

You may, or probably may not, be disappointed that space limitations preclude an exhaustive discussion of everything. No doubt some clever reviewer will point this out, happy to refer to this, that, or the other missing book, or to opine that the full historical context of every reference to past authors is not spelled out in detail. However, the longer the tome, the fewer the readers, and proportionately less will be read. Gone are the days when a fourteen-volume *Church Dogmatics* could stream off the press as from a conveyor belt. In a multivolume systematic theology, the first volume is likely to be remaindered before the last one is released. However, I will address some issues in more detail, since they are matters that have been disputed recently.

This of itself prevents extensive biblical exegesis. I do not write out biblical passages that readers can easily locate for themselves, although there are exceptions to every rule. Theology is more than the accumulation of biblical texts. It involves the interaction of a range of realities to which the cumulative witness of the Bible directs us. It is the entailment of "the sense of Scripture," as Gregory of Nazianzus described it, a theoretical and metatheoretical account of the overall interrelationship and inherent connections of the holistic biblical teaching. I hope something of this may become clear as we go along. That does not preclude focus on key passages, nor does it set aside reference to the overall biblical witness on each matter. The Bible is the Word of God, the supreme authority in all matters of faith and practice. It simply means that we need to consider the whole teaching of Scripture.

Integr-ation

---

6. Oliver D. Crisp, *God Incarnate: Explorations in Christology* (London: T&T Clark, 2009), 17 (italics original).

So my method is based on Scripture, but in dialogue with important voices from the church.

More basic than this is the question of whether and how we can speak about God. In part, we will consider this in the first chapter. For now, my answer is that we can speak about him since he has spoken to us, in our world, in our words. Even more, in his Son he has lived as one of us, taking our humanity as his own. We can think his thoughts after him and so speak, falteringly but truly, with the aid of the Holy Spirit.

In what follows, a few features differ from what is often encountered. I have already mentioned the absence of prolegomena. Additionally, I begin not with the doctrine of Scripture but with the Trinity. This stems from the overall arrangement of the book, which is centered on God and feeds thereafter into the works of God in creation, providence, and grace. While many, if not most, recent systematic theologies take Scripture as their starting point, so as to provide an epistemological foundation, it has struck me that to say that the Bible is the Word of God begs the question, in today's world, of the identity of the God whose Word it is. Moreover, God precedes his revelation. He brought all other entities into existence. For this reason, if you read sequentially, you may wish to leave chapters 6–8, on Scripture, until after the chapters on election and the covenant. Since God inspired Scripture after his acts of redemption (WCF, 1.1), it would be legitimate to hold back discussion of the Bible until later. The basic premise of the book is the living God, who communicates contingent life to his creatures, which humanity abandoned by sin—a choice for death—but which is renewed and superabundantly enhanced in Christ. Again, I deal with the Trinity before the divine attributes. While the revelation of the unity of God came first historically, God's ultimate self-revelation is as the Father, the Son, and the Holy Spirit in indivisible union. This is the Christian doctrine of God.

However, the main innovation is that I attempt to integrate soteriology and ecclesiology. The doctrine of salvation has long been treated in isolation from the doctrine of the church. In Roman Catholic theology the church comes first, with the sacraments at its heart; individual salvation is tacked on at the end. In contrast, in Reformed theology, individual soteriology is discussed in great detail, but the church and sacraments come later. In reality they stand together, since outside the church "there is no ordinary possibility of salvation" (WCF, 25.2). We are saved not merely as discrete individuals but as the one church of Jesus Christ. Consequently, I have long thought that the two should be treated together.

There are historical factors behind this separation of individual salvation from the church. First is the obvious dominance of individualism in Western society. Beginning in the Renaissance and gaining ground in the Enlightenment, the focus on the individual has become pervasive and often unrecognized. Descartes's famous search for certainty began with the assumption of the thinking self—"I think, therefore I am." Whereas the New Testament places the salvation of the individual in the context of the church, both evangelical theology and its practical outworking have detached the two, viewing church and sacraments as effective optional extras.[7] Aiding and abetting this trend have been analytic modes of thought, in which realities are broken down into discrete elements, focusing on distinctions. Hence, the doctrine of salvation is seen as not only distinct but in some cases separate from the doctrine of the church, in stark contrast to WCF, 25.2. We need a reorientation of mind to think these great realities together, and so to implement a more thoroughly ecclesial practice. Such would be closer to the focus of the apostles and the great tradition of the church.

In line with this, I seek to connect the preaching of the Word of God and the sacraments with the outworking of salvation by the Holy Spirit. From the analytic thinking I have outlined has arisen the idea that the sacraments are merely material and external rites, symbolic at best, to be distinguished from the work of the Spirit in the individual. Hence, the distinction of water baptism from Spirit baptism has become something of a commonplace. The Reformers and successive generations thereafter knew no such classification. That the Spirit's work was not to be restricted was clear in their writings, as was their resistance to any suggestion that he operated automatically on the performance of church ordinances. However, underlying their belief and practice was the fact that since God created the heavens and the earth, he uses material means to convey spiritual grace to his people. It was not by mistake that baptism came first in Jesus's last instructions to his apostles for their ongoing work (Matt. 28:19–20). It is no accident

---

7. Robert Letham and Donald Macleod, "Is Evangelicalism Christian?," *EQ* 67 (1995): 3–33. I am using "evangelical" to refer to conservative theology that acknowledges, among other things, the supreme authority of Scripture, which includes but is not restricted to the Reformed, rather than—as is common in North America—being viewed in distinction from the Reformed.

that Jesus was crucified at the Passover or that the Spirit came on the day of Pentecost rather than any other day. God honored the feasts he had established. He keeps his appointments. Those appointments are now related to his church.

On a more basic note, when referring to the Greek or Hebrew text, I have normally provided a translation and put a transliterated version as a footnote, so as to avoid disrupting the reading. I use the original text where it appears important to do so, if significant terms are used, or if there is an important exegetical question that depends on it. Readers may be amused to find that there are fewer of these in the early chapters than in the later ones. This is because of the subject matter; there happen to be more such questions arising the further we progress in the book.

An acquaintance, on hearing I was writing a systematic theology, remarked with a yawn, "Do we need *another* one?" As with biblical commentaries, theologies can give insight into different ways of understanding the faith. For nearly two hundred years after the Reformation they were coming off the press almost as quickly as one could say "Martin Luther." I set this volume before you with the hope and prayer that it may be of some little help to your faith and to your ministry. I write for the church, intending it to be read by laypeople as well as students, ministers, and professional scholars, with the aim that we will deepen and broaden our understanding of the Christian faith and so advance in faith and love for Christ, his church, and those around us, and articulate it effectively in a rapidly changing world. I hope you will join me on this journey.

You probably will not agree with me on every point; that's your freedom. Of necessity, any such book is inadequate to the task, to the vastness of the mystery. Owing to the scope of a systematic theology and the necessary restrictions of space, it is not feasible to discuss each matter in the detail that would be possible in a book devoted expressly to any one of them. However, we will grapple with questions arising from the greatest and most astounding story ever told. I hope you enjoy it; theology should be enjoyed, for our greatest privilege is "to glorify God, and to enjoy him for ever" (WSC, 1).

PART 1

THE TRIUNE GOD

Almighty and everlasting God, who has given to us your servants grace by the confession of a true faith to acknowledge the glory of the eternal Trinity, and in the power of the divine Majesty to worship the Unity; we beseech you, that you would keep us stedfast in this faith, and evermore defend us from all adversities, who lives and reigns, one God, world without end. Amen.

Collect for Trinity Sunday, Book of Common Prayer (1662) — Anglican!

1

The Revelation of God

Opens w/ a strong pressing claim.

The Bible never attempts to prove that God is. Attempts to do so by logic fall short of establishing the God and Father of our Lord Jesus Christ. God exists necessarily—there is no possibility that he cannot exist. The existence of God is not rationally attained, though it can be rationally explained and defended. Rather, God reveals himself in the world around us and has implanted a knowledge of his existence in all people, evidenced in the almost universal recognition of the need to worship a higher being. This implanted revelation is clear and fulfills the purpose God has for it, but it does not disclose the gospel and so cannot lead us to salvation. Nevertheless, it is essential as a basis for knowing God.

A few years ago, a group of atheists, which included the British Humanist Association, paid for a poster on the sides of London double-decker buses. The poster said: "There's Probably No God. Now Relax and Enjoy Your Life."[1] Along similar lines, the geneticist Richard Dawkins has argued that the claim that there is a god has a very low probability, though Dawkins stopped short of zero. "I think God is very improbable and I live my life on the assumption that he is not there," he acknowledged.[2] Again, "I am agnostic only to the extent that I am agnostic about fairies at the bottom of the garden."[3]

---

1. "Atheists Launch Bus Ad Campaign," BBC News, January 6, 2009, http://news.bbc.co.uk/1/hi/7813812.stm; and "Atheist Bus Campaign," Humanist UK (website), https://humanism.org.uk/campaigns/successful-campaigns/atheist-bus-campaign/; accessed December 9, 2017.

2. Richard Dawkins, *The God Delusion* (London: Black Swan, 2007), 73.

3. Dawkins, *Delusion*, 74.

I couldn't agree more. If anything, the advertisers didn't go far enough. The god who is a product of the constructions of human thought and the predication of whose existence depends on human reasoning does not and cannot exist, since in any argument the premises have a higher degree of certainty than the conclusion to which the argument leads. Such argumentation could never establish that the God and Father of our Lord Jesus Christ is.

The Bible nowhere attempts to argue for the existence of God. It assumes that God is and that he has revealed himself; God is the necessary presupposition for human life, so much so that it is the fool who has said in his heart that there is no God (Ps. 14:1). Centuries ago the then archbishop of Canterbury, Anselm (1033–1109), wrote that God is that than which none greater can be thought. Necessary existence is entailed in that. If one were to conceive of a being that might not exist, one would not have conceived of One who is the greatest that can be thought, since it would be possible to conceive of a greater, about whom nonexistence is not predicable.

R. C. Sproul has gone a stage further, arguing strongly and correctly that, in an important sense, God does not exist.[4] From a different angle, if one has a hankering for etymological fallacies[5]—one does from time to time, doesn't one?—we can see how this works out. Our verb "to exist" is ultimately derived from the Latin verb *exsistere*, meaning, among other things, to come into view, to come forward, to come into being.[6] This entails being out of or from another entity. All things created are what they are in this way, derived from something else. We exist from our parents, our children exist from us, my desk comes from a tree, which in turn is derived from an acorn, which fell from another tree, and so on. The building in which I work was produced from a range of materials. The air we breathe, our planet, and its galaxy are all brought about by other entities. All such entities are in a constant process of change, growth, retraction, and flux. All things in the universe exist contingently. Once they did not exist; their present existence depends on God, while the possibility of their ceasing to be is ever present. This is not the case with Yahweh, the God of Israel, the God and Father of our

4. Nathan W. Bingham, "R. C. Sproul Proves That God Does Not Exist," Ligonier Ministries, May 29, 2014, http://www.ligonier.org/blog/rc-sproul-proves-god-does-not-exist/.

5. See D. A. Carson, *Exegetical Fallacies* (Grand Rapids, MI: Baker, 1984), 34–36.

6. P. G. W. Glare, *Oxford Latin Dictionary* (Oxford: Oxford University Press, 1996), 656.

Lord Jesus Christ. He *is*. He is life itself. Created entities *exist*; but God *is*. As Aquinas wrote, God is his own existence—he is above existence and exceeds every kind of knowledge.[7] He subsists, for "those things subsist which exist in themselves, and not in another."[8]

With these important provisos, we will accommodate ourselves to popular usage. There are a range of arguments devised to prove or to explain that God is.

1.1 Arguments for the Existence of God

One class of arguments for the existence of God might be intended to persuade an unbeliever. Not only does the Bible not follow this method, but it will not lead to the desired conclusion. Another type of argument is one presented to believers to disclose the rationality of what they hold already by faith. These can be helpful in establishing a rational basis for what is believed on other grounds. Among this second type, foremost is Anselm's proof, often misleadingly called the ontological argument.

1.1.1 Anselm's Proof for the Existence of God

Anselm had a distinctive line of thought. In his *Proslogion* he did not intend to prove to an unbeliever that God exists. He may never have met such a person. Instead, he wrote for his fellow monks, to demonstrate that their belief in God could be established on a rational basis without recourse to Scripture.[9] This purpose is vital to note, for his case must not be assessed as if it were intended to accomplish something he never had in mind. Moreover, he couched his proof in an attitude of prayer, addressing God in the flow of discussion. He assumed God but sought reasons to support what he already knew.[10] The context of the entire book, and the *Monologion* that preceded it, places it within a commitment to Christ. In the *Monologion* Anselm indicates that his work is grounded on Augustine's treatise on the Trinity.[11] Barth comments that Anselm is

---

7. Aquinas, *ST* 1a.12.1.

8. Aquinas, *ST* 1a.29.2.

9. Anselm, *Proslogion*, preface, in Eugene R. Fairweather, *A Scholastic Miscellany: Anselm to Ockham* (New York: Macmillan, 1970), 69. See Karl Barth, *Fides Quaerens Intellectum: Anselm's Proof of the Existence of God in the Context of His Theological Scheme* (Pittsburgh: Pickwick, 1975), 64.

10. Anselm, *Proslogion* 1, in Fairweather, *A Scholastic Miscellany*, 70. See Ian Davie, "Anselm's Argument Reassessed," *DRev* 112 (1994): 103–20.

11. Lydia Schumacher, "The Lost Legacy of Anselm's Argument: Re-Thinking the Purpose of Proofs for the Existence of God," *MTheol* 27 (2011): 87–101.

seeking not to prove logically but to understand in order to establish validity,[12] as the outcome of faith, a faith that impels us to understand and to delight in what we understand.[13] It is "the nature of faith that desires knowledge. *Credo ut intelligam* means: It is my very faith itself that summons me to knowledge."[14] Hogg reflects that *probare* (to prove) can mean "to probe" or "to test."[15]

When Anselm speaks of God existing necessarily, "*necessitas* means the attribute of being unable not to be, or of being unable to be different. . . . The *necessitas* that is peculiar to the object of faith is the impossibility of the object of faith not existing or of being otherwise than it is."[16] Anselm does not pursue this on the basis of autonomous human reason[17] but seeks to let the truth disclose itself.[18] As I have indicated, he does not argue on the terms of unbelievers[19] but seeks to establish the certainty of what he already believes.[20] His argument can be summed up fairly concisely, but it is so dense that it requires a treatise properly to unpack it and, in effect, a library to discuss it.

The crucial point in the Proslogion is the name of God that Anselm presupposes. In prayer, he sought the name of God, and eventually it was revealed to him that God is "that than which none greater can be thought."[21] This goes beyond God being the greatest entity ever conceived by humans, or the greatest that is possible to conceive. Rather, as Barth indicates, God is entirely independent of whether humans do or do not so conceive.[22]

It follows that existence is an attribute of perfection, since perfection could not be present in an entity that did not exist. Since God is "that than which none greater can be thought," existence is entailed. Anselm argues that if a thing is in the mind but not in reality, nonexistence is implied; but if it is in reality, it exists apart from our thoughts.[23] For

12. Barth, *Fides Quaerens Intellectum*, 13–14. Barth regarded this as his greatest work.
13. Barth, *Fides Quaerens Intellectum*, 15–17.
14. Barth, *Fides Quaerens Intellectum*, 18.
15. David S. Hogg, *Anselm of Canterbury: The Beauty of Theology* (Aldershot: Ashgate, 2004), 91.
16. Barth, *Fides Quaerens Intellectum*, 49.
17. Barth, *Fides Quaerens Intellectum*, 52–53, 63.
18. Barth, *Fides Quaerens Intellectum*, 64.
19. Barth, *Fides Quaerens Intellectum*, 69.
20. Hogg, *Anselm*, 92.
21. Anselm, *Proslogion* 2, in Fairweather, *A Scholastic Miscellany*, 73.
22. Barth, *Fides Quaerens Intellectum*, 74.
23. Anselm, *Proslogion* 2, in Fairweather, *A Scholastic Miscellany*, 73–74; Barth, *Fides Quaerens Intellectum*, 91.

tricky

Anselm "the object then is first of all in reality, then following from that it exists, then as a consequence of that it can be thought."[24] Anselm's purpose in *Proslogion* 2–4 is to demonstrate the impossibility of thinking of God as merely a conception in the mind.[25] For Anselm, God is in a unique category.[26] It is impossible to conceive of a being as God who exists in the mind alone since God is that than which none greater can be thought.[27] Therefore, God exists in reality as well as in the mind, since it is impossible that he exist in the mind alone.[28] God is not merely the greatest being, or the greatest being about which we can think. There is no greater entity possible, nor can one possibly be conceived to be.

Opponents pointed out what to them was an obvious flaw: an idea of an absolutely perfect being does not entail that such a being exists. Anselm's fellow monk Gaunilo, playing the devil's advocate, objected on the grounds that one can have an idea of the existence of a perfect island, but that does not establish its existence.[29] Centuries later, Immanuel Kant used a similar line of reasoning, only in his case the perfect island was replaced by a hundred possible thalers.[30] However, what both objections missed is that God is not on the same footing as creatures. He cannot be compared to islands or currencies. Creatures exist contingently; they may or may not exist. But God is, and is of necessity, and is of necessity because of who he is. Since he is that than which none greater can be thought, his nonexistence is inconceivable, for any conception of his nonexistence would not be a conception of that than whom none greater can be thought; it would be a conception of an entity that could not be God. Neither Gaunilo nor Kant touch this central nerve of Anselm's case.

Barth continues, *"God exists in such a way (true only of him) that it is impossible for him to be conceived of as not existing."*[31] "The Name of God as it is heard and understood compels the more precise

24. Barth, *Fides Quaerens Intellectum*, 92.
25. Barth, *Fides Quaerens Intellectum*, 94–95.
26. Barth, *Fides Quaerens Intellectum*, 96.
27. Barth, *Fides Quaerens Intellectum*, 126.
28. Barth, *Fides Quaerens Intellectum*, 128.
29. Gaunilo of Marmoutiers, *Pro Insipiente (On Behalf of the Fool)*, in Brian Davies, *Anselm of Canterbury: The Major Works* (Oxford: Oxford University Press, 1998), 105–10, esp. 109. For Anselm's reply, see Anselm, *Reply to Gaunilo*, in Davies, *Anselm of Canterbury*, 110–22.
30. Immanuel Kant, *Immanuel Kant's Critique of Pure Reason* (Norman Kemp Smith, 1933; repr., London: Macmillan, 1970), 504–7.
31. Anselm, *Proslogion* 3, in Fairweather, *A Scholastic Miscellany*, 74; Barth, *Fides Quaerens Intellectum*, 132 (my italics).

definition that God does not exist as all other things exist. . . . God exists—and he alone—in such a way that it is impossible even to conceive the possibility of his non-existence."[32] The contrast is now advanced, Barth argues, to that "between something that certainly exists objectively as well as in thought but yet which is conceivable as not existing and on the other hand something existing objectively and in thought but which is not conceivable as not existing."[33] We could paraphrase this by saying that if a person were to predicate the nonexistence of God, it could not possibly be God—the God who created the world and who has revealed himself in Jesus Christ—about whom this was predicated. In this light, Barth concludes, God "exists as the reality of existence itself, as the criterion of all existence and non-existence."[34] Again, "The positive statement: God so exists that his non-existence is inconceivable."[35]

Graham Oppy, an agnostic philosopher, concludes that ontological arguments can neither prove nor disprove the existence of God and so are worthless.[36] Correctly, he points to the presuppositions that underlie the arguments: "Only those who make the relevant presuppositions will suppose that ontological arguments are sound; but there is nothing in ontological arguments that establishes a case for those presuppositions from the standpoint of those who do not share them."[37] Anselm, however, was never attempting to convince those who differed with his commitments, nor am I suggesting that his argument be used in such a context.[38]

Anna Williams remarks, "It is a curious feature of arguments for the existence of God that they presume an identity for that which they seek to prove."[39] In reality, "God" denotes different things to different people, posing difficulties for Christians, for whom God is Trinity. The doctrine of the Trinity affirms that God is personal, his actions being those of a personal agent, which other religious conceptions cannot allow.[40]

---

32. Barth, *Fides Quaerens Intellectum*, 134–35.
33. Barth, *Fides Quaerens Intellectum*, 141.
34. Barth, *Fides Quaerens Intellectum*, 142.
35. Barth, *Fides Quaerens Intellectum*, 150.
36. Graham Oppy, *Ontological Arguments and Belief in God* (Cambridge: Cambridge University Press, 1995), 199.
37. Oppy, *Ontological Arguments*, 198.
38. For discussions of Anselm's argument and its critics, see G. R. Evans, *Anselm* (London: Geoffrey Chapman, 1989), 49–55; Hogg, *Anselm*, 89–124.
39. A. N. Williams, "Does 'God' Exist?," *SJT* 58 (2005): 468.
40. Williams, "Does 'God' Exist?," 468–84.

Along the same lines, Aquinas did not accept Anselm's argument as convincing for those who do not share his presuppositions.[41] Until recently, it has been thought that he took a different tack and sought to convince unbelievers, in the mode of the first type of argument I mentioned above. However, a newer school of thought holds that Aquinas, like Anselm, was explaining how the Christian faith was rationally defensible.[42] Brian Davies comments:

> Aquinas is not at all worried about making out a case for God's existence. . . . It is most unlikely that he ever encountered an atheist in the modern sense. . . . He thinks it perfectly proper for someone to start by taking God's existence for granted. At the end of the day his basic position is roughly that of St Anselm . . . : "I do not seek to understand so that I may believe; but I believe so that I may understand."[43]

It has been suggested that, in the face of the challenge of the Islamic scholarship of Averroes (1126–1198) and Avicenna (ca. 980–1037) and their interpretation of Aristotle, some Latin Averroists held to "double truth," the idea that contradictories could be true. Thus, for example, the Christian account of creation could be true on religious grounds while false scientifically. Hence, the need for Aquinas to demonstrate the compatibility of faith with reason.[44] So, in terms of the doctrine of the Trinity, for Aquinas, "though . . . it cannot be rationally demonstrated, it can still be rationally discussed."[45]

Aquinas considered that the existence of God could be supported both a priori, from the cause to the effect, and a posteriori, from the effect to the cause. If the effect is more familiar to us, then we can reason from the effects of God, his works in the world, back to God as their cause.[46] From this, Thomas thought, the existence of God can be established in

41. Aquinas, *ST* 1a.2.1; Brian Davies, *Thomas Aquinas's* Summa Theologiae: *A Guide and Commentary* (Oxford: Oxford University Press, 2014), 30.

42. Schumacher, "Lost Legacy," 97–99; Aquinas, *ST* 1a.2.1–2; David Braine, *The Reality of Time and the Existence of God: The Project of Proving God's Existence* (Oxford: Clarendon, 1988); Leo Elders, *The Philosophical Theology of St. Thomas Aquinas* (Leiden: Brill, 1990); Anthony Kenny, *The Five Ways: St. Thomas Aquinas; Proofs for God's Existence* (London: Routledge, 2008); Fergus Kerr, "Theology in Philosophy: Revisiting the Five Ways," *International Journal for Philosophy of Religion* 50, no. 1/3 (2001): 115–30; Mark Jordan, *Rewritten Theology: Aquinas after His Readers* (Oxford: Blackwell, 2006). All cited in Schumacher.

43. Brian Davies, *The Thought of Thomas Aquinas* (Oxford: Clarendon, 1992), 21–22.

44. Ralph McInerny, ed., *Thomas Aquinas: Selected Writings* (London: Penguin, 1999), xi–xiii.

45. Davies, *Aquinas*, 191.

46. Aquinas, *ST* 1a.2.2.

five ways.[47] (1) *From motion*, which requires that an entity be put in motion by another. From this, one can reason back to God as the first mover. Here there are echoes of Aristotle's unmoved mover.[48] (2) *From the nature of the efficient cause.* It is not possible to have an infinite regression, since if there were no first cause, neither could there be intermediate causes or an ultimate cause, which is false. (3) *From possibility and necessity.* It is impossible for everything to be merely possible, such that all things may or may not be, since if it were possible for everything not to be, then at some time there would have been nothing in existence. If at some time there were nothing in existence, it would be impossible for anything to come into existence. Therefore, not all beings are merely possible. Since some beings necessarily exist and it is impossible for all such beings to derive their necessity from another, as was discussed in the second argument from causality, there must be a necessary being that has its necessity from itself. (4) *From the gradation found in things.* Some beings are more or less good, true, and so forth. This assumes that there is a standard alongside which their goodness is measured, which is the best in all instances. (5) *From the government of the world.* Since unintelligent things work toward their end, it follows that they are governed by an intelligent being by whom all beings are directed. All changeable things must be traced back to an immovable first principle, which is God.[49]

Aquinas held that we can also come to know God by "demonstration," an argument that starts from true premises and establishes its conclusion validly; a syllogism.[50] He denied that "God exists" is an article of faith, since the Nicene Creed presupposes it.[51]

From these, the following arguments have been developed, leaving ontological arguments aside. While, as I argued, they cannot of themselves prove God is, nevertheless they are not useless, as they have a certain value in supporting the rational nature of what we recognize by faith.

1.1.2   *The Cosmological Argument*

The cosmological argument reasons that everything in the universe has a cause, and therefore the universe must have a cause. The rejoinder to

---

47. Aquinas, *ST* 1a.2.3.
48. Aristotle, *Metaphysics*, trans. John Warrington, Everyman Library (London: Dent, 1955), 333–47, cited by Colin Brown, *Philosophy and the Christian Faith* (London: Tyndale, 1969), 16.
49. Aquinas, *ST* 1a.2.3.
50. Aquinas, *ST* 1a.2.2.
51. Aquinas, *ST* 2a2ae.1.8; Davies, Summa Theologiae: A Guide, 32.

this argument is that one can end up with an infinite causal regression. What caused the cause of the universe? Moreover, the argument begs the question as to the nature of the originator of the universe. It does not lead to or demand a personal Creator. It requires something in the order of Anselm's argument to bolster it; Anselm's proof was undertaken in prayer. This argument has affinities with Aquinas's second way and perhaps with the others.

1.1.3 The Teleological Argument

The universe reveals harmony and purpose, implying that an intelligent and powerful being started it. This may be so, but the identity of the intelligent designer is left unclear, as is the possibility that there may be another, yet more intelligent designer behind it. This line of thought has resurfaced recently with the Intelligent Design movement. While its exponents recognize the biblical teaching that the heavens declare the glory of God, the argument stops short of requiring belief in the God who has revealed himself in Scripture and in Jesus Christ. Here there are connections with Aquinas's fifth way.

1.1.4 The Moral Argument

From the universal existence of moral values it is inferred that there is a lawgiver and judge with the absolute right to command humans, and to whom humans are responsible. All we are left with here is an overlord who may or may not be beneficent, leaving the possibility of a frightening despot ready to crush its subordinates. Again, this does not arrive at the conclusion that the judge is the God and Father of our Lord Jesus Christ.

———

Do these arguments establish the existence of the living God of the Bible in the face of skeptical criticism? They do not. They cannot convince someone who does not already believe in God. They might be used to demonstrate what an unbeliever is suppressing (Rom. 1:19–20). They can have some utility from the perspective of faith, as *ex post facto* confirmations of what is believed on the basis of revelation, creation, and Scripture.

There are other problems with using such arguments to establish God's existence for unbelievers. Foremost is the point that, simple deductive arguments apart,[52] the original premise has greater certainty than the conclusion toward which the argument heads. Moreover, in the cases we have discussed, the projected conclusions exceed the scope of the premises.[53] Hence, the assumptions shared by the participants have a surer basis than the god about whom the discussion is concerned. The quest is doomed from the start.

We can probe a stage further. Is logical argumentation the appropriate mode for the knowledge of God? In personal interactions, we relate to people not by logic but by recognition and communion. When we see a friend walking down the street, we do not engage in a carefully structured series of syllogisms to persuade ourselves of his or her presence. Facial recognition is more instinctive and intuitive than logic. Moreover, friendship and love emerge through communion with another. They are no less real than formal or logical propositions. Relations with persons operate in a different dimension than mathematical theorems, scientific evidence, or logical debates. The problem that keeps many from recognizing this is not logic but personal alienation. When we have had a serious problem with someone, we often do our best to avoid contact. Likewise, on a greater stage, sin keeps people from recognizing God. In this light, it is significant to note that Anselm's argument is based on the premise of Christian belief and communion in prayer, and includes a discussion of the nature of God later in the *Proslogion*.[54]

This does not rule out logic but limits it, locating it in its appropriate place. It can fulfill a role as an after-the-fact support for what is believed on other grounds. James Loder and Jim Neidhardt discuss questions such as these. Drawing on a range of disciplines, from physics and mathematics to the arts, including M. C. Escher's line drawings and the Mobius curve, they argue that at the boundaries of knowledge logic breaks down before the realities of things as they are.[55]

---

52. In such cases, if the premises are true, then the conclusion must also be true, provided the form of the argument is valid. Socrates is mortal, we can be certain of, *if* it's true that all men are mortal and Socrates is a man. I am grateful to Paul Helm and Ron Di Giacomo for this observation. The law of noncontradiction is operative in instances like this.

53. Ron Di Giacomo pointed this out in personal correspondence.

54. Anselm, *Proslogion* 5–26, in Fairweather, *A Scholastic Miscellany*, 75–93.

55. James E. Loder and W. Jim Neidhardt, *The Knight's Move: The Relational Logic of the Spirit in Theology and Science* (Colorado Springs: Helmers & Howard, 1992).

Returning to Aquinas, Thomas placed limits on reason and its powers to plumb the depths of God and his works. For him, revelation was necessary to lead us beyond our own innate capacities.[56] As Augustine wrote, "God is more truly thought than he is uttered, and exists more truly than he is thought."[57] However, Aquinas still held that revelation could be rationally explained and defended.[58] Like Anselm, he presupposed the existence of God; he was no Enlightenment rationalist before the time.

Calvin's teaching on the universal *sensus divinitatis* is helpful at this point.[59] He says that "no long or toilsome proof is needed to elicit evidences that serve to illuminate and affirm the divine majesty."[60] In fact, "there is within the human mind . . . an awareness of divinity,"[61] "a sense of divinity which can never be effaced."[62] He adds, "God has sown a seed of religion in all men. But scarcely one in a hundred is met with who fosters it."[63] Helm describes this as, for Calvin, "part of what it means to be really or fully human,"[64] "an innate endowment triggered by factors which are not innate."[65] Helm notes that there are limitations on human nature; humans "cannot hear sounds beyond a certain frequency range, but bats can"; so "there are sounds created in the world such that they cannot be heard by normal human beings." In this case he considers that, for Calvin, there are moral or emotional preconditions that enable persons to receive the evidence without eroding its objectivity.[66]

Daniel von Wachter indicates that in recent years there has been a move away from discussion of "proofs" for the existence of God, requiring absolute conclusions, toward "arguments" for the existence of God, with probabilistic results on both sides. Indeed, he says, German philosophers and theologians have been increasingly questioning former prejudices about arguments for God's existence.[67] Ironically, in a chapter entitled "Why There Almost Certainly Is No God," Dawkins seriously

56. Aquinas, *ST* 1a.32.1.
57. Augustine, *De Trinitate* 7.4 (*NPNF*[1], 3:109).
58. Aquinas, *ST* 1a.27–43; Davies, Summa Theologiae: *A Guide*, 96–97.
59. See Paul Helm, *John Calvin's Ideas* (Oxford: Oxford University Press, 2004), 209–45.
60. Calvin, *Institutes*, 1.5.9.
61. Calvin, *Institutes*, 1.3.1.
62. Calvin, *Institutes*, 1.3.3.
63. Calvin, *Institutes*, 1.4.1.
64. Helm, *Calvin's Ideas*, 222.
65. Helm, *Calvin's Ideas*, 229–30.
66. Helm, *Calvin's Ideas*, 239.
67. Daniel von Wachter, "Has Modernity Shown All Arguments for the Existence of God to Be Wrong?," *JRT* 10 (2016): 257–61.

considers the possibility of multiverses.[68] While the theory of infinite universes and infinite cosmic inflation has significant following among physicists, there is no concrete evidence in its favor. Besides, it leaves the same questions on the agenda, pushing them back further to the point of why universes come into being *ad infinitum*, and what brings them into existence in the first place, which is a question of metaphysics, not science, and is "the height of irrationality" according to Richard Swinburne.[69]

1.2   General Revelation

The Bible declares that God has made himself known in creation (Ps. 19:1–6; Rom. 1:18–20). He has taken the initiative. Moreover, he created humanity in his image and gave him responsibility to govern the earth, to subdue it, and, in doing so, to understand it (Gen. 1:26–27; 2:15–25). This revelation and this task are universal and indiscriminate, given to humanity as a whole. However, this general revelation stops short of declaring the way of salvation. It does not disclose the character of God, beyond "his eternal power and divine nature" (Rom. 1:19–20). Before discussing this, we should note some significant deviations.

Pantheism is an identification of creation or nature with God: all things are divine. This has surfaced in recent decades in the West through the environmental movement, New Age spirituality, and the like, with talk of Mother Nature.

Panentheism does not go as far as pantheism in identifying God with creation. Instead, it posits codependency. God is in the world and the world is in God. There is a continuum. As the world depends on God, so God depends on the world. He is deeply enmeshed in history; the history of the world is, in effect, the history of God, impinging on him and changing him. In turn, the future is open-ended and indeterminate. Jürgen Moltmann is effectively a panentheist,[70] as are many contemporary theologians who envisage God as involved in a process, in becoming, in a dynamic interplay with cosmic forces.

In pantheism, the classic distinction between Creator and creature is erased; in panentheism it is blurred. Effectively, God is remote and unknowable, and so practically irrelevant to us, with the corollary that

---

68. Dawkins, *Delusion*, 137–89, esp. 169–76.
69. Richard Swinburne, *Is There a God?* (Oxford: Oxford University Press, 1995), 68.
70. See Jürgen Moltmann, *God in Creation: A New Theology of Creation and the Spirit of God* (San Francisco: HarperSanFrancisco, 1991).

we are autonomous and the masters of our fate. Conversely, in an immanent sense, God is bound up with the events of the world, codependent, cosuffering, and weak. In both cases, he has been dethroned, and humanity is the master.

Polytheism is the belief in a plurality of divine beings. In the ancient world, the gods were held to preside over particular territories. In the Old Testament, the Philistines think the ark of the covenant must be returned to Israel to appease its God (1 Sam. 4:1–5:12) This widespread belief helped protect the church in its early years as the Roman authorities believed it to be a Jewish sect and thus under the protection of Israel's deity. When it became evident that it was international, cutting across ethnic and tribal boundaries, the church was seen to pose a threat to all the deities throughout the empire. Even after Christianity was made the official religion of the Roman Empire by Theodosius in AD 380, the sack of Rome was blamed on the Christians for this reason, among others.

Monotheism is the belief that there is only one God, who is thereby clearly distinguished from the creation. Christianity, orthodox Judaism, and Islam alike are monotheistic. However, there are radical differences between the Christian doctrine of God and the Islamic doctrine of Allah. The Christian Trinity is relational. The three are one, indivisible in mutual love. For Islam, Allah is a solitary monad. Allah cannot be love, for love presupposes more than one person. Neither can Allah be personal. In fact, Allah is power and will, to which his followers are responsible to submit. Christianity maintains that the heart of the universe is personhood and love, placed there by the tripersonal God.

Deism, dominant from the Enlightenment, holds that while God is Creator, he is remote from the world. The cosmos operates under the laws he gave it, effectively autonomously. There can be no place for the incarnation or for miracles in such thinking

1.2.1 The Extent of God's Revelation in Creation and Providence

How far does God reveal himself in his works of creation and providence? The Bible asserts that there is inescapable evidence of God in the world around us (Ps. 19:1–6; Rom. 1:18–21; Heb. 1:3). His presence is unavoidable (Ps. 139:1–12). Bavinck comments, "Now the fact that the world is the theatre of God's self-revelation can hardly be denied."[71] As

---

71. Bavinck, *RD*, 2:56.

John of Damascus wrote, "God . . . did not leave us in absolute igno-rance. For the knowledge of God's existence has been implanted by him in all nature. This creation, too, and its maintenance, and its govern-ment, proclaim the majesty of the divine nature."[72] The Psalms are full of praise to God for the wonders he has done in creating the world and maintaining it, displaying his glory. All creation is called on to praise Yahweh (e.g., Psalm 148).

God's self-revelation is self-evident. The invisible nature of God is clearly visible in the created order (Rom. 1:19–20). Like a bomb that leaves behind a huge crater, it needs no lengthy process of argument, no concoction of syllogisms to establish that a hole has emerged. More remarkably, it is vivid for all to see in the beauty and order of all he has made and sustains.

General revelation is infallible since it is God who reveals himself. It is revelation, supremely self-revelation. Through the creation we see a reflection of his glory. It is a window through which we recognize the greater glory of its Creator. Even our daily food marks the interface be-tween the humdrum material world and the beneficence of the God who provides for us. Our daily bread should be the occasion for thanksgiving, praise, and communion (1 Tim. 4:1–5).

WCF, 1.1, points to the ways God reveals himself in the natural world: through the light of nature, the works of creation, and the works of providence, covering the production of the universe and its mainte-nance. "The light of nature" refers to the realization God has implanted in our minds that all around is a signal of his eternal being. Calvin's *sensus divinitatis* is an expression of that reality.[73] There are things to be known of God by human beings in general regardless of whether they are Christian—for example, his goodness, wisdom, and power.

1.2.2   The Limits of General Revelation

What are the limits of general revelation? Creation, providence, and the *sensus divinitatis* are inadequate when it comes to salvation. There is a twofold insufficiency.

First, because of sin humans resist such revelation. The noetic and ethical effects of sin incapacitate us from recognizing and responding,

---

72. John of Damascus, *The Orthodox Faith* 1.1 (NPNF², 9/2:1).
73. See Helm, *Calvin's Ideas*, 218–45.

and debar any attempt on our part to reach God (1 Cor. 2:5–16). Calvin argued that we need Scripture as "spectacles" through which to view the creation rightly, together with the Holy Spirit to enlighten the mind and dissipate the mists that cloud it; otherwise we are led captive to various forms of idolatry.[74]

Second, the revelation is not designed to deliver from sin. It discloses God's power but does not make known his grace.[75] It reveals that God is and displays his eternal power and deity; it does not go beyond that. It does not reveal the Trinity.[76] It simply leaves people without excuse for unbelief (Rom. 1:19–20).

Still, general revelation is reliable within its limitations,[77] and in terms of God's intention, for it declares plainly that there is a God (WLC, 2). In this it is utterly infallible; it achieves God's purpose. Since God reveals himself, his revelation is without defect as far as it goes; but after the fall, it is impossible to attain salvation through it, no matter how diligently one may follow its leading (WLC, 60), for that is not its purpose. As Barth puts it, the light of nature "refers to the inner light of the inborn image of God in the human. The light of nature appears as a source of knowledge, but immediately is placed beneath Scripture as ineffective and incapable of revealing to us the will of God."[78]

1.2.3   General Revelation and Natural Theology

General revelation differs from natural theology. *General revelation* refers to what God makes known of himself through creation. It is accepted and understood in faith. It proceeds from God and reaches us. On the other hand, *natural theology*, as it is called, refers to attempts by humans to argue for the existence and nature of God based on what is known or observed in creation and providence. It assumes that we have the capacity to know a great deal about God on the basis of our

74. Calvin, *Institutes*, 1.6.1.
75. Even before the fall, Adam was given word revelation in order for him to understand his place in the created order. His task and responsibilities were spelled out verbally (Gen. 1:28–30; 2:16–17), while God's walking in the garden and calling out to Adam immediately after the fall implies that communion between God and man was part of the original created order and that this included verbal communication.
76. Aquinas, *ST* 1a.32.1. I understand Paul in Rom. 2:14–15, "the work of the law is written on their hearts," to refer to Gentile Christians, rather than to pagans.
77. Benjamin B. Warfield, *The Westminster Assembly and Its Work* (New York: Oxford University Press, 1934), 193.
78. Karl Barth, *The Theology of the Reformed Confessions: 1923*, trans. Darrell L. Guder and Judith J. Guder (Louisville: Westminster John Knox, 2002), 48.

own powers of reason and observation. This may, theoretically, have been possible before the fall, but even then, Adam depended on verbal revelation to understand his place in creation. God's word interpreted God's world (Gen. 1:26–27; 2:15–17). In the church, human reason has a place, but under the authority and leadership of God's Word revelation.

Barth famously said no to natural theology. Everything depended on his idea of revelation, refracted through God's primal decision to be God in Christ. For him, everything is frozen in this eternal determination. Since revelation is exclusively in Christ, he determinedly rejected all attempts to construct an independent theology.

There are clear limits to general revelation. Aquinas remarks that "our natural knowledge can go as far as it can be led by sensible things," but from this the whole power of God cannot be known. But because "they are his effects . . . we can be led from them so far as to know of God *whether he exists*," that he is the Creator, and that he differs from created things, super-exceeding them.[79] Again,

> It must be said that God's being three in one is only believed and in no way can be demonstratively proved, though some arguments of a non-necessary kind and of little probability except to the believer can be fashioned. This is evident from the fact that we know God in this life only from his effects. . . . Therefore, we can know of God from natural reason only what is perceived of him from the relation of effects to him, such as those which indicate his causality and eminence above what is caused. . . . The trinity of persons cannot be perceived from the divine causality itself, since causality is common to the whole trinity.[80]

1.2.4 *The Interrelationship between General and Special Revelation*

General revelation in the light of special revelation. We noted Calvin's comment that God's revelation in creation cannot be known rightly apart from Scripture.[81] We need special revelation, the Word of God, to understand general revelation properly. This was true before the fall, when Adam received verbal revelation from God as to the nature of his task. It is doubly so once sin entered, the human mind and heart now being inherently biased against God and his goodness.

---

79. Aquinas, *ST* 1a.12.12.
80. Thomas Aquinas, "The Exposition of Boethius's *On the Trinity*, Art. 4," in *Thomas Aquinas: Selected Writings*, ed. Ralph McInerny (London: Penguin, 1998), 124.
81. Calvin, *Institutes*, 1.6.1.

However, with Scripture and in its light, we can understand creation in perspective. Calvin writes that in the light of Genesis, we see creation as the theater of God's glory, the clothes he wears to display his beauty and glory.[82] It is semiotic. Through creation, in faith, we perceive that beyond it is its wonderful Creator. Without faith, such a perception is impossible; by faith we understand (Heb. 11:3). This is due not to any inadequacy in creation or in God's self-revelation in it but to our obtuseness and unbelief. Indeed, God cannot be seen by any organ of sense, for he is Spirit. He can be known only through faith.[83] *Having faith*, we can approach the creation with thanksgiving and gratitude to God, its Creator (Ps. 148:1–14; Col. 1:15–20; 1 Tim. 4:1–5).[84]

Bavinck asserts that general revelation continues in God's providential dealings with creation and is not limited to creation itself. Since it comes from God, it is supernatural.[85] So "the supernatural is not at odds with human nature, nor with the nature of creatures; it belongs, so to speak, to humanity's essence. Human beings are images of God and akin to God and by means of religion stand in a direct relation to God."[86] Indeed, God revealed himself to pagans after the fall in dreams (Gen. 20:1–7; 31:24; 40:1–23; 41:1–36; Judg. 7:13–14; Dan. 2:3ff.).[87] More widely, this reflects on all human effort that in some way refracts the truth. Augustine affirmed this in *De doctrina Christiana*, writing, "If those who are called philosophers, and especially the Platonists, have said aught that is true and in harmony with our faith, we are not only not to shrink from it, but to claim it for our own use from those who have unlawful possession of it."[88] However, he recognized that it does not lead to salvation and is only useful for a few.[89]

Calvin had a generally negative attitude toward other religions and toward general revelation apart from the lens of Scripture.[90] Yet he was

---

82. John Calvin, *Commentaries on the First Book of Moses Called Genesis*, trans. John King (Grand Rapids, MI: Eerdmans, 1979), argument.

83. Aquinas, *ST* 1a.12.3–5.

84. St. John of Damascus, *Three Treatises on the Divine Images*, trans. Andrew Louth (Crestwood, NY: St Vladimir's Seminary Press, 2003), 21–28 (1.4–14).

85. Bavinck, *RD*, 1:307.

86. Bavinck, *RD*, 1:308.

87. Bavinck, *RD*, 1:311.

88. Augustine, *On Christian Doctrine* 2.40.60 (NPNF[1], 2:554).

89. Augustine, *City of God* 9.20 (NPNF[1], 2:176–77). See also Aquinas, *ST* 1a.1.1; Calvin, *Institutes*, 1.3.1–3; Francis Turretin, *Institutes of Elenctic Theology*, trans. George Musgrave Giger, ed. James T. Dennison Jr. (Phillipsburg, NJ: P&R, 1992), 1:6–16.

90. John Span, "John Calvin's View of 'the Turks' and of Finding Truth in Non-Biblical Texts," *Hapshin Theological Review* 4 (December 2015): 187–228.

not averse to citing pagan writings when it suited him and reflected on the goodness of creation in the most striking ways. Bavinck agrees that pagan religions contain elements of truth passed down from creation. However, they have been distorted. The oneness of God was lost, polytheism developed, and the distinction between the Creator and creature was blurred to the extent that these religions are idolatrous, with demonic powers at work.[91] However,

> with their Christian confession, accordingly, Christians find themselves at home also in the world. They are not strangers there and see the God who rules creation as none other than the one they address as Father in Christ. As a result of this general revelation, they feel at home in the world; it is God's fatherly hand from which they receive all things also in the context of nature.

It is a common basis on which to meet non-Christians, "a point of contact with all those who bear the name 'human.'"[92]

Special revelation in the light of general revelation. While the revelation of God in creation and providence is incapable of leading us to salvation, given the presence of sin, it is still necessary in order to understand special revelation. The two elements interact, so much so that neither is complete without the other. As we need Scripture rightly to appreciate general revelation, so creation informs our grasp of special revelation; without it we could not understand the Bible at all. The history of the world and the church, geography, politics, economics, personal interactions, and psychology are necessary ingredients so as to appreciate what God says in Scripture. The biblical books were composed at definite times and places. To grasp what the Spirit says in these books, we need to understand the languages in which they were written, the situations that occasioned their production, the place each occupies in the ongoing history of redemption, the particular cultural and environmental factors that surround them, political and military events, and so on.

Furthermore, redemption is the renewal and transformation of the creation. Special revelation is given by God in order that we may appreciate the place he has assigned for the created order. In the long run, the sphere currently delimited by general revelation is the locus of God's ultimate pur-

---

91. Bavinck, *RD*, 1:315.
92. Bavinck, *RD*, 1:321.

poses. This unity of general and special revelation reflects the unity of God's plans (Eph. 1:10), where he is to head up all things under the rule of Christ. These two spheres, while distinct, are inseparably conjoined. Having been grasped by redemption in Christ, believers can take a totally different view of creation than was possible beforehand. The world is ours because it belongs to God. The arts are there to develop and be enjoyed. Music, fine art, poetry, politics, science, literature—these are areas to be conquered and reclaimed. Christ is the Mediator of creation (Col. 1:15–20).[93]

As Bavinck explains:

> Hence the object of revelation cannot only be to teach human beings, to illuminate their intellects (rationalism), or to prompt them to practice religious virtue (moralism), or to arouse religious sensations in them (mysticism). God's aim in special revelation is both much deeper and reaches much farther. It is none other than to redeem human beings in their totality of body and soul, with all their capacities and powers; to redeem not only individual, isolated human beings but humanity as an organic whole. Finally, the goal is to redeem not just humanity apart from all the other creatures but along with humanity to wrest heaven and earth, in a word, the whole world in its organic interconnectedness, from the power of sin and again to cause the glory of God to shine forth from every creature.[94]

C. S. Lewis stated that there can be no neutral territory in the universe.[95] The Dutch theologian and prime minister of the Netherlands Abraham Kuyper famously declared, "There is not a square inch in the whole domain of our human existence over which Christ, who is Sovereign over *all*, does not cry: 'Mine!'"[96] Atheists, adherents of other religions, and all unbelievers are, in the final analysis, squatters. Notwithstanding, due to God's common grace, by which he grants gifts and abilities to humanity as such, they have many things to say that are true. I am not deterred from appreciating Mahler's *Das Lied von der Erde* because he did not subscribe to the Westminster Confession of Faith, nor Beethoven's great C-sharp minor string quartet because he was a

---

93. See Chul Won Suh, *The Creation-Mediatorship of Jesus Christ* (Amsterdam: Rodopi, 1982).
94. Bavinck, *RD*, 1:346.
95. Cited in N. T. Wright, *The Epistles of Paul to the Colossians and to Philemon* (Leicester: Inter-Varsity Press, 1986), 79.
96. Inaugural address at the opening of the Free University of Amsterdam, October 20, 1880, cited in *Abraham Kuyper: A Centennial Reader*, ed. James D. Bratt (Grand Rapids, MI: Eerdmans, 1998), 488.

rationalist. When I watched from the terraces the great Tottenham football (soccer) team of the sixties (Blanchflower, White, Mackay, Greaves), I did not stop to ask whether they had made professions of faith.

1.3   Special Revelation[97]

Calvin stresses the necessity of Scripture, since something more is needed if we are to know the Creator even in creation.[98] Scripture, Calvin writes, is the preservative against idolatry and polytheism.[99] Moreover, the human mind is ceaselessly prone to conjure up new and artificial religions.[100] Even Psalm 19, which extols the glory of God in creation (vv. 1–6), proceeds to focus on the law of God (vv. 7–12).[101] As Bavinck wrote, "Not a single religion can survive on general revelation alone."[102] A classic statement on the necessity of special revelation—in particular, Scripture—was given in the WCF (1647).

> Although the light of nature, and the works of creation and providence do so far manifest the goodness, wisdom, and power of God, as to leave men inexcusable; yet they are not sufficient to give that knowledge of God, and of his will, which is necessary unto salvation. Therefore it pleased the Lord, at sundry times, and in divers manners, to reveal Himself, and to declare that His will unto His Church; and afterwards, for the better preserving and propagating of the truth, and for the more sure establishment and comfort of the Church against the corruption of the flesh, and the malice of Satan and of the world, to commit the same wholly unto writing: which maketh the Holy Scripture to be most necessary: those former ways of God's revealing His will unto His people being now ceased. (1.1)

1.3.1   Revelation Is from the Living God

Aquinas makes a crucial statement: "It is said of God that he is life itself, and not only that he is a living thing."[103] Prior to his bringing into

---

97. This will be the mode underlying the rest of the book. I will probe the church's confession and various key figures in its transmission, asking questions of Scripture and attempting to explain its witness. As for special revelation itself, I will simply define it here and leave it until after the discussion of God.
98. Calvin, *Institutes*, 1.6.1.
99. Calvin, *Institutes*, 1.6.2.
100. Calvin, *Institutes*, 1.6.3.
101. Calvin, *Institutes*, 1.6.4.
102. Bavinck, *RD*, 1:324.
103. Aquinas, *ST* 1a.3.3.

[handwritten margin note: Letter has been blacked-out - quietly his way through a fair.]

existence life other than himself, he himself was eternally brimful of life. Revelation—general as well as special—underlines this point; it entails the fact that God himself is the active agent making himself known. This lies behind Bavinck's comment that the eternal generation of the Son is necessary in order for God to create; that God is fullness of life, overflowing fecundity, establishes the ground for his decision to create.[104] The same applies to revelation. Revelation is subsequent to creation, for there needed to be creatures for God to reveal himself to them.

By definition, revelation is not the product of human ingenuity or attainment; it is solely from God. Barth argued that it is impossible for humans to reach up to God and discover him or his plans. Rather, revelation works the other way, from the side of God. The impossibility is possible for God.[105] "Nothing is too wonderful for God."[106] God takes the initiative. He reveals himself.

Special revelation existed from the time humans existed, before the question of salvation ever came into purview. Prior to the fall, Adam needed word revelation from God defining him as "Adam," as made in the image and likeness of God, with a task to fulfill of procreation and government (Gen. 1:26–28), tilling the ground (Gen. 2:15), and acting as a priest-king on behalf of God.

After the fall, God encountered Adam and his wife with words of reproof, judgment, and yet hope (Gen. 3:8–19). To the patriarchs God frequently appeared in human or angelic form. These theophanies were prominent in the Pentateuchal period and on into the time of the judges (Gen. 3:8–19; 15:1–21; 18:1–33; 32:22–32; Ex. 3:1ff.; 13:21–22; 19:16–25; 24:9–11; 33:7–34:9; Josh. 5:13–15; Judg. 2:1–5; 13:2–23). During this time, he often chose dreams and visions to make his will known (Gen. 15:1–21; 28:10–22). Later, with the prophets, God used both written and oral communication. Miracles occurred on various occasions, normally in connection with redemptive deeds: the exodus, the start of the prophetic era, the ministry of Jesus and the apostles. Miracles were signs, not drawing attention to themselves but reaching a climax with the incarnation of the Son (John 1:1–4, 14–18; 14:1–11; Heb. 1:1–4), his saving work on the cross, his resurrection, and his ascension to the right hand of the Father. These events are all part of a great unified plan, for

---

104. Bavinck, *RD*, 2:420.
105. Barth, *CD*, I/1:340.
106. Bavinck, *RD*, 1:336.

ιck says, "The revelation that Scripture discloses to us does not just consist in a number of disconnected words and isolated facts but is one single historical and organic whole."[107]

1.3.2 How Far Can God Be Known? — *Does he answer this Q?*

God is knowable and he makes himself known. He made humanity in his own image, and he reveals himself by his works and words, and in the person of his Son incarnate, who is not merely the revealer but the revelation (John 14:1–9).

The central purpose of special revelation is gracious: to bring salvation. Unfolding progressively over wide epochs, it is rooted in human history and historical events. Above all, revelation centers in Jesus Christ, the eternal Son (John 14:1–9; Col. 1:15–20; Heb. 1:1–14). He is apprehensible (known truly) but incomprehensible (not known exhaustively, nor enclosed by our thought), for God has accommodated himself to our capacity, coming and living among us as man (John 1:18; 1 Tim. 1:17). The incomprehensibility of God is crucial for the whole of theology. It alerts us to our limitations, our finitude, while simultaneously asserting the reality of God's revelation as a faithful testimony to who he is and all that he has done. The staggering point is that Jesus Christ, the eternal Son of the Father, one with him from eternity, is also man. This is the supreme and overwhelming pledge that we can and do know God, for Christ, the eternal Son, has taken humanity into perfect union.

1.3.3 The Nature of Our Knowledge of and Language about God

Our knowledge of God is not *univocal*, identical to his in manner or content. If it were, it would yield a precise identity between God's knowledge and ours. His knowledge of this or that, from 2×2=4 to more complex realities, would not differ in principle from the way we know things. This would be rationalism. It would erode the Creator-creature distinction. God transcends his creation.

Conversely, neither is our knowledge of God or creation, in relation to God's knowledge, to be understood as *equivocal*, in principle totally different. If it were, there would be no correspondence between our knowledge and God's knowledge, an unbridgeable gap between God

---

107. Bavinck, *RD*, 1:340.

and ourselves. We could not know God at all, nor know his creati(
accurately.

Instead, our knowledge of God is *analogical*, with both a correspondence and a difference between our knowledge of God and who he is in
himself, between our knowledge of this or that created entity and God's
knowledge of the same entity. This is based on the biblical revelation that
God is the infinite Creator, knowing all things instantaneously and comprehensively, and we are his creatures, yet made in his image for partnership, with a correspondence between him and us. This is even clearer in
the light of the incarnation, whereby the eternal Son took human nature
into permanent indivisible personal union. The assumed nature is forever
distinct from the Son who assumes it, but it is also his, inseparable and
indivisible from him. Thus, Jesus can say to Philip, "Whoever has seen
me has seen the Father" (John 14:9). If there were no correspondence
between God and humanity, this would not have been possible.

This is of monumental importance. It affects the way we interpret
the Bible. God speaks to us in ways we can understand. His revelation
is true. He reveals himself in a manner that we can grasp, like a father
speaking to his young child. Yet the reality transcends the revelation. The
same applies to our knowledge of creation, whether through Scripture,
science, or personal observation. Aquinas considered this at length and
in some detail.[108]

1.3.4 *Revelation and the Bible*
God's revelation was committed to writing in Scripture.

> Therefore it pleased the Lord, at sundry times, and in diverse man-
> ners, to reveal Himself, and to declare that His will unto His Church;
> and afterwards, for the better preserving and propagating of his truth,
> and for the more sure establishment and comfort of His Church
> against the corruption of the flesh, and the malice of Satan and of the
> world, to commit the same wholly unto writing; which maketh the
> Holy Scripture to be *most necessary*. (WCF, 1.1, my italics)

Therefore, the Lord revealed himself and his will freely ("it pleased the
Lord") *to his church*. Notice the distinction between this written revelation and God's revelation in creation; that is universal, this is focused.

---

108. Aquinas, *ST* 1a.13.1–12, esp. 1a.13.5.

God made himself and his will known in two distinct but inseparable ways, as the WCF notes. He revealed himself and his will in *acts* of revelation; following that, he committed it to *writing* in Holy Scripture. The Bible as a written record is necessary for the better preserving of God's revelation. Failing that, we would be left high and dry, ignorant of God, inexcusable for our sin, destitute of God's grace.

The WCF distinguishes between the Lord revealing *himself* to his church and, in doing so, revealing *his will*. While the two are inseparable, the distinction is important, for at all stages of redemptive history God progressively reveals who he is. It also distinguishes between revelation and inscripturation. The revelation precedes the Bible. However, the revelation and the writing are the same, in that what was committed to writing was what the Lord revealed of himself and of his will. We cannot drive a wedge between revelation and the Bible. The same Lord who revealed himself committed his revelation to writing and preserved it. Between the acts of God in the history of salvation, from Adam to the apostles, and the written record and explanation of those acts there is both a distinction but an identity, a unity-in-diversity. We distinguish between the Bible and God's actions in revelation; it is equally vital to maintain their unity and identity. This is a strong bulwark against bibliolatry, on the one hand—e.g., hymns addressed to the Bible, such as "Holy Bible, book divine, / precious treasure thou art mine"—and the neoorthodox separation of revelation and the Bible, on the other.[109]

This revelation, in both deed and word, contains both personal and propositional elements. The Lord reveals *himself,* and he also reveals *his will* relating to salvation. At each stage of covenant history, God reveals his name alongside his covenanting. God's committing of his revelation to writing is necessary for us to know him and his will for us since it preserves the record. While God could have chosen some other way for us to receive his will, his permanent recording in writing surpasses oral transmission, which can more readily be corrupted.[110] Because of the enormous importance of the Bible as the definitive record of God's revelation, breathed out by the Spirit in the words of the human authors, utterly reliable and without error on all it pronounces, we shall discuss this in detail in chapters 6–8. However, special revelation comes to its

---

109. See Warfield, *Assembly*, 194.
110. See a similar argument in Amandus Polanus, *Syntagma theologiae Christianae* (Basel, 1609), 69. Muller also cites this passage in Muller, *PRRD*, 2:171.

highest expression as God reveals himself to be Trinity (Matt. 28:19–20). This is the apex of covenant history. It is the supreme revelation of God's name. It is the theme of the next three chapters.

Further Reading

Anselm. *Proslogion*. In *Anselm of Canterbury: The Major Works*, edited by Brian Davies and G. R. Evans, 82–104. Oxford: Oxford University Press, 1998.

Barth, Karl. *Fides Quaerens Intellectum*. Pittsburgh: Pickwick, 1975. This advanced work requires knowledge of Latin.

Calvin, John. *Institutes of the Christian Religion*. 1.3.1–1.6.2.

Helm, Paul. "Natural Theology and the *Sensus Divinitatis*." In *John Calvin's Ideas*, 209–45. Oxford: Oxford University Press, 2004.

Study Questions

1. The Bible never attempts to prove the existence of God; it is assumed. In the light of this, consider what value, if any, arguments for God's existence may have.

2. How far is general revelation necessary for our understanding of special revelation?

3. To what extent is the *sensus divinitatis*, as Calvin termed it, evident in atheistic ideologies?

4. "Although they knew God" (Rom. 1:21), Paul writes of unbelievers who suppress the truth. How did they know God, to what extent did they know him, and what was the impact of their suppression of the truth? Was this suppression final and irrevocable? What might it say regarding contemporary Western society?

2

The Trinity (1)

Biblical Basis

God is Trinity from eternity. The Trinity is revealed in the Old Testament in latent form and in the New Testament implicitly and pervasively, but the full-fledged *doctrine* awaited prolonged reflection by the church. The Old Testament stresses that Yahweh is unique, but there are hints of plurality in the creation account, in the angel of the Lord, in certain psalms, and elsewhere. The New Testament presents Jesus as the Son in relation to God as his Father, distinct from him and yet one, as the Creator, Judge, and Savior, equal to and identical with God, the object of worship. The risen Christ is called Lord, the effective functional equivalent of *YHWH* (Yahweh), God's covenant name. To the Holy Spirit are ascribed the characteristics and functions of God. The Spirit is linked with the Father and the Son as one in the baptismal formula and elsewhere. The question of the Trinity was being raised and answered in the later New Testament.

We must distinguish between the doctrine of the Trinity and the Trinity itself. God always is, and he always is triune. From eternity he is the Father, the Son, and the Holy Spirit, one indivisible being, three irreducible persons.

The doctrine of the Trinity is the developed formulation of what the church understands God to have revealed in the history of revelation

about
his
personhood

and redemption, as recorded in Scripture. Responding to erroneous ideas that imperiled the gospel, the church used refined concepts, language stretched to express the reality God had disclosed.

The Trinity is revealed in the Old Testament in latent form and in the New Testament implicitly but pervasively. However, the full-fledged *doctrine* awaited prolonged reflection on the biblical record. As Wainwright observes: "In so far as a doctrine is an answer, however fragmentary, to a problem, there is a doctrine of the Trinity in the New Testament. In so far as it is a formal statement of a position, there is no doctrine of the Trinity in the New Testament."[1] Here we must differ from Warfield, who wrote that the New Testament "is not the record of the development of the doctrine" for "it everywhere presupposes the doctrine as the fixed possession of the Christian community";[2] indeed, "this doctrine underlies the whole New Testament as its constant presupposition."[3] The issue turns on how one defines a doctrine. My understanding is that it is to be regarded as a carefully formulated statement by the church of the overall teaching of Scripture, perhaps closer to dogma. Warfield is correct that the Trinity is revealed in the Old and New Testaments; however, the precise formulation awaited later thought.

2.1   Progressive Revelation of the Trinity

The doctrine of the Trinity is latent in the Old Testament. The evidence for the Trinity in the Old Testament is best seen in retrospect, much as we might read a detective novel and miss many of the clues, then reread it and, knowing the eventual outcome, recognize the evidence we overlooked the first time. In this sense, the Trinity is present in the Old Testament, but the evidence is scattered and somewhat opaque, awaiting the clearer light of the New Testament and its cumulative pointers.

The major reason for this is the pervasive monotheism of the Old Testament. Israel was time and again taught that there is one God

1. Arthur Wainwright, *The Trinity in the New Testament* (London: SPCK, 1963), 4. A fuller discussion of the themes in this chapter and the following can be found in Robert Letham, *The Holy Trinity: In Scripture, History, Theology, and Worship* (Phillipsburg, NJ: P&R, 2004) and in a second edition, 2019.
2. Benjamin B. Warfield, "The Biblical Doctrine of the Trinity," in *Biblical and Theological Studies*, ed. Samuel Craig (Philadelphia: Presbyterian and Reformed, 1952), 32.
3. Warfield, "Biblical Doctrine of the Trinity," 36.

only—Yahweh, who had taken his people into covenant with him. Deuteronomy 6:4–5 was central to Israel's faith. "Hear, O Israel: The LORD our God, the LORD is one. You shall love the LORD your God with all your heart and with all your soul and with all your might." These words, and the whole law, repudiate pagan polytheism. Canaanite religions would prove to be a challenge to Israel. A cafeteria of divinities lurked in the ancient Near East, lifeless territorial deities with authority over their own people. In this confusion, it was imperative that Israel realize—often the hard way—that Yahweh was the one true and living God, supreme over the entire creation (Pss. 115:4–8; 135:4–7, 15–18). The lesson was finally learned only through the painful tragedy of exile.[4] Isaiah is full of assertions of the uniqueness of Yahweh:

> Thus says the LORD, the King of Israel
>   and his Redeemer, the LORD of hosts:
> I am the first and I am the last;
>   besides me there is no god.
> Who is like me? Let him proclaim it.
>   Let him declare and set it before me,
> since I appointed an ancient people.
>   Let them declare what is to come, and what will happen.
> Fear not, nor be afraid;
>   have I not told you from of old and declared it?
>   And you are my witnesses!
> Is there a God besides me?
>   There is no Rock; I know not any. (Isa. 44:6–8; cf. 40:9–31;
>   42:8; Zech. 14:9)

The creation account in Genesis was itself a powerful counter to the axiomatic assumption in the ancient Near East that the nations' gods were territorial, presiding over the area where their devotees lived but without jurisdiction beyond. In this light the conflict between the great king Sennacherib the Assyrian and the prophet Isaiah is crucial (2 Kings 18–19). Recorded three times in the Old Testament, it demonstrates Yahweh's universal domain. The central point is the duel between

---

4. "All idolatrous worship had been abolished by that time." Jules Lebreton, *History of the Dogma of the Trinity: From Its Origins to the Council of Nicea*, 8th ed., trans. Algar Thorold (London: Burns Oates and Washbourne, 1939), 74.

the word of the great king, backed up by all the political and economic muscle and military might of the greatest power on earth, and, on the other hand, the word of Yahweh, his human agents utterly powerless, completely at the great king's mercy. There is no contest. The word of Yahweh triumphs with ease!

In the light of this monotheistic faith, the Pentateuchal passages concerning the angel of the Lord and various hints of distinction within God's being fitted a monotheistic framework, not a polytheistic one. This axiom of Israel's belief made claims to deity on the part of Jesus a matter of blasphemy in the eyes of the establishment.

The doctrine of the Trinity is implicit in the New Testament. The New Testament was written following the great events of the incarnation of the Son and the sending of the Holy Spirit. The apostolic writings look back on the momentous change that these acts of revelation introduced. Clearly, Jesus Christ is the Son of the Father, one with him from eternity; and the Holy Spirit, sent by the Father and the Son, is one with them. The baptismal formula spelled this out (Matt. 28:19–20). From the start, it was the central element in the faith and worship of the church.

Yet the New Testament writers proceed with caution and do not state explicitly that God is triune, still less spell out a doctrine of the Trinity. For the church to assert that Jesus Christ is one with God from eternity, distinct from the Father yet one indivisible being, had to be handled with great care. The message needed to be presented in a way that was not misconstrued.

Furthermore, when the gospel was taken into the Gentile world, it faced a catalog of religions, each with its own deity, sometimes with a plurality. While these traditional religions were on the wane and not often taken seriously, the church had to exercise prudence in expressing the truth about Christ and the Holy Spirit, so that it was not taken to mean that Christ was merely one divine being among many.

For these reasons, we rarely encounter anything like an express statement in the New Testament that God is Trinity. That is no problem. The information needed to piece together such a teaching is pervasive, all the more powerful in being presented without the slightest self-consciousness, but incidentally and under the surface, with no need for explanation or defense.

2.2   The Old Testament Foundation

2.2.1   *Hints of Plurality in the Old Testament*

While a Jewish reader looking at the Old Testament will see monotheism writ large, in the light of the fullness of revelation in Christ as recorded in the New Testament, we can see clues that were there all along but are clearer now. In Genesis 1:1–5, God creates, the Spirit of God broods over the waters, and God speaks his creative word. Later, when he determines to create humanity, God engages in self-deliberation: "Let us make man in our image, after our likeness" (Gen. 1:26).[5] While the New Testament never refers to this statement, it is by no means unwarranted to see here a proleptic reference to the Trinity. The New Testament does not refer to *everything*, but it provides the principle that the Old Testament contains in seed form what is more fully made known in the New. In terms of the *sensus plenior* (the fuller sense or meaning) of Scripture, God's words here attest a plurality in God, later expressed in the doctrine of the Trinity. The original readers would not have grasped this, but we, with the full plot disclosed, can revisit the passage and see the clues.

This vital point is underlined by other—poetic—accounts of creation. Creation is said to be "by the word of the LORD . . . / and by the breath of his mouth" (Ps. 33:6). Job acknowledges that the Spirit of God made him (Job 33:4; cf. 27:3), and the psalmist also talks of God's Spirit as Creator (Ps. 104:30).

Genesis 1 itself indicates a threefold manner of creation; by direct fiat (vv. 3, 9, 11, 14–15), by labor (vv. 7, 16, 21, 25), and through the ministerial cooperation of the creation itself (vv. 11, 24).

---

5. Von Rad comments that this signifies the high point and goal to which all God's creative activity is directed. But what does it mean? A variety of interpretations have been advanced to explain it. Some suggest God is addressing the angels and placing himself in the heavenly court, so that man is made like the angels. Gerhard von Rad, *Genesis: A Commentary*, rev. ed. (Philadelphia: Westminster, 1961), 57–59. However, the agents addressed are invited to share in the creation of man, and this is never attributed to the angels elsewhere in the Bible. Second, Driver is one of those who suggest a plural of majesty, a figure of speech underlining God's dignity and greatness. S. R. Driver, *The Book of Genesis: With Introduction and Notes* (London: Methuen, 1926), 14. However, this is no longer as favored as once it was. Among other things, plurals of majesty are rarely if ever used with verbs. Third, Westermann and many recent interpreters favor a plural of self-deliberation or self-encouragement. Yet few parallels support it. Wenham puts forward a variant on the theme of the heavenly court, except that he argues for God inviting the angels to witness the creation of man rather than to participate in it. He points to Job 38:4–7, where, at creation, the morning stars are said to sing together and all the sons of God (angels?) shout for joy. Gordon J. Wenham, *Genesis 1–15*, Word Biblical Commentary 1 (Waco, TX: Word, 1987), 28.

Later, the angel of the Lord is both distinguished from and identified with God. The angel sometimes speaks as God (Gen. 16:7–13; 21:17–18; 22:11–18; cf. 12:1–3; 31:11–13). This also happens after the conquest (Judg. 2:1–5). The angel appears to Moses in the burning bush, while out of the bush the Lord sees, speaks, and identifies himself as God (Ex. 3:4–6). Appearing to Gideon, the angel of the Lord *is* the Lord (Judg. 6:12, 14ff., 20–24).

[handwritten margin note: 9? an angel. or proxy.]

Three men visit Abraham and are at various stages identified as angels, humans, and God in a puzzling juxtaposition (Gen. 18:1–19:22). When he appears to Samson's parents, an angel of the Lord is equated with a man of God by Manoah's wife at his first showing (Judg. 13:3–8), while the second time he is the angel of God, the Lord, and also a man (Judg. 13:9–20). Yahweh addresses Yahweh (Pss. 45:6–7; 110:1). These passages have puzzled rabbinic scholars.

While the distinctive covenant name of God, *YHWH* (יהוה), occurs nearly seven thousand times in the Old Testament, God calls himself "Father" on just over twenty occasions, and is not invoked as Father. Both the stress on monotheism and the commandment against images for worship explain why the name is so scarce, and also why feminine images and metaphors for God are absent.[6] Indeed, *Father* usually refers to the covenantal relationship of Yahweh to Israel (Ex. 4:22–23; Hos. 11:1).

The Spirit of God is mentioned nearly four hundred times in the Old Testament. Generally, the Spirit is seen as the power of God at work, but mostly as little more than a divine attribute. Sometimes poetic parallelism implies that the Spirit of God is identical to Yahweh (Ps. 139:7), but there is little hint of the Spirit as a distinct person. Rather, the Spirit is God's divine power or breath,[7] "God's manifest and powerful activity in the world."[8]

Frequently, we encounter anthropomorphisms. The Spirit has characteristics—guiding, instructing, being grieved—that hint at personhood. The Spirit, or breath, of God gives life (Gen. 1:2; Pss. 33:9; 104:29–30), coming upon the inert bones in Ezekiel's vision to animate them (Ezek. 37:8–10). The Spirit of God empowers people for various forms of

6. Gerald O'Collins, SJ, *The Tripersonal God: Understanding and Interpreting the Trinity* (London: Geoffrey Chapman, 1999), 12.

7. Wainwright, *Trinity*, 30.

8. O'Collins, *Tripersonal God*, 32.

service in God's kingdom (Ex. 31:3; 35:31–34; Num. 27:18; Judg. 3:10; 1 Sam. 16:13) and is the protector of God's people (1 Sam. 19:20, 23; Isa. 63:11–12; Hag. 2:5), indwelling them (Num. 27:18; Ezek. 2:2; 3:24; Dan. 4:8–9, 18; 5:11; Mic. 3:8), as well as resting upon and empowering the Messiah (Isa. 11:2; 42:1; 61:1). The most remarkable actions of the patriarchs and prophets are all due to the Spirit of God, whether they be those of Gideon, Samson, Saul, or Joseph, who is able to interpret dreams by the Spirit (Gen. 41:38). All these events were to protect Israel or to develop its relationship to Yahweh. However, the Spirit's action, not his nature, is in view.[9] Yahweh acts through the Spirit.[10] To suggest the contrary would have challenged the insistence of Deuteronomy that there is only one God, for no tools existed at that time to distinguish such a putative claim from the pagan polytheism Israel was bound to reject. In these contexts, the Spirit is seen as the power of God at work, no more.

However, a development helps pave the way for the Christian teaching. Generally, the Spirit comes only intermittently on the prophets and on select persons, such as Samson and Saul, besides his general presence with his people (Ps. 51:11). However, later the Spirit is seen as a permanent possession (Isa. 11:2; Zech. 12:10),[11] is linked with the Messiah (Isa. 11:1–2; 42:1; 61:1), and is expected as a future gift to all God's people (Ezek. 11:19; 36:26; 37:14; Joel 2:28ff.; Zech. 12:10). Thus "the developing idea of the Spirit provided a climate in which plurality within the Godhead was conceivable."[12]

Warfield's comments are important.[13] He considers the work of the Spirit in connection with the cosmos, the kingdom of God, and the individual, concluding that the Spirit was at work in the Old Testament in all the ways he works in the New. However, what is new in the New Testament are the miraculous endowments of the apostles and the Spirit's worldwide mission, promised in the Old Testament but only now realized. The Old Testament prepared for the New Testament, the Spirit preserving the people of God, whereas now he effects the fulfillment of God's promises, producing "the fruitage and gathering of the harvest."[14]

---

9. Lebreton, *Trinity*, 88.
10. Wainwright, *Trinity*, 31.
11. Wainwright, *Trinity*, 32.
12. Wainwright, *Trinity*, 32–33.
13. Benjamin B. Warfield, "The Spirit of God in the Old Testament," in *Biblical and Theological Studies*, 127–56.
14. Warfield, "Spirit of God," 155–56.

2.2.2 The Word and Wisdom of God

After the exile, God is seen to work through a variety of heavenly figures, with divine attributes and powers: wisdom, Word, and principal angels like Michael (Dan. 10:1–12:13). Wisdom and Word provide the closest hints that Yahweh is not a solitary monad.

Wisdom is mentioned in Job 15:7–8 and 28:12, implying preexistence but hardly personal distinction. Wisdom is the chief figure in two poems in Proverbs. In Proverbs 8, wisdom addresses human beings, promising the same things God gives.[15] In chapter 9, wisdom presents herself as "a personified abstraction," in antithetical parallel with folly (v. 13ff.). However, from 8:22 more than metaphor is present, for wisdom cries aloud, advises, instructs, hates and loves, and is portrayed as God's master workman. Wisdom is identified with God, yet also distinguished.[16] These themes are repeated in the intertestamental literature. Wisdom has a role in creation, is frequently identified with the law, and is clearly distinguished from God.[17] The idea of wisdom is used by Paul in 1 Corinthians 1:18–24 and Colossians 2:1–3, and by the early Christians to explain who Christ is.[18]

The psalmist presents the Word of God as active in creation, in parallel with God's Spirit (Ps. 33:6–9). God spoke (Ex. 3:4ff.; Ps. 33:6–9). But the Word is never personified in the Old Testament as wisdom is. It was Philo, with the aid of Hellenistic influence present in Alexandria, who thought of the Logos in a personalized way.[19] Lebreton suggests that "if these various obscure and elementary conceptions are not sufficient of themselves to constitute a doctrine of the Trinity, they at least prepare the soul for the Christian revelation."[20]

2.2.3 The Expectation of the Coming of the Messiah

The prophets occasionally hold out the prospect of a future deliverer. Yahweh himself was to come and save his people and bring them to an age of peace and prosperity. Isaiah speaks of a child, a son who would rule, whose dominion was to be of unending peace, security, and justice.

15. Lebreton, *Trinity*, 91–92; O'Collins, *Tripersonal God*, 24.
16. Lebreton, *Trinity*, 92–94; Wainwright, *Trinity*, 33–34.
17. Lebreton, *Trinity*, 94–98.
18. See James D. G. Dunn, *Christology in the Making: A New Testament Inquiry into the Origins of the Doctrine of the Incarnation* (Philadelphia: Westminster, 1980), 163–212.
19. Wainwright, *Trinity*, 35–36; Lebreton, *Trinity*, 99–100.
20. Lebreton, *Trinity*, 81.

Interactive but forgetable section on Trinity & OT.

This son was to sit on the throne of David and be called, among other things, "Mighty God" (Isa. 9:6). Micah foretells a ruler over Judah, born in Bethlehem, of superhuman origins, "whose coming forth is from of old, / from ancient days" (Mic. 5:2–5), associated with God but not identical to him. In Daniel, the Son of Man (Dan. 7:13–14) is given universal, everlasting, and impregnable dominion. The exact identity of this figure, presented in Daniel without recourse to any other source, is unclear. Neither the prophet's contemporaries nor later generations grasped the full meaning of these oracles, and it is only with the presence of Jesus, and the reality of who he was and what he did, that their full meaning is disclosed, for then the New Testament writers apply to Jesus the prophetic statements referring to Yahweh.[21]

———

Very clear quote of O'Collins here?

The Old Testament provides the essential foundation without which the full Christian doctrine of God could not exist.[22] As O'Collins puts it, "The OT contains, in anticipation, categories used to express and elaborate the Trinity. To put this point negatively, a theology of the Trinity that ignores or plays down the OT can only be radically deficient"[23] while, from the positive angle, "the New Testament and post–New Testament Christian language for the tripersonal God flowed from the Jewish Scriptures"; for though deeply modified in the light of Jesus's life, death, and resurrection, naming God as Father, Son, and Spirit "found its roots in the OT."[24]

This is not to say that by the first century there had emerged in Israel a clear and coherent picture of plurality within the one being of God. These ideas in the Old Testament were scattered and had not formed into a coherent pattern.[25] Notwithstanding, the Old Testament provided the means both to distinguish and to hold together the role of Son/wisdom/ Word and Spirit, since these were vivid personifications, not abstract

---

21. Lebreton, *Trinity*, 101.
22. For further reading, see Matthew W. Bates, *The Birth of the Trinity: Jesus, God, and Spirit in New Testament and Early Christian Interpretations of the Old Testament* (Oxford: Oxford University Press, 2015).
23. O'Collins, *Tripersonal God*, 11.
24. O'Collins, *Tripersonal God*, 32.
25. Lebreton, *Trinity*, 102–3.

principles. The ultimate acknowledgment by the church of the triunity of God was "providentially prepared" by these foreshadowings.[26] The Old Testament personalizations helped lay the ground for the eventual leap to persons, for "the post-exilic Jews had an idea of plurality within the Godhead," and so "the idea of plurality within unity was already implicit in Jewish theology."[27]

However, there is no evidence in the Old Testament that the question the church had to answer had been raised. That problem was that Christ was not a mere emanation from God, and he was more than a personalized concept. He was a man with whom the apostles conversed and with whom they worked. Indeed, they had eavesdropped on "an interaction within the divine personality," "a dialogue within the Godhead" of which there is little if any trace in the Old Testament. Wainwright continues, "The idea of extension of divine personality is Hebraic. The idea of the interaction within the extended personality is neither Hebraic nor Hellenistic but Christian."[28] This is the great leap forward that the New Testament contains and that the church was to develop.

As so often, Gregory of Nazianzus gives us a superbly appropriate summary, ingeniously pointing to the historical outworking of revelation, to explain its cautious, gradual, and progressive unfolding of who God is:

> The Old Testament proclaimed the Father openly, and the Son more obscurely. The New manifested the Son, and suggested the deity of the Spirit. Now the Spirit himself dwells among us, and supplies us with a clearer demonstration of himself. For it was not safe, when the Godhead of the Father was not yet acknowledged, plainly to proclaim the Son; nor when that of the Son was not yet received to burden us further . . . with the Holy Spirit. . . . It was necessary that, increasing little by little, and, as David says, by ascensions from glory to glory, the full splendour of the Trinity should gradually shine forth.[29]

2.3 Jesus and the Father

Of first importance is the constant and unprecedented way in which Jesus talks of God. He calls him his Father, with the corollary that he is the Father's Son. While the title "son of God" was used in the Old Testament for

26. O'Collins, *Tripersonal God*, 33–34.
27. Wainwright, *Trinity*, 37.
28. Wainwright, *Trinity*, 38–40.
29. Gregory of Nazianzus, *Oration 31* 26 (NPNF², 7:326).

the Messiah, and on occasion for Israel itself, it was without precedent for an individual to speak in this way, let alone for it to be his normal usage. "Father," an occasional designation of God in the Old Testament, is in the New his personal name, known in relation to Jesus Christ his Son.[30]

The relation between Jesus the Son and the Father is unique. Human fatherhood derives from God the Father and is to be measured by him, not vice versa (Eph. 3:14–15). The name Father refers to the unique relations of the Father to the Son, which are mutual relations within the being of God. God's revelation as the Father does not refer to a general fatherhood of all his creatures, nor to the way human fathers relate to their sons. Moreover, as Toon comments, the name "the Father" is not merely a simile (as if God is simply *like* a father) or even a metaphor (an unusual use of language drawing attention to aspects of God's nature in surprising and odd terms), but it is a definite personal name. In contrast, maternal language for God is a simile in the Old Testament but never a metaphor,[31] and is completely absent in the New Testament. Father is the proper name for God and does not merely describe what he is like.

Jesus refers to his relation with the Father in all four Gospels. He speaks of the temple as "my Father's house" (Luke 2:49; John 2:16). At Jesus's baptism, the Father declares him to be his Son (Matt. 3:17), setting his seal upon him (John 5:27). Repeatedly Jesus asserts that he was sent into the world by the Father (John 5:30, 36; 6:38–40; 8:16–18, 26, 29) and that he shares with the Father in raising the dead (John 5:24–29) and in judging the world (John 5:27). All will honor him just as they honor the Father (John 5:23). The Father gives him his disciples and draws them to him (John 6:37–65). The Father knows him and loves him, while he fulfills the Father's charge (John 10:15–18). In turn, Jesus prays to the Father (Matt. 6:9; John 17:1–26). "Abba" is his normal way of addressing God (Matt. 16:17; Mark 13:32; Luke 22:29–30), a familiar form of address, the Aramaic for father, though it does not mean "daddy."[32] In Gethsemane and on the cross Jesus calls on the Father, *in extremis* (e.g., Matt. 26:39–42; Luke 23:34).[33]

---

30. Wainwright, *Trinity*, 171–95. Forty times in Paul, God is said to be the Father. John uses θεός (God) for Father 122 times.

31. Peter Toon, *Our Triune God: A Biblical Portrayal of the Trinity* (Wheaton, IL: BridgePoint, 1996), 145–48.

32. James Barr, "Abba Isn't Daddy," *JTS* 39 (1988): 28–47.

33. Thomas F. Torrance, *The Christian Doctrine of God: One Being, Three Persons* (Edinburgh: T&T Clark, 1996), 54.

In John 17, Jesus speaks of the glory he shared with the Father before creation, anticipating creation's renewal (vv. 5, 22–24), having completed the work the Father gave him (v. 4). He reflects on his union and mutual indwelling with the Father (vv. 20ff.). Earlier he defended his equality and identity with the Father (John 10:30; 14:6–11, 20), an indivisible union, so that his own word would be the criterion the Father uses in the judgment (John 5:22–24; 12:44–50). Jesus tells Mary Magdalene he will ascend to his Father (John 20:17; cf. 14:1–3; 16:10, 17, 28).

On the other hand, Jesus also says that he is less than the Father (John 14:28). This refers to his incarnation, in which he restricts himself to human limitations. So, he does nothing other than he sees the Father doing (John 5:19). As the Father raises the dead, so the Son gives life to whoever he wills (John 5:21). As the Father has life in himself, so he has given to the Son to have life in himself and to exercise judgment (John 5:26–29). The Son derives certain things from the Father, yet Jesus puts this in the context of their indivisible union. Thus, to Thomas he says that to know him is to know the Father, and to Philip, "Whoever has seen me has seen the Father" (John 14:6–9). Behind this is the fact that he and the Father are one (John 10:30), and that he is, with the Father, the object of the disciples' faith (John 14:1). No one can come to the Father except through Jesus. Throughout John 14–16 Jesus refers to himself in relation to both the Father and the Holy Spirit. He mentions the mutual indwelling of the three. The Father will send the Spirit in response to Jesus's own request (John 14:16ff., 26; 15:26). So the disciples' prayer to the Father is to be made in the name of Jesus (John 15:16).

In Matthew, Jesus claims mutual knowledge and sovereignty with the Father.

> At that time Jesus declared, "I thank you, Father, Lord of heaven and earth, that you have hidden these things from the wise and understanding and revealed them to little children; yes, Father, for such was your gracious will. All things have been handed over to me by my Father, and no one knows the Son except the Father, and no one knows the Father except the Son and anyone to whom the Son chooses to reveal him." (Matt. 11:25–27)

H. R. Mackintosh described this passage as "the most important for Christology in the New Testament," speaking as it does of "the unqualified correlation of the Father and the Son."[34] Jesus describes himself as the Son and thanks the Father for hiding "these things" [the things Jesus did and taught] from the wise, while revealing them instead to babes. The Father is, he says, sovereign in revealing himself. However, Jesus immediately claims that he, the Son, has this sovereignty too. To know the Father is a gift given by the Son to whomever *he* chooses. As the Father reveals "these things" concerning the Son to whomever he pleases, so the Son reveals the Father—and "all things" the Father has committed to him—to whomever *he* pleases. Moreover, Jesus shares fully in the Father's comprehensive knowledge. Only the Father knows the Son, and only the Son knows the Father. Jesus shares fully in the sovereignty of God the Father, and his knowledge, with the Father's, is comprehensive and mutual. On the other hand, in passages such as Matthew 24:36, where Jesus says he is ignorant of the time of his parousia, which the Father alone knows, he refers to the voluntary restrictions of his incarnate state.

In short, Jesus as Son claims a relation of great personal intimacy with the Father, exclusive and unique, and marked by his full and willing obedience to the Father.[35] Jesus is distinct from the Father and yet one with him. As Bauckham comments, "Jesus is not saying that he and the Father are a single person, but that together they are one God."[36] This oneness distinguishes him from the prophets and, in the writings of Paul, entails his participation in God's attributes, sharing in his glory, so that the Son is "worthy to receive formal veneration with God in Christian assemblies."[37]

Paul, in his important statement about the Son[38] in Romans 1:3–4, distinguishes between the Son of God "of the seed of David according to the flesh" and the Son as he is "appointed Son of God with power by the Holy Spirit since the resurrection of the dead" (my trans.). Both phrases refer to Jesus Christ, God's Son (v. 3). God's Son was descended from David by his incarnation; he was resurrected by the Spirit to a new, transformed state—Son of God with power. As God's Son before the

---

34. H.R. Mackintosh, *The Doctrine of the Person of Jesus Christ* (Edinburgh: T&T Clark, 1912), 27.

35. D. R. Bauer, "Son of God," in *DJG*, 769–75.

36. Richard Bauckham, *Jesus and the God of Israel* (Milton Keynes: Paternoster, 2008), 104.

37. L. W. Hurtado, "Son of God," in *DPL*, 900–906.

38. On Jesus as the Son of God, see Donald Guthrie, *New Testament Theology* (Leicester: Inter-Varsity Press, 1981), 303–21; Richard Bauckham, "The Sonship of the Historical Jesus in Christology," *SJT* 31 (1978): 245–60.

crucifixion, he was in weakness, having "the form of a servant" (Phil. 2:7). Now that he has risen, he is exalted to the right hand of God the Father (Acts 2:33–36; Eph. 1:19–23; Phil. 2:9–11; Col. 1:18; Heb. 1:3–4) and reigns over the whole cosmos (Matt. 28:18), directing all things till all his enemies submit (1 Cor. 15:24–26), at which point death will finally be eliminated, and he will hand back the kingdom to the Father (1 Cor. 15:24–28). This dominating focus on Jesus as the Son in relation to the Father reveals a communion of life and love between the Father and the Son in the being of God, a distinction and an identity. In Toon's words, "It is in the relation of 'the Father and the Son' and 'the Son and the Father' that the true identity of Jesus is known and salvation is available. To take away the words is also to take away the reality."[39]

2.4 Jesus's Equality and Identity with God

Wainwright concludes that the evidence "favours the view that Jesus Christ was called God in Christian worship during New Testament times." But how would one articulate this in the face of Jewish monotheism and pagan polytheism?[40]

Jesus asserts his equality and identity with God in the face of blasphemy charges by the Jewish leaders. He is charged, among other things, with making himself equal with God (John 5:16–47) and, later, with identifying himself with God (John 10:25–39). His accusers threaten the penalty for blasphemy. In both cases, Jesus denies the charge, citing the plurality of witnesses required by Jewish law. His claims are true, not false. In John 14:1, Jesus coordinates himself with God as the object of faith: "Believe in God; believe also in me." Similarly, like frames around a picture, John opens his Gospel by referring to him as "God" (1:18), and in the end has Thomas confessing him as "my Lord and my God" (20:28).[41]

Paul's characteristic name for Jesus Christ is "Lord" (κύριος),[42] the Greek word commonly used for the tetragrammaton יהוה (*YHWH*), the

---

39. Toon, *Our Triune God*, 171. This is done by abandoning the vocabulary of Christian Trinitarianism, drawn from the Scriptures, in favor of impersonal epithets such as *Creator, Redeemer, sanctifier*; or *parent, child, spirit*; or some other human construction.

40. Wainwright, *Trinity*, 68–69; see 54–72.

41. For further reading, see Richard B. Hays, *Echoes of Scripture in the Gospels* (Waco, TX: Baylor University Press, 2016).

42. *Kyrios*. See Guthrie, *New Testament Theology*, 291–301; Wainwright, *Trinity*, 757–92; O'Collins, *Tripersonal God*, 54–59; Lebreton, *Trinity*, 267–80, 303–6; and from an Eastern perspective, Boris Bobrinskoy, *The Mystery of the Trinity: Trinitarian Experience and Vision in the*

covenant name of God in the Old Testament. In using it not occasionally or casually but pervasively, Paul shows he regards Jesus as having the status of God, fully and without abridgment. He makes no attempt to explain or defend it, mentioning it so unselfconsciously that, as Hurtado comments, it implies everyday currency among the early Christians. Paul's letters, the earliest of the New Testament documents, testify to belief in the full deity of Jesus Christ from the very start of the Christian church as its basic axiom, not as a point of contention. It was assumed as a given in Palestinian Christianity. This, Hurtado points out, is confirmed by the Aramaic acclamation in 1 Corinthians 16:22, μαράνα θά (*maran atha*: "Lord, come!"). Paul uses this in a Gentile context without explanation or translation, addressing Christ in a corporate, liturgical prayer, with the same reverence shown to God. Moreover, the roots of this prayer are Palestinian, widely familiar beyond its original source and probably pre-Pauline.[43] Bauckham writes of "its very early origin."[44] This fits well with the thesis of Seyoon Kim that the origins of Paul's gospel go back to the very earliest days of Christianity, a thesis Kim has defended strongly against his critics, particularly Dunn.[45] Hurtado refers to a range of places where Paul applies the tetragrammaton to Christ via κύριος "without explanation or justification, suggesting that his readers were already familiar with the term and its connotation."[46] In Witherington's words, John "is willing to predicate of Jesus what he predicates of the Lord God, because he sees them as on the same level."[47] In Romans 9:5 it is likely that Paul expressly designates Jesus Christ as θεός (God).[48]

Biblical and Patristic Tradition, trans. Anthony P. Gythiel (Crestwood, NY: St Vladimir's Seminary Press, 1999), 114ff.

43. Larry Hurtado, *One God, One Lord*, 3rd ed. (London: T&T Clark, 2015), 110–12; Hurtado, "Lord," in *DPL*, 560–69.

44. Bauckham, *Jesus and the God of Israel*, 128.

45. Seyoon Kim, *The Origin of Paul's Gospel* (Grand Rapids, MI: Eerdmans, 1982); Kim, *Paul and the New Perspective: Second Thoughts on the Origin of Paul's Gospel* (Grand Rapids, MI: Eerdmans, 2002).

46. Certainly in the following passages: Rom. 4:8 (Ps. 32:1–2); 9:28–29 (Isa. 1:9; 28:22); 10:16 (Isa. 53:1); 11:34 (Isa. 40:13); 15:11 (Ps. 117:1); 1 Cor. 3:20 (Ps. 94:11); 2 Cor. 6:17–18 (Isa. 52:11; 2 Sam. 7:14); probably in the following: Rom. 10:13 (Joel 2:32); 1 Cor. 1:31 (Jer. 9:23–24); 10:26 (Ps. 24:1); 2 Cor. 10:17 (Jer. 9:23–24); and possibly in a range of others. See Hurtado, "Lord," 563.

47. B. Witherington III, "Lord," in *DLNT*, 672.

48. See C. E. B. Cranfield, *A Critical and Exegetical Commentary on the Epistle to the Romans*, 2 vols., International Critical Commentary (Edinburgh: T&T Clark, 1975), 2:464–70; William Sanday and Arthur C. Headlam, *A Critical and Exegetical Commentary on the Epistle to the Romans*, International Critical Commentary (Edinburgh: T&T Clark, 1905), 233–38; B. M. Metzger, "The Punctuation of Rom. 9:5," in *Christ and Spirit in the New Testament: Studies in Honour of C. F. D. Moule*, ed. Barnabas Lindars and Stephen S. Smalley (Cambridge: Cambridge University Press, 1973), 95–112.

The author of Hebrews, too, in his argument for Christ's supremacy, cites Psalm 45 to support the incarnate Son as possessing the status of God (Heb. 1:8–9). This is underlined in the rest of the chapter. The Son is the brightness of the Father's glory, the express image of his being. All angels are to worship him. Since the Son is superior to the angels, Bauckham comments, "he is included in the unique identity of the one God."[49] Psalm 102, referring to the Creator of the universe, is here (Heb. 1:10–12) applied directly to Christ.[50] As T. F. Torrance puts it, Christ is "not just a sort of *locum tenens*, or a kind of 'double' for God in his absence, but the incarnate presence of *Yahweh*."[51]

Towering over all else in the New Testament is Jesus's resurrection. The resurrection discloses that Jesus is Lord, and from there the deity of Christ becomes "the supreme truth of the Gospel . . . the central point of reference consistent with the whole sequence of events leading up to and beyond the crucifixion."[52] At the center of the New Testament message is the *unbroken* relation between the Son and the Father.[53] It distinguishes the New Testament witness from intertestamental references to a range of heavenly figures, including the archangel Michael.[54]

2.5 Jesus as Creator, Judge, and Savior

To Jesus Christ are attributed works God alone can do. In particular, he is the Creator of the universe, the Judge of the world, and the Savior of his people.

John declares that Jesus Christ is identical with the eternal Word, who made all things, who is with God, and who is God (John 1:1–18). Jesus is the Word who became flesh. Not one thing came into existence apart from that Word. The Word who is "in the beginning" (note the allusion to Gen. 1:1) is "with God," is directed toward God, and, moreover, is God. This entails preexistence.[55] John points to the unity, equality, and distinction of the Word (λόγος) and God (θεός). He underlines that the

49. Bauckham, *Jesus and the God of Israel*, 24.
50. See P. E. Hughes, "The Christology of Hebrews," *SwJT* 28 (1985): 19–27.
51. Torrance, *Christian Doctrine of God*, 51.
52. Torrance, *Christian Doctrine of God*, 46; see also 52; Toon, *Our Triune God*, 159.
53. Torrance, *Christian Doctrine of God*, 49.
54. Toon, *Our Triune God*, 114–15. See also the letter to the Hebrews, where the author proves that Christ is superior to all human, superhuman, and angelic figures.
55. Jehovah's Witnesses point to the absence of a definite article and argue that John means the Word is "a god." However, nominative predicate nouns preceding the verb, as is the case here, normally lack the definite article. The issue is one of Greek syntax. John points to the unity, equality, and distinction of the Word (*logos*) and God (*theos*).

Word created all things (John 1:3–4), and that he became flesh (1:14). He is the only-begotten God (1:18).[56] Paul echoes this (Col. 1:15–20). And Hebrews 1:1–4 says the same, for the Son is the one through whom the world was made, and who directs it toward his intended goal. In 1 Corinthians 8:6, Paul couples God the Father "from whom are all things" and the Lord Jesus Christ "through whom are all things," referring to their respective work in creation.

This throws light on many incidents in the Gospels. Jesus's walking on water is the action of Yahweh, the God of Israel, described in the Old Testament as the one whose path lies through the waters (Matt. 14:22–33; cf. Job 9:8; Ps. 77:19). Moreover, Yahweh has the power to calm the raging storm (Job 26:11–14; Pss. 89:9; 107:23–30). Jesus displays the functions of deity in sovereign charge of the elements. Jesus's miraculous power over sickness and disease, his creation of food to sustain thousands at one sitting, and the like, while presented as signs of the kingdom of God, point to his lordship over the world as its King.

In John 5:22–30, Jesus describes himself as the Judge of the world; this can only be God. In Matthew 25:31–46, as the son of man in Daniel 7:13–14 presides over the eschatological judgment, so Jesus as the Son of Man will judge the nations with righteousness (cf. Mark 8:38). Paul is emphatic (1 Thess. 3:13; 5:23; 2 Thess. 1:5–10); we must all appear before the judgment seat of Christ (2 Cor. 5:10).

The Old Testament stresses that deliverance could come only from Yahweh, not man (Ps. 146:3–6).[57] The name Jesus, which the angel required Joseph to use, means "savior." He was to save his people from their sins (Matt. 1:21). His healings demonstrate him to be the Lord of life. The cumulative impact of his creative and healing miracles indicates deliverance from all that enslaves. Beyond that, he delivers from sin and death.[58] Since salvation is a work of God, Paul's persistent description of Jesus as Savior is an implicit attribution of deity (Phil. 3:20; 2 Tim. 1:10; Titus 1:4; 2:11–13; 3:6; 2 Pet. 1:11). The once-common view that New Testament teaching about Christ was purely functional misses the point; in Bauckham's words, "Jesus' participation in the unique divine sovereignty is not just a matter of what Jesus does, but of *who Jesus is*

---

56. On Christ as Creator in the New Testament, see Wainwright, *Trinity*, 130–54.
57. Wainwright, *Trinity*, 155–70, on Christ as Savior.
58. Robert Letham, *The Work of Christ* (Leicester: Inter-Varsity Press, 1993), esp. chaps. 7, 10, and 11.

in relation to God." As a result, "it becomes unequivocally a matter of regarding Jesus as *intrinsic* to the unique identity of God."[59]

2.6   Worship of Jesus

A number of New Testament passages express praise to Jesus Christ. Each has a hymnic meter. They indicate Christ to be an object of worship, entailing recognition that Christ is one with God (John 1:1–18; Phil. 2:5–11; Col. 1:15–20; 2 Tim. 2:11–13; Heb. 1:3–13). However, Dunn argues that these passages are *about* Jesus rather than hymns addressed *to* him, and that we find the latter only in Revelation.[60] Notwithstanding, the way Jesus is described in these passages *requires* that hymns be addressed to him. Not needing any special explanation, and so assuming wide, if not universal, familiarity in the church, the hymns in Revelation were probably based on a practice in existence already. Hurtado considers that "the practice of singing hymns in Christ's honor goes back to the earliest stratum of the Christian movement."[61] Moreover, he notes, there is not the slightest sign of objection from any of the Jewish churches of the day.[62] Furthermore, since Christ is the Son of the Father, worship of him is simultaneously worship of the Father (Phil. 2:9–11). Again, the link between the churches in Asia Minor and the church triumphant in heaven indicates a correlation between heavenly and earthly worship. Wainwright lists a range of New Testament doxologies addressed to Christ, two of which he considers "clear examples" (2 Pet. 3:18; Rev. 1:5–6), and two (Rom. 9:5; 2 Tim. 4:18) very probable.[63] Hurtado points to the church's hymns addressed *to the Lord* (Eph. 5:19), contrary to Dunn, showing that "the devotional life of early Christianity involved the hymnic celebration of the risen Christ in the corporate worship setting."[64] Bauckham concludes that the bearing of the divine name *YHWH*, via κύριος, by the risen Jesus "signifies unequivocally his inclusion in the unique divine identity, recognition of which is precisely what worship in the Jewish monotheistic tradition expresses."[65]

59. Bauckham, *Jesus and the God of Israel*, 31 (italics original).

60. James D. G. Dunn, *The Parting of the Ways between Christianity and Judaism and Their Significance for the Character of Christianity* (Philadelphia: Trinity Press International, 1991).

61. Hurtado, *One God, One Lord*, 106.

62. Hurtado, *One God, One Lord*, 107.

63. Wainwright, *Trinity*, 93–97.

64. Hurtado, *One God, One Lord*, 107–8.

65. Bauckham, *Jesus and the God of Israel*, 200.

Prayer is also offered to Christ. Stephen calls out to the Lord Jesus as he is being stoned to death (Acts 7:59–60). His cry "Lord Jesus, receive my spirit" parallels Jesus's own words "Father, into your hands I commit my spirit!" which Luke also records (Luke 23:46). Paul too prays to the Lord (the risen Christ) that his thorn in the flesh might be removed (2 Cor. 12:8–9). He refers to an apparently common cry "Our Lord, come!" or *maranatha* (1 Cor. 16:22; cf. Rev. 22:20). We noted that this Aramaic phrase recognizes Jesus as equal in status to Yahweh, right from the start. Moreover, Paul also appeals to both "our God and Father" and "our Lord Jesus" to direct his way (1 Thess. 3:11–12). He calls on the name of the Lord Jesus (Acts 9:14, 21; 22:16), following the Old Testament pattern of calling on the name of Yahweh. Salvation consists in confessing Jesus Christ as κύριος (Rom. 10:9–13; 1 Cor. 12:1–3; Phil. 2:9–11). While in first-century Judaism, prayers may have been offered to angels as intermediaries, the angels were never the objects of devotion.[66] These prayers to Christ distinguish him clearly from any intermediaries, placing him on the same level as the Father.[67] Bauckham writes, "The worship of Jesus serves to focus in conceptuality, as well as making most obvious in religious practice, the inclusion of Jesus in the unique identity of the one God of Jewish monotheism."[68]

2.7   The Preexistence of Christ

A revision is needed of the consensus held until recently that belief in Christ's personal preexistence was a gradual development, crystallizing only relatively late in the composition of the New Testament. Certainly the later New Testament contains much such material (Heb. 1:3–4, 8–9; 1 Pet. 1:20; Rev. 1:17; 3:14; 22:13).[69] However, there is ample evidence that it was known earlier.[70]

Typical of this flawed consensus is James Dunn, who argues that a full view of Christ's personal preexistence is found not in Paul but only later in Hebrews and John. In particular, Philippians 2:5ff. is said not to refer to the pretemporal existence of Christ at all. Instead, Paul contrasts Christ with Adam. Adam wanted to be like God and grasped the forbidden fruit.

---

66. Hurtado, *One God, One Lord*, 112.
67. Wainwright, *Trinity*, 100–101.
68. Bauckham, *Jesus and the God of Israel*, 181.
69. D. B. Capes, "Pre-Existence," in *DLNT*, 955–61.
70. Douglas McCready, *He Came Down from Heaven: The Pre-Existence of Christ and the Christian Faith* (Downers Grove, IL: InterVarsity Press, 2005).

In contrast, Christ refused to act like this. Therefore, there is n̶
to seek any pretemporal reference there.[71] Seyoon Kim opposes Dunn,
considering Paul to be the author of the teaching of preexistence.[72] Ralph
Martin regards Paul as teaching preexistence here.[73] Hurtado points out
the logical fallacy of assuming that even if Paul refers to Adam, preexistence is precluded. Moreover, the Adamic reference is not conclusive, and
most exegetes maintain that preexistence is in view.[74] Hurtado considers
that, if this passage is an early Christian hymn, it was probably in wide
use and its teaching commonplace before Paul wrote Philippians. Thus,
belief in Christ's preexistence came "remarkably early" and was "an un-
contested and familiar view of Christ in Paul's churches."[75]

This sheds light on other Pauline passages. Romans 8:3 and Galatians
4:4 can be seen afresh to refer to the coming of the preexistent Christ
for our salvation. Together with the prologue to the Gospel of John and
the introduction to Hebrews, they reflect a belief present in the church,
from the very start, that Jesus's birth at Bethlehem was *incarnation*, the
coming into the world of God the Son as man. Paul was giving voice,
clarity, and development to what was already believed.

These developments are crucial for the Christian doctrine of God. In
Lebreton's words:

> They show us very clearly that, in all the theses presented by the
> Christian religion from the very first days, there was something new
> and something traditional; the belief in Christ, the worship of Christ
> appears in the foreground, and yet the ancient faith in Jahve is not
> supplanted by this new belief, nor is it transformed into it, nor placed
> side by side with it; Christian worship is not addressed to two Gods
> or to two Lords, and yet it is offered, with the same confidence and
> the same love to Jesus and his Father.[76]

Hurtado argues that "elaborate theories of identifiable stages of Christological development leading up to a divine status accorded to Christ
are refuted by the evidence."[77]

71. Dunn, *Christology in the Making*, 117ff.
72. Kim, *Origin*.
73. Ralph Martin, *Philippians*, The New Century Bible Commentary (Grand Rapids, MI: Eerdmans, 1980), 94–96.
74. L. W. Hurtado, "Pre-Existence," in *DPL*, 743–46.
75. Hurtado, "Pre-Existence," 746.
76. Lebreton, *Trinity*, 277.
77. L. W. Hurtado, "Christology," in *DLNT*, 178–79.

As T. F. Torrance says, we rely for our belief in the deity of Christ not on various incidents recorded in the Gospels or on particular statements but

> upon the whole coherent evangelical structure of historical divine revelation given in the New Testament Scriptures. It is when we indwell it, meditate upon it, tune into it, penetrate inside it, and absorb it into ourselves, and find the very foundations of our life and thought changing under the creative and saving impact of Christ, and are saved by Christ and personally reconciled to God in Christ, that we believe in him as Lord and God.[78]

In consequence, Torrance continues, we pray to Jesus as Lord, worship him, and sing praises to him as God. No wonder Thomas, confronted with the very tangible evidence of Jesus's resurrection, could say in response, "My Lord and my God" (John 20:28).

2.8   The Holy Spirit

There are comparatively few references in the Old Testament to the Spirit of God. The Spirit is active in creation (Gen. 1:2), providence (Ps. 139:7), and redemption (Isa. 63:10) but is presented not as person but as "the executive name of God."[79] While רוח[80] is used roughly ninety times for the Spirit of God in the entire Old Testament, Paul alone uses πνεῦμα[81] for the Spirit 115 times.[82] Pentecost was a momentous event. The presence of the Spirit is overwhelmingly clear in Acts. The church's dynamism comes not from human direction but from the Spirit's overwhelming power.

Owing to the invisibility and anonymity of the Spirit, his presence is not normally noted but is known by what he does. The baptismal formula identifies all three persons as bearing the one new covenant name of God (Matt. 28:19–20).

The Spirit is active at every stage of redemption, especially in the life and ministry of Jesus.[83] Jesus is conceived by the Holy Spirit. Joseph is

---

78. Torrance, *Christian Doctrine of God*, 53.
79. Warfield, "Spirit of God," 131.
80. *ruah*.
81. *pneuma*.
82. Toon, *Our Triune God*, 123.
83. On the Holy Spirit in the New Testament, see Guthrie, *New Testament Theology*, 510–72; Lebreton, *Trinity*, 252–58, 280–84, 314–31, 352–54, 398–407; Wainwright, *Trinity*, 199–234; Toon, *Our Triune God*, 175–94; Bobrinskoy, *Mystery*, 95–136.

informed that Mary's pregnancy is a result of the Spirit's work (Matt. 1:20). Gabriel tells Mary, "The Holy Spirit will come upon you, and the power of the Most High will overshadow you: therefore the child to be born will be called holy—the Son of God" (Luke 1:35). The angel compares the Spirit's involvement in Jesus's conception to his work in creation, where he brooded over the primeval waters (Gen. 1:2). Jesus is to be the author of a new creation, begun, as the first, through the overshadowing action of the Spirit of God. In turn, the holiness of the child is the result of his conception by the Holy Spirit.

In Luke's account, the Spirit surrounds the events at the nativity. The Russian theologian Boris Bobrinskoy writes of "an exceptional convergence between the outpouring of the Spirit and the birth of Christ," and describes the outpoured Spirit as "the Spirit of the incarnation, the One in whom and through whom the Word of God breaks into history."[84] When Mary visits her cousin, Elizabeth is filled with the Holy Spirit and her baby leaps for joy in her womb (Luke 1:41–44). Elizabeth's husband, Zechariah, is also filled with the Spirit when he prophesies concerning his son (Luke 1:67ff.). After Jesus's birth, Simeon receives Jesus, the Holy Spirit having come upon him. Simeon was forewarned by the Spirit that he would see the Christ in person, and on that day he entered the temple with "the Spirit . . . upon him" (Luke 2:25–28).

At the outset of Jesus's public ministry, the Spirit pervades all that happens. John announces that the one who is to come will baptize "with the Holy Spirit and fire" (Luke 3:16). At Jesus's baptism the Spirit descends on him in the form of a dove (Luke 3:22 and parallels; John 1:32–33). Bobrinskoy calls this "a revelation of the eternal movement of the Spirit of the Father who remains in the Son from all eternity," the Savior's entire being defined "in a constant, existential relation with the Father in the Spirit."[85] This baptism manifests the eternal rest of the Spirit on the Son.[86] Jesus returns from the Jordan "full of the Holy Spirit" and in turn is led by the Spirit into the wilderness to be tempted by the devil (Luke 4:1). Afterward, under the direction of the Spirit, Jesus returns to Galilee "in the power of the Spirit" (Luke 4:14). There in the synagogue he reads from the prophet Isaiah, who refers to the Spirit of the Lord resting on the Messiah for his work (Luke 4:17ff.), and Jesus declares that this is now

84. Bobrinskoy, Mystery, 87.
85. Bobrinskoy, Mystery, 88, 91.
86. Bobrinskoy, Mystery, 94, 99.

fulfilled in himself. Luke informs his readers that Jesus was directed by the Spirit in all he did. Beforehand, Jesus, in all his human development (Luke 2:40–52), was under the leading of the Spirit.

This does not of itself establish that the Spirit is a third person in addition to the Father and the Son. These are circumstantial factors, but they stop short of direct proof. The Spirit's divine status is clearer in Jesus's teaching in John 14–16 on his coming at Pentecost, where Jesus links the Spirit expressly with the Father and the Son, entailing identity of status and consequently of being. Here Jesus calls the Spirit "another παράκλητος"[87] (John 14:16), like himself. A παράκλητος is akin to a defense attorney, one who speaks for us against an accuser, represented by the διάβολος.[88] Jesus brings the Spirit into the closest possible connection with the Father and the Son. The Father will send the Spirit on the Son's request (John 14:16, 26). Jesus identifies the Spirit's coming with his, for it is as if Jesus himself were to come (John 14:18). John commented earlier that the Spirit would come only when Jesus had been glorified (John 7:37–39; cf. 16:7). When the Spirit comes, he will enable the disciples to recognize the mutual indwelling of the Father and the Son (John 14:20). The Spirit's coming to those who love Jesus is the same as the Father's and the Son's coming (John 14:21, 23). This connection is indivisible union. The Spirit will bring to the apostles' minds all that Jesus has said to them (John 14:26). So close is the connection that the Spirit's presence and work are interchangeable with those of the Father and the Son.

This interchangeability is clear when Jesus says that it is he who sends the Holy Spirit from the Father (John 15:26; 16:7), rather than the Father who sends the Spirit in response to Jesus's request. Later, Jesus breathes the Spirit on his disciples (John 20:21–23). In the earlier utterance, Jesus also refers to the Spirit proceeding from the Father, a continuous procession (present tense), distinct from his impending coming at Pentecost. In view of this inseparable union, one of the Spirit's tasks after Pentecost is to convince the world of sin, righteousness, and judgment (John 16:8–11), each in connection with the Father and the Son. The Spirit convicts the world of sin because it does not believe in the Son, and convicts the world of righteousness, seen in the Son going to

---

87. *paraclētos*, "advocate."
88. *diabolos*, "devil." See Bertrand de Margerie, SJ, *The Christian Trinity in History*, trans. Edmund J. Fortman, SJ (Petersham. MA: St. Bede's, 1982), 32–34.

the Father. Only one of identical status with the Father and the Son could do this. Finally, the judgment facing the world following the judgment of the ruler of the world cannot be detached from the Father or the Son. John has already spoken of the prince of this world cast out in connection with the cross of Jesus (John 12:31–32). The Father has shown his immeasurable love for this wicked world by giving his Son. Yet the world faces judgment if it continues impenitent; the Spirit convicts it of this.

Jesus makes this identity explicit in his final instructions to the apostles (Matt. 28:18–20). The church is to make the nations disciples, beginning with baptism. This baptism is to be "in the name of the Father and of the Son and of the Holy Spirit." Behind this lies the point that at each stage of the outworking of God's covenant, he names himself. In the Abrahamic covenant he names himself as אל שדי (Gen. 17:1).[89] In the Mosaic covenant he reveals himself as יהוה (Ex. 6:2–3).[90] Matthew has shown how Jesus fulfills all the successive covenants God made (Matt. 1:1; 26:27–29). Jesus has inaugurated the new covenant (Matt. 26:27–29), in which all nations participate (Matt. 8:11–12). Now, in this climactic revelation of the new covenant in Christ, God reveals his covenant name in its fullness, the *one* name of the Father, the Son, and the Holy Spirit. The Spirit is equal to the Father and the Son in the one identical being of God.

Paul also refers to the Spirit in the same breath as the Father and the Son. In writing of the gifts of the Spirit, he refers to "the same Spirit," "the same Lord," and "the same God" (1 Cor. 12:4–6), the Spirit being on a par with both God (the Father) and the Lord (the Son). A similar pattern is present in Ephesians 4:4–6. Most obvious of all in Paul's letters is his apostolic benediction in 2 Corinthians 13:14 (Greek v. 13), where he associates "the fellowship of the Holy Spirit" with "the grace of the Lord Jesus Christ" and "the love of God [the Father]." In Romans 8:9–11, Paul connects Jesus's resurrection with our resurrection on the last day, both works of the Father accomplished by the Holy Spirit. The Spirit transforms us into the glory of the Lord (2 Cor. 3:18); only one who is God can do that.

Added to this are the personal characteristics attributed to the Spirit throughout the New Testament. He grieves over human sin (Eph. 4:30),

89. *El Shaddai*, "God Almighty."
90. *YHWH*, Yahweh.

persuades and convicts (John 14–16), intercedes for us with groanings that cannot be uttered (Rom. 8:26–27), testifies (John 16:12–15), cries (Gal. 4:6), speaks (Mark 13:11 and parallels), creates (Gen. 1:2; Luke 1:35), judges, leads Jesus throughout his life and ministry (Luke 1:35; 4:15ff.), and tells evangelists like Philip and apostles like Paul what to do (Acts 8:29, 39; 16:6–10). He has a mind (Rom. 8:27) and so does not lead us in ways that detour our own intellects (1 Cor. 12:1–3). He can be blasphemed (Matt. 12:32; Mark 3:28–29; and parallels). Peter equates him with God; lying to the Holy Spirit is lying to God (Acts 5:3–4). He is self-effacing, drawing attention to Christ the Son, not to himself (John 16:14–15; cf. 13:31–32; 17:1ff.). He creates the confession that Jesus is Lord (1 Cor. 12:3). He is invisible, unlike Jesus, for he does not share our nature.

Moreover, the Holy Spirit is mentioned in triadic statements linking him with the Father and the Son (Rom. 15:30; 1 Cor. 12:4–6; 2 Cor. 13:14; Gal. 4:4–6; Eph. 2:18; Col. 1:3–8; 2 Thess. 2:13–14; Titus 3:4–7). He is called "the Spirit of Christ" (Rom. 8:9; 1 Pet. 1:11) and "the Spirit of [God's] Son" (Gal. 4:6). He is personally distinct from the Father and the Son while having divine status himself, since he reveals them. Furthermore, the baptismal formula has an ongoing and powerful effect on the entire church. At every baptism there is the reminder that the God the church worships and serves is the Father, the Son, and the Holy Spirit.

Recognition of the Spirit's divine status sprang from Christian experience. The power of God displayed in the gift of faith, his support in the face of opposition and suffering, the deep sense of communion with God, and, with it, the knowledge that the risen Christ shared in the being of God were all overwhelming realities of Christian experience. Concurrently, four factors had a cautionary impact, restraining an immediate, outright statement of the Spirit's deity. First, there was the overwhelming importance attached to the unity of God, which we noted. Second, the danger of misunderstanding in the polytheistic Gentile world was very real. Third, there is what Torrance calls the

> diaphonous self-effacing nature of the Holy Spirit . . . enlightening transparence. . . . We do not know the Holy Spirit directly in his own personal Reality or Glory. We know him only in his unique spiritual mode of activity and transparent presence in virtue of which God's self-revelation shines through to us in Christ, and we

are made through the Spirit to see the Father in the Son and the Son in the Father.[91]

The point is that only the Son became incarnate and shares our nature; the Spirit did not become flesh. There are irreducible distinctions between the persons. Therefore, hypostatically the Spirit is distinctly different from the realm in which we live. Fourth, the comparative reticence of the New Testament writers to attribute personality to the Spirit is understandable; personality was not understood then and is hardly known now. The concept of the person actually *followed* the formulation of the doctrine of the Trinity. However, while Warfield overstates the case in saying that the doctrine of the Trinity is in the New Testament "already made,"[92] it is still true that the New Testament "exhibits a coherent witness to God's trinitarian self-revelation imprinted upon its theological content in an implicit conceptual form."[93] While the overt pattern of Christian worship was at first binitarian (God the Father and our Lord Jesus Christ), behind it lay a tacit Trinitarianism.

2.9 Trinitarian Formulae and Triadic Patterns

Triadic patterns are *pervasive* throughout the New Testament, unselfconsciously so. In the New Testament θεός is often used for the Father, κύριος for the Son, the ascended Christ, and πνεῦμα for the Spirit.[94] This provides what Wainwright calls a Trinitarian pattern, "a strong body of evidence which shows that the writers of the New Testament were influenced in thought and expression by the triad 'Father, Son, and Holy Spirit.'" However, there are no doctrinal comments in these passages on the relations of the three and how this fits into the received teaching. The writers assume that the readers will know what they mean without explanation. Into such a category Wainwright places, among many others, the baptismal formula.[95] Other such passages include 1 Corinthians 12:4–6 and Ephesians 4:4–6.

Galatians 4:4–6 is a striking example: "But when the fullness of time had come, God sent forth his Son, born of woman, born under the law, to redeem those who were under the law, so that we might receive

---

91. Torrance, *Christian Doctrine of God*, 66.
92. Warfield, "Biblical Doctrine of the Trinity," 30.
93. Torrance, *Christian Doctrine of God*, 49.
94. Wainwright, *Trinity*, 237–47.
95. Wainwright, *Trinity*, 245–46.

adoption as sons. And because you are sons, God has sent the Spirit of his Son into our hearts, crying, 'Abba! Father!'" Paul sees the whole of redemptive history from a Trinitarian perspective; triadic patterns pervade his letters.

Paul describes himself as "an apostle, set apart for the gospel of God . . . concerning his Son . . . who was declared to be the Son of God in power according to the Spirit of holiness by his resurrection from the dead" (Rom. 1:1–4). The consequences of salvation are that "we have peace with God through our Lord Jesus Christ" and "God's love has been poured into our hearts through the Holy Spirit" (Rom. 5:1, 5). We have "died to the law through the body of Christ . . . in order that we may bear fruit for God . . . [serving] in the new life of the Spirit" (Rom. 7:4–6). Consequently, "there is therefore now no condemnation for those who are in Christ Jesus. For the law of the Spirit of life has set you free in Christ Jesus from the law of sin and death. For God has done what the law . . . could not do" (Rom. 8:1–3a). By sending his own Son, he has condemned sin and enables us to fulfill the righteous requirement of the law as we walk according to the Spirit (Rom. 8:3b–4). Christian believers "live according to the Spirit," "set their minds on the things of the Spirit," and are "in the Spirit," for "the Spirit of God dwells in [them]." The Spirit is "the Spirit of Christ," and so Christ dwells in them. The Spirit is also called "the Spirit of him who raised Jesus from the dead," referring to the Father, who will also raise us from the dead "through his Spirit who dwells in you" (Rom. 8:5–11).

The following section, on Israel's privileges (Rom. 9:1–5), also contains reference to Christ as God, and to the Spirit. Paul describes the kingdom of God as "righteousness and peace and joy in the Holy Spirit" for "whoever thus serves Christ is acceptable to God" (Rom. 14:17–18). He describes himself as "a minister of Christ Jesus . . . in the priestly service of the gospel of God, so that the offering of the Gentiles may be acceptable, sanctified by the Holy Spirit" (Rom. 15:16), and then appeals to his readers "by our Lord Jesus Christ and by the love of the Spirit, to strive together with me in your prayers to God on my behalf" (Rom. 15:30).

These features occur in all Paul's letters and in Peter's too. Thiselton's comment is apt that "an overreaction against an earlier naïve dogmatics has made us too timid in what we claim for Paul's respective understandings of Christ, the Holy Spirit, and God."[96] The author of Hebrews considers the cross in a triadic context: "How much more [than the Old Testament sacrifices] will the blood of Christ, who through the eternal Spirit offered himself without blemish to God, purify our conscience from dead works to serve the living God" (Heb. 9:14). As for "eternal spirit" (πνεύματος αἰωνίου), the mention of Christ and God, evidently the Father, supports a reference to the Holy Spirit. The human spirit can hardly be called eternal.

These paradigms vary. Most prominent is the pattern *from the Father through the Son in or by the Holy Spirit*. This is clear in the work of salvation and in the baptismal formula. From our side, in response to salvation—in prayer, worship, and the Christian life—is a reverse pattern *by the Holy Spirit through the Son to the Father* (Eph. 2:18). However, these are not the only such triads. Paul's apostolic benediction runs *Son–Father–Holy Spirit* (2 Cor. 13:14 [Greek v. 13]), suggesting the Johannine model of the Son revealing the Father and promising the Spirit. In 1 Corinthians 12:4–6 and Ephesians 4:4–6, Paul writes of *the Spirit–the Son–the Father*. John refers in Revelation 1:4–6 to *the Father–the Spirit–the Son*, following the revelation at the Jordan, where the Spirit proceeded from the Father and rested on the Son. That also mirrors the messianic passage quoted by the Father at that time (Isa. 42:1), and the pattern at Jesus's conception. And it was followed by the Syrian tradition.[97]

There is no inflexible pattern. Understanding unfolds from the experience of salvation; conceptualization comes later. The expression of the Trinity is rooted in salvation and Christian experience, not speculation. Bobrinskoy suggests that the most common formula, Father–Son–Holy Spirit, points to the need for the Orthodox to reflect on the fact that the Son is not only the one on whom the Spirit rests but also the one who gives the Spirit. Nevertheless, he argues that this formula should be balanced by the one from the Jordan, "by the vision of Christ as the One on whom the Spirit rests, the One who is obedient to the Spirit, the One who is sent by the Spirit, who speaks and acts by the Spirit."[98] This

---

96. Anthony C. Thiselton, *The First Epistle to the Corinthians: A Commentary on the Greek Text* (Grand Rapids, MI: Eerdmans, 2000), 1238.

97. See Emmanuel Pataq Siman, *L'expérience de l'Esprit par l'Église d'après la tradition syrienne d'Antioche* (Paris, 1971), cited by Bobrinskoy, *Mystery*, 67.

98. Bobrinskoy, *Mystery*, 70. The whole section 65–72 is particularly stimulating. Bobrinskoy calls for a balance between what he terms *filioquism* and *Spirituque*, a participation and presence of the Spirit in the Father and the Son.

flexibility shows there is, in Torrance's words, "an implicit belief in the equality of the three divine Persons." Torrance maintains that it was the baptismal formula, in accordance with the "irreversible relation of the Father to the Son," that established the Trinitarian order regularly used in the church's proclamation, worship, and tradition, and that these triadic patterns "give expression to the three-fold structure of God's astonishing revelation of himself through himself."[99] In the light of the cross and resurrection, and the sending of the Spirit at Pentecost, we can see that God is inherently triune.[100]

2.10   Trinitarian Questions

Wainwright sees an awareness of a Trinitarian problem—the question of how to relate the deity of the Son and the Spirit to the unity and uniqueness of God—as coming later. Paul, the author of Hebrews, and particularly John were aware of it.[101] Given that the Son and the Spirit are fully God, how can they—together with the Father—be one God? How are they related the one to the other? The problem focuses on the relation of the Father to the Son. The Spirit does not pose such difficulties. Although it does not expressly call the Spirit God, the New Testament sees him as distinct. It is also clear that if a second person shares the divine nature, there should be no insuperable difficulties in a third doing so.

John's Gospel is the only place in the New Testament where the three-fold problem is clearly articulated and an explanation is attempted.[102] Wainwright suggests that it is one of the major themes of John.[103] That he starts and ends his Gospel by equating Jesus with God (John 1:1–18; 20:31) is neither accidental nor unpremeditated. The Word who is "in the beginning" is "with God" or directed toward God and, moreover, is also equated with God. John points to the unity, equality, and distinction of the Word and God, and then underlines that the Word is the Creator of all things (1:3–4), and that he became flesh (1:14). To cap it all, he is the only-begotten God (1:18). The "I am" sayings and the consistent stress on the relation between the Father and the Son support this. The Spirit is clearly distinct from the Father and the Son, especially in the

---

99. Torrance, *Christian Doctrine of God*, 71–72.
100. Torrance, *Christian Doctrine of God*, 54.
101. Wainwright, *Trinity*, 248ff.
102. Wainwright, *Trinity*, 250.
103. Wainwright, *Trinity*, 264–65.

Paraclete sayings in chapters 14–16. True worship is to be directed to the Father in Jesus, the truth (John 1:17; 14:6) by the Spirit (John 4:21–24).

In summary, the Father loves the Son, sends the Son, and glorifies the Son. He also sends the Holy Spirit in Jesus's name and in response to his request, and is worshiped in the Son and in the Spirit. He and the Son indwell one another. He has life in himself and has given to the Son to have life in himself. He is Judge and has committed judgment to his Son.

The Son was with God in the beginning, in the bosom of the Father, and was/is God. He made all things. He was sent by the Father, became flesh, lived among his disciples, obeyed the Father, prayed to the Father, and after his resurrection ascended to the Father. He asked the Father to send the Holy Spirit, and also sends the Spirit himself, and breathes out the Spirit on his disciples. He and the Father indwell one another. He receives from the Father life in himself and the right to judge.

The Holy Spirit proceeds from the Father, is sent by the Father on the day of Pentecost in response to the Son's request, and is also sent at that time by the Son. He is breathed out by the Son. He testifies to the Son and brings glory to him.

The three work together in harmony. Together they come by the Spirit to the disciples, who consequently live in the Father and the Son.

Wainwright concludes that John not only is aware of the problem but also provides an answer to it. There is no formal statement of the doctrine of the Trinity in the Bible as we find it in the later church councils, but an answer to the problem is there. "The problem of the trinity was being raised and answered in the New Testament,"[104] arising from Christian experience, worship, and thought, based on the life of Jesus and his reception of the Holy Spirit upon his resurrection, and his subsequent impartation of the Spirit to his church.[105]

Further Reading

Bates, Matthew W. *The Birth of the Trinity: Jesus, God, and Spirit in New Testament and Early Christian Interpretation of the Old Testament.* Oxford: Oxford University Press, 2015.

---

104. Wainwright, *Trinity*, 266.
105. See Toon, *Our Triune God*, 197–246; Lebreton, *Trinity*, 408–14; de Margerie, *Christian Trinity*, 8–56.

Bauckham, Richard. *Jesus and the God of Israel: God Crucified and Other Studies on the New Testament's Christology of Divine Identity.* Milton Keynes: Paternoster, 2008.

Hurtado, Larry W. *One God, One Lord: Early Christian Devotion and Ancient Jewish Monotheism.* 3rd ed. London: Bloomsbury T&T Clark, 2015.

Letham, Robert. *The Holy Trinity: In Scripture, History, Theology, and Worship.* 2nd ed. Phillipsburg, NJ: P&R, 2019.

Study Questions

1. How far is it appropriate to talk about the revelation of the Trinity in the Old Testament?

2. Consider whether it is valid to distinguish between the Trinity and the doctrine of the Trinity.

3. After reading the proposals of Bates, to what extent would or should our own exegesis be guided by prosopological interpretation? See the brief discussion in chapter 8, page 256.

3

The Trinity (2)

Church Formulation

The doctrine of the Trinity was formally developed in the fourth century. It followed decades of controversy and confusion. The problem was how to conceive of God as one while according to the Son and the Spirit the status given them in the Bible. It required the forging of linguistic tools to express what the church had believed and confessed. Eventually, at Constantinople I the church confessed that God is one indivisible being, three irreducible persons or hypostases; the Father, the Son, and the Holy Spirit are each fully God, equal in power and glory, indivisible, and inseparable in all their works, while the Father generates the Son from eternity, and the Spirit proceeds from the Father. Generation and procession demonstrate that God is infinite superabundance of life and vitality and are the basis from which he freely and sovereignly creates.

3.1 From the New Testament to Constantinople I

3.1.1 *Two Main Heresies*

Until the early fourth century there were two potentially deviant tendencies affecting the church's grasp of the Trinity. The first of these was modalism, which blurred the distinctions of the three persons. In

modalism [handwritten annotation]

the third century, Sabellius held that the Father, the Son, and the Spirit were merely ways in which the one God revealed himself, like an actor taking on different roles. He maintained that the only God, Father in the Old Testament, had become Son in the New and sanctified the church as Holy Spirit after Pentecost. The three were successive modes of the unipersonal God. Consequently, Christ was merely an appearance of the one God but did not have any distinct identity of his own.[1] With modalism, God's revelation in human history as the Father, the Son, and the Holy Spirit did not reveal who he is eternally, and so Christ gives us no true knowledge of God. Moreover, the effect was to undermine God's faithfulness, for we could not rely on him if what he disclosed of himself in Christ did not truly reflect who he eternally is. Indeed, for those determined to maintain the unity of God and resist anything savoring of a dual or threefold god, there was a constant danger of regarding the Son and the Spirit as identical to the Father, as appearances of the one God at different times. Tertullian countered modalism in his book *Contra Praxeas*, calling those who held this position "monarchians," who insisted that God's rule (*monarchia*) was one. Later, Paul of Samosata was condemned on these grounds at the Council of Antioch in 268.

On the other side of the spectrum were those who, recognizing the distinctions of the three, accorded a lower status to the Son and the Spirit. Seeking to maintain the unity of God, they held that God was a hierarchical being, with the Father imparting deity to the Son and the Spirit. This was endemic at the time, for the conceptual and linguistic resources did not exist to distinguish between the way God is one and the way he is three. This tendency was generally held within bounds by placing the relations of the three firmly within God, as opposed to the creature. However, it was an unstable situation, for unless the Son and the Spirit were held to be fully God, there could be no viable proclamation of the gospel, for we would not have true knowledge of God. If Christ were not unimpaired God, he could not save us. Many have held that Origen was a subordinationist. However, it is at least equally clear that he understood the Son to be God, together with the Father, a view

---

1. Bertrand de Margerie, SJ, *The Christian Trinity in History*, trans. Edmund J. Fortman, SJ (Petersham. MA: St. Bede's, 1982), 85–87; Boris Bobrinskoy, *The Mystery of the Trinity: Trinitarian Experience and Vision in the Biblical and Patristic Tradition*, trans. Anthony P. Gythiel (Crestwood, NY: St Vladimir's Seminary Press, 1999), 217–20.

underlined by his doctrine of eternal generation.[2] Thus, there is enough evidence to see Origen's basic orthodoxy. Ayres agrees that to suggest Origen was a subordinationist is implausible.[3]

[handwritten margin note: Why speak into this debate?]

Both modalism and subordinationism were attempts to make the Trinity intelligible to human reason. We would be left with either the one God, with the Son and the Holy Spirit as temporary appearances, or a graded deity, with the Son and the Spirit as semidivine. A metaphorical time bomb was destined sooner or later to explode. The chief problem was how to reconcile the unity of the one God with the status of Christ. While modalism was officially suppressed, the subordinationist issue was unresolved.

3.1.2 The Fourth-Century Crisis

Suddenly bursting on the scene in 318 was an Alexandrian presbyter called Arius. He maintained that the Son was not coeternal with the Father but came into existence out of nothing and was a creature. Arius was an effective propagandist and attracted a large following. The dangers for the church were great.[4] For Arius, God was not Father eternally any more than a man is a father before he begets his son. The Son had an origin, ex nihilo. At some point he did not exist, and now he exists by the will of God. God used the Son as an intermediary to create other entities; so God is effectively at arm's length from the creation. Hence, the Son is a different *ousia* (being) from the Father, for the Father is his God. There is another Word of God besides the Son, and it is because the Son shares in this that he is called, by grace, Word and Son.[5] Jesus's statement "I and the Father are one" (John 10:30) was taken to mean a harmonious agreement of will, not identity of being. The Son was an assistant to the Father, operating under orders. The monarchy of God, his oneness in rule, was preserved by insisting that the Son was and is not true God.[6] Arius's identification of the Son with humans severed the

---

2. E.g., Origen, *De principiis* 1.2.9 (*PG*, 11:138); Origen, *Homily on John* 13.25 (*PG*, 14:411–14); Henri Crouzel, *Origen*, trans. A. S. Worrall (Edinburgh: T&T Clark, 1989), 102–3, 186–92; Letham, *The Holy Trinity: In Scripture, History, Theology, and Worship* (Phillipsburg, NJ: P&R, 2004), 101–7; Peter Widdicombe, *The Fatherhood of God from Origen to Athanasius* (Oxford: Clarendon, 1994), 63–92.

3. Lewis Ayres, *Nicaea and Its Legacy: An Approach to Fourth-Century Trinitarian Theology* (Oxford: Oxford University Press, 2004), 20–23.

4. In many ways, Arius was a precursor of the modern Jehovah's Witnesses.

5. See Athanasius, *Of Synods* 16, for Arius's profession of faith.

6. Robert C. Gregg, *Early Arianism—a Way of Salvation* (Philadelphia: Fortress, 1981), 1–129.

Son's connection with God. Arius's views were outlawed as heretical by the Council of Nicaea in 325. The council affirmed that the Son is *homoousios*, of the identical being, with the Father.

The controversy erupted again in the 350s and was bedeviled by political intrigue and terminological confusion. The pro-Nicenes termed all their opponents "Arians," whatever the nuances of their views. The words that eventually were chosen to resolve the crisis—*ousia, hypostasis*—were used in a variety of ways in Greek thought, as well as by figures in the church. People spoke past one another. A coherent and agreed language was lacking.[7] Ayres comments, "Nicaea's terminology is thus a window onto the confusion and complexity of the early fourth-century theological debates, not a revelation that a definitive turning-point had been reached."[8] Certainly, terms such as *East* and *West* are not appropriate to describe the confusion at this stage.[9]

The theological, political, personal, and ecclesiastical differences were bewildering. The controversy did not arise from any intrusion of Greek thought to supplant biblical faith, but it erupted out of questions basic to the gospel—belief in one God together with the recognition that Jesus Christ is divine. Since all sides cited the Bible in support, "the theologians of the Christian Church were slowly driven to a realization that the deepest questions which face Christianity cannot be answered in purely biblical language, because the questions are about the meaning of biblical language itself."[10]

Later, Eunomius—more able than Arius, and a bishop rather than a presbyter—advocated similar ideas in his *Apology*. The Eunomians were rationalists, confident in the extensive capacities of human logic. They assumed a correspondence between the respective minds of God and humans such that meaning is identical for both. Because of this identity between God's mind and ours, the Son's generation from the Father is to be understood in terms of human generation. Since eternal generation

---

7. R. P. C. Hanson, *The Search for the Christian Doctrine of God: The Arian Controversy 318–381* (Edinburgh: T&T Clark, 1988), 99–675; Ayres, *Nicaea and Its Legacy*, passim.

8. Ayres, *Nicaea and Its Legacy*, 92.

9. Ayres, *Nicaea and Its Legacy*, 123–30.

10. Hanson, *Search*, xxi. On the conflict, see also de Margerie, *Christian Trinity*, 87–91; J. N. D. Kelly, *Early Christian Doctrines* (London: Adam & Charles Black, 1968), 226–31; Bobrinskoy, *Mystery*, 220–21; Basil Studer, *Trinity and Incarnation: The Faith of the Early Church*, trans. Matthias Westerhoff, ed. Andrew Louth (Collegeville, MN: Liturgical, 1993), 103–5; Gregg, *Early Arianism*, 1–129; Charles Kannengiesser, *Arius and Athanasius: Two Alexandrian Theologians* (Aldershot, Hampshire: Variorum, 1991); Rowan Williams, *Arius: Heresy and Tradition* (London: Darton, Longman, & Todd, 1987).

is inconceivable, the Son's generation must have had a beginning. There was a point when the Son did not exist. He was the first to be created and was the instrument by which God created the world. He is unlike the Father.

For the Arian tradition, the line between God and creation came between the Father and the Son, with the Son on the side of the creature. Conversely, the supporters of Nicaea drew the line between the triad—the Father, the Son, and the Spirit—and all other beings.[11] However, Eunomius did not think the Son was a creature like all others, for he created all others.[12] The Arian triad was a hierarchy consisting of the one God who became the Father, plus two different, subordinate, and noneternal beings.

Eunomius was opposed initially by Athanasius and later by the Cappadocians—Basil the Great, his brother Gregory of Nyssa, and Gregory of Nazianzus—who argued that the Son and the Holy Spirit were one being with the Father from eternity. Athanasius wrote that the Word comes from the being of the Father and is emphatically not a creature.[13] The Son is consubstantial with the Father, "out of the being of the Father." Whatever the Father has, the Son has.[14] This phrase, more than *homoousios*, was prominent in Athanasius's writings.

The Eunomians, on the basis of human relationships, argued that fathers are not fathers before they beget sons, who in turn come into being on being begotten; therefore, the Son began to be at some point. The pro-Nicenes replied that the names Father and Son denote identity of nature, and it is fallacious to argue from human experience back to God.

The Cappadocians have been criticized for making the Father the cause of the deity of the Son and the Holy Spirit, so that the Father is the source of the divine essence. Gregory of Nazianzus, in his *Theological Orations*, shows that nothing could be further from his mind. Torrance argues that, for Gregory, the monarchy, the divine rule, belongs to the whole Trinity and is not limited to one person, so that there is no severance of essence.[15] Here is an advance that offsets any possible tendency

---

11. Richard Paul Vaggione, *Eunomius of Cyzicus and the Nicene Revolution* (Oxford: Oxford University Press, 2000), 123–24.
12. Vaggione, *Eunomius of Cyzicus*, 124–26.
13. Athanasius, *On the Decrees of the Synod of Nicea* 19 (PG, 25:447–50).
14. Athanasius, *Letters to Serapion on the Holy Spirit* 2.5 (PG, 26:616).
15. Thomas F. Torrance, *The Christian Doctrine of God: One Being, Three Persons*, 2nd ed. (Edinburgh: T&T Clark, 2016), 180–85.

to subordinate the Son and the Spirit to the Father. The Father is the source, the begetter and emitter, the Son is the begotten, and the Holy Spirit the emission, but this concerns the hypostatic relations.[16] Equality of the three and identity of being are preserved.[17]

3.1.3   The Crisis Resolved

Some held that the Son is *homoiousios* (of like being) with the Father. Athanasius had the breadth of mind to recognize that differences of terminology should not prevent agreement if the intention behind those terms was the same, and that what matters is right belief even though words and phrases are not precisely what he might want. At the Council of Alexandria (AD 362) he allowed that *ousia* and *hypostasis* can be used in different senses, and that it is possible to speak of three hypostases and be orthodox.[18] This was a major breakthrough, paving the way for the eventual resolution of the crisis at the Council of Constantinople in AD 381, spearheaded by the Cappadocians. Eunomianism was rejected as heresy, as was a development known as Macedonianism or pneumatomachianism, the adherents of which accepted the deity of the Son but balked at calling the Holy Spirit "God." A number of treatises were written on the Spirit in opposition to the *pneumatomachii*, establishing his deity from, among other things, the fact that only one who is God can unite us to the Son and makes us partakers of the divine nature.[19] The three Cappadocians together brought about an open recognition of the deity of the Spirit as well as the Son, and so cleared the decks for a definitive settlement of the crisis.[20]

A number of factors lay behind this resolution. First, the Cappadocians used terms, hitherto bedeviled by confusing philosophical baggage,

---

16. Gregory of Nazianzus, *Oration 29* 15 (*PG*, 36:93); T. A. Noble, "Paradox in Gregory Nazianzen's Doctrine of the Trinity," *StPatr* 27 (1993): 94–99; Ayres, *Nicaea and Its Legacy*, 247–48.

17. Gregory of Nazianzus, *Oration 29* 2 (*PG*, 36:76); Gregory of Nazianzus, *Oration 31* 13f. (*PG*, 36:148f.); Gregory of Nazianzus, *Oration 39* 12 (*PG*, 36:348).

18. Athanasius, *To the Antiochenes* 5–8 (*PG*, 26:799–806); Hanson, *Search*, 644–45.

19. Athanasius, *Serapion*; Didymus, *On the Holy Spirit*, both in *Works on the Spirit: Athanasius and Didymus*, trans. Mark DelCogliano, Andrew Radde-Gallwitz, and Lewis Ayres (Yonkers, NY: St Vladimir's Seminary Press, 2011); Basil of Caesarea, *On the Holy Spirit*; Gregory of Nazianzus, *Oration 31*. Later, Cyril wrote, "It is inconceivable that created being should have the power to deify. This is something that can be attributed only to God." Cyril of Alexandria, *Dialogue on the Most Holy Trinity*, vii.644d, in Norman Russell, *The Doctrine of Deification in the Greek Patristic Tradition* (Oxford: Oxford University Press, 2004), 195.

20. For a discussion of the meaning of "pro-Nicene" for those who paved the way for the eventual settlement at Constantinople, see Ayres, *Nicaea and Its Legacy*, 236–40.

in a nontechnical way to express the reality. This simplified the discussion. Second, Basil proposed to reserve *ousia* for the way God is one, and *hypostasis* for the way he is three. This helped communication. Third, appeal was made to "the sense of Scripture" rather than to precise proof texts, so as to clarify meaning. This provided context. It was widely recognized that the Son is one identical being with the Father and that this was integral to the gospel itself. So the Council of Constantinople unequivocally rejected the claim that the Son and the Spirit are simply intermediaries between God and humanity. Such an idea would have destroyed the gospel. Jesus Christ would not have given us true knowledge of God, as he would not have been one with God from eternity. As such he could not have saved us.[21]

3.1.4 *The Niceno-Constantinopolitan Creed (C)*

The Niceno-Constantinopolitan Creed, probably dating from the Council of Constantinople (381), states:

> We believe in one God the Father Almighty, maker of heaven and earth and of all things visible and invisible;
>
> And in one Lord Jesus Christ the Son of God, the Only-begotten, begotten by his Father before all ages, Light from Light, true God from true God, begotten not made, consubstantial with the Father, through whom all things came into existence, who for us men and for our salvation came down from the heavens and became incarnate by the Holy Spirit and the Virgin Mary and became a man, and was crucified for us under Pontius Pilate and suffered and was buried and rose again on the third day in accordance with the Scriptures and ascended into the heavens and is seated at the right hand of the Father and will come again with glory to judge the living and the dead, and there will be no end to his kingdom;
>
> And in the Holy Spirit, the Lord and life-giver, who proceeds from the Father, who is worshipped and glorified together with the Father and the Son, who spoke by the prophets;
>
> And in one holy, catholic and apostolic Church;
>
> We confess one baptism for the forgiveness of sins;
>
> We wait for the resurrection of the dead and the life of the coming age. Amen.

---

21. Letham, *The Holy Trinity*, 167–83.

C emphatically affirms that Christ, the Son, is eternally identical in being to the Father. In the context of pneumatomachianism, it teaches the deity of the Holy Spirit guardedly, giving as little offense as possible. First, the title "Lord" is applied to the Spirit. Κύριος is the Greek word customarily used for יהוה, the God of Israel. Second, the Spirit is said to be "worshipped . . . together with the Father and the Son." The persons are real distinctions, but the worship is identical. While the Spirit is not specifically called *homoousios*, everything relevant to that term is present, explicitly or by entailment.[22] Not all the orthodox as yet felt at ease about calling the Holy Spirit God in so many words, but the synodic letter the following year removed all ambiguity. It said, "We believe that there is one substance [*ousia*] of the Father and of the Son and of the Holy Spirit in three most perfect hypostases or three perfect persons [*prosōpois*]."[23]

The creed asserts the Father as the source from whom the Holy Spirit proceeds.[24] In this it refutes the Macedonians, placing the Spirit outside those things made by the Son.[25] Additionally, the Spirit's personality is implied in his speaking through the prophets.[26] He is also coordinate with the Father and the Son in creation and grace. The Father is the Maker of all things, the Lord Jesus Christ is the one through whom all things came into existence, and the Holy Spirit is the Lord and giver of life. Creation is a work of the whole Trinity. In these, the Spirit is placed unequivocally in the category of what is God.

J. N. D. Kelly sums up the profound achievements of the fourth century, culminating in C:

> What is not always noticed, however, is the profound intellectual revolution which the triumph of the new orthodoxy at the two great councils implied. To make my point as clearly and as simply as I can, prior to Nicaea the accepted Christian doctrine of God was an Origenistic one of a holy Triad, of an ineffable Godhead with two subordinate and, in the last resort, disparate hypostases; but after Nicaea the pressure group which pushed through the introduction of the *homoousion* dragged, if you will forgive the crude metaphor,

---

22. De Margerie, *Christian Trinity*, 105–6; Studer, *Trinity*, 157.
23. De Margerie, *Christian Trinity*, 107, citing J. Alberigo, *Conciliorum Oecumenicorum Decreta* (Rome: Herder, 1962), 24. See Studer, *Trinity*, 158.
24. Bobrinskoy, *Mystery*, 249–50.
25. Studer, *Trinity*, 157.
26. Studer, *Trinity*, 157–58; Bobrinskoy, *Mystery*, 249–50.

these two inferior hypostases within the divine essence. During the four or five decades following Nicaea the predominant view in the church continued to be Origenistic, pluralistic. . . . But once the creed of Constantinople both reaffirmed and supplemented the Nicene creed proper, there could be no future for such pluralism. The Son and the Spirit were "one in being" (as we now translate *homoousion*) with the Father, and the Godhead was an indivisible unity expressing itself in three eternal modes differing only in their relations. The Nicene creed, in its original form N and its more mature development C, symbolised this far-reaching revolution.[27]

Later, this theology was further elaborated in systematic form by Augustine, in his *De Trinitate*, his *Tractates on John*, and some of his letters. All this should be seen against the prior background described by Georges Florovsky, that *"the classical world did not know the mystery of personal being."*[28]

3.2 One *Ousia*, Three Hypostases

That God is one indivisible being (essence, from *esse*, "to be") is, biblically, axiomatic. Basic is the simplicity of God, he is not divisible into parts. That entails indivisibility; the three hypostases are not detachable for they are each and together identical with the one indivisible being of God. That the one being of God consists eternally of three distinct persons is a matter the fathers saw is essential to salvation, for if it were not so, the truth and reliability of God's revelation would be destroyed. Creation and salvation are presented in the Bible as works of God. Since the Son and the Holy Spirit are, together with the Father, direct and distinct personal actors in both realms, it follows that all three have the status of deity.

Since all three persons are the one God, from one side God is one being, three persons, while from another angle he is three persons, one being.[29] Both are equally ultimate.

When the church says that the Son or the Holy Spirit is fully God, it means that all that is God, all that can ever be said to be God, without

---

27. J. N. D. Kelly, "The Nicene Creed: A Turning Point," *SJT* 36 (1983): 38–39.
28. Georges Florovsky, *The Eastern Fathers of the Fourth Century*, vol. 7 of *Collected Works of Father Georges Florovsky*, ed. Richard S. Haugh (Vaduz: Büchervertriebsanstalt, 1987), 32 (italics original).
29. See Torrance, *Christian Doctrine of God*, 112–67, for a developed exposition of this point.

dilution or subtraction, constitutes the person of the Son and in turn the person of the Spirit, just as is so with the person of the Father. Each person of the Trinity, when considered in himself, is 100 percent God without remainder. The whole God is in each person, and also each person is the whole God.

Simultaneously, the one God is simple, not divisible. It is impossible to cut off and detach part of God, as can be done with any created being. That is why each of the Father, the Son, and the Holy Spirit comprises all of God both severally and together. It follows that none of the three is less than all three together. This is so because there is but one divine essence or being. Nor is the divine being a fourth entity; it is the Father, the Son, and the Holy Spirit. So, being simple, God is not divisible into parts less than the whole of who he is. Augustine maintains, "Some things are even said about the persons singly by name; however, they must not be understood in the sense of excluding the other persons, because this same three is also one, and there is one substance and godhead of the Father and Son and Holy Spirit."[30] While Augustine has been particularly noted for his defense of divine simplicity, he was following in the footsteps of the Cappadocians.[31]

Above all, the debates acknowledged the divine incomprehensibility, that in all this is mystery, the reality infinitely outstripping the powers of the human mind, so requiring worship and an appropriate caution.[32]

3.2.1 Consubstantiality

It follows that all three persons are of one substance (consubstantial), of the one identical being (*homoousios*). Further, each person is God in himself. There is nothing in the creed (C) to suggest that the Son or the Spirit derives his deity from the Father. If this idea was present in Origen or others, by the time of the Council of Constantinople it had been cor-

---

30. Augustine, *De Trinitate* 1.19, in *The Works of Saint Augustine: A Translation for the 21st Century: The Trinity*, trans. Edmund Hill, OP (Hyde Park, NY: New City, 1991), 79. See also Augustine, *On the Gospel of John* 77.2 (NPNF[1], 1:339).

31. Gregory of Nyssa, *Against Eunomius* 1.19 (NPNF[2], 5:57); Gregory of Nyssa, *On the Holy Spirit against the Macedonians* 6 (NPNF[2], 5:317); Gregory of Nazianzus, *Oration 29* 17 (NPNF[2], 7:307); Gregory of Nazianzus, *Oration 31* 14 (NPNF[2], 7:322); *St. Gregory of Nazianzus: On God and Christ: The Five Theological Orations and Two Letters to Cledonius*, trans. Frederick Williams and Lionel Wickham (Crestwood, NY: St Vladimir's Seminary Press, 2002), 84–85, 127–28; Lewis Ayres, *Augustine and the Trinity* (Cambridge: Cambridge University Press, 2010), 208–16.

32. See Gregory of Nazianzus, *Oration 27* 3–7 (PG, 36:13–21).

rected. While at times Gregory of Nyssa appears to suggest a chain of causal dependency, Gregory of Nazianzus corrects him, and both stress that the relations of origin (begetting and procession) refer to the relations between the persons. The theme, present in Athanasius, taken up by the two Gregorys—that the Son is all that the Father is except for being the Father—entails the full status of deity *a se* (of himself). Gregory of Nazianzus could not have been more emphatic on this point.[33] Even statements taken by some to refer to remnants of subordination—"light of light," "true God of true God"—are understood by contemporaries and the tradition to refer to the *homoousion*.[34] It follows that all the divine attributes are possessed comprehensively by all three persons. Each person of the Trinity, when considered in himself, is totally and comprehensively God, and is the whole God.

Why take as "absolute" statement.

3.2.2 *Hypostatic Distinctions*

Stephen Holmes remarks, "The three divine *hypostases* are distinguished by eternal relations of origin—begetting and proceeding—and not otherwise."[35] If Holmes is referring simply to the immanent Trinity, the Trinity in its eternal state, this is acceptable. However, as an absolute statement it needs nuancing, since the missions in human history disclose significant distinctions that reflect on the eternal immanent relations. There is a difference between the Spirit appearing temporarily as a dove and the Son becoming permanently incarnate.[36] The Spirit indwells the church, whereas the Son assumed a human nature into hypostatic union. The Father was not sent and does not proceed. These clear differences indicate eternal distinctions. Yet, since all three persons act together inseparably in all God's works, these distinctions are not divisions but point to harmony and indivisibility. They are distinctions not of opposition but of congruity. Brian Davies refers to Aquinas's conviction that, since God is simple and the relations between the persons are real, as are

---

33. Gregory of Nazianzus, *Oration 30* 20 (*PG*, 36:128–32); Gregory of Nazianzus, *Oration 31* 14, 16 (*PG*, 36:148–52); Gregory of Nazianzus, *Oration 40* 43 (*PG*, 36:420–21).

34. Gregory of Nyssa, *Against Eunomius* 3.4; Saint Photios, *On the Mystagogy of the Holy Spirit* (n.p.: Studion, 1983). In view of this, it is puzzling, to say the least, to read Warfield's comments on "the subordinationism which entrenched itself in the Nicene Fathers." Benjamin B. Warfield, "Calvin's Doctrine of the Trinity," in *Calvin and Augustine* (Philadelphia: Presbyterian and Reformed, 1974), 267.

35. S. R. Holmes, *The Holy Trinity: Understanding God's Life* (Milton Keynes: Paternoster, 2012), 200. "Personae enim divinae, quum in essentia conveniant, non possunt distingui nisi per relationem originis." Aquinas, *SCG* 4.26.

36. See Augustine, *De Trinitate* 2.11.

the distinctions, not existing merely in our minds, it follows that they are coextensive with God's essence, with who God is.[37]

Can a thing be numerically the same without identity? Scott Williams refers to Henry of Ghent, who wrote that a divine person is constituted by a real relation (*relatio*) and is numerically the same thing (*res*) as the divine essence without being identical to it.[38] He provides the example of a bronze statue of Athena. The lump of bronze occupies the same space-time where the statue is: are there two objects or one? The bronze is precisely identical to the statue formed from the bronze. However, Rea and Brower argue that they are not identical. The statue can be melted down and recast into a different statue, whereas the piece of bronze would remain.[39] Clearly, this analogy has limitations, but it does shed light on the point at issue.

3.2.3 Perichorēsis

Although this precise word is not used in Trinitarian discourse until later, the truth it signifies, mutual indwelling, is already in vogue. Athanasius and the Cappadocians brought to the forefront the idea of the full mutual indwelling of the three persons in the one being of God. Although C does not use the idea, it is entailed by all that C openly expresses. It follows from the *homoousial* identity of the three and the indivisible divine being. Since all three persons are fully God, and the whole God is in each of the three, the three mutually contain one another. As Gerald Bray puts it, all three occupy the same infinite divine space.[40]

This idea was developed, and the term introduced, by John of Damascus (ca. 675–ca. 749).[41] It is entailed in the pervasive reference to the three persons as inseparable, their union unbreakable. None of them occupies space, so to speak, that the others do not. Here divine and human persons differ, as the Leiden Synopsis explains. Human persons do not

---

37. Aquinas, *ST* 1a.28.1–3, cf. 1a.28–32; Brian Davies, *Thomas Aquinas's* Summa Theologiae: *A Guide and Commentary* (Oxford: Oxford University Press, 2014), 100–101. Also, Aquinas, *SCG* 4.2–26; Davies, *Thomas Aquinas's* Summa contra Gentiles: *A Guide and Commentary* (Oxford: Oxford University Press, 2016), 300–304.
38. Scott M. Williams, "Henry of Ghent on Real Relations and the Trinity: The Case for Numerical Sameness without Identity," *RTPM* 79 (2012): 109–48.
39. Williams, "Henry of Ghent," 112–13.
40. Gerald Bray, *The Doctrine of God* (Leicester: Inter-Varsity Press, 1993), 158.
41. Charles C. Twombly, *Perichoresis and Personhood: God, Christ, and Salvation in John of Damascus* (Eugene, OR: Pickwick, 2015).

exist in one another.[42] As human beings, we are not only distinct but apart. We act differently; we go our separate ways; some live a long time while others die young. Moreover, there are a vast number of different human beings, and the sum total increases or diminishes as time goes by. But the divine persons are three, no more and no less, and are so eternally without change. That is why the generic analogy of three men sharing a common human nature could never remotely approximate the Trinity.

3.3   Inseparable Operations and Distinct Appropriations

The theme of inseparable operations is a constant leitmotif in the fourth and fifth century pro-Nicenes of both Greek and Latin churches.[43] From it comes the phrase *opera Trinitatis ad extra indivisa sunt* (the external works of the Trinity are indivisible). Since God is one indivisible being, in all his works all three persons operate inseparably.

Creation was a work of the whole Trinity. Genesis 1:1–5 hints at that: "In the beginning God created. . . . The Spirit of God was hovering over the face of the waters. . . . And God said . . ." There is God, the Spirit, and the Word. The idea surfaces in Psalm 33:6–9, reinforced by the New Testament teaching on Christ and the Spirit (John 1:1–3; Eph. 1:11; Col. 1:15–17; Heb. 1:1–3). The same passages include providence in their scope. The incarnation involved the Father sending the Son (John 3:16–17; 5:23–24, 37–39), the Son taking human nature into union, conceived by the Holy Spirit (Luke 1:34–35). At Jesus's baptism, the Father speaks, declaring him to be his Son, while the Spirit descends as a dove and rests upon him (Matt. 3:13–17). On the cross, the Son offers himself through the eternal Spirit to the Father (Heb. 9:14), after which he is raised from the dead by the Spirit of the Father (Rom. 8:10–11). This is underlined by Paul as he surveys the whole field of redemption (Gal. 4:4–6; Eph. 1:3–14). Thus, we have access to God the Trinity by the Spirit, through Christ, to the Father (Eph. 2:18).

The inseparability of the Trinitarian actions was a major theme of Augustine, but it was also held by the Cappadocians.[44] Augustine

---

42. Johannes Polyander et al., *Synopsis purioris theologiae, disputationibus quinquaginta duabus comprehensa* (Leiden: Ex officina Elzeverianus, 1625), 77.

43. Athanasius, *Serapion* 1.17–18, 28, 30–31; Didymus the Blind, *On the Holy Spirit* 75–80; Gregory of Nazianzus, *Oration 31*; Gregory of Nyssa, *On "Not Three Gods"*; Augustine, *De Trinitate* 1–2, 6.

44. Augustine, *John* 20.3, 8 (NPNF[1], 7:132–34); *Letter 169, to Evodius* 2.5–7 (NPNF[1], 1:540–41).

strenuously affirms, "Just as Father and Son and Holy Spirit are inseparable, so do they work inseparably."[45] Yet, as the three are eternally distinct, each work is specifically attributed—or *appropriated*—to one of them. The Son is sent by the Father and is conceived by the Spirit, but only he becomes flesh. Only the Spirit comes at Pentecost, while sent by the Father and the Son. In Augustine's words, "although in all things the divine persons act perfectly in common, and without possibility of separation, nevertheless their operations behoved to be exhibited in such a way as to be distinguished from each other."[46] We might say they work in harmony rather than in unison.

This was expressed well by Maximus the Confessor, referring to the mystery of the incarnation:

> This mystery was known to the Father by his approval . . . to the Son by his carrying it out . . . and to the Holy Spirit by his cooperation . . . in it. For there is one knowledge shared by the Father, the Son, and the Holy Spirit because they also share one essence and power. The Father and the Holy Spirit were not ignorant of the incarnation of the Son because the whole Father is by essence in the whole Son who himself carried out the mystery of our salvation through his incarnation. The Father himself did not become incarnate but rather approved the incarnation of the Son. Moreover, the Holy Spirit exists by essence in the whole Son, but he too did not become incarnate but rather cooperated in the Son's ineffable incarnation for our sake.[47]

Within these boundaries Trinitarian reflection should take place.[48]

Aquinas's treatment has been influential in the Western tradition. Since, he reasons, because of the divine simplicity, the essence is the same as the person, "it follows that in God essence is not really distinct from person; and yet that the persons are really distinguished from each other." Persons are distinguished from each other because they are real relations of opposition.[49] Hence, "the divine persons are not distinguished as regards being, in which they subsist, or in anything absolute,

45. Augustine, *De Trinitate* 1.7, in Hill, *Augustine*, 70.
46. Augustine, *Letter 11, to Nebridius* 4 (NPNF¹, 1:230).
47. Maximus the Confessor, *Ad Thalassium* 60, in Paul M. Blowers, *On the Cosmic Mystery of Jesus Christ: Selected Writings of St. Maximus the Confessor* (Crestwood, NY: St Vladimir's Seminary Press, 2003), 127.
48. Aquinas, *ST* 1a.28, 1a.43; Davies, Summa Theologiae: A Guide, 100ff.
49. Aquinas, *ST* 1a.39.1.

but only as regards something relative. Hence relation suffices for their distinction."[50] Consequently, the word *God* is sometimes used for the essence and sometimes for the person.[51]

There is no evidence that any of the pro-Nicenes "take as their point of departure the psychological intercommunion of three distinct people."[52] To do so would open the door to heresy.

3.4 The *Taxis* (Τάξις)[53]

In terms of the *relations* between the three, there is a clear order: *from the Father through the Son by the Holy Spirit*. These relations cannot be reversed—the Son does not beget the Father, nor does the Father proceed from the Holy Spirit. In this sense only, the Father is the first, the Son the second, and the Holy Spirit the third. However, some Eastern theologians—following hints in Basil and Gregory of Nyssa—refer to the Father as the source or origin of the deity of the Son and the Spirit, language with subordinationist overtones. T. F. Torrance's argument that the monarchy should be seen as that of the whole Trinity rather than the person of the Father, on the grounds that all three persons are coequally God while retaining the distinctive relations of the persons, was a basis for agreement between Orthodox and Reformed churches recently, although it is not universally accepted.[54] It was also taught by Gregory of Nazianzus,[55] who regarded the Father as the source of the hypostatic subsistence of the Son and Spirit.[56]

---

50. Aquinas, *ST* 1a.40.2.

51. Aquinas, *ST* 1a.39.4.

52. Ayres, *Nicaea and Its Legacy*, 292.

53. *Taxis* has a range of meanings. It was often used in military contexts and had the idea of rank, entailing a hierarchy of some kind. This fit well with the Arian view of a gradation between the Father and the Son, with the latter of a lower and subordinate status. However, the term was also used of role, office, class, orderliness and regularity of the stars, order in the church or monastery, or an ordered constitution. It is in the sense of order, not rank, closer to what is fitting and suitable rather than any hierarchy, that the orthodox use the term. See G. W. H. Lampe, ed., *A Patristic Greek Lexicon* (Oxford: Clarendon, 1961), 1372–73.

54. For the limitations of this agreement, see 4.3, p. 131.

55. Torrance, *Christian Doctrine of God*, 168–202; Thomas F. Torrance, *Trinitarian Perspectives: Toward Doctrinal Agreement* (Edinburgh: T&T Clark, 1994); Gregory of Nazianzus, *Oration 29* 2 (PG, 36:76); Gregory of Nazianzus, *Oration 31* 13–16 (PG, 36:148–52); Gregory of Nazianzus, *Oration 39* 12 (PG, 36:348).

56. Gregory of Nazianzus, *Oration 25* 18; Noble, "Gregory Nazianzen"; Christopher A. Beeley, *Gregory of Nazianzus on the Trinity and the Knowledge of God: In Your Light We Shall See Light* (Oxford: Oxford University Press, 2008), 206–10. Giles's proposal that "monarchy" be reserved for the authority of the whole Trinity and *archē* for the Father as the source of the hypostases of the Son and the Spirit is worth heeding in view of the semantic confusion that generally prevails. Kevin Giles, "The Father as the *Mia Archē*," *Colloquium* 46, no. 2 (2014): 175–92.

While the three are one indivisible being, they are not identical to one another. It was modalism that confused them; this still surfaces whenever the personal distinctions are in any way blurred or confined to human history. The *relations* the three sustain to each other are inseparable from their identity and so are eternal and unchangeable. Thus, the Father is the Father of the Son, and the Son is the Son of the Father. The Father begets the Son, the Son is begotten by the Father. This eternal relation is neither interchangeable nor reversible. *Mutatis mutandis*, the Spirit proceeds from the Father (the West adds "and the Son"), while the Father (and the Son, according to the West) spirates the Spirit. This is never reversed. The Father is neither begotten, nor does he proceed; the Son neither begets nor proceeds; the Spirit neither begets nor spirates. These relations exist in connection with the mutual indwelling of the three (*perichorēsis*). Indeed, the Spirit is the Spirit of the Son, which entails that the Father is the Father of the Son, while the relation of the Father and the Son is in the midst of the perichoretic relations of the three, and thus in the Holy Spirit. There is a distinction—not a division—between the three as they distinctly and together constitute the one undivided being of God and the three in their eternal and distinct personal relations.

Torrance points to the foundational work of Gregory of Nazianzus. Gregory effected a shift from the concept of "modes of being" found in Basil to a view of

> interrelations that belong intrinsically to what Father, Son, and Holy Spirit are coinherently in themselves and in their mutual objective relations with and for one another . . . [relations that are] just as substantial as what they are unchangeably in themselves and by themselves. . . . "Person" is an onto-relational concept.[57]

Calvin sums this up when he says of the Son that he is God of himself (*ex seipso esse*), whereas in terms of his personal subsistence he is from the Father (*ex Patre*).[58]

In this light, that the Son is *under* the Father in his incarnate lowliness according to the flesh is compatible with his being *from* the Father eternally in the unity of the indivisible Trinity. Nowhere is this

57. Torrance, *Christian Doctrine of God*, 157.
58. Calvin, *Institutes*, 1.13.25; cf. 1.13.17–19.

Does this make sense?

expressed more vividly than by Paul in Philippians 2:5–8: "Have this mind among yourselves which is yours in Christ Jesus," he says. The incarnate Christ followed a path of obedience and humiliation, leading to the cruel and—especially for those in Philippi, a Roman colony—shameful death of the cross. He looked not to his own interests but to those of others. This loving self-sacrificial obedience was the fruit of his decision in eternity, expressing the indivisible will of God in its hypostatic manifestation in the Son, not to exploit his status "in the form of God" for his own advantage.[59] "Being in the form of God, he did not use his status of equality with God for his own advantage[60] but emptied himself, taking the form of a slave" (2:6–7, my trans). His self-emptying involved an addition, not a subtraction. He emptied himself not by ceasing to be who he eternally was and is but by becoming man, and following a path of obedience that led to the death of the cross. He added the form of a servant to the form of God. However, his determination not to exploit his true and real status for his own advantage was made in eternity. His human obedience expresses his divine commitment to self-emptying, not by his ceasing to be who he eternally is but by adding lowly humanity.[61]

Then how what was emptied "emptied"?

The latter no more detracts from his full deity than does his post-resurrection exaltation diminish his full humanity. His human obedience *under* the Father flows from his free decision, in the indivisible will of the Trinity, and comports with his eternal hypostatic relation *from* the Father. Hebrews 5:1–10 runs along similar lines, referring to Christ's refusal to claim the office of High Priest for himself as, instead, he accepted his appointment by the Father. While his office as High Priest began on earth, this statement cannot be restricted in scope to his incarnate life

---

59. On the phrase ἐν μορφῇ θεοῦ, see, among others, Ralph P. Martin, *Carmen Christi: Philippians ii.5–11 in Recent Interpretation and in the Setting of Early Christian Worship* (Grand Rapids, MI: Eerdmans, 1983).

60. The word ἁρπαγμός has been the subject of intense debate through the years. See Roy W. Hoover, "The Harpagmos Enigma: A Philological Solution," *HTR* 64 (1971): 95–119; Ralph Martin, *Philippians*, The New Century Bible Commentary (Grand Rapids, MI: Eerdmans, 1980), 96–97; N. T. Wright, "Harpagmos and the Meaning of Philippians ii.5–11," *JTS* 37 (1986): 321–52.

61. Lossky comments that there is a twofold *kenosis* (self-emptying). In the first place, the Son submitted his will to the will of the Father. This is actually the will of the whole Trinity, for the Father's will is the source of will, the will of the Son is expressed in obedience, and the will of the Spirit in accomplishment. The Son's submission led to his incarnation. Second, there is also the kenosis of the deified humanity of Christ, by which he submitted to the fallen condition of humanity, which entailed suffering and death. The first *kenosis* is the basis of the second. Vladimir Lossky, *The Mystical Theology of the Eastern Church* (London: James Clarke, 1957), 144–46. Lossky here appears to divide the one indivisible will.

since the appointment preceded the work. John Owen, among others, referred this to the covenant of redemption in eternity.[62]

This is what God is like. When he seeks his glory, he is not pursuing self-interest like a celestial bully. The Trinity is an indivisible union, a union of love, each seeking the interests of the other. Thus, the Father allows the Son to bring in the kingdom, the Son leads us to the Father, while the Spirit does not speak of himself but testifies of the Son.[63] This was articulated originally by Gregory of Nyssa when he wrote that in their mutual indwelling, the three seek the glory of the others. There is, he says,

> a revolving circle of glory from like to like. The Son is glorified by the Spirit; the Father is glorified by the Son; again the Son has his glory from the Father; and the Only-begotten thus becomes the glory of the Spirit. . . . In like manner . . . faith completes the circle, and glorifies the Son by means of the Spirit, and the Father by means of the Son.[64]

3.5   Eternal Generation, Eternal Procession

Since Irenaeus, the church has held that the Father begat the Son in eternity. This comes to expression in C and is repeated in later confessions.[65] Constantinople II (553) anathematized those who rejected it.[66] This doctrine has come under fire on both biblical and theological grounds. Since the nineteenth century, many New Testament scholars have held that this teaching does not find biblical support, since the word μονογενής[67] means "only" or "one and only." It is also held that the passage in Psalm 2:7, "You are my Son; / today I have begotten you," is cited in the New Testament with reference to Jesus's resurrection (Acts 13:33) and so does not refer to the relation between the Father and the Son in eternity. From the theological angle, it is argued that the eternal generation of the Son implies a subordinate status for the Son, and that its roots are Neoplatonic. Similar arguments have been advanced on the eternal procession of the Holy Spirit.

---

62. *The Works of John Owen*, ed. William H. Goold, 23 vols. (1850–1855; repr., London: Banner of Truth, 1965–1968), 19:77–86.

63. Wolfhart Pannenberg, *Systematic Theology*, trans. Geoffrey W. Bromiley, 3 vols. (Grand Rapids, MI: Eerdmans, 1991–1998), 1:315–17.

64. Gregory of Nyssa, *On the Holy Spirit against the Macedonians* (NPNF[2], 5:324).

65. WCF, 2.3; WLC, 10.

66. *Capitulum* 2 (NPNF[2], 14:312).

67. *monogenēs*, "only-begotten" in older New Testament translations.

Let us look first at the biblical criticisms, although the doctrine was not developed on those grounds, nor is it hostage to the meaning of any one word or to biblical exegesis alone. It is a theological predicate grounded in the eternal relations of the Son and the Father in the one being of God.

First, the older idea of μονογενής has never entirely been eclipsed. Although B. F. Westcott, B. B. Warfield, and the majority of twentieth- and twenty-first-century exegetes abandoned it,[68] the idea that it means "only-begotten" has continued support from, for example, F. Büchsel, J. V. Dahms, C. H. Dodd, M.-J. Lagrange, F. F. Bruce, John Frame, and Roger Beckwith.[69] Moreover, it is important to consider the contexts where the word occurs. Μονογενής refers to the Son of God only in the writings of John, in John 1:14, 1:18, 3:16, 3:18, and in 1 John 4:9. Common to each context is that the force of the passage relates to Christian believers being born or begotten by God. The verb γεννάω[70] is used in each place.

John 1:14 reads, "And the Word became flesh and dwelt among us, and we have seen his glory, glory as of the [μονογενής] from the Father, full of grace and truth." This refers to the Son's incarnation and to his life and ministry. John has recorded that those who believed in his name were given authority to become children of God. These believers or children of God were born of God (ἐκ θεοῦ ἐγεννήθησαν). The focus here is the regeneration of believers, sharply distanced from physical generation. The idea of birth or begetting is pervasive, and directly connected with God's Son; he is the μονογενής from the Father, and they are the children (τέκνα) of God. As God has become the Father of believers in

---

68. Robert L. Reymond, *A New Systematic Theology of the Christian Faith* (New York: Nelson, 1998), 326ff.; Raymond E. Brown, *The Gospel according to John (i–xii)*, The Anchor Bible (Garden City, NY: Doubleday, 1966), 13–14; Brooke Foss Westcott, *The Gospel according to St. John: The Greek Text with Introduction and Notes* (London: John Murray, 1908), 1:23; B. B. Warfield, "The Biblical Doctrine of the Trinity," in *Biblical and Theological Studies*, ed. Samuel G. Craig (Philadelphia: Presbyterian and Reformed, 1952), 52; C. H. Turner, "O UIOS MOU O AGAPH-TOS," *JTS* 27 (1926): 113–29; Dale Moody, "God's Only Son: The Translation of John 3:16 in the Revised Standard Version," *JBL* 72 (1953): 213–19; Otto Betz, *What Do We Know about Jesus?* (London: SCM, 1968).

69. John V. Dahms, "The Johannine Use of Monogenēs Reconsidered," *NTS* 29 (1983): 222–32; M. Theobald, *Die Fleischwerdung des Logos* (Münster: Aschendorf, 1988), 250–54; F. Büchsel, "μονογενής," in *TDNT*, 4:737–41; C. H. Dodd, *The Interpretation of the Fourth Gospel* (Cambridge: Cambridge University Press, 1953), 305; M.-J. Lagrange, *Evangile selon Saint Jean* (Paris: Gabalda, 1948), 413; F. F. Bruce, *The Gospel of John* (Grand Rapids, MI: Eerdmans, 1984), 65n26; John M. Frame, *The Doctrine of God* (Phillipsburg, NJ: P&R, 2002), 710–11; Roger Beckwith, "The Calvinist Doctrine of the Trinity," *Churchman* 115 (2001): 308–16.

70. *gennaō*, "beget" or "give birth."

their generation or birth, the Word stands in relation to the Father as his μονογενής. His relation to the Father is in view, not any particular event in his life or saving work. In John 1:18, the Word is described as "[μονογενής] God [or Son], who is at the Father's side," who has made the unseen God known. The same contextual considerations apply, and again the immediate reference is to his being in the most immediate proximity to the Father, a relation that self-evidently transcends the purely temporal.

In John 3:16–18, John's comments follow his account of Jesus confronting Nicodemus with his need for a radical rebirth by the Holy Spirit, without which he will not see the kingdom of God. The regenerative work of the Spirit is indispensably necessary to eternal life. The similarities with 1:14–18 are obvious. In both passages, God is the author of life or of a new status as his children. Again, γεννάω occurs seven times in 3:4–7. Jesus talks of birth or begetting by the Spirit, mysterious and inscrutable. These are heavenly things, not earthly (3:12), connected with his incarnation, crucifixion, and ascension (3:13–14). In this context John says that the Father sent his μονογενής Son to give eternal life to all who believe (3:16). Lack of faith in the μονογενής will debar a person from life (3:18). John uses the term, as in chapter 1, to refer to the Son in relation to the Father, in immediate connection with regeneration to life by the Holy Spirit.

In 1 John 4:7–9, John urges his readers to love one another. Everyone who loves has been begotten by God (again the verb is γεννάω) and so knows God. Again, begetting by the Holy Spirit is in view, the outset of spiritual life. Then John says, "In this the love of God was made manifest among us, that God sent his [μονογενής] Son into the world, so that we might live through him." The same features are present here too; the μονογενής Son is in relation to God the Father. Those who love and know God, receive life from God, compared to being begotten.

In 1 John 5:18, John says, "Everyone who has been begotten [γεγεννημένος] of God does not sin, but he who was begotten of God [γεννηθείς] keeps him, and the evil one does not touch him" (my trans.). The difference in tenses between the perfect, referring clearly to those begotten to new life by God, and the aorist supports the idea that the latter refers to a different subject than does the former, and thus to Christ. The reference again is to eternity, the relation between the Father and the Son, and the connection is again to regeneration.[71]

In each case no particular episode in the Son's career is in view. Certainly, Peter connects our regeneration with Christ's resurrection, since we are raised to new life in union with Christ, who was raised from the dead (1 Pet. 1:3); and so too does Paul (Rom. 6:1–11). But John has in focus the Son's relation with the Father, existing throughout his earthly life, in effect when he is sent into the world. Moreover, this relation is eternal, preceding creation (John 1:1–3, 18; 8:58; 20:31). The invariable connection with spiritual generation makes it impossible to eliminate any reference to begetting in connection with the Son. While the doctrine of eternal generation does not stand or fall or even depend on this one word, it is important to recognize that claims that it has no bearing on the question are exaggerated.

As for the statement in Psalm 2:7, "I will tell of the decree: / The LORD said to me, 'You are my Son; / today I have begotten you,'" while it denotes a royal reference in the context of Israel, it comes to full expression in the resurrection of God's Son to reign over his enemies. Paul cites it in this way in his speech in Acts 13, and that is the probable sense in Hebrews 1:5. However, it points beyond that. Psalm 2:7 refers to the relation between Yahweh and the one he calls "my Son," signifying the nature of the one who speaks (Yahweh) and the one addressed (Yahweh's Son). As such, while it reaches fulfillment in Jesus's resurrection, it can hardly be limited to that. Moreover, further support is found in the overall witness to the Son as the radiance of the Father's glory (Heb. 1:3) and the like.[72]

The attacks on eternal generation on biblical grounds need to be reconsidered. Its validity is related to the teaching of the eternal relation of the Son to the Father in the undivided being of God.

Additionally, criticisms have been made of eternal generation on theological grounds. Some have claimed that the teaching posits a lesser

---

71. See the translations of the RSV (1946, 1952), NEB, and NIV; John R. W. Stott, *The Epistles of John: An Introduction and Commentary* (London: Tyndale Press, 1964), 192; Kenneth Grayston, *The Johannine Epistles*, The New Century Bible Commentary (Grand Rapids, MI: Eerdmans, 1984), 145. In Stott's words, "It is the high privilege of the Christian to be like Christ . . . begotten of God and therefore sons of God." He adds that our begetting and sonship are different from his, which are unique and eternal, but they are sufficiently similar to make it possible for John to use almost identical expressions to cover both.

72. See the intriguing comments of Matthew W. Bates, *The Birth of the Trinity: Jesus, God, and Spirit in New Testament and Early Christian Interpretations of the Old Testament* (Oxford: Oxford University Press, 2015), 64–73.

status for the Son, as an emanation from the Father in Neoplatonic guise. However, this is not how the framers of C understand the matter.[73] Indeed, it is difficult to make a case that Origen saw it that way, for he countered gnostic ideas of emanation and asserted the Son's identity with the Father. Widdicombe observes that Origen's twin aim is to stress the Son's real individual existence and also his sharing the divine nature of the Father. Origen aims to keep a balance between these two fundamental ideas.[74] The fathers, including Origen, consistently urge that all ideas of human generation be removed from the picture. Human begetting entails a beginning of existence; human fathers exist before their sons are begotten. This is not the case here. The Father is always the Father, the Son is always the Son.[75] In the *Expositio fidei*, a work attributed to Athanasius[76] but with all the marks of Marcellus of Ancyra,[77] the author states that the Son is "true God of true God . . . omnipotent from omnipotent . . . whole from whole."[78] This was to be the basis of the relevant section in C. Marcellus, of all people, can hardly be accused of subordinationism; rather the reverse. But the argument is not materially affected if Athanasius was the author. Later, Photios argues too that the creedal statements connected with eternal generation underline the *homoousios* of the Father and the Son.[79]

Similar principles apply to the procession of the Spirit. It is often claimed that the *locus classicus*, John 15:26, refers purely to the history of salvation, to the coming of the Spirit at Pentecost, and so any projection back into eternity is not only exegetically improper but also mere speculation. However, while Jesus's comments clearly do refer to Pentecost, they cannot be restricted to it. In keeping with the rest of the pericope, John uses the future [πέμψω] to refer to Jesus's sending the Spirit at that particular time, but says that he "proceeds [ἐκπο-

---

73. Cf. Gregory of Nyssa, *Against Eunomius* 3.4.

74. Widdicombe, *The Fatherhood of God*, 85–86.

75. On the eternal generation of the Son and its application to the relations of the persons, not the divine essence, see Francis Turretin, *Institutes of Elenctic Theology*, trans. George Musgrave Giger, ed. James T. Dennison Jr. (Phillipsburg, NJ: P&R, 1992), 1:278–302, esp. 292–302.

76. *PG*, 25:199–208.

77. Hanson, *Search*, 231.

78. *PG*, 25:201.

79. Photios, *On the Mystagogy of the Holy Spirit*, 92, 170. For other examinations of the question see Paul A. Rainbow, "Orthodox Trinitarianism and Evangelical Feminism," ResearchGate, https://www.researchgate.net/publication/265623530_Orthodox_Trinitarianism_and_Evangelical _Feminism; and Lee Irons, "The Eternal Generation of the Son," The Upper Register, http://www .upper-register.com/papers/monogenes.html.

ρεύεται—present indicative] from the Father." The Spirit's sending at Pentecost, in which the Son is the sender, is distinct from the Spirit's procession, which is continuous and for which the Father is the spirator. Even if this were a Hebraic parallelism, we are again in the realm of the relation between two distinct agents, the Father and the Spirit. The nature of these agents should govern our view of the relation between them. As D. A. Carson agrees, the early creedal statement on the procession of the Spirit is "eminently defensible" since the clause here in John 15:26 (allowing for John's theology in this Gospel) presupposes this ontological status.[80] As with the Son, the parameters indicate clearly that neither the Son nor the Spirit is subordinate in being or status, and that the begetting and procession apply to their relations as persons.

The strategic significance of the doctrine. As Bavinck states, "God's fecundity is a beautiful theme." The doctrine of the generation of the Son displays God as "no abstract, fixed, monadic, solitary substance, but a plenitude of life. It is his nature to be generative and fruitful."[81] Indeed, "without generation, creation would not be possible. If, in an absolute sense, God could not communicate himself to the Son, he would be even less able, in a relative sense, to communicate himself to his creature."[82] In this, Bavinck reflects the classic Trinitarian doctrine, that the persons are oriented to each other. The Father is the Father of the Son; the Son is the Son of the Father. The three are inherently relational. This relationality underlies God's free determination to create—an act of his will, exercised in harmony with his nature.[83]

Generation is ineffable and incomparable. Eternal generation reflects the incomprehensibility of God and is a transcendent mystery, beyond the grasp of our minds. It is a matter of faith. This poses no problem, or else faith would be based on our own capacities. This was uniformly recognized by the fathers; for them it was a great mystery. The idea that

---

80. D. A. Carson, *The Gospel according to St John* (Leicester: Inter-Varsity Press, 1991), on 15:26.

81. Bavinck, *RD*, 2:308.

82. Bavinck, *RD*, 2:420.

83. This connection between the generation of the Son and creation has also been considered by Athanasius, *Contra Arianos* 2.2; Aquinas, *ST* 1a.14.8, 1a.19.1–4; Hans Urs Von Balthasar, *Theo-Drama: Theological Dramatic Theory*, trans. Graham Harrison (San Francisco: Ignatius, 1994), 4:323–31. See Eugene R. Schlesinger, "Trinity, Incarnation and Time: A Restatement of the Doctrine of God in Conversation with Robert Jenson," *SJT* 69 (2016): 189–203, esp. 200.

they were given to speculative attempts to explain it is not borne out by the sources.

Generation is in contrast to creation; the Son is of the same nature as the Father, yet distinct. The doctrine of eternal generation obviates any notion of the Son as a creature. In the creed the positive "begotten" and the negative "not made" are equally vital. Simultaneously, the dogma asserts identity of nature and personal distinctions—the heart of the doctrine of the Trinity. What is generated is identical in nature to the one who generates. The Father and the Son are numerically one. Yet the Son is not the Father, the Father is not the Son, and the Holy Spirit is neither the Father nor the Son. And yet the three are one. That the Father is not the Son is a matter not of difference or diversity but of distinction. So, as Aquinas says, the Father is other than the Son but not something else, while they are one thing but not one person.[84] Citing Augustine, he holds that the Father is the principle (*principium*),[85] "that whence another proceeds." Aquinas argues against calling the Father the cause of the Son, since it implies diversity of substance, but "principle" entails simply an order between them, a procession and no inferiority. The word signifies not priority but origin.[86] Eternal generation underlines the point that the Father is the Father of the Son in eternity before he is ever Father of the creature in time.[87]

Generation highlights an irreversible hypostatic order. We saw that the New Testament authors refer to the three persons in differing orders (Matt. 28:19–20; 1 Cor. 12:4–6; 2 Cor. 13:14; Eph. 4:4–6; Rev. 1:4–5), but that there is a general pattern evident throughout the economy of creation, providence, and grace; *from the Father through the Son by the Spirit* (Matt. 28:19). In turn, our response to God's grace is enabled by the Spirit, offered through the Son, and resting on the Father (Eph. 2:18). God's revelation in human history reflects eternal antecedent realities, for he is faithful to himself. He acts in conformity with who he is. Thus, the Father sends the Son, while the Spirit proceeds from the Father and is sent by the Son, never the reverse. The relations of sending and being sent reflect the order of begetting and being begotten. There is a distinction, although the two are inseparably related.

---

84. Aquinas, *ST* 1a.31.2.
85. Augustine, *De Trinitate* 4.20.
86. Aquinas, *ST* 1a.33.1; Calvin, *Institutes*, 1.13.18.
87. Aquinas, *ST* 1a.33.3. For a fuller discussion, see Aquinas, *SCG* 4.10–14.

The dogma of eternal generation is crucial. The generation is eternal, since the Father and the Son are eternal. As Bavinck puts it, "Rejection of the eternal generation of the Son involves not only a failure to do justice to the deity of the Son, but also to that of the Father"; and, "It is not something that was completed and finished at some point in eternity, but an eternal unchanging act of God, at once always complete and eternally ongoing. . . . The Father is not and never was ungenerative; he begets everlastingly."[88] Since God is eternal and transcends time—which he created—the Trinitarian relations are eternal. There is not a punctiliar moment when the Father begets the Son, for that would place generation within the parameters of space-time and be contrary to its place within the eternal life of the indivisible Trinity. It follows that eternal generation is emphatically opposed to subordination.[89] The order—from the Father through the Son by the Holy Spirit—is not hierarchical, nor is it patterned after human relationships. Rather, it is an order of equals, in the identity of the indivisible Trinity.[90]

3.6   The Processions and the Missions

The sendings of the Son and the Spirit by the Father in human history (the missions) are distinguishable from their eternal antecedent relations (the processions). Yet, at the same time, the missions reflect the processions.[91] Gilles Emery writes of "a profound correspondence between . . . the eternal property of the Son and the Holy Spirit and . . . their visible missions." Thus, the sending of the Holy Spirit reflects his eternal procession.[92]

This brings us close to the relationship between the Son in eternity and the Son in human history, between his relation to the Father in the indivisible Trinity and his mission here for us and our salvation. Emery comments:

> The patristic and medieval tradition will be especially attentive to the correspondence between the sending of the Son into the world and his eternal origin: in the same way that the Son is sent by the Father,

---

88. Bavinck, *RD*, 2:310.
89. Contra John V. Dahms, "The Generation of the Son," *JETS* 32 (1989): 493–501; Dahms, "The Subordination of the Son," *JETS* 37 (1994): 351–64.
90. "In the divine life there is therefore no line on which the relation describable as God's sending and Jesus' obedience could occupy a position 'after' anything." Robert Jenson, "Once More the *Logos Asarkos*," *IJST* 13 (2011): 133. This is colored by Jenson's identification of the Son with the history of Jesus of Nazareth and the problems this creates for the freedom of God, eternity, and the preexistence of the Son. On eternal generation, see Kevin Giles, *The Eternal Generation of the Son: Maintaining Orthodoxy in Trinitarian Theology* (Downers Grove, IL: IVP Academic, 2012).
91. Aquinas, *ST* 1a.43.2.
92. Gilles Emery, *The Trinity: An Introduction to Catholic Doctrine of the Triune God*, trans. Matthew Levering (Washington, DC: Catholic University of America Press, 2011), 183.

he has his existence from the Father. In other words, when Trinitarian doctrine speaks of the divine person in terms of "relation of origin," it is not a speculation detached from the economy of salvation, but rather it proposes a doctrine grounded on the teaching of the Gospels about Jesus, whose existence is always relative to his Father. The *mystery* of the Father and the Son is present and revealed in the *economy*.[93]

So Emery adds:

This teaching makes manifest a profound correspondence between, on the one hand, the eternal property of the Son and the Holy Spirit and, on the other hand, their "visible mission." The Son is begotten from all eternity by the Father. As Son, he receives from the Father his being the principle of the Holy Spirit, along with the Father: with the Father, the Son spirates the Holy Spirit. It therefore pertains to the Son, in his very quality as Son, to be sent by the Father as *Author of sanctification*—that is to say, as *Giver of the Holy Spirit*. This is a dimension of the "fittingness" of the Son's incarnation that we discover here.[94]

Aquinas comments that sending implies not inferiority but procession of origin, which is according to equality.[95] Since mission is according to procession of origin, and the Father is the principle of the Trinity and is not from another, "in no way is it fitting for him to be sent."[96] Thus, also, the missions of the Son and the Holy Spirit are distinct, as generation is distinguished from procession.[97]

This highlights the connection between the economic Trinity and the immanent Trinity, concepts for our benefit, since there can be only one Trinity. If the economic Trinity, the Trinity as revealed in history, did not reveal the immanent Trinity, the Trinity in itself, we would have no true knowledge of God and could not be saved. There can be no possibility of God being other than he has revealed himself to be.

3.7   The Father as the Source of the Son and the Spirit

The East has typically been seen as basing its Trinitarian doctrine on the Father as the source of the personal subsistence of the Son and the Spirit,

---

93. Emery, *The Trinity*, 27.
94. Emery, *The Trinity*, 183–84 (italics original).
95. Aquinas, *ST* 1a.43.1.
96. Aquinas, *ST* 1a.34.4.
97. Aquinas, *ST* 1a.43.5.

in contrast to the Western stress on the unity of the one divine essence. This characterization is overdone; both hold to the indivisibility of the Trinity, both regard the Father as the *archē* (East) or *principium* (West).[98]

Among the Cappadocians, Gregory of Nazianzus saw this as the fundamental element of his theological system.[99] In Beeley's words, "The unity or oneness of the Trinity . . . is constituted by the Father's begetting of the Son and sending forth of the Spirit." Reflecting on the confusion among modern historians and theologians, who think that the monarchy of the Father, the generation of the Son, and the procession of the Spirit conflict a priori with their unity and equality in being,[100] Beeley argues, "To put it more sharply, Gregory is firmly rejecting the notion that the monarchy of the Father in any way conflicts with the equality of the three persons— on the grounds that it is precisely what brings about that equality!"[101]

T. F. Torrance agrees that Gregory regarded the monarchy to be that of the whole Trinity.[102] However, the evidence for that claim must be qualified. Some passages seem to support the case, but others do not. T. A. Noble highlights a distinction Gregory makes that explains this apparent ambiguity. On the one hand, the monarchy resides in the whole Trinity—being indivisible—but the Father is the *principium* in terms of the hypostatic relations.[103] These two perspectives are not contradictory, since they refer to distinct aspects.

As Ayres suggests, Gregory's emphasis is the harmony of unity and diversity in God.[104] We noted the confusion of terminology relating to monarchy earlier.

3.8 Augustine and the Niceno-Constantinopolitan Settlement

While the inseparability of the Trinitarian actions was to be a major theme of Augustine, and has rightly been highlighted in the literature, it was equally maintained by the Cappadocians.[105] Gregory joined

98. On Augustine and the Trinitarian *taxis* and the Father as *principium*, see Ayres, *Augustine and the Trinity*, 178–83, 263–65.

99. Gregory of Nazianzus, *Oration 25* 15–18; Beeley, *Gregory of Nazianzus*, 206.

100. Beeley, *Gregory of Nazianzus*, 209.

101. Beeley, *Gregory of Nazianzus*, 209–10. See Giles, "The Father as *Mia Archē*," who proposes reserving monarchy for the indivisible rule of the Trinity and *mia archē* for the Father in relation to the Son and the Spirit.

102. Torrance, *Christian Doctrine of God*, 180–85.

103. Noble, "Gregory Nazianzen." See also Calvin, *Institutes*, 1.13.18–20.

104. Ayres, *Nicaea and Its Legacy*, 245–47.

105. Augustine, *Tractates on John* 20.3, 8 (*NPNF*[1], 7:132–34); *Letter 169, to Evodius* 2.5–7 (*NPNF*[1], 1:540–41); Gregory of Nyssa, *On "Not Three Gods" to Ablabius* (*NPNF*[2], 5:331–36; *PG*, 45:115–36); Gregory of Nazianzus, *Oration 29* 16–17 (*PG*, 36:93–97).

Athanasius and Basil in stressing the oneness of the Son with the Father, the indivisibility of the Trinity, and the inseparable works. In this, they were at one with Augustine.[106]

As noted earlier, Augustine strenuously affirms that "just as Father and Son and Holy Spirit are inseparable, so do they work inseparably."[107] Yet, as the three are eternally distinct, each work is specifically attributed—or *appropriated*—to one of them. The Son is sent by the Father and is conceived by the Spirit, but only he becomes flesh. The Spirit alone comes at Pentecost, while sent by the Father and the Son. In Augustine's words, "Although in all things the divine persons act perfectly in common, and without possibility of separation, nevertheless their operations . . . [are] . . . distinguished from each other."[108] The three work in harmony rather than in unison. Moreover, as Ayres comments, throughout his career Augustine insists that the three persons are real and irreducible, and that he founds the unity of God in "the Father's eternal act of giving rise to a communion in which the mutual love of the three constitutes their unity of substance."[109]

Thus, Ayres explains, Augustine places at the heart of his theology the eternal generation of the Son from the being of the Father.[110] Moreover, Augustine contends that the missions of the Son and the Spirit depend on the Father being the source of both.[111] Simultaneously, because of the inseparable operations, both the processions and missions are Trinitarian, with all three persons involved. Consequently, there can be no question of subordination in the relations, for these are grounded in the indivisible being of God. The order in which the Father is manifested as the source of the Son and the Spirit is indicative of equality and inseparability.[112] It is an order without hierarchy.[113]

Further Reading

Anatolios, Khaled. *Retrieving Nicaea: The Development and Meaning of Trinitarian Doctrine.* Grand Rapids, MI: Baker, 2011.

---

106. Ayres argues strongly that analysis of fourth-century Trinitarianism into Eastern and Western models is inappropriate. Ayres, *Nicaea and Its Legacy*, 344–45 and passim.
107. Augustine, *De Trinitate* 1.7, in Hill, *Augustine*, 70.
108. Augustine, *Letter 11, to Nebridius* 4 (NPNF¹, 1:230).
109. Ayres, *Augustine and the Trinity*, 319.
110. Ayres, *Augustine and the Trinity*, 180.
111. Ayres, *Augustine and the Trinity*, 181.
112. Ayres, *Augustine and the Trinity*, 182–87.
113. Ayres, *Augustine and the Trinity*, 197.

Ayres, Lewis. *Augustine and the Trinity.* Cambridge: Cambridge University Press, 2010.

Ayres, Lewis. *Nicaea and Its Legacy: An Approach to Fourth-Century Trinitarian Theology.* Oxford: Oxford University Press, 2004.

Gregory of Nazianzus. *The Five Theological Orations.*

Hanson, R. P. C. *The Search for the Christian Doctrine of God: The Arian Controversy, 318–381.* Edinburgh: T&T Clark, 1988.

Letham, Robert. *The Holy Trinity: In Scripture, History, Theology, and Worship.* 2nd ed. Phillipsburg, NJ: P&R, 2019.

Muller, Richard A. *Post-Reformation Reformed Dogmatics: The Rise and Development of Reformed Orthodoxy, ca. 1520 to ca. 1725.* Vol. 4, *The Triunity of God.* Grand Rapids, MI: Baker, 2003. An exhaustive discussion of Reformed Trinitarianism up to the eighteenth century.

Twombly, Charles C. *Perichoresis and Personhood: God, Christ, and Salvation in John of Damascus.* Eugene, OR: Pickwick, 2015.

Study Questions

1. Given that the Trinity is revealed in Scripture and believed in the church, why did it take the church so long to arrive at a considered decision about its parameters?

2. To what extent are the twin problems of modalism and subordinationism a continuing reality?

3. Consider how far the Niceno-Constantinopolitan Creed, viewed as the distillation of biblical exegesis of the church of the day, should feature prominently in church life.

4

The Trinity (3)

Ongoing Questions

Over the centuries a range of questions have arisen on the Trinity. How useful is the word *person* to describe the three hypostases? Can we find analogies of the Trinity in the creation? Is there a difference in the doctrines of the Trinity in the Eastern and Western churches? What is the relation of the Holy Spirit to the Son? How does the Trinity as revealed in human history relate to eternal antecedent realities? Could any of the three hypostases have become incarnate? What is the relationship between the Trinity and election?

4.1 Is the Term *Person* Adequate?

The idea that *person* is inadequate for expressing God's threeness has been around since Augustine. God's incomprehensibility precludes a comprehensive understanding of him (John 1:18; 1 Tim. 1:17; 6:16). The modern idea of personality relates to centers of self-consciousness, separate and autonomous. This has fed much social Trinitarianism, but it is incompatible with the indivisibility of the Trinity. Yet, as Augustine wrote, we have to say something. The fathers, he said, "could not find any other more suitable way by which to enunciate in words that which they understood without words." So "the answer . . . is given, three 'persons,' not that it might be completely spoken, but that it might not be left wholly unspoken."[1] Still, pressure has continued for some other term.

Barth came up with *Seinsweise* (way of being).[2] He thought that, besides its confusion with the modern idea, which has tritheistic connotations, *person* or *hypostasis* was not sufficiently clear in the Patristic debates. The issue was muddied for the English reader since the translator used "mode of being" for *Seinsweise*. Those without knowledge of German often concluded that Barth was a modalist. However, Bromiley, the translator, considered this absurd, since Barth consistently opposes modalism.[3] Notwithstanding, accusations of modalist tendencies remain, largely due to his paradigms for the Trinity: the priority of lordship; his description of God "in threefold repetition"; and the paradigm of revealer, revelation, and revealedness. These features have a whiff of unipersonality. Ironically, in the later volumes, Barth's use of the Augustinian theme of the Spirit as the bond of unity between the Father and the Son points in the opposite direction, as if the Father and the Son need the Spirit to unite them.[4]

Karl Rahner, recognizing the same problem as Barth addressed, proposed as an alternative "distinct manner of subsisting." Rahner intended this to be used as an *explanation* for person and not a replacement.[5] If anything, the tendency since Rahner wrote has been in the opposite direction, to adopt human personhood as a model for the doctrine of the Trinity and to see the Trinity as an analogy of a human family.

Neither proposal by Barth or Rahner has gained acceptance. Indeed, Rahner himself recognized it, acknowledging that "the expression 'distinct manner of subsisting' needs more explanation. . . . This-there is what subsists."[6] It is hard to see how either this or *Seinsweise* could resonate at a pastoral level. How meaningful would it be to inform a congregation that God is one in three "distinct manners of subsisting"? Or to refer to the Son or the Spirit as "this-there"? The insuperable problem is trying to define God while eradicating the element of mystery. *Person* has an ambiguity that enables it to function in a variety of ways,

---

1. Augustine, *De Trinitate* 5.9 (*NPNF*[1], 3:92).
2. Barth, *CD*, I/1:353–68.
3. Geoffrey W. Bromiley, *An Introduction to the Theology of Karl Barth* (Grand Rapids, MI: Eerdmans, 1979), 16.
4. Robert Letham, *The Holy Trinity: In Scripture, History, Theology, and Worship* (Phillipsburg, NJ: P&R, 2004), 271–90.
5. Karl Rahner, *The Trinity*, trans. Joseph Donceel (New York: Crossroad, 1997), 103–15.
6. Rahner, *Trinity*, 110.

especially in popular, pastoral terms.[7] The incarnation signals a congruity, a compatibility, between human nature and personhood (whatever *that* is) and the *hypostasis* of the Son. However, Rahner's point that *person* requires explanation, as far as it can be done, is valid in order to distinguish it from the idea of a human community that undermines the indivisibility of God.

Once again, Aquinas has wise words that in many ways foreshadow and should forestall these questions:

> Although the word *person* is not found applied to God in Scripture, either in the Old or New Testament, nevertheless what the word signifies is found to be affirmed of God in many places of Scripture; as that he is the supreme self-subsisting being, and the most perfectly intelligent being. If we could speak of God only in the very terms themselves of Scripture, it would follow that no one could speak of God in any but the original language of the Old or New Testament. The urgency of confuting heretics made it necessary to find new words to express the ancient faith about God. Nor is such a kind of novelty to be shunned; since it is by no means profane, for it does not lead us astray from the sense of Scripture.[8]

The Trinity means love is at the heart of the cosmos that God made. It is not a cold, heartless, universe of pointlessness and futility, but it has a purpose that God has designed for it from eternity. Since God is personal, he is love, the living God, for life and love go together. It is not that God has life or even that he is the author of life: he is life itself.

4.2   *Vestigia Trinitatis?*

Augustine considered whether there is something in humans that reflects the Trinity. More precisely, he wanted to know how three things, separately displayed, could work indivisibly.[9] Eventually, he focused on memory, understanding, and will in the human mind. He disclaimed the idea that these represent the three persons, and was aware of the severe limitations of such analogies. However, his discussion has proved very

---

7. For a further elaboration of the problem, see Christopher Lombard, "Problems concerning the Term *Person* in Karl Barth's *Church Dogmatics* (I/1) and Karl Rahner's *The Trinity* (MTh thesis, Middlesex University, 2014).

8. Aquinas, *ST* 1a.29.3.

9. Augustine, *Letter 169* (*NPNF*[1], 1:541; *PL*, 33:740–41); Augustine, *On the Gospel of John* 23 (*NPNF*[1], 7:155; *PL*, 35:1582–92); Augustine, *De Trinitate* 8–14 (*NPNF*[1], 3:115–98; *PL*, 42:943ff.).

influential and has been heavily criticized for modalist tendencies, giving paradigmatic significance to a single mind and encountering problems over the distinctiveness and integrity of the persons.[10] This criticism is unfair, as the reason for his constructing the illustrations was to see in creation whether there were three things that work inseparably.[11] Recently, scholarship has presented a revised and more sympathetic picture of Augustine's Trinitarianism.[12]

Gregory of Nazianzus had, earlier, been skeptical. He said, "Though I have examined the question in private so busily and so often, searching from all points of view for an illustration of this profound matter, I have failed to find anything in this world with which I might compare the divine nature."[13] Each possibility he considered had elements that led to false conclusions.[14] Indeed, such a quest supposes a comprehensive knowledge of God's nature, which is beyond us.

Aquinas, reflecting on Augustine, writes, "As Augustine says, *De trin.* 15.6, there is a great difference between the trinity in ourselves and the Divine Trinity. Therefore, as he there says: *We see, rather than believe, the trinity which is in ourselves; we believe rather than see that God is Trinity.*"[15] Again, referring to Augustine *De Trinitate* 6.10, he writes, "The trace of the trinity is found in every creature, according *as it is one individual*, and according *as it is formed by a species*, and according as it *has a certain relation of order*."[16] In answer to the question of whether the doctrine of the Trinity can be known by natural reason, Aquinas says no, it is impossible, since "by natural reason we can know what belongs to the unity of the essence, but not what belongs to the distinction of the persons." He argues against attempts to prove the Trinity by reason, arguing that it undermines faith and, by the lack of cogency in such arguments, incites the ridicule of unbelievers. "Therefore, we must not attempt to prove what is of faith, except by authority alone, to those who receive the

10. Colin Gunton, "Augustine, the Trinity, and the Theological Crisis of the West," *SJT* 43 (1990): 33–58.

11. Letham, *The Holy Trinity*, 195–98.

12. See Lewis Ayres, *Augustine and the Trinity* (Cambridge: Cambridge University Press, 2010).

13. Gregory of Nazianzus, *Oration 31* 31, in *St. Gregory of Nazianzus: On God and Christ*, trans. Frederick Williams and Lionel Wickham (Crestwood, NY: St Vladimir's Seminary Press, 2002), 141 (also *NPNF²*, 7:328).

14. Gregory of Nazianzus, *Oration 31* 33, in Williams, *Gregory*, 143.

15. Aquinas, *ST* 1a.93.5 (italics original to the translation).

16. Aquinas, *ST* 1a.45.7 (italics original to the translation).

authority; while, as regards others, it suffices to prove that what faith teaches is not impossible."[17]

More recently, Barth has famously addressed the topic.[18] While he agrees that those who accepted the possibility of reflections of the Trinity in the world were trying "to explain the world by the Trinity in order to be able to speak about the Trinity in this world,"[19] the Trinity "is the very thing that cannot be proved from these *vestigia*."[20] Instead, we are to look nowhere else than the true *vestigium Trinitatis in creatura* that God himself has assumed, his threefold revelation as the Father, the Son, and the Spirit in the threefold form of his Word—in his revelation, in Holy Scripture, and in proclamation.[21] In this Barth is close to Calvin, who insists that we should not be "inquiring about [the Trinity] elsewhere than from his Word,"[22] and warns against "too subtly penetrating into the sublime mystery to wander through many evanescent speculations."[23]

Bavinck does not share the Reformer's reluctance, still less those of Barth. He writes, "There is much truth in the belief that creation everywhere displays to us vestiges of the Trinity. And because these vestiges are most clearly evident in 'humanity,' so that human beings may even be called 'the image of the Trinity,' 'humanity' is driven from within to search out these vestiges." He adds, "The higher a thing's place in the order of creation, the more it aspires to the triad."[24] He affirms that all creatures "display the footsteps or vestiges of God."[25] However, he prefers not to search for triads in creation but instead focuses on the themes of diversity-in-unity and unity-in-diversity.[26] Eglinton argues that it was "an attempt to redeem, rather than react against, Augustine's position."[27] On balance, "in Bavinck's understanding of the Trinity and the cosmos, *the Trinity is wholly unlike anything else, but everything else is like the Trinity*."[28]

---

17. Aquinas, *ST* 1a.32.1.
18. Barth, *CD*, I/1:333–47.
19. Barth, *CD*, I/1:341.
20. Barth, *CD*, I/1:343.
21. Barth, *CD*, I/1:347.
22. Calvin, *Institutes*, 1.13.21.
23. Calvin, *Institutes*, 1.13.19.
24. Bavinck, *RD*, 2:333.
25. Bavinck, *RD*, 2:562.
26. See the discussion in James Eglinton, *Trinity and Organism: Towards a New Reading of Herman Bavinck's Organic Motif* (London: Bloomsbury, 2012), 82–89. I have written elsewhere that unity-in-diversity is evident everywhere and is indicative of the unity-in-diversity of God; see Letham, *The Holy Trinity*, 434–42.
27. Eglinton, *Trinity and Organism*, 87.
28. Eglinton, *Trinity and Organism*, 89 (italics original).

4.3 Eastern and Western Doctrines

Over time, differences emerged between the Eastern and Western churches. The West added the word *filioque* to C, asserting that the Spirit proceeds from the Father and the Son. The East objected as, in its eyes, with the Father as the personalizing source of the Son and the Spirit, this blurred the distinction between the Father and the Son. This has been the main factor behind the East-West schism.

Recently theologians have disputed whether there is such a divide between East and West. The paradigm is said to rely on the work of Théodore de Régnon. This criticism was spearheaded by M. R. Barnes.[29] In fact de Régnon's main thrust was a temporal distinction between what he called Patristic and Scholastic Trinitarianism, both categories encompassing both Greeks and Latins. Those influenced by the paradigm of East and West developed it to a far greater extent than he did. How far is such a distinction valid? Ayres argues that it is inapplicable to the fourth century, and stresses continuity between Augustine and the Cappadocians.[30] Holmes dismisses such a distinction altogether.[31]

These questions can be debated by theologians, but the acid test with the Eastern church is the liturgy, which, more than anything else, is at the heart of Orthodox belief and practice. The writings of individual theologians are considered simply *theologoumena*, theological

---

29. Théodore de Régnon, *Études de théologie positive sur la Sainté Trinité* (Paris: Retaux, 1898); Michel René Barnes, "De Régnon Reconsidered," *AugStud* 26 (1995): 51–79; Barnes, "Re-reading Augustine on the Trinity," in *The Trinity: An Interdisciplinary Symposium on the Trinity*, ed. Stephen T. Davis, Daniel Kendall, SJ, and Gerald O'Collins, SJ (Oxford: Oxford University Press, 1999), 143–76.

30. Lewis Ayres, *Nicaea and Its Legacy: An Approach to Fourth-Century Trinitarian Theology* (Oxford: Oxford University Press, 2004).

31. Stephen R. Holmes, *The Holy Trinity: Understanding God's Life* (Milton Keynes: Paternoster, 2012), 164. On discussion relating to this theme, the Eastern paradigm of essence and energies, the *filioque*, and so on, see Ayres, *Nicaea and Its legacy*; Sarah Coakley, "Introduction: Disputed Questions in Patristic Trinitarianism," *HTR* 100 (2007): 125–38; John Behr, "Response to Ayres: the Legacies of Nicaea, East and West," *HTR* 100 (2007): 145–52; Lewis Ayres, "Nicaea and Its Legacy: An Introduction," *HTR* 100 (2007): 141–44; Khaled Anatolios, "Yes and No: Reflections on Lewis Ayres: Nicaea and Its Legacy," *HTR* 100 (2007): 153–58; Lewis Ayres, "A Response to Critics of Nicaea and Its Legacy," *HTR* 100 (2007): 159–71; John Behr, "Final Reflections," *HTR* 100 (2007): 173–75; Kristin Hennessy, "An Answer to De Régnon's Critics: Why We Should Not Speak of 'His' Paradigm," *HTR* 100 (2007): 179–97; Volker Henning Drecoll, "Lewis Ayres, Augustine and the Trinity," *SJT* 66 (2013): 88–98; M. Edmund Hussey, "The Palamite Trinitarian Models," *SVTQ* 16 (1972): 83–89; Jeremy D. Wilkins, "'The Image of His Highest Love': The Trinitarian Analogy in Gregory Palamas's Capita 150," *SVTQ* 47 (2003): 383–412; Aristotle Papanikolaou, "Is John Zizioulas an Existentialist in Disguise? Response to Lucian Turcescu," *MTheol* 20 (2004): 601–7; Robert Letham, "The Trinity between East and West," *JRT* 3 (2009): 42–56; Letham, "Old and New, East and West, and a Missing Horse," in *The Holy Trinity Revisited: Essays in Response to Stephen R. Holmes*, ed. T. A. Noble and Jason S. Sexton (Milton Keynes: Paternoster, 2015), 27–41.

opinions. In contrast to the West, for which originality refers to something new, in the East originality means faithfulness to the originals.[32] The Eastern liturgy—whether of St. Basil or St. Chrysostom—contains a profusion of Trinitarianism; prayers and doxologies abound, saturated in a repeated recognition of the three persons in indivisible union. Worship and theology are inseparable; the liturgy is the heart of its belief. While to Eastern Christians Trinitarian worship is axiomatic, to the vast majority of Westerners the Trinity is something approaching an abstruse mathematical conundrum.

Moreover, the claim that East and West diverged was not new with de Régnon. It was firmly held over a millennium earlier by the patriarch of Constantinople, Photios. In his treatise on the Holy Spirit he denounced Augustine and his Latin followers as effective heretics by their modalistic blurring of the distinctions between the Father and the Son. Later developments that arose with Gregory Palamas, particularly the distinction between God's essence and energies, were not shared in the West. Eastern apophatic theology differs significantly from its Western counterpart, being largely a negation of rational thought and an exercise in prayer and mystical contemplation, rather than a cognitive, rational positing of qualities in God differing from those in humanity.[33] Additionally, converts to Orthodoxy from Rome or Protestantism—before their chrismation—have been required to renounce, among other things, the *filioque* clause. Together, these features demonstrate that East and West do not see the Trinity identically and that such differences as there are have been and are matters of significant disagreement, affecting worship, thought, life, and ecclesial relations.

Certainly, this distinction can be overplayed. The West has had a strong focus on the simplicity of God—in a very strong form in Aquinas—and the inseparable operations, but the Cappadocians maintained both too. Augustine may have proposed psychological illustrations to help in grasping aspects of the Trinity—while Gregory of Nazianzus ruled out attempts to seek created analogies—but his purpose was to

---

32. Andrew Louth, *John Damascene: Tradition and Originality in Byzantine Theology* (Oxford: Oxford University Press, 2002).

33. Dumitru Staniloae, *The Experience of God: Orthodox Dogmatic Theology*, vol. 1, *Revelation and Knowledge of the Triune God*, trans. Iona Ionita (Brookline, MA: Holy Cross Orthodox Press, 1994), 95–97; Vladimir Lossky, *Mystical Theology of the Eastern Church* (London: James Clarke, 1957).

affirm his agreement with the Trinitarian settlement reached in the East, not to distance himself from it.

4.4 The *Filioque* Clause[34]

Communion between the Eastern and Western churches was ruptured in 1054 and confirmed after the collapse of the Byzantine Empire in 1453. By far the most important of a number of serious disagreements was, and is, the *filioque* clause added by the West to the Niceno-Constantinopolitan Creed (C).[35] In 1965, as part of a long path toward rapprochement, Pope Paul VI and patriarch Athenagoras I withdrew the anathemas of 1054.

C states that the Holy Spirit "proceeds from the Father." There is no mention of his proceeding from the Son as well. However, in Spain, owing to the rise of Arian views, an addition emerged in liturgies—*a Patre Filioque*—"from the Father *and the Son.*" This addition spread and was adopted by the Council of Toledo (589),[36] was accepted by the French church in the late eighth century, but was not inserted into the creed by Rome until 1014 under Pope Benedict VIII. The Fourth Lateran Council of 1215 mentioned it, and the Council of Lyons in 1274 proclaimed it as dogma. The East objected to this development on ecclesiastical grounds, since a change should require another ecumenical council. Theologically, they held that the West was undermining the monarchy of the Father and the unity of the Trinity.

---

34. Much of the following section was originally a lecture given at Mid-America Reformed Seminary on November 10, 1999, subsequently published in *MAJT* 13 (2002): 71–86, and republished with permission in my book *The Holy Trinity* (Phillipsburg, NJ: P&R, 2004). It has been edited, adapted, and abridged.

35. The best place to begin consideration of this important matter is, in support of the East, the excellent article by Nick Needham, "The Filioque Clause: East or West?," *SBET* 15 (1997): 142–62, and, in support of the *filioque*, Gerald Bray, "The Filioque Clause in History and Theology," *TynBul* 34 (1983): 91–144. Bray's article is an extensive historical discussion with penetrating theological comment. A valuable collection of essays from Orthodox, Roman Catholic, and Protestant perspectives is Lukas Vischer, ed., *Spirit of God, Spirit of Christ: Ecumenical Reflections on the Filioque Controversy* (London: SPCK, 1981). A further symposium that takes the later ecumenical discussions into consideration is Myk Habets, ed., *Ecumenical Perspectives on the Filioque for the Twenty-First Century* (London: Bloomsbury, 2014). The most comprehensive and recent works on the whole issue are Bernd Oberdorfer, *Filioque: Geschichte und Theologie eines ökumenischen Problems* (Göttingen: Vandenhoeck & Ruprecht, 2001); A. Edward Siecienski, *The Filioque: History of a Doctrinal Controversy* (New York: Oxford University Press, 2010).

36. But see Richard S. Haugh, *Photius and the Carolingians: The Trinitarian Controversy* (Belmont, MA: Norland, 1975), 160–61, who questions this explanation and argues that it "first entered the Ecumenical Creed in the Latin West by a simple method of transposition and not by any willful act of interpolation in conscious violation of the Ecumenical decrees." Sergei Bulgakov rightly argues that the phrase was unnecessary, for Arianism could have been rebutted quite readily without it; "pour rejeter l'arianisme et reconnaître l'équi-divinité et la consubstantialité du Fils au Père, on n'a nul besoin de cette surérogation." Sergei Nikolaevich Bulgakov, *Le Paraclet*, trans. Constantin Andronikof (Paris: Aubier, 1946), 125.

4.4.1   Biblical Teaching on the Procession of the Holy Spirit

Jaroslav Pelikan famously quipped:

> If there is a special circle of the inferno described by Dante reserved
> for historians of theology, the principal homework assigned to that
> subdivision of hell for at least the first several eons of eternity may
> well be the thorough study of all the treatises . . . devoted to the in-
> quiry: Does the Holy Spirit proceed from the Father only, as Eastern
> Christendom contends, or from both the Father and the Son (*ex Patre
> Filioque*), as the Latin Church teaches?[37]

In the *locus classicus*, John 15:26, Jesus says he will send the Paraclete
at Pentecost, who *proceeds from* (ἐκπορεύεται) the Father. Much modern New Testament scholarship argues that the procession here refers
to economic activity only. De Margerie rightly calls this restriction to
the temporal mission "a simplistic exegesis that lacks a theological
background."[38] It posits the idea that what God does economically does
not necessarily reveal who he is.

The Spirit proceeds from the Father; the question in dispute concerns
whether this procession is from the Son also. Jesus refers to the Father's
sending the Spirit at Pentecost in response to his request or in his name
(John 14:16, 26). However, Jesus also says he himself will send the Spirit
at Pentecost (John 16:7), and later he breathes on the disciples and says,
"Receive the Holy Spirit" (John 20:22). So he shares with the Father in
the sending of the Spirit. Moreover, he says he and the Father are one
(John 10:30). It may be asked whether the Son does not also share with
the Father in spirating the Spirit?

The Bible paints a complex picture of the relations of the Spirit to
the Father and the Son. The Spirit hears the Father, receives from the
Father, takes from the Son and makes his truth known to the church,
proceeds from the Father, is sent by the Father in the name of the Son,
is sent by the Son from the Father, rests on the Son, speaks of the Son,
and glorifies the Son. The relation between the Spirit and the Son is
not one-directional but mutual and reciprocal. The Spirit plays an in-

---

37. Jaroslav Pelikan, *The Melody of Theology: A Philosophical Dictionary* (Cambridge, MA:
Harvard University Press, 1988), 90.

38. Robert. L. Reymond, *A New Systematic Theology of the Christian Faith* (New York: Nelson,
1998), 331f.; Bertrand de Margerie, SJ, *The Christian Trinity in History*, trans. Edmund J. Fortman,
SJ (Petersham. MA: St. Bede's, 1982), 169.

strumental role in the coming of Christ and in his resurrection, and is active throughout his earthly life. While Christ sends the Spirit, he lives in union with the Spirit and in dependence on the Spirit.[39] The Spirit is called the Spirit of God, referring to the Father, but he is also the Spirit of Christ, the Spirit of God's Son, and the Spirit of the Lord.

4.4.2 *Differences between the Eastern and the Western Churches*

In the East, stress falls on the Father as the source of the personal subsistence of the Son and the Spirit. The Father is the guarantor of unity in the Godhead, the source, and the cause of the Son and the Spirit. Thus, the Spirit proceeds from the Father. In the West, the Arian threat led to an emphasis on the oneness of the Father and the Son. The *filioque* is intended to undergird this; the dual procession serves to safeguard the Son's status. Following Augustine, the Spirit is the bond of union between the Father and the Son.[40]

Augustine broached the subject in *De Trinitate*:

> It is not without meaning that in this Trinity only the Son is called the Word of God, only the Holy Spirit is called the gift of God, and God the Father is the only one by whom the Son is generated and from whom the Spirit principally proceeds. I added "principally" because we discover that the Spirit proceeds also from the Son. This also the Father gives to him [the Son], not that he exists at any point without having it, but whatever he gave to his only-begotten Word he gave in begetting him. Therefore, he begat him so that the common gift should proceed from him also, and the Holy Spirit should be the Spirit of both.[41]

For Augustine, the Spirit proceeds from the Father and the Son as one principle of origination. The Father is the sole principle of deity, the Son is begotten by the Father, and from their common love proceeds, as a single principle, the Holy Spirit.[42] The Spirit proceeds first from the Father and by the Father's gift at no interval from both in common.[43]

---

39. John 14:26; 15:26; 16:7, 13–15; cf. Matt. 1:18–20; Mark 1:10; Luke 1:34–35; 3:22; 4:1, 14; Rom. 1:3–4; 8:11.
40. See Vischer, *Spirit of God, Spirit of Christ*, 12–16, for a clear and incisive evaluation of these differences.
41. Augustine, *De Trinitate* 15.29 (my trans. of *PL*, 42:1081). See also 15.47.
42. Augustine, *De Trinitate* 15.27.
43. Augustine, *De Trinitate* 15.47.

Eastern objections to the *filioque* are not that it implies two separate sources for the Holy Spirit or that the clause might subordinate the Holy Spirit to the Son. The main concern is that the Western view compromises the monarchy of the Father. The Greek fathers held that the Holy Spirit is the treasure, and the Son is the treasurer; the Son receives and manifests the Spirit, but the Father is the source, origin, or cause of both through ineffably different but united acts.

Another problem for the East is that the clause confuses the Father and the Son. The Father is not the Son. Thus, the relation between the Spirit and the Father differs from the relation between the Spirit and the Son. Since the Son and the Father are not the same, their respective relations to the Holy Spirit cannot be the same. Therefore, to talk of the Spirit proceeding from the Father *and* the Son is to confuse the two. This is underlined by Augustine's teaching that the Spirit proceeds from both as from a common source. By avoiding the suggestion that there are two separate sources of the Spirit, which would divide the Trinity, the West confuses the distinctiveness of both the Father and the Son in modalist fashion. However, the West has never intended to compromise the monarchy of the Father and has consistently affirmed it; the *filioque* was never directed against this. Stylianopoulos agrees but adds, "The *que* (and) of the *filioque* does not seem to relinquish the 'monarchy' of the Father in the Augustinian context but unintentionally does relinquish it in the Cappadocian context."[44]

From the Western side, the Eastern repudiation of the *filioque* leaves no clear relation between the Son and the Spirit. This contrasts with the Patristic teaching of *perichorēsis*, whereby the persons of the Trinity indwell and interpenetrate one another. The West holds that this exhibits subordinationist tendencies, for in the East the Son and the Spirit are commonly said to receive their deity from the Father, and so both seem to be derivative. Instead, the *filioque* affirms the intimate relation between the Son and the Spirit. The West claims that the East has created a chasm between theology and piety. Theology, grounded on the Logos, is separate from worship, mediated by the Spirit, Bavinck claims, and thus Eastern piety is dominated by mysticism.[45]

44. Theodore Stylianopoulos, ed., *Spirit of Truth: Ecumenical Perspectives on the Holy Spirit* (Brookline, MA: Holy Cross Orthodox Press, 1986), 50.

45. Herman Bavinck, *The Doctrine of God*, trans. William Hendriksen (repr., Edinburgh: Banner of Truth, 1977), 313–17.

The claim that the East's rejection of the *filioque* holds apart the Son and the Spirit is wrong. The Eastern church accepts the phrase "from the Father through the Son" as a valid expression of C. It argues that the Spirit rests on the Son—as at Jesus's baptism—is received by him, and in turn is sent by him.[46] The East presupposes the relation in the Trinity between the Father and the Son, for the Father is the Father of the Son, the Son is eternally in and with the Father, and the Father is never apart from the Son.[47] The Cappadocian teaching on mutual indwelling offsets the Western argument. C is not silent on the relation of the Spirit and the Son, for the Spirit is worshiped and glorified together with the Father and the Son, and is the author and giver of life, as are the Father and the Son, "through whom all things came into existence." The East affirms that the Son participates in the Holy Spirit's procession from the Father both immanently and economically.

On the criticism of Eastern piety, the Jesus prayer is thoroughly Christocentric: "Lord Jesus Christ, Son of God, have mercy on me a sinner" can hardly be more evangelical or Christological in tone. Moreover, the East has no monopoly on unbridled mysticism.

A third objection carries greater weight. Following John of Damascus, the East tends to consider the essence of God unknowable, in that only God's energies or operations are revealed ("All that we can affirm concerning God does not shew forth God's nature, but only the qualities of his nature").[48] A sympathetic critic like T. F. Torrance argues that this claim drives a wedge between the inner life of God and his saving activity in history, ruling out any real access to knowing God in himself.[49] It also departs from earlier Greek Patristic thought, which rejected this distinction.[50] Besides opening a yawning chasm between the economic Trinity and the immanent Trinity, the tendency points to a quaternity— the unknowable divine essence plus the three revealed persons

Earlier Eastern views can address this impasse. Basil held that true religion teaches us to think of the Son together with the Father.[51] The

---

46. Wolfhart Pannenberg, *Systematic Theology*, trans. Geoffrey W. Bromiley (Grand Rapids, MI: Eerdmans, 1998), 1:317–19.

47. See the references to Athanasius below. Jürgen Moltmann's proposal that the Spirit proceeds "from the Father of the Son" assumes a consensus would form in the East in support; see his volume *The Trinity and the Kingdom: The Doctrine of God* (London: SCM, 1991), 185–87.

48. John of Damascus, *The Orthodox Faith* 1.4 (NPNF², 9/2:4).

49. Thomas F. Torrance, *The Christian Doctrine of God: One Being, Three Persons*, 2nd ed. (Edinburgh: T&T Clark, 2016), 187.

50. Athanasius, *On the Decrees of the Synod of Nicea* 22; D. Wendebourg, "From the Cappadocian Fathers to Gregory Palamas: The Defeat of Trinitarian Theology," *StPatr* 17 (1982): 194–98.

51. Basil of Caesarea, *On the Holy Spirit*, 14.

good things that come from God reach us "through the Son."[52] The Son's will is in indissoluble union with the Father's.[53] Thus, *mutatis mutandis*, the Spirit is inseparable from the Father and the Son.[54] Moreover, "the way of the knowledge of God lies from one Spirit through the one Son to the one Father, and conversely the natural goodness and the inherent holiness and the royal dignity extend from the Father through the only-begotten to the Spirit."[55] Hence, the Spirit shares in the works of the Father and the Son.[56] In short, the Father is the sole principle of deity. From the Father, the Holy Spirit proceeds through the Son. The deity communicates itself from the Father through the Son to the Holy Spirit.

Further, John of Damascus teaches that the Spirit is "the companion of the Word and the revealer of His energy . . . proceeding from the Father and resting in the Word, and shewing forth the Word, neither capable of disjunction from God in Whom it exists, and the Word Whose companion it is . . . being in subsistence the likeness of the Word."[57] Never at any time was the Father lacking in the Word, nor the Word in the Spirit. The Holy Spirit proceeds from the Father and rests in the Son, is communicated through the Son, is inseparable and indivisible from the Father and the Son, possessing all the qualities the Father and the Son possess, except that the Spirit is not begotten or born. Both the Son and the Spirit have their being from the Father. The three are in each other, having the same essence and dwelling in each other, being the same in will, energy, power, authority, and movement. They cleave to each other and have their being in each other, without coalescence or commingling. The Son and the Spirit, therefore, do not stand apart. The relationship is like three suns cleaving to each other without separation and giving out light mingled and conjoined into one. The Spirit is manifested and imparted to us through the Son.[58]

4.4.3 *Problems of East and West*

Criticism has been made that the *filioque* debate centers on the persons understood in terms of relations of origin. In contrast, Pannenberg points

52. Basil of Caesarea, *On the Holy Spirit*, 19.
53. Basil of Caesarea, *On the Holy Spirit*, 20.
54. Basil of Caesarea, *On the Holy Spirit*, 37.
55. Basil of Caesarea, *On the Holy Spirit*, 47.
56. Basil of Caesarea, *On the Holy Spirit*, 53.
57. John of Damascus, *The Orthodox Faith* 1.7 (NPNF[2], 9/2:5).
58. John of Damascus, *The Orthodox Faith* 1.8.

to the rich complexity in the New Testament that indicates these relations are subtler than the formulas of East and West give us to believe.[59] This is true, but this is the classic Trinitarian doctrine.

From the split between God's essence and his energies, certainly as taught by Gregory Palamas, Eastern apologists can say that references to the Son sending the Spirit apply only to the energies. Moltmann, in rebuttal, answers that we can speak of only one Trinity and of its economy of salvation, and so "the divine Trinity cannot appear in the economy of salvation as something other than it is in itself. Therefore, one cannot posit temporal trinitarian relations within the economy of salvation which are not grounded in the primal trinitarian relations." Thus, Moltmann continues, the relation between the Son and the Spirit cannot be restricted to the temporal sending. If it could, there would be a contradiction in God. This cannot be, for God remains true to himself. What holds true in his revelation is true in his being.[60]

The doctrine of the procession of the Holy Spirit must take the hypostatic distinctions fully into account. Moreover, there could be a tendency to subordination of the Holy Spirit if the *filioque* is needed to support the consubstantiality of the Son. If the deity of the Son requires him to be the spirating source of the Spirit, where does that leave the Spirit, who is the source of no other *hypostasis*? Is not a basic principle of Trinitarian theology flouted? The divine attributes are shared by all three persons, while each divine property is held by one person. Here a property (spiration) is shared by two persons while the third is excluded.[61]

Both lines of approach have weaknesses, highlighted when exposed to dialogue with the other. Can this division be overcome, preserving the best intentions of both sides?

4.4.4 Historical Reconstruction

Before the Cappadocians and Augustine set the stage for future discussion, Athanasius made some crucial points, followed in the next century by Cyril of Alexandria. In his *Letters to Serapion on the Holy Spirit,*

---

59. Pannenberg, *Systematic Theology*, 1:320.
60. Jürgen Moltmann, "Theological Proposals towards the Resolution of the Filioque Controversy," in Vischer, *Spirit of God, Spirit of Christ*, 165–66.
61. Photios argues, "Everything not said about the whole, omnipotent, consubstantial, and supersubstantial Trinity is said about one of the three persons. The procession of the Spirit is not said to be common to the three, consequently it must belong to one of the three." Saint Photios, *On the Mystagogy of the Holy Spirit* (n.p.: Studion, 1983), 36.

Athanasius considers at length the Trinitarian relations. The Son is consubstantial with the Father, out of the being of the Father. Whatever the Father has, the Son has.[62] The Trinity is indivisible, so wherever the Father is mentioned, the Son should also be understood; and—by the same token—where the Son is, the Holy Spirit is in him.[63] The Spirit is never apart from the Word, the Son, a point Athanasius repeats time and time again.[64]

Moreover, as the Son's particular property is in relation to the Father, so the Spirit is in relation to the Son.[65] The Son is the image of the Father, and so too the Spirit is the image of the Son.[66] Athanasius denies a rejoinder that there are consequently two sons, maintaining the distinctiveness of the Spirit in doing so. That he makes such a point indicates how close he understands the relation of the Son and the Spirit to be. Indeed, the Spirit has the same order and nature toward the Son as the Son has toward the Father. The Son is in the Father and the Father is in the Son, and so also the Holy Spirit is in the Son and the Son is in the Holy Spirit. Thus, the Spirit cannot be divided from the Word.[67] The Spirit is in God the Father and from the Father.[68] As the Son comes in the name of the Father, so the Holy Spirit comes in the name of the Son.[69] There is one efficacy of the Trinity, for the Father makes all things through the Word by the Holy Spirit.[70] The intimate, unbreakable relation between the Son and the Spirit is patently clear in Athanasius's thought. The three persons indwell one another; this applies as much to the Son and the Spirit as to the Son and the Father or the Father and the Spirit.

Cyril writes similarly. In the *Dialogus II de SS. trinitate* he explains that the whole divinity is common to each person, so the Father, the Son, and the Spirit are of one identical essence. The Son and the Spirit are no less than the Father and are equal in all things except for their relations, the Spirit proceeding from the Father, flowing or pouring forth *through* the Son.[71] In his *Thesaurus de sancta et consubstantiali*

---

62. Athanasius, *Serapion* 2.5 (*PG*, 26:616).
63. Athanasius, *Serapion* 1.14 (*PG*, 26:566).
64. Athanasius, *Serapion* 1.14, 17, 20, 31, 3.5, 4.4 (*PG*, 26:565–66, 572, 576–77, 601, 632–33, 641).
65. Athanasius, *Serapion* 3.1 (*PG*, 26:625).
66. Athanasius, *Serapion* 4.3 (*PG*, 26:640–41).
67. Athanasius, *Serapion* 1.20–21 (*PG*, 26:580).
68. Athanasius, *Serapion* 1.25 (*PG*, 26:588).
69. Athanasius, *Serapion* 1.20 (*PG*, 26:580).
70. Athanasius, *Serapion* 1.20, 28, 30 (*PG*, 26:580, 596, 600).
71. Cyril of Alexandria, *Dialogue on the Most Holy Trinity* (*PG*, 75:721–23).

trinitate he writes that the Spirit is according to nature God, from the being of the Father. The creation was made through the Son by the Holy Spirit.[72] The Spirit is not alien to the divine essence, for he is of the essence, for he *inexists* (*enhypostatos*), proceeding from it and remaining in it.[73] So the Spirit is from the Father *and* the Son, since it is clear that he proceeds *in* and *from* the divine being.[74] Hence, the Spirit is from the being of the Son as well as the being of the Father.[75] While he naturally proceeds from the Father,[76] because of his enhypostatic relations, he is *in* the Son and *from* the Son[77] and so can be said to proceed from the Father *in* the Son.[78] Cyril also says that the Spirit is sent from the Father *through* the Son (citing John 15:26 and 14:26)[79] and that he proceeds from the Father *and* the Son.[80] Here, as Torrance has remarked, is a way to undercut the controversy.

4.4.5 Recent Developments

Renewed interest in the matter was generated by the attention given to it by Barth.[81] Since then a range of Western theologians have expressed dissatisfaction with the *filioque*. Among them are Moltmann and Pannenberg. Moltmann attempts to bridge the divide by his proposal that the Spirit proceeds *from the Father of the Son*. He points to the Son being both conceived by the Spirit and baptized by the Spirit in salvation history. Here the Spirit precedes the Son. Moltmann stresses the reciprocal relations of the persons. He wants to preserve the procession of the Spirit from the Father while recognizing the Son's participation. He seems to concede the case to the East and, from the West's perspective, does not adequately express the place of the Son.[82] Pannenberg rejects the *filioque* on the grounds that it implies the subordination of the Spirit and that Scripture says the Son receives the Spirit from the Father, so undermining the idea that the relation of the Son and the Spirit is unilateral.[83]

---

72. Cyril of Alexandria, *Thesaurus on the Holy and Consubstantial Trinity* (PG, 75:565).
73. Cyril, *Thesaurus* (PG, 75:577).
74. Cyril, *Thesaurus* (PG, 75:585).
75. Cyril, *Thesaurus* (PG, 75:587, 589).
76. Cyril, *Thesuarus* (PG, 75:597).
77. Cyril, *Thesaurus* (PG, 75:581).
78. Cyril, *Thesuarus* (PG, 75:577).
79. Cyril, *Thesaurus* (PG, 75:581).
80. Cyril, *Thesaurus* (PG, 75:585).
81. Barth, *CD*, I/1:546–57.
82. Moltmann, *Trinity*, 178–90.
83. Pannenberg, *Systematic Theology*, 1:319–21.

On the other hand, Gerald Bray defends the *filioque*. The different positions disclose differing views of salvation. The East has inadequately connected the Spirit and the Son according to its soteriology, in which deification by the Spirit is central, rather than the West's focus on the work of Christ, applied by the Spirit.[84] Under Western eyes the Eastern paradigm undermines the gospel by its failure to place the atoning work of Christ in center stage and to integrate it with the work of the Spirit. This is a crucial point. Athanasius has little to say about the atonement; the key for him is Christ, in the incarnation, assuming our humanity and uniting it with God, thus healing it. As Hanson describes, for Athanasius, salvation is by means of a kind of sacred blood transfusion.[85]

For the East, death is the great enemy, bringing about the disorder of sin. Sin is subordinate to death. Christ's resurrection defeats death. Salvation is a conquest of mortality, the risen Christ bringing life in its place. The cross is not ignored, but it is seen from the standpoint of the resurrection. The idea of sin as a transgression of the law of God, for which Christ on the cross makes atonement is found hardly at all. For the West, salvation is at its root moral and ethical, for the East it is cosmic. For the West, a holy God delivers his people from sin, while for the East, the risen Christ delivers the human race from death.[86] The gulf between East and West, according to Bray, is wider than the *filioque*. Referring to Calvin, he suggests that "the work of the Holy Spirit is to remake us in the image of Christ, so that we might enjoy the benefits of Christ's relationship to the Father," and so "He is remaking us in the image of Christ's *person* . . . [to do which, the Spirit] must share in the hypostasis of the Son, and therefore proceed from Him." Thus, Bray argues, "without a living appreciation of the *Filioque* clause . . . evangelical faith becomes incomprehensible."[87] Barth reinforces these criticisms by taking Eastern Trinitarianism to task for isolating individual verses of the Bible—he has John 15:26 in mind—from others that speak of the Spirit of the Son.[88]

Clearly, both atonement for sin and conquest of death should be prominent in any biblically faithful theology, and so the entail of the *fil-*

---

84. Bray, "Filioque," 139–44.

85. R. P. C. Hanson, *The Search for the Christian Doctrine of God: The Arian Controversy 318–381* (Edinburgh: T&T Clark, 1988), 450–51.

86. Timothy Ware, *The Orthodox Church* (London: Penguin, 1969), 230–34; John Meyendorff, *Byzantine Theology: Historical Trends and Doctrinal Themes* (New York: Fordham University Press, 1979), 159–65. Since the late sixties, Timothy Ware has been known as Kallistos Ware.

87. Bray, "Filioque," 142–43.

88. Barth, CD, I/1:480.

ioque cannot be discarded.[89] However, Bray overlooks the rich reflection in the East on the baptism of Jesus. In Staniloae's words:

> The sending of the Spirit by the Son to men rather signifies that the Spirit rests in those who are united with the Son, since he rests in the Son. The Spirit does not go beyond the Son, even when we say improperly that he is sent to men. The Son is the only and ultimate resting place of the Spirit. The Spirit dwells in us insofar as we are raised up in the Son. This saves us from a theological rationalism on the one side and a purely sentimental enthusiasm on the other.[90]

Various ecumenical agreements have been brokered in recent years. Of particular interest is the 1991 agreement between Orthodox and Reformed Churches.[91] This is limited in its scope. The Western representatives were from the World Alliance of Reformed Churches, one particular strand of Reformed theology. There was no adequate representation of Augustinian Trinitarianism; the Reformed participants were already sympathetic, though not uncritically, toward the East. The leading figure, T. F. Torrance, had already adopted the Athanasian soteriology, refracted through his reading of Calvin and Barth, and his interaction with modern physics. That said, the agreement represents progress of sorts. Torrance's commentary indicates a thorough recognition of all the main theological parameters: the *homoousion* of all three persons; their full mutual indwelling, the *perichorēsis*; the equal ultimacy of the one being of God and the three persons; the rejection of an impersonal divine essence and a concurrent recognition of the living, dynamic personal being of God; and the order and relationality of the persons. The monarchy is the whole Trinity, not the Father alone. Any idea of subordinationism is eliminated. The procession of the Holy Spirit is seen in the light of the full homoousial and perichoretic relations of the three persons in the one divine essence. So the Spirit proceeds from the being of God inseparably from the Father and the Son.

---

89. See Robert Letham, *The Work of Christ* (Leicester: Inter-Varsity Press, 1993), esp. chap. 7.

90. Dumitru Staniloae, "The Procession of the Holy Spirit from the Father and His Relation to the Son, as the Basis for Our Deification and Adoption," in Vischer, *Spirit of God, Spirit of Christ*, 179.

91. For the official text, see Thomas F. Torrance, *Theological Dialogue between Orthodox and Reformed Churches* (Edinburgh: Scottish Academic Press, 1993), 2:219–32; or "Agreed Statement on the Holy Trinity between the Orthodox Church and the World Alliance of Reformed Churches," *Touchstone* 5, no. 1 (1992): 22–23. For commentary on the agreement, see Thomas F. Torrance, *Trinitarian Perspectives: Toward Doctrinal Agreement* (Edinburgh: T&T Clark, 1994), 110–43.

Bobrinskoy points to the perichoretic relations of the three as providing a way out of the dilemma.[92] The Cyrilline phrase *from the Father in the Son* seems to me to express the mutual indwelling of the three, avoids any residual subordination, and also directs us to Jesus's baptism. It also avoids a focus on the Spirit apart from Christ, for we receive the Spirit *in Christ*. The West's concern for the relation between the Son and the Spirit is maintained, and the confusion of the *filioque* avoided. The Father is clearly the *principium* or *archē*. Weinandy agrees, suggesting a nonsequential order based on mutually coinherent, reciprocal, and related eternal acts.[93] Kathryn Tanner also argues that the perichoretic relations of the three provide a solution to the impasse, going behind the clause and rendering the differences redundant, affirming the positive dimensions of both sides.[94]

4.5   Rahner's Axiom and the Social Trinity

Rahner, in probing the relationship between the Trinity and the incarnation, points out that since Augustine Western theologians have generally assumed that any one member of the Trinity could have become incarnate.[95] This is mirrored by the common perception that God as such became man. If that were so, Rahner insists, the incarnation of the Son would tell us nothing distinctive about the Son himself.[96] Instead, it is *the Son* who became man.[97] This leads Rahner to the heart of his argument, the axiomatic unity of the economic Trinity and the immanent Trinity.[98] The basic thesis that establishes that the Trinity is a mystery of salvation and not simply a doctrine is that *"The 'economic' Trinity is the 'immanent' Trinity and the 'immanent' Trinity is the 'economic' Trinity."*[99] This entails the unity of the Trinity with the history of salvation and roots it in the Bible. The economic distinctiveness of Jesus Christ the Son and of the Holy Spirit in our salvation reflects real antecedent eternal distinctions.

92. See chap. 2, n. 98, referring to Boris Bobrinskoy, *Mystery*, 65–72.

93. Thomas G. Weinandy, "The *Filioque*: Beyond Athanasius and Thomas Aquinas: An Ecumenical Proposal," in Habets, *Ecumenical Perspectives*, 185–97.

94. Kathryn Tanner, "Beyond the East/West Divide," in Habets, *Ecumenical Perspectives*, 198–210.

95. But see Anselm, *De fide Trinitatis et de incarnatione Verbi* 3.27–29, in Brian Davies, *Anselm of Canterbury: The Major Works* (Oxford: Oxford University Press, 1998), 251–52 (also *PL*, 158:276–77).

96. Rahner, *Trinity*, 11.

97. Rahner, *Trinity*, 12.

98. Rahner, *Trinity*, 21ff.

99. Rahner, *Trinity*, 22 (italics original).

Rahner points to the incarnation. Jesus is God the Son—there is at least one mission that is not simply *appropriated* to the Son "but is proper to him." This is not just a work of the Trinity that is specially the part of the Son but in which the other two share. Rather, this is something that belongs to the Logos alone and can be predicated of one person only.[100] It is unique and not an example of a general principle.[101] It cannot be demonstrated that any person of the Trinity could have become incarnate, and it is false to claim that each could.[102] If any of the three could, there would be no connection between the missions and the intra-Trinitarian life, and so "that which God is for us would tell us absolutely nothing about that which he is in himself, as triune." So "we cling to the truth that the Logos is really as he appears in revelation, that he is *the one* who reveals to us (not merely *one* of those who might have revealed to us) the triune God."[103]

Rahner does not deny that the Father and the Spirit share in their distinctive ways in the incarnation, nor does he question that the work of the Trinity is indivisible. He means that only the Son became man, and that this is the way it had to be.[104] Rahner goes on to apply the dogmas of *anhypostasia* and *enhypostasia* to the question, concluding that the Logos reveals himself in and through his humanity.[105] Thus, "each one of the three divine persons communicates himself to man in gratuitous grace in his own personal particularity and diversity."[106] The self-communication of God has a threefold aspect.[107] Economic Sabellianism is false.[108] In the Son and the Spirit the immanent Trinity is already given. The Trinity is not merely a doctrine; it is rooted in experience.[109]

Rahner wants to follow the biblical order of events.[110] However, he sees the biggest danger, like Barth, as tritheism rather than modalism.[111]

---

100. Rahner, *Trinity*, 23.
101. Rahner, *Trinity*, 24–28.
102. Rahner, *Trinity*, 28–30.
103. Rahner, *Trinity*, 30.
104. On this see Athanasius, *On the Incarnation* 13–14; Anselm, *De fide* 3.27–31, in Davies, *Anselm*, 250–52 (also *PL*, 158:276–79); Aquinas, *ST* 3a.3.8; Thomas G. Weinandy, "The Eternal Son," in *The Oxford Handbook of the Trinity*, ed. Gilles Emery and Matthew Levering (Oxford: Oxford University Press, 2011), 390–94.
105. Rahner, *Trinity*, 31–33.
106. Rahner, *Trinity*, 34–35.
107. Rahner, *Trinity*, 36.
108. Rahner, *Trinity*, 38.
109. Rahner, *Trinity*, 39.
110. Rahner, *Trinity*, 40–42.
111. Rahner, *Trinity*, 43.

He shares Barth's reservations about the term *person*, concedes there is no better word, and so uses it; but he begins not with the persons but with the one God.[112] Understanding of the immanent Trinity comes by way of the economic Trinity.[113] It follows that the Father, Son, and Holy Spirit are identical with the one Godhead but relatively distinct from one another.[114]

There are both valid and invalid uses of Rahner's axiom. Positively, it can indicate that God reveals himself in history as he is in himself in eternity. In this sense, the economic Trinity differs not in the slightest from the immanent Trinity. There is only one Trinity; the triune God *reveals* himself and in so doing reveals *himself*. He is faithful; we can count on his revelation being true to who he eternally is.

Nevertheless, the most frequent use of the axiom has been by social Trinitarians, effectively eliminating the immanent Trinity altogether.[115] In this line of thought the economy is all there is, connected with the panentheism of process theology, in which God and the world are mutually dependent. For such thinking, the economic Trinity is the immanent Trinity, since there is nothing else, for all is governed by history. Moltmann, Pannenberg, Catherine Mowry LaCugna, and Robert Jenson come into this category.[116] When one depicts the Trinity as a community, akin to a human family, as social Trinitarianism does, the indivisibility of the Trinity is at best threatened, and the door opened to tritheism.

Seung Goo Lee proposes a refinement of Rahner's axiom that guards against its abuses.[117] He writes, "The classic understanding of the Trinity lies in asserting the following proposition without any reservation and without any condition: *The ontological Trinity is the ground of being for the economic Trinity; and the economic Trinity is the ground of cognition for the ontological Trinity.*"[118] Professor Lee has made an incisive contribution, provided it is clear that there is only one Trinity.

---

112. Rahner, *Trinity*, 44. See also 56–57.
113. Rahner, *Trinity*, 65–66.
114. Rahner, *Trinity*, 72.
115. Paul D. Molnar, *Divine Freedom and the Doctrine of the Immanent Trinity: In Dialogue with Karl Barth and Contemporary Theology*, rev. ed. (London: T&T Clark, 2017). Citations are from the first edition, 2002.
116. Molnar, *Divine Freedom*.
117. Seung Goo Lee, "The Relationship between the Ontological Trinity and the Economic Trinity," *JRT* 3 (2009): 90–107.
118. Lee, "The Ontological Trinity and the Economic Trinity," 106–7 (italics original).

4.6 Was It Necessary That the Son, Not the Father or Spirit, Become Incarnate?

As Rahner points out, there is one mission that is not simply *appropriated* to the Son "but is proper to him."[119] If it were possible that any one of the Trinity could become incarnate, there would be no connection between the missions and the intra-Trinitarian life, and so "that which God is for us would tell us absolutely nothing about that which he is in himself, as triune." So "we cling to the truth that the Logos is really as he appears in revelation, that he is *the one* who reveals to us (not merely *one* of those who might have revealed to us) the triune God."[120]

Long before, Athanasius argued that the renewal of man in God's image could be achieved only "by the coming of the very image himself"; and so "the Word of God came in his own person, because it was he alone, the image of the Father, who would re-create man made after the image." This only the Word could do.[121] Anselm agreed that "no divine person other than the Son ought to become flesh since there cannot be any least inappropriate thing in God."[122] Both considered it necessary that the Son be incarnate.

Aquinas held that the Father and the Holy Spirit could have become incarnate,[123] but concluded that "it was most fitting that the person of the Son should become incarnate" by virtue of the union to be established with his people, and since "he has a particular agreement with human nature." Moreover, Aquinas added that salvation is adoption to the likeness of his natural sonship,[124] which renders it fitting that the Son become incarnate. This fittingness is tantamount to necessity, not a necessity of external constraint on God, of which there could be none, but a necessity corresponding to his character. If anything, Athanasius and Anselm had gone further in talking of necessity, for they insisted that while the works of the Trinity are inseparable, only the Son became man, and that this is the way it had to be.[125] We might add that the Son's taking into personal union human nature, in its lowliness and obedience,

---

119. Rahner, *Trinity*, 23.
120. Rahner, *Trinity*, 28–30.
121. Athanasius, *Incarnation* 13–14, in Athanasius, *On the Incarnation: The Treatise De Incarnatione Verbi Dei*, trans. Sister Penelope Lawson (New York: Macmillan, 1946), 23–24.
122. Anselm, *De fide* 3.27–31, in Davies, *Anselm*, 251 (also *PL*, 158:276).
123. Aquinas, *ST* 3a.1.2, 3a.3.5.
124. Aquinas, *ST* 3a.3.8. Thus, it was not fitting that the Father be sent, *ST* 1a.43.5.
125. On this see Athanasius, *Incarnation* 13–14; Anselm, *De fide* 3.27–31, in Davies, *Anselm*, 250–52 (also *PL*, 158:276–79); Aquinas, *ST* 3a.3.8; Weinandy, "Eternal Son," 390–94.

is congruous with his being from the Father. As Augustine wrote, "He was not sent in respect to any inequality of power, or substance . . . but in respect of this, that the Son is from the Father, not the Father from the Son."[126]

4.7   Did God Elect to Be Triune?

Recently, a debate has erupted among Barth scholars on whether God exists eternally as Trinity and freely determines to elect or he elected to be triune. Which is primary? Does God elect to be Trinity? Or does the triune God elect? The question raises a number of crucial issues and is expressed on two levels: as interpretation of Barth and as substantive Trinitarian theology.

The controversy stems from Barth's volume on the doctrine of election in *Church Dogmatics.*[127] The issue was first raised by Bruce McCormack toward the end of his major book on Barth.[128] He later developed the theme in his article in the *Cambridge Companion to Karl Barth.*[129] The background to the debate is Barth's comment that he revised his doctrine of election after hearing a paper by Pierre Maury at the International Calvin Congress in 1936. As a result, he proposed a radically Christo-centric doctrine in which Christ is both electing God and elect man. He wanted to avoid any idea of a decree by God in himself about man in himself and a focus on the election of individuals. Rather, Christ is both the subject and the object of election. In light of Barth's discussion of John 1 concerning the Word "in the beginning" and so with God and God himself, it follows that the Word is the electing God. Moreover, he is also elect man. In election, the beginning of all God's ways and works, God elects to be God in Christ, in this man Jesus of Nazareth and in no other way.[130]

So instead of focusing on God's choice of certain persons and his re-jection of others, Barth expanded the traditional doctrine so as to become virtually all-embracing. The decree of election, in eternity or in God's

---

126. Augustine, *De Trinitate* 4.27 (*NPNF*[1], 3:83; *PL*, 42:862–63).

127. Barth, *CD*, II/2:3–506.

128. Bruce L. McCormack, *Karl Barth's Critically Realistic Dialectical Theology: Its Genesis and Development 1909–1936* (Oxford: Clarendon, 1995), 459.

129. Bruce L. McCormack, "Grace and Being: The Role of God's Gracious Election in Karl Barth's Theological Ontology," in *The Cambridge Companion to Karl Barth*, ed. John Webster (Cambridge: Cambridge University Press, 2000), 92–110.

130. Barth, *CD*, II/2:95–121.

time, encompasses creation, the incarnation, the cross, the resurrection, the entire creation, covenant, and redemption. It entails God himself taking on reprobation in Christ and in Christ electing man. As such, all people are elect in Christ while Christ became reprobate for them. The reconstructed doctrine has clearly universalist undertones, since the decisive point is in eternity, in the primal decision made by God, and involves a form of substitution between Christ and humanity as a whole, rather than a sharp and ineradicable distinction between two large groups of individuals within humanity. However, Barth refused to follow through to what appears to be the logical outcome of universal salvation.[131] In this eternal decree, encompassing the entirety of the human narrative, God elected to be God in Jesus Christ, in his incarnation and in no other way. This was the point that McCormack developed, arguing that God, in determining to be God in Christ, determined to be Trinity, election being logically prior.[132]

McCormack's argument is that this decree of election is an eternal determination of God *to be God in Christ*, in the incarnate Christ, and thus to be Trinity. God constitutes himself as triune in election. This is what McCormack understands Barth to mean. It represents a stark contrast to the traditional understanding that God is eternally Trinity, and his decree of election is his free and sovereign choice. McCormack is critical of this construction on the grounds that it posits an abstract notion of God prior to his action in election and incarnation, together with a distinction between the *Logos asarkos* (the Logos apart from the flesh, in eternity) and the *Logos ensarkos* (the Logos incarnate in human history), who consequently has no bearing on the identity of God. For McCormack, election has priority over the works of God *ad intra*, the eternal processions. He holds that God's freedom is preserved, since God has freely determined to be triune; it is not a matter of necessity binding him as it would otherwise be.

McCormack has been criticized strongly by Edwin van Driel, Paul Molnar, and George Hunsinger.[133] His critics believe he makes God necessarily dependent on creation, since God is God in no other way

---

131. Barth, *CD*, II/2:417–22, 475–77.
132. McCormack, "Grace and Being."
133. Edwin Chr. Van Driel, "Karl Barth on the Eternal Existence of Jesus Christ," *SJT* 60 (2007): 45–61; Molnar, *Divine Freedom*, 61–64; George Hunsinger, "Election and the Trinity: Twenty-Five Theses on the Theology of Karl Barth," *MTheol* 24 (2008): 179–98.

than in relation to humanity and the world.[134] This effectively removes the immanent Trinity and the *Logos asarkos*, thus abolishing the freedom of God. Molnar, opposing McCormack, cites Barth to the effect that God in himself is Trinity, distinct from and prior to his becoming Creator and Redeemer in relation to us.[135] According to McCormack's proposals, humans would be a predicate of God, since God's being would be constituted by his decision to be incarnate for our salvation.[136] Barth, we must say, emphatically rejects any idea that God exists only in relation to the world, as this would undermine his independence and destroy any revelation of himself.[137] Hunsinger adds that, if McCormack were right, it would entail the Son and the Spirit being subordinate to the Father. The Father alone would be the active subject in election, since generation and procession would be subsequent to election.[138] Moreover, an abstract deity would precede the Trinity.[139] Allied with these criticisms is a denial that McCormack's position is what Barth intended to say.[140]

While the criticisms are on the level of Barth interpretation as well as Trinitarian theology, our interest here is more with the latter. Barth on many occasions stresses that God is the Father, the Son, and the Holy Spirit antecedently to his revelation and to his work in reconciliation and redemption.[141] McCormack replies that the evidence advanced by his critics antedates Barth's changed doctrine of election.[142] However, there is also such evidence from the later volumes of the *Church Dogmatics*.[143] Moreover, McCormack argues that by making God's will subsequent to his nature, as the traditional doctrine does, God is restricted, since his choice to be Trinity is subsequent to the reality. He is, and only subsequently chooses to be who he is. McCormack thinks this is alien to Barth, and behind it there are strong theological objections. Instead, he

---

134. Molnar, *Divine Freedom*, 63, 152–54.
135. Molnar, *Divine Freedom*, x.
136. Molnar, *Divine Freedom*, 63.
137. Barth, *CD*, II/1:330, citing G. Thomasius and J. A. Dorner, *Christi Person und Werk* (1886), 1:38.
138. George Hunsinger, "Election and the Trinity: Twenty-Five Theses on the Theology of Karl Barth," in *Trinity and Election in Contemporary Theology*, ed. Michael T. Dempsey (Grand Rapids, MI: Eerdmans, 2011), 110.
139. Molnar, *Divine Freedom*, 63.
140. For detailed criticism of the McCormack proposal, see Paul D. Molnar, *Faith, Freedom and the Spirit* (Downers Grove, IL: IVP Academic, 2015), esp. 129–86.
141. Dempsey, *Trinity and Election*, 11–12.
142. Dempsey, *Trinity and Election*, 13.
143. E.g., Barth, *CD*, IV/1:201.

identifies God's being with the acts of Jesus in history.[144] McCormack's opponents regard this as destructive of the Trinity, since there would be no Son or Holy Spirit in eternity, and God would be dependent on the world and unable to save us.[145]

It boils down to these alternatives: For McCormack, God's nature is determined by his will. This is intended to preserve God's freedom but appears to posit a God who is arbitrary. Moreover, there is no place for the immanent Trinity or for the *Logos asarkos*. For Molnar, Hunsinger, and the traditional doctrine, God's nature is prior to his decree to be who he is. This might seem to limit God's freedom, but it avoids the problems with the McCormack thesis.

The classic position is persuasive. McCormack has raised profound questions that can be answered in ways that refine that position. However, his proposals open the door to devastating consequences. It seems to me that *God is eternally triune and he elects to be so*. It is a matter of the relationship between God's nature and his will. His will is an aspect of his nature; he chooses in accordance with his character. Both are eternal as he is. But to prioritize will over nature is to suggest that he is arbitrary. If God's nature were to follow from his decree—if he had elected to constitute himself as *a*, *b*, and *c* in distinction from *x*, *y*, and *z*—it would be hard to eliminate the idea of arbitrariness, all flowing from a choice that could have gone another way. Moreover, it would undermine the Trinity, for the status of the Son and the Spirit would depend on an act of will. God in himself would be dependent on the creation.

There is no reason to abandon the classic position. With Anselm[146] and Aquinas[147] and the Reformed tradition, God is necessarily and eternally Trinity. In contrast, he was free to create and elect or not; that he did so was a decision of his free will by which he determines everything outside himself.[148] The creation is contingent; it might not have been, and its actual existence depends on God's will.

144. Dempsey, *Trinity and Election*, 15; Bruce L. McCormack, "Divine Impassibility or Simply Divine Constancy: Implications of Barth's Later Christology for Debates over Impassibility," in *Divine Impassibility and the Mystery of Human Suffering*, ed. James F. Keating and Thomas Joseph White (Grand Rapids, MI: Eerdmans, 2009), 178–80.
145. Dempsey, *Trinity and Election*, 15–16.
146. Anselm, *Cur Deus homo?* 1.10; Anselm, *Monologion* 33–34.
147. Aquinas, *ST* 1a.19.3; Aquinas, *SCG* 1.80: ". . . sequitur quod Deus de necessitate velit suum esse et suam bonitatem, nec possit contrarium velle. . . . Necesse igitur est quod velit suum esse et suam bonitatem."
148. Richard A. Muller, *Dictionary of Latin and Greek Theological Terms* (Grand Rapids, MI: Baker, 1985), 331.

Certainly, Barth has drawn attention to a crucial point. We shall observe later that Genesis 1 directs attention to Christ. The whole chapter is centered on God preparing the world for humans, transforming a dark, wet, uninhabitable environment into one that is light, dry, and suitable for human life. The chief point is that Adam was *made* in the image of God, while in the New Testament, Christ *is* the image of God. The weight of the account is placed on the seventh day, mentioned three times in two verses (Gen. 2:2–3), indicating that the focus of creation is on its eschatological fulfillment, which will be in Christ. This supports the claim that central to God's purpose in creating was that, in the Son, he become man as Jesus Christ, and in him his work of creation be consummated.[149]

4.8   The Trinity in Contrast to Islam

The doctrine of the Trinity tells us that God is personal and relational; love is at the heart of who God is. C. S. Lewis remarked that the Trinity is required for God to be love. "The words 'God is love' have no meaning unless God contains at least two persons. . . . If God was a single person, then before the world was made, he was not love."[150]

This contrasts with the other monotheistic religions—Islam and Judaism—where the deity is considered a unitary monad. As such, the god who is worshiped cannot be inherently relational and so cannot love. Since it cannot love, it cannot in any sense be said to be personal. With Islam, Allah is sheer power. This makes an enormous difference to life and culture. In Islam, diversity is suppressed, the *umma* being one undifferentiated polity, and polyphonic music regarded with abhorrence.

It is vital to see how the Trinity discloses itself preeminently in Christ, sent by the Father, endowed with the Holy Spirit. With Irenaeus, we can see this at Jesus's baptism in the Jordan, accompanied by the Father's voice and the Spirit's descent.[151] The Trinity is the Christian doctrine of God, which the unfolding of biblical revelation discloses in Christ.

---

149. For further discussion, in addition to Dempsey, *Trinity and Election*, see Brandon Gallaher, *Freedom and Necessity in Modern Trinitarian Theology* (Oxford: Oxford University Press, 2016), 117–61.

150. C. S. Lewis, *Mere Christianity* (San Francisco: Harper, 1960), 174.

151. Irenaeus, *Against Heresies* 3.17.1–3, 3.18.2–3 (PG, 7:929–34); Letham, *The Holy Trinity*, 94.

4.9 Recent Evangelical Discussions

Recently there has been heated discussion online in conservative circles over whether, and to what extent, the incarnate obedience of Christ may reflect eternal Trinitarian realities. Some, speaking of the will of the Son and the will of the Father, argue that the Son is eternally subordinate to the Father, and, until recently, they opposed the eternal generation of the Son. In this regard, the line drawn by Constantinople I between orthodoxy and heresy had temporarily been crossed. Others oppose anything that appears to undermine the equality of the persons but reflect little on the relationship between the Trinity and Christology. The following is an edited email I wrote in response to questions I was asked arising from a book I had not read. I have altered the names to preserve anonymity.

Dear Maximus

Thanks for this. I have not followed the controversy, both by accident and design, although a number of people have mentioned it. Nor have I read much of what Theodore has written. So my comments are more generalized and are questions that may be relevant and might need addressing.

Does Theodore affirm the indivisibility of the trinity and the inseparable operations? That is a key question, from which the indivisible will follows.

There *is* a danger of imposing human relations on to the trinity; that was what the Arians did, abusing the generation of the Son to conclude that he began to be.

If someone were to speak of "subordination" how could he or she still maintain the indivisibility of the trinity?

By speaking of the will of the Father and the will of the Son some explanation seems required so as to avoid the previous problem.

On the other hand, if it was said that the Father or the Spirit could have become incarnate as the Son did, would this not make God arbitrary?

Since the economic missions reflect the eternal processions, since the Son became incarnate was this appropriate or not? Was it necessary—a necessity of God's nature—that this be so?

Jesus obeyed the Father as incarnate; this was appropriate to humanity. However, if it was not appropriate for the Son to follow the Father (not in the sense of sequence but in that the Father is the source, as per Calvin) how could Nestorianism be avoided? In that case there would appear to be a gulf between the Son and the assumed humanity.

It is ironic that some of those correctly concerned about subordinationist language also hold to the covenant of redemption, which has strongly subordinationist themes.

As in any controversy, polarization can occur and problems surface on both sides.[152]

Further Reading

Dempsey, Michael T., ed. *Trinity and Election in Contemporary Theology.* Grand Rapids, MI: Eerdmans, 2011.

Habets, Myk, ed. *Ecumenical Perspectives on the Filioque for the 21st Century.* London: Bloomsbury, 2014.

Letham, Robert. *The Holy Trinity: In Scripture, History, Theology, and Worship.* 2nd ed. Phillipsburg, NJ: P&R, 2019.

Molnar, Paul D. *Faith, Freedom and the Spirit: The Economic Trinity in Barth, Torrance and Contemporary Theology.* Downers Grove, IL: IVP Academic, 2015.

Torrance, Thomas F. *The Christian Doctrine of God: One Being Three Persons.* Edinburgh: T&T Clark, 2016.

Study Questions

1. To what extent do attempts to rename the persons of the Trinity produce impersonal titles or names that describe God's work in creation and grace, making God dependent on the creation?

2. How far does the *filioque* controversy indicate differing perspectives on the Trinity?

3. Does McCormack's argument that God's decision to be Trinity has priority over his being Trinity suggest arbitrariness in God? Does it actually limit his freedom?

4. What are the basic differences between Christianity and Islam over the doctrine of God?

---

152. For a fuller discussion of this question, see Robert Letham, *The Holy Trinity: In Scripture, History, Theology, and Worship.* 2nd ed. (Phillipsburg, NJ: P&R, 2019).

5

The Attributes of God

What is meant by the attributes of God? What various classifications have been made of them? This chapter discusses the names of God, the beauty of God, the will of God, and his decrees, including predestination, election, and reprobation, together with forms of relational and noncoercive doctrines of God.

5.1   What Are the Attributes of God?

The attributes of God are particular aspects of what he is like.[1] They describe his character as he has revealed it. John Frame considers the attributes of God to be "perspectives on his whole being."[2] Frame correctly draws a connection with the simplicity of God. Since God is simple, not divisible into parts, his attributes are coextensive with who he is. As such, they are comprehensively possessed by each Trinitarian *hypostasis*. The Father does not possess them to any greater extent than does the Son or the Spirit.

Moreover, the attributes are not abstract qualities, existing in their own right and somehow independent of God. Rather, God himself defines these qualities. There is no entity called "love" floating around in the cosmos, by which God is measured; on the contrary, love is to be understood in the light of who God himself is.

---

1. On this, see Muller, *PRRD*, 3:1–589.
2. John M. Frame, *The Doctrine of God* (Phillipsburg, NJ: P&R, 2002), 388.

My plan in this chapter is to be concise and relatively sparse. In this, my model is Calvin, who largely eschewed discussion of God's attributes as a discrete topic in his *Institutes*, although he referred to them where the occasion required in that work and elsewhere.

In distancing himself from some earlier theologians who, like me, had begun with a discussion of the Trinity before moving to the attributes, Bavinck writes that "in order for us to understand in the locus of the Trinity that Father, Son, and Spirit share in the same divine nature, it is necessary for us to know what that divine nature comprises and in what way it differs from every created nature." Bavinck supports his case with the fact that in Scripture "the nature of God is shown us earlier and more clearly than his trinitarian existence."[3] Indeed, that is the far more common procedure.

However, the demographic changes in the Western world since Bavinck's time, with the upsurge of Islam and the proliferation of other religions, call for a stronger assertion of the distinctly *Christian* doctrine of God. Moreover, while the revelation of God as Trinity emerged in its fullness at a later time than the revelation of his unity, one can argue that what is last in revelation is first in importance, since it sums up and crystallizes all that has gone before. The one new covenant name of the Father, the Son, and the Holy Spirit brings to a climax the whole movement—the *organic* movement, to borrow Bavinck's favorite category—of the biblical and Christian revelation. Furthermore, while the Trinitarian debates were founded on the premise of the indivisibility of God, his one nature, the treatment of the Trinity up front ensures that there is no confusion with a general monotheism.

Returning to our theme, Frame states that "God is a person."[4] This appears to suggest that God is one among others, or alternatively that there is something to be seen as "person" to which God conforms. Frame can hardly mean that. It would be better to say that God is "personal" or "personhood." Even then, such a claim creates problems with the Trinity. Are the three hypostases (persons) to be reduced to attributes?

Frame is cogent when he deals with the philosophical conundrum of Plato, who "poses the question of whether piety is what the gods say it is, or whether the gods command piety because of its intrinsic nature."[5]

---

3. Bavinck, *RD*, 2:149–50.
4. Frame, *Doctrine of God*, 388.
5. Frame, *Doctrine of God*, 405–10.

Frame recognizes that when dealing with God, we are inevitably going to have circularity, and that this applies to atheistic arguments as well. Ultimately the actions of God display his goodness; revelation, not logic, is the key.

I am using the following terms thus: *essence* refers to who God *is* (from *esse*, "to be"), and *nature* to what God is *like*. When we think of the divine attributes, we are working with this latter category. This very roughly corresponds to the Eastern distinction between essence and energies or powers. Often in fourth-century Trinitarian discussions, *essence* and *nature* were used interchangeably.

Since the attributes are aspects of God's nature possessed by all three persons of the Trinity, not only are they mutually interpenetrating but they are also coextensive with the essence, since God is simple and cannot be divided into portions less than the whole of who he is. Viewed from our perspective, love and justice appear distinct, yet in God they are not only indivisible but identical to God due to his simplicity.

By *simplicity* I mean that God is one and indivisible, not composite.[6] He is not composed of distinct and independent elements. He is not 50 percent good and 50 percent just but 100 percent good and 100 percent just. He is not partly love, partly good, partly just. He is exhaustively good, righteous, loving, and so on. There can be nothing in God that is less than himself, less than the whole of who he is; neither can there be anything in him that is removable or adventitious.[7] By the same token, the attributes are not only indivisible but also identical; the distinctions between them are for our benefit. As Bavinck comments, "If God is in any sense composite, then it is impossible to maintain the perfection of his oneness, independence, and immutability."[8]

How can God be simple and yet have a range of attributes? The answer lies in that the attributes are identical with who he is.[9] From our angle, it appears that they are mutually defining: his justice is loving justice, his goodness is omnipotent, righteous, and just; and so on. From this it follows that his love is almighty, righteous, good, and holy love. His wrath is his settled holy and righteous antagonism toward sin.

---

6. See James E. Dolezal, *God without Parts: Divine Simplicity and the Metaphysics of God's Absoluteness* (Eugene, OR: Pickwick, 2011).

7. Frame, *Doctrine of God*, 226.

8. Bavinck, *RD*, 2:149; also 2:176.

9. Aquinas, *ST* 1a.3.3–4, 7.

This has significant pastoral implications. It differs from the doctrine of *perichorēsis* as applied to the persons of the Trinity,[10] each
of whom is eternally distinct; the Father is not the Son and so forth.
Indeed, the simplicity of God is perfectly compatible with the Trinity,
since all three persons are God exhaustively, indivisibly occupying the
same "infinite divine space."[11] All three persons have all the attributes
without exception. The attributes describe in limited form—accommodated to our capacity—what God is like. However, we are not to
understand what God is like from our own limited grasp of such things
as goodness and love, for these qualities are not autonomous but are
understood from who God is. Furthermore, "we can speak of simple
things only as though they were like the composite things from which
we derive our knowledge."[12]

5.2 Classifications

Various attempts have been made over the years to distinguish God's
attributes, whether in relation to his decree to create the universe or in
terms of the possibility of, and degrees to which, the creature can participate in them on a finite level.

5.2.1 *Communicable and Incommunicable Attributes*

One classification relates to what divine attributes can and cannot be
shared in some measure by humans. Righteousness, truth, goodness,
and mercy are communicable to us. In some way, by the grace of God,
we are enabled to share these characteristics through the indwelling of
the Holy Spirit (Gal. 5:22–26). Clearly, God himself defines goodness;
goodness is what God is. However, in some measure we can be said to be
good, insofar as the Spirit transforms us into the image of Christ. There
is not an identity between human and divine goodness; there is more an
analogy. God is good infinitely and himself defines what goodness is.

---

10. Charles C. Twombly, *Perichoresis and Personhood: God, Christ, and Salvation in John of Damascus* (Eugene, OR: Pickwick, 2015).
11. Gerald Bray, *The Doctrine of God* (Leicester: Inter-Varsity Press, 1993), 158; Bavinck, *RD*, 2;177, who indicates that *simplicity* is an antonym not of *trinity* but of *composite*.
12. Aquinas, *ST* 1a.3.3. Richard Cross argues that Duns Scotus (1266–1308) held, contrary to Aquinas and the West and in agreement with John of Damascus, that there is a mind-independent distinction between the essence and attributes of God. Scotus takes from the West that we can speak of the divine essence, and from John that we can signify the divine attributes in distinction from the essence. Richard Cross, "Duns Scotus on God's Essence and Attributes: Metaphysics, Semantics, and the Greek Patristic Tradition," *RTPM* 83 (2016): 353–83.

We are given to share in goodness to a limited, finite extent, and in this world we are never wholly good, since even while being transformed, we retain "some remnants of corruption in every part" (WCF, 13.2), "the remnants of sin abiding in every part" (WLC, 78).

On the other hand, attributes such as infinity, eternity, self-existence, and immutability are possessed, and can be possessed, only by God. They are incommunicable. Since we are finite, living in time and space, in one place at one time, with limited knowledge, subject to growth, change, and decay, we cannot share these features. However, they are essential to who God is. If he were finite, he could not be God. Nor could he be God if he were subject to the possibility of change into who he is not, or to a progression from one degree to another; any change of this kind would entail that at one point he was less than who he became or who he had been. Moreover, it would negate his faithfulness, his being true to himself.

This classification has its limitations. Even though God is omnipresent and we are in one place, we nevertheless share presence. Our knowledge is limited and puny in contrast to God's omniscience, but it is still true knowledge. So, it would be a mistake to press this distinction overmuch. Notwithstanding, the classification does show us ways in which we are like God and ways in which God is unique. It underlies the point in chapter 1 about our knowledge of God being analogical.

5.2.2 Absolute and Relative Attributes

There is another way in which theologians have categorized God's attributes. Absolute attributes are those without which God would not be God; infinity, spirituality, eternity, omnipotence, omniscience, and omnipresence are intrinsic to God himself.

Relative attributes are those involved in God's relationship to the creation: he is holy, patient, merciful, creator, and preserver. To be *manifested*, these attributes require the existence of other entities. Since holiness at root is God's distinction and separateness from the creature,[13] without the existence of the creature there was nothing in relation to which God could be holy. However, upon his free determination to create, *by the very fact of who he eternally was and is*, he was holy in relation to the entities to which he gave life and existence. God did not

---

13. Bavinck, *RD*, 2:217–21.

change; it was not that he was potentially holy, becoming holy in relation to creation; he brought the creation into existence, which now reflects what he always is inasmuch as it differs from him.

Some attributes are related purely to sin: wrath is the prime example. Apart from human sin, God would not exercise wrath, for there would be nothing about which to be wrathful. However, once he had created humanity and Adam had disobeyed his law, with the consequent devastating effects on the human race and the cosmos itself, God—being holy and righteous—reacted with settled hostility to the emergence of rebellion in his prime creature. This was no change in God; it was the creature that had changed.

However, the relative attributes, as well as the absolute ones, are characteristics without which God would not be God. He *is* patient and merciful, even though patience and mercy entail other entities about which to be patient and merciful; if he were not so, he would not be who he is; he would not be God. Moreover, patience is an aspect of his eternity; since he transcends time, which he brought into existence, he sees the end from the beginning, and in relation to the creature he takes his time. Again, mercy is an outflow of his goodness. Since he is eternally good, in relation to the creatures he displays his goodness in showing mercy and grace to them. So, too, holiness and wrath, which we considered earlier, are the responses of God's inherent goodness to the existence and the sin of the creature.

5.3   The Names of God

5.3.1   Proper Names

God's proper names are designations by which he chose to reveal himself. They go beyond similes, whereby God compares himself to some element of his creation in order to highlight a particular facet of his character as it impinges on a particular historical circumstance. In Hosea God compares himself to a lion, a moth, and dry rot (Hos. 5:12, 14). Of course, God is not a moth; his actions toward Judah are what compare to the disruptive effect of a moth on cloth, eating away at the fabric. So too, when he is compared to a lion, his power and fearsomeness are in view. With dry rot, there is the idea of an insidious spread of an ultimately destructive mold. In each case, these figures of speech indicate that Yahweh is acting in judgment on the corruption and decadence of his people.

The proper names also go beyond metaphor. A metaphor describes one thing in terms of another, as in "Bill is a pig." The juxtaposition of entities is unusual. It is less clearly comparative than a simile is, positing a kind of identity; but it has limitations, being specific to a particular situation, circumstance, or character trait. Hence, Hebrews says, "Our God is a consuming fire" (Heb. 12:29), referring to the future judgment when his wrath will be evidenced unstoppably.

However, when God *names* himself, he is announcing who he is. Names are substantive declarations that relate to God himself rather than to a particular feature of his nature or actions. His principal names are as follows: *Elohim* is a generic name for God, used also for the angels and for human rulers in Psalm 82. *El Shaddai*, "God Almighty," is used in connection with the Abrahamic covenant in Genesis 17:1. *Yahweh, YHWH*, is the Old Testament covenant name of God. The Jews regarded it with such reverence that they refused to pronounce it but instead used *Adonai* (Lord).

God's self-naming reaches its climax in his new covenant name of *the Father, the Son, and the Holy Spirit* (Matt. 28:19).[14] At the institution of the Mosaic covenant, Moses read the book of the covenant and sprinkled the people with the blood of the sacrificial oxen while declaring, "Behold the blood of the covenant" (Ex. 24:1–8). In Matthew, Jesus inaugurates the new covenant in his own blood by saying, "This is my blood of the covenant," bringing to a climax the entire Gospel (Matt. 26:26–29). Matthew started with Jesus Christ, announced as the son of David, the son of Abraham (Matt. 1:1), inheritor of the Davidic and Abrahamic covenants. There followed a royal genealogy—three sets of fourteen generations each, corresponding to the rabbinical system of gematria, whereby numerical values were accorded to Hebrew letters, the values of the name David being fourteen.[15] As the Abrahamic covenant anticipated worldwide blessing (Gen. 12:1–3), so Matthew looks to the time when the nations will be included (Matt. 8:11–12). The Syro-Phoenecian woman is a prime example (Matt. 15:21–28). So in the new covenant the nations are to be made disciples, with initiation into the covenant by the sacrament of baptism in the one name of the Father, the Son, and the Holy Spirit (Matt. 28:18–20; cf. 26:26–29).

---

14. Robert Letham, *The Holy Trinity: In Scripture, History, Theology, and Worship* (Phillipsburg, NJ: P&R, 2004), 59–60.

15. W. D. Davies and Dale C. Allison Jr., *A Critical and Exegetical Commentary on the Gospel according to Saint Matthew* (Edinburgh: T&T Clark, 1988), 1:63–65.

5.3.2   *Essential Names*

God's essential names are those by which he is described absolutely: Spirit, love, light, life (John 4:24; 1 John 1:5; 4:8). These are foundational to who God is. God is the living God, brimful of life, overflowing with irrepressible vitality. He is pure love; the three delight in one another in the indivisible Trinity. God is light, shining in the darkness of human sin and wretchedness, shining with such power and penetration as to overcome and ultimately banish it. He is also Spirit, transcending and permeating all that he has brought into existence.

Only God can name himself, just as only God can reveal himself. No created entity has the power or right to name him; it is outside our capacity; it is his prerogative entirely. As T. F. Torrance remarks, "Knowledge of God is impossible on any ground other than that which God himself is, for as God is of himself alone, so he is known through himself alone," since we can know him only because he reveals himself.[16] Torrance concludes that to alter the Trinitarian formula is "to suggest that the Lord Jesus Christ was mistaken and indeed quite wrong in teaching us to hallow the name of the 'Father' and to believe in himself as the 'Son' of the Father." Indeed, "any person or any church that departs from the centrality of the Father-Son relation in faith and worship thereby rejects the particularity and finality of God's self-revelation in the Lord Jesus Christ and puts in question any claim to be authentically Christian."[17]

Recently, feminism has voiced some concerns of a societal nature, which theologians have developed in various ways. Feminist theologians have been re-imagining God. Seeking to eradicate what they see as irredeemable patriarchalism, in which powerful men have written the rules to the detriment of women, they see the names of God—Father and Son—as bearing the marks of this patriarchalism. From this has come the attribution of feminine names to God. Elisabeth Schüssler Fiorenza's seminal book *In Memory of Her*[18] is an example, as is Elizabeth Johnson's *She Who Is*.[19] Milder versions use names such as *creator*, *savior*, and *sanctifier*. Such are de facto attempts to seize a privilege that

---

16. Thomas F. Torrance, "The Christian Apprehension of God the Father," in *Speaking the Christian God: The Holy Trinity and the Challenge of Feminism*, ed. Alvin F. Kimel Jr. (Grand Rapids, MI: Eerdmans, 1992), 121.

17. Torrance, "God the Father," 142.

18. Elisabeth Schüssler Fiorenza, *In Memory of Her: A Feminist Theological Reconstruction of Christian Origins* (New York: Crossroad, 1983).

19. Elizabeth Johnson, *She Who Is* (New York: Crossroad, 1996).

belongs to God alone.[20] Moreover, they are names relating to the works of God *ad extra* and to the creation, implying a blurring or eradicating of the Creator-creature distinction, making God dependent on his works. Rather, God is to be worshiped exclusively in his own image, Jesus Christ, who is the eternal Son of the Father. Feminist renaming misses the point that, since God is not sexual, his names do not relate to gender. Besides, all attempts to rename God end up with descriptors that are less than personal; even *creator, redeemer,* and *sanctifier* are abstract, referring to the works of God, to the economic Trinity in isolation from any conception of the immanent Trinity.

5.4   The Beauty of God

Barth considers that the beauty of God is an aspect of his glory:

> It is to say that God has this superior force, this power of attraction, which speaks for itself, which wins and conquers, in the fact that he is beautiful, divinely beautiful, beautiful in his own way. . . . He does not have it . . . as a fact or a power. . . . He acts as the One who gives pleasure, creates desire and rewards with enjoyment. And he does this because he is pleasant, desirable, full of enjoyment, because . . . he alone is that which is pleasant, desirable and full of enjoyment. God loves us as the One who is worthy of love as God. This is what we mean when we say that God is beautiful.[21]

It is an explanation of his glory, a subordinate and auxiliary idea.[22] It is not that there is a concept of beauty to which God conforms; that would be to dethrone God. Rather, God in himself and all his works is glorious and, in this, beautiful. "God's being itself speaks for his beauty in his revelation"[23] seen in his attributes, his triunity, and the incarnation.[24]

This is a theme from which Reformation and Reformed theology has shied away with some mistrust, Barth suggests. But that is not entirely so. Bavinck points to the glory of God. He adds that while creaturely beauty is transitory and changeable, God is "the pinnacle of beauty, the beauty toward which all creatures point."[25] He prefers to speak of the glory and

---

20. Torrance, "God the Father"; Frame, *Doctrine of God*, 378–86.
21. Barth, *CD*, II/1:650–51.
22. Barth, *CD*, II/1:653.
23. Barth, *CD*, II/1:657.
24. Barth, *CD*, II/1:657–64.
25. Bavinck, *RD*, 2:254.

majesty of God. The Westminster Shorter Catechism famously begins by asserting that the chief end of man is "to glorify God, and to enjoy him for ever" (WSC, 1). God is supremely enjoyable. His glory is to be our greatest delight; it is seen in Jesus Christ (2 Cor. 4:6). Our greatest enjoyment in this life and the next is, and should be, to be animated by the beauty of God in the face of Jesus Christ. From this, all appreciation of aesthetics in the creation flows. Music, art, the dazzling beauty of landscapes are all pointers to the supreme glory of the Creator, the holy Trinity, revealed in Christ. Indeed, the creation account in Genesis 2 introduces us to the beauty of God's creation as iconic; the pursuit of beauty independent of him is perverse.

5.5   Biblical Foundations

Spirituality. Jesus said: "The hour is coming and now is, when true worshipers will worship the Father in Spirit and Truth, for the Father seeks such people to worship him. God is Spirit, and those who worship him must worship in Spirit and Truth" (John 4:23–24, my trans.). Jesus indicates that the nature of God is quite different from our bodily existence. He is Spirit, not material. He lives in a realm strange to us. References to God's body—his mighty arm—are anthropomorphisms. God describes himself in this way so that his revelation will be readily intelligible to humans of all kinds. It is typical that God accommodates himself to our capacities; otherwise we would be unable to bear his revelation. As Calvin put it, "Now the mode of accommodation is for him to represent himself to us not as he is in himself, but as he seems to us."[26] The apostle Paul tells of the one "who dwells in unapproachable light, whom no one has ever seen or can see" (1 Tim. 6:16). His being Spirit also denotes invisibility (1 Tim. 1:17), that he is not bound by the limitations of enfleshed humanity or by the nature of the cosmos that he created. God is infinite and not limited by created spacial or temporal categories.

However, God does now have a body! How? Of what kind? While God is in himself invisible—for his very nature is of another dimension than is ours—yet he has made himself visible to us (John 1:18; 2 Cor. 4:4; Col. 1:15). The Son has taken our flesh and blood as his own. The infinite, supreme one has a *human* body and soul, now and forever,

---

26. Calvin, *Institutes*, 1.17.13; cf. Aquinas, *ST* 1a.19.7.

and thereby we are called into fellowship and union with him—in Jesus Christ, the living God, the truth, who is now one with us, and in the Spirit, who elicits such worship.

Infinity. God, who permeates his creation, vastly transcends it. In relation to space, he is immense (1 Kings 8:27). In relation to time, he is eternal (Pss. 90:2; 102:26–28). In relation to creation, he is omnipresent:

> Where shall I go from your Spirit?
> Or where shall I flee from your presence?
> If I ascend to heaven, you are there!
> If I make my bed in Sheol, you are there! (Ps. 139:7–8)

> Am I a God at hand, declares the LORD, and not a God far away? Can a man hide himself in secret places so that I cannot see him? declares the LORD. Do I not fill heaven and earth? declares the LORD. (Jer. 23:23–24)

Eternity. Aquinas wrote that eternity is nothing else but God himself, for he is not to be measured by anything else than himself. Measurements are simply in order for us to be able to understand.[27] It follows that eternity is without time. Eternity is simultaneously whole, whereas time has a "before" and "after"; only God transcends time.[28]

Immutability. An aspect of God's eternity is that he is unchangeable.[29] He cannot cease to be who he eternally is. Immutability has come under attack in recent times as presenting a static conception of God in contrast to the dynamic portrayal in the Bible. This objection is not sustainable. God's immutability is not to be portrayed in such a way, for he is the *living* God (Mal. 3:6; Heb. 13:8). Immutability entails that God is not subject to outside forces; if he were, he would be at the mercy of elements of his creation, which is impossible. Nor is God in a process of becoming, contrary to process theology. If God were in a state of constant flux so that his identity would continuously change and develop, it would mean that at some stage he would be less than who he was eventually to

---

27. Aquinas, *ST* 1a.10.2.

28. Aquinas, *ST* 1a.10.4; Paul Helm, *Eternal God: A Study of God without Time*, 2nd ed. (New York: Oxford University Press, 2011).

29. Thomas G. Weinandy, *Does God Change? The Word's Becoming in the Incarnation* (Still River, MA: St. Bede's, 1985); Weinandy, *Does God Suffer?* (Notre Dame, IN: University of Notre Dame, 2000).

be, or become less than he previously was. God cannot change. This is not as an inhibition upon his freedom but rather it is his freedom to be eternally who he is, for there is never a point at which he is less. God's immutability is his freedom to be himself.[30]

The living God. Throughout the Bible God presents himself as the God who speaks and acts, who loves from eternity, who is indivisibly relational. He is depicted as the living God, in contrast to pagan idols.

> Our God is in the heavens;
>> he does all that he pleases.
>
> Their idols are silver and gold,
>> the work of human hands.
> They have mouths, but do not speak;
>> eyes, but do not see.
> They have ears, but do not hear;
>> noses, but do not smell.
> They have hands, but do not feel;
>> feet, but do not walk;
>> and they do not make a sound in their throat.
> Those who make them become like them;
>> so do all that trust in them. (Ps. 115:3–8)

God is the Creator of contingent life, of all entities other than himself, and he offers us to share in everlasting and eternal life. Bavinck argues that this is possible only because the Father generates the Son and spirates the Spirit eternally, indicating that he is himself infinitely superabundant life.

Omnipresence, omnipotence, omniscience. All these attributes are aspects of God's infinity. He is not limited by anything outside himself, since he is independent. All other entities were brought into existence by him and are completely dependent on his sovereign will for their continuation. He is omnipresent, since he cannot be confined spatially. All other entities are located in space. God transcends space. Psalm 139:7–12 presents a vivid poetic account of his omnipresence. Wherever we go, he is there. Says Bavinck, "Neither space nor location can

---

30. I will discuss God's impassibility, in passing, later in this chapter.

be predicated of God."[31] Instead, "God fills to repletion every point of space and sustains it by his immensity."[32] Similarly, his knowledge is infinite and comprehensive. He knows all things in one instantaneous act of cognition. We will consider this later. In turn, he can do all things that are consistent with his character, with who he is. As the pagan king came to realize, "He does according to his will . . . and none can stay his hand" (Dan. 4:35).

Incomprehensibility. Further, since he is infinite, God cannot be boxed in, or encompassed. In short, we are unable to know God exhaustively. Indeed, our knowledge of God is limited to what he has chosen to reveal of himself and, beyond that, to what the Spirit enables us to understand of that revelation. There remains a vast mystery, in the colloquial sense of what lies beyond our comprehension. Aquinas cites Augustine to the effect that comprehension entails seeing something in such a way that nothing of that thing is hidden. Even though God can be known, he cannot be known fully or comprehended as a whole by any creature.[33] Psalm 139 speaks of his exhaustive knowledge, his omnipresence, his transcendence; in every sense God is beyond our capacities. We can know him, and know him truly, but only as he makes himself known to us on our own level. Solomon's prayer at the dedication of the temple sums it up: "But will God indeed dwell on the earth? Behold, heaven and the highest heaven cannot contain you" (1 Kings 8:27).

This is taken to the point of agnosticism in the Palamite strand of Orthodoxy. Vladimir Lossky, focusing on apophatic knowledge as it had been taught by Dionysius, considers that it entails emptying ourselves of all concepts and, in mystical contemplation, ascending to the unknown divine essence in the darkness of total ignorance.[34] Lossky has been questioned within Orthodoxy as to his choice of Dionysius and Palamas. Moreover, as McGuckin comments, "What is it that apophatic awareness of God contributes to the ecclesial tradition if it exceeds speech and thought? Can such a profoundly silent theological tradition actually teach?"[35] He records that one of Lossky's teachers said, "If you really

---

31. Bavinck, *RD*, 2:167.
32. Bavinck, *RD*, 2:168.
33. Aquinas, *ST* 1a.12.7.
34. Vladimir Lossky, *The Mystical Theology of the Eastern Church* (London: James Clarke, 1957), 23–43.
35. J. A. McGuckin, "On the Mystical Theology of the Eastern Church," *SVTQ* 58 (2014): 393.

are an apophatic theologian, the least you can do is: Shut up!"[36] Paul
Gavrilyuk observes:

> Both Lossky and Meyendorff turn the normative claim about the
> ideal relationship between mystical theology and dogmatic theology
> into a descriptive generalization about the historical development
> of Byzantine theology. Such a conflation of theological desideratum
> with what purports to be a historical description is a peculiar tempta-
> tion of the Orthodox reading of the patristic past.[37]

In the same place he writes of the reception of Dionysius as a Trojan
horse in the Orthodox camp.[38]

5.6   The Will of God

The will is an aspect of self-determination. It entails the one who wills,
choosing freely between a number of possible alternatives or making
decisions that reflect his or her wishes. In the case of God, his will is an
aspect of his omnipotence and sovereignty—indeed, of all other attributes—and as such is inherently effective in accomplishing his purposes.
However, the complex nature of the world, especially since the fall,
means that the ramifications of God's willing have their own complexities, owing to the complexities introduced by the rebellious creature and
their effects upon the cosmos.[39] We noted in previous chapters that God's
will is an aspect of his nature and so is one and indivisible. The classifications that follow are simply tools to aid us in our human understanding
and neither can nor do imply any division in the will of God.

5.6.1   Decretive and Preceptive

God's decretive will is what he has determined to be. His preceptive
will is what is conformable to his demands, ethical and otherwise. Such
a distinction is due to the entrance of sin into the world. Ethical rebellion and physical catastrophes pose a problem, since some things that

---

36. McGuckin, "Mystical Theology," 395.
37. Paul L. Gavrilyuk, "The Reception of Dionysius in Twentieth-Century Eastern Orthodoxy,"
MTheol 24 (2008): 720.
38. For a judicious discussion of the relationship between apophatic and cataphatic theology in
Patristic and Orthodox theology, see Verna E. F. Harrison, "The Relationship between Apophatic
and Kataphatic Theology," *PrEccl* 6 (1995): 318–32.
39. See Richard A. Muller, *Divine Will and Human Choice: Freedom, Contingency, and Necessity in Early Modern Reformed Thought* (Grand Rapids, MI: Baker Academic, 2017).

humans choose are out of line with the law of God and contrary to what he has prescribed for human flourishing.

God's decretive will. The stress throughout Scripture is that all that happens is a consequence of God's decretive will, his particular determination that this or that will transpire. Paul speaks of "him who works all things according to the counsel of his will" (Eph. 1:11). This includes random events, such as when a Syrian soldier fired his arrow at random and killed the king of Israel, who had taken every precaution to make himself *incognito*, having heard the word of the Lord that he was to fall in battle that day (1 Kings 22:13–36, esp. 34). It also covers the casting of lots (Prov. 16:33). Acts intended to bring evil and harm can nevertheless be part of God's overriding purpose to accomplish good (Gen. 50:20; Acts 2:23). Each thought and policy of the most powerful ruler is ordered by God to fulfill *his* will (Prov. 21:1; Rev. 1:5). The book of Esther is full of seemingly fortuitous events, lucky breaks, all clearly— if subtly and implicitly—testifying to the sovereignty of God, who is not mentioned by name in the entire book. The ultimate destiny of the universe, the earth, its inhabitants, and the church is all to work out in line with the eternal plan of God.

God's preceptive will. God's preceptive will is seen particularly in the Decalogue (Ex. 20:1–17) and in legislation and commands that flow from it in both the Old and the New Testaments. Various ethical exhortations occurring in the New Testament, grounded as they are in the Decalogue and its application, are features of the preceptive will of God. They show us the way God wants us to live, the pattern for Christian behavior. Sadly, due to sin, we do not always live in accordance with God's preceptive will.

5.6.2 God's Decretive Will and the Problem of Sin and Evil

Because of the fall, humans disobey God and do not follow his precepts. The impact of the fall on the creation is such that tragic natural disasters are frequent. Seemingly random evils occur—the screech of brakes, the ambulance siren, the plane crash, the stillborn child, the degenerative disease. God has willed all that comes to pass, and some events are evil. Does this mean that God's sovereignty trumps his love and grace? On the one hand, since he is good and holy, God cannot be the author of sin. Clearly, God allows a vast number of material, ethical, and personal evils to occur. The world is full of them. Yet he has foreordained all that comes to pass. How, then, can he escape responsibility for these happenings? On the other hand, if one were to say that God has no part in such things, God would be a helpless bystander, unable to change the contorted way the human race had developed or to curb natural disasters; he would not be the sovereign ruler of the universe.

There are a number of factors that we need to take into account.

The first coordinate is human responsibility. The Bible holds that we have no escape clause. We are fully responsible for our actions in the sight of God. When sin entered the world, the first instinct of the fallen couple was to try to pass the blame elsewhere. The woman attributed the sin to the serpent; the man blamed the woman. Neither was prepared to face his or her own responsibility (Gen. 3:8–13).

Second, there is compatibility between God and humans. God created the human race in his image (Gen. 1:26–27). There was communication between them. The man and the woman were put in the garden, on behalf of God, to maintain it and to extend its reach to the rest of creation. They were to share in God's rule over the earth (Gen. 1:28–30; 2:15–25). The free agency of the human race and the sovereignty of God operate on different levels. God and humanity are partners, not competitors.

Third, our perspective is necessarily limited. We can see only the immediately evident context; God sees the whole in one instantaneous act of cognition. Tony Lane compares this relationship to a beautiful work of art such as a tapestry. On one side, it seems to be a mess, with a mass of threads sticking out of the fabric in a seemingly disordered way; on the other side, beauty and clarity abound.[40]

The limited resolution currently possible lies along the lines of the compatibility of the sovereignty of God over all things together with the free agency of humans; a fuller resolution occurs eschatologically, at the last judgment, when God will set all things right.

Frame has a useful practical section on questions often asked about the will of God for one's life.[41] The bottom line is that we need to exercise wisdom to determine what is the best course of action for ourselves within the bounds of God's preceptive will. Whom should I marry? Should I ac-

---

40. Tony Lane, *Exploring Christian Doctrine* (London: SPCK, 2013), 90.
41. Frame, *Doctrine of God*, 539–42.

cept this job offer? What plans should we make for retirement? There may
be a variety of possible and valid courses of action. We must act within
the bounds laid down by God in Scripture, on the basis of a realistic assessment of the gifts God has given us and the prevailing circumstances.

5.6.3   *The Will of God as Desire*

Sometimes the will of God is expressed as a desire that this or that take
place, even though the desired outcome does not occur. Two examples
will suffice. Ezekiel 18:30–32 says:

> Therefore I will judge you, O house of Israel, every one according
> to his ways, declares the Lord GOD. Repent and turn from all your
> transgressions, lest iniquity be your ruin. Cast away from you all the
> transgressions that you have committed, and make yourselves a new
> heart and a new spirit! Why will you die, O house of Israel? For I
> have no pleasure in the death of anyone, declares the Lord GOD; so
> turn, and live.

Despite Yahweh's deep desire that the house of Israel should repent and
live, they remained obstinate in their unbelief, and Jerusalem was soon
overthrown.

Again, 2 Peter 3:9 declares, "The Lord is not slow concerning his
promise, as some count slowness, but he is patient toward you, not willing that anyone perish but that all reach repentance" (my trans.). This
expresses the overall desire of God that all people be saved. Evidently not
all will be saved. According to Paul's argument in Ephesians 1:11, this
outcome has been planned by God. Yet he derives no pleasure in anyone
perishing. Indeed, the statement here in 2 Peter is held out as an example
of what we are to do on our part (2 Pet. 3:11–12).

5.6.4   *Absolute and Conditional Will*

God's absolute will is his will to create and to redeem by Christ, with
all that this entails. In this no action of the creature is contemplated. It
is a determination that involves God alone, contingent on nothing. In
contrast, his conditional will is related to actions on the part of creatures;
this or that decree is to be fulfilled in conjunction with actions by humans or angels or other created entities. In each case, the actions of the
creatures are themselves part of the eternal plan of God, the result of his

decretive will. So, God willed that humans be saved, and in that will he purposed that their salvation be brought about through repentance and faith in Jesus Christ. Their salvation is brought about by means, without which they would not be saved, means that themselves are ordained by God. This distinction recognizes that God is sovereign and yet not the author of sin; he allows room for humans as responsible free agents, with eternal consequences riding on their decisions.[42]

In this we need to remember that these paradigms are constructed by theologians to obtain some kind of understanding of the variegated manifestations of the will of God. God has one will, since he is one indivisible being. If will were a predicate of persons rather than nature, God would have three wills, and we would be on the road to tritheism. These classifications relate more to the relationship between the will of God and the creation, the latter being changeable. They lead us toward a discussion of the works of God, which will occupy the rest of the book.

5.7   The Decrees of God

Opera ad intra refers to intra-Trinitarian works, the relations between the three persons, generation and procession. *Opera ad extra* are the works of God relating to his creation, whether immanent (decrees) or emanant (flowing out: creation, providence, and grace). Precisely because God is the living Trinity, these works are possible and rendered actual.

A variety of terms are used in the New Testament, including *counsel, will, good pleasure, purpose, foreknowledge, election,* and *predestination.* I will refer to some of the different nuances as we proceed.

God's decrees are eternal. Since God is eternal, transcending time and space, his decree has logical priority over its execution in time. However, God's decree is to be distinguished from God's eternity, which is necessary, whereas he is free to decree or not decree as he sees fit. His decree depends on his sovereign will, while his will is an attribute, coextensive with who he is.

Are God's decrees unconditional? God's purpose is settled and sure. There are no factors over which God does not have control. His decree is immutable (Ps. 33:9–11; Isa. 14:14, 27; 46:9–10; Dan. 4:34–35; Rom.

---

42. James Dolezal suggests that it is better to talk of God's will for conditionals rather than his conditional will, not of God willing conditionally but of his unconditional will for conditionals.

9:11–12, 19–21; Heb. 6:17–18). On the other hand, as with the absolute and conditional wills of God, some of his decrees take into consideration and include the actions of his creatures. In that subsidiary sense, they are conditional. For instance, God offers salvation on condition of faith in Jesus Christ. Suppose God has decreed to save Fred. From one perspective, whether Fred receives salvation depends on whether he exercises faith in Christ. However, Fred's believing response to the gospel is also decreed in eternity by God as an aspect of God's decree to save Fred.[43]

The decrees *ad extra* can be apportioned to creation (the bringing into existence of the universe), providence (God's maintenance and government of it), which we will consider in chapters 9 and 10, and grace (God's deliverance of humanity following sin, and the concomitant consummation of the cosmos), which will occupy us thereafter.

5.8 Predestination, Election, and Reprobation

5.8.1 The Meaning of the Terms

Predestination should be distinguished from foreknowledge. The latter is an aspect of God's omniscience and refers to his knowing all things comprehensively in one instantaneous act of cognition. David marveled:

> O Lord, you have searched me and known me!
> You know when I sit down and when I rise up;
>   you discern my thoughts from afar.
> You search out my path and my lying down
>   and are acquainted with all my ways.
> Even before a word is on my tongue,
>   behold, O Lord, you know it altogether. (Ps. 139:1–4)

However, sometimes in the New Testament "foreknow" is the equivalent of "foreordain," as in Romans 8:29–30.[44] *Predestination* refers to God's ordaining this or that immutably from eternity. It is comprehensive and includes providence (his government of all things). However, it usually refers to his foreordination of the eternal destinies of humans, in election and reprobation.

---

43. For a brilliant, concise summary on the divine counsel, see Bavinck, *RD*, 2:337–41.

44. See C. E. B. Cranfield, *A Critical and Exegetical Commentary on the Epistle to the Romans*, 2 vols., The International Critical Commentary (Edinburgh: T&T Clark, 1975), 1:431; Rudolph Bultmann, "προγινώσκω, πρόγνωσις," in *TDNT*, 1:715–16, who remarks that God's foreknowledge "is an election or foreordination of his people."

Election is that aspect of predestination that relates to those whom God ordains to salvation in Christ. Election is made by the Father in Christ the Son.

> Blessed be the God and Father of our Lord Jesus Christ, who blessed us with every blessing of the Spirit in the heavenly realms in Christ, as he chose us in him before the foundation of the world that we should be holy and without blame before him. (Eph. 1:3–4, my trans.)

> [God the Father] saved us and called us with a holy calling, not in accordance with our works but according to his own purpose and grace, which he gave us in Christ Jesus before eternal ages. (2 Tim. 1:9, my trans.)

> Those he [God the Father] foreknew, he foreordained to be conformed to the image of his Son. (Rom. 8:29, my trans.)

> Therefore, it is not of him who wills nor of him who runs, but of God who gives mercy. . . . Therefore, he has mercy on whomever he wills, and he hardens whomever he wills. (Rom. 9:16, 18, my trans.)

> Everyone the Father has given me will come to me, and he who comes to me I will never cast out. (John 6:37, my trans.)

The whole tenor of Scripture in a broader sense testifies to election. God's calling Abraham, his choosing Isaac and rejecting Ishmael, his choice of Jacob and rejection of Esau, and his election of Israel and rejection of the nations until the new covenant are all aspects of his electing purpose.

The decree of election is made by the God who is good and wise. It is made in Christ; Christ is central to it. It is an act of grace and love; it is a miracle that he chose us, since we have done nothing to warrant it—rather the reverse.

Reprobation refers to God's decree to pass by the nonelect and ordain them to wrath on account of their sins in accord with his justice (WCF, 3.7). I will discuss this portentous theme more fully in chapter 14.

5.8.2 *The Order of Decrees in the Mind of God*

This rather abstruse debate does not relate to the order between the decree of God and what happens in human history. All agree that the decree has priority over its historical outworking; the standard way Reformed theologians have discussed that is by distinguishing between the decree and the execution of the decree. Rather, the question revolves around which aspect of God's eternal plan has priority in his own mind.[45]

Supralapsarianism argues that first in God's mind was his decree to elect some to salvation. The order runs *election, creation, fall, grace* (the work of salvation). The decree of election precedes the decree to permit the fall—hence, it is *supra* (above) the fall. Thus, God elects those who are potentially creatable. They are not considered fallen at the point the decree is made.

Infralapsarianism maintains the order *creation, fall, election, grace*. The decree of election follows or is under (*infra*) the decree of the fall. This is an attempt to do justice to the historical outworking of redemption and so follows the order of the biblical record. The elect are considered to be both created and fallen at the point the decree is made.

All Reformed confessions adopt an infralapsarian position; none have chosen supralapsarianism. However, supralapsarians are not beyond the pale of Reformed orthodoxy. Franciscus Gomarus, a supralapsarian, was a key participant at the Synod of Dort. The first prolocutor of the Westminster Assembly was the supralapsarian William Twisse. Another prominent supralapsarian, Samuel Rutherford, a Scots commissioner though not a member of the assembly as such, was an active and influential participant in debates.

Supralapsarianism tends to govern the whole theological spectrum by the decree of election. This has an impact on creation, common grace, and the free offer of the gospel. Karl Barth came down in favor of a reconstituted form of supralapsarianism, which we will consider in chapter 14.[46]

Arminius (1560–1609) held to the order *creation, fall, grace, election*. Here election follows grace as well as the fall. God elects those he foresees will respond to the gospel in repentance and faith. The outworking of grace has priority over the decree of election. God's election of us is effectively to rubber stamp our election of him. Human action is effectively determinative.

---

45. The most compendious treatment of the question is J. V. Fesko, *Diversity within the Reformed Tradition: Supra- and Infralapsarianism in Calvin, Dort, and Westminster* (Greenville, SC: Reformed Academic Press, 2003).

46. Barth, *CD*, II/2:127–45.

This whole question can seem a recondite matter, conjured up by theologians with too much time on their hands. That may be so. Yet decisions here can have far-reaching consequences; many supralapsarians, by no means all, are opposed to the free offer of the gospel, since it is governed by election. What supralapsarianism has in its support is the principle that what is last in execution is usually first in intention. In the design and construction of a house, the first thing that comes to mind is the kind of house one wants to build. Then follow the architect's plans, the foundations, the superstructure, and finally the internal parts: the electric wiring, the floors, and so on. The final goal comes first, then the practical execution. In this way, supralapsarianism approaches salvation strictly from the side of God, insofar as we are falteringly able to grasp that. Infralapsarianism looks from our side, from the historical outworking of the decree. The relationship between time and eternity is a large and perhaps unacknowledged factor in the debate. Both positions have strengths and weaknesses. Both are recognizably in the Reformed camp, but only infralapsarianism has confessional status.

5.9   Open Theism

In the recent past, a view known as open theism emerged in opposition to the traditional understanding of God as omniscient and omnipotent. Open theists have included evangelicals Clark Pinnock, John Sanders, Gregory Boyd, and David Basinger. While the movement has tended to fade, the issues it raised are not likely to go away for some time, and the answer to them highlights the importance of God's omniscience.

5.9.1   Open Theism's Major Claims

Open theists argue that the Christian doctrine of God was influenced by Greek thought. Theology became philosophical rather than biblical. God was seen to be impassible (incapable of suffering) and immutable. Lost was the dynamic interaction between God and the creature. In the Bible, so the argument runs, God responds to human actions and is even said to repent of what he planned. In the book of Jonah, God warns Nineveh of its impending destruction, whereupon he repents and relents once the city abandoned its ungodliness. In contrast, the doctrine of omniscience reduces humans to robots, so open theists claim. Genuine relationships entail mutuality, give and take, which is missing if God is seen as the almighty, all-knowing ruler. Instead of a loving God who feels human suffering, the church has taught that he is remote and aloof.

Clark Pinnock, one of open theism's leading exponents, wrote that his former Calvinism was nonsense:

> To say that God hates sin while secretly willing it, to say that God warns us not to fall away though it is impossible, to say that God loves the world while excluding most people from an opportunity of salvation, to say that God warmly invites sinners to come knowing all the while that they cannot possibly do so—such things do not deserve to be called mysteries when that is just a euphemism for nonsense.[47]

Instead, God is love. This implies reciprocity and mutuality, since these are inherent in all personal interaction.

Hence, God does not have certain knowledge of future events. His eternity is not timelessness. He may be taken by surprise by events in the world. He knows a lot, but it is impossible for him to know everything that will happen in the future. He is very resourceful, but there is no guarantee his plans will succeed. Like a chess grandmaster, he is able to respond to unusual moves by his creatures, but there is always the possibility that he will be taken by surprise. This is seen as an immense stimulus for us, since we can have real interaction with God and contribute to the relationship.

5.9.2 Evaluating Open Theism

Open theism rejects the historic teaching of the church. This is the hallmark of sects and cults down through the ages. In rejecting the insistence of the church—Rome, Orthodoxy, and Protestant alike—on the immutability and omniscience of God, open theists value their own exegesis of the Bible above that of the church of the last fifty generations.

Open theism takes a radical approach to the Bible. This is particularly clear with prophecy. The prophetic writings, and prophetic utterances in general, indicate that God *does* have comprehensive knowledge of the future. If he were ignorant of the future, prophecy in its predictive mode could not exist. The interpretive problem surfaces also with language in which God is said to have human emotions. Open theists

---

47. In Clark Pinnock et al., *The Openness of God: A Biblical Challenge to the Traditional Understanding of God* (Downers Grove, IL: InterVarsity Press, 1994), 115n33.

make much of statements that God regretted this or that, or repented of what he had intended to do. In this, he is said to display emotions and changeableness. However, open theists do not apply such a strategy to statements attributing human body parts to God. It is generally recognized that these statements are anthropomorphisms. Yet the psychological, emotional, and physical are so closely related in humans that it is arbitrary for open theists to stress one aspect but ignore another.

Open theist scholarship is outdated. The idea that the church was overcome by Greek philosophy was popularized by Adolf von Harnack (1851–1930) but has been debunked many times over. Scholars such as Aloys Grillmeier, J. N. D. Kelly, and Jaroslav Pelikan, among others, have undermined it.[48] Recent work on Augustine has brought about a major reassessment of the extent to which he was influenced by Neoplatonism.[49] Even Origen has been enjoying a posthumous rehabilitation (I hope he is enjoying it).[50] The Greek fathers were forced to reply to the heretics' use of the Bible by recourse to Greek philosophical terms. However, they adapted the language to make it an effective vehicle for the communication of biblical truth, stretching it to accommodate new meaning that expressed what had always been believed.[51] Moreover, it was the Christian theology of the fathers that came up with the concept of personhood that open theists are so keen on using. Furthermore, the exponents of open theism seem unaware that they have resuscitated the sixteenth- and seventeenth-century aberration of Socinianism.[52]

Open theism's knowledge of the fathers is inadequate. This surfaces in the treatment of the impassibility of God. They argue—in common

---

48. Aloys Grillmeier, SJ, *Christ in Christian Tradition*, vol. 1, *From the Apostolic Age to Chalcedon (451)*, 2nd ed., trans. John Bowden (Atlanta: John Knox, 1975); J. N. D. Kelly, *Early Christian Doctrines* (London: Adam & Charles Black, 1968); Jaroslav Pelikan, *The Christian Tradition*, vol. 1, *The Emergence of the Catholic Tradition (100–600)* (Chicago: University of Chicago Press, 1971).

49. Basil Studer, *Trinity and Incarnation: The Faith of the Early Church*, trans. Matthias Westerhoff, ed. Andrew Louth (Collegeville, MN: Liturgical, 1993), 167–85; Studer, *The Grace of Christ and the Grace of God in Augustine of Hippo: Christocentrism or Theocentrism?* (Collegeville, MN: Liturgical, 1997), 104–9; Michel René Barnes, "Rereading Augustine on the Trinity," in *The Trinity: An Interdisciplinary Symposium on the Trinity*, ed. Stephen T. Davis, Daniel Kendall, and Gerald O'Collins (Oxford: Oxford University Press, 1999), 145–53; Lewis Ayres, *Augustine and the Trinity* (Cambridge: Cambridge University Press, 2010).

50. Cf. Henry Crouzel, *Origen*, trans. A. S. Worrall (Edinburgh: T&T Clark, 1989). Scholars are divided over whether this is possible.

51. Letham, *The Holy Trinity*, 146–83.

52. See "Socinianism," in *The Oxford Encyclopedia of the Reformation*, ed. Hans J. Hillerbrand, 4 vols. (New York: Oxford University Press, 1996), 4:83–87.

with much recent theology, following Moltmann—that only a God who suffers can be of help to us in our predicaments. In contrast, the fathers, so they say, presented a God who was detached from suffering. Thomas Weinandy has refuted these claims. The fathers did not support such ideas at all, he indicates. Instead, in affirming that God could not suffer, they meant that he could not be constrained from outside, but they held that in the incarnation the Son took our humanity and in our flesh experienced *human* suffering. As such, God is able to help us, since he is impregnable and qualified to help us since he has suffered *as man.*[53]

Open theism has a distorted view of God. Its focus is on God as suffering love (Moltmann) but not on his justice or holiness. Thus, the simplicity of God is threatened, as one attribute is extracted at the expense of others. Sin is downplayed. Biblical statements about the love of God are taken out of context. Richard Rice, in *The Openness of God* (Downers Grove, IL: InterVarsity Press, 1994) ignores developments in linguistics relating to ἀγαπάω, propounding a special *agapē* love that God exercises in distinction from *phileō* love, an idea undermined by the work of Robert Joly, who had long demonstrated that by the first century the verbs were used interchangeably.[54] Rice's view of reconciliation also proceeds without reference to the work of Leon Morris, who established that God is the primary one to be reconciled in the atoning death of Christ.[55]

Moreover, to say that God does not change is to affirm that he does not change in himself, not that his relationships *ad extra* with his creatures do not change. Since creatures change in themselves, such changes bring them into new and potentially differing relationships with God. Bray indicates that true statements about God can be false or meaningless if taken outside their proper context, the context of his covenant. God's love toward his covenant people is of a different order than his love toward the creation in general.[56]

Open theism has striking similarities to process theology. God is in a mutually dependent relationship with his creation, one of dynamic

---

53. See Weinandy, *Does God Suffer?*
54. Robert Joly, *Le vocabulaire Chrétien de l'amour est-il original? Filein et agapan dans le Grec antique* (Bruxelles: Presses Universitaires de Bruxelles, 1968).
55. Leon Morris, *The Apostolic Preaching of the Cross* (London: Tyndale Press, 1955), 214–50.
56. Gerald Bray, *The Personal God* (Carlisle: Paternoster, 1998), 45.

change and development. It has a decided similarity to panentheism in this regard.

Open theism implies that God's plans could be endlessly frustrated. The implication of open theism is that the incarnation and atonement were reactions to an unforeseen emergency. Indeed, God has no certain knowledge that his purposes will succeed; neither have we. This uncertainty could even extend to the eschaton. Since he does not have exhaustive knowledge of future events, how can even God be sure that there will not be a sinful rebellion of his people in heaven?

Open theists' claims that their theology enables a dynamic and exciting view of prayer are untenable. The claim is that this interactive relationship enables us to play an integral role in the unfolding of events in the world. But since God's plans are merely provisional, how can this be? Basinger writes that God has no certain knowledge of how the economy will perform over the next five to ten years; he thinks this makes prayer a dynamic and exciting spiritual journey.[57]

Open theism is an example of postmodernism. It is simply a perspective that some may find more helpful. Basinger thinks one should choose the conceptualization of God that one finds most appealing. So, he says, "I personally find [the open theism model] to be the most . . . appealing conceptualization of this relationship."[58] One basically pays one's money and takes one's choice. This is a matter of reimagining God in one's own image, the very essence of idolatry.[59]

An even more radical proposal, advanced by Thomas Jay Oord, oversteps the bounds of the Christian faith. Oord proposes that God is essentially and preeminently uncontrolling love. Oord's focus is on the problem of evil, which we will address in chapter 10. It is based on an understanding of Philippians 2, in which Christ's self-emptying is not restricted to the incarnation but is definitive of the nature of God. God is inherently and necessarily self-emptying love, which empowers others, the *kenosis* involving self-emptying so as to be powerless to prevent evil actions or events. These cannot be attributed to him, since he is love.

57. Pinnock et al., *Openness*, 161–65.
58. Pinnock et al., *Openness*, 76.
59. For a later work on similar lines, see John Sanders, *The God Who Risks: A Theology of Divine Providence* (Downers Grove, IL: IVP Academic, 2007).

Moreover, he is uncontrolling love, so he does not and cannot coerce anyone.

By elevating love over all other attributes, Oord has disrupted the unity of God. The authority for Oord is not Scripture but human culture and experience. In positing an autonomous evil, he allows a deep ontological dualism at the heart of his view of the creation. Moreover, if God is powerless to prevent evil, how can that be loving? Such a view of God is radically opposed to the Bible and to the belief of the entire church, Catholic, Orthodox, and Protestant.[60]

Further Reading

Dolezal, James E. *All That Is in God: Evangelical Theology and the Challenge of Classical Christian Theism.* Grand Rapids, MI: Reformation Heritage, 2017.

Dolezal, James E. *God without Parts: Divine Simplicity and the Metaphysics of God's Absoluteness.* Eugene, OR: Pickwick, 2011.

Muller, Richard A. *Divine Will and Human Choice: Freedom, Contingency, and Necessity in Early Modern Reformed Thought.* Grand Rapids, MI: Baker Academic, 2017.

Weinandy, Thomas G. *Does God Suffer?* Notre Dame, IN: University of Notre Dame Press, 2000.

Study Questions

1. The simplicity of God is a doctrine historically held as vital in both Eastern and Western churches, yet it has come under attack in recent years. What would be the impact if God were divisible into parts?

2. The understanding that holiness is God's separateness from his creatures might seem to imply that holiness comes into effect only after God creates. Why is this not the case?

3. How are biblical statements about God repenting or changing his mind best understood?

4. Discuss whether it is valid to isolate some attributes of God and view them as definitive to the exclusion of the whole biblical picture?

---

60. Thomas Jay Oord, *The Uncontrolling Love of God: An Open and Relational Account of Providence* (Downers Grove, IL: IVP Academic, 2015).

PART 2

THE WORD OF GOD

Blessed Lord, who has caused all holy Scriptures to be written for our learning; grant that we may in such wise hear them, read, mark, learn, and inwardly digest them, that by patience, and comfort of your holy Word, we may embrace, and ever hold fast the blessed hope of everlasting life, which you have given us in our Saviour Jesus Christ. Amen.

Collect for the second Sunday in Advent, Book of Common Prayer (1662)

6

The Doctrine of Scripture

Due to sin and the limitations of general revelation, Scripture is necessary in order to preserve the record of God's redemptive deeds and to teach us of God's glory and our salvation, faith, and life. Originating from God, who, by the Holy Spirit, used the contributions of the human authors, Scripture is the Word of God in servant form, the supreme authority in all matters of faith and life. While in part it is hard to understand, its central message of salvation in Christ can be grasped by everyone, given the due use of the ordinary means. As such, it is sufficient for its purpose and needs no supplementation.

There are objections and conundrums in every science. Those who do not want to start in faith will never arrive at knowledge. . . . Those who do not want to embark on scientific investigation until they see the road by which we arrive at knowledge fully cleared will never start. Those who do not want to eat before they understand the entire process by which food arrives at their table will starve to death. And those who do not want to believe the Word of God before they see all problems resolved will die of spiritual starvation.[1]

Theological statements as such are contested statements—challenged by the sheer incomparability of their subject. . . . There is one, and only one, apparent exception to this rule: the theologian speaks absolutely

---

1. Bavinck, *RD*, 1:442.

when his statements coincide with the text, or with the necessary inferences from the text, of the sacred authority.[2]

There may be times . . . when it is right to begin one's theology with the doctrine of Scripture. . . . However, the doctrine of Scripture itself is often distorted by this approach. . . . Its every aspect is shaped from the bottom up by the character and actions of God.[3]

6.1   The Necessity of Scripture[4]

We considered why Scripture is necessary in our discussion of general and special revelation. God's revelation in creation is insufficient to bring us to salvation since sin entered the picture. Sin blinds the mind to the goodness of God all around us. Scripture is necessary to bring the church to the destiny God has for it, because it is a written and permanent record of his redemptive deeds. It is also needed to teach us authoritatively about the glory of God and salvation, faith, and life (WCF, 1.4). As Calvin wrote, "No one can get even the slightest taste of right and sound doctrine unless he be a pupil of Scripture."[5]

6.2   The Canon of Scripture

This raises the question of where Scripture can be found. Athanasius, in his *Paschal Letter* of 367, lists a New Testament canon identical to ours,[6] although lists of authoritative books were given from the second century, following Marcion's rejection of the Old Testament and much of the New, and the appearance of spurious "Gospels" from various Gnostic groups. The Muratorian fragment of AD 170 has a list substantially, although not completely, identical to that of Athanasius.[7] However, the canon was again a matter of debate after the Reformation. Luther rejected James and relegated Hebrews, Jude, and Revelation—

2. Karl Barth, *Fides Quaerens Intellectum: Anselm's Proof of the Existence of God in the Context of His Theological Scheme* (Pittsburgh: Pickwick, 1975), 30–31.

3. Timothy Ward, *Words of Life: Scripture as the Living and Active Word of God* (Nottingham: Inter-Varsity Press, 2009), 19.

4. This chapter is an edited, condensed version, with additions, of material in my book *The Westminster Assembly: Reading Its Theology in Historical Context* (Phillipsburg, NJ: P&R, 2009).

5. Calvin, *Institutes*, 1.6.2. See John Webster, *Holy Scripture* (Cambridge: Cambridge University Press, 2003), 11–17.

6. *NPNF²*, 4:551–52.

7. J. Stevenson, ed., *A New Eusebius: Documents Illustrating the History of the Church to 337*, rev. by W. H. C. Frend (London: SPCK, 1987), 123–25. See also R. Giordani, "Scripture, Holy," in *EECh*, 2:762–63; C. F. D. Moule, *The Birth of the New Testament* (New York: Harper & Row, 1962), 178–209.

with James—to deuterocanonical status in his September Bible of 1522. Zwingli also rejected Revelation. Calvin believed that doctrinal content justified canonicity, and, while he disputed the authorship of some New Testament books, he did not oppose their place in the canon.[8] Moreover, Protestants rejected Rome's inclusion of the Apocrypha in the canon, although they were not averse to citing or alluding to it in debate.

The Reformed confessions of the sixteenth century generally find canonicity in the testimony of the Holy Spirit and not in the authority of the church. The listing of the biblical books and the rejection of those not considered biblical in the Thirty-Nine Articles and the Westminster Confession of Faith demonstrate Barth's point that such listing distinguishes Reformed confessionalism from Lutheranism, as the latter put church councils roughly level with Scripture, and so the list of canonical books was settled, whereas the Reformed "with these lists . . . wanted to document their fundamental right to reject what non-biblical history and even the church might prescribe as canonical, and to make such decisions themselves as the ancient church had done."[9]

The WCF states that the origin of the canonical books of Scripture is from God—"given by inspiration of God." Inspiration is its definition of Scripture.[10] The phrase "immediately inspired" (WCF, 1.8) denotes that the Father breathed Scripture out by the Spirit *in the origination* of the original manuscripts. This, again, refers to the *origin* of Scripture rather than its eventual production, for human means were clearly used. The Bible was composed by human hands, human thought, and often historical research, but its ultimate origin was from God. However—qualifying the WCF at this point—inspiration of itself can hardly be Scripture's *defining* characteristic, since other statements were inspired by God, and yet were not Scripture—for example, the letter of Paul to Laodicea, and a wide range of prophetic utterances where the Holy Spirit spoke directly.

Protestant lists exclude all other books, notably the Apocrypha.[11] Since canonical books are inspired by God, the reason why the Apocrypha is not considered canonical is that its books are purely human

---

8. Barth, *CD*, I/2:476–78.

9. Karl Barth, *The Theology of the Reformed Confessions: 1923*, trans. Darrell L. Guder and Judith J. Guder (Louisville: Westminster John Knox, 2002), 50.

10. Benjamin B. Warfield, *The Westminster Assembly and Its Work* (New York: Oxford University Press, 1934), 202.

11. The Council of Trent had included under the books of the Old and New Testaments Tobit, Judith, Ecclesiasticus, Baruch, Wisdom, and 1 and 2 Maccabees. Additionally, it stated that it received and venerated with reverence equal to that owed the written books the traditions dictated

compositions and, Rome and Orthodoxy notwithstanding, "are of no authority in the church of God."[12] This exclusion is based, among other things, on the absence of direct New Testament citations from the Apocrypha, in contrast to the plethora from the Old Testament;[13] it is based, as well, on the opinions of a range of fathers and ancient councils.[14] There is clearly a connection between inspiration and canonicity, yet, for the reasons considered above, inspiration, while a necessary condition of canonicity, is not of itself sufficient.

Nor is canonicity based on the decision of the church, as Rome maintains. The church *recognized* the canon; it did not *confer* it. Long before official lists were compiled or conciliar decisions were made, the existence of a New Testament canon was recognized.[15] The four Gospels and the writings of Paul were acknowledged early, while other books like Hebrews and Revelation took longer to receive universal acceptance. Paul probably refers to the Gospel of Luke as Scripture (1 Tim. 5:18), as does Peter to the writings of Paul (2 Pet. 3:16). Underlying these assessments was the commission Jesus gave to the apostles, conferring his own authority on them in their teaching (John 16:12–15).

In turn, apostolicity does not of itself guarantee canonicity either, nor does its absence preclude it. I have mentioned Paul's lost letter; it would be surprising if there were not others from his hand. These are not in the canon, nor are apostolic oral communications to their churches. Some New Testament books were not written by apostles; if apostolic authorship were required, it would rule out Mark, Luke, Acts, Hebrews, James, and Jude.

Nor does doctrinal content constitute canonicity, although, like inspiration, it is a necessary element. We must assume apostolic writings

either by Christ's own word of mouth or by the Holy Spirit, and preserved in the Catholic Church by a continuous succession. It anathematized any who did not receive all the books in their entirety.

12. WCF, 1.3. By this the confession places the Apocrypha on a par with "other human writings, some of which may have a certain authority. Evidently, it means that they are not to be received as the Word of God." Robert Letham, *Through Western Eyes: Eastern Orthodoxy: A Reformed Perspective* (Fearn: Mentor, 2007), 179–87.

13. On the Old Testament canon, see Roger Beckwith, *The Old Testament Canon of the New Testament Church and Its Background in Early Judaism* (Grand Rapids, MI: Eerdmans, 1985).

14. Muller, *PRRD*, 2:413. Although Jerome included the Apocrypha in the Vulgate, he warned against its being placed on a par with Scripture. His judgment was shared "by a litany of church fathers." Kenneth J. Collins and Jerry L. Walls, *Roman but Not Catholic: What Remains at Stake 500 Years after the Reformation* (Grand Rapids, MI: Baker Academic, 2017), 35–36.

15. The Muratorian fragment, dating from around 190, in Stevenson, *A New Eusebius*, 123–25; Irenaeus, *Against Heresies* 3.1.1–3.2.2, 3.11.1–9 (ANF, 1:414–15, 426–29); Clement of Alexandria, *Stromata* 7.16–17 (ANF, 2:550–55).

outside the canon were in conformity doctrinally with the rest of Scripture, as I hope my writings are; but this does not make them canonical.

Some of these putative criteria—inspiration and doctrinal conformity—are necessary components of what makes the canonical books canonical. Nonetheless, by themselves they are insufficient. None of these categories provides a watertight explanation. Indeed, if there was a criterion to determine canonicity, that criterion would take precedence over the canonical books and be a tool in the hands of the church to stamp its own authority over the Bible. It would function as a gauge against which to measure the qualifications of a document. Effectively, it would place power in the hands of the church over the Word of God.

Ultimately, the canon imposed itself on the church. The church recognized it, although it took longer for some books to receive acceptance than others. Behind this is the principle that only God can adequately attest the works of God, and so the canon, notwithstanding the many external evidences in support, is self-attesting.[16]

6.3   The Inspiration and Authority of Scripture

Inspiration refers to the origin of Scripture; it is God-breathed (2 Tim. 3:16; 2 Pet. 1:20–21). The classic Reformed statement of the doctrine of Scripture is WCF, 1. It asserts that we believe Scripture and obey it on the basis of its authority. This derives from its own inherent qualities, preeminently that it comes from God.[17] "The authority of the Holy Scripture, for which it ought to be believed, and obeyed, dependeth not upon the testimony of any man, or Church; but wholly upon God (who is truth itself) the author thereof: and therefore it is to be received, because it is the Word of God" (WCF, 1.4). The origin of Scripture, its being inspired by God, is the basis of its authority over the church. It is independent of the church's testimony. Scripture's authority depends wholly on God, its author.

The author of Hebrews, demonstrating that God continues to speak in Scripture, cites Psalm 95:7–11 with the comment "as the Holy Spirit says" (Heb. 3:7) and describes the Word of God as "living and active, sharper than any two-edged sword" (Heb. 4:12). Scripture is not to

---

16. See, for further discussion, Michael J. Kruger, *The Question of Canon: Challenging the Status Quo in the New Testament Debate* (Nottingham: Apollos, 2013); Webster, *Holy Scripture*, 42–67.

17. See Webster, *Holy Scripture*, 30–39.

be seen in a deistic sense, as if the Spirit has wandered off and left it. Bavinck expressed this well: "It was not only 'God-breathed' at the time it was written; it *is* 'God-breathing.' It was divinely inspired, not merely while it was written, God breathing through the writers; but also, whilst it is being read, God breathing through the Scripture," so that "divine inspiration, accordingly, is a permanent attribute of Holy Scripture."[18] God continues to speak in and through Scripture today.

New Testament revelation is grounded on the authority Jesus gave to his apostles. Whereas the prophets said, "Thus says the Lord," he, the eternal Son, spoke in his own name and with his own supreme authority (Matt. 5:17–18, 21–22, 27–28, 31–32, 33–34, 38–39, 43–44; 6:2, 5, 16, 25; John 1:1–4, 14). In turn, he delegated his authority to the apostles such that their teaching was to be the equivalent of his own (John 16:12–15; cf. Gal. 1:11–24). In the background was the Jewish institution of the שליח,[19] one sent under orders of another, a rabbinical summary being, "The one sent by a man is as the man himself."[20]

Thus, the Scriptures of the Old and New Testaments as the Word of God are our "only rule of faith and obedience" (WLC, 3), teaching us how we may glorify God and enjoy him forever (WSC, 1). Since the Bible is God's revelation to his church concerning salvation, it also determines what we are to believe concerning him, and what we are to do in obeying him. The Scriptures are the *authority* for our faith and life. In contrast to the decrees and decisions of church councils, which cannot be the rule of faith and practice, since they are inherently capable of error (WCF, 31.4), Scripture is free from error.[21]

6.3.1 Inerrancy

Inerrancy has been embraced throughout the ages. The claim that the Bible is without error in all it pronounces emerged prominently in the nineteenth century. Yet, as Warfield demonstrated, the church down through the centuries held this position, whether explicitly or implicitly.[22]

---

18. Bavinck, *RD*, 1:385.
19. *shaliyakh.*
20. *TDNT*, 1:414–20.
21. On the authority of Scripture, in the context of an overall doctrine of Scripture, see Matthew M. Barrett, *God's Word Alone: The Authority of Scripture* (Grand Rapids, MI: Zondervan, 2016).
22. Benjamin B. Warfield, "The Church Doctrine of Inspiration," *BSac* 51 (1894): 614–40; Warfield, "The Church Doctrine of Inspiration," in *The Inspiration and Authority of the Bible*, ed. Samuel G. Craig (Philadelphia: Presbyterian and Reformed, 1970), 105–28.

Augustine wrote to Jerome repeatedly, upbraiding him for saying that Paul wrote something false about his differences with Peter as described in Galatians 2. For instance: "For it seems to me that most disastrous consequences must follow upon our believing that anything false is found in the sacred books: that is to say, that the men by whom Scripture has been given to us, and committed to writing, did put down in these books anything false." Again, in the same letter:

> For if you once admit into such a high sanctuary of authority one false statement as made in the way of duty, there will not be left a single sentence of those books which, if appearing to any one difficult in practice or hard to believe, may not by the same fatal rule be explained away, as a statement in which, intentionally, and under a sense of duty, the author declared what was not true.[23]

Aquinas also argued that faith rests upon infallible truth. The canonical Scriptures are incontrovertible truth, whereas the writings of the doctors of the church, while useful, are merely probable. Citing the above letter from Augustine, he said that the canonical Scriptures are without error, whereas he approaches other writings with an attitude of critical scrutiny.[24]

Dowey remarks that throughout Calvin's writings there is no hint that he contemplated the possibility of errors in the original text.[25] Indeed, Dowey observes that there is nothing in Calvin remotely approximating the neoorthodox distinction between the Word and the words, the former inspired, the latter not. Dowey is right, and to look for such ideas is anachronistic. In the *Argumentum* to his commentary on John, Calvin goes so far as to say that God "so dictated to the four evangelists what they should write that, while each had his own part, the whole formed one complete body."[26] Commenting on 2 Timothy 3:16 he states that the law and the prophets are "dictated by the Holy Spirit."[27] This is

---

23. Augustine, *Letter 28* 3 (*NPNF*[1], 1:251–2). See also *Letter 82* 5, 7, 22, 24 (*NPNF*[1], 1:351, 357, 358).

24. Aquinas, *ST* 1a.1.8.

25. Edward A. Dowey Jr., *The Knowledge of God in Calvin's Theology* (Grand Rapids, MI: Eerdmans, 1994), 100.

26. John Calvin, *Calvin's Commentaries: The Gospel according to St. John 1–10*, trans. T. H. L. Parker (Grand Rapids, MI: Eerdmans, 1961), 6; Calvin, *In evangelium secundum Johannem commentarius pars prior*, Ioannis Calvini opera exegetica (Geneva: Droz, 1997), 9.

27. John Calvin, *Calvin's Commentaries: The Second Epistle of Paul the Apostle to the Corinthians and the Epistles to Timothy, Titus and Philemon*, trans. T. A. Smail (Grand Rapids, MI: Eerdmans, 1964), 330.

not a dictation theory in which the human authors were merely cyphers. Dowey agrees with Warfield that the term is figurative and that Calvin was intending to stress the purity of the Word of God as delivered, the effects rather than the mode of inspiration.[28] "The result was a series of documents errorless in their original form."[29] Calvin did occasionally attribute error to the text of Scripture, but the mistake always lay with the copyist. God providentially preserved the text, but now and then the copyist slipped up. Calvin drew no theological conclusions from this.[30] At root he saw the Bible in the context of God's work of salvation. So, "we may perceive how necessary was such written proof of the heavenly doctrine, that it should neither perish through forgetfulness nor vanish through error nor be corrupted by the audacity of men."[31]

The WCF considers Scripture the rule of faith and life (WCF, 1.2). In contrast, all councils of the church may err and therefore cannot be made the rule of faith or practice (WCF, 31.4). Implied in this is that, since Scripture *is* the rule of faith or practice, it cannot err. It does not depend for its authority on the testimony of the church; it is the ultimate authority in the church. Synods and councils are to make decrees and determinations that are "consonant to the Word of God," and these decrees are to be received with reverence and submission, provided they are in "agreement with the Word" (WCF, 31.3).

Rome also acknowledges the inspiration and inerrancy of Scripture. At Vatican II, *Dei Verbum*, 3, states that both Testaments, in all their parts and in the whole, are canonical because they were "written under the inspiration of the Holy Spirit . . . [and] have God as their author."[32] God chose men and used their abilities so that they wrote exclusively everything he wanted.[33] Therefore, "the books of Scripture must be acknowledged as teaching firmly, faithfully, and without error that truth which God wanted put into the sacred writings for the sake of our salvation." Reference is made to 2 Timothy 3:16–17 in the Greek text.[34] However, the statement is ambiguous, as it is qualified by "whatever

---

28. Dowey, *Knowledge of God*, 101–2; Benjamin B. Warfield, "Calvin's Doctrine of the Knowledge of God," in *Calvin and Augustine* (Philadelphia: Presbyterian and Reformed, 1974), 62–64.
29. Dowey, *Knowledge of God*, 102.
30. Dowey, *Knowledge of God*, 103.
31. Calvin, *Institutes*, 1.6.3.
32. *Dei Verbum*, 3.11, in Walter M. Abbott, *The Documents of Vatican II* (New York: Guild, 1966), 118.
33. *Dei Verbum*, 3.11, in Abbott, *Documents*, 119.
34. *Dei Verbum*, 3.11, in Abbott, *Documents*, 119.

God wanted to put into the sacred writings," leaving open the possibility that inerrancy may be partial, and the truth limited to what God wanted to put into the sacred writings for our salvation.

Warfield had reason to address this question in 1894. Charles Augustus Briggs and others, influenced by German higher-critical theories, distinguished between the Word of God and the written words of the Bible, between the thoughts, which were inspired, and the words, which were not, between the saving message of the Bible and the rest of the historical and cosmological details. Warfield, in rebuttal, established that inerrancy is the church doctrine. He cited in support Irenaeus, Polycarp, Origen, Augustine, Luther, Calvin, Rutherford, Baxter, and Westcott, as well as the WCF, in contrast to rationalism and mysticism, and argued that such a view was held by the writers of the New Testament and by Jesus.[35] This was certainly the position of the Westminster Assembly and definitely not a novelty introduced by the Princeton theology.[36]

Inerrancy is derived from inspiration. Freedom from error in what it pronounces does not make the Bible the Word of God; inspiration does that. Scripture is the Word of God because God originated it and speaks in and through it. Moreover, not everything recorded in the Bible is itself true and reliable. The speech and actions of Satan and of wicked people, as well as the advice of Job's friends, are hardly themselves words from God on which we can rely. They are faithfully and inerrantly reported; the account of them is reliable, but the content of the reported speech and actions is far from it.

Inerrancy can apply only to whatever the Bible itself intends to state. Scripture contains "the whole counsel of God . . . for God's glory, man's salvation, faith and life" (WCF, 1.6). It was not given to tell us where to drill for oil or as a manual for civil government. The Bible does not pronounce on everything. While it states that the whole world is God's, it does not pretend to be an encyclopedia. Furthermore, the inerrancy of the Bible is not to be confused with particular interpretations of what

---

35. Warfield, "Church Doctrine," in Warfield, *Inspiration*, 108–14; Benjamin B. Warfield, "Inspiration," in *The International Standard Bible Encyclopedia*, ed. James Orr (Chicago: Howard-Severance, 1915), 1473–83, reprinted as "The Biblical Idea of Inspiration," in Warfield, *Inspiration*, 131–66.

36. Warfield, *Assembly*, 280–333. Alan Strange remarks that the PCUSA issued the Portland Deliverance at its 1892 General Assembly in opposition to Briggs and in favor of infallibility and inerrancy, while the next year Pope Leo XIII issued *Providentissimus Deus*, also affirming inerrancy, *inter alia*.

this or that passage is saying. A passage may seem to a reader to have a clear and obvious meaning; that does not make that the correct interpretation, still less invest it with an unchallengeable authority.

Furthermore, not all literary forms in the Bible are ones in which precision is necessary or desired. Much is poetry, evocative in nature. Events are reported in ways that do not accord with twenty-first-century historiography, since they were not set down in the twenty-first century. Often round numbers are given; the Bible is not a statistical manual. In cricket, it is perfectly accurate to say that a batsman scored a hundred when he made 119, even though it would be an error if a statistician reported it in that form.[37] The Bible refers to the world in the language of everyday observation rather than modern scientific precision. It is not pedantic.

In view of these caveats, one may well ask exactly how useful is the concept of inerrancy. After all, it is equally maintained by Jehovah's Witnesses. Being incapable of error or of misleading us does not itself make something the Word of God. Books of statistics can be free from error; they are no more the Word of God than is an accurate railway timetable. Inerrancy is an entailment of the Bible being intrinsically the Word of God. Following that, inerrancy affirms positively that the Bible sits in judgment on all human opinions, in the church and outside it, and is the final arbiter of all claims to spiritual experience or constructive thought. It affirms that we can totally rely on it for our relationship to God and our life in the world. However, these things follow *from its being inspired by God as canon for the church*, not directly from the fact that it is free from error, understood in the way I have described. It is because God is its author and has given it as canon and authority for the church that these consequences follow. As Bavinck indicated, inspiration is more than the preservation of the writer from error; it is God speaking by the mouths of the apostles and prophets.[38]

6.3.2 *Organic Inspiration*

What I have said does not discount the human authorship, with all the particular contributions each writer made. The idea of organic inspiration takes this fully into account. A. A. Hodge wrote:

---

37. And I am told that in baseball, someone with a .312 batting average may be called a .300 hitter.

38. James Eglinton, *Trinity and Organism: Towards a New Reading of Herman Bavinck's Organic Motif* (London: Bloomsbury, 2012), 172.

The human agency . . . is everywhere apparent. . . . It is not merely in the matter of verbal expression or literary composition that the personal idiosyncracies of each author are freely manifested by the untrammeled play of all his faculties, but the very substance of what they write is evidently for the most part the product of their own mental and spiritual activities.[39]

The Scriptures, Hodge remarks, are

an organism consisting of many parts, each adjusted to all the rest. . . . Each sacred writer was by God specially formed, endowed, educated, providentially conditioned, and then supplied with knowledge naturally, supernaturally, or spiritually conveyed, so that he, and he alone could, and freely would, produce his allotted part.[40]

So, as Warfield comments, "If God wished to give his people a series of letters like Paul's, he prepared a Paul to write them, and the Paul he brought to the task was a Paul who spontaneously would write just such letters."[41]

The idea of Scripture as an organism was developed at roughly the same time on the other side of the Atlantic by Herman Bavinck.[42] Bavinck affirms that human authors "retain their powers of reflection and deliberation, their emotional states and freedom of the will. Research . . . reflection, and memory . . . the use of sources, and all the ordinary means that an author employs in the process of writing a book are used."[43] For him this "implies the idea that the Holy Spirit, in the inscripturation of the word of God, did not spurn anything human to serve as an organ of the divine."[44] This is so since "Christianity is not antithetically opposed to that which is human but is its restoration and renewal."[45]

Effectively the idea of organic inspiration as unfolded by Hodge and Bavinck took two related but integrally connected forms. It expressed the concursive operation of the Holy Spirit with the free thoughts and

---

39. A. A. Hodge, "Inspiration," *Presbyterian Review* 2 (April 1881): 225–60; reprinted in Mark Noll, *The Princeton Theology 1812–1921: Scripture, Science, and Theological Method from Archibald Alexander to Benjamin Breckinridge Warfield* (Phillipsburg, NJ: Presbyterian and Reformed, 1983), 218–32; see 223.
40. Noll, *The Princeton Theology*, 224.
41. Warfield, *Inspiration*, 155.
42. See Eglinton, *Trinity and Organism*, 155–82.
43. Bavinck, *RD*, 1:433.
44. Bavinck, *RD*, 1:442.
45. Bavinck, *RD*, 1:443.

actions of the human authors as they engaged in research and writing, and it also sought to place the compilation of Scripture firmly in the context of the historical outworking of redemption. Both these strands exemplify the work of God as conjoined with human thought and action, God's providential direction harmonizing with human freedom. This superintending and harmonizing underlines the need for the doctrine of Scripture to be indissolubly related to the rest of the theological spectrum; the Bible cannot be considered as a separate stand-alone item.

Bavinck's use of the incarnational analogy is valuable. This connection has been misused—I will note an egregious abuse of it shortly—but as Bavinck properly understands it, the analogy sheds a great deal of light. Bavinck notes that the incarnation consisted of the Son taking into union a human nature. There was full humanity but not symmetry, for the initiative and action lay on the divine side. As Christ lived in the state of humiliation, in lowliness and as a servant, so the Scriptures bear "that dimension of weakness and lowliness, the servant form." Again, "just as Christ's human nature, however weak and lowly, remained free from sin, so also Scripture is 'conceived without defect or stain'; totally human in all its parts but also divine in all its parts."[46] The Scriptures are God's Word in servant form.[47]

6.3.3   *Scripture and the Word of God*

WSC, 2, states that the Word of God "is contained in the scriptures of the Old and New Testaments." This might be taken in the neoorthodox sense, in which the Word of God is not equated with the text of Scripture, but to do so would be anachronistic, importing ideas that only emerged centuries later. Indeed, the Westminster divines affirm *both* that Scripture is the Word of God *and* that it contains the Word of God. God's speech in Scripture cannot be confined to the written text alone, since it reverberates onward through the Holy Spirit. The Word of God is living and active (Heb. 4:12–13), going beyond the printed page to sit in judgment on us. Precisely because Scripture *is* the Word of God, so it also contains the Word of God.[48] The Assembly was using "contains" in a different way than the neoorthodox, indicating that this is the place where the

---

46. Bavinck, *RD*, 1:435.
47. Bavinck, *RD*, 1:380–81.
48. Cf. the Irish Articles 1.6; the French Confession, 5; the Belgic Confession, 7.

Word of God is to be found. The distinction between the text of Scripture as the Word of God written, its continuing and ongoing efficacy, and the Word of God eternal, essential, and unwritten was a commonplace among seventeenth-century Reformed theologians. As Muller states:

> The assumption of a radical discontinuity between the Reformation and the orthodox doctrine of the Word [with Westminster in this latter group], thus, rests on a profound and dogmatic misunderstanding that falsifies both the teaching of the Reformers and the doctrine of their orthodox successors. Whereas it is incorrect to claim, on the one side, that the Reformers so stressed the concept of Christ as the living Word witnessed by Scripture that they either lost or diminished the doctrine of Scripture as Word of God written, it is equally incorrect to claim, on the other side, that the orthodox, by developing a formal doctrine of Scripture as Word, lost the Reformers' conception of Scripture as living Word. Theologically, such claims arise out of a mistaken either/or approach to the problem, where Word of God is taken to indicate either Christ or Scripture but not both. A multilevel understanding of Word is, however, quite typical of both the Reformers and the post-Reformation orthodox.[49]

Timothy Ward adds, "To say of God that he spoke, and to say of God that he did something, is often one and the same thing."[50] Since God is the living God, his speech is dynamic and accomplishes what he intends (Isa. 55:10; Heb. 4:12–13). It brings life out of death (Gen. 1:2–5; James 1:18; 1 Pet. 1:23).

6.3.4 *Barth and the Threefold Form of the Word of God*

There are various meanings for the phrase "the word of God" in the Bible. It is used for Jesus Christ the incarnate Word, for the eternal Word, for Scripture, and for the preached Word, besides which Augustine famously referred to the sacraments as "a kind of visible word of God."[51] In the first half volume of his *Church Dogmatics*, Karl Barth develops his theology of revelation and integrates it with the doctrine of the Trinity. He proceeds then, in the next half volume, to advance the idea of the Word of God in threefold form: the incarnate Word, Jesus Christ;

---

49. Muller, *PRRD*, 2:185–86.
50. Ward, *Words of Life*, 22.
51. Augustine, *On the Gospel of John* 80.3 (NPNF[1], 7:344; *PL*, 35:1840).

the written Word, Scripture; and the proclaimed Word, preaching. The three interpenetrate each other in perichoretic form, analogous to the Trinitarian *perichorēsis*.[52]

The positive gains of this threefold form are that, as in Bavinck, Scripture is seen in integral connection with the whole theological spectrum. Moreover, the perichoretic model not only encourages this but also enables us to see that each element "indwells" each other. These are not three elements connected as beads on a string, conjoined but discrete; they pervade each other. Their relationship is not symmetrical, since Christ, the eternal Word, incarnate for our salvation, is the source and subject of both the written and proclaimed Word.

Thus, Scripture has Christ as its beginning, center, and goal. Christ himself is the author of Scripture through the Holy Spirit. Scripture is the foundation of preaching; Christ is the focus of preaching, present throughout. By noting this integral mutual indwelling, we have a preventative against the Bible being isolated from Christ and the history of redemption while, positively, such an organic relation is demanded.

Barth's contribution is intriguing but mixed. His threefold perichoretic model is important for locating the Bible in the relationship between God and humans, and in its place in the work of redemption. However, by viewing the human authors as fallible witnesses, he takes away with one hand what he has given with the other. For him, the Bible is and remains "witness to revelation."[53] It consists of the words of fallible men. It is not to be equated with revelation. To equate the Bible and revelation in this way would place God under our control, for it would become, as a static given, an object over which we would form a critical jurisdiction. However, we can say that it is the Word of God, but we do so in a dynamic sense, in the form of a miracle insofar as, despite the impossibility from the human side, we have heard the Word of God in it and we believe that we will hear the Word of God in it in the future.[54]

In response, many will resonate with this remark by Peter Lewis:

> Whenever I read the *Church Dogmatics* I feel like someone entering a
> great cathedral but walking in constant fear of falling masonry! I am

---

52. Barth, *CD*, I/1:88–124.
53. Barth, *CD*, II/2:457–59. The English translation has "a witness to divine revelation," suggesting it may be one among others, but there is no article in the German; see Geoffrey W. Bromiley, *An Introduction to the Theology of Karl Barth* (Grand Rapids, MI: Eerdmans, 1979), 34.
54. Barth, *CD*, I/1:530.

deeply aware not only of a great mind but of a worshipful spirit and many passages and sentences thrill me. However besides finding very much of it above my head I am also aware of what look suspiciously like cracks and fissures and do not stay too long![55]

Here the Christological analogy of Bavinck will help. The relationship between the divine and human in Scripture shows a parallel with that relation in Christ. It is not symmetrical. God's action has priority. As the eternal Son took human nature into union, the humanity sinless, so the sovereign action of the Spirit takes the humanity of the biblical authors into a relationship that undergirds the utter reliability, indefectibility, and truthfulness of what they affirm. As such the Bible is the Word of God. It is God speaking to us in human language, in servant form, such that we do not worship it, but God encounters us in it.

6.4   How We Believe Scripture Is the Word of God

Given that Scripture is the final authority in Christ's church for all aspects of faith and practice, how do we recognize it as such? Calvin writes that "the Scriptures obtain full authority among believers only when men regard them as having sprung from heaven."[56] There are various ways Scripture displays its exalted nature, each of which has a certain degree of persuasiveness but by itself stops short of convincing us. As WCF, 1.5, says, the testimony of the church, through its preaching, or factors inherent to the Bible—its doctrine, its style, and internal harmony—all demonstrate its perfection. Such "excellencies" have inspired some of the greatest creative work of human history. Yet they do not convince readers of its infallible truth and divine authority. That comes only from "the inward work of the Holy Spirit bearing witness by and with the Word in our hearts."

Why is this? One reason is our sinful indisposition to receive God's revelation; our sin makes us slow to recognize the voice of the Spirit. Second, since the Spirit is the prime author of Scripture, it follows that he is best equipped to convince us of its truth. Jesus said that this would be one of the main features of the Spirit's ministry (John 16:12–15); lacking this, we flounder. Here is the conjunction of the Holy Spirit, the primary author of Scripture, with the Word written (*cum verbo*), which

---

55. Peter Lewis, personal email, June 27, 2015, with permission.
56. Calvin, *Institutes*, 1.7.1; Webster, *Holy Scripture*, 68–106.

is distinctive of Reformed theology. As Spear comments, Calvin is convinced that the Spirit "does not give new revelation, or a purely mystical experience, but opens a person's spiritual vision to appreciate the marks of truth which were objectively present in Scripture all along."[57]

Calvin's teaching on the testimony of the Spirit is crucial. He says, "We ought to seek our conviction in a higher place than human reasons, judgments, or conjectures, that is, in the secret testimony of the Spirit."[58] This is because "the testimony of the Spirit is more excellent than all reason. For as God alone is a fit witness of himself in his Word, so also the Word will not find acceptance in men's hearts before it is sealed by the inward testimony of the Spirit."[59] So "Scripture indeed is self-authenticated; hence, it is not right to subject it to proof and reasoning. And the certainty it deserves with us, it attains by the testimony of the Spirit . . . [for] it seriously affects us only when it is sealed upon our hearts through the Spirit."[60]

Neoorthodox interpreters understand the authority of Scripture to rest upon the witness of the Spirit in our hearts, confusing our reception of Scripture as authoritative with the basis of its authority, which is its origin from God. Consequently, avoiding a static idea of the Bible opens the door, as with Barth, to viewing Scripture as the fallible words of men. It confuses inspiration with illumination.

6.5   The Sufficiency of Scripture

6.5.1   *What Is the Sufficiency of Scripture?*

Since Scripture is the Word of God, what does it contain? WCF, 1.6, provides the answer: "the whole counsel of God concerning all things necessary for His own glory, man's salvation, faith and life." Note the order; first the glory of God (WSC, 1), then our salvation, which in turn comprises first faith and then our life (WLC, 5). We must recognize what Scripture does *not* teach. The Bible does not contain all truth. It is not a scientific textbook. The works of creation and providence disclose the eternal power and deity of God; general revelation provides the basis for the vast range of human knowledge. The Bible is complete *for the pur-*

---

57. Wayne Spear, "Word and Spirit in the Westminster Confession," in *The Westminster Confession into the 21st Century*, ed. Ligon Duncan III (Fearn: Mentor, 2003), 1:50. See n. 7.
58. Calvin, *Institutes*, 1.7.4.
59. Calvin, *Institutes*, 1.7.5.
60. Calvin, *Institutes*, 1.7.5.

pose for which it is given. It talks of many things—"of ships and shoes and sealing wax, of cabbages and kings"[61]—but not of everything. Its message concentrates on God's glory and our salvation, faith, and life. Scripture is sufficient for this purpose.[62]

How is this message of Scripture to be sought? According to WCF, 1.6, it is found "expressly set down in Scripture." There are clear and explicit statements in the Bible where the glory of God is unfolded and our salvation is explained. Second, the whole counsel of God "by good and necessary consequence may be deduced from Scripture."

This is a profoundly important statement. Thoughtful reading and preaching, and extended reflection on the implications and interconnections of the Bible's content, are imperative. The whole counsel of God includes legitimate deductions from the Bible. Orderly thought is a sine qua non. Anti-intellectualism undermines Scripture and begins to unravel the message of salvation.[63] Systematic theology is indispensable. How else can the church defend itself against heresy or evangelical anti-intellectualism? The church fathers found that the gospel was threatened by unthinking repetition of biblical words and phrases. A challenging intellectual response was required in order to defend "the sense of Scripture" from those who would use its words to overturn essential elements of the faith.[64]

This statement raises the question of the relationship between Scripture and tradition, which we will explore in the next chapter. It also preserves the role of human reason, enlightened by the Holy Spirit, in our reflecting on Scripture, and guards us against a literalistic fundamentalism. It rules out a requirement that proof texts be produced for everything.[65] Warfield remarks,

> The re-emergence in recent controversies of the plea that the authority of Scripture is to be confined to its express declarations, and that human logic is not to be trusted in divine things, is, therefore, a direct denial of a fundamental position of Reformed theology, explicitly

61. From Lewis Carroll, "The Walrus and the Carpenter."
62. Warfield, *Assembly*, 84–85.
63. See 2 Cor. 10:3–5, where spiritual warfare is described in terms of reasoning and argumentation.
64. Robert Letham, *The Holy Trinity: In Scripture, History, Theology, and Worship* (Phillipsburg, NJ: P&R, 2004), esp. 108–83.
65. It does not negate the legitimate use of proof texts to support doctrine where it is "expressly set down in Scripture."

202 *The Word of God*

affirmed in the Confession, as well as an abnegation of fundamental reason, which would not only render thinking in a system impossible, but would discredit at a stroke many of the fundamentals of the faith, such e.g. as the doctrine of the Trinity, and would logically involve the denial of the authority of all doctrine whatsoever, since no single doctrine of whatever simplicity can be ascertained from Scripture except by the use of the process of the understanding.[66]

Beyond the sense of Scripture found in its explicit statements and by deduction, nothing is to be added. Scripture is the complete and utterly sufficient revelation of God for the salvation of his church (2 Tim. 3:16–17). There are two main potential sources for claiming additions to Scripture. First, mysticism proposes new revelations from the Holy Spirit. To suppose that such are needed is to regard Scripture as less than sufficient to disclose God's glory and to unfold our salvation, faith, and life. Second, traditionalism is another threat, chiefly in the Church of Rome with its body of dogmatic accretions, reinforced by its stress on the supremacy of churchly authority. Instead, we are to look to Scripture as our only rule of faith and life (Isa. 8:19–20).

In no way does this eliminate the need for the Holy Spirit. We need his illumination in order to understand the Bible in a saving manner. Rationalism is as damaging as mysticism. The Spirit, who authored Scripture, enables us to recognize that it is the Word of God and helps us to interpret it correctly.

Nor should we reject tradition as such.[67] However, the bottom line is that there is no truth required by God to be believed for salvation or duty required of us to perform other than what is found in Scripture. The Bible,

---

66. Warfield, *Assembly*, 226–27. I am grateful to Sherman Isbell for pointing out the following works, which address the question of inferences from Scripture: George Gillespie, *A Treatise of Miscellany Questions* (Edinburgh: Gedeon Lithgow for George Swintoun, 1649), 243. Wing / G371; Aldis, H.G. Scotland /1367. For the Westminster Assembly's use of necessary consequence, see John R. de Witt, *Jus Divinum: The Westminster Assembly and the Divine Right of Church Government* (Kampen: Kok, 1969), 130. Important discussions of the role of necessary consequences in the interpretation of Scripture are found in James Bannerman, *Inspiration: The Infallible Truth and Divine Authority of the Holy Scriptures* (Edinburgh: T&T Clark, 1865), 582–88, and Francis Turretin, *Institutes of Elenctic Theology*, trans. George Musgrave Giger, ed. James T. Dennison Jr. (Phillipsburg, NJ: P&R, 1992), 1:37–43. See also John Owen, *The Works of John Owen*, ed. William H. Goold, 23 vols. (1850–1855; repr., London: Banner of Truth, 1965–1968), 2:379, 20:147; William Cunningham, *Theological Lectures* (London: James Nisbet, 1878), 457–58; James Bannerman, *The Church of Christ* (Edinburgh: T&T Clark, 1868), 2:409–13; Warfield, *Assembly*, 226–27.

67. By "tradition" I mean the past teaching of the church, together with the cumulative thought of its leading theologians. This could be false, as in the dogma of transubstantiation, or valid, in the Trinitarian and Christological dogmas. The Westminster Assembly referred constantly to past theologians and fathers. The point is that Scripture has supremacy over all since it originates with God.

as Warfield puts it, is more than *a* rule of faith and practice; it is more than *the* rule of faith and practice; it is more than a *sufficient* rule of faith and practice; it is *the only* rule of faith and practice.[68] This is the charter guaranteeing Christian liberty, freedom from all forms of human tyranny.

6.5.2   *The Charismatic Movement and the Sufficiency of Scripture*

Scripture was given so that we may be thoroughly equipped for every good work (2 Tim. 3:17). Everything needed for us to persevere in faith and attain final salvation is provided in Scripture, under the illumination of the Holy Spirit and with the guidance of the teaching of the historic church. Into this context has come the charismatic renewal, claiming that the Spirit speaks directly to the church today. There seems to be no way to avoid the implication that continuing prophecy would mean Scripture needs substantive supplementation.

Wayne Grudem believes that claims for continuing revelation can be compatible with the sufficiency of Scripture. He argues that there are three strands of prophecy in the Bible. The first two are commonly recognized. False prophecy, which encourages worship of pagan deities or is shown to be spurious by its failed predictions, is strenuously condemned in the Bible (Deut. 13:1–5). True prophecy, where the prophet speaks under the direction of God, is borne out by events or by its faithful application of the law.[69]

However, what is distinctive about Grudem's proposal is his third category. It concerns speech inspired by the Spirit that conveys advice which need not be accepted. Often such prophecies are given to specific people in particular situations, though in language that may be imprecise. They are not infallible or inerrant or canonical or binding in their details. Among a range of arguments in support, Grudem cites the warnings of Agabus to Paul in Acts 21:10–14.[70] This example was well answered by Edmund Clowney.[71]

In the Acts account, Agabus binds his own hands and feet with Paul's belt and declares, "Thus says the Holy Spirit, 'This is how the Jews in Jerusalem will bind the man who owns this belt and deliver him into

---

68. Warfield, *Assembly*, 225.
69. Wayne A. Grudem, *The Gift of Prophecy in the New Testament and Today* (Westchester, IL: Crossway, 1988); Grudem, *Systematic Theology* (Grand Rapids, MI: Zondervan, 1994), 1049–61.
70. Grudem, *Systematic Theology*, 1052–55.
71. Edmund P. Clowney, *The Church* (Downers Grove, IL: InterVarsity Press, 1995), 255–68.

the hands of the Gentiles'" (Acts 21:11). Despite this warning and the entreaties of his friends, Paul is not diverted from his plan to go to Jerusalem. He does not consider this message from the Holy Spirit to be binding. So Grudem argues that the prophecy is not fulfilled accurately. Paul is not taken prisoner by the Jews and handed over to the Roman authorities; instead, he risks being lynched by the Jews, is rescued by the Romans, and is taken into protective custody. The Romans, not the Jews, bind him. This kind of inaccuracy, Grudem thinks, would have condemned a prophet in the Old Testament. Moreover, Paul disregards the prophecy and goes to Jerusalem regardless. Evidently, he feels free to set aside a warning delivered in the name of the Holy Spirit. Thus, this is a prophecy from the Spirit that is wrong in its details and can legitimately be disregarded.[72]

However, it seems pedantic to say that the prophecy is inaccurate. The Spirit is not urging Paul to abandon his plans but simply warning him of the danger into which he is heading and the eventual outcome of his journey. The situation is reminiscent of Jesus's repeated warnings to his disciples that he would be arrested in Jerusalem and put to death.

Ultimately the claim of continued prophecy inevitably collides with the sufficiency of Scripture. There seem to me to be only three alternatives: (1) The prophecy contradicts Scripture, in which case it is false and must be rejected. (2) It repeats the words of Scripture, rendering it unnecessary and disqualifying it of the status of new prophecy, for the Bible has already spoken on the matter. While the words would be self-evidently edifying and clearly the Word of God, it could not be said to be new, direct revelation. Or (3) it adds to Scripture, in the context of the closed canon of the New Testament, contradicting the words of the apostle that Scripture has been given "that the man of God may be equipped [ἄρτιος (*artios*), "complete," "capable"] for every good work" (2 Tim. 3:17), and implying that the Bible is not sufficient to guide us to heaven.

Of course, the claim can be adjusted. Preaching is a form of prophecy in declaring the Word of God. The Spirit accompanies the Word in preaching. People often acknowledge that the Spirit spoke to them through the words of a sermon. Yet a preacher cannot say that his words are direct, fresh revelation; they are a declaration of the Word of God

---

72. Grudem, *Systematic Theology*, 1052–53.

as it has been definitively given. Again, one may give useful counsel ("ghostly counsel and advice" as the prayer book says), which may be exactly the right words at the right time for a person. Yet, however edifying, however in harmony with the will of God, the advice has no demonstrable standing as direct words of the Holy Spirit. One can agree that they might bear a relation to prophecy, insofar as they convey the Word of God as given. Later, we will consider biblical preaching as the Word of God; it is so in a derivative sense. However, if Grudem's position were to be understood in this light, it would undercut the claim for a third strand of prophecy in terms of "thus says the Holy Spirit."

Grudem's argument also raises questions about the extraordinary gifts of the Spirit. This is conventionally discussed as *cessationism* versus *continuationism*. The exponents of continuationism argue that the special gifts of the Spirit mentioned in the New Testament are of ongoing validity and exist in the church today. Those in the cessationist camp maintain that they ceased with the passing of the apostles, since such gifts were "the signs of a true apostle" (2 Cor. 12:12).

The choice of nomenclature can easily prejudice a case. The term *cessationism* implies that these gifts were, to varying degrees, normal in the covenant community but suddenly stopped. They ceased. Implied in cessation is a previous ongoing presence and operation. The hiatus requires explanation, and the burden of proof lies there.

However, any idea that extraordinary gifts were the norm for the covenant community is untenable. Miracles and similar phenomena never happened on an ongoing basis. They occurred only at particular points in the history of redemption: in the exodus and the conquest, at or following the ministry of Moses; at the beginning of the prophetic period with Elijah and Elisha; and with the ministry of Jesus and the apostles. Talk of "continuationism" and "cessationism" is misleading, for the norm was the absence, not presence of miracles. Only at three key hinges of redemptive history did the miraculous punctuate the narrative. The terms of the discussion are misplaced and need to be recalibrated.

Following the ascension of Christ and the apostolic foundation of the church, there are no significant redemptive-historical events to precede the parousia. God has spoken in Christ (Heb. 1:1–4). Christ is his definitive Word; there is nothing more that God can say. The ministry of Christ and the apostles, under the direction of the Spirit, accompanied by the signs and wonders appropriate to the clinching action of God in the cross, resurrection, and ascension, is the last word. This is definitively interpreted to us in the New Testament. The next item on the agenda is the consummation of salvation at the parousia. While unusual happenings may well occur and sometimes do, especially in pioneer missionary situations—for God is sovereign, free to act as and how he wishes—no theological or redemptive significance can be attached to them. God has given us all we need to get to heaven—the Spirit empowering the Word, the sacraments, and prayer, the means of grace for that purpose (WSC, 88).[73]

6.6 The Clarity of Scripture

A difficulty arises in the discussion of Scripture: how intelligible is Scripture, and to which kind of reader? Rome still maintains that Scripture must be interpreted by the church authorities.[74] More recently, it has encouraged the study of Scripture on a wide basis by the laity. Historically, translations into vernacular languages were frowned on, since they opened the door to aberrant theologies through unskilled interpreters who would set at naught the sacred teaching of the church. Ironically, the base version of the Bible Rome used was a Latin translation, the Vulgate. However, at Vatican II translations were encouraged.[75]

Conversely, based on their belief that Scripture is the highest authority, Protestants, ever since Luther and Tyndale, insisted on translating the Bible into the common language of the people. In this they were at one with the Orthodox, for whom the vernacular translation of the Bible and the liturgy was always of first importance in all missionary endeavor.

A number of crucial distinctions must be made. There are varying degrees of clarity in the Bible. First, this is intrinsic to Scripture itself, since "all things in Scripture are not alike plain in themselves" (WCF, 1.7). Some things are difficult to understand, as Peter comments of the letters of Paul, which he found difficult himself (2 Pet. 3:16). A prominent example in the Bible is 1 Chronicles 26:18: "And for the *parbar* on the west there were four at the road and two at the *parbar*" (my trans.).

---

73. I have been told by a critic that there is not a single reputable New Testament scholar who would agree with me. If so, so be it. When I began my doctoral dissertation in 1976, there was barely a scholar of Calvinism who would have agreed with me; the tide has since turned.
74. *Dei Verbum*, 21, 25; CCC, 85–90.
75. *Dei Verbum*, 21–26; CCC, 131–33, 2653–54.

It would be helpful to know what is meant by *parbar*! Again, 2 Thessalonians 2:5 is a puzzle; in order to understand what Paul means in the early part of the chapter, we need to have been at Thessalonica to hear his oral teaching to the church.

Second, the relative clarity of Scripture also depends on the capacity of the reader; "all things in Scripture are . . . not alike clear unto all" (WCF, 1.7). Some readers are less able to understand than others, whether by lack of knowledge or education, lack of Christian experience, or a deficit of intelligence. Peter refers to those who are "ignorant and unstable," who twist the Scriptures to their own destruction (2 Pet. 3:16). This clearly acknowledges the difficulty of interpreting some of the Bible. Hard work is needed to explain it. The role of the human interpreter, the knower in the process of knowing, is significant.[76] A level of maturity is needed, a point stressed by some of the fathers.[77]

However, the Protestant doctrine of the perspicuity, or clarity, of Scripture acknowledges these difficulties but nevertheless asserts that its saving message is clear. "Those things which are necessary to be known, believed, and observed for salvation," on which the Bible focuses, are clearly and openly propounded (WCF, 1.7). However, this does not occur uniformly; the teaching of salvation can be found "in some place of Scripture or other," here or there. There has to be some effort expended; the places of Scripture have to be sought out. "Ordinary means" are to be used in this process—the ministry of the Word, the sacraments, and prayer, which the Assembly says are the principal means God uses for the salvation of his elect (WCF, 1.7; WSC, 88; WCF, 25–29). This task of encountering the message of salvation in "some place or other" of Scripture, conducted through the use of "ordinary means," is open to all, whatever their education. The common person can come to a clear knowledge of the gospel through the Word of God propounded in the ordinary way, through the ministry of the church.

Not all of the Scriptures is of equal weight or significance. Some things—those necessary to be known, believed, and observed for

---

76. Note the crucial discussions of these issues in Michael Polanyi, *Personal Knowledge: Towards a Post-Critical Philosophy* (Chicago: University of Chicago Press, 1958), and Polanyi, *The Tacit Dimension* (Chicago: University of Chicago Press, 1958).

77. Origen, *On First Principles* 4.1.8–4.1.14 (*ANF*, 4:355–63); Peter W. Martens, *Origen and Scripture: The Contours of the Exegetical Life* (Oxford: Oxford University Press, 2012), 89–106, 161–91; Gregory of Nazianzus, *Oration 27* 3, in Williams and Wickham, *St. Gregory of Nazianzus*, 26–27 (also *NPNF*², 7:285).

salvation—have a strategic significance and shed light on the rest. They are paradigmatic for the whole. Moreover, saving truth is set forth "in some place of Scripture or other," not in every single place. Additionally, these things are set forth so that a "sufficient"—not exhaustive—understanding may result. Nor are they equally intelligible to all. The reason the saving message is reliable is that the whole comes from God. The Reformed doctrine of perspicuity refers to the saving message of salvation.

The variety of Scripture is evident; the Bible is sometimes obscure and difficult, at other times clear as crystal, but it always points beyond itself to the God who gave it. Furthermore, Scripture is open to all through the use of ordinary means; there is no need for an infallible teaching authority, special inner light, or extra revelation. Yet the teaching of the church has an integral place; the means of grace lead us to the knowledge of salvation, with the illumination of the Holy Spirit indispensable for a right understanding. In short, the Bible has to be interpreted; it needs a human interpreter and the divine illuminator.

6.7   The Text of Scripture

In what form do the Scriptures come? To what texts should we go? How do vernacular translations fit the picture? How should we discern the transmission of the text down through the centuries? These were important questions in the seventeenth century in view of the claims of Rome, the development of textual criticism since Erasmus, and the work of Levita and Cappel on the vowel points of the Hebrew text.

The WCF presents a nuanced and layered approach. First, the Hebrew text of the Old Testament and the Greek text of the New Testament were "immediately inspired by God" (WCF, 1.8). The Scriptures as first penned, in the original *autographa*, were directly inspired by the Holy Spirit. Divine authorship is paramount. It logically precedes the human contribution without overriding or discounting it. That these originals are immediately inspired by God is the ground of the conviction that the church is to appeal to the original languages of Scripture in any doctrinal controversy.

Second, this text has been transmitted over the centuries. It was "by [God's] singular care and providence, kept pure in all ages," and is therefore "authentical" (WCF, 1.8). The originals were immediately inspired by God, and the text thereafter has been kept pure by special providential care. The WCF makes no discrimination between manuscripts; the Greek text as a whole has been preserved. Some later argued that since what is now known as the "Byzantine text" was the standard in the 1640s, the statement refers to these manuscripts rather than others. But there is little justification for this claim. God's "singular care and providence" has never gone into remission. With the discovery of large numbers of new manuscripts in later years, it was not as if God had gone to sleep; the same "singular care and providence" was evident in the discovery and analysis of them. The distinction between the original documents and later copies is connected with the inevitability of errors in transmission through hand-copying. God's "singular care and providence" does not exclude errors from all copies; it refers to the text as a whole. Thus, as Warfield comments, "Our Tischendorfs and Tregelleses, and Westcotts and Horts . . . are all parts of God's singular care and providence in preserving His inspired Word pure."[78] Textual criticism has yielded a text that gets us as close to the original as it may be possible to come, a text more complete than possessed by anyone in the first century.

The third layer identified in WCF, 1.8, refers to translations, including the LXX. These are required so all can read and hear the Word of God in their own language, so that every nation may worship God in an acceptable manner. This is a far cry from Islam, for which the Qur'an is the Qur'an only in its Arabic original. In contrast, the universality of the gospel, together with the inability of most people to read the original languages requires translations, and these translations—while distinct from the Bible in its original languages, and further distinct from the original manuscripts—are still the Word of God, conveying clearly that knowledge required for salvation. The result of Bible translation is that "the Word of God dwelling plentifully in all," they may worship him in an acceptable manner and, through patience and comfort of the Scriptures, may have hope. In religious controversies, where precision is required, appeal must be to the original languages, but translations are sufficient for all ordinary purposes.[79]

There emerges a twofold layering to the Bible: (1) what is clear to all by the use of ordinary means, which is central to what the Scriptures as a whole teach concerning salvation, and (2) things inherently difficult to

---

78. Warfield, *Assembly*, 237–39.
79. Warfield, *Assembly*, 240–41.

grasp, which many are unable to understand. Moreover, (1) translations are needed for the common person, and when made, are the Word of God, while (2) the Hebrew and Greek texts are to be the basis for settling religious disputes. Knowledge of the Hebrew of the Old Testament and the Greek of the New Testament is essential for church leaders, especially ministers of the Word. Since study of the original languages is increasingly being marginalized, this is a trenchant warning. Where ministry is not well founded in the languages of Scripture, the church will flounder. This sad reality puts in perspective the strident voices of fundamentalists who insist on particular English translations of the Bible.[80] As one notable Puritan is said to have written in a presentation copy of the Bible given to a fellow minister upon his ordination, "Thou art a minister of the Word; know thy business."

6.8   Modern and Postmodern Challenges

6.8.1   The Princeton Theology

In late nineteenth-century America, influenced by German higher criticism, Charles Augustus Briggs, among others, argued that inspiration is basically a quality of the biblical text. This put the Bible in a category similar to a great work of literature, an inspired human production, whereas the church position was that inspiration related to its origin from God. A. A. Hodge and B. B. Warfield, of Princeton Theological Seminary, addressed this question in a joint article in the *Presbyterian Review*.[81] They based inerrancy, in all matters on which the Bible speaks, on the original autographs.

Hodge defined inspiration as "the constant attribute of all the thoughts and statements of Scripture."[82] He distinguished the origin of Scripture—including its historic processes and interaction of divine and human factors—from inspiration itself, or God's superintendence

---

80. In a biting jibe at his Anabaptist opponents, the Westminster divine Daniel Featley proposes this syllogism: "First, by Authority, if you will dispute in Divinity, you must be able to produce the Scriptures in the Originall Languages; For no Translation is simply authenticall, or the undoubted word of God. In the undoubted word of God there can be no Error. But in Translations there may be, and are errors. The Bible Translated therefore is not the undoubted word of God but so farre only as it agreeth with the Originall, which (as I am informed), none of you understand." Daniel Featley, *The Dippers Dipt, or the Anabaptists Duck'd and Plung'd Over Head and Eares, at a Disputation in Southwark* (London: Nicholas Bourne and Richard Royston, 1645), 2.

81. *Presbyterian Review* 2 (April 1881): 225–60; reprinted in Noll, *Princeton Theology*, 218–32.

82. Noll, *Princeton Theology*, 221.

of the human authors in their writing, "which accounts for nothing whatever but the absolute infallibility of the record . . . in the original autograph."[83]

Hodge recognized that inspiration is basic to valid biblical interpretation, but the truth of Christianity does not depend on any doctrine of inspiration.[84] Ultimately our view of inspiration depends on our view of God and his relation to the world, his involvement in human affairs, and his concursive operation with human agents.[85] Human agency is everywhere apparent in literary forms and distinctive personal features, but the agency of God operates through the human authors, since salvation is rooted in history.[86] As noted earlier, Hodge maintained that "each sacred writer was by God specially formed, endowed, educated, providentially conditioned, and then supplied with knowledge naturally, supernaturally, or spiritually conveyed, so that he, and he alone, could, and freely would, produce his allotted part." Moreover, "each writer was prepared precisely for his part in the work by the personal dealings of the Holy Spirit with his soul."[87] The human authors were free and active in their thinking and writing, conscious of what they were doing and the purpose of their utterances, the result being "an errorless record of the matters he designed them to communicate, and hence constituting the entire volume in all its parts the word of God to us."[88]

Inspiration is verbal, not in the sense of dictation but rather that it extends beyond the mere thoughts of the authors to their forms of expression. The divine authority extends to the human words, and so the Bible in its entirety is free from error.[89] The line between fallible and infallible can never rationally be drawn between the thoughts and words of Scripture.[90] The basis for these assertions is not scholarship but the teaching of Christ and the apostles.[91] The Bible is accurate, not pedantic.[92] Warfield, at this time close to the start of his career, commented

---

83. Noll, *Princeton Theology*, 221.
84. Noll, *Princeton Theology*, 222.
85. Noll, *Princeton Theology*, 223.
86. Noll, *Princeton Theology*, 223–24.
87. Noll, *Princeton Theology*, 224.
88. Noll, *Princeton Theology*, 225.
89. Noll, *Princeton Theology*, 226–27.
90. Noll, *Princeton Theology*, 228.
91. Noll, *Princeton Theology*, 228.
92. Noll, *Princeton Theology*, 229–30.

toward the end of the article that the New Testament constantly asserts that the Old Testament is the Word of God.[93] He stressed that the burden of proof rests with those who assert errors.[94]

Warfield later made his own weighty contributions. In 1893, in the face of growing criticism from Old Testament scholars, he tackled the question of whether the doctrine held by the church is what was taught by the biblical writers.[95] He answered in the affirmative. In turn, he amassed evidence to show that the biblical writers are trustworthy as doctrinal guides.[96] Warfield advanced beyond scholarship to what he regarded as the hub of the matter. If we abandon the doctrine of inspiration taught by Jesus and the apostles, we abandon them as doctrinal teachers and guides.[97] Attempts to play off Christ against the apostles, Jesus versus Paul, are untenable, Warfield insisted, since we have no Christ except the one whom the apostles have given us.[98] Christ has bound his trustworthiness with indissoluble bands to the trustworthiness of his accredited agents (John 16:12–15).[99]

In the following year, Warfield addressed the doctrine of inspiration taught by the historic church.[100] He cited Irenaeus, Polycarp, Origen, Augustine, Luther, Calvin, Rutherford, Baxter, Westcott, and the WCF, 1,[101] contrasting them with rationalism and mysticism.[102] He argued that the church doctrine was held by the writers of the New Testament and Jesus.[103] Against the counterclaim that the case for inspiration argues in a circle, he indicated that the question is not what the Bible teaches but whether what the Bible teaches is true.[104] Ultimately it comes down to this: were Christ and the apostles deceived? He concluded:

> We believe this doctrine of the plenary inspiration of the Scriptures
> primarily because it is the doctrine which Christ and his apostles

93. Noll, *Princeton Theology*, 230.
94. Noll, *Princeton Theology*, 232.
95. "The Real Problem of Inspiration," *The Presbyterian and Reformed Review* 4 (1893): 177–221. In Warfield, *Inspiration*, 169–226.
96. Warfield, *Inspiration*, 174.
97. Warfield, *Inspiration*, 180.
98. Warfield, *Inspiration*, 187.
99. Warfield, *Inspiration*, 188.
100. Warfield, "Church Doctrine," *BSac* 51 (1894): 614–40, and in Warfield, *Inspiration*, 105–228.
101. Warfield, *Inspiration*, 108–10.
102. Warfield, *Inspiration*, 111–14.
103. Warfield, *Inspiration*, 114.
104. Warfield, *Inspiration*, 118.

believed, and which they have taught us. It may sometimes seem difficult to take our stand frankly by the side of Christ and his apostles. It will always be found safe.[105]

Later, in 1915, Warfield dealt with the foundation of the doctrine of inspiration in the Bible itself.[106] The English usage of *inspiration* implies an influence from without. However, in biblical terms, inspiration is a supernatural influence exerted on the human authors by the Spirit of God, by virtue of which their writings are given divine trustworthiness.[107] Paul, in 2 Timothy 3:16, uses θεόπνευστος to speak of this.[108] The word does not mean inspired but breathed out by God, literally "God-breathed."[109] The result is that the Scriptures are a divine product, the means by which God produced them unaddressed.[110] In Warfield's exposition of 2 Timothy 3:16 and 2 Peter 1:20–21, he said that Jesus regards Scripture as law; it is impossible for it to be annulled or for its authority to be withstood or denied.[111] He continued, "In the Saviour's view the indefectible authority of Scripture attaches to the very form of expression of its most casual clauses."[112] On the phrase, "Scripture cannot be broken" in John 10:35, Jesus's use of Scripture as authority rests on God as its author.[113] The writers of the New Testament have the same view.[114] For them, what Scripture says, God says.[115] "When thus Scripture is adduced by the names of its human authors, it is a matter of complete indifference whether the words adduced are comments of these authors or direct words of God recorded by them."[116] This is a much more intimate process than can be described as dictation.[117] Warfield recognized the long-term preparation of the human authors, bringing into conjunction God the primary author and the full freedom of the human writers.[118] Moreover, the New Testament writers place other

---

105. Warfield, *Inspiration*, 128.
106. Warfield," Inspiration," in *The International Standard Bible Encyclopedia*, 3:1473–83; and Warfield, "The Biblical Idea of Inspiration," in *Inspiration*, 131–66.
107. Warfield, *Inspiration*, 131.
108. *theopneustos*.
109. Warfield, *Inspiration*, 132–33.
110. Warfield, *Inspiration*, 133.
111. Warfield, *Inspiration*, 139.
112. Warfield, *Inspiration*, 140.
113. Warfield, *Inspiration*, 143.
114. Warfield, *Inspiration*, 144.
115. Warfield, *Inspiration*, 146–50.
116. Warfield, *Inspiration*, 152.
117. Warfield, *Inspiration*, 153.
118. Warfield, *Inspiration*, 155.

New Testament writings in the category of Scripture. Paul in 1 Timothy 5:18 cites Deuteronomy and the Gospel of Luke; 2 Peter 3:16 cites Paul's letters as Scripture.[119]

Some might argue against Warfield that his doctrine is based on documents to which we do not have access and so has no practical use. However, it follows that, Scripture being originated by God, those documents were without error and absolutely reliable in all on which they pronounce. In the case of copying, human errors do enter the picture, but in God's singular care and providence they cannot erode the original reality and do not touch important doctrines. Again, it is said that this is a circular argument. However, so too are counterarguments; they are based on the premise that God cannot have direct dealings with humanity, and so they arrive at conclusions in line with that premise. Another criticism is that, whereas Calvin places his confidence in the testimony of the Spirit as more excellent than reason, Warfield is using logic to support his case. The difference is explained by the very different contexts. Calvin was opposing church authority that had overreached itself, whereas Warfield was answering skeptical arguments. Calvin did not avoid using reason, nor elsewhere did Warfield distance himself from reliance on the Spirit.

Andrew McGowan argued that Warfield's defense of biblical inspiration was not reciprocated by the contemporary Dutch theologians Abraham Kuyper and Herman Bavinck.[120] This cannot be sustained. Bavinck approached the matter from his principle of organicism, unity-in-diversity modeled to an extent on a Christological analogy, rather than Warfield's accumulation of exegetical, historical, and phenomenological evidence. Bavinck considered that inerrancy did not go far enough, for it failed to express the divine-human concursus that his organic motif, as it was related to Scripture, required. However, both A. A. Hodge and Warfield wrote along similar lines, though without the more wide-ranging application of organic development through the theological spectrum that Bavinck produced.[121]

---

119. Warfield, *Inspiration*, 164–65.
120. Andrew T. B. McGowan, *The Divine Spiration of Scripture: Challenging Evangelical Perspectives* (Downers Grove, IL: InterVarsity Press, 2007), 158.
121. Bavinck, *RD*, 1:380–85, 435–48; Eglinton, *Trinity and Organism*, 155–82.

6.8.2 *J. I. Packer and Fundamentalism*

Packer's book *"Fundamentalism" and the Word of God*[122] was written in response to a raft of criticisms of British evangelicals by theologians such as Alan Richardson and A. M. Ramsey, and by Anglo-Catholics such as A. G. Hebert in his book *Fundamentalism and the Church of God* (1957). These criticisms, in which evangelicals were charged with fundamentalism, had been stimulated by the growth of the Inter-Varsity Fellowship on university campuses in the United Kingdom after World War II, spearheaded by missions led by John Stott, as well as by the evangelistic visit of Billy Graham in 1954.

Packer distances evangelicalism from the label *fundamentalism*. He stresses that the real question, unasked by the critics—an oversight displaying their ignorance—is that of authority. Christianity is built on truth; this raises the issue of the basis for truth. Packer distinguishes evangelicalism (truth is found supremely in the Bible, with tradition and reason subordinate) from traditionalism (the official teaching of the church is the arbiter of truth) and subjectivism (mysticism or reason is basic). The teaching of Christ is that the Old Testament is the authoritative Word of God; he submitted to it in his own life. The apostles followed suit, as did the early church. Church tradition and private theological speculations can never be identified with the Word of God, he insists.

Packer considers the divine origin of Scripture. To call it dictation is wrong. On the other hand, the critics have a mistaken notion of accommodation, believing that it includes human error. Their mistake is to deny that the Bible can be simultaneously a fully divine and fully human product. They fall into a form of Nestorianism, radically separating deity and humanity. Evangelicalism preserves the Christological analogy in accordance with orthodox theology. Packer rehearses the common arguments in support of divine inspiration, the unity of Scripture, and propositional revelation, the Word of God consisting of revealed truths. Scripture is both infallible (never deceiving) and inerrant (wholly true). It is to be interpreted literally (in accordance with the natural meaning of the passage), with Scripture interpreting Scripture. Ultimately the Holy Spirit is its interpreter. This is to be

---

122. J. I. Packer, *"Fundamentalism" and the Word of God: Some Evangelical Principles* (London: Inter-Varsity Fellowship, 1958).

received in faith. Packer was following in the line of Warfield, adapted to a new situation.

6.8.3   Excursus: Peter Enns on Scripture

With Peter Enns, the doctrine of Scripture faced a postmodern challenge, a radical argument undercutting the fabric of the Christian faith. For Enns, Christian doctrine is to be reviewed constantly and is merely provisional, to be realigned according to the latest insights of biblical scholars.[123] Enns's expressed aim is to bring what he terms "the evangelical doctrine of Scripture" into conversation with biblical scholarship. Such a conversation has not taken place, he claims. We need to engage the doctrinal implications of biblical studies, since many think an evangelical faith is untenable. Enns is ready to affirm "that many evangelical instincts are correct."[124] However, when new evidence comes to light "we must be willing to . . . *adjust our doctrine accordingly.*"[125]

Enns focuses on three issues, which we may summarize as follows:

1. *The Old Testament and other ancient literature.* Why does the Bible look a lot like the literature of its neighbors? The creation and flood accounts and the Old Testament law code are similar to accounts elsewhere in the ancient Near East that predated them. If the Bible is the Word of God, why is it so much like the ancient world?[126]
2. *Theological diversity in the Old Testament.* Why do different parts of the Old Testament say different things about the same things, such as the different interpretations of 1–2 Samuel and 1–2 Kings, compared with 1–2 Chronicles?
3. *The New Testament's handling of the Old Testament.* Why are Old Testament passages taken out of context?[127]

Enns has constructed arbitrary categories into which Scripture is to fit. First is the idea that Scripture, as the Word of God, must be in all ways unique, unlike anything else. This is absent from the history of reflection on the Bible; its human and historical dimensions have always been recognized. Second is an assumption that the Bible must speak in unison in all

---

123. Peter Enns, *Inspiration and Incarnation: Evangelicals and the Problem of the Old Testament* (Grand Rapids, MI: Baker, 2005).
124. Enns, *Inspiration and Incarnation,* 13.
125. Enns, *Inspiration and Incarnation,* 14 (italics mine).
126. Enns, *Inspiration and Incarnation,* 15–16.
127. Enns, *Inspiration and Incarnation,* 16.

its parts. This flies in the face of the unity-in-diversity of God's creation, which reflects that he is triune and not monadic. Third, while Enns commendably wants to disabuse his readers of the anachronistic assumption that biblical writers must fit twenty-first-century ideas on history and textual interpretation,[128] he fails to recognize that, as Warfield demonstrated, the evangelical doctrine of Scripture is the church's doctrine.

Enns's starting point for his argument is an incarnational analogy: *"as Christ is both God and human, so is the Bible."*[129] He continues, "The human dimension of Scripture is, therefore, part of what makes Scripture Scripture."[130] Unfortunately, Enns is not aware of the church's developed Christology. The dogma of *enhypostasia* does not enter the picture. He cites Chalcedon but does not understand it in context—something he insists should be done with the historical background to the Old Testament.

The church came to the considered conclusion that the two natures of Christ were not equal entities that came together. When we ask who Jesus of Nazareth is, the church's answer is that he is the eternal Son of God. Regarding the further question of what he consists of, the answer is that he took into indivisible and permanent personal union a human nature conceived by the Holy Spirit in the womb of the Virgin Mary. Christ is fully human, but it is *the person of the Son* who takes into union a human nature. Christ is not a composite; the incarnation is asymmetrical. The humanity of Christ is the humanity of the eternal Son of the Father. It has no independent existence. With the incarnational analogy applied to Scripture the movement is from the side of God. So Scripture is fully human, produced in particular historical contexts, but what makes it Scripture is its origination and outbreathing by the Spirit, constituting it canon for the church.

Throughout, Enns is preoccupied with the Bible's uniqueness. If there are possible parallels with other ancient literature, or if that literature preceded the Old Testament, this "makes it look less special in some respects."[131] Thus, he argues that Genesis adopts, with some variations, previous mythical descriptions of creation and the flood. Enns wants to avoid a history-versus-myth polarity and wants a new word for explanatory purposes (Barth used "saga," but Enns does not refer to it.) He defines *myth* as "an ancient, premodern, prescientific way of addressing questions

128. Enns, *Inspiration and Incarnation*, 16.
129. Enns, *Inspiration and Incarnation*, 17.
130. Enns, *Inspiration and Incarnation*, 18.
131. Enns, *Inspiration and Incarnation*, 32.

of ultimate origins and meaning in the form of stories: Who are we? Where do we come from?" This idea has been around for a long time. Enns wonders why history—as understood in the modern Western world—is regarded as better than myth or a plain story. The Bible, he states, should be understood in terms of the cultural context in which it was given.[132]

To Enns, it is a problem for the doctrine of Scripture that the New Testament cites or alludes to extrabiblical literature and rabbinical interpretations based not on the Old Testament but on legends. Why is this a problem? There is a very significant difference in the way they use these sources. The New Testament reserves the introductory formulae *legein, graphein, hoti,* "it is written," for the Old Testament Scriptures. Enns equates a high view of Scripture with a refusal to recognize any other theological source than Scripture. But the latter does not follow from the former. Instead of accepting Scripture on the basis that Christ and the apostles are reliable teachers of doctrine, he appears to treat modern biblical scholarship as the determiner of canon.

Enns argues that there was no constructive engagement in the nineteenth century between defenders of the "evangelical" doctrine of Scripture and discoveries from the ancient world. He overlooks the work of Westcott, Hort, and others. He assumes that "the evangelical doctrine of Scripture" is one among other options; it is the church's doctrine, shared with Rome and Orthodoxy. Enns refers us to a guild of biblical scholars for their latest hypotheses. Since the academic world feeds on novelty, this suggestion removes any firm foundation for the faith and renders it hostage to the constantly shifting fads of academia. For Enns, everything is provisional—our biblical interpretation, our doctrine of Scripture, our theology, which is always revisable in the light of the latest theories of biblical scholars. He argues, "Our confession of the Bible as God's word has a provisional quality to it."[133]

Does our postmodern confession of Christ also have a provisional quality to it? And if not, why not? Paul Helm considers these arguments "monstrous."[134] As Helm concludes:

> Enns's problems have little or nothing to do with the discoveries and claims of Old Testament scholarship. Instead, they are due to two basic failures. A failure in theological method, that of starting from

132. Enns, *Inspiration and Incarnation,* 41.
133. Enns, *Inspiration and Incarnation,* 168.
134. Paul Helm, review of *Inspiration and Incarnation: Evangelicals and the Problem of the Old Testament,* by Peter Enns, *Reformation 21,* April 2006, http://www.reformation21.org/shelf-life/inspiration-and-incarnation-evangelicals-and-the-problem-of-the-old-testament.php.

difficulties instead of from dogma. And a failure in epistemology, a commitment to the idea of universal cultural bias that makes objectivity and finality about our faith impossible.[135]

6.9　Conclusion

The church through the ages has confessed that the Bible is the infallible and inerrant Word of God, given in human, servant form. Protestants maintain it to be the only infallible rule of faith and practice, by which all human teaching and every claim to spiritual experience is to be judged. Throughout, it testifies of Jesus Christ, God's Son, our Savior. He committed his authority to his apostles. We believe because of the Spirit's work in us attesting his words given through the apostles and prophets. Commitment to Scripture is defensible and explicable in scholarly terms, but ultimately it is a matter of discipleship, for we maintain that Christ and the apostles are reliable in their teaching.

Further Reading

Barrett, Matthew M. *God's Word Alone: The Authority of Scripture*. Grand Rapids, MI: Zondervan, 2016.

Kruger, Michael J. *The Question of Canon: Challenging the Status Quo in the New Testament Debate*. Nottingham: Apollos, 2013.

Ward, Timothy. *Words of Life: Scripture as the Living and Active Word of God*. Nottingham: Inter-Varsity Press, 2009.

Warfield, Benjamin B. *The Inspiration and Authority of the Bible*. Edited by Samuel G. Craig. Philadelphia: Presbyterian and Reformed, 1970.

Study Questions

1. Is there a disparity between Calvin's use of the testimony of the Holy Spirit in persuading us of the divine authorship of Scripture and Warfield's focus on reasons to believe it?

2. How would you understand the relationship between the Bible, on the one hand, and Christ, on the other? To what extent should our view of the production of Scripture be related to the history of redemption?

3. Consider how faith and discipleship should shape our understanding of Scripture and our allegiance to it.

4. In what sense is the Bible inerrant? Since this doctrine has been maintained by some heretical sects, of what value is it?

---

135. Helm, review of *Inspiration and Incarnation*.

7

Scripture and Tradition

The relationship between Scripture and the accumulated teaching of the church has varied according to historical context. While the apostles were alive and for some time afterward, their written and oral teachings formed a seamless web. But as time went on, with greater distance from the apostles, this inevitably changed. Before long, the unwritten traditions were distinguished from Scripture and were accorded an authority. During the Middle Ages, tradition was seen to supplement Scripture and acquired equal standing. However, it became evident that some tradition was biblically insupportable. The Reformers did not jettison tradition but set it under the supreme authority of the Bible. As Rome's historical claims were undermined, Newman proposed the idea of the development of doctrine, which enabled papal and ecclesiastical authority to be buttressed by an appeal to implicit and explicit tradition. While Rome has lately become more positive on the reading of Scripture, the issues of the Reformation are still with us. The modern world has posed a threat to the authority of both Scripture and tradition.

Someone said: "the dead writers are remote from us because we *know* so much more than they did." Precisely, and they are that which we know.[1]

Tradition is "an extension of the franchise" by "giving votes to the most obscure of all classes, our ancestors."[2]

---

1. T. S. Eliot, *Selected Essays*, 3rd. ed. (London: Faber and Faber, 1951), 16.
2. Jaroslav Pelikan, *The Vindication of Tradition* (New Haven, CT: Yale University Press, 1984), 17, quoting G. K. Chesterton, *Orthodoxy*, chap. 4.

Tradition is the living faith of the dead, traditionalism is the dead faith of the living. And, I suppose I should add, it is traditionalism that gives tradition such a bad name.[3]

Tradition can be described as vicarious experience. An old proverb states that "experience is the wisdom of fools." This may appear to be counter-intuitive, but the point is simple. Fools learn from experience that fire burns your fingers; wise people learn this by heeding what they are taught—and by observing fools! The biggest fools do not learn even from their experience. As the saying goes, there is not much to learn from the second kick of the mule. There is no need to reinvent the wheel in every generation.[4]

7.1 The Meaning of *Tradition*[5]

In New Testament usage, *tradition* refers to what has been passed on or handed down (παράδοσις).[6] Insofar as it depicts the sayings of Jesus or the content of the apostolic gospel, it is viewed positively. Paul received the gospel and handed it down to the church at Corinth (1 Cor. 15:1–11), including instruction about the Lord's Supper (1 Cor. 11:23–34). The yardstick for right faith and conduct is to live and believe according to the written or oral Pauline traditions (2 Thess. 2:15). The apostolic faith is to be passed down the generations in a line of faithful leaders (2 Tim. 2:2). On the other hand, other traditions run contrary to the faith. The traditions of the elders were often used to evade the teaching of the Law (Matt. 15:1–20). Then, too, there were "human traditions," pagan and opposed to the truth, from which Gentile converts were to turn (Col. 2:8). Tradition is positive when in harmony with apostolic doctrine but in other settings is to be rejected.

A group arose in the nineteenth century that wanted to jettison church traditions and the edicts of church councils, and get back to the simplicity of the Bible. They published the journal *Studies in the Scriptures*. We know them now as the Jehovah's Witnesses. Such a cry is shorthand for a desire to dispense with the accumulated biblical exegesis of the history of the church and replace it with one's own. Instead, the

---

3. Pelikan, *Vindication of Tradition*, 65.
4. Anthony N. S. Lane, *Exploring Christian Doctrine* (London: SPCK, 2013), 17.
5. The general outline of what follows is indebted to A. N. S. Lane, "Scripture, Tradition and Church: An Historical Survey," *VE* 9 (1975): 37–55.
6. *paradosis.*

Bible requires us to submit "to one another out of reverence for Christ" (Eph. 5:21). Tradition in some form is inescapable. Even the smallest fundamentalist sects base their beliefs on the teachings of their leaders, which eventually become a tradition, often a highly idiosyncratic or deviant one.

My discussion here will be historical, focusing mainly on the Western tradition, although I will also examine the way Orthodoxy views the relationship.

Tradition can be seen as the sum total of the teaching and practices of the church. Within this, there is the rule of faith that summarizes the apostolic teaching and is expressed in various ways in its creeds and councils, and the writings of leading theologians. However, through the years, elements in apparent conflict with the apostolic writings, whether in teaching or practice, entered to cloud the picture. The Reformation erupted in part due to this discrepancy. Yet, since tradition represents the cumulative biblical exegesis of the church, its relation to Scripture cannot be ignored.

7.2   Changing Relationships between Scripture and Tradition

7.2.1   *The First Two Centuries: Scripture and Oral Apostolic Teaching, a Seamless Whole*

During the first two centuries AD, either some of the apostles were still alive or some leading figures had known them and had been taught by one or another of them. We know that Paul gave oral instruction to the churches he planted (2 Thess. 2:1–2, 5). Not only his writings but also reports of his teaching were in circulation. The same undoubtedly applied to churches founded by other apostles, like Thomas, who, it is claimed, planted the church in India. The martyr Polycarp (69–155) had been taught by the apostle John.[7] Hence, in this period there was little distinction between the apostolic writings—not all of which were possessed by all the churches—and the transmission of oral apostolic teaching. In the ancient world information was mainly conveyed by word of mouth, and generally people had more retentive memories than they do today. Thus Ignatius, ca. 110–115, urged the Smyrneans, "Follow, all of you, the bishop,

---

7. This is on the testimony of Irenaeus, who in his youth had met him. Irenaeus, *Against Heresies* 3.3.4 (*ANF*, 1:416). There has been controversy over the date of Polycarp's martyrdom. Some have placed it in AD 167, but others in 155. He was eighty-seven at the time of his death, although even this is problematic, and he claimed to have known John the apostle.

as Jesus Christ followed the Father."[8] For Ignatius, the gospel taught by the church was the same as that taught by the apostles and by Jesus.

7.2.2 Tradition Supplements Scripture

As time passed, the connection with the apostles faded and disappeared. A new perspective was required and evolved. The main problem facing the church was how to defend itself against heresy. The apologists found themselves defending the faith on the basis that the church, in contrast to the heretics, had the right interpretation of the apostolic writings because it was in unbroken continuity with the apostolic churches.

According to Irenaeus, tradition shows how Scripture is to be interpreted. The Holy Spirit preserves the church from error, with the result that the apostolic teaching is found in the apostolic Scriptures and in the apostolic tradition found in the apostolic churches.[9] This line of defense was developed by Tertullian. He maintained that the truth is found in the teaching of the churches the apostles founded, which have a continuous succession to the present. So "we hold communion with the apostolic churches because our doctrine is in no respect different from theirs."[10] Vincent of Lerins's famous slogan to the effect that authentic Christianity is *quod ubique, quod semper, quod omnibus creditum est* (what is believed everywhere, always, and by all) stressed the universal consensus of the church. The idea of "the rule of faith" emerged, a summary of apostolic doctrine that was the yardstick by which any teaching or exegesis was to be measured.

In this light, the great ecumenical councils addressed and answered challenges to the heart of the gospel, those on the Trinity and the person of Christ.[11] The assembled bishops were conscious of confessing the faith, of measuring their response on the basis of what had been handed down by the apostles in their writings.

However, tendencies were emerging that would undermine the supremacy of Scripture. By the fourth century, Basil was stating that "we are not, as is well known, content with what the apostle or the Gospel has recorded, but . . . we add other words as being of great importance to the

---

8. Ignatius, *To the Smyrnaeans* (ANF, 1:89).
9. Irenaeus, *Against Heresies* 4.26.2–4 (ANF, 1:497).
10. Tertullian, *On Prescription against Heretics* 21 (ANF, 3:252–53).
11. See chaps. 3 and 17.

validity of the ministry, and these we derive from unwritten teaching."[12]
These "other words" related to blessing the baptismal waters, anointing
with oil, renunciation of Satan, praying to the east in anticipation of
the resurrection, and the like. For Basil, the beliefs and practices of the
church were based both on the written teaching of the apostles and on
the unwritten apostolic precepts handed down in a secret mystery. Both
were of the same force. He added, "I hold it apostolic to abide by the
unwritten traditions."[13] While the examples he cited were in themselves
trivial, the publicly accessible written apostolic teaching was relativized.

With far-reaching implications, Gregory of Nyssa claimed that visual
revelation had priority over verbal. The visual was clearer to a wider
range of people. In his opposition to the heretic Eunomius, he followed
Psalm 19:1–6 and Romans 1:20, pointing to the creation declaring the
glory and power of God. From this, he argued that "this is not given in
articulate speech, but by the things which are seen, and it instills into our
minds the knowledge of Divine power more than if speech proclaimed
it with a voice." For Gregory, the visible revelation of God in creation
is superior to a verbal declaration by God's voice. This is because "we
are not told that God is the creator of words, but of things made known
to us by the signification of our words."[14] In keeping with the visual
emphasis, iconography developed, particularly in the Greek church. We
considered the limitations of general revelation in chapter 1 (cf., e.g.,
Deut. 4:9–12; 8:1–3).

Against the Manicheans, Augustine took the position "I should not
believe the gospel except as moved by the authority of the Catholic
Church."[15] In turn, he believed that many things practiced by the whole
church must be supposed to be apostolic although they are not contained
in the apostolic writings.[16] In a letter to Januarius, he remarked that these
consisted of "the annual commemoration of the Lord's passion, resurrection, and ascension, and of the descent of the Holy Spirit from heaven,
and whatever else is in like manner observed by the whole Church wherever it has been established."[17] Augustine here placed controls on the unwritten traditions—universality of practice and centrality to the gospel.

---

12. Basil of Caesarea, *On the Holy Spirit* 27.66 (NPNF[2], 8:41–42).
13. Basil, *Holy Spirit* 29.71 (NPNF[2], 8:45).
14. Gregory of Nyssa, *Contra Eunomius* 2 (NPNF[2], 5:272–73).
15. Augustine, *Against the Epistle of Manichaeus Called Fundamental* 5.6 (NPNF[1], 4:131).
16. Augustine, *On Baptism* 12; *Against the Donatists* 23.31 (NPNF[1], 4:430, 475).
17. Augustine, *Letter 54* 1.1 (NPNF[1], 1:300).

7.2.3   *The Reformation: The Paths Diverge*

Clearly, not all that was handed down in the church had biblical warrant. While biblical teaching was transmitted, other elements were dubious. Problems arose in the Middle Ages when it became obvious that some church practices and beliefs contradicted Scripture, and when the claims of Rome to ecclesiastical supremacy were shown to rest on forged documents, not on unwritten apostolic tradition. The Reformation was not a conflict between Scripture and tradition but a conflict between Scripture and the contemporary church with its assumption of unwritten tradition and its adoption of beliefs and practices at variance with the apostolic writings. The Reformers consistently used tradition, in the sense of the ecumenical creeds and the writings of the chief theologians, in support of their claims. Bullinger argued forcefully that the Reformation had its roots in the ongoing history of the church and, behind that, in God's covenantal revelation reaching back to Abraham and Adam.[18] However, they regarded tradition not as a supplement to Scripture but rather as a help to understanding it; it was not on a par with the written Word but was a commentary of sorts, subordinate and under its authority.

Calvin is clear that the authority of the Scriptures derives from their origin and not from the church. They "spring from heaven as if there the living words of God were heard."[19] While Rome believed the Bible to be the indefectible Word of God, it considered its authority to rest on the consent of the church, its only reliable interpreter. Calvin calls it "a pernicious error" to say that "Scripture has only so much weight as is conceded to it by the consent of the church. As if the eternal and inviolable truth of God depended upon the decision of men!"[20] Rome asserted that the church had power to determine the extent of the canon and to pronounce on Scripture's divine origin. This, for Calvin, was "sacrilegious" and led to "an unbridled tyranny." It was to mock the Holy Spirit.[21] In Calvin's understanding, the church receives Scripture and

---

18. Heinrich Bullinger, *De testamento seu foedere Dei unico et aeterno brevis expositio* (Zürich, 1534); Heinrich Bullinger, *Antiquissima fides et vera religio* (Zürich, 1534).

19. Calvin, *Institutes*, 1.7.1. See also John Calvin, *Calvin's Commentaries: The Epistle of Paul the Apostle to the Hebrews and the First and Second Epistles of St. Peter*, trans. William B. Johnston (Grand Rapids, MI: Eerdmans, 1963), 343; John Calvin, *Commentarii in epistolas canonicas*, Ioannis Calvini opera exegetica (Geneva: Droz, 2009), 344.

20. Calvin, *Institutes*, 1.7.1.

21. Calvin, *Institutes*, 1.7.1–2.

recognizes it as such; it does not and cannot render authentic what is otherwise doubtful. On the contrary, because of its divine origin, Scripture is self-authenticating. It "exhibits fully as clear evidence of its own truth as white or black things do of their color, or sweet and bitter things do of their taste."[22] Calvin cites Augustine in support, contrary to Rome's use of him.[23] Calvin considers it "a damnable blasphemy of the Papists to imagine that the light of Scripture does nothing but dazzle the eyes, so that they frighten off the simple from reading it."[24]

Foundational to Calvin's argument is that the Holy Spirit, the author of Scripture, convinces us of its truth. Human argumentation cannot convince, but "the testimony of the Spirit is more excellent than all reason."[25] At the same time, while rejecting the claims of Rome, Calvin's writings regularly referred to authorities—Patristic and medieval—in support. He rejected the argument that tradition was on a par with Scripture, which would grant the church of Rome the sole right to interpret the Bible, but he recognized the value and need to reinforce his teaching by citing those who preceded him.[26]

A succinct summary of this principle is found in article 8 of the Thirty-Nine Articles, on the three creeds: the Apostles', Nicene, and Athanasian Creeds. These "ought thoroughly to be received and believed: for they may be proved by most certain warrants of holy Scripture."[27] The creeds of the church confessed throughout the ages are to be believed thoroughly since they are fully in accord with Scripture; if they were not, it would follow that they were not to be accepted. Church statements of whatever kind are to be judged by the Word of God; the Word of God can be judged by no one. Notwithstanding, such faithful statements, confessions, and creeds are not to be dismissed but, rather, are to be received and believed *thoroughly*. They are an aid, an invaluable one.

The acceptance of tradition, under the authority of Scripture, is also evident in the proliferation of confessions and creeds put together by

22. Calvin, *Institutes*, 1.7.1.
23. Calvin, *Institutes*, 1.7.3.
24. Calvin, *Hebrews and First and Second Peter*, 342; Calvin, *In Epistolas Canonicas*, 343.
25. Calvin, *Institutes*, 1.7.4; see also 1.9.2; Calvin, *Calvin's Commentaries: The Second Epistle of Paul the Apostle to the Corinthians and the Epistles to Timothy, Titus and Philemon*, trans. T. A. Smail (Grand Rapids, MI: Eerdmans, 1964), 330.
26. In his *Institutes* Calvin frequently cited the fathers, especially Augustine, and the medieval theologians. Concerning the early church councils, he commented, "I venerate them from my heart, and desire that they be honored by all." *Institutes*, 4.9.1.
27. Philip Schaff, *The Creeds of Christendom* (Grand Rapids, MI: Baker, 1966), 3:492.

both the Lutherans and the Reformed, reaching its apogee at the West-minster Assembly (1643–1652). Here the Reformation and its aftermath were adding to the cumulative witness of the church and producing what would be regarded in future years as part of that tradition. It was doing so gladly. The debates at the Westminster Assembly are full of references to Latin and Greek fathers, medieval theologians, and more-recent voices on both sides of the Reformation divide.[28]

Much had changed over the intervening centuries. For Irenaeus and Tertullian, at around AD 200, church teaching was apostolic. But the Reformers saw some church teaching as being opposed to apostolic teaching. The two were no longer identical. Tradition is neither a supple-mentary nor an equal authority. It is a tool to help understand Scripture.

7.2.4   The Anabaptists

Generally, the Anabaptists rejected tradition. As G. H. Williams remarks, "The basic opposition of the whole of the Radical Reformation to the intrusion of the state into the realm of conscience found doctrinal ex-pression also in the opposition of the anti-Nicenes to conciliar decisions enforced by the Roman Empire."[29] The doctrinal commitments of the church post-Constantine were all suspect in their eyes. So,

> when the whole of Christian doctrine became subject to both learned and popular scrutiny in the light of the Scriptural and solafideist and antischolastic, but still "catholic," stress of the Magisterial Refor-mation, it was inevitable that within the Radical Reformation there would be diverse attempts to return to what would be considered a more Biblical interpretation [*sic*] of the doctrine of the Trinity.[30]

Similarly, "common to certain spokesmen in all three groupings of the Radical Reformation were . . . a distinctive Christology (the celestial flesh or body of Christ); . . . in almost all cases an espousal of the free-dom of the will in striving for sanctification . . . a perfectionist view of the church."[31] The result of this rejection of tradition was a virtual

---

28. On the debates on the three creeds at the Westminster Assembly in its initial work when it discussed the Thirty-Nine Articles, see Robert Letham, *The Westminster Assembly: Reading Its Theology in Historical Context* (Phillipsburg, NJ: P&R, 2009), 153–58.
29. George Huntston Williams, *The Radical Reformation* (Philadelphia: Westminster, 1975), 320.
30. Williams, *Radical Reformation*, 321.
31. Williams, *Radical Reformation*, 325.

recapitulation of all the major heresies, together with a range of new ones.[32] I believe it was Alister McGrath who coined the term "tradition zero" for this position.[33] It is misnamed the Radical *Reformation*, for it was a departure from not only the Reformation but, in many cases, the consensus of the historic church.[34]

Much fundamentalism and large swathes of evangelicalism have imbibed this view. The subtitle of Douglas Kelly's *Systematic Theology* sums up the classic Reformed relationship between Scripture and tradition: *Grounded in Holy Scripture and Understood in the Light of the Church*. In contrast, the Anabaptist viewpoint is clearly expressed by a well-known British evangelical: "I am not convinced that many 'Evangelicals' are truly evangelical. . . . Where are the people who are truly willing to think through this question with nothing in front of them except an open Bible?"[35] This perspective values what the Holy Spirit putatively makes known to us at the expense of what he has made known to the church of Jesus Christ over the last two thousand years. Moreover, it is impossible to come to the Bible with a blank mind, unaffected by philosophical or cultural presuppositions, or previously received teaching. It is better to acknowledge these factors than to pretend that one's biblical interpretation is pure and unalloyed when it may be far from it.

7.2.5   Renewal of the Roman Catholic Position

In 1546, in response to the pressing demands occasioned by the Protestant Reformation, the Council of Trent reiterated the normative position of the Roman church in a statement that remains authoritative to this day:

> Following the example of the orthodox Fathers, the church receives and venerates *with an equal affection of piety and reverence* all the books of the Old and New Testaments, of which the one God is the author, and also the traditions—relating to faith and life—as having

---

32. See, e.g., Williams, *Radical Reformation*, 320–40.

33. Alister E. McGrath, *Reformation Thought: An Introduction*, 2nd ed. (Oxford: Blackwell, 1993), 144.

34. See my discussion of Anabaptist Christology in *Reformation Theology: A Systematic Summary*, ed. Matthew Barrett (Wheaton, IL: Crossway, 2017), 340–43.

35. Stuart Olyott, "Some Personal Thoughts on Ministerial Training," *The Evangelical Magazine* 48, no. 1 (2009): 16–17. On another matter, see Keith G. Stanglin, "The Rise and Fall of Biblical Perspicuity: Remonstrants and the Transition towards Modern Exegesis," *CH* 83 (2014): 38–59, who argues that the stress among the Remonstrants for the perspicuity of Scripture in opposition to both Rome and the Reformed led to a divorce between scholarship and the church.

been dictated either by Christ's own mouth, or by the Holy Spirit, and preserved in the Catholic Church by a continuous succession.[36]

Over the following centuries the phrase "with equal affection of piety" (*pari pietatis affectu*) became the focus of immense debate. Whatever the niceties, it implied that Protestants had strayed from the historic position of the church that Scripture is not the only source of revelation; the traditions are also included. Moreover, the Protestant canon was defective, since it did not include the apocryphal books. At a time when Protestantism had been spawned by critical textual work on the original languages, Rome held the Latin Vulgate translation to be authoritative. In the face of the perceived rampant individualism of the Protestants, the church maintained its authority to interpret Scripture. Robert Bellarmine wrote: "The holie Church is the spouse of God, and hath the holy Ghost for her master. And therefore there is no danger that she should be deceived, or that she doe teach others to do anything that were against the commandements of God."[37] Bellarmine lists, in addition to doctrines, precepts of the holy church—attendance at Mass, confession, fasting in Lent, abstinence from flesh on Fridays and Saturdays, payment of tithes—and counsels of our Lord—voluntary poverty, chastity, and obedience.[38]

7.3   Newman and the Development of Doctrine

Increasingly, it became evident that Rome's belief that it rested on unbroken apostolic traditions was fragile. It had been long recognized that the growth of church authority depended on claims in documents that were fabrications and forgeries, most notably *The Donation of Constantine* and the *Pseudo-Isidiorian Decretals*. Even before he defected to Rome in 1845, John Henry Newman had been exercised about this problem. He coined an explanation in the form of a distinction between explicit and implicit tradition. In this way he could account for the absence of explicit justification for the current teaching of the church by arguing

---

36. My translation and italics: ". . . orthodoxorum Patrum exempla secuta, omnes libros tam Veteris quam Novi Testamenti, cum utriusque unus Deus sit auctor, nec non traditiones ipsas, tum ad fidem tum ad mores pertinentes, tanquam vel oretenus a Christo, vel a Spiritu Sancto dictatas et continua successione in Ecclesia catholica conservatas, pari pietatis affectu ac reverentia suscipit et veneratur." *DS*, 1501.

37. Robert Bellarmine, *An Ample Declaration of the Christian Doctrine*, trans. Richard Hadock (Roan: n.p., 1604), 124.

38. Bellarmine, *Declaration*, 174–79.

that it was present in *implicit* form earlier. In effect, this represented a loss of confidence not only in Scripture but also in tradition; Scripture was not the supreme authority and tradition itself needed saving from clear vulnerabilities.

7.3.1 Newman's Theory of Development

In his landmark book *An Essay on the Development of Doctrine* (1845),[39] Newman expounded his ideas. The rocks between which he attempted to steer were, on the one side, the weakness of Rome's claims, owing to their spurious foundations, and, on the other, Protestantism's stress on the supremacy of the Bible. Newman wrote at the wake of the Romantic movement (1760–1830), with its notion of organic development, which spawned a range of evolutionary theories in philosophy (Hegel), theology (Nevin, Newman), and biology (Darwin), and gave rise to a heightened awareness of the historical process. Newman, like Darwin, was a child of his times.

His main argument can be summarized as follows. Protestantism is incompatible with history. This is because, in the words of the less-than-orthodox William Chillingworth, "The Bible I say, the Bible only, is the religion of Protestants." Protestants, Newman argued, "are forced . . . to fall back upon the Bible as the sole source of revelation, and upon their own personal private judgment as the sole expounder of its doctrine." In contrast, "the Christianity of history is not Protestantism. If ever there were a safe truth, it is this." Consequently, "to be deep in history is to cease to be a Protestant."[40] This was a necessary device to eliminate Protestant arguments and to clear the deck for Newman's recasting of the Roman defense of implicit apostolic tradition, a defense that needed to be based on a historical argument, not an expressly biblical one. However, it was done by setting up a straw man. We have seen that classic Protestantism had a strong view of church tradition, insofar as it conformed to Scripture, and an awareness of history due to its covenant theology.

From this, Newman spent the rest of the treatise applying the idea of development. Doctrine requires our going beyond the letter of Scripture.

---

39. John Henry Newman, *An Essay on the Development of Christian Doctrine* (Notre Dame, IN: University of Notre Dame Press, 1989).
40. Newman, *Development*, 6–8.

Scripture leaves some questions unresolved, requiring our investigation. Indeed, the Bible itself shows development. An infallible authority is needed to adjudicate its questions. Here Newman points to the infallibility of the church—a permanent authority in matters of faith, found in the Greek and Latin churches, which stretch right back to apostolic times. This argument has not been rebutted, Newman argues; the lack of a positive reply to Trent establishes the point. The developments in view are the doctrines propounded by successive popes and councils. Inevitably, there have been conflicts between the fathers and the councils. The key is the pope; an arbiter has been provided.

It seems that Newman's ideas have enabled Rome to argue that whatever it teaches now is the church's tradition. Present teaching has developed from the past and so must always have been part of that tradition. This is the consequence of infallibility plus development. Oberman describes this as the Roman Catholic "magisterium of the moment."[41]

Most modern Orthodox theologians consider development incompatible with Orthodoxy.[42] Orthodoxy's claim is that it has preserved the faith once for all delivered, and that this faith is expressed in the ecumenical councils, the creeds, and the liturgy.

7.3.2 Development Developed

In his major works *History of Dogma*[43] and *What Is Christianity?*,[44] Adolf von Harnack presented his famous argument that Christianity had been corrupted by Greek philosophy. The pure religion of Jesus related to the fatherhood of God, ethics, and the value of the soul. Paul instead taught about Christ. Furthermore, Greek thought soon entered, with the Logos doctrine, via Clement of Alexandria and Origen. Faith was equated with doctrine. Rome perverted the gospel. The Reformation was the greatest movement in church history, but it produced state churches, emotionalism, and the abandonment of the monastic spirit. In short, for

---

41. Heiko Augustinus Oberman, *The Dawn of the Reformation: Essays in Late Medieval and Early Reformation Thought* (Grand Rapids, MI: Eerdmans, 1992), 295. Thanks to Keith Mathison for pointing me to this.

42. See Daniel J. Lattier, "The Orthodox Rejection of Doctrinal Development," *PrEccl* 20 (2011): 389–410, who argues that this view is not uniform and suggests that Newman's view of development is in harmony with the Orthodox commitment to tradition.

43. Adolf von Harnack, *History of Dogma*, trans. James Millar (London: Williams & Norgate, 1897).

44. Adolf von Harnack, *Das Wesen des Christentums: Sechzehn Vorlesungen vor Studierenden aller Facultäten Im Wintersemester 1899/1900 an der Universität Berlin gehalten* (Leipzig: Hinrichs, 1901).

Harnack, the history of the church was a sad tale of departure, decay, and decline. This was not an account of *development* of doctrine so much as the *dissolution* of the original religion of Jesus. The theory has had a lasting impact and still lingers on the semipopular level and among some New Testament scholars, even though it has been refuted many times over. What is significant for our purposes is that it provoked a response asserting a Protestant theory of development.

James Orr, in *The Progress of Dogma*, a series of lectures given in America in 1897 and published in 1901, argued that Christianity unfolded historically according to its own inner logic, under God's providence. This inner development served to vindicate orthodox doctrines. The historical development mirrored the logical, and the logical reflected the inner coherence of the discipline of systematic theology.[45]

First on the agenda was the doctrine of the Trinity. In this the church was compelled by the logic of the gospel to come to an agreement on the way Jesus Christ the Son could be God while not jeopardizing the unity or uniqueness of the one God. From this the next major question naturally emerged; how could Christ as God also be fully human, as the Gospel records made clear he was. So the questions of Christology followed logically and historically in the wake of those relating to the Trinity.

In turn, the relationship of the grace of God to human sin and its effects came to the surface. Much of the Middle Ages was taken up with matters of sin and grace, at first in the Pelagian crisis of the fifth century and then in protracted discussions on the atonement. Following these considerations, justification rose to prominence at the Reformation, a logical outflow of the previous preoccupation with atonement. All these questions revolved around the work of Christ, propelling the sacraments—especially the Eucharist—to the center of attention.

The tests of valid doctrine, as far as Orr was concerned, consisted of organic unity with the whole body of Christian doctrine, correlation with Christian experience, and the practical effects a doctrine had. Together these provide the inner coherence to, and the litmus test of, what is a valid development. Overall, the test of history is unerring; it unfolds according to the inner logic of the gospel as taught by Christ and

---

45. James Orr, *The Progress of Dogma: Being the Elliot Lectures, Delivered at the Western Theological Seminary, Allegheny, Penna., USA* (Grand Rapids, MI: Eerdmans, 1901).

the apostles. From one angle, Orr recognized that Newman's theories were valid; there is a genuine development as church history proceeds. Notwithstanding, Orr differed in application and claimed Newman's principles can be used so as to refute him. Development can be explained from within the context of classic and historic Protestantism without sacrificing the supremacy of Scripture or according the church a comparable authority.

The doctrine of Scripture in the WCF allows room for the development of doctrine in the church. "The whole counsel of God concerning all things necessary for his own glory, man's salvation, faith and life, is either expressly set down in Scripture, or by good and necessary consequence may be deduced from Scripture" (WCF, 1.6). This permits deductions, considered theological exegesis of the Bible that, if shown to be a legitimate development from Scripture, is part of the whole counsel of God for our salvation.

Furthermore, the idea held by many Catholics and Orthodox that Reformed theology has no doctrine of the church but is purely individualistic is pure myth. Central to Reformed theology is the covenant, focusing on God's commitment to his people, expressed in the promise repeated at each stage in its historical development: "I will be your God, and you shall be my people" (see Gen. 17:7–8; Jer. 11:4; 24:7; 30:22; 31:31–34; 32:38; Ezek. 34:24; 37:21–28; Rev. 21:3). Covenant theology is as far from individualism as night from day. It is expressed classically in the WCF, from chapter 7 onward, with an extensive section on the church and sacraments in chapters 25–31. In the Reformed confessions, church and sacraments are integral, making up a sizeable proportion of these documents.[46] Calvin devotes the whole of book 4 in his *Institutes* to the church.

It needs to be restated forcefully that the idea of "the right of private interpretation" is *not* a Reformation principle. This notion supposes that any individual has the right, privilege, and duty to interpret the Bible as he or she sees fit. A striking example is the case of the Particular Baptists in Nottinghamshire, who "followed the common Particular

---

46. The following instances refer to Schaff, *Creeds*: the Heidelberg Catechism (1563), 65–85 (Schaff, 3:328–38); the Belgic Confession (1561), 27–35 (Schaff, 3:416–31); the Scots Confession (1560), 16–23, 25 (Schaff, 3:458–74, 476–79); the French Confession (1559), 24–38 (Schaff, 3:373–81); the Thirty-Nine Articles of Religion of the Church of England (1563, 1571), 8, 19–36 (Schaff, 3:492, 499–512); the Second Helvetic Confession (1562, 1566), 17–28 (Schaff, 3:868–905).

Baptist practice of constituting themselves into a church in a solemn ceremony in which participants covenanted with one another and with God to live in church fellowship according to the will of God as they saw it."[47] However, God gave the Bible not to private persons but to the church. Hence, the celebrated first chapter of the Second Helvetic Confession roots the preaching of the Word of God in the life of the church: "Wherefore when this Word of God is now preached in the church by preachers lawfully called, we believe that the very Word of God is preached, and received of the faithful."[48] It is preachers lawfully called—called by the church and preaching in the church—whose preaching is the Word of God. Alongside this we note the rigorous stipulations for those who preach in the Westminster Assembly's "Directory for the Publick Worship of God" and "The Form of Presbyterial Church-Government."[49] This body was called by Parliament to provide a confession of faith and ordinances for the government of the church, and had as its task the licensing and ordaining of ministers. To categorize Reformed theology as individualistic with no doctrine of the church is a monumental error.

Allied to this is the false notion, held widely, that the slogan *sola Scriptura* means that the Bible is the only source for theology. Though it is said to be one of the central pillars of the Reformation, there is no evidence of such a phrase in sixteenth-century Reformed theology. It probably did not appear until the eighteenth century at least, when it affirmed that the Bible is the highest court of appeal in all matters of religious controversy, which is what the Reformers and their successors actually held. The slogan itself, still less the reality to which it pointed, never meant that the Bible was the only source for theology.[50] The dangers of such a position are most clearly seen in the Socinians, the Jehovah's Witnesses, and in the early Plymouth Brethren, who, in their first decade, recapitulated many of the heresies of the early church.

---

47. F. H. W. Harrison, "The Nottinghamshire Baptists: Polity," *BQ* 25 (1974): 212–31; see 217.

48. Schaff, *Creeds*, 3:832.

49. *The Confession of Faith, the Larger and Shorter Catechisms with the Scripture Proofs at Large together with The Sum of Saving Knowledge* (Applecross, Ross-shire: Publications Committee of the Free Presbyterian Church of Scotland, 1970), 369–93, 394–416.

50. See Lane, "Scripture."

7.4   Modern Developments

7.4.1   *Developments within Protestantism*

The discussion of the relationship between Scripture and tradition in the last two hundred years has been affected greatly by the rise of the historical-critical method. This led to a widespread loss of acceptance of the authority of Scripture, particularly in Protestantism.[51] The Bible began to be treated like any other book, rather than the divinely given canon for the church. Its connection to the church was undermined, and the university effectively hijacked the right of interpretation. This took the Bible out of the context God had given it; while it is capable of academic defense and explanation, it was meant for the church, not the university.

A second trend has been the rise and increasing sophistication of historical study. Overall, the positives outweigh the negatives. Christianity is historical; God has revealed himself in Christ in the muck and mire of the human condition in a fallen and disordered world. Some, like Wolfgang Pannenberg, have used this to defend the central theme of the resurrection.[52]

Third, the last fifty or more years have seen a focus on hermeneutics, drawing attention to the place of the interpreters and readers of Scripture. This in turn has set past interpreters in a new light and so fostered an understanding of the development and interaction of various forces in forging the doctrinal solutions needed at different stages. The turn to hermeneutics has been a by-product of the developments I have noted. This has been heightened by the emergence of postmodernism since around 1970.

Finally, the controversy between Rome, the Reformers, and the Anabaptists is still the same as in the sixteenth century. Despite agreements reached by the Lutheran World Federation and others with the Roman Catholic Church, as well as by representatives of Rome and disparate individual evangelicals—leaders answerable only to themselves—the foundational hermeneutical and theological issues are unchanged. There has been some movement, it is true.[53] However, the Reformation and the issues surrounding it are not over.

---

51. Henning Graf Reventlow, *The Authority of the Bible and the Rise of the Modern World* (Philadelphia: Fortress, 1984).

52. Wolfhart Pannenberg, *Jesus—God and Man*, trans. Lewis L. Wilkins (Philadelphia: Westminster, 1968); Pannenberg, *Systematic Theology*, trans. Geoffrey W. Bromiley, 3 vols. (Grand Rapids, MI: Eerdmans, 1991–1998).

53. See Anthony N. S. Lane, *Justification by Faith in Catholic-Protestant Dialogue: An Evangelical Assessment* (London: T&T Clark, 2002).

7.4.2   Roman Catholic Developments

At Vatican II, the Dogmatic Constitution on Divine Revelation (*Dei Verbum*) made some departures from previous practice but left the more substantive issues unaltered. After summarizing the doctrine of Scripture,[54] the document discusses the transmission of divine revelation. In order to perpetuate and transmit his revelation, Christ committed the task to the apostles to preach the gospel, by oral preaching and writing. To keep the gospel alive, they appointed bishops as their successors. The apostolic preaching is expressed in a special way in their writings and by a continuous succession of preachers. The apostles warn the faithful to hold on to what they learned, whether by word of mouth or by letter (2 Thess. 2:15). This tradition develops in the church by the Holy Spirit. There is a growth in the understanding of "the living presence of this tradition" through which the canon is known and the sacred writings are more fully understood.[55] Hence, there is a close connection between sacred tradition and sacred Scripture. Both flow from the same divine wellspring. "Consequently, it is not from sacred Scripture alone that the Church draws her certainty about everything which has been revealed. Therefore both sacred tradition and sacred Scripture are to be accepted and venerated with the same sense of devotion and reverence." Again, "sacred tradition and sacred Scripture form one sacred deposit of the word of God, which is committed to the Church."[56] Formally, there is no change in this matter from Trent or Vatican I.

Further, the task of authentically interpreting the Word of God, whether written or handed on, has been entrusted exclusively to the living teaching office of the church, whose authority is exercised in the name of Jesus Christ. This teaching office is not above the Word of God, but serves it.[57] Sacred Scripture and tradition are so joined together "that one cannot stand without the others, and that all together and each in its own way under the action of the one Holy Spirit contribute effectively to the salvation of souls."[58] Again, there is no change, although the statement can be taken in various ways and has engendered much debate.

---

54. Walter M. Abbott, *The Documents of Vatican II* (New York: Guild, 1966), 111–14.
55. Abbott, *Documents*, 116.
56. Abbott, *Documents*, 117.
57. Abbott, *Documents*, 117–18.
58. Abbott, *Documents*, 118.

In discussing sacred Scripture in the life of the church, the council forcefully encouraged the laity to read the Bible, in contrast to previous practice. Here there is very noticeable change. The document continues by affirming that the church has always venerated the divine Scriptures: "She has always regarded the Scriptures together with sacred tradition as the supreme rule of faith, and will ever do so." All the preaching of the church must be nourished and ruled by sacred Scripture. Moreover, easy access to sacred Scripture should be provided for all the faithful.[59] Suitable and correct translations are to be made, especially from the original texts. And if these are made in cooperation with the separated brethren, all Christians will be able to use them. The church also encourages the study of the fathers of both East and West, together with the liturgy. In pursuance of these goals, the church encourages its sons who are biblical scholars to continue energetically.[60] So, once again, "sacred theology rests on the written word of God, together with sacred tradition, as its primary and perpetual foundation."[61] The sacred Scriptures contain the Word of God and, because they are inspired, actually are the Word of God. It follows that ignorance of the Scriptures is ignorance of Christ.[62]

While it was promising to see how the reading of Scripture was so positively encouraged by Vatican II, the leveling of Scripture and tradition remains, together with the sole right of the magisterium over biblical interpretation. Ultimately the church as the sacramental bearer of grace is the de facto authority, the vehicle through which tradition and Scripture are channeled. As Pius IX said to Gregory II Yousef, the Greek Catholic patriarch of Antioch, "I am tradition!"[63]

7.4.3 *Scripture and Tradition in Orthodoxy*

For Orthodoxy, tradition means the whole teaching of the church, whether in church councils, the Bible, official dogma, or the liturgy. As Kallistos Ware puts it, tradition has a broad, comprehensive meaning:

> To an Orthodox Christian . . . it means the books of the Bible; it means the Creed; it means the decrees of the Ecumenical Councils and the writings of the Fathers; it means the Canons, the Service Books,

---

59. Abbott, *Documents*, 125.
60. Abbott, *Documents*, 126.
61. Abbott, *Documents*, 127.
62. Abbott, *Documents*, 127.
63. Olivier Clément, *You Are Peter* (New York: New City, 1997), 64–65.

the Holy Icons—in fact, the whole system of doctrine, Church government, worship, and art which Orthodoxy has articulated over the
ages. The Orthodox Christian of today sees himself as heir and guardian to a great inheritance received from the past, and he believes that
it is his duty to transmit this inheritance unimpaired to the future.[64]

In the West, Scripture and tradition tend to be seen as separable entities; Protestants view them as contrasting and in some way competing
with each other. For the Orthodox, there has never been a conflict. In
part, this is because authority has not been so dominant, as Orthodoxy
has not had the ecclesiastical hierarchy that Rome has. The great councils simply recognized the truth. No one bishop has had jurisdiction
beyond his own diocese, whereas in Rome the pope has authority over
the worldwide church, an authority he claims to have received from
Christ. The East has always considered Scripture to be part of the living
apostolic tradition. The liturgy and the writings of the fathers were the
basis for understanding the Bible.[65] As Lossky explains, tradition is not
merely the aggregate of the dogmas, rites, and institutions of the church.
It is dynamic and living, the revelation of the Holy Spirit in the church.
Dogma cannot be understood apart from spiritual experience. Doctrine
and experience go together, mutually conditioning one another.[66]

Yet, Orthodox theologians recognize that given this, Scripture has
a prime place within the living tradition. Stylianopoulos acknowledges
the superior (but not supreme) authority of Scripture, for "the very fact
of a biblical canon clearly implies recognition of the unique authority
of what is received as divine revelation and thus the superior authority of the Bible in the general tradition." So "it is essential therefore
to acknowledge the authority of Scripture for tradition."[67] As Thomas
Hopko writes:

> Once the Bible has been constituted as the scripture of the church, it
> becomes its main written authority within the church and not over
> or apart from it. Everything in the church is judged by the Bible.

---

64. Timothy Ware, *The Orthodox Church* (London: Penguin, 1969), 204.
65. John Meyendorff, *Byzantine Theology: Historical Trends and Doctrinal Themes* (New
York: Fordham University Press, 1979), 8.
66. Vladimir Lossky, *The Mystical Theology of the Eastern Church* (London: James Clarke,
1957), 236–37.
67. Theodore G. Stylianopoulos, *The New Testament: An Orthodox Perspective*, vol. 1, *Scripture, Tradition, Hermeneutics* (Brookline, MA: Holy Cross Orthodox Press, 1997), 47–55.

Nothing in the church may contradict it. Everything in the church must be Biblical; for the church, in order to be the church, must be wholly expressive of the Bible; or, more accurately, it must be wholly faithful to and expressive of that reality to which the Bible is itself the scriptural witness.[68]

Nevertheless, this is not the same as the Reformed position. For the Orthodox, according to Hopko, the Bible is the church's *main* written authority; it is not over the church but within it; and the church must reflect the reality to which the Bible bears witness. The Bible is part of the picture, a very significant part, but it is not the highest authority.

However, the Orthodox understanding of the place and context of the Bible raises some important points that can help clarify our own appreciation of the origins and authority of Scripture. I have argued that the biblical books imposed themselves on the church as canon. Does this mean that the Bible preceded the church, as some have argued, in contrast to the Orthodox idea that the church gave us the Bible? Is either of these proposals adequate?

Clearly, the church was produced by the Holy Spirit, who is also the ultimate author of the Bible. The church was born through the preaching of the Word. But who preached the Word? It was the apostles, beginning with Peter on the day of Pentecost. Peter was himself part of the church! So too the biblical books were composed by apostles and others, all part of the church. These books, as canon, were products, on the human level, of members of the church! In that sense, the church *did* produce the Bible. It is not the whole story, of course, but it is still part of the story. Again, to whom was the Bible given? To private individuals, to universities and scholars, or to the church?

There is a dynamic interplay here between the church and the Bible. The common notion that the Bible came into existence independently of, and prior to, the church is untenable. At the same time, the Orthodox tend to overstate their position as if the church created the Bible or approved it. The reality was that the Spirit formed the church, empowered the preaching of the gospel, and inspired Scripture. In turn, the church, formed and enlightened by the Holy Spirit, recognized the Scriptures that the same Spirit had inspired through the agency of its apostles and

---

68. Cited in Stylianopoulos, *New Testament*, 55–56.

leaders. The Holy Spirit is the source of both, originating *both* Scripture *and* the church.

We should not forget the central place the Bible has in the belief and worship of Orthodoxy. Ware points out that the Bible is the supreme expression of God's revelation to man. It is the church alone that can interpret the Bible with authority.[69] Reformed readers may be reassured by the following remarks of St. Peter of Damaskos (probably alive in the eleventh or early twelfth centuries): "There is no contradiction in Holy Scripture. . . . Every word of Scripture is beyond reproach. The appearance of contradiction is due to our ignorance. . . . We should attend to them [the words of Scripture] as they are." The person who searches for the meaning of Holy Scripture will not put forward his own opinion but will take as his teacher not the learning of the world but Scripture itself.[70] Protestants need to remember that the church, not the university or some scholarly society, is the custodian of Scripture.

The words of one of the leading Orthodox thinkers of the last century, Georges Florovsky, are of significance. An advocate of a rediscovery of the fathers in terms of not merely a repristination but a renewal of their witness to the catholic faith and its transfiguration of the human spirit, he states regarding the fathers' authority: "This was, however, secondary to the authority of the Scriptures and their reception in the tradition of the Church: it is as interpreters of the Scriptures that the Fathers possess what authority they have."[71]

7.5 Conclusion

Sola Scriptura, a post-Reformation slogan, was intended to assert that the Bible is the supreme authority in the church. As the Westminster Confession stated, Scripture is the supreme rule of faith and practice. In contrast, all church synods and councils may err and so are not to be made the rule of faith and practice, but are merely a help. In this way, it is the Bible that sits in judgment on the church; the church can never sit in judgment on the Word of God.

69. Ware, *Orthodox Church*, 205–7.
70. St. Nikodimos of the Holy Mountain, *The Philokalia*, trans. Kallistos Ware, G. E. H. Palmer, and Philip Sherrard (London: Faber and Faber, 1983), 3:144.
71. Andrew Louth, *Modern Orthodox Thinkers: From the Philokalia to the Present* (London: SPCK, 2015), 87.

However, the Bible was given by God to the church. It is to be read, preached, believed, and followed in the church's life and ministry. As a general guide to the varied levels of authority, with Scripture as the supreme court of appeal, the citation from Oliver Crisp in the introduction is as good a summary as I can find (see p. 34). The various books of the Bible were produced by prophets, apostles, and others who themselves were part of the church, as they were moved, consciously or unconsciously, by the Holy Spirit. There is an inseparable interplay between the revelation of God in Jesus Christ the Son—the head of the church—the words he enabled to be written in witness to this stupendous fact, and the ongoing direction and interpretation of this canon. This will be the subject of the next chapter.

> Was du ererbt von deinen Vätern hast,
> erwirb es, um es zu besitzen.
>
> What you have as heritage,
> take now as task;
> for thus you will make it your own!
>
> Goethe, *Faust*.[72]

Further Reading

Mathison, Keith A. *The Shape of Sola Scriptura*. Moscow, ID: Canon, 2001.
Newman, John Henry. *An Essay in the Development of Christian Doctrine*. Notre Dame, IN: University of Notre Dame Press, 1989.
Orr, James. *The Progress of Dogma*. Grand Rapids, MI: Eerdmans, 1901.

Study Questions

1. Discuss and evaluate what Jaroslav Pelikan means by the following: "Tradition is the living faith of the dead, traditionalism is the dead faith of the living."

2. Is it desirable, or even possible, to read the Bible entirely in isolation from the past teaching of the church?

3. To what extent should the historic teaching of the church function in our reading of Scripture and in our grappling with its implications?

---

72. Quoted in Pelikan, *Vindication of Tradition*, 82.

8

The Interpretation of Scripture

In this chapter we consider major lines of biblical interpretation in the history of the church. Some, while having certain merits, were scarred by glaring weaknesses. It is easy to spot deficiencies in contexts other than our own and to miss what may distort our own reading of the Bible. The focus of Scripture is Christ. The main methodological questions surrounded how far to interpret the Bible according to the literal sense, and what exactly is the literal sense. For centuries, Origen's allegorical methods were dominant, but not to the exclusion of other approaches. Aquinas brought a more rigorous paradigm to bear, paving the way for Calvin's concern to determine the mind of the original author. Even so, there were considerable differences between Calvin and Augustine on how to interpret the Old Testament and to what extent it refers to Christ. Recent developments in hermeneutics and the employment of tools such as speech-act theory have been helpful but have their own limitations. Whatever the methodology, the illumination of the Holy Spirit is needed in interpretation.

✠

We sought to do the composer's bidding. . . . In all our work we saw ourselves as servants of the composer.[1]

Both of us felt that lucid brevity constituted the particular value of an interpreter. Since it is almost his only task to unfold the mind of the

---

1. Norbert Brainin, commenting on the work of the Amadeus String Quartet, BBC2, September 5, 1987, following the disbandment of the Quartet after thirty-nine years, upon the death of Peter Schidlof, the violist. The members of the quartet, in their discussions on the interpretation of a work, aimed to allow the intention of the composer to disclose itself or, as Martin Lovett, the cellist, remarked, until "the truth" disclosed itself.

writer whom he has undertaken to expound, he misses the mark, or at least strays outside his limits, by the extent to which he leads his readers away from the meaning of his author.[2]

Biblical authority is an empty notion unless we know how to determine what the Bible means.[3]

It is important to distinguish between the doctrine of Scripture and the interpretation of Scripture. Genesis 1 is a good example; it teaches that God created the universe, bringing into existence all entities other than himself, with the pinnacle of creation being the human male and the human female, made in his image. He did this in six "days." That, in a nutshell, is what is said in the chapter. However, there have been a wide range of interpretations of what various aspects of Genesis 1 mean. I discuss these differing views in appendix 1. These questions relate to the *interpretation* of Scripture rather than to the doctrine of Scripture. Interpreters are influenced by their cultural and philosophical assumptions. Interpretations of this or that cannot possess the same authority as the text itself.

In this chapter we will consider major lines of interpretation in the history of the church. Some, while having certain merits, were beset with glaring weaknesses that overshadowed the good they might have achieved. It is easy to spot deficiencies in contexts other than our own. This raises the question of what impinges on our own reading of the Bible and thus distorts it.

8.1   Christ as the Focus of Scripture

Christ is the key to the relationship between the Old Testament and the New. Jesus affirmed that the Old Testament is directed to him, his sufferings and glory (Luke 24:25–27, 44–47); the prophets foretold the coming of the Christ but did not receive the full revelation (Matt. 13:17). Abraham saw Christ's day (John 8:56). The apostles and evangelists followed. Stephen, when asked by the Ethiopian about the meaning of Isaiah 53, preached Jesus (Acts 8:26–35). The letter to the Hebrews considers that the whole Old Testament comes to a head and is fulfilled

2. John Calvin, to Simon Grynaeus, in *Calvin's Commentaries: The Epistles of Paul the Apostle to the Romans and to the Thessalonians*, trans. Ross MacKenzie (Grand Rapids, MI: Eerdmans, 1973), 1; Calvin, *Commentarius in epistolam Pauli ad Romanos*, in CO2 (1999), 3.
3. James Packer, "Hermeneutics and Biblical Authority," *Them* 1 (1975): 3.

244 The Word of God

in Christ (Heb. 1:1–3). Peter says that the prophets prophesied of the New Testament times (1 Pet. 1:10–12). Paul similarly states that the Old Testament was written for our benefit (Rom. 15:4) and that the gospel was disclosed in advance to Abraham (Gal. 3:8).

From its earliest times (Gen. 3:15) the Old Testament had an eschatological outlook.[4] From this came the typological interpretation in the New Testament, which was common in the first centuries of the church. New Testament typology posits a correspondence between the Old Testament type and the New Testament antitype, with the Old Testament consisting of promise and the New Testament of fulfillment. Christ was foreshadowed in the Old, Christ is revealed in the New. Behind this was the context of sin, judgment, the covenant, and its promises of a deliverer. Christ is the organic center of Scripture, as Bavinck maintained.[5] However, typology as practiced in the early church was sometimes overdone.

God intends that Christ have the preeminence. The principal ministry of the Holy Spirit is to testify of Christ (John 14:18–20, 26; 15:26; 16:7–15). The apostles were commissioned by Christ to teach, and their teaching was to be tantamount to his (John 16:12–15) as the Spirit accompanied their witness to him. Moreover, the Father determined that the Son should have the preeminence (Phil. 2:9–11; Col. 1:15–20). It is the concerted purpose of the indivisible Trinity that God should be glorified in Christ, the incarnate Son; this is the Spirit's work and the Father's glory. In keeping with the undivided purpose of the Trinity, the Word of God written, among the many things to which it refers, testifies above all concerning the sufferings and glory of Christ.

The relationship between Scripture and proclamation. I have suggested that the perichoretic interpenetration of the revealed Word, the Word written, and the Word proclaimed points to an integrated grasp of the relationship between Christ, the Bible, and preaching.[6] Christ is the central theme of Scripture and thus of preaching. Scripture testifies of Christ and is the basis of preaching. Preaching itself must be grounded on Scripture and testify of Christ. The three are integrally and inseparably interconnected.

---

4. John V. Fesko, *Last Things First: Unlocking Genesis 1–3 with the Christ of Eschatology* (Fearn: Mentor, 2007).
5. James Eglinton, *Trinity and Organism: Towards a New Reading of Herman Bavinck's Organic Motif* (London: Bloomsbury, 2012), 171.
6. Barth, *CD*, I/1:88–124, esp. 121.

Preaching shares in the Word of God in a derivative sense. Calvin regards preaching as at the heart of the church's life. He states that "doctrine is the mother from whom God generates us [*Doctrina enim mater est, ex qua nos Deus generat*]."[7] Again, in the *Institutes* he affirms that "the saving doctrine of Christ is the soul of the church [*salvifica Christi doctrina anima est Ecclesiae*]." The context is about preaching; a few lines later he mentions "the preaching of doctrine [*ad doctrinae praedicationem*]."[8]

Reformed theology has consistently maintained that preaching and the sacraments together are the outward means God uses to bring his people to salvation (WSC, 8; WLC, 154). Yet the Word has priority over the sacraments; the sacraments are nothing without it (WCF, 27.3; WLC, 169).[9] As Barth says of the Reformed, "They could not and would not assign to the sacrament the place which falls to preaching," for "the former must exist for the sake of the latter, and therefore the sacrament for the sake of preaching, not *vice-versa*."[10] A number of biblical passages support this claim.

In Romans 10:14, where Paul insists on the urgency of preachers being sent to his compatriots, the Jews, the subjective genitive is to be preferred, yielding the clause "how are they to believe him whom they have not heard?" (my trans.). In short, Christ is heard in the preaching of the gospel.[11] When the Word is truly preached, Christ is present.[12] That Paul refers to the preacher as sent indicates the ministerial nature of preaching; the preacher is subservient to the Word and is commissioned by the church.[13]

---

7. John Calvin, *Commentarii in Pauli epistolas ad Galatas, ad Ephesios, ad Philippenses, ad Colossenses*. Ioannis Calvini opera exegetica (Geneva: Droz, 1992), 108; Calvin, *Calvin's Commentaries: The Epistles of Paul to the Galatians, Ephesians, Philippians, and Colossians*, trans. T. H. L. Parker (Grand Rapids, MI: Eerdmans, 1965), 85.

8. Calvin, *OS*, 5:212; Calvin, *Institutes*, 4.12.1.

9. See also "The Directory for the Publick Worship of God" (1645), in *The Confession of Faith, the Larger and Shorter Catechisms with the Scripture Proofs at Large, Together with The Sum of Saving Knowledge* (Applecross, Ross-shire: Publications Committee of the Free Presbyterian Church of Scotland, 1970), 383, 385.

10. Barth, *CD*, I/1:70.

11. John Murray, *The Epistle to the Romans* (Grand Rapids, MI: Eerdmans, 1965), 2:58; C. E. B. Cranfield, *A Critical and Exegetical Commentary on the Epistle to the Romans*, 2 vols. International Critical Commentary (Edinburgh: T&T Clark, 1975), 2:533–34; James D. G. Dunn, *Romans 9–16*. Word Biblical Commentary 38B (Dallas: Word, 1988), 620; Leon Morris, *The Epistle to the Romans* (Grand Rapids. MI: Eerdmans, 1988), 389–90. In this and the following paragraph, see Robert Letham, "The Authority of Preaching," *Baptist Reformation Review* 3, no. 4 (1974): 21–29.

12. Hughes Oliphant Old, *The Reading and Preaching of the Scriptures in the Worship of the Christian Church*, vol. 1, *The Biblical Period* (Grand Rapids, MI: Eerdmans, 1998), 186–87.

13. Old, *Reading and Preaching*, 1:184.

In Ephesians 2:17, Christ is said to have preached peace to the Gentiles at Ephesus: "He came and preached peace to you who were far off and peace to those who were near." Jesus never visited Ephesus; Paul refers to his own preaching in founding the church. In Paul's preaching, Christ himself preaches.

In Luke 10:16, Jesus sends the apostles to preach and heal, saying, "The one who hears you hears me, and the one who rejects you rejects me, and the one who rejects me rejects him who sent me." The apostles are Jesus's special representatives in their preaching ministry; their preaching is his own, their words are his. Acceptance or rejection of their words is the acceptance or rejection of Jesus. The intrinsic quality of their preaching is not in view—their status depends on their having been commissioned by Jesus.

In John 5:25 the voice of the Son of God raises the dead. This means spiritual resurrection in the present rather than the physical resurrection in the future mentioned in verses 28–29. Already present ("and now is"), it comes through hearing the voice of the Son of God, or hearing the word of Christ and believing (v. 24).

Finally, Paul states in 2 Corinthians 5:19–20 that God makes his appeal through us. Paul and all true preachers are ambassadors of Christ, thus possessing the authority of the one they represent. Behind this is the figure of the שליח,[14] a personal emissary, whom the Talmud considered to carry the authority of the one who sent him.[15] In line with this, Calvin regarded preaching as both a human and a divine activity, the Holy Spirit working sovereignly through the words of the preacher.[16] Calvin states that "God himself appears in our midst, and, as author of this order, would have men recognize him as present in his institution."[17]

Moreover, the Westminster Assembly viewed the Bible not in isolation but integrally bound up with the whole of God's revelation. Thus, when the object of saving faith (WCF, 14.2) is presented as whatsoever God has revealed in his Word *and* Christ, whom we receive and rest on for salvation, the confession does not intend some dualistic sense, as if

---

14. *shaliyahk.*
15. *TDNT,* 1:414–20.
16. See the discussion by John H. Leith, "Calvin's Doctrine of the Proclamation of the Word and Its Significance for Us Today," in *John Calvin and the Church: A Prism of Reform,* ed. Timothy George (Louisville: Westminster John Knox, 1990), 210–12.
17. Calvin, *Institutes,* 4.1.5.

Christ and the Bible were competing for our attention. For the Assembly, Scripture is subordinate to Christ as the means by which God draws us to himself in Christ. As Muller indicates, "There is a continuity between the Reformation and Protestant orthodox language of Word that does not look in the direction of the neo-orthodox usage."[18] In fact, Muller concludes, "The orthodox tread a fine doctrinal balance in their distinction between the essential, the unwritten and written, the external and internal Word."[19]

8.2   Scripture as Self-Interpreting

The WCF, 1.9, states, "The infallible rule of interpretation of Scripture is the Scripture itself: and therefore, when there is a question about the true and full sense of Scripture (which is not manifold, but one), it must be searched and known by other places that speak more clearly."

The meaning of much of Scripture is not immediately apparent; this requires thought and interpretation. Meaning is to be sought in Scripture's overall teaching. The basis for this assertion of Scripture as self-interpreting is that the Bible was immediately inspired by God. Scripture is authoritative on all on which it pronounces. Therefore, it is authoritative over its own interpretation. If some other principle than Scripture were the key to its interpretation, it would not be the ultimate authority.

An assumption here is the unity, as well as diversity, of Scripture. There is a common theme holding the various parts together, which justifies and requires interpreting it as a whole. Thus, "the true and full sense of any Scripture" is one. This may also be a sideswipe against the threefold interpretive model of Origen, which we will consider shortly. Questions about the meaning of any particular Scripture are to be sought from the whole. Difficult passages are to be understood in the light of clearer ones.[20]

Moreover, Scripture's voice is not confined to the precise letter of the text but also includes its sense, what may be deduced from the text

---

18. Muller, *PRRD*, 2:181.
19. Muller, *PRRD*, 2:183.
20. In view of recent discussions in hermeneutics, the reader may ask where the interpreter fits into the picture. It is a matter of much debate as to how far meaning in a text is to be sought in the intention of the author, the text itself, or the contribution of the reader and whether the reader shapes the meaning in decisive fashion. To impose these discussions on the WCF would be anachronistic, for these were not matters of debate at that time.

(WCF, 1.6). This mandates interpretation. Ever since the time of Athanasius and Basil it had been recognized that doctrine was founded not by appeal to the letter of this or that text but by understanding the overall sense of Scripture, an approach pioneered by Origen.[21] Interpretation was a key issue before, during, and after the Reformation.[22]

The Bible can be understood not in isolation but only in reference to itself. Extrabiblical sources are necessary to interpret it. Historical, geographical, political, and linguistic contexts are indispensable. I argued in chapter 1 that general revelation is necessary for us to begin to grasp special revelation. However, there is an opposite danger of conceding to such sources a controlling, paradigmatic influence. I will discuss two such examples in later chapters.

Clearly, the historical context is vital, but when faced with a difficult passage, we are to see it in the light of clearer ones. This rules out any obsession with eschatology in Daniel 9, 2 Thessalonians 2, and Revelation 20. These texts are at best abstruse. For us to know what Paul meant by "the man of sin," "the apostasy," and so forth in 2 Thessalonians, we would need to have been privy to his oral teaching in the three weeks he was present there after planting the church (2 Thess. 2:5). Rather, clearer didactic passages should inform the more difficult ones.

In order to understand any biblical passage, we must grasp the literary genre. The Bible includes long stretches of historical narrative, wisdom literature, poetry, letters, and apocalyptic. Each passage needs to be interpreted in accordance with its nature and how it would have been understood in the time of its original composition. Poetic and evocative utterances are to be seen in a different light than factual reports. The book of Proverbs, with wise sayings to guide everyday life, is not to be equated with the Law. Apocalyptic, with vivid and dramatic imagery often relating to divine judgment, cannot be understood in a literal manner. In short, the Bible is a rich and varied collection of documents; while this sounds trite and self-evident, many mistakes result from failure to recognize diverse genres.

21. Origen, *The Philocalia of Origen: A Compilation of Selected Passages from Origen's Works Made by St. Gregory of Nazianzus and St. Basil of Caesarea*, trans. G. Lewis (Edinburgh: T&T Clark, 1911), 2:3; Origène, *Philocalie, 1–20 sur les Écritures: Introduction, texte, traduction et notes par Marguerite Harl*, Sources Chrétiennes 302 (Paris: Les Éditions du Cerf, 1983), 447–57; Peter W. Martens, *Origen and Scripture: The Contours of the Exegetical Life* (Oxford: Oxford University Press, 2012), 61–62.
22. Muller, *PRRD*, 2:465–543.

8.3   Word and Spirit

The Word and the Holy Spirit are coordinate at every point in salvation: the Spirit who authored Scripture employs the Word to effect his saving purposes. The Word and Spirit effectually reveal God (WLC, 2). God effectually calls by his Word and Spirit (WCF, 10.1, 4; WLC, 2, 43), as the ministry of the Word is effectual and saving faith is produced through the Spirit (WCF, 14.1; WLC, 67, 72, 155). In turn, Christ governs the hearts of his elect by his Word and Spirit (WCF, 8.8). Sanctification is by the Holy Spirit through the Word (WCF, 13.1). Good works are such as are commanded by the Word (WCF, 16.1), and the ability to do them comes wholly from the Spirit of Christ (WCF, 16.3).

The Word of God, committed to writing in Holy Scripture, is the source of our knowledge of God, together with the Spirit, who makes effectual God's salvation. Scripture reveals what is pleasing to God. It is determinative for worship and Christian living. It provides the epistemological basis of the Christian faith. In it are made known the covenant of grace, the mediation of Christ, the way of salvation.

8.4   The History of Biblical Interpretation

8.4.1   The Fathers[23]

Typology. In typology, certain people or things in the Old Testament have definite parallels with corresponding people or things in the New Testament, in the fulfillment of God's covenantal purposes in Christ. Typology rests on the unity of redemptive history, the flow in the history of salvation from promise to fulfillment. Typology is particularly evident in Hebrews. It requires a considerable degree of correspondence between the Old Testament type and its fulfillment in the New Testament. Hence, the animal sacrifices are types of Christ to the extent that they were sacrificial victims, slain in connection with atonement for sins, offered on behalf of the people of Israel. So Jesus was killed on behalf of those he represented.

---

23. See Bertrand de Margerie, SJ, *An Introduction to the History of Exegesis*, 3 vols. (Petersham, MA: Bede, 1991–1995); Manlio Simonetti, *Biblical Interpretation in the Early Church: An Historical Introduction to Patristic Exegesis*, trans. John A. Hughes (Edinburgh: T&T Clark, 1994); Henri de Lubac, SJ, *Medieval Exegesis*, trans. Mark Sebanc, 3 vols. (repr., Grand Rapids, MI: Eerdmans, 1998–2009); John J. O'Keefe and R. R. Reno, *Sanctified Vision: An Introduction to Early Christian Interpretation of the Bible* (Baltimore: Johns Hopkins University Press, 2005); Stephen Westerholm and Martin Westerholm, *Reading Sacred Scripture: Voices from the History of Biblical Interpretation* (Grand Rapids, MI: Eerdmans, 2016).

Justin Martyr, in his *Dialogue with Trypho the Jew*, trawls through the Old Testament, arguing from copious places that the ultimate reference is to Christ. Jesus fulfills the Law and the Prophets.[24] In this, Justin builds on the letter to the Hebrews. There the law, including the priesthood, the sacrifices, and the covenant, all came to its fullest expression in Christ, who is both Priest and victim, and who embodies in himself the covenant made by Yahweh with Abraham and later with Israel. This method was followed across the board by Patristic authors, including Origen.[25] Its application in particular cases may have been valid or not; any method is open to abuse. The fact that the New Testament uses typology under such constraints does not give a carte blanche to adopt such procedures ourselves.

However, it is clear that the fathers believed that God had revealed himself in Scripture, and that consequently the Bible has a unity to it that enables us to see connections throughout. In contrast, Fairbairn comments:

> Modern exegesis as a whole, with its almost fanatical commitment to each individual text and its exhaustive probing of all possible backgrounds to that text, is wedded to a view of reality in which the Bible is not the self-revelation of God, is not trustworthy, and is definitely not to be seen as a unity. To put it another way, the painful search for "objective" methods of exegesis in the modern world may actually be an attempt to discover a foundation for truth outside of the Bible itself, since the theological conviction that God has revealed himself to humanity in the words of Scripture is deemed to be either false or irrelevant.[26]

Allegory. Origen, in *On First Principles*, book 4, is the most notable, and definitely the most influential, exponent of allegory.[27] He defined the exegetical agenda for centuries, whether those who came afterward were favorable or opposed. His impact lingers today on the popular level. Though he had some positive impact, the general consensus is that his methods opened the door to arbitrary and uncontrolled exegesis.

---

24. Justin, *Dialogue with Trypho the Jew* 13–139 (ANF, 1:200–269).
25. Origen, *On First Principles* 4.1.9 (ANF, 4:357); Martens, *Origen and Scripture*, 156–60, 216–21.
26. Donald Fairbairn, "Patristic Exegesis and Theology: The Cart and the Horse," *WTJ* 69 (2007): 1–19, quoting 13.
27. For Origen as a biblical interpreter, see R. P. C. Hanson, *Allegory and Event: A Study of the Sources and Significance of Origen's Interpretation of Scripture* (1959; repr., Louisville: Westminster John Knox, 2002); Martens, *Origen and Scripture*.

At root, Origen argued that the Bible is to be interpreted in a three-fold method, based on Proverbs 22:20–21 (LXX), where the text reads καὶ σὺ δὲ ἀπόγραψαι αὐτὰ σεαυτῷ τρισσῶς: "and you portray them in a threefold manner." The impetus for Origen's interpretative principles was apparent moral difficulties and impossibilities in the Old Testament. Jewish objections to the Christian reading of the Old Testament were a problem owing to literal interpretation by the rabbis. Not seeing the wolf feeding with the lamb or the lion eating straw like the ox, they assumed the Messiah had not yet come. Moreover, they continued to adhere to a literal observance of the Mosaic ceremonial law. In turn, the pagans had their own objections.[28] According to Origen, the problem was that both groups failed to understand Scripture according to its spiritual meaning.[29] A literal reading of the text would lead to absurdities. The way to understand the Bible, he wrote, is by following the rule established by Solomon in Proverbs—"portray them in a threefold manner."

> The individual ought, then, to portray the ideas of holy Scripture in a threefold manner . . . in order that the simple man may be edified by the "flesh," as it were, of the Scripture, for so we name the obvious sense; while he who has ascended a certain way (may be edified) by the "soul." . . . The perfect man again . . . (may receive edification) from the spiritual law, which has a shadow of the good things to come. For as man consists of body, and soul, and spirit, so in the same way does Scripture.[30]

This method is based on a trichotomic view of the human being as consisting of body, soul, and spirit. Behind this lay a dualistic view of the superiority of the spiritual over matter. The three levels of interpretation are related to stages in the experience and ability of believers. "The first 'sense' . . . is profitable in this respect, that it is capable of imparting edification, is testified by the multitudes of genuine and simple believers; while of that interpretation which is referred back to the 'soul' there is an illustration in Paul's [use of Deut. 25:4 in 1 Cor. 9:9]." These

---

28. Origen, *On First Principles* 4.1.8 (*ANF*, 4:356. References are to the translation from the Greek text.

29. Origen, *On First Principles* 4.1.9 (*ANF*, 4:357–58); Origen, *Against Celsus* 5.60 (*ANF*, 4:569); Martens, *Origen and Scripture*, 135–56.

30. Origen, *On First Principles* 4.1.11 (*ANF*, 4:359).

senses edify those unable to understand profounder meanings.[31] "But the interpretation is 'spiritual,' when one is able to show of what heavenly things the Jews 'according to the flesh' served as an example and a shadow, and of what future blessings the law contains a shadow."[32] This sounds to our ears elitist. However, it reflects an age where copying the Scriptures was time-consuming and expensive, so that very few had their own editions, and the vast majority consequently relied on portions of the Bible in the liturgy and exposition of Scripture in church services.[33]

The object of the Spirit was to convey "ineffable mysteries" concerning humans ("those souls that make use of bodies"). Primary are those doctrines about God and his only-begotten Son.[34] A second object, for the sake of those "unable to endure the fatigue of investigating matters so important," was "to conceal the doctrine . . . in expressions containing a narrative which conveyed an announcement regarding the things of the visible creation . . . and other histories relating the acts of just men and the sins occasionally committed." This was capable of "improving the multitude, according to their capacity."[35] To this end, "the word of God has arranged that certain stumbling-blocks . . . offences . . . and impossibilities, should be introduced into the midst of the law and the history" so that we would not be led astray from seeking the spiritual meaning by the attractiveness of the language. This concealed the deeper meaning from the multitude. Consequently, Scripture introduced "some event that did not take place, sometimes what could not have happened; sometimes what could, but did not. And sometimes a few words are interpolated which are not true in their literal acceptation." This is so that the more skillful may give themselves to the toil of investigation.[36] Examples are the days of creation in Genesis 1—it is impossible to take these literally. The events of Genesis 1–4 are undoubtedly figurative, as is the temptation narrative in the Gospels.[37] In the histories, "circumstances that did not occur are inserted."[38] Origen cites numerous examples from the Mosaic legislation and the Gospels.[39] However, the historical account

31. Origen, *On First Principles* 4.1.12 (ANF, 4:360–61).
32. Origen, *On First Principles* 4.1.13 (ANF, 4:361).
33. Martens, *Origen and Scripture*, 25–28.
34. Origen, *On First Principles* 4.1.14 (ANF, 4:362).
35. Origen, *On First Principles* 4.1.14 (ANF, 4:363).
36. Origen, *On First Principles* 4.1.15 (ANF, 4:364).
37. Origen, *On First Principles* 4.1.16 (ANF, 4:365).
38. Origen, *On First Principles* 4.1.16 (ANF, 4:365–66).
39. Origen, *On First Principles* 4.1.17–18 (ANF, 4:366–67).

is far more often true, keeping passages with a purely spiritual meaning in a clear minority.[40] "Therefore the exact reader must, in obedience to the Saviour's injunction to 'search the Scriptures,' carefully ascertain how far the literal meaning is true, and how far impossible."[41] In short, many passages in the Bible are symbols of something else.[42]

Overall, Origen believes "it must be our object to grasp the whole meaning," relating the literal meaning to the spiritual. "For . . . our opinion is that the whole of it has a 'spiritual,' but not the whole a 'bodily' meaning, because the bodily meaning is in many places proved to be impossible."[43] Origen did not wish to remove the historical sense. He spent much time in Palestine investigating historical sites. He produced the *Hexapla*, a monumental compilation of biblical texts and translations. But he felt there were limitations to it and, lacking the equipment to deal with those issues, he appealed to a higher level. All Scripture has a spiritual meaning, but not all has a bodily sense.

The method implies that there is a spiritual elite who alone have access to the mysteries. On the other hand, our own egalitarian age may have blinded us to the reality that there are a range of abilities. The Bible recognizes this (Heb. 6:1–4; 2 Pet. 3:16; 1 John 2:12–14).

The method often gave rise to speculative exegesis that bore no relation to the text. This is particularly noteworthy in Origen's *Homily on Numbers 33*. The text records the place names of the various stopping points of the Israelites as they journeyed through the wilderness. Origen understands the names to refer to stages in spiritual experience. For instance, *Rameses* means "agitation of the worm," denoting disorder and corruption; and from there the next stop was *Succuth*, meaning "tabernacles," so signifying sojourning, readiness for battle.[44] Hanson suggests that these methods reduce the significance of history, rendering it a parable for the soul to learn eternal truths.[45] However, to what extent can we recognize the cultural influences on our own biblical

---

40. Origen, *On First Principles* 4.1.19 (ANF, 4:368).
41. Origen, *On First Principles* 4.1.19 (ANF, 4:369).
42. Origen, *Homilies on Numbers*, trans. Thomas P. Scheck, ed. Christopher A. Hall, Ancient Christian Texts (Downers Grove, IL: IVP Academic, 2009), 168–83; Origen, *On First Principles* 4.2.2; Origen, *The Commentary of Origen on S. John's Gospel: The Text Revised with a Critical Introduction and Indices*, ed. A. E. Brooke (Cambridge: Cambridge University Press, 1896), 1–2; Martens, *Origen and Scripture*, 64, 90–92.
43. Origen, *On First Principles* 4.1.20 (ANF, 4:369).
44. Origen, *Homily on Numbers* 27.9.1, in Scheck, *Homilies on Numbers*, 176.
45. Hanson, *Allegory and Event*, 364–65.

interpretation? At least we can say that Origen ultimately sought a Christocentric reading. Moreover, the Bible itself adopts something like allegory on occasions,[46] although, again, that does not justify our following in Origen's footsteps.

Like other fathers, such as Gregory of Nazianzus and Augustine, Origen insists that piety and discipleship are necessary in order to interpret Scripture aright.[47] He reflects Jesus's words "If anyone is willing to do [the Father's] will, he shall know whether my teaching is from God or from myself" (John 7:17, my trans.). Genuine piety trumps *detached* academic study of the kind that imagines the Bible to be just another book and thus subject to the kind of criticism whereby the scholar acts as arbiter over the text.

Origen's interpretative principles impacted the church for centuries and still find echoes today. Henri de Lubac notes a wide range of such perspectives. Discussing the law in Deuteronomy 21:10–13 that enables a Hebrew soldier battling in a far country to capture a beautiful woman, bring her home, make her shave her head, pare her nails, change her clothes, and become his wife, de Lubac notes Origen's comments:

> I too have often gone forth to war . . . and I have found among my spoils a beautiful woman. . . . If, therefore, we read wise and knowledgeable words in one of them, we must purify them, we must remove and cut away everything in this knowledge that is deadly and vain. . . . Thus we shall make her our wife. . . . If we find a beautiful woman in the camp of our adversary, that is to say, some rational discipline, in that case we shall purify her.[48]

De Lubac also cites a later writer, Sidonius Apollinaris, who praises the work of Faustus of Riez:

> You have joined a beautiful woman to yourself, my lord bishop. . . . While you were yet young, you caught sight of her amid the enemy troops, and loving her as you did in the battle-line of the opposing

---

46. For instance, in Ezekiel 40–48; in Paul's application of Deut. 25:4 in 1 Cor. 9:9–10 and 1 Tim. 5:17–18; of circumcision in Rom. 2:28–29; in his comparison of marriage to the union of Christ and the church in Eph. 5:31–32; and in his comparisons of the crossing of the Red Sea to baptism and of water from the rock to Christ in 1 Cor. 10:3–4, to say nothing of Gal. 4:21–31. See Martens, *Origen and Scripture*, 158.

47. See Gregory of Nazianzus, *Oration 27* 1–3 (NPNF², 7:284–85); Augustine, *On Christian Doctrine* 27.59–60, 30.63 (NPNF¹, 2:595–97); Martens, *Origen and Scripture*.

48. De Lubac, *Medieval Exegesis*, 1:213.

forces, you were not put off by the warriors who stood in your way, but you snatched her away with the powerful, conquering arm of desire. Philosophy was violently removed from the number of the sacrilegious arts. The hair of unnecessary religion was shorn, together with the eyebrows of secular knowledge. . . . Now she has joined her cleansed members with yours in a mystic embrace. . . . She has been the inseparable companion by your side. . . . She has been your partner in the Athenaeum and at the monastery. In your company, she rejects worldly disciplines, while proclaiming heavenly ones. Once you are joined in marriage to the one who urged you on and gave you that impetus, you will have the impression that Plato's Academy is in the service of the Church and that you are philosophizing more nobly.[49]

Others rejected these ideas. Basil the Great railed against allegory and argued for the literal sense. In his *Hexaemeron*, a series of sermons on Genesis 1, he says:

I know the laws of allegory, though less by myself than from the works of others. There are those truly, who do not admit the common sense of the Scriptures, for whom water is not water, but some other nature, who see in a plant, in a fish, what their fancy wishes, who change the nature of reptiles and of wild beasts to suit their allegories, like the interpreter of dreams who explain visions in sleep to make them serve their own ends. For me grass is grass; plant, fish, wild beast, domestic animal, I take all in the literal sense. "For I am not ashamed of the gospel."[50]

While we may look askance at some of the exegesis of Origen and those influenced by him, nevertheless he accomplished two significant things. First, he saved the Old Testament for the church in the face of its cultured despisers, showing that it had an ongoing meaning.[51] Second, he pointed to the richness and depth of Scripture, that it is not to be reduced to a monochrome level, for it is pregnant with meaning at every point. These were no mean achievements.

In stark contrast to Origen, and close to Basil's approach, Chrysostom, in his homilies, followed a phrase-by-phrase exegesis, with very direct and uninhibited moral exhortations, which eventually proved his

---

49. Cited in de Lubac, *Medieval Exegesis*, 1:215–16.
50. Basil of Caesarea, *The Hexaemeron* 9.1 (NPNF[2], 8:101).
51. Martens, *Origen and Scripture*, 216–21.

undoing when he fell foul of the empress Eudoxia. He was a preacher more than anything else.[52]

These differences gave rise to the claim that there were two broad schools of interpretation in the early centuries. The Alexandrian school was said to be prone to allegorizing, whereas the school of Antioch adopted literal exegesis and was the forerunner of more modern methods. However, recently this model has been undermined. Allegory was a common practice that cannot be rooted in any one location, and Alexandrians also interpreted the Bible in a plain and straightforward way. In fact, exegesis was driven by theology, and those held to be exemplars of the Antiochene school—Diodore, Theodore, and Nestorius—were condemned by the church as heretics. Most Patristic scholars have abandoned the paradigm.[53]

Prosopological interpretation. Matthew Bates has recently argued that person-based interpretation of the Old Testament by the New Testament and early Christian exegetes was instrumental in preparing the way for the formulation of the doctrine of the Trinity.[54] He makes a convincing case that it was a far more widespread interpretative strategy than typology and was probably used by Jesus himself, as well as the apostles. It regarded certain discourses in the Old Testament as dialogues between the persons of the Trinity. Hence, in Psalm 110:1, David reports a setting in which God addresses "my Lord," the Christ. Mark and other Synoptic writers relate how Jesus deduced "via scriptural exegesis that God (*the Father*) via a script authored by the *Holy Spirit* had spoken directly to him after the dawn of time about his origin before time began."[55] In this way the prophets were on occasions swept up to hear intra-Trinitarian discourse referring to events that were to occur at a later date. In turn, the incarnate Son would enact these events performatively in the course of his life and ministry.

This interpretative method went beyond typology even as it differed from it. Whereas typology required a correspondence between the Old and New Testament entities, here there is a major difference, for proso-

---

52. See the wide selection of homilies in *NPNF*[1], vols. 9–14; J. N. D. Kelly, *Golden Mouth: The Story of John Chrysostom—Ascetic, Preacher, Bishop* (Grand Rapids, MI: Baker, 1995), 55–71.

53. Fairbairn, "Patristic Exegesis," 14–15.

54. Matthew W. Bates, *The Birth of the Trinity: Jesus, God, and Spirit in New Testament and Early Christian Interpretations of the Old Testament* (Oxford: Oxford University Press, 2015).

55. Bates, *Birth*, 44–62; here 62.

pological meaning demands that the discourse cannot refer to the Old Testament prophet or any mere mortal. Often the identity of the referent in the passage is a puzzle if taken to be a human. It can only refer to divine persons; indeed, it does not *refer* to them, nor is it simply *about* them, for the divine persons are themselves the actors in the drama. To appreciate this, we must recognize the widest context of Scripture, including the sovereignty of God, his transcendence over time, and his purposes in revelation and redemption. Consequently, the Son is in conversation with the Father about later events in human history in his incarnate life that are yet to happen from the perspective of the prophet; in the New Testament he or the apostles recount these discourses as referring to him.

These proposals have been called "stunningly important," "a compelling game changer" (Joel Green), "an important contribution" (Larry Hurtado), "a stream of early Trinitarian thinking that has all too often been forgotten" (Lewis Ayres), "bold and erudite" (Matthew Levering).[56] Bates is aware of the dangers of using such a method ourselves and provides some clear guidelines as controls to keep it within bounds. It was used when the natural meaning could not apply to the human author. Bates contends that it is a valid mode of interpretation, casting light on the Trinitarian relations that go beyond generation and procession, a method he deems to have been well-nigh essential to the emergence of the doctrine of the Trinity, greatly facilitating the church's recognition of the personal nature of God. Moreover, this method sheds light on the meaning of the literal sense of Scripture, for it attests that the widest theological context should be taken into consideration.

Augustine. Augustine, in *De doctrina Christiana*, discusses the interpretation of signs. Difficulties in understanding Scripture arise from unknown or ambiguous signs. We can remove the unknown element by learning the original languages and attending to the context.[57] In figurative language we need to know about things as much as words, scientific knowledge being particularly valuable. Indeed, anything valid in pagan science and philosophy can be useful in interpreting Scripture.[58] On whether something is to be taken literally or figuratively, Augustine says:

---

56. Bates, *Birth*, back cover.
57. Augustine, *On Christian Doctrine* 2.11.16 (NPNF[1], 2:540).
58. Augustine, *On Christian Doctrine* 2.12.17–2.42.65 (NPNF[1], 2:546–55).

> Whatever there is in the word of God that cannot, when taken literally, be referred either to purity of life or soundness of doctrine, you may set down as figurative. Purity of life has reference to the love of God and one's neighbour; soundness of doctrine to the knowledge of God and one's neighbour.[59]

Love for God and one's neighbor is the fulfillment of Scripture. So a reading that promotes love is not wrong even if it is technically faulty.[60]

> Whoever takes another meaning out of Scripture than the writer intended, goes astray, but not through any falsehood in Scripture. Nevertheless . . . if his mistaken interpretation tends to build up love, which is the end of the commandment, he goes astray in much the same way as a man who by mistake quits the high road, but yet reaches through the fields the same place to which the road leads. He is to be corrected, however, and to be shown how much better it is not to quit the straight road, lest, if he get into a habit of going astray, he may sometimes take cross roads, or even go in the wrong direction altogether.[61]

Nevertheless, one can end up with readings that cannot be harmonized properly with the text, and so one's confidence in the text may be eroded, faith may falter, and love may grow cold.[62] Consequently, the interpreter of Scripture requires faith, hope, and love.[63] Ultimately, the correct interpretation will point to Christ and promote love; this is more important than whether the particular text has been exegeted correctly, although that too is needed.

From this, Augustine can say that statements representing God as severe are intended to pull down the dominion of lust.[64] For figurative expressions we are to arrive at an interpretation "that tends to establish . . . love." If a literal reading promotes love, the text should be read literally.[65] If a command prohibits a sin and promotes prudence, it is to be understood literally, whereas if it seems to encourage a crime and prohibits prudence, it is to be taken figuratively.[66] In general, words should

59. Augustine, *On Christian Doctrine* 3.10.14 (NPNF[1], 2:560–61).
60. Augustine, *On Christian Doctrine* 1.35.39 (NPNF[1], 2:532–33).
61. Augustine, *On Christian Doctrine* 1.36.41 (NPNF[1], 2:533).
62. Augustine, *On Christian Doctrine* 1.37.42 (NPNF[1], 2:533).
63. Augustine, *On Christian Doctrine* 1.38.42–1.40.44 (NPNF[1], 2:533–34).
64. Augustine, *On Christian Doctrine* 3.11.17 (NPNF[1], 2:561).
65. Augustine, *On Christian Doctrine* 3.15.23 (NPNF[1], 2:563).
66. Augustine, *On Christian Doctrine* 3.16.24 (NPNF[1], 2:563).

be understood in context, with obscure passages interpreted by clearer ones.[67] Where the meaning of a passage is ambiguous, any interpretation in harmony with sound doctrine is acceptable; it is safer to interpret it with reference to another biblical passage than by reason.[68]

While the idea that Augustine was governed by Neoplatonism has been undermined in recent years,[69] he used elements of it for his own purposes.[70] He shows clear influence at times from the Origenist line of thought, seen in his treatment of Genesis 1.[71] However, compared with Origen and the allegorists, Augustine was far more careful. He was predominantly Christological, showing perhaps more influence from typology.

On the Psalms, Augustine generally goes straight to Christ. On Psalm 22 he writes of the inscription, "For his own resurrection, the Lord Jesus Christ himself speaketh." What follows, Augustine says, "is spoken in the person of the crucified."[72] Psalm 47 is about the crucifixion and ascension of Christ. On verse 5, "God has gone up with a shout," he states that "even he, our God, the Lord Christ, is gone up with jubilation."[73] Psalm 85, with the inscription "A Psalm for the end, to the sons of Core," elicits from Augustine this response: "Let us understand no other end than that of which the Apostle speaks: for, 'Christ is the end of the law.'"[74] While he had a strong sense of the centrality of Christ, here and elsewhere he pays scant attention to the historical setting.

Yet, strangely, in view of this, Augustine hesitated to view the Old Testament theophanies as Christophanies, contrary to the preceding tradition. He suggested that they could have been appearances of any one of the three Trinitarian persons.[75] This reluctance was part of the

---

67. Augustine, *On Christian Doctrine* 3.25.34–3.26.37 (NPNF[1], 2:566).
68. Augustine, *On Christian Doctrine* 3.27.38–3.28.39 (NPNF[1], 2:567).
69. John M. Rist, "Basil's 'Neoplatonism': Its Background and Nature," in *Basil of Caesarea: Christian, Humanist, Ascetic: A Sixteen-Hundredth Anniversary Symposium*, ed. Paul Jonathan Fedwick (Toronto: Pontifical Institute of Medieval Studies, 1981), 1:137–220; Michel René Barnes, "Rereading Augustine on the Trinity," in *The Trinity: An Interdisciplinary Symposium on the Trinity*, ed. Stephen T. Davis, Daniel Kendall, and Gerald O'Collins (Oxford: Oxford University Press, 1999), 145–76.
70. Lewis Ayres, *Augustine and the Trinity* (Cambridge: Cambridge University Press, 2010).
71. Augustine, *St. Augustine: The Literal Meaning of Genesis*, trans. John Hammond Taylor, 2 vols. (New York: Paulist, 1982). See appendix 1.
72. NPNF[1], 8:58–60.
73. NPNF[1], 8:160–64.
74. NPNF[1], 8:405.
75. John Thomas Slotemaker, "'"Fuisse in Forma Hominis" Belongs to Christ Alone': John Calvin's Trinitarian Hermeneutics in His Lectures on Ezekiel," *SJT* 68 (2015): 421–36.

reason for Colin Gunton's attack on Augustine, suggesting that he had difficulty in understanding the incarnation and the real human embodiment of the Son.[76] Nonetheless, biblical exegesis was the ultimate basis of Augustine's theology. His Trinitarianism was exegetically rooted, not only in the *Homilies on John* but in *De Trinitate* as well. His principle that if in doubt, a reference to Christ and to love was to be preferred, while it might yield bad exegesis, would do so by pointing to the heart of the Christian faith and, from that most important perspective, would by no means be harmful.

8.4.2   Later Clarifications

Aquinas, in the *Summa theologia* 1a.1.9–10, makes a major breakthrough; the literal sense is what the human author intended, whether that be literal and historical or figurative. God conveys his meaning not only by words but also by things signified by the words. The literal sense is whatever the words signify. Where the things signified by words in turn signify yet other things, the meaning conveyed is called "the spiritual sense, which is based on the literal, and presupposes it." This spiritual sense has a threefold division. The allegorical sense consists in things in the Old Testament signifying things in the New Testament. There is also the moral sense, in which things that signify Christ signify what we are to do. Finally, there is the anagogical sense, in which things signify eternal glory. At the root of it all, "the literal sense is that which the author intends." One word in Scripture can have multiple senses, but these must all be based throughout on the literal sense, understood in this way. Consequently,

> no confusion results, for all the senses are founded on one—the literal—from which alone can any argument be drawn, and not from those intended in allegory. . . . Nevertheless, nothing of holy Scripture perishes on account of this, since nothing necessary to faith is contained under the spiritual sense which is not elsewhere put forward by the Scripture in its literal sense.[77]

Aquinas's major insight explains and supports the richness and multilayered nature of the Bible, but ensures that it is based on a secure founda-

---

76. Colin Gunton, "Augustine, the Trinity, and the Theological Crisis of the West," *SJT* 43 (1990): 33–58.
77. Aquinas, *ST* 1a.1.10.

tion, the literal sense—what the author intended—acting as a brake on undue speculation.[78]

Aquinas's proposal found wide acceptance among Reformation exegetes,[79] demonstrated by the citation from Calvin at the head of this chapter (see p. 242). This was a lynchpin of Calvin's own interpretation to the extent that he frequently distanced himself from Augustine's eager Christological exegesis of the Old Testament. Calvin refused to recognize that Abraham's offering of Isaac was a type of the sacrifice of Christ and preferred to see Old Testament passages in their own historical context, keeping strictly to this rule. While Augustine can be faulted for sometimes evading the immediate context and proceeding straight to Christ, Calvin was unduly cautious. Because of this, he has sometimes been accused of "Judaizing."[80] However, after the 1559 *Institutes*, faced with the anti-Trinitarianism of Blandrata and Gentile, he revised his practice and drew up rules for the interpretation of Old Testament theophanies that argued—contrary to Augustine and Jerome—that they should be seen as manifestations or likenesses of Christ.[81]

Hans-Joachim Kraus, in his influential article on Calvin's exegetical principles, listed eight major emphases. First is brevity and clarity, with the exclusion of allegory. Calvin mentions this in the extract from his letter to Grynaeus, where he chides contemporaries like Bucer for prolixity, and Melanchthon for focusing more on doctrinal *loci* than on the text. The clarity of the interpreter should match the clarity of Scripture. Second, in Kraus's estimation, is the determination of the author's intention. Third comes investigation of the historical and geographical context. Fourth, the original meaning must be set out, entailing knowledge of the Hebrew and Greek. Fifth, the context of the passage must be investigated. Sixth, the interpreter should discuss how far exegesis should go beyond the literal biblical wording. Seventh, the possible use of metaphor must be considered. And finally, the passage should be seen in its ultimate relation to Christ.[82]

---

78. See also Christopher T. Baglow, "Sacred Scripture and Sacred Doctrine in Saint Thomas Aquinas," in *Aquinas on Doctrine: A Critical Introduction*, ed. Thomas G. Weinandy, Daniel A. Keating, and John P. Yocum (London: T&T Clark, 2004), 1–25.

79. See Robert B. Strimple, in *Three Views on the Millennium and Beyond*, ed. Darrell L. Bock (Grand Rapids, MI: Zondervan, 1999), 261–63.

80. Slotemaker, "Calvin's Trinitarian Hermeneutics."

81. Slotemaker, "Calvin's Trinitarian Hermeneutics."

82. Hans-Joachim Kraus, "Calvin's Exegetical Principles," *Interpretation* 31 (1977): 8–18.

We should note that from the 1539 *Institutes* onward Calvin indicated that henceforth his commentaries were to be brief and clear, with longer doctrinal discussions kept for the *Institutes*. This plan he followed for the rest of his career. To find Calvin's thought on any major topic, it is necessary to consider both the *Institutes* and the commentaries and to follow both as they progress, bearing in mind the occasion and the purpose for which they were written.[83]

8.4.3   Rome

Recognizing the divine origin of Scripture, Vatican II allows that human interpretation is needed. The context, literary genre, authorial intention, and rhetorical style must all be investigated, as well as the unity of Scripture and the living tradition of the church.[84] Rome had not permitted its clergy to engage in critical biblical scholarship until Pius XII's encyclical *Divino afflante Spiritu* in 1943. Despite these developments, all interpretation is still ultimately subject to the judgment of the church.[85] Some Protestants may balk at this claim, but ultimately it is the same for them. All biblical interpretation must and will be accountable to the church and finds acceptance or rejection there, magisterium or no magisterium. Genuine biblical interpretation will find a resonance among the people of God, for they will hear the voice of the Shepherd and follow him. On the human level, it is to the church, not the academy, that interpreters of the Bible are accountable.

However, in the case of Rome, since Scripture and tradition are equal in status, and since the magisterium has the decisive voice, it is the church that has effective authority. The catechism asserts that tradition, Scripture, and the magisterium cannot stand by themselves, since they are so closely connected.[86] Consequently, Scripture does not stand by itself; according to the declaration of papal infallibility by Pius IX in 1870, ultimate authority in dogma and biblical interpretation rests with the pope.[87]

---

83. See his comments on Rom. 3:21 and 3:28, where, in reference to doctrinal issues arising from the text, he writes, "De qua re vide Institutionem nostram." Calvin, *Romans*, 73, 79; *ad Romans*, 70, 77. Note also, Richard A. Muller, *The Unaccommodated Calvin: Studies in the Foundation of a Theological Tradition* (New York: Oxford University Press, 2000), 111–16.

84. Walter M. Abbott, *Documents of Vatican II* (New York: Guild, 1966), 120.

85. Abbott, *Documents*, 121. Kenneth J. Collins and Jerry L. Walls, *Roman but Not Catholic: What Remains at Stake 500 Years after the Reformation* (Grand Rapids, MI: Baker Academic, 2017), 33–34.

86. CCC, 95.

87. Collins and Walls, *Roman but Not Catholic*, 41–43.

8.4.4 Postmodern Developments

The complexities of postmodernism are beyond the scope of this book. Readers can pursue them elsewhere.[88] In the past fifty years the theories of postmodern philosophers and literary critics have influenced Western culture, impinging on biblical interpretation and theology in passing. The ideas of Jacques Derrida, Roland Barthes, Michel Foucault, and others have given rise to the question of whether objective meaning is possible. Regarding totalizing discourses as a bid for power, the Christian claim to objective, universal authority is seen as bigotry. In terms of biblical interpretation, there have been some helpful consequences or accompaniments. Postmodern criticism has drawn attention to the particular contexts of participants—author, text, and reader—and to intertextual discourse. This has opened new vistas obscured by the historical-critical method.

Nevertheless, the development has had some negative results for theology. Meaning is forever undecidable. While seeking the intention of the original author of an ancient text is frequently elusive, the idea that meaning is largely determined by the reader effectively promotes human authority over Scripture.[89]

Somewhat in tandem with postmodernism's privileging of diversity over unity is a noticeable tension between biblical studies and orthodox theology. Biblical scholars currently operate largely under the premise that each biblical document is to be considered in isolation. This precludes seeing them as part of a larger whole, with God as the primary author, in concursive and organic relation with the human authors. T. F. Torrance, in a lecture entitled "Theological Questions to Biblical Scholars," raised pointed questions on the relationship of language to things in a way that challenges biblical scholars to adopt methods appropriate to the reality the Scriptures disclose.[90]

8.4.5 Speech-Act Theory

Speech-act theory has been influential in recent decades. The major influences on theology have come from John R. Searle and J. L. Austin.[91]

---

88. Anthony C. Thiselton, *New Horizons in Hermeneutics* (Grand Rapids, MI: Zondervan, 1992); Thiselton, *Interpreting God and the Post-Modern Self: On Meaning, Manipulation, and Promise* (Edinburgh: T&T Clark, 1995); Kevin J. Vanhoozer, *Is There Meaning in This Text? The Bible, the Reader, and the Morality of Literary Knowledge* (Leicester: Apollos, 1998).

89. See Thiselton, *Interpreting God*, esp. 127–35, where he traces the consequences of breakdown in rational discourse.

90. T. F. Torrance, *Reality and Evangelical Theology* (Philadelphia: Westminster, 1983), 52–83.

91. J. L. Austin, *How to Do Things with Words: The William James Lectures Delivered in Harvard University in 1955* (Oxford: Oxford University Press, 1976); John R. Searle,

Speech-act theory distinguishes between a *locution*, something that is being said; an *illocution*, something that is being *done* through the words; and a *perlocution*, the effect that the words have on the hearers. Its main application to theology, and in particular to Scripture and its interpretation, is that it enables us to think of the relationship between God and humans in distinctly personal ways. Its main affirmation, that words and language do not merely communicate information but also do something between persons, fits into theology very effectively. Words inform, promise, warn, threaten, convey personal attitudes—from love to anger—can be designed to get people to act in certain ways, and so on.

Speech-act theory has been applied to the Bible since the 1990s by, among others, Kevin Vanhoozer, Nicholas Wolterstorff, John Frame, Timothy Ward, and Anthony Thiselton.[92] Ward treats this in the context of God's covenant in which he promises and warns. As such, God's speech acts are the expression of God himself, the Bible being a covenantal document that brings people into a real existential relation with him. Our response, in one way or another, to God speaking in the Bible is effectively a response to God himself. This is a helpful use of speech-act theory.

Ward acknowledges his debt to Wolterstorff.[93] However, Brevard Childs is highly critical of Wolterstorff for his distinctive construction of double-agency discourse, in which one person performs something by another's illocutions.[94] In this way God speaks in Scripture through human illocutions. Wolterstorff maintains by this proposal the unity of Scripture rather than splintering it into a disparate collection of books, and he does so by maintaining the infallibility of God's locutions without attributing infallibility to human words. However, Childs argues, he

Expression and Meaning: Studies in the Theory of Speech-Acts (Cambridge: Cambridge University Press, 1979).

92. Anthony C. Thiselton, *The Two Horizons: New Testament Hermeneutics and Philosophical Description with Special Reference to Heidegger, Bultmann, Gadamer, and Wittgenstein* (Grand Rapids, MI: Eerdmans, 1980); Thiselton, *New Horizons in Hermeneutics*; Vanhoozer, *Is There a Meaning in This Text?*; Kevin J. Vanhoozer, "God's Mighty Speech-Acts: The Doctrine of Scripture Today," in *A Pathway into the Holy Scripture*, ed. Philip E. Satterthwaite and David F. Wright (Grand Rapids, MI: Eerdmans, 1994), 143–81; Timothy Ward, *Words of Life: Scripture as the Living and Active Word of God* (Nottingham: Inter-Varsity Press, 2009); Ward, *Word and Supplement: Speech Acts, Biblical Texts, and the Sufficiency of Scripture* (Oxford: Oxford University Press, 2002); Nicholas Wolterstorff, *Divine Discourse: Philosophical Reflections on the Claim that God Speaks* (Cambridge: Cambridge University Press, 1995).

93. Ward, *Words of Life*, 59.

94. Brevard Childs, "Speech-Act Theory and Biblical Interpretation," *SJT* 58 (2005): 375–92.

makes God the sole author, undermines the human element, and misses the fact of canon, a corollary of inspiration.

In contrast, Thiselton, who is expert both in philosophy and New Testament interpretation, uses speech-act theory but does so sparingly. He stays within the bounds of Pauline theology and confessional Christian theology. The problem for Childs is that Wolterstorff's model pulls human speech apart from its divine appropriation. Childs concludes, "Under the broad umbrella of speech-act theory fundamentally different hermeneutical applications to biblical interpretation can be defended." Because Wolterstorff's claims are deeply flawed and not hermeneutically successful, they do not offer a fruitful direction. So "it would be sad indeed if a new generation of evangelicals would . . . commit themselves uncritically to a new and untested philosophical model, allegedly designed for the twenty-first century."[95]

Vanhoozer writes of language as a vehicle for interpersonal, covenantal communication. In the Bible God communicates as the Spirit illuminates the text.[96]

There are limitations with speech-act theory. It operates with simple speech-acts. Yet the process of verbal communication is extremely complex, as Poythress points out.

> The decision to start with atomic propositions is a decontextualizing move, and all such moves are problematic when, as is the case with human language, context is essential to meaning. In this case, the context includes the complexity of human beings, who are the speakers and conversationalists, and the complexity of their environment, which includes world history and the God who rules it.[97]

This complexity affects speech itself, which can function on a range of levels simultaneously, together with the multiplicity of factors in the human environment. Poythress continues:

> The difficulty here is that meaning in the world of persons and personal action is so rich and multidimensional that no theory can master it. Therefore analysts, in their desire to be "scientific" and precise,

---

95. Childs, "Speech-Act Theory," 392.
96. Vanhoozer, *Is There a Meaning in This Text?*, 219, 456.
97. Vern S. Poythress, "Canon and Speech Act: Limitations in Speech-Act Theory, with Implications for a Putative Theory of Canonical Speech Acts," *WTJ* 70 (2008): 339.

266 The Word of God

run the risk of neglecting all but some one dimension, or a small number of dimensions, that can be selected out and flattened enough so that one can be "rigorous."[98]

This complexity, Poythress continues, has been recognized by Searle and Roman Jakobson, who acknowledge the pervasive presence of multiple communication levels. This difficulty may be true of the Bible too. Poythress comments:

> The challenges increase when we move from considering sentences to considering the canon as a whole. The canon constitutes an exceedingly rich and complex product. It is easy to oversimplify if we try to fit it into a theory initially developed to deal with simple sentence-length utterances.[99]

Thus he points to the gain in philosophical rigor at the expense of artificiality.[100]

> The genius of speech-act theory is to teach us to pay attention to the meaning that utterances receive through embedding in a larger context of human purposeful action. But context, its strength, is also its weakness. Sentence level utterances occur in the context of larger discourses. Discourse takes place in the context of human action. Human purposeful action takes place within the context of culture, and culture in the context of cultures, in the plural. And cultures occur in a context of a world and a world history whose interpretation differs from culture to culture. . . . Therefore, though speech-act theory may be helpful . . . we cannot commit ourselves to its keeping, as if it were a completely trustworthy, independent source for telling us what is and what is not taking place in the Bible.[101]

Further Reading

Bates, Matthew W. *The Birth of the Trinity: Jesus, God, and Spirit in New Testament and Early Christian Interpretations of the Old Testament.* Oxford: Oxford University Press, 2015.

De Lubac, Henri. *Medieval Exegesis*, 3 vols. Grand Rapids, MI: Eerdmans, 1998–2009.

---

98. Poythress, "Canon and Speech Acts," 341–42.
99. Poythress, "Canon and Speech Acts," 344–45.
100. Poythress, "Canon and Speech Acts," 349.
101. Poythress, "Canon and Speech Acts," 354.

Martens, Peter W. *Origen and Scripture: The Contours of the Exegetical Life*. Oxford: Oxford University Press, 2012.

Simonetti, Manlio. *Biblical Interpretation in the Early Church: An Historical Introduction to Patristic Exegesis*. Edinburgh: T&T Clark, 1994.

Vanhoozer, Kevin. *Is There Meaning in This Text? The Bible, the Reader, and the Morality of Literary Knowledge*. Leicester: Apollos, 1998.

Westerholm, Stephen, and Martin Westerholm. *Reading Sacred Scripture: Voices from the History of Biblical Interpretation*. Grand Rapids, MI: Eerdmans, 2016.

Study Questions

1. Distinguish between typology, allegory, and prosopological exegesis. Discuss their validity in particular biblical contexts.

2. What weaknesses are evident in post-Enlightenment historical-critical interpretation?

3. To what degree should we develop an attitude of self-criticism toward our own exegetical strategies? Can we avoid the danger of lapsing into skepticism?

PART 3

THE WORKS OF GOD

Great are the works of the Lord,
  studied by all who delight in them.
Psalm 111:2

9

Creation

The works of God *ad extra* consist of creation, providence, and grace. Creation is ex nihilo, neither an emanation from the Supreme Being nor made out of preexistent material. It is a free and sovereign act of the living God, bringing into existence all other entities and granting them contingent life in dependence on him. God is the focus of the creation account and is revealed as relational, creating in a threefold manner; the New Testament develops the Trinitarian nature of creation. As such, the creation is an icon through which we perceive something of the beauty and grandeur of its Maker. God charged humans with the task of investigating the creation and governing it. From this arises questions about the relationship of the Bible to science and whether there are other intelligent life forms in the universe.

We are now discussing the works of God *ad extra*—outside or beyond himself—rather than the works of God *ad intra*—the generation of the Son and the procession of the Holy Spirit.

9.1 Creation ex Nihilo

Everything that exists was brought into being by God; this was a free act of God's will, not an emanation from his being, and there was no preexisting material. Consequently, all that is not God is contingent, dependent on him for its existence and continuation. God is not merely the giver of life but also life itself—overflowing, superabundant life. In generating the Son and spirating the Spirit, the Father is the fountain of the life that forever is brimming over in God by necessity of his nature. In creation, God freely determined to bring into existence entities other than himself with which to share life on a creaturely level. Creation ex nihilo (out of nothing) was a stark contrast to ideas prevalent in paganism, where the universe was often held to be a emanation from a Supreme Being, or matter to be preexistent. In such cases, any Supreme Being would be in some sense dependent on the world. As Georges Florovsky comments, "The idea of creation was a strikingly Christian innovation in philosophy. The problem itself was alien and even unintelligible to the Greek mind."[1]

Paul Gavrilyuk argues that the problem for the Gnostics was the origin of evil,[2] which they explained variously: evil was rooted in preexistent matter; or the perfect god delegated creation to a committee of lesser gods or a subcommittee of angels; or the world of matter resulted from a cosmic fall; or the material world was a mistake or an afterthought.[3] Tatian was the first explicitly to reject the eternality of matter.[4] However, 2 Maccabees 7:28 indicates that creation ex nihilo was part of pious Jewish belief during the second century BC, evidence that the doctrine antedated the New Testament and the Patristics. Some biblical passages support it explicitly (John 1:3; Rom. 4:17; Col. 1:16; Heb. 11:3);[5] all things were created by the one God, and as Creator, God is different from everything in creation.[6] As such, he is sovereign, independent of the creature.

According to Gavrilyuk, the next major breakthrough occurred in the fourth century, with Athanasius's treatise *De incarnatione.*[7] Florovsky outlines the background.[8] For Origen it was impossible to think of God

---

1. Georges Florovsky, "St. Athanasius' Concept of Creation," in *The Collected Works of Georges Florovsky*, vol. 4, *Aspects of Church History*, ed. Richard S. Haugh (Vaduz: Büchervertriebsanstalt, 1987), 39.

2. *Gnosticism* is a broad, amorphous term referring to a range of philosophical and syncretistic religious worldviews at the time of the early church, having in common—among other things—the positions described below.

3. Paul Gavrilyuk, "Creation in Early Christian Polemical Literature: Irenaeus against the Gnostics and Athanasius against the Arians," *MTheol* 29, no. 2 (2013): 22–32.

4. J. C. O'Neill, "How Early Is the Doctrine of *Creatio ex Nihilo*?," *JTS* 53 (2002): 449–65.

5. Gavrilyuk, "Creation," 27.

6. Gavrilyuk, "Creation," 29.

7. Gavrilyuk, "Creation," 30.

8. Florovsky, "Athanasius," 39–62.

apart from his being Creator. There is nothing potential in God—he is always the Father of the Son, the Son coeternal with the Father. Creation was eternal, since to call God almighty entails something in relation to which he exercises power.[9] This left some unresolved problems for theology.

In response, Athanasius rejected the eternal nature of the world. Relating creation to the incarnation in *De incarnatione*, he argued for a radical cleavage between the absolute being of God and the contingent existence of the world.[10] In contrast to Epicureanism, Athanasius insisted that the world does not exist by chance. He rejected the idea of preexistent matter, since that makes God dependent, besides implying the dualistic notion that the Creator is different from the God revealed by Jesus. The world is no accident; it is created by God's Word so that the creatures are ontologically different from the Creator.[11] The Logos as the only-begotten God is absolutely different from all creatures (*De incarnatione* 17).[12] The Logos is God before he is the Creator;[13] even if there were no creation, he would have been with God, and the Father in him (*Contra Arianos* 2.31). This freed Athanasius to define creation properly.[14] God is more than Creator: he is eternally the Father of the Son. His Fatherhood antedates his creatorship.[15] Athanasius's opponents collapsed the generation of the Son into creation, whereas he distinguished the generation of the Son sharply from creation; the Son was generated out of the Father's essence,[16] flowing from the Father's being, while the world is external and contingent.[17] Nicaea indirectly canonized creation ex nihilo, and was vindicated at Constantinople.[18] Cyril followed suit (*Thesaurus* 15, 18, 32 [*PG*, 75:276, 313, 564–65]),[19] with John of Damascus summing up the consensus (*De fide orthodoxa* 1.8 [*PG*, 94:812–13]).[20]

Augustine, in his confrontation with the Manicheans, took the matter further. The Manicheans, radical dualists, held that there were two

---

9. Florovsky, "Athanasius," 42–46.
10. Florovsky, "Athanasius," 49.
11. Gavrilyuk, "Creation," 30.
12. Florovsky, "Athanasius," 50.
13. Florovsky, "Athanasius," 51.
14. Florovsky, "Athanasius," 52.
15. Florovsky, "Athanasius," 52–53.
16. Gavrilyuk, "Creation," 31.
17. Florovsky, "Athanasius," 53.
18. Gavrilyuk, "Creation," 32.
19. Florovsky, "Athanasius," 60.
20. Florovsky, "Athanasius," 61.

coequal principles of good and evil. This was a denial of God's universal authority. Augustine refuted these ideas in a range of works.[21]

López-Farjeat points to Aquinas as having two distinct views of creation. The first was philosophical, inspired by Avicenna. In created things, nonbeing is prior to being, and therefore created things are nonbeing in nature. Consequently, they receive their being from another, from God. This proves to Aquinas that the world needs a first cause, or it would not be. The second perspective is a matter of faith, since it is indemonstrable whether creation is eternal or temporal; neither contradicts the ontological dependence of every possible being on God. Aquinas sees the act of creation and its temporal or eternal character as two quite different problems. In the latter, if creation were eternal, that would not rule out creation ex nihilo, since creation is not in the realm of time but of being.[22] On the act of creation, Aquinas held that whether the world had a beginning cannot be demonstrated; we believe it in faith on the basis of revelation. "And it is useful to consider this, lest anyone, presuming to demonstrate what is of faith, should bring forth reasons that are not cogent, so as to give occasion to unbelievers to laugh, thinking that on such grounds we believe things that are of faith."[23]

Creation, we may say, is God's free and sovereign bestowal of existence to all other entities, and of contingent life appropriate to those entities. That it is a free act of God, not an emanation of his nature, is underlined by Étienne Gilson in a remark reported by Georges Florovsky: "A God whose very existence it is to be a Creator is not a Christian God at all."[24] If he were, God would be beholden to the creation. Or, as Burrell writes, "Creation can only be creation if God can be God without creating. No external incentive or internal need can induce God to create."[25]

21. Augustine, *Reply to Faustus* (NPNF[1], 4:155–345; *PL*, 42:207–518); Augustine, *Against the Epistle of Manichaeus Called Fundamental* (NPNF[1], 4:129–50; *PL*, 42:173–206); Augustine, *Acts or Disputation against Fortunatus* (NPNF[1], 4:113–29; *PL*, 42:111–30); Augustine, *On Two Souls* (NPNF[1], 4:95–107; *PL*, 42:93–112).
22. Luis Xavier López-Farjeat, "Avicenna's Influence on Aquinas' Early Doctrine of Creation," *RTPM* 79 (2012): 305–37.
23. Aquinas, *ST* 1a.46.2.
24. Andrew Louth, *Modern Orthodox Thinkers: From the Philokalia to the Present* (London: SPCK, 2015), 90.
25. David B. Burrell, "Act of Creation with Its Theological Consequences," in *Aquinas on Doctrine: A Critical Introduction*, ed. Thomas G. Weinandy, Daniel A. Keating, and John P. Yocum (London: T&T Clark, 2004), 28.

Further, our knowledge of God as analogical impacts our knowledge of his revelation in both general and special revelation and has to be factored into our knowledge of creation. Hence, our knowledge has a certain correspondence, but the reality transcends our abilities. For Calvin, God's revelation is accommodated to our own capacities, given in such a way that anyone, of whatever intelligence, education, or cultural situation, can grasp it. It does not come as a modern scientific paper, accessible to a mere handful. Its form and literary genre must be understood so as to determine what it intends to teach us.

9.2 The Trinity and Creation

All three persons of the Trinity are inseparably involved in creation.

9.2.1 *Biblical Foundation*

In Genesis 1 the act of *creation* itself is direct and immediate (vv. 1–2), distinct from the work of formation that follows.[26] The result is a cosmos formless, empty, dark, and wet—unfit for human life. The rest of chapter 1 describes the world's *formation* (or *distinction*) and *adornment*, God introduces order, light, and dryness, making it fit for life to flourish. First, God creates light and sets boundaries to the darkness (vv. 3–5). Second, he shapes the earth so that it is no longer formless (vv. 6–10). Third, God separates the waters and forms dry land so that it is no longer entirely wet (vv. 9–10). Subsequently, he populates the earth, ending its emptiness (vv. 20–30), with fish and birds, then with land animals, and, finally—as the apex of the whole—by humans made in his image. This order is clear from the parallels between two groups of days, the first three and the second three.[27] In this, God shows his sovereign freedom in naming and blessing his creation. He sees it as thoroughly good. Finally comes the unfinished seventh day, when God enters his rest, which he made to share with humanity, whom he created in his own image. Entailed is an implicit invitation for us to follow.[28]

---

26. Herman Bavinck, *In the Beginning: Foundations of Creation Theology*, ed. John Bolt, trans. John Vriend (Grand Rapids, MI: Baker, 1999), 100ff. See also the discussion in Aquinas, *ST* 1a.66.1–4 and the entire section QQ. 66–74 in general.

27. See chap. 1. This pattern was discerned at least as long ago as the thirteenth century. See Robert Grosseteste, *On the Six Days of Creation: A Translation of the Hexaëmeron*, trans. C. F. J. Martin, Auctores Britannici Medii Aevi (Oxford University Press, 1996), 160–61 (5.I.3–5.II.1); Aquinas, *ST* 1a.74.1. See Robert Letham, "'In the Space of Six Days': The Days of Creation from Origen to the Westminster Assembly," *WTJ* 61 (1999): 149–74.

28. Heb. 3:7–4:11.

Particularly striking is God's sovereign and variegated ordering of his creation. He forms the earth in a threefold manner. First, he issues direct fiats. He says, "Let there be light," and there is light (Gen. 1:3). He brings the expanse into existence with effortless command (v. 6), as well as the dry ground (v. 9), the stars (vv. 14–15), the birds, and the fish (vv. 20–21). It is enough for God to speak; his edict is fulfilled.

Second, he works. He separates the light from the darkness (v. 4); he makes the expanse and separates the waters (v. 7); he makes the two great lights, the sun and the moon (v. 16), and sets them in the expanse to give light on the earth (v. 17); he creates the great sea creatures and birds (v. 21); he makes the beasts of the earth and reptiles (v. 25); and, finally, he creates man—male and female—in his own image (vv. 26–27). The thought is of focused, purposeful action by God, of divine labor accomplishing his ends.

Third, God uses the activity of the creatures themselves. God commands the earth to produce vegetation, plants and trees (vv. 11–12). He commands the lights to govern the day and night (vv. 14–16), the earth to bring forth land animals (v. 24). Here the creatures follow God's instructions and contribute to the eventual outcome. God's order is unified and varied; it is threefold but one. His work shows diversity in its unity and unity in its diversity.[29]

This reflects what the Genesis 1 records of God himself. He is relational. There is a distinction between God (v. 1), the Spirit of God (v. 2), and the speech or word of God (v. 3). Wenham is sound when he suggests that verse 2 presents a vivid image of the Spirit of God.[30] The New Testament personalizing of the Spirit of God is a congruent development from this statement. Furthermore, with the creation of humanity there is the unique deliberation "Let us make man in our image," expressing a plurality in God (vv. 26–27). Von Rad suggests that this signifies the goal to which all God's creation is directed.[31] Since Scripture has a fullness that goes beyond the horizons of the original authors, the fathers who saw a latent reference to the Trinity were on the right track. The New Testament gives us the principle that the Old Testament contains

---

29. Francis Watson, *Text, Church and World: Biblical Interpretation in Theological Perspective* (Edinburgh: T&T Clark, 1994), 142–43.

30. Gordon J. Wenham, *Genesis 1–15*, Word Biblical Commentary 1 (Waco, TX: Word, 1987), 15–17.

31. Gerhard von Rad, *Genesis: A Commentary*, rev. ed. (Philadelphia: Westminster, 1961), 57.

in seed form what is more fully made known in the New. In terms of the *sensus plenior* (the fuller meaning) of Scripture, these words of God attest a plurality in God, which came later to be expressed in the doctrine of the Trinity.

In short, God, for whom communion and communication are inherent to who he is, in creating the world, made us for communion with himself in a universe of ravishing beauty and ordered variety. On the seventh day he ceased from his works in contemplation of their ordered beauty and goodness, and invites us to join him. This chapter declares that Yahweh, the God of Abraham, Isaac, and Jacob, the God of Moses, created all things. He who made his covenant with Israel is not some merely territorial divinity but is the one to whom all nations are accountable, for he is their Maker. There is a clear unity between creation and redemption. The mandate to multiply and subdue the earth (vv. 26–29) embraces the whole creation and is the basic building block for the unfolding structure of salvation after the fall. Reflecting on this, Athanasius writes of creation *in Christ*.[32] Since Genesis, as any other part of the Bible, is to be read in the context of the whole, New Testament references to Christ and the Spirit in creation reinforce this (John 1:1ff.; Col. 1:15–20; Heb. 1:3; 11:3).[33] It is impossible to think of creation apart from its Maker being relational, and thus triune, as Bavinck cogently argues.[34] Bavinck goes further, saying that

> without generation [the generation of the Son by the Father] creation would not be possible. If in an absolute sense God could not communicate himself to the Son, he would be even less able, in a relative sense, to communicate himself to his creature. If God were not triune, creation would not be possible.[35]

God, who is life itself, freely granted life to other entities, which he brought into existence sovereignly by his will.

The New Testament develops this further by its unequivocal claim that Christ, the eternal Son of God, is Creator. All things were made by him and for him. He is the one who holds everything together. God's

---

32. Athanasius, *On the Incarnation* 1, 3, 12, 14 (*PG*, 25:97–102, 115–22).
33. This is reinforced by poetic accounts of creation in Ps. 33:6, Prov. 8:22–23, and Job 33:4 (cf. 26:13), and by references to the Spirit of God as Creator in Ps. 104:30.
34. Bavinck, *In the Beginning*, 39–45.
35. Bavinck, *In the Beginning*, 39.

ultimate purpose for the universe is that Christ be the Head, the one in supreme authority over the redeemed and renewed cosmos (John 1:1–3; Eph. 1:10; Col. 1:15–20; Heb. 1:1–3). This is the background to events where Jesus displays his authority over creation. By walking on the water and calming the raging storm (Matt. 14:22–33), he demonstrates that he has the full authority of Yahweh, of whom the psalmist declared,

> Your way was through the sea,
>> your path through the great waters;
>> yet your footprints were unseen. (Ps. 77:19)

Athanasius compares the creation to the printing of the name of a king's son on every building of the town that his father builds, implying that the Son's name is imaged throughout creation.[36] Hallmarks of God's unity-in-diversity are evident throughout.

> The heavens declare the glory of God,
>> and the sky above proclaims his handiwork. (Ps. 19:1)

9.2.2   Basic Principles[37]

Gunton lists a number of distinctive features in the Christian account of creation. In its historical context, the teaching of creation ex nihilo is unique, "one of the most momentous developments in all the history of thought,"[38] in stark contrast to all forms of monism, such as ancient Gnosticism and recent pagan spirituality. Moreover, this act of God was not arbitrary but purposive, deriving from his love, heading somewhere, in contrast to the Islamic doctrine of fate, which cannot derive from love, since Allah is conceived as unitary, with power and will dominant. A Trinitarian theology of creation enables the universe to be closely related to God and yet free to be itself. It also opposes deism, which envisions a remote god with no ongoing contact with creation, and scientific materialism, which posits purely immanent causes for all that is.

Gunton points out the Bible's assertion that God created time, with the corollary that our world and its history have ultimate value. Creation, incarnation, and resurrection underline the fact that to God, mat-

---

36. Athanasius, *Orations against the Arians* 2.79 (PG, 26:314).
37. This section is a version of part of a chapter in my book *The Holy Trinity: In Scripture, History, Theology, and Worship* (Phillipsburg, NJ: P&R, 2004).
38. Colin Gunton, *The Triune Creator* (Grand Rapids, MI: Eerdmans, 1998), 65f.

ter matters.[39] We need, Gunton propounds, a *theological* interpretation of creation, an account that integrates the whole biblical witness, not just Genesis alone, and sees it in the light of its triune Maker.[40] A theology of creation must not limit its biblical basis to Genesis 1.[41] This is an argument in line with classic Reformed theology and its sixteenth-century confessions.[42] Since the triune God created, we cannot understand creation apart from the reality of the incarnation in Jesus Christ in history, and of the Trinity who created all things. This line of thought follows a basic principle of biblical interpretation; any passage of Scripture must be seen in the light of the whole. The fact that Genesis 1 comes first in the Hebrew, Greek, and English Bibles does not legitimize viewing it in isolation. Both biblically and theologically, the Christian view of salvation cannot be separated from a Christian view of creation.

Irenaeus strongly affirmed the goodness of creation, including matter, and had a clearly Trinitarian perspective. God (the Father) created by means of his two hands (the Son and the Holy Spirit), needing neither angels nor any inferior power to assist him.[43] Despite the pre-Nicene subordinationism, which seems to relegate the two hands to instruments of the Father, the positive point is that God does not require intermediaries between himself and the universe to achieve his ends. There are two realities only—God the Creator and his creation. The creation is real but only in relation to the God who upholds it by his two hands. It is precisely Trinitarianism that enables Irenaeus to affirm creation ex nihilo.[44] Because creation is a work of the Trinity, it is an act not only of will and power but also of love. God the Father enters into personal relations with the created order through the Son and the Spirit. The eternal union and communion of Father, Son, and Holy Spirit underlies the work of creation.

Moreover, creation is *relatively* perfect. It was made very good but destined for fulfillment in the end. This differs from some versions of the big bang theory, where—dependent on its density—an expanding universe either will eventually wind down and collapse back into nothingness,[45] or

---

39. Gunton, *Triune Creator*, 44–50, 57–61.
40. Gunton, *Triune Creator*, 62–64.
41. Gunton, *Triune Creator*, 64.
42. Letham, "The Space of Six Days."
43. Irenaeus, *Against Heresies* 2.2.4 (*PG*, 7:714–15).
44. Irenaeus, *Against Heresies* 4.20.1 (*PG*, 7:1032).
45. Stephen W. Hawking, *A Brief History of Time: From the Big Bang to Black Holes* (New York: Bantam, 1988).

else will continually expand and grow increasingly cold. Indeed, without the providential direction of the Trinity, the cosmos would have no power to prolong its existence. But a Trinitarian view of creation entails that the cosmos was made not for ultimate futility but to become something even greater than at first.

Gunton points out that the eternity of the Creator and the time of the creature meet in the incarnate Christ, in human time.[46] The link between creation and the incarnation is something I have explored elsewhere.[47] Creation and redemption are in continuity, Christ the Mediator of both. Earlier, I noted that Bavinck argues that creation could not occur if God were not triune. By eternal generation God communicates his full image to his Son, while by creation he communicates a weak image to the creature. The latter depends upon the former as both prior and eternal. Without generation, creation would be impossible.[48] Correspondingly, the procession of the Spirit from the Father and the Son is the basis of the willing of that world. The creation proceeds from the Father through the Son by the Spirit in order that, by the Spirit and through the Son, it may return to the Father.[49] This continuity also allows for genuine distinction, thus avoiding the cosmic soup served in the kitchens of New Age pantheism.

Christianity stresses the incarnation as God's supreme affirmation of his creation. And the resurrection clinches this. The Apostles' Creed and the Nicene Creed (C) both summarize the plan of salvation, grounded on the Trinity. However, this entails the renewal of creation. God the Father created all things (C makes the Trinitarianism explicit); the Son became incarnate, died on the cross, and rose for us and our salvation (in this God reaffirms his creation by taking part of it into personal union); while the resurrection is itself the renewal of creation and the beginning of the kingdom that shall have no end. There is an unbreakable unity between creation and redemption. All things declare the glory of the holy Trinity.

9.3   Creation and the Revelation of God

9.3.1   Vestigia Trinitatis *Again?*

The Bible attests that all creation reveals the glory of God. The Psalms are full of such comments; creation is an image, something through

---

46. Gunton, *Triune Creator*, 68–96.
47. Robert Letham, *The Work of Christ* (Leicester: Inter-Varsity Press, 1993).
48. Bavinck, *In the Beginning*, 39.
49. Bavinck, *In the Beginning*, 45.

which we perceive the reality of God. It is not itself God, but it points to him.

> The heavens declare the glory of God,
>   and the sky above proclaims his handiwork. (Ps. 19:1)

Paul also reflects on creation in this way. The invisible things of God are clearly visible in the world around us, he says, through the things that have been made, leaving humans inexcusable for rejecting him (Rom. 1:19–20).

Calvin, in his Genesis commentary, emphasizes this point. Moses's intention is "to render God, as it were, visible to us in his works." The Lord, "that he may invite us to the knowledge of himself, places the fabric of heaven and earth before our eyes rendering himself, in a certain manner, manifest in them." The heavens "are eloquent heralds of the glory of God, and . . . this most beautiful order of nature silently proclaims his admirable wisdom." He "clothes himself, so to speak, with the image of the world . . . magnificently arrayed in the incomparable vesture of the heavens and the earth." In short, the world is "a mirror in which we ought to behold God."[50] There is a symmetry in God's works to which nothing can be added.[51] The divine artificer arranged the creation in such a wonderful order that nothing more beautiful in appearance can be imagined.[52] In the Catechism of the Church of Geneva (1541), Calvin foreshadows his comments on Genesis in saying that the world is a kind of mirror in which we may observe God. The account here is given for our sake, to teach us that God has made nothing without a certain reason and design.[53]

These brilliant images point to the connection and yet distinction between God and his creation. The beauties of the world are the clothes God wears to display his glory, but its riveting beauty is not to be identified with him.

In this God speaks to us on our own level. Considering the separation of light and darkness on the first day in Genesis 1, and reflecting on the differences in the ancient world in reckoning when the day actually

---

50. Calvin, *Commentaries on the First Book of Moses Called Genesis*, trans. John King (Grand Rapids, MI: Baker, 1979), argument.
51. Calvin, *Genesis*, on 1:31.
52. Calvin, *Institutes*, 1.14.21.
53. In *Calvin: Theological Treatises*, ed. J. K. S. Reid (Philadelphia: Westminster, 1966), 93–94.

282 The Works of God

ended and began, Calvin says that Moses accommodated his discourse to the received custom. God accommodates his works to our capacity, fixing our attention and compelling us to pause and reflect. Everything here relates to the visible world, the theater he places before our eyes.[54] It has been persuasively argued that, for Calvin, God not only accommodates his revelation to our level but also accommodates himself, speaking to us in the prattling babble of baby-talk (*balbutire*, "to prattle," is a favorite verb of Calvin's in this connection).[55]

If the world was made by the holy Trinity, and it also declares the glory of God, it seems reasonable to suppose that there are hints all around us in creation pointing to the Trinity. Ever since Augustine propounded his Trinitarian illustrations, this has been debated. We considered earlier that illustrations drawn from the world cannot *prove* the doctrine of the Trinity; rather, they lead to some form of heresy. The most such analogies give is evidence of diversity-in-unity and unity-in-diversity. Hints of the relational character of God and his unity-in-diversity are all around us. However, these are not proofs in a logical sense, nor do they portray the Trinity as such.

Frame suggests a number of Trinitarian analogies. He points to a wide range of triadic patterns. His argument bears careful consideration, but no pattern can reflect all the contours of the doctrine of the Trinity, nor does he claim they do.[56] Frame succeeds in underlining the point that all around us are inescapable evidences of unity-in-diversity and diversity-in-unity. At the far end of the spectrum, Barth's rejection of the *vestigia Trinitatis* flows from his programmatic rejection of natural theology.

9.3.2 Creation as an Icon

Creation reveals God. Though it does not bring us salvation in our fallen condition, it does not leave God without a witness. In consequence, the human race is left inexcusable for its continued rejection of its Creator.[57]

---

54. Calvin, *Genesis*, on 1:3–5.
55. David F. Wright, "Calvin's Accommodating God," in *Calvinus Sincerioris Religionis Vindex: Calvin as the Protector of the Purer Religion*, ed. Wilhelm H. Neuser, Sixteenth Century Essays and Studies 36 (Kirksville, MO: Sixteenth Century Journal Publishers, 1997), 3–19.
56. John M. Frame, *The Doctrine of God* (Phillipsburg, NJ: P&R, 2002), 726–32, 743–50. However, this is the best case I have yet encountered for this position, especially the article he cites by Vern S. Poythress, "Reforming Ontology and Logic in the Light of the Trinity: An Application of Van Til's Idea of Analogy," *WTJ* 57 (1995): 187–219.
57. WCF, 1.1.

Creation itself is, as Calvin said, an *eikōn* (image), a window through which we can perceive something of its Maker. While the Trinity may not be directly discerned through the creation, Paul points to God's "eternal power and deity" as clearly evident.

Eastern Christianity is particularly identified with its icons. These are not intended to be worshiped.[58] They are teaching devices, windows through which to perceive greater realities that lie beyond. Thus, Leontius of Neapolis said that icons are "opened books to remind us of God."[59] The Reformed differ from the East, considering the Eastern view too restrictive. For the Reformed, the whole of creation is an icon. All around us the trees, plants, grass, and sky, the contours of the earth, the sumptuously variegated and ever-changing colors of the landscape, and the sights and sounds of the world cry out with a loud roar, or quietly and soothingly breathe a gentle whisper to the effect that "the hand that made us is divine."[60] They are not to be worshiped, for they are created. But since God made them, he reveals himself through them. These are the clothes God wears to display his glory.[61]

9.3.3   Unity-in-Diversity

Bavinck writes that unity-in-diversity and vice versa in creation are reflections of the Trinity. "The Christian mind remains unsatisfied until all of existence is referred back to the triune God."[62] From this flows unity and diversity in the cosmos.

> There is a most profuse diversity and yet, in that diversity, there is also a superlative kind of unity. The foundation for both diversity and unity is in God. . . . Here is a unity that does not destroy but rather maintains diversity, and a diversity that does not come at the expense of unity, but rather unfolds it in its riches. In virtue of this unity the world can, metaphorically, be called an organism, in which all the parts are connected with each other and influence each other reciprocally.[63]

58. Timothy Ware, *The Orthodox Church* (London: Penguin, 1969), 38–40, 41ff., 277f.; John Meyendorff, *Byzantine Theology: Historical Trends and Doctrinal Themes* (New York: Fordham University Press, 1979), 42–53.

59. *PG*, 94:1276a, cited by Ware, *Orthodox Church*, 40.

60. From the hymn "The Spacious Firmament on High," by Joseph Addison (1712).

61. Robert Letham, *Through Western Eyes: Eastern Orthodoxy: A Reformed Perspective* (Fearn: Mentor, 2007), 143–62.

62. Bavinck, *RD*, 2:330.

63. Bavinck, *RD*, 2:435.

Indeed, Bavinck argues that the imprints of God are evident everywhere; all creatures "display the footsteps or vestiges of God."[64] Yet God and the cosmos are distinct, radically so, for the latter has been brought into existence by God. Along these lines, Eglinton suggests that "in Bavinck's understanding of the Trinity and the cosmos, *the Trinity is wholly unlike anything else, but everything else is like the Trinity.*"[65]

Music demonstrates unity-in-diversity very clearly. Western classical music emerged in a culture formed by Christianity, and its central features mirror the works of God—purpose, movement toward a goal, and resolution. Its unity-in-diversity is heard in a variety of instruments combining to play one integrated score. This is obvious in chamber music, where the various instruments can be heard distinctly within the overall ensemble. String quartets feature this prominently, especially those of the Classical period of Haydn, Mozart, and the early quartets of Beethoven, when they were composed for private performance, written in a conversational style, the voices interacting. However, it is also obvious as the genre develops with the radical changes Beethoven makes.[66]

The two major challenges to the Christian faith today—the postmodern thinking of our own culture and Islam—are both deviations from the created order of unity-in-diversity and diversity-in-unity that the holy Trinity has embedded in the world he made. In Islam, unity trumps diversity. Allah is one, and the Muslim world is theoretically one *umma*, in which the religious and the political are indivisible. Western music, with its polyphony, different instruments playing different notes in one integrated score, is unacceptable. Hence, Islam's opposition to Western democracy. In contrast, postmodernism opposes universalizing and totalizing discourse, truth claims that are applicable at all times and in all places. Its tendency is for unity to be fragmented, and meaning de-centered.[67]

---

64. Bavinck, *RD*, 2:561; James Eglinton, *Trinity and Organism: Towards a New Reading of Herman Bavinck's Organic Motif* (London: Bloomsbury, 2012), 88.

65. Eglinton, *Trinity and Organism*, 89.

66. See Robert Winter, *The Beethoven Quartet Companion* (Berkeley: University of California Press, 1994), especially the article by Joseph Kerman, "Beethoven Quartet Audiences: Actual, Potential, Ideal," 7–27.

67. I have written elsewhere at greater length on this theme; see Letham, *The Holy Trinity*, 439–57. See also Bernard Lewis, *What Went Wrong? Western Impact and Middle Eastern Response* (New York: Oxford University Press, 2002); on postmodernism, see Anthony C. Thiselton, *Interpreting God and the Post-Modern Self: On Meaning, Manipulation and Promise* (Edinburgh: T&T Clark, 1995).

9.4   The Bible and Science on the Origin of the Universe

The Bible is the Word of God, utterly reliable and without error in all that it pronounces. The question is this: on what does it pronounce? Its relationship to science is based on the following factors.

Science is mandated by God (Gen. 1:26ff.; 2:15ff.). The first command God gave to humanity was to multiply and govern the earth, subduing it to his glory. Integral to the human task as God gave it is that the world be investigated, understood, governed, and developed in a way conducive to displaying the glory of its Maker. Adam was to till the garden and to extend its boundaries to cover the whole earth. He classified the animals, noting their distinctive characteristics. The New Testament presents the incarnate, risen Christ, the second Adam, sovereignly ruling the new creation as our forerunner (Heb. 2:5–9; cf. Ps. 8:3–8; Col. 2:1–3).

God reveals himself in creation (Ps. 19:1–6.; Rom. 1:18–20). The world displays the glory of God and expresses his creative will. Humanity, made by God in his image to be compatible with him, is given the task of ruling the world that itself manifests God's glory. There is an inbuilt affinity between the mind of God, the mind of humans, and the universe around us.[68] It makes science natural to us, from the moment that a toddler discovers the law of gravity by repeatedly throwing everything on the floor. Adam's zoological classification is an example (Gen. 2:19ff.). Afterward, technology, agriculture, industry, and the arts developed rapidly (Gen. 4:17–26).

The purpose of the Bible. As Bavinck says, the Bible was intended for theological purposes, not to provide a history of Israel or a biography of Jesus. "Inspiration was evidently not a matter of drawing up material with notarial precision," for "Scripture does not satisfy the demand for exact knowledge in the way we demand it in mathematics, astronomy, chemistry, etc. This is a standard that may not be applied to it."[69] Nevertheless, while its intent is to make us wise to salvation, it has much to say to science, for "it claims authority in all areas of life."[70] In doing so, "it

---

68. Thomas F. Torrance, *Transformation and Convergence in the Frame of Knowledge: Explorations in the Interrelations of Scientific and Theological Enterprise* (Grand Rapids, MI: Eerdmans, 1984), 215–42.
69. Bavinck, *RD*, 1:444.
70. Bavinck, *RD*, 1:445.

speaks the language of observation and daily life"[71] and so "it speaks of the earth as the center of God's creation and does not take sides between the Ptolemaic and Copernican world-view," for it speaks "in language intelligible to the most simple person."[72] Moreover, it was not written by the rules of contemporary historical criticism; but "it surely does not follow that the historiography of Scripture is untrue and unreliable."[73] Truth is expressed differently in different literary genres.[74] Since the Bible is the supreme authority in all matters of faith and practice, if there is a conflict with scientific theory, or anything else for that matter, the Bible carries the day. However, one's biblical interpretation might need revision too.[75]

Creation and evolution. Space precludes anything more than a cursory summary of a huge topic. Evolutionary theory first appeared as an explanation for biological diversity. Darwin lived and wrote during the aftermath of Romanticism, when development was the theme in a range of disciplines.[76] Later, his ideas were developed into a paradigm that went far beyond its original claims, to be an embracive explanation for everything. In this, it has taken on the air of a religious commitment. The leading Chinese paleontologist Jun-Yuan Chen, on a visit to the United States in 1999, remarked, "In China we can criticize Darwin, but not the government; in America you can criticize the government, but not Darwin."[77]

Naturalistic evolution is the idea that the universe, together with its component parts, has developed from purely immanent factors. In naturalistic evolutionary theories humans are advanced animals—merely a stage on the evolutionary process—who may in time be overtaken and deposed, perhaps by intelligent robots. Philosophically, on the metaphysical level, such an idea entails either full-blown determinism or indeterminism, since it accords no place to a transcendent Creator. The chances of the universe having occurred on the basis of naturalistic evo-

---

71. Bavinck, *RD*, 1:445.
72. Bavinck, *RD*, 1:446.
73. Bavinck, *RD*, 1:447.
74. Bavinck, *RD*, 1:447..
75. A well-known example is pre-Copernican exegesis of passages like Pss. 93:1, 96:10, and 104:5, which commonly understood the earth to be fixed and cosmic geocentrism to prevail.
76. Examples include philosophy (Hegel) and theology (Newman, Nevin).
77. Cited in John C. Lennox, *God's Undertaker: Has Science Buried God?* (Oxford: Lion, 2007), 93.

lution are mathematically remote. This is recognized by atheists, from the astrophysicist and mathematician Fred Hoyle, who compared the chances of a random origin to a tornado sweeping through a junkyard and spontaneously assembling a Boeing 747,[78] to Richard Dawkins, who has said that an eye or a hemoglobin molecule would take from here to infinity to self-assemble by mere higgledy-piggledy luck.[79] Dawkins himself recognizes that "if the laws of physics had been even slightly different, the universe would have developed in such a way that life would have been impossible."[80] John Lennox, professor of mathematics at the University of Oxford, remarks, "Is it not to be wondered at that . . . some scientists, when faced by the 3.5 billion letter sequence of the human genome, inform us that it is to be explained solely in terms of chance and necessity?"[81]

Theistic evolution agrees that God is the Creator of all entities other than himself. However, it asserts that he then superintends a cosmic process of evolution that includes humans. Theistic evolution has more connection to providence than to creation as it refers not so much to the beginning of the cosmos as to its development and maintenance.[82] I will refer to it in the next chapter.

Christians have responded in differing ways. Some have ruled out evolution entirely, except for microevolution within species. Others have gone to the opposite extreme by accepting science uncritically, while attempting to maintain a place for God. A third reaction has been to adopt some form of theistic evolution. The issue raises questions not only about science but also about biblical exegesis. (I discuss major interpretations of Genesis 1 in appendix 1.)

At root, the conflict—such as there may be—is not between theology and science. The biblical and theological basis for science is clear, as we have noted. The doctrine of creation provides a grounding for investigation of the natural world, since it establishes that there is order and rationality in the universe, such as is discoverable by reasoned and empirical inquiry. A significant proportion of practicing scientists

---

78. Cited by Lennox, *God's Undertaker*, 123.
79. Cited by Lennox, *God's Undertaker*, 155, from Richard Dawkins, *Climbing Mount Improbable* (New York: Norton, 1996), 67.
80. Richard Dawkins, *The God Delusion* (London: Black Swan, 2007), 169–70.
81. Lennox, *God's Undertaker*, 172.
82. Denis Alexander and Robert S. White, *Beyond Belief: Science, Faith and Ethical Challenges* (Oxford: Lion Hudson, 2004), 120–23.

are Christian believers. Ultimately the conflict is over worldviews and relates to questions underlying the origin of the universe, on which science as such cannot pronounce. It is, as Plantinga argues, a conflict not between science and faith but between science and naturalism; naturalism is unable to provide or account for the necessary preconditions for the intelligibility of science.[83] Ultimately, as Polanyi argued, all knowing rests on unprovable axioms and acceptance of the real existence of what is known.[84]

9.5   Extraterrestrial Intelligent Life?

While the creation of humanity is central to Genesis 1, we will consider it in chapter 11. For now, we will look briefly at whether there is intelligent extraterrestrial life in the universe.

Some argue that there is no extraterrestrial intelligence (ETI) anywhere in the universe. The vast size of the cosmos, it is said, is necessary for humans to be able to live here on the earth. Good scientific reasons have been advanced to explain that the existence of the earth as it is requires a vast universe. A stable universe with gravity must expand or else it will collapse. A universe with human life requires an increasingly vast and old cosmos.[85]

On the other hand, a counterargument suggests that ETI exists, since it is inconceivable that in such a vast universe we are the only such life form. With billions upon billions of galaxies, it is hardly unlikely that there is not a planet somewhere with conditions similar to our own that can support life forms, some of which may have capabilities similar to, or in advance of, ours.[86] This would be no threat to the faith, since all it would entail is that such ETI would be incidental to God's purposes for the human race.[87]

---

83. Alvin Plantinga, *Where the Conflict Really Lies: Science, Religion, and Naturalism* (Oxford: Oxford University Press, 2011). Thanks to Alan Strange for directing me to this source.

84. Michael Polanyi, *Personal Knowledge: Towards a Post-Critical Philosophy* (Chicago: University of Chicago Press, 1958); Thomas F. Torrance, *Reality and Evangelical Theology* (Philadelphia: Westminster, 1983), esp. 42–49, 63–83, 150–54.

85. Stephen M. Barr, "Anthropic Coincidences," *First Things*, June–July 2001, https://www.firstthings.com/article/2001/06/anthropic-coincidences; Fred Heeren, "Home Alone in the Universe?," *First Things*, March 2002, https://www.firstthings.com/article/2002/03/home-alone-in-the-universe-36.

86. Anthony N. S. Lane, "Is the Truth Out There? Creatures, Cosmos and New Creation," *EQ* 84 (2012): 291–306; 85 (2013): 3–18, for an assessment of these arguments.

87. On speculations about multiple incarnations, see Oliver D. Crisp, *God Incarnate: Explorations in Christology* (London: T&T Clark, 2009), 155–75.

What, we may ask, if such forms were moral? Would they worship God? Would or could they have sinned? If so, would God have redeemed them? Would there be other incarnations?

The Bible does address these questions obliquely. There definitely *is* ETI in the vast cosmos. The answers are: yes, they are moral beings; yes, they worship God; no, those that fell await God's judgment; no, there are no other incarnations. Clearly, we know there are angels. These moral beings, about which we know little, either worship and serve God or have sinned and are left to judgment. The unfallen angels serve the heirs of eternal life (Heb. 1:14). They exist not necessarily on other planets but in other realms. The angel Gabriel came "from God to a city of Galilee named Nazareth" in order to visit Mary and to speak to her in her own language (Luke 1:26). These creatures are very powerful (Isa. 37:36; Dan. 10:10–14, 20; 12:1–2) and fast moving (Dan. 9:20–21); and when they appear to humans, great terror results (Daniel 10; Matt. 28:2–5; Luke 1:26–30). Some fell into sin and are kept under lock and key, awaiting judgment (2 Pet. 2:4; Jude 6), of whom the chief is Satan (Rev. 12:9ff.; 20:1–6). However, there is only one incarnation. When the Son came for salvation, he did not take angelic nature into union but became human (Heb. 2:5ff., 16–18).

Then again, in the visions in Revelation, John saw "living creatures" representative of the creation gathered around the throne of God in worship of the Lamb. These are distinct from the twenty-four elders and the angels (Rev. 4:1–5:14). This was a vision, but we must suppose it represents a reality. The Lamb receives homage and praise from throughout the created order, now taken up into the new heavens and the new earth. While we are not given a detailed answer to our question and must leave it in the hands of the all-wise God, it seems that eternity will be filled with praise and obedient faithfulness from throughout the animate and intelligent cosmos.

9.6 The Goodness of God in Creation

The sixth day of creation is capped by the observation that God saw all he had made and pronounced it very good (Gen. 1:31). There was not a single discordant note. Psalm 104 reflects on God's government of his world and his bountiful provision for all manner of creatures. Aquinas attacks those who hold that matter is inferior: "Corporeal creatures according to their nature are good" and come from God.[88] Matter as well as spirit displays the Father's benevolence. This is reinforced by the incarnation, the resurrection, the creation mediatorship of Christ, and the final reconstitution of the cosmos. Together, these great moments in redemption establish God's commitment to all that he made. It is his purpose that all things be headed up under the rule of Christ, his Son (Eph. 1:10).

Today created things are either idolized, as with technology, or else disparaged, as in the case of some radical feminists "who hate their own bodies and reproductive systems."[89] The disparagement of created things is evident also in the culture of death and dissolution engulfing the Western world via abortion, assisted suicide, the homosexual agenda, the redefinition of marriage to exclude procreation as integral, and the campaign for the acceptance of gender fluidity. In contrast, the creation should lead us to God, as Paul indicates in Romans 1:19–20, and to life in communion with him. If the creatures lead us away from God, that is due to humans suppressing the truth in foolishness and godlessness, not an outflow of creation itself. Creation is not to be despised but used to the glory of God and thoroughly enjoyed (1 Tim. 6:17). As I indicate in appendix 1, the weight of Genesis 1 falls at its end, directing us forward to the consummation, the unending seventh day, in Christ the Mediator of creation (Eph. 1:10). God's eternal electing purpose to be God in Christ, governing the cosmos, in union with humanity, is the great underlying theme.

Barth comments brilliantly concerning "the appearance of man at the summit of creation," created in the image of God, tasked with multiplying and ruling, that it is not he who brings the history of creation to an end. Rather,

> it is God's rest . . . God's free, solemn, and joyful satisfaction with that which has taken place and has been completed as creation, and his invitation to man to rest with him. . . . The goal of creation . . . is the event of God's Sabbath freedom, Sabbath rest, and Sabbath joy, in which man, too, has been summoned to participate. . . . Everything that precedes is the road to this supreme point.

---

88. Aquinas, *ST* 1a.65.1.
89. Peter Kreeft, *A Summa of the Summa: The Essential Philosophical Passages of St. Thomas Aquinas'* Summa Theologica *Edited and Explained for Beginners* (San Francisco: Ignatius, 1990), 219.

Indeed, "rightly to understand this passage, it is necessary to read it backwards."[90]

Wenham comments:

> The Bible versus science debate has, most regrettably, sidetracked readers of Gen 1. Instead of reading the chapter as a triumphant affirmation of the power and wisdom of God and the wonder of his creation, we have been too often bogged down in attempting to squeeze Scripture into the mold of the latest scientific hypothesis or distorting scientific facts to fit a particular interpretation. When allowed to speak for itself, Gen 1 looks beyond such minutiae. Its proclamation of the God of grace and power who undergirds the world and gives it purpose justifies the scientific approach to nature. Gen 1, by further affirming the unique status of man, his place in the divine program, and God's care for him, gives a hope to mankind that atheistic philosophies can never legitimately supply.[91]

Further Reading

Bavinck, Herman. *Reformed Dogmatics*, ed. John Bolt, trans. John Vriend. Vol. 2, *God and Creation*. Grand Rapids, MI: Baker Academic, 2004.

Gunton, Colin E. *The Triune Creator*. Grand Rapids, MI: Eerdmans, 1998.

Plantinga, Alvin. *Where the Conflict Really Lies: Science, Religion, and Naturalism*. Oxford: Oxford University Press, 2011.

Study Questions

1. Distinguish the Christian doctrine of creation from emanationism, pantheism, and naturalistic evolution.

2. To what extent is it valid to say that the Bible is in conflict with science?

3. In what ways is creation an icon?

---

90. Barth, *CD*, III/1:98–99.
91. Wenham, *Genesis 1–15*, 40.

10

Providence

Providence refers to God's preservation and government of creation. It is comprehensive, relating to human affairs, the animate world, and the entire universe, from subatomic particles to galaxies. Normally, God rules through created means, whether the free choices of free agents, the instinct of other creatures, or the natural processes governing inanimate entities. He also uses angelic powers, about which we know very little. He has a special care for his church and has promised to protect and build it. At various times he works directly in miracles, signs of his kingdom. Because of the fallen state of the world, many events such as tragedies, disasters, and atrocities are inexplicable from our present perspective and will be resolved only eschatologically.

✠

10.1 Biblical Discussion

The biblical doctrine of providence opposes *deism*, which regards God as allowing the world to operate under its own immanent laws without his ongoing involvement. Instead, God actively governs the world and is not an absentee landlord. Moreover, God's government respects the integrity of secondary causes, those immanent relationships that are the object of scientific analysis and everyday observation. These are preserved according to their respective natures. Humans and animate creatures, as free agents, operate according to choice or instinct, whereas inanimate entities work according to the laws that govern their processes, while at a higher level God sovereignly implements his purposes (WCF, 5). Divine, created, and human actions function at different levels.

Providence is also opposed to *occasionalism* as taught by Jonathan Edwards. Edwards held that God creates the world every nanosecond. Edwards writes, "The existence of created substances, in each successive moment, must be the effect of the *immediate* agency, will, and power of God" or "from the immediate *continued* creation of God."[1] Edwards explains what he means: "God's upholding created substance, or causing its existence in each successive moment, is altogether equivalent to an *immediate production out of nothing*, at each moment. . . . So that this effect differs not at all from the first creation."[2] It is literally a re-creation of all entities over and over again. "God produces the effect as much from *nothing*, as if there had been nothing *before*."[3]

With Edwards, there is no room for secondary causes, since all that happens is a result of a direct creative act of God. Nothing in the world can be said to be the cause of any other thing in the world. God is the immediate author of all events, including sin. This is not providence but only creation repeated on a continuous basis. Indeed, with Edwards there can be no stable doctrine of creation at all. This is a radical departure not merely from Reformed but even from Christian orthodoxy. Crisp notes that by dispensing with secondary causes, Edwards makes God the author of all human actions, including sin, and in doing so moves in the direction of pantheism or at least panentheism, affirming that the world is the necessary output of God's creativity. The only way Edwards could escape this problem, Crisp argues, is by surrendering the simplicity of God.[4] Edwards may have been overreacting to deism. If so, he directly created more problems than he was trying to solve.

The biblical doctrine is also opposed to a risky doctrine of providence associated with Arminianism and open theism. For Arminianism, God ordains those things he foresees his creatures will perform. In effect, he rubber-stamps the decisions and actions of the creature. For the latter, an extreme version of Arminianism, God ordains only some things and so there is no guarantee as to how events will work out; not even God

---

1. Jonathan Edwards, "The Great Christian Doctrine of Original Sin Defended," in *The Works of Jonathan Edwards* (1834; repr., Edinburgh: Banner of Truth, 1974), 1:223.
2. Edwards, *Works*, 1:224.
3. Edwards, *Works*, 1:224.
4. Oliver Crisp, "On the Orthodoxy of Jonathan Edwards," *SJT* 67 (2014): 304–22.

knows this. Helm suggests that these ideas were born out of a concern for human freedom.[5] Moreover, open theism's claim that God does not have certain knowledge of future events entails that God is in time.[6] We considered this error in chapter 5.

The doctrine of God's providence is also opposed to some forms of the theory of middle knowledge. This theory holds that God knows of all theoretically possible future actions (1 Sam. 23:7–13; Matt. 11:20–24). If middle knowledge were held with the assumption of indeterministic human freedom, it would follow that God could not know with certainty what individuals will do in particular circumstances.[7] According to Dabney, middle knowledge is compatible with a Reformed doctrine of providence if it is not committed to human libertarian freedom and accords no contingency to God.[8]

10.1.1   Preservation: The Noachic Covenant

Integral to the doctrine of providence is the covenant God established with the entire human race, as part of the cosmos, recorded in Genesis 8–9. "Noah and his sons" (Gen. 9:1) are the human race following the flood. The covenant entails the restoration and renewal of the created order, encompassing procreation, dominion, and the food supply. It comes in a new context, after the fall, the ravages of sin, and judgment. It is therefore with the *fallen* human race that this covenant with Noah is enacted, together with the rest of creation, animate and inanimate. In this covenant, God promises preservation from universal judgment by a flood.

This covenant addresses the modern-day threat that humanity will be destroyed by a nuclear war, of great concern at times such as the Cuban missile crisis of 1962, the cold war confrontation of the mid-1980s, and escalating tensions relating to North Korea. The human race could now be wiped out within an hour or two on a Friday afternoon. Environmental catastrophe is another threat; Moltmann comments, "The standard of living in the USA, Japan and the European Community cannot be universalized without ecologically exterminating humanity."[9] The No-

---

5. Paul Helm, *The Providence of God* (Leicester: Inter-Varsity Press, 1993), 39–68.

6. Helm, *Providence*, 54–55.

7. Helm, *Providence*, 55–62.

8. Robert L. Dabney, *Lectures in Systematic Theology* (1878; repr., Grand Rapids, MI: Zondervan, 1972), 289. Thanks to Ron Di Giacomo for pointing out Dabney's comments.

9. Jürgen Moltmann, *The Coming of God: Christian Eschatology*, trans. Margaret Kohl (Minneapolis: Fortress, 1996), 225.

achic covenant counters this notion, as well as the fear of universal annihilation through a collision with a large asteroid or an eventual cosmic
implosion. God affirms that he is in charge of the universe and covenants
to preserve it so as to bring his purposes to realization.[10]

No doubt there will continue to be major catastrophes; this is in part
the result of sin (Rom. 8:20–23). Pandemics and wars have eliminated one-
third of the world's population on occasions. The Black Death and World
War I are stark examples of such horrors. However, in the Noachic covenant God promises that a *universal* judgment will not occur throughout
the age until his planned final judgment. This requires, on our part, active
care for the environment, responsible political leadership, and prayer.

The Noachic covenant does not promise simply a restoration of the
Adamic state. The gifts of creation are extended. The human food supply is increased to include animal flesh as well as fruit and vegetables.
The original creation was but the beginning, not the goal. Moreover, it
establishes the covenantal responsibility of all people to God. None can
evade it, for it relates to Noah *and his sons*. It underlines the responsibility of humanity to care for the environment.

Moreover, the Noachic covenant is linked with redemption, the goal
of which is the renovation of the cosmos. The New Testament affirms that
Christ is the Mediator of creation, who upholds all things by the word
of his power (Eph. 1:10; Col. 1:15–20; Heb. 1:1–3; Revelation 21–22).
This covenant displays common grace; God's benevolence extends to the
whole human race, irrespective of the redemptive status of any part of it:
"God blessed Noah and his sons" (Gen. 9:1). This is compatible with a
curse issued against Ham (Gen. 9:24–25), for the blessing and the curse
operated at different levels. Helm thinks that grace may imply active approval by God,[11] but the context does not lend itself to such a conclusion.

10.1.2 Government

God's government is universal. It is comprehensive, including all things
(Eph. 1:10–11). God's eternal purpose is worked out in events, great
and small, of the earth and the cosmos. It extends over the whole of nature (Matt. 5:45; 6:30; 10:29; Acts 14:17): climate, harvests, economic

---

10. See Moltmann, *The Coming of God*, 202–35, for an extensive and brutally realistic discussion of exterminism.
11. Helm, *Providence*, 99–100.

performance, war and peace (Gen. 8:21–22), sun and rain (Matt. 5:44–45). The animal world is included too, down to the smallest sparrow (Ps. 104:21, 27–28; Matt. 6:26).

This rule is over nations and international politics (Ps. 66:7; Isa. 10:5–7, 15; Dan. 2:21; 4:35). The plans and intentions of world leaders and the policies they devise and implement are in the hands of the Lord (Prov. 21:1). The fortunes of the most powerful rulers (Dan. 4:1–37; 5:1–31) and the rise and fall of nations and kingdoms, empires and principalities, economic communities and power blocs are all under his control (Isa. 13:1–24:23). Christ is the ruler of kings (Rev. 1:5).

God's providence directs not only the high and mighty but also the humblest individuals and families (1 Sam. 2:6–7; Est. 1:1–10:3; Ps. 75:6–7; Prov. 16:9; Isa. 45:5; Acts 17:25–26), as well as the details of their lives, including what appear to be concatenations of chance circumstances (Matt. 6:25–34). This entails God's appointment of acts freely chosen by responsible agents (Ex. 3:21; 1 Kings 22:13–36; Prov. 16:1; 21:1; Ezek. 7:27)—the drawing of lots, lucky breaks, random and apparently purposeless actions.

10.2   The Meaning of *Providence*

The WCF, 5, the fullest Protestant definition of *providence*, sees it as God's upholding and governing of all things. Helm considers this chapter of the confession to preserve the centrality of God, as the divines sought to be faithful to Scripture by arguing not from logic but from the Bible. The distinction between primary and secondary causes was drawn from Aristotelian philosophy, but as a means of understanding the entailments of biblical teaching.[12]

Providence is more than God's preservation of the universe; it is his directing and governing of it. He actively rules his creation. His government accords with his character; it is wise, good, and holy. His foreknowledge is infallible, and his will unchangeable. Morris remarks of WCF, 5: "No definition of providence so exact and so comprehensive as this can be found elsewhere in Protestant symbolism."[13] In creation God brings entities into existence, whereas in providence he governs and directs those entities in an ordered, coherent, and purposive undertaking.

---

12. Paul Helm, "Westminster and Protestant Scholasticism," in J. Ligon Duncan III, *The Westminster Confession into the 21st Century* (Fearn: Mentor, 2005), 2:99–116.

13. Edward D. Morris, *Theology of the Westminster Symbols: A Commentary Historical, Doctrinal, Practical on the Confession of Faith and Catechisms, and the Related Formularies of Presbyterian Churches* (Columbus, OH: n.p., 1900), 216.

WCF, 5.2, portrays God as the first cause; he created and governs. The various elements of creation are secondary causes. Thus, God determined that India would win the Fourth Test Match yesterday in Mumbai. However, God's government takes fully into account the weather, the state of the wicket, and the contributions of the various players. The outcome of the game depends on those who participate in it. While God decreed infallibly and immutably that India should win, it happened in harmony with the human factors that produced the victory. The nature of this concatenation changes when we consider inanimate forces that interact in producing the weather. Hence, "by the same providence, He ordereth them to fall out, according to the nature of second causes, either necessarily, freely, or contingently."[14]

The created order does not have its existence of itself; existence entails that what an entity is derives from some other source than itself. Recall the point at the start of chapter 1 that God is not to be conceived as belonging to the realm in which those created things find themselves.

10.3 Ordinary Providence

God uses means. He deploys the free participation of what, in Aristotelian terms, are called "secondary causes." He determined that it should rain this morning in Bridgend, Wales—he frequently decides this. His plan is implemented through air pressure, the direction of winds, temperature, dew point, and so on, factors which, singularly and together, can explain why it is raining. The integrity of these secondary sources is maintained; a weather report represents this. But these forces are all directed in accordance with the eternal will and purpose of God.

In the natural world, God makes the grass grow for the cattle (Ps. 104:14), and he does so through rain and the climatic conditions that produce it. Similarly, with human actions, God decreed that the Allies should win the Second World War, defeating Nazi Germany. However, this did not occur apart from the efforts of millions of soldiers and

---

14. For further reading, see Richard A. Muller, *Divine Will and Human Choice: Freedom, Contingency, and Necessity in Early Modern Reformed Thought* (Grand Rapids, MI: Baker Academic, 2017). Among other things, Muller argues, with vast scholarship, that current categories of libertarianism and compatibilism are inadequate to describe historical discussions of the relationship between divine sovereignty and human choice, working as such discussions were with Aristotelian categories of primary and secondary causation that provided a conceptual basis for flexibility and nuancing of the complexities of the interaction of God's government and human free agency. This is essential reading for advanced discussion.

civilians from many countries, and the leadership of Churchill, Roosevelt, Stalin, and a range of others. God's sovereignty and human action work together, the former being the driving force.

In terms of salvation, Paul exhorts his readers, "Work out your own salvation . . . for it is God who works in you, both to will and to work for his good pleasure" (Phil. 2:12–13). In his own case, Paul asserts that the grace of God toward him was not in vain, for "I worked harder than any of them" (1 Cor. 15:10). Once again, this stands in stark contrast to the fatalism of Islam.

10.4   Extraordinary Providence

Sometimes there is a very unusual concatenation of events, eliciting the thought that it is a lucky sequence: "What a coincidence!" Israel's crossing of the Red Sea is a case in point, for it happened in conjunction with a strong east wind (Ex. 14:21). The forces at work appear natural, yet the primary actor is God, and the conjunction at that particular time remarkable. The book of Esther does not mention God at all, yet the constant series of coincidences demonstrates his invincible purpose throughout.

The episode in 1 Kings 22 is striking. There Micaiah prophesies that wicked King Ahab will be killed by the Syrians in battle (vv. 13–23). Ahab takes every precaution, disguising himself as an ordinary soldier. The Syrians instead target Jehoshaphat, king of Judah, allied with Ahab, since he wears his royal robes. Realizing that Jehoshaphat is not Ahab, the Syrians withdraw, since they aim to kill Ahab (vv. 29–33). At that point, a Syrian bowman fires an arrow aimlessly and randomly into the air and it happens to strike and mortally injure the disguised king (vv. 34–36). This is a normal use of human and inanimate means in accord with their respective modes of operation but in ways that appear to us to transcend the usual course. They involve a highly unusual interconnection, indicative of a higher purpose beyond the thoughts of the actors.

WCF, 5.3, recognizes that, while he normally uses creaturely means, God is not bound to his creation. He is free and sovereign and can dispense with means if he so wishes. He is free to work above means or against them too. Miracles come into this category; we will discuss these shortly. The resurrection is contrary to the normal process of secondary causation; yet God can reconstitute the body as and how he pleases. On a lower level, someone may contract a terminal illness beyond the power of medicine to cure. Yet God is able to heal without the intervention of medical professionals just as he heals through surgery, therapeutic chemicals, or a cup of tea and an aspirin. This contradicts the Enlightenment view that the world operates purely from immanent causes, from which the miraculous is in principle excluded.[15] It equally counters the notion that we are to look for the miraculous, since God ordinarily makes use of means.

10.5   Supernatural Providence: The Ministry of Angels

There is little that we know about angels, other than that they are immensely powerful spirits. In the Old Testament, some bore messages from God to the patriarchs. The angel of the Lord slaughtered the firstborn of animals and humans in one night (Ex. 11:1–12:30). Other angelic beings were engaged behind the scenes in administering human affairs, battling the political leaders of the day (Isa. 37:36–38 and parallels; Dan. 9:20–23; 10:1–12:13). In the New Testament, they are present at the birth of Jesus, strengthening him in his temptations (Matt. 4:11; Mark 1:13; Luke 22:43), at the resurrection (Matt. 28:2–7; Mark 16:5–8; Luke 24:4–7), and at his ascension (Acts 1:10–11). An angel assists in rescuing Peter from prison and imminent execution (Acts 12:1–17). The early church apparently believed that an angel is assigned to each believer (Acts 12:12–15; Heb. 13:2), a view backed up by Jesus's reference to children (Matt. 18:1–6; 19:13–15). Angels are deployed in the service of the elect (Heb. 1:14). It follows that particular aspects of God's providential care for the church are delegated to the creaturely agency of angels. It is equally clear that we know nothing specific about this topic, for the details have not been disclosed. Some of us may have had experiences highly suggestive of the intervention of angelic powers, but we cannot be precise or speak with authority, since it is a mystery beyond our grasp, being from another realm. Furthermore, the Bible affirms that we are of greater significance to God than are angels (Heb. 1:14; 2:5–16).

10.6   Providence and Human Sin

Sinful actions cannot occur without God's permission. Indeed, he decrees that they take place and that they fulfill his ultimate purposes.

---

15. Morris, *Westminster Symbols*, 219.

Humans sin; God intends very different outcomes. Joseph commented to his brothers, "You meant evil against me, but God meant it for good" (Gen. 50:20). The pinnacle of evil was the crucifixion of the Son of God. God had determined it, yet the Jewish leaders arranged it through the instrumentality of the Roman governor (Acts 2:23).

This raises the old question of whether God is thereby the author of sin. This cannot be. He restrains sin within prescribed bounds (2 Kings 19:28; Ps. 76:10). Sin originates from humans; God is not its author (Jer. 17:9; James 1:13; 1 John 2:16). The conundrum has been expressed by saying that while God is sovereign, he could not be the author of sin, because he is holy. On the other hand, if his sovereignty is understood as permission, this is effectively the same as performance, since it assumes he knows about sins and evils in advance but is either powerless to prevent them or determines not to prevent them.[16]

How we view this affects the study of history. Before Christianity, classical thought understood events to be either due to fate or else random. Consequently, either human action was of no account or the study of history was nugatory.[17] Christianity, based on the Bible, gives a proper place to human actions and motives. The appropriate focus of the historian is the interplay of human agents, since this interplay reflects the concursive relations between God and humans in the course of world history.

10.7   Special Providence

All I have discussed hitherto is what is called "general providence," relating to the government of the whole universe. Special providence refers to God's particular care for his church and those who belong to it. This is evident from the whole of Scripture. Examples are the following.

Yahweh's protection and preservation of the covenant seed is a recurrent theme in the Old Testament. Joseph was sent ahead to Egypt for the survival of the covenant community during the impending famine; "God meant it for good, to bring it about that many people should be kept alive" (Gen. 50:20; see also Ps. 105:16–22). The baby Moses was protected from the murderous plans of Pharaoh by a curious turn of

---

16. Helm, *Providence*, 101.
17. Andrew Louth, *Modern Orthodox Thinkers: From the Philokalia to the Present* (London: SPCK, 2015), 91.

events that resulted in Israel's deliverer being raised in the very household that had selected him for destruction and that, much later, he would overthrow (Ex. 1:6–2:10).[18] Frequently, judges were provided to deliver Israel from domination by the surrounding tribes. A long series of seemingly fortuitous and entirely unlikely coincidences resulted in a Jewess, Esther, becoming queen in the Medo-Persian Empire at a time when the Jews were about to be subjected to genocide.

Very striking is the cryptic comment in Daniel 5:31: "And Darius the Mede received the kingdom, being about sixty-two years old." The Jews had been sent into exile. Later the Babylonian Empire was overthrown by the more benevolent Medo-Persians under the leadership of Darius. He was sixty-two years old. Why alone is his age mentioned in the book? He was born at the same time that the exile began! In Judah's darkest days, when its fortunes were at their lowest ebb, there was born the man who would instigate its restoration!

The struggling churches in Asia Minor are presented as under the scrutiny and protection of the glorified Christ (Rev. 2:1–3:22), who had promised that the gates of hell would never prevail against his church (Matt. 16:18; Rom. 8:28; Phil. 1:6). Nothing that occurs to the elect is outside his control. All he sends is for our good. It is not by accident that great trials befall us. Not even death itself is beyond the Creator's care and disposal. While God's providence extends to the whole of creation, he takes special care of his church (Matt. 6:25–34; WCF, 5.7).

On the other hand, a very different picture is painted concerning the wicked (WCF, 5.6). In their case, God withholds his grace. Sometimes he withholds his gifts, thus giving the wicked over to their sins and to the power of Satan so that they harden themselves in their impenitence (Rom. 1:24–28; 11:7–8).

10.8   Evolution

Theistic evolutionists believe that God created the universe ex nihilo but thereafter brought about an evolutionary development that included the origin of the human race.[19] In this view, evolution relates to providence rather than creation.

---

18. What comedic irony!

19. Denis Alexander and Robert S. White, *Beyond Belief: Science, Faith and Ethical Challenges* (Oxford: Lion Hudson, 2004), 120–23.

Evolution has many different aspects. Microevolution, whereby species develop and change over time, is unexceptionable. My father, a member of the Rose Society in the United Kingdom, cultivated—among other things—the Queen Elizabeth rose, pink in color, a cross between a floribunda and a hybrid tea, which was developed in 1954 to celebrate Elizabeth II's coronation the previous year. From it, the grandiflora range of roses was created. The rose itself is still in production and still immensely popular. Other types have been formed from it. However, these are still roses. They represent an evolution within a particular species, brought about by human intervention rather than an unguided process.[20] Few would dispute such instances of evolution.

Macroevolution raises large questions. It refers to such things as the development of new genetic material, with new body structures. Leaving scientific questions aside,[21] the biblical and theological factors are crucial. I remarked that theistic evolution makes room for creation and regards evolution as an aspect of *providence*, as the way God directs the created order to bring about his purposes. However, it faces problems relating to the uniqueness of the human being and the historicity of Adam, which we will consider in chapter 11. Significantly, Alexander and White, while operating within a biblical framework of creation, fall, and redemption, do not address the question of Adam. This, to my mind, is the sticking point.

Overall, macroevolution entails an ongoing progress, the fittest and most adaptable surviving and advancing, with an upward gradient from creation onward. The Christian paradigm is creation, fall, and redemption, applying not only to humanity but to the whole cosmos (Rom. 8:18–23). While there are clearly ways in which these paradigms can coexist on different levels, as explanations that relate to the wider context of God and humanity, they collide.

10.9 Miracles

10.9.1 Defining Terms

New Testament terms. The words used in the New Testament for the miraculous are δύναμις (*dynamis*, "power"), τέρας (*teras*, "wonder"

---

20. See John C. Lennox, *God's Undertaker: Has Science Buried God?* (Oxford: Lion, 2007), 99–100.
21. Lennox, *God's Undertaker*, esp. 99–109. Lennox disputes the claim that macroevolution comes from a lengthy process of microevolution.

or "portent"), which never appears by itself, and σημεῖον (*sēmeion*, "sign"), indicating that the miraculous is never intended to draw attention to itself but instead points to something signified.

Some common characteristics surround the events described by these terms. First, each healing miracle was in response to a clear illness or disease—sometimes a death. Second, in each case an obvious event occurred that defied explanation. The healing was irrefutable. Not even Jesus's opponents could deny it. The signs were both immediate and self-evident, public and dramatic. Third, the change was lasting and not ephemeral. Miracles were signs pointing to a reality, like signposts directing travelers toward a destination, signs of the kingdom of God. In this regard, I am excluding Old Testament theophanies, which are in their own category.

The problem of a working definition. The Bible does not define a sign or wonder. Nor does it rigidly distinguish between natural and supernatural.[22] Hodge defined a miracle as an event in the external world brought about by the immediate efficiency of God.[23] For better or worse, I will adopt that.

Events in the material world. Miracles, signs, and wonders were visible. There was never any question that the events had occurred. Hodge does not consider invisible things such as regeneration in this connection. We cannot comment on something hidden from our sight. Lydia's heart was opened by God, but humans can only observe the evident consequences—in her case, faith (Acts 16:14–15).

The result of the immediate efficiency of God. These were not events of ordinary providence, in which God used secondary causes, such as Israel's crossing of the Red Sea, when Yahweh used a strong east wind (Ex. 14:21). Extraordinary providence must also be distinguished since, while an unusual concatenation, such providence involved creaturely activity. Virginal conception could be said to be a miracle in this sense, although in part secondary causality was present.

The miraculous is also distinguished from supernatural providence, in which God used angels to accomplish his purposes. Apart from revelation, we cannot possibly distinguish between an event brought about by

---

22. Helm, *Providence*, 106.
23. Charles Hodge, *Systematic Theology* (Grand Rapids, MI: Eerdmans, 1977), 2:617–18.

angelic instrumentality and one caused by the direct, unmediated action of God. Hodge's definition has the merit of excluding events where God used secondary causality of whatever kind, besides events on which we are not competent to pronounce.

Does God ever operate directly? WCF, 5.3, suggests he may do so and in fact does. "God, in His ordinary providence, maketh use of means, yet is free to work without, above, and against them, at His pleasure." It would be improper to suggest that God cannot work this way. There is a distinction between what God is *able* to do and what he *wills* to do; and, beyond this, what he *reveals himself to have done*. God is *able* to do all things in accordance with his nature. However, what he *chooses* to do is the result of his free and sovereign determination. He is under no obligation to do this or that, or anything at all. God has *revealed* what he has determined insofar as he has seen it to be necessary for his glory and our salvation. There are a vast number of things about which he has not seen fit to inform us. In such cases, we are invited to trust him on the basis that he has revealed himself to be wise, loving, and good, and that all he has planned and effected is for our ultimate benefit, whatever means he may or may not have used.

10.9.2   *The Purpose of Miracles*

Miracles serve the redemptive purpose of God. Miracles are not isolated displays of power. Neither Jesus nor the apostles were wonderworkers putting on a show. Jesus's miracles were signs of the kingdom of God (Mark 1:14–15; John 2:1–3:2; 4:46–54). They signified something. The sign corresponded to the reality and indicated its transcendent nature. Moreover, the signs were material. They effected dramatic change in people's physical health, created food, or calmed a raging storm (e.g., Matt. 14:13–20; 15:21–39; Luke 8:22–25). They were not hidden from view; they were public events. The healings were not merely changes in mental or psychological states—although such changes happened to those healed or to those who observed healings—but they delivered from real organic disease. Moreover, in every case it was immediately obvious and indisputable to all that healing had occurred.

Accumulations of miracles mark climactic points in the history of redemption. Miracles are not evenly spread throughout Scripture. There are batches of them at the exodus, at the start of the ministry of the prophets, and with Jesus and the apostles. Paul calls them "signs of a true apostle" (2 Cor. 12:12). This is crucial when we consider the question of their cessation or continuance.

Miracles are connected to redemption and revelation. The miracles of Elisha follow his request for a double portion of Elijah's spirit on his ascension into heaven. Elijah informs him that this will happen if Elisha sees him as he departs. This Elisha does. Afterward, he performs twice as many recorded miracles as Elijah (2 Kings 2:1–14). In turn, the apostles are promised the gift of the Spirit following Jesus's ascension. After they see him ascend, the Spirit is poured out with a profusion of miracles following, attending the rapid expansion of the church (Acts 1:1–11). Again, the changing of the water into wine points to the superiority of Jesus to Moses, who changed water into blood (John 2:1–11).

10.9.3 Have Miracles Ceased?

There is no reason—theoretically—why God might not perform miracles at any time. He is able to do so if he chooses (WCF, 5.3). If this were not so, he would not be sovereign. However, the work of Christ is complete, and the canon of Scripture is closed (Heb. 1:1–3). We await the return of Christ and the consummation of salvation. In that context, given their function in the history of redemption, signs and wonders are *theologically* superfluous. The reality has already definitively happened. God has spoken his final word. There is nothing more he can say. He has said it all. He has left two vivid and effectual signs, baptism and the Lord's Supper, together with the Word, all pointing to the incarnate Word, Jesus Christ, the eternal Son of the Father. Miracles may happen; if so, they do not have the same function as they once did.

On another note, we need to take account of the ministry of angels and the reality of extraordinary providence. We do not know the agents underlying much that happens. Angels are "ministering spirits sent out to serve for the sake of those who are to inherit salvation" (Heb. 1:14; cf. Acts 12:1ff.). They operate behind the scenes, and we are unaware of what they do. Additionally, in many cases an amazing range of co-incidences occur to protect God's people or to advance the work of the kingdom. Some extraordinary accounts of protection from danger or of deliverances in times of need defy normal explanation.

Does God heal today? Yes. He normally uses means, varying from a cup of tea and an aspirin to proven home remedies, medication, the body's recuperative powers, surgery, and factors beyond our knowledge. In every case, God heals, usually through created means. On occasions, he may heal directly or, instead, have determined that we die, effecting a permanent and irreversible deliverance from the causes, medical and ethical, of disease.

10.10   Providence, Disasters, and Human Responsibility

Aquinas's discussion of the relationship between providence and evil is helpful to guide us when we consider major incidents and disasters. He considered evil to be a defect, an absence of good. We will consider this further in chapter 13. A defect of action is always caused by a defect in the agent. But in God there is no defect. His intention for the universe is its good order. The corruption of things occurs *per accidens*, incidentally. God does not will this *for its own sake*.[24]

God is not the author of sin. However, this does not mean that there is an abstract principle of evil. Aquinas argues that since God is the cause of every being,[25] there cannot be any supreme principle of evil in opposition. Nothing can be bad in terms of its being since every being is good, for evil can exist only in what is good. Moreover, while evil lessens good, it never overcomes good. Citing Aristotle (*Ethics* 4.5), Aquinas argues that if something could be wholly evil, it would destroy itself. Since evil is parasitic on the good, anything wholly evil would destroy the good and so annihilate itself.[26] Since evil is absence of participation in the good and thus only has an accidental—an incidental, nonsubstantial—cause, there can be no essential evil, no positive entity as such.[27]

Evils, atrocities, major disasters. It was a foggy autumn morning, the sun soon to break through the mist to give a bright and mellow day. I was a few weeks short of five years old. It was just after 8:15 and my father had left for work. The back door was open, my mother outside, while I stood on the steps, waiting until she took me to school. Suddenly we heard a strange sound through the fog, the sound of what seemed

24. Aquinas, *ST* 1a.49.2.
25. Aquinas, *ST* 1a.2.3, 1a.6.4.
26. Aquinas, *ST* 1a.49.3.
27. Aquinas, *ST* 1a.49.3.

to me to be the clash of a large pile of saucepans. "What was *that?*" my mother, turning suddenly, exclaimed with some alarm. A strange puzzlement came over us. A few seconds later came another loud clatter of saucepans, perhaps louder and longer, together with a deep rumbling. Very strange, very sinister, very foreboding.

We soon knew the answer. We had heard the sound, a mile and a half away, of the terrifying Harrow and Wealdstone train crash of October 8, 1952. The Perth to London express, ninety minutes late, had plowed into a suburban train standing in the station at the height of the morning rush hour. There were no automatic early warning signals in those days, and the fog was thick. The driver had gone through the red light; had he even seen it? The wreckage spewed across the adjacent line. Less than thirty seconds later the London Euston to Liverpool express, powered by two steam engines, tore into the tangled mass of the first collision, mounted the opposite platform, roared into the waiting crowds, brought down the covered passenger bridge overhead, and ended up lying at a drunken angle high on the platform. In all, 112 people died and around 350 were seriously injured or maimed. It remains the worst civilian train crash in British history. Everyone in the area knew multiple people who died. A five-year-old classmate of mine lost his father that morning. The following day he stood in the class, bawling his eyes out. There was no counseling, no time off, for at five you just gritted your teeth, kept a stiff upper lip, and got on with life; the Second World War had ended only seven years earlier, and there was no time for mourning then.

Tragedies, disasters—we cannot make sense of them. Today, I still feel the sense of numbness that hit me a few years later when eight of the Manchester United team were killed in the Munich air crash in February 1958. A brilliant young team, about to conquer Europe it seemed, gone after a third attempt to get in the air when the plane was iced up and the runway full of snow.

Tragedies involving human moral responsibility. Individual sins can bring devastation, ranging from minor to severe. Among the latter sort would be murder, cannibalism, adultery, theft, physical assault, rape, and slander. These can destroy individual lives and families. Human sin also has its effects on the environment, with the degradation of resources too commonly resulting. Wars, genocide, terrorism are immense moral evils.

Notwithstanding, WCF, 5.4, states that within the bounds of God's providence is included the fall of humanity and the angels into sin. This he not only permitted but ordered and governed with "a most wise and powerful bounding." God was not a passive spectator watching help-lessly. Sin was part of his greater purpose, "to his own holy ends." He kept it within the limits he had ordained, eschatologically, for his glory and our greater good. Accountability rests squarely with fallen angels and humans; God himself cannot be held responsible. This of course raises big questions, but it is the consensus of the Christian tradition.

Disasters stemming from the effects of sin on the creation. Here are to be considered natural disasters such as volcanic eruptions, earthquakes, hurricanes, and tsunamis, together with human accidents, like plane crashes and train wrecks.[28]

Human sin and the providence of God. The connection between human suffering (disease, bereavement, and the like) and the providence of God is a perpetual conundrum, frequently agonizing. Why was the brilliant cellist Jacqueline du Pré struck down by multiple sclerosis at the age of twenty-eight? Why was the all-conquering Torino football (soccer) team that supplied the entire Italian national side wiped out in an air crash in 1949? Why were thousands upon thousands killed in the Indian Ocean tsunami in 2004? Why are there countless private human tragedies? Why? We do not know.

We do know that human disease and death owe their existence to sin and its impact (Rom. 5:12). That does not mean that this or that death, illness, or tragedy is the direct result of sin in the one who suffers it. Sometimes, this may be so, but usually it is not.

If God is loving and sovereign, how can these things happen? Either he is love and not sovereign and is unable to stop them, or he is sovereign and decrees that they happen but is not loving, so the argument runs. In both putative cases, he would not be the God of Scripture. The book of Job wrestles with these problems. Since these things happen on a seemingly random basis, there is no ready-made solution, other than the promise and expectation that God will put things right at the final

---

28. For a thorough exploration of a theological approach to major incidents, see Roger Philip Abbott, *Sit on Our Hands, or Stand on Our Feet? Exploring a Practical Theology of Major Incident Response for the Evangelical Catholic Christian Community in the U.K.* (Eugene, OR: Wipf & Stock, 2013).

judgment. One preacher I know used to refer frequently in sermons to "this hospital of a world," an apt description of a world torn by sin and discord, and a cosmos groaning in disorder. Paul in Romans 8:18–23 looks ahead in hope to the redemption of the body. Then justice will be done; now injustice prevails. It is a mystery. Many attempts have been made to address this question. We do not have space to consider them in detail; this is systematic theology not a volume on ethics.

The free will defense. Held by Arminian theology, this attributes all ills to human free will and so attempts to relieve God of any connection with evil events. However, it relinquishes God's sovereignty, asserting that he does not infallibly foreordain everything that happens. He leaves space for human freedom, the power of contrary choice, the freedom to choose evil. In this view, God may not even know all that will occur. It pits God against humanity, the freedom of the one limiting the freedom of the other, contrary to their created compatibility. At the extreme, open theism argues that God does not have certain knowledge of the future. Even further along the spectrum, outside the historic Christian tradition, are the views of Thomas Jay Oord, who considers God to be self-emptying, uncontrolling love. Oord's God cannot prevent evil, does not know future possibilities, and cannot act directly in the world. This view is the logical conclusion of abandoning the supreme authority of Scripture, relinquishing the sovereignty of God, and setting up an imagined ontological dualism in which evil has necessary existence. I discussed this in passing in chapter 5.[29]

Middle knowledge. This is an attempt to marry divine sovereignty and human freedom. In contrast to the advocates of the free will defense, God foreknows not only everything that will happen but also all possible outcomes. Knowing these possibilities, God brings about what he purposes by arranging circumstances that will implement them. Craig believes that opponents "have not shown that . . . counterfactuals of freedom cannot be true or that they cannot be logically prior to God's decision to actualize a world or that God cannot know them at such a moment."[30] Moreover, he contends that middle knowledge

---

29. Thomas Jay Oord, *The Uncontrolling Love of God: An Open and Relational Account of Providence* (Downers Grove, IL: IVP Academic, 2015), passim.
30. William Lane Craig, *Divine Foreknowledge and Human Freedom: The Coherence of Theism: Omniscience* (Leiden: Brill, 1991), 278.

is compatible with divine freedom, since the counterfactuals relate to human freedom. As such, "God's sovereignty and man's freedom are logically consistent."[31] Nevertheless, this is a compromise and does not work, since its default position is human autonomy, indeterministic freedom, the power to choose or not to choose. Therefore, there is no guarantee that humans will act in particular ways for, under the premise of indeterministic freedom, they are free to act in any way, and if so, God will not have certain advance knowledge of such acts.[32]

Risk-free providence. God's providential government is comprehensive. This is the most common view in the church, from Augustine to Aquinas, Calvin, and the Westminster Assembly. It seems most in harmony with the Bible.[33] It is by no means incompatible with human freedom.

Our perspective is necessarily limited. We can see only the immediately evident context; God sees the whole in one instantaneous act of cognition. Tony Lane compares this relationship to a tapestry. On one side is a disordered mass of threads sticking out of the fabric; on the other side is a beautiful work of art.[34] The resolution, such as we are able presently to reach, lies along the lines of the compatibility of the sovereignty of God with the free agency of humans, the resolution being eschatological, at the last judgment, when God will set all things right.

As mentioned earlier, Frame has a useful section on questions often asked about the will of God for one's life.[35] In the end, we need to exercise wisdom to determine the best course of action for ourselves within the bounds of God's revealed will. Whom should I marry? What job should I accept? How should I spend my free time? There may be a wide variety of valid alternatives. We need to act within the bounds of Scripture, informed by a realistic assessment of the gifts God has given us and the circumstances in which he has placed us.

Providence and prayer. Prayer relates to this scenario, as it is part of human responsibility. God has planned all things from eternity, yet we

---

31. Craig, *Divine Foreknowledge*, 278. See also William Hasker, David Basinger, and Eef Dekker, *Middle Knowledge: Theory and Application* (Frankfurt am Main: Peter Lang, 2000).

32. See Helm, *Providence*, 55–61, for a fuller discussion. Note that the scenario changes without the premise of human indeterministic freedom and divine contingency, as Helm notes.

33. See the exposition in Helm, *Providence*, 209–15.

34. Anthony N. S. Lane, *Exploring Christian Doctrine* (London: SPCK, 2013), 90.

35. John M. Frame, *The Doctrine of God* (Phillipsburg, NJ: P&R, 2002), 539–42.

are to pray. How do these elements cohere? Aquinas again has a helpful comment, bringing the themes together:

> Divine providence not only disposes what effects will take place, but also the manner in which they will take place, and which actions will cause them. Human acts are true causes, and therefore people must perform certain actions, not in order to change divine providence, but in order to obtain certain effects in the manner planned by God. What is true of natural causes is also true of prayer, for we do not pray in order to change the decree of divine providence, rather we pray in order to obtain by our prayers those things which God has planned to bring about by means of prayers.[36]

Therefore, human action, prayer in particular, has a real part in God's providential ordering of the world. This leads on to grace, the saving action of God, which is also part of providence. But that, and prayer as part of it, will be reserved for later discussion.

Further Reading

Helm, Paul. *The Providence of God.* Leicester: Inter-Varsity Press, 1993.
Muller, Richard A. *Divine Will and Human Choice: Freedom, Contingency, and Necessity in Early Modern Reformed Though.* Grand Rapids, MI: Baker Academic, 2017.

Study Questions

1. God is good and he is sovereign over the entire universe. Why, then, do evils and atrocities occur?

2. Discuss whether we should expect miracles to happen.

3. Is it legitimate to suggest that we can know God's attitude toward this or that event from the way he allows things to transpire in the world?

---

36. Aquinas, *ST* 2a2ae.83.2; see the Blackfriars translation in Brian Davies, Summa Theologiae: *A Guide and Commentary* (Oxford: Oxford University Press, 2016), 261–62.

PART 4

THE IMAGE OF GOD

For it was not to angels that God subjected the world to come, of which we are speaking. It has been testified somewhere,

> "What is man, that you are mindful of him,
>   or the son of man, that you care for him?
> You made him for a little while lower than the angels,
>   you have crowned him with glory and honor,
>   putting everything in subjection under his feet."

Hebrews 2:5–8

11

Humanity in Creation

Humanity is central to God's purposes in creation. He who is life granted contingent, finite life to his special creature. Adam was created by God as head of the human race. Male and female were made equally in the image of God. The image has often been understood to consist in characteristics intrinsic to humans, such as righteousness and holiness. In recent years, it has been viewed in a relational manner or in terms of dominion. However, the paradigm of the first and second Adams may be closer to the mark. This will help us avoid the problem arising from whether fallen humanity is still in the image of God and, if so, in what sense. Questions relating to the composition of human psychology (trichotomy, dichotomy) and the origin of the soul are seemingly abstruse yet have a significant bearing on a range of issues, including Christology and the origin of human life.

11.1 Adam as a Historical Person, Unique Creation, and Original Progenitor

It has become common for some evangelical scholars to posit the idea that Adam was not a historical person or, if he was, he was simply a member of some hominin species who was elevated by God to be his image. In either theory, Adam is something other than the unique, historical, special creation of God. These ideas have emerged out of the growing interest in human origins fueled by archaeological discoveries, the application of DNA to ancient skeletal remains, the genome project, and the like. Science has, to many, challenged the viability of the Genesis account. Ways have been sought to bring the two into some kind of harmony. This is nothing new, although recent developments have intensified it. Long ago, in AD 418, Augustine wrote: "For how could I now possibly *prove* that a man was made of the dust, without any parents, and a wife formed for him out of his own side? And yet faith takes on trust what the eye no longer discovers."[1]

As I have remarked, Genesis does not tell us everything that happened. It does not mention the creation of angels. It is based in the world of ancient Near Eastern agrarian societies, not our own. It does not address questions that were to arise millennia afterward. It is not a complete history of the origins of humanity or its early development. Much as we might wish that it did, it does not tell us how old the earth is or how long ago Adam lived.

The crucial point, based on its treatment in the rest of the Bible, is the historical existence of Adam as the progenitor of the race, his being in the image of God, his relationship to the rest of the human race, and his responsibility for sin and its transmission to all his descendants. Questions relating to the covenant and sin I will discuss later. For now, we confine ourselves to the origin of humanity as created by God.

William Stone, in his discussion of the current status of paleoanthropology, mentions that the existing evidence of human origins in terms of skeletal remains and the corresponding genetic evidence is fragmentary, susceptible to problems owing to the passage of time and the resulting degradation, and open to wide varieties of interpretation. However, he concludes that there is clear evidence on the basis of current scholarship to distinguish "between the genus *Homo* and the *australopithecine* genera."[2] He places Adam at the head of the genus *homo* 1.8 million years ago. That may possibly move toward a resolution of scientific issues as currently understood, but it raises questions over the comparative duration of the human race before God instituted the covenant of grace with Abraham approximately 1,796,000 years later. On the other hand, another alternative is to declare the entirety of geology and paleoanthropology mistaken—which it could be—and to date Adam

---

1. Augustine, *On the Grace of God and Original Sin* 2.40.35 (NPNF[1], 5:252).
2. William Stone, "Adam and Modern Science," in *Adam, the Fall, and Original Sin: Theological, Biblical, and Scientific Perspectives*, ed. Hans Madeume and Michael Reeves (Grand Rapids, MI: Baker Academic, 2014), 80.

only a few thousand years back. Such a proposal requires clear, cogent, peer-reviewed, and publicly sustainable explanations on the part of its advocates to account for fossil records indicating apparent diversity and interbreeding. It would threaten to overthrow much modern science. In between, we may need to live with varying tensions between current scientific theories and biblical understanding.[3]

However, such theories are provisional. The Bible is God's revelation and utterly trustworthy, but our understanding is often lacking and, in turn, revisable. Moreover, science is directed, openly or subtly, by the prevailing philosophical and cultural assumptions of those who practice it. Darwin's theories were propounded in an era when organic development was the governing paradigm in philosophy, inherited from Romanticism and Hegel, and was being applied in various disciplines, including theology, with Newman's idea of the development of dogma and Nevin's doctrine of church and sacraments. A significant part of the conflict, if conflict there be, is between current scientific theories and some current exegetical theories. In short, there is a need to disentangle those elements that reside in interpretative theory from those that represent clear theological truth.

Vern Poythress has some pertinent comments.[4] He analyzes the common claim that there is a 99 percent identity between human and chimpanzee DNA. This figure emerged due to a range of restrictions and has led to differing conclusions. "If the comparison focuses only on substitutions within aligned protein-coding regions, the match is 99 percent. Indels constitute roughly a 3 percent difference in addition to the one percent for substitutions, leading to the figure of 96 percent offered by the NIH."[5] Poythress continues:

> But we have only begun. The 96 percent figure deals only with DNA regions where an alignment or partially matching sequence can be found. It turns out that not all the regions of human DNA align with chimp DNA. A technical article in 2002 reported that 28 percent of the total DNA had to be excluded because of alignment problems, and that "for 7% of the chimpanzee sequences, no region

3. Hans Madueme, "'The Most Vulnerable Part of the Whole Christian Account': Original Sin and Modern Science," in Madueme and Reeves, *Adam*, 225–49.
4. Vern S. Poythress, "Adam versus Claims from Genetics," *WTJ* 75 (2013): 65–82. In addition to being a theologian and New Testament scholar, Poythress is also a scientist and mathematician, with a PhD from Harvard.
5. Poythress, "Claims," 66–67.

with similarity could be detected in the human genome." Even when there is alignment, the alignment with other primate DNA may be closer than the alignment with chimp DNA: "For about 23% of our genome, we share no immediate genetic ancestry with our closest living relative, the chimpanzee. This encompasses genes and exons to the same extent as intergenic regions." The study in question analyzed similarities with the orangutan, gorilla, and rhesus monkey, and found cases where human DNA aligns better with one of these than with chimpanzees."[6]

Among Poythress's conclusions, he comments:

> In the midst of rapidly expanding research, popular claims made in the name of science easily fall victim to one of three failings: they overreach or exaggerate the implications of evidence, they misread the significance of technical research, or they argue in a circle by assuming the principle of purely gradualistic evolution at the beginning of their analysis.[7]

The distinct existence of Adam and his being the originally created human and head of the race are vital matters. The New Testament presents powerful theological reasons as to why this is so. The apostle Paul founds the biblical account of the fall of humanity and redemption in Christ on the parallel and contrast between Adam and Christ, the first and second Adams (Rom. 5:12–21; 1 Cor. 15:19–26). If one side of the equation is false, the other will follow, so the argument goes. Moreover, Jesus also based important teaching on the existence of Adam (Matt. 19:1–6). In the light of this, Collins's suggestion, advanced no more than tentatively, and considered by Frame, that Adam may have been the covenant head of a tribe of humans, while interesting, should be treated with considerable reserve.[8]

---

6. Poythress, "Claims," 67.

7. Poythress, "Claims," 80. Poythress cites, for example, Ingo Ebersberger et al., "Genomewide Comparison of DNA Sequences between Humans and Chimpanzees," *American Journal of Human Genetics* 70 (2002): 1490–97, esp. 1492–93, http://www.cell.com/AjHG/abstract/S0002-9297%2807%2960701-0; Ingo Ebersberger et al., "Mapping Human Genetic Ancestry," *Molecular Biology and Evolution* 24 (2007): 2266, http://mbe.oxfordjournals.org/content/24/10/2266.full.pdf; referenced by Casey Luskin, "Study Reports a Whopping '23% of Our Genome' Contradicts Standard Human-Ape Evolutionary Phylogeny," *Evolution News*, June 3, 2011, http://www.evolutionnews.org/2011/06/study_reports_a_whopping_23_of047041.html. For a clear exposition of different meanings of "evolution," see John C. Lennox, *God's Undertaker: Has Science Buried God?* (Oxford: Lion, 2007), 100–108, cited by Poythress, "Claims," 68.

8. John M. Frame, *Systematic Theology* (Phillipsburg, NJ: P&R, 2013), 805–6.

In his work on John of Damascus, Andrew Louth obliquely refers to the Christological implications of Adam. In the monothelite controversy,

> it soon became clear that, since human willing as we know it is bound up with the consequences of the Fall, which makes a free choice of the good well nigh impossible, it would be necessary to form some concept of what the unfallen experience of free will would be like, if one were not to misconstrue the moral experience of the Incarnate One.[9]

Adam is crucial for Christology as well as soteriology.

11.2   Features of Human Origins

God's self-deliberation (Gen. 1:26). The reported speech of God and the comment that follows are the highlights of Genesis 1. It is the only occasion in the narrative where God engages in self-deliberation. It is followed immediately by the only example of parallelism, apart from the repeated refrain ("there was evening and there was morning . . ."). The section stands out in bold relief, highlighted as a distinct element, a pointer to the significance of the whole account. In Barth's words, "The totality of creation reaches its terminus and goal, the meaning and pre-supposition of all God's creative utterances and actions from the very outset."[10]

The unique deliberation "Let us make man in our image" expresses a plurality in God (vv. 26–27). Von Rad comments that this signifies the high point and goal to which all God's creative activity is directed. But what does it mean? A variety of interpretations have been advanced to explain it. First, some suggest that God addresses the angels and places himself in the heavenly court, so that humanity is made like the angels.[11] However, the agents addressed are invited to share in the creation, something never attributed to angels elsewhere in the Bible. Second, the idea of a plural of majesty, underlining God's dignity and greatness,[12] is no longer as favored as it once was. Third, Westermann and many recent

---

9. Andrew Louth, *John Damascene: Tradition and Originality in Byzantine Theology* (Oxford: Oxford University Press, 2002), 154.

10. Barth, *CD*, III/1:183.

11. Gerhard von Rad, *Genesis: A Commentary*, rev. ed. (Philadelphia: Westminster, 1961), 57–59.

12. S. R. Driver, *The Book of Genesis: With Introduction and Notes* (London: Methuen, 1926), 14.

interpreters favor a plural of self-deliberation or self-encouragement. Yet few parallels support it.

Wenham puts forward a variant on the theme of the heavenly court, except that he argues that God invites the angels to witness the creation of man rather than to participate in it. He points to Job 38:4–7, where at creation the morning stars are said to sing together and all the sons of God (angels?) shout for joy.[13] Collins considers that in this statement God addresses himself, a latent Trinitarian reference, the *sensus plenior*, the sense of the full canon pointing unmistakably in that direction.[14] Barth took a similar line; it is "a divine soliloquy . . . a divine decision resting on it. . . . It is a summons to intra-divine unanimity of intention and decision,"[15] and represents "a genuine plurality in the divine essence."[16]

The unique nature of humanity as made in the image of God. I will discuss this at greater length later. For now, the image of God entails compatibility with God. Humans are finite creatures but are given a nature oriented toward God, in some way reflecting him. The first humans were "an obvious copy," and there is "a genuine counterpart in God himself." This means that "in God's sphere and being, there exists a divine and therefore self-grounded prototype to which this being can correspond."[17]

Dominion given to humanity over the whole of creation. This is implied in the previous statement. Humans have clear similarities with the animals, fish, and birds. All are created by God; all inhabit the earth and its environment. But humanity is in charge, commissioned to be so by God, the Creator. It is our responsibility to govern the animal world.

The unique procedure in humanity's formation (Gen. 2:7). Nowhere else is the creative process described in any detail. What we have indicates our kinship with the earth. *Adam* is related to *adamah*, the earth. Adam is formed from the dust of the ground, compatible not only with

13. Gordon J. Wenham, *Genesis 1–15*, Word Biblical Commentary 1 (Waco, TX: Word, 1987), 28.
14. C. John Collins, *Genesis 1–4: A Linguistic, Literary, and Theological Commentary* (Phillipsburg, NJ: P&R, 2006), 59–61.
15. Barth, *CD*, III/1:182.
16. Barth, *CD*, III/1:191.
17. Barth, *CD*, III/1:183.

God but also with the creation, particularly the very earth that he is given to work, with the nonanimate as well as the animate world.

Yet there is another dimension setting Adam apart from the rest of the creatures, some of which have a similar kinship with the earth. There is an inbreathing from God,[18] akin to Jesus's breathing out the Holy Spirit (John 20:22). Adam becomes a living creature with the breath of life directly from God. Murray is clear that Adam's becoming living being coincides with his being constituted human, *adam*: "Genesis 2:7 does not refer to any supposed animate progenitor of man," for he is already defined in Genesis 1:26.[19] The formation of Eve has striking similarities, being entirely different from the way the animals were made. Moreover, Adam names the animals, demonstrating authority over them, for "name-giving in the ancient Orient was primarily an exercise of sovereignty, of command."[20]

11.3   Humanity as Male and Female

The last fifty years have seen a transformation of thought on the nature of humanity instigated by the rise of feminism. It is a vital area for ongoing consideration by the church.

11.3.1   *Equal and Different*

Male and female are equally made in the image of God (Gen. 1:26–27). At the same time, God intends male and female to be different (Gen. 2:18–23). There is unity, equality, and difference. Humanity—male and female—is in the image of God, related to God and to each other. This prompted Barth to identify the image of God with sexual differentiation.[21] While this may be going beyond the evidence, there is a clear relationality within humanity, as there is in God, and the two are related to each other.

The distinction is clear in Genesis 2. Adam was given the task of tilling the ground, of cultivating the garden; Eve was formed as a helper for Adam. The man was created directly by God; the woman was taken out of the man. Yet, to both the task was given of subduing the earth to

---

18. John Murray, *Select Lectures in Systematic Theology*, vol. 2 of *Collected Writings of John Murray* (Edinburgh: Banner of Truth, 1977), 7.
19. Murray, *Writings*, 2:8.
20. Von Rad, *Genesis*, 83.
21. Barth, *CD*, III/1:181–206.

the glory of God (Gen. 1:26–31); both together are in the image of God, not the one without the other.

In the wider context of Scripture, the covenant of grace treats the raising and nurturing of the covenant seed as a primary responsibility (Gen. 12:1–3; Deut. 6:1–9; Ps. 78:1–8; Mal. 2:13–16). That means the task of women in giving birth and nurturing children is crucial for the advancement of the church and the gospel (1 Tim. 2:15).This is what has come under attack in the Western world, with the undermining of marriage, childbearing, and the family, together with social and economic changes that give parents far less time for this responsibility.

Marriage is a creation ordinance, given for the benefit of humanity as a whole. It is not peculiar to the church. Yet it is the foundation on which the church is based and a means through which the gospel is handed down from one generation to the next. It is a prime case of God using created means. It should be obvious too that marriage is between man and woman. Since the chief purpose of marriage is procreation, it cannot be otherwise. While marriage is also a means of companionship (Gen. 2:18, 20), this is not its *distinguishing* characteristic, as there are other ways in which companionship can be established and fostered.

Ideally, marriage is between one man and one woman. This has not always been the case, even in the covenant community. Polygamy was tolerated in the Old Testament, as in the case of no less than David, while Abraham had a wife and two concubines; Solomon had hundreds of both. However, this was a concession in which God accommodated himself to the barbaric nature of the times. The New Testament reiterates the purpose as it was laid down at creation (Matt. 19:1–9; Mark 10:2–12). Church leaders are to be monogamous, but there is no call for others in the church to divorce a second wife, it there were any.

It has been remarked that God created Adam and Eve, not Adam and Steve. Humans are sexual beings, male and female made for each other, to be united in marriage (Gen. 2:23–24). That marriage is between a man and a woman is obvious from the biblical record and has been assumed by almost every society since creation. In past epochs, with high mortality rates, the need to gather the harvest in precarious economic and climatic conditions, together with the depredations of wars, childbirth was vital to a people's continuance. In modern Western societies, people have time on their hands. While ethics is outside our purview, we should note that the biblical ordinance is opposed to bigamy, polyamory, bestiality, and homosexuality.

In the New Testament, Paul records that in marriage the husband is the head of the wife (Eph. 5:22–33), that an order exists mirroring the relationship between Christ and the church. This requires the wife to submit to the husband. However, simultaneously it places far greater responsibility on the husband, who is to love his wife as Christ loved the church—with sacrificial love in which he is to lay down his life on her behalf, nourishing and cherishing her as himself. Those who wish to eliminate the part of the wife must also be prepared to reject the responsibilities of the husband. In Christ, believers are called to mutual submission (Eph. 5:21). Paul is simply spelling out what mutual submission looks like in marriage; the husband lays down his life for his wife; the wife, in response to such love, is to submit willingly. It is evident that, due to sin, these features often do not take place. Finally, there are indications that marriage is for this world only (Matt. 22:23–33).

11.3.2   Feminist Theology[22]

Feminist theology covers a wide spectrum, from those with evangelical sympathies to others committed to witchcraft. Elsewhere, I have made a broad-brush description in terms of *evangelical feminism*, those committed to the authority of Scripture and the historic creeds; *Christian feminism*, where there is some identification with the Christian faith but in a critical form; and *religious feminism*, with no explicit commitment to Christianity but rather to various forms of paganism, including witchcraft and goddess worship.[23] In this last camp are authors such as Carol P. Christ, who wrote, "I found god in myself and I loved her fiercely,"[24] and

---

22. On the incompatibility of Christianity and feminism, see Daphne Hampson, *Theology and Feminism* (Oxford: Basil Blackwell, 1990). Hampson, Professor Emerita of Divinity at the University of St Andrews, had been a leading activist for the ordination of women in the Church of England but subsequently abandoned the Christian faith. She is on record as saying, in a 1997 conference speech: "I am a Western person, living in a post-Christian age, who has taken something with me from Christian thinkers, but who has rejected the Christian myth. Indeed, I want to go a lot further than that. The myth is not neutral; it is highly dangerous. It is a brilliant, subtle, elaborate, male cultural projection, calculated to legitimise a patriarchal world and to enable men to find their way within it. We need to see it for what it is. But for myself I am a spiritual person, not an atheist." See Hampson, "An Ethic for the 21st Century," Sea of Faith Network (website), http://www.sofn.org.uk/conferences/hamps97.html. Accessed 22 March 2016.

23. R. Letham, "The Hermeneutics of Feminism," *Them* 17 (1992): 4–7.

24. Carol P. Christ, "Why Women Need the Goddess: Phenomenological, Psychological, and Political Reflections," in *Womanspirit Rising: A Feminist Reader in Religion*, ed. Carol P. Christ and Judith Plaskow (San Francisco: Harper & Row, 1979), 273.

Mary Daly, who prefers to speak of goddess rather than "the hopelessly male identified term God."[25] At the conservative end of the spectrum, *evangelical feminism* has gained ground through many voices.

Any movement that raises new questions suggests prior imbalances that require correction. Among these imbalances is the past evangelical assumption that women could be overseas missionaries but not undertake the same forms of service at home. Leaving cultural factors aside, what is permissible or not in biblical terms in the one place must also be so in the other. If it is impermissible for women to assume leadership in the church in one country on biblical and theological grounds, it can hardly be acceptable elsewhere. Besides, the church has tended to relegate women to lower status despite Paul's listing of ten women out of the twenty-six persons to whom he sent personal greetings as his fellow laborers in Romans 16. In answer to one minister who complained that my seminary had a woman teaching a module on female spirituality, I suggested he get into the TARDIS, go back to the first century, and tell the apostle Paul to ask Priscilla to keep her big mouth shut, or else become an expert on female spirituality so that he could teach it himself! Are there any male experts on female spirituality?

The broad category of what I have termed *Christian feminism* is the most immediately relevant. Among prominent advocates have been theologians such as Elisabeth Schüssler Fiorenza, Rosemary Radford Ruether, Elisabeth Moltmann-Wendel, and Elizabeth Johnson. The basic premises of the movement are as follows: Fiorenza writes that the Bible and the historic Christian church are incorrigibly patriarchal, reflecting cultures dominated by men, with texts and histories written by men, who were the winners. Women's experience has been ignored. The Bible and the church have been oppressive to women. Evidence of the prominence of women in church leadership has been suppressed.[26] Jesus appointed Mary Magdalene as an apostle, but she was ousted after a row with Peter and thereafter written out of the history.[27] An imaginative reconstrual of history is needed, correcting this imbalance and placing women back into the center of the story.[28] Indeed, Sheila Collins prefers to talk of "herstory"

25. Mary Daly, "Why Speak about God?," in Christ and Plaskow, *Womanspirit Rising*, 210.
26. Elisabeth Schüssler Fiorenza, *In Memory of Her: A Feminist Theological Reconstruction of Christian Origins* (New York: Crossroad, 1983), xiii–xxiii.
27. Fiorenza, *In Memory of Her*, 332ff.
28. Fiorenza, *In Memory of Her*, 68f., 167–68.

rather than history. Thus, the feminist herstorian can overcome the imperialism of the historical event.[29]

In this view, only feminist interpretation can do justice to the historical reality of the suppressed leadership of women. A feminist theologian must question whether a man, Jesus, can be a model for contemporary women. The Bible cannot be the canon for Christian feminism, since it was written by men in patriarchal cultures. It perpetuates violence and alienation for women. Only elements that transcend patriarchalism can be accepted as canonical.[30] A paradigm shift is needed, with an avowed advocacy stance in favor of women.[31] Letty Russell thinks that the Bible itself needs liberation.[32]

Ultimately, anything that contradicts feminist convictions is unacceptable. Into this category are the household codes of Ephesians and Colossians, while Genesis 2 raises the question of control over women's bodies.[33] Feminists should therefore adopt a hermeneutic of suspicion toward the Bible, for it refers to women only when they were a problem or were exceptional.[34] Thus, Fiorenza considers the Gospel of John to be anti-Semitic with its vituperative language, not literally true, and marked by androcentric dualism and Christological exclusivism. Its use of the metaphors of light and darkness has bequeathed a long history of racist interpretation that provides a context for racist readings today. Similarly, the Pauline tradition is thoroughly androcentric.[35] To avoid sexist language, Fiorenza writes of *the*logy*, the asterisk circumventing the problem that *theos* is masculine and *thea* feminine.[36] Biblical language is androcentric and kyriocentric, focused on an elite of powerful men, to the exclusion of women; she argues for a non-kyriarchal approach so as to liberate all people.[37]

---

29. Sheila Collins, "Reflections on the Meaning of Herstory," in Christ and Plaskow, *Womanspirit Rising*, 68–73.

30. Elisabeth Schüssler Fiorenza, "Toward a Feminist Biblical Hermeneutics: Biblical Interpretation and Liberation Theology," in *A Guide to Contemporary Hermeneutics*, ed. Donald K. McKim (Grand Rapids, MI: Eerdmans, 1986), 377–79; Fiorenza, *In Memory of Her*, 32–33.

31. Fiorenza, "Feminist Biblical Hermeneutics," 358–64.

32. Letty M. Russell, ed., *Feminist Interpretation of the Bible* (Philadelphia: Westminster, 1985), 11.

33. Susan Brooks Thistlethwaite, "Every Two Minutes: Battered Women and Feminist Interpretation," in Russell, *Feminist Interpretation of the Bible*, 96, 104–6.

34. Fiorenza, *In Memory of Her*, 107–9, 332ff.

35. Elisabeth Schüssler Fiorenza, *Changing Horizons: Explorations in Feminist Interpretation* (Minneapolis: Fortress, 2013), 181–94.

36. Elisabeth Schüssler Fiorenza, *Jesus: Miriam's Child, Sophia's Prophet: Critical Issues in Feminist Christology*, 2nd ed. (London: Bloomsbury, 2015), xxix.

37. Fiorenza, *Jesus*, x.

Connected with this is a generally positive attitude toward paganism. There is an overlap between feminists who identify in some sense
with Christianity and those who, in the interests of women's experience, practice goddess worship and witchcraft. If priority is accorded to
women's experience, goddess worship is not far off, since the God of the
Bible allegedly supports the abhorrent patriarchal system. Fiorenza and
Ruether have contributed to symposia together with practicing witches.[38]
Indeed, Ruether wrote that a female messiah is needed. She describes
God as "the empowering Matrix; She, in whom we live and move and
have our being—She comes; She is here."[39] In line with this hermeneutic,
Letty Russell argues for cooperation, community, and interdependence,
rather than doctrine, which is a very male and patriarchal obsession.[40]

Such ideas are distant from the historic Christian faith. Daphne
Hampson, a prominent feminist theologian and member of the divinity faculty at the University of St. Andrews, concluded that Christianity
and feminism are incompatible, and so she abandoned Christianity.[41] It
betrays a radical gynocentrism, a dualist version of the anthropocentrism
of the post-Enlightenment world. Women, rather than God, are at the
center; God is now goddess. The feminist community is the criterion
of truth, such as there may be. Russell, Ruether, Fiorenza, and Thistlethwaite all acknowledge that the Bible is against them.

It is true that Fiorenza's rejection of the claim to value-free neutrality
is correct. We all come to the text of the Bible with our own presuppositions. The knower has an integral part in knowledge, as Polanyi
convincingly demonstrated.[42] However, feminists go beyond that; the
advocacy stance, far from being a tool to aid interpretation, has become
master (better, mistress). The personal commitments of the interpreter
assume dominance. As George Tyrell described Adolf von Harnack as
gazing down the well of history and seeing at the bottom the reflection of
a liberal bourgeois German face, so the exponent of feminism can hardly
fail to see merely the reflection of a professional middle-class feminist.

38. I say this with a certain reserve since I have contributed to at least one symposium on which I was at odds with many of the other contributors, whose identity was not known to me at the time of writing.

39. Rosemary Radford Ruether, *Sexism and God-Talk: Toward a Feminist Theology* (Boston: Beacon, 1983), 266.

40. Russell, *Feminist Interpretation of the Bible*, 137–46.

41. Hampson, *Theology and Feminism*.

42. Michael Polanyi, *Personal Knowledge: Towards a Post-Critical Philosophy* (Chicago: University of Chicago Press, 1958).

The feminist critical principle entails not only a radically new view of humanity—some dislike this term since it has *man* in it—but a new doctrine of god and a new model for redemption. Ruether suggests a new Christology in which Christ is not necessarily male, in order to avoid distancing women from representation in the new humanity. We need a woman-Christ.[43] Fiorenza agrees with a reviewer that orthodox Christology is not based on objective facts but has been formulated by powerful men under a system of male domination.[44] Elizabeth Johnson claims that Jesus is the embodiment of Wisdom (Sophia). Sophia is feminine. The early church understood it variously to be "sister, mother, bride, hostess, female beloved, woman prophet."[45] So Jesus was "the incarnation of Sophia herself." The patriarchal tendencies of the early church substituted Logos.[46] Johnson has some interesting and useful things to say. However, the drift of her argument is that "women's reality has been excluded from the discourse and consequently suppressed." She continues, "I do not think that we can overestimate the seriousness of the feminist charge brought against christology, that of all the doctrines of the church it is the one most used to suppress women."[47] Woman Christology directs us to a nonsexist version: "Sophia in all her fullness was in Jesus so that in all his particularity he manifests her divine mystery."[48] In Christ, "God revealed herself, her power as Creator, her love as Savior, in a full and final way."[49] The Spirit of Jesus has not dried up for "she moves everywhere throughout the world to heal and redeem and liberate. May she teach us in her ways to go."[50] You can draw your own conclusions as to whether this is a new religion.

---

43. Rosemary Radford Ruether, *Womanguides: Readings Toward a Feminist Theology* (Boston: Beacon, 1986), 105, 111–12; Radford Ruether, *Sexism*, 116–38. That the incarnation is not sexist is argued strongly by Thomas Oden. He writes, with copious references to Augustine, Gregory of Nazianzus, and others, "*If the mother of the Savior must necessarily be female, the Savior must be male, if both sexes are to be rightly and equitably involved in the salvation event,* according to classical interpretation." Thomas C. Oden, *The Word of Life,* vol. 2 of *Systematic Theology* (New York: Harper & Row, 1989), 117–18 (italics original). He cites Augustine, who, for example, remarked that God has concern for both sexes—not only the sex he assumed but also the one by which he did assume the other; and Paul in Gal. 4:4, who writes that the Son was born of a woman "without male assistance, not born of woman and man."
44. Fiorenza, *Jesus,* xiii.
45. Elizabeth A. Johnson, *Jesus-Sophia: Ramifications for Contemporary Theology: Mary Ward Lecture, 1999* (Cambridge: Margaret Beaufort Institute for Theology, 1999), 2.
46. Johnson, *Jesus-Sophia,* 3.
47. Johnson, *Jesus-Sophia,* 11.
48. Johnson, *Jesus-Sophia,* 11.
49. Johnson, *Jesus-Sophia,* 12.
50. Johnson, *Jesus-Sophia,* 13.

Fiorenza's principle of imaginative reconstrual opens the door to the destruction of history—if not herstory. If imagination trumps evidence, it is questionable whether there can be any limit to the rewriting of the past. Moreover, despite the talk of being nonsexist, the drift of the feminist critique is thoroughly dualist. Male and female are virtually two separate creatures with interests and concerns diametrically opposed, locked in irreconcilable conflict. While the differences between men and women are obvious, the Bible (not to mention experience and old-fashioned common sense) indicates that the features held in common far outweigh the distinctions. Both male and female are *adam*, "man" (Gen. 1:26–28), made in the image of God. Both together fell into sin (Gen. 3:1–6). Both need salvation. Male and female are complementary, not competitive.

Evangelical feminism, on the other hand, maintains a determination to work within the bounds of the biblical teaching, although it achieves this aim with varying degrees of success. Much effort has been spent to attain equality in public ministry through the ordination of women to teaching and ruling offices in the church, a matter I address in chapter 27.

11.4   Humanity as Made in the Image of God

There is a certain tension in the biblical record regarding the image of God. Some passages suggest that fallen people remain in God's image despite the effects of sin (Gen. 5:1–3; 9:6; 1 Cor. 11:7; James 3:9). These statements make no discrimination between those who are faithful to God and those who are not. However, other passages suggest that being in the image of God is relational and so belongs to those who are renewed by the Holy Spirit (Eph. 4:24; Col. 3:10).

11.4.1   *Differing Interpretations*

Debate has focused on how to reconcile these apparently diverse readings. The tension has been faced either by positing a dual aspect to the image of God or by collapsing one side of the tension.

Pelagius. With his strongly moralistic theology, Pelagius taught that the image of God consists in reason and free will. These are possessed by all people, and so all are still in the image of God. This is connected with his minimalist view of sin. All retain the power of contrary choice after the fall; all are innately able to do good and respond to the gospel.[51] However, the proposal fails to do justice to the Pauline teaching on renewal in the image by the Holy Spirit. It was condemned as heresy at the Council of Carthage in 418.

Classic Arminianism. Here the solution was sought in the dominion given to humanity over the creation (Gen. 1:26–31). As with Pelagius's view, all people since the fall are in the image of God. Again, this diminishes the Pauline focus on renewal in Christ.[52]

Lutheranism. Luther and Lutheranism took the reverse position to Pelagius. Here, the image consisted in solely spiritual qualities—righteousness, knowledge, and holiness—that were lost in the fall. Consequently, fallen humans retain merely vestiges or remnants of the divine image, while the essence of humanity is unchanged.[53] Since it is the mirror opposite of the Pelagian view, this view's weakness is the reverse. It does not do justice to passages that affirm that humans remain in the image of God regardless of their redemptive status.

What these three perspectives have in common is that one side of the biblical evidence tends to trump the other. In Pelagianism, the statements of Paul are diminished in the belief that all people are in the image of God, more or less unimpaired, whereas for Lutheranism, the Pauline teaching restricts the image and negates the evidence that being in the image of God is something inherent to all people. Thus we turn our attention to two positions—those of Rome and the Reformed—that attempt to do justice to both elements.

Rome. Rome, from Genesis 1:26, draws a distinction between the image and the likeness of God. It shares this distinction with Orthodoxy, although the respective conclusions are not identical. For Rome, the image of God consists of reason, free will, moral agency, and civic virtues. These were possessions of Adam and Eve at creation, in the state of pure nature (*in puris naturalibus*), and are inherent to humans. Additionally, at creation God gave a superadded gift (*donum superadditum*) consisting

---

51. Pelagius, *De libero arbitrio* (*PL*, 48:611–13); Pelagius, *De natura* (*PL*, 44:247–90).

52. G. C. Berkouwer, *Man: The Image of God*, trans. Dirk W. Jellema (Grand Rapids, MI: Eerdmans, 1962), 54–56, 70–72.

53. Formula of Concord, art. 1–2, in Philip Schaff, *The Creeds of Christendom* (Grand Rapids, MI: Baker, 1966), 3:97–114; see Berkouwer, *Man*, 129–37.

of holiness and spiritual virtues. This was the likeness of God. With it was original righteousness, in which the sensuous aspects of human nature were kept in check and in harmony. It was agreed that these distinct elements were given simultaneously at creation, although the Scotists thought that an interval elapsed (Lombard, Bonaventure). The likeness of God—the *donum superadditum*—was lost in the fall, but the image of God was retained. Hence, Rome's position is an attempt to grapple with the biblical tension.

Aquinas argued that man is the image of God due to his intellectual nature, which is most perfectly like God.[54] In the rational creature alone is there a likeness of the image—"a procession of the Word in the intellect, and a procession of the love in the will."[55] Likeness is more general than image, relating to more common things. It is found in the soul's incorruptibility. Citing John of Damascus, Aquinas thought it could also be viewed as an expression of the image.[56] Intellectually, Adam did not know God according to his essence, for if he had, he would not have turned away from him. However, his knowledge was better than ours, midway between us now and the knowledge we will have in heaven. Adam's lower powers were subject to the higher, and the higher nature was made so as not to be impeded by the lower.[57] The rectitude of the primitive state was that "the soul remained subject to God, the lower faculties in man were subject to the higher, and were no impediment to their action." The intellect is never deceived of itself, "but whatever deception occurs must be ascribed to some lower faculty, such as the imagination or the like."[58] This requires that Adam was created in grace, since, "his reason being subject to God, the lower powers to reason, and the body to the soul," this was not according to nature, nor could it be a natural gift, for the effect cannot be greater than the cause. Since the loss of grace resulting from the fall dissolved the obedience of the flesh to the soul, it follows that the lower powers were originally subjected to the soul by grace.[59] For Aquinas, "while in all creatures there is some kind of likeness to God, in the rational creature alone we find a likeness of *image*."[60]

---

54. Aquinas, *ST* 1a.93.4.
55. Aquinas, *ST* 1a.93.6.
56. Aquinas, *ST* 1a.93.9.
57. Aquinas, *ST* 1a.94.1.
58. Aquinas, *ST* 1a.94.4.
59. Aquinas, *ST* 1a.95.1.
60. Aquinas, *ST* 1a.93.6.

Bavinck, reflecting on the Roman argument, believes that it entails conflict between flesh and spirit in creation. This concupiscence was not sinful but a disease arising from materiality. Since after the fall there was a reversion to this, it led to original sin being understood as the loss of the superadded gift, to a negative rather than something positive. Trent was cautious on the matter, adding that Adam was changed for the worse. Concupiscence arises from sin but is not in itself sinful; the free will is not lost but weakened. Consequently, nothing is left for original sin except the imputation of Adam's sin and the loss of original righteousness. Bellarmine openly stated this in *De gratia primi hominis*. The state into which humans are born after the fall is identical to the situation before the fall, with the exception of the loss of the supernatural gift. The natural state remains intact.[61]

While the *Catechism of the Catholic Church* speaks of "the inner harmony of the human person" and states that "the original man was free from the triple concupiscence that subjugates him to the pleasures of the senses," this was due to the *donum superadditum*.[62]

Rome has attempted to grapple with the tension in the biblical material. As with the Reformed view, discussed below, it tries to take both sides of the question into consideration. As Thiselton remarks, contemporary Christians tend to devalue reason and rationality, in contrast to the Christian tradition.[63] However, the Roman argument is beset by weaknesses.

First, its distinction between image and likeness, shared with the Eastern church, is despite the fact that these are used interchangeably in the early chapters of Genesis. Collins indicates that there is no conjunction joining the two words in Genesis 1:26–27. Moreover, whereas "the image of God" occurs in verse 27, in Genesis 5:1 man is said to be made "in the likeness of God." On semantic grounds and in terms of usage, *image* and *likeness* are interchangeable.[64]

Second, it teaches that body and soul are intrinsically in conflict. Aquinas held that supernatural grace was required to prevent sinful concupiscence. Implied is that there was something lacking in humanity at creation. There is no biblical support for this dualistic construction.

---

61. Bavinck, *RD*, 3:96–97. On the narrow question of the relationship of Adam's sin to the race, the views of Rome were not strikingly different from the Reformed—a natural or representative connection, or a combination of the two. CCC, 388–89, 402–4.

62. CCC, 374–79.

63. Anthony C. Thiselton, *Systematic Theology* (London: SPCK, 2015), 138.

64. Collins, *Genesis 1–4*, 61–67.

Third, it leads to a truncated view of the fall. Human sin led merely to a return to the state of nature, which was not in itself a sinful condition but only potentially sinful. The fall did not directly result in a corrupted nature. Sin was regarded as primarily bodily, with the mind relatively less affected; this is contrary to the biblical view that sin has affected every area of the human being.

Reformed. As with Rome, the Reformed have tried to do justice to the dual aspect of the image of God. The solution has been a distinction between the image in the broader sense and in the narrow sense, between moral agency (which is distinctive of being human) and moral excellence (lost in the fall and regained in Christ). This is close to certain aspects of the Roman position.[65]

Calvin holds that "the proper seat of [God's] image is in the soul" and rejects Rome's distinction between image and likeness, since repetitions were common among the Hebrews.[66] He is close to the Lutherans when, dealing with Christ as second Adam, he says that man's nature was so corrupted by the fall that whatever remains is "frightful deformity." The beginning of restoration is obtained in Christ, the second Adam, since he restores us to true and complete integrity (Eph. 4:24; Col. 3:10). Christ is the most perfect image of God. If we are conformed to him, we bear God's image.[67] The image is the perfect excellence of human nature in Adam before the fall, vitiated and almost blotted out at the fall, in some part manifest now in the elect, attaining its full splendor in heaven.

The Belgic Confession is much to the point. The fall has corrupted humanity's entire nature. "And being wicked and perverse, and corrupt in all his ways, he has lost all his excellent gifts he had received from God, and only retained a few remains [*petites traces*]," which are enough to leave him without excuse.[68]

Criticisms of the Reformed view of humanity in the image of God. The criticisms by Barth and Berkouwer are examples of a shift in the last

---

65. See Luca Baschera, "Total Depravity? The Consequences of Original Sin in John Calvin and Later Reformed Theology," in Calvinus Clarissimus Theologus: *Papers of the Tenth International Congress on Calvin Research,* ed. Herman J. Selderhuis (Göttingen: Vandenhoeck & Ruprecht, 2012), 37–59, esp. 57–59.

66. Calvin, *Institutes,* 1.15.3.

67. Calvin, *Institutes,* 1.15.4.

68. Belgic Confession, 14, in Schaff, *Creeds,* 3:398–99.

century to a more relational view of humanity. Instead of looking for some particular features intrinsic to, and definitive of, human nature, the drift of thought was toward dynamic and relational categories. While reason, freedom, and holiness are involved, the image consists preeminently in representing God in the world, reflecting the glory of Christ, and being transformed by the Spirit to be like Christ.[69]

Barth. Barth approaches the question on the basis of his Christology, a stance integral to his whole theology. Central to human existence is the relation to God. In this, Barth sees the context in Genesis 1 as significant. The image of God is humanity's creation as man and woman (Gen. 1:27). It is a unity in plurality that reflects the nature of God, whose image man is.

> It is not a quality of man. Hence there is no point in asking in which of man's peculiar attributes and attitudes it consists. It does not consist in anything man is or does. It consists as man himself consists as the creature of God. . . . He is the image of God in the fact that he is man. . . . [God] willed the existence of a being which in all its non-deity and therefore its differentiation can be a real partner.[70]

Man is no more solitary than God. In the duality of man and woman he is a copy and imitation of God. In his confrontation between God and himself, man repeats the confrontation in God.[71]

> This correspondence of the unlike is what takes place in the fact that the being of man represents, in the form of the coexistence of the different individuals of male and female, a creaturely and therefore a dissimilar repetition of the fact that the one God is in Himself not only I but also I and Thou, i.e., I only in relation to Himself who is also Thou, and Thou only in relation to Himself who is also I.[72]

It is an *analogia relationis*; there is no question of anything more than an analogy.[73] Ultimately, "man has reason to look for the man who will be different from him, but who for this reason will be real man for him, in the image and likeness of God male and female in his place and on his behalf, namely, Jesus Christ and his community." The image is fulfilled

69. Thiselton, *Systematic Theology*, 140.
70. Barth, *CD*, III/1:184.
71. Barth, *CD*, III/1:186.
72. Barth, *CD*, III/1:196.
73. Barth, *CD*, III/1:196.

in Christ and the church (the *totus Christus*).[74] Christ is God for us: God is God in Christ: all people are in Christ. For Barth, classic Reformed theology missed this entirely, viewing man as the image of God independently of Christ.

Berkouwer. Berkouwer claimed that the Reformed teaching is dualistic. In this, it tends to minimize the radical totality of human corruption. In its place, he argued for a dynamic and relational position somewhat akin to Barth's, but he failed to provide adequate exegetical support.[75] Besides, we have seen that the Reformed—and Rome for that matter— were grappling with a dual aspect that is present in the Bible itself.

Another instance of a trend away from the traditional approach has been to see the image of God as consisting in dominion, as the remaining section of Genesis 1 spells out. Calvin thought that such a view had no probability to it; God's image was to be sought within man, not outside him—"indeed, it is an inner good of the soul."[76] However, this is no new theme, as one might expect, given the context in Genesis 1, which suggests the idea.[77]

11.4.2   A Resolution of the Question

There is nothing wrong with the Reformed interpretation, provided it is viewed in a wider context. It reflects the tension found in the Bible, with which Rome was grappling from another angle though yielding less-than-satisfactory results. This wider context was provided by the Greek and Syrian fathers.

Athanasius. In *De incarnatione* Athanasius connects humanity's creation in the image of God with Christ. Athanasius declares that the Son was forever being worshiped by the angels and the whole creation, which he had made, before ever he became incarnate.[78] Athanasius brilliantly integrates the deity of the Son, his incarnation, and the sweep of salvation/deification.[79] Christ, the Son, is the image of God in whom we were created. God "did not barely create man . . . but made them after his own image, giving them a portion even of the power of his own Word;

---

74. Barth, *CD*, III/1:190.
75. Berkouwer, *Man*, 38–40, 45–48, 51–56.
76. Calvin, *Institutes*, 1.15.4.
77. Berkouwer, *Man*, 70–72.
78. Athanasius, *Orations against the Arians* 1.42 (NPNF[2], 4:331).
79. Athanasius, *Against the Arians* 2.70 (NPNF[2], 4:386).

so that having as it were a kind of reflexion of the Word, and being made rational, they might be able to abide even in blessedness."[80] Adam was created by the Word, God giving us freely, by the grace of the Word, a life in correspondence with God (in creation), "partaking of the Word."[81] So "the most holy Son of the Father, being the image of the Father, came to our region to renew man once made in his likeness."[82] He was made man that we might be made God.[83]

For Athanasius, the Son, "considered as Wisdom is the wisdom which is implanted in us an image." "Whereas he is not himself created, being creator, yet because of the image of him created in the works, he says this as of himself."[84]

> Moreover, that the Son should be speaking of the impress that is within us as if it were himself, should not startle any one, considering . . . that when Saul was persecuting the church, in which was his [the Son's] impress and image, he said, as if he were himself under persecution, "Saul, why persecuteth thou me?"[85]

St. Peter Chrysologus (380–449 or 458). Writing about the two men Adam and Christ, St. Peter Chrysologus states that "the second Adam stamped his image on the first Adam when he created him. That is why he took on himself the role and the name of the first Adam, in order that he might not lose what he had made in his own image."[86] The *Catechism of the Catholic Church* also affirms that "it is only in the mystery of the Word made flesh that the mystery of man truly becomes clear."[87]

John of Damascus. In his work on the divine images, John states that an image is a likeness of something. The image is one thing, what is depicted is another.[88] Every image makes manifest hidden things, since we do not have direct knowledge of the invisible realm.[89] The first image of the invisible God is the Son, in himself showing the Father (John 1:18;

80. Athanasius, *On the Incarnation* 3 (NPNF², 4:37).

81. Athanasius, *Incarnation* 4–5 (NPNF², 4:38).

82. Athanasius, *Incarnation* 14 (NPNF², 4:43).

83. Athanasius, *Incarnation* 54 (NPNF², 4:65).

84. Athanasius, *Against the Arians* 2.78 (NPNF², 4:390–91).

85. Athanasius, *Against the Arians* 2.80 (NPNF², 4:391). See also Athanasius, *On the Decrees of the Synod of Nicea* 3.14 (NPNF², 4:159).

86. St. Peter Chrysologus, Sermo 117 (PL, 52:520–21), cited in CCC, 359.

87. CCC, 359.

88. St. John of Damascus, *Three Treatises on the Divine Images*, trans. Andrew Louth (Crestwood, NY: St Vladimir's Seminary Press, 2003), 95.

89. St. John of Damascus, *Divine Images*, 96.

6:46; 14:8–9; Col. 1:15; Heb. 1:3).[90] "The Son is the Father's image, natural, undeviating, in every respect like the Father, save for being unbegotten and possessing fatherhood,"[91] while, following Athanasius, the Holy Spirit is the image of the Son (1 Cor. 12:3). "It is therefore because of the Holy Spirit that we know Christ, the Son of God, and God, and in the Son behold the Father."[92] While the second kind of image is God's pre-eternal will, the third kind of image is brought about by God through humankind. Since this is effected by God, John implies that it is connected with *theōsis*.[93]

As Hughes argues, Adam was created *in* the image of God (Gen. 1:26).[94] What—or *who*—is the image of God? The New Testament's answer is clear. *Christ* is the image of God (2 Cor. 4:4; Col. 1:15; Heb. 1:3). Creation was made by Christ, for Christ, and in Christ. Christ is the image of God as the second or last Adam.[95] Hence, the context for the image of God is the connection between the first and second Adams. The attributes of knowledge, righteousness, and holiness (Eph. 4:24) fit here as derivative.[96] The focus is not on inherent properties of humanity but on the history of redemption and preeminently with Christ and union with him.

The first Adam was brought into existence endowed with natural life, with the prospect of everlasting life upon continued obedience. The second or last Adam is the *giver* of resurrection life, eternal and everlasting (1 Cor. 15:45). Adam was formed in the image and likeness of God. Sin marred the image but did not eradicate it, for all people indiscriminately are still in the image of God, with a created dignity, but part of the fallen Adamic condition. In redemption, we are renewed in the image of God, *in union with Christ, the second Adam.* Thiselton summarizes the point well by stating that the image of God signifies "humankind as God *had intended and called* humans to be. It signifies the *potential of human be-*

---

90. St. John of Damascus, *Divine Images*, 96.

91. St. John of Damascus, *Divine Images*, 97.

92. St. John of Damascus, *Divine Images*, 97.

93. St. John of Damascus, *Divine Images*, 98.

94. Philip Edgcumbe Hughes, *The True Image: The Origin and Destiny of Man in Christ* (Grand Rapids, MI: Eerdmans, 1989), 281–86.

95. Some say that Christ is *not* the second Adam, since that might imply a range of Adams beyond the second, but is the last Adam. While the latter is true and is the term Paul uses in 1 Corinthians 15:45, he also in the same place describes him as "the second man [or Adam]." Besides, the Westminster divines used the term when affirming that "the covenant of grace was made with Christ as the second Adam" (WLC, 31).

96. Hughes, *The True Image*, 29.

ings for the future. Its measure is Jesus Christ, the person who actually bears God's image."[97]

The foundation for this is that humanity has a created compatibility with God, preeminently demonstrated by the incarnation of Christ. We do have a *commonality* with other entities; with trees, clouds, and planets, which were also created; with plants, birds, and slugs, which are created entities with life; with cows, cats, and pigs, which are equally mammals; and with angels, intelligent creatures related to God. However, we have a *compatibility* with one other entity, God: the uncreated, self-existent, eternal Creator. While we share a good deal with other creatures, God made us to be like him on a creaturely level. The incarnation establishes this. Deification, or *theōsis*, is the result.[98]

The importance of the created condition of humanity is evident throughout the theological spectrum. One's view of our original condition will impact the seriousness with which sin is viewed and, consequently, the need for grace and the depth of that need. The roots of the conflict between Augustine and the Pelagians lie here.

11.5   Monism, Dichotomy, or Trichotomy

The Old Testament presents humans as a psychosomatic unity; different elements are apparent, but there is no hint of a polarity between them.[99] The early Christians, let alone the Bible, never disparaged the body; it was the Greeks who did that. Running through much pagan thought was a radical disjunction between the spiritual and the material.

11.5.1   *Trichotomy*

Some claim that humans consist of three elements—body, soul, and spirit—based on New Testament references (1 Thess. 5:23; Heb. 4:12–13). It is highly questionable whether Platonic influence underlay Patristic ideas, since the fathers generally taught trichotomy of the whole person, whereas Plato related it to the soul (intelligence, anger, covetousness), and Origen based his understanding on biblical language.[100] Leading Patristic exponents of trichotomy were Clement of Alexandria,

---

97. Thiselton, *Systematic Theology*, 137 (italics original).
98. See chaps. 26 and 31 for more on this.
99. Wolfhart Pannenberg, *Systematic Theology*, trans. Geoffrey W. Bromiley, 3 vols. (Grand Rapids, MI: Eerdmans, 1991–1998), 2:181–202.
100. Henri Crouzel, *Origen*, trans. A. S. Worrall (Edinburgh: T&T Clark, 1989), 87–88.

who distinguishes between the body, the rational mind, and the carnal spirit,[101] and Origen, whose threefold principles of biblical interpretation were based on a reading of Proverbs 22:20–21 (LXX) reinforced by a trichotomic division into body, soul, and spirit.[102] Apollinaris's Christology, condemned at Constantinople I, was also based on trichotomy.[103] Gregory of Nyssa also distinguished between the rational and passionate elements of the nonmaterial aspects of humans.[104]

More recently, A. J. Mason, in the Ellicott commentary on 1 Thessalonians 5:23, stated that the spirit apprehends things intuitively without reasoning, whereas the soul includes the intellect, affections, and will, the gospel forcing a sharp distinction between them.[105] Others have elevated trichotomy to a cardinal principle. Delitzsch, discussing passages such as Hebrews 4:12,[106] states that "we regard the dualism of nature and spirit as strenuously as we maintain the dualism of God and the world."[107] The Scofield Reference Bible, in notes on 1 Thessalonians, claims that "to assert . . . that there is no difference between soul and spirit is to assert that there is no difference between the mortal body and the resurrection body."[108] The connection is difficult to see and the stakes wildly overinflated.

The Chinese writer Watchman Nee thought that humans are like onions, with a series of layers. The outer layer is the body or outermost man, within is the soul or outer man, and the inner man is the spirit.[109] It is the spirit, the inner man, that relates to God. The soul and the body are like clothes in relation to a person, the outward shell that conceals the reality. Anyone who works for God effectively is one whose inner spirit is released.[110] This is done only by being broken as the alabaster box was broken preparatory to Jesus's death and burial.[111] This is necessary because the spirit, not the soul or the body, has contact with God.

101. Clement, *Stromata* 6.16 (*ANF*, 2:511–12).

102. Origen, *On First Principles* 4.1.11–4.1.23 (*ANF*, 4:359–73); see also Origen, *On First Principles* 2.10.7 (*ANF*, 4:296). On Origen's trichotomy, see Crouzel, *Origen*, 87–92.

103. Hughes, *The True Image*, 287–93.

104. Gregory of Nyssa, *On the Soul and the Resurrection* (*NPNF*², 5:441–42); *The Making of Man* 14.2, 15.1–3 (*NPNF*², 5:402–4).

105. Charles John Ellicott, *A Bible Commentary for English Readers* (London: Cassell, 1897).

106. Franz Delitzsch, *A System of Biblical Psychology*, 2nd ed., trans. Robert Ernest Wallis (1899; repr., Grand Rapids, MI: Baker, 1977), 109–14.

107. Delitzsch, *Biblical Psychology*, 113–14.

108. *Scofield Reference Bible* (n.p., n.d. [ca. 1917]), 1270.

109. Watchman Nee, *The Release of the Spirit* (Bombay: Gospel Literature Service, 1965), 6.

110. Nee, *Release*, 10.

111. Nee, *Release*, 12.

Nee's construction displays a diluted view of the effects of sin and, correspondingly, a truncated and eviscerated account of sanctification and the nature of human beings. The spirit becomes a privileged part of the human constitution, while the mind and body are devalued. Sin has affected the spirit less than the outer shell. In turn, the soul and the body are less equipped to relate to God. It is a schizoid view of humanity. It suggests that what we do with our bodies is of lesser moment, theoretically opening the door to a *laisser faire* attitude toward behavior.[112] Such ideas encourage quietism, mysticism, and anti-intellectualism. It so happened that in London in 1969 I met a close relative of Nee, who shared his views. When I mentioned that I was planning on studying theology, he remonstrated forcefully with me that I must not do it. Theology is soulish! It engages the mind! (So now you know, though it's a bit late if you have read this far!) This suggests a possible influence from Buddhism.

There are powerful exegetical objections to trichotomy. Many of these are expounded by John Murray.[113] On Hebrews 4:12–13, he indicates that, contrary to Delitzsch, μερισμός (dividing asunder) refers to a dividing within an entity rather than a division between two distinct entities. Soul and spirit are thereby aspects of a single reality. Μερισμός occurs in Hebrews 2:4 and there means "distributions" or "impartation," not division. The verb means to impart or to divide up, to distribute, not to separate one entity from another.[114] Indeed, Murray insists there is "no instance in which the idea of distinguishing or separating two things is apparent."[115] Here it means that the Word of God "penetrates to the inmost parts of our being and like a sharp sword can rend them asunder." No aspect of our being is hidden from the Word of God. Moreover, the text also speaks of the penetration of the Word to the joints and marrow, the thoughts and intents of the heart: why should the trichotomist stop at soul and spirit, ignoring joints and marrow? As Hughes remarks, "Our author is not concerned to provide here a psychological or anatomical analysis of the human constitution, but rather to describe in graphic terms the penetration of God's word to the innermost depth of man's personality."[116]

---

112. Nee himself would have been aghast at this, I am sure.
113. Murray, *Writings*, 2:23–33.
114. Murray, *Writings*, 2:2:30.
115. Murray, *Writings*, 2:2:31.
116. Philip Edgcumbe Hughes, *A Commentary on the Epistle to the Hebrews* (Grand Rapids, MI: Eerdmans, 1977), 165.

In 1 Thessalonians 5:23, Paul says, "May the God of peace himself sanctify you completely, and may your whole spirit and soul and body be kept blameless at the coming of our Lord Jesus Christ." He accumulates terms to express completeness, a common idiom, as in Jesus's summary of the Law (Mark 12:30). Paul prays that the Thessalonians will be thoroughly preserved by God; he is not defining the inner structure of the human personality. H. Wheeler Robinson refers to "the stately and wholly artificial structure of Pauline 'trichotomy.'" The passage, he says, "is not a systematic dissection of the distinct elements of personality; its true analogy is such an Old Testament sentence as Deut. vi.5, where a somewhat similar enumeration emphasizes the totality of the personality."[117] Thiselton remarks that "the words simply mean 'wholly' or 'through and through.' They no more refer to 'parts' of humans than Mary refers to 'parts' in 'My soul magnifies the Lord, and my spirit rejoices in God' (Luke 1:46–47). They are an example of Hebrew synonymous parallelism, even when rendered into Greek."[118]

In the New Testament, *soul* and *spirit* express the same reality from differing perspectives. *Spirit*, πνεῦμα,[119] tends to be used when referring to "the principle of life as derived from God," while *soul*, ψυχή,[120] is commonly used for "the animating entity as life constituted in a body." Indeed, humans in their entirety are viewed as a "living soul."[121] From these distinct angles, soul or spirit is "the substrate, centre, and seat of human personality."[122]

For Christians, the body belongs to the Holy Spirit and so must not be devalued. The biblical treatment of the body is to contrast not the material to the immaterial but rather what is visible in the eyes of the world to what is invisible. J. A. T. Robinson made a good distinction, allowing for contextual usage, when he referred σάρξ,[123] "flesh," to man in solidarity with creation in his distance from God, and σῶμα,[124] "body," to man in solidarity with creation as made for God.[125]

The *Catechism of the Catholic Church* rejects trichotomy.[126]

117. H. Wheeler Robinson, *The Christian Doctrine of Man*, 3rd ed. (Edinburgh: T&T Clark, 1926), 108.
118. Pannenberg, *Systematic Theology*, 142.
119. *pneuma*.
120. *psychē*.
121. Murray, *Writings*, 2:32.
122. Murray, *Writings*, 2:33.
123. *sarx*.
124. *sōma*.
125. Cited by Thiselton, *Systematic Theology*, 143.
126. CCC, 367.

11.5.2 *Monism*

In part a reaction to dualist or trichotomist analyses, in the last hundred years or so the idea has grown that the Bible presents a holistic view of man. Humans are unities. At root, this is a materialist perspective; the mind or soul is material, explicable in purely physical terms. With advances in brain science, it is argued that humans are merely products of nerve cells, molecules, and electrical impulses.[127] This widespread idea has influenced Christian thought. Consequently, the existence of the soul has been disputed or rejected. Humans are regarded as nothing but a collection of material elements, the psychological and spiritual dimensions being functions of the brain.

Various attempts have been made to build on neuroscientific theories while not relinquishing entirely the biblical commitment to a nonmaterial aspect of the human being.[128] The key is to maintain the unity of the person while recognizing the Bible's teaching on a dual aspect, signaled especially by what happens at death. Then the body decays in the grave as conscious existence continues, which for the Christian is "far better," since it is residence with Christ (Phil. 1:21–24). Frame attempts this, trying to avoid an untenable dualism but allowing for distinct aspects of human existence, and expressing a correct agnosticism on the details.[129] Frame thinks this avoids arcane discussions veering toward dualism, such as dichotomy and trichotomy, and creationism versus traducianism. While he preempts the latter, for his strongly unitary position entails some form of traducianism, the important Christological dimensions thrown up by that debate are unaddressed.[130]

At root, materialistic determinism is effectively reductionism—humans are nothing but a collection of molecules and electrical impulses. How can this be known and established? The existence of the soul is beyond the competence of neuroscience. Humans are material; that is certain. But for scientists devoted to the material to claim that there is nothing other than what they investigate is an imperialist claim and insupportable. As Lane indicates, it is tantamount to the

---

127. Francis Crick, *The Astonishing Hypothesis: The Scientific Search for the Soul* (New York: Simon & Schuster, 1994), 3. Try telling that to your wife, husband, or friends.
128. See Nancey Murphy's argument for "non-reductive physicalism" and William Hasker's "emergent dualism," discussed in Greg R. Allison, *Historical Theology: An Introduction to Christian Doctrine* (Grand Rapids, MI: Zondervan, 2011), 340–41.
129. Frame, *Systematic Theology*, 796–802.
130. Frame, *Systematic Theology*, 801–2.

assertion that this book is nothing more than a series of marks made by ink on paper or that a credit card is nothing other than plastic and metal.[131]

11.5.3   Dichotomy—Unity in Duality

2 Corinthians 5:1–10. I will discuss this crucial text in detail in chapter 28 in relation to Paul's understanding of what happens after death. In 2 Corinthians 5:1–5, he uses verbs conveying emotional intensity; we deeply long for our permanent resurrection body. However, from verse 6 the language is restrained. Here, as we face death, we are of good courage. This lacks eager anticipation, since we will be absent from the body. There are compensating factors; we will take up residence with the Lord, which elsewhere Paul says is "far better" (Phil. 1:23). However, we will be in a less-than-ideal position. Our present bodies will have died, and we will not have received the resurrection body for which we yearn. There is conscious existence, since we will be present with the Lord. However, Paul's prime choice is to be embodied, particularly with the resurrection body (2 Cor. 5:1–5). Paul points to the debilitating effect of the dissolution of the body but simultaneously indicates that our conscious existence will continue and, from another angle, be advantageous, since we will be with Christ.

Philippians 1:21ff. Being with Christ and therefore, by entailment, absent from the body is "far better" from the purely personal angle. However, Paul prefers to live on in an embodied state, although not "with Christ" in the way he mentions here. This preference is so that Paul will have "fruit of work" (my trans.), since it will be for the good of the Philippians and others. This is what he later recommends of all— to look not to one's own interests but to the interests of others, for this is the way of love, the path Christ himself trod (Phil. 2:1–6).

Revelation 6:9–11. The martyrs are seen here as "souls," slain for their testimony to Christ. They are conscious, aware of the passage of time, and able to communicate, although disembodied.

Each of these strategic passages represents the tenor of Scripture on this question, that humans are a duality in unity. Tertullian argues that

---

131. Anthony N. S. Lane, *Exploring Christian Doctrine* (London: SPCK, 2013), 257.

we are "one in a twofold condition," even teaching the corporeality of the soul.[132] In turn, he points to the identity of soul and spirit.[133] The body is ancillary to the soul in sin, the flesh blamed since it is the instrument by which we sin.[134] So, as a consequence, death "is the separation of body and soul."[135] For Aquinas, "man is not a soul only, but something composed of soul and body."[136] Davies remarks that Thomas is not dualistic, as there is only one "thing" of which the soul is an aspect. He thinks Aquinas is attempting to describe what it means for humans to be alive in comparison with cats.[137] The *Catechism of the Catholic Church*, in rejecting trichotomy, adopts duality in unity.[138] Calvin too asserts, "That man consists of a soul and a body ought to be beyond controversy. Now I understand by the term 'soul' an immortal yet created essence, which is his nobler part. Sometimes it is called 'spirit.' . . . when 'spirit' is used by itself, it means the same thing as soul."[139]

11.6 The Origin of the Soul

The question of how each individual human soul comes into existence seems as obscure a matter as can be. However, its significance has surfaced in discussions relating to abortion; the commencement of human life is a key issue. In turn, it bears on the incarnation and the relation between the Son and the humanity he assumed. Seemingly arcane theological discussions can bear directly on crucial issues relating to life and salvation. We will mention three attempts to identify the nature of the soul's origin.[140]

11.6.1 Preexistence

On the basis of Genesis 1:1, Origen held that God created, before all other things, "so great a number of rational or intellectual creatures . . . as he foresaw would be sufficient." This was a definite number—from Wisdom 11:20: "you have ordered all things in measure, number, and

---

132. Tertullian, *De anima* 9 (*ANF*, 3:188–89).
133. Tertullian, *De anima* 10 (*ANF*, 3:189–90).
134. Tertullian, *De anima* 40 (*ANF*, 3:220).
135. Tertullian, *De anima* 51 (*ANF*, 3:228–29).
136. Aquinas, *ST* 1a.75.4.
137. Brian Davies, Summa Theologiae: *A Guide and Commentary* (Oxford: Oxford University Press, 2016), 126–34.
138. CCC, 367.
139. Calvin, *Institutes*, 1.15.2.
140. See J. F. Bethune-Baker, *An Introduction to the Early History of Christian Doctrine to the Time of the Council of Chalcedon*, 6th ed. (London: Methuen, 1938), 302–6.

weight"—to which God applied bodies.[141] This idea was condemned in 553 at Constantinople II.[142]

11.6.2 Creationism

Creationism maintains that God creates each individual soul directly.[143] Lactantius, in the late third century, wrote that a body can be produced from a body, but not a soul from a soul. Hence, the creation of souls is not to be identified with generation.[144] Jerome also dismissed the idea that as body springs from body, so soul from soul. Instead, he argued, "Surely (as the church teaches in accordance with the Saviour's words, 'my Father worketh hitherto and I work'; and the passage in Isaiah, 'who maketh the spirit of man in him,'; and in the Psalms, 'who fashioneth one by one the hearts of them,') God is daily making souls."[145] Pope Leo affirmed that this was the teaching of the Catholic faith.[146]

Aquinas, addressed the question of whether the intellectual soul is produced by the semen and thus has a material cause.[147] In dependence on Aristotle,[148] he distinguished between the sensitive soul, which is produced by bodily means, and the intellectual soul. He rejected the idea that the latter is produced by the former on the grounds, among others, that "the intellectual soul is created by God at the end of human generation"; for "to say that the intellectual soul is caused by the begetter, is nothing else than to hold the soul to be non-subsistent, and consequently to perish with the body."[149] Aquinas considered a subsistent to be identifiable as "this particular thing." So "souls were not created before bodies, but are created at the same time as they are infused into them."[150] Rome adopted creationism and explicitly rejected traducianism.[151] Calvin tended to support creationism too, writing that "souls are just as much created

---

141. Origen, *On First Principles* 1.8.2, 2.9.1 (*ANF*, 4:265, 289–90.
142. *NPNF²*, 14:318–20.
143. Here is an example of how a term, established for centuries or millennia, can be highjacked by groups that know little about the history of theology.
144. Lactantius, *On the Workmanship of God* 19 (*ANF*, 7:298–99).
145. Jerome, *To Pammachius against John of Jerusalem* 22 (*NPNF²*, 6:434).
146. Leo the Great, *Letter 15* 11 (*NPNF²*, 12:23).
147. Aquinas, *ST* 1a.118.2–3.
148. Davies, *Summa Theologiae: A Guide*, 152–53.
149. Aquinas, *ST* 1a.118.2.
150. Aquinas, *ST* 1a.90.2, 1a.118.1, 1a2ae.81.1.
151. *CCC*, 366.

as angels are. But creation is not the inpouring, but the beginning of essence out of nothing."[152] Reformed theology has leaned strongly toward creationism. Charles Hodge was a powerful advocate,[153] with Louis Berkhof very cautiously so.[154] Turretin affirmed it and opposed traducianism.[155]

Arguments in support cover a range, from the distinctness of soul and body (Berkouwer) to the simplicity of the soul (Berkhof). Creationism avoids difficulties with Christology, according to Berkhof, since it obviates the problem of Christ inheriting original sin from his mother. However, this argument proves too much, for it requires original sin to be conveyed to each individual person separately when God creates their souls and so makes God the transmitter of sin to every person. Moreover, creationism tends not to duality-in-unity but to a dualism, with body and soul having separate and independent origins, akin to Platonism. Since at death there is a disruption between body and soul, it implies that there was a corresponding disruption of sorts as we were originally created, owing to the putatively separate origins of the constituent elements of the person. Furthermore, it yields only a physical solidarity for humanity, for our parents transmit only our bodies.

11.6.3 Traducianism

Traducianism maintains that the soul, together with the body, is derived from parents. There is a possible Stoic origin here.

Tertullian mounts a cogent and persuasive argument for the simultaneous transmission of soul and body in the act of generation. He writes of "soul and body conceived, formed and perfected in element simultaneously." This argument is based on what happens at death:

> As death is defined to be nothing else than the separation of body and soul, life, which is the opposite of death, is susceptible of no other definition than the conjunction of body and soul. If the severance happens at one and the same time to both substances by means of death, so the law of their combination ought to assure

---

152. Calvin, *Institutes*, 1.15.5.
153. Charles Hodge, *Systematic Theology* (Grand Rapids, MI: Eerdmans, 1977), 2:69–76.
154. Louis Berkhof, *Systematic Theology* (London: Banner of Truth, 1958), 196–201.
155. Francis Turretin, *Institutes of Elenctic Theology*, trans. George Musgrave Giger, ed. James T. Dennison Jr. (Phillipsburg, NJ: P&R, 1992), 1:477–82.

us that it occurs simultaneously to the two substances by means of life.

So, retrospectively, as the clay and the breath combined in the creation of Adam,

> they then both amalgamated and mixed their proper seminal rudiments into one, and ever afterwards committed to the human race the normal mode of its propagation, so that even now the two substances, although diverse from each other, flow forth simultaneously in a united channel. . . . Accordingly, from the one (primeval) man comes the entire outflow and redundance of men's souls.[156]

Gregory of Nyssa also writes in support of traducianism. "But as man is one, the being consisting of soul and body, we are to suppose that the beginning of his existence is one, common to both parts, so that he should not be found to be antecedent and posterior to himself, if the bodily element were first in time, and the other were a later addition," for "there is one beginning of both."[157] W. G. T. Shedd is a leading advocate for traducianism.[158] Bethune-Baker favors it,[159] as does Donald Macleod.[160]

In its support, the corporate solidarity of the race is clear in Scripture, feeding into the solidarity of the tribe, the nation, and the household. This relation of the individual to the corporate is evident throughout the Bible. When one man sinned, all Israel sinned (Josh. 7:11–12). When Adam sinned, we all sinned (Rom. 5:12). The relational character of humanity is seen in the Old Testament, from Genesis 1:26 onward. You were A, the son of B, of the tribe of C. This is strange to Westerners but taken for granted in most parts of the world without any need for explanation. It is the basis for God dealing with successive generations, as in the second commandment. In short, traducianism accounts better for the solidarity of the race.

Augustine was noncommittal on the issue. In his *Letter 166*[161] to Jerome, on the origin of the human soul, he refers to Jerome's opinion

---

156. Tertullian, *De anima* 27 (ANF, 3:207–8); also *De anima* 37 (ANF, 3:218).
157. Gregory of Nyssa, *The Making of Man* 29 (NPNF², 5:420–21).
158. W. G. T. Shedd, *Dogmatic Theology* (Grand Rapids, MI: Zondervan, 1971), 2:75–81.
159. Bethune-Baker, *Early History of Christian Doctrine*, 302–6.
160. In Madeume and Reeves, *Adam*, 144–47.
161. Augustine, *Letter 166* (NPNF¹, 1:523–32).

that God creates each soul separately,[162] stating his "hesitation to embrace any definite view on this subject."[163] Nevertheless, as Robinson remarks, it fits well with Augustine's theology, despite his revulsion at its materialism.

An argument against traducianism suggests that it undermines the simplicity of the soul. However, this is a philosophical construct, not a biblical one. More significantly, it has been charged with making Christ inherit corruption from his mother, since she would have passed on his soul to him, thus opening the door to the idea of Mary's immaculate conception in defense. However, the sanctifying work of the Spirit in Jesus's conception overcomes that problem (Luke 1:34–35).

11.7 Other Questions

At this juncture, we could address questions raised by bioethics on the nature of being human. But this is not a book on ethics, nor is there space. There is the rapid development of Artificial Intelligence, with its benefits and possible threats. A race of supercomputers, it is feared, could overtake us and threaten our existence; these are not created by God in his image. At the other end of the spectrum, many ethicists regard humans as no better than chimpanzees or insects; it is only a matter of time before people are treated accordingly in law and daily life. Both mind-sets have a diminished view of humanity. Indeed, the post-Enlightenment West has increasingly, and with exponential effect, promoted a culture of death— abortion, euthanasia, and assisted dying are all symptoms of rebellion against the *living* God, who is the Creator and sustainer of contingent life and the giver of eternal life. We are living in a culture of meaninglessness and death, in which humans are merely a cluster of molecules of no more value than an insect. Thankfully, this is not the last word.

Further Reading

Hughes, Philip E. *The True Image: The Origin and Destiny of Man in Christ.* Grand Rapids, MI: Eerdmans, 1989.

Madueme, Hans, and Michael Reeves, eds. *Adam, the Fall, and Original Sin: Theological, Biblical, and Scientific Perspectives.* Grand Rapids, MI: Baker, 2014.

---

162. Augustine, *Letter 166* 3.7 (NPNF¹, 1:525).
163. Augustine, *Letter 166* 3.8 (NPNF¹, 1:526).

Murray, John. *Collected Writings*. Vol. 2, *Select Lectures in Systematic Theology*. Edinburgh: Banner of Truth, 1977.

Study Questions

1. What is at stake in the question of the historicity of Adam as the progenitor of the race?

2. Consider the benefits and limitations of feminist theology.

3. What are the strengths and weaknesses of the various attempts to identify what is meant by humanity being created "in the image and likeness of God."

12

Humanity in Covenant

That the relationship between God and Adam in creation was covenantal is determined by extrapolation from covenants God established after the fall. There were two parties, responsibilities given to Adam, a warning of death in the case of disobedience, with an implied promise of life for continued faithfulness, together with a sacrament related to that promise. Ultimately, the living God promises eternal life for faithful obedience. This covenant relationship is also to be seen in connection with the work of Christ as second Adam, who, having obeyed God, was resurrected to everlasting life and enthroned in vindication. This covenant with Adam was established by God in grace, while being regulated by law. To reject this covenant on the grounds that it was legal is to misconstrue the function of law and the justice of God, while to assert that it is a purely legal covenant entails a range of problematic consequences.

12.1 The Pre-fall Covenant

> The LORD God took the man and put him in the garden of Eden to work it and keep it. And the LORD God commanded the man, saying, "You may surely eat of every tree of the garden, but of the tree of the knowledge of good and evil you shall not eat, for in the day that you eat of it you shall surely die." (Gen. 2:15–17)

The claim that the pre-fall situation was covenantal emerged in Reformed theology in the late sixteenth century,[1] although clear antecedents

---

1. Robert Letham, "The *Foedus Operum*: Some Factors Accounting for Its Development," *SCJ* 14 (1983): 63–76; David A. Weir, *The Origins of Federal Theology in Sixteenth-Century Reformation Thought* (Oxford: Clarendon, 1990).

existed.[2] A variety of terms were used for this covenant. Zacharias Ursinus, in 1562, used *foedus naturae*.[3] Caspar Olevian, more hesitant on the covenantal status of Genesis 2, wrote in 1585 of a *primus foedus* made by God with man.[4] The Puritan Dudley Fenner was the first to speak of a *foedus operum* in 1585,[5] and the Basel theologian Amandus Polanus followed suit the next year.[6] Johannes Piscator wrote of a *foedus legale* in 1590.[7] In 1594 Franciscus Gomarus called it the *foedus naturale*, in contrast to the *foedus supernaturale* made by God after the fall.[8]

This terminological variety still existed at the time of the Westminster Assembly (1643–1652). The WCF uses the phrase "covenant of works" (WCF, 7.2). The WSC refers only to the "covenant of life" (WSC, 12). The WLC also prefers "covenant of life" (WLC, 20), but acknowledges that it is commonly called the "covenant of works" (WLC, 30). The "covenant of life" focuses on God's promise of everlasting life for continued obedience by Adam, while "covenant of works" draws attention to the means by which this promise was to be attained, although even here in WCF, 7.2, the spotlight is still on the promise of life: "The first covenant made with man was a covenant of works, wherein life was promised to Adam; and in him to his posterity, upon condition of perfect and personal obedience." Classic Reformed theology did not construe the pre-fall covenant in uniform terms.

Neither in his Genesis commentary nor in the *Institutes* does John Calvin (1509–1564) describe the condition of Adam before the fall as covenantal, still less as a covenant of works. Peter Lillback argues that all the ingredients for such a view are present in Calvin and that he has an *inchoate* (just begun) covenant of works,[9] but I prefer the word *incipient* (about to begin), since, while the elements for such a covenant are present, the formulation itself is not. While Calvin has all the ingredients laid out on the counter, he has not yet put them in the oven, whereas Lillback thinks they are in the oven, just about to be brought out and put

---

2. Muller, *PRRD*, 2:458–63; Peter A. Lillback, *The Binding of God: Calvin's Role in the Development of Covenant Theology* (Grand Rapids, MI: Baker Academic, 2001).

3. Zacharias Ursinus, "*Summa Theologia*," in *Opera Theologia* (Heidelberg, 1612), 1:10.

4. Caspar Olevian, *De substantia foederis gratuiti inter Deum et electos* (Geneva, 1585).

5. Dudley Fenner, *Sacra theologia, sive veritas quae secundum pietatem* (Geneva, 1585), 88.

6. Amandus Polanus, *Partitiones theologiae*, 2nd ed. (Basel, 1590), 79–80.

7. Johannes Piscator, *Aphorismi doctrinae Christianae* (1590; repr., Oxford, 1630), 50.

8. Franciscus Gomarus, "Oratio de Foedere Dei," in *Opera Theologica omnia* (Amsterdam, 1664), 2.

9. Lillback, *Binding of God*.

on the plate. Whatever one's conclusion, Calvin used the first-and-second Adams paradigm in his soteriology.[10] Kline's claim that this connection stands or falls with an acceptance of the pre-fall covenant of works cannot be sustained.[11] Indeed, all Reformed theologians before Fenner operated without a pre-fall covenant; the integrity of Reformed theology was not tied to the construction.

12.2 Was the Pre-fall Situation Covenantal?

It has been argued that there is no mention of a covenant in Genesis 2. However, the whole counsel of God is not confined to express biblical statements. It also includes what "by good and necessary consequence may be deduced from Scripture" (WCF, 1.4).

In Genesis 2 there are two parties present, as in any covenant made by God. They are God and Adam. Paul later indicates that Adam represented the entire human race (Rom. 5:12–21; 1 Cor. 15:19–26, 35–49). For now, it is sufficient to concentrate on Adam.

Genesis 2:15–17 discloses that God gave Adam a warning not to eat of the fruit of the tree of the knowledge of good and evil, together with a threat that if he were to do so, he would certainly die. The meaning of "die" in this context becomes clear only as the narrative proceeds; I will discuss it in the next chapter. Warning and threat are clear. Elsewhere, where God gives a promise or a warning, the reverse also applies. God offers eternal life through faith in Christ; the obverse is that unbelief will bring death. So here the reverse of the threat is an implied promise. In contrast to the certain death following disobedience is assurance of life for continued obedience. This is underlined after the fall when God prevents Adam from returning to the garden by locating the cherubim and the flaming sword in the way, "lest he reach out his hand and take also of the tree of life and eat, and live forever" (Gen. 3:22).

This is the reason for the title "covenant of life," for the promise of life transcends the means of its attainment. This is its ultimate purpose, to be confirmed and share in the life God gives in fellowship with himself. God, the giver of contingent life, is life itself, and so communion with him is communion in an inexhaustible and overflowing fountain of life.

---

10. Calvin, *Institutes*, 2.12.3.
11. Meredith G. Kline, "Covenant Theology under Attack," *NH*, February 1994, 4.

The tree of life is thus a sacrament. An implied promise is attached to it. Eating from this tree brings everlasting life. The sign is appropriate to the reality, for God is the giver of life, being life itself (Genesis 1). Much is confirmed by later references to the tree of life (Rev. 22:1–2, 18–19).

These features are shared by the later covenants God made after the fall: two parties, a promise and a warning, blessing and judgment, with a sacrament suitable to the reality to which it points.

Furthermore, there is a close parallel with Christ and the covenant of grace. Christ, as the second Adam, obeyed the Father and was exalted as Mediator in his resurrection and ascension. The first Adam disobeyed when tested in a beautiful garden, paying the penalty of death, together with all humanity he represented. The last Adam proved faithful, tested in a barren desert, and was publicly vindicated by God, raised to his right hand, and made the author of eternal life for all united to him in that covenant.

12.3   Arguments against the Pre-fall Covenant

12.3.1   James B. Torrance

According to James Torrance, *the pre-fall covenant is legal and so places law before grace.* Torrance was deeply critical of federal theology as it developed in Scotland. He understood the covenant of works to be a purely legal covenant and therefore opposed it since, he argued, it bases God's dealings with humanity on law, not grace. Consequently, this puts the covenant of grace in a legal frame, subserving the ends of law, with disastrous consequences for theology and piety. "God's prime purpose for man is legal, not filial, but this yields an impersonal view of man as the object of justice, rather than primarily the object of love." Torrance asked whether it is appropriate to interpret creation in terms of natural law and to restrict grace to redemption.[12] He was prepared to see the pre-fall situation as covenantal, but not if it was defined in legal terms.

Torrance's opposition flowed from his recasting of theology along the lines of his brother T. F. Torrance's theology and that of Karl Barth. At

---

12. James Torrance, "The Concept of Federal Theology—Was Calvin a Federal Theologian?," in *Calvinus Sacrae Scripturae professor: Die Referate des Congres International des Recherches Calviniennes*, ed. Wilhelm H. Neuser (Grand Rapids, MI: Eerdmans, 1994), 15–40, esp. 23, 35; James B. Torrance, "Covenant or Contract? A Study of the Background of Worship in Seventeenth-Century Scotland," *SJT* 23 (1970): 51–76; Thomas F. Torrance, *Scottish Theology: From John Knox to John McLeod Campbell* (Edinburgh: T&T Clark, 1996), 214ff.

root is a radical interpretation of the atonement stemming from the all-encompassing eternal decree of God to be God in Christ, which encompassed creation, covenant, incarnation, and atonement. God fully reveals himself in Christ as the God who loves every person. Legal categories governing atonement and covenant blur and eviscerate the revelation of God's love in Christ. I cannot answer all these questions here, but Torrance's objections to the pre-fall covenant fail to do justice to the full weight of biblical revelation. They signal a divorce of sorts between law and grace, in contrast to the WCF, which maintains that the two "sweetly comply" (WCF, 19.7).

12.3.2 *John Murray*

In John Murray's estimation, *the pre-fall covenant fails to highlight the elements of grace present in creation.* Murray disliked the term "covenant of works" because he did not find a covenant in Genesis 1–2 and since "the elements of grace entering into the administration are not properly provided for by the term 'works.'"[13] Generically, he understood God's covenants to be sovereign administrations of grace.[14] As a result, he preferred to express the pre-fall situation as the Adamic administration.

Murray showed commendable caution. However, that may have imposed too great a brake on his articulation of the Adamic situation. All the ingredients for a covenant are present, and an analogy or parallel exists between Adam and Christ, while Adam's disobedience and Christ's faithfulness are integrally related to the covenant of grace. Besides, as we saw, other terms were available giving greater prominence to the gracious elements of the administration without changing its substance.

12.4   Misleading Arguments for the Pre-fall Covenant

Meredith Kline believed that *the pre-fall covenant is essential to getting the gospel right.* From the end of the spectrum opposite to Torrance, differing from Murray and drawing on ancient Near Eastern parallels, Kline saw biblical covenants as essentially law covenants. "A truly systematic formulation of the theology of the covenant will define covenant generically in terms of law administration." The satisfaction of divine law underscores

---

13. John Murray, *Select Lectures in Systematic Theology*, vol. 2 of *Collected Writings of John Murray* (Edinburgh: Banner of Truth, 1977), 49.
14. John Murray, *The Covenant of Grace* (London: Tyndale Press, 1954).

every administration of covenant promise. Thus, the promises are, in effect, ancillary to law. For Kline, this reflects on the character of God; "merciful he may be according to his sovereign will but all his works are in righteousness and truth."[15] The priority of law is an outflow of who God is. Mercy is an act of God's will, whereas justice is inherent in his nature.

Kline argued that the active obedience of Christ underlying the atonement and justification is unintelligible without a commitment to the pre-fall covenant of works. Adam would have been confirmed in life if he had been obedient. Christ was obedient and so merited life for those he represented. Remove this obedience, and the ground is undercut from atonement and justification. The objective heart of the gospel depends on the pre-fall covenant of works.

I will interact more with the argument of Kline later. For now, we may note that while there are antecedents of a pre-fall covenant in Augustine and in medieval theologians, the idea did not emerge fully until 1586. However, Reformed theologians before that date could hardly be said to have undermined the gospel. Indeed, Lutheranism has no confessional commitment to the pre-fall covenant but still holds to justification only by faith, its central plank ever since Luther.

Moreover, Kline was arguing that things clearly revealed—the atonement and justification only by faith—depend for their stability on something inferred. This cannot be so. Furthermore, the historical process was exactly the reverse of what Kline supports; the pre-fall covenant was deduced from the clear revelation of the covenant of grace, the atonement, and justification. Historically and theologically, his argument fails.

12.5   Sustainable Arguments for the Pre-fall Covenant of Life

Much opposition to the pre-fall covenant dissipates if it is seen in terms of the living, fecund, triune God granting life to his creature and promising eternal life upon his continued obedience.

The WCF, 7.1, sets all God's covenantal dealings with humanity in the context of his free condescension:

> The distance between God and the creature is so great, that although reasonable creatures do owe obedience unto him as their Creator, yet they could never have any fruition of him as their blessedness and

15. Meredith G. Kline, *By Oath Consigned: A Reinterpretation of the Covenantal Signs of Circumcision and Baptism* (Grand Rapids, MI: Eerdmans, 1968), 33.

reward, but by some voluntary condescension on God's part, which he hath been pleased to express by way of covenant.

God's covenants express his "voluntary condescension," which is the only way we can come into communion with him. This condescension applies as much to the first covenant as it does to the covenant of grace, made after the fall (WCF, 7.3). It is clear how the latter, in both the Old Testament and the New, expresses the free condescension of God (WCF, 7.3–6). However, the pre-fall covenant equally expresses God's gracious condescension. John Leith, reflecting on the Assembly's portrayal of the prelapsarian covenant, indicates, "This was not simply a covenant of merit, for the covenant itself was a gracious act of God, the great disparity between God and man prohibiting any possibility of man's works by their own merit earning salvation."[16]

Much earlier, Athanasius writes of God that "he secured the grace given them by a law."[17]

In WCF, 7.1, the divines outline general principles underlying God's covenant. The focus is on the great distance between God and his creatures. His morally responsible creatures—angels and humans—owe him obedience. God's covenant expresses his sovereignty, his stooping low to grant blessings to which we had no inherent claim. However, what exactly does the Assembly mean by "some voluntary condescension on God's part"?

The minutes of the Assembly do not record any details.[18] In Protestant Scholasticism, *condescensio* was used for God's accommodation of himself to human ways of knowing in order to reveal himself. This was closely related to the *gratia Dei*, the goodness and undeserved favor of God toward man and to *gratia communis*, his nonsaving, universal grace by which he bestows his favor on creation in blessings of physical sustenance and moral influence for the good.[19] These are the clearest senses of the terms for the Assembly, for it saw grace as fully compatible with law. Law is present in the covenant

---

16. John H. Leith, *Assembly at Westminster: Reformed Theology in the Making* (Richmond, VA: John Knox, 1973), 92.
17. Athanasius, *On the Incarnation* 3.4 (NPNF², 4:38).
18. Alex F. Mitchell, *Minutes of the Sessions of the Westminster Assembly of Divines (November 1644 to March 1649): From Transcripts of the Originals Procured by a Committee of the General Assembly of the Church of Scotland* (Edinburgh and London: William Blackwood and Sons, 1874), 148, 172; Chad Van Dixhoorn, "Reforming the Reformation, Vol. 6: Minutes of the Westminster Assembly; Folio 293v– ; 18 November 1644–14 April 1648" (PhD diss., Cambridge University, 2004), 6:196, 231.
19. Richard A. Muller, *Dictionary of Latin and Greek Theological Terms Drawn Principally from Protestant Scholastic Theology* (Grand Rapids, MI: Baker, 1985), 19, 130.

of grace in the time of the law and the gospel (WCF, 7.5).[20] In the covenant of grace, grace and law are not competing ways of salvation; they fulfill different functions: grace constitutes, law regulates. The covenant is pervasively gracious, yet we receive the promise through the obedience of Christ, and the law continues to regulate the Christian life (WCF, 20.2, 5–7). By extension, grace and law are also present in the covenant of life. The gracious promise of everlasting life is in the foreground, even defining the Assembly's view of the covenant. Simultaneously, law regulates Adam's situation. The promise is received through obedience. In reviewing the law from before the fall until now, WCF, 20.7, underlines this compatibility, supporting Paul's argument in Galatians 3 that law serves the purposes of God's grace, rather than vice versa: "Neither are the aforementioned uses of the law contrary to the grace of the gospel, but do sweetly comply with it."

Since Genesis does not comment explicitly on many of these issues, the fathers of the Reformed churches saw no covenant here. In addition to Calvin, others such as Zwingli, Bullinger, Bucer, Vermigli, and Zanchi never adopted a dual covenant system. Nor is the construction present in the great Reformed confessions and catechisms prior to the Westminster Assembly, such as the French Confession (1559); the Scots Confession (1560), composed by John Knox; the Belgic Confession (1561); the Heidelberg Catechism (1563); the Second Helvetic Confession (1566)—the most widely approved of all Reformed confessions—and the Canons of the Synod of Dort (1619). The covenantal construction of the pre-fall situation only developed in the 1580s in response to questions surrounding the relationship between predestination and the fall.[21] Although almost universally accepted, the pre-fall covenant is a distinguishing feature of confessional Presbyterianism, not of the confessional Reformed tradition as a whole.[22]

12.6   Biblical Considerations

12.6.1   *The Context of the Pre-fall Covenant*

The terms of the covenant are to be seen in relation to creation.[23] Adam's original state contemplated this covenantal relationship with God. Never

---

20. See the chapters on the mediatorial work of Christ (8.4–5), justification (11.3), and the law of God (19.1–7).

21. Weir, *Origins*.

22. See my article, "Reformed Theology," in *NDT*, 569–72.

23. The WCF, WLC, and WSC do *not* imply an interval of time between creation and the inception of a covenant by God with Adam. WSC, 12, speaks of the covenant being made "when God

was he outside that relationship. The human race, under his headship, was given the task of ruling the earth, as wide-ranging a mandate as the realm in which it was to be exercised (Gen. 1:26–31).

Genesis 2 portrays Adam as placed in an environment abounding in beauty, with a profusion of lush vegetation, an ideal irrigation system, mineral resources, and superabundant food, with more besides. God gave him a vast area of personal freedom for his own benefit and enjoyment (v. 16). Calvin remarks on Genesis 2:8: "What a happy and pleasant habitation was allotted to him [Adam] . . . a place which he [God] had especially embellished with every variety of delights, with abounding fruits, and with all other most excellent gifts . . . the fairest scene of fruitfulness and delight."[24] Calvin adds that God hereby proved his benevolence toward the human race. On verse 9, Calvin suggests that the tree of life pointed to the kindness of God, the sign teaching Adam that he could claim nothing for himself, as if it were his own, but instead that he must depend wholly on the Son of God. Calvin indicates that Adam's creation in the image of God itself comprised the knowledge of God, who is the chief good.[25] Adam's freedom commends God's liberality.[26]

Moreover, to crown all these rich expressions of God's goodness, God provided a woman for the man to be his assistant, companion, and wife. She was made from him, as one corresponding to him. In short, humanity was created by God as relational, like him on a creaturely level. As Elohim was relational, disclosing a plurality in unity and creating as God, the Spirit of God, and the speech of God (Gen. 1:1–3), so he made humanity not solitary but as male and female, in communion with each other and with him their Maker. In the midst of the variety and bounty of the garden, humans bore a profound relationality mirroring their Creator. The woman was made for the man, the man cleaved to her, both were placed in the midst of creation to rule it, and (chief of all) both were made by God and for him.

12.6.2 The Parties to the Pre-fall Covenant

Man was made in the image of God, placed over creation to exercise dominion over it (Gen. 1:26–27). He was in relationship with God,

---

had created man"—at the same time. Conceptually creation comes first, since the covenant could not be made if Adam did not exist!

24. John Calvin, *Commentaries on the First Book of Moses Called Genesis*, trans. John King (Grand Rapids, MI: Eerdmans, 1979), 113–14.

25. Calvin, *Genesis*, 114–18.

26. Calvin, *Genesis*, 125–28.

himself a relational being. Suggestions that this is a plural of majesty, often found in the ancient Near East where a king speaks in the plural, or an address by Elohim to his heavenly court do not carry the weight sometimes suggested.[27]

In turn, man is created as a plurality, male and female, made for relationship with God as created in his image. Moreover, his creation as male and female is a relationship of distinction-in-equality. Creating is an act of God's sovereign freedom and grace. Our very breath is due to his free grace, the gift of life flowing from the giver of life, who is life himself. It is also an act of God's sovereign freedom and grace to create man in his image, to represent him, to be like him on a creaturely level, and to live in communion with him.

Adam's creation in the image of God directs our attention to the One who is "the image of the invisible God, the firstborn of all creation" (Col. 1:15). Paul, on many occasions, draws a connection between the first Adam of Genesis and Christ as the second Adam. In each case, the second Adam is the archetype. The first Adam was created *in* the image of God; Christ *is* the image of God. This grounding of humanity in Christ at creation demonstrates the high calling of the race and points to its ultimate destiny—expressing the grace of God.

Thus, the God who creates is disclosed as bountiful beyond imagination, beautiful in the immense variety and sumptuous splendor of his works, amazing in his grace and goodness toward his creature. To have made him is itself an act of grace; to have made him to be in Christ his Son, to have fellowship with him and enter into the communion he himself enjoys, is grace beyond calculation.

12.6.3   *The Terms of the Pre-fall Covenant*
Genesis 2:15–17 refers to the heart of the covenant of life. God places Adam in the garden, giving him the responsibility to cultivate it. He grants him freedom to eat of all the trees of the garden, a rich abundance. Then comes the warning: Adam is responsible to obey God. He has received much. In response, he has an obligation to follow faithfully the path God has for him. The heart of the covenant is a promise of everlast-

---

27. See the discussion in the previous chapter. Karl Barth is forthright: "A trinitarian understanding of Genesis 1:26 . . . is both nearer to the text and does it more justice than the alternative suggested by modern exegesis in its arrogant rejection of the exegesis of the Early Church." *CD*, III/1:192.

ing life for continued obedience after an undefined period of probation, with a warning of death if Adam disobeys.

While the promise is not explicit in Genesis, it is entailed on at least two counts. First, as Murray acknowledges, when God issues a promise, normally implied is a warning for failing to fulfill the condition attached to the promise, and vice versa.[28] For example, the Ten Commandments not only forbid certain actions but support and reinforce positive ones. The command "You shall not commit murder" reinforces the value of human life; "you shall not commit adultery" is designed to safeguard marriage; and so on. The negative form of the Decalogue expresses positive intent. In Genesis 2, the warning attached to the ban on eating from the tree points to a corresponding promise for continued obedience. Hence, the covenant is a covenant of life in which this promise is the chief point.

Second, while the pre-fall situation is not explicitly covenantal, we are justified in construing it this way by extension from the new covenant and the work of Christ as second Adam. As the fathers saw from the days of Irenaeus, Christ, by his obedience, repaired the damage done by Adam's disobedience. He recapitulated Adam. Where Adam had sinned in connection with a tree, Christ obeyed on a tree.[29] Christ fulfilled God's covenant. He took our place, and by his righteousness we have eternal life. Therefore, the first Adam's disobedience was also related to a covenant instituted by God. This connection with the second Adam, planned by God from eternity, requires that Adam's situation was covenantal; from that, we see it in the light of its ultimate fulfillment in Christ.

12.7 Theological Considerations

12.7.1 *By Law or by Grace Regulated by Law?*

The question arises of whether God related to man in this original covenant by law or by grace regulated by law. This has a profound impact throughout the rest of theology. If God related to Adam in creation exclusively by law, our view of the covenant of grace will be dominantly legal, for grace will serve the purposes of law, and this will color the way we relate to God now. At the same time, we must stress the

28. Murray, *Writings*, 2:54.
29. Irenaeus, *Against Heresies* 5.16.3 (*ANF*, 1:544).

need for caution. We view the Adamic situation as covenantal largely by extrapolation from the work of Christ, the second Adam. We do not view Christ's work primarily through a construal of a relatively dimly revealed relationship in Genesis 2. The movement of thought is from the work of Christ as the whole of Scripture portrays it backward to the Adamic covenant.[30] We are to interpret the less clear in the light of fuller revelation. I have written elsewhere that Christ's work cannot be understood apart from its roots in the Old Testament.[31] Thus, we move from the whole Old Testament forward to the fulfillment in Christ, then return to Genesis, to find that Christ as the second Adam casts a fresh and fuller light on what went on before.

12.7.2   Grace and Law as Complementary, Not Competitive

Lutheranism tended to see law and gospel in dialectical tension, as polar opposites. Indeed, when they are construed as ways of salvation, the Bible demonstrates a radical incompatibility (Rom. 4:4–5, 13ff.; 11:5–6; Gal. 2:21). The Reformed, on the other hand, have viewed law and grace as complementary. Both exist together, fulfilling different functions. Grace constitutes, law regulates. If the Adamic covenant was exclusively legal, with grace excluded, Adam on fulfilling the covenantal stipulations would have had something about which to boast, something other than God (Rom. 4:1–4). The man would have gloried in himself! This is the essence of sin! It is far from the appropriate attitude of the creature made for partnership with the triune God. Even Christ, the second Adam, exercised a humble submission to, utter dependence on, and grateful faith in his Father. He, uniquely, was marked by the fear of the Lord. He, preeminently, sang the Psalter as the one who fulfilled it, with the psalmists confessing his faith and expressing his gratitude in Yahweh's gracious deliverance. Christ, in his vicarious human priesthood, demonstrated the proper human response to God.

In this connection, Paul Helm makes a valuable point in his discussion of Calvin's treatment of the *sensus divinitatis* (SD), which Calvin, as a matter of factual observation, deemed all people to have. Helm writes,

---

30. This was the way the historical development of the pre-fall covenant occurred. See Letham, "The *Foedus Operum*"; Weir, *Origins*; Michael C. McGiffert, "From Moses to Adam: The Making of the Covenant of Works," *SCJ* 19 (1988): 131–55.

31. Robert Letham, *The Work of Christ* (Leicester: Inter-Varsity Press, 1993), 19ff.; Thomas F. Torrance, *Reality and Evangelical Theology* (Philadelphia: Westminster, 1983).

"Using Immanuel Kant's terminology we might say that each person with a properly-working SD in a properly-working environment has a 'holy will,' a will that loves and respects God, and which willingly meets obligations to do so, while not recognizing these *as* obligations."[32] In short, in the absence of sin and a personality disordered resulting from it, God's requirements are not burdensome obligations so much as aspects of joyful service and fellowship. Again, while law is clear in the Adamic covenant, it does not exclude all else.

Advocates of the view that the Adamic covenant was purely legal argue that if grace was present, merit would necessarily have been denied, consequently threatening the second Adam's meritorious obedience. This concern stems from a polarized view of law and grace, and puts law prior to grace. It creates precisely the problem John McLeod Campbell (1800–1872) faced. Campbell argued that Scottish Calvinism had made justice an essential attribute of God and love purely arbitrary. The consequence, he argued, was the priority of the legal over the filial, with devastating effects on piety and assurance. He was wrong in terms of the sixteenth and much of the seventeenth century but has a point here. To speak of grace in the Adamic covenant as rendering meaningless Christ's fulfillment of God's righteous law clouds the issue and makes meaningful discourse difficult.

12.7.3 *Harmony with God's Subsequent Covenantal Operations*

If the pre-fall covenant expresses grace regulated by law, it will harmonize with God's subsequent covenantal dealings. In Galatians 3, Paul argues that the law given by God through Moses was added to serve the interests of his covenant with Abraham, made centuries earlier. Law serves the promise. The promise to Abraham was fulfilled in Christ, the law acting as custodian of the covenant people until Christ came, the seed promised to Abraham. The Abrahamic and Mosaic covenants existed side by side; the law was *added* (v. 19). Law and grace coexisted, fulfilling distinct functions. The Mosaic covenant itself supports Paul. The law was given to a people already in covenant with God. In Exodus 20:2–3, first comes the record of the grace of God, where he says, "I am the LORD your God, who brought you out of the land of Egypt, out of the house of slavery." The community was already under the gracious

---

32. Paul Helm, *John Calvin's Ideas* (Oxford: Oxford University Press, 2004), 228.

covenantal protection of Yahweh. Then comes the law, "You shall have no other gods before me."

12.7.4   Implications for Union with Christ

If God's primary dealings with man are by grace regulated by law, a purely legal covenantal understanding that reduces union with Christ to external contractual relations is avoided. This is a problem that crept into Reformed theology after the Westminster Assembly. Whereas union with Christ, understood in real, spiritual terms, was central to Calvin's view of salvation and was at the heart of the soteriology of the WLC, by the time of Charles Hodge (1797–1878), American Presbyterianism externalized that relationship. This externalization also affected sacramental theology. Where the WCF talks of the faithful feeding on Christ truly and spiritually in the Lord's Supper, and Calvin writes of Christ communicating his substance to us, in a sense mysteriously pouring himself into us,[33] nineteenth-century worthies like William Cunningham (1805–1861) and Robert Dabney (1820–1898) could not make rhyme or reason of such thoughts and reverted to a form of Zwinglian memorialism. Whole tracts of John's Gospel, like chapters 13–17, will make little sense if this point is missed, and the adoption of believers as the children of God will fail to make the impact in piety and Christian living that it should.

12.7.5   The Covenant of Life and the Revelation of God

The answer to the question of whether the covenant of life was gracious reflects on the character of God. The Father, the Son, and the Holy Spirit are from eternity in indivisible union, in love, goodness, and blessedness. If God had related to man in creation exclusively by law, then his revelation of himself to Adam would not have been a true self-revelation at all, and creation would not express the character of God. He would be, behind his revelation, something other than Adam was given reason to believe him to be. The being and acts of God would be in radical disjunction. If, on the other hand, we were to hold that this supposed nongracious revelation was a true revelation of who he is, we then would be in the exceedingly dangerous position of holding that the relations between

---

33. *Calvin's Commentaries: The Epistles of Paul to the Galatians, Ephesians, Philippians, and Colossians*, trans. T. H. L. Parker (Grand Rapids, MI: Eerdmans, 1965), 208–10, commenting on Eph. 5:30–32; John Calvin, *Commentarii in Pauli Epistolas*, Ioannis Calvini opera exegetica (Geneva: Droz, 1992), 271–74; WCF, 29.7.

the persons of the Trinity were purely legal, with the unity of God legal and contractual rather than ontological.

12.7.6 *Christological Questions*

Christ, the second Adam, was and is the eternal Son of the Father, one of the Trinity, who united to himself a human nature conceived in the womb of the Virgin Mary. As Constantinople II (553) held, the *person* of the Son took into union a full human *nature*. There were, of course, obvious legal aspects to what Christ came to do, for our salvation is established according to divine justice and in fulfillment of God's law. But this does not exhaust the meaning of the incarnation. In becoming incarnate, the Son took human nature into union, and thus we *in union with Christ* are given to share in communion with God. Has anyone ever expressed this more eloquently than John Henry Newman?[34]

> O loving wisdom of our God!
> When all was sin and shame,
> a second Adam to the fight,
> and to the rescue came.
>
> O wisest love!—that flesh and blood,
> which did in Adam fail,
> should strive afresh against their foe,
> should strive and should prevail;
>
> And that a higher gift than grace,
> should flesh and blood refine,
> God's presence and his very self,
> and essence all-divine.

Calvin, commenting on Genesis 2:22ff., with reference to Ephesians 5, cites Adam's pre-fall life with the woman in marriage as pointing to the church's union with the Son of God. We can hardly construe the relationship between God and humanity in creation in abstraction from grace if his primary provision for Adam's need, as he stood in covenant with God, speaks so vividly of our union with the Son.

Additionally, we need to consider the Christological ground of creation. In common with many other fathers, Athanasius held that creation

---

34. The hymn "Praise to the Holiest in the Height" (1865).

was grounded in Christ. This is in line with Paul's teaching that Christ is the Mediator of creation (Col. 1:15–17): "He is the image of the invisible God, the firstborn of all creation. For in him all things were created, in heaven and upon the earth, visible and invisible . . . all things were created through him and for him. He is before all things and in him all things hold together" (my trans.). As such, man was created *in* the image of God, who is Jesus Christ.[35] From day one, humanity in general and Adam in particular stood in and under the grace of God. To repeat Calvin's comment, Adam could claim nothing for himself as if it were his own but was taught to depend solely on the Son of God. This *in no way* negates the law or the obligation but simply underlines that it was never isolated from the wonders of Trinitarian grace. This is what makes Adam's sin so heinous—it was sin not only against the law of God but also against the grace of God.[36]

12.7.7   *Avoidance of a Nature-Grace Dualism*

If there were no grace in the covenant of life, God would have related to humanity differently in creation than he does in all subsequent stages of history. God would relate to man in creation by law but in redemption by grace. Such a radical separation between creation and redemption is belied by the central truths of the incarnation and resurrection. In both, in achieving reconciliation and redemption, God affirms his creation. In the incarnation, the Son assumes our whole nature (body and soul) into permanent union. In the resurrection, in which we share by grace, our whole person (body as well as soul) is raised from death and transformed to be like Christ. We are saved as whole people in psychosomatic unity, including our bodily existence. Indeed, Christ at the right hand of God has a glorified human body and rational soul. Redemption is the redemption of creation, humanity centrally included. Christ is both the Creator and the Mediator of creation. Creation thus has *as its goal* the redemption he has brought. God's first covenant with Adam, that of life, cannot be regarded in isolation from this grand purpose, for it signifies God's original and teleological relations to the human race.

---

35. Philip Edgcumbe Hughes, *The True Image: The Origin and Destiny of Man in Christ* (Grand Rapids, MI: Eerdmans, 1989), 1–69, 211–316, esp. 276–80.

36. Cf. John of Damascus, *The Orthodox Faith* 2.30 (NPNF[2], 9/2:43): "Man then the creator made male, giving him to share in his own divine grace, and bringing him thus into communion with himself."

In conclusion, the evidence does not support a radical distinction between law in the creation covenant and grace thereafter. Nor does it suggest that grace, in some undifferentiated sense, operates both before and after the fall, with law relegated to a minor role. Rather, in accordance with the WCF, God initiates his law as an outflow of his gracious benevolence and his righteous nature in the creation covenant. With various nuances, which we will explore, his subsequent covenant of grace is regulated by law.

Further Reading

Lillback, Peter A. *The Binding of God: Calvin's Role in the Development of Covenant Theology*. Grand Rapids, MI: Baker, 2001.

Venema, Cornelis P. *Christ and Covenant Theology: Essays on Election, Republication, and the Covenants*. Phillipsburg, NJ: P&R, 2017.

Study Questions

1. On the assumption that the creation situation was covenantal, consider the nature of the promise implied in the threat for disobedience.

2. What consequences may follow from rejecting the legal element of the creation covenant? Similarly, identify weaknesses in the case that grace is excluded from this covenant.

13

Humanity in Sin

Sin is any transgression of the law of God and thus is directed principally against God. It is an absence of good, not a positive entity; this is a reflection of the New Testament terms for sin, which are mainly negative—*transgression, disobedience, lawlessness, lovelessness, unrighteousness, godlessness.* The consequences of sin are guilt, broken relationships with God and others, death, and condemnation. Since it is a choice directed against the living God, it is a choice for death. All humanity is implicated in guilt from the first sin of Adam; various attempts have been made to identify the basis for such a connection. The consequence of the guilt of sin is a corrupt nature, inherited through the generations. This renders humans unable, because unwilling, to respond in themselves to the offer of the gospel.

✠

Adam chose death rather than life by disobeying God's commandment. The covenant was to lead him to everlasting life. Instead, he chose a different path, one of his own making, in rebellion against the living God, and so propelled himself straight to death, in all its various forms. "The wages of sin is death" (Rom. 6:23).

In the later stages of Anthony Powell's twelve-novel masterpiece *A Dance to the Music of Time*, we are introduced to a novelist called X. Trapnel, whose major work was called *Camel Ride to the Tomb*, a title drawn from a childhood experience.

The novel's title referred to an incident in Trapnel's childhood there described; one, so he insisted, that had prefigured to him what life—anyway his own life—was to be. In the narrative this episode had taken place in some warm foreign land, the name forgotten, but a good deal of sand, the faint impression of a pyramid, offering a strong presumption that the locale was Egyptian. The words that made such an impression on the young Trapnel . . . were intoned by an old man whose beard, turban, nightshirt, all the same shade of off-white, manifested the outer habiliments of a prophet; just as the stony ground from which he delivered his tidings to the Trapnel family party seemed the right sort of platform from which to prophesy.

"Camel ride to the Tomb . . . Camel ride to the Tomb . . . Camel ride to the Tomb . . . Camel ride to the Tomb."

Trapnel, according to himself, immediately recognized these words, monotonously repeated over and over again, as a revelation.

"I grasped at once that's what life was. How could the description be bettered? Juddering through the wilderness, on an uncomfortable conveyance you can't properly control, along a rocky, unpremeditated, but indefeasible track, towards the destination crudely, yet truly, stated."[1]

What a graphic illustration of the human plight following the fall!

13.1   Adam and the Fall

I discussed the historicity of Adam earlier. Now there are questions to consider relating to the historicity of the fall. Reeves and Madeume argue that if there were no historic fall, the alternatives would be either radical dualism, as in Manicheism, for which evil is an equally ultimate principle with the good, or monism in which God is above good and evil, both coming from him, and thus is the author of evil.[2] They discuss the proposals of John Hick (1966) that Irenaeus held to an upward, teleological trajectory for the world, which included within it sin and evil as a means toward its perfecting. Reeves and Madeume demonstrate that Hick not

---

1. Anthony Powell, *Books Do Furnish a Room*, in *A Dance to the Music of Time: Fourth Movement* (1971; repr., Chicago: University of Chicago Press, 1995), 108–9.
2. Hans Madeume and Michael Reeves, "Threads in a Seamless Garment: Original Sin in Systematic Theology," in *Adam, the Fall, and Original Sin: Theological, Biblical, and Scientific Perspectives*, ed. Hans Madeume and Michael Reeves (Grand Rapids, MI: Baker Academic, 2014), 210–11.

only has taken a mere incidental comment out of context but also has ignored Irenaeus's strategy of opposing gnosticism. Besides, if Hick were correct, the point of the death and resurrection of Christ would be lost entirely, since death would be an integral part of God's creation and his intentions. They refer to other similar arguments that the original creation was imperfect, sin and evil being part of the evolutionary process leading to the ultimate perfecting of creation. Such arguments pose similar problems.[3]

In Genesis 3, we are confronted by a surprising anomaly. A serpent speaks; something has happened out of harmony with the settled order of creation (v. 1). Humanity was given authority over the animals but here is a reversal (Gen. 1:26–28; 2:18–20), to be followed by a sequence of disorder and rebellion.

First, the woman listens to the serpent, acquiescing in the breach of the created order, tacitly accepting the serpent's usurpation of humanity's authority and God's purpose (3:1–2). Second, the serpent questions whether God has issued the command not to eat from the tree; it turns a clear divine command into a matter for debate and dialog (v. 1). Third, the woman adds to the word of God. Not only does she engage in this illicit discussion, but she thinks she can perfect what God has already given. "Neither shall you touch it" is an erroneous human embellishment, implying that God is stricter than he is, that human regulations trump the word of God (vv. 2–3). Already the seeds of unbelief appear as distorted shoots from the soil of the garden. Fourth, the serpent makes explicit what was previously implicit, outrightly denying the truth and reliability of God's word—"you will not surely die" (vv. 4–5). The serpent implies that God is lying or her interpretation is wrong: God is jealous, since they will be like God if they eat this fruit. It is an invitation to *theōsis* by human effort rather than the grace of God, a temptation to be autonomous, a blurring of the Creator-creature distinction.

For her part, the woman sees the attractiveness of the forbidden fruit. It looks delicious, aesthetically pleasing, and intellectually empowering (v. 6). That this is not the woman's fault alone is clear insofar as the man is with her throughout and thus is complicit in everything (v. 6). Indeed, he abdicates his responsibilities and allows himself to be led, knowingly, by the serpent and Eve. The tree of the knowledge of good and evil en-

---

3. Madeume and Reeves, "Threads," 211–14.

ables humans to know evil, but from active engagement in it, not from the standpoint of the knowledge of God.[4]

The results are immediate. First comes shame, with the pair's attempt to cover their nakedness (v. 7). Later God provides coverings (v. 21); their own attempt is human self-effort. The shame is also evident in the attempt to hide from God amid his creation (v. 8), a harbinger of humanity's ongoing evasion of God and immersion in its control of creation.

Connected with the shame is evasion of responsibility. Blame is cast elsewhere, personal accountability avoided. The man blames the woman and, implicitly, God, who provided her; the woman blames the serpent (vv. 12–13). Social relationships are eroding, communion with God is broken.

Then there are the penalties. The woman is to undergo pain in childbearing, together with domestic strife (v. 16). The man suffers the curse on the ground with its hard labor and unfruitful toil (vv. 17–19). There will be a perpetual conflict with the serpent (vv. 14–15). Eventually, physical decay and death will result (vv. 18–19); there will be no return to Eden (vv. 22–24).

Yet, in the midst of this dismal scene there is hope of ultimate deliverance through the offspring of the woman who will deal a mortal blow to the serpent (v. 15). The fall is not the finale, for God provides covering, life continues, and offspring are born, one of whom will bring eventual victory (v. 20). Indeed, the prohibition on any return to the *status quo ante* is an act of God's mercy so that the fallen state could not be perpetuated. There is not, nor can there ever be, a restoration of the original condition. Paradise will never be restored; it was provisional, but the end product will be far superior.

The following chapters depict a flowering of economic and cultural development but also an exponential escalation of violence until God acts in judgment, renewing creation with developed safeguards (Gen. 4:1–9:17).

13.2 The Origin of Sin

Sin appears to have originated in the angelic world (Job 1:6–2:10; John 8:43–44; Rom. 16:20; 2 Cor. 2:10–11; 11:3; 1 Pet. 3:19–20; 2 Pet. 2:4;

---

4. Edward J. Young, *Genesis 3: A Devotional and Exegetical Study* (London: Banner of Truth, 1966), 36–38.

1 John 3:8; Jude 6, 9; Rev. 12:7–17), a definite sin, a free choice by some angels by which they rejected God, seeking to be like God themselves (John 8:44; 1 John 3:8). No repentance is possible for them, but they are kept in chains awaiting judgment.[5] Unfallen angels are spirits, immensely powerful creatures (Isa. 37:36) who can travel swiftly (Dan. 9:20–21; Luke 1:26) and to whom the Old Testament attributes governmental functions (Dan. 10:13–14, 20–21; 12:1). In the New Testament, angels are presented as serving the people of God (Acts 12:6–15; Heb. 1:14). Those that sinned have "no power against anyone except what God in his dispensation has conceded to them."[6] It is this that may explain the serpent speaking, "the infiltration of a spiritual superterrestrial power," as Bavinck hints.[7]

However, seeking the origin of sin is dangerous, as Berkouwer stresses, because of sin's inherent deceitfulness and the temptation to exculpate our own guilt. He points to Bavinck's contention that sin had no origin, only a beginning. "An explanation for sin is truly impossible," Berkouwer states.[8] Sin is deceitful; the responsibility for human sin lies entirely with ourselves. We cannot blame the devil or vainly attempt to pass off responsibility to some prior cause. Ultimately sin is an anomaly, its origin a mystery. As Augustine wrote, "I sought from where evil comes and I found no solution."[9]

Aquinas argues that good is the cause of evil. Here the nuances of Aristotelian causality are important in helping us distinguish ways in which various elements are connected. Evil is caused by an agent *per accidens*, Thomas argues.[10] The action of evil is caused by some deficiency in action due to weakness or ineptitude. It is caused by an agent's action when that agent's intention is to deprive, as when a fire deprives of air or water, but it does so adventitiously. He cites Augustine's argument (*Letter to Julian* 1) that the movement of an evil will is caused by a rational creature that is good; thus, good is the cause of evil. But evil has no direct cause, only an accidental, or adventitious, one.[11] Since evil is attributable to a defect in action or in the agent, it cannot be attributed

---

5. John of Damascus, *The Orthodox Faith* 2.4 (NPNF², 9/2:21; PG, 94:877).

6. John of Damascus, *The Orthodox Faith* 2.4 (NPNF², 9/2:20; PG, 94:877).

7. Bavinck, *RD*, 3:34.

8. G. C. Berkouwer, *Sin* (Grand Rapids, MI: Eerdmans, 1971), 11–26, here 26.

9. Augustine, *Confessions* 7.7 (NPNF¹, 1:106–7; PL, 32:739); my translation.

10. Adventitiously, not as its primary aim but as something that happens incidentally, in passing.

11. Aquinas, *ST* 1a.49.1.

to God, in whom is no defect.[12] Nor can there be a first principle of evil, like a first principle of good, since evil is parasitic on the good. Referring to Aristotle, Thomas argues that evil cannot triumph, for if it did it would destroy itself, since it requires good on which to be parasitic.[13] In short, good is original. Sin is the absence of good, whereas good is not the absence of evil. Thus, sin is the negation of God's requirement for human life; God's requirement is the standard against which sin is measured. Since sin is primarily a negative, it cannot triumph, for that would be self-destructive. This leads us to ask what sin is.

13.3 The Nature of Sin

13.3.1 Biblical Terms for Sin

The principal words for sin in the New Testament are ἁμαρτία (*sin*), ἀνομία (*lawlessness*), ἀδικία (*unrighteousness* or *injustice*), παράβασις (*transgression*), παρακοή (*disobedience*), and πίπτω (the verb *fall*). All these terms have in common a deviation from the law or requirements of God. The range of words used for sin warns us against viewing it by one term alone. It is described as lawlessness and lovelessness in 1 John. Love is the fulfilling of the law; therefore, lawlessness is the absence of love. There is no antithesis between love and the law of God.

13.3.2 The Deceitfulness of Sin

Sin is contrary to truth (Jer. 17:9; Matt. 23:28). Sin promises a great reward, but its actual return is death (2 Cor. 11:13–15). This was clear in Genesis 3. The original pair thought disobedience to God would be intellectually fulfilling and make them like God; the reverse was true.

> There is a way that seems right to a man,
>   but its end is the way to death. (Prov. 16:25)

13.3.3 Sin Is Directed against God

All terms for sin come back to this point, even when sin is committed against another human being in violation of the fifth to ninth commandments. Sin, being a transgression of God's command (Gen. 2:15–17), is ultimately against God himself (Ps. 51:4). God's law reveals sin in its true

---

12. Aquinas, *ST* 1a.49.2.
13. Aquinas, *ST* 1a.49.3.

colors (Rom. 1:18–3:20; 7:7–8). It defines what is pleasing to God and what is not. Powerless of itself to effect any change in us, for it is diagnostic rather than palliative, the law demonstrates our great plight and the state of condemnation in which humanity is implicated. If sin were an offense against law alone, the yardstick would be abstract. But this is the law of God, and so at root, sin is an attack against God, a personal affront, not merely a legal one. It is apostasy and rebellion, stemming from the desire to be God, autonomous, and free from his jurisdiction. Since God is holy and just, his law discloses that our sin is an affront to him and deserves his just retribution (Rom. 3:9–20).

As Calvin wrote, "The very name of the tree [of the knowledge of good and evil] shows the sole purpose of the precept was to keep [Adam] content with his lot and to prevent him being puffed up with wicked lust." The promise of eternal life and the threat of death "served to prove and exercise his faith." Consequently, disobedience was the beginning of the fall; the root was contempt of God's word. The sin not merely was apostasy but was joined with vile reproaches against God.[14] Since sin is directed against God, who is life itself and love, it is a choice for death, a decision for hatred, discord, and disorder.

13.3.4   *Sin Is against Justice and the Law of God*

Augustine writes that "sin is the will to retain and follow after what justice forbids, and from which it is free to abstain."[15] Taking it a stage further he adds: "Sin . . . is any transgression in deed, or word, or desire, of the eternal law. And the eternal law is the divine order or will of God."[16] It is an offense against the natural order God has established. "Sin is not the striving after evil nature but the desertion of better."[17] It comes from the will of those who sin,[18] and it is "nothing else than corruption, either of the measure, or the form, or the order, that belong to nature."[19] Similarly, Aquinas considers sin to be "a word, deed, or desire which is against eternal law," that is, God in his government of the world.[20] It is departure from the goodness of God, for all offenses are

---

14. Calvin, *Institutes*, 2.1.4.
15. Augustine, *On Two Souls, against the Manicheans* 11 (NPNF¹, 4:103).
16. Augustine, *Reply to Faustus, the Manichean* 27 (NPNF¹, 4:283).
17. Augustine, *Concerning the Nature of the Good, against the Manicheans* 34 (NPNF¹, 4:358).
18. Augustine, *Concerning the Nature of the Good* 35 (NPNF¹, 4:359).
19. Augustine, *Concerning the Nature of the Good* 4 (NPNF¹, 4:352).
20. Aquinas, *ST* 1a2ae.91.1, 1a2ae.93.1–6.

against God.[21] It is self-love, which is ultimately self-hatred, as Augustine notes: "It is inherent in the sinful soul to desire above all things, and to claim as due to itself, that which is properly due to God only. Now such love of itself is more correctly called hate."[22]

13.3.5   *Sin as* Privatio

Augustine holds sin to be a negative, an absence of good, rather than a thing in itself.[23] John of Damascus, summing up the Patristic consensus, considers that "evil is nothing else than the absence of goodness."[24] Aquinas too denies that evil is either a being or a nature. It is relative to good but good is not relative to evil. Hence, evil must be known from the nature of the good so that "by the name of evil is signified the absence of good."[25] It is real and not illusory; it is an absence, an actual deprivation, of good.[26] If evil were correlative with good, a good God could not be. Sin therefore is a failure, a privation of the good that should be there. Therefore, God is not the cause of sin.[27] To propose sin and evil as positive realities is to posit a dualism akin to Manicheism.

To say that sin is an absence of good is not to say that it does not exist. Rather something is missing that ought to be there. Brian Davies remarks on this in Aquinas, quoting Herbert McCabe:

> If I have a hole in my sock, the hole is not anything at all, it is just an absence of wool or cotton or whatever, but it is a perfectly real hole in my sock. It would be absurd to say that holes in socks are unreal and illusory just because the hole isn't made of anything and is purely an absence. *Nothing* in the wrong place can be just as real and just as important as *something* in the wrong place. If you inadvertently drive your car over a cliff, you will have nothing to worry about; it is precisely the nothing that you will have to worry about.[28]

---

21. Aquinas, *ST* 1a2ae.72.7; Brian Davies, *Thomas Aquinas's* Summa Theologiae: *A Guide and Commentary* (Oxford: Oxford University Press, 2014), 202–4.

22. Augustine, *On Christian Doctrine* 1.23.23 (*NPNF*[1], 2:528); see Augustine, *De Trinitate* 14.18 (*NPNF*[1], 3:192–93).

23. Augustine, *City of God* 12.7 (*NPNF*[1], 2:230); Augustine, *Of Free Will* 2.20.54.

24. John of Damascus, *The Orthodox Faith* 2.4 (*NPNF*[2], 9/2:20; *PG*, 94:877).

25. Aquinas, *ST* 1a.48.1.

26. Peter Kreeft, *A Summa of the Summa: The Essential Philosophical Passages of St. Thomas Aquinas'* Summa Theologica *Edited and Explained for Beginners* (San Francisco: Ignatius, 1990), 208–9.

27. Aquinas, *ST* 1a2ae.79; Davies, Summa Theologiae: *A Guide*, 204.

28. Herbert McCabe, OP, *God Matters* (London: Chapman, 1987), 29, cited by Brian Davies, *The Thought of Thomas Aquinas* (Oxford: Clarendon, 1992), 91.

Indeed, Kreeft is correct that, for Aquinas, sin is worse than hell, since moral evil is worse than physical evil; "it is plain that fault has more evil in it than pain has."[29]

When loved ones die, their absence is real. My mother was a convivial person. When I was a small child, she invariably took two or three hours on trips to the local shops, stopping to talk with whoever was passing by. After she died, the house was strangely silent. Her absence was the dominating presence; it was a gap, a nothing, immensely real.

Bavinck correctly distinguishes *privatio* from pure negation. "Nothing" as such is simply nothing. However, the "nothing" that is sin is a deprivation of the good, of what is essential to life. Sin is described in the Bible in active terms, as a corrupting and destructive power. As such, it can also be called transgression of the law, as Augustine taught, an active privation.[30] The hole in the sock is a deprivation resulting from a tear or erosion, a real, although trivial, problem, while the gap left by my mother was a dominant nothingness, a deep loss. This reflects the biblical definition of sin as lawlessness, unrighteousness, injustice, godlessness, the absence of what is good and right, the lack of love—all negations (Rom. 1:29–31; 2 Tim. 3:2–3, 5). Death itself is the absence of life.

Helm comments:

> What determines [an evil action] . . . are the normal causes of action, human intentions and the like, which God ordains and upholds as he ordains and upholds everything. But what determines the action insofar as it is an *evil* action is a divine *withholding*. God withholds his goodness or grace, and forthwith the agent forms a morally deficient motive or reason and acts accordingly. . . . Because sin or moral evil is a privation, the only cause or author of a morally evil act is whoever is the immediate author of it.[31]

13.4   The Consequences of Sin

13.4.1   *Death*

Since sin is rebellion against God, who is life, it inescapably entails death. This includes spiritual death (Eph. 2:1ff.), severance of relations with

---

29. Aquinas, *ST* 1a.48.6; Kreeft, *Summa of the Summa*, 212.
30. Bavinck, *RD*, 3:136–41.
31. Paul Helm, *The Providence of God* (Leicester: Inter-Varsity Press, 1993), 170.

God, evident instantly in the attempt of Adam and Eve to hide from him. It also includes the breakdown of healthy human relationships, as both the man and the woman, filled with shame, evade responsibility for their sin. The following chapters of Genesis recount an escalating cycle of violence and disorder, eventually threatening the existence of the human race. Physical death is recorded meticulously in Genesis 4 and 5. Together these various aspects of the absence of the life God gave to the race culminate in eternal death—the confirmation of the fallen state and the choices humans have made.

13.4.2 Guilt

In Romans 5:12ff. Paul establishes that the penalty of Adam's first sin fell upon the whole human race and is seen in death. In verse 12, Paul makes an unfinished comparison, breaking off with a parenthesis (vv. 13–17), which is divided into two sections, (vv. 13–14 and vv. 15–17). The interjection is needed because of the statement in the latter part of verse 12, that death spread to the entire race since all had sinned. There is an active sinning in which all participated, with the consequence of death. W. G. T. Shedd points out that the sinners' act is the reason for the punishment.[32] In what way had all sinned so as to incur death? The latter section of Paul's parenthesis (vv. 15–17) is necessitated by the reference to Adam as a type of Christ (v. 14); in what ways are Adam and Christ to be compared, and how does this affect the argument begun in verse 12?

The governing thought in verse 12 is not properly resumed until verses 18–19, when the explanatory interlude is over. The most crucial clause is at the end of verse 12: "sin spread to all since all sinned" (my trans.). The question arises, In what way did all sin?

The Pelagian interpretation argues that the penalty of death on all occurs as a result of *imitation* of Adam's sin; and since all of us commit sins, we all die because of those sins. This claim cannot be correct, in that it fails to account for infants who die prematurely, before they have any chance to sin in actual ways, whether knowingly or unknowingly. Nor does it apply to people who have not sinned against an express command of God, such as those Paul notes who lived after Adam and before the law was given to Israel through Moses (v. 14). These all died even

---

32. W. G. T. Shedd, *Dogmatic Theology* (Grand Rapids, MI: Zondervan, 1971), 2:184.

though they were not imitating disobedience to an explicit command of God. Furthermore, the Pelagian claim ignores the stress, later in the paragraph, on the *one* sin of the *one* man, referring to the first sin committed by Adam. All die as a consequence of that first sin of Adam, regardless of their own circumstances or their relationship to the history of redemption, and despite whether they had or had not sinned as Adam had done, in a voluntary manner against a published law.

Nor is Paul thinking of the *transmission* of original sin; the aorist (ἥμαρτον) undermines that notion, since original sin, conveyed by propagation, is a continuous process. The connection is between the one sin of Adam and its impact of death on the entire human race. The one sin of the one man is identified with all people having sinned; it is one and the same. It entails a solidarity between the one man and the rest of the race. Again, Shedd writes of the indivisibility of guilt in this matter.[33]

Given that Paul is discussing the effects of Adam's sin on the whole human race, what exactly was the nature of the relationship between Adam and his descendants? There are two broad lines of interpretation, with variations within both, which are not necessarily incompatible. In general terms, they can be called *realist* and *federal* interpretations.

The realist interpretation. In the first line of interpretation human nature is considered a numerical unity that constantly subdivides. Hence, each person who lives is part of a vast ontological reality, of which Adam was the first of the kind called human. The situation is akin to an enormous intergalactic pizza cut into innumerable slices. You and I are slices, but the whole pizza is first. Hence, when Adam sinned, the whole race participated, rather like the tomato sauce or the cheese being spoiled, contaminating the huge pizza and so damaging each and every piece that is subsequently cut.

Discussing Romans 5, Shedd refers to "the human nature existing in Adam and subsequently individualized by propagation." Whatever is predicable of Adam is predicable of his posterity, and in precisely the same way.[34] As Shedd remarks, "If two individual men commit a murder, each is chargeable with the whole guilt of the act. One-half of the guilt cannot be imputed to one, and one-half to the other."[35] He

33. Shedd, *Dogmatic Theology*, 2:185.
34. Shedd, *Dogmatic Theology*, 2:30.
35. Shedd, *Dogmatic Theology*, 2:185.

bases his argument on a commitment to traducianism.[36] The first sin corrupted the nature of the posterity simultaneously with its commission, prior to the imputation to the posterity. Shedd is suggesting not an aggregate of individuals but a specific nature not yet individualized. He argues that imputation based solely on Adam having been appointed as a representative would be "an arbitrary act of sovereignty, not a righteous judicial act which carries in it an intrinsic morality and justice."[37] He sees Turretin as marking a transition from a theory of Adamic union to one of Adamic representation.[38] Shedd argues strongly against the imputation of Adam's sin being an exact parallel with the imputation of Christ's righteousness.[39] He sees this as necessary to maintain justification by faith, since, if the parallel were exact, the imputation of Christ's righteousness would be grounded on an antecedent infusion of grace. He sees the indivisibility of Christ's righteousness as corresponding, since each believer is as completely justified as the other; for "as the unmerited imputation of Christ's obedience conveys the total undivided merit of this obedience to each and every believer, so the merited imputation of Adam's disobedience conveys the total undivided guilt of this disobedience to each and every individual of the posterity." This is so because sin is justly imputed on the basis that it was committed by those to whom it is imputed.[40]

Bavinck objects that this would require us to be responsible for all of Adam's sins and, indeed, all the sins of the human race before us, which clearly is not the case.[41] This objection is invalid. The point at issue is the transition from righteousness to corruption. Once the ingredients of the pizza are spoiled, the whole pizza is corrupted and the game is up. What may follow later is of no account, since the covenant of life was irretrievably broken, the pizza already spoiled. Bavinck assumes that realist and federal interpretations are incompatible. It is defensible to argue that they are compatible, addressing the subject from differing directions. This was the position of Turretin, who recognized that the representative union between Adam and the race rested on a union of origin.[42]

---

36. Shedd, *Dogmatic Theology*, 2:31.
37. Shedd, *Dogmatic Theology*, 2:36.
38. Shedd, *Dogmatic Theology*, 2:36; see also 2:43.
39. Shedd, *Dogmatic Theology*, 2:57–66.
40. Shedd, *Dogmatic Theology*, 2:185–86.
41. Bavinck, *RD*, 3:103.
42. Francis Turretin, *Institutes of Elenctic Theology*, trans. George Musgrave Giger, ed. James T. Dennison Jr. (Phillipsburg, NJ: P&R, 1992), 1:616.

Throughout the Bible particular individuals are held to exist in union with others independently of any federal relation, usually with their ancestors but also with contemporaries of the same social entity. When Achan sinned, all Israel sinned (Josh. 7:11). Jesus, as High Priest according to the order of Melchizedek, is superior to the Levitical priests, since Abraham, his ancestor, paid tithes to Melchizedek (Heb. 7:10); the natural solidarity between Abraham and Levi is the basis. Throughout the Old Testament, a man is seen as A, the son of B, the son of C, of the tribe of D. The difference is that these are not numerical unities.

This idea is foreign to Western individualism, but it is commonplace to many cultures in Africa or Asia. You are who you are in relation to others. You are not an isolated island, all by yourself. If you were, it would be high time to see a clinical psychiatrist.

Inheritance of a corrupt nature by means of natural generation. The generality of Reformed theologians before the covenant of works was proposed in 1585 held to this interpretation, or some variation of it. Calvin was one, Bucer another. This has similarities with the realist position insofar as it assumes the genetic unity of the race but it differs in denying that human nature is a particular and numerical unity. In this line of thought, Adam by his sin was corrupted in nature and so passed on that corrupt nature to his offspring, they to theirs, and so on down through time by means of natural propagation. As physical characteristics and character traits are transmitted through the generations, so too is the corrupt nature occasioned by sin. On this basis, the whole human race is objectively guilty of Adam's sin, participant in it, owing to the corruption they inherit from conception.

The federal interpretation. The second broad line of interpretation envisions a legal imputation by God of Adam's sin in consequence of his appointment as the head and representative of the human race. According to this perspective, God constituted Adam as the covenant head and representative of the race. Consequently, we were all *in Adam* when he sinned. This was and is a legal and representative relationship. It involves a headship somewhat akin to that of an ambassador to a foreign country, who acts on behalf of his or her government. In this way, Adam represented the entire race. By God's appointment his actions were those of the race he represented. This interpretation came in the wake of the emergence of the doctrine of the covenant of works/life.

The federal interpretation is not incompatible with the realist inter-pretation. Both assume the genetic unity of the race. The federal interpre-tation also affirms the transmission of corruption. What distinguishes it is the specific reason why Adam's sin is the sin of the race, and why the entire race participates in both the guilt of his sin and its penalty: he was appointed its representative head. The one major difference is that the federal view does not accept that human nature was a numerical unity subsequently subdivided. For this reason, there is a closer affinity with the theory of corruption transmitted through natural propagation.

It seems to me that the federal interpretation is of itself incomplete and needs to be understood in conjunction with one or both of the al-ternative views. We shall see why shortly.

Murray believes that a representative, federal relation is required in order to explain the connection between Adam and Christ in 1 Co-rinthians 15, for it goes beyond the natural union on which all these interpretations are agreed. Adam is the first man; the risen Christ is the second. Moreover, Christ is also the last Adam. There are two, and only two, structural relationships of this kind. Since the relationship between Christ and those he represents is forensic, not natural or genetic, so Murray argues, it requires something similar to explain the relationship between Adam and those he represents.[43]

However, neither side of the Adam-Christ paradigm precludes ele-ments relating to the condition of the respective members. On the one side, there is the corrupt nature transmitted from Adam to the race; on the other side, Christ, by the Holy Spirit, gives life and transformation to those in union with him. Notwithstanding, the corrupt nature is not the *cause* of guilt in Adam's offspring, nor is the renewed nature the *basis* for the righteous status in Christ's people; these are the results, the concomitants, not the originating causes or the fundamental bases.

Corporate personality. The idea of corporate personality is com-patible with both the realist and federalist views. It may fall short of providing a full explanation of the connection between Adam's sin and the race, but it is a concept upon which both these interpretations in some measure rely. It is based on the nature of humans as relational beings rather than individualists. This is evident throughout the Old

---

43. John Murray, *The Imputation of Adam's Sin* (Grand Rapids, MI: Eerdmans, 1959), 39–40.

Testament, particularly in 2 Samuel 21:1–14, Deuteronomy 25:5, the second commandment, and the consequences of Achan's sin (Josh. 7:24–26). H. Wheeler Robinson stresses this.[44]

The idea of "person" only emerged in the context of the Christian faith, in the fourth century Trinitarian debates. In speaking of the Trinitarian hypostases, the church recognized that the three are in indivisible union, each in relation to the others. Since there is something of an analogous relation between divine and human persons, the inference is that human persons too exist in relation to others, in their particular networks.

This is similar to the connection between a team and its members. If the score is 2–2 and the goalkeeper makes an error and concedes a goal in the last minute, the whole team loses, despite the quality of the other members' play. This analogy demonstrates the unity of a corporate entity acting through one of its members, and how the actions of the one can be those of the whole, but no further. However, it is a stronger and more realistic connection than a purely legal one. It suggests a reality that grounds other ideas.

All these interpretations agree that in some way when Adam sinned, all sinned. All inherit the guilt of Adam's first sin. All are born in a state of covenantal death (Eph. 2:1), for with Adam and in Adam they have opted for antagonism against God and so voted against the life he gives. Together with that, all inherit a nature inherently biased against God, corrupted at its roots and in all its facets.

To my mind, it is not necessarily a case of choosing between these interpretations; each sheds light on the other and thus on the connection with Adam. On both sides of Paul's paradigm, each aspect contributes. There is a representative connection seen in Adam's disobedience to the law and Christ's obedience being reckoned ours; this concerns our status. There is a realist aspect, as we inherit a corrupt nature and, conversely, are transformed by the Holy Spirit into the image of Christ; this concerns our condition. Finally, there is corporate personality, as Adam and the race, as well as Christ and his church, are one body; this concerns our relations. None of these images can or should be taken beyond the particular way in which they are appropriate.

---

44. H. Wheeler Robinson, *The Christian Doctrine of Man*, 3rd ed. (Edinburgh: T&T Clark, 1926), 27–30.

13.4.3 Original Sin

The term *original sin* has been used in various ways. It can refer to the first sin committed by Adam. Some, such as Bavinck, speak of the first sin as "originating sin."[45] More frequently it means the corrupt moral nature we all inherit from Adam. It entails "captivity under the power of him who thenceforth had the power of death, that is, the devil."[46] Bavinck describes this inherited corruption as "originated sin" in order to distinguish it from the first sin.[47] This corrupt disposition is called "sin" in Scripture (Rom. 6:12–17; 7:15–24; Gal. 5:17, 24; Eph. 4:18–19; James 1:14–15) and in classic Protestant theology.[48] Many of the fathers agreed.[49] It contrasts with the Roman Catholic view of *concupiscence*, an inclination to sin that is not itself culpable.[50] Original sin is therefore more than a lack of original righteousness; it is a definite in-built bias to sin. In itself it is sin. Furthermore, it is wrong to identify it with the process of natural propagation. While original sin is inherited from our parents, the process by which we originate from our parents is good.

It is widely agreed that Augustine did not invent the doctrine of original sin but that there were clear antecedents in Tertullian, Origen, Ambrose, and the Greeks.[51] In Augustine, forged against Pelagius's trust in human ability and moral effort to respond to the gospel apart from the grace of God, the doctrine had four main bases: (1) Adam's sin and its punishment are inherited, although the nature of the connection is not clear; (2) the infant soul is guilty; (3) infant sins are real and inherited by way of generation; and (4) baptism is the necessary means of salvation for all, including infants.[52] Augustine held that sin passes to

---

45. Bavinck, *RD*, 3:106.
46. CCC, 407, citing Heb. 2:14 and the Council of Trent (1546); *DS*, 1511.
47. Bavinck, *RD*, 3:106.
48. See the list of authorities cited by Shedd, *Dogmatic Theology*, 2:198–203.
49. See Irenaeus, *Against Heresies* 4.13 (*ANF*, 1:477–78); Tertullian, *De pudicitia*, cited by Shedd, *Dogmatic Theology*, 2:200; Maximus the Confessor, *Ambigua* 10 (*PG*, 91:1156C–1157); Maximus the Confessor, *Ad Thalassium* 61, in Corpus Christianorum: Series Graeca (Turnhout: Brepols, 1977–), 22:85–105; Maximus the Confessor, *On the Cosmic Mystery of Jesus Christ: Selected Writings from St. Maximus the Confessor*, trans. Paul M. Blowers and Robert Louis Wilken (Crestwood, NY: St Vladimir's Seminary Press, 2003), 131–44.
50. CCC, 1264.
51. See Tertullian, *De anima* 40–41 (*ANF*, 3:220–21), together with the sources cited in Allan D. Fitzgerald, *Augustine through the Ages: An Encyclopedia* (Grand Rapids, MI: Eerdmans, 1999), 607. Peter Sanlon, "Original Sin in Patristic Theology," in Madeume and Reeves, *Adam*, 86–88, refers to a range of predecessors cited by Augustine in support. A sophisticated, nuanced discussion of the question is Anthony Dupont, "Original Sin in Tertullian and Cyprian: Conceptual Presence and Pre-Augustinian Content," *RÉAug* 63 (2017): 1–29.
52. Fitzgerald, *Augustine*, 608.

all people by natural descent, not by imitation.[53] If Paul had meant the latter, Augustine wrote, he would have referred to the sin of the devil, not Adam, since the devil sinned first. Therefore, Paul regards Adam as the propagator of the race. No doubt many imitate Adam, but he is one thing as an example and another as a progenitor. Many imitate Christ, but illumination and justification come by grace.[54] Indeed, "the catholic Church maintains against those very Pelagians . . . that it is original sin, the guilt of which, contracted by generation, must be remitted by regeneration."[55] Infants are bound by original sin.[56] That corruption remains in children of the regenerate is seen in that "a regenerate man does not regenerate, but generates, sons according to the flesh; and thus he transmits to his posterity, not the condition of the regenerated, but only of the generated."[57]

Aquinas agreed with Augustine and made his own additions.

> According to the Catholic faith we are bound to hold that the first sin of the first man is transmitted to his descendants, by way of origin. For this reason children are taken to be baptized soon after their birth, to show that they have to be washed from some uncleanness. The contrary is part of the Pelagian heresy, as is clear from Augustine in many of his books.[58]

How does this happen? Aquinas rejected a genetic view, since sin involves guilt and consequently voluntary action. But inasmuch as we did not sin voluntarily when Adam sinned, how do we inherit sin? Aquinas answered that we inherit human nature from our first parents.

> Therefore we must explain the matter . . . by saying that all men born of Adam may be considered as one man, inasmuch as they have one common nature, which they receive from their first parents; even as in civil matters, all who are members of one community are reputed as one body, and the whole community as one man. . . . . Accordingly

---

53. Augustine, *On the Merits and Forgiveness of Sins, and on the Baptism of Infants* 9 (NPNF¹, 5:18).

54. Augustine, *On the Merits and Forgiveness of Sins, and on the Baptism of Infants* 10 (NPNF¹, 5:18).

55. Augustine, *On the Gift of Perseverance* 11 (NPNF¹, 5:536).

56. Augustine, *On the Gift of Perseverance* 12 (NPNF¹, 5:537). See also *On the Merits and Remission of Sins* 1.10; *City of God* 13.14.

57. Augustine, *On the Grace of God and Original Sin* 2.39.45 (NPNF¹, 5:253).

58. Aquinas, *ST* 1a2ae.81.1.

the multitude of men born of Adam, are as so many members of one body.[59]

This does not rule out the part played by human generation. The semen is not able to cause the rational soul, but its motion is a disposition to the transmission of the rational soul, so that the semen by its power transmits the soul from parent to child, and with that nature the stain that infects it. The offspring inherit the parent's guilt by inheriting the parent's nature by the act of generation.[60]

The later sins of the first parent and others are not so transmitted, since "a man begets his like in species but not in individual." So things that relate to the individual are not transmitted, but only those that concern the nature of the species.[61] So, according to the Catholic faith, "Christ alone excepted, all men descended from Adam contract original sin from him."[62] Christ is the exception in that he was miraculously, not directly, descended from Adam.[63]

Rome introduced modifications to the positions of Augustine and Aquinas. Original sin is first of all the imputation of Adam's trespass to all humans, since they were all included in him. First comes guilt, then punishment.[64]

Then, whereas Augustine had located the consequent moral state in concupiscence, with its seat in the sex drive, another view gained ground: that it consisted in the loss of the *donum superadditum*, from which concupiscence followed.[65] As created, flesh and spirit were in conflict, with concupiscence a disease arising from a material condition. Original sin was seen as the loss of the superadded gift after the fall, a negative rather than a positive. Trent was cautious; concupiscence arises from sin but is not in itself sinful; the free will is not lost but weakened. There was nothing left for original sin except the imputation of Adam's sin and the loss of original righteousness.[66] Bellarmine stated that the state into which humans are born after the fall is identical with the situation before the fall, with the exception of the

---

59. Aquinas, *ST* 1a2ae.81.1.
60. Aquinas, *ST* 1a2ae.81.1. See Davies, Summa Theologiae: *A Guide*, 208.
61. Aquinas, *ST* 1a2ae.81.2.
62. Aquinas, *ST* 1a2ae.82.3.
63. Aquinas, *ST* 1a2ae.81.3–4.
64. Council of Trent, 5.2; see Bavinck, *RD*, 3:95.
65. Bavinck, *RD*, 3:95–96.
66. Bavinck, *RD*, 3:96.

loss of the supernatural gift. The natural state remains intact.[67] On the imputation of sin the views were similar to the Reformed; it was either a natural or a federal and representative connection—or a combination of the two.

Rome is committed to the doctrine of original sin: "The Church, which has the mind of Christ, knows very well that we cannot tamper with the revelation of original sin without undermining the mystery of Christ." It is the reverse side of the good news that Jesus is the Savior.[68] However, since Rome restricts original sin to the loss of the superadded gifts and a return to prelapsarian concupiscence, its position is drastically weaker than either Scripture or the Reformed tradition.

Calvin maintained that original sin consists in "the depravation of a nature previously good and pure."[69] "We must surely hold that Adam was not only the progenitor but, as it were, the root of human nature; and that therefore in his corruption mankind deserved to be vitiated."[70] Thus, on the Adam-Christ comparison,

> if it is beyond controversy that Christ's righteousness, and thereby life, are ours by communication [not imitation, as with the Pelagians], it immediately follows that both were lost in Adam, only to be recovered in Christ; and that sin and death crept in through Adam, only to be abolished though Christ.

Calvin makes no attempt to explain it but simply adds that Adam plunged our race into destruction "not due to the guilt of himself alone, *which would not pertain to us at all*, but . . . because he infected all his posterity with that corruption into which he had fallen."[71] Calvin's focus is on guilt stemming from propagation, a natural connection rather than a federal one. Later, he defines original sin as "a hereditary depravity and corruption of our nature, diffused into all parts of the soul, which first makes us liable to God's wrath, then also brings forth in us those works which Scripture calls 'works of the flesh.' And that is properly what Paul calls sin."[72] We are justly condemned before God for this corrupted nature.

---

67. Robert Bellarmine, *De gratia primi hominis*, 5; Bavinck, *RD*, 3:97.
68. *CCC*, 389.
69. Calvin, *Institutes*, 2.1.5.
70. Calvin, *Institutes*, 2.1.6.
71. Calvin, *Institutes*, 2.1.6 (my italics).
72. Calvin, *Institutes*, 2.1.8.

> And this is not liability for another's transgression . . . not as if we,
> guiltless and undeserving, bore the guilt of his offense but in the sense
> that, since we through his transgression have become entangled in the
> curse, he is said to have made us guilty. Yet not only has punishment
> fallen upon us from Adam, but a contagion imparted by him resides
> in us, which justly deserves punishment.

So infants are guilty from their own fault, not from another.[73]

The WLC, 26, agrees that original sin "is conveyed from our first
parents unto their posterity by natural generation."

Original sin marks the embedding of death in the human race.
Adam's rejection of life, in his rejection of God, is transmitted down
through the generations. In terms of the pizza analogy, if the ingredients
are contaminated, every single slice is affected. Original sin marks, as
Augustine taught, a return to nothingness, a diminishing of creation. It
has metaphysical roots. And thus redemption will be the renewal of life,
its entry to a higher and indestructible plane.[74]

Orthodoxy does not give dogmatic significance to original sin, nor
does it accept the Augustinian doctrine. As Kallistos Ware writes, "Most
Orthodox theologians reject the idea of 'original guilt,' put forward by
Augustine and still accepted by the Roman Catholic Church," owing to
a far less somber view of the state of humanity.[75] This, Ware explains,
is why most Orthodox reject the Roman dogma of the immaculate conception of Mary, since in their eyes it rests on a defective view of sin.[76]
Meyendorff states that the consensus of the Orthodox takes Romans 5 to
refer to a solidarity of the race in death, a cosmic disease that makes sin
inevitable, an inheritance of mortality rather than sinfulness. He refers
to Maximus, who held that inherited guilt is impossible.[77]

While the Augustinian doctrine has spread to the East, it is alien to the
Eastern tradition as such.[78] There are definite similarities with the Western
doctrine, as Ware remarks,[79] and the East has mirrored the West in its

---

73. Calvin, *Institutes*, 2.1.8.
74. See Simon Heans, "Original Sin or Original Sinfulness? A Comment," *Heythrop Journal*
54 (2013): 55–69.
75. Timothy Ware, *The Orthodox Church* (London: Penguin, 1969), 229.
76. Ware, *Orthodox Church*, 263–64.
77. John Meyendorff, *Byzantine Theology: Historical Trends and Doctrinal Themes* (New
York: Fordham University Press, 1979), 143–46.
78. David J. Melling, "Adam and Eve," in *The Blackwell Dictionary of Eastern Christianity*,
ed. Ken Parry and David J. Melling (Oxford: Blackwell, 2001), 4–6.
79. Ware, *Orthodox Church*, 222–23.

reaction to evolutionary theory: some opposing evolution, others accommodating it, and others dismissing the historicity of Genesis. However, as Ladouceur remarks, most twentieth-century Orthodox theologians take for granted the existence of Paradise, the expulsion of Adam and Eve, and the introduction of death as a result of sin.[80] For Ladouceur himself, these are not essential Christian dogmas; no ancient pronouncement surrounded them, and so a relativization of the fall and its consequences has, for him, no effect on Christian dogma. All that is undermined is the doctrine of original sin, which the Greek church never adopted.[81]

From the West, the answers are quite different. As Newman remarked in a sermon at Oxford University, "All teaching about duty and obedience, about attaining heaven and about the office of Christ towards us is hollow and unsubstantial, which is not built here, in the doctrine of our original guilt and helplessness; and, in consequence, of original guilt and sin."[82] Newman was right. How humanity's plight is conceived will directly impact how one understands the deliverance. Rome agrees, for, again, "the Church, which has the mind of Christ, knows very well that we cannot tamper with the revelation of original sin without undermining the mystery of Christ."[83]

Original sin entails the unity of the race, that all have a common origin. As Reeves and Madeume argue, this provides a theoretical ground for the rejection of racism, a basis lacking when the unity of the race is disputed, since, if the common ancestors numbered thousands, we today would not have a single ancestor who is common to the entire race. Moreover, it would raise questions as to whether Christ took *my* nature.[84] It would make the gospel a matter of law,[85] sinners being "not helpless addicts in need of outside rescue [but] more like spiritual slobs who need to be told to buck up."[86]

Rome contends that Mary is a second exception, additional to Christ, to the universality of original sin, by virtue of her immaculate conception. The dogma intends to preserve Christ from inherited cor-

80. Paul Ladouceur, "Evolution and Genesis 2–3: The Decline and Fall of Adam and Eve," *SVTQ* 57 (2013): 135–76.
81. Ladouceur, "Evolution and Genesis 2–3," 172–73.
82. John Henry Newman, *Parochial and Plain Sermons* (London: Longman, Green, 1901), 134–35.
83. CCC, 389.
84. Madeume and Reeves, *Adam*, 215–16.
85. Madeume and Reeves, *Adam*, 224.
86. Madeume and Reeves, *Adam*, 220.

ruption by preserving his mother. However, no biblical evidence supports it. The idea was relatively late to arise. Duns Scotus (1266–1308) appears to be the first to propound it.[87] Aquinas, while holding that Mary was born without sin and did not sin, did not suggest she was conceived without sin.[88]

There is another exception to the dominion of original sin. While, as Shedd suggests, it is an ongoing *crescendo* in the fallen Adamic world, it is a *diminuendo* among believers, who no longer accept it as the desirable state of affairs, since the Holy Spirit "more and more" transforms them into the image of Christ. It rules over us no longer, for we are absolved from the results of sin by the mediation of Christ. Thanks be to God![89]

13.4.4   *The Imputation of Adam's Sin*

Following the emergence of the pre-fall covenant of works/life with Adam as federal head and representative of the race, there is a clear development in classic Reformed theology on this question. In the decades after the Reformation, the original consensus was that the race participates in Adam's sin by virtue of the natural connection all have with him through generation.

During the time of development, the following questions presented themselves:

1. Was the connection between the first sin and the rest of the race based on natural propagation and thus to be understood as inherited corruption (original sin)?
2. Was this connection also due to a determination by God that Adam was the representative of the race and so his sin was reckoned or imputed to his posterity?
3. If the answer to 2 was positive, what was the connection between 1 and 2?
4. Was *Adam's* sin imputed to the race, or was it the sin *of the first parents*? The former points to a representative relationship, although it does not require it, while the latter is more clearly based on natural descent and so places the transmission of original sin in the primary position. The latter is the position of the WCF, 6.2–3.

---

87. Bavinck, *RD*, 3:120.
88. Aquinas, *ST* 3a.27.1; Davies, Summa Theologiae: *A Guide*, 309–10.
89. Shedd, *Dogmatic Theology*, 2:212–13.

5. Related to 3, on what basis was the sin imputed? Was it by natural propagation? Was it on the grounds of a decree by God? Was it related to a covenant God made with Adam?

6. A subsidiary question is whether obedience before the fall was meritorious or something God accepted through grace? The important book by John Ball, *A Treatise on the Covenant of Grace* (1645), favorably received by the Westminster divines, denies that Adam's works were meritorious and insists on the grace of God as permeating his covenant.[90]

For imputation, it is clear that there must be a previously established union between Adam and his posterity. As Shedd remarks, Adam's sin could not be imputed to the fallen angels, nor theirs to us, nor the sin of the angels to all the angels: "Men must sin in Adam, in order to be justly punished for Adam's sin. And participation requires union with Adam."[91] The question is, what kind of union must this be? For most of the sixteenth century the natural union was considered the ground of our connection. When the pre-fall covenant emerged, the representative dimension assumed prominence, and the connection was seen in covenantal terms.

The emergence of the doctrine of the imputation of Adam's sin in Reformed theology.[92] In the half century following the first major treatise on the covenant of grace,[93] the dominant focus was on the transmission of sin based on natural propagation. Bucer understood the relationship in this way.[94] Calvin recognized that Adam's sin was imputed, but this was not his principal point: "We are condemned by Adam's sin not by imputation alone . . . but we suffer his punishment because we too are guilty, since God holds our nature, which has been corrupted in Adam, guilty of iniquity."[95] Fesko claims that Calvin speaks of imputation in

---

90. John Ball, *A Treatise of the Covenant of Grace* (London: Simeon Ash, 1645), 6–12.

91. Shedd, *Dogmatic Theology*, 2:186–87.

92. This section is an abbreviated version of an excursus in my book *The Westminster Assembly: Reading Its Theology in Historical Context* (Phillipsburg, NJ: P&R, 2009).

93. Heinrich Bullinger, *De testamento seu foedere Dei unico et aeterno brevis expositio* (Zürich, 1534).

94. Martin Bucer, *Metaphrasis et enarrationes in perpetuae epistolarum D. Pauli apostoli: Tomus primus* (Strassburg, 1536), 253–58.

95. "Prior est, quod peccato Adae non per solam imputationem damnatur, acsi alieni peccati exigeretur a nobis poena; sed ideo poenam eius sustinemus, quia et culpae sumus rei, quatenus scilicet natura nostra in ipso vitiata, iniquitatis reatu obstringitur apud Deum." Calvin, *Commentarius in epistolam Pauli ad Romanos*, in CO2 (1999), on 5:17.

the *Institutes* 2.1.7.[96] However, Calvin refers to the contagion of sin and its transmission, not the guilt of sin and its imputation. The connection is natural before it is federal.[97] Both Bullinger and Musculus focused on the connection with Adam as hereditary depravity[98] occurring by natural propagation.[99] Vermigli says the same thing;[100] he implicitly acknowledges imputation, but it rests on inherited corruption.[101] A realist perspective underlies this. Adam "was as a certaine common lumpe or masse, wherein was conteined all mankind: which lumpe being corrupted, we cannot be brought forth into the world, but corrupted and defiled."[102]

When the doctrine of the imputation of Adam's sin emerged, it was initially based on this natural connection. As the covenant of works became increasingly recognized after 1585–1590, the focus began to shift from our first parents as the root of sin to Adam in particular. Eventually, not only was it thought that corruption was reckoned to humanity by a divine decree, but Adam was seen as a representative, the guilt of his sin being imputed.

Fenner, in *Sacra theologia* (1585), adopts the earlier consensus position[103] but also writes of all who were in the person of Adam by that contract (*illo contractu*),[104] introducing the term *foedus operum*, if not the concept,[105] suggesting both realistic and representative elements. Rollock, in his Romans commentary, gives no hint of a federal relationship,[106] nor

96. J. V. Fesko, "The Westminster Confession and Lapsarianism: Calvin and the Divines," in *The Westminster Confession into the 21st Century*, ed. J. Ligon Duncan III (Fearn: Mentor, 2005), 2:521.

97. ". . . ita corruptionis exordium in Adam fuit, ut perpetuo defluxu, a prioribus in posteros transfundatur. Neque enim in substantia carnis aut animae causam habet contagio: sed quia a Deo ita fuit ordinatum." Calvin, *OS*, 3:236.

98. The Rev. Thomas Harding, *The Decades of Henry Bullinger*, ed. Thomas, trans. H. I—— (Cambridge: Cambridge University Press, 1850), 2:358–432.

99. Wolfgang Musculus, *In epistolam D. apostoli Pauli ad Romanos commentarii* (Basel: Sebastian Henric Petri, 1555), 94; *idem*, *Loci communes theologiae sacrae* (Basel: Sebastian Henric Petri, n.d.), 20.

100. Pietro Martire Vermigli, *In epistolam S. Pauli apostoli ad Romanos, commentarii doctissimi* (Basel: Petrum Pernam, 1558), 158, 162–63.

101. Vermigli, *Ad Romanos*, 170.

102. Peter Martyr Vermigli, *The Common Places of the Most Famous and Renowned Doctor Peter Martyr*, trans. Anthonie Marten (London: Denham, Chard, Broome, and Maunsell, 1583), 242.

103. Dudley Fenner, *Sacra theologia* (Geneva, 1585), 78–79.

104. "Reatus illius peccati est reatus poenae de toto illo contractu in Adami persona ad posteritatem totam, lege praedicta propogando." Fenner, *Sacra theologia*, 78–79.

105. Robert Letham, "The *Foedus Operum*: Some Factors Accounting for Its Development," *SCJ* 14 (1983): 63–76.

106. Robert Rollock, *In epistolam S. Pauli apostoli ad Romanos* (Geneva: Franc. LePreux, 1596), 94.

of imputation, despite adopting the pre-fall covenant.[107] In his *Tractatus de vocatione efficaci*,[108] Rollock views original sin as hereditary[109] and universal[110] but transmitted "by reason of that word and covenant which God made with Adam in his creation."[111] In view is the transmission of corruption rather than the imputation of guilt. Rollock dismisses as "grosse" the opinions of the Schoolmen that Adam's sin is ours only by imputation.[112] Piscator, in 1590, takes the earlier position, imputation being on the basis of hereditary propagation,[113] but by 1609 he thinks the principal part is our participation in the sin of our first parents by imputation,[114] not a bare imputation, for that first sin is really and actually ours.[115]

William Perkins, in *A Golden Chaine*,[116] says that Adam represented all people, who are implicated in guilt as well as corruption through natural descent.[117] By 1595, in his *Exposition of the Symbol or Creed of the Apostles*, he argues that Adam was "a public person, representing all his posteritie, and therefore when he sinned, all his posteritie sinned with him; as in a Parliament whatever is done by the Burgesse of the shire, is done by every person in the shire."[118] It is unclear whether Perkins sees the connection as imputative.[119] Adam was appointed by God to be the root of his posterity.[120] What is implicit becomes explicit in Perkins's *A Cloud of Faithfull Witnesses, Leading to the Heavenly Canaan*.[121] Perkins sees a realistic and organic connection between Adam and the race, and brings the covenant into the equation, with Adam representing all. Imputation is not mentioned, but all the ingredients are present. He spells out imputation precisely

107. Rollock, *Ad Romanos*, 99–102.

108. Robert Rollock, *Tractatus de vocatione efficaci* (Edinburgh: Robert Waldegrave, 1597).

109. Robert Rollock, *A Treatise of God's Effectual Calling*, trans., Henry Holland (London: Felix Kyngston, 1603), 133.

110. Rollock, *A Treatise*, 134–35.

111. Rollock, *Tractatus*, 193–94.

112. Rollock, *Tractatus*, 196; Rollock, *A Treatise*, 143.

113. Johannes Piscator, *Epistolarum Pauli ad Romanos, Corinthios, Galatas, Ephesios, Philippenses, Colossenses, Thessalonicenses* (London: George Bishop, 1590), 44–45, 48–49.

114. Johannes Piscator, *De iustificatione hominis coram Deo* (Leiden: Andreas Clouquius, 1609), 78.

115. Piscator, *De iustificatione*, 78–79.

116. *Armilla aurea*, Latin ed. (1590); first English edition, 1600.

117. *The Workes of That Famous and Worthie Minister of Christ, in the Universitie of Cambridge, Mr. W. Perkins* (Iohn Legate, 1608), 1:19–20.

118. Perkins, *Workes*, 1:164.

119. Perkins, *Workes*, 1:165.

120. Perkins, *Workes*, 1:166.

121. Second ed. (London: Humfrey Lownes for Leo. Greene, 1607); Perkins, *Workes*, 3:2:415.

in *A Godly and Learned Exposition upon the Whole Epistle of Jude* (1606).[122] Why God allowed this is "a iust iudgement of God silently to be with reverence rested in, and not with curiositie to be searched out."[123]

After 1600, it takes time to fit these questions into a covenantal framework. Polanus explicitly argues that Adam's sin was imputed to his posterity but based on propagation. He deals with *the sin of our first parents*.[124] He writes of the imputation of Adam's sin in a legal, contractual way but based on his natural connection to his posterity. We sinned in Adam, since he was the root of the human race; his sin was imputed to us due to the contract.[125]

The Leiden Synopsis (1625) stresses the natural connection with posterity. However, God made a covenant with Adam.[126] Yet all sinned in the sin of both parents and inherited corruption. Thysius, the author of the section, distinguishes between the responsibility for sin, in Adam,[127] and the inheritance of a corrupt nature from both parents.[128]

Confessional documents such as the Irish Articles (1615) and the Canons of Dort (1618–1619) mention original corruption, not imputation. This does not mean that their authors did not believe in the latter; rather, they did not see fit to put it into a confession.[129] Surprisingly, WCF, 6, affirms that what is imputed is the guilt not of Adam's sin but of "our first parents," Eve included, based on their being "the root of all mankind." Imputation is grounded on genetic solidarity rather than a judicial or covenantal appointment. The placement in the chapter on sin rather than in the one on the covenant emphasizes this contrast. Covenant theology was still developing in the 1640s. Not everything, or all that may be true, is appropriate for a confession.[130]

---

122. First English edition, 1606.
123. Perkins, *Workes*, 3:2:75b.
124. Amandus Polanus, *Syntagma theologiae Christianae* (Geneva: Petri Auberti, 1612), 6.3.10.
125. "Nam transgressio Adae nobis imputatur, alioqui reque iniquitate inde contracta, neque reatu ullo teneremur." Polanus, *Syntagma*, 6.3.12.
126. "In quo Deus omnes homines, tanquam in primario parente, pro rationis pacti cum ipso initi, censuerit." Johannes Polyander et al., *Synopsis purioris theologiae, disputationibus quinquaginta duabus comprehensa* (Leiden: Ex officina Elzeverianus, 1625), 152.
127. Polyander et al., *Synopsis*, 161.
128. Polyander et al., *Synopsis*, 157.
129. Philip Schaff, *The Creeds of Christendom* (Grand Rapids, MI: Baker, 1966), 3:530, 564, 588.
130. Letham, *Westminster Assembly*, 198–206.

Charles Hodge's doctrine of immediate imputation. Hodge held that the sin of Adam is imputed to the race independently of guilt.[131] It is a *peccatum alienum* (an alien sin, a sin of another) and is the judicial ground of the condemnation of the human race. He regarded this as fundamental to Protestant theology, seeing the relationship between Adam and Christ in Romans 5 as an exact parallel and warning that opposition to this idea of the imputation of Adam's sin would lead to a rejection of the biblical doctrine of the atonement and justification.[132]

Consequently, Hodge maintained that the imputation was purely gratuitous, in parallel with the imputation of Christ's obedience. Adam's sin was exclusively his own and not ours. All the evils Adam's descendants suffer are penal inflictions on account of Adam's purely personal sin. Hodge denied that we participated in this sin; it could only be imputed to us forensically, prior to which there is no incurred guilt whatsoever. The one offense of the one man led to the rest having "a judicial obligation to satisfy justice." It is imputed to us as something not our own in parallel to the imputation of Christ's righteousness.[133] Hodge's theory was shared by William Cunningham, for whom "there was no *actual* participation by them in the . . . blameworthiness of [Adam's] sin," but "God, on the ground of the covenant, regarded and treated them as if they themselves had been guilty of the sin whereby the covenant was broken."[134]

Hodge's claim entails a violation of the justice of God, in conflict with the repeated statements in the Old Testament that Yahweh abominates the judge who condemns the innocent and clears the guilty. According to Hodge, the human race would have been declared guilty without participating in any wrongdoing. The implication is that God is arbitrary and acts contrary to his justice as he has revealed it.

Moreover, Hodge misread Romans 5. Paul is *not* making an exact parallel between Adam and Christ. There are two reasons for this. First, there is a clear antithesis between the two. "The free gift is *not* like the trespass" (v. 15); "the free gift is *not* like the result of that one man's sin" (v. 16). Second, the effect of what Christ has done far outweighs what Adam did. The argument is from the lesser to the greater. "For if many died through one man's trespass, *much more* have the grace of God and

---

131. Charles Hodge, *Systematic Theology* (Grand Rapids, MI: Eerdmans, 1977), 2:192–240.
132. Hodge, *Systematic Theology*, 2:194.
133. Hodge, *Systematic Theology*, 2:194.
134. William Cunningham, *Historical Theology* (Edinburgh, 1870), 1:515.

the free gift . . . abounded" (v. 15). "If, because of one man's trespass, *death* reigned through that one man, *much more* will *those who receive the abundance of grace and the free gift of righteousness* reign in life through the one man Jesus Christ" (v. 17). In this last instance, whereas *death* reigned through Adam, *those who receive the abundance of grace* will reign. It is not a parallel; it is a wildly uneven contrast, the only common factors being the respective heads of the two solidaric groups and the far-reaching outcomes of what they did. Shedd points to the different kinds of union that Hodge missed: Adam's sin was grounded on a natural union, in contrast to the union with Christ. All people were in Adam when he disobeyed; not all were in Christ when he obeyed. All are propagated from Adam; no one is propagated from Christ. Union in Adam is substantial and physical; in Christ, it is spiritual and mystical. In Adam, it is by creation; in Christ, by regeneration.[135]

Hodge was strenuously opposed by Robert W. Landis (1809–1883).[136] Landis was able to prove that Hodge's idea was a novelty among the Reformed churches and had no confessional support. It was a departure from the Augustinian doctrine of original sin and its transmission and rested on the assumption of a judicial verdict by God that, if true, would be thoroughly unjust, conflicting with the evidence of his revelation in the Bible.

Murray points out Hodge's exegetical errors. Hodge thought that "all sinned" meant all were placed under an obligation to satisfy justice.[137] But this is incompatible with verse 19, where they are said to have been "constituted sinners," and with the other side of the analogy, being "constituted righteous," where not merely the judicial benefit of Christ's righteousness is imputed but Christ's righteousness itself.[138]

Murray cites Owen (*Works*, 5:325) in support, who states that there can be no obligation to the penalty of sin unless there is an antecedent sin. Consequently, the imputation of Adam's sin cannot be defined in terms of obligation to its penalty.[139] Instead,

---

135. Shedd, *Dogmatic Theology*, 2:188.
136. Robert W. Landis, *The Doctrine of Original Sin Received and Taught by the Churches of the Reformation Stated and Defended, and the Error of Dr. Hodge in Claiming That This Doctrine Recognizes the Gratuitous Imputation of Sin, Pointed Out and Refuted* (Richmond, VA: Whittet & Sheperson, 1884).
137. Hodge, *Systematic Theology*, 2:194.
138. Murray, *Adam's Sin*, 73–76.
139. Murray, *Adam's Sin*, 79.

the most representative of Reformed theologians were jealous to maintain that . . . *reatus* and *poena* and, if we will, *reatus poenae*, always presuppose *culpa* and that therefore, our involvement in the *reatus*, the obligation to penalty, of Adam's sin means that we were also involved in the *culpa* of his sin.[140]

Murray's doctrine of immediate imputation. Murray argues that we were all implicated in the sin of Adam, and so all became sinners.

We did not personally and voluntarily participate in his sin. Nor was Adam's character transferred to us. But there was a real involvement, not just a judicial liability. Adam's sin was both *peccatum alienum* and *peccatum proprium*.[141] It is a forensic matter, involving a radical change of relationship to law and justice. We came to have property in Adam's disobedience in such a way that the judicial status belongs to the disobedience in which we have property.[142] So "there is as truly an imputation of the disobedience of Adam as there is of the obedience of Christ." In the one the benefit follows the imputation, so here the liability follows the imputation.[143] In turn, "as representative solidarity with Christ . . . secures and insures subjective renewal in regeneration, so representative solidarity with Adam in his sin involved for posterity their subjective depravity as well as the forensic judgment of their being 'constituted sinners.'"[144] This depravity is an implication of the imputation of Adam's sin, not a consequence.[145]

Hutchinson's evaluation. George Hutchinson identifies the two most crucial questions. First, what is the mode of the union between Adam and the race? Following this, what is the justice of the imputation of Adam's sin to the race?[146] Hutchinson thinks that the answer to the first question determines the answer to the second.

The first question revolves around the moral foundation of the union signified by ἐν τῷ Ἀδάμ (in Adam) in 1 Corinthians 15:22 and δι' ἑνὸς ἀνθρώπου (through one man) in Romans 5:12. It concerns the identities of, and the relationship between, the natural union and the legal union

---

140. Murray, *Adam's Sin*, 83.
141. Murray, *Adam's Sin*, 85–86.
142. Murray, *Adam's Sin*, 86–87.
143. Murray, *Adam's Sin*, 88.
144. Murray, *Adam's Sin*, 89.
145. Murray, *Adam's Sin*, 92.
146. George P. Hutchinson, *The Problem of Original Sin in American Presbyterian Theology* (Nutley, NJ: Presbyterian and Reformed, 1972), 98.

sustained by Adam to the race. Hutchinson correctly highlights the biblical realism of Augustine, whose focus was the natural unity of the race such that, when God created humanity, he created a man, Adam, and the race, humankind, so that Adam's sin was simultaneously the sin of humanity. Later, Scholastic theology, influenced by nominalism, in which reality exists only in the particular, sought the union in legal terms, since, in its estimation, corruption could not be based on a natural connection. Calvin and the Reformers reverted to the Augustinian tradition.[147]

The emergence and rise of covenant theology did not bring a return to the late medieval nominalist idea of a purely legal union but superimposed the covenant on the natural relationship so that the two coexisted, seeing no contradiction between the two elements, the natural and the federal. Hutchinson thinks this explains how the federal and representative approach only took over in the late seventeenth century.[148] The evidence I have presented supports this claim. The lack of definitive confessional comment on the matter gave rise to the vehement differences in the nineteenth century between Hodge and Landis, aided and abetted by attacks on federal theology from Albert Barnes.[149]

Hodge failed to see that the natural relation of Adam to the race had any bearing on the matter, and, following that, he conceived imputation to be gratuitous and forensic. Moreover, he was forced to conclude that the imputation was not of the guilt of Adam's sin, which was entirely his own, but rather of the judicial liability for the punishment of that sin. Adam alone sinned; we all are liable to be punished for it.

Overall assessment. Some, like Shedd, in contrast point to the natural union as primary to our sharing in the common human nature, with the federal relation of no immediate consequence. Others, such as Landis, maintain that both elements are of equal significance and cannot be played off one against each other. This is an attempt to provide a just basis for the covenantal imputation. A third school of thought agrees with Hodge that the forensic relation is paramount, but departs from him in recognizing that it must not be divorced from the natural relation. Murray is an exponent of this line of thought.

---

147. Hutchinson, *Original Sin*, 100–101.
148. Hutchinson, *Original Sin*, 101–2.
149. Hutchinson, *Original Sin*, 104.

It seems to me that Hodge was wrong, for the reasons I have given. For a judicial decision of itself to condemn the human race appears to be, and is, unjust on a biblical basis, as well as in natural justice. A decision to condemn must, if it is to be just, rest upon the reality that those condemned are deserving of condemnation, since they share in the guilt and, consequently, the sin that brought about the guilt. At the other end of the spectrum, Shedd does not provide a legal foundation for the imputation. It seems clear that both the forensic and the natural relationships are mutually necessary.

Both guilt and corruption imply a prior act from which they are derived. First comes sin; guilt and corruption follow. Thinking further, it would seem appropriate that guilt should have precedence over corruption. Guilt relates to the fact of the sin; it is present immediately, concurrent with the offense. It is objective in that a person is either guilty or not. Corruption involves the nature and characteristics of the person who is guilty. Guilt relates to status and is absolute; corruption relates to condition and may be variable.

Here Murray is correct to affirm that judicial guilt is prior to depravity. However, as justification arguably has a certain precedence to sanctification while, nevertheless, the two are inseparable, so with the imputation of Adam's sin, the guilt and the corruption are inseparably connected even while it may be correct to point to the priority of the forensic declaration of guilt.

Underlining this last point is the earlier observation that a purely legal declaration, without regard to the condition of those concerning whom it is made, is inherently unjust—not only according to commonly understood human conceptions but also in terms of divinely revealed standards, for we know that God judges according to the case (Gen. 18:25; Matt. 25:31–46; Rev. 20:12–13). Hence, the natural, seminal relationship Adam sustained to the race must be the basis both for the covenant relationship established by God and for the imputation of his sin and guilt. It is not a question of either–or, in an analytic sense, but of both–and synthetically.[150]

---

150. We will consider how this applies to justification in chap. 24. For a recent evaluation of the imputation of Adam' sin, see J. V. Fesko, *Death in Adam, Life in Christ: The Doctrine of Imputation* (Fearn: Mentor, 2016).

13.4.5 Total Depravity

Depravity, a corrupt condition of human nature, is a concomitant of original sin. The solidarity of the race is the necessary presupposition on which the doctrine rests. Without it, depravity does not make sense. The modifier *total* denotes that sin affects every facet of our nature. It does not mean that everyone is as bad as he or she possibly could be or that any one person is as bad as he or she possibly could be. Nor does it mean that fallen humans lack a conscience. It means that there is no part of the personality that is not corrupted: the mind, the emotions, or whatever. In Shedd's words, it means "the entire absence of holiness, not the highest intensity of sin."[151]

This is in contrast to Aquinas. For him, original sin wounded human nature.[152] It does not take away various God-given powers, nor does it render us disinclined to virtue, although it weakens us in this regard[153] and brings the penalty of death.[154] Death and all that leads to it come from our inheriting Adam's loss of original innocence.[155] Sin stains us[156] and makes us guilty and deserving of punishment.[157] Sin is like an illness. Some sins are curable; others are mortal. It stains us, wounds us, weakens us, and brings death but does not do the extent of damage that Protestants maintain. Indeed, Rome increasingly defined corruption in purely negative terms as the loss of original righteousness (the *donum superadditum*). The Reformers stressed that it was positive, total corruption.[158] The biblical basis is clear as to its universality (Gen. 6:5; Rom. 1:18–3:20), its rendering humans blind to the gospel (1 Cor. 2:14; 2 Cor. 4:1–6) and enemies of God (Rom. 8:7; Eph. 2:1–3), its deceitfulness and wickedness (Jer. 17:9), and its being the source of evil thoughts and actions (Matt. 15:16–20).

However, there were differences between the Lutherans and the Reformed. According to the Formula of Concord, humans after the fall are "nothing sound, nothing incorrupt in the body and soul of man, or in his

---

151. Shedd, *Dogmatic Theology*, 2:257.
152. Aquinas, *ST* 1a2ae.85.3; Davies, Summa Theologiae: A Guide, 209.
153. Aquinas, *ST* 1a2ae.85.1–2.
154. Aquinas, *ST* 1a2ae.85.5.
155. Aquinas, *ST* 1a2ae.85.6.
156. Aquinas, *ST* 1a2ae.85.6, 1a2ae.86.
157. Aquinas, *ST* 1a2ae.87.
158. Calvin, *Institutes*, 2.1.8.

mental or bodily powers."[159] Early Lutheran statements were often ex-treme, sometimes implying that original sin was the essence of humans.[160]

Calvin refused to accept the early Lutheran statements, although he agreed, in opposition to Rome, that corruption is positive as well as negative. All parts of the soul are possessed by sin,[161] he maintained in contrast to Peter Lombard, who thought that sin resides in the flesh, since the flesh most clearly manifests it. In distinction from Lutheran-ism, Calvin qualified the matter, since a depravity of nature is involved, not a defect in human nature as such, in that God is the author of our nature.[162] This means that humans are corrupted through natural vitia-tion, but this did not flow from nature. Sin is natural in that it is an adventitious quality, not something implanted from the beginning.[163] Later, WCF, 6.2, takes a stern line in affirming that humanity is "wholly defiled in all the parts and faculties of soul and body." It means that at the deepest level fallen humans are totally alienated from God.

At seventeenth-century Saumur, Placaeus held that corruption had priority to imputation. Adam's sin was imputed only because humans have a corrupt nature. This was a reversal of the standard order that we are born corrupt because original sin is imputed to us.[164] Placaeus's proposal was rejected by the Synod of Charenton in 1645 but became widely accepted elsewhere, including by Edwards.[165]

13.4.6   *Total Inability*

Another consequence of original sin is that fallen people cannot rescue themselves from their guilt and depravity. This is an ethical "cannot"; they cannot because they will not. Those who are in the flesh cannot please God (Rom. 8:6–8), cannot receive the revelation of God (Matt. 16:17; John 6:44–45, 64–65; 1 Cor. 2:14), cannot submit to the law of God (Rom. 8:7), and cannot rescue themselves, because they are dead (Ezek. 36:16; Eph. 2:1). This is "a free self-determination or inclining to

---

159. Formula of Concord, 1: Affirmative 3, in Schaff, *Creeds*, 3:100.
160. Bavinck, *RD*, 3:98.
161. Calvin, *Institutes*, 2.1.9.
162. Calvin, *Institutes*, 2.1.10.
163. Calvin, *Institutes*, 2.1.11.
164. Placaeus, *Two-Part Disputation concerning Adam's First Sin* (1655).
165. Jonathan Edwards, "Original Sin Defended," in *The Works of Jonathan Edwards*, ed. Perry Miller, John E. Smith, and Harry S. Stout, 26 vols. (New Haven, CT: Yale University Press, 1957–2008), 3:305–10.

evil, in the sinner's will," an inability that "is culpable, because it is the product of the sinner's agency."[166]

Fallen people can do much good of a moral, social, and cultural nature. They can show love to family members, do works of kindness, display civic virtues, produce great works of art, and make major contributions to the well-being of their fellow citizens. However, apart from regeneration by the Spirit, they cannot do this intentionally for the glory of God.

Augustine put his finger on the consequences that arise from denial of original sin and its corollaries. In *Against Two Letters of the Pelagians* he identified three main elements of the Pelagian heresy. The first was a denial of original sin.[167] The second, as a direct consequence, was that the grace of God by which we are justified is not given freely but granted according to our merits. The third was that forgiveness of sins is not necessary after baptism. Instead, Augustine maintained, the Catholic faith opposes both Manicheism and Pelagianism in saying human nature is healable, since, according to the Pelagians, it does not need to be healed, whereas according to the Manicheans it cannot be healed, because evil is held to be coeternal and immutable.[168] In his *Letter 188 to the Lady Juliana* (AD 416), Augustine underlined the consequences of Pelagianism. "For the possession . . . of a will inclined to what is good . . . they hold that we are not indebted to the aid of God, but affirm that we ourselves of our own will are sufficient for these things." And again, "Understand, then, how greatly and how fatally that man errs who does not acknowledge that this is the 'great gift of the Saviour.'"[169] For Pelagianism, fallen people have the ability to do spiritual good of themselves, and therefore faith and obedience are to be attributed to the person who exhibits them, while failure is due to not trying hard enough. J. I. Packer warns us that Pelagianism is the default position of zealous Christians with little interest in doctrine.[170]

Jonathan Edwards made a distinction between natural ability and moral ability.[171] This is valid insofar as fallen humans still have a will

---

166. Shedd, *Dogmatic Theology*, 2:256.
167. This is a commonplace in much Protestant theology of the last two hundred years. See Carl Trueman, "Original Sin in Modern Theology," in Madeume and Reeves, *Adam*, 167–86.
168. Augustine, *Against Two Letters of the Pelagians* 24–25 (NPNF¹, 5:414–15).
169. Augustine, *Letter 188* 1.3 (NPNF¹, 1:549).
170. James I. Packer, "'Keswick' and the Reformed Doctrine of Sanctification," *EQ* 27 (1955): 153–67.
171. *The Works of Jonathan Edwards* (Edinburgh: Banner of Truth, 1974), 1:4–11.

and exercise it. The problem is not that they cannot believe but that they will not believe. It is an ethical problem rather than a physical or psychological one. They refuse to choose the good and have an inbuilt antipathy toward God. The will is there, but it requires a radical change altering its inclinations in order to respond positively to the gospel. Bavinck points out that, taken out of its context, Edwards's argument encouraged the supposition that the natural ability of the will was un-impaired.[172] The root of the Pelagian controversy was the assertion of fallen people's ability to respond to the gospel unaided by divine grace, a view resting on the assumption that a command of God entailed the ability of those commanded to fulfill it, together with a concomitant denial of original sin. Augustine argued in reply that we humans respond but do so because God makes us willing by changing our hearts, and so we believe freely.[173] As Barth comments, "The man who is saved in the person of another, and only in that way, is obviously in himself a lost man."[174]

13.4.7   Condemnation

The ultimate consequence of sin is eternal death, and the sufferings of hell. What this means is beyond us, something we do not wish to experience. We will discuss this in chapter 30. For now, as Bavinck comments, "believers are willing to look at the disturbing reality of life; they do not scatter flowers over graves, turn death into an angel, regard sin as mere weakness, or consider this the best of all possible worlds. Calvinism has no use for such drivel."[175] What a somber note on which to end the chapter; it is also a realistic one.

Further Reading

Fesko, John V. *Death in Adam, Life in Christ: The Doctrine of Imputation.* Fearn: Mentor, 2016.

Hutchinson, George P. *The Problem of Original Sin in American Presbyterian Theology.* Nutley, NJ: Presbyterian and Reformed, 1972.

Murray, John. *The Imputation of Adam's Sin.* Phillipsburg, NJ: P&R, 2012.

---

172. Bavinck, *RD* 3:121–22.
173. Augustine, *On Grace and Free-Will* (*NPNF*[1], 5:443–65).
174. Barth, *CD*, IV/1:413.
175. Bavinck, *RD*, 2:341.

Study Questions

1. Given the range of biblical terms for sin, how legitimate is it to restrict a definition to only one?

2. What are some reasons to prefer one solution or a combination of proposed solutions to the relationship between the sin of Adam and the race.

3. What historical factors may have encouraged the emergence of the doctrine of the imputation of Adam's sin in the Reformed theology of the sixteenth and seventeenth centuries?

4. What possible implications are there for any particular position on the extent to which sin has affected the human person? What views on the process of salvation are each likely to yield?

PART 5

THE COVENANT OF GOD

Blessed be the God and Father of our Lord Jesus Christ . . . even as he chose us in him before the foundation of the world, that we should be holy and blameless before him.

Ephesians 1:3–4

14

Election and the Counsel
of Redemption

Election is God's eternal sovereign decree to save his people, bestowing life
on them in Christ. It is a Trinitarian decree founded in Christ and includes
God's determination for the Son to become incarnate and so take human
nature into permanent union. The doctrine has roots going back at least as
far as Augustine and is built on biblical foundations in Jesus, Paul, and the
Old Testament. Classic Reformed theology reflected on election being in
Christ. Debates arose on the order of decrees in the mind of God; although
abstruse, these have significant implications. Controversy erupted over the
proposals of Arminius and has reverberated through the years. Within the
Reformed church, various nuances have been proposed, including hypothetical universalism. Latterly, Barth reconstructed the doctrine in a radical and
all-encompassing manner, giving rise in recent years to the astonishing claim
of some that election has priority over the Trinity.

14.1   Election

14.1.1   Biblical Teaching

Election and reprobation equally depend on the will of God. However,
there is a disparity between them. Election is in Christ and is according
to God's grace, whereas reprobation is according to God's justice and
takes into consideration the judgment of God and his wrath against sin;
it is deserved (WCF, 3.5–7).

Paul discusses these themes in considering Israel's unbelief. He traces everything back to God's choice of Isaac, not Ishmael, and of Jacob, not Esau. Inevitable questions arise: Is God just? Is he fair? Paul's emphatic retort is "Silence!" God has a perfect right to do as he chooses with his creatures. We have no place to question his eternal decrees (Rom. 9:6–24).

Election is a Trinitarian event, seen against the backdrop of sin and its consequences. As such, it is an eternal, gracious, sovereign, and loving determination (Jer. 31:3; Mal. 1:2–3). It entails the election and reprobation of individuals but goes beyond that, for it is also the point where Christ is constituted Mediator and Redeemer, and includes the fact that God chooses not to be in isolation but to be incarnate in his Son. Hence, Scripture teaches election from beginning to end. Election follows from creation and salvation being works of God. Bucer described it as "the first locus of theology."[1]

The separate lines of Seth and Cain (Gen. 4:17–5:32) vividly contrast the godly and the wicked. The genealogies are parallel, the names strikingly similar, yet the conduct glaringly different. This chasm remains throughout the Old Testament. Out of the whole human race, God calls one man, Abram, who simply responds; the subject throughout is "the Lord" (Gen. 12:1–3). God's covenant is made with Abraham and his offspring, by-passing millions. Later come distinctions in Abraham's own family—between Isaac and Ishmael, Jacob and Esau—not of human devising or based on the character of the human agents but based on God's determination.

Yahweh's choice of Israel as his people left the rest of the nations aside. This is put memorably in Amos 3:2:

> You only have I known
>   of all the families of the earth.

Jesus is the strongest of all proponents of election (John 6:37–40; 17:2–3, 6–12, 24). He stresses his coordinate sovereignty and knowledge with the Father (Matt. 11:25–27), followed immediately by an uninhibited appeal for faith and discipleship! Paul unfolds God's sovereignty in salvation, including election (Rom. 8:28–11:36; Eph. 1:3–5, 11; 2 Tim. 1:8–10). So does Peter (1 Pet. 1:3–5, 17–21; 2:9–10; 2 Pet. 1:3–10).

---

1. Martin Bucer, *In epistolam D. Pauli ad Ephesios* (Basel, 1561), 19c.

There is no need to belabor this point. Implied and entailed is the obverse that in choosing some, others were passed by. From our perspective, we are not God and do not know human hearts, and so should entertain hope for all that they may believe in Christ. Can we say for certain that Esau or even Judas are reprobate? The content of the decrees of election and reprobation are hidden from us—Calvin frequently refers to them as secret—and are not the basis of faith and practice (Deut. 29:29).

That reprobation is taught in Scripture is evident not only in these entailments but also in clear passages (Rom. 9:17–23; 1 Pet. 2:8; Jude 4) and in Jesus's prayer thanking the Father for hiding "these things" from the wise (Matt. 11:25–26). Notwithstanding, it is not prominent in Scripture, since the message is of good news and salvation. Rejection and eventual condemnation are true but occur *per accidens*, incidentally to the main purpose. We are reminded of the question and answer on hell in Calvin's Geneva Catechism. The minister asks, "Why, then, is there mention only of eternal life and not of hell?" to which the child replies, "Since nothing is held by faith except what contributes to the consolation of the souls of the pious . . . therefore it is not added what fate may await the impious."[2]

Election and reprobation are asymmetrical. They equally depend on the will of God but with crucial differences. Reprobation is a matter of divine justice and contemplates the sins and eventual just condemnation of those passed by (WCF, 3.7). Each of the reprobate will receive what he or she deserves, for "the wages of sin is death." In graphic contrast, election is entirely according to God's grace, undeserved and unearned. Election is *in Christ*; reprobation is in ourselves.[3]

Election contemplates God's choice of not only the church but also individuals within it. The distinction between Jacob and Esau is an obvious instance.

Election is not based on God's foreknowledge of our faith, as Arminius and the Remonstrants held.[4] As Jewett remarks, the Arminian view would mean not that God chooses us but that he foresees our choosing him: "Instead of a free *divine* election *in* Christ, there is a free *human*

---

2. In *Calvin: Theological Treatises*, ed. J. K. S. Reid (Philadelphia: Westminster, 1954), 104; Calvin, *OS*, 2:92.
3. Primum doctrinae caput, *The Canons of the Synod of Dort*, in Philip Schaff, *The Creeds of Christendom* (Grand Rapids, MI: Baker, 1966), 3:551–58.
4. James Nichols and William Nichols, *The Works of James Arminius* (London, 1825–1828; repr., Grand Rapids, MI: Baker, 1996), 1:589.

election *of* Christ."[5] Arminians refer to Romans 8:29, where Paul says that those whom God foreknew he foreordained to be conformed to the image of Christ. However, the verb προγινώσκω, a derivative of γινώσκω (know), refers here not to having knowledge of future events but to knowing *persons*. The idea is equivalent to that in Amos 3:2, where Yahweh's knowledge of Israel is a deep personal knowledge.[6] Besides, the biblical focus is that election is an act of God's grace, while Arminianism makes it depend on foreseen human faith.

The biblical doctrine of election is far removed from fatalism, such as in Islam. The Bible always affirms human responsibility as well as God's sovereignty.[7] The covenant brings these into focus, with its blend of gracious divine promises and consequent human obligations. Historically, too, whatever one thinks of Max Weber's thesis,[8] Calvinism was associated with an outburst of unprecedented energy in society. Moreover, in contrast to fatalism, the Father's love is the basis of our foreordination (Eph. 1:4–5); election is *personal*—not some blind force but the gracious decision of the loving Father to give us to his Son by the Spirit's work. After reflecting on foreordination, Paul immediately turns to the Father's not sparing his Son but giving him up for us all (Rom. 8:29–32).

Critics commonly argue that election is unfair. On the contrary, fairness would demand that God send us all to hell, for that is what we deserve. Moreover, no one will go to hell against his or her will. Jesus confronts his opponents by exposing the fact that by their own choice they do not believe (John 8:43–44). Election neither limits human choice nor shuts out of heaven a single person who wishes to repent. The sad reality is that humanity is given over to autonomous rebellion against its Creator (Rom. 3:9–20).

In contrast to hyper-Calvinism, the decree of election is not a basis for logical deductions that control other areas of theology and practice. The Bible presents it to reinforce assurance, to stress that salvation is of grace; wherever it surfaces, the response is thanksgiving, praise, and prayer (Matt. 11:25–27; John 17:1–26; Rom. 11:33–36). These are the appropriate contexts in which to consider election.

---

5. Paul K. Jewett, *Election and Predestination* (Grand Rapids, MI: Eerdmans, 1986), 72–73.

6. The verb ידע is used on occasions elsewhere in the Old Testament for marital relations.

7. See Richard A. Muller, *Divine Will and Human Choice: Freedom, Contingency, and Necessity in Early Modern Reformed Thought* (Grand Rapids, MI: Baker Academic, 2017).

8. Max Weber, *The Protestant Ethic and the Spirit of Capitalism* (New York: Charles Scribner's Sons, 1958).

How can we question election—since we were so bad (depravity), since God is so good (all his decisions are wise, just, good, and holy), and since Christ is so central (so election is intimately tied to the gospel)? Election is in the context of sin and grace, the character of the God who chooses, and the gospel (in Christ). It is a loving choice by the Father to rescue us in Christ, his Son, by the power of the Holy Spirit.

That election takes place *in Christ* is clear in the New Testament. Where Paul writes of our election, he invariably identifies it this way. He states that "[the God and Father of our Lord Jesus Christ] chose us *in him* before the foundation of the world" (Eph. 1:4). Paul attributes election to the God and Father of Christ, and affirms that it was an eternal decision prior to creation and is in Christ. As in the rest of the paragraph (1:3–14), since he unfolds the panorama of salvation as occurring in Christ at every stage, it follows that election too is in union with Christ. Paul says the same in 2 Timothy 1:9, where he refers to God's grace "which he gave us in Christ Jesus before the ages began." In the great chain of salvation, God's predestining us was so that we are "to be conformed to the image of his Son, in order that he might be the firstborn among many brothers" (Rom. 8:29–30). This echoes Jesus's words that the Father had given him certain people who in time come to him, and whom he would never cast out (John 6:37–40). Election cannot be understood biblically and theologically in abstraction from Christ. It is a Trinitarian decree, bears an inseparable connection to the person and work of Christ, cannot be severed from the gospel, and is the root of all the ways union with Christ is worked out in the life experience of the faithful. It is as far from fatalism as could be imagined.[9] How is it to be understood? To help us, we will explore the history of discussion in the church.

14.1.2   *Historical Development*

Augustine. Augustine has been associated with a developed doctrine of predestination and election, largely through his later writings against the Pelagians. Pelagius, and Julian of Eclanum, who followed, denied original sin and held that fallen humans are able to respond to the gospel

---

9. For further discussion of this, see Robert Letham, *The Work of Christ* (Leicester: Inter-Varsity Press, 1993), 53–56; R. A. Muller, *Christ and the Decree: Christology and Predestination in Reformed Theology from Calvin to Perkins* (Grand Rapids, MI: Baker, 1986).

apart from the grace of God. Since humans have free will, with the power to choose what is good, there is no room for predestination.

In *On Rebuke and Grace (De correptione et gratia)*, written in AD 426, Augustine emphasizes that election is of grace and is unmerited.[10] He distinguishes predestination from foreknowledge. God not only knows who will be good but also makes them so.[11] Indeed, the number of the predestined is certain and fixed, "so certain that one can neither be added to them nor taken from them."[12] Referring to Romans 8:29–30, Augustine affirms that none of the elect can perish.[13] Why perseverance to the end is given to one and not to another is a mystery, about which he expresses ignorance.[14]

In *On the Predestination of the Saints (De praedestinatione sanctorum)*, AD 429, Augustine focuses on the distinction between the elect and the rest. God's grace distinguishes one person from another and "makes the good differ from the wicked." That some are elected is of God's mercy. Mercy and judgment are manifest in the wills of those who believe and do not believe.[15] The reasoning behind this mystery is that the gift of faith is not given to all. Since all are in a state of condemnation, it is by grace that any are delivered. Why God delivers some and not all is an unsearchable mystery known only to him.[16] Predestination and grace differ in this respect: "predestination is the preparation for grace, while grace is the donation itself."[17]

The most illustrious example of predestination is Jesus; there were no preceding merits in the assumed human nature.[18] So election is prior to the realization of grace; no one is elected because he or she has believed, but people are elect in order that they may believe. If it were otherwise, they would have been elected by believing and so would have deserved it. Reflecting on John 15:16, Augustine concludes, "They did not choose him that he should choose them, but he chose them that they might choose him; because his mercy preceded them according to grace, not

---

10. Augustine, *Rebuke and Grace* 13 (NPNF[1], 5:477).
11. Augustine, *Rebuke and Grace* 36 (NPNF[1], 5:486).
12. Augustine, *Rebuke and Grace* 39 (NPNF[1], 5:488–89).
13. Augustine, *Rebuke and Grace* 14 (NPNF[1], 5:477); see also, *Rebuke and Grace* 23 (NPNF[1], 5:481).
14. Augustine, *Rebuke and Grace* 17 (NPNF[1], 5:478).
15. Augustine, *Predestination of the Saints* 10–11 (NPNF[1], 5:503–4).
16. Augustine, *Predestination of the Saints* 16 (NPNF[1], 5:506).
17. Augustine, *Predestination of the Saints* 19 (NPNF[1], 5:507).
18. Augustine, *Predestination of the Saints* 30 (NPNF[1], 5:512).

according to debt."[19] So God chose the righteous—not those he foresaw would be righteous but those whom he predestined to make righteous,[20] and not because they were going to be holy but in order that they might be so.[21]

In *On the Gift of Perseverance (De dono perseverantia)*, also written in 429, Augustine rebuts the charge that predestination is inimical to preaching. It is not, since it was taught by the apostles.[22] Both Cyprian and Ambrose knew that few receive salvation without any human preaching to them. Whatever the circumstances, "from man to hear it in such a way as to obey it, is God's gift."[23] Therefore predestination must be preached so that those who hear may glory in the Lord and not in themselves.[24] Augustine comments that he preached and wrote that faith was God's gift before the Pelagian crisis arose; this was not a response to a crisis.[25]

Again, *foreknowledge* in Scripture sometimes means foreordination, as in Romans 11:2, where the context requires "predestinated."[26] Grace precedes faith since, if faith were to precede grace, will would also precede grace, inasmuch as there cannot be faith without a will.[27] So Augustine cites his *Confessions*: "Give what you command, and command what you will."[28] Conversely, a person who deserts the faith does so by his own fault. Hence, perseverance is a gift of God, as seen in the prayer "lead us not into temptation."[29] God gives both the means and the end. What is more ungrateful to God than to deny his grace by saying that it is given according to our merits? "Whoever as a faithful catholic is horrified to say that the grace of God is given according to our merits, let him not withdraw faith itself from God's grace . . . and thus let him attribute perseverance to the end to God's grace." "But between the beginning of faith and the perfection of perseverance there are those means whereby we live righteously," all which God gives to his elect.[30]

---

19. Augustine, *Predestination of the Saints* 34 (NPNF¹, 5:514–15).
20. Augustine, *Predestination of the Saints* 36 (NPNF¹, 5:515–16).
21. Augustine, *Predestination of the Saints* 37 (NPNF¹, 5:516).
22. Augustine, *Gift of Perseverance* 34 (NPNF¹, 5:538–39).
23. Augustine, *Gift of Perseverance* 48 (NPNF¹, 5:545).
24. Augustine, *Gift of Perseverance* 51 (NPNF¹, 5:546–47).
25. Augustine, *Gift of Perseverance* 52 (NPNF¹, 5:547).
26. Augustine, *Gift of Perseverance* 47 (NPNF¹, 5:544–45).
27. Augustine, *Gift of Perseverance* 41 (NPNF¹, 5:542).
28. Augustine, *Gift of Perseverance* 53 (NPNF¹, 5:547).
29. Augustine, *Gift of Perseverance* 46 (NPNF¹, 5:544).
30. Augustine, *Gift of Perseverance* 56 (NPNF¹, 5:548–49).

Augustine gives some careful pastoral advice on how the doctrine should be preached and taught.[31] It is to be applied with discrimination. Some receive the will to believe while others, not predestinated to God's kingdom, may endure for a while but not continue to the end.[32] To those who have not yet come to faith, the exhortation to believe must be given, and the church encouraged to pray for them.[33] Consequently, when we refer to the nonelect, the third person should be used rather than the second person, since the latter will encourage fatalism and would be "abominable . . . excessively harsh . . . hateful," "to fly into the face of an audience with abuse," "very monstrous, very inconsiderate, and very unsuitable," not because it is false but because it does not consider "the health of human infirmity." The preacher must not say, "If any of you obey, if you are predestined to be rejected, the power of obeying will be withdrawn from you, that you may cease to obey."[34] Last but certainly not least, the most eminent instance of predestination is Jesus Christ. God predestined both him and us, so that he might be the head and we his members.[35]

With Augustine, it is clear that salvation in its entirety stems from God's electing decree. Augustine held to reprobation, though not as prominently. When Jesus describes his opponents as not his sheep, he means "they are predestined to everlasting destruction."[36] Elsewhere Augustine refers to "those whom in his justice he has predestined to punishment . . . [and] those whom in his mercy he has predestined to grace."[37]

Aquinas. During the Middle Ages, semi-Pelagianism gained ground. It held that sin had merely weakened fallen humans, such that they retained the ability to take the first steps in response to the gospel, God's grace then assisting them. Election was generally reduced to God's foreknowledge of those who believe. However, other voices maintained an essentially Augustinian position. Most prominent among them was Aquinas.

31. Augustine, *Gift of Perseverance* 57–65 (NPNF[1], 5:549–51).
32. Augustine, *Gift of Perseverance* 58 (NPNF[1], 5:549).
33. Augustine, *Gift of Perseverance* 59–60 (NPNF[1], 5:549).
34. Augustine, *Gift of Perseverance* 61 (NPNF[1], 5:550).
35. Augustine, *Gift of Perseverance* 67 (NPNF[1], 5:552).
36. Augustine, *Gospel of John* 48.4 (NPNF[1], 7:267).
37. Augustine, *Enchiridion* 100 (NPNF[1], 3:269); see also Augustine, *City of God* 15.1 (NPNF[1], 2:284–85).

Aquinas makes some considerable refinements. He sets predestination in the context of providence, as part of God's government of the cosmos. Since all things are predestined by God, this includes humans. In providence God directs rational creatures to their end, whether according to nature or exceeding nature, in predestination, which "is a part of providence."[38]

Aquinas develops Augustine's thought on double predestination and considers carefully its implications. Since God predestines some to eternal life, it follows that it is part of his providence to permit some to fall away from that end. "Thus reprobation implies not only foreknowledge, but also something more . . . the will to permit a person to fall into sin, and to impose the punishment of damnation on account of that sin." Reprobation differs from predestination in its causality. The latter is the cause of grace in this life and eternal life in the future, but reprobation is not the cause of what occurs in this life—that belongs to sin, which proceeds from human free will—although it is the cause of abandonment by God and future punishment. The elect, for their part, will necessarily be saved, by a conditional necessity that does not abolish the freedom of choice.[39]

Election springs from the love of God, Aquinas agrees. Predestination implies election, choice by God, and election presupposes love, being the result of the love and the will of God. It is from love, since it flows out of the desire of God to do us good; it is from his will, since he determines this good to come to some rather than others. However, in God love has precedence, for while we love those in whom we detect good, God's love brings about the good.[40]

Consequently, Aquinas comments, election is not based on anything in us but is due to the sheer goodness of God. God's foreknowledge of human merits is not the cause of predestination; instead God predestined us so that we would be saved. Grace foreknown by God cannot be the cause of his conferring grace. The reason must be sought in the goodness of God, election and reprobation displaying God's goodness, whether in mercy or in justice. This is the case entirely by his will. It is no affront to his justice, for predestination is a matter of grace,

---

38. Aquinas, *ST* 1a.23.1.
39. Aquinas, *ST* 1a.23.3.
40. Aquinas, *ST* 1a.23.4.

and something entirely gratuitous cannot be unjust.[41] Aquinas, citing
Romans 1:3–4, agrees with Augustine that Christ was predestinated
according to his humanity.[42]

> We can say both that the Son of God was predestinated to be man,
> and that the Son of Man was predestinated to be the Son of God. But
> because grace was not bestowed on the Son of God that he might be
> man, but rather on human nature, that it might be united to the Son
> of God, it is more proper to say that *Christ, as man, was predesti-
> nated to be the Son of God.*[43]

In this sense, his election is gracious and an exemplar of ours.[44]

Aquinas insists that predestination does not undermine human freedom. Predestination infallibly takes effect but not from necessity. Since it
is a part of providence, in which some things happen from contingency,
respecting the integrity of secondary causes, the order of predestination
is certain while free will is preserved.[45] As to the relationship between
predestination and prayer, Aquinas warns of two errors: fatalism, rendering prayer superfluous, and the idea that prayer can change predestination. Prayer cannot alter God's preordination, but it can help the
effects of predestination, since providence does not override the integrity
of secondary causes, and it is through these means that predestination
is fulfilled.[46]

From the time of the Reformation until the present, Rome has not followed Augustine. It has sought to accommodate a range of views within
what is basically a semi-Pelagian context. Predestination and election
feature little. The catechism has effectively nothing to say other than that
God predestines no one to hell.[47]

Although there was a Calvinist patriarch of Constantinople, Cyril
Lukar (1638–1643), the Eastern church has a synergistic and voluntarist
view of salvation, the reverse of Augustinianism. It would be wrong to
call this Pelagian, as that was a Western phenomenon, and there is evidence that the Council of Ephesus (431) may have repudiated the views

---

41. Aquinas, *ST* 1a.23.5.
42. Aquinas, *ST* 3a.24.1.
43. Aquinas, *ST* 3a.24.2 (italics original to the translation).
44. Aquinas, *ST* 3a.24.3–4.
45. Aquinas, *ST* 1a.23.6.
46. Aquinas, *ST* 1a.23.8.
47. CCC, 1037. Its teaching on providence is found in 302–14.

of "Celestine," probably Celestius, a leading Pelagian. At the risk of an anachronism, it is perhaps closer to a form of semi-Pelagianism.[48]

Calvin. Calvin develops the inherited Augustinian doctrine by a clear treatment of reprobation and by pointing to election in Christ, to which I will refer in the next section. Calvin remarks that the preaching of the covenant of life is not accepted by all. This is according to God's own judgment, for it is freely offered, but some are barred from access to life. Calvin recognizes the difficult questions that arise when some "are predestined to salvation, others to destruction."[49] However, the chief point is that "we shall never be clearly persuaded, as we ought to be, that our salvation flows from the wellspring of God's free mercy until we come to know his eternal election."[50] It is a great mystery, hidden in

> the sacred precincts of divine wisdom. If anyone with carefree assurance breaks into this place, he will not succeed in satisfying his curiosity and he will enter a dark labyrinth from which he can find no exit. For it is not right for man unrestrainedly to search out things that the Lord has willed to be hid in himself.[51]

We must keep close to the Word of God, opening our minds to all he has revealed, but when he closes his lips, we immediately close our inquiries.[52] Calvin refers to God's election of Israel and, within Israel, the election and reprobation of individuals.[53] This election is prior to all human action and virtue.[54] Moreover, God did not merely permit the fall or the destruction of the wicked, for—per Augustine—God's will of necessity comes to pass. However, this is just because the wicked fall by their own choice, and their condemnation is just.[55] Therefore, we should find the cause of their destruction in their own corrupt nature, "for of

---

48. Henry R. Percival, *Seven Ecumenical Councils of the Undivided Church: Their Canons and Dogmatic Decrees*, A Select Library of Nicene and Post-Nicene Fathers of the Christian Church: Second Series (repr., Edinburgh: T&T Clark, 1997), 229; Robert Letham, *Through Western Eyes: Eastern Orthodoxy: A Reformed Perspective* (Fearn: Mentor, 2007), 78.
49. Calvin, *Institutes*, 3.21.1.
50. Calvin, *Institutes*, 3.21.1.
51. Calvin, *Institutes*, 3.21.1.
52. Calvin, *Institutes*, 3.21.2–3.
53. Calvin, *Institutes*, 3.21.6.
54. Calvin, *Institutes*, 3.22.2–5.
55. John Calvin, *Concerning the Eternal Predestination of God*, trans. J. K. S. Reid (London: James Clarke, 1961), 156.

those things which it is neither given nor lawful to know, ignorance is learnèd; the craving to know, a kind of madness."[56]

14.1.3   Election in Christ

Election in Christ merits additional emphasis in that it has often been overlooked. Calvin[57] and Zanchius[58] taught it vividly. So too did Thomas Goodwin later.[59] All God's blessings are received in union with Christ, from before creation. Election must therefore be seen foremost as in Christ from eternity. This is far removed from a cold, abstract display of logic. It is not present in Turretin, whose construction of election in Christ raises questions over his Christology.[60] He was reacting against Arminius, for whom Christ was the foundation of election on which basis God elected individuals whom he foresaw would believe, and against Amyraut, who asserted that the merits of Christ were the foundation of election, the decree relating to the atonement being prior to election.

John Calvin (1509–1564). For Calvin, because election is in Christ, assurance of election is to be sought in Christ. Any attempt to probe the mysteries of election is futile, for it is beyond us. However, God has revealed himself in his Son, in whom we have salvation.

> Accordingly, those whom God has adopted as his sons are said to have been chosen not in themselves but in his Christ [Eph. 1:4] for unless he could love them in him, he could not honor them with the inheritance of his Kingdom if they had not previously become partakers of him. But if we have been chosen in him, we shall not find assurance of our election in ourselves; and not even in God the Father, if we conceive him as severed from his Son. Christ, then, is the mirror wherein we must, and without self-deception may, contemplate our own election. For since it is into his body the Father has destined those to be engrafted whom he has willed from eternity to be his own, that he may hold as sons all whom he acknowledges to be

---

56. Calvin, *Institutes*, 3.23.8.
57. Calvin, *Institutes*, 3.24.4–5.
58. Jerome Zanchius, *Omnium operum theologicorum* (Geneva: Samuel Crispin, 1619), 2:535–40 (6.1.11–13).
59. Thomas Goodwin, *An Exposition of Ephesians Chapter 1 to 2:10* (n.p.: Sovereign Grace Book Club, 1958), 69–80.
60. Francis Turretin, *Institutes of Elenctic Theology*, trans. George Musgrave Giger, ed. James T. Dennison Jr. (Phillipsburg, NJ: P&R, 1992), 1:350–55. See also Oliver D. Crisp, "The Election of Jesus Christ," *JRT* 2 (2008): 131–50, who probes weaknesses in the doctrines of election of Turretin and others.

among his members, we have a sufficiently clear and firm testimony that we have been inscribed in the book of life [cf. Rev. 21:27] if we are in communion with Christ.[61]

Calvin is convinced that election in Christ has definite practical implications. Faith in Christ mirrors the eternal electing purpose of God, since the latter was undertaken with Christ as our Head. Calvin believes that Christ "claims for himself, in common with the Father, the right to choose."[62] Furthermore, following Augustine, he talks of Christ as the first of the elect, since he himself was chosen to the office of Mediator. He is "the clearest light of predestination and grace," appointed Mediator solely by God's good pleasure.[63] The Father has gathered us together in Christ the head and joined us to himself "by an indissoluble bond." Consequently, the members of Christ "engrafted to their head . . . are never cut off from salvation."[64] Election cannot be properly conceived in separation from Christ, for

> since the certainty of salvation is set forth to us in Christ, it is wrong and injurious to Christ to pass over this proffered fountain of life from which supplies are available, and to toil to draw life out of the hidden recesses of God. . . . Let no one then seek confidence in his election elsewhere, unless he wishes to obliterate his name from the book of life in which it is written.[65]

Hence, "If Pighius asks how I know I am elect, I answer that Christ is more than a thousand testimonies to me" (*Christus mihi pro mille testimoniis sufficit*).[66] For this reason, election "is not a subtle and obscure speculation. . . . It is rather a solid argument excellently fitted to the use of the godly. For it builds up faith, trains us to humility, elevates us to admiration of the immense goodness of God towards us, and excites us to praise this goodness."[67]

Jerome Zanchius (1516–1590). Zanchius, a native of Italy, wrote at length of election in Christ in his massive treatise *De natura Dei.*

61. Calvin, *Institutes*, 3.24.5.
62. Calvin, *Institutes*, 3.22.7.
63. Calvin, *Institutes*, 3.24.5.
64. Calvin, *Institutes*, 3.21.7.
65. Calvin, *Eternal Predestination*, 126.
66. Calvin, *Eternal Predestination*, 130; *Ioannis Calvini: Scripta Ecclesiastica*, vol. 1, *De aeterna praedsetinatione Dei: De la praedestination eternelle*, in CO2 (1998), 160.
67. Calvin, *Eternal Predestination*, 56.

Discussing Ephesians 1:4, he reasons that the Father elected not as the Father only but as God, since election is a work common to the whole Trinity, including of course the Son. As for our election "in him," Zanchius says we were chosen in Christ, considered neither as God nor as man but as the God-man (*theanthropos*). As God, he chose us himself (John 13:18). Nor can he be considered purely as man. Paul, in Ephesians 1, means that in election there is a conjunction between the elect and the One who elected, man with God. The Redeemer needs to be God and man simultaneously in his office as Mediator.[68] The Son was predestined and appointed to this office, including his human nature, which he was to assume into union. So Christ, according to his humanity, was chosen that in union with the Logos he was to be born the Son of God, Mediator and Savior of the elect.[69] Furthermore, in Christ all the elect were foreknown, loved, chosen, and predestined to be given the Spirit of adoption and regenerated.[70]

We note, Zanchius continues, that there are three relations to Christ in this connection—in him, through him, on account of him (*in Christo, per Christum, propter Christum*)—often used interchangeably. The first signifies Christ as Head of the church, in whom all the blessings of the Father rest and are given to us from eternity. God loves us *in Christ* and owns us as his sons. The second phrase, *through him*, refers to his office of Mediator, for through Christ we are reconciled to God.[71] In short, God did not choose us because Christ died for us, but Christ died for us because God chose us in him.[72] Therefore, we are not elect on account of Christ's merits, since election has priority over what he did and includes his merit in its purview.[73]

Zanchius relates the atonement to election in Christ. Christ expiated the sins of those for whom he died, freeing them from death. Since the elect were chosen to these things *in Christ*, those who were not chosen lack these benefits.[74]

---

68. "Itaque cum sit Apostolus, nos electos fuisse in Christo: Christus proponitur considerandus, non ut purus Deus, neque ut simplex homo: sed ut Deus & homo simul, cum officio Mediatoris aeterno." Hieronymous Zanchius, *Operum theologicorum omnium* (Amsterdam: Stephanus Gamonentus, 1613), 2:535.
69. Zanchius, *Operum*, 2:536.
70. Zanchius, *Operum*, 2:536.
71. Zanchius, *Operum*, 2:536.
72. Zanchius, *Operum*, 2:536–37.
73. Zanchius, *Operum*, 2:537.
74. Zanchius, *Operum*, 2:498.

Amandus Polanus (1561–1610). Polanus, a significant theologian of the Reformed church, based at Basel, was a synthesizer of Reformed doctrine. He provides an example of what ministers were being taught in the Reformed churches at that time.[75] For Polanus, the election of Christ is an aspect of predestination "by which God, from eternity, designated his only-begotten Son to be also Son of God according to his human nature, and head of angels and humans."[76] The whole Trinity made this decree, and so was the efficient cause. The Father elected us, not as the Father but as God, because election is a work not strictly of the person of the Father but of the whole Trinity, of which the Father is the *principium*, the source. The Son (John 13:18; 15:16, 19) and the Spirit (John 3:6; Acts 13:2; 1 Cor. 6:11; 12:3, 13; Eph. 4:4) also chose us in union with the Father.[77] This election was entirely gratuitous, not for any merit of ours. Its end is the glory of the Father. Christ is contemplated as the Son of God according to both natures. He is not chosen as Son of God, since he is from the Father eternally by generation. According to his humanity, however, he is eternally elected, as the image of God, to the grace of personal union with the eternal Son. This election of Christ is the foundation of the election of angels and humans.[78] Christ is chosen as our Mediator.[79]

The election of humans can be divided into two parts, Polanus thinks.[80] There is the general election of a nation, such as Israel, and there is special election, by which God ordains to eternal life whomever he chooses in his free goodwill.[81] Polanus cites Athanasius, *Orationes contra Arianos* 3.1, in support, in his statement that our life is founded

75. Robert Letham, "Amandus Polanus: A Neglected Theologian?," *SCJ* 21 (1990): 463–76. Muller calls him "a theologian of considerable stature," in *Christ and the Decree*, 130, and "the most compendious systematic theologian of the early orthodox period" of Reformed Scholasticism, in Richard A. Muller, *After Calvin: Studies in the Development of a Theological Tradition* (Oxford: Oxford University Press, 2003), 148.
76. "Est praedestinatio qua Deus Filium suum unigenitum designavit ab aeterno, ut etiam quo ad suam humanam natura esset Filius Dei & caput Angelorum & hominesque." Amandus Polanus, *Syntagma theologiae Christianae* (Geneva: Petri Auberti, 1612), 1:678. He cites in support Isa. 42:1, Matt. 12:18, and 1 Pet. 1:20, 2:5.
77. Polanus, *Syntagma*, 1:681.
78. Polanus, *Syntagma*, 1:679.
79. "Electionis subjectum . . . in quo electi sumus, est Christus, non quatenus Deus, nec quatenus nudus homo, sed quatenus *theanthrōpos* & Mediator noster. . . . Ita Christus est vinculum, quo Deus & electi coniunguntur." Polanus, *Syntagma*, 1:689–90.
80. Polanus was strongly influenced by the philosophical methodology of Petrus Ramus (1514–1572), in which knowledge was divisible into component parts, usually dichotomous. See Letham, "Polanus"; Walter J. Ong, *Ramus, Method, and the Decay of Dialogue* (Cambridge, MA: Harvard University Press, 1958); Donald K. McKim, *Ramism in William Perkins' Theology* (New York: Peter Lang, 1987).
81. Polanus, *Syntagma*, 1:680.

in no other way than in Christ before the ages existed, for it is through Christ that the ages were created.[82] Polanus insists that not only is Christ chosen as the means by which we were to be saved but also the election took place *in him* (*Nec enim Paulus dicit, elegit nos per ispum, sed elegit nos in ipso*).[83]

Polanus answers the charge of Arminius that this doctrine of election has no regard for Christ: "Certain people accuse us of having an absolute election . . . by which God, without respect to Christ, chooses some to salvation, and that we oppose election as founded in Christ," he complains. On the contrary, "we acknowledge with all our heart through the grace of God and openly profess that God chose us in Christ to be acknowledged through faith and that our election to salvation was founded in Christ, in whom as our head we are chosen as members of his mystical body."[84]

Polanus agrees with Zanchius that election consists, first, in the entire Trinity's choice of Christ as Mediator and Savior. This includes the Son's assumption of human nature in the incarnation, and his entire work for us and our salvation; all of it is embraced by the term *in Christ*. Then, second, God chose to salvation in union with Christ those upon whom he sets his free and sovereign love. At no time are they contemplated in any other state than in him.

Thomas Goodwin (1600–1680). Goodwin, a prominent member of the Westminster Assembly, wrote similarly to Zanchius and Polanus. In election, Christ was a common person, as Head of the elect. He was chosen first, and simultaneously we in him. As a common person, he was the Son of God who was to become incarnate; by the decree of God he was "pitched upon and singled out to assume our nature, and to sustain the person of a Head before God in the meanwhile."[85] God, in the act of choosing, gave us to Christ, and in giving us to Christ he chose us.

As in the womb head and members are not conceived apart, but together, as having relation each to the other, so were we and Christ,

---

82. Polanus, *Syntagma*, 1:686; see also Athanasius, *Orations against the Arians* 2.70.
83. Polanus, *Syntagma*, 1:686.
84. "Atqui nos agnoscimus toto corde per Dei gratiam & aperte profitemur, quod Deus nos elegerit in Christo per fidem agnoscendo ac quod electio nostra ad salutem aeternam fundata sit in Christo, in quo tanquam in capite nos tanquam membra mysticii corporis eius gratiose electi sumus." Polanus, *Syntagma*, 1:690.
85. Goodwin, *Ephesians*, 69–72.

as making up one mystical body unto God, formed together in that eternal womb of election. So that God's choice did completely terminate itself on him and us; us with him, and yet us in him.[86]

The Westminster Confession (1647). The Westminster divines expressed their belief that election is in Christ, although this is not a strong emphasis in the confession. It is seen in the confession's presentation of a marked disparity between election and reprobation. The latter is directly connected with sin and is in accord with God's justice. Conversely, election is entirely a matter of grace and love. The elect are chosen in Christ, the nonelect left to their sins. Election is "to the praise of His glorious grace," while preterition is "to the praise of His glorious justice." In the latter, the nonelect receive what is due to them for their own sin. In the former, the elect receive what is due to Christ, in whom they are chosen. Both reflect justice; in election, the justice is gracious because freely given in and through the Mediator (WCF, 3.5–7).[87]

Herman Bavinck (1854–1921). Bavinck agrees with Zanchius and Polanus that "the church and Christ are jointly chosen, in one and the same decree, in fellowship with and for each other (Eph. 1:4)."[88] Moreover,

> the elect are not viewed separately, that is, atomistically, but as a single organism. They constitute the people of God, the body of Christ, the temple of the Holy Spirit. They are, accordingly, elect *in Christ* (Eph. 1:4), to be members of his body. Hence both Christ and the church are included in the decree of predestination.[89]

Bavinck is clear that Christ, unlike us, was not the recipient of God's mercy regarding sin and misery but agrees that it is appropriate to speak of him being elected in that he was ordained to the office of Mediator and to assume human nature into union. Additionally, there is the consistent witness of Scripture to our being chosen *in Christ*.[90] Reformed theologians were agreed that Christ and his church, the mystical Christ, together constitute the real object of election. To include angels in

---

86. Goodwin, *Ephesians*, 74–75.
87. Robert Letham, *The Westminster Assembly: Reading Its Theology in Historical Context* (Phillipsburg, NJ: P&R, 2009), 186–87.
88. Bavinck, *RD*, 2:401.
89. Bavinck, *RD*, 2:402–3.
90. Bavinck, *RD*, 2:403–4.

election, as Polanus did, served only to indicate their strong conviction that election embraces not only the redemption of humanity but also the renovation of the cosmos.[91]

14.1.4   The Order of Decrees

The lapsarian debate concerns the order of decrees in the mind of God in eternity. It is not a question of the relation of election to its historical outworking. Both sides—supralapsarianism and infralapsarianism—agree that the decree of election is prior to creation and the fall. The question relates to whether, in election, God contemplated humans as already fallen, which was the infralapsarian claim (the decree of election being below—*infra*—the decree relating to the fall) or whether he considered them as not yet created and fallen (the decree of election being above—*supra*—the decree relating to the fall).

In many ways, this is a highly abstruse question. The inner workings of the mind of God are beyond us. However, it indicates ultimate priorities in God's plan and has quite extensive ramifications. Infralapsarianism attempts to do justice to the historical nature of redemption. It has confessional support and has easily been the majority position in the Reformed church. Supralapsarianism seeks to prioritize the ultimate purpose of God; what is last in execution is first in intention. In planning to build a house, the first thing that comes to mind is the house that one intends to build. From that the various stages in planning and construction follow. While supralapsarianism has never been confessionally adopted, neither has it ever been outlawed. So this is a discussion within Reformed confessional boundaries.

There was disagreement at Dort between supralapsarians and infralapsarians. Franciscus Gomarus fought a virtually lone battle on behalf of supralapsarianism. Walter Balcanqual wrote of the session on March 8, 1619,

> My Lord this is worth the observing, that there is no Colledge yet which hath not overthrown *Gomarus* his opinion of the subject of Predestination; for though none of them did directly dispute against it, yet all of them expressly took it as granted, that not *homo creabilis*, but *homo lapsus* was *subjectum* both of Elec-

---

91. Bavinck, *RD*, 2:404–5.

tion and Reprobation, which I think doth trouble *Gomarus* not a little.[92]

Later, of the session on March 11 he wrote,

> Since all the forraign Divines, without exception, and likewise all the Belgick professors except *Gomarus*, had already delivered their judgements for *homo lapsus*, and that he doubted not but the Provincials would determine the same; it were very fit that the Synod should likewise determine so of it; neither was it any reason that for the particular opinion of one professor, who in this did disassent from the judgement of all the Reformed Churches, the Synod should abstain from determination of the question.[93]

The following day saw the provincial delegations all support infralapsarianism "and it is to be noted that all of them determined *homo lapsus* to be the subject of Predestination; except *Gomarus* whom all men know to be against it; and the South-*Hollandi*, who only said they would determine nothing of it."[94] Hence, while not explicitly rejecting supralapsarianism, the canons clearly support infralapsarianism.[95]

Barth's treatment of the historical positions is long, detailed, and perceptive. He has some strong criticisms of supralapsarianism.

> Obviously the sick man cannot be cured unless he exists as a man and is sick. But obviously, too, his existence as a man and his sickness cannot be regarded as a means to cure him. . . . The supralapsarian view . . . [is] open to the severest criticism because it implies the impossible belief that God rejected some men even before they existed in his own consciousness as reprobates, and that he allowed them to become worthy of rejection simply in order that he might as such reject them.[96]

Nevertheless, Barth eventually preferred a reconstructed supralapsarianism, which I will discuss shortly.

Supralapsarianism, while having a high view of the sovereign plan of God, can have the tendency to freeze everything by the decree, and so

---

92. Walter Balcanqual, *Letters of Walter Balcanqual from the Synod of Dort to the R. Honourable Sir D. Carlton, L. Embassador* (London, 1659), 20.
93. Balcanqual, *Letters*, 24.
94. Balcanqual, *Letters*, 25.
95. Canons of Dort, 1.1, 7, 15, in Schaff, *Creeds*, 3:551–55.
96. Barth, *CD*, II/2:131.

to relativize creation. The distinction between elect and reprobate dominates, affecting the free offer of the gospel and undermining the idea that God demonstrates his goodness indiscriminately to all people. On the other hand, the issue does not correlate with the respective positions the doctrine of election may occupy within the theological spectrum. It might seem that supralapsarianism leads to a consideration of predestination up front, under the doctrine of God—since election has priority over all other areas—rather than later, in Christology or soteriology. However, Muller has demonstrated that the positioning of the doctrine has no direct bearing upon, or is not necessarily indicative of, any inclination to one or another of these perspectives.[97] He says, "From the perspective of the various definitions of predestination offered by the Reformed theologians of the sixteenth and seventeenth centuries, it becomes immediately clear that the placement of the doctrine does not, shall we say, predetermine its meaning."[98] I'll leave you to work this out yourself.

14.1.5   Arminius and the Synod of Dort

At the heart of the turmoil over Arminius was his radical view of predestination. His attack arose in response to the supralapsarianism of Beza and Perkins.[99] In his declaration before the States General of Holland on October 30, 1608,[100] he attacked a perceived lack of Christocentrism in this system. He claimed that in that teaching God's decree has no regard to righteousness or sin. It is not the decree by which Christ was appointed Savior, head, and foundation of the elect. It affirms that individuals were predestined before Christ was elected to save them; consequently, Christ is not the foundation of election. Moreover, it denies that he is the meritorious cause of election, since he is only a subordinate cause of a salvation already foreordained, an instrument to apply that salvation.[101]

Second, Arminius attacked what he saw as a split between election and salvation. Election in that formulation cannot be the foundation of salvation, since it is not identical with the decree on which our salvation

---

97. Richard A. Muller, "The Placement of Predestination in Reformed Theology: Issue or Non-Issue?," *CTJ* 40 (2005): 184–210.
98. Muller, "Placement," 204–5.
99. William Perkins, *De praedestinationis modi et ordine: et de amplitudine gratiae divinae Christiana & perspicua disceptatio* (Cambridge, 1598).
100. Nichols and Nichols, *Arminius*, 1:516–668.
101. Nichols and Nichols, *Arminius*, 1:566.

depends. Nor can it be the foundation of our certainty of salvation, for that rests on God's promise of salvation to those who believe, which supralapsarianism subordinates to the decree. This decree contains no gospel—neither its promises nor its commands. Instead of a promise of everlasting life *if* we believe, the gift of faith is promised *because* God has already chosen to give us eternal life.[102]

This concern to safeguard the centrality of Christ and the gospel led Arminius to invert the order of decrees. Supralapsarianism proposed the order *election, creation, fall, grace (faith and perseverance)*. Infralapsarianism placed election after the fall but prior to grace—*creation, fall, election, grace*. Franciscus Junius had, in 1593, proposed a compromise—*creation, election, fall, grace*. All three proposals made the historical manifestation of grace dependent on election. But then Arminius proposed *creation, fall, grace (faith and perseverance), election*; the gospel does not depend on the election of individual persons.

For Arminius, the decree first in order is the absolute decree by which God determines the salvation of sinners in appointing Jesus Christ as Mediator. The object of the decree is not the elect but Christ. He is more than the executor of election; he is its foundation. Second, God decrees to receive into favor all who repent and believe. He determines *in Christo, propter Christum*, and *per Christum* to save all who persevere in faith to the end and to reject and to damn all the impenitent and unbelieving. Third, God appoints the means of salvation—the sincere call of the gospel—and decrees to administer it with grace sufficient for people to believe. Finally, he decrees to save and to damn particular persons. This rests on his foreknowledge; foreknowing who will repent and believe, he decrees to save them.[103] Arminius contends that this order safeguards the primacy of Christ and the order of gospel proclamation (the requirement of repentance and faith *followed by* the promise of salvation).[104] For Arminius, God chooses believers, and he reprobates unbelievers, for "he resolved from eternity to condemn to eternal death unbelievers who, by their own fault and the just judgment of God, would not believe."[105]

A number of corollaries follow from Arminius's construction. First, the election of individuals is based on God's foreseeing their faith and

102. Nichols and Nichols, *Arminius*, 1:554–55, 567–68.
103. Nichols and Nichols, *Arminius*, 1:589.
104. Nichols and Nichols, *Arminius*, 1:591.
105. Nichols and Nichols, *Arminius*, 2:228.

perseverance. We are not chosen so that we might believe, but we believe and persevere so that we might be elect. God does not choose anyone in particular, but he foresees that we choose him and elects us on that basis. It follows that Arminius has no doctrine of perseverance. Although he denies ever having taught that a true believer can "either totally or finally" fall away and perish, he says,

> Yet I will not conceal, that there are passages of Scripture which seem to me to wear this aspect; and those answers to them which I have been permitted to see, are not of such a kind as to approve themselves on all points to my understanding. On the other hand, certain passages are produced for the contrary doctrine . . . which are worthy of much consideration.[106]

His equivocation indicates an unwillingness to commit to a doctrine that his opponents affirm and defend. Against Perkins, he argues for the possibility of a living member of Christ falling from grace and perishing, since a living member of Christ remains such *if* he or she perseveres in the faith of Christ.[107] A believer who ceases to trust God is no longer a believer.[108] A believer and an elect person are not identical.[109] Therefore perseverance is *conditional* on continued faith. It is not undergirded by election, since election is *subsequent* to perseverance. For Arminius, believers no longer have confidence that God has purposed to preserve them in faith to the end. On the contrary, they may fall from grace.

Precisely because Arminius inverts the order of decrees and thus makes perseverance conditional, so he destroys assurance of salvation. He wants to say believers can have assurance of present salvation. However, as Carl Bangs notes, "There is no present assurance of final salvation."[110] Or, as Arminius himself states:

> No one can believe that his future sins will likewise be remitted, unless he knows that he will believe to the end: For sins are forgiven to him who believes, and only after they have been committed; wherefore the promise of forgiveness, which is that of the NT, must be

---

106. Nichols and Nichols, *Arminius*, 1:603.
107. Nichols and Nichols, *Arminius*, 3:470.
108. Nichols and Nichols, *Arminius*, 1:281.
109. Nichols and Nichols, *Arminius*, 1:385.
110. Nichols and Nichols, *Arminius*, 1:255, 384–85, 3:540; Carl Bangs, *Arminius: A Study in the Dutch Reformation* (Nashville: Abington, 1971), 348.

considered as depending upon a condition stipulated by God, that is FAITH, without which there is no [*pactum*] covenant.[111]

In subordinating election to Christology and soteriology, Arminius undermines certainty of the salvation on which he intends to focus.

When, at the Synod of Dort, Martinius of Bremen propounded Christ as the foundation of election, the staunch supralapsarian Gomarus challenged him to a duel! Gomarus understood Martinius to be voicing the ideas of the Remonstrants. The Remonstrants, following Arminius, had stressed Christ as the foundation of election. Consequently, the Dutch at the synod were averse to this expression. Some foreign delegates, not having direct contact with the Remonstrants, sought to do justice to election in Christ by acknowledging that Christ is not only the executor of election but also its foundation.[112] That was what provoked Gomarus. The synod eventually testified to election in Christ but was silent on how Christ is its foundation.[113]

14.1.6 *Amyraldianism*

Moïse Amyraut (1596–1664) held that Christ died on the cross for all people on condition of their faith. However, God the Father elected some to salvation. In turn, the Spirit grants repentance and faith to the elect. As Reymond points out, for Amyraldianism, "the actual execution of the divine discrimination comes not at the point of Christ's redemptive accomplishment but at the point of the Spirit's redemptive application."[114] Essentially, Amyraldianism sought to maintain the particularity of election and the application of redemption by the Spirit, while also having a universal atonement. For this reason, Warfield classes it as inconsistent Calvinism.[115] Unlike Arminianism, its doctrine of election was not based on God's foreknowledge of the human response to the gospel. However, its view of the efficacy of Christ's work was split—he died for all but intercedes for the elect. It appears

---

111. Nichols and Nichols, *Arminius*, 2:70.
112. John Hales, *Letters from the Synod of Dort to Sir Dudley Carlton, the English Embassador at the Hague* (Glasgow, 1765), 137–38.
113. "Ad salutem elegit in Christo," "Canones Synodi Dordrechtanae" (1.6), in Schaff, *Creeds*, 3:553. The English translation fails to convey the meaning, making *in Christo* qualify *ad salutem* rather than describe the manner of God's electing.
114. Robert L. Reymond, *A New Systematic Theology of the Christian Faith* (New York: Nelson, 1998), 477.
115. Benjamin B. Warfield, *The Plan of Salvation*, rev. ed. (Grand Rapids, MI: Eerdmans, 1973), 89–95.

to drive a wedge between the decree of election, the atonement, and the particularity of application.

14.1.7   Hypothetical Universalism

Some English theologians proposed a slightly different argument than Amyraut.[116] Again, the point of disagreement lay more on the intent of the atonement than on election and reprobation. Edmund Calamy (1600–1666), a member of the Westminster Assembly, held that Christ died absolutely for the elect and conditionally for the reprobate, in case they believe. In this context, Calamy preserved the congruence in the works of the Trinity and avoided a split between the atonement and the intercession of Christ.[117] Calamy distinguished his position from Arminianism. Arminians say Christ paid a price placing all in an equal state of salvation. Calamy insisted his views "doth neither intrude upon either [the] doctrine of speciall election or speciall grace." He argued that Arminianism asserted that Christ simply suffered; all people are placed in a potentially salvable situation, so that any who believe will be saved. In contrast, he believed Christ's death saves his elect and grants a conditional possibility of salvation to the rest.[118] In distinction from Amyraut, Calamy held that the atonement is efficacious for the elect. Calamy's views were not seen as posing a major threat to the Reformed consensus.

This general position is evidenced in John Davenant (1576–1641), a member of the influential British delegation to Dort. From the premise of the need for universal gospel preaching to be grounded on a coterminous provision, he taught that the death of Christ was the basis for the salvation of all people everywhere. The call to faith, given indiscriminately, presupposes that the death or merit of Christ is applicable to all who are promised the benefit on condition of faith. Therefore, the scope and intent of the atonement is universal. Christ paid the penalty for the whole human race, grounded on an evangelical covenant in which he promises everlasting salvation to all on condition of faith in Christ. This sufficiency is ordained by God in the evangelical covenant but is overshadowed by another decree whereby God determined salva-

---

116. See Jonathan D. Moore, *English Hypothetical Universalism: John Preston and the Softening of Reformed Theology* (Grand Rapids, MI: Eerdmans, 2007).
117. Chad Van Dixhoorn, "Reforming the Reformation, Vol. 6: Minutes of the Westminster Assembly; Folio 293v– ; 18 November 1644–14 April 1648" (PhD diss., Cambridge University, 2004), 202–3.
118. Van Dixhoorn, "Reforming the Reformation, Vol. 6," 202–3.

tion for the elect. No actual reconciliation or salvation comes before a person believes. In this, God makes available or withholds the means of application of salvation to nations or individuals, according to his will. Only the elect receive saving faith. This decree of election, differentiating between elect and reprobate, conflicts with God's decision that Christ atone for each and every person by his death. God decides first one thing, then another.[119]

14.1.8 Karl Barth

Barth was strongly opposed to an absolute decree by God in himself concerning man in himself, and a concentration on the election and rejection of individuals as such. Instead, Barth saw election as the primal decision of God to be God in Christ and in no other way. "From all eternity he elects and decides one way or another about the being and nature of the creature," and so we cannot distinguish this from his Word and decree in the beginning, as in John 1.[120] This is "God's decision that as described in Jn. 1:1–2 the Word which is 'the same,' and is called Jesus, should really be in the beginning, with himself, like himself, one with himself in his deity."[121] Since Jesus Christ is in the beginning, he is the electing God. God determines to be God in this man, Jesus. In that decree Jesus Christ is also elect man. "Primarily, then, electing is the divine determination of the existence of Jesus Christ, and election (being elected) the human."[122] As such, Christ is the sole object of God's good pleasure.[123] While Christ elects together with the Father and the Holy Spirit, he is both elector and elected, more than the means of reconciliation between God and man, for he is himself the reconciliation.[124] In effect, the election encompasses creation, covenant, incarnation, and atonement, for it is an election by and of Jesus Christ. Controversy has been raised around whether Barth regarded election as God's election to be triune, as a primal decision to be God in Christ and in no other way. I referred to this debate in chapter 4 (see 4.7, p. 148); you may want to refresh your memory by returning to it.

---

119. John Davenant, *Dissertationes duae* (Cambridge: ex officinia Rogeri Danielis, 1650), 11–17, 55–87.
120. Barth, *CD*, II/2:100.
121. Barth, *CD*, II/2:101.
122. Barth, *CD*, II/2:103.
123. Barth, *CD*, II/2:104.
124. Barth, *CD*, II/2:105.

That election is all-encompassing for Barth is evident when he states,

> The eternal divine decision as such has as its object and content the existence of this one created being, the man Jesus of Nazareth, and the work of this man in his life and death, his humiliation and exaltation, his obedience and merit . . . the execution of the divine covenant with man, the salvation of all men.[125]

There are no other elect but those who are "in him," in his person, in his own choice, for this is more than his being the executor of salvation, and it is more than merely being with him, in his company.[126] His election carries with it the election of the rest.[127] Election has priority over all else, for it includes within it all else. Christ is both electing God and elect man. He also took on rejection, reprobation, in being judged in our place.[128] So,

> man cannot evade his responsibility by complaining that God required too much of him, for what God required of himself on man's behalf is infinitely greater than what he required of man. In the last analysis, what God required of man consists only in the demand that he should live as the one on whose behalf God required the very uttermost of himself.[129]

This has a noticeable universalistic flavor to it, although Barth denied universalism.[130] Oliver Crisp has argued that Barth is incoherent. With covenant, incarnation, and atonement all located in Christ, it is hard to see how the incorporation of humanity in Christ can, given the efficacy of Christ's death, fail to issue in universal salvation. Barth's denial of this conclusion is a triumph for his recognition of biblical teaching; it also renders his overall argument self-contradictory.[131] Barth's construction was adopted in all salient details by T. F. Torrance. I have written about this elsewhere, my conclusions agreeing with Crisp's discussion of Barth.[132]

---

125. Barth, *CD*, II/2:116.
126. Barth, *CD*, II/2:116–17.
127. Barth, *CD*, II/2: 117.
128. Barth, *CD*, IV/1:211–83.
129. Barth, *CD*, II/2:166.
130. Barth, *CD*, II/1:264, 553; Geoffrey W. Bromiley, *An Introduction to the Theology of Karl Barth* (Grand Rapids, MI: Eerdmans, 1979), 97–98.
131. Oliver D. Crisp, "On Barth's Denial of Universalism," *Them* 29 (2003): 18–29.
132. Robert Letham, "The Triune God, Incarnation, and Definite Atonement," in *From Heaven He Came and Sought Her: Definite Atonement in Historical, Biblical, Theological, and Pastoral*

431 Election and the Counsel of Redemption

14.2   The Covenant of Redemption (the *Pactum Salutis*)

14.2.1   Development of Covenant Theology

While the next chapter will focus on covenant, it is important to summarize its emergence now so as to appreciate the background to the appearance of the covenant of redemption. The covenant of grace began to be a distinct theme in Reformed theology as early as the 1520s, with Heinrich Bullinger writing the first major treatise on the subject in 1534.[133] Initially it was prompted by the emergence of Anabaptists and the need to respond to their separation of old and new covenants in opposing infant baptism.

Eventually, in tandem with reflection on how the covenant related to the ongoing administration of the law, thought turned to the prelapsarian situation. A number of suggestions were made about a creation covenant, but the first to propose formally a covenant of works was Dudley Fenner in 1585.[134] By 1590 the doctrine was widespread and it received confessional status in the Westminster Assembly documents in 1647. Facilitating the prelapsarian covenant was the continuity of law and grace throughout redemptive history. Clearly, biblical exegesis played a large part. In particular, it was noted that all the ingredients of a covenant are present in Genesis 2 even if the term itself is not. Then, taking the wider context of Scripture into account, there is the connection between the first and second Adams; what Adam lost Christ regained—and more. Moreover, the threat for disobedience entailed a corresponding promise for obedience, a promise of life, in conjunction with the tree of life, for God is the living God, the source of created life.

From this, some began to construe the eternal counsels of God in covenantal terms. Caspar Olevian wrote of an eternal *pactum* as early as 1585,[135] but the idea of a pretemporal covenant between the Father and the Son emerged more clearly in the 1630s. Muller has identified the idea as broached by Arminius in 1603 and taken up by Paul Bayne in 1618, by Edward Reynolds in 1632, by David Dickson from 1635, on the Continent by Johannes Cloppenburg in 1643, in England again

---

Perspective, ed. David Gibson and Jonathan Gibson (Wheaton, IL: Crossway, 2013), 447–59. See J. V. Fesko, *The Trinity and the Covenant of Redemption* (Fearn: Mentor, 2016), 195–207, 225–39.

133. Heinrich Bullinger, *De testamento seu foedere Dei et aeterno brevis expositio* (Zürich, 1534).

134. Dudley Fenner, *Sacra theologia, sive veritas quae secundum pietatem*(Geneva, 1585).

135. Caspar Olevian, *De substantia foederis gratuiti inter Deum et electos* (Geneva, 1585).

by John Owen in 1647, and famously and idiosyncratically by Johannes Coccecius the following year.[136] Unlike the pre-fall covenant, it has not attained confessional status and so, while commonly expounded and defended, is still more of a theological opinion, although widely held.

14.2.2   Outlines of the Pactum Salutis

As generally explained the *pactum salutis* is an agreement reached within the Trinity, a pact between the Father and the Son. While some of the more acute theologians recognized that the Spirit must be included, many constructions of this covenant have confined themselves to the Father and the Son without reference to the Spirit.

The Sum of Saving Knowledge, coauthored by David Dickson and James Durham, one of the earliest statements, refers to "the covenant of redemption . . . made and agreed upon between God the Father and God the Son, in the counsel of the Trinity, before the world began." In this, God gave "a certain number of lost mankind"—freely chosen before time— to God the Son, "appointed Redeemer, that, upon condition he would humble himself [etc.]. . . . This condition the Son of God . . . did accept before the world began." We have here the problem of two agents, two wills, two parties to a contractual agreement. The document continues, "But by virtue of the aforesaid bargain . . . he is still upon the work of applying actually the aforesaid benefits unto the elect." Apart from its reading like the terms of an insurance policy, its description as a "bargain" entails negotiations, more than one party, a business arrangement. And where, in all this, is the Holy Spirit?[137] Following this, "by the sacraments, God will have the covenant sealed for confirming the bargain on the foresaid condition."[138] A foundational axiom of Trinitarian theology, the inseparable operations, grounded on the indivisibility of the Trinity, has been broken.

Much the same is seen in A. A. Hodge, *Outlines of Theology*. While Hodge makes a passing reference to the three persons, when he describes the covenant, the Holy Spirit is absent.[139] Berkhof's exposition of the covenant also omits reference to the Spirit, other than a brief comment

---

136. Richard A. Muller, "Toward the Pactum Salutis: Locating the Origins of a Concept," *MAJT* 18 (2007): 11–65.
137. "The Sum of Saving Knowledge," in *The Confession of Faith, the Larger and Shorter Catechisms with the Scriptural Proofs at Large, Together with The Sum of Saving Knowledge* (Applecross, Ross-shire: Publications Committee of the Free Church of Scotland, 1970), 324.
138. "Saving Knowledge," 325.
139. A. A. Hodge, *Outlines of Theology* (Grand Rapids, MI: Eerdmans, 1972), 372.

that, as a reward for his finished work, the Son would "send out the Holy Spirit for the formation of his spiritual body."[140]

The emergence of the *pactum salutis* was based on a collation of biblical passages. Muller points out that while Zechariah 6:13 is often seen as a primary text for the *pactum*, it was not used in support in the seventeenth century. Each author supported his claims by a different set of passages. Many were drawn from the Old Testament (e.g., Pss. 2:7; 40:5–6; 89:27; 110:1; Isa. 42:1–4; 49:4–6; 50:4–9; 52:13–53:12). From the New Testament, there was Luke 22:29.[141] However, what was not noted is that these texts refer to the incarnate Christ, not to an eternal intra-Trinitarian pact.

Hugh Martin, one of the more acute exponents, sums up the rationale for the *pactum*: "On no scheme whatever that shall be true to the leading contents of Scripture, concerning the work of the incarnate Redeemer, can we possibly avoid coming to the conclusion that he acts according to a covenant with the Father."[142] Again, the Spirit takes a back seat.

The *pactum salutis* is a *theologoumenon* (theological opinion) rather than a dogma. It has no confessional support from either the WCF or the Formula Consensus Helvetica (1675). In contrast, the WCF and the WLC maintain that there are two covenants, the covenant of works or life and the covenant of grace (WCF, 7.2–3; WLC, 30), the covenant of works being the first. Some of the ingredients for the *pactum* are present in the confession's chapter on Christ the Mediator (WCF, 8.1–5) but the focus is on the relationship between God the Father and *the incarnate Christ*. This is further underlined by WLC, 31; this covenant of grace "was made [by God] with Christ *as the second Adam*, and in him with all the elect as his seed" (italics mine).

14.2.3 Evaluation

The basic premise—the inescapable axiom—to which we must constantly pay attention is the indivisibility of the Trinity: one being, three persons. From this it follows that in all the works of the Trinity, the three persons operate inseparably: creation (Gen. 1:1–5; Ps. 33:6–9), providence (Ps 104:29–30; Col. 1:18; Heb. 1:3), and grace (the incarnation,

---

140. Louis Berkhof, *Systematic Theology* (London: Banner of Truth, 1958), 265–71, see 270.
141. Muller, "Toward the Pactum Salutis," 25–46.
142. Hugh Martin, *The Atonement: In Its Relations to the Covenant, the Priesthood, the Intercession of Our Lord* (Edinburgh: Lyon and Gemmell, 1877), 35.

the baptism of Jesus, the cross, and the resurrection). Redemption rests on God's eternal determination in which all three persons are engaged (Rom. 8:29–30; Eph. 1:4–5; 2 Tim. 1:9). Jesus refers to the Father's having given people to him (John 6:37) and having sent him (John 3:16; 5:36–37, 43), and to his own fulfilling the work the Father had given him to do (John 4:34; 17:4; Heb. 10:5–10). In all this, while he is not explicitly mentioned, the Holy Spirit is implicitly included, while in John his work is described in detail later.

Hugh Martin, arguing for the *pactum*, writes of election as a cold, dispassionate decree in contrast to the covenant of redemption, which he sees as more evidently personal: "It is not enough to consider this [covenant] oneness as decreed; we must consider it as specially and expressly covenanted."[143] He adds that a decree may honor the Godhead, but does it honor the Trinity? The covenant reveals the distinct actings of the persons of the Godhead. There can be no excuse for regarding this as a consequence of a simple decree. It would be to overlook love as the motive of redemption. "There is a certain aspect of coldness about a mere decree."[144]

However, can election—an action of the Trinity, with all three persons inseparably engaged—ever be cold or dispassionate? Eternal election is not a simple or bare decree: it is by the Father in Christ and is the source of "every spiritual blessing" from the Holy Spirit (Eph. 1:3–4). To make a distinction between a non-Trinitarian election and a Trinitarian covenant seems to me to be at best splitting hairs, at worst to have far-reaching consequences. Martin's argument itself has Trinitarian implications, since "a simple decree" is in his thinking of lesser import than a covenant, a contractual agreement being required to overcome its coldness. How can a determination of the indivisible Trinity, pulsating with life and love, be regarded as cold and abstract? How can it require a contractual agreement to make it personal?

Moreover, this has further worrying implications. Martin writes of "the will of the Father" and "the will of the Son."[145] However, the Trinity is simple, with one indivisible will. Owen recognized the problem when, in his exposition of the *pactum*, he wrote of the one will in its distinct

---

143. Martin, *Atonement*, 43–44.
144. Martin, *Atonement*, 44–45.
145. Martin, *Atonement*, 45.

manifestations in the Father, the Son, and the Spirit.[146] Martin does not make these qualifications.

Notwithstanding, there is much of great value in Martin's exposition. His emphasis that God's purpose underlying the covenant of grace has priority over its historical execution is vital. The incarnation, the atonement, and our union with Christ would indeed be abstractions were it not for the fact that the Trinity had planned the work of redemption and provided the context that alone gives it meaning. The atonement and union with Christ are grounded on the unity of the work of God, which in turn derives from his eternal Trinitarian counsel. In terms of details, the covenant of redemption attests to the vital eternal foundation of the whole work of redemption in all its elements—cosmic, ecclesial, individual—and all its outworking in history. Therefore, the intent of the *pactum salutis* is closely related to election and is in that sense commendable. However, its advocates clearly differentiate the two. Election concerns the ultimate goal; the *pactum* considers the means.

But if election is understood in Trinitarian terms, is a distinction from the *pactum salutis* valid? Positively, the *pactum salutis* was intended to express that the eternal counsel of God underwrites the covenant of grace, atonement, and justification, and so provides for us the meaning that it has. *But is this best expressed by covenant?* Is it *rightly* expressed by covenant?

Even more importantly, are the formulations of the *pactum salutis* compatible with historic Christian orthodoxy? There are clear Trinitarian problems involved in the *pactum salutis as it has frequently been constructed*, in the form present in *The Sum of Saving Knowledge*, for example. The most striking point in many such accounts is that the Holy Spirit is not mentioned! A. A. Hodge describes what, in effect, is a divine committee meeting, the Spirit apparently having sent apologies for absence, but those apologies are not even noted.[147] Such constructions are binitarian.

Furthermore, inevitable problems arise in applying covenant concepts to God. There are two kinds of covenant in the Bible. The first kind is a one-sided imposition. Applied to the relations of the Father and the

---

146. *The Works of John Owen*, ed. William H. Goold, 23 vols. (1850–1855; repr., London: Banner of Truth, 1965–1968), 19:88.

147. Hodge, *Outlines*, 372.

Son (leaving the Holy Spirit aside!), this would mean subordination. The other covenant type is a *quid pro quo*, a voluntary contract between two or more persons. This requires the parties to be autonomous agents. Applied to the Trinity, this type of covenant implies that each person has his own will, entailing something approaching Tritheism. Both of these elements are present in the *pactum salutis*. In short, in constructions like this its compatibility with classic Trinitarian theology is questionable. It veers toward either subordinationism or tritheism. John Owen recognized this when he made a significant caveat in discussing the *pactum*, of which he was one of the earliest exponents, referring to the one will of God as it comes to distinct expression in the three persons.[148] However, Bavinck—perhaps its best exponent[149]—states that the Son as Mediator is subordinate to the Father (which is uncontroversial) and that this relation existed in eternity also.[150]

Hoeksema is emphatic in his criticisms:

> It is of the utmost importance that we distinguish sharply between the covenant that God establishes with Christ as the Servant of the Lord, standing at the head of those whom the Father gave him, and the eternal covenant of the three persons of the Holy Trinity. Failure to make this distinction became the cause that the covenant of redemption was presented as a relation or agreement between the Father and the Son, and that no place was found in this covenant for the Holy Spirit, and that the result was practically a denial of the Holy Trinity and of the co-equality of the Son with the Father.[151]

Furthermore, the biblical texts cited in support of the *pactum salutis* all refer to the incarnate Christ in his work as Mediator. In doing so, they do not apply to the intra-Trinitarian relations as such. Hoeksema again states, "When we pay attention to all those Scriptural passages

---

148. Goold, *Works*, 19:86–88.
149. See Laurence R. O'Donnell III, "Not Subtle Enough: An Assessment of Modern Scholarship on Herman Bavinck's Reformulation of the *Pactum Salutis* contra 'Scholastic Subtlety,'" *MAJT*, 22 (2011): 89–106, who defends Bavinck against charges of ontologizing the *pactum salutis* by importing covenant concepts into the being of God, making the *pactum* a necessity of his being. Bavinck avoids most of the dangers I have pinpointed, but his distinction between the decree, involving the undivided Trinity, and the counsel or *pactum*, relating to the persons, has evident problems. See also Cornelis P. Venema, "Covenant and Election in the Theology of Herman Bavinck," *MAJT* 19 (2008): 69–115.
150. Bavinck, *RD*, 2:214.
151. Herman Hoeksema, *Reformed Dogmatics* (Grand Rapids, MI: Reformed Free Publishing Association, 1966), 297.

which former dogmaticians quoted as proof for the counsel of peace, or the *pactum salutis*, it becomes evident that they all, without exception, refer to the covenant which God establishes with Christ as the Head of the elect."[152]

The focus of the *pactum salutis* on contractual agreement misses the heart of what God's covenant is about. Such a construction generally overlooks the point that central to the covenant is the promise of living fellowship, communion, and union. This is expressed in the repeated promise "I will be your God, and you shall be my people" (see Gen. 17:7–8; Jer. 11:14; 24:7; 30:22; 31:1, 33; 32:28; Rev. 21:3). At the heart of the Trinity is an infinite superabundance of life. The eternal generation of the Son and the eternal procession of the Holy Spirit indicate that God is immeasurable life and fecundity. As Bavinck states, creation would be impossible if the Son were not generated from eternity. The three are inherently relational. This relationality underlies God's free determination to create—a sovereign act of his will, all three persons engaged, exercised in harmony with his nature. It also underlies his initiation of his covenant. Its heart is living, vibrant personal fellowship, communion and union; we are invited to share this relation, to participate in God's everlasting Sabbath rest. This is akin to marriage; as marriage is buttressed by law, so is God's covenant. This element cannot be ignored. However, to construe this covenant in *purely* legal terms is to miss the relation of the most intimate communion or friendship in which God reflects his covenant life in his relation to the creature.[153] It is a living relationship of friendship.

Atonement and justification are grounded in the eternal purpose of God. While the *pactum salutis* bears witness to this, so too does the WLC's construction, avoiding the dangers inherent in the *pactum*.

Historical consequences followed its deployment. English Presbyterianism soon became infected with Arianism and Unitarianism in the half century after the Restoration. Did constructions of the *pactum salutis* that implied the subordination of the Son play a part in this precipitous collapse? It is difficult to establish.[154] Some might argue that

---

152. Hoeksema, *Reformed Dogmatics*, 298.
153. Martin, we have noted, wanted to avoid this danger.
154. Elsewhere I discuss critically Patrick Gillespie's attempt to avoid some of the problems mentioned above, arguing that he created others of a Christological kind; see Robert Letham, *The Holy Trinity: In Scripture, History, Theology, and Worship*, 2nd ed. (Phillipsburg, NJ: P&R, 2019), chap. 12.

Enlightenment rationalism was the direct cause and that there is no demonstrable connection with the *pactum*. However, a construction in which the Son is subordinate to the Father could hardly have helped avert such an outcome.

Iain Campbell attempted to overcome some of these difficulties. To my mind, Campbell succeeded in being consciously Trinitarian.[155] J. V. Fesko has produced a defense of the doctrine, wide-ranging and thorough, with most of which I am in agreement and which, in many ways, meets the reservations I have had ever since, back in 1972, I read Thomas Goodwin's remarkable exegesis of Ephesians 1.[156] However, the nagging suspicion remains that the application of covenant concepts to the eternal life of the Trinity loses more than it gains, even if one recognizes that analogical predication is involved and an exact equivalence is ruled out. To talk of *the eternal Trinitarian counsel* avoids these problems, maintaining the indivisibility of the Trinity as well as the hypostatic distinctions, while achieving all that was intended by the *pactum salutis*.

14.2.4 *Positive Statement of the* Consilium Salutis

God, from eternity, before the foundation of the world, determined salvation for the human race and the renewal and consummation of the cosmos. The Father, in his wise and inscrutable counsel, chose in Christ the Son, that he would be the Head of his church and to that end become incarnate as man, make atonement for sin, rise from the dead, ascend, and reign with the Father and the Holy Spirit in the indivisible unity of the Trinity forever. This was a determination that the Son would take human nature, thus binding himself to humanity in permanent and indissoluble union.

Since the Trinity is indivisible, the Father's choice was inseparably the Son's and the Spirit's too, for they have one will. The Son's determination to take human nature was indivisibly that of the Father and the Holy Spirit. In this indivisible determination, the holy Trinity chose in Christ to save—by pure, free, and sovereign grace—a vast number out of the fallen human race from every nation of the world, as integral to his pur-

---

155. Iain D. Campbell, "Re-Visiting the Covenant of Redemption," in *The People's Theologian: Writings in Honour of Donald Macleod*, ed. Iain D. Campbell and Malcolm MacLean (Fearn: Mentor, 2011), 173–94.

156. Fesko, *The Trinity and the Covenant of Redemption*, passim. This is the most thorough treatment.

pose of renewing and consummating in Christ his entire creation, leaving the rest to the consequences of their sinful rebellion, to the praise of his glorious justice. *Mutatis mutandis*, the undivided Trinity also determined that the Holy Spirit should bring into effect this plan in inseparable working with the Father and the Son, by upholding the incarnate Son in his earthly life and ministry, raising him from the dead, granting faith to those elected to salvation, sustaining them in the course of their lives, and energizing the renewal of the cosmos. In this great plan, entailing the establishment of the covenant of grace with his chosen people, the will and purpose of God was one, the three acting together in distinct ways in all its aspects.

Further Reading

Crisp, Oliver D. "On Barth's Denial of Universalism," *Them* 29 (2003): 18–29.

Molnar, Paul D. *Faith, Freedom and the Spirit: The Economic Trinity in Barth, Torrance and Contemporary Theology*. Downers Grove, IL: IVP Academic, 2015.

Muller, Richard A. *Christ and the Decree: Christology and Predestination in Reformed Theology from Calvin to Perkins*. Grand Rapids, MI: Baker, 2008.

Venema, Cornelis P. *Chosen in Christ: Revisiting the Contours of Predestination*. Fearn: Mentor, 2019.

Study Questions

1. How is the doctrine of election a catholic doctrine?

2. What is meant by "election in Christ"?

3. In what contexts is election mentioned in the New Testament, and what are the purposes of the New Testament writers in referring to it?

4. Evaluate the weaknesses of some of the presentations of the *pactum salutis*. In your estimation, is it best expressed in terms of a covenant or is it preferable to call it the *consilium salutis*?

15

The Covenant of Grace

Covenant theology emerged in Reformed theology in the sixteenth century but had antecedents and is rooted in the Bible. God deals with humanity redemptively by covenants, from Abraham, through Moses, to the new covenant in Christ. These are all manifestations of God's grace, regulated by law. There is a unity throughout, justifying the singular term *covenant of grace*. A particular area of debate has surrounded the place of the Mosaic covenant, in relation both to the pre-fall covenant of life and to the new covenant. While there has been a diversity of views on both aspects, it is clear that the dominant position is that the pre-fall covenant came to an end on Adam's fall but that the Mosaic covenant is in continuity with the new covenant, the moral law expressed in the Decalogue being of perpetual and universal validity.

15.1   The Emergence and Development of Covenant Theology

15.1.1   *Origins of Reformed Covenant Theology*

In Reformed theology, attention to the covenant of grace began soon after the Reformation. A major impetus was the Anabaptists' opposition to infant baptism, which encouraged Zwingli, in response, to stress the unity of God's covenant in the Old and New Testaments, linking circumcision and baptism. In 1523, Zwingli was the first to write about the covenant. His successor at Zurich, Heinrich Bullinger, wrote the first treatise expressly devoted to the covenant of grace.[1] From that time on, it was a commonplace. At first, the focus was on the one postlapsarian covenant from Adam onward, but later the pre-fall situation was understood to be covenantal. While these developments were rooted in biblical exposition, precedents in medieval times may have helped to pave the way, although the extent to which this was so has been disputed.

15.1.2 Medieval Antecedents?

Until the eleventh century there was a consensus in Europe that all classes of society, including the king, were under the authority of law, principally the law of God. This was nowhere better expressed than by the thirteenth-century English jurist, Bracton; the king was under the law (*sub legem*). If he failed to keep the law, his kingship was invalid.[2]

The relation of king to church came to a head in the Investiture Contest in 1075, in which Pope Gregory VII (Hildebrand) and the Holy Roman emperor, Henry IV, exchanged excommunications and depositions.[3] This clash of civil and religious authority was mirrored by increasing disputes over the powers of the king in relation to the people. Royalists pointed to the *lex regia*, part of the Institute of Justinian (483–565), which claimed—spuriously as it was later proved—that the Roman people had transferred their power to the emperor. Conflicting interpretations among jurists followed,[4] with the counterclaim of Manegold of Lautenbach that there was nothing to stop the people from revoking this transfer, rendering the king a dismissable functionary.[5] For Manegold, the king had a right to rule as a servant had a right to his wages. As long

---

1. Heinrich Bullinger, *De testamento seu foedere Dei unico et aeterno brevis expositio* (Zürich, 1534).

2. "The king . . . ought to be subject to God and the law, since law makes a king (*Ipse autem rex non debet esse sub homine sed sub deo et sub lege, quia lex facit regem*). Therefore let the king render to the law what the law has rendered to the king, lordship and power, for where will rules and not law there is no king." *Bracton: De legibus et consuetudinibus Angliae*, ed. George E. Woodine, 4 vols. (1255–1268; New Haven, CT: Yale, 1922), 2:33. Bracton argues that the king's task is patterned on Christ, who put himself under the law to redeem those under the law (Gal. 4:4–5).

3. Geoffrey Barraclough, *The Medieval Papacy* (London: Thames and Hudson, 1968), 82–84; Gerd Tellenach, *Church, State and Christian Society at the Time of the Investiture Contest* (Oxford: Basil Blackwell, 1940); J. P. Whitney, *Hildebrandine Essays* (Cambridge: Cambridge University Press, 1932); Z. N. Brooke, "Lay Investiture and Its Relation to the Conflict of Empire and Papacy," *Proceedings of the British Academy* 25 (1939): 217–47.

4. See R. W. Carlyle and A. J. Carlyle, *A History of Medieval Political Theory in the West*, 6 vols. (Edinburgh, 1892–1936), 6:19–29.

5. J. W. Gough, *The Social Contract: A Critical Study of Its Development*, 2nd ed. (Oxford: Clarendon, 1957), 32.

as the king fulfilled his side of the contract, he got paid.[6] The rule of law was now a law of contract. From 1300 on, contract theory posed a serious limitation on the power of rulers, Magna Carta having provided an outstanding precursor.

A parallel development occurred in the church, with a struggle for power between the papacy and the Conciliar Movement. Meanwhile, the publicists held that power in the church, as in the civil realm, was derived from the people.[7] With the feudal system, groups formed for mutual defense and protection against external threats. In Scotland, the practice of bonding or banding by local lairds was common. Similar features were present in Switzerland and the German protectorates.[8]

Social changes led to new perspectives in theology. Gabriel Biel held that God's *potentia absoluta* (absolute power) is restrained by his *potentia ordinata* (ordained power), to which he had committed himself by *pactum*. Biel's theology was not immediately related to the emergence of covenant theology in Switzerland and the Rhineland, for which the Bible was clearly the main source. However, the covenant idea in Scripture had indirectly affected medieval society, providing fertile ground for later biblical and theological development.

15.2   Biblical Covenants after the Fall

The Bible describes five covenants that God made after the fall. The Noachic covenant was nonredemptive, made with all humanity and the totality of the animate creation (Gen. 8:20–9:17).[9] It consisted of a unilateral, sovereign promise by God never again to inundate the whole earth by a flood. It promised the continuation of the regular order of day and night, summer and winter, and the production of resources to sustain life. In evidence of this promise was the sacrament of the rainbow, a sign principally for God himself even before it was for humanity (Gen. 9:14). This covenant reinstituted and reaffirmed creation.

---

6. Fritz Kern, *Kingship and Law in the Middle Ages* (Oxford: Basil Blackwell, 1939), 120.

7. Antony Black, "The Conciliar Movement," in *The Cambridge History of Medieval Political Thought c. 350–c. 1450*, ed. J. H. Burns (Cambridge: Cambridge University Press, 1988), 573–87, here 574.

8. J. N. Figgis, *Studies of Political Thought from Gerson to Grotius, 1414–1625: Seven Studies*, 2nd ed. (Cambridge: Cambridge University Press, 1916), 10; Gough, *Social Contract*, 34; R. Van Caenegem, "Government, Law and Society," in Burns, *Medieval Political Thought c. 350–c. 1450*, 210.

9. In Noah's entering the ark with his family, an ultimately redemptive purpose was present (Gen. 6:18). I am grateful to Keith Mathison for this observation.

This was a thoroughly gracious covenant. God would have been justified in effecting a final and permanent judgment for the sins and unbridled violence that preceded the flood (Gen. 6:5). However, after the deluge, "God blessed Noah and his sons" (Gen. 9:1), a blessing on the human race without regard to the status or attitude of its members toward him. One of Noah's sons disregarded the dignity of his father and came under judgment (Gen. 9:20–27), yet God's blessing rested upon him. This blessing, while limited to the ordinary life of the creature in the world, is the basis for both common grace and redemption. In the first case, its blessing represents a curtailment of judgment. Second, it is the necessary prelude to the redemptive covenants that follow, for they could not be given if humanity did not survive and flourish. The Noachic covenant finds fullest expression in the blessing that God gives to the race viewed as a totality—the incarnation of his Son and salvation for a countless concourse from every nation on the face of the globe.

I will discuss later the respective content of the redemptive covenants: the Abrahamic (Gen. 12:1–3; 15:1–21; 17:1–14), the Mosaic (Ex. 19–20; 24:1ff.), the Davidic (2 Samuel 7), and the new (Jer. 31:31–33; Matt. 26:26–29; 28:18–20).

15.3 The Covenant of Grace

Murray wrote that biblical covenants were sovereign administrations of grace to man. In this he included the Mosaic covenant. In each case the covenants were both initiated and implemented by God.[10] Conversely, Meredith Kline argued that biblical covenants were at root law covenants, with promise ancillary. His basis was his assessment of the Hittite suzerainty treaties that he saw as underlying the Mosaic covenant.[11] Michael Horton has written that there are two types of covenant—royal grants, exemplified by the Abrahamic covenant, and suzerainty treaties, with legal requirements, such as the Mosaic covenant.[12] Whatever one's conclusions, God's covenants consist of promises he makes, mediation he provides, obligations to which his people are committed, and sacraments that sign and seal the covenant. Although the Bible describes a

---

10. John Murray, *The Covenant of Grace* (London: Tyndale Press, 1954), 1954.

11. Meredith G. Kline, *By Oath Consigned: A Reinterpretation of the Covenantal Signs of Circumcision and Baptism* (Grand Rapids, MI: Eerdmans, 1968).

12. Michael S. Horton, *Covenant and Salvation: Union with Christ* (Louisville: Westminster John Knox, 2007).

wide variety of covenants, God's redemptive covenants are marked by oath-bound promise (Heb. 6:13ff.). I will discuss these questions below.

15.3.1   The Unity of the Covenants

In the face of the series of covenants in Scripture, are we justified in talking of one covenant of grace? Yes, there is an underlying unity to them, taken together and as parts of the ongoing flow of redemptive history. This unity is seen in the following ways.

The promise. Again, the central promise found throughout these covenants is the affirmation "I will be your God, and you shall be my people," a promise of fellowship and union. At root God's covenant is relational, reaffirmed, and ultimately fulfilled. It is expressed in the Abrahamic covenant (Gen. 17:7–8), by Jeremiah referring to the Mosaic covenant (Jer. 11:1–5), with the returned exiles from Babylon (Jer. 24:7; 30:22; 32:38), with the promise of a new covenant (Jer. 31:33), by Ezekiel (Ezek. 37:23–28), and in terms of the church in the new covenant (Rev. 21:3).

Galatians 3:15–22 sketches the relationship between the Abrahamic, Mosaic, and new covenants. We will consider this connection shortly.[13] Between these covenants there are differences but also an ongoing thread of continuity. In 2 Corinthians 3:4–11, Paul, in refuting his Judaizing opponents, focuses on the superiority of his apostolic ministry to that of Moses. However, with the differences there is commonality. While the law was written externally on stone tablets at Sinai and could only condemn, it was still attended with glory. Further, Paul's ministry results in God's law being written on the heart by the Holy Spirit, bringing to fulfillment what Moses's ministry foreshadowed.

The Mediator. Throughout there is mediation, ultimately realized when the incarnate Son, Jesus Christ, came to reconcile us to God. In the Mosaic covenant, this was presaged by the priesthood and the sacrificial system. In themselves, these were weak and ineffective. They merely portrayed visually what was to come.

The contrast between the old covenant and the new is starker in Hebrews 8:6–13, where the author points to the supremacy of Christ the

---

13. Robert Letham, *The Work of Christ* (Leicester: Inter-Varsity Press, 1993), 39–53, 106–10.

Mediator. His person, his sacrifice, and the promises given in, by, and through him far surpass what preceded. The priestly, sacrificial ritual of the Mosaic covenant has been fulfilled, superseded, and rendered obsolete by the priestly sacrifice of Christ, who made once-for-all atonement for sin.

The required response. At each stage, faith and obedience are the obligations required of those with whom God enters into covenant. Abraham was told to walk before God and be perfect (Gen. 17:1); he believed God (Gen. 15:6) and performed the covenantal sign (Gen. 17:1ff.). Also, in the new covenant, we are to believe in Jesus Christ and turn from sin (Acts 2:37–41).

As Calvin described it, the covenant is one in substance, differing in administration. In terms of its content, there is but one way of salvation, one means of redemption and consummation for the human race and the cosmos. This is revealed, expressed, and administered in the covenant of grace. Yet the manner in which it is administered shows significant differences before and after Christ. We will consider such questions where they surface in relation to the Mosaic covenant.

15.3.2 *With Whom Is the Covenant Made?*

The Abrahamic covenant is made with Abraham and his offspring, later narrowed to Isaac, not Ishmael, and to Jacob, not Esau. In the New Testament Paul affirms that those with faith inherit the promises made to Abraham (Gal. 3:6–29).

Credobaptists consider this to mean that the new covenant is made with the believer only. They highlight individual responsibility. The New Testament pattern is of entrance to the covenant through faith (Acts 2:37–39; 3:16; 13:39; 15:5–9; Rom. 1:16–17; 10:8–17; Gal. 2:20; 3:26–29).

Paedobaptists maintain that the covenant is made with believers and their children, arguing that in the Bible individuals live in a corporate context; the Old Testament sees a man as A, the son of B, the son of C, of the tribe D, and so the sin of Achan is the sin of Israel, while the household unit continues as the basis of covenant administration. Paul's treatment of believers' children is cited in support (Eph. 6:1–3). If the children of believers were excluded from membership in the new covenant when they had been an integral part of the old covenant, Pentecost would have been a day of mass excommunication.

This difference is more a question of hermeneutics than of exegesis. As one professor of philosophy remarked when walking down the street and observing two women polishing their doorsteps on opposite sides of the street while having a furious dispute, "It's no use; you'll never come to an agreement—you're arguing from different premises."

The heart of this disagreement surrounds respective commitments on three levels. First is the relationship between the individual and the corporate. Are the corporate structures in the Old Testament carried over into the New Testament? Credobaptists assert that each person is considered purely as an individual in the New Testament, whereas paedobaptists maintain that the household unit is still the basis for covenantal administration.

Second, allied with this difference is the question of covenantal continuity or discontinuity. Credobaptists argue for a greater element of discontinuity between the Testaments than do paedobaptists, who recognize that there are discontinuities but maintain that there is a basic continuity between them.

A third layer of relevance is the respective priority of grace to faith. The credobaptist position suggests that the human response of faith is decisive for each person in terms of covenant membership; covenantal grace is conditioned on the individual response. Paedobaptists argue that God's grace precedes the human response, that grace constitutes membership.

Beyond this, there has been some disagreement in Reformed churches about whether the covenant of grace is made by God with believers and their children or, alternatively, with Christ as the second Adam and the elect in him. Both positions were represented at the Westminster Assembly (WCF, 7.3; WLC, 31). There is also the question of whether the infants of believers are baptized in order to become covenant members or are baptized because they are covenant members, and therefore Christians, already.[14]

---

14. Both these positions were also represented at the Westminster Assembly: so, "children, by baptism, are solemnly received into the bosom of the visible church," and shortly afterward, "they are Christians, and federally holy before baptism, and therefore are they baptized." "The Directory for the Publick Worship of God," in *The Confession of Faith, the Larger and Shorter Catechisms with the Scripture Proofs at Large, Together with The Sum of Saving Knowledge* (Applecross, Rossshire: Publications Committee of the Free Presbyterian Church of Scotland, 1970), 383.

15.4   The Abrahamic Covenant

Basic to the flow of redemptive history is God's covenant with Abraham. God took Abram—whom he renamed—and his family out of Ur to Canaan via Haran and Egypt. God promised him innumerable descendants, the land of Canaan, and that he would be a worldwide blessing through his offspring (Gen. 12:1–3). Throughout the narrative, the initiative is entirely God's, and Abraham follows. The stress in Genesis 12:1–3 is on the action of God: "Go . . . to the land I will show you. . . . I will make of you a great nation . . . I will bless you and make your name great. . . . I will bless those who bless you . . . him who dishonors you I will curse." On Abram's part, he was required to obey God (Gen. 17:1); he was accounted righteous through his faith, believing God and resting on him (Gen. 15:6). As the covenant was formally made, God required that all males in his household be circumcised (Gen. 17:9–14). In the mysterious ceremony in Genesis 15:7–21 God, appearing as a flaming torch, took a self-maledictory oath, calling on himself the curses of the covenant, should he prove unfaithful to his promise. It was a gracious covenant through and through.

In the New Testament, this covenant finds its fulfillment in the new covenant in Christ. Matthew begins his Gospel with a genealogy establishing that Jesus is the son of Abraham and so the inheritor of the promise, the offspring to whom it was made (Matt. 1:1). Later, Jesus describes the kingdom of God in terms of a feast in the company of Abraham (Matt. 8:11–12). Paul considers Christian believers to inherit the promise of life in the Abrahamic covenant through faith (Gal. 3:26–29). Indeed, God preached the gospel beforehand to Abraham (Gal. 3:8), and Jesus could say that Abraham saw his day and rejoiced (John 8:56). Therefore, the Abrahamic covenant was not replaced by the Mosaic covenant that followed four hundred years later (Gal. 3:19–21).

15.5   The Mosaic Covenant

Yahweh made the Mosaic covenant with Israel, with whom he was already in covenant (Ex. 20:1–2). The Mosaic was added to the Abrahamic covenant and so the two existed side by side. Paul argues that it was, from one perspective, inferior, since it was given through an intermediary, whereas God spoke directly to Abraham (Gal. 3:18–20). It was also a gracious covenant, since it preserved the covenant people until Christ should come—the offspring to whom the promise of the Abrahamic covenant had been made (Gal. 3:19–21)—protecting them from the surrounding pagan environment. Moreover, its sacrificial system declared Yahweh's forgiveness of sins. It contained a legal system to govern the nation, and a moral law that defined what was pleasing to God and what was sin (Ex. 20:1–17; Deut. 5:1–21). It was a means of administering the covenant community until the arrival of the Christ.

Recently, discussions have surrounded the question of how the Mosaic covenant relates to the covenant of grace? Some have argued that it is in some way a republication of the pre-fall covenant of works. This has been strongly advocated by Meredith Kline, Michael Horton, and others. Reformed theologians, particularly before the Westminster Assembly, were never of one mind on the question.[15]

In the covenant of works, as outlined in WCF, 7.2,[16] there were two parties: God, who laid down the terms, and Adam, with the entire human race in him, its head and representative. God gave Adam the task of keeping the garden, with complete freedom but for one requirement: he was not to eat the fruit of the tree of the knowledge of good and evil, on penalty of death. To rebel against the living God was to choose death. Conversely, if Adam continued in obedience, life would follow; the presence of the tree of life suggests eternal life, for eating its fruit is connected with everlasting life (Gen. 3:22), a theme also in the New Testament (Rev. 22:1–2). The resurrection of Christ, the second Adam,

---

15. Apart from the works of Kline, cited below, others have addressed the matter in some detail: Mark W. Karlberg, "The Search for an Evangelical Consensus on Paul and the Law," *JETS* 40 (1997): 563–79; Karlberg, "Recovering the Mosaic Covenant as Law and Gospel: J. Mark Beach, John H. Sailhammer, and Jason C. Meyer as Representative Expositors," *EQ* 83 (2011): 233–50; D. Patrick Ramsey, "In Defense of Moses: A Confessional Critique of Kline and Karlberg," *WTJ* 66 (2004): 373–400; Brenton C. Ferry, "Cross-Examining Moses' Defense: An Answer to Ramsey's Critique of Kline and Karlberg," *WTJ* 67 (2005): 163–68; J. Mark Beach, *Christ and the Covenant: Francis Turretin's Federal Theology as a Defense of the Doctrine of Grace* (Göttingen: Vandenhoeck & Ruprecht, 2007); Michael S. Horton, *Covenant and Salvation: Union with Christ* (Louisville: Westminster John Knox, 2007), 9–36; James T. Dennison Jr., Scott F. Sanborn, and Benjamin W. Swinburnson, "Merit or 'Entitlement' in Reformed Covenant Theology: A Review," *Kerux* 24, no. 3 (2009): 3–152; David VanDrunen, "Natural Law and the Works Principle under Adam and Moses," in *The Law Is Not of Faith: Essays on Works and Grace in the Mosaic Covenant*, ed. Bryan D. Estelle, J. V. Fesko, and David VanDrunen (Phillipsburg, NJ: P&R, 2009), 283–314; VanDrunen, "Israel's Recapitulation of Adam's Probation under the Law of Moses," *WTJ* 73 (2011): 303–24; Cornelis P. Venema, "The Mosaic Covenant: A 'Republication' of the Covenant of Works?," *MAJT* 21 (2010): 35–101; Robert Letham, "'Not a Covenant of Works in Disguise' (Herman Bavinck): The Place of the Mosaic Covenant in Redemptive History," *MAJT* 24 (2013): 143–77. What follows is a compression of the substance of the last-named article, with permission. See also Cornelis P. Venema, *Christ and Covenant Theology: Essays on Election, Republication, and the Covenants* (Phillipsburg, NJ: P&R, 2017), 3–144.

16. See the discussion in chap. 12.

supports this. Adam sinned, he was expelled from the garden, the way back was barred, and death resulted. Covenantally, he and the race were dead in sins. The only hope was another covenant, one on a different basis altogether.

The covenant of works according to the republication theory. Advocates of republication argue that the covenant of works was transacted on the exclusive basis of justice. Kline opposes any idea of grace being present in this covenant as this would undermine the doctrines of justification and atonement.

> Adam would have fully deserved the blessings promised in the covenant, had he obediently performed the duty stipulated in it. Great as the blessings were to which the good Lord committed himself, the granting of them would not have involved a gram of grace. Judged by the stipulated terms of the covenant, they would have been merited in simple justice.[17]

Kline understands grace as operating only after the fall, against the background of demerit.[18] He argues, "Simple justice was the governing principle in the pre-fall covenant,"[19] so that continuity between the creation and redemptive covenants is not grace but justice.[20] Ironically, in an earlier work Kline acknowledged that "in another sense grace is present in the preredemptive covenant. For the offer of a consummation of man's original beatitude . . . was a display of the graciousness and goodness of God to this claimless creature of the dust."[21]

Later, according to the republication theory, the Mosaic covenant was based on the same principle as the pre-fall covenant, inheritance by works, insofar as it signified redemptive blessings typologically. It existed side by side with the Abrahamic promise covenant but was radically different.[22] Israel was disobedient and so forfeited the promised blessing in the land of Canaan. In what sense was this a covenant of works? According to Kline, alongside the gracious promises to Abraham it reiterated the works principle, which related to the administration of

---

17. Kline, "Covenant Theology under Attack," *NH*, February 1994, 4.
18. Kline, "Covenant Theology," 3.
19. Kline, "Covenant Theology," 3.
20. Kline, "Covenant Theology," 4.
21. Kline, *By Oath Consigned*, 36.
22. Kline, *By Oath Consigned*, 22–25.

the covenant—to Israel's reception of the covenantal blessings of the Mosaic covenant—rather than to its substance. These covenantal blessings were to be earned by obedience to the law and were typological of the consummate blessings of the covenant of grace.

Israel, due to disobedience, was disinherited and exiled, its national identity destroyed. Israel's failure prepared the way for Christ, who took Adam's place and obeyed God. By Christ's obedience he fulfilled the demands of the covenant of works, and so merited salvation for all united to him. He was vindicated in the resurrection and confirmed in everlasting life for himself and all his people. Kline summarizes, "Coherence can be achieved in Covenant theology only by the subordination of grace to law."[23] Hence, God's covenant is "an administration of God's lordship, consecrating a people to himself under the sanctions of divine law."[24]

The basis of this claim, that God deals with humanity primarily by law and justice, is supported by parallels in ancient Near Eastern treaty forms; these posit two sorts of covenant—vassal suzerainty treaties, with legal stipulations made by a victor to a vassal king, and royal grants, marked by sovereign favor.[25] The Abrahamic covenant was a royal grant; the Mosaic covenant and the covenant of works, suzerainty treaties. The two forms operated together from Moses until Christ, exemplifying opposing principles. Salvation was based on grace, while Israel's possession of the temporal blessings was based on the works-inheritance principle but also signified Christ's meriting salvation for his people.

The covenants of works (or life) and of grace in relation to the first and second Adams. Can these arguments be sustained? In the covenants of works and of grace there are covenant heads—Adam and Christ. Both represent others: Adam, the human race; Christ, the new humanity, the elect. Both were without sin. For both there was a promise of everlasting life on faithful completion of a period of obedience. Whereas Adam was tempted to sin in the beautiful garden, with a profusion of food, and failed, the second Adam, tempted in a desolate wilderness, without food, remained faithful. Adam sinned by eating from the tree; the second Adam achieved atonement and reconciliation by his obedience on the

23. Kline, *By Oath Consigned*, 35.
24. Kline, *By Oath Consigned*, 36.
25. Kline, *By Oath Consigned*, 14–22; Horton, *Covenant and Salvation*, 12–29.

tree. For both there is judgment—on Adam, the consequence of sin; on Christ, in his mediatorial work on behalf of sinners. Whereas Adam was cast out of the garden and the return journey was debarred for him and his posterity (Gen. 3:22), Christ was openly vindicated in his resurrection and his elect people were raised in him.

Can the covenant of works continue in any form after the fall? Allowing for Christ's fulfilling the covenant of works as the second Adam, is that covenant operative for the fallen human race after the first Adam broke it? In the Mosaic covenant, the parties are Yahweh and Israel. Israel was already in covenant with Yahweh through the Abrahamic covenant. The land was given to Israel freely *by promise* (Gen. 12:1–3). In turn, the law was given to a people in covenant already by God's free grace. The preamble to the Ten Commandments reads:

> I am the LORD your God, who brought you out of the land of Egypt, out of the house of slavery.
> You shall have no other gods before me. (Ex. 20:2–3)

The process was not "do this and live" but "you are my people; therefore you shall do this, and in doing this you shall live."

Further, there was no sinless covenant head in the Mosaic covenant; it was made not with a representative person but with a community. The first Adam had forfeited God's favor; the second Adam was yet to come.

Third, this covenant did not proceed on the works principle requiring meritorious obedience. As soon as the covenant was enacted on Mount Sinai, Israel at the foot of the mountain was worshiping the golden calf. If this were a works covenant, it would have been over immediately. The subsequent history is one of continued and repetitive unfaithfulness on Israel's part and continued mercy and grace, patience, and forgiveness from the side of Yahweh. The land was given by free promise (Gen. 12:1, 7; 15:7–21) and retained despite repetitive rebellion.[26]

Fourth, if the Mosaic covenant had been based on a works principle, a schizoid character would have dogged the rest of the Old Testament—which aspect was Abrahamic and which Mosaic? Yet Kline embraces this

---

26. See, among many places, Psalm 78 for a catalog of such scenes, and the book of Judges for a record of decline and deliverance. Psalm 106 is also pertinent; in the face of the unrelenting disobedience of Israel, Yahweh, "for their sake . . . remembered his covenant, / and relented according to the abundance of his steadfast love" (v. 45).

point. He says, "The Sinaitic Covenant in itself, as a covenant ratified by Israel's oath, made law obedience by the Israelites themselves the way of life-inheritance, and yet in the Mosaic revelation as a whole law was accompanied by promise sealed by divine oath and offering *an alternative way of inheritance.*"[27] Kline reiterated this point—how clear it could have been at the time?—when he says "the administrative compatibility of the law and promise principles of inheritance, as joint elements within a single covenant, is explained by the fact that *they were alternates to one another.*"[28]

Were there ancillary consequences of the violated pre-fall covenant of works? After the covenant of works was broken, it expired. As Bavinck comments, "When humans broke the covenant of works, God replaced it with the greatly improved covenant of grace."[29] However, the effects of the broken covenant remained. The whole race participated in the death Adam earned. All in Adam are covenantally dead, children of wrath, inheriting condemnation, under the curse of the covenant of works (Eph. 2:1); only in Christ, in the covenant of grace, are they released. Notwithstanding, this did not represent an ongoing covenantal situation in which everlasting life was held out as a possibility on obedience. All were born as covenant breakers in a state of disobedience and condemnation. There were no further probationary periods. The sacrament of the covenant of life was no more; no promises remained from that covenant.

However, while that covenant was abolished, no mortal is outside its reach.[30] A war may be fought and ended, but the results for the losers, the wounded, and the bereaved continue. J. H. Heidegger (1633–1698) comments similarly when he says that the rule of God and his law cannot be overthrown by sin. But, Heidegger adds, man's obligation was as a creature to his Creator, by creation and prior to the covenant. So his continuing obligation is as a creature.[31] There is no way back to the garden after Adam was cast out, no chance to take his place and try again. Given this, there can be no active covenant of works.

---

27. Kline, *By Oath Consigned*, 32 (my italics).
28. Kline, *By Oath Consigned*, 33 (my italics).
29. Bavinck, *RD*, 3:65.
30. Francis Turretin, *Institutes of Elenctic Theology*, trans. George Musgrave Giger, ed. James T. Dennison Jr. (Phillipsburg, NJ: P&R, 1994), 2:191–92.
31. Joh. Heinrici Heidegger, *Corpus theologiae Christianae* (Zurich: Joh. Henrici Bodmeri, 1700), 371–72 (11.1).

However, the law of God, given in the covenant of works, remains. While the particular law in Genesis 2 is no longer applicable, nevertheless the law of God—of which it was a specific instance—reveals his perpetual requirements for the human race. It is expanded in the Decalogue, was obeyed by Christ on behalf of all under his headship, and remains the rule of life for all who are in him. It condemns all in Adam, who fell from the covenant of life. It transcends and outlasts that covenant. Apart from its relation to the obedience of the second Adam, its presence in subsequent covenants cannot denote a principle of inheritance by meritorious works as in the first covenant. The law still applies as a rule of life for believers in the new covenant, but their personal works are not the efficient cause of their obtaining the heavenly inheritance.

Failure to recognize this distinction between the law as it functioned in the covenant of works and the law as such is the root of a confusion that dogs this debate. Because the law of God was at the heart of the covenant of works/life, and since it continues to be operative, some conclude wrongly that the first covenant also remains in effect.

The relationship of law and gospel is complex and requires careful definition. The law and gospel were carefully distinguished by the Reformed. *Law* itself has several meanings in the Bible. It can refer to whatever God has instituted, to the doctrine of the Old and New Testaments, to the Old Testament as a whole, to God's demands, to the moral or ceremonial or civil law, to the Levitical priestly ministry, to a principle of seeking salvation by self-effort versus a principle of life led by the Holy Spirit, to the first five books of the Old Testament, to the Mosaic covenant, to the law of nature impressed on human hearts at creation, or to human law.[32] I refer here to the moral law.

First, as ways of salvation, law and gospel are in direct antithesis. Adam was in a very different situation than we who live under the covenant of grace; in his sinlessness, he was promised life by works of obedience, while for us it is—and can only be—by grace; for the breaking of the covenant of life excludes all possibility of our achieving salvation by our own efforts.

---

32. See Johannes Polyander's treatment *De lege Dei*, in Johannes Polyander et al., *Synopsis purioris theologiae, disputationibus quinquaginta duabus comprehensa* (Leiden: Ex officina Elzeverianus, 1625), 204–10.

Second, and on the other hand, our gratuitous salvation was achieved by Christ by means of his obedience to the law of God as second Adam. This reflects an inherent compatibility between law and grace.

Third, the law had the aim of convicting of sin and so leading sinners to Christ. From this, we are freed to obey the law, its righteous demands being met in those who live according to the Spirit (Rom. 8:3–4). Here again, law and gospel work together in a complementary manner. As Augustine wrote, "It is not by the law that the ungodly are made righteous but by grace. . . . The law was therefore given, in order that grace might be sought; grace was given, in order that the law might be fulfilled."[33]

Fourth, the law, in the sense of the Old Testament as a whole, contains the gospel. It is seen in the promises God made in his covenants, the provision for atonement in the sacrificial system, and the forbearance of God in the face of Israel's rebellious obstinacy. Indeed, the sacraments of the Mosaic covenant spoke of grace and deliverance, the Passover recalling rescue by Yahweh from Egypt, circumcision signifying regeneration by the Spirit.

Fifth, the New Testament, revealing the gospel in greater clarity, maintains and preserves the law as the rule of life for believers. In all but the first sense, the law and the gospel are complementary, not competitive.

However, it does not follow that because God's law is constant, the covenant of works is perpetually and universally operative, as—for example—Robert Rollock taught.[34] If it were, believers now would be subject to a "works principle" too. Alternatively, if believers are not subject to a works principle but the law is identified as a covenant of works, the law would cease to apply to them, as Venema considers VanDrunen to suggest is true outside the civil sphere.[35]

Calvin strongly opposed comparing law and gospel based upon a contrast between free imputation and the works principle. He wrote, "We refute those who always erroneously compare the law with the gospel by contrasting the merit of works with the free imputation of righteousness." And, in the same section, "the gospel did not so supplant the law as to bring forward a different way of salvation" for "where the whole law is

33. Augustine, *On the Spirit and the Letter* 19.43 (NPNF[1], 5:97).

34. Robert Rollock, *A Treatise of God's Effectual Calling*, trans. Henry Holland (London: Felix Kyngston, 1603), 1–27. Note Rollock's confusion between the law and the covenant of works, p. 17.

35. VanDrunen, "Natural Law and the Works Principle," esp. 313–14. See the critical comments of Venema, "The Mosaic Covenant," 96–98.

concerned, the gospel differs from it only in clarity of manifestation."[36] Therefore in the words of the WCF, law and grace or gospel are not polar opposites in the redemptive economy of God for they "sweetly comply."[37]

Differing views on the Mosaic covenant. There were four major views in classic Reformed theology on the status of this covenant, according to John Ball and Francis Turretin. Both comment that the standard teaching among the Reformed was that the covenant of grace "for manner of administration . . . is divers . . . but for substance it is one,"[38] for at all stages it has the same Mediator, faith, promises, and way of reconciliation.[39] The four positions are as follows:

1. *The Mosaic covenant was a covenant of works.* Rollock,[40] Perkins,[41] and Piscator took this position. Ball thought it unsound.[42] Turretin concludes, "It is one thing to live under a legal economy; another, however, to be under the law as a covenant or to be of the works of the law."[43]

2. *The Mosaic covenant was a subservient covenant to the covenant of grace.* John Cameron (1579–1625) was a leading exponent of this idea.[44] The subservient covenant prepared Israel for faith and the promise of the gospel covenant. It was neither a covenant of grace nor a covenant of works.[45] It agreed with the covenant of nature in terms of the parties, the condition, the stipulation, and the promise—both covenants leading to Christ—but the covenant of nature was made with all, whereas the subservient covenant was only with the Israelites.[46] They differed, among other ways, in the contrast between the law of nature and the Mosaic ceremonies.[47]

---

36. Calvin, *Institutes*, 2.9.4.
37. WCF, 19.7.
38. John Ball, *A Treatise of the Covenant of Grace* (London: Simeon Ash, 1645), 23.
39. Turretin, *Institutes*, 2:192–205.
40. Rollock, *Effectual Calling*, 21–24; Rollock, *Quaestiones et responsiones aliquot de foedere Dei, deque sacramento quod foederis Dei sigillum est* (Edinburgh: Henricus Charteris, 1596), A4b–A5b.
41. William Perkins, *Workes* (London: Iohn Legat, 1608), 1:32, 70; William Perkins, *Workes* (London: John Legat, 1631), 2:235.1c–2b, 2:237.1b, 2:245.1b, 2:251.1a.
42. Ball, *Treatise*, 93.
43. Turretin, *Institutes*, 2:255–56. This view is also opposed by the Formula Consensus Helvetica (1675), 25, composed by Heidegger and Turretin: "We disapprove therefore of the doctrine of those who fabricate for us three Covenants, the Natural, the Legal, and the Gospel Covenant, different in their whole nature and pith"; quoted in A. A. Hodge, *Outlines of Theology* (Grand Rapids, MI: Eerdmans, 1972), 663.
44. John Cameron, *The Threefold Covenant of God with Man*; bound with Samuel Bolton, *The True Bounds of Christian Freedome* (London: J. L. for Philemon Stephens, 1645), 353–401.
45. Cameron, *Threefold Covenant*, 381.
46. Cameron, *Threefold Covenant*, 382.
47. Cameron, *Threefold Covenant*, 383.

Cameron lists seventeen ways in which the Mosaic covenant differs from the covenant of grace.[48] In summary,

> The Old [subservient] covenant is that, whereby God doth require from the people of Israel, obedience of the Morall, Ceremoniall and Iudiciall Law; and to as many as doe give it to him, he promises all sorts of blessings in the possession of the land of Canaan; on the contrary, to as many as deny it him, he denounces, most severely, curses and death; and that for this end, that he might bring them to the Messias which was for to come.[49]

Cameron was regarded by some as close to Arminianism, but Muller correctly rebuffs this argument.[50] Cameron's distinction between absolute and conditional covenants was more in alignment with the hypothetical universalism that was within the bounds of Reformed orthodoxy at the time.[51] Ball concludes that it appears "the Divines of this opinion, make the Old Covenant differ from the new in substance, and kind."[52] Turretin states, "We do not think that the received opinion (which retains the twofold division . . .) ought to be discarded."[53] The proposal received no confessional support.

3. *The Mosaic covenant was part of the covenant of grace but differed in degree.* Most divines, Ball says, "hold the old and new Covenant to be one in substance and kind, to differ only in degrees: but in setting down the differences they speake so obscurely, that it is hard to find how they consent with themselves."[54] Some whose comments sound like what Ball describes are Amandus Polanus (1561–1610)[55] and Johannes Polyander (1568–1646).[56] Polyander distinguishes between the Old Testament and New in a strict sense, in which two alternative ways of salvation are offered, but restricts this to the circumstances and accidents,

---

48. Cameron, *Threefold Covenant*, 392–95.

49. Cameron, *Threefold Covenant*, 400–401.

50. Richard A. Muller, "Divine Covenants, Absolute and Conditional: John Cameron and the Early Orthodox Development of Reformed Covenant Theology," *MAJT* 17 (2006): 11–56.

51. Jonathan D. Moore, *English Hypothetical Universalism: John Preston and the Softening of Reformed Theology* (Grand Rapids, MI: Eerdmans, 2007); Robert Letham, "The Triune God, Incarnation, and Definite Atonement," in *From Heaven He Came and Sought Her*, ed. David Gibson and Jonathan Gibson (Wheaton, IL: Crossway, 2013), 437–60.

52. Ball, *Treatise*, 92–95.

53. Turretin, *Institutes*, 2:218; see also 2:262–69.

54. Ball, *Treatise*, 95; see also 95–102.

55. Amandus Polanus, *Syntagma theologiae Christianae* (Geneva: Petri Auberti, 1612), 2:321–23.

56. Polyander et al., *Synopsis*, 279–86.

The Covenant of Grace

holding simultaneously to the unity of the covenant in substance. He, like Polanus, foreshadows some of the interests of Kline.

4. *The Mosaic covenant was the covenant of grace accommodated to the time and the people.* This is Ball's position, contrary to Muller, who erroneously argues that Ball held that the Mosaic covenant was a subservient covenant, the second of the four alternatives.[57] Ball opposes the idea that anything after the fall can be called a covenant of works, and dismisses the idea of a subservient covenant, since "they make the Old Covenant differ from the new in substance, and kind, and not in degree."[58] Rather, Ball concludes:

> Some Divines hold the Old Testament, even the Law, as it was given upon Mount Sinai, to be the Covenant of Grace for substance, though propounded in a manner fitting to the state of that people, time and condition of the Church. . . . This I take to be the truth, and it may be confirmed by many and strong reasons out of the word of God.[59]

This is the position taken by WCF, 7.5.

Other views. Other theologians did not mention the pre-fall covenant and so could never have envisaged the possibility of the Mosaic covenant being a repetition of it.[60] The WCF, 7.5, regards the Mosaic covenant as an administration of the covenant of grace, adapted to the time of the law (cf. WLC, 33). This redemptive-historical distinction relates to the administration of the covenant, not to its substance. This point was brought out clearly by Calvin.[61] There is a difference between law and gospel, but also a basic compatibility.

Turretin (1623–1687) asserts that the covenant of grace is one in substance in the Old and New Testaments,[62] though dispensed in different ways.[63] The Decalogue is part of the covenant of grace; Turretin distances himself from any idea that it is a covenant of works.[64] In his

---

57. Muller, "Divine Covenants," 50.
58. Ball, *Treatise*, 93–95.
59. Ball, *Treatise*, 102; see also 103–37.
60. William Bucanus, *Institutions of Christian Religion, Framed out of Gods Word, and the Writings of the Best Divines* (London: George Snowdon and Leonell Snowdon, 1606), 104–11; Franciscus Junius, *Opera theologica* (Geneva, 1613), 1:2051–55; James Ussher, *A Body of Divinitie, or The Summe and Substance of Christian Religion* (London, 1645), 124–25, 157–59; Anthony Tuckney, *Praelectiones theologicae* (Amsterdam, 1679), 170–73. The list includes all who wrote before the doctrine of the covenant of works emerged, including Bucer, Bullinger, Calvin, and Vermigli.
61. Calvin, *Institutes*, 2.9.1–2.11.14.
62. Turretin, *Institutes*, 2:192–205.
63. Turretin, *Institutes*, 2:216–18.
64. Turretin, *Institutes*, 2:226–37.

Corpus theologiae Christianae (1700), J. H. Heidegger argues that the covenant of works was interrupted by sin but remains in terms of human obligation to obedience.[65] But this obligation was as a creature to the Creator, by creation and prior to the covenant of works, and so endures beyond that covenant.[66] Heidegger recognizes that there are many legal requirements in the Mosaic covenant.[67] But the Sinaitic covenant was not a law of works as in the covenant of works. Treating it that way was the error of the Jewish people. The Decalogue includes a law of works as a rule of sanctification.[68] After the fall, justification by works is impossible, and, according to Heidegger, it was impossible for God to make a covenant from which his people could inherit Canaan as a type of the heavenly inheritance.[69] More recently, A. A. Hodge[70] and Herman Bavinck[71] have taken the same position.

Clearly, a position with formal similarities to Kline's was held in Reformed orthodoxy, though it was a minority report. It was not adopted by any Reformed confession; confessions do not address every issue, nor do they exclude views that many might consider wrong but that may be within the bounds of acceptable doctrine.

Does law have priority? Underlying the claim that the Mosaic covenant is a covenant of works, in some sense or other, is the notion that God *primarily* and consistently relates to humanity on the basis of law and justice. Kline bases this notion on his doctrine of God: "Merciful he may be according to his sovereign will; but all his works are in righteousness and truth."[72] In this he makes justice an essential attribute while relegating love, goodness, and grace to arbitrary attributes. This is the account of Calvinism that was at the heart of James Torrance's unfortunate strictures, which we have seen to be misleading and wrong.[73]

---

65. Heidegger, *Corpus*, 370.
66. Heidegger, *Corpus*, 372.
67. Heidegger, *Corpus*, 461.
68. Heidegger, *Corpus*, 462.
69. "Praeterea Deus non potuit cum populo Israel sub conditione legis operum foedus pangere." Heidegger, *Corpus*, 463.
70. Hodge, *Outlines*, 370–77.
71. Bavinck, *RD*, 3:219–28.
72. Kline, *By Oath Consigned*, 33.
73. See chap. 12. James B. Torrance, "Covenant or Contract? A Study of the Theological Background of Worship in Seventeenth-Century Scotland," *SJT* 23 (1970): 51–76; Torrance, "The Incarnation and Limited Atonement," *EQ* 55 (1983): 82–94; taking a critical position against Torrance is Paul Helm, "The Logic of Limited Atonement," *SBET* 3 (1985): 50. See also Letham,

Although Kline wants to restrict the works principle to Israel's inheritance of Canaan and associated temporal blessings, he regards these as typological of the blessings of the covenant of grace. These blessings, received by grace through faith, are founded on Christ's meritorious obedience to the covenant of works as the second Adam. Israel would have received the typological blessings, such as Canaan, by meritorious law keeping according to a works principle. These, Kline has stated, are two alternative, antithetical ways of inheritance. But a type corresponds to the antitype. If the one is a type of the other, either the blessings of the covenant of grace are received by law keeping on the part of the recipients—in which case there is no gospel—or the temporal blessings of the Mosaic covenant were to be received by grace. The only other possibilities are either that law and grace work together, in distinct ways, or that the typical relationship is untenable.[74]

Moreover, there are two far-reaching problems with this position. First, it has consequences for the doctrine of God. If the claim that God's relationship to Adam before the fall was purely on the basis of law, justice, and merit were true, then one of two alternatives is possible. Either God revealed himself truly to Adam before the fall or he did not. If he did not reveal himself truly before the fall, the underlying structure of redemption would be undermined and God's faithfulness would be in question; how could we rely on him thereafter? Conversely, if God did reveal himself truly to Adam, and if this revelation was purely by law and justice, it suggests that the persons of the Trinity relate purely on the basis of law. Kline affirms that the relations between the Trinitarian persons in the pretemporal covenant are those of "simple justice."[75] This would seem to threaten the indivisibility of God. If, in order to act, the three persons must engage in a contractual manner, how can the doctrine of the inseparable operations be maintained? Behind that doctrine is the indivisibility of the Trinity and the identity of the essence. This claim needs further thought. Moreover, if justice is elevated above other attributes, how does this impinge on the simplicity of God, a doctrine held

The Work of Christ, 238. There is, of course, a vital point in what Kline says—one I support in the above reference—that by their natures neither can justice be abrogated nor mercy be required.

74. As James Dennison and others remark, "The mainstream Reformed tradition . . . is very uneasy with any construction that places God's people simultaneously under two antithetical principles of obedience. It is either works, or it is faith. It is either grace, or it is merit. It cannot be both at the same time." James T. Dennison Jr., Scott F. Sanborn, and Benjamin W. Swinburnson, "Merit or 'Entitlement' in Reformed Covenant Theology: A Review" *Kerux* 24, no. 3 (2009): 81.

75. Kline, "Covenant Theology," 4.

not only by Augustine and the West but also by the Cappadocians,[76] as recent scholarship has highlighted.[77]

A second problem is the dominance of extrabiblical material. Rather than such sources being used as secondary supports for scriptural doctrine, they are deployed as structural markers into which biblical teaching is placed. The Hittite suzerainty treaties are in view here. This in the face of the stern warnings by Yahweh to Israel to have nothing to do with the culture and practices of the Hittites![78] From a sharp contrast between suzerainty treaties and royal grants there thus arises a radical antithesis between the Mosaic and Abrahamic covenants. If the doctrine of the covenants must be mediated via the Hittites, what sources should govern our doctrine of atonement? This predilection for ancient Near Eastern parallels, while all the rage in the fifties and sixties of the last century, has for some time been eclipsed among Old Testament scholars.[79] Mendenhall's theories,[80] which Kline adopted,[81] have been all but abandoned since.[82]

Weeks argues that "the simple borrowing models that have been used . . . do not do justice to the complexity of the data."[83] The evidence suggests that in the late second millennium BC there is a lack of evidence of treaty forms in Canaan.[84] It is "practically impossible to judge whether covenants in Israel have any relation to treaties in the world outside."[85] Evidence from historians points to something more complex than a single covenant form.[86] Stephen Dempster follows Brevard Childs

76. Bavinck, *RD*, 2:173–77.
77. Robert Letham, *The Holy Trinity: In Scripture, History, Theology, and Worship* (Phillipsburg, NJ: P&R, 2004); Lewis Ayres, *Nicaea and Its Legacy: An Approach to Fourth-Century Trinitarian Theology* (Oxford: Oxford University Press, 2004); Ayres, *Augustine and the Trinity* (Cambridge: Cambridge University Press, 2010), 208–16; Bradley G. Green, *Colin Gunton and the Failure of Augustine: The Theology of Colin Gunton in the Light of Augustine* (Eugene, OR: Pickwick, 2011).
78. Ex. 23:23–24; Lev. 18:2–4; Deut. 7:1–5.
79. Noel Weeks, *Admonition and Curse: The Ancient Near Eastern Treaty/Covenant Form as a Problem in Inter-Cultural Relationships* (London: T&T Clark, 2004), 1.
80. G. F. Mendenhall, *Law and Covenant in Israel and the Ancient Near East* (Philadelphia: Biblical Colloquium, 1955).
81. Meredith G. Kline, *The Structure of Biblical Authority* (Grand Rapids, MI: Eerdmans, 1972).
82. Weeks, *Admonition and Curse*, 135.
83. Weeks, *Admonition and Curse*, 9.
84. Weeks, *Admonition and Curse*, 163.
85. Weeks, *Admonition and Curse*, 139.
86. Kenneth A. Kitchen, *On the Reliability of the Old Testament* (Grand Rapids, MI: Eerdmans, 2003). See Ronald S. Hendel, William W. Hallo, and Kenneth A. Kitchen, "The Kitchen Debate," *Biblical Archaeology Review* 31, no. 4 (2005): 48–53, for polarized views on Kitchen's work. Kitchen, an eminent Egyptologist, berates Old Testament scholars for being behind the times in their knowledge of historical learning in Ancient Near East studies. See James K. Hoffmeier,

in warning against the overuse of information about the wider historical context when he writes, "Childs makes an important point that the burgeoning information about the historical context needs to be carefully evaluated before it is automatically appropriated since uncritical acceptance can lead to hermeneutical distortions."[87] Ernest Nicholson, in a review, considers Weeks's book "an invaluable contribution, which, indeed, had it been written forty to fifty years ago would have spared much paper and print."[88] In short, there are significant problems with the republication theory.

15.6 The New Covenant

The new covenant fulfills all the preceding redemptive covenants. They all point to Christ, the Son made flesh. He is the offspring, featured in the Abrahamic covenant, in whom all the nations are blessed (Matt. 1:1; Gal. 3:16). He fulfilled the law, expressed in the Mosaic covenant, for he obeyed God's law throughout, his is the one sacrifice effective for sins, and he is the temple, the place where God and his people meet. He also is the One who inherits the throne of David and whose kingdom stands and grows forever (2 Sam. 7:8–16). He is the Son of David as much as the son of Abraham (Matt. 1:1).[89] In Christ all God's promises meet; in Christ all requirements of God's covenant from our side were fulfilled.

The new covenant was inaugurated through the sacrificial death of Jesus. As Moses sprinkled the people with the blood of the covenant, so Jesus instituted the Supper with the words "this is my blood of the covenant" (Matt. 26:26–29). Jeremiah had looked for the new covenant, with its promise of permanence, in contrast to the Mosaic economy, which was marked by rebellion on the part of Israel. The knowledge of

---

Ancient Israel in Sinai: The Evidence for the Authenticity of the Wilderness Tradition (New York: Oxford University Press, 2011), and Kenneth A. Kitchen and Paul J. N. Lawrence, *Treaty, Law and Covenant in the Ancient Near East* (Weisbaden: Harrassowitz, 2012), for important recent works of relevance here.

87. Stephen Dempster, "A Member of the Family or a Stranger? A Review Article of Jeffrey A. Niehaus, *Ancient Near Eastern Themes in Biblical Theology*," *Them* 35 (2010): 228–37.

88. Ernest Nicholson, "Review of Noel Weeks, *Admonition and Curse: The Ancient Near Eastern Treaty/Covenant Form as a Problem in Inter-Cultural Relationships*," *JTS* 57 (2006): 608–10.

89. Hence, the division of his genealogy: Abraham to David, David to the exile, and the exile to his birth. According to the Rabbinic practice of *gematria*, the numerical value of the Hebrew consonants in David's name adds up to fourteen, indicating that the three divisions of fourteen generations (there were many more than these in actuality) signify it is a Davidic genealogy. The inclusion of Gentiles (Rahab, Ruth) highlights the promise to Abraham of blessing to the nations.

God would be universal among God's people, and effective atonement made, the memory of sins being ultimately removed (Jer. 31:31–33).

The letter to the Hebrews reflects on this. Jesus is the Mediator of a better covenant, founded on better promises, having offered one sacrifice for all time that deals once and for all with human sin (Heb. 8:1–10:14). In Hebrews 8, the Old Testament priestly system is in view. Its sacrifices could never have been intrinsically efficacious, given that they were animal offerings. In contrast, Christ is both the Creator God (Heb. 1:1–14) and fully man (Heb. 2:5–18; 4:14–16), holy and obedient, and thus qualified to make atonement. This he has done effectively and definitively. In stark contrast, the Mosaic covenant was old, obsolete, and about to be ended; the events of AD 70 were public evidence of the fact.

That this is not an absolute contrast is evident from Paul's comments in 2 Corinthians 3. There he compares and contrasts his own apostolic ministry and that of Moses. Paul is a second Moses.[90] The Mosaic covenant, as a covenant, was distinguished by the law engraved on stone tablets. As a covenantal administration, it was powerless to change people. It pronounced what pleased God and what was sin, but it could do nothing to effect change. It could only condemn the sinner. In contrast Paul's ministry is one of life, for it is a ministry of the Holy Spirit transforming us into the glory of God (v. 18). Moreover, the law which was written on stone, is now written on human hearts by the Holy Spirit; in covenantal terms, there is a quantum advance. Yet there is also continuity. Moses's face shone with the glory of God when he returned from the mountain, even though the glory was fading. While there is immeasurably greater glory in the new covenant ministry (v. 18), it is a matter of degree rather than kind, for there is glory in both.

The new covenant comes to its consummate realization in the new heavens and the new earth (Rev. 21:1–3). Its members are the elect people of God, drawn from every nation on the face of the earth, with Christ, the second Adam, as their leader (WLC, 31, 87, 90). In terms of the present day, the visible church consists of all who profess faith in Christ and their children (WCF, 25.2).

This is in contrast to the arguments proposed by dispensationalism and the self-styled new covenant theology. Both these positions maintain

---

90. Peter R. Jones, "The Apostle Paul: Second Moses to the New Covenant Community," in *God's Inerrant Word: An International Symposium on the Trustworthiness of Scripture*, ed. John Warwick Montgomery (Minneapolis: Bethany Fellowship, 1974), 219–41.

that there was a radical break with the past in the coming of Christ. Consequently, the moral law, exemplified in the Decalogue, being part of the Mosaic covenant, is jettisoned in the new covenant, since that is a covenant of grace. Instead, we fulfill "the law of Christ," although it is difficult to see what the content of that may be if it is not to be identified with the Ten Commandments. That requires a discussion of the law.

15.7   The Law

The threefold classification of *ceremonial*, *civil*, and *moral laws* has become the standard understanding in the Reformed churches. However, its roots are far more extensive than that. It is the uniform Christian understanding and reaches back into the Old Testament itself for its theological basis.[91]

All ten commandments relate to ordinances or circumstances found in creation: humanity's relationship to God, the family, life, marriage, property, personal reputations, and internal desires. The Sabbath commandment was based on the work of God, in whatever manner the six days of creation are understood.

In turn, the Decalogue anticipates the eschaton; the Sabbath is now prospective, as we look for the resurrection of the dead and the life everlasting (Heb. 4:9) and thus is at the start of the week rather than the end. Christ's promise of rest to those who labor anticipates our sharing God's eternal rest (Matt. 11:28–30; cf. Gen. 2:1–3; Rev. 14:13). The new covenant consists, in part, of God's law being written on our hearts (Jer. 31:31–33).

15.7.1   *The Law in the Covenant of Grace*[92]

In Reformed theology, the law is seen as the rule of life for believers. Calvin described this as its principal use. Here we are talking about the Decalogue and its entailments, not the ceremonial or the civil law, nor the law in covenantal terms.

This does not mean that the law has any inherent power to change us. Paul establishes this point in Romans 7:1–8:8. The law was weak, not

---

91. Philip Ross, *From the Finger of God: The Biblical and Theological Basis for the Threefold Division of the Law* (Fearn: Mentor, 2010).

92. This section and the next build on Robert Letham, "Lighting the Way: The Didactic Use of the Law," Ligonier Ministries, March 1, 2011, https://www.ligonier.org/learn/articles /lighting-way-didactic-use-law/.

because of any defect in it but because of our sinful nature. It exposes our sin but does not provide the remedy; it exacerbates our sinful inclinations not by its own intent but incidentally due to the wickedness of our hearts. Only the Holy Spirit can give us new hearts and enable us, in union with Christ, to obey God.

The "third use of the law" asserts that the law is our rule of life as Christian believers. This is because—as noted above—it is based on creation ordinances concerning the worship of God, work and rest, marriage and the family, life, private property, and so on. It is rooted in the law of nature impressed on the human heart at creation and so is applicable to all people at all times. The law exposes what sin is and so warns us to avoid it. Simultaneously and conversely, its negations express positive requirements and point us to what is pleasing to God. The first four commandments relate to the worship of the one living God; in the image he has chosen (Jesus Christ); in sincerity, faith, and awe; and on his appointed day. The rest of the commandments require appropriate respect for those in God-given authority; the preservation of life, marriage, property, and personal reputations; and contentment with God's gracious provisions. These are expressions of love—toward God our Creator and Redeemer, and toward people, in supporting and developing their well-being.

As such, the law expresses the unchanging will of God for his creatures and is no more open to change than God himself is. Not only does the Decalogue express God's will for humanity in creation, but it also continues to the end of the age. The promise of the new covenant given through Jeremiah affirms that God will write his laws on our hearts (Jer. 31:31–33; Rom. 8:1–9; 2 Cor. 3:1–4:6). Jesus intensifies the law in the Sermon on the Mount against rabbinic externalization, applying it to thoughts, words, and attitudes. He severely warns any who think it is abrogated (Matt. 5:17–20). His reduction of the law to two great commandments (Matt. 22:34–40) is not meant to replace the Decalogue; instead, "Matthew probably interpreted the double commandment to love as a summary of the Decalogue,"[93] for the rest of the commandments depend on the two greatest.[94] Jesus summarizes the whole law in

---

93. W. D. Davies Jr. and Dale C. Allison, *A Critical and Exegetical Commentary on the Gospel according to Saint Matthew* (Edinburgh: T&T Clark, 1988), 3:245.

94. R. T. France, *The Gospel according to Matthew: An Introduction and Commentary* (Leicester: Inter-Varsity Press, 1985), 318–20.

a couple of comprehensive statements, placing it in the context of love. Obedience to the law in the true sense is indicative of love for God and other people. It describes how the grace of love is to be expressed.

New Testament writers also reiterate the "ten words" and apply them to their contexts. Paul affirms that the law is spiritual: holy, just, and good (Rom. 7:12). However, by nature we are sinful and weak and cannot keep it. Notwithstanding, the Holy Spirit changes us and enables us to fulfill its righteous requirements (Rom. 8:1–4). James uses it to stress the details of Christian living; every commandment is of vital significance (James 2:8–12). The author of Hebrews indicates that the Sabbath commandment remains, pointing us to the future eternal rest we will share with God in Christ, entering the rest he enjoyed at creation (Heb. 3:7–4:11). Since the Sabbath explicitly looks back to creation (Ex. 20: 8–11), it is far more extensive in its realm of authority than to Israel alone and so anticipates the consummation of the new creation in which the redeemed will share the delight God has in his transcendent and finished work.

This has been the consistent teaching of the Christian church. It is not a prerogative of a certain branch of Reformed theology.[95] Despite popular misconceptions, Luther taught that while believers were no longer under the law, they continue to need the preaching of the law. Melanchthon took this further, and the Formula of Concord (1576) expressed believers' need for the law insofar as they are still fleshly.[96] Similarly, the Thirty-Nine Articles of the Church of England (1563, 1571) state that "no Christian man whatsoever is free from the obedience of the commaundementes, which are called morall."[97] Rome argues similarly, in its catechism, and earlier at the Council of Trent, referring back to Augustine as an authority.[98] Indeed, as Sofia Cavelletti remarks, "From the start the church assigned the Decalogue a special place in catechesis, as a privileged and universally valid expression of the divine will."[99] As early as Irenaeus, there was an insistence that the Decalogue was of permanent validity.[100] As Augustine wrote, "Grace is pointed at by the law, in order that the law may be fulfilled by grace."[101] This is evidenced

---

95. WCF, 19.
96. Art. 6, Schaff, *Creeds*, 3:130–35.
97. Art. 7. Schaff, *Creeds*, 3:492.
98. CCC, 1961–64, 2052–50.
99. EECh, 1:222.
100. Irenaeus, *Against Heresies* 4.16 (ANF, 1:480–82).
101. Augustine, *On the Grace of God and Original Sin* 1.10.9 (NPNF[1], 5:221). See Matt. 5:17–19.

in that the Ten Commandments are one of the three integral features of Christian catechetical literature through the centuries.

At various times, antinomian groups have arisen to trumpet the claim that Christ has ended the law. This would strike at the heart of the gospel, for the atonement and justification are based on the continuing validity of the moral law, which Christ obeyed for us in union with us. This is pertinent today, with the rise in evangelical circles of the "new covenant theology," a movement contrary to the Christian tradition and its distillation of biblical exegesis through the ages, whether in Protestantism, Rome, or the Patristic era.

15.7.2   A Brief Summary of the Law

The first commandment requires worship to be directed to Yahweh, the God and Father of our Lord Jesus Christ alone. All other foci that dominate us are idolatrous.

The second commandment, in forbidding worship through man-made images, directs us to worship God in the image he has presented, Jesus Christ his Son, one with the Father from eternity.

The third commandment prohibits taking the name of the Lord our God in an empty manner; it directs us to sincerity, faith, and reverent awe in addressing him.

The fourth commandment requires us to observe God's own patterns of work and rest. He labored in creating the universe and then rested, delighting in all he had done. Now that Christ has come, the commandment is more prospective than retrospective. To those who are weary he gives rest as he is one with the Father (Matt. 11:25–30). We look forward to the resurrection and the life of the world to come, in the consummated new creation. There remains a *sabbatismos* (σαββατισμός) for the people of God (Heb. 4:9). We do so on the first day of the week with the covenanted people of God.

The fifth commandment requires age-appropriate respect for our parents and, by extension, respect for properly constituted authority ordained by God. God has determined that authority be exercised on his behalf by humans, and we are to give the intelligent respect due to the family and to other organs of legitimate rule. There is a promise attached to this command; the implication is that settled order is a good provided by God, intended as a means for the preservation of life.

The sixth commandment points to the sanctity of human life, which is not to be taken, outside of just, public contexts such as wars and certain capital offenses. This commandment directs us to do all we can to preserve and enhance human life.

The seventh commandment defends the creation ordinance of marriage between a man and a woman. This is intended by God for the good of the human race. Adultery, fornication, and homosexuality are all instances of an attack on marriage. Same-sex "marriage" is a figment of social engineering; procreation is an integral part of marriage and requires a male and a female to participate. The commandment directs us to enhance the creation ordinance of marriage and its particular instances.

The eighth commandment safeguards private property. God is the owner of all creation and has entrusted small segments of it to humans as stewards. This commandment declares that not only is the seizure of what belongs to another offensive in God's sight, but also the expropriation of property by private or public corporate entities or by one country over another is sin.

The ninth commandment is intended to protect personal reputations. It forbids false witness against another in a law court. It requires us to do all we can to maintain the good name of other people.

The tenth commandment explicitly applies to our inward attitudes. It warns against greed and a desire to possess what rightfully belongs to someone else. It urges upon us contentment with the circumstances in which God has placed us.

By giving us his law, God has set us free from bondage to human opinions; it is a charter for Christian liberty. That is why the WCF's chapter on the law of God is followed directly by one on Christian liberty; bound in conscience to God's law, we are free from human dictates when they conflict with it or seek to usurp it (WCF, 19–20). In short, the law defines for us what is pleasing to God and what is sin. It is a map, explaining to us how our sanctification is to take shape. Consequently, Paul writes that living according to the Spirit entails the just requirement of the law to be fulfilled in us (Rom. 8:1–8). We are set free from the law of sin and death in order to obey God. The Spirit uses the law for that purpose. We neglect it to our eternal peril. It marks the path of life; all other ways are ways of death.

Further Reading

Murray, John. *The Covenant of Grace*. London: Tyndale Press, 1954.

Venema, Cornelis P. *Christ and Covenant Theology: Essays on Election, Republication, and the Covenants*. Phillipsburg, NJ: P&R, 2017.

Study Questions

1. How would you describe the continuity between the Abrahamic and new covenants?

2. What relationship, if any, does the Mosaic covenant have to the pre-fall creation covenant, otherwise called the covenant of life or of works?

3. What is at stake in the question of the continuity of the Decalogue in the new covenant?

4. Who are the members of the covenant of grace?

PART 6

CHRIST, THE SON OF GOD

Thou art the everlasting Word,
the Father's only Son;
God manifestly seen and heard,
and heaven's beloved one.
Worthy, O Lamb of God art thou
that every knee to thee should bow.

Josiah Conder

16

Incarnation (1)

Biblical Teaching

The incarnation is a great mystery, transcending our capacities to comprehend. It entails the eternal Son taking into union a human nature, conceived by the Holy Spirit and born of the Virgin Mary. Why was it necessary that the Son, rather than the Father or the Spirit, become incarnate? The biblical evidence for Jesus's humanity is overwhelming, and there is no dispute about its reality. The text of John 1 and Luke 1 indicates that in becoming man, the Son or Logos remained who he eternally was and is. In taking human nature into permanent union, the Son grants eternal life to the human race.

⳨

For it was fitting for the creator of the universe, who by the economy of his incarnation became what by nature he was not, to preserve without change both what he himself was by nature and what he became in his incarnation. . . . This is the great and hidden mystery, at once the blessed end for which all things are ordained. It is the divine purpose conceived before the beginning of created beings. In defining it we would say that this mystery is the preconceived goal for which everything exists, but which itself exists on account of nothing . . . a super-infinite plan infinitely preexisting the ages.[1]

---

1. Maximus the Confessor, *Ad Thalassium* 60, in *On the Cosmic Mystery of Jesus Christ: Selected Writings from St. Maximus the Confessor*, trans. Paul M. Blowers and Robert Louis Wilken (Crestwood, NY: St Vladimir's Seminary Press, 2003), 124–25.

> While the incarnation falls within the structures of our spatio-temporal humanity in this world, it also falls within the Life and Being of God—that is its astounding implication which needs to be thought out very carefully.[2]

We discussed the deity of Christ in chapter 2. You might want to refresh your memory by returning there. At the center of the gospel is the incarnation. This dominating fact that "the Word became flesh and dwelt among us" (John 1:14) bestrides the pages of the New Testament. As Paul describes it, "in Christ God was reconciling the world to himself" (2 Cor. 5:19). Without the incarnation, we could not be saved. It was the incarnate Christ who died on the cross, rose from the dead, ascended into heaven, and is now at God's right hand making intercession for us. In the words of Christopher Wordsworth,

> You have raised our human nature,
> in the clouds to God's right hand.[3]

Aquinas wrote, "Nothing more marvelous can be thought of than this divine work: that the true God, the Son of God, should become true man."[4]

Underlying this mystery is the astonishing point that God alone could not save us. Putting it another way, apart from the Son's coming among us as man, we could not be saved. This is not for any lack or deficiency on God's part; he has the power to do as he pleases. But since he declares himself to be just, salvation by fiat would have been inconsistent with his character. The first question in our deliverance from sin and death was the satisfaction of God's own justice. Being who he is, he could save us only in accordance with the dictates of his own character. His freedom is to act in harmony with who he is and not be constrained by anything external. Atonement for sin accords with divine justice. The sin of the first Adam could be atoned only by a second who did not bear the guilt and corruption inherited from the first. The Savior needed to be man, a perfect and righteous man. This is expressed eloquently by the Heidelberg Catechism (1563):

---

2. Thomas F. Torrance, *The Christian Doctrine of God: One Being, Three Persons*, 2nd ed. (Edinburgh: T&T Clark, 2016), 95.

3. From the hymn "See the Conqueror Mounts in Triumph" (1862).

4. "Nihil enim mirabilius excogitari potest divinitus factum quam quod verus Deus Dei Filius fieret homo verus." Aquinas, *SCG* 4.27.1.

Q. 15. What kind of mediator and deliverer should we look for then?

A. He must be truly human and truly righteous, yet more powerful than all creatures, that is, he must also be true God.

Q. 16. Why must he be truly human and truly righteous?

A. God's justice demands it: man has sinned, man must pay for his sin, but a sinner can not pay for others.

Q. 17. Why must he also be true God?

A. So that, by the power of his deity, he might bear the wrath of God in his humanity and earn for us and restore to us righteousness and life.

Discussion has surrounded whether *any* of the Trinitarian persons could have become incarnate.[5] It is hardly beyond God's capabilities. However, in *De incarnatione Verbi*, Anselm argues that it was supremely fitting, or appropriate, for the Son to become incarnate, rather than the Father or the Holy Spirit. In effect, Anselm deems it more than appropriate, effectively necessary, not through any external constraint on God but by necessity of his nature. First, Anselm establishes *that* only the Son became incarnate. Later, he argues that *if* either the Father or the Holy Spirit had become flesh, there would have been two Sons. If the Father were incarnate, the Son would be the virgin's grandson, and the Father would be the grandson of the virgin's parents. This would be inappropriate for God, and "there cannot be any least inappropriate thing in God."[6]

We must bear in mind the context of the incarnation. The human race was plunged into the mire of sin, guilty before God, and under his wrath. There was no other way for it to be delivered other than by the incarnation, life, atoning death, and ascension of the incarnate Son.

Maximus the Confessor summarizes the received teaching of the church:

The only-begotten Son, one of the holy and consubstantial Trinity, who is perfect God by nature, has become a perfect human being in accordance with his will, by truly assuming flesh that is consubstantial with us and endowed with a rational soul and mind from the holy

5. Anselm, *De fide Trinitatis et de incarnatione Verbi* 3.27–29 (PL, 158:276–77).

6. Anselm, "On the Incarnation of the Word," in Brian Davies, *Anselm of Canterbury: The Major Works* (Oxford: Oxford University Press, 1998), 250–51. "Quoniam ergo quamlibet parvum inconveniens in Deo est impossibile, non debuit alia Dei persona incarnari quam filius" (PL, 158:276).

Theotokos and ever-Virgin. He united it properly and inseparably to himself in accordance with the hypostasis, . . . Remaining God and consubstantial with the Father, when he became flesh, he became double, so that being double by nature, he had kinship by nature with both extremes, and preserved the natural difference of his own parts each from the other.[7]

16.1 The Eternal Son and the Incarnation

It was necessary that the Son become incarnate rather than the Father or the Holy Spirit. Anselm's argument that only the Son could become incarnate refuted Roscelin's idea that either the three are three separate things or the Father and the Spirit became incarnate with the Son. Anselm sees the latter as Sabellian; it gives no grounds for any personal distinctions.[8] Contrary to Roscelin, he maintains that the fact that the Son alone became incarnate does not mean that the three persons are three things. Nor does it imply that if the three persons are one thing, all three became incarnate.[9]

Anselm proceeds to discuss the reasons why it was the Son who became incarnate. No other divine person could have become incarnate since there is nothing inappropriate in God.[10] Since the Son was incarnate, and God acts in a suitable way, no other course of action was viable. Underlying this is that God always does what is best. Furthermore, since the incarnate one was to intercede for humanity, it is more intelligible *for us* that that person be the Son pleading with his Father.[11] Further, Anselm cites Philippians 2:7, stating that none of the three more appropriately emptied himself than the Son.[12] In this, Anselm affirms what Augustine said centuries earlier in reply to a question from Nebridius.[13] What was fitting or appropriate was effectively a moral necessity, Anselm using *oportet* and *convenio*, not to imply any constraint on God but, rather, as a corollary of God's character, the relation of the Son to the Father in

7. Maximus, *Opusculum* 7 (*PG*, 91:73B-C), cited in Christopher A. Beeley, *The Unity of Christ: Continuity and Conflict in Patristic Tradition* (New Haven, CT: Yale University Press, 2012), 297.
8. Anselm, *De fide* 3, in Davies, *Anselm*, 241–43.
9. Anselm, *De fide* 6, in Davies, *Anselm*, 245–47.
10. Anselm, *De fide*, 10; Davies, *Anselm*, 250–52; *PL*, 158:276.
11. "Est et aliud, cur magis conveniat Filio incarnatio quam alii." Anselm, *De fide* 10, in Davies, *Anselm*, 251; *PL*, 158:277.
12. "Nulla igitur trium personarum Dei congruentius semetipsum exinanivit formam servi accipiens . . . quam Filii." *Anselm, De fide* 10, in Davies, *Anselm*, 252; *PL*, 158:277.
13. Augustine, *Letter 11* 2 (*NPNF*[1], 1:229).

the indivisible Trinity, and the nature of redemption.[14] Others, such as Athanasius, Augustine, and Aquinas, held that it was simply appropriate or "fitting" for the Son to become incarnate.[15]

The incarnation establishes the compatibility of God and humanity. As Anselm argued against Roscelin, in Christ there is not One who is God and one who is a human being. Instead, the very same One who is the human being is God.[16] The Son assumed into union *a human nature*, not a human person; the Son and the assumed human nature are the same person. While the Creator is infinite and the creature finite—the Creator-creature distinction remains inviolable—God has established a compatibility between himself and humanity, such that the humanity of Christ is the humanity of the eternal Son.

This is crucial. If the Creator-creature distinction applied absolutely, an infinite chasm would preclude that unbreakable union between God and humanity in Christ; we would end up with Nestorianism and could not be saved.

Since the Son found it possible to live as man, we must conclude that God made humanity in such a manner as to be capable of union with him in Christ. This is a vast mystery; human personality is analogous to the divine, neither identical or mingled nor alien. The creation of humanity, in which God breathes into Adam's nostrils the breath of life (Gen. 2:7), and the final goal of participation in the divine nature (2 Pet. 1:4) point to this.[17]

There is personal continuity between the eternal and the incarnate Son. Following the Christological controversies, the church affirmed that the eternal Son had taken into union a human nature, body and soul, conceived by the Holy Spirit in the womb of the Virgin Mary. This is not a case of two separate natures coming together but rather the assumption into unbreakable union by the person of the Son of a human nature. We will consider this in the next chapter.

---

14. G. R. Evans, *Anselm* (London: Geoffrey Chapman, 1989), 79; David S. Hogg, *Anselm of Canterbury: The Beauty of Theology* (Aldershot: Ashgate, 2004), 157–60, 167–70.

15. Athanasius, *On the Incarnation* 13–14; Athanasius, *On the Incarnation: The Treatise De Incarnatione Verbi Dei*, trans. Sister Penelope Lawson (New York: Macmillan, 1946), 23–24; Augustine, *De Trinitate* 4.27 (NPNF[1], 3:83; *PL*, 42:862–63); Aquinas, *ST* 1a.43.5, 3a.3.8.

16. Anselm, *De fide* 11 (*PL*, 158:279).

17. Sergius Bulgakov, *The Wisdom of God: A Brief Summary of Sophiology* (London: Williams and Norgate, 1937), 126–31. Bulgakov was highly speculative and controversial, but in this he has some important things to say, among others.

The most significant architect of this settlement was Cyril of Alexandria. He wrote of an ontological union that involved no change in the Son himself, for "the Word who is God came down out of heaven and entered our likeness . . . while ever remaining what he was."[18] The result is an "inseparable union," "an indissoluble union."[19] Referring to Cyril's writings before the Nestorian crisis ever arose, Weinandy puts it like this: for Cyril, "Jesus is one ontological entity, and the one ontological entity that Jesus is is the one person of the Son of God existing as a complete and authentic man."[20] So "the incarnational act does not bring about a union of natures, but rather it is an act by which the humanity is united substantially to the person of the Word."[21] Jesus is the same Son who existed eternally with the Father and who came to exist as man.[22] Hence, in terms of his personal identity—*who* he is—he is the eternal Son, one of the Trinity according to the flesh, and his humanity—both body and soul—is that of the Son.

16.2   The Word Became Flesh: John 1:14[23]

In the incarnation, eternity and time intersect, Creator and creature are conjoined, God and man are united. Athanasius wrote these immortal words:

> It is, then, proper for us to begin the treatment of this subject by speaking of the creation of the universe, and of God its artificer, that so it may be duly perceived that the renewal of creation has been the work of the self-same Word that made it at the beginning. For it will appear not inconsonant for the Father to have wrought its salvation in Him by whose means he made it.[24]

The use of ἐγένετο,[25] "became," in John 1:14 indicates something new for the Word (Logos). He remained the same, but he entered a new

---

18. Cyril of Alexandria, *On the Unity of Christ*, trans. John Anthony McGuckin (Crestwood, NY: St Vladimir's Seminary Press, 1995), 61 (also *PG*, 75:1269); Thomas G. Weinandy, "Cyril and the Mystery of the Incarnation," in *The Theology of St. Cyril of Alexandria: A Critical Appreciation*, ed. Thomas G. Weinandy (London: T&T Clark, 2003), 27–28.
19. Cyril, *The Unity of Christ*, 77 (*PG*, 75:1289).
20. Weinandy, "Cyril," 30.
21. Weinandy, "Cyril," 41.
22. Weinandy, "Cyril," 43; See Cyril, *The Unity of Christ*, 107–16.
23. This section, on John 1, and the following one, on Luke 1, are abbreviated versions of sections in my book *The Message of the Person of Christ: The Word Made Flesh* (Nottingham: Inter-Varsity Press, 2013).
24. Athanasius, *Incarnation* 1.4 (*NPNF*², 4:36).
25. *egeneto*.

realm. In verses 1–4, John uses the imperfect of εἰμί for the Word, indicating continuance, but employs γίνομαι,[26] "become," for the creation (v. 3); all things *became* through him. John uses γίνομαι again for John the Baptist (v. 6). In verse 14 the Word is also said *to become*, existing as all other things he had created. Yet his becoming is, as Schnackenburg insists, a unique event.[27]

The difference is this. The Word's becoming did not happen to him, as John's becoming happened to him; the Word chose the becoming in view in John 1. The subject is ὁ λόγος, the Word, and continues to be so in the following clauses. The Word is the active agent throughout. He who always was and is, who is with God and who is God, the Creator who is life itself, became flesh but continues to be who he always was.

Superficially, it might seem that the Word changed into flesh, into humanity, by ceasing to be the Word, a metamorphosis like that of a caterpillar changing into a butterfly. But this is excluded by the fact that the Word continues to be the subject of all that follows. Again, it might be suggested that the Word mingled with flesh, so forming a third substance, an amalgam, the way ingredients in a recipe are mixed and become something other than what they were. However, such a mixture would be of a different kind. Again, John states that it was the Word, not some composite entity, that lived and was seen.

What, then, does John mean by the Word's becoming *flesh*? The physicality of humanity is evidently included, but there is something more than simply the flesh and blood of a human body. The flesh represents humanity in its weakness and dependence, creaturely existence in its fragility in contrast to the living Creator, human nature in its trajectory of decay.[28] The Jews considered humans to be psychosomatic unities, body and soul, and this Jesus most certainly was. He grew tired and hungry (John 4:4). He was distressed in the presence of death (John 11:33–35). He conversed with others (1 John 1:1). He assumed and incorporated human nature, body and soul, into union with himself such that it was his own. He remained the Word. What is there, and who is there, after the ἐγένετο, the becoming, is the same as what was there and who was there before.

---

26. *ginomai.*

27. Rudolf Schnackenburg, *The Gospel according to St John*, vol. 1, *Introduction and Commentary on Chapters 1–4*, trans. Kevin Smyth (Tunbridge Wells, Kent: Burns & Oates, 1968), 266.

28. Barnabas Lindars, *The Gospel of John*, The New Century Bible Commentary (Grand Rapids, MI: Eerdmans, 1972), 93–94; Schnackenburg, *John*, 267–68.

The difference is that there is now an addition. The Word now has a full human nature.[29] In the words of Paul, he who was—and eternally is—"in the form of God" has now added "the form of a servant" (Phil. 2:6–8). He has not ceased to be in the form of God. There is no subtraction, only addition. It is the Word who is the subject of the whole event.

As to the question of *who* is Jesus of Nazareth, what is his personal identity, he is the eternal Word of the Father, the Son of God, one with the Father from eternity. If we change the question and ask of *what* he consists, what is the manner of his existence, he is the Son of God incarnate in human nature.[30] The Word is the personal subject; it is flesh that *is added—permanently.*

He lived in a tent among us. In the Old Testament Yahweh dwelt in the tabernacle inserted into the innermost part of the temple, at the heart of the covenant relationship with Israel. Now the Word has his permanent tent dwelling among his people; Jesus Christ is the place where God and they meet, the center and focus of covenant worship. True worship is in the Spirit and in the truth, the incarnate Christ (John 4:21–24).[31] God takes the initiative; it is his work throughout. Jesus displays the grace and truth of God, pointing to God's loyalty to his covenant and its promises.[32]

He was seen by apostolic witnesses. "We have seen his glory," wrote John (John 1:14). The law required two or three witnesses to establish a matter as true; here there is a superfluity. First are the apostles, including John himself. He refers here to the transfiguration, where, together with Peter and James, John saw Jesus's appearance changed into dazzling glory, a preview of his glorification.[33] Yahweh's glory, revealed in part to Israel, is now fully embodied in Jesus Christ. Humans could not look on the glory of Yahweh and live (Ex. 33:20), but in Jesus this is a reality.

However, Jesus's glory was radically different than expected. He did not seek his own advancement, for he came as a servant, washing his

---

29. The idea of flesh (*sarx*) as corrupt and sinful, a theme prominent in Paul and evident in 1 John 2:16, is not in view here; see Schnackenburg, *John*, 267–68.

30. The best description of the Christology of John that I have read is Thomas Weinandy's description of the Christology of Cyril of Alexandria, in Weinandy, "Cyril."

31. Note Basil's striking turn of phrase, referring to the Spirit as the place of the saints, mentioning expressly John 4:21–24; Basil of Caesarea, *On the Holy Spirit* 26.62.

32. Lindars, *John*, 95.

33. C. K. Barrett, *The Gospel according to St John: An Introduction with Commentary and Notes on the Greek Text*, 2nd ed. (London: SPCK, 1978), 166.

disciples' feet, the action of a Gentile slave, the lowest of the low (John 13:1–20). His glorification was at the cross where he hung as a condemned criminal (John 12:20–33). The Word, in becoming flesh, freely gave himself to self-abandonment by the Father so that we might become the children of God (John 20:31).

The incarnation is the ultimate revelation of God. We cannot know God as God. No one has seen God as he is in himself. He is invisible (Ex. 33:20; 1 Tim. 1:17; 6:16). He revealed himself as man, on our level, in our nature. Jesus Christ has made God known. The expression "only begotten God" (ὁ μονογενὴς Θεός) has greater textual support than the variant "only begotten Son," supported as it is by both the Nestlé-Aland 28th edition and the UBS 4th edition. The reference is to the unique and only Son, begotten of the Father before all ages.[34] He is in an intimate and indivisible relation to the Father. There is a fellowship and union of love within the Trinity from eternity.[35] From this, the Son has interpreted[36] the mystery of God to us, making known the indivisible love in the Trinity in self-sacrificial love to us. Nowhere is this expressed better than in the words of John Henry Newman:

> O wisest love! that flesh and blood
> Which did in Adam fail,
> Should strive afresh against their foe,
> Should strive and should prevail;
>
> And that a higher gift than grace
> Should flesh and blood refine,
> God's presence and his very self,
> And essence all-divine.[37]

16.3   Biblical Evidence for Christ's Humanity

We saw the biblical evidence for the deity of Christ in chapter 2.[38] The New Testament is replete with evidence for the genuineness and reality

---

34. Barrett, *John*, 169; Lindars, *John*, 98; Leon Morris, *The Gospel according to John: The English Text with Introduction, Exposition and Notes* (London: Marshall, Morgan & Scott, 1971), 113–14; Schnackenburg, *John*, 269–71.

35. Barrett, *John*, 169–70; D. A. Carson, *The Gospel according to St John* (Leicester: Inter-Varsity Press, 1991), 135.

36. Barrett, *John*, 170; Lindars, *John*, 99.

37. From the hymn "Praise to the Holiest in the Height" (1865).

38. See also Letham, *Message of the Person of Christ*, 111–17, for a fuller account.

of Christ's human nature. He is portrayed as undergoing normal human growth; experiencing weariness, hunger, and thirst; being filled with normal human emotions; being horrified at the prospect of death; engaging in regular relationships with family and friends; aging; trusting and obeying God; undergoing temptation and suffering; dying and being buried. He ate and drank, grew from infancy to maturity, and progressed in wisdom and stature in favor with God and man (Luke 2:42, 52). While a child, he was subject to his parents (Luke 2:51), and later entered the family business as a carpenter.

His development from embryo to birth to infancy, childhood, and maturity is charted in the Gospels. Luke chronicles the announcement of his conception, the progress of Mary's pregnancy, and the birth, infancy, childhood, and later developments of Jesus (Luke 1–2). Like the rest of us, he experienced weariness, hunger, and thirst (John 4:1–7). Later, on the cross, Jesus cried out in anguish, "I thirst" (John 19:28). He experienced the gamut of human emotions. Faced with sudden bereavement, he wept in grief, inwardly in turmoil as he confronted the grim horrors of a friend's death (John 11:32–38). Contemplating the even greater ordeal of his own death, he was in deep sorrow (Matt. 26:38 and parallels). He provided for the care of his mother after his departure (John 19:25–27). He had a group of friends—Peter, James, and John—within the circle of the apostles. His close friendship with Mary, Martha, and Lazarus is evident in John 11. His opponents noted that he was not yet fifty years old when he was actually in his early thirties (John 8:57; cf. Isa. 53:3–4).

He trusted Yahweh, his Father, and obeyed him (Heb. 5:8; 10:1–10). His suffering and temptation are addressed in Matthew 4:1–10 and parallels, while Hebrews reflects on their significance (Heb. 2:18; 4:14–5:10). He died (Matt. 27:50–56 and parallels). He was buried (Matt. 27:57–66 and parallels; 1 Cor. 15:3–4). His resurrection was, of course, resurrection *from the dead*. As a result he is able to sympathize with us in our weakness (Heb. 4:14–16), interceding for us at the right hand of the Father (Heb. 7:25).[39] In short, as a result of having a common nature with us, he shares a common faith, common temptations, common sufferings, and a common death (Heb. 2:10–18).

---

39. As for what exactly is a human nature and in what sense it applies to Christ, see Oliver D. Crisp, *Divinity and Humanity: The Incarnation Reconsidered* (Cambridge: Cambridge University Press, 2007), 34–71.

16.4 The Virginal Conception: Mary as *Theotokos*

However, immediately we are confronted by a singularity—Jesus's unique conception. This appears to set him apart from the rest of us. It has also faced critical attacks on the assumption that the records are mythological and reflect similar stories in other religions. We will ask what exactly is entailed, within the parameters of what is revealed. Most skeptical assaults assume something different from the reality.

The expression *virgin birth* does not make sense; Jesus's birth was a normal human delivery. His mother was pregnant for nine months and then gave birth in the usual way. What was unique was the conception. This took place without the involvement of a human father. For this reason, the term *virginal conception* more adequately describes the reality.

16.4.1 The Narratives in Matthew and Luke[40]

Matthew 1:18–25. Matthew's account is from Joseph's perspective. Joseph is considered Jesus's father since he accepted legal responsibility as his father. The narrative makes clear that Joseph was not Jesus's biological father (v. 18). In the genealogy in Luke 3:23, Joseph is entered as the supposed father of Jesus. Since betrothal was legally binding, Joseph had a right to divorce Mary when he discovered that she was pregnant. Because he was a good man, he determined to do this privately rather than shaming Mary in public. Only after the information provided by the angel did he relent.[41]

Luke 1:26–38. The Lukan material presents the events from Mary's perspective and in a fuller way. No wonder she was shocked and perturbed! Suddenly she had an unexpected visitor. "The angel Gabriel was sent *from God to a city of Galilee named Nazareth.*" His departure point was God; his destination was an obscure village in northern Israel. This was a conjunction of the spiritual and the material, heaven and earth. This great spirit appeared in bodily form. He left the presence of God; he spoke to Mary in Hebrew. Mary was shaken. She was young—"a virgin betrothed to a man whose name was Joseph"—legally married to Joseph, as betrothal entailed, although the usual period before the marriage was consummated had not yet passed.

---

40. Material in this section is condensed from Letham, *Message of the Person of Christ*, 81–88.

41. R. T. France, *The Gospel according to Matthew: An Introduction and Commentary* (Leicester: Inter-Varsity Press, 1985), 77–80; W. D. Davies Jr. and Dale C. Allison, *A Critical and Exegetical Commentary on the Gospel according to Saint Matthew* (Edinburgh: T&T Clark, 1988), 1:196–223.

Twice in verse 27 Luke records that Mary was a παρθένος, a virgin.[42] This was an obvious barrier to the promised child, just as Elizabeth's barrenness was to the birth of John the Baptist.[43] Both events resulted from the sovereign power of God. However, Joseph was "of the house of David." Consequently, the family was in David's line, qualified to inherit the promises given to David in 2 Samuel 7.

Gabriel's first words—words *from God*—were greetings. "Hail, highly favored one, the Lord be/is with you" (Luke 1:28–29, my trans.). Mary was the passive receiver of God's grace. Yahweh was with her. There is not the slightest hint that Mary was a conduit of grace to others.[44] The participle is passive—if Mary represents anything, it is the faithful who *receive* the bountiful goodness of God. Gabriel's statement reassured her in the face of agitation and declared that her status with God was secure.

Mary was still confused (v. 29) and terrified, in need of further solace (v. 30). There were good reasons for Mary to rejoice (vv. 30–33, cf. 46–55). She would conceive a son. He would be called *Jesus*, which means "Yahweh saves."[45] This was an explicit declaration from Gabriel, sent directly from God, that *this* child would be the deliverer and Savior. The connection with the conception of John is significant, for he was to prepare the way for the Savior. Mary knew of this; she and Elizabeth were cousins, and she visited Elizabeth shortly afterward.

Mary's child would be great. John was to be "great before the Lord" (v. 15), but Jesus's greatness would surpass all others. "He will be great and will be called Son of the Most High"—the lack of definite article in Greek indicates the quality of the term, demonstrating his uniqueness. The phrase "the Most High" is often used in the Old

---

42. *Parthenos* could mean "a young woman of marriageable age" (LN, 1:109), but, as we shall see, the passage points unmistakably to virginity. As Morris writes, "The evidence of the Gospel as we have it is plain." Leon Morris, *Luke: An Introduction and Commentary* (Leicester: Inter-Varsity Press, 1997), 79. Fitzmyer regards "the normal understanding" of *parthenos* to be "virgin"; Joseph A. Fitzmyer, SJ, *The Gospel according to Luke (I–IX)*, The Anchor Bible (New York: Doubleday, 1970), 343. See also Joel B. Green, *The Gospel of Luke* (Grand Rapids, MI: Eerdmans, 1997), 85–86. The context—see v. 34—establishes this beyond question. For a detailed discussion of competing interpretations see I. Howard Marshall, *The Gospel of Luke: A Commentary on the Greek Text*, The New International Greek Testament Commentary (Exeter: Paternoster, 1978), 68–70. Besides, a young woman of marriageable age would be assumed to be a virgin in first-century Israel.

43. John Nolland, *Luke 1–9:20*, Word Biblical Commentary 35 (Dallas: Word, 1989), 49.

44. The Jesuit scholar Fitzmyer acknowledges that the later Scholastic tradition went beyond the Lucan perfect participle; Fitzmyer, *Luke (I–IX)*, 345–46. See Marshall, *Luke*, 65.

45. On the meaning, see Fitzmyer, *Luke (I–IX)*, 347.

Testament to refer to God. In the background is Isaiah 9:6–7, where the child born to deliver the covenant people of God is called "the mighty God."

Additionally, "the Lord God will give to him the throne of his father David" (Luke 1:32). Jesus would inherit the promises of the Davidic covenant (2 Sam. 7:12–16; Ps. 89:26–29). Contrary to the Davidic kings, most of whom failed to follow Yahweh, Jesus "will reign over the house of Jacob forever, and of his kingdom there will be no end" (Luke 1:33). Additionally, in view may be the Son of Man in Daniel 7, who is given a universal and unending kingdom. The point Luke makes in 1:27 about Joseph becomes clear. Since Joseph would become Jesus's legal father, Jesus would beyond dispute be in the line of David, since in Israel, legal paternity decided the matter. Jesus's opponents never questioned his Davidic claim; his relatives boasted of it. For Paul, it would be a significant theme in his view of Christ, "who was descended from David according to the flesh" (Rom. 1:3). What a staggering announcement for Mary to take in! Furthermore, her marriage was not yet consummated, and the penalty for sexual infidelity by a betrothed woman was death![46]

As if the identity of her son were not enough to astonish her, the fact itself was barely comprehensible. She was still a virgin; the conception was physically impossible. Mary's question demonstrates this. "How can this be, since I do not know a man?" (Luke 1:34, my trans.). Green remarks that "her question plays a vital theological role, for it accents the fact that she is still a virgin."[47] People in first-century Israel were no more gullible or credulous than people today; they may have been less so. One of the three main religious groups at the time, the Sadducees, were antisupernaturalists, rationalists who opposed the idea of the resurrection and angels. For them, the very idea that the angel Gabriel had visited Nazareth was in the realm of fairy tales, to say nothing about the details of his message. Mary was not taken in; she questioned the angel. However, it was not a question stemming from skepticism—her faith is evident in verse 38—for it was the question of one who believed but needed to understand. How could these things be? She believed but did not grasp its meaning.[48] This did not suggest any resolve to remain

46. Deut. 22:23–24.
47. Green, *Luke*, 89.
48. Green, *Luke*, 89; Nolland, *Luke 1–9:20*, 55; Fitzmyer, *Luke (I-IX)*, 348.

a virgin. There is no textual support for the claim of perpetual virginity, a position from which Roman Catholic exegetes are increasingly retreating.[49]

Gabriel explained. His comment was poetic, presented in parallelism:

The Holy Spirit will come upon you,
and the power of the Most High will overshadow you.

The parallelism indicates deep mystery, beyond definition. The truth cannot be captured in prose. The imminent pregnancy would be due to the Holy Spirit. The language reminds us that "the Spirit of God was hovering over the face of the waters" of creation like a mother bird (Gen. 1:2). The Spirit, in overshadowing Mary, would bring about a new creation, a new creative act on the part of God, the start of a new humanity of which the child would be the head, a new creation that would stand and flourish for eternity.[50] This was the decisive point in the history of redemption, in world history as a whole. As with the original creation—and all the direct mighty acts of God—no one was there to observe the mechanics of it, to see what occurred at the instant it happened. It remains a mystery, known only by revelation (cf. Job 38:1ff.). To reinforce this, we now know that parthenogenesis can only produce a female, since, without the participation of a male, the Y chromosome is missing. This required a supervening action of God to create what otherwise would have been absent.

The consequence of the Spirit's sovereign, creative action was that the child to whom Mary would give birth would be called the holy Son of God. There are several possible word orders here. The stress falls on the last words, υἱὸς θεοῦ, "Son of God"[51] (Luke 1:35). In his humanity Jesus would be the Son of God. Israel had been called God's son (Ex. 4:22; Hos. 11:1). The Davidic king was the embodiment of sonship (Ps. 2:7), and Israel was anticipating this to be developed by great David's greater Son. Since Luke has already described Jesus as "the son of the

---

49. Fitzmyer, *Luke (I-IX)*, 348–49.
50. Most commentators draw attention to a kindred phrase in Acts 1:8, to manifestations of the glory of God in the exodus and wilderness period, or to the transfiguration, but miss this point. Green is right, however, in that "these parallel affirmations do not suggest sexual activity, but do connote divine agency." Green, *Luke*, 90. However, what element of divine agency is more compelling in this case than creation? Barth expresses it well when he describes the virgin birth as "a creative act of divine omnipotence." Barth, CD, IV/1:207.
51. *huios theou.*

Most High" (Luke 1:32), against the backcloth of Isaiah 9:6–7, where the Son born is "the mighty God," an attribution of deity to the child can hardly be excluded. The church has recognized this throughout the ages in calling Mary *theotokos*, God-bearer. Overall, Jesus's divine sonship follows from the miraculous divine conception due to the work of the Spirit. It is this that fit him for the throne of David.[52]

However, other descriptions of the child Jesus are present here. He was a child and had a mother, so he was human. He was holy (ἅγιος): set apart for God in his call and his purposes. Entailed is separation from sin. In Matthew's account Jesus is to "save his people from their sins" (Matt. 1:21). To do this he must be free from the entanglements that sin brought into the world.

Gabriel went out of his way to reassure Mary that this was to be her future. First, there was Elizabeth's remarkable pregnancy. Both Zacharias and Elizabeth were "advanced in years" (Luke 1:7). Zacharias affirmed this to the angel, calling himself πρεσβύτης "an old man" (v. 18). Elizabeth herself was called "barren"—a term of reproach for a woman (vv. 7, 25)—and when the child was eventually born, a great celebration was held (vv. 57–58). Yet, into this situation the power of God came with overwhelming force. Gabriel's news was already foreshadowed.

Second, the angel pointed to the invincible power of the word of God (v. 37). No word from God is powerless; he always accomplishes what he says he will do. With the Spirit of God hovering over the waters, God said, "Let there be light," and there was light (Gen. 1:1–5). He spoke; it was done. For Mary, what in human terms was impossible—to conceive a male child without the participation of a male—could be effected by the word of God in an instant. Luke points to the Spirit and the word of God working together, inseparably, powerfully, effectively, effortlessly.

For Mary, this was to be extremely difficult. Her immediate future was problematic. Besides the obvious changes that come with pregnancy there were the resulting social problems, the comments and the gossip that would reverberate for years. The resulting suspicions were raised against Jesus by some of his opponents (John 8:41). Yet Mary's reply was one of faith, "Let it be to me according to your word" (Luke 1:38), echoing David's response concerning the promises about his dynasty,

---

52. Green, *Luke*, 91.

"Do as you have spoken" (2 Sam. 7:25). Mary believed God's word, submitted, and followed it.

Faith is a matter of denying oneself, taking up one's cross and following Jesus. Far from being a co-redemptrix, Mary is a pattern of saving faith. The whole scene, as Barth stressed, portrays the relationship between the regenerating work of the Spirit and the consequent response of faith.[53] Additionally, the virginal conception stands at the start of the Gospels with the resurrection at the climax, like bookends framing the whole, pointing to the mighty acts of God constituting and establishing the entire drama of salvation.[54]

16.4.2   Allusions to the Virginal Conception in the Rest of the New Testament[55]

It is sometimes said that, outside the accounts in Matthew and Luke, there are no other references to the virginal conception in the New Testament. However, Mark describes Jesus as "the son of Mary" (Mark 6:3); in first-century Jewish society, a man would normally be seen in relation to his father. Paul uses γεννάω[56] for human begetting of sons and does so three times in Galatians 4, but when in the same context (Gal. 4:4) he refers to the birth of Jesus, he uses γίνομαι; evidently, he knows there is something unusual about it. He also uses γίνομαι in Romans 1:3. In keeping with the fathers of the first five centuries, around AD 200 Tertullian insists on a reading of John 1:13 in the singular, thus *qui . . . natus est,* "who was born," referring to the birth of Jesus, and castigates the Valentinian Gnostics for corrupting the text by intruding the plural in reference to believers.[57] In John 8:19 and 41, Jesus's opponents appear to mock him asking, "Where is your father?"

16.4.3   The Significance of the Virginal Conception

What is the significance of the virginal conception? There seem to me to be five major factors:

---

53. Barth, *CD*, I/2:138–41.
54. The finest exposition of the doctrine of the virgin birth is Thomas F. Torrance, *Incarnation: The Person and Life of Christ* (Milton Keynes: Paternoster, 2008), 88–104.
55. I am indebted to Torrance, *Incarnation*, in this section.
56. *gennaō.*
57. Tertullian, *De carne Christi* 19, 24 (ANF, 3:537–38).

1. There are two sides to the virginal conception—Jesus was born of the Virgin Mary but conceived by the Holy Spirit. There are a normal gestation and birth but also a dimension beyond our knowledge, an act of God as Creator. Biological explanations will produce only biological answers.

2. The virginal conception comes in the context of the incarnation and is to be seen in connection with the resurrection. Both events are like bookends enclosing the events recorded in the Gospels and pointing to the sovereign creative power of God. Christ's birth is not something under human power. It is the union of God and man achieved entirely by God.

3. Christ's birth displays his true humanity—he was born of a human mother after the normal period of gestation. The docetists, in the process of opposing the full humanity of Christ, denied the virgin birth.

4. It indicates that human capacity is disqualified and that salvation is from the Lord. The initiative is God's. Mary is believingly receptive (Luke 1:37). She is a picture and pattern of God's grace in regeneration and faith.

5. The virginal conception is a new creation—a renovation of the old (Luke 1:34–35). As in the original creation and the resurrection, we understand by the Holy Spirit in faith, not by a process of human logic and argumentation, even though it can be logically defended.

John of Damascus, the great synthesizer of the orthodox fathers, understood three things to have occurred simultaneously. First was the assumption of human nature by the Logos; second, its coming into being; and third, its being made divine by the Word.[58] By the last category we should understand the sanctification of the assumed humanity, with the endowment of the Holy Spirit. Crisp argues along similar lines:

> The Virginal Conception teaches us that, at a certain moment in time, the Word becomes incarnate. So the human nature he assumes at the Virginal Conception, he assumes "into" his person. . . . And, of course, all of this happens at one-and-the-same-time, according to most orthodox accounts of the Incarnation. . . . There is no time lapse between the generation of the human body in the womb of the Virgin by the Holy Spirit, the creation and "attachment"/ integration

---

58. John of Damascus, *The Orthodox Faith* 3.12 (NPNF², 9/2:56–57).

of the soul to the body, and the assumption and "personalization" of this complete human nature (the body + soul composite) by the Word of God. All these events take place simultaneously at the Virginal Conception. If there were any delay between these different "moments" of the Virginal Conception and Incarnation, the result, I suggest, would be something other than an orthodox account of the Incarnation.[59]

The Damascene also refers to Christ's two begettings.[60] Here the virginal conception corresponds not so much to the resurrection, as in Matthew and Luke, as to the eternal generation by the Father. In eternity, the Son is generated by the Father without a mother, while in time he is generated through the mother without a father. Charles Twombly refers to John's discussion of whether someone can be human lacking a human father. His answer points to Adam and Eve, who are regarded as truly human.[61]

Barth comments:

In the Creeds the assertion of the Virgin Birth is plainly enough characterised as a first statement about the One who was and is and will be the Son of God. It is not a statement about how He became this, a statement concerning the basis and condition of his divine Sonship. It is a description of the way in which the Son of God became man.[62]

Further, "It is the sign which accompanies and indicates the mystery of the incarnation of the Son, marking it off as a mystery from all the beginnings of other human existences." It is a creative act of God from which the will of man is excluded. It is an inconceivable act of grace, comparable to the miracle of the empty tomb.[63]

Calvin supports the idea that it is not the virgin birth as such that guarantees Christ's holiness but rather the work of the Spirit. "For we make Christ free of all stain not just because he was begotten of his mother without copulation with a man, but because he was sanctified

59. Oliver Crisp, *God Incarnate: Explorations in Christology* (London: T&T Clark, 2009), 86. See also *idem, Divinity and Humanity*, 62.
60. John of Damascus, *The Orthodox Faith* 3.7 (NPNF², 9/2:51).
61. Charles C. Twombly, *Perichoresis and Personhood: God, Christ, and Salvation in John of Damascus* (Eugene, OR: Pickwick, 2015), 68.
62. Barth, *CD*, IV/1:207.
63. Barth, *CD*, IV/1:207.

by the Spirit that the generation might be pure and undefiled as would have been true before Adam's fall."[64]

Further Reading

Bauckham, Richard. *Jesus and the Eyewitnesses: The Gospels as Eyewitness Testimony*. 2nd ed. Grand Rapids, MI: Eerdmans, 2017.

Macleod, Donald. *The Person of Christ*. Leicester: Inter-Varsity Press, 1998.

Torrance, Thomas F. *Incarnation: The Person and Life of Christ*. Milton Keynes: Paternoster, 2008.

Study Questions

1. Why was Jesus born of a virgin?

2. Does the New Testament present Jesus as in any sense less than human? Indicate some of the ways in which his humanity is demonstrated.

3. Why was it necessary that the Son become man? Could not God have saved us by some other means?

---

64. Calvin, *Institutes*, 2.13.4.

17

Incarnation (2)

Church Formulations

The Christological controversies of the fifth to seventh centuries ultimately recognized a number of factors as essential to the biblical portrayal of Christ and thus to the gospel, factors that were already believed but that required formal elaboration in the wake of erroneous teaching. These were that Christ is one indivisible person, having taken into union a human nature, not a separate human person; that the humanity is not swamped by the deity but retains its distinctive properties; that the humanity has no existence independently of the incarnation and as such is the human nature of the Son; and that Christ has a human will as well as a divine one, the two working in perfect harmony, or else he would not be properly human.

17.1 The Battle for Orthodoxy

Docetism was the earliest Christological heresy. It denied the reality of Christ's humanity. The name derives from the Greek verb *dokeō*, "seem" or "appear." Docetism claimed that the human nature of Christ was only apparent and not real. The underlying assumption was that the divine could have no dealings with the world of matter. The material world was inferior and the spiritual realm would be contaminated by contact with it. Today the humanity of Christ is hardly controversial; the major questions since the Enlightenment have concerned Christ's deity. Nevertheless, docetic tendencies are hard to shrug off and still appear from time to time.

For much of the last century the received paradigm was that there were two schools of thought on Christology in the fifth century, based in Alexandria and Antioch. The Alexandrian school held to the unity of Christ, whereas the Antiochenes stressed the humanity and had a looser grasp of the unity of the person.[1] Fairbairn demonstrates that this reading is misleading and has fallen out of favor, much as the comparable claim for two schools of biblical interpretation has been undermined. Indeed, the main representatives of the putative Antiochene school were condemned as heretics by the church.[2]

17.2   Christ Is One Indivisible Person: The Council of Ephesus (431)[3]

17.2.1   *The Nestorian Crisis*

In the early fifth century, a major crisis erupted over the identity of Jesus Christ. Since he was and is the eternal Son of God, how does this relate to his being human? How are his deity and humanity related? How does this affect our reading of the Gospels? What is its significance for salvation?

These questions were thrust onto center stage in 428 by Nestorius, patriarch of Constantinople.[4] He attacked the term *theotokos* (God-bearer), a popular liturgical title for Mary. Since he distinguished sharply between the deity of Christ and his humanity,[5] he held that Mary could be called mother only of *the man* Jesus. She could be termed *christotokos* (Christ-bearer) with no qualms, since in this there was no danger of confusing deity and humanity. Talk of Mary as *theotokos* conjured up

1. E.g., J. N. D. Kelly, *Early Christian Doctrines* (London: Adam & Charles Black, 1968), 280–309; Jaroslav Pelikan, *The Christian Tradition*, vol. 1, *The Emergence of the Catholic Tradition (100–600)* (Chicago: University of Chicago Press, 1971), 243–66.

2. Donald Fairbairn, "The One Person Who Is Jesus Christ: The Patristic Perspective," in *Jesus in Trinitarian Perspective: An Introductory Christology*, ed. Fred Sanders and Klaus Issler (Nashville: B&H Academic, 2007), 86–94; Fairbairn, *Grace and Christology in the Early Church* (Oxford: Oxford University Press, 2003); Fairbairn, "Patristic Soteriology: Three Trajectories," *JETS* 50 (2007): 298–310.

3. The material in this chapter was presented, in fuller form, in my books *Through Western Eyes: Eastern Orthodoxy: A Reformed Perspective* (Fearn: Mentor, 2007) and *The Message of the Person of Christ: The Word Made Flesh* (Nottingham: Inter-Varsity Press, 2013).

4. On Nestorius, see G. L. Prestige, *Fathers and Heretics* (London: SPCK, 1940), 120–49; Kelly, *Early Christian Doctrines*, 310–17.

5. See D. S. Wallace-Hadrill, *Christian Antioch: A Study of Early Christian Thought in the East* (Cambridge: Cambridge University Press, 1982).

in his mind the specter of Arianism, a refusal to accord deity to Christ, a blurring of the Creator-creature distinction, a mixture of deity and humanity. Nestorius wanted to maintain the integrity of the human nature.

Nestorius was also alert to the danger of Apollinarianism. Apollinaris (ca. 315–ca. 390), a strong supporter of the Council of Nicaea, had wandered into heresy by teaching that the Logos—the Son—took the place of a human soul in the incarnate Christ; the Word assumed flesh, a body, only. Apollinaris was condemned by Constantinople I (381). The problem with Apollinaris's teaching, in Gregory of Nazianzus's words, was that "whatever is not assumed cannot be healed."[6] As John of Damascus later wrote of Christ, "He in his fullness took upon himself me in my fullness, and was united whole to whole that he might in his grace bestow salvation on the whole man."[7] If the Son did not take into union a full humanity, including a soul, there was no incarnation. We could not then be saved, since Christ would have been less than human, since a human being minus a soul is not human. Nestorius's correct concern against Apollinarianism was to affirm the full integrity of Christ's human nature. Nestorius's problem was that, while he had a firm grasp of the distinctiveness of Christ's divinity and humanity, he was less sure of the unity of his person. So he spoke of a "conjunction" of the divinity and humanity rather than a "union." This conjunction resulted in a πρόσω-πον[8] of union, a single object of appearance, which was identical with neither of the two natures. The πρόσωπον of union, not the Logos or Word, was thought to be the subject of the incarnate Christ.

Nestorius was vehemently opposed by Cyril of Alexandria, who began from the premise of Christ's unity.[9] For Cyril, Nestorius threatened not only the unity of Christ's person but also the incarnation, effectively denying a real participation by the Son of God in our humanity. The two na-

6. *Letter 101, to Cledonius,* in *St. Gregory of Nazianzus: On God and Christ,* trans. Frederick Williams and Lionel Wickham (Crestwood, NY: St Vladimir's Seminary Press, 2002), 158.

7. John of Damascus, *The Orthodox Faith* 3.6 (NPNF[2], 9/2:50). In relation to recent monistic approaches to anthropology, based on developments in neuroscience, and a resultant new warmth to Apollinarian interests by such as J. P. Moreland and William Lane Craig, see Mark Harris, "When Jesus Lost His Soul: Fourth-Century Christology and Modern Neuroscience," *SJT* 70 (2017): 74–92.

8. *prosōpon.*

9. See Cyril of Alexandria,, *On the Unity of Christ,* trans. John Anthony McGuckin (Crestwood, NY: St Vladimir's Seminary Press, 1995); J. A. McGuckin, *St. Cyril and the Christological Controversy* (Crestwood, NY: St Vladimir's Seminary Press, 2010); Prestige, *Fathers,* 150–79; Kelly, *Early Christian Doctrines,* 317–23; Norman Russell, *Cyril of Alexandria* (London: Routledge, 2000); Thomas G. Weinandy, ed., *The Theology of St. Cyril of Alexandria: A Critical Appreciation* (London: T&T Clark, 2003), 23–74.

tures, it seemed, were more like two pieces of board held together by glue. Cyril stressed that salvation was a work of God, that the man Jesus could not defeat sin and death by his human nature alone. To overcome sin and death, the eternal Logos assumed into *union* the human nature of Christ.[10]

In his *Second Letter to Nestorius* Cyril states that the Word "united to himself . . . flesh enlivened by a rational soul, and in this way became a human being." There is an "unspeakable and unutterable convergence into unity, one Christ and one Son out of two." To reject this personal union is to fall into the error of positing two sons. "We do not worship a human being in conjunction with the Logos, lest the appearance of a division creep in. . . . No, we worship one and the same, because the body of the Logos is not alien to him but accompanies him even as he is enthroned with the Father." The Word did not unite himself to a human person. The Virgin Mary is *theotokos* since it is *the Word* that united himself to this human body and soul.[11]

In his *Third Letter to Nestorius*, Cyril again stressed the personal union of the Word with the flesh. All expressions in the Gospels refer to *the one incarnate person of the Word*. Mary is *theotokos* since she "gave birth after the flesh to God who was united by *hypostasis* with flesh," man ensouled with a rational soul.[12] Cyril adds twelve anathemas to this letter. In these, he declares that "if anyone will not confess that the Emmanuel is very God, and that therefore the Holy Virgin is the Mother of God (*theotokos*), in-asmuch as in the flesh she bore the Word of God made flesh . . . let him be anathema." He insists, among other things, that it is the Word who suffered, was crucified, and died *according to the flesh*.[13] For Cyril, the Word who existed before the incarnation is the same person after the incarnation, now enfleshed. This union excludes division but does not eliminate difference.

17.2.2 *The Council of Ephesus*

The council called to Ephesus to resolve the matter expelled Nestorius from the episcopal office and the priesthood,[14] declaring that Christ's

---

10. John Meyendorff, *Christ in Eastern Christian Thought* (Crestwood, NY: St Vladimir's Seminary Press, 1975), 18–19.

11. Leo Donald Davis, *The First Seven Ecumenical Councils (325–787)* (Collegeville, MN: Liturgical, 1990), 149–50; Richard A. Norris Jr., *The Christological Controversy* (Philadelphia: Fortress, 1980), 131–35, esp. 133.

12. Edward Roche Hardy, *Christology of the Later Fathers* (Philadelphia: Westminster, 1954), 349–54, esp. 352–53.

13. Hardy, *Later Fathers*, 354; Davis, *Councils*, 150–51; NPNF[2], 14:206.

14. Davis, *Councils*, 160.

humanity, wholly human, was appropriated by the Word as his own, and so forms the basis for our own salvation.[15] A conjunction between deity and humanity—existing side by side—is not incarnation and could not save us.[16]

17.3   The Humanity of Christ Is Not Absorbed by the Deity: The Council of Chalcedon (451)

17.3.1   *Eutyches and the Council of Chalcedon*[17]

Before long a fresh crisis arose, generated by Eutyches from Alexandria, whom Kelly calls an "aged and muddle-headed archimandrite."[18] Eutyches was an extreme exponent of Cyrilline Christology, without Cyril's theological sophistication. For Eutyches, before the incarnation the Son was of two natures, but after it he is one nature, one Christ, one Son, in one *hypostasis* and one πρόσωπον. Christ's flesh was not identical with ordinary human flesh, since Eutyches thought this would entail the Word assuming an individual man, thus destroying the union. Behind this, he understood nature to mean concrete existence— so Christ could not have two natures or he would have two concrete existences and so be divided.[19] Thus, Eutyches had an overpowering emphasis on the unity of Christ's person, exactly the opposite of Nestorius. Where Nestorius had sought to uphold the distinctness of the two natures and so threatened the unity of Christ, Eutyches so underlined Christ's unity that he blurred the distinctness of the two natures, his humanity swamped by his deity—although, to be fair, Eutyches did insist on the full and complete humanity. His ideas raised problems similar to those of Apollinaris, for our salvation depends on the reality of the incarnation, of a real assumption of unabbreviated humanity by the Son of God. If Christ were not truly and fully man, we could not

---

15. Meyendorff, *Christ*, 21.
16. The conciliar affirmation of Mary as *theotokos*, a Christological issue, should not be confused with later Mariological developments. The later Roman dogma of Mary's immaculate conception, by which she was allegedly preserved from original sin, designed to offset any idea that Christ himself inherited original sin, effectively undermines Christ's humanity, since not only was he without a human father but his mother would have been unlike the rest of humanity. Besides, it requires a progression of immaculate conceptions through successive previous generations to negate the proposed problem.
17. See Aloys Grillmeier, SJ, *Christ in Christian Tradition*, vol. 1, *From the Apostolic Age to Chalcedon (451)*, 2nd ed., trans. John Bowden (Atlanta: John Knox, 1975), 520–57; Pelikan, *The Christian Tradition*, 1:263–66.
18. Kelly, *Early Christian Doctrines*, 331.
19. See Kelly, *Early Christian Doctrines*, 330–34; Davis, *Councils*, 171.

be saved, for only a second Adam could undo the damage caused by the first.

Eventually Marcian, the emperor, called a council to be held at Nicaea, but switched to Chalcedon, across the Bosphorus, due to invasions by the Huns. Pope Leo sent three legates.[20] The bishops reaffirmed Cyril's *Second Letter to Nestorius* and Pope Leo's *Tome*, addressed to the council. A commission was appointed to draw up a doctrinal statement. In composing the Definition of Chalcedon, the bishops drew on a variety of sources, Leo's *Tome* the single most decisive contributor, even though there were more quotations from Cyril.[21] The Definition clearly distinguishes between one person and two natures.

> Therefore, following the holy Fathers, we all with one accord teach men to acknowledge one and the same Son, our Lord Jesus Christ, at once complete in Godhead and complete in manhood, truly God and truly man, consisting also of a reasonable soul and body; of one substance with the Father as regards his Godhead, and at the same time of one substance with us as regards his manhood; like us in all respects, apart from sin; as regards his Godhead, begotten of the Father before the ages, but yet as regards his manhood begotten, for us and for our salvation, of Mary the Virgin, the God-bearer; one and the same Christ, Son, Lord, Only-begotten, recognized in two natures, without confusion, without change, without division, without separation; the distinction of natures being in no way annulled by the union, but rather the characteristics of each nature being preserved and coming together to form one person and subsistence, not as parted or separated into two persons, but one and the same Son and only-begotten God, the Word, Lord Jesus Christ; even as the prophets from earliest times spoke of him, and our Lord Jesus Christ himself taught us, and the creed of the Fathers has handed down to us.

The affirmation that Christ subsists in two natures is a decisive rejection of Eutyches. The Definition rejects any notion of the union that might erode or threaten the differences of the natures. At the same time, it also

---

20. For the Council of Chalcedon, see R. V. Sellers, *The Council of Chalcedon: A Historical and Doctrinal Survey* (London: SPCK, 1953), 209ff.; Kelly, *Early Christian Doctrines*, 338–43; Davis, *Councils*, 180–82; Henry R. Percival, *Seven Ecumenical Councils of the Undivided Church: Their Canons and Dogmatic Decrees*, A Select Library of Nicene and Post-Nicene Fathers of the Christian Church: Second Series (repr., Edinburgh: T&T Clark, 1997), 243–95.

21. Pelikan, *The Christian Tradition*, 1:263–64; Sellers, *Chalcedon*, 209–10.

insists that Christ is not divided or separated into two persons, as the Nestorian heresy implied.

The anti-Nestorian stance is evident in a number of ways. The repetition of the phrase "the same" and the reaffirmation of the Virgin Mary as *theotokos* are two obvious points. Again, toward the end, the Definition denies that Christ is parted or separated into two persons, but rather asserts that the two natures "come together to form one person and subsistence," echoing Cyril's *Second Letter to Nestorius*. In all these ways the Definition clearly affirms the unity of the person of Christ. On the other hand, it equally repudiates the Eutychian heresy, which occasioned the council in the first place. Christ is "complete in manhood," so much so that he is "of one substance with us." The distinction of natures is in no way annulled by the union. There are also clear restatements of opposition both to Apollinarianism, in that Christ has "a reasonable soul and body," and also to Arianism, in that Christ is "of one substance with the Father."

Above all, the famous four privative adverbs together form the central hinge of the Definition.[22] The incarnate Christ is "in two natures, without confusion, without change." Here is an explicit rejection of Eutyches. The union neither changes Christ's humanity into anything else nor absorbs it into the divinity. The humanity remains fully humanity. On the other side of the spectrum, the natures are "without division, without separation." By this it is impermissible so to focus on either nature of Christ that the personal union is undermined as Nestorius has done. These four phrases outlaw both Nestorianism and Eutychianism.

The council also anathematizes those who talk of two natures of the Lord before the union but only one afterward. This is directed at Eutyches, probably at the behest of Pope Leo and the papal legates,[23] and was to cause problems later, for the monophysites (proponents of "one nature") were accustomed to thinking of "nature" as synonymous with what we would now call "person" and so considered Chalcedon a capitulation to Nestorius. However, the problem was a lack of knowledge of Greek by the Latins, who had pressed this point. Taking φύσις (Greek)[24] to mean *natura* (Latin), Leo and his legates thought that the

---

22. The words in question are adverbs in Greek.
23. Sellers, *Chalcedon*, 224–26.
24. *physis*.

Alexandrian mantra of one incarnate φύσις of the Logos was a heretical belief in only one *natura*. They failed to appreciate that the difference was semantic, since the Greeks used φύσις and *hypostasis* interchangeably. Another century passed before Emperor Justinian I brought a clear distinction between these two terms. In reality, the real objection in this anathema is, as Sellers observes, to Eutyches's false interpretation of the formula, not to Cyril's position, which was not in view at the time.[25] It was in defense of the gospel that the council rejected any idea that Christ's humanity was truncated or absorbed by deity; if that had been so we could not be saved.

17.3.2 Assessment of Chalcedon

Chalcedon failed to do justice to some real concerns of some of the Cyrillians. The point that "the distinction of natures being in no way annulled by the union but rather the characteristics of each nature being preserved and coming together" could be taken to mean that human attributes must be predicated only of the human nature, and the divine of the divine. This sounded Nestorian to these people. It gave the impression that Christ was some form of schizoid, for whom some things could be related only to one part of him and other things to another part. Their strong concern for the unity of Christ seemed to have been given short shrift. It seemed as though the idea that salvation begins by the union of the human nature with the person of Christ was under attack.[26]

Moreover, despite the repeated stress on the incarnate and eternal Son as "one and the same," Chalcedon left the concept of the personal union unclear. For instance, it did not specify *who* exactly had suffered and been crucified. Nor did it say—a vital theme for Cyril's supporters—that the deification of man began in the union of Christ's humanity with his divinity. It also appeared that the two natures were seen as prior to the person, for they were said to come together to form the person. This would make Christ's person distinct from the eternal Son and so destroy the incarnation. The monophysites later thought that Chalcedon was soft on Nestorianism by asserting "two natures after the union," precisely because it made no mention of the hypostatic (personal) union,

---

25. Sellers, *Chalcedon*, 226.
26. Sellers, *Chalcedon*, 224.

refusing to include the confession "out of two." Chalcedon satisfied the West but divided opinion in the East.[27]

Furthermore, two passages in Leo's *Tome*, effectively canonized by Chalcedon, were held by the monophysites to be indisputably Nestorian, passages where, they argued, "Leo so separates, and personalizes, what is divine and what is human in Christ that the hypostatic union is dissolved."[28] Leo states that the properties of both natures are kept intact so that "one and the same mediator between God and human beings, the human being who is Jesus Christ, can at one and the same time die in virtue of the one nature and, in virtue of the other, be incapable of death."[29] As a result, the final version stated that Christ is recognized "*in* two natures" rather than "*out of* two natures," as the original draft prior to the acceptance of Leo's *Tome* had claimed.[30] In the absence of mention of the hypostatic union, many followers of Cyril were loath to accept Chalcedon. Moreover, they strongly held to the personal identity of the incarnate Christ with the preexistent Son, considering that the council did not affirm it,[31] although the repeated phrase "one and the same" must be borne in mind in response to this claim. Consequently, "the West supported it, but many in the East rejected it."[32]

Chalcedon was never intended to be the final, definitive verdict on Christology. As Sellers points out, "it allows deductions to be made from its dogmatic decisions, and, in effect, encourages enquiry into the mystery."[33] "It is intended to explain just one definite question of the church's Christology, indeed the most important one. It does not lay claim to having said all that may be said about Christ." It was far from innovative but, rather, was in line with the preceding tradition.[34] However, it left a good deal of unfinished business on the table.

There is some disagreement on the nature and scope of the Definition.[35] Following the general consensus, Crisp argues that it was mainly negative,

---

27. Sellers, *Chalcedon*, 256–60; Davis, *Councils*, 187; Meyendorff, *Christ*, 28; Pelikan, *The Christian Tradition*, 1:265–66.

28. Sellers, *Chalcedon*, 266.

29. Norris, *Controversy*, 148.

30. Andrew Louth, *John Damascene: Tradition and Originality in Byzantine Theology* (Oxford: Oxford University Press, 2002), 150.

31. Davis, *Councils*, 196–97.

32. Louth, *John Damascene*, 151.

33. Sellers, *Chalcedon*, 350.

34. Grillmeier, *Christ in Christian Tradition*, 1:550.

35. Sarah Coakley, "What Does Chalcedon Solve and What Does It Not? Some Reflections on the Status and Meaning of the Chalcedonian Definition," in *The Incarnation*, ed. Stephen T. Davis, Daniel Kendall, and Gerald O'Collins (Oxford: Oxford University Press, 2002), 148.

outlawing heresy and identifying the boundaries for reflection while leaving a wide area of ambiguity.[36] He contends that it does not give us a complete account of the person of Christ or of his natures and is ambiguous because it was more concerned to rule out what was not orthodox than to make positive statements.[37] It does not say what a person is or what a nature is, nor does it address how someone fully human can be of the identical essence as God. It is minimalist.[38] Its positive comment, Crisp contends, is limited to affirming that Christ is one person who has two natures that retain their integrity, are distinct, and are united in the person of Christ.[39] On the other hand, Fairbairn argues against the view that Chalcedon was a negative statement and presses the point that the Definition of Chalcedon has on eight occasions the phrase "the same one" or "one and the same," stressing that the personal identity of Jesus Christ is the eternal Son.[40]

Central to these discussions was that the incarnation is essential for our salvation. Recall the words of Gregory of Nazianzus, "Whatever is not assumed cannot be healed."[41] Unless Christ came in our own flesh and blood, we cannot be saved. The gospel was at stake. An appearance of God in human form was not enough. An assumption of human nature that remained separate from personal union with God would have left us with a divine messenger or a highly inspired man, not a Savior. Only the union established in the incarnation could avail. Thus, the supreme mystery of the incarnation can be summed up in the following way: The eternal Son of God took into union a human nature created in the womb of the Virgin Mary by the Holy Spirit. This union continues for the whole of eternity, so that the humanity is permanently united to the Son and remains human; it is the humanity of the Son of God. So Torrance remarks, "As Cyril of Alexandria used to point out with reference to the burning bush, just as the bush was not consumed by the fiery presence of God, so the humanity of Christ is not consumed by his deity."[42]

---

36. Oliver D. Crisp, "Desiderata for Models of the Hypostatic Union," in *Christology Ancient and Modern: Explorations in Constructive Dogmatics*, ed. Oliver D. Crisp and Fred Sanders (Grand Rapids, MI: Zondervan, 2013), 19–41.

37. Crisp, "Desiderata," 26.

38. Crisp, "Desiderata," 27.

39. Crisp, "Desiderata," 29.

40. Fairbairn, "The Patristic Perspective." While this is clearly true, it does not explain the century-long controversy that followed. If Chalcedon had been understood in that way at that time, much of the discord may have been alleviated.

41. Gregory of Nazianzus, *Letter 101, to Cledonius* (PG, 37:181c).

42. Thomas F. Torrance, *Incarnation: The Person and Life of Christ* (Milton Keynes: Paternoster, 2008), 9.

17.4   How Is Christ to Be Understood as One
Indivisible Person? Constantinople II (553)[43]

17.4.1   *The Monophysites and the Chalcedonians*

Twombly comments that what was lacking in the fifth century was an
extra-Chalcedonian rationale that could provide a plausible explanation of how one subject could be in possession of two natures.[44] Given
Chalcedon's rejection of the idea that the Son absorbs the humanity,
how was the union of the two natures of Christ to be understood and
proclaimed? Did it happen by metamorphosis? Was it akin to ingredients in soup?

English pancakes are made of flour, milk, and eggs beaten and mixed
together, and then fried in a frying pan. Each ingredient is a necessary
part of the finished product; without them all, one does not have an English pancake. Yet none of the ingredients on its own makes a pancake.
All must be added together and mixed. Put the eggs, flour, and milk side
by side in separate containers and there is no pancake. Moreover, the
pancake differs from each of the ingredients; it is something other than
any one, or all, of its constituent elements.

Is Christ like that, composed of deity and humanity but not to be
identified with either but instead a third thing, a mixture? The answer
is clearly no. This would not be incarnation; neither the deity nor the
humanity would be preserved and so we could not be saved.

Sections of the church went into a schism over whether Chalcedon,
by stressing the integrity of the two natures and the appropriate at-
tributions to be made to either one, left the door open to a Nestorian
interpretation that undermined the unity of Christ's person. Many were
disconcerted that not nearly enough emphasis was laid on Christ's unity
and on his personal identity with the eternal, preexistent Logos. These
people, known as *monophysites* (those holding to "one nature") insisted
on the absolute unity of the person of Christ and his continuity with the

43. Aloys Grillmeier, SJ, *Christ in Christian Tradition*, vol. 2, *From the Council of Chalcedon (451) to Gregory the Great (590–604)*, pt. 2, *The Church of Constantinople in the Sixth Century*, trans. Theresia Hainthaler, and John Cawte (London: Mowbray, 1995), 438–75, 503–13; Sellers, *Chalcedon*, 254–350; Herbert M. Relton, *A Study in Christology: The Problem of the Relation of the Two Natures in the Person of Christ* (London: SPCK, 1917); Timothy Ware, *The Orthodox Church* (London: Penguin, 1969), 37; Pelikan, *The Christian Tradition*, 2:49–61; Pelikan, *The Christian Tradition*, 1:277, 337–41; W. H. C. Frend, *The Rise of the Monophysite Movement* (Cambridge: Cambridge University Press, 1972); Meyendorff, *Christ*.

44. Charles C. Twombly, *Perichoresis and Personhood: God, Christ, and Salvation in John of Damascus* (Eugene, OR: Pickwick, 2015), 57.

preincarnate Logos. Conceptually, Chalcedon appeared incongruous to them; they held that a nature must be related to a person and so, since Christ was one person, he could have only one nature.

The Chalcedonians, on the other hand, were fearful of minimizing the humanity of Christ. Their leading exponents (including the monk Leontius of Byzantium and, more importantly, the Emperor Justinian) used an obscure facet of Aristotelian philosophy to argue that a nature does not have to be personalized separately but can be granted personhood, enveloped, and instantiated from another. Moreover, they argued, the eternal Son is capable of providing the personhood of the human nature because he is the divine Creator, and humans were made in the image of God, compatible with him on the creaturely level. So Constantinople II came up with the dogma of *enhypostasia*, which affirmed that the Son personalized the assumed humanity. The human nature—body and soul—was taken into union by the deity. It was not a case of two separate natures somehow meeting one another and coalescing into one. It was asymmetrical; as Paul said, "God was in Christ." God was the active agent, the humanity was conceived. The result is a union in which the humanity has its own personal integrity, but is not in any way separate or apart by itself. In answer to the question of *who* Christ is, he is the eternal Son of God. This is rooted in humanity being made in the image of God, with a created compatibility with God. The Son is able to embrace and enclose the humanity in union without violating its created integrity. Thus, the humanity of Christ has no separate existence—*anhypostasia*—of its own apart from this personal union.[45]

Earlier scholarship attributed the developments that led to the framing of the doctrine of *enhypostasia* to Leontius of Byzantium.[46] However, this is now generally considered to be the work of Leontius of Jerusalem.[47] He was emphatic that the one subject in Christ is clearly

---

45. See Relton, *A Study in Christology*. But note Louth, *John Damascene*, 157–79, where Louth makes an important point about *enhypostasia* against Relton and others. The term does not mean *in-hypostatic*; there is no process of "enhypostatization." The word is not *en* + the adjective formed from *hypostasis*, but instead it is the simple adjective from *hypostasis*, the prefix affirming the quality designated by the root in contrast to the prefix *an*, which denies it. *Enhypostasis* thus means "real," possessing concrete reality. Louth acknowledges that his argument comes from an unpublished paper of Brian Daley at the 1979 Eighth International Conference on Patristic Studies in Oxford, which was taken up by Grillmeier, *Christ in Christian Tradition*, 2/2:187n14, 193–98.

46. Sellers, *Chalcedon*, 308–20, esp. 316–19; Relton, *A Study in Christology*, 69–83.

47. Grillmeier, *Christ in Christian Tradition*, 2/2:276–312; Angelo Di Berardino, ed. *Patrology: The Eastern Fathers from the Council of Chalcedon (451) to John of Damascus (†750)*, trans. Adrian Walford (Cambridge: James Clarke, 2008), 288–89.

the *hypostasis* (person) of the Logos.[48] He came up with the idea of Christ's humanity as *enhypostatos* (existing in a *hypostasis* of another nature). Thus, the human nature in Christ is both *anhypostatos*—having no independent existence[49]—and *enhypostatos*—subsisting *in* the single *hypostasis* (person) of Christ, the Word. All operations of both natures are attributed to the *hypostasis* (person) of the divine Word.[50] Grillmeier comments that there is thus complete identity of the person before and after the incarnation. The preexistent Son himself is the subject of the incarnation. He assumes a human nature and so is the subject of both divine and human natures.[51] This was an absolutely crucial point, and "the chief merit for this identification seems to belong to Leontius of Jerusalem."[52] Borrowing from the Scythian monks, he used the phrase "one of the Trinity suffered in the flesh."[53]

Thus, for Leontius, the humanity becomes the source of divine life, since it is the Word's own flesh. Because Christ's humanity has divine life as the humanity of the eternal Son, we can, in union with Christ, receive divine life by grace and participation.[54] Later, Calvin affirmed that since Christ's human nature is the human nature of the eternal Son of God; it is suffused by the divine qualities of the Son, *while remaining human.*[55] The biblical evidence for this is evident, for example, in the angel's words in Luke 1:34–35 that the Holy Spirit's overshadowing Mary and bringing

---

48. Grillmeier, *Christ in Christian Tradition*, 2/2:277.

49. This is often rather unhelpfully called "the impersonal humanity." It is impossible to contemplate humanity that does not have personhood. What this idea attests is that the assumed humanity of Christ exists only as the humanity of the Son of God. In turn, *enhypostasia* underlines the point that this humanity *is* that of the eternal Son of the Father.

50. Davis, *Councils*, 234; Meyendorff, *Christ*, 61–68.

51. Grillmeier, *Christ in Christian Tradition*, 2/2:279.

52. Meyendorff, *Christ*, 73.

53. Meyendorff, *Christ*, 77; Grillmeier, *Christ in Christian Tradition*, 2/2:317–43.

54. Meyendorff, *Christ*, 78–79; Leontius of Jerusalem, *Adversus Nestorius*, 1.49 (*PG* 86/1:1512b). But see comments by Louth, *John Damascene*, 160–61.

55. Calvin, *Institutes*, 4.17.9. This statement is based on my reading of the Patristic source. Bill Evans has pointed me to the penetrating observations of Bruce McCormack to the effect that for Reformed theology the Holy Spirit, not the hypostatic union, preserves the incarnate Christ from the taint of sin. This is indeed so, as I have affirmed elsewhere. Robert Letham, *The Work of Christ* (Leicester: Inter-Varsity Press, 1993), 114–15; Letham, *The Holy Trinity: In Scripture, History, Theology, and Worship* (Phillipsburg, NJ: P&R, 2004), 56–57. However, the work of the Holy Spirit and the personalization of the incarnate one by the eternal Son are not at loggerheads, as if they were from disparate sources. The Son and the Spirit act distinctly, yet harmoniously and indivisibly in all the ways and works of God. Both are involved, with this distinction—the assumed humanity is in *personal union* not with the Holy Spirit but with the eternal Son. See Bruce L. McCormack, *For Us and Our Salvation: Incarnation and Atonement in the Reformed Tradition*, Studies in Reformed Theology and History (Princeton: Princeton Theological Seminary, 1993), 17–22. Evans discusses this question himself in William B. Evans, *Imputation and Impartation: Union with Christ in American Reformed Theology* (Eugene, OR: Wipf & Stock, 2008), 167–68.

about the new creation would result in Jesus's being called "holy—the Son of God."

Another contributor to the resolution of the post-Chalcedon Christological problem was the Emperor Justinian I (483–565, reigned from 527), in many ways the principal architect of the resolution of the crisis. His interest in theology propelled him onto the stage as a force to be reckoned with theologically as well as politically.[56] Grillmeier remarks that Justinian had "a commendable understanding of the problems of incarnational theology" and that "in Justinian we find for the first time the sketch of a complete interpretation of Christ's person and its union of divine and human nature in the one divine *hypostasis* of the Logos."[57] He had a strong grasp of the union, owing to the presence of Cyrilline elements and Leontius's model.

17.4.2   *The Second Council of Constantinople (553)*[58]

Justinian called the council "to unite the churches again, and to bring the Synod of Chalcedon, together with the three earlier, to universal acceptance."[59] A series of anathemas stressed the unity of Christ, and another series defended the distinction, not separation or division, of the natures.[60]

Canon 2 ascribes two births to the God-Logos, the one from eternity from the Father, without time and without body, and the other his being made flesh of the holy and glorious Mary, mother of God. The next three canons are all strongly anti-Nestorian. Canon 3 says that the God-Logos who works miracles and the Christ who suffered should not be separated, for it is one and the same Jesus Christ our Lord, the Word, who became flesh and a human being.[61] Behind this is the fact that Christ's unity is a true union, not a mingling or division. Canon 5 asserts that there is only one subsistence or person. The incarnation is to be seen solely from the *hypostasis* of the Son, who is one of the Trinity. Thus, "one of the trinity has been made man." Canon 8, on the other hand,

---

56. Davis, *Councils*, 225–29; Kenneth Paul Wesche, *On the Person of Christ: The Christology of Emperor Justinian* (Crestwood, NY: St Vladimir's Seminary Press, 1991), 165–66, 178–79.

57. Grillmeier, *Christ in Christian Tradition*, 2/2:438.

58. See Richard Price, "The Second Council of Constantinople (553) and the Malleable Past," in *Chalcedon in Context: Church Councils 400–700*, ed. Richard Price and Mary Whitby (Liverpool: Liverpool University Press, 2009), 117–32.

59. Percival, *Seven Ecumenical Councils*, 302.

60. Davis, *Councils*, 244–46; Sellers, *Chalcedon*, 330; Hardy, *Later Fathers*, 378–81.

61. Grillmeier, *Christ in Christian Tradition*, 2/2:446; Percival, *Seven Ecumenical Councils*, 312.

guards against monophysitism, pronouncing that both natures remain what they were: "For in teaching that the only-begotten Word was united hypostatically [to humanity] we do not mean to say that there was made a mutual confusion of natures, but rather each [nature] remaining what it was, we understand that the Word was united to flesh."[62] Canon 9 declares that the worshiping of Christ in two natures is in fact one act of worship directed to the incarnate God-Logos with his flesh.[63]

Grillmeier concludes that Constantinople II is "not a weakening of Chalcedonian terminology, but its logical clarification. . . . Nevertheless the use and application of the main concepts were clearer and more un-ambiguous than at Chalcedon."[64] Fairbairn agrees:

> When one recognizes that the fundamental issue of the controversy was *who* the one person of Christ was, and when one accepts the centrality of Cyril's place in the controversy, then it becomes clear that the Council of Chalcedon in 451 and the Second Council of Con-stantinople in 553 were consistent with each other and were Cyrillian in substance, even though they did not use Cyril's terminology.[65]

Crisp, exploring the logic of *enhypostasia*, concludes:

> Take away the Word and, assuming the remaining parts of the person of Christ can form a human being, the product of such a union is not the person of Christ, even if the person thus formed is called Jesus and lives in Nazareth. For without the hypostatic union with the Word, what we have is not Christ, the God-man.[66]

He points out that it is the Word who is the personal subject of the in-carnation and who assumes the human nature and personalizes it.[67] The human nature is only ever the natural endowment of a person. Thus, it is *the Word's* human soul and body and cannot be the human nature of another.[68] Crisp refers to Brian Daley's comment that *person* in the Greek fathers is not an independent subject with unique self-consciousness

---

62. Percival, *Seven Ecumenical Councils*, 313.

63. Percival, *Seven Ecumenical Councils*, 314–16; Grillmeier, *Christ in Christian Tradition*, 2/2:447–53.

64. Grillmeier, *Christ in Christian Tradition*, 2/2:456.

65. Fairbairn, "The Patristic Perspective," 82.

66. Oliver D. Crisp, *Divinity and Humanity: The Incarnation Reconsidered* (Cambridge: Cam-bridge University Press, 2007), 66.

67. Crisp, *Divinity and Humanity*, 82.

68. Crisp, *Divinity and Humanity*, 83.

and psychological freedom but more a particular individual within a universal species, with characteristics all its own so that one could call it by name. Crisp considers it essential to say that Christ is the second person of the Trinity, the subject to whom the human nature is joined. The natures exist in Christ, possessed or instantiated by him. The divine nature is essential to him, the human nature contingently related as the nature he assumed.[69]

There are implications here. Fairbairn rightly points to the impasse many find when talking about the cross. *Who* suffered there? Most today say either Christ suffered or the human nature suffered (betraying an implicit Nestorianism), or else they deny the impassibility of God and say God suffered. The point, Fairbairn stresses, is that suffering and death do not happen to a nature but to a person.[70] As Barth put it, "He exists as man so far and only so far as he exists as God"; and "the human nature acquires existence (subsistence) . . . in the mode of being (*hypostasis*, 'person') of the Word."[71] This is what Georges Florovsky terms "asymmetrical Christology" with union occurring from the side of the Logos.[72]

John of Damascus summed this up succinctly by saying that the nature is called *enhypostaton* that has been assumed by another *hypostasis* and in that has existence.[73] Twombly argues that *perichorēsis*, a term first used in the Christological debates, and especially by John, signifying mutual indwelling, is more dynamic than *enhypostasia*, the latter implying a state of rest whereas the former indicates movement toward the human object.[74] "The underlying anthropological vision here is one in which human nature, whether Christ's or ours, far from being diminished by its union with the divine nature, actually becomes fully itself."[75] He continues, "What gives licence to say of one nature what is antecedently true of the other nature is the hypostatically grounded unity of the

---

69. Crisp, "Desiderata," 29–35. See also Fred Sanders's comment, stressing the continuity of the councils, "This one divine person (Ephesus 431) who is fully divine and fully human (Chalcedon 451) is the second person of the trinity (Constantinople II 553)." Fred Sanders, "Introduction to Christology: Chalcedonian Categories for the Gospel Narrative," in *Jesus in Trinitarian Perspective: An Introductory Christology*, ed. Fred Sanders and Klaus Issler (Nashville: B&H Academic, 2007), 32.

70. Fairbairn, "The Patristic Perspective," 106–8.

71. Barth, *CD*, I/2:163.

72. Georges Florovsky, *The Byzantine Fathers of the Fifth Century*, vol. 8 of *The Collected Works of Father Georges Florovsky*, ed. Richard S. Haugh (Vaduz: Büchervertriebsanstalt, 1987), 197.

73. Cited by Twombly, *Perichoresis and Personhood*, 68–69.

74. Twombly, *Perichoresis and Personhood*, 70.

75. Twombly, *Perichoresis and Personhood*, 71.

one person of the incarnate Logos."[76] For John, in mutual indwelling, both the human nature and the human will were deified without being transformed into something else.[77] Twombly asks how a human mind can will if it is not at the same time a person. The answer is that it is a person, the person of the Son. *Anhypostatos* does not mean that Christ's humanity is impersonal but rather means that it has its existence in another.[78] To grant the human nature a *hypostasis* other than the Logos would be Nestorian, whereas to identify the *hypostasis* with the single nature of other heretics would be to erode the humanity.[79] In the words of the Damascene, "The Word of God serving as the person of the flesh . . . the very Word became person to the body."[80] Christ's humanity is complete; the person is God and not an autonomous human or some combination such as a "God-man."

17.5   Christ Has a Human Will as Well as a Divine Will: Constantinople III (680–681)[81]

That the declarations of Constantinople II did not stifle debate on Christ's humanity is evident by the issue of whether he had two wills or only one. Theodore of Pharan argued that there was in the incarnate Christ only one energy and one will, that of the Word. "The Incarnate Word was thus the agent and subject of all action, whether this was appropriate to his divine or human nature."[82] The Syrians accepted *monoenergism* (the claim that Christ had only one energy) and later *monotheletism* (the teaching that Christ had only one will). This was an extreme version of the Alexandrian stress on the oneness of Christ's person. All action was attributed to the person of Christ, not the natures. It seemed to be a belated triumph and vindication of the monophysites.[83]

However, Sophronius of Jerusalem, in opposition, insisted that action springs from the natures. At the Synod of Jerusalem in 634, the doctrine of two operations was defined; either nature works what is proper to itself. But Sophronius insisted that while there are two opera-

---

76. Twombly, *Perichoresis and Personhood*, 75.
77. Twombly, *Perichoresis and Personhood*, 83.
78. Twombly, *Perichoresis and Personhood*, 81.
79. Twombly, *Perichoresis and Personhood*, 61.
80. John of Damascus, *The Orthodox Faith* 3.2 (NPNF², 9/2:46), cited by Twombly, *Perichoresis and Personhood*, 60–61, from the Chase translation.
81. Pelikan, *The Christian Tradition*, 2:62–90; Meyendorff, *Christ*; Davis, *Councils*, 260–89.
82. Davis, *Councils*, 261.
83. Davis, *Councils*, 262–63.

tions, there is only one agent. This statement was limited to a rebuttal of monoenergism. Sophronius did not speak of two wills in Christ; the question had not yet surfaced. It was in 636 that Sergius, bishop of Constantinople, a monoenergist, issued an edict, the *Ecthesis*, signed by Pope Honorius in 638, to the effect that there is one Christ who works both divine and human effects, with one will. According to Sergius, the human nature is merely a docile instrument with no initiative of its own.[84]

Suddenly, in 638, the Muslims invaded. Within ten years much of the territory of the Eastern church was overrun. Because the Muslims treated all Christians equally, there was no longer any pressure on Christian heretics to conform to a prescribed standard of orthodoxy. At once monophysitism spread from Syria into Persia and Mesopotamia. The Nestorians remained strong in Persia and engaged in missionary activity beyond its borders. Orthodoxy shrank to the Byzantine lands, Greek in language under the patriarch of Constantinople. Many Greek monks fled to the West, including most notably Maximus the Confessor, who had already moved to Carthage in 628.[85] A huge controversy erupted, with many who embraced dyothelitism—the view that Christ had two wills—either mutilated or executed. Among them was Maximus.

For Maximus, the incarnation is the central factor in deification. Christ is the meeting point of God's reaching down to humanity, and of humanity's God-given tendency toward the divine. If the natures of Christ are two, Maximus concluded, the operations of those natures must be two. Consequently, Christ has two natures, operations, and wills. His wills proceed from the divine and human natures but always act in harmony because the single divine person assures that they choose the good.[86] For Maximus, since the union comes from the divine side, the eternal Word being the active agent, God is the cause of the natural harmony between Christ's divine and human wills. Christ is the superessential Word who gives his humanity the very right to exist.[87]

Maximus argued that since the incarnate Son is free from sin—which is the cause of conflict between God and humans—there can be no

---

84. Davis, *Councils*, 264–68.
85. Davis, *Councils*, 269–71.
86. Davis, *Councils*, 272–73; Maximus the Confessor, *On the Cosmic Mystery of Jesus Christ: Selected Writings from St. Maximus the Confessor*, trans. Paul M. Blowers and Robert Louis Wilken (Crestwood, NY: St Vladimir's Seminary Press, 2003), 173–76.
87. Maximus, *Disputatio cum Phyrro* (*PG*, 91:297B).

conflict between the divine and human wills of Christ.[88] Unlike us, he had no "gnomic will," which, after a process of deliberation, made its choice out of desire; this could not be so with Christ for there can be no process in the divine will. While we may think this erodes freedom, Maximus meant the reverse, for deliberation entails uncertainty, a clouded moral vision, which would be ethically unacceptable and indicate lack of freedom.[89] The Word sustains the distinctness and compatibility of both natures; if this were not so, Maximus argued, it would be a defect in the Son's deity.[90] Indeed, in assuming the human nature into union, the Son heals and divinizes it and does not overpower it.[91]

For Maximus, Jesus chooses in a human manner exactly what he wills as God. So the divine Son is the subject of all Jesus's deeds as the one who wills while Jesus chooses to have the same objective as God wills.[92] Thus, the Son of God wills divine things together with the Father who begot him, and he also wills naturally human things.[93] Jesus's struggle in Gethsemane shows he has a human will and that it is in harmony with the divine will. Maximus concluded, "His will in no way contradicts God, since it has been completely deified"[94]

In discussing Gethsemane, Maximus again referred to Gregory, who asked whether Jesus's prayer means resistance, courage, agreement, or disagreement? He acknowledged that it reflects perfect harmony, but this in turn raises the question of who is the subject of the prayer. If it were from a man just like us, it would entail some degree of resistance to the divine will. However, if it is a prayer of the man who is the Savior, it expresses

> ultimate concurrence of his human will with the divine will, which is both his and the Father's; and you have demonstrated that with the duality of his natures there are two wills and two operations respective to the two natures, and that he admits of no opposition between them, even though he maintains all the while the differ-

---

88. Maximus, *Disputatio cum Phyrro* (PG, 91:292A-B).
89. Louth, *John Damascene*, 168.
90. Maximus, *Opusculum 7* (PG, 91:73C-D).
91. Maximus, *Opusculum 7* (PG, 91:77C).
92. Maximus, *Opusculum 7* (PG, 91:77C-80A). See Christopher A. Beeley, *The Unity of Christ: Continuity and Conflict in Patristic Tradition* (New Haven, CT: Yale University Press, 2012), 299.
93. Maximus, *Opusculum 7* (PG, 91:77C).
94. Maximus, *Opusculum 6.1*, in Maximus the Confessor, *Cosmic Mystery*, 173, citing Gregory of Nazianzus, *Oration 30* 12 (PG, 91:65A).

ence between the two natures from which, in which, and which he is by nature.[95]

In this, as Blowers and Wilken remark in a note on this statement, Maximus asserts that Christ *is* as those two natures. Maximus argues that this demonstrates the harmony between Christ's human will and the indivisible will he shares with the Father from eternity; for, "having become like us for our sake, he was calling on his God and Father in a human manner . . . inasmuch as, being God by nature, he also in his humanity has, as his human volition, the fulfillment of the will of the Father."[96] Thus, "as God, he approved that salvation along with the Father and the Holy Spirit; as man, he *became* for the sake of that salvation *obedient* to his Father *unto death*."[97]

On a wider base, Maximus stated that "nothing natural is in conflict with God since God created it."[98] Maximus opposed any idea that the incarnation might involve an ontological conflict with the creation. What may seem a problem from the human perspective is nothing of the kind for God, since he created human nature. Maximus considered sin an aberration, a corruption and perversion rather than an intrinsic quality of nature as such.[99]

In 649, Pope Martin I called a council, with Maximus present, which adopted a clear dyothelite position, that in Christ there are two wills, in harmony with Maximus's teaching.[100] This did not settle the matter, and controversy lingered, eventually resolved at the Third Council of Constantinople in 680–681.

The definition produced by that council specified that in Christ there are "two natural wills and two natural operations, indivisibly, incontrovertibly, inseparably, inconfusedly." These two wills "are not contrary the one to the other . . . but the human will follows . . . as subject to his divine and omnipotent will."[101] With similar language, the council affirmed two natural operations in the one Lord Jesus Christ, divine and human. As Sellers points out, "For as his most holy and immaculate animated soul was not destroyed because it was deified, but continued in its own measure

---

95. Maximus, *Opusculum* 6.2, in Maximus the Confessor, *Cosmic Mystery*, 174 (also *PG*, 91:68A).
96. Maximus, *Opusculum* 6.4, in Maximus the Confessor, *Cosmic Mystery*, 176 (also *PG*, 91:68C).
97. Maximus, *Opusculum* 6.4, in Maximus the Confessor, *Cosmic Mystery*, 176 (also *PG*, 91:68D).
98. Maximus, *Opusculum* 7 (*PG*, 91:80A, my trans.).
99. Maximus, *Opusculum* 7 (*PG*, 91:80A).
100. Davis, *Councils*, 275–78.
101. Davis, *Councils*, 283; Percival, *Seven Ecumenical Councils*, 345.

and order . . . so also his human will, though deified, was not suppressed but rather preserved."[102] So close was the harmony in which the natures acted together that the human will "willed of its own free will those things which the divine will willed it to will."[103] This was not a parallelism, in which the two wills willed separately but in agreement. Rather, it was a synthesis, concurring into the one πρόσωπον of Jesus Christ.[104]

Ultimately, monotheletism was defeated for much the same reasons as monophysitism. To deny the existence of a human will was to adopt a truncated view of Christ's humanity. The lack of a human will would raise huge questions over whether Christ was truly human, and consequently over the gospel itself. Thus, the will is a predicate of the nature, and since Christ has two natures, he also has two wills. However, since his two natures are in inseparable union, so his two wills will in harmony and synthesis. The ecumenical nature of the decision is seen in that Pope Leo II approved the definition, had it translated into Latin, and distributed it to all bishops in the West.[105]

Later, John of Damascus reflected that

> since . . . Christ has two natures, we hold that he has also two natural wills and two natural energies. But since his two natures have one subsistence, we hold that it is one and the same person who wills and energises naturally in both natures of which, and in which, and also which is Christ our Lord: and moreover that he wills and energises without separation but as a united whole.[106]

Hence, although the monothelites accepted Chalcedon while the monophysites did not, John of Damascus would treat the former more sternly, since their error struck more closely at the heart of Christ's humanity and thus of salvation.[107]

The issue has arisen again recently in the writings of William Lane Craig[108] and J. P. Moreland, together with Garrett J. DeWeese. DeWeese ar-

---

102. Sellers, *Chalcedon*, 346.
103. John of Damascus, *The Orthodox Faith* 3.18 (NPNF², 9/2:67).
104. Sellers, *Chalcedon*, 346.
105. Davis, *Councils*, 284.
106. John of Damascus, *The Orthodox Faith* 3.14 (NPNF², 9/2:57).
107. Louth, *John Damascene*, 172; John of Damascus, *The Orthodox Faith* 3.13–15 (NPNF², 9/2:57–64).
108. William Lane Craig, "The Incarnation," in J. P. Moreland and William Lane Craig, *Philosophical Foundations for a Christian Worldview* (Downers Grove, IL: InterVarsity Press, 2003), 599–611.

gues, on the basis of recent discussions in analytical philosophy, that Christ has one will and, as a corollary, God has three. Apart from undermining the simplicity and indivisibility of God—both axioms of Trinitarian theology—such a construction veers close to Apollinarianism and is a modern form of monotheletism. Granted that DeWeese is aware of the problems and seeks to avoid them, it is only late in his case that he uses the dogma of *enhypostasia* to explain how the one will of Christ can be simultaneously divine and human.[109] On the other hand, Oliver Crisp has written in defense of the historic position of the church. "All dyothelitism claims," he remarks, "is that if Christ is fully human, he must have a human will that is distinct from a divine will. To deny this is to deny the full humanity of Christ."[110]

So much for the Christological questions posed in the early church. A number of other issues have surfaced since. We will consider them in the next chapter.

Further Reading

Crisp, Oliver D. *Divinity and Humanity: The Incarnation Reconsidered.* Cambridge: Cambridge University Press, 2007.

Crisp, Oliver D. *God Incarnate: Explorations in Christology.* London: T&T Clark, 2009.

Crisp, Oliver D. *The Word Enfleshed: Exploring the Person and Work of Christ.* Grand Rapids, MI: Baker Academic, 2016.

McGuckin, John A. *Saint Cyril of Alexandria and the Christological Controversy.* Crestwood, NY: St Vladimir's Seminary Press, 2010.

Twombly, Charles C. *Perichoresis and Personhood: God, Christ, and Salvation in John of Damascus.* Eugene, OR: Pickwick, 2015.

Weinandy, Thomas G. "Cyril and the Mystery of the Incarnation." In *The Theology of St. Cyril of Alexandria: A Critical Appreciation*, edited by Thomas G. Weinandy, 23–54. London: T&T Clark, 2003.

Study Questions

1. What was at stake in the Nestorian and Eutychian teachings?

2. Consider how best to express the dogma of *enhypostasia* in contemporary terms while remaining within the bounds of its meaning.

---

109. Garrett J. DeWeese, "One Person, Two Natures: Two Metaphysical Models of the Incarnation," in *Jesus in Trinitarian Perspective: An Introductory Christology*, ed. Fred Sanders and Klaus Issler (Nashville: B&H Academic, 2007), 114–53.

110. Crisp, *Divinity and Humanity*, 63.

3. "One of the Trinity died according to the flesh." This was voiced by the Scythian monks to express the unity of Christ's person and the distinctiveness of his human nature. How might this impact the question of Christ's obedience?

4. Why is it vital to maintain that Christ has two wills?

18

Incarnation (3)

Ongoing Questions

Since the Christological controversies of the early church, a number of related matters have garnered attention. Is the person of Christ confined to the hypostatic union or does he exist beyond its bounds? Granted Jesus's sinlessness, was it possible that he might have sinned? What kind of human nature was assumed in the incarnation—was it a nature exactly like ours, fallen and corrupt, then cleansed and sanctified from within? How were the divine attributes of omnipotence, omnipresence, and omniscience compatible with Christ's genuine humanity and his lowly state? In what ways are we able to make predications concerning Christ? How is the incarnation to be understood in the modern world?

18.1 The *Communicatio Idiomatum* and the *Extra-Calvinisticum*[1]

> When, then, we speak of his divinity we do not ascribe to it the properties of humanity. For we do not say that his divinity is subject to passion or created. Nor, again, do we predicate of his flesh or of his

---

1. A fuller account of the differences between Lutheran and Reformed Christologies can be found in my chapter "The Person of Christ," in *Reformation Theology: A Systematic Summary*, ed. Matthew Barrett (Wheaton, IL: Crossway, 2017), 313–45.

humanity the properties of divinity: for we do not say that his flesh or his humanity is uncreated. But when we speak of his subsistence, whether we give it a name implying both natures, or one that refers to only one of them, we still attribute to it the properties of both natures. For Christ, which name implies both natures, is spoken of as at once God and man, created and uncreated, subject to suffering and incapable of suffering: and when he is named Son of God and God, in reference to only one of his natures, he still keeps the properties of the co-existing nature, that is, the flesh, being spoken of as God who suffers, and as the Lord of Glory crucified, not in respect of his being God but in respect of his being at the same time man. . . . And this is the manner of the mutual communication, either nature giving in exchange to the other its own properties through the identity of the subsistence and the interpenetration of the parts with one another.[2]

18.1.1   *Lutheran Christological Innovations*

The foundation of Luther's Christology was that there is no God apart from Christ.[3] Consequently, Christ's humanity is omnipresent. The right hand of God is not to be located in one place but is everywhere: "Where is the Scripture which limits the right hand of God in this fashion to one place?" Luther asks.[4] He states:

> The Scriptures teach us . . . that the right hand of God is not a specific place in which a body must or may be . . . but is the almighty power of God, which at one and the same time can be nowhere and yet must be everywhere. . . . For if it were at some specific place, it would have to be there in a circumscribed and determinate manner . . . so that it cannot meanwhile be at any other place. But the power of God cannot be so determined and measured, for it is uncircumscribed and immeasurable, beyond and above all that is and may be. . . . On the other hand it must be essentially present at all places, even in the tiniest tree leaf.[5]

Luther concludes that Christ is present simultaneously in heaven and in the Lord's Supper, for "it is contrary neither to Scripture nor to the

---

2. John of Damascus, *The Orthodox Faith* 4.3 (NPNF², 9/2:48).
3. Martin Luther, "That These Words of Christ, 'This Is My Body,' Etc., Still Stand Firm against the Fanatics," in *LW*, 37:56.
4. Luther, "This Is My Body," in *LW*, 37:56.
5. Luther, "This Is My Body," in *LW*, 37:57.

articles of faith for Christ's body to be at the same time in heaven and in the Supper."[6]

Luther based his ideas on there being three forms of presence. First, an object is locally or circumscriptively in a place, where the object and the space fit precisely. People, for instance, occupy particular locations. Second, an object is present definitively or in an uncircumscribed way, where it can occupy more room or less. The risen Christ, passing through locked doors, and angels are not confined to particular spaces. Third, God alone occupies places repletively, being present in all places at all times, filling them while not being measured by any one location. Therefore, Christ is not confined to one mode of presence only.[7] Since the risen Christ was present definitively, it makes sense to take "this is my body" as it stands.[8] Wherever Christ is, he is present as God and as man; if this were not so, he would be divided.[9] Rather, he is one person with God, besides which there is nothing higher.[10] Since he is one indivisible person with God, wherever God is, he must be also. This is a mystery; Luther wanted to show "what crass fools our fanatics are."[11]

18.1.2 *Zwingli, Chemnitz, and Calvin*

In contrast, Zwingli argued that things are attributed figuratively to one nature that are accomplished by the other, based on the unity of Christ's person. This is not an actual transfer of attributes; he described this as *alloiosis*, meaning that where one nature is mentioned the other is understood, or where both are named, only one is understood.[12] Consequently, Zwingli resisted Luther's belief in the ubiquity of Christ's humanity. Luther held together the two natures to an extent that it is questionable whether he did justice to the humanity, while Zwingli distinguished them to a point where the unity of the person was suspect.

Martin Chemnitz, the leading Lutheran of the next generation, considered there to be a threefold aspect to the communication of attributes. The first type, resulting from the hypostatic union, entails the attribution of

---

6. Luther, "This Is My Body," in *LW*, 37:55.

7. Luther, "Confession concerning Christ's Supper," in *LW*, 37:215–16.

8. Luther, "Confession," in *LW*, 37:217.

9. Luther, "Confession," in *LW*, 37:218.

10. Luther, "Confession," in *LW*, 37:221–22.

11. Luther, "Confession," in *LW*, 37:223. This is a reference to Zwingli and those who thought like him.

12. Ulrich Zwingli, *Commentary on True and False Religion*, ed. Samuel Macaulay Jackson (1929; repr., Durham, NC: Labyrinth, 1981), 205.

516 Christ, the Son of God

properties of Christ's natures to his person *in concreto*.[13] Second are things attributed to the person according to both natures, when both natures perform in communion with the other what is proper to them.[14] Chemnitz's third category is that "countless supernatural qualities and qualities even contrary to the common condition of human nature are given and communicated to Christ's human nature."[15] Scripture testifies that the humanity assumed in the incarnation retains its essential attributes but because of the hypostatic union is exalted above every name and given all power in heaven and earth, so that the flesh is life-giving.[16] Since Christ's divine nature dwells personally in the assumed nature, it would be blasphemous to think that in this hypostatic union the humanity of Christ is left only in its merely natural state and that it had received nothing beyond its essential attributes, powers, and faculties. Scripture asserts that Christ was anointed above his fellows. These infused gifts are not the essential attributes of the divine nature but are his external workings infused into the human nature so that they inhere in it formally, habitually, and subjectively, an instrument suitable for the deity.[17]

Chemnitz agreed that there is no mixture or change in either nature.[18] The divine attributes communicated to the humanity are not possessed essentially by the human nature, or the divine nature would be commuted. Properties of one nature cannot become the properties of the other. There is no equalization of natures, no communication of essences or natures.[19] On the other hand, Chemnitz also rejected any denial that the assumed humanity has no share in divine attributes. He opposed the claim that the divine attributes relate only to the person and are only given verbally to Christ as man, the humanity having no communion in them at all.[20]

Chemnitz had a better grasp than Zwingli of the classic doctrine of the incarnation. As in the Patristic resolution, his basic premise was the hypostatic union, rather than the two natures. His view of ubiquity was nuanced too. Christ *is able to be present* when, where, and how he pleases, a hypothetical or optional omnipresence, as Bruce calls it.[21]

13. Martin Chemnitz, *The Two Natures in Christ*, trans. J. A. O. Preus (1578; repr., Saint Louis: Concordia, 1971), 215–31.
14. Chemnitz, *The Two Natures*, 231–40.
15. Chemnitz, *The Two Natures*, 241–42.
16. Chemnitz, *The Two Natures*, 243–44.
17. Chemnitz, *The Two Natures*, 247–48.
18. Chemnitz, *The Two Natures*, 267.
19. Chemnitz, *The Two Natures*, 270.
20. Chemnitz, *The Two Natures*, 278–79.
21. A. B. Bruce, *The Humiliation of Christ* (Edinburgh: T&T Clark, 1905), 99.

Chemnitz saw this as following from the hypostatic union, after which the Logos is not outside the flesh, so that Christ's human nature is always intimately and inseparably present to the Logos, with the possibility of being present at will to any part of the creation.[22] Chemnitz acknowledged that Jesus only occasionally used these gifts but after his ascension entered their full use. Brenz, in contrast, thought that Christ possessed them from conception but used them furtively.[23]

Calvin, in expounding the *communicatio idiomatum*, held that Christ was free from all corruption primarily "because he was sanctified by the Spirit that the generation might be pure and undefiled as would have been true before Adam's fall." Calvin added, "Here is something marvelous: the Son of God descended from heaven in such a way that, without leaving heaven, he willed to be borne in the virgin's womb, to go about the earth, and to hang upon the cross; yet he continually filled the world even as he had done from the beginning!"[24] This is what Lutherans were to call the *extra-Calvinisticum*, the claim that the person of Christ exists beyond the bounds of the assumed humanity.

However, Calvin so much stressed the two natures that he appears to have flirted with Nestorianism. Christ's divinity is so joined and united with his humanity that each retains its distinctive nature unimpaired, and yet these two natures constitute one Christ.[25] Calvin appears to equalize the natures, implying that the humanity existed prior to the union inasmuch as the union is formed out of the two. This impression is reinforced, in the same section, by his considering the *communicatio* to be a figure of speech. The Lutherans considered this a reality rather than a trope.

While Calvin says that passages that comprehend both natures at once set forth Christ's true substance most clearly of all (John 1:29; 5:21–23; 8:12; 9:5; 10:11; 15:1), he remarks that "the name 'Lord' exclusively belongs to the person of Christ only in so far as it represents a degree midway between God and us [*Nec alio respectu peculiariter in Christi personam competit Domini nomen, nisi quatenus medium gradum statuit inter Deum et nos*]."[26] *Medium gradum* raises

22. Bruce, *The Humiliation of Christ*, 100.
23. Bruce, *The Humiliation of Christ*, 101–2.
24. Calvin, *Institutes*, 2.13.4.
25. Calvin, *Institutes*, 2.14.1.
26. Calvin, *Institutes*, 2.14.3.

the question of how far Calvin understands the eternal Son to be the person of Christ or whether he thinks the person is a union of two natures, almost a third entity "midway between God and us." Then he adds:

> To him was lordship committed by the Father, until such time as we should see his divine majesty face to face. Then he returns his divine lordship to his Father so that—far from diminishing his own majesty—it may shine all the more brightly. Then, also, God shall cease to be the head of Christ, for Christ's own deity will shine of itself, although as yet it is covered by a veil.

Elsewhere he opposes Nestorianism very effectively.[27]

Yet the same tendency is particularly evident in Calvin's comments on 1 Corinthians 15:27. There, where Paul writes of the Son handing back the kingdom to the Father after his parousia, Calvin states that the Son "will transfer it in some way or other (*quodammodo*) from his humanity to his glorious divinity,"[28] as if the natures have some degree of autonomy.[29] It is this that lies at the root of the Reformed notion that the union of natures and the works performed by Christ are attributable to the Holy Spirit rather than to the union established in the Son himself; for if the incarnation was simply a coalescence of two natures, the union is subsequent to the natures, almost a conjunction, and so requires an outside agent to effect and maintain it.

Crisp discusses strong and weak views of the *communicatio idiomatum*, arguing in favor of a weak view in which attributes of both natures are predicable of the person, rather than the Lutheran position in which there is a transfer of attributes from one nature to the other, at least as far as the nonglorified humanity of Christ is concerned. Person-*perichorēsis* (in the Trinity) and nature-*perichorēsis* (in the incarnation, in which the divine omnipresence is transferred to the human nature) Crisp considers to be a mystery.[30]

---

27. Calvin, *Institutes*, 2.13.5.

28. John Calvin, *Calvin's Commentaries: The First Epistle of Paul the Apostle to the Corinthians*, trans. John W. Fraser (Grand Rapids, MI: Eerdmans, 1960), 327.

29. See the discussion in Marvin P. Hoogland, *Calvin's Perspective on the Exaltation of Christ in Comparison with the Post-Reformation Doctrine of the Two States* (Kampen: Kok, 1966), 168; Hoogland refers to E. Emmen and H. Quistorp, who both took this to imply that Calvin thought Christ's humanity is not eternal, but rejects this interpretation.

30. Oliver D. Crisp, *Divinity and Humanity: The Incarnation Reconsidered* (Cambridge: Cambridge University Press, 2007), 1–33.

18.1.3 *The* Extra-Calvinisticum

As a corollary, the Reformed maintained that the person of the Logos is not confined to the union established with the assumed humanity. As God, he transcends the bounds of the incarnate union. Conversely, Lutheranism, with its idea of the transference of divine attributes to the humanity, strenuously held that since the humanity partakes of omnipresence, the Son is never beyond its bounds. In calling the Reformed formulation the *extra-Calvinisticum* or "the Calvinistic beyond," Lutherans contended that it was a departure from orthodox Christology.

However, Luther and the Lutherans were the innovators. While Chemnitz had a surer grasp of the hypostatic union, and the Reformed sought to do justice to the genuineness of the assumed humanity, the weight of Patristic statements supports the latter. David Willis's classic work on Calvin's Christology concludes that it would be better to have called his formulation the "extra-Catholicum."[31] At least as early as Athanasius, this idea was commonplace. In his *De incarnatione* he wrote:

> For he was not, as might be imagined, circumscribed in his body, nor, while present in the body, was he absent elsewhere; nor, while he moved the body, was the universe left void of his working and providence; but, thing most marvellous, Word as he was, so far from being constrained by anything, he rather contained all things himself; and just as while present in the whole of creation, he is at once distinct in being from the universe, and present in all things by his own power . . . even when present in a human body and himself quickening it, he was, without inconsistency, quickening the universe as well, and was in every process of nature, and was outside the whole, and while known from the body by his works, he was none the less manifest from the working of the universe as well. . . . For he was not bound to his body, but rather was himself wielding it, so that he was not only in it, but was actually in everything, and while external to the universe, abode in his Father only. And this was the wonderful thing that he was at once walking as man, and as the Word was quickening all things, and as the Son was dwelling with his Father.[32]

31. Edward David Willis, *Calvin's Catholic Christology: The Function of the So-Called Extra Calvinisticum in Calvin's Theology* (Leiden: Brill, 1966). See, further, Andrew M. McGinnis, *The Son of God beyond the Flesh: A Historical and Theological Study of the Extra-Calvinisticum* (Edinburgh: T&T Clark, 2014).
32. Athanasius, *On the Incarnation* 17.1–5 (NPNF[2], 4:45).

Indeed, Origen had written that God the Word was incarnate but "not in such a way as to confine therein all the rays of his glory; and we are not to suppose that the light of him who is God the Word is shed forth in no other way than this."[33]

18.2   The Sinlessness of Christ

Jesus's sinlessness has occasioned little controversy in the history of the church. The witness of the New Testament is consistent and unambiguous. He challenged his opponents to convict him of sin, a challenge they found unanswerable (John 8:46). Whereas Adam was tempted in a beautiful garden and succumbed, Jesus was tempted in a bleak desert and triumphed (Matt. 4:1–10). His life was devoted to the will of the Father (e.g., Matt. 26:39; John 4:34; 17:4; Rom. 5:12–21; Heb. 10:5–10). Repeatedly, the New Testament affirms that he was without sin (2 Cor. 5:21; Heb. 4:14–16; 5:7–10; 7:26–27; 1 Pet. 1:19–24; 3:18). All sections of the church recognize this, and it is a basic axiom of the historic faith. As Barth comments, the sinlessness of Jesus "consisted in his actual freedom from sin itself, from the basis of all sins. That is why he was not a transgressor and committed no sins. That is why he could take on himself and deliver up to death the sins of all other men. That is why he could forgive sins and transgressions."[34] However, a question has arisen over whether it was *possible* for Jesus to sin.

18.3   Was It Possible for Jesus to Sin?

Given that Jesus did not sin, *could* he have sinned? The majority position in the history of the church is impeccability, that it was not possible. However, since the nineteenth century there has been a growing consensus that, although he did not sin, it was possible that, when tempted, he *could* have sinned—peccability.[35]

18.3.1   *Arguments for Peccability*

The thought is that, given Christ's full and complete humanity and the reality of his temptations, it must have been possible for him to have

---

33. Origen, *Against Celsus* 7.17 (ANF, 4:617).
34. Barth, *CD*, IV/1:258.
35. For a rigorous and incisive exposition of impeccability from the angle of analytic philosophy, see Oliver D. Crisp, *God Incarnate: Explorations in Christology* (London: T&T Clark, 2009), 122–36.

succumbed. If that were not so, would he not be less than human? Furthermore, could the temptations have been real if there was no chance of his capitulating? Would that not create an unbridgeable chasm between the incarnate Son and us such that he could not identify with us in our present condition? If so, it would seem that our salvation would be in jeopardy.

Two factors are prominent among those who support peccability. The obvious point is the full and unabbreviated humanity of Christ. From this is a second and related concern to maintain the likeness between Christ's humanity and ours. This is necessary for salvation. If Christ did not assume our humanity, how could he identify with us and represent us before the Father? Jesus is our Great High Priest, tempted in every point as we are, and thus qualified to help us in our situations. In order for him to do this, his temptations must have been like ours, or he would have been unable to identify with us. In our temptations there is always the possibility of our sinning, Therefore, it must have been the case with him. If not, we would have a hollow Savior. If it was impossible for him to sin, the force of his temptations would have been nullified since the outcome would never have been in the balance.

Charles Hodge argued that sinlessness does not entail impeccability, and the reality of Christ's temptations implies the possibility of sinning.[36] Hodge equally asserted that Christ was sinless and acted at all times in obedience to the Father. Hodge was concerned to avoid any idea that Christ was bound by some necessity that prevented him acting as a free agent. If he were, his temptations could not have been real, for "temptation implies the possibility of sin."[37] Others in the nineteenth century took a similar line, notably Edward Irving.

In more recent years, Karl Barth argued that Christ

> was a man as we are. His condition was no different from ours. He took our flesh, the nature of man as he comes from the fall. In this nature he is exposed every moment to the temptation to a renewal of sin. . . . His sinlessness was not therefore his condition. It was the act of his being in which he defeated temptation in his condition which is ours, in the flesh.[38]

---

36. Charles Hodge, *Systematic Theology* (Grand Rapids, MI: Eerdmans, 1977), 2:457.
37. Hodge, *Systematic Theology*, 2:457.
38. Barth, *CD*, IV/1:258–59.

Barth asked, "How else could he represent them except in a serious entering into their whole situation?"[39] He pointed to Hebrews 5:8, "He learned obedience through what he suffered," meaning that Christ's sinlessness was not an automatic result but was worked out in his acts.[40] The difference between Barth and Hodge on this point was that Barth held that Christ assumed a fallen human nature; I will discuss that matter shortly.

18.3.2   Arguments for Impeccability

One of the most incisive advocates of impeccability was the brilliant nineteenth-century American Presbyterian theologian W. G. T. Shedd.[41] Shedd argued that the question does not surround the supposed peccability of the human nature, since the humanity never exists independently of the personal union into which it was taken. Rather, it concerns Christ's *personal* impeccability. So "Christ while having a peccable human *nature* in his constitution was an impeccable *person*."[42] Herman Hoeksema took a similar line.[43] In short, the issue concerns whether it was possible for the *person* of Christ, the incarnate Son of God, to sin. Due to the hypostatic union, Christ's human nature does not exist of itself but is the human nature of the eternal Son of God. Bavinck concluded that if it were possible for Christ to have sinned, it would follow that it was possible for God to have sinned, or else we would be driven to deny the hypostatic union.[44]

McKinley lists at least nine major models proposed to explain impeccability. Four date from the Patristic era, one is medieval, one developed in the Reformation, and three are modern.

The Patristic models are based on the deity of Christ. First, since Jesus is God, impeccability is inherent and necessary to who he is. A second proposal, one that has persisted in Orthodox thought, is that Christ's humanity was in the process of deification, precluding the possibility of sin. Others held that the deity predominated and directed the assumed humanity. Additionally, it was argued that Jesus was upheld by divine grace. The claim that he lived in dependence on the Holy Spirit was

---

39. Barth, *CD*, IV/1:259.
40. Barth, *CD*, IV/1:260.
41. W. G. T. Shedd, *Dogmatic Theology* (Grand Rapids, MI: Zondervan, 1971), 2:330–49.
42. Shedd, *Dogmatic Theology*, 2:333.
43. Herman Hoeksema, *Reformed Dogmatics* (Grand Rapids, MI: Reformed Free Publishing Association, 1966), 358.
44. Bavinck, *RD*, 3:314.

anathematized at Ephesus, since it was associated with Nestorius and therefore the idea that the Spirit was other than his own.[45] In the medieval period some propounded the idea that Jesus was sinless by created grace.[46] Luther and Calvin, building on the preceding models, added new dimensions, based on Christ's human experience. Calvin developed the idea that Christ's deity and its attributes were concealed during the time of his humiliation. This resulted in his feeling the full force of temptation, but in this he was supported by the Spirit.[47]

Among modern proposals, in response to the kenosis theory that Christ divested himself of certain divine attributes in his incarnation, Macleod has pointed to a psychological restriction on Jesus's part: he did not know the whole truth about himself and so, when tempted, he did not know whether he would withstand it.[48] It does not follow, Macleod argues, that Christ was aware of his impeccability. It is unwise to conclude that at every point he knew all that there was to be known about himself.[49] As McKinley indicates, there are weaknesses in all of these proposals, but taken in combination they have a cumulative force.

18.3.3   What Are the Main Issues?

The main questions that need to be answered regarding Christ's sinlessness are as follows.

How real were Christ's temptations? Is there a distinction between his temptations and ours? Temptation cannot be defined in terms of the capacity of the one tempted to succumb. Temptation is enticement to sin from whatever source. On this basis, Christ endured stronger temptations than we do, since no one has resisted them as he did. A person walking into the teeth of a force 9 gale feels the stresses and strains far more than the one who goes with the flow. Moreover, Christ took the form of a servant, humanity in a low condition, living in a world torn by sin and decay (Heb. 2:13–18).[50]

---

45. John E. McKinley, *Tempted for Us: Theological Models and the Practical Relevance of Christ's Impeccability and Temptation* (Milton Keynes: Paternoster, 2009), 131–43; Anathematism 9, Council of Ephesus AD 431, in Henry R. Percival, ed. *The Seven Ecumenical Councils*, 214–15.
46. McKinley, *Tempted for Us*, 144–68.
47. McKinley, *Tempted for Us*, 169–88.
48. Donald Macleod, *The Person of Christ* (Leicester: Inter-Varsity Press, 1998), 220–30.
49. MacLeod, *Christ*, 230.
50. Herman Bavinck, *Our Reasonable Faith*, trans. Henry Zylstra (Grand Rapids, MI: Baker, 1977), 329.

Shedd, addressing the objection of whether a person who cannot sin can really be tempted to sin, says: "This is not correct; any more than it would be correct to say that because an army cannot be conquered, it cannot be attacked. Temptability depends upon the constitutional *susceptibility*, while impeccability depends upon the *will*."[51] Crisp has a sporting analogy: it is a foregone conclusion that an invincible boxer will win, but in order to do so he must put up a fight against a real opponent.[52]

This simply refers us back to the question of the nature of temptation and what its sources are. As a working definition, I have proposed that temptation is incitement to sin, from whatever source that incitement arises. We face onslaughts from three sources: the world, the flesh, and the devil. The key for us is the flesh. Temptations from without meet an answering response from within. There is always something within us that finds such inducements attractive in varying ways, depending on our differing predilections for particular sins. Often we do not need external stimuli to draw us to sin. There is enough within us to lead us astray without our looking elsewhere.

With Jesus, temptation came from without—from the devil and from the world around him. Nevertheless, this was still temptation. It was still inducement to break the law of God. If anything, he felt it more fiercely than anyone else. He endured the uninhibited fury of the devil seeking to divert him from the course prepared by the Father (Matt. 4:1–10). The stronger the resistance, the more forceful the buffeting, and no one felt temptation more than he. It is enough that he was induced to sin. The twin forces of the devil and militant human opponents were quite sufficient, for his steadfast resistance made their enticements unremitting in their fury.[53]

Is there a distinction between impeccability and temptability? Yes; temptability relates to the capacity to face an incitement to sin, whereas impeccability refers to the impossibility of responding positively to such incitement. As Bavinck indicates, the struggle Christ faced in temptation was not nullified by his being impeccable, since the latter was ethical and had to be demonstrated in an ethical manner.[54] Crisp draws attention

51. Shedd, *Dogmatic Theology*, 2:336.
52. Crisp, *God Incarnate*, 133.
53. For a detailed analysis of temptations of various kinds, see Crisp, *God Incarnate*, 122–36.
54. Bavinck, *RD*, 3:315.

to the argument of Anselm that Christ had the capacity to lie but was incapable of doing so.[55] Anselm considers that Christ could have told a lie if he had willed to do so. However, he could not will to lie.[56] In this there is a distinction between Christ having the capacity to sin, since he was human, and the impossibility of his sinning due to his obedient will. Crisp compares this to a fragile champagne glass, capable of breaking but protected by secure wrapping that prevents this outcome.[57]

Is the possibility of sinning a defining characteristic of humanity? This is not sustainable. The redeemed in heaven can hardly have the possibility of sinning, as their status is secure. Yet this, apart from its exemplification in Christ, will be the quintessence of what it means to be human, freedom consisting in the total deliverance from sin.

However, Bruce Ware and John McKinley suggest the possibility that temptation may still exist in heaven, but they agree that the redeemed will resist it.[58] If we suppose that such temptation might occur, it would support the point that genuine temptation is compatible with impeccability. However, the idea is entirely speculative, and there are strong countervailing reasons. From what source would such temptations arise? It could hardly be from a corrupt nature, which would be eradicated by glorification. The world, in its rebellion against God, would no longer be present, while the devil would be cast into eternal fire. It is hard to see what forces there might be that could pose such a threat. However, the point at issue if peccability for the redeemed were involved in that scenario would be the possibility of the failure of eschatological salvation, of being cast out of heaven, of another fall. The whole sense of Scripture is that this is ruled out. If the quintessence of being human is found in heaven and consists, among other things, in freedom from the possibility of sinning, it follows that impeccability of itself does not undermine the humanity of Christ in his state of incarnate weakness prior to the resurrection.

Thomas Morris has an important proposal in his distinction between an *individual essence*, a cluster of properties essential for an individual to be the entity it is, and a *kind essence*, which he considers to be a cluster of properties without which an individual could not belong to the natural

---

55. Crisp, *God Incarnate*, 132–33.
56. Anselm, *Cur Deus homo?* 2.10, in Brian Davies, *Anselm of Canterbury: The Major Works* (Oxford: Oxford University Press, 1998), 326.
57. Crisp, *God Incarnate*, 132.
58. McKinley, *Tempted for Us*, 272n22.

kind it exemplifies. In terms of the latter, he suggests that "there are properties which happen to be *common* to members of a natural kind, which may even be *universal* to all members of that kind, without being *essential* to membership in the kind." Many critics have employed what Morris calls "the look around town approach." As you look around town, you observe that every human being has certain properties in common, among which is the property of being sinful. To conclude that being sinful is an essential part of human nature is to miss this distinction. Being sinful is common to humans as they are, universally so, but it does not follow that it is essential to being human.[59] We may conclude that since a sinful condition is not essential to being human, the argument that impeccability undermines the reality of Christ's humanity and the genuineness of his temptations fails.

18.4   Did Christ Assume a *Fallen* Human Nature?[60]

18.4.1   *Are There Differences between Christ's Humanity and Ours?*

The question remains—what kind of human nature did Christ assume in the incarnation? Was it the nature of Adam before the fall, a sinless nature but with the potential to disobey God and fall into sin? Or did he take a fallen nature, like Adam and his successors after the fall, with an in-built bias to sin? Or was it a nature preserved from sin and its associated contamination, and, if so, how could he still be one with us?

In the last two centuries, an increasing number (including Edward Irving,[61] most notably Karl Barth,[62] and T. F. Torrance[63]) have argued that, for Christ to identify with us in our fallen condition, it was necessary for him to have a fallen human nature. By assuming humanity in its fallenness, he redeemed it from where it actually is. Unless he has done this, he cannot have saved us in our actual state as fallen human beings. Nor can he effectively sympathize or intercede for us if he has no experience of our own condition.

59. Thomas V. Morris, "The Metaphysics of God Incarnate," in *Oxford Readings in Philosophical Theology*, vol. 1, *Trinity, Incarnation, and Atonement*, ed. Michael Rea (Oxford: Oxford University Press, 2009), 216.

60. See the excellent discussion in Macleod, *Christ*, 221–30.

61. Edward Irving, *Collected Writings* (London: Alexander Strahan, 1864–1865), 5:126, 129, 137.

62. Barth, *CD*, I/2:151–55.

63. Thomas F. Torrance, *The Mediation of Christ* (Grand Rapids, MI: Eerdmans, 1983), 48–52; Torrance, *Incarnation: The Person and Life of Christ* (Milton Keynes: Paternoster, 2008), 60–65, 204–6.

Barth argues that "[Christ's] condition was no different from ours. He took our flesh, the nature of man as he comes from the fall. . . . His sinlessness was not therefore his condition. It was the act of his being in which he defeated temptation in his condition which is ours, in the flesh."[64] Consequently, Christ reversed the effects of the fall. Barth cites Hebrews 2:11–18, 4:15, and 5:8. In contrast to us, Christ suffers temptation on the offensive.[65] At root, the Word is flesh, "all that we are and exactly like us even in our opposition to him."[66] "He did nothing that Adam did. But he lived life in the form it must take on the basis and assumption of Adam's act."[67] So "there must be no weakening or obscuring of the saving truth that the nature which God assumed in Christ is identical with our nature as we see it in the light of the Fall. If it were otherwise, how could Christ be really like us?"[68] In short, "he entered the concrete form of our nature, under which we stand before God as men damned and lost."[69] Barth acknowledges that this was the position of Gottfried Menken (1812) and Edward Irving (1827).[70] Earlier, in 1912, H. R. Mackintosh refuted Irving. He suggested that Irving had misunderstood the Patristic use of *flesh* as a synonym for humanity, leading him to conclude that because Christ was liable to death, his humanity was fallen. He also thought Irving had a loose idea of sinlessness.[71]

The advocates of Christ's having a fallen human nature want to avoid any tendency to docetism. An unfallen nature, it is held, would mean his humanity was not real, for it would be detached from the world we live in. Instead, they claim, Christ acted in redeeming love from within our own nature, sanctifying it and offering it up to the Father. T. F. Torrance cites Cyril approvingly to the effect that the Son penetrated into the disobedient sonship of our Adamic humanity and restored it to proper sonship in the image of God by living out within it a life of continuous and perfect obedience.[72]

---

64. Barth, *CD*, IV/1:258–59.

65. Barth, *CD*, IV/1:260–61.

66. Barth, *CD*, I/2:151.

67. Barth, *CD*, I/2:152.

68. Barth, *CD*, I/2:153.

69. Barth, *CD*, I/2:153.

70. Barth, *CD*, I/2:154.

71. H. R. Mackintosh, *The Doctrine of the Person of Christ* (Edinburgh: T&T Clark, 1912), 276–78.

72. Thomas F. Torrance, *Theology in Reconciliation* (Grand Rapids, MI: Eerdmans, 1975), 170; Torrance, *Incarnation*, 82.

Torrance cites Gregory of Nazianzus's famous dictum "Whatever is not assumed cannot be healed" to argue that if Christ did not have the same nature as ours, we could not be saved. "One thing should be abundantly clear, that if Jesus Christ did not assume our fallen flesh, our fallen humanity, then our fallen humanity is untouched by his work—for '*the unassumed is the unredeemed*,' as Gregory Nazianzen put it."[73] However, Torrance overlooks the point that this was written against Apollinaris, who claimed that the Son took the place of a human mind in the incarnate Christ. Gregory was opposing an ontological claim, not asserting an ethical one.[74]

Similarly, Thomas Weinandy appeals to Aquinas in support of this position.[75] However, Aquinas refers to Christ's assuming the defects of fallen nature, such as hunger, thirst, and death—the penalties of sin but not sin itself.[76]

The case has been supported recently in evangelical circles by John C. Clark and Marcus Peter Johnson.[77] They refer to a range of historical sources in support.[78] Their citation from Basil has the most substance to it, but he is opposing the idea that Christ has a heavenly body. He is dealing with flesh and soul, or with the soul using a body, with ontological realities without any reference to sin.[79] Clark and Johnson's reference to Irenaeus does not require a fallen or corrupt nature but requires a nature bearing the ravages of the fall.[80] Tertullian writes that the flesh of Christ is called the nature of that which had sinned. It is so in its nature, not in the corruption coming from Adam, for "there was in Christ the same flesh as that whose nature in man is sinful," and "in putting on our flesh, he made it his own; in making it his own, he made it sinless."[81] But Tertullian does not address the same question as Clark and Johnson pose.

---

73. Torrance, *Incarnation*, 62.

74. "Whoever has set his hope on a human being without mind is actually mindless himself and unworthy of being saved in his entirety. The unassumed is the unhealed." Gregory of Nazianzus, *Letter 101, to Cledonius*, in *St. Gregory of Nazianzus: On God and Christ*, trans. Frederick Williams and Lionel Wickham (Crestwood, NY: St Vladimir's Seminary Press, 2002), 158.

75. Thomas G. Weinandy, "The Marvel of the Incarnation," in *Aquinas on Doctrine: A Critical Introduction*, ed. Thomas G. Weinandy, Daniel A. Keating, and John P. Yocum (London: T&T Clark, 2004), 84n9.

76. Aquinas, *ST* 3a.4.6., 3a.14.1–4, 3a.15.1. *SCG* 29, citing Rom. 8:3, says, "Christus veram quidem carnem habuit, sed non carnem peccati, quia in eo peccatum non fuit; sed similem carni peccati."

77. John C. Clark, *The Incarnation of God: The Mystery of the Gospel as the Foundation of Evangelical Theology* (Wheaton, IL: Crossway, 2015).

78. Clark, *Incarnation*, 114–17.

79. Basil, *Letter 261, to the Sozopolitans* (NPNF[2], 8:300).

80. Irenaeus, *Against Heresies* 3.18.7 (ANF, 1:448).

81. Tertullian, *On the Flesh of Christ* (ANF, 3:335–36).

Neither does Calvin write of these issues. Rather, he ma
scent undertaken in the incarnation and the lowly conditi
Christ came, a matter not in dispute.[82] Thus, "[Christ] m
self as but a lowly and despised man" and in "a lowly
condition," neither of which requires the assumption of a fallen nature.[83]
Similarly in the same section Calvin argues that what Peter wrote in
1 Peter 3:18 would have been meaningless unless the Son of God in his
humanity had been weak. Indeed, he was "true man but without fault or
corruption." He was free of all stain by virtue of the sanctifying operation of the Spirit.[84] Calvin makes similar comments on Colossians 1:22.[85]

Barth cites Calvin on John 1:14, where he talks of the "low and abject
state" to which the Son of God descended, taking to himself "that flesh
addicted to so many wretchednesses." However, Calvin immediately
qualifies this, adding: "'Flesh' here is not used for corrupt nature (as in
Paul), but for mortal man. It denotes derogatorily his frail and almost
transient nature."[86]

All the references cited by Clark and Johnson are anachronistic, used
to address a question posed later in the nineteenth century. As Kelly comments, "I have not yet found a passage in the Fathers that clearly shows
they taught Christ's participation in fallen flesh."[87]

The argument that Christ assumed a fallen nature raises more questions than it purports to solve, for it requires Christ's own assumed humanity to be healed. Clark and Johnson also cite Kuyper, who appears
to insist that Christ took a human nature that was fallen, just like us.[88]
However, the wider context indicates what Kuyper means. He points
out that corruption inherited from Adam is a by-product of the guilt
incurred. The question involves whether Christ was guilty of the sin of
Adam and whether he inherited original sin. The answer Kuyper gives

---

82. Calvin, *Institutes*, 4.17.2.
83. Calvin, *Institutes*, 2.13.2.
84. Calvin, *Institutes*, 2.13.4.
85. ". . . corpus humanum quod nobiscum habuit commune Filius Dei . . . eandem nobiscum naturam induisse Filium Dei . . . humile, terrenum et infirmitatibus multis obnoxiam corpus
gestasse." John Calvin, *Commentarii in Pauli Epistolas*, Ioannis Calvini opera exegetica (Geneva:
Droz, 1992), 406.
86. John Calvin, *Calvin's Commentaries: The Gospel according to St. John 1–10*, trans. T. H. L.
Parker (Grand Rapids, MI: Eerdmans, 1961), 20.
87. Douglas F. Kelly, *Systematic Theology*, vol. 2, *Grounded in Holy Scripture and Understood
in the Light of the Church: The Beauty of Christ: A Trinitarian Vision* (Fearn: Mentor, 2014), 312.
88. Abraham Kuyper, *The Work of the Holy Spirit*, trans. Henri De Vries (Grand Rapids, MI:
Eerdmans, 1975), 84.

is an emphatic no. This "does not imply the least participation of our sin and guilt." Christ is like us in one sense and not like us in another. What Kuyper means is that the nature Christ took is identical to ours in the effects of the fall that engulf it so that it is "susceptible to its temptations," but, on the other hand, "he is completely cut off from all fellowship with its sin."[89]

The argument that Christ assumed a fallen nature has a certain appeal. It appears to paint a satisfying picture of Christ living a sinless life within the precise conditions we are in, thus achieving a complete and thorough deliverance for us. Not only Irving but also Barth and Torrance defend Christ's sinlessness. Indeed, they argue that his triumph is *magnified* by his living a sinless life from out of the depths of our fallen nature. However, all is not as straightforward as it seems.

Macleod thinks the problems with the claim that Christ took a fallen nature are as follows: First, it implies a Nestorian separation of the human nature from Christ's person. Second, its understanding of what "fallen" means entails that Christ inherits original sin, for a sinful nature and original sin are inextricably linked. Third, it ignores the state of humiliation; Christ assumed into union not a nature like Adam's before the fall but one bearing the consequences of the fall.[90]

18.4.2 *What Is at Stake?*

1. A crucial factor is that our fallen nature is inherently sinful. We inherit corruption from the moment of our conception. This contaminated nature we receive from our parents, and they from theirs, and so on back to Adam. It entails an unavoidable, in-built propensity to disobey God. We cannot but do wrong. Even if we do what is intrinsically good (obeying our parents when children, doing acts of kindness), we do so from wrong motives and not with a view to the glory of God.

Moreover, we are guilty of the first sin of Adam. Adam's actions led the whole race into ruin, including even the youngest infants. The guilt Adam incurred is shared by every member of the race. So too is its penalty, death.

Therefore, we all share three things as members of the human race in solidarity with Adam: first, the guilt of his first sin, in which we partici-

---

89. Kuyper, *Holy Spirit*, 84–85.
90. Macleod, *Christ*, 224–29.

pated; second, the penalty of that sin, death; and third, the inheritance of a corrupt nature.

The Bible describes fallen human nature as corrupt. If Christ had a fallen nature, he unavoidably would be included in the sin of Adam and its consequences. Even if he had not sinned throughout the course of his life, he would still have been guilty of the sin of Adam and have inherited the corruption shared by the rest of the race. He could not have saved us, since he would have needed atonement himself, if only for his inclusion in the sin of Adam. Since Christ's humanity never exists by itself in separation from his person, any attribution of fallenness to that nature is a statement about Christ. If his human nature was fallen, Christ was fallen, corrupt, and subject to the penalty faced by Adam and the rest of the race.

In contrast, the letter to the Hebrews stresses that he did not need to atone first for his own sins and then, afterward, for the sins of others. This is the great point of difference between Christ and the high priests of old Israel. None of them could effect our salvation, since they were sinners. If Jesus had needed atonement himself, he could not have been the Mediator of a better covenant. On the other hand, Jesus, needing no atonement, is able to save us completely. Thus, there is this twofold discontinuity between Christ and us: he did not commit actual sins, and he was also separate from the need for atonement for sin (Heb. 4:15; 7:26).

Some might think at this point that the virginal conception is in some way connected with his avoidance of "the entail of consequence" resulting from the sin of Adam. This may be so, but it seems sounder to consider this matter safeguarded by the creative, sanctifying work of the Holy Spirit in setting him apart from sin and corruption and thus beginning a new humanity with Christ, the second Adam, as its Head (Luke 1:34–35).

2. It follows that those who advocate the assumption of a fallen human nature by Christ and also wish to preserve his sinlessness abandon covenant theology and the claim that the race participates in the sin of Adam as its covenant head. By cutting the ties between Adam and the race, such advocates seek to offset the possibility that Christ inherited sin and guilt.

However, if this relationship of solidarity with the first Adam is jettisoned, the other side of the equation is threatened too—the participation of the new humanity in Christ, the second Adam. It is no surprise that Barth, Torrance (as Irving before them), and Gunton have doctrines of the atonement significantly different from Reformed orthodoxy. Irving described the doctrine of penal substitutionary atonement as "stock-exchange divinity," a pejorative phrase cited approvingly by Gunton.[91]

It follows that if Christ had a fallen human nature yet committed no actual sins himself, sooner or later he would have died—perhaps from pneumonia or of old age—as a consequence of being under the covenant headship of Adam. This death could never have saved us, for only by his substitutionary sufferings on the cross could atonement be made.[92] A natural death would contradict his testimony that his death was voluntary (John 10:11, 14–15, 17–18). Thus, I will argue for the necessity of the cross. That alone could save us.

3. The claim that, to sympathize effectively with us, Christ needed to share our fallenness and corruption sounds rather like the argument that to counsel a person who has committed adultery, one must have committed adultery oneself. Christ's sympathy as High Priest is directly connected to his ability. His sympathy is *effective* sympathy. He sends us grace to help us in time of need. He is able to do so precisely because he has been tempted and has emerged without stain. It is *his conquest of temptation* that qualifies him as our High Priest, not any possibility that he was subject to it.

A basic premise for the idea that Christ had a fallen human nature is that anything other than a propensity to sin would diminish his humanity. We have considered this argument above and rejected it. A fallen nature is a necessary part of what it means to be a *fallen* human being, but it is not definitive of a human being per se. In fact, being human is being in relation to God as his image bearers. That was how Adam was first created and how the second Adam preeminently is. We gain our humanity by being *rescued* from sin and corruption, not by wallowing in it.

Christian theology is interrelated. New developments in one area inevitably impinge on others. If you enter a room, by opening the door, you set in motion new wind currents. Objects on the other side of the room will be disturbed or displaced by the draft. If windows are open, curtains will billow, and your favorite lamp may come crashing to the floor and

---

91. Colin Gunton, *The Actuality of Atonement* (Edinburgh: T&T Clark, 1988), 128–37.
92. Robert Letham, *The Work of Christ* (Leicester: Inter-Varsity Press, 1993).

smash to smithereens without your laying so much as a finger on it. Here, a claim concerning the humanity of Christ has the most profound results. The gospel itself is at stake. Entailed in that gospel are the eternal deity of Christ and his unabbreviated humanity, with its assumption into personal union by the Son. Following all this comes his conquest of sin and death. If he had assumed a fallen human nature, he could not have achieved this, for he would have needed a savior himself.[93]

18.5 The Kenosis Theory

"There are obvious difficulties in supposing that, in the plain and obvious sense of the words, the human mind of the Babe of Bethlehem was thinking, as he lay in the manger, of the Procession of the Holy Ghost, the theorems of hydrodynamics, the novels of Jane Austen, and the Battle of Hastings."[94] Questions arise over the compatibility of the omniscience of deity with the limited knowledge of human nature: How can these coexist in one person? Will not the deity swamp the human limitations?

18.5.1 *Historical Background*

The nineteenth century saw an increasing interest in human psychology, personhood, and consciousness. This raised the issue of how these ideas could be related to orthodox Christology. Lutheran theologians proposed, in a variety of ways, that in the incarnation Christ divested himself of certain divine attributes, especially omniscience, omnipotence, and omnipresence. The verb κενόω, "empty,"[95] in Philippians 2:7 was at one time the focus, from which the movement got its name. However, the main issues are theological and would remain regardless of the exegetical conclusions drawn from Philippians 2:7.

18.5.2 *Theological Arguments for the Kenosis Theory*

Since some have considered it impossible for limitations of human knowledge to coexist with omniscience, on the grounds that the latter would swamp the former, they have argued that, in order for Christ to

93. For further reading, see Crisp, *Divinity and Humanity*, 90–117; Darren O. Sumner, "Fallenness and Anhypostasia: A Way Forward in the Debate over Christ's Humanity," *SJT* 67 (2014): 195–212; Kelly Kapic, "The Son's Assumption of a Human Nature: A Call for Clarity," *IJST* 3 (2001): 154–66.
94. E. L. Mascall, *Christ, the Christian and the Church* (London: Longmans, Green and Co., 1946), 53.
95. kenoō.

be fully human, divine attributes incompatible with human limitations were relinquished. These attributes, again, are specifically omnipotence, omnipresence, and omniscience. To save us, Christ needed to undergo the temptations and sufferings common to humans. This would be rendered impossible if, during his incarnate life on earth, he were omnipotent, had comprehensive knowledge of the future, or could transcend the restrictions of time and space. It is clear that the issues involved here reach to the heart of the saving work of Christ. Moreover, the theory raises large questions connected to the relationship between divine and human knowledge.

18.5.3   General Theological Objections

The world-ruling functions of the Son. With the kenosis theory, the Son, in emptying himself of these attributes when becoming incarnate, abandoned his rule over the universe. This would entail a disruption in the Trinity. As William Temple observed, "To say that the creative Word was so self-emptied as to have no being except in the infant Jesus, is to assert that for a certain period the history of the world was let loose from the control of the creative Word."[96] Donald Baillie observes that Temple's comment is predicated on the kenosis theory's own premises that postulate a division between the persons of the Trinity.[97]

The immutability of God. Following this, the theory implies that God is no longer true to himself, for certain aspects of his character could be suspended, curtailed, or abandoned, whether for a time or permanently. If that were so, Christ would not convey to us a genuine and true knowledge of God, since God himself would lurk behind a restricted revelation. Jesus could hardly have said to Philip, "Whoever has seen me has seen the Father" (John 14:9).

Incarnation is not metamorphosis. Baillie's estimate of the theory is that it implies a metamorphosis. Underlying the theory is the assumption that God and man cannot coexist uncurtailed in the person of Christ. As such, the eternal Son existed as fully God before the incarnation and as fully man during his earthly life and ministry, with crucial elements

---

96. William Temple, *Christus Veritas*, 142f., cited in D. M. Baillie, *God Was in Christ: An Essay on Incarnation and Atonement* (New York: Charles Scribner's Sons, 1948), 96.
97. Baillie, *God Was in Christ*, 96.

of his deity relinquished. In the assumption of human nature in the incarnation, the eternal Son would contract to less than who he is. The imagery would then be of a caterpillar transitioning into a butterfly. The problem for the theory is merely postponed to the postascension state. If unabbreviated deity will swamp humanity in the incarnate Christ from conception to the cross, how can his humanity coexist after the ascension? If aspects of deity are divested in the first instance, is not humanity obliterated in the second? An alternative scenario would consist of such a transforming change to the humanity as to transmute it into the divine, an apotheosis rather than an exaltation.

18.5.4 Relevant New Testament Passages

John 1:14. I noted in chapter 16 that the subject in John 1:14 who became flesh is the Word, who has already been identified as God and the Creator (vv. 1ff.). Yet he becomes flesh and lives as man, while his glory is revealed (vv. 15, 18).

Philippians 2:6–8. While the kenosis theory takes its name from the verb in Philippians 2:7, it does not stand or fall on the exegesis of this or any other passage. The theological arguments are the most crucial. However, the theory requires that we give attention to Philippians 2.

Main interpretations of Philippians 2:6–8. Problems have surrounded the noun ἁρπαγμός (v. 6),[98] which occurs only here in the Bible. Many proposals have been advanced, while commentators have often been confused and inaccurate. The word occurs in the clause at the end of verse 6, "[He] did not count equality with God [ἁρπαγμός]." It would connote something like booty, a prize, a piece of good fortune, or the like.[99]

Res rapienda—a prize to be seized. This line of interpretation considers ἁρπαγμός to have the sense of "a prize to be seized." It would follow that Christ was not eternally equal with God and was offered the opportunity to seize such a status, like Adam, but declined to do so, unlike Adam. Instead, Christ arrived at this status by humbling himself and living in human obedience. This view drives a wedge between Christ's being in the form of God, which generally it accepts, and his being equal

---

98. *harpagmos.*
99. BAG, 108.

with God. Some like Dunn have argued that there is a contrast here with Adam, who grasped at being like God, whereas Christ, the second Adam, took another route, refusing this way of proceeding and instead emptied himself.[100] The interpretation is at odds with the overall New Testament teaching that Christ is eternally one with God.

Res rapta—a prize to be retained. This idea understands ἁρπαγμός as "a prize to be clutched, or eagerly retained." Here Paul would be saying that Christ refused to regard his equality with God as something to be clutched or retained but instead took the form of a servant (v. 7). This interpretation agrees that in terms of preexistence, Christ was in the form of God and equal with God. Some, such as J. B. Lightfoot, held that in refusing to do this, Christ became man and so emptied himself "not of his divine nature . . . but of the glories, the prerogatives of Deity."[101] While this view fits the New Testament evidence better, it is still not entirely satisfactory.

Neither of these two strands *requires* a particular position on the key verb in verse 7, although both could and often did point to some form of kenosis.

A third possibility. Roy Hoover, in a seminal article in 1971, proposed a different meaning from either of the two main lines of interpretation.[102] He built on earlier work by Werner Jaeger (1915), who concluded that ἁρπαγμός, when used as a predicate accusative in double-accusative structures such as here, connotes a piece of good fortune, a lucky find, a treasure trove that can be exploited to one's personal advantage. Hoover identified the predominant use of the word in classical and first-century Greek as referring to something within one's power that can be exploited. He maintained that there was no element of fortuitousness in the term in this context, but rather ἁρπαγμός should be seen simply as referring to something to be seized upon and used to one's advantage. Christ, who was in the form of God, equal with God, chose not to use his position, status, and nature for his own ends, did not look after his own interests, but rather attended to the interests of others (cf. v. 4), in contrast to Adam and the triumphalists at Philippi. This was his path to exaltation

---

100. James D. G. Dunn, *Christology in the Making: A New Testament Enquiry into the Origins of the Doctrine of the Incarnation*, 2nd ed. (London: SCM, 1989), 114–21.

101. J. B. Lightfoot, *Saint Paul's Epistle to the Philippians: A Revised Text with Introduction, Notes, and Dissertations* (London: Macmillan, 1881), 112.

102. Roy W. Hoover, "The Harpagmos Enigma: A Philological Solution," *HTR* 64 (1971): 95–119.

as Lord (vv. 9–11). A key to the passage is the adversative ἀλλά[103] at the start of verse 7, which puts a barrier between what precedes and what follows, contrasting the two thoughts. As such, the clause is best translated "did not exploit [his status of] equality with God to his own advantage." Hoover's work has been developed further by N. T. Wright and has fed its way into the literature.[104]

Supporting this interpretation is the present participle ὑπάρχων,[105] "being," in verse 6. This may be timeless and therefore not necessarily indicative of continuance grammatically,[106] but the overall statement requires continuance. Christ's being in the form of God is something that continues; it was, it is, and it continues to be. Paul is saying very much what John states when he says, "In the beginning was the Word, and the Word was with God, and the Word was God" (John 1:1).

Does ἀλλὰ ἑαυτὸν ἐκένωσεν,[107] "but emptied himself" (Phil. 2:7), refer to something ontological or ethical? The verb occurs five times in the New Testament and on all other occasions is used metaphorically (Rom. 4:14; 1 Cor. 1:17; 9:15; 2 Cor. 9:3). The phrase is harsh—"himself he emptied"—the following clauses being modal, showing *how* he did this: by taking the form of a servant, becoming in the likeness of a man, being found in form as a man. The first aspect exemplifies what the Philippians were to do (Phil. 2:3–5). This is reminiscent of Isaiah 53:12 and has led some to see the servant of the Lord in Isaiah as the background and the word δοῦλος, "servant" or "slave," to refer to that. However, while this cannot be far from Paul's mind, the sequence would be out of order if that were so. Moreover, since Philippi was a Roman colony, priding itself on its Roman citizenship and lacking a synagogue or any Jewish presence, a Greco-Roman reference to a slave is more than likely, although both could be in view. The following clauses are effectively parenthetical, describing the way Christ emptied himself in his incarnation, leading up to the cross, which for Roman citizens was the lowest place

---

103. *alla.*

104. N. T. Wright, "Harpagmos and the Meaning of Philippians ii.5–11," *JTS* 37 (1986): 321–52; Crisp, *Divinity and Humanity*, 118–53.

105. *hyparchōn.*

106. "The principle of a timeless *present* participle needs very careful application, since alternative explanations are often possible, and grammar speaks to exegesis here with no decisive voice." James Hope Moulton, *A Grammar of New Testament Greek*, vol. 1, *Prolegomena*, 3rd ed. (Edinburgh: T&T Clark, 1908), 127. However, Fee thinks there is a temporal reference, as in 2 Cor. 8:9. Gordon D. Fee, *Paul's Letter to the Philippians* (Grand Rapids, MI: Eerdmans, 1995), 203. In this he is in agreement with Lightfoot, *Philippians*, 110–11.

107. *alla heauton ekenōsen.*

anyone could occupy, that of a condemned slave. Thus Christ had two contrasted forms: the form of God and the form of a servant or slave. He emptied himself not by ceasing to be what he always was but by becoming what he previously was not, not by subtraction but addition. This analysis of the passage indicates that there are no cogent reasons why it should be read in terms favorable to the kenosis theory. Torrance indicates that unless there is a real and essential relation between the union of God and man on earth and the eternal union of God the Father, the Son, and the Holy Spirit in heaven, we are not assured of real eternal relations with God.[108]

It is clear that the kenosis theory points to a real question. How is this best resolved? Evidently, Jesus did not exercise the full prerogatives of deity in his incarnate life; God came among us *as man*. Yet he did not relinquish such prerogatives. The most common approach to this question in Reformed theology has been *krypsis*, something hidden; Jesus's deity was concealed. He was *incognito*, as John the Baptist remarked (John 1:26).[109]

18.6   Predication regarding Christ

Augustine held that there are three forms of predication of Christ. "There are some statements of scripture about the Father and the Son which indicate their unity and equality of substance. . . . And there are others which mark the Son as lesser because of the form of a servant. . . . Lastly, there are others which mark him as neither less nor equal, but only intimate that he is from the Father."[110]

18.6.1   *Christ as God*

Augustine maintained that the Son is equal to, and indivisible with, the Father[111] and that the same applies to the Holy Spirit.[112] There is little need to belabor this point; it was established by the Trinitarian controversy, and Augustine was demonstrating his agreement with the church's

---

108. Torrance, *Incarnation*, 177.

109. "Christ . . . did not renounce his divinity, but he kept it concealed for a time." John Calvin, *Calvin's Commentaries: The Epistles of Paul to the Galatians, Ephesians, Philippians, and Colossians*, trans. T. H. L. Parker (Grand Rapids, MI: Eerdmans, 1965), 248; John Calvin, *Commentarii in Pauli Epistolas*. Ioannis Calvini opera exegetica (Geneva: Droz, 1992), 322. See also Crisp, *Divinity and Humanity*, 118–53.

110. Augustine, *De Trinitate* 2.3 (*NPNF*[1], 3:38).

111. Augustine, *De Trinitate* 1.12.

112. Augustine, *De Trinitate* 1.13.

resolution of the crisis. In this he followed in the footsteps of Hilary of Poitiers. For Hilary, the eternal generation of the Son establishes his identity of nature with the Father. It is different from human generation. Hilary explained:

> It is One from One; no partition, or withdrawing, or lessening, or efflux, or extension, or suffering of change, but the birth of living nature from living nature. It is God going forth from God, not a creature picked out to bear the name of God. His existence did not take its beginning out of nothing, but went forth from the Eternal; and this going forth is rightly entitled a birth, though it would be false to call it a beginning. For the proceeding forth of God from God is a thing entirely different from the coming into existence of a new substance.[113]

As Hilary contended, birth produces offspring identical in nature.[114] As such, the generation of the Son is different from a beginning; he is begotten, not created. There is unity of nature of the begetter and the begotten.[115] If the property of fatherhood is coeternal with the Father, then necessarily also the property of sonship must be coeternal with the Son.[116]

Some things, then, are predicated of Christ in terms of his personal identity as the eternal Son of God, in the form of God, equal with God, of one being with the Father (e.g., John 10:30). Among many others, the prologue of John's Gospel identifies the Word as distinct from ὁ θεός but yet identical with him. Jesus is there identified personally with the eternal Son of the Father (John 1:14–15, 18). He reveals God (John 1:18), since whoever has seen him has seen the Father (John 14:9).

18.6.2 *Christ as Man*

Many things said in Scripture "suggest, or even state openly that the Father is greater than the Son," Augustine observes.[117] He remarks that these have misled many to transfer what is said of Christ as man to his everlasting substance. These statements are predicated of Christ in his incarnate lowliness, his life in the flesh (Rom. 1:3–4). Scripture is clear

113. Hilary of Poitiers, *De Trinitate* 6.35 (NPNF², 9/1:111).
114. Hilary, *De Trinitate* 7.14 (NPNF², 9/1:123–24).
115. Hilary, *De Trinitate* 9.51 (NPNF², 9/1:173).
116. Hilary, *De Trinitate* 12.23 (NPNF², 9/1:223–24).
117. Augustine, *De Trinitate* 1.14, in *The Works of Saint Augustine: A Translation for the 21st Century: The Trinity*, trans. Edmund Hill, OP (Hyde Park, NY: New City, 1991), 74.

that there are things God cannot do: being conceived, being carried in the womb, being born, undergoing childhood, growing physically and mentally, and being subject to weariness, hunger, thirst, sorrow at bereavement, death, burial, and the like. In this category is the Son's obedience to death as the second Adam. Here he took the form of a servant. That is why Scripture says both that the Son is equal to the Father and the Father is greater than the Son. It does not mean, Augustine says, that when Paul writes in 1 Corinthians 15:27 that the Son will hand the kingdom over to the Father, he will take it away from himself.[118] Along similar lines, the Lutheran Martin Chemnitz cites Theodoret, who in turn cited Athanasius to say that whatever Christ was given in time relates to the humanity rather than the divinity.[119] Chemnitz calls this the rule of Leo.[120] If these lowly elements were not compatible with his being the eternal Son of the Father, one in being, equal in status, power, and authority, we would be driven toward a Nestorian separation in the person of Christ.

18.6.3   *Christ as Sent by the Father*

Augustine comments that some statements in Scripture are unclear on whether we should "take the Son as less than the Father in the created nature he took on" or

> take him as equal to the Father, while still deriving from him his being God from God, light from light. We do, after all, call the Son God from God, but the Father we simply call God, not from God. Thus, it is clear that the Son has another from whom he is and whose Son he is, while the Father does not have a Son from whom he is.[121]

Augustine believes that any reference in Scripture where there is doubt about which of these categories is applicable can be put in either category without any harm.[122]

Augustine maintains that order in the Trinity does not entail hierarchy, with superiority or inferiority. The Son and the Spirit are not less

---

118. Augustine, *De Trinitate* 1.16, 1.18.
119. Chemnitz, *The Two Natures*, 259–60, citing Theodoret, *Dialogus* 1 (*PG*, 83:92–93). Chemnitz also refers to Leo, *Epistola* 124 (*PL*, 54:1066–67); Origen, *In Iohannem* 13 (*PG*, 14:812–13); Cyril, *Thesaurus* 4.13 (Basel edition, 2:71); Cyril, *In Iohannem* 2.114, 4.14–15, 18, 221 (Basel edition, 1:134–35, 201–9).
120. Chemnitz, *The Two Natures*, 282.
121. Augustine, *De Trinitate* 1.2, in Hill, *Augustine*, 98.
122. Augustine, *De Trinitate* 1.4.

because they are sent.[123] The sending of the Son is brought about by the indivisible working of the Father and the Son with the Spirit.[124] The sender and the sent are equal. One is not greater and the other less, but one is the Father and the other the Son, the Son being from the Father, not the Father from the Son.[125] The two are one.[126] These are things predicable of God in terms not of his essence but of the relations of the three persons.[127] This is because there is an appropriate order or τάξις.[128] The Son is sent because he is begotten by the Father; the begetter and the begotten are of the identical being. The congruity of the processions and the missions is crucial. The sending is congruous with the eternal procession and is the basis of the action of the incarnation. In turn, the Father is not sent, since he has no one from whom he proceeds.[129]

18.7 Wolfhart Pannenberg on Jesus, History, and the Resurrection

Wolfhart Pannenberg (1928–2014), a leading figure of the late twentieth century, is a good example of recent theological trajectories, particularly since he is a more conservative figure than many. Throughout his work, he exhibits prodigious, careful scholarship, avoiding unbridled speculation.

For Pannenberg, Christology is grounded on universal history. Jesus's deity is established retroactively by his resurrection. In his early work *Jesus—God and Man* (1964), Pannenberg goes so far as to argue that the existence of God is only to be established by the eschatological resurrection. One dense but pregnant passage sums it up:

> That an element of God's becoming and being in the other, in the reality differentiated from himself, is one with his eternity requires that what newly flashes into view from time to time in the divine life can be understood at the same time as having always been true in God's eternity. This can be expressed in the form of the concept that the "intention" of the incarnation had been determined from all eternity in God's decree. However, the truth of such an assertion is dependent upon the temporal actuality of that thing, thus in this case

---

123. Augustine, *De Trinitate* 2.7.
124. Augustine, *De Trinitate* 2.9.
125. Augustine, *De Trinitate* 4.27.
126. Augustine, *De Trinitate* 4.29.
127. Augustine, *De Trinitate* 5.3–6.
128. *taxis.*
129. Augustine, *De Trinitate* 4.28.

the incarnation. *What is true in God's eternity is decided with retro-active validity only from the perspective of what occurs temporally with the import of the ultimate.* Thus, Jesus' unity with God—and thus the truth of the incarnation—is also decided only retroactively from the perspective of Jesus' resurrection for the whole of Jesus' existence on the one hand . . . and thus also for God's eternity on the other. Apart from Jesus' resurrection, it would not be true that from the very beginning of his earthly way God was one with this man. That is true from all eternity *because* of Jesus' resurrection. Until his resurrection, Jesus' unity with God was hidden not only to other men but above all . . . for Jesus himself also. It was hidden because the ultimate decision about it had not been given.[130]

Much of this work is taken up by arguing that the resurrection of Jesus is to be established on the basis of general history, and thus by the methodology of historical research.

In short, Pannenberg stresses the historicity of the resurrection: "We cannot separate the question whether the resurrection is part of the basis of faith from that of the facticity or historicity of the event."[131] He approaches the records of the Gospels as instances of historical narrative. However, he approaches these documents much as he would any other historical record.

The impact of Hegel is clear. Hegel considered history a process, unfolding in a dialectical manner, from thesis to antithesis to synthesis, and so on. There is constant flux, opposing forces come into conflict, a resolution of sorts results, and so on into the future. Undergirding these ideas were Trinitarian assumptions, with the result that God becomes part of the cosmic process, in some ways interdependent—codependent—with the world, as dependent on it as it is dependent on him. This is panentheism and is also seen in the theologies of Moltmann and Robert Jenson.

In the case of Pannenberg, as the above extract shows, the future determines the present in this process, the resurrection of Jesus having retroactive effect on all that went before. World history determines who Jesus is. The ultimate decision about his identity is given in his resurrection in space and time.

---

130. Wolfhart Pannenberg, *Jesus—God and Man*, trans. Lewis L. Wilkins and Duane A. Priebe (Philadelphia: Westminster, 1968), 321 (italics mine).

131. Wolfhart Pannenberg, *Systematic Theology*, trans. Geoffrey W. Bromiley, 3 vols. (Grand Rapids, MI: Eerdmans, 1991–1998), 2:285.

In his *Systematic Theology*, Pannenberg denies that the Son of God is antecedently the Son of God in himself, for Christ's eternal deity is a reflection of his humanity. The Easter event does not simply *disclose* who Jesus was in his relation to God but *determines* the meaning of his pre-Easter history.[132] Pannenberg implies that the Son needed to become incarnate to actualize his eternal sonship.[133] Thus, it is Jesus's message, not his person, that is central. With unmistakable echoes of Harnack, Pannenberg claims: "In the debate about the figure of Jesus it is of decisive importance that we should not put his person at the center. The center, rather, is God, the nearness of his rule, and his fatherly love."[134] Jesus's claim and message needed confirmation by the resurrection, since during his earthly ministry Jesus did not have this confirmation.[135] Although Pannenberg acknowledges the eternal deity of the Son and that this preceded the incarnation,[136] yet Jesus's identity depends on the resurrection.[137] Statements referring to the eternal deity are possible only in the light of the resurrection.[138]

Christ's identity as the eternal Son of the Father is thoroughly historicized. Here is another example of the panentheist turn taken from Rahner's axiom in Trinitarian theology, which I noted in chapter 4. The consequent move there to abandon the immanent Trinity—making the economic Trinity all there is—is mirrored here in the historical and economic determining the eternal.

Further Reading

Crisp, Oliver D. *Divinity and Humanity: The Incarnation Reconsidered.* Cambridge: Cambridge University Press, 2007.

Crisp, Oliver D. *God Incarnate: Explorations in Christology.* London: T&T Clark, 2009.

Crisp, Oliver D. *The Word Enfleshed: Exploring the Person and Work of Christ.* Grand Rapids, MI: Baker Academic, 2016.

Macleod, Donald. *The Person of Christ.* Leicester: Inter-Varsity Press, 1998.

---

132. Pannenberg, *Systematic Theology*, 2:345–46; Paul D. Molnar, *Divine Freedom and the Doctrine of the Immanent Trinity: In Dialogue with Karl Barth and Contemporary Theology* (London: T&T Clark, 2002), 153–54.

133. Pannenberg, *Systematic Theology*, 2:325, 367.

134. Pannenberg, *Systematic Theology*, 2:335.

135. Pannenberg, *Systematic Theology*, 2:337.

136. Pannenberg, *Systematic Theology*, 2:367.

137. Pannenberg, *Systematic Theology*, 2:345.

138. Pannenberg, *Systematic Theology*, 2:371.

McKinley, John E. *Tempted for Us: Theological Models and the Practical Relevance of Christ's Impeccability and Temptation*. Milton Keynes: Paternoster, 2009.

Study Questions

1. How do differences over the *communicatio idiomatum* impact the church's life?

2. What would be the consequences if Christ were to have taken into union a fallen human nature?

3. In what ways did Christ empty himself, and how may that affect the way we live?

19

Christ Our Great High Priest

The work of Christ fulfills the threefold office of Prophet, Priest, and King, with roots in the Old Testament. His priestly work consists of atonement, intercession, and benediction. The New Testament presents the atonement from a variety of complementary angles—as obedience, sacrifice, expiation, propitiation, reconciliation, redemption, and conquest. Each perspective contributes to the overall picture. Various theories have been produced to explain the atonement. Perhaps the most common and strategically central are penal substitution and representation. Both of these, as with the whole biblical presentation, need to be seen in the context of union with Christ, which overcomes the distance between a substitute and the ones for whom substitution is intended and thus offsets criticisms of injustice that could legitimately be made. The question of the intent of the atonement is best approached from the basis of its nature.

The fact that a later age may find it hard to understand traditional ideas is not sufficient reason for replacing them. It simply shows how necessary it is to open up their ideas to later generations by interpretation and thus to keep their meaning alive.[1]

19.1 The Threefold Office

Consideration of the work of Christ in terms of the offices of Prophet, Priest, and King in ancient Israel has been characteristic of Reformed

---

1. Wolfhart Pannenberg, *Systematic Theology*, trans. Geoffrey W. Bromiley, 3 vols. (Grand Rapids, MI: Eerdmans, 1991–1998), 2:422.

theology,[2] but not exclusively. It was foreshadowed in Aquinas and has been adopted by the *Catechism of the Catholic Church*.[3]

Prophet. The prophets spoke or wrote the word of God, applying covenantal requirements to Israel in their own day. Sometimes this included making predictions, but this was not the distinguishing mark of prophecy. Jesus also spoke the word of God. He contrasted rabbinic interpretation of the Torah with his own words, authority clearly resting with him (Matt. 5:21–42). However, Jesus was immeasurably greater than any other prophet, since he is one with the Father from eternity. Whereas the prophets said, "Thus says the Lord," Jesus speaks in his own name, "I say to you." While God spoke in many different ways by the prophets, now that the last days have arrived, he has spoken definitively by his Son (Heb. 1:1–3). He is the last word God has given and can give, since he is God incarnate. WLC, 43, states that Christ's prophetic office consists "in his revealing to the church, in all ages, by his Spirit and word, in divers ways of administration, the whole will of God, in all things concerning their edification and salvation." This occurs in the written Word, Scripture, produced by human agents under the direction of the Holy Spirit, sent by the ascended Christ.[4]

Priest. WLC, 44, states that Christ's priestly ministry is seen "in his once offering himself a sacrifice without spot to God, to be a reconciliation for the sins of his people, and in making continual intercession for them."

King. As King, Christ rules

> in calling out of the world a people to himself, and giving them officers, laws, and censures, by which he visibly governs them; in bestowing saving grace upon his elect . . . and powerfully ordering all things for his own glory, and their good; and also in taking vengeance on the rest, who know not God, and obey not the gospel. (WLC, 45; cf. 51–54)

---

2. Calvin, *Institutes*, 2.15.1; WCF, 8.1; WLC, 42–45; Charles Hodge, *Systematic Theology* (Grand Rapids, MI: Eerdmans, 1977), 2:459–609.
3. Aquinas, *ST* 3a.7.8, 3a.22.1–2, 3a.26; Brian Davies, *The Thought of Thomas Aquinas* (Oxford: Clarendon, 1992), 310, 327–30; CCC, 436. On Christ as Priest, CCC, 1544–51; as Prophet, CCC, 436; as King, CCC, 436–51.
4. See chap. 6.

19.2   Functions of a Priest

The priestly office in the Old Testament was restricted to the descendants of Aaron, of the tribe of Levi. Other Levites were excluded (Num. 3:10). The high priest was Israel's representative in the presence of God. His breastplate bore the names of the sons of Israel to bring them to remembrance before Yahweh (Ex. 28:15–30). He had prophetic functions too (Ex. 28:30; Lev. 10:9–11) and pronounced a benediction (Num. 6:24–27). On the annual day of atonement the high priest alone would enter the Most Holy Place to make atonement for the people (Lev. 16:1–27). How could Jesus be a Priest, since he was of the tribe of Judah? Under the Old Testament system this was impossible. Instead, he was a Priest of a different order. He is called a High Priest according to the order of Melchizedek (Heb. 5:6–10; 7:1–10:18), based on an intertextual reading (Gen. 14:17–20; Ps. 110:1–4).

19.3   Aaron and Melchizedek[5]

In Genesis 14, Melchizedek, a sacral king, king of Salem and priest of God Most High, receives tithes from Abram, who recognizes his priesthood as legitimate. Melchizedek blesses Abram. Sacral kingship was forbidden in Israel; no priest could be king. But Melchizedek appears startlingly different.

Psalm 110 takes up the theme. Here the Lord is both King (v. 1) and Priest forever (v. 4). Because this union of priestly and kingly offices was outlawed in Israel, Uzziah was struck with leprosy when attempting to usurp priestly functions (2 Chron. 26:16–21). David, to whom the psalm is attributed, was aware that as king that he could not be a priest. Yet Melchizedek's priesthood was instituted by a decree and an oath together, denoting permanence and irrevocability. Moreover, it was a more ancient priesthood than Aaron's.

Consequently, there were two priesthoods in the Old Testament. The Aaronic was based on genealogy—birth in the tribe of Levi and descent from Aaron—and ended with death. Conversely, Melchizedek's birth, ancestry, and death go unmentioned in Genesis. The Aaronic priest was a sinner who needed to offer sacrifice first for himself. Appalling sins were committed by some of these priests (Ex. 32:1–6; Lev. 10:1–7; 1 Sam.

---

5. Much of the material in this chapter can be found in fuller form in my book *The Work of Christ* (Leicester: Inter-Varsity Press, 1993).

2:22–25). There is no record of Melchizedek's sins. He must have been a sinner, but the biblical record ignores it.

Aaron was the prototypical high priest of the Mosaic covenant, while Melchizedek could be said to be high priest in relation to the Abrahamic covenant. Moreover, the Abrahamic covenant continues into the new covenant, whereas the Mosaic covenant was temporary and is now obsolete.[6]

19.4   Jesus's Qualifications as High Priest

Jesus never explicitly claimed priesthood. Being from Judah he could not be an Aaronic priest. However, he had a close relation to the temple (Matt. 24:1; Luke 2:46–52; John 2:13–22). Intercession was prominent throughout his earthly ministry (John 17:1–26). His death is portrayed as the shedding of covenantal blood (Matt. 26:26–29). He was sinless, a Lamb without blemish (1 Pet. 1:17–19). His death was a sacrifice (1 Cor. 5:7; Heb.10:14; 1 Pet. 1:19–21; 2:22–24). He was and is fully human (Heb. 2:5–18).

Superior to the Aaronic high priests, he annulled the Aaronic priesthood (Heb. 7:1–10:18). At his ascension he parts from the apostles while offering a benediction (Luke 24:50–51), and he continues to make intercession for us (Heb. 7:25).

19.5   Vicarious Humanity

According to the Nicene Creed, Christ became incarnate "for us and our salvation." As a Priest, he represents his people. This vicarious work is not confined to the cross but extended throughout his ministry and on into his heavenly session. As our High Priest, he represents us in every facet of his life and work.

His human obedience is vicarious throughout, remedying the failure of Adam. It is essential to our justification that he obeyed the Father; he had no need to do it for himself. Thus, whereas Adam was tempted in a beautiful garden, with a profusion of food available, and fell into sin, Jesus was tested brutally in a barren desert, going without physical sustenance, and succeeded.[7]

---

6. Letham, *The Work of Christ*, 106–10.
7. Thomas F. Torrance, *Theology in Reconciliation* (Grand Rapids, MI: Eerdmans, 1975), 139–214; Christian D. Kettler, *The Vicarious Humanity of Christ and the Reality of Salvation* (Lanham, MD: University Press of America, 1991).

For us baptized, for us he bore
his holy fast, and hungered sore;
for us temptations sharp he knew,
for us the tempter overthrew.

For us to wicked men betrayed,
scourged, mocked, in crown of thorns arrayed;
for us he bore the cross's death,
for us at length gave up his breath.

For us he rose from death again,
for us he went on high to reign;
for us he sent his Spirit here
to guide, to strengthen, and to cheer.[8]

19.6   Atonement

19.6.1   Covenant and Atonement

Was atonement necessary for salvation? There have been two main answers to this question in Reformed theology.

Consequent hypothetical necessity. The first answer to this question takes the position that, given that God decreed to save his elect, he could have done so in any way he chose. However, once he determined to do so by means of the atoning death of Christ, the death of the cross was a necessity. It is a necessity consequent not only to the decree to save but also to the decree to save by atonement, following it and dependent on it. It is hypothetical, since its necessity is not absolute but contingent on the decree that chose this means to redeem us. In short, God, having decreed to save us, could have chosen some other means to do so. However, having chosen this means, it was necessary for our salvation.

Many significant theologians adopted this position. Calvin has been cited in support, inasmuch as he wrote that "there has been no simple . . . or absolute necessity. Rather, it stemmed from a heavenly decree, on which man's salvation depended."[9] However, Calvin discusses here why the Mediator must be both true God and true man. It is unclear whether the decree he mentions is the decree to save us or the decree to save us in

---

8. From "O, Love, How Deep, How Broad, How High," a Latin hymn of the fifteenth century, trans. Benjamin Webb (1854, 1871).

9. Calvin, *Institutes*, 2.12.1.

the particular way God did save us. If the former, Calvin cannot be said to hold to consequent hypothetical necessity. Indicating that he cannot is the string of statements in the subsequent sections in which he insists that this or that had to be. These all suggest that, once God decreed to save us, this way alone was consistent with God's character.

John Owen, early in his career (1647), argued in *The Death of Death* that it was "false and erroneous . . . that God could not have mercy on mankind unless satisfaction were made by his Son" and that "to assert positively, that absolutely and antecedently to his constitution he could not have done it, is to me an unwritten tradition, the Scripture affirming no such thing, neither can it be gathered from thence in any good consequence." He thought God chose this way because it was the most convenient.[10] But by 1653 he had changed his position on the matter, possibly (as Trueman suggests) in response to the rising threat of Socinianism.[11]

Thomas Goodwin argued that God's purpose was to save people according to "his depths of wisdom." God could have done so by pardoning the rebels. But

> to punish sin being an act of his will . . . may therefore be suspended as he himself pleaseth. To hate sin is his nature; and that sin deserves death is also the natural and inseparable property, consequent, and demerit of it; but the expression of this hatred, and of what sin deserves by actual punishment, is an act of his will, and so might be suspended.

To pardon sin without punishing it would not have produced the best results or shown "such depths of love."[12] Goodwin makes the atonement contingent on the will of God. The decree was not dependent on his nature, for he could have chosen some other means. Goodwin seems to me to be arbitrary. If God could have chosen another way, why should he have chosen *this* way, one that led the Son to the intense suffering of the cross? Furthermore, it detaches the work of Christ from the nature of God.

---

10. John Owen, "Salus Electorum, Sanguis Jesu; or The Death of Death in the Death of Christ: A Treatise of the Redemption and Reconciliation That Is in the Blood of Christ," vol. 10 in *The Works of John Owen*, ed. William H. Goold (1647; repr., London: Banner of Truth, 1967), 205.

11. Carl R. Trueman, *John Owen: Reformed Catholic, Renaissance Man* (Aldershot: Ashgate, 2007), 42.

12. Thomas Goodwin, *Christ Our Mediator* (1692; repr., Grand Rapids, MI: Sovereign Grace, 1971), 14–15.

Consequent absolute necessity. This position asserts that, given that God decreed to save his elect, there was no other way he could do this in a manner compatible with his nature than by the death of his Son. Since God is righteous and just, he must bring about salvation in a form that is righteous and just. Of paramount importance is that the disobedience of Adam be overcome in a just way, by the obedience of a second Adam, the eternal Son (Rom. 3:25–26).

The necessity of the atonement under this line of thought is consequent upon God's determining to save his people. Once he had decreed that, it was necessary that it be achieved by the atoning death of Christ on the cross. The atonement was necessary in an absolute sense, contingent on the foregoing decree to save. The necessity rests on God's nature, a free and sovereign outflow of who he is. This is no limitation on God, for he is not constrained by external necessity.

Those who have held to this include J. H. Thornwell.[13] He wrote:

> The two great principles on which the doctrine of atonement rests are—the inseparable connection between punishment and guilt, and the admissibility under proper restrictions of a surety to endure the curse of the law. The unpardonable nature of sin, the practicability of legal substitution, these are the pillars of the Christian fabric.[14]

The necessity of the atonement is as a means to an end. The end itself is not necessary apart from the free purpose of God's grace.[15] It is mercy that gives rise to atonement, not the reverse.[16] The purpose of the atonement was not to make God merciful but to render the exercise of mercy consistent with righteousness.[17]

19.6.2   Obedience

Why was obedience necessary, and how does it relate to the atonement? In the covenant of life before the fall, Adam disobeyed God, breaking his law. The penalty was death and condemnation (Gen. 2:15–17), the consequence of rejecting God, who is life itself and the author and giver of contingent, creaturely life. Consequently, the entire

---

13. James Henley Thornwell, *The Collected Writings of James Henley Thornwell* (1875; repr., Edinburgh: Banner of Truth, 1974), 2:209–13.
14. Thornwell, *Collected Writings*, 2:209.
15. Thornwell, *Collected Writings*, 2:210.
16. Thornwell, *Collected Writings*, 2:210.
17. Thornwell, *Collected Writings*, 2:211.

race was covenantally dead in "trespasses and sins" (Eph. 2:1–2). The remedy was for another Adam to take his place, living in obedience to God and suffering the consequences that had accrued. Among Adam's descendants, none could do this. Each one conceived was disqualified, guilty under the covenantal headship of Adam, inheriting a corrupt and sinful nature.

It is at this point that the loving decree of God enters the picture. Again, the words of John Henry Newman bear quoting:

> O loving wisdom of our God!
> When all was sin and shame,
> a second Adam to the fight,
> and to the rescue came.
>
> O wisest love!—that flesh and blood,
> which did in Adam fail,
> should strive afresh against the foe,
> should strive and should prevail.[18]

Consequently, Christ the second Adam obeyed, bringing righteousness and life (Rom. 5:12–21). In Luke 1:34–35, Jesus's conception is likened to a new creation, the Holy Spirit the agent of generation, akin to his brooding over the creation at its inception. As his public ministry began, Jesus was led by the Spirit into the wilderness to be tempted by the devil. The parallel with Adam is unmistakable. Yet there is a colossal difference. Adam was tempted in a beautiful garden, with a profusion of trees, beautiful to the eyes, an aesthetic delight. From these trees and the lush attendant vegetation was an abundance of food. Adam had no lack of resources, only one commandment to keep, with the run of the place. Yet he fell into sin. Jesus, on the other hand, was tempted when utterly alone, in a desert, bereft and without resources. Having gone without sustenance for forty days and at his weakest, he faced the devil and triumphed. Adam disobeyed God's word; Jesus submitted to it (Matt. 4:1–10). Whereas the first Adam's sin brought death and condemnation, the second Adam obeyed the Father and received the inheritance of life. Adam's sin plunged all humanity into ruin; Christ, the second Adam, received life for himself and his new humanity.

---

18. From the hymn "Praise to the Holiest in the Height" (1865).

This corporate language is difficult for Westerners to grasp, since we are dominated by individualism. Such language poses no problem for people from Africa and Asia. Theirs are cultures in which corporate solidarity is as much a feature of everyday life as it was in the ancient Near East. This is the pattern in the Bible, and to understand the gospel from within the biblical context, we need to grasp this vital point.

The dual aspect of Christ's obedience. Christ's obedience has been considered in twofold form. His *active obedience* was his complete conformity to the law of God throughout his life. This went beyond sinlessness; not only was he without sin, but he also rendered complete, positive, faithful, and intentional obedience to God (Rom. 5:12–21; Heb. 4:14–16; 7:25–26; 10:1–5) from day one. When he was an infant, all the requirements of the law were performed regarding him (Luke 2:21–39). Throughout his life he obeyed his Father (Heb. 10:5–10). Not one of his vehement opponents could convict him of sin (John 8:46).

There was also his *passive obedience*. This does not denote passivity in the contemporary sense of inactivity, being acted upon from without, limp and ineffective. The term *passive* derives from the Latin verb *patior* (*passus, passa, passum*), meaning "suffer." It entailed Jesus's suffering the consequences of our having broken the law of God. "The wages of sin is death" (Rom. 6:23); we earned the penalty, he received it, and he did so in union with us. He suffered what we deserved, being delivered up for our offenses (Rom. 4:25). He learned obedience through what he suffered (Heb. 5:7–10). He emptied himself, becoming obedient to death, even the death of the cross (Phil. 2:7–8). He did so with tears and agony (Luke 22:39–46; Heb. 5:7–8). On the cross, he uttered the cry of dereliction (Matt. 27:46).

Active and passive obedience are not two sets of obedience but one obedience with two dimensions. There is an inextricable connection between atonement and justification; he was "delivered up for our trespasses [atonement for sin] and raised for our justification [vindication]" (Rom. 4:25). Christ's obedience is the indispensable backcloth for the atonement as it qualified him as our Priest and representative; only a sinless and obedient second Adam could receive the life that was to come in the vindication of resurrection. It is the necessary ground for our justification, as we shall see in chapter 24.

19.6.3   *Expiatory Sacrifice*

The Old Testament sacrifices present a picture of expiation (Lev. 4:1–7:38; 16:1–34). The occasion of the sacrificial system was sin, with the guilt and defilement that follow. The process is simple. The offerer is declared guilty. An animal—lamb, bull, or goat—is involved. The offerer lays his hands on the animal, identifying personally with the sacrifice, transferring guilt to the offering. The animal is slain, and its blood is shed and spread on the altar. There follows the pronouncement—he is forgiven.

This is most vividly expressed on the Day of Atonement (Leviticus 16). Of the two goats to be offered, the one for Azazel was sent alive into the wilderness to a remote location from which it could never return, bearing the sins of Israel upon it (Lev. 16:5–8, 15–16, 20–22). Thus, Psalm 103:8–12 and Micah 7:18–19 pronounce that our sins are separated far from us, buried in the depths of the sea.

Christ, suffering in our place, fulfilled this ritual, canceling our sins and erasing the consequent guilt. The Old Testament background is vicarious expiation, the removal of sin. The contrast is the limitation and inadequacy of animal sacrifices versus the efficacy of Christ's sacrificial offering.

19.6.4   *Propitiation*

Propitiation is closely related to the ideas of expiation and sacrifice and refers to the averting of God's wrath. For some time in the West this theme aroused aversion. C. H. Dodd famously argued that, in the New Testament, ἱλάσκεσθαι[19] and related verbs should be translated "expiate" rather than "propitiate." The same should apply to the cognate noun ἱλαστήριον.[20] The LXX did not regard כפר[21] as conveying the idea of propitiation, which Dodd regarded as indicative of the pagan idea of conciliation of a capricious and angry deity, ready to crush us in fierce anger. Behind this, Dodd did not accept that God had wrath; instead, wrath was the natural outcome of sin.[22]

Dodd was right to warn against the idea that God is capricious or arbitrary. This is not how he has revealed himself in the Old Testament

---

19. *hilaskesthai.*
20. *hilastērion.*
21. *ciper.*
22. C. H. Dodd, "*Hilaskesthai,* Its Cognates, Derivatives, and Synonyms in the Septuagint," *JTS* 32 (1931): 352–60.

or the New. However, Dodd's argument has been refuted many times on both linguistic and theological grounds. In linguistic terms, his case was undermined by Leon Morris[23] and Roger Nicole.[24] They questioned Dodd's assumptions of the alleged unity of the LXX, and the relationship of the LXX to the New Testament. Dodd claimed that in the New Testament we encounter an unusual variant of the ἱλάσκεσθαι group. Indeed, it is so unusual as to be irrelevant. Moreover, the verb means "propitiate," and its cognate noun ἱλαστήριον a "place of propitiation."[25] In cases such as Hebrews 2:17, where the verb is followed by an accusative, it is likely an accusative of respect.[26]

On theological grounds, R. V. G. Tasker countered Dodd with his monograph *The Biblical Doctrine of the Wrath of God*.[27] Dodd did not accept that God had active wrath against the sinner for his sin. He held that sin brings its own penalty in terms of an immanent law. In turn, to describe the atonement as propitiation was to compare the God of the Bible with the capricious and arbitrary tyrants worshiped by the ancient Near Eastern tribes. Both Tasker and Morris insisted that the Bible teaches that the wrath of God is his settled and holy antagonism toward sin and that this is a cardinal doctrine.[28] Dodd failed to see that in the New Testament, propitiation is the result of God's love, and he himself provides it, the Son suffering his wrath in himself: "This is love, not that we loved God, but that he loved us and sent his Son to be the propitiation with respect to our sins" (1 John 4:10, my trans.). It also demonstrates his righteousness (Rom. 3:25–26). The entire undivided Trinity was engaged in accomplishing our salvation. The cross was the concerted action of the three persons inseparably. Christ's death was a loving act whereby our salvation was won in accord with God's justice, and a grievous penalty was taken willingly on our behalf by God the Son, upheld by the loving Trinity.[29]

---

23. Leon Morris, *The Apostolic Preaching of the Cross* (London: Tyndale Press, 1955), 144–213.
24. Roger Nicole, "C. H. Dodd and the Doctrine of Propitiation," *WTJ* 17 (1955): 117–57.
25. C. E. B. Cranfield, *A Critical and Exegetical Commentary on the Epistle to the Romans*, The International Critical Commentary (Edinburgh: T&T Clark, 1975), 1:214–18.
26. Philip Edgcumbe Hughes, *A Commentary on the Epistle to the Hebrews* (Grand Rapids, MI: Eerdmans, 1977), 121n123.
27. R. V. G. Tasker, *The Biblical Doctrine of the Wrath of God* (London: Tyndale Press, 1951).
28. Tasker, *Wrath of God*, passim; Morris, *Apostolic Preaching*, 147–54, 158f., 174–84, 208–13.
29. Contra scholars who propound a nonviolent theory of the atonement, such as Denny Weaver, "The Nonviolent Atonement: Human Violence, Discipleship, and God," in *Stricken by*

19.6.5   Reconciliation

Reconciliation takes us a stage further than propitiation. In propitiation, enmity is removed; in reconciliation, friendship is established. The one is the prelude to the other. Propitiation involves the aversion of God's wrath, which he initiates and fulfills. Reconciliation is God's establishment of peace and friendship with us. Both assume a prior state of enmity due to sin.

Who needs to be reconciled? Popular preaching often assumes it is we who need to be reconciled and that God does not need to be. This has become an axiom. Pannenberg remarks:

> Only after the destruction of the satisfaction theory by the rational criticism of the Socinians and the adoption of this criticism by the Protestant theology of the Enlightenment did attention begin to focus more widely on the difference between the thought of reconciliation in the New Testament (including Paul) and later theological usage. *God* did not have to be reconciled; the *world* is reconciled by God in Christ (2 Cor. 5:19).[30]

However, as Leon Morris has shown, this is not the normal meaning. In nonsoteriological contexts, reconciliation is the removal of the enmity of the person offended. For instance, in Matthew 5:23–24, the worshiper must prioritize reconciliation over worship, the removal of enmity of the one offended bringing the reconciliation.[31]

In soteriological contexts, this is the case too. In Romans 5:8–11, Paul parallels justification (v. 9) and reconciliation (v. 10). He uses an *a fortiori* argument, from the greater to the lesser, pointing to the definitive action as having already occurred in the death of Christ. Justification is grounded in the death of Christ; so is reconciliation. These are both actions of God. His enmity is removed before ours.

In 2 Corinthians 5:18–21, reconciliation is again what God has accomplished. Human reconciliation is also in view (v. 20), but when it occurs, it is a consequence of what God has already done in Christ. In Ephesians 2:11–19, Christ accomplished peace between God and humanity and between Jew and Gentile at the cross, creating one new man.

God? Nonviolent Identification and the Victory of Christ, ed. Brad Jersak and Michael Hardin (Grand Rapids, MI: Eerdmans, 2007), 316–55.

30. Pannenberg, *Systematic Theology*, 2:407.
31. Morris, *Apostolic Preaching*, 214–50.

The same applies in Colossians 1:18–19. In each of these passages God is reconciled to us; the reconciliation is definitive, having taken place in the death of the Son. The overriding point is that it is God himself who has taken the initiative to do this. In love, the Son took our place and in union with us satisfied the justice of God.

19.6.6 Redemption

Redemption involves deliverance from slavery by the payment of a price. It is connected to adoption, which is the consequence of this deliverance.[32] The New Testament words for redemption all have commercial connotations. Many dislike this, including Colin Gunton, who refers with approval to Edward Irving's remark about "stock-exchange divinity."[33] However, commercial language is in the text; why should it be rejected? Is some language privileged while others are to be avoided? The sticking point is that redemption means more than simply deliverance; it is effected on the payment of a ransom price.[34]

Israel was delivered from slavery in Egypt by the mighty power of Yahweh (Ex. 6:5–7) for life with him in the covenanted land. Passover, the classic paradigm of redemption, as Thiselton remarks, recalls God's deliverance of Israel from death so as to grant safe passage to the Promised Land.[35] Later, Yahweh delivers Israel from oppression by a savior, a judge, into a state of peace and security.[36]

To whom is the price paid? For Origen and others in the early church, the ransom is paid to the devil. This is foreign to the Bible; the devil has no such rights. Rather, the key New Testament passages include 1 Corinthians 6:19–20, where the church is said to have been bought with a price, placing an onus on us to live for Christ. Colossians 1:13 states that we were delivered from the devil and transferred to the kingdom of the Father's Son. Ephesians 1:7 locates redemption occurring through the blood of Christ.[37] In the context, Jesus implies this in Mark 10:45.

---

32. Tim Trumper, "The Metaphorical Import of Adoption: A Plea for Realisation: II: The Adoption Metaphor in Theological Usage," *SBET* 15 (1997): 98–115; Trumper, "The Metaphorical Import of Adoption: A Plea for Realisation: I: The Adoption Metaphor in Biblical Usage," *SBET* 14 (1996): 129–45.

33. Colin Gunton, "Two Dogmas Revisited: Edward Irving's Christology," *SJT* 41 (1988): 367.

34. Morris, *Apostolic Preaching*, 18–27, 38–62.

35. Anthony C. Thiselton, *Systematic Theology* (London: SPCK, 2015), 184.

36. Thiselton, *Systematic Theology*, 188.

37. A. M. Stibbs, *The Meaning of the Word "Blood" in Scripture* (London: Tyndale Press, 1948).

19.6.7   Conquest

By his death and resurrection, Christ destroyed the power of the devil. The idea is related to redemption. The idea of conquest is related to redemption and is close to a theory revived by Gustaf Aulén in his book *Christus Victor* (1931), who called it the classic theory.[38]

It has biblical support. The first intimation of redemption is in Genesis 3:15, where it is said that the offspring of the woman will deal a death blow to the serpent and its offspring. Paul understands this to refer to Satan (Rom. 16:20; 2 Cor. 11:3–4; cf. vv. 14–15). Jesus speaks of his death as marking the overthrow of "the ruler of this world" (John 12:31–33). Paul considers the cross as marking the overthrow of the principalities and powers (Col. 2:14–15). Jesus came to destroy the works of the devil (1 John 3:8). Peter agrees that this was a conquest by Christ in which he proclaimed judgment upon the fallen angels (1 Pet. 3:18–22, with 19–21 as a parenthesis).

This perspective brings the cross into harmony with the resurrection. John 12:31–33 connects the cross with Jesus's glorification. Christ's victory over Satan was decisive; it awaits the eschaton for the final touches. It facilitates the conquest of various ills. However, it was propounded by Aulén and others in contradiction of the other models of atonement in the New Testament, for "the classic type stands by itself, in opposition to both the other two."[39] Yet its validity is in conjunction with these perspectives. Besides, a question arises as to whether it is an aspect of the atonement or a consequence of it.

19.6.8   Penal Substitution

The theory of penal substitution derives its name from *poena* (penalty), the penalty of the law due to sin (Rom. 6:23), and substitution, where one takes the place of another. It is closely connected to representation.

Effectively, Christ took our place and submitted to the curse of the law on our behalf. Garry Williams states, "An author can be held to teach penal substitution if he plainly states that the punishment deserved by sin from God was borne and dealt with by Jesus Christ in his death

---

38. Gustaf Aulén, *Christus Victor: An Historical Study of the Three Main Types of the Idea of Atonement* (1931; repr., New York: Macmillan, 1969).

39. Aulén, *Christus Victor*, 155.

on the cross."[40] Williams has established that this was held from the days of the fathers.[41] The Old Testament background is the substitutionary nature of the sacrificial system (Lev. 1:4; 4:20, 26, 31; 6:7). It is pervasive in the New Testament (2 Cor. 5:21; Gal. 3:13; Heb. 9:28; 1 Pet. 2:21–24; 3:18; cf. Mark 10:45 and its parallel, Matt. 20:28; Rom. 5:8; 8:32; 1 Cor. 15:3; 2 Cor. 5:14; Eph. 5:2, 25; 1 Tim. 2:6; Heb. 7:26–27; 1 John 3:16).

Many criticisms have been leveled at the doctrine. It has been labeled "divine child abuse," with Christ a helpless bystander on whom violence was inflicted against his will. Such criticism overlooks that the cross was the provision of God's love, the atonement being the work of the entire Trinity (Heb. 9:14).

Williams has addressed recent attacks on penal substitution.[42] Some argue that Christ's suffering was limited to six hours, in contrast to the eternal consequences of sin; this misses the point that his sufferings were infinitely more intense in that he is the sinless Son of God. Again, it is held to be inherently unjust to punish the innocent and let the guilty go free; I will consider this shortly. Others object to the idea of God delighting in an innocent person suffering, ignoring the point that the Son is God; God takes the penalty himself. Still more object to the prominence of law. Gunton's objection to "stock-exchange divinity" superficially reflects his aversion to commercial language.[43]

Penal substitution is to be seen in connection with union with Christ. Union sets substitution and representation in a fuller context. Christ is our substitute. He took our place throughout his life and ministry, the cross, his resurrection, and his ascension. Jesus's words at the Last Supper (Luke 22:19), repeated by Paul (1 Cor. 11:24), stress that he came to give his life as a ransom for many (Matt. 20:28; Mark 10:45), to give his flesh for the life of the world (John 6:51). Paul remarks that the gospel is, among other things, that Christ died for our sins (1 Cor. 15:3). In this he died for all (2 Cor. 5:14–15), being made sin for us (2 Cor. 5:21). Christ died for

40. Garry J. Williams, "Penal Substitutionary Atonement in the Church Fathers," *EQ* 83 (2011): 196.

41. Garry J. Williams, "Penal Substitution: A Response to Recent Criticisms," *JETS* 50 (2007): 80–81. He cites Eusebius of Caesarea, *Demonstratio Evangelica* 10.1, in *The Proof of the Gospel*, ed. and trans. W. J. Ferrar (Eugene, OR: Wipf & Stock, 2001), 2:195–96, which can be found in *PG*, 22:723–26; and Cyril, *De adoratione et cultu in spiritu et veritate* 3.100–102 (*PG*, 68:293, 296).

42. Williams, "A Response."

43. Gunton, "Two Dogmas Revisited," 367.

us (Rom. 5:8), the Father not sparing his Son but giving him up for us all (Rom. 8:32), a ransom for all (1 Tim. 2:6). Peter has the same doctrine as Paul (1 Pet. 2:21–24; 3:18), as does the letter to the Hebrews (Heb. 9:28).

Christ is our representative. All he did and does is on our behalf. While a substitute takes the place of another, a representative acts on behalf of that person. His actions are regarded as those of the ones he represents. In Britain, a member of Parliament votes on behalf of his or her constituents, voicing their interests in Parliament. Ambassadors represent their countries with words regarded as reflecting their governments' policies. Christ did not act on his own account but represented us (Rom 5:12–21). In this sense, Paul describes Christ as being handed over for our offenses and raised for our justification (Rom. 4:25). Christ, on the cross, took our place and endured the full brunt of the wrath of God for us. He represented us and in his ascension to the Father acts on our behalf. Consequently, his righteousness is reckoned to us.

As both substitute and representative, Christ is distinct from those who benefit from what he did. A substitute is another person than the one he replaces. While his actions are legally those of the ones he represents, a representative is distinct from them too. With union, we are taken a stage further; all Christ did and does we do, since we are one with him. The "otherness" of a substitute or representative is in eclipse. Because of the union between us and Christ, his actions *are* ours.

This is of immense importance in connection with the argument that it would be unjust for God to acquit the guilty and charge the innocent. This argument is correct. God abominates those who clear the guilty and punish the innocent. Such practices are severely condemned in the Old Testament (Ex. 23:6–8; 34:7; Deut. 27:25; Prov. 17:15; cf. Prov. 17:26; 18:5; 24:24; Isa. 5:23). However, because of the union established between Christ and his elect people, the wrongs done by the guilty parties have become Christ's as well. In turn, the righteousness of the one who bears the punishment actually belongs to the other, since both are regarded as one. One recent defense of penal substitution spends successive chapters answering a range of criticisms, all variations on this theme. Only late in the book is union with Christ introduced; if it were considered earlier, these objections could be answered at once.[44]

---

44. Steve Jeffery, Michael Ovey, and Andrew Sach, *Pierced for Our Transgressions: Recovering the Glory of Penal Substitution* (Wheaton, IL: Crossway, 2007).

It follows that when Christ died on the cross and rose from the dead, *we* died and rose with him (Rom. 6:1ff.). It also follows that when he died, our sin was utterly and definitively dealt with, since Christ died in union with us and we with him. Because he was raised from the dead and ascended to the Father, demonstrating the conclusive conquest of sin and its entail, sin can no longer have dominion over us!

19.6.9 Historical Theories

Irenaeus and recapitulation. In his famous recapitulation theory, Irenaeus held that Christ united himself with us in the incarnation in order that we might become what he is.[45] He united himself to humanity that we might be united to God.[46] There are two moments in this union: the incarnation and the work of the Spirit. In the incarnation Christ became what we are, took Adam's place, and crushed the enemy that had led us captive in Adam.[47] He obeyed the Father and so restored humanity to the likeness of God. He conquered Satan by his obedience. Adam had been led astray through food; Christ overcame Satan by hunger in the wilderness. Adam disobeyed; Christ obeyed.[48] Adam disobeyed through a tree; Christ obeyed on the tree.[49] Christ's whole life was one of obedience, recapitulating and annulling the disobedience of Adam.[50] As a result, humanity is set free, Satan bound by the same fetters with which he bound us.[51]

As Thiselton remarks, Irenaeus saw God as *"recapitulating our bad fate in Adam by a new creation in Christ. . . . Christ reverses the effects of Adam's fall."*[52] Redemption is a drama, set against the backdrop of disobedience and bondage to Satan. It involves conflict. The work of Christ is conquest of Satan. The obedience of Christ is central and crucial. While the atonement is ransom from the devil, above all the context is obedience to God. The atonement is in continuum with the whole of Christ's incarnate life, with the result that Christ overcomes corruption and death, and humanity is elevated.

---

45. Irenaeus, *Against Heresies* 5: preface (*ANF*, 1:526).
46. Irenaeus, *Against Heresies* 5.1.1 (*ANF*, 1:527).
47. Irenaeus, *Against Heresies* 5.21.1 (*ANF*, 1:549).
48. Irenaeus, *Against Heresies* 5.21.2 (*ANF*, 1:549).
49. Irenaeus, *Against Heresies* 5.16.3 (*ANF*, 1:544).
50. Irenaeus, *Against Heresies* 3.18.1, 7, 3.21.10, 5.17.1 (*ANF*, 1: 446, 448, 454, 544).
51. Irenaeus, *Against Heresies* 5.21.3 (*ANF*, 1:550).
52. Thiselton, *Systematic Theology*, 207 (italics original).

The ransom theory. Gustaf Aulén described this as "the classic theory" of the atonement. It held that the devil had humanity in his power, but Christ came into the world to destroy the devil's works. Satan thought Christ was in his power by destroying the humanity but was deceived by the hidden deity, like a fish deceived through bait. This was a work of God. Consequently, humanity is freed from the grip of the devil.

There are hints of the ransom idea in Irenaeus.[53] However, it emerges strongly with Origen, although the element of deception comes later. For Origen, Christ gives his soul as a ransom to Satan and destroys Satan by the resurrection. God in Christ destroys the devil's power, but it is also a process that will be finalized when the last enemy is destroyed.[54] Origen based his teaching on New Testament passages relating to the resurrection and exaltation of Christ.[55]

Gregory of Nyssa wrote of Christ as the bait, and Satan as duped and hooked by the hidden deity:

> In order to secure that the ransom on our behalf might be easily accepted by him who required it, the Deity was hidden under the veil of our nature, that so, as with ravenous fish, the hook of the Deity might be gulped down along with the bait of the flesh, and thus, life being introduced into the house of death, and light shining in darkness, that which is diametrically opposed to light and life might vanish.[56]

Gregory acknowledged that deception was used and defended it on the ground of justice;[57] the biter bit![58] Gregory combined this theory with the idea of the incarnation paving way for deification: "He was transfused throughout our nature, in order that our nature might by this transfusion of the divine become itself divine."[59] Ambrose also wrote of our having been in debt to the devil but Christ having paid the debt.[60]

---

53. Irenaeus, *Against Heresies* 5.21.3 (*ANF*, 1:550).
54. Origen, *Against Celsus* 1.31, 7.17 (*ANF*, 4:410, 617), where he refers simply to Christ overcoming the devil.
55. Origen, *On First Principles* 1.6:1–2 (*ANF*, 4:260–61; *GCS*, 22:79–80). See also citations in Benjamin Drewery, *Origen and the Doctrine of Grace* (London: Epworth, 1960), 122–25, from Origen's commentaries on Matt. 16:8, 1 Corinthians 6, Ephesians 4, and John 6, and Josh. 8:3–4, 6 ("the cross as a trophy of victory over the devil").
56. Gregory of Nyssa, *The Great Catechism* 24 (*NPNF²*, 5:494).
57. Gregory of Nyssa, *The Great Catechism* 26 (*NPNF²*, 5:495).
58. Ivor H. Evans, *Brewer's Dictionary of Phrase and Fable* (London: Cassell, 1981), 120.
59. Gregory of Nyssa, *The Great Catechism* 25 (*NPNF²*, 5:495).
60. Ambrose, *Letter 41, to His Sister* 7 (*NPNF²*, 10:446; *PL*, 16:1115).

As time passed the realization dawned that Satan had no rights over humanity, and so God was under no obligation to pay a ransom to him. Ethical questions arose over the theory's assumption of duplicity. Gregory of Nazianzus dealt a crippling blow to it: "Now, since a ransom belongs only to him who holds in bondage, I ask to whom was this offered, and for what cause? If to the evil one, fie upon the outrage!"[61]

The theory saw atonement as a work of God, the author and object of reconciliation. It aimed to preserve the unity of redemption. Deliverance from sin, evil, and the devil is simultaneously deliverance from the wrath of God due to sin. The idea of evil overreaching itself is true to the Bible and to experience. However, there can be no question in Scripture of Satan having any rights, still less of Christ making payment to him.

Penal substitution. It has been argued that penal substitution was a theory devised in the sixteenth century and that, as a formulated doctrine, it was absent from the fathers.[62] Others have claimed that evidence produced from this period for penal substitution is mistaken and that the fathers cited taught the conquest theory rather than penal substitution.[63] These arguments have been effectively rebuffed by Williams[64] and Ensor.[65] Thiselton is emphatic:

> For the first seventy years after the New Testament era . . . *precisely the same gospel of the atonement was written about, preached, and taught* as that of the apostles themselves. The earliest writings emphasized especially substitution. Christian tradition had its roots firmly in the soil of the New Testament from the very beginning.[66]

Thus, Justin cited Christ's death for the sins of the people.[67] In the West, Tertullian advocated Christ's death as a satisfaction to God for human sin.[68] It was a sacrifice in terms of Isaiah 53.[69] Reconciliation is two-sided rather than one-sided. The Mediator reconciles God to man, and man to God.[70]

---

61. Gregory of Nazianzus, *Oration 45* 22 (*NPNF²*, 7:431).
62. Jersak and Hardin, *Stricken by God?*, 358, 435; P. Fiddes, *Past Event and Present Salvation* (London: Darton, Longman & Todd, 1989), 102.
63. Derek Flood, "Substitutionary Atonement and the Church Fathers: A Reply to the Authors of *Pierced for Our Transgressions*," *EQ* 82 (2010): 142–59.
64. Williams, "Penal Substitutionary Atonement."
65. Peter Ensor, "Justin Martyr and Penal Substitutionary Atonement," *EQ* 83 (2011): 217–32.
66. Thiselton, *Systematic Theology*, 205–6.
67. Justin, *Dialogue with Trypho the Jew* 89, 94–95 (*ANF*, 1:244, 246–47).
68. Tertullian, *On Penitence* 5.9, 7.14, 8.9 (*CCSL*, 1:328–29, 334, 336; *PL*, 1:1234–43).
69. Tertullian, *Against the Jews* 13.21 (*CCSL*, 2:1388–89; *PL*, 2:634–36).
70. Tertullian, *On the Resurrection of the Flesh* 63 (*ANF*, 3:593).

Hilary had a clear treatment of penal satisfaction.[71] Origen held that Christ suffered for sins as a Priest offering a sacrifice in which he himself was the victim.[72] For Athanasius, the theme of satisfaction to God is clearly evident.[73] Gregory of Nazianzus spoke of Christ taking away the world's sin by enduring the curse for us.[74] Ambrose demonstrated what Thiselton calls an unprecedented focus on the death of Christ and stated that Christ was made sin and a curse not on his account but on ours.[75] The teaching is also present in Augustine,[76] the grace of God at its root.[77] Cyril wrote of Christ's death as a sacrifice of penal substitution.[78] According to Kelly, it was a mainstream view of the atonement in the East in the fourth century.[79] Apart from the more recent exponents from Calvin onward, both Barth (see below) and Pannenberg have strong doctrines of penal substitution.[80]

Anselm's doctrine of satisfaction. Anselm is famous for his doctrine of satisfaction to God's honor. He argues that if a person violates another, he must repay what is owed, plus an amount for restitution for pain and injury. So all who sin against God must pay their debt together with an amount to cover the violation of his honor.[81] It is not fitting otherwise.[82] Sin is followed by either satisfaction or punishment.[83] For someone to be saved, satisfaction must be made for human sin.[84] Humans cannot

---

71. Hilary of Poitiers, *Homilies on the Psalms* 53.4, 13–14 (*NPNF²*, 9/1:244–47; Corpus Scriptorum Ecclesiasticorum Latinorum, 22:137, 144–45; *PL*, 9:344).

72. Origen, *Homily on Numbers* 24.1.3–6 (*PG*, 12:755–59); Origen, *Homilies on Numbers*, trans. Thomas P. Scheck, ed. Christopher A. Hall, Ancient Christian Texts (Grand Rapids, MI: Baker Academic, 2009), 148–49; Origen, *Homily on John* 28.19 (*PG*, 14:732–37); Origen, *Homily on Luke* 14.4, cited in Thiselton, *Systematic Theology*, 209.

73. Athanasius, *On the Incarnation* 9–10, 24, 27 (*NPNF²*, 4:40–41, 49, 51).

74. Gregory of Nazianzus, *Oration 30* 5, in Williams and Wickham, *St. Gregory of Nazianzus*, 96 (also *NPNF²*, 7:311).

75. Thiselton, *Systematic Theology*, 213; Ambrose, *On the Christian Faith* 5.14 (*NPNF²*, 10:306).

76. Augustine, *On the Merits and Forgiveness of Sins, and on the Baptism of Infants* 1.61 (*NPNF¹*, 5:39).

77. Thiselton, *Systematic Theology*, 213.

78. Cyril of Alexandria, *On Adoration and Worship in Spirit and in Truth* 3 (*PG*, 68:293f.); Cyril, *On John* 2 (*PG*, 73:192); Cyril, *Letter 50* (*PG*, 77:264).

79. J. N. D. Kelly, *Early Christian Doctrines* (London: Adam & Charles Black, 1968), 375–77. On Irenaeus, see Joshua Schendel, "'That Justice Might Not Be Infringed Upon': The Judgment of God in the Passion of Christ in Irenaeus of Lyons," *SJT* 71 (2018): 212–25.

80. Wolfhart Pannenberg, *Jesus—God and Man*, trans. Lewis L. Wilkins and Duane A. Priebe (Philadelphia: Westminster, 1968), 247.

81. Anselm, *Cur Deus homo?* 1.11, in *A Scholastic Miscellany: Anselm to Ockham*, ed. Eugene R. Fairweather (New York: Macmillan, 1970), 100–83; Brian Davies, *Anselm of Canterbury: The Major Works* (Oxford: Oxford University Press, 1998), 260–356.

82. Anselm, *Cur Deus homo?* 1.12–13.

83. Anselm, *Cur Deus homo?* 1.14–15.

84. Anselm, *Cur Deus homo?* 1.19.

do this by themselves.[85] This requires satisfaction for sin by One who is not himself a sinner.[86] God does not do this under any external necessity; the necessity arises from his own nature.[87] Only a God-man can make this satisfaction, since he must be greater than anything other than God, and since it is a human responsibility to pay the debt; hence the necessity of the incarnation.[88] The God-man is not obliged to die, since only the corrupt deserve death and, as God, Christ cannot sin; so he dies from his own free choice.[89] It is also a conquest of the devil,[90] but nothing is owed to the devil, for all that is owed is owed to God.[91] The atonement is a payment of the debt of the human race to God by a substitute whom God himself provides.

Does this introduce necessity into God? Not external necessity, for God acts according to his nature. Is there a logical necessity in his argument? Is it rationalistic? No, not in any sense that Anselm's basis is reason cut free from revelation. Anselm writes for the benefit of his fellow monks in dialogue form on the basis that he is to establish his point to someone who will not believe unless it is explained by reason.[92] The context is monastic, "faith seeking understanding" (*fides quaerens intellectum*). The reasoning is the outflow of faith. He repeatedly says that "it is fitting" for God to act in this way; but he rules out any external necessity, for God remains true to his character; it is a necessity of nature, inasmuch as God acts in accordance with who he is and does not act in any other way.[93] Is the atonement seen through the prism of medieval feudalism? Perhaps, although penance is as much the backdrop. But since Anselm was living in that context, it is a case of contextualization, with the strengths and weaknesses that this involves. As Thiselton remarks, "To dismiss Anselm because he also drew on the feudal imagery would be a mistake: every theologian has to consider hermeneutical bridges to the readers of the day."[94] Certainly, Anselm linked incarnation and atonement well. Atonement is a work of the undivided Mediator,

---

85. Anselm, *Cur Deus homo?* 1.20–25.
86. Anselm, *Cur Deus homo?* 2.4.
87. Anselm, *Cur Deus homo?* 2.5.
88. Anselm, *Cur Deus homo?* 2.6–7.
89. Anselm, *Cur Deus homo?* 2.7–11.
90. Anselm, *Cur Deus homo?* 6.7.
91. Anselm, *Cur Deus homo?* 2.19.
92. Anselm, *Cur Deus homo?* 1.10.
93. Thiselton, *Systematic Theology*, 216–17.
94. Thiselton, *Systematic Theology*, 215.

according to both natures. It is the provision of God from first to last. Moreover, Anselm effectively laid to rest the old ransom theory.

Luther's emphasis. Aulén's claim that Luther was a major protagonist of the "classic" theory was misplaced. Luther referred to the death of Christ as a sacrifice whereby he took on himself all our sins and obtained forgiveness and reconciliation for us.[95] It was a satisfaction of God's justice.[96] Christ was our substitute. He "shed his blood for me," wrote Luther, for "we can and must say: 'God was crucified and died for me.' And if anyone projects a God who did not suffer and die for me, I will have no truck with him."[97] Christ died for us so that we will not die for all eternity.[98] Thiselton agrees that Aulén underrated "Luther's emphasis on sacrifice, expiation, and substitution."[99] In his "Lectures on Galatians" (1535), Luther has some characteristically vivid and shocking comments:

> The merciful Father . . . said to [his Son]: "Be Peter the denier; Paul the persecutor, blasphemer, and assaulter; David the adulterer; the sinner who ate the apple in Paradise; the thief on the cross. In short, be the person of all men, the one who has committed the sins of all men. And see to it that you pay and make satisfaction for them."[100]

Calvin's view. Calvin's dominant theme on the atonement is satisfaction of the justice of God.[101] Christ has abolished sin, banished the resulting separation from God, and acquired righteousness for us "by the whole course of his obedience," although peculiarly and properly by his death.[102] Even in death "his willing obedience is the important thing because a sacrifice not offered voluntarily would not have furthered righteousness."[103] He offered himself to the Father as an expiatory sacrifice.[104] By his obedience he acquired and merited grace for us

---

95. Martin Luther, "Psalm 110," in *LW*, 13:319; "Sermons on the Gospel of St. John," in *LW*, 23:195.

96. Luther, "The Misuse of the Mass," in *LW*, 36:177; "Psalm 51," in *LW*, 12:365; "Eight Sermons at Wittenberg, 1522," in *LW*, 51:92.

97. Luther, "Sermons on the Gospel of St. John," in *LW*, 24:98.

98. Luther, "Lectures on Romans," in *LW*, 25:45; "Eight Sermons at Wittenberg, 1522," in *LW*, 51:92.

99. Thiselton, *Systematic Theology*, 220.

100. In *LW*, 26:280.

101. Calvin, *Institutes*, 2.16.1–2.

102. Calvin, *Institutes*, 2.16.5.

103. Calvin, *Institutes*, 2.16.5.

104. Calvin, *Institutes*, 2.16.6.

with his Father.[105] The substitutionary nature of Christ's death is clear, as Calvin cites Matthew 20:28, John 1:29, Romans 4:25 and 5:19, and Galatians 4:4–5.[106] Christ's offering renders "the Father favorable and propitious to us,"[107] this propitiatory sacrifice being a provision of God's love.[108] Calvin affirms, "Christ's grace is too much weakened unless we grant to his sacrifice the power of expiating, appeasing, and making satisfaction."[109] The righteousness he acquired for us when he reconciled us to God is as if *we* had kept the law.[110] The link to justification is clear.

The governmental theory. Hugo Grotius (1583–1645), a Dutch jurist, in his *Defence of the Catholic Faith concerning the Satisfaction of Christ*, reasoned that God ordained the atoning work of Christ in order to maintain the moral order of the universe. He opposed the Socinian denial of the appropriateness of God punishing sin. However, he thought God did this on pragmatic grounds. Punishment is appropriate in order to prevent corruption of human morals and to promote the common good.[111] God chose it out of his goodness, because of his wrath against sin, and particularly in his wisdom. By this he upholds his law and deters from sin. The cross is a free decision of God for prudential reasons. It is an act of God's will, not an outflow of his nature. He could have chosen differently, but this was the most prudent course of action. God was acting like a wise jurist.

Grotius evidently had a truncated view of God's justice. For him, God's rectoral justice trumped retributive justice. God is a wise administrator. Absent is any idea of the biblical connection between sin and punishment as a matter of just deserts. A break in this connection, as Thornwell argued, is at the root of divergences from the biblical doctrine of atonement. Grotius posited an atonement that rested on an arbitrary

---

105. Calvin, *Institutes*, 2.17.3.
106. Calvin, *Institutes*, 2.12.2–3, 2.16.6, 2.17.2–4; Calvin, *Commentarius in epistolam Pauli ad Romanos*, in CO2 (1999), 72–74.
107. Calvin, *Institutes*, 2.15.6.
108. Calvin, *Institutes*, 2.12.1; 2.15.6; 2.16.6, 14; 2.17.2–4; Calvin, *Calvin's Commentaries: The Epistles of Paul the Apostle to the Romans and to the Thessalonians*, trans. Ross MacKenzie (Grand Rapids, MI: Eerdmans, 1973), 74–77; Calvin, *Ad Romanos*, 72–74; Calvin, *Calvin's Commentaries: The Second Epistle of Paul the Apostle to the Corinthians and the Epistles to Timothy, Titus, and Philemon*, trans. T. Smail (Grand Rapids, MI: Eerdmans, 1964), 78–80; Calvin, *in Commentarii in Pauli Epistolas*, Ioannis Calvini opera exegetica (Geneva: Droz, 1992), 101–3.
109. Calvin, *Institutes*, 2.17.4.
110. Calvin, *Institutes*, 2.17.5.
111. Hugo Grotius, *Opera omnia theologica* (London: Moses Pitt, 1679), 3:306–9, 315–17.

decision. Crisp describes Grotius's theory as penal nonsubstitution.[112] John Stott took a favorable attitude toward Grotius, even referencing Warfield in support.[113] This was a blemish on a fine book as, far from granting approval, Warfield considered Grotius to occupy a position halfway between an objective view of the atonement and outright rationalism.[114]

McLeod Campbell's theory. Campbell developed his ideas in a pastoral situation in the Church of Scotland, where many lacked assurance of salvation. He was eventually expelled from the kirk. In *The Nature of the Atonement* (1856), he launched an attack on Calvinism, particularly as expressed by John Owen (1616–1684) and Jonathan Edwards (1703–1758). He contended that they made justice an essential attribute of God and relegated mercy to an arbitrary attribute by their insistence that God is necessarily just but displays mercy only to those he chooses. Campbell considered this to be a reversal of the nature of the atonement, which reveals God as love. For Owen and Edwards, God is primarily a stern judge, Campbell claimed. Consequently, they imposed a limit on the warrant of the gospel, which calls all who hear it to trust Christ. Instead, Campbell argued that in the incarnation Christ identified himself with us, living a life of self-sacrificial love and confessing his full concurrence in God's wrath against human sin. Christ repented on our behalf, freely acknowledging his identification with us by suffering the brunt of divine wrath.[115]

The deficiencies of Campbell's views are clear. Helm has argued that justice that can be abrogated is not justice, and mercy that cannot be abrogated is not mercy.[116] Campbell effectively inverted justice and mercy by making mercy a necessary attribute and justice arbitrary.[117] He appears to have undermined the simplicity of God by setting attribute against attribute. Furthermore, it is difficult to understand what vicarious repentance is. With other theories that undermine the biblical doctrine, this one mistakenly severs the connection between human sin and the judgment

---

112. Oliver D. Crisp, "Penal Non-Substitution," *JTS* 59 (2008): 140–68.

113. John Stott, *The Cross of Christ* (Leicester: Inter-Varsity Press, 1986), 122.

114. B. B. Warfield, *The Person and Work of Christ* (Philadelphia: Presbyterian and Reformed, 1970), 363–66, 373–87.

115. John McLeod Campbell, *The Nature of the Atonement and Its Relation to Remission of Sins and Eternal Life* (1856; repr., London: James Clarke, 1959).

116. Paul Helm, "The Logic of Limited Atonement," *SBET* 3 (1985): 50.

117. Letham, *The Work of Christ*, 169–70, 237–39.

and wrath of God. Leon Morris has remarked, such "theories of the atonement are right in what they affirm, but wrong in what they deny."[118] However, in Campbell's case it is more difficult to see positive elements.

Moral influence theory. Peter Abelard (1079–1142) is perhaps wrongly associated with the idea that the essence of the atonement is the love of God shown to us in Christ, which in turn elicits love in us. This is based on a short extract from his Romans commentary and sidesteps the fact that Abelard's primary thought on the atonement is related to God's action. As Thiselton remarks, it is inconceivable that this was the sum of Abelard's doctrine.[119] The theory is more to be associated with the liberal theology that existed before the First World War, seen in Hastings Rashdall.[120] It held that the cross demonstrates the love of God, constraining an answering love in us. While this is clearly a New Testament theme (John 13:15, 34; 1 John 4:9–11, 19), it is not intrinsic to the atonement but is an appropriate consequence. Moreover, the theory was constructed in opposition to the full range of New Testament motifs.[121] The events of 1914–1918 dealt a fatal blow to the theory, predicated as it was on inherent human goodness and perfectibility.

Karl Barth's and T. F. Torrance's constructions. For both Barth and Torrance, there is an integral connection between the incarnation and the atonement. Behind both lies God's primal decree of election, in which God elects to be God in Christ—God for us—to be no other than in Jesus Christ. This decree embraces creation, covenant, incarnation, atonement, and resurrection, all determined supratemporally in God's time. Since Christ assumes human nature, the same nature as every person, his atoning death is for all people. Grounded in election, it is also effective. Atonement, justification, and reconciliation are all accomplished realities in the death of Christ. Atonement is effective for all people at all times.

Barth holds that the atonement is both substitutionary and penal: "The judge judged in our place."[122] However, a robust doctrine of penal

---

118. Leon Morris, *The Cross in the New Testament* (Exeter: Paternoster, 1967), 399.

119. R. O. P. Taylor, "Was Abelard an Exemplarist?," *Theology* 31 (1935): 207–13; R. E. Weingart, *The Logic of Divine Love: A Critical Analysis of the Soteriology of Peter Abelard* (Oxford: Clarendon, 1970); Thiselton, *Systematic Theology*, 218; Letham, *The Work of Christ*, 166–67.

120. Alister McGrath, "The Moral Theory of the Atonement: An Historical and Theological Critique," *SJT* 38 (1985): 205–20.

121. Letham, *The Work of Christ*, 166–67; McGrath, "The Moral Theory," 205–20; Weingart, *The Logic of Divine Love*; Taylor, "Was Abelard an Exemplarist?," 207–13.

122. Barth, *CD*, IV/1:211–14, 230–31.

substitution by itself is not enough, for in Barth's case it is colored by his dominant doctrine of election, which means that in this case penal substitution plus effective atonement points logically toward universal salvation, which Barth himself wishes to avoid. However, Torrance regards the use of logic in this instance as a symptom of an uncrucified epistemology. As the high priest entered the Most Holy Place within the veil, out of sight, in a mystery, so too with the atonement; it takes place in the heart of God. To us it is a mystery. Logic here is inappropriate; we need to bow before the mystery. Torrance states, "The innermost mystery of atonement and intercession remains mystery; it cannot be spelled out."[123] So, avoiding the logical consequences of their doctrine of incarnation and atonement, both Barth and Torrance deny universal salvation. This position is at root incoherent. Crisp has argued this regarding Barth,[124] as I have done with Torrance.[125]

19.7   The Scope of the Atonement

19.7.1   Theological Considerations

The scope of the atonement concerns God's intention. When Christ went to the cross, who were the intended beneficiaries of his sacrifice? Here, the nature of the atonement is related to its scope. Hence, penal substitution is not held by Arminianism; penal substitution requires that the atonement was definitively achieved at the cross, where Christ made effective atonement for sinners. Arminianism denies this. For Arminius (1560–1609), Christ simply suffered. His sufferings were sufficient so that all who believe will be saved.[126] It follows that the efficacy of Christ's atoning death is contingent on the response of repentance and faith by each sinner. The Arminian doctrine of atonement places its fulcrum in the human response of faith.

19.7.2   Historical Background

Augustine's disciple Prosper of Aquitaine held to definite atonement in the fifth century. However, the scope of the atonement was not a matter

---

123. Thomas F. Torrance, *Atonement: The Person and Work of Christ*, ed. Robert T. Walker (Milton Keynes: Paternoster, 2009), 2–4.

124. Oliver Crisp, "On Barth's Denial of Universalism," *Them* 29 (2003): 18–29.

125. Robert Letham, "The Triune God, Incarnation, and Definite Atonement," in *From Heaven He Came and Sought Her: Definite Atonement in Historical, Biblical, Theological, and Pastoral Perspective*, ed. David Gibson and Jonathan Gibson (Wheaton, IL: Crossway, 2013), 437–60.

126. J. K. Grider, "Arminianism," in *Evangelical Dictionary of Theology*, ed. Walter A. Elwell (Basingstoke: Marshall Pickering, 1985), 79–81.

of major interest at the time. Later, Peter Lombard argued that Christ's atoning death was "sufficient for all, efficient for some."[127] However, the extent—or intent—of the atonement only became a major question at the Colloquy of Montbéliard in 1586, where Theodore Beza clashed with the Lutheran Jacob Andraeus.[128] From then until the Synod of Dort (1618–1619), it was a live issue.[129]

Four main positions

Universal salvation. This position claims that Christ made effective atonement for each and every person. Consequently, everyone is saved. The atonement effects the intention behind it. However, the Bible is clear that not everyone will be saved. Barth and Torrance both imply universal salvation, as we saw, while denying that each and every person will be saved. For them, atonement and incarnation are integrally connected; Christ took human nature and made atonement for everyone. His atonement is effective, yet some can reject the love of God expressed and effected for them.

Arminianism. For classic Arminianism, Christ suffered on the cross. His sufferings are sufficient for all who believe. Since God elects those he foresees will believe, the fulcrum is the response of believers. The atonement is therefore provisional, contingent on the response of faith and repentance.

Limited/definite/effective atonement. Christ died with the purpose of making full and effective atonement for all his people, who had been chosen to salvation from before the foundation of the world. While many consider the value of Christ's death to be infinite, due to the nature of Christ who suffered and its sufficiency, which would be more than adequate were the whole world to believe, yet its saving purpose is directed to the elect.

Hypothetical universalism. Here there are two variants. Moïse Amyraut (1596–1664) held that Christ died equally for all people, on condition that they believe, but God, foreseeing that not all would believe, elected

---

127. Peter Lombard, *The Sentences*, bk. 3, *On the Incarnation of the Word* (Toronto: Pontifical Institute of Medieval Studies, 2008), 3.20.5.

128. Jill Raitt, *The Colloquy of Montbéliard: Religion and Politics in the Sixteenth Century* (New York: Oxford University Press, 1993).

129. W. Robert Godfrey, "Tensions within International Calvinism: The Debate on the Atonement at the Synod of Dort" (PhD diss., Stanford University, 1974); Stephen Strehle, "The Extent of the Atonement and the Synod of Dort," *WTJ* 51 (1989): 1–23.

some to salvation and applied this to them by the Holy Spirit.[130] Another
line of thought was English hypothetical universalism, one of its chief
spokesmen being John Davenant, a member of the British delegation to
the Synod of Dort. From the premise of the need for the universal preaching of the gospel to be grounded on a coterminous provision, he taught
that the death of Christ was the basis for the salvation of all people everywhere. Christ paid the penalty for the sins of the entire race, grounded
on an evangelical covenant in which God promises salvation on condition
of faith in Christ. This universal provision precedes and overshadows a
decree by which God determined salvation for the elect, who alone are
saved. Consequently, there is a dual aspect to the covenant of grace: universal and conditional for sinners, effective for the elect. While it is not its
official position, there are echoes of this in WCF, 7.3. In the seventeenth
century, hypothetical universalism was considered to be within the bounds
of the Reformed faith. I have argued elsewhere that its constructions are
incoherent and, in Amyraut's case, posit a disjunction within the Trinity.[131]

19.7.3 Arguments for Definite Atonement

The following factors all speak in favor of definite atonement. The electing purpose of God suggests that, in view of the indivisibility of the
Trinity, the intent of the atonement is in harmony with both election and
its application by the Spirit. Moreover, union with Christ, at the heart
of salvation, requires that Christ's death be in union with his covenant
people. Furthermore, the nature of the atonement as penal substitution
underlines the atonement's intrinsic efficacy.

There is also biblical support. Jesus spoke of laying down his life
for his sheep, in the same context saying that his unbelieving opponents
were not his sheep (John 10:11–16, 25–29). Paul preached that Christ's
blood was shed for his church (Acts 20:28) and wrote the same (Eph.
5:25–27).[132]

19.7.4 Arguments against Definite Atonement

A number of biblical passages suggest that Christ died for all (John
3:16; 1 Tim. 2:6; 1 John 2:2). If these are not given due weight, op-

---

130. Moïse Amyraut, *Brief traité de la prédestination et des ses principales dépendances* (Saumur, 1634).
131. Letham, "The Triune God, Incarnation, and Definite Atonement," 438–44.
132. Letham, *The Work of Christ*, 225–47.

ponents of definite atonement say, we will place limits on the offer of the gospel, since it will not be possible to tell people that Christ died for them.

Theologically, it is argued that the atonement reveals God as love; but limiting its scope makes justice and will primary, which would not properly reflect God's character. This thought was favored by McLeod Campbell and James Torrance. Additionally, T. F. Torrance argued that, as the high priest in the Old Testament disappeared when he entered the Most Holy Place on the Day of Atonement, so the atonement is a mystery. Limited atonement is seen as a rationalist attempt to reduce a mystery to the bar of human logic, and so is impermissible. Moreover, the incarnation and atonement are coherent; since Christ took the nature of all people, therefore he died to save all people.[133]

19.7.5 Counterarguments

The biblical arguments for universal atonement are also open to debate. John 3:16 has to be seen in terms of John's uses of κόσμος.[134] Previously John has used the word ethically, for the world in rebellion, which did not receive the Word made flesh (John 1:10–11). Warfield argues that John means not that the world is so big that it takes a great deal of love to love it but that the world is so bad that it is a wonder that God loves it at all.[135]

First John 2:2 more clearly means the whole world in contrast to the Jews; Christ is the propitiation not merely for Israel, the Old Testament people of God, but also for the nations.

The context of 1 Timothy 2:6 is conduct in public worship, in prayer (v. 8ff.), and in church leaders (3:1ff.). Paul has asked for prayer for all kinds of people, including rulers and government officials (2:1–2). This suggests that he means all kinds of people rather than every single individual.

Moreover, Christ's atoning work is in harmony with his intercession. He prays for his people, not for the world (John 17:9). Consequently, his atoning death is intended to benefit them.

---

133. Torrance, *Atonement*, xxxv–lxxxiii, 70–75, 181–85; Letham, "The Triune God, Incarnation, and Definite Atonement," 447–60.

134. *kosmos.*

135. B. B. Warfield, "God's Immeasurable Love," in *Biblical and Theological Studies*, ed. Samuel G. Craig (Philadelphia: Presbyterian and Reformed, 1952), 505–22.

19.8   Intercession and Benediction

Christ's priestly work continues now that he has ascended. One recent writer has remarked that "the ascension is, I think, a subject richer and more instructive than is commonly recognized."[136] A description of the event occurs in only two places in the New Testament, both written by Luke; that may lead us to assume that it lacks a significant place in the teaching of the Bible. Yet, the New Testament refers to it in many places, and it is also foreshadowed in the Old Testament.

19.8.1   *Old Testament Background to the Ascension*[137]

The psalms of enthronement (Psalms 24; 47; 68; 110) feature the installation of the royal king, behind which lie the events in 2 Samuel 6 and 1 Chronicles 13–16, where David brings the ark of the covenant up to Jerusalem with shouts of joy. The ark was central to Israel's worship, where Yahweh met his people. Years before, it had been captured by the Philistines (1 Sam. 4:1–22) and hastily returned to Israelite territory (1 Sam. 5:1–7:2), but it had not been brought to Jerusalem. David led the triumphant procession. These psalms reflect those events. Psalms 24, 47, 68, and 110 portray an ascent to royal sovereignty, the enthronement of Yahweh as King.

Earlier, Moses had repeatedly ascended Mount Sinai, on Yahweh's invitation, to meet him in the clouds on behalf of the people (Ex. 19:3, 20, 24; 24:1–2, 9–18; 32:30ff.; 34:4). At the establishment of the Mosaic covenant, Moses and Aaron, Nadab and Abihu, and seventy of the elders of Israel ascended Sinai (Ex. 24:9–10), saw the God of Israel, and ate and drank.

Even earlier, at creation, "a river flowed out of Eden to water the garden, and there it divided and became four rivers" (Gen. 2:10). The location of Adam's fellowship with God was elevated, with rivers flowing down to lower ground.[138]

Later, Elijah ended his ministry by ascension. He was aware that he was to be taken from Elisha and "chariots of fire and horses of fire sepa-

---

136. Douglas Farrow, *Ascension and Ecclesia: On the Significance of the Doctrine of the Ascension for Ecclesiology and Cosmology* (Edinburgh: T&T Clark, 1999), x.

137. This is the substance of a lecture given in the Faculty Lecture Series at Calvin College, Grand Rapids, Michigan, in September 2004, later published in my book *The Message of the Person of Christ: The Word Made Flesh* (Nottingham: Inter-Varsity Press, 2013).

138. John V. Fesko, *Last Things First: Unlocking Genesis 1–3 with the Christ of Eschatology* (Fearn: Mentor, 2007).

rated the two of them. And Elijah went up by a whirlwind into heaven" (2 Kings 2:11). Elijah ascended "into heaven," where Yahweh dwells. He was no longer found (2 Kings 2:15–18), removed from his contemporaries to the realm of God, a deeply mysterious event beyond our grasp.

These events indicate that God's place is far above ours, that to worship and commune with him, we are to ascend beyond our own sphere, elevated by the mighty hand of God.

19.8.2   *The Ascension in Luke-Acts*

Luke 24:50–53. Only Luke describes the details of the ascension. He concludes his first volume with these details: (1) Jesus lifts up his hands and blesses his disciples; (2) while he blesses them, he is parted from them; (3) he is carried up into heaven. Benediction, parting, being taken up into heaven—these are the salient features.

Benediction is a priestly act, the last thing the apostles see Jesus doing. It defines his ongoing ministry. It signals that his effective blessing rests on his disciples. *The parting* is decisive and differentiates this event from the resurrection appearances. Then Jesus disappeared for a time; this is permanent. Then he returned after a few days; now the interaction of the previous years has ended. It is an ongoing departure. In *being taken up into heaven*, Jesus is *passive*; the Father takes him up to his right hand. The movement originates from God. Jesus is God incarnate; he depends on the Holy Spirit and follows the Father's will. Here the pattern is underlined. The ascension mirrors the virginal conception (Luke 1:26–38), where the incarnation is described as a new creation; the Spirit takes the initiative in both cases.

Acts 1:9–11. Luke recounts the ascension from another angle. First at the end of Luke and now at the beginning of Acts, he pinpoints its pivotal significance in relation to all that precedes and follows. This, as Douglas Farrow says, is "the hinge" upon which the two volumes turn.[139]

Jesus has taught the apostles of the imminent coming of the Spirit and their task as his witnesses. After this Jesus is lifted up, and a cloud receives him as he passes out of the apostles' sight. During this sequence, they look on. He is taken up into heaven. Again, the Father takes him to be with himself, the seal of divine approval on all he has done.

---

139. Farrow, *Ascension and Ecclesia*, 16.

There is a physical removal, a lifting up. We must ask, first, about the other elements of this unique scene.

The reference to *the cloud receiving him* is more than a weather report. The language is reminiscent of the Son of Man (Dan. 7:13–14), who comes "with the clouds of heaven" and to whom is given "dominion and glory and a kingdom, that all peoples, nations, and languages should serve him." Jesus, in his ascension as the Son of Man, receives his kingdom, which shall embrace "the end of the earth" (Acts 1:8). The rest of Acts records how this process begins. Luke has, in his Gospel, explained the things "Jesus began to do and teach" (Acts 1:1); now his focus is on the things he continues to do and teach through his apostles, ending at Rome, the heart of the leading world power (Acts 28).

Throughout Scripture *the clouds are associated with the glory of God*. In the transfiguration (Luke 9:34–35), a cloud overshadows the three disciples, who are struck with fear. From the cloud comes the voice saying, "This is my Son, my Chosen One; listen to him!" The Father speaks, referring to his Son; the cloud that envelopes Jesus is the glory of the Father and in this context the apostles are to listen to Jesus. John writes of Jesus at his parousia, his coming "with the clouds" (Rev. 1:7), in line with the angels' announcement that Jesus will return as he has gone—with the clouds (Acts 1:10–11). His return will be in glory. His disappearance, concealed by a cloud, is his passing into the presence of God.

The disciples see this—Luke stresses the point—taking us back to the ascension of Elijah (2 Kings 2:1–14). There Elijah promises Elisha a double portion of his spirit—the portion of the firstborn—*if* he sees Elijah taken up to heaven. And so he does: "And Elijah went up by a whirlwind into heaven. And Elisha saw it" (2 Kings 2:11–12). Thereafter twice as many miracles by Elisha are recorded. He receives the double portion. Here, the apostles—promised the Holy Spirit—see Jesus taken up by the Father to the glory of God in the cloud. They gaze intently. They are "looking on . . . gazing into heaven" (Acts 1:9–11). Then, a few days later, the Spirit of Jesus is unleashed in power, with consequences reported throughout Acts.

Farrow's comment on the centrality of the ascension to Luke-Acts is very perceptive.[140] It follows that Peter's sermon on the day of Pentecost

---

140. Farrow, *Ascension and Ecclesia*, 16.

(Acts 2:14–36) is a sermon on the ascension of the risen Jesus to the throne, from where the Spirit goes forth.

The physics of the ascension. There are boundaries to keep us from viewing the mystery of the ascension in unhelpful ways. *It is not to be reduced to the level of a primitive form of space-travel.* Again, the reference to the clouds was not intended as a weather update. As Yahweh in the wilderness goes before Israel in a pillar of cloud by day (Ex. 13:21), as Moses in ascending to his meeting with Yahweh enters the clouds (Ex. 24:18), as Yahweh rides on a swift cloud (Isa. 19:1), as the Son of Man comes with the clouds of heaven (Dan. 7:13), and as the Father speaks from the cloud at the transfiguration (Luke 9:35–36), so Luke points us to Jesus's removal from the immediate realm of human interaction to the presence and place of God.

However, *we must avoid the opposite danger of reading Christ's ascension in an entirely spiritual manner.* As he parted, Jesus's hands were raised in priestly blessing. The physicality of the event is clear. The ascension affirms, par excellence, Jesus's continuing humanity. Our human flesh is taken to the right hand of God, invested with the glory of God, and received by the Father. That this event took place in our own time and space was *necessary* since what is at stake is the continuation of our humanity.

In summary, *the ascension bridges our present world and that of the age to come.* It is a movement, in T. F. Torrance's words, "from man's place to God's place."[141] Jesus moved from regular interaction with his contemporaries to the place where God dwells, in the clouds of glory. It was an event that occurred in this world at a definite time and place but with extra dimensions to it. There is the departure, but there is also the cloud; the severance of fellowship, and the reception by the Father; Jesus's consequent absence until his parousia, and his presence through the Spirit, whose sending followed the ascension. It is a happening in this world that can be dated, but it is also an event that occurs in the life of God and so has eternal significance

The resurrection and the ascension. The ascension was not simply the last of Jesus's resurrection appearances. There is an obvious connection between the two. The interaction immediately before the ascension occurred

---

141. Thomas F. Torrance, *Space, Time and Resurrection* (Grand Rapids, MI: Eerdmans, 1976), 106–58.

during the last of the resurrection appearances. However, the ascension is qualitatively different. In all the resurrection appearances, Jesus suddenly disappears, later reappearing at another place. In the ascension, his departure is not a sudden vanishing but a concealment that takes place while the apostles watch, a diminishing into the distance. Moreover, it is confirmed by the angels as a continuous absence until his parousia. After the resurrection, Christ appears in recognizable form, with enhanced powers; Mary Magdalene thinks he is a gardener; the disciples on the road to Emmaus talk with him as though he were another traveler; he cooks breakfast by the lakeside. But after his ascension he is transformed (Acts 9:1–19; Rev. 1:9–20), so suffused with glory that those to whom he appears cannot bear it. If the ascension were simply the ending of the last of a sequence of resurrection appearances, we would miss the goal toward which Jesus was heading as man: the glory of God at the right hand of the Father. We would miss too the connection with Pentecost and what follows, severing the connection between the present world and the new creation in Christ.

The ascension and reception by the Father. The ascension is a definitive parting, for an indefinite time, to be ended only at Jesus's return. As Farrow states, it is "a real departure, the exchanging of a shared . . . history for an altogether distinct and unique one," a liturgical act (according to Venerable Bede) that was the link between our fallen world and the new creation.[142] In this, the act of benediction—paradigmatic for all that follows—conveys divine blessing into our place.

Moreover, we must bear in mind that all Jesus did is done in union with us, his people. We were *in him* as he ascended to the right hand of the Father. As he disappeared into the glory of God, so in union with him do all who believe go also. We too are ascended in Christ; our life is hid with Christ in God (Col. 3:1–4). We are seated with him in heavenly places (Eph. 2:6–7), in the closest union and communion with Christ, reigning with him even as we suffer and struggle in our present condition. This is a pledge of our ultimate salvation, a tonic in the face of dispiriting circumstances, a vast encouragement to faithfulness to Christ and to perseverance in adversity. Bishop Christopher Wordsworth expresses it this way:

You have raised our human nature
in the clouds to God's right hand;

---

142. Farrow, *Ascension and Ecclesia*, 39.

there we sit in heavenly places,
there with you in glory stand!

Jesus reigns, adored by angels,
man with God is on the throne;
mighty Lord, in your ascension
we by faith behold our own.[143]

19.8.3   The Ascension and Christ as Priest

Luke records Jesus's parting words and gesture. There at Bethany, "lifting up his hands he blessed them. *While he blessed them*, he parted from them and was carried up into heaven" (Luke 24:50–51). His final act was the priestly act of benediction (Num. 6:24). This priestly act is characteristic of his continuing ministry after his ascension. In parting from them he blesses them and continues to do so. As the author of Hebrews states it, Jesus, the Son of God, has "passed through the heavens" and so is able to send us grace and help in time of need (Heb. 4:14–16).

His continuing priestly ministry following his ascension is threefold: intercession, benediction, and communion. First, it is important to understand what Christ's intercession is not. He does not plead on our behalf before a reluctant Father: this would have, among other things, enormous consequences for the Trinity. Nor is it to be equated with the kinds of intercession we make here and now. When we pray, there is an element of uncertainty; we ask God to heal someone, but he may have determined that the person die a slow and painful death. The ascended Christ's intercession has no caveats. It is to be compared with the high priest in the Old Testament, who entered the Most Holy Place once a year, wearing the prescribed breastplate—containing twelve jewels, representing the twelve tribes of Israel. In his representative capacity he was, so to speak, bringing the twelve tribes with him into the sanctuary of God. In an analogous way, Christ, having passed through the heavens, brings us, his people, with him into the presence of God, at the right hand of the Father, and he does this since he himself not merely represents man but *is* man himself. In his incarnation he, the Son of God, permanently unites to himself our nature, our flesh and blood, and so carries it before the Father on a permanent, everlasting basis. As the

---

143. From the hymn "See the Conqueror Mounts with Triumph" (1862).

WLC, 55, puts it, his intercession is "his appearing in our nature continually before the Father in heaven." The ascended Christ's continuing intercession is his constant presence with the Father *as man*. Thus, in the words of Charitie Lees Bancroft,

> When Satan tempts me to despair,
> and tells me of the wrong within,
> upwards I look and see him there,
> who made an end of all my sin.[144]

Second, Jesus's final *benediction*, while characteristic of the ascended Christ's continuing ministry, also differs from prayer. While intercessory prayer is the expression of a desire that this or that happen, if it be God's will, a benediction is a declaration of a state of affairs that actually exists and a bestowing of that reality on those to whom it belongs. There is none of the hesitation or uncertainty of our own intercessions. In the case of the ascending and ascended Christ, this uncertainty is entirely absent, for as King, he has ascended far above all heavens, that he might fill all things. Christ's priestly benediction grants to his people all they need for salvation both in this life and in what follows; in it he guards, protects, and nourishes his church, governs the world, and brings his sovereign judgments to bear on its inhabitants. This includes all that is entailed in the author of Hebrews's description of him as our forerunner (Heb. 6:19–20), foreshadowed in John (John 14:1–3). Christ has gone before, we follow: we follow because he has gone before; in going before he brings us there by the Holy Spirit, whom he has sent. Indeed, all that occurs consequent to the sending of the Spirit—his blessing of his church, his ministry to its members, his witness to the world—is entailed in this.

Third, there is *union and communion*. Jesus refers to his ascension immediately after the Bread of Life Discourse, which has often been associated with the Eucharist (John 6:47–58, 62).[145] From this, and from the fact of communion with Christ in the Lord's Supper—evident elsewhere in the New Testament beyond this one passage—it follows that the ascension and the Eucharist are closely linked. Calvin saw this clearly. Jesus is absent from us. Yet we feed on his body and drink his

---

144. From the hymn "Before the Throne of God Above" (1863).
145. Robert Letham, *The Lord's Supper: Eternal Word in Broken Bread* (Phillipsburg, NJ: P&R, 2001), 7–15.

blood. How? Through the Spirit (John 6:63), who lifts us up to heaven. Similarly, the author of Hebrews writes that we have come now to Mount Zion, to the city of the living God, to an innumerable company of angels, and to Jesus (Heb. 12:18–24). The bodily ascension of Jesus is the basis for our communion with him—according to both natures— through the Holy Spirit, who unites things separated by distance. The Eucharist is for the church until Christ's parousia. It is coterminous with his ascended ministry. So long as he intercedes for us and blesses his church, so we feed on him in the Eucharist. It points to our destiny: union with God in Christ; the ascended Christ has sent the Spirit to unite us to him and thus to the Father. It is the ascension that makes room for this to occur. As Jesus said, "It is to your advantage that I go away" (John 16:7).

19.8.4 *The Ascension in the New Testament beyond Luke-Acts*

It is mistaken to assume that the ascension was a matter for the writings of Luke alone.

First, the ascension is mentioned a number of times in John. Jesus links his incarnation with the ascension: "No one has ascended into heaven except he who descended from heaven, the Son of Man" (John 3:13). Then Jesus asks the disciples, as they grumble over the hard saying of the Bread of Life Discourse, perplexed by Jesus's crude imagery of eating his flesh and drinking his blood, "What if you were to see the Son of Man ascending to where he was before?" (John 6:62). He makes the point that it is more difficult for us to comprehend the ascension than the imagery of the discourse. Later, Jesus reassures his disciples, who are disturbed by his announcement of his impending departure, with these words: "I go to prepare a place for you," and "I will come again and will take you to myself, that where I am you may be also" (John 14:2–3). Jesus gives a lengthy, detailed account of the coming of the Spirit and the Spirit's ministry subsequent to his departure (John 14:16–16:33). In particular, Jesus says he is going to the One who sent him—the Father (John 16:5). This he reiterates to Mary Magdalene in the garden after his resurrection (John 20:17). The Spirit's indwelling of the disciples will be the permanent indwelling of all three persons of the Trinity (John 14:23). Earlier in John, Jesus refers to the gift of the Holy

Spirit following his glorification (John 7:37–39). Those who believe in him will have rivers of living water flowing out of their inmost beings, a reference to the Holy Spirit.

Second, Peter refers to the ascension in 1 Peter 3:18–22. Leaving aside the complexities of this passage, if—as is probable—verses 19–21 are a parenthesis, we have a progression in Peter's thought from the crucifixion ("put to death in the flesh," v. 18, "flesh" in the redemptive-historical Pauline sense of the old aeon), to the resurrection ("made alive in the Spirit," v. 18, my trans.; i.e., by the Spirit and in the new age of the Spirit), to the ascension ("who has gone into heaven and is at the right hand of God," v. 22).[146]

Third, Paul refers specifically to the ascension in Ephesians 4:8–10.[147] Citing Psalm 68, he argues that the church is founded on the basis of Christ's ascension. The ascended Christ has given gifts to his church, gifts of *persons*, including the apostles, for particular strategic tasks. Again, in the hymnic citation in 1 Timothy 3:16, which refers to the incarnation, the resurrection, and the preaching of the apostles, comes the phrase "taken up in glory."

Fourth and finally, the ascension is absolutely crucial for the author of Hebrews. There are many implicit references among a number of explicit ones. Jesus is our Great High Priest, "who has passed through the heavens" (Heb. 4:14–16) and so is able to help us in our time of need, and to sympathize with us in light of his own experience of temptation; he is our forerunner, who has entered into "the inner place behind the curtain" (Heb. 6:19–20), from where he is able to save to the uttermost those who draw near to God through him (Heb. 7:25–26). He has entered "once for all into the holy places" (Heb. 9:11–12), "into heaven itself, now to appear in the presence of God on our behalf" (Heb. 9:24). He has sat down at the right hand of God (Heb. 10:12–13). All these passages trace the journey of Jesus from the cross to the right hand of God without reference to the resurrection but instead focusing on the

---

146. William J. Dalton, *Christ's Proclamation to the Spirits: A Study of 1 Peter 3:18–4:6* (Rome: Editrice Pontifico Instituo Biblico, 1989).

147. Elsewhere I have written on the authorship of Ephesians: Robert Letham, *The Holy Trinity: In Scripture, History, Theology, and Worship* (Phillipsburg, NJ: P&R, 2004), 73–74; see also C. E. Arnold, "Ephesians," in *Dictionary of Paul and His Letters*, ed. Gerald F. Hawthorne (Downers Grove IL: InterVarsity Press, 1993), 238–49.

ascension as portraying his passage into the Most Holy Place, the presence of God.

19.8.5 *The Ascension and Our Present Life*

The ascension marks the boundary between two closely related contrasts. *First, there is the redemptive-historical contrast of two ages*: the world in Adam, from the fall onward, subject to sin, corruption, and death, an age that is passing away; and the world in Christ, from the incarnation, resurrection, and ascension onward, which is being renewed and is marked by life that will last for eternity. *Second, this contrast is evident in relation to creation.* The creation, as made by God, was good, made in Christ,[148] but it was affected by human sin and is described by Paul as currently in bondage. On the other hand, there is the new creation, from the resurrection and ascension, renewed in Christ and ultimately destined for his eternal rule. These two contrasts intersect, distinct but inseparably related.

> Grant, we beseech thee, Almighty God, that like as we do believe thy only-begotten Son our Lord Jesus Christ to have ascended into the heavens; so we may also in heart and mind thither ascend, and with him continually dwell, who liveth and reigneth with thee and the Holy Ghost, one God, world without end. Amen.

> Collect for Ascension Day, Book of Common Prayer (1662)

Further Reading

Letham, Robert. *The Work of Christ*. Leicester: Inter-Varsity Press, 1993.

Stott, John. *The Cross of Christ*. Leicester: Inter-Varsity Press, 1986.

Torrance, Thomas F. *Space, Time and Resurrection*, 106–58. Grand Rapids, MI: Eerdmans, 1976.

Study Questions

1. How is the doctrine of the atonement best articulated?

2. In what ways is the ascension of Christ crucial to an understanding of his work?

---

148. Athanasius, *Incarnation* 1, 3, 12, 14 (*PG*, 25:97–102, 115–22).

20

Christ Our King

Christ's mediatorial kingship is consequent upon his ascension to the right hand of the Father and his enthronement. The scope of his kingdom is universal, coextensive with the universe that he created. His government is in tandem with his headship over his church and is for the ultimate establishment, growth, and triumph of his people over all the forces of evil. There is nothing outside his domain. His rule over church and world is of a piece. There is only one King, and there can be only one kingdom, albeit in distinct realms. Suggestions that the creation is neutral represent a retraction of the sovereign authority of Christ.

20.1 The Ascension and Christ as King

Jesus, as recorded in the Gospels, proclaimed the kingdom of God as being near, about to burst forth in the world (Matt. 4:17; Mark 1:15). The kingdom required repentance on the part of Israel. With Jesus's self-description as the Son of Man, it was reminiscent of the visions of Daniel of a kingdom that would overthrow all human rulers and be established forever (Dan. 2:31–45; 7:9–14). The significance of this is seen after Jesus's resurrection when he taught the apostles about the kingdom of God (Acts 1:3). It represented a powerful demonstration of the rule of God over the whole of human life.

However, in the rest of the New Testament this theme disappears. Instead, the apostles draw attention to Jesus Christ. He is the subject of the sermons of Peter and Paul (Acts 2:14–36; 3:12–16; 17:2–3). The primary focus of the gospel is on the death, burial, and resurrection of Christ (1 Cor. 15:3–4). The kingdom is equated with the whole counsel of God (Acts 20:25–27). It is identified with the totality of apostolic teaching after the resurrection, the main point of which is precisely Christ's resurrection. The kingdom of God is embodied in the risen Christ, who has been given plenipotentiary powers over the entire universe (Matt. 28:18–20; Rom. 1:3–4; Eph. 1:18–23; Phil. 2:9–11; Col. 1:15–20; Heb. 1:1–4; Rev. 1:5). The mediatorial kingdom of Christ comes into view as the fulfillment of what Jesus proclaimed. Paul declares, "He must reign until he has put all his enemies under his feet" (1 Cor. 15:20–25).

Underlying this is that creation is a work of the undivided Trinity and thus of the Son. In turn, there is personal identity and continuity between the eternal Son and Jesus of Nazareth. Consequently, Paul describes creation as a work of Christ (Col. 1:15–17). As I have written elsewhere, "Christ (as in Heb. 1:3) reflects the glory of God both in the time of revelatory history but also too in the relations of the eternal Godhead."[1]

This again is the corollary of the incarnation, for, as Torrance puts it, unless there is a real and essential relation between the union of God and man on earth and the eternal union of God the Father, the Son, and the Holy Spirit in heaven, we are not assured of real or eternal relations with God.[2] Barth expresses it well in writing that Christ became wholly and utterly one with man,

> not in an act of secret or even public condescension, like a king for a change donning a beggar's rags and mingling with the crowd, but by belonging to them in every way, by being no more and no less than one of them, by having no point of reference except to them. He became one of them, not in order to renounce fellowship with them when the game was over, like the king exchanging again the beggar's rags for his kingly robes, not in order to leave again the table where He had seated Himself with the publicans and sinners, and to find a better place, but in order to be one of them definitively as well as

---

1. Robert Letham, *The Work of Christ* (Leicester: Inter-Varsity Press, 1993), 200.
2. Thomas F. Torrance, *Incarnation: The Person and Life of Christ* (Milton Keynes: Paternoster, 2008), 177.

originally, unashamed to call them brethren to all eternity because
He was their brother from all eternity.[3]

From this, the incarnate Christ, "gentle and lowly in heart" (Matt.
11:28–30), remaining man, is the one exalted to the highest place as
ruler of all things.

Paul writes that Jesus was highly exalted and given the supreme name
of κύριος (Phil. 2:9–11). It is not a case of a man being promoted to God-
hood, since he was eternally in the form of God and equal to God (v. 6),
and continued to be so in the days of his incarnate lowliness. Rather, as
the incarnate One, the Savior and Mediator, nailed to the cross and now
risen, he was exalted to be given the name of κύριος.

In Romans 1:3–4, Paul writes that Christ was descended from the seed
of David according to the flesh and appointed Son of God with power by
the Spirit of holiness since his resurrection from the dead. Is Paul referring to
the two natures of Christ or to stages in redemptive history? The latter is to
be preferred. His status as God's Son our Lord did not begin at the resurrection, which might be implied if the reference were to his divine nature. The
expressions κατὰ σάρκα and κατὰ πνεῦμα are best understood to express
two states rather than two natures.[4] Jesus Christ is God's Son both in the
state of lowliness from conception to crucifixion (of the seed of David according to the flesh) and in his risen exaltation (appointed Son of God with
power by the Spirit of holiness since his resurrection from the dead). In both
cases he is God's Son, in weakness and in power.[5] The resurrection marks the
decisive center point in redemptive history. At the ascension, he is received
by the Father and invested with sovereign, plenipotentiary authority. In that
sense, it is expedient that he leaves the disciples (John 14:1–4, 28; 16:7–15).
The work of redemption reaches its culmination when Christ returns and
hands over the kingdom to the Father (1 Cor. 15:27–28). However, since he
is one with the Father, his kingdom never ends.

20.2   The Cosmic Scope of Christ's Kingdom

Christ is heir to the cosmos (Col. 1:16). It was created in him, through
him, and for him. He maintains it and directs it to its appointed goal.

---

3. Barth, CD, IV/4:58–59.
4. *kata sarka* (according to the flesh), *kata pneuma* (according to the [Holy] Spirit).
5. C. E. B. Cranfield, *A Critical and Exegetical Commentary on the Epistle to the Romans*, The
International Critical Commentary (Edinburgh: T&T Clark, 1975), 1:57–65; Ernst Käsemann,
Commentary on Romans, trans. Geoffrey W. Bromiley (Grand Rapids, MI: Eerdmans, 1980), 11–
14; James D. G. Dunn, *Romans 1–8*, Word Biblical Commentary 38A (Dallas: Word, 1988), 11–16.

The reconciliation he achieved relates not only to the church but to the entire universe (Col. 1:19–20). This inheritance he received at his resurrection, his ascension to the Father effecting his enthronement as King. While, as Son, he ruled inseparably with the Father and the Holy Spirit in the unity of the indivisible Trinity, this was his investiture as King in his incarnational, mediatorial office. "The scene and context is different, the personal actor is the same."[6]

We have already seen how Luke regards the ascended Christ as our High Priest, blessing his people in the act of departure. Now we will concentrate on the point that Christ's ascension establishes that he rules the universe. In it he publicly displays his conquest of his enemies, as in a triumphant victory procession. In Ephesians 4:8–10, citing Psalm 68:18, Paul teaches that the ascended Christ has pervasive authority. A victorious king would travel throughout his territory establishing and confirming his rule in every place throughout his domain.[7] So Christ's realm is universal. He has ascended far above the heavens and now fills all things. He has passed through his territory and has won the authority throughout his realm. Athanasius wrote along these lines, as did Abraham Kuyper.[8] From this, the cosmos will be liberated when Christ returns (Rom. 8:18–23). Meanwhile, he rules the new heavens and the new earth (Heb. 2:5–9).

20.3 The Corporate Nature of Christ's Kingdom

We can take this a stage further. By Christ's ascension he establishes the church, granting gifts to it for its preservation and advancement (Eph. 4:11ff.). All that he did and does is not only for us, in our place, and on our behalf but also in union with us. We were in him in his ascension. We too have ascended to the right hand of the Father in Christ. We too sit with him in heavenly places.

This is why, from chapter 22, I will be connecting the *ordo salutis* with the church and the means of grace. Soteriology (the doctrine of salvation) and the doctrine of the church (ecclesiology) are in reality

---

6. Letham, *The Work of Christ*, 204.

7. Markus Barth, *Ephesians: Translation and Commentary on Chapters 4–6*, The Anchor Bible (New York: Doubleday, 1974), 472–77; Charles Hodge, *A Commentary on the Epistle to the Ephesians* (London: Banner of Truth, 1964), 212–19.

8. Athanasius, *Orations against the Arians* 2.79 (*PG*, 26:314). Abraham Kuyper, inaugural address at the opening of the Free University of Amsterdam, October 20, 1880, cited in *Abraham Kuyper: A Centennial Reader*, ed. James D. Bratt (Grand Rapids, MI: Eerdmans, 1998), 488.

inseparably conjoined. Christ is King not merely over a collection of disparate individuals but over his covenant people, of which individuals are a part. Correspondingly, salvation does not occur independently from the covenant community.

20.4   The Two-Kingdoms Theory

Does Christ's kingdom cover all things or only the church? Some claim that his kingdom is synonymous with the church. The rest of creation, it is said, is a "common kingdom," directed by God's providential rule, and is to be distinguished sharply from the sphere in which God's redemptive purposes are unfolded. This is known as the two-kingdoms theory, associated with David VanDrunen, Darryl Hart, and others.[9] It has affinities with Lutheranism. I will focus on VanDrunen, the most prominent voice of this school of thought. He has many valuable things to say, much wise counsel, but space forbids my commenting on them; rather, I will address the distinctive features of his case.

Broadly, the argument advanced for the idea of two kingdoms is as follows. The mandate given by God to Adam to govern creation and subdue it was a task given to the human race as a whole. After the flood, it was reiterated in the Noachic covenant, in the new context of a fallen world that had been subject to divine judgment. The covenant of grace, instituted by God with Abraham and administered in distinct ways thereafter, is a redemptive covenant and came to fulfillment in Jesus Christ. It is now located in the church. As a redemptive covenant, it is of a different order from the Noachic. Christian believers belong to the church, in which God's plans for his new creation are worked out. Christ is Mediator of the new covenant, and he is also Mediator of creation; however, these are different realms. The redemptive covenant is governed by special revelation, in the Bible, whereas the common kingdom is regulated by natural law, written on the consciences of all people. Ultimately the common kingdom will end when the existing creation is destroyed by fire (2 Pet. 3:1–13), and everything in it, including all human culture as we have known it, will be annihilated.

---

9. David VanDrunen, *A Biblical Case for Natural Law* (Grand Rapids, MI: The Acton Institute, 2006); VanDrunen, *Natural Law and the Two Kingdoms: A Study in the Development of Reformed Social Thought* (Grand Rapids, MI: Eerdmans, 2009); VanDrunen, *Living in God's Two Kingdoms* (Wheaton, IL: Crossway, 2010); Darryl G. Hart, *A Secular Faith: Why Christianity Favors the Separation of Church and State* (Chicago: Ivan R. Dee, 2006).

Hence, there is a radical dualism between the realms of creation and redemption. The world operates in the common kingdom, in which believers and unbelievers alike function. Its basic mode of operation is natural law, written on human hearts from creation. Its destiny is not redemption but ultimate destruction. Christians are to work in it, to do good works, to use their gifts, but they do so alongside unbelievers. Special revelation, found in the Bible, is not applicable to this realm, and any attempt to "redeem" it for Christ is futile; indeed, it can savor of an attempt to earn salvation by good works. It is in the church that the redemptive kingdom of Christ is to be found. This is the realm of the new covenant, the new creation, governed by Christ through his Word and Spirit. The only element of the common kingdom that will last into the eternal state is the resurrection of the bodies of believers at the last day.

The two-kingdoms idea has the merit of pointing to two radically different eternal destinies. It also highlights the reality that, until Christ returns, the church and its members are pilgrims and strangers in a world that has been deeply affected by sin and rebellion against God. However, it is in contrast to Herman Bavinck, who held that Christians of all people are, in another sense, at home in the world, since it was created and is directed by the triune God, with Christ its Mediator.[10] Moreover, as Beach remarks, the two-kingdoms view splits the Christian believer into a dualism: under Christ's authority in the kingdom of God but neutral in the common kingdom.[11] It appears to undermine the Bible as the supreme authority in *all matters of faith and practice.*

Moreover, it is not apparent that such a dualism is sustainable in the programmatic way that the two-kingdoms theory holds. We have noted that Christ is exalted as King over the universe. His rule over his church is connected integrally with his cosmic authority. He is Head over all things *for the church* (Eph. 1:20–23). The Lion of the tribe of Judah, who alone has authority to govern the world and to execute the judgments of God, is at the same time the Lamb who was slain on the cross for our salvation (Rev. 5:1ff.). As ruler of kings on earth, he is also the one who

---

10. Bavinck, *RD*, 1:321; James Eglinton, *Trinity and Organism: Towards a New Reading of Herman Bavinck's Organic Motif* (London: Bloomsbury, 2012), 149.

11. J. Mark Beach, "A Tale of Two Kingdoms: Some Critics of the Lutheran Doctrine of Two Kingdoms," *MAJT* 25 (2014): 52.

has freed his church from its sins by his blood and made us a kingdom of priests (Rev. 1:5–6).[12]

There is a serious Christological problem with the two-kingdoms theory—there is only one King and there can only be one kingdom in two distinct realms, not two separate kingdoms. Indeed, Christ's redemptive work is portrayed as a progressive subjugation of his enemies until the very last enemy is abolished at his parousia (1 Cor. 15:20–26). During this time, the church destroys opposing arguments and leads every thought captive to obey Christ (2 Cor. 10:1–6). It is more than doubtful that the devil considers the world of human culture to be a "common kingdom." It is even less likely that Christ, given all authority in heaven and earth, will restrict his lordship to the religious sphere only or consider the world he created and maintains to be a lost cause. While the church is indeed distinct from the world, Christ rules both in coordinated coherence (Eph. 1:20–23).

Behind this theory, in the case of VanDrunen, lies a literalist interpretation of Scripture akin to dispensationalist hermeneutics. He considers the language of 2 Peter 3 to indicate that the present world is to be destroyed literally by fire, all vestiges of human culture wiped out. He writes, "The New Testament teaches that the natural order as it exists will come to a radical end and that the products of human culture will perish along with the natural order."[13] The present order "will be burned up, melt, and dissolve." The earth will remain no more.[14] However, Peter uses the same language with reference to the world of Noah's day, which was destroyed by water. That world was not annihilated. The destruction related to the judgment of God on human sin; the earth remained. The human race and the various nonhuman species were preserved. Peter writes in the language of apocalyptic, with graphic visual imagery relating to the judgment of the wicked. The creation is no more to be eradicated than, at the overthrow of Babylon, did the stars cease to emit their light or was the earth shaken off its axis (Isa. 13:9–13).

In order to escape the consequences of his position, VanDrunen has to agree that there is one exception—believers are resurrected. Beyond this, "asserting that anything else in this world will be transformed and taken up into the world-to-come is speculation beyond Scripture."[15]

---

12. VanDrunen passes over such passages in his book *Living in God's Two Kingdoms*.
13. VanDrunen, *God's Two Kingdoms*, 64.
14. VanDrunen, *God's Two Kingdoms*, 65.
15. VanDrunen, *God's Two Kingdoms*, 66.

Indeed, VanDrunen continues, "The New Testament teaches that the entirety of present cultural activities and products will be brought to a radical end . . . at the second coming of Christ."[16] "The flood indicates that the products of present human culture are doomed to destruction with the natural order itself."[17] Christians cannot expect to see the fruit of their labors in the New Jerusalem.[18] The only part of creation that will remain is believers themselves.

However, humans are part of creation. If we escape the conflagration, creation itself has escaped too, since humanity is its chief part. As Venema points out, reflecting on Romans 8:18–23, "the redemption for which the children of God eagerly await and the redemption of the creation itself are intimately connected. Individual eschatology and cosmic eschatology are so joined together that what is true for believers holds true for creation."[19] Since the whole cosmos groans like a woman in labor anticipating its redemption and glory, how can it be brought to a radical end (Rom. 8:18–23)? The whole creation cannot therefore be annihilated. VanDrunen's argument sounds plausible only if we ignore the evidence against it, much like a legal advocate charged to make the best case on behalf of his client. Moreover, one assumes VanDrunen holds that the wicked will also be raised from the dead to face judgment, and that he is not an annihilationist but believes that they will suffer the eternal consequences of their sins. Under even a cursory cross-examination, the argument that the whole creation will be extinguished begins to evaporate.[20]

Mark Beach, in criticizing the Lutheran view of two kingdoms, demonstrates its remarkable convergence with the ideas propounded by Van-Drunen. Its quietist tendency, in encouraging passivity toward the status quo, paved the way for tyranny.[21] Beach comments:

> As has been frequently noted, an unforeseen implication of the Lutheran understanding of the two-kingdoms doctrine emerged with

---

16. VanDrunen, *God's Two Kingdoms*, 67.
17. VanDrunen, *God's Two Kingdoms*, 68.
18. VanDrunen, *God's Two Kingdoms*, 70.
19. Cornelis P. Venema, "Christ's Kingship in All of Life: Butchers, Bakers, and Candlestick Makers in the Service of Christ," *MAJT* 25 (2014): 17.
20. For further critical evaluation of the two-kingdoms theory, see Cornelis P. Venema, "One Kingdom or Two? An Evaluation of the 'Two Kingdoms' Doctrine as an Alternative to Neo-Calvinism," *MAJT* 23 (2012): 77–129; and the essays in Ryan C. McIlhenny, ed., *Kingdoms Apart: Engaging the Two Kingdoms Perspective* (Phillipsburg, NJ: P&R, 2012).
21. Beach, "A Tale of Two Kingdoms," 50.

Hitler's rise to power and the ideology of National Socialism. The German Christians, accustomed to a Lutheran doctrine of the two kingdoms, readily capitulated to the *Führer* and accommodated the church to function in support of the state. However, the confessing church [mainly Reformed] viewed matters quite differently. This difference was aptly expressed in Dietrich Bonhoeffer's words of resistance, when he said, "we must deny that there are God-willed autonomous spheres of life which are exempt from the lordship of Christ, and do not need to listen to this Word. What belongs to Christ is not a holy sacred district of the world, but the whole world."[22]

As Beach continues, the crucial question is not God's sovereignty but the scope of the lordship of Christ as the incarnate Mediator. There is no part of life exempt from his lordship, no sphere beyond his authority. The world is not autonomous.[23] Beach concludes that for the two-kingdoms theory, Christ's redemptive rule, expressed in the Bible, is not relevant to civil government or the common kingdom.[24] Christ's work as Savior is restricted to the ethical-religious.[25] Venema shares this concern:

> The service of Christians in the common kingdom is of a piece with the service of non-Christians, and it has no vital connection with the gospel or Christ's work of redemption. It is, strictly speaking, a "secular" and not a "spiritual" service. The problem with this perspective is that . . . it can only encourage the secularizing of human life in God's world and the privatizing of the claims of Christ upon it.[26]

Elsewhere, in the late 1980s, long before the two-kingdoms theory surfaced, I wrote, "To separate creation and redemption is, so to speak, a Nestorian position. Just as Nestorius held the two natures of Christ apart without doing adequate justice to the unity of his person . . . there is potential for a disruption in understanding the works and ways of God."[27] Rather, they are like two concentric circles in which Christ reigns supreme.[28] Again:

---

22. Beach, "A Tale of Two Kingdoms," 36. Beach cites Dietrich Bonhoeffer, *Werke*, 11:331.
23. Beach, "A Tale of Two Kingdoms," 36.
24. Beach, "A Tale of Two Kingdoms," 38.
25. Beach, "A Tale of Two Kingdoms," 56.
26. Venema, "Christ's Kingship," 33.
27. Letham, *The Work of Christ*, 204. That book was part of a series. I finished the manuscript in 1989, but it and another completed title were held back from publication until the other volumes were near completion, so as to maintain momentum in the series.
28. Letham, *The Work of Christ*, 74.

> If Christ is creator and sustainer of the universe, and he is to remould it . . . no realm is out of bounds to the Christian faith. All things—education, politics, business, sport, the arts, family life, economic conditions . . . scientific inquiry, the legal profession . . . —are to be seen from the perspective of the creation mediatorship of Jesus Christ. This represents not just one way of looking at the world. Since he made it, to view the universe from any other perspective will result in distortion.[29]

Indeed, as mentioned above, the two-kingdoms theory has Christological implications. It represents a retraction of Christ's sphere of authority.

Furthermore, the two-kingdoms theory runs counter to the historic Reformed attitude toward the created realm. As I have suggested, it has more in common with Lutheranism. It was in Reformed circles that resistance theory emerged and flourished in the sixteenth and seventeenth centuries. It had a profound effect, facilitating the emergence of responsible and democratic government, not only in Europe but also in North America. This required Reformed thinkers and activists to suppose that the political realm, among others, was of direct consequence to the gospel and to apply the Word of God to every area of life. They were cognizant of the reality that the civil ruler is accountable ultimately to God (Rom. 13:1–7) and that the kings of the earth are warned to "serve the Lord with fear," to

> kiss the Son,
> lest he be angry, and you perish in the way. (Ps. 2:10–12)

This does not seem like a "common kingdom," shared with a usurper. All areas of life are under Christ's authority (Matt. 28:18–20; Eph. 1:22–23); not a blade of grass is excluded from his rightful realm.

The position betrays a naïve and complacent view of the propensities of fallen people. We are in a war. There is an enemy. That enemy is no gentleman, prepared to play by rules and on a level playing field. When the world around us is relinquished to a supposedly neutral "common kingdom," that enemy will seize control, and in many ways has done so and is increasingly advancing.

John Wind makes a valiant attempt to suggest that much of the disagreement concerning the two-kingdoms view is misunderstanding.[30] In

---

29. Letham, *The Work of Christ*, 208–9.
30. John Wind, "The Keys of the Two Kingdoms: Covenantal Framework as the Fundamental Divide between VanDrunen and His Critics," *WTJ* 77 (2015): 15–33.

part, this may be so, but it cannot hide radical differences. Wind correctly points to the major conflict on the relationship of biblical covenants, stemming from the theories of Meredith Kline. He highlights the point that VanDrunen makes continual contrasts between various covenants (creation and Noachic, Noachic and Abrahamic, Abrahamic and Mosaic, Mosaic and new, new covenant inaugurated and new covenant consummated). To my mind, this is a type of Reformed dispensationalism.[31]

Further Reading

Beach, J. Mark. "A Tale of Two Kingdoms: Some Critics of the Lutheran Doctrine of Two Kingdoms." *MAJT* 25 (2014): 35–73.

VanDrunen, David. *Living in God's Two Kingdoms*. Wheaton, IL: Crossway, 2010.

VanDrunen, David. *Natural Law and the Two Kingdoms: A Study in the Development of Reformed Social Thought*. Grand Rapids, MI: Eerdmans, 2009.

Venema, Cornelis. "Christ's Kingship in All of Life: Butchers, Bakers, and Candlestick Makers in the Service of Christ." *MAJT* 25 (2014): 7–33.

Venema, Cornelis. "One Kingdom or Two? An Evaluation of the 'Two Kingdoms' Doctrine as an Alternative to Neo-Calvinism." *MAJT* 23 (2012): 77–129.

Study Questions

1. According to the New Testament, how extensive is the rule of Jesus Christ?

2. How should Christian believers act in the world? Is it legitimate to distinguish between long-term aspirations and immediate realities?

3. In what ways is the kingdom of Christ principally advanced?

---

31. See Richard C. Gamble, *The Whole Counsel of God*, vol. 2, *The Full Revelation of God* (Phillipsburg, NJ: P&R, 2018), 512–20.

PART 7

THE SPIRIT OF GOD AND
THE PEOPLE OF GOD

God, who at this time did teach the hearts of your faithful people, by the sending to them the light of your Holy Spirit; grant us by the same Spirit to have a right judgment in all things, and evermore to rejoice in his holy comfort; through the merits of Jesus Christ our Saviour, who lives and reigns with you, in the unity of the same Spirit, one God, world without end. Amen.

Collect for Whit-Sunday, Book of Common Prayer (1662)

21

Union with Christ

Union with Christ is central to soteriology. It is rooted in the great Trinitarian events of creation, incarnation, and Pentecost. The creation account demonstrates, besides the Creator-creature distinction, the inherent compatibility of God and humanity. In the incarnation the Son takes a human nature of his own into permanent union. At Pentecost the Holy Spirit comes to indwell or saturate Christ's church and so to bring us into living union with Christ the Son. This union is expressed both in representational terms, in atonement and justification, and transformatively, as the Spirit conforms us to Christ gradually in this era and fully at the eschaton. Currently, he uses the Word and sacraments as means to effect this transformation, which is hidden from the world and not yet fully known to us.

✠

Union with Christ is at the heart of the biblical doctrine of salvation. For Paul (Eph. 1:3–14), John (John 14:12ff.; 17:21–24; 1 John 3:1–2), and Peter (1 Pet. 1:1–4) it is vividly prominent. It is grounded on three foundational acts of God: creation, incarnation, and Pentecost.[1]

---

1. For a fuller discussion of union with Christ, see Robert Letham, *Union with Christ: In Scripture, History, and Theology* (Phillipsburg: P&R, 2011).

21.1   Creation: The Creator-Creature Distinction and Compatibility

Union with Christ rests on the creation of humanity as compatible with God. While the Creator-creature distinction is vast, God the Creator is a relational being, with humanity made in his image reflecting this (Gen. 1:26–27). This points forward to Jesus Christ, who *is* the image of the invisible God.

Flowing from the biblical presentation of creation as a work of the whole Trinity comes the New Testament assertion of the creation mediatorship of Jesus Christ. In John 1, the Logos is described as existing "in the beginning," a phrase reminiscent of Genesis 1:1. This Logos, who was with God and who was God, who became flesh and lived among us, is the Creator of all things (John 1:3). Not only is he the author of created life, as if life were something independent and autonomous, but he himself *is* life (v. 4).

Paul expounds a similar theme in Colossians 1:16–17, where he affirms that "all things were created in him, things in heaven and on earth, things visible and invisible, whether thrones and dominions, rulers and authorities; all things were created through him and to him. And he is before all things, and in him all things hold together" (my trans.). Paul argues that Christ, as the preexistent Son (v. 13–15), is the Creator of the universe. "All things" is comprehensive, excluding nothing. He created them all, but he did so in such a way that he is their Head. Creation was *in Christ*. In turn, the cosmos has a purpose; it is held together by the Son. He sustains it at every moment and directs it toward the end he intends. That end is himself. All things were created and are sustained *for Christ*. The goal toward which the universe is heading is conformity to him; it will be under his headship and rule for eternity (Eph. 1:10).[2] A similar theme is present in Hebrews 1:1–3.

We noted that Paul remarks that Christ *is* the image of God (2 Cor. 4:4; Col. 1:15). In discussing the resurrection of the body, Paul compares Adam with the risen Christ. From Adam we inherit the image of the earthly, in weakness and mortality, whereas in Christ we receive the image of the heavenly, under the direction and domination of the Holy Spirit (1 Cor. 15:45–49).[3] In Paul's thought, Christ *is* the image of God as

---

2. Robert Letham, *The Work of Christ* (Leicester: Inter-Varsity Press, 1993), 198–202.

3. Richard B. Gaffin Jr., *The Centrality of the Resurrection: A Study in Paul's Soteriology* (Grand Rapids, MI: Baker, 1978).

the second Adam. Adam was created *in* Christ, then fell from that estate, but now, in grace, we are being renewed in the image of God, *in Christ the second Adam*, and thus in knowledge, righteousness, and holiness. So also says Hebrews 1:3, where the Son, by whom God has spoken his final and ultimate word, is "the brightness of his [God's] glory and the express image of his being" (my trans.).

Consequently, from one angle there is a *difference* between God and humans. God is the Creator; we his creatures. God is infinite and eternal, sovereign and all-powerful; humanity is weak and finite, limited to one place at one time, subject to the rule of God the Creator, derivative and not creative in the sense outlined in Genesis. From another angle, there is an inherent *compatibility* between God and man.[4] Humanity has been created *in* the image of God, made for union and communion with God.

21.2 Incarnation: Christ's Union with Us

The New Testament witness is that Jesus Christ is the eternal Son of God. Yet Jesus was also born, grew, and developed from infancy to childhood and adulthood. Jesus's humanity is real. The basis of our union with Christ is Christ's union with us in the incarnation. We can become one with him because he first became one with us. By taking human nature into personal union, the Son joined himself to humanity. He now has a human body and soul, and will never jettison either. We considered this in chapter 16.

The central promise of God's covenants is the repeated statement in each covenantal administration "I will be your God, and you shall be my people" (see Gen. 17:7–8; Jer. 11:4; 24:7; 30:22; 31:33; 32:38; Rev. 21:3). All these promises come to a head in Jesus Christ, who fulfills all God's covenants. *God is our God in Jesus Christ.* Furthermore, *in Christ we are God's people*—he perfectly replies as man to God in faith and obedience. We cannot be God's people in ourselves, since we are naturally sinners, deserving of God's wrath. Thus, our election before the foundation of the world is *in Christ* and so our whole salvation is *in Christ* too. Here Christ's work as our Great High Priest fits. In the incarnation, he took our place and bore our sins, rising for our justification and ascending in our flesh to the right hand of the Father. He is one

---

4. An instance of this is the concurrence of the attitude of Yahweh and Samuel to Saul's delinquency (1 Sam. 15:11, 35); Yahweh regrets, Samuel is angry; Samuel grieved, Yahweh regretted.

with us. He everlastingly took our nature into personal union. He is at the Father's right hand in our flesh. The incarnation is the indispensable basis for union with Christ; since Christ has united himself to us in the incarnation, we can be united to him by the Holy Spirit.

However, something more was needed, distinct from the incarnation but inseparable from it. This movement of God's grace consists of the Holy Spirit coming at Pentecost.

21.3   Pentecost: The Holy Spirit Unites the Church to Christ

Bavinck points in this direction: "After creation and the incarnation, the outpouring of the Holy Spirit is the third great work of God."[5] Luke highlights the activity of the Spirit in the conception and life of Jesus. Bobrinskoy comments about "an exceptional convergence between the outpouring of the Spirit and the birth of Christ."[6] Later, at the outset of Jesus's public ministry, the Spirit pervades all that happens. As Bavinck puts it:

> At this point it is important to note that this activity of the Holy Spirit with respect to Christ's human nature absolutely does not stand by itself. Though it began with the conception, it did not stop there. It continued throughout his entire life, even right into the state of exaltation. Generally speaking, the necessity of this activity can be inferred already from the fact that the Holy Spirit is the author of all creaturely life and specifically of the religious-ethical life in humans. The true human who bears God's image is inconceivable even for a moment without the indwelling of the Holy Spirit.[7]

The sending of the Spirit is the central theme of the Upper Room Discourse in John 14–17. Jesus was to depart, but he would not abandon his disciples. He would come to them in the παράκλητος[8] following his ascension. The Spirit was to unite believers to Christ and indwell them. In John 14:1–11, Jesus affirms his identity with the Father while remaining distinct. He and the Father are coordinate objects of faith (v. 1). Whoever has seen him has seen the Father (vv. 8–10), since he and the

---

5. Bavinck, *RD*, 3:500.
6. Boris Bobrinskoy, *The Mystery of the Trinity: Trinitarian Experience and Vision in the Biblical and Patristic Tradition*, trans. Anthony P. Gythiel (Crestwood, NY: St Vladimir's Seminary Press, 1999), 87.
7. Bavinck, *RD*, 3:292.
8. *paraklētos*.

Father indwell one another (vv. 10–11): "Do you believe that I am in the Father and the Father is in me? The words that I say to you I do not speak on my own authority, but the Father who dwells in me does his works. Believe me that I am in the Father and the Father is in me." This refers to the Trinitarian *perichorēsis*, discussed in chapter 3. The three occupy the same infinite divine space,[9] in indissoluble union, with no infringement of the distinctness of any.

Jesus says that when the Spirit comes to indwell his disciples, they will know for themselves that he and the Father are in each other. They will also know that Christ is in them (John 14:20). There is an analogy between the indwelling of the Father and the Son, on the one hand, and Christ and his disciples, on the other. There is an obvious difference between the two relationships: the Father and the Son are one in being, eternal, and immense, while Christ and his disciples are separate beings. The Spirit is the agent of the indwelling. He indwells countless people, who remain individuals, although individuals in communion, in union with God the Spirit, who indwells them.

Jesus says more. Having indicated that anyone who loves him will be loved by him and his Father, he adds, "If anyone loves me, he will keep my word, and my Father will love him, and we will come to him and make our home with him" (John 14:23). Both the Father and the Son will come to the one who loves Jesus. In the coming of the Spirit to indwell, the Father and the Son are indivisibly present. The loving disciple will have intimate communion and union with the whole Trinity, in the person of the Holy Spirit. Behind this are the inseparable operations of the Trinity, while each work is specifically attributable to one of them. In the indwelling of the Spirit, the Father and the Son are inseparably involved. Jesus insists that he and the Father will make their permanent residence with this one; μονή denotes a secure dwelling, in contrast to a tent. This great event occurred at Pentecost, but the result is permanent.

The Holy Spirit inseparably continues the ministry of the Father and the Son. He was sent in place of the physical presence of Jesus. The ministry of the apostles and the early church in the power of the Spirit continued Jesus's ministry (Acts 1:1–2; 2:47; cf. John 16:12–15). Again, Paul reflects on the Father sending the Son in his incarnation and so also

---

9. Gerald Bray, *The Doctrine of God* (Leicester: Inter-Varsity Press, 1993), 158.

the Spirit at Pentecost; not only is the Spirit sent by the Father, but he is also called "the Spirit of [the Father's] Son" (Gal. 4:4–6). The Father also is said to send the Spirit (John 14:26), while the Son also sends him, having received him from the Father (Acts 2:33). Much in the New Testament supports the Orthodox point that the Spirit is sent by the Father and received by the Son, here and at his baptism, with the Son then pouring him out on his church.

Pentecost thus marks a new era in the history of redemption. It fulfills Old Testament prophecy. The Spirit is now present in a heightened way. He *was* present in the Old Testament (he could hardly have been absent) but not in the foreground as in the New. How and in what ways was the Spirit active in the Old Testament? Warfield, in considering the work of the Spirit in the cosmos, the kingdom of God, and the individual, concluded that he was at work in all the ways in which he is at work in the New Testament.[10] However, there is something new: first, the miraculous endowments of the apostles, together with the churches they founded; second, the worldwide mission of the Spirit, promised in the Old Testament but only now realized; and, third and principally, the fact that the Old Testament was preparatory for the New Testament, the Spirit then preserving the people of God, whereas now he produces "the fruitage and gathering of the harvest."[11]

The distinction is not between his presence now compared with a putative absence in the Old Testament but rather between the falling away of what was preparatory and temporary (the Old Testament) and the emergence of what is final, binding, and permanent (the New). Galatians 4:4–6 is again pertinent. Israel was God's son in the Old Testament, but it was so in a way little short of servant status. It was a child in its minority, under the protection of a pedagogue, a slave entrusted with its care and upbringing (Gal. 3:24). With Christ's coming and the Spirit's sending at Pentecost, God's people have been adopted as mature sons. So significant is the sending of the Spirit that Paul describes this transition in absolute terms, as elsewhere does John (John 1:17; 4:24). Hence, in the Old Testament the Spirit came intermittently on the prophets, whereas now he is poured out on all flesh (Acts 2:16–21). Then his presence with

---

10. B. B. Warfield, "The Spirit of God in the Old Testament," in *Biblical and Theological Studies*, ed. Samuel G. Craig (Philadelphia: Presbyterian and Reformed, 1952), 154.
11. Warfield, "Spirit of God," 155–56.

his people was spasmodic (Ps. 51:11); now he is given permanently (John 14:17, 23).

The Old Testament describes him as the giver of life (Gen. 1:2; Pss. 33:9; 104:29–30), the One who empowers for various forms of service in God's kingdom (Ex. 31:3; 35:31–34; Num. 27:18; Judg. 3:10; 1 Sam. 16:13), as the protector of God's people (1 Sam. 19:20, 23; Isa. 63:11–12; Hag. 2:5), indwelling them (Num. 27:18; Deut. 34:9; Ezek. 2:2; 3:24; Dan. 4:8–9, 18; 5:11; Mic. 3:8), and above all resting on and empowering the Messiah (Isa. 11:2–3; 42:1; 61:1).

In the New Testament the Spirit is presented as the One who purifies and sanctifies (Matt. 3:11; Rom. 8:13; Gal. 5:22–23; 1 Cor. 6:11; 2 Cor. 3:18; 1 Pet. 1:2); reveals truth to the apostles and prophets, teaches and, illumines all God's people (Luke 12:12; John 14:26; 16:13; 1 Cor. 12:10ff.; 1 Tim. 4:1; 1 John 2:19–27); directs the apostles, evangelists, prophets, and other church leaders (Acts 8:29; 10:19–20; 13:2; 15:28; 20:22–23); and grants assurance (Rom. 8:16; 1 John 3:24; 4:13) and unity (1 Cor. 12:7–21; 2 Cor. 13:14; Eph. 2:18–22; 4:3–6; Phil. 2:1–2). There is continuity but also a more lavish outpouring and a wider ministry in the New Testament.

The church of Jesus Christ is a Pentecostal church. The church was sent to baptize, teach, and disciple in the power of the Holy Spirit. The Bible is the Word of the Spirit and therefore the objective bearer of the Spirit's power, and thus it is the Word of Christ. The Spirit unites people to Christ by and through his Word.

The actions of Ananias and Sapphira in misleading the apostles are described as lying to the Holy Spirit, which brought upon them swift and unmistakable discipline enforced not by the human leaders but by the Spirit himself (Acts 5:1–11). The Spirit disciplines the church. Administrative and judicial discipline and the considered decisions of the Council of Jerusalem are also the decisions of the Spirit (Acts 15:28).

There is a conjunction between the calling, ordaining, and sending of the church at Antioch and the actions of the Spirit (Acts 13:1–7). The Spirit set Saul and Barnabas apart for missionary labors and made this known to the church leaders, who in turn set the two apart by prayer and the imposition of hands and so sent them away, a sending that was ultimately by the Holy Spirit. Church action and action by the Spirit were coordinate. Indeed, throughout Acts the Spirit directs Paul's missionary labors (Acts 16:6ff.). Paul's apostolic authority is the Spirit's work. Although he has no instructions from Jesus from his earthly ministry on a matter, yet Paul's apostolic advice is of equal weight, since he has the Spirit of God to direct him as an apostle (1 Cor. 7:10–12, 40).[12]

The Holy Spirit brings about our union with Christ in our life history, doing this by grace through faith. Our faith and all that flows from it in the Christian life are due to the Spirit, who renews us in the image of God and transforms us into Christ (2 Cor. 3:18). Eventually, when Christ returns in glory, we will be like him (1 John 3:1–2). This entire process occurs through faith. Faith is "the principal work of the Holy Spirit," as Calvin said.[13] The Spirit unites us to Christ. As a house benefits from electricity when hooked up to the grid, so we benefit from the work of Christ when it becomes ours as the Spirit unites us to him.[14]

21.4   Union with Christ and Representation

There is a legal aspect to union with Christ. As we saw in chapter 19, Christ fulfilled the law on our behalf, as our representative. He did this in what is termed his *active obedience*—his obedience to the demands of God's holy law—and his *passive obedience*, by which he underwent for us the penalty of the broken law. We had sinned in Adam, resulting in death and condemnation. In order for us to be restored to God's favor, at the very least the penalty of that broken law had to be suffered in Christ.[15]

Christ is perfectly suited to be our representative for two overwhelming reasons. First, he is the eternal Son of God. He is *able* to help us in time of need because of who he is. Second, he has taken our nature into union, and so he is *qualified* to be so. He was "in every respect . . . tempted as we are, yet without sin" (Heb. 4:14–16). Since the Spirit unites us to Christ through faith, Christ's substitutionary and representative work is effectively applied to us. We will examine its relation to justification in chapter 24.

---

12. H. B. Swete, *The Holy Spirit in the Ancient Church: A Study of Christian Teaching in the Age of the Fathers* (1912; repr., Eugene, OR: Wipf & Stock), 80, cites Tertullian, who remarks on the power of the Holy Spirit in the discipline of the church and on the newness of the New Testament.

13. Calvin, *Institutes*, 3.1.4.

14. An image used in Anthony N. S. Lane, *Justification by Faith in Catholic-Protestant Dialogue: An Evangelical Assessment* (London: T&T Clark, 2002), 23.

15. The alternative is to bear that penalty ourselves, eternal death and condemnation, the just and holy wrath of God.

21.4.1   Union with Christ and Atonement

Christ took our place throughout his life and ministry, especially on the cross and in his resurrection and ascension. In chapter 19, we considered how Christ's substitutionary and representative work is best seen in the context of his union with us.[16] Since we are united with Christ, God regards us in the identical way he does Christ; the Father treats us as he does his Son.

21.4.2   Union with Christ and Justification

Since justification is only by faith, it is grounded in Christ's obedience, received by no other means than faith. This excludes anything in us, including the grace of God imparted to us by the Holy Spirit. Paul makes clear that justification is only through faith since it is only by Christ. Luther and Calvin, Lutherans and the Reformed as a whole, all stressed that the work of God's grace in us does *not* have regard to justification. This is because justification is a legal or forensic matter that affects our status, not our condition, and *it is grounded on Christ*, on his obedience and righteousness. This is outside us and independent of our personal accomplishments. It is *received* by faith since, in faith, we abandon self-reliance, and we trust in Christ alone for salvation. Since we were by nature dead in sin, nothing in us enables us to attain a right status with him. God's impartation of grace, transforming us into his image in Christ, is a tremendous reality, but it is not pertinent to our attaining a right *status* with God. Only faith, because it looks entirely outside us, is *appropriate* for receiving the gift of justification.[17]

That justification is in union with Christ points us to Christ's own experience. Having been delivered up and condemned for our sins, dying as a vile criminal, he was raised for our justification (Rom. 4:25), vindicated by the Father. United to him by the Spirit we are joined to

---

16. Mark A. Garcia, "Imputation and the Christology of Union with Christ: Calvin, Osiander, and the Contemporary Quest for a Reformed Model," *WTJ* 68 (2006): 219–51.

17. I am not talking here about what Calvin describes as God's justification of our good works, those works of obedience that are the result of the gracious operation of the Holy Spirit within us and are nevertheless in some way soiled by our own continued sinfulness. That relates more to sanctification; such works can in no way secure for us a right status with God, for they are rather evidences of the grace of God, pardoned and accepted by God in virtue of our union with Christ. See Calvin, *Institutes*, 3.17.5–10; Lane, *Justification by Faith*, 33–36; William B. Evans, *Imputation and Impartation: Union with Christ in American Reformed Theology* (Eugene, OR: Wipf & Stock, 2008), 30–32; Mark A. Garcia, *Life in Christ: Union with Christ and Twofold Grace in Calvin's Theology* (Milton Keynes: Paternoster, 2008), 74–78.

him in both his death and his resurrection (Rom. 6:1ff.), and we now sit with him in the heavenly places (Eph. 2:4–7). When he died, we died with him; when he rose from the dead, we rose with him. In tandem with that, we are adopted as sons, sharing with the Son, by grace, the identical relation to the Father that he has by nature and thus calling on God as "our Father in heaven."

21.5   Union with Christ and Transformation

Our union with Christ also transforms us. When Christ died and rose from the dead, we died and rose with him, and so not only our status but also our existence was dramatically changed. Since, following Christ's ascension, the Holy Spirit was sent to give us life, indwell us, and renew us, our participation in Christ's death and resurrection is dynamic and transformative.

In Ephesians 1:15ff., Paul prays that the power of God in the resurrection of Christ would be at work in the life experience of those united to him. God raised Jesus from the dead; it was a new creation. He raised him far above all angels, far above the entire creation, so that he might be all in all. Paul asks the Father that this same power would be displayed in the Ephesian church. Union with Christ is a real and dynamic experience. Elsewhere Paul describes the resurrection of Christ as effected by the Father through the Spirit (Rom. 8:10–11). This resurrection from death in sin (Eph. 2:1–7) is an action in which all three persons of the Trinity are engaged, as they were when Christ was raised at the first Easter. The Father raises us in union with Christ the Son, effected by the Holy Spirit.

In 2 Corinthians 3:18, Paul writes that we all are being transformed into the image of God. Christ is the image of God (2 Cor. 4:4; cf. Col. 1:15). We are therefore being changed to be like the glorified Christ, the second Adam. This happens gradually and progressively, "from one degree of glory to another." Glory is what belongs exclusively to God; it is closely connected with the image of God. Our transformation happens as we behold "the glory of the Lord," the risen Christ. The one who brings this about is "the Lord . . . the Spirit," who is inseparably identified with the risen Christ (2 Cor. 3:17–18). We are united to Christ in the sense that we are in the process of being made to be like him.

At root, sanctification is a spatial concept. It involves being purchased by Christ and thus being the property of God. We have been transferred from the domain of darkness to the kingdom of God's Son (Col. 1:13). We have been bought with a price, we are not our own (1 Cor. 6:19–20). We have been separated from sin and the world and belong to God (Rom. 6:1–23). We belong to God in Christ—we are with him and in him. In this manner, sanctification is definitive; it has already taken place in Christ by the power of the Spirit. Because Christ died, we have died to sin in union with him. Because he rose from the dead, we have risen to newness of life in him.

By the power of the Spirit this is also a dynamic and objective reality. Sanctification in its most commonly recognized aspect is understood in ethical terms. The letters of Paul are replete with instructions on how we are to live. That we can obey God is due to the Spirit's work within us, transforming us into his image (Eph. 4:24; Col. 3:10). The dynamic of union with Christ is expressed in the life experience of believers. Christ has risen, never again to die. So we, in union with him, are no longer subject to the domain of sin and death, and so grow "more and more" (WCF, 13.1) in conformity to Christ by the Spirit through the means God has provided: the ministry of the Word, the sacraments, and prayer (WSC, 88).

21.6 Union with Christ and the Sacraments

The central substantive affirmation of the chapter on the Lord's Supper in the WCF is that the faithful, or "worthy receivers," "receive and feed on Christ" (WCF, 29.7). They are enabled to do this "really and truly"; it is no fiction, for the sacraments are more than symbolic. It is spiritual, not corporeal, and so depends on the Holy Spirit and requires faith on our part. The Assembly opposed the Roman Catholic position that the sacraments worked *ex opere operato*, by the fact of being performed. However, in keeping with the Reformed tradition, it equally opposed the Anabaptist claim that they were simply symbols and memorials. For the Reformed, the sacraments are signs and seals of the covenant of grace, exhibiting the grace signified, which grace is conferred by the Spirit in his own time to those to whom it applies (WCF, 27.3; 28.6). Baptism exhibits our ingrafting into Christ, in regeneration, justification, and sanctification, which the Spirit confers in due time. In the Lord's Supper, Christ gives himself for us to feed and nourish us to everlasting life.

Salvation therefore consists in our being united with Christ. The Father unites us to the incarnate Son, who effects our salvation, by the Holy Spirit. This is one movement of God's grace, for all three persons work in harmony and indivisible unity.

The means the Spirit uses, from our side, is faith. This is because our salvation is the result of grace, something achieved for us, not anything we ourselves could do. It therefore comes to us from outside ourselves. However, saving faith does not occur in a vacuum. We are brought to salvation in the context of the church. There is an outward side to what happens within. Union with Christ comes to external expression in baptism, as we are united with Christ's church. We shall see later the close connections drawn in the New Testament between baptism and regeneration, faith, the Spirit, and union with Christ. Just as it is impossible to separate faith, the Spirit, and union, so is it impossible to abstract these from baptism.

Baptism marks the start of the Christian life and in the New Testament was administered when a person could first be considered a Christian—at the moment of conversion for an adult convert or at birth for an infant born within a Christian home. Thus, there is a close connection between baptism and union with Christ (Rom. 6:1ff.; 1 Cor. 10:1ff.; Col. 2:11–13). The close nexus—baptism, the Spirit, membership of the body of Christ, and union with Christ its Head—is seen in 1 Corinthians 12:13, where Paul states, "For in one Spirit we were all baptized into one body . . . and all were made to drink of one Spirit."

Union with Christ is to be cultivated, developed, nourished. To that end, the Father has appointed that our union with the Son be matured by the Holy Spirit through means he has appointed for that purpose. This is where the preaching of the Word, the sacraments, and prayer come into play (WSC, 88). Transformation in union with Christ occurs through the means of grace, until the church is entirely conformed to Christ, when it sees him as he is and is like him in glory.

21.7　Union with Christ in Death and Resurrection

The New Testament portrays our union with Christ as grounded on his death and resurrection. In that sense, when he died on the cross, we were present *with him* and *in him* there and then. In short, all that we now possess and enjoy of union with Christ is based on something that happened two thousand years ago. Paul unfolds some implications of this in Romans 6. There is also a sense in which this union reaches back into eternity, for Paul explains that our election was in Christ before the foundation of the world. It is, of course, virtually impossible for us to conceive what eternity is, being creatures of time and space.

Paul argues in 1 Corinthians 15 that the resurrection of Christ and the future resurrection of his church are one reality (vv. 12–19). Paul argues back and forth from one to the other. If Christ is not raised, there can be no resurrection of believers. If there is no general resurrection, Christ cannot have been raised himself. The two stand together. In fact, Christ has been raised—and so, therefore, will we be. Christ is the first-fruits of the resurrection of believers at his return (vv. 19–23). Not only is his resurrection first in time, but also, as firstfruits, it is of the same kind as the full harvest. Hence, not only is it the guarantee that the full harvest will be gathered, but also, both his resurrection and ours are identical. From this, the resurrection of believers at the parousia is a resurrection *in Christ*. The resurrections are effectively the same (vv. 35ff.). Christ's resurrection and the resurrection of the righteous, separated by indefinite time, are identical because the latter occurs in union with the former.

A similar pattern occurs in Romans 8:10–11. Here Paul says that the Father raised Christ from the dead by the Holy Spirit. Moreover, the Father will raise us from the dead in union with Christ by the Spirit. Meanwhile, the Spirit by whom the resurrection occurs, who is the author and giver of life, dwells within us.

Union with Christ in his death and resurrection also has a present impact on the life experience of Paul in his apostolic ministry. He experiences the death of Christ in his body as he suffers in union with him. The persecutions, the rejection, the imminence of death on so many occasions all exhibit Paul's sharing in the sufferings of Christ on behalf of his body (2 Cor. 1:8–11; Phil.1:12–26; Col.1:24). Concurrently, he also experiences the life of Christ and the power of his resurrection in the midst of his sufferings (2 Cor. 4:7–18). Paul does not limit this to his own account. On the contrary, this is something common to regular Christian experience. He presents his own experience as a model and an encouragement.

21.8   Union with Christ and the Trinity

A basic premise underlying all we know of God, the principle *opera Trinitatis ad extra sunt indivisa* (the external works of the Trinity are indivisible) was carefully articulated by Augustine in the early chapters of *De Trinitate*.[18] Since God is one, all three persons work together in indivisible union. Examples are plentiful:

1. *In creation* (Gen. 1:1–3, 26ff.; Ps. 33:6); in the New Testament in relation to the Son (John 1:1–4; Col. 1:15–20; Heb. 1:1–4), and the Spirit, by inference from Luke 1:35–36, where the Spirit begins the new creation in terms reminiscent of Genesis 1:2, as in John 3:3–8, the connection between the Holy Spirit and life (John 6:63; Rom. 8:6–11; 1 Cor. 15:45).
2. *In providence*, concerning the Son (Col. 1:17–18; Heb. 1:3–4) and the Spirit (Ps. 104:29–30).
3. *In salvation*: (i) The incarnation was a Trinitarian event. Note how frequently Jesus speaks of his being sent by the Father (John 5:17, 19–27, 37–43). Simultaneously, he was conceived by the Spirit (Luke 1:35). His earthly ministry fulfilled the Father's will (John 4:34; 17:4), but at each stage he was led and enabled by the Spirit (Matt. 3:16–17; 4:1ff.; Luke 4:1ff., 14ff.; 10:21). (ii) At the cross, his sufferings were in relation to the Father (Matt. 27:46; Luke 23:46). This is brought into a Trinitarian context in Hebrews 9:14. (iii) Jesus's resurrection was by the power of the Father effected by the Holy Spirit (Rom. 8:8–11). And so on.

It is not wrong to talk of this as the work of the Holy Spirit, for this is where the classic doctrine of the *divine appropriations* comes in. While all three persons are engaged in every aspect of our creation, preservation, and salvation, each action is most appropriate to one of the three rather than the others. Only the Son became incarnate, not the Father or the Holy Spirit. Only the Son died on the cross, not the Father or the Spirit. Only the Spirit was sent at Pentecost, not the Father or the Son—although the Spirit was sent by the Father through the Son. All three were engaged at Pentecost, but only the Spirit came upon the church in the form of a powerful wind and tongues of fire.

The application of redemption in union with Christ is a Trinitarian event. The gifts of faith, hope, and love are all gifts of the Spirit, sent at Pentecost. From "life's first cry to final breath,"[19] the Spirit effects the eternal purposes of the Father, which were realized for us by his Son in

---

18. Augustine, *Trinity* (NPNF[1], 3:17–114).
19. From the song "In Christ alone," by Keith Getty and Pete Townend, copyright Capitol Christian Music Group, 2002.

his death and resurrection. Yet he was sent by the Father through the Son (John 14:14–20; Acts 2:33–36) and so executes what the Father intended and the Son achieved, while each is active in each element. Calvin is helpful when he says, "To the Father is attributed the beginning of activity, and the fountain and wellspring of all things; to the Son, wisdom, counsel, and the ordered disposition of all things; but to the Spirit is assigned the power and efficacy of that activity."[20] That efficacy will be the theme of the next few chapters.

Further Reading

Billings, J. Todd. *Union with Christ: Reframing Theology and Ministry for the Church*. Grand Rapids, MI: Baker, 2011.

Letham, Robert. *Union with Christ: In Scripture, History, and Theology*. Phillipsburg, NJ: P&R, 2011.

Macaskill, Grant. *Union with Christ in the New Testament*. Oxford: Oxford University Press, 2013.

Study Questions

1. How does union with Christ come to expression in the New Testament?

2. Union with Christ is a multifaceted reality—not surprisingly, since it has to do with union with the Son of God effected and developed by the Holy Spirit. How do these various elements hold together?

3. What encouragement does union with Christ give us as we face suffering and death?

---

20. Calvin, *Institutes*, 1.13.18.

22

Salvation and the Church

Recent discussions have surrounded the relationship between the *ordo salutis* and redemptive history. These two elements are complementary rather than competitive. More far-reaching problems concern the relationship between the church and the salvation of the individual. Here there is a large difference between the Roman church and evangelical Protestantism, and between both and the Bible. The influence of Enlightenment individualism has been profound. This chapter explores the biblical relationship between the individual and the corporate, including biblical metaphors for the church, before an extensive examination of preaching and the sacraments as means of grace through which we are brought into union with Christ and enabled by the Holy Spirit to grow and develop in union.

22.1   The *Ordo Salutis* and Biblical Theology

The *ordo salutis* is a theological construction whereby the application of salvation is unfolded in an orderly, analytical manner. There are biblical examples of such an order (Rom. 8:29–30; Eph. 1:3–14). Confessions such as the WCF include an order in logical progression, while the WLC, 65–90, identifies it as aspects of union and communion with Christ. In general, the Reformed order runs in logical rather than temporal fashion, from regeneration and effectual calling, to faith and repentance, justification and adoption, and on to sanctification, perseverance, and glorification.

There are clear limitations to such patterns. They can miss the redemptive-historical dimension of Scripture. A logical conundrum surrounds the relationship between regeneration, faith, and justification: since justification is only by faith, faith precedes justification; but since faith is the result of regeneration, the latter precedes faith. So we are left to conclude that regeneration precedes justification, a result that seemingly undermines justification only by faith by making it depend on a prior work of the Spirit within us. I will address this problem shortly. Moreover, a focus on the order can eclipse union with Christ, diverting attention away from Christ to the benefits of Christ.

Clearly, there are elements present at the start of Christian life—regeneration, effectual calling, faith, and justification. Other elements are ongoing, such as adoption, sanctification, and perseverance. Further, glorification is only realized in the future. However, to muddy the waters a little, each has past, present, and future dimensions.

22.1.1 Biblical Texts

Paul provides a clear order in Romans 8:29–30. He moves from foreordination to calling, justification, and glorification. Assuring his readers of the unbreakable chain of salvation, he stresses that those whom God has foreordained to salvation will be brought to this goal. Foreordination is based on foreknowledge—not the foreknowledge envisaged by Arminius, which is simply God's knowledge of the future actions of his creatures, but rather his knowledge of persons. The verb προγινώσκω[1] is used here not so much for advance knowledge of this or that but as the equivalent of electing love.[2] Such people are called powerfully into fellowship with God's Son, are justified, and are certain of glorification.[3]

In Ephesians 1:3–14, Paul explains how our whole salvation is in union with Christ. He begins with election in eternity (v. 4), moves to foreordination to adoption (v. 5), and advances to redemption through the death of Christ (v. 7) and then sealing by the Holy Spirit (vv. 13–14). While the underlying leitmotif is Trinitarian and consists in union, there are clearly discernible aspects that Paul treats in progressive order.

1. *proginōskō.*
2. Rudolf Bultmann says that it is "an election or foreordination of his people," in *TDNT*, 1:715.
3. ἐδόξασεν is an aorist.

22.1.2   *The* Ordo Salutis *and Union with Christ*

Recently, there has been discussion of how union with Christ relates to the *ordo salutis*. Usually effectual calling and regeneration are placed first. Calling is the powerful action of the Father drawing us from death to life in Christ, embracing the whole process of what popularly is called "conversion." Regeneration is the hidden action of the Holy Spirit in renewing us, making us a new creation (2 Cor. 5:17), and giving us faith. There are various explanations of how effectual calling relates to regeneration. Some believe calling has priority, while others think regeneration comes first.[4] Calvin terms our whole reception of salvation *regeneration*. We will discuss the identity of and relationship between these elements more fully in later chapters.

Faith, justification, and adoption all occur at the start of the Christian life. Faith, as a gift of God, is a consequence of regeneration. This is counter to Arminianism and semi-Pelagianism, which hold that fallen humans retain the ability to believe the gospel, with assistance from divine grace, after taking the first step. Conversely, the Reformed maintain that fallen people are dead in sin and so have no ability of themselves to attain spiritual life; it requires a work of God to raise the dead, which the Spirit does in regeneration. The newly regenerate person will then respond in faith to the gospel and be justified on the basis of the work of Christ. Simultaneously with justification, he or she will become a child of God, adopted into his family and enabled to call God "Father" (Rom. 8:15–16; Gal. 4:6). Justification is mainly legal and juridical, adoption is primarily filial.

Lifelong sanctification follows, buttressed by perseverance. We "by God's power are being guarded through faith" (1 Pet. 1:5). We are responsible to persevere in faith; the ability comes from God. So we grow in the grace and knowledge of Christ throughout our lives, through temptation, suffering, and trials. Hence, the phrase "the perseverance of the saints" is appropriate; those who are sanctified will prevail. Finally, glorification occurs at the resurrection and the return of Christ, when we are finally brought to the destiny God has planned from eternity, transformation into the image of God in Christ.

This *ordo salutis*—effectual calling, regeneration, faith, justification, adoption, sanctification, glorification—or some such arrangement

---

4. R. W. A. Letham, "Calling," in *NDT*, 119–20.

is expressed in the WCF, 10–18. Nevertheless, union with Christ does not seem to fit very easily. Indeed, John Murray, in his book *Redemption Accomplished and Applied*, included a chapter at the end where he wrote that it was difficult to decide how to handle it.[5] In fairness, the Westminster Assembly, in the WLC, 65–90, considered the entire *ordo salutis* under the umbrella of union and communion with Christ in grace and glory.

Influenced by the biblical theology of Geerhardus Vos, Richard B. Gaffin Jr. raised questions about the *ordo salutis*. He cautiously suggested that it needed recasting in the light of Paul's insistence that biblical salvation be centered on the death and resurrection of Christ and our union with him, viewed in the eschatological terms Paul gives them.[6] Gaffin has not intended to undermine the *ordo salutis*; he considers it compatible with the Pauline view of redemptive history. Others, influenced by Gaffin, have voiced similar concerns.[7] Earlier I highlighted a logical problem on the relationship between regeneration, faith, and justification. This riddle demonstrates the limitations of logic divorced from the wider and deeper context in which doctrine is found.[8]

While such concerns are important, it would be a serious mistake to abandon the *ordo salutis*. Gaffin does not advocate this. The fact that each element of salvation is received in Christ does not negate a relationship between these constituent elements. There are connections and relative priorities that each sustains to the others. There are elements at the start of the Christian life (regeneration, saving faith, justification, adoption, sanctification in its definitive sense), each continuing to have significance and reality thereafter. Again, some aspects of salvation exist mainly in an ongoing way (perseverance, sanctification in its progressive sense, adoption). Other elements are to be fulfilled only at the return of Christ (resurrection of the body, glorification). Yet the final and eschatological aspects of salvation have a present reality to them even as those

---

5. John Murray, *Redemption Accomplished and Applied* (London: Banner of Truth, 1961), 161–62.

6. Richard B. Gaffin Jr., *The Centrality of the Resurrection: A Study in Paul's Soteriology* (Grand Rapids, MI: Baker, 1978), 135–43; Gaffin, *By Faith, Not by Sight: Paul and the Order of Salvation* (Milton Keynes: Paternoster, 2006).

7. William B. Evans, *Imputation and Impartation: Union with Christ in American Reformed Theology* (Eugene, OR: Wipf & Stock, 2008); Tim J. R. Trumper, "Covenant Theology and Constructive Calvinism," *WTJ* 64 (2002): 387–404.

8. See James E. Loder and W. Jim Neidhardt, *The Knight's Move: The Relational Logic of the Spirit in Theology and Science* (Colorado Springs: Helmers & Howard, 1992).

largely associated with the commencement of Christian experience are fulfilled only at the end. Paul writes of us having been glorified, using the aorist in Romans 8:30. Isaac Watts expressed it well when he wrote, "The men of grace have found glory begun below."[9] The Spirit has been given as an earnest of the final redemption (2 Cor. 1:21–22; Eph. 1:13–14).[10] The paramount placement of union with Christ, far from requiring that we dispense with the *ordo salutis*, preserves and enhances it by pointing to its integrating feature. The Westminster divines knew this when combining a logical *ordo salutis* in the WCF, 9–18, with the same topics as aspects of union and communion with Christ in WLC, 65–90.[11] Moreover, it is debatable whether we are to follow slavishly the same pattern as Paul did. He was not the only biblical author.

22.2   The Church and the Means of Grace

A major problem in the West is the separation of individual salvation from the church. For Rome, the church and sacraments have priority, with personal salvation tacked on at the end. The structure of the *Catechism of the Catholic Church* follows the traditional catechetical order of the Apostles' Creed, the Ten Commandments, and the Lord's Prayer. There is discussion of the church in the section on the creed (748–963), followed by more on the sacraments and the church as a sacramental economy (1076–1690). Personal elements occur only in the third major section (1699–2051), with discussion of moral virtues and sin (1699–1877), and then grace and justification (1987–2029).[12]

Protestantism adopts a reverse procedure. The *ordo salutis* relates to the salvation of the individual, with church and sacraments considered later and separately; every systematic theology has this order. At grassroots level, church membership is effectively a de facto optional extra, following faith at an indefinite interval. This reaches an extreme among many Western missiologists, who advocate insider movements and churchless Christianity, where inquirers or those who make professions

---

9. From the hymn "Come We That Love the Lord" (1707).

10. Vos writes of the Spirit's proper sphere as "the future aeon; from thence, he projects himself into the present, and becomes a prophecy of himself in his eschatological operations" and as "the element, as it were, in which, as in its circumambient atmosphere the life of the coming aeon shall be lived." Geerhardus Vos, *The Pauline Eschatology* (Grand Rapids, MI: Eerdmans, 1972), 165, 163.

11. Robert Letham, *The Westminster Assembly: Reading Its Theology in Historical Context* (Phillipsburg, NJ: P&R, 2009), 242–92.

12. CCC.

of faith are sent back to the temple or mosque to be better Muslims or Hindus and witness to Christ within their own social structures. They are often called "Christ followers," although following Christ in the New Testament required simultaneously being members of the visible church. Here anthropology and sociology trump theology and the Bible. Instead, we need to see the individual outworking of salvation in the church, without granting to the church instrumentality in salvation.[13] McGuckin expresses it well: "The western Church since the high middle ages has, according to Lossky, introduced a damaging distinction between ecclesial dogmatic theology and personal mystical apprehension: 'Me and God' on the one side; 'organized religion' on the other."[14]

In both the WCF and the WLC the church is connected to the *ordo salutis* and the work of Christ. The WLC distinguishes between the *visible church*—all who profess the true religion and their children—and the *invisible church*—the whole number of the elect. Not all in the visible church will be saved, since their profession of faith may be spurious and they may abandon it. However, the visible church enjoys God's protection and preservation against all enemies. In it, the saints have communion with one another, and there are found the ordinary means of salvation, while in and through it the gospel is heard (WLC, 60–63). The invisible church, the elect present and future, enjoy union and communion with Christ in grace, now in this life, and in glory, in the future eternal kingdom (WLC, 64–65).

Elsewhere I have argued that this stress on the church as the place where salvation is to be found is at the heart of the historic Christian faith,[15] as seen in the Apostles' Creed: "I believe in . . . the holy catholic church, the communion of saints, the forgiveness of sins." These phrases are expanded in the Niceno-Constantinopolitan Creed: "And in one holy, catholic and apostolic Church; We confess one baptism for the forgiveness of sins." There the latter phrase sheds light on the more cryptic "in the forgiveness of sins" of the Apostles' Creed, pointing to baptism and thus to the sacraments in general. Calvin, I have argued, follows this line of thought in his *Institutes*, where church and sacraments are the particular focus of book 4. He refers approvingly to Cyprian's comment that he cannot have God for his Father who does not have the church for

---

13. Robert Letham, *The Work of Christ* (Leicester: Inter-Varsity Press, 1993), 211–20.
14. J. A. McGuckin, "On the Mystical Theology of the Eastern Church," *SVTQ* 58 (2014): 382.
15. Letham, *The Work of Christ*, 211–20.

his mother. However, post-eighteenth-century evangelicalism moved into new territory, focusing on the individual and his or her personal faith, in abstraction from a churchly mooring.[16] The validity of the historic position is that even if one becomes a Christian seemingly in isolation by reading the Bible, it is the message of the apostles and prophets that brings faith—and the apostles and prophets were the foundation of the church.

The statement in WSC, 88, is important:

> Q. 88. What are the outward means whereby Christ communicateth to us the benefits of redemption?
>
> A. . . . his ordinances, especially the word, sacraments, and prayer, all of which are made effectual to the elect for salvation.[17]

These are found in the church. For all the church's flaws—at the time this was written there was no properly constituted church in England—the church is where we hear the gospel and are nurtured in our faith.

22.2.1   The Church

Chapter 25 of the WCF expands on these matters. It distinguishes between the visible church of believers and their children,[18] on the one hand, and the invisible church, composed of the elect of all ages and places, on the other. Outside the visible church "there is no ordinary possibility of salvation." The confession identifies the church with the kingdom of the Lord Jesus Christ. To the visible church "the ministry, oracles, and ordinances of God, for the gathering and perfecting of the saints, in this life, to the end of the world" have been committed. This, despite the fact that these churches are only "more or less visible," that even the purest churches "are subject both to mixture and to error." The efficacy of the Word, sacraments, and prayer is therefore not due to the church itself, nor to the relative level of its purity; it depends entirely on the presence of Christ and the Holy Spirit according to his promise.

Some churches have degenerated, the confession states, so as to become no churches of Christ but synagogues of Satan (WCF, 25.5). In

---

16. Robert Letham and Donald Macleod, "Is Evangelicalism Christian?," *EQ* 67 (January 1995): 3–33.

17. Cf. WLC, 154.

18. In contrast to the various types of credobaptist, who claimed that the church is restricted to believers only.

view is the church of Rome and probably also the Church of England under Archbishop William Laud. However, this is less than a blanket condemnation of the Roman church. The Assembly accepted baptism in the triune name; those baptized in the Roman church were not to be rebaptized. Hence, Rome possessed one of the marks of the church and so could not be said to be no church at all. Moreover, the Assembly's debates were replete with references not only to the fathers but also to a range of medieval and recent Roman theologians, cited as authorities on particular points. Meanwhile, the vigorous defense of the Reformation against Rome in the Thirty-Nine Articles was assumed.

The threats from France and Spain seen in the Armada, the Gunpowder Plot, and the feared "Popish Plot" were perceived as real. The more immediate pressures from Laud were still fresh in mind. Foremost were the papal claims, addressed in WCF, 25.6, this way: "There is no other head of the Church but the Lord Jesus Christ. Nor can the Pope of Rome, in any sense, be head thereof: but is that Antichrist, that man of sin, and son of perdition, that exalteth himself, in the Church, against Christ and all that is called God."

22.2.2 *The Communion of Saints*

Union and communion with Christ are foundational to the communion the saints have with one another. This is explicit in WCF, 26.1; union with Christ in grace and glory entails union with one another in love. This expands on the phrase in the Apostles' Creed "I believe in . . . the communion of saints."

The connection between union with Christ and love for all united to him is evident in WCF, 26.2. This extends to practical matters, the relief of material needs as well as ministry and communion in the worship of God and "other spiritual services." The communion the church enjoys in Christ extends to all who call on the name of the Lord Jesus, whether they are in full agreement on every point of doctrine or not. Indeed, that love and union on the human level reflect the union the saints have in Christ.[19]

19. Robert Letham, "The Westminster Assembly and the Communion of Saints," in *Learning from the Past: Essays in Reception, Catholicity, and Dialogue in Honour of Anthony N. S. Lane,* ed. Jon Balserak and Richard Snoddy (London: T&T Clark, 2015), 131–45. See also Takeshi Kodama, "The Unity and Catholicity of the Church: A Comparison of Calvin and the Westminster Assembly" (PhD diss., University of Wales, Trinity Saint David, 2011).

22.2.3   *Biblical and Theological Background*

Concerning the relationship between the individual and the corporate, the Western focus on the individual began at the time of the Renaissance but developed in a big way in the Enlightenment. Most hymns composed after 1700 have this slant: "It is well with my soul . . ." "Break thou the bread of life, dear Lord, to me." The Bible presents a fuller picture. Individuals find their place within the community. The New Testament letters were read to churches, not printed separately for private reading. This differs not only from Western preoccupations but also from Marxist corporatism.

In Joshua 7:11 the sin of one man, Achan, is the sin of Israel, and so the nation suffers. There is a relational understanding of humans throughout the Old Testament. You were A, the son of B, the son of C, of the tribe of D; you were who you were in connection with your ancestors, descendants, and tribe. In Genesis 1, God reveals himself in a threefold pattern: God (v. 1), the Spirit of God (v. 2), and the word of God (v. 3). Similarly, he creates in a threefold manner: by fiat (v. 3), by working (vv. 7, 16, 21), and by co-opting the ministerial functions of the created order (vv. 11, 24). In creating humanity, he makes them in his image as male and female, living in relation to God and to the creation (vv. 26–27). Both the singular and plural are used of both God and man in 1:26–27. Both the Trinity and humanity are relational. Isolated individuals they are not. Thus women are included in the reference to men.

In the New Testament, salvation in Christ is connected inextricably to the community of the church, in parallel with the solidarity of the race in sin in Adam (Rom. 5:12–21; 1 Cor. 15:20–23, 35–49). Hence, the means of the salvation of individuals is the Word of Christ through the apostles and their colleagues, the Word and the sacraments (for preaching, Rom. 10:1–17; Eph. 2:17; 1 Cor. 1:18–2:5; for the sacraments, Matt. 26:26–28; 28:19–20; John 6:47–58; Rom. 6:1–9; 1 Pet. 3:18–22). The New Testament letters, for the most part, were addressed to churches rather than individuals, to be read to the assembled congregation. Individuals are addressed within these letters but in this churchly context. In Ephesians, Paul writes to the church and then talks to groups within it. In Romans, within the church, Paul focuses on both Jewish and Gentile elements. This corporate dimension is of immense significance. Without it we will not understand baptism or come to grips with the New Testament understanding of salvation. "In Christ" is a dominant theme throughout and it is located and expressed in the church.

What a contrast to post-eighteenth-century evangelicalism! Both church and sacraments are integral to the ecumenical creeds, to Calvin, and to the WCF.[20] The confession of "one holy, catholic and apostolic Church," made at Constantinople I and repeated down through the centuries, is based on Ephesians 2:19–22.[21] It is well expressed by Bavinck, flowing from his view that unity in diversity flows from the Trinity, in whom unity has precedence over diversity:

> The oneness of all the churches does not just come into being a posteriori by the establishment of a creed, a church order, and a synodical system. Neither is the church an association of individual persons who first became believers apart from the church and subsequently united themselves. But it is an organism in which the whole exists prior to the parts; its unity precedes the plurality of local churches and rests in Christ.[22]

And again: "The assertion that the universal ecclesia precedes the local churches is correct in the sense that while it is not historically prior it is logically so."[23]

In this regard, election in Christ should not be taken as excluding the election of individuals but rather as affirming that the church has its origin in the eternal counsel of God. God created the world for the sake of the church. The church was instituted by Christ. Jesus chose the Twelve, the foundation of the church. His death and resurrection are the basis of the church's existence and of his individual people's salvation. Moreover, at Pentecost the Holy Spirit baptized the disciples into one body (1 Cor. 12:13). He gives gifts to the church (Eph. 4:7–16), gifts of persons in particular offices (Rom. 12:3–8), specific gifts to a variety of people (1 Cor. 12:1ff.).

22.2.4 Metaphors for the Church

The church is described in a variety of ways in the New Testament. Each metaphor highlights a particular facet of its identity. No one metaphor presents a complete picture; they are mutually dependent.

The body of Christ. The stress here is on union with Christ and our consequent communion with him, seen especially in the Eucharist. This

---

20. Letham and Macleod, "Evangelicalism."
21. Robert Letham, "Catholicity Global and Historical: Constantinople, Westminster, and the Church in the Twenty-First Century," *WTJ* 72 (2010): 43–57.
22. Bavinck, *RD*, 4:280.
23. Bavinck, *RD*, 4:281.

union is through the Holy Spirit. It is unbreakable; Head and body are mutually indispensable. Entailed is the unity of all members with each other (1 Cor. 12:12–30; Eph. 2:11–22), which is fully compatible with their diversity (Rom. 12:4–8; 1 Cor. 12:12–30; Eph. 4:1–6). Christ is the Head of the body (Eph. 1:22; Col. 1:18); he unites us to himself and provides for our growth (Eph. 5:23–32). In this sense, Christ and his church, the Head and the body, have been seen as the *totus Christus* (the whole Christ). Thus Augustine writes:

> Let us rejoice, then, and give thanks that we are made not only Christians, but Christ. Do you understand . . . and apprehend the grace of God upon us? marvel, be glad, we are made Christ. For if he is the head, we are the members: the whole man is he and we . . . Head and members, what is that? Christ and the church.[24]

The people of God. The church is given to share in the prophetic, priestly, and kingly office of Christ. The prophetic task is seen in preaching the gospel, baptizing, and making disciples; the priestly office, in intercession and serving the needy; the kingly office, in subduing the earth for God's glory (Gen. 1:26ff.) and in judging the world and fallen angels (1 Cor. 6:1–3). "The people of God" conveys a more communal perspective than "Head and body" does.

An indestructible army. In Ephesians 6:10–18, Paul portrays the church as an army, equipped with weapons for defense and attack. However, the efficacy of the church militant does not come from any human power but is found "in the Lord" (v. 10), and its potent weapon is "the sword of the Spirit, which is the word of God" (v. 17). The Old Testament background of the kingdom of God advancing against all comers is evident (Psalms 2, 110). Again, in 2 Corinthians 10 Paul stresses that the church's weaponry for the battle is not of human origin. Notwithstanding, the battle requires human effort and consists in the refutation of opposing arguments, "tak[ing] every thought captive to Christ" (vv. 3–6). This reminds us that Paul's evangelism consisted in reasoning, persuading his hearers of the truth and validity of the gospel.[25]

---

24. Augustine, *On John* 21.8 (*NPNF*[1], 7:140; *PL*, 35:1568).
25. Anti-intellectualism undermines the gospel; it has dominated large sections of British and American evangelicalism.

Images from agriculture and shepherding. These were close at hand in the first century. The church is *a sheepfold* (Isa. 40:11; Ezek. 34:11–31; John 10:1–30; 1 Pet. 5:4), *a cultivated field* (1 Cor. 3:9), *an olive tree* (Rom. 11:13–26), *a vineyard* (Isa. 5:1–7; Matt. 21:33–43 and parallels; John 15:1–5). These all require hard work in care, nurture, feeding, leading, and protection.

Images from architecture. The church is *the building of God* (Ps. 118:22; Matt. 21:42 and parallels; Acts 4:11; 1 Cor. 3:9, 11; 1 Pet. 2:7), *a house* (1 Tim. 3:15), and especially *a holy temple* (Eph. 2:19–22), *the dwelling place of God* (1 Cor. 3:16–17; 1 Pet. 2:5; Rev. 21:1–3). These are structures, built on secure foundations, that take time to build. Each stone is an integral part of the whole.

Relational imagery. Here the church is *the New Jerusalem, our mother, the spotless bride of the spotless Lamb* (Gal. 4:26; Eph. 5:25–26, 29; Rev. 21:2, 9; 22:17; 12:17; 19:7), pointing to the ongoing flow of redemptive history, from the Old Testament on into the final consummation. The bridal imagery, very prominent throughout the Old Testament and consummated in the New, where the church is *the bride of Christ*, displays two distinct entities within a personal relationship—as Augustine says, an indestructible union.[26]

No one metaphor comprehends the whole, but taken together they present a holistic picture. Amid the church's real existential struggle, there is a tension between two powerful realities. In one realm, the church is persecuted and suffers (Heb. 10:32–39; 1 Pet. 4:12–19; Rev. 12:1–14:5). Yet, simultaneously and in another realm, it is triumphant (Rev. 14:1–4; 19:11–21).

They suffer with their Lord below,
they reign with him above.[27]

22.3 Preaching as a Means of Grace
22.3.1 The Necessity of Preaching
Behind the Word as a means of grace lies the classic statement of the Second Helvetic Confession, 1, and its marginal note "the preaching

---

26. Augustine, *On Psalm 74* (*PL*, 36:948–49).
27. From the hymn "The Head That Once Was Crowned with Thorns," by Thomas Kelly (1820).

of the Word of God is the Word of God."[28] Anthony Tuckney argues that the Word of God is the normal means of conversion to salvation. However, it is not the efficient cause of salvation, as if it had power in itself to bring sinners to faith. Rather, it is the mode, means, occasion, and condition—the instrumental means—through which faith is engendered. There is nothing automatic. Conversion does not always follow preaching; the parable of the sower demonstrates that. The word preached is powerless of itself (*destitutum*) without the internal operation of the Holy Spirit.[29] Moreover, the preached word may not bear fruit for many years.[30]

Why is preaching necessary?[31]

The nature of God. At the heart of the Christian doctrine of the Trinity are love and communication. God is relational and personal. Jesus talks of the glory he shared with the Father in eternity (John 17:22–24). The Father advances his kingdom through the Son, for it is his will that the Son should have preeminence in all things (Col. 1:19). The Father loves the Son (John 3:35; 17:23–24; Rom. 8:32), the Son honors the Father (John 17:4), and the Spirit glorifies the Son (John 16:14–15). The eternal generation of the Son tells us that God is not at all lonely, even without the world and us.[32] Apart from the generation of the Son, creation would be inconceivable.[33] The eternal vibrance of the living Trinity—an indivisible union of life communicated, received, and mutually possessed, instanced in the relations of the three, in eternal generation and procession—grounds the free and sovereign determination of the Trinity to bring into existence what is contingent and other. God is life itself, overflowing vitality, inherently fecund.[34] Communication is at the heart of who God is and what he does.

---

28. Philip Schaff, *The Creeds of Christendom* (Grand Rapids, MI: Baker, 1966), 3:233–306. See 1.4, which lacks the marginal reference that appears in the original text.

29. Anthony Tuckney, *Praelectiones theologicae*, 258–62.

30. There is the remarkable tale of Luke Short, a farmer in New England, who came to faith at the age of one hundred as he reflected on a sermon he heard preached by John Flavel in Devon eighty-five years earlier. John Flavel, *The Mystery of Providence* (1678; repr., London: Banner of Truth, 1963), 11.

31. The following, through 22.3.2, builds on my essay "The Necessity of Preaching in the Modern World," parts 2 and 3, *Ordained Servant*, November and December 2013, which was originally a paper given at the International Conference of Reformed Churches, Cardiff, August 2013.

32. Barth, *CD*, II/1:139–40.

33. Bavinck, *RD*, 2:420.

34. On the eternal generation of the Son, see Kevin Giles, *Eternal Generation of the Son: Maintaining Orthodoxy in Trinitarian Theology* (Downers Grove, IL: IVP Academic, 2012); Robert Letham, "The Doctrine of Eternal Generation in the Church Fathers," in *One God in Three Per-*

The incarnation. While Adam was created *in* the image of God, the second Adam, the Word become flesh, *is* the image of God (2 Cor. 4:4; Col. 1:15; Heb. 1:3).[35] In the incarnation, the Son took our nature into union. In terms of personal identity, Jesus of Nazareth is the eternal Son of the Father.[36] Hughes Oliphant Old recognizes that the Pauline statement that faith comes from Christ speaking through his Word follows from the doctrine of grace. God saves us because he loves us and has spoken to us, revealing himself and opening up communion with him.[37]

The personal nature of humankind. Humans are personal beings; while this is an elusive concept, it establishes that we have been made by God for partnership, fellowship, communion, and union with him. Preaching is the means God uses to bring the gospel, as personal address is utterly suitable for the purpose.

Preaching as personal communication is at the heart of God's covenant. As we have seen, central to the whole flow of covenant history is the constantly repeated promise "I will be your God, and you shall be my people" (see Gen. 17:7–8; Jer. 11:4; 24:7; 30:22; 31:33; 32:38; Rev. 21:3).[38] Verbal communication was necessary even before the fall; it disclosed the meaning of creation and the purpose of human existence.[39] God announced to humans the nature of their task (Gen. 1:26–29), instructing Adam about his agricultural responsibilities—a function both priestly and kingly[40]—and the outcome if he proved disobedient (Gen. 2:15–17). The record after the fall, when God walked in the garden and called out to Adam, suggests that such communication was a regular feature in the original setting of creation.

---

sons: *Unity of Essence, Distinction of Persons, Implications for Life,* ed. Bruce A. Ware and John Starke (Wheaton, IL: Crossway, 2015), 109–25.

35. Robert Letham, *Union with Christ: In Scripture, History, and Theology* (Phillipsburg, NJ: P&R, 2011), 13–14; Gaffin, *Centrality of the Resurrection;* Philip Edgcumbe Hughes, *The True Image: The Origin and Destiny of Man in Christ* (Grand Rapids, MI: Eerdmans, 1989), 281–86.

36. Cyril of Alexandria, *On the Unity of Christ,* trans. John Anthony McGuckin (Crestwood, NY: St Vladimir's Seminary Press, 1995); J. A. McGuckin, *Saint Cyril and the Christological Controversy* (Crestwood, NY: St Vladimir's Seminary Press, 2010); Thomas G. Weinandy, "Cyril and the Mystery of the Incarnation," in *The Theology of St. Cyril of Alexandria: A Critical Appreciation,* ed. Thomas G. Weinandy (London: T&T Clark, 2003), 23–54; Donald Fairbairn, *Grace and Christology in the Early Church* (Oxford: Oxford University Press, 2003), 63–132; John Meyendorff, *Christ in Eastern Christian Thought* (Crestwood, NY: St Vladimir's Seminary Press, 1975).

37. Hughes Oliphant Old, *The Reading and Preaching of the Scriptures in the Worship of the Christian Church,* vol. 1, *The Biblical Period* (Grand Rapids, MI: Eerdmans, 1998), 183.

38. Herman Hoeksema, *Reformed Dogmatics* (Grand Rapids, MI: Reformed Free Publishing Association, 1966), 285–336; Letham, *The Work of Christ,* 39–49.

39. Gregory Edward Reynolds, *The Word Is Worth a Thousand Pictures: A Resource for Preaching in the Twenty-First Century* (Eugene, OR: Wipf & Stock, 2001), 316.

40. John V. Fesko, *Last Things First: Unlocking Genesis 1–3 with the Christ of Eschatology* (Fearn: Mentor, 2007).

Thereafter, verbal communication of God's word is pervasive. In the Old Testament, preaching was at the heart of worship. The prophets constantly engaged the community by word written or spoken. Over the centuries, preaching developed "both theological depth and literary refinement," Old remarks.[41] In the New Testament, more than thirty verbs describe it.[42] Once upon a time, documents such as the New Testament Gospels and its letters were read aloud in public to groups. While later, with the invention of the printing press and the wider spread of books, reading became increasingly a private, individual, and silent matter, in earlier times preaching would have regularly accompanied the reading of the biblical books.

The suitability of speech. Speech is the normal means God uses to communicate to us. Arguing to the contrary, Gregory of Nyssa favors the primacy of sense knowledge, of the visual over words, which he suggests are inherently ambiguous.[43] Indeed, Gregory says, visible objects are more readily comprehensible, while God needs no words to make known his mind.[44] Gregory's argument has had ongoing effect in the Eastern church, where worship is very strongly visual, with icons everywhere, the comings and goings of the priest into and out of the sanctuary symbolizing Christ's coming to feed his people, the entrance into the kingdom of heaven, the opening of the gates of paradise, and so on.[45] However, this is not the normal way God communicated to his people. On God's appearance to Israel at Sinai, Moses recorded: "The LORD spoke to you out of the midst of the fire. You heard the sound of words, but saw no form; there was only a voice" (Deut. 4:12). Whereas the visual can be evocative, *it* is inherently ambiguous. If the president of the United States were to declare war, he would not likely announce it by means of a troupe of dancers, actors performing a skit, or an artist drawing a picture on an easel.

Speech-act theory reinforces this argument.[46] Words are uniquely adaptable. Words can promise, warn, encourage, rebuke, inform, elicit, express sorrow or thanksgiving, praise, advise or command, and many

41. Old, *Reading and Preaching*, 1:102.
42. Klaas Runia, "Preaching, Theology Of," in *NDT*, 527–28.
43. Gregory of Nyssa, *Answer to Eunomius' Second Book* 44 (NPNF², 5:273).
44. Gregory of Nyssa, *Answer to Eunomius' Second Book* 45–46 (NPNF², 5:273).
45. Robert Letham, *Through Western Eyes: Eastern Orthodoxy: A Reformed Perspective* (Fearn: Mentor, 2007), 143–62.
46. J. L. Austin, *How to Do Things with Words: The William James Lectures Delivered in Harvard University in 1955* (Oxford: Oxford University Press, 1976), 176.

such things besides. Words can effect actions and bring about change. The urgent shout "Fire!" will usually result in a rapid exodus from a building; an inconsiderate comment will produce anger or bitterness.

Confessional support. The French Confession (1559), 25, in which Calvin played a central role, stresses in no uncertain terms the importance of preaching: "We detest all visionaries who would like, so far as lies in their power, to destroy this ministry and preaching of the Word and sacraments."[47] The Scots Confession (1560), 18, drawn up by John Knox, states, "The notes therefore of the trew Kirk of God we beleeve, confesse, and avow to be, first, the trew preaching of the Worde of God."[48] The Belgic Confession (1561), 29, agrees, stating that "the marks by which the true Church is known are these: If the pure doctrine of the gospel is preached therein."[49]

The Heidelberg Catechism (1563) places preaching in the context of our deliverance from sin:

Q. 65. Since, then, we are made partakers of Christ and all his benefits by faith only, whence comes this faith?
A. The Holy Ghost works it in our hearts by the preaching of the holy Gospel, and confirms it by the use of the holy Sacraments.[50]

The Second Helvetic Confession (1566) declares in a celebrated passage:

Wherefore when this Word of God is now preached in the church by preachers lawfully called, we believe that the very Word of God is preached, and received of the faithful [*credimus ipsum Dei verbum annunciari et a fidelibus recipi*]; and that neither any other Word of God is to be feigned, nor to be expected from heaven: and that now the Word itself which is preached is to be regarded, not the minister that preaches; who, although he be evil and a sinner, nevertheless the Word of God abides true and good. (1.4)[51]

There is here a marginal reference—*praedicatio verbi Dei est verbum Dei* (the preaching of the Word of God is the Word of God). The efficacy of preaching depends not on the minister but on the Word of God itself.

---

47. Schaff, *Creeds*, 3:374.
48. Schaff, *Creeds*, 3:460–61.
49. Schaff, *Creeds*, 3:419.
50. Schaff, *Creeds*, 3:328.
51. Schaff, *Creeds*, 3:237, 872.

Another significant stress here is on the lawful calling of the preacher; there is a twofold check, preventing the idea that anyone standing up and spouting off about the Christian faith can say that he is preaching the Word of God. First is the comment "when this Word of God is now preached"; the content of the preaching must be within the boundaries of the rule of faith. Second is the stipulation that he preaching is done "by preachers lawfully called," referring to church authority, in harmony with the New Testament correlation of the Holy Spirit and the church, where the sending of Saul and Barnabas by the church is equated with their sending by the Holy Spirit (Acts 13:3–4), and with the Council of Jerusalem's comment that "it has seemed good to the Holy Spirit and to us" (Acts 15:28).

The WCF, 1.1, refers the propagation of the truth—later defined as through the ministry of the Word—to the revelation by the Lord that has been committed wholly to writing in the Scriptures: "It pleased the Lord . . . to reveal himself, and to declare that his will unto his Church; and afterwards, for the better preserving *and propagating* of the truth, and for the more sure establishment and comfort of the Church . . . to commit the same wholly unto writing." In this the preaching of the church, properly understood, is not detached from the Lord's revelation of himself and his will to the church, nor from the written record of that revelation in Scripture, which in turn is wholly identified with that prior revelation.

What barriers exist to preaching today? A point Old makes repeatedly is that the church's health is directly related to the vibrancy of its preaching. In turn, the quality of the preaching largely depends on the level of education in society.[52] Referring to the Benedictines and their cultivation of learning, Old remarks:

> If the Church was to worship as it always had, there needed to be a steady supply of young men who knew how to speak in public, how to use words, and how to read and understand a written text. If there was to be a ministry of the Word, then the culture of words, the arts of literature, and the preservation and distribution of books had to be cultivated.[53]

---

52. Old, *Reading and Preaching*, 3:190.
53. Old, *Reading and Preaching*, 2:400–401.

Besides a lack of education, another barrier to preaching is the contemporary hostility toward all forms of authority. Reynolds remarks that in our age, when authority of all kinds is being repudiated, the monologue is anathema. However, he adds, biblical preaching has never been acceptable to the autonomous mind.[54] Furthermore, preaching—as presented in Scripture—is not a monologue; it is dialogical because it is covenantal.[55] It is personal address by God, demanding a response from the hearer. As Carrick comments, the interrogative is as much a vital element of preaching as the indicative and imperative.[56]

Indeed, as face-to-face encounter, preaching is in vivid contrast to the direction of today's social media. Reynolds observes that these are marked by attempts to transcend space and time.[57] Electronic technology connects us to remote locations but is in itself disincarnational. It aims to transcend the limits of human finitude but at the expense of normal human relationships. Recent social media have encouraged connections remotely but have undermined face-to-face human contact. In contrast, preaching is inescapably personal. We can close a book, switch off the computer, or exit social media, but the Word of God reaches our innermost being (Heb. 4:12–13).

Preaching is peculiarly adapted by God for the purpose he has for it. Alan Strange remarks that the plays of Euripides, Sophocles, and Aeschylus were very popular in the ancient world, but the apostles made no use of the medium.[58] The same applies to the Greek predilection for rhetoric and oratory.[59] Paul makes a point of saying to the Corinthians that he gave no attention to such matters but rather preached simply and directly, relying on the Holy Spirit to give understanding (1 Cor. 1:18–2:5). There was plenty of intellectual content, but it was shorn of extraneous adornments, devoted entirely to presenting Christ clearly and directly.

22.3.2 *Preaching and the Holy Spirit*

The Reformed confessions uniformly witness to the inseparability of Word and Spirit in all the means of grace, preaching included. This is directly

---

54. Reynolds, *The Word*, 335.
55. Reynolds, *The Word*, 335–36.
56. John Carrick, *The Imperative of Preaching: A Theology of Sacred Rhetoric* (Edinburgh: Banner of Truth, 2002), 56–81.
57. Reynolds, *The Word*, 340.
58. Alan D. Strange, "Comments on the Centrality of Preaching in the Westminster Standards," *MAJT* 10 (1999): 194n12.
59. Strange, "The Centrality of Preaching," 217n28.

counter to the Anabaptist separation of the two, a view that is rife in the wider evangelical world. It also stands in distinction from a purely instrumentalist view of preaching, often questionably associated with Lutheranism. Whereas the Anabaptists and their heirs focus on the distinction between Word and Spirit at the expense of their inseparability, the "Lutheran" idea stresses their inseparability but minimizes their distinctness.

Here the WLC (1648) is of great help.

Q.155. How is the word made effectual to salvation?

A. The Spirit of God maketh the reading, but especially the preaching of the word, an effectual means of enlightening, convincing, and humbling sinners; of driving them out of themselves, and drawing them unto Christ; of conforming them to his image, and subduing them to his will; of strengthening them against temptations and corruptions; of building them up in grace, and establishing their hearts in holiness and comfort through faith unto salvation.

Q.158. By whom is the word of God to be preached?

A. The word of God is to be preached only by such as are sufficiently gifted, and also duly approved and called to that office.

Q.159. How is the word of God to be preached by those that are called thereunto?

A. They that are called to labour in the ministry of the word, are to preach sound doctrine, diligently, in season and out of season; plainly, not in the enticing words of man's wisdom, but in demonstration of the Spirit, and of power; faithfully . . . wisely . . . zealously, with fervent love to God and the souls of his people. . . .

According to the catechism, the demonstration of the Spirit and of power is evidenced by the faithful preaching of sound doctrine, wisdom, zeal, and, above all, fervent love. Preaching is an effectual means of grace; diligent and faithful preaching is the instrumental cause, while the Holy Spirit is the efficient cause. The Word without the Spirit is ineffective; the Spirit without the Word is inaudible. The Spirit is the author of Scripture and continues to speak in it today (Heb. 3:7). The Word and the Spirit go together. However, the Spirit is sovereign and free to work as he wills. Moreover, the Word, whether the text of Scripture or the message proclaimed by the preacher, does not have power of itself.

In this, there is a contrast with the idea that the Word works grace invariably unless it is resisted, the position associated—debatably so—with Lutheranism. The Augsburg Confession (1530), 5, states that, "by the Word and sacraments, as by instruments, the Holy Spirit is given: who worketh faith, where and when it pleaseth God, in those that hear the Gospel";[60] the same article condemns the Anabaptists, "who imagine that the Holy Spirit is given to men without the outward word." The confession's view of the Word as the instrument of the Spirit has commonly been connected with Lutheran sacramental theology, perhaps wrongly, in which grace is given objectively and is efficacious unless there is resistance. It seems to some that this minimizes the work of the Spirit by holding that the Spirit works *through* the Word, rather than *with* the Word. However, this statement in the Augsburg Confession is unexceptionable.

More recently, under the impact of the eighteenth-century revivals, a doctrine of preaching similar to that of the Anabaptists has arisen. The prominent British evangelical Stuart Olyott argues that the preaching of the gospel is often powerless, and he urges the faithful to "strive and agonise and prevail in prayer," to "storm the throne of grace, determined that by sheer importunity they will persuade God to accompany the word to be preached."[61] This school of thought refers to 1 Thessalonians 1:5 ("Our gospel came to you not only in word, but also in power and in the Holy Spirit and with full conviction") to assert that the preaching of the Word may be unaccompanied by the Spirit. However, in saying that his preaching at Thessalonica was accompanied by the Spirit, Paul hardly implies that on other occasions this was not so. Rather, he highlights the grounds for the Thessalonians' assurance, since they were subject to persecution (Acts 17:1–9; 1 Thess. 2:13; 2 Thess. 1:1–12). This persecution came from Jewish sources; he is probably contrasting the Spirit's power in gospel preaching with the empty words of the synagogue. In the similar passage in 1 Corinthians 1:18–2:5, Paul obviously contrasts his preaching with the Greek hankering for rhetoric. In both cases, "word only" and reliance on "human wisdom" refer to pagan or Jewish sources, not to Christian preaching.

---

60. Schaff, *Creeds*, 3:10.
61. Stuart Olyott, "Where Luther Got It Wrong—and Why We Need to Know About It," *The Banner of Truth*, December 2009, 27. See in reply, George M. Ella, "Where Olyott Got It Wrong," *Biographia Evangelica*, http://www.evangelica.de/articles/where-olyott-got-it-wrong/, accessed December 21, 2012; idem, "Where Luther Puts Olyott Right," *Biographia Evangelica*, http://www.evangelica.de/articles/where-luther-puts-olyott-right/, accessed December 21, 2012.

This approach to preaching has a dynamic similar to Barth's doctrine of Scripture. For Barth, revelation was an act of God, unpredictable and outside our control, to which the Bible bears witness in a human and fallible way. For this school of thought, preaching is second-rate if it is unaccompanied by "the Holy Spirit and power." In short, true preaching occurs when the Spirit comes in power, an event similarly unpredictable, outside our control, which we are to seek and for which we are to pray, an experience that may just as suddenly and inexplicably be withdrawn.[62] As with Barth, where God can make the Scriptures be the Word of God in this or that circumstance, so preaching can become the Word of God with power on occasions entirely at his free and sovereign determination. Ordinary preaching may bear little fruit; when these visitations of the Holy Spirit come, transformation occurs. Many in this camp refer to the Spirit as a "visitor."

For the Reformed, the Spirit and the Word are distinct but inseparable. "Lutheranism" stresses the inseparability at the expense of the distinction; the Anabaptists and revivalists stress the distinctness at the expense of the inseparability. This revivalist view implies that the Spirit is free not only to leave the Word unaccompanied by his presence but also to work independently. In contrast, we assert that God's Word carries the authority of God himself and cannot be detached from him. According to Scripture, the Word of God shares in all the works of God; it creates (Gen. 1:3; Ps. 33:6, 9; Heb. 11:3), maintains the universe (Heb. 1:3), brings about regeneration (John 5:24–25; Rom. 10:17; 1 Pet. 1:23), is spirit and life (John 6:63), raises the dead (John 5:28–29), and will not pass away (Matt. 24:35). As Jesus said, "Whoever is ashamed of me *and of my words*, of him will the Son of Man be ashamed when he comes in his glory and the glory of the Father" (Luke 9:26).

The New Testament attributes efficacy to the Word (John 5:25; Rom. 10:17; James 1:23; 1 Pet. 1:23). It is the Word of the Spirit, the Word of Christ, the living Word. The Spirit, who breathed out the words of Scripture, accompanies the reading and proclamation of those words. He and his words are inseparable. "Faith comes from hearing, *and hearing through the word of Christ*" (Rom. 10:17). The Spirit uses means; he does not speak, only to wander off and leave his ambassadors in the

---

62. D. Martyn Lloyd-Jones, *Preaching and Preachers* (Grand Rapids, MI: Zondervan, 1971), 304–25.

lurch. Nor does he speak in disjunction from the Word he has already and definitively spoken.

There is a close connection with the sacraments. The sacraments in themselves have no efficacy, for it is the Spirit who makes them effective for the elect (WCF, 27.3; 28.6; 29.7; WLC, 155, 161). However, the Spirit works in and through the sacraments so that the faithful feed on Christ in the Eucharist; this is not evanescent or unpredictable.[63]

Expectations for preaching. Consequently, we *expect* the blessing of God upon the preaching of his Word. This is not presumption; it is simply faith, confidence that what he has promised he performs, and will continue to perform. This blessing can cut both ways; in some instances, it is a form of judgment (2 Cor. 2:14–16). Hughes cites Calvin to the effect that the gospel is never preached in vain but is effectual, leading either to life or to death.[64] Indeed, Calvin states that "wherever there is pure and unfeigned preaching of the gospel, there this strong savour that Paul mentions [in 2 Cor. 2:15–16] will be found . . . not only when they [faithful and sincere ministers] quicken souls by the fragrance of salvation but also when they bring death to unbelievers."[65] Hodge comments, "The word of God is quick and powerful either to save or to destroy. It cannot be neutral. If it does not save, it destroys."[66] It is best to say, with Strange, that the Spirit makes the Word efficacious to different people in different ways at different times, according to his sovereign will.[67]

Certainly, preachers of the gospel are called and required to exemplify in their lives the work of the Spirit and to be examples to the flock (1 Tim. 3:1–7; 4:16; 2 Tim. 2:1–26; 1 Pet. 5:1–4). That is self-evident. But the Reformed confessions are clear that the efficacy of Word and sacrament does not depend on the piety and godliness of the ones who administer them (WCF, 27.3; WLC, 161). If that were so, the church would be hostage to the daily uncertainties of individuals' lives. Rather, their efficacy depends on the One who has established them, Christ,

---

63. Ralph Cunnington, *Preaching with Spiritual Power: Calvin's Doctrine of Word and Spirit in Preaching* (Fearn: Mentor, 2015).

64. Philip Edgcumbe Hughes, *Paul's Second Epistle to the Corinthians: The English Text, with Introduction, Exposition and Notes* (London: Marshall, Morgan & Scott, 1961), 80.

65. John Calvin, *Calvin's Commentaries: The Second Epistle of Paul the Apostle to the Corinthians and the Epistles to Timothy, Titus, and Philemon*, trans. T. Smail (Grand Rapids, MI: Eerdmans, 1964), 34.

66. Charles Hodge, *A Commentary on the Second Epistle to the Corinthians* (London: Banner of Truth, 1959), 46.

67. Strange, "The Centrality of Preaching," 199.

to whom they inextricably point, and to the Holy Spirit, who works through them.

For the congregation, receiving the Word as blessing is connected to the extent to which its members have prepared themselves to hear it. In an age of egalitarianism, it is not uncommon for professing believers to exhibit a critical attitude toward anything that resembles authoritative speech.[68]

How significant is the preaching of Christ? Preaching concerns not only this life but also eternity. It points to the chief purpose of human existence (WSC, 1). It relates to the glory of God. It points forward to the cosmic panorama of the redeemed universe. Hence, Jeremiah's profound turmoil when, for a time, he refrained from declaring the Word of the Lord to Judah (Jer. 20:7–9). So, too, Paul records in words that should resonate deep in the conscience of every preacher, "Woe to me if I do not preach the gospel!" (1 Cor. 9:16).

Anything that diverts the hearers' attention from the Word of God is counter to the nature and intent of preaching. The proclaimer is there to witness to Christ, not himself: "What we proclaim is not ourselves, but Jesus Christ as Lord" (2 Cor. 4:5). No personal anecdote can be allowed to compete; these can convey the idea that the preacher's own activities are of greater importance, the message God has called him to declare not so urgent after all. So Paul's final, parting charge to his protégé Timothy—the charge that was most vital for him and all his successors—was to preach the Word, in season and out of season, when it seemed productive and when it met resistance, indifference, or hostility (2 Tim. 4:1–3). Whatever the circumstances, preach the Word!

22.4   The Sacraments

22.4.1   *The Sacraments and God's Covenant Promises*

Together with the Word, and under it, are the sacraments, supporting and reinforcing the verbal message. At each stage of covenant history God reinforces his promises by material signs by which he assures us of the truth of what he has said and done. Underlying this is the first sentence in the Bible: "In the beginning, God created the heavens and the

---

68. Strange, "The Centrality of Preaching," 228–31; WLC, 160.

earth" (Gen. 1:1). God created both matter and spirit and thus can use matter as a vehicle for transmitting spiritual grace. Christianity is not something confined to the "spiritual" dimension; it involves the whole of life. The creation, incarnation, and bodily resurrection are proof of this. The biblical account of creation focuses attention on the material world. We read little or nothing about the creation of the angels. While God created all things, including the spiritual realm, the physical and visible world takes center stage. The incarnation points in the same direction. The eternal Son experienced the world of matter and consequently redeemed it. We are material beings, and the entire creation awaits its glorious liberation at Christ's return. Both now and forever the Son has a human body.

Moreover, the physical aspect of creation and redemption is underlined by the resurrection from the dead. On the third day, Jesus rose from the tomb *bodily*. It is wonderfully true that Christ's body was transformed, now glorified beyond our current conceptions, yet it was and forever is the same body that bore the nail prints from the cross. While, as Paul says, he entered a new phase of life according to the Spirit, κατὰ πνεῦμα (Rom. 1:3–4; 1 Cor. 15:19–58),[69] Jesus expressly denied that it was as a spirit, emphasizing this by eating a piece of broiled fish (Luke 24:36–43; John 20:24–29).

We believe in the resurrection of the body. We are embodied creatures, and salvation includes the redemption of the body. Christianity is earthy and physical as well as spiritual. Neglect of the material nature of the gospel is akin to Gnosticism, which regarded matter as inherently inferior to the spiritual. If it were inferior, and if our salvation consisted merely in existence in a spiritual state, *we ourselves* would not be saved. As Anthony Cross indicates, much contemporary thought has lapsed into a form of gnosticism, "with its matter-spirit dualism, which is found in the writings of both Zwingli and Barth."[70] He also identifies biblical scholars such as James Dunn and Gordon Fee as falling into the same category by their setting water baptism in opposition to Spirit baptism.[71]

---

69. *kata pneuma.*
70. Anthony R. Cross, "Baptism in the Theology of John Calvin and Karl Barth," in *Calvin, Barth and Reformed Theology*, ed. Neil B. MacDonald and Carl Trueman (Eugene, OR: Wipf & Stock, 2008), 82–83.
71. Cross, "Calvin, Barth," 80.

Correspondingly, God uses material signs to reinforce his promises. In the garden of Eden, before the fall, was the tree of life (Gen. 2:9; cf. Rev. 22:1–2, 19). Eating of this tree was associated with everlasting life (Gen. 3:22–24). This is reinforced in Revelation 22:1–2, where the leaves of the tree of life are for the healing of the nations. In the Noachic covenant, which reestablished the creation order after the flood, God appointed the rainbow as a sign that he would never again flood the earth (Gen. 8:20–22; 9:8–17). God instituted circumcision in the Abrahamic covenant (Gen. 17:3–14). As flesh was removed in circumcision, so God removes the heart of unbelief and grants a new heart and a new spirit (Ezek. 36:25–28; Rom. 2:25–29; 4:9–12; Phil. 3:3). In the Mosaic covenant, the Passover commemorated Yahweh's mighty deliverance of Israel from bondage in Egypt on its way to inheriting the promises of the Abrahamic covenant (Ex. 12:1–13:16); the exodus looked forward to the new exodus to be accomplished later. In the new covenant, Jesus appointed baptism in the name of the Trinity (Matt. 28:19–20) to portray cleansing from sin and union with him in his death and resurrection. The Supper he introduced was to nourish his people to eternal life (John 6:47–58; 1 Cor. 10:16–17). He appeals not only to our ears, through the words he utters, but also to our eyes, by the sacramental signs.

The signs and the reality. Each of these signs accompanied a new stage in the outworking of God's covenant purposes. His actions and words in his covenants were reinforced by the signs. The signs were not the reality; they pointed to the reality, much as a signpost directs us to a destination other than itself. The reality and the sign differ. However, in each case the sign is appropriate to the reality, with a definite and visible connection. The tree of life gives everlasting life. The rainbow denotes the triumph of grace over judgment. The Passover indicates Yahweh's passing over and sparing his people from wrath, and guiding them to their inheritance. Washing with water in baptism portrays cleansing from the greater filth of sin. Bread and wine in the Lord's Supper demonstrate Christ's feeding and nourishing us to eternal life. Sign and reality are distinct, but the connection is inseparable.

The sacraments are crucial because they present Christ to us. Robert Bruce remarked concerning the Lord's Supper: "If Christ is not both eaten and digested, he can do us no good, but this digestion cannot exist where there is not a greedy appetite to receive him."[72] He added that in the Supper we get something new: "We get Christ better . . . than we could have before."[73] That is what makes the neglect of the sacraments so devastating. Moreover, since Christ is the theme of the sacraments, the gospel is presented vividly before our eyes whenever baptism or the Lord's Supper takes place.

In each case the major point is not what we do but what God does. It may be tempting to think of the sacraments as merely human rites. However, the sacraments are preeminently signs for God, indicating what he has done or will do. They go beyond the surface appearance and bring us into direct contact with eternal realities in which the grace of God is powerfully at work.

Consider two examples. First, the tree of life in the garden was not expressly forbidden to Adam until after the fall, when Adam reaped the covenant penalty of death. He and Eve were expelled from Eden, and the way back was barred by cherubim who guarded the tree of life, lest Adam eat of it and live forever (Gen. 3:22–24). There was a connection between eating the fruit of the tree and living forever, as there was between eating the fruit of the tree of the knowledge of good and evil and experiencing sin and death (Gen. 2:16–17; 3:6–7, 11–22). This was not magic, which never occurs in God's dealings. The most plausible implication is that, should Adam have remained obedient, he would have been granted access to the tree of life and thus to eternal life for himself and all under his headship.

The tree of life appears again in Revelation 22:1–2, located beside the river flowing from the heavenly city. Its leaves are "for the healing of the nations." Again, the tree brings healing and, with it, life and blessing (Rev. 22:14). Eternal salvation consists in eating from it, while those forbidden to do so are under God's curse (Rev. 22:18–19). Again, the tree is connected with eternal life in a signifying and instrumental sense. Only God gives life. He put the tree in the garden and placed it alongside the heavenly river. He grants and forbids access to it. Only

---

72. Robert Bruce, *The Mystery of the Lord's Supper: Sermons on the Sacrament Preached in the Kirk of Edinburgh in A.D. 1589*, ed. and trans. Thomas F. Torrance (London: James Clarke, 1958), 56.
73. Bruce, *Mystery*, 84–85.

he gives life, because he himself is life. Only he has life in himself (John 5:26). The sign of the tree of life points us to God.

Second, in the Noachic covenant, God puts the rainbow in the sky as a sign that he will never again judge the earth by means of a flood. Every time we see, it we can recall this covenant promise to the human race. However, this is a sign to God before it is a sign to us. God says:

> This is the sign of the covenant that I make between me and you and every living creature that is with you, for all future generations: I have set my bow in the cloud, and it shall be a sign of the covenant between me and the earth. When I bring clouds over the earth and the bow is seen in the clouds, *I will remember my covenant that is between me and you and every living creature of all flesh.* And the waters shall never again become a flood to destroy all flesh. When the bow is in the clouds, *I will see it and remember the everlasting covenant between God and every living creature of all flesh that is on the earth.* (Gen. 9:12–17)

The sign is something God himself notes. His own recognition of the sacraments he has appointed impacts his fulfillment of those signs.

In both cases the major point in the sacrament is not what we do but what God does. These are signs for God. Likewise, the focus of circumcision and the Passover, as with baptism and the Lord's Supper, is on the mighty acts of God. Baptism is into the one name of the Father, the Son, and the Holy Spirit; it belongs to God. The indivisible action of all three persons of the Trinity is the theme. In the sacraments we have to do with the living God.

God keeps his appointments. God is not arbitrary or capricious. He is faithful. When he commits himself, he remains committed, now and forever. He is not some unpredictable despot. The coming of the Spirit at Pentecost was not as some evanescent or transitory "visitor" but as a permanent resident (John 14:14–23). Not only are the sacraments signs in which God is at work, but behind them is the glorious reality that God keeps his appointments.

When Christ died on the cross, it was not on any random day, for it was on the day of the Passover (1 Cor. 5:7), "when the fullness of time had come" (Gal. 4:4). He was the Passover Lamb. The Passover dramatically foreshadowed him and his work. He offered himself by the eternal Spirit to the Father (Heb. 9:14). The slaughter of the sacrificial lamb signified the deliverance Yahweh gave from the bondage of Egypt. At the cross a greater deliverance arrived, from sin and death, effected not on any day but on *this* day.

When Christ rose from the dead, it was on the first day of the week. It marked a new epoch, a new creation, foreshadowed by the angel announcing to Mary the conception of Jesus as akin to the creation account in Genesis (Luke 1:34–35). This new creation broke through on the *first* day of the week.

The Holy Spirit came when the day of Pentecost had fully come (Acts 2:1ff.)—not a day earlier, not a day later, but precisely on time. It did not happen on the spur of the moment; it was a day fixed by God from eternity that coincided with one of the great festivals he had set up centuries earlier with precisely this in mind. This day was not simply an occasion for a human ritual. It was selected by God for a decisive staging point in the history of redemption, planned from before the foundation of the earth.

God honored the feast days he had set in the Old Testament. These were not accidental dates on the calendar. God invested them with great significance. From our side, the ritual was no empty repetition. It pointed to a reality to be fulfilled expressly in and through the ritual. When God promises, and seals these promises in his appointed signs, he does not deceive us. He honors his appointments, he comes as he promised, and the reality to which the signs point is effected through them.

22.4.2 *The Sacraments in the Confessions of the Church*

The term *sacrament* derives from the Latin *sacramentum*, which at one point meant an oath of allegiance. However, this has no real significance for its ecclesiastical usage, although some of the Latin fathers used it this way. In the church it came to refer to a sacred mystery, the equivalent of the Greek μυστήριον, "mystery," something hidden until it was revealed.[74]

Augustine defined a sacrament as "a visible sign of invisible grace."[75] Article 25 of the Thirty-Nine Articles of the Christian Religion calls sacraments "sure witnesses and effectual signs of grace and of God's good will to us." The WLC, 162–63, says they "signify, seal and exhibit . . .

---

74. A. Hamman, *"Sacramentum,"* *EECh*, 2:751.
75. Augustine, *On John* 26.11 (*NPNF*[1], 7:171); Augustine, *On 1 John* 6.11 (*NPNF*[1], 7:498–99).

the benefits of Christ's mediation." The Council of Trent saw them as "something presented to the senses which has the power by divine institution not only of signifying but also of conveying grace." The differing emphases here represent differing sacramental theologies.

Murray argues that a sacrament is something that (1) was ordained by Christ in the days of his flesh, (2) uses material elements, (3) represents spiritual blessing, and (4) is a seal of the covenant of grace. Furthermore, (5), the sacraments are to be observed by the church until Christ returns. They are not occasional ceremonies or designed for a short period, nor illustrative actions to indicate the way believers are to live, like foot washing in John 13, which Jesus did not require to be repeated.[76] Essentially, there are two main things in a sacrament: the outward sign and the reality signified.

Rome. Rome places the sacraments in a strongly Trinitarian context that Protestantism would do well to emulate.[77] The *Catechism of the Catholic Church* states: "'Seated at the right hand of the Father' and pouring out the Holy Spirit on his Body which is the Church, Christ now acts through the sacraments he instituted to consummate his grace."[78] The sacraments are not magic, nor do they have power of themselves. It is the risen Christ who conveys his grace by the Holy Spirit. They are perceptible signs, and by the action of Christ and the power of the Spirit they make present efficaciously the grace that they signify. In the sacrament, Christ baptizes, while he himself speaks when the Scriptures are read in the church. Every liturgical and sacramental action is an encounter between Christ and the church.[79] The sacraments are actions of the Holy Spirit at work in his body, the church, masterworks of God in the new and everlasting covenant.[80] The ordained priesthood is the bond between Christ and the liturgical actions, guaranteeing that it really is Christ acting by the Holy Spirit in his church. "The ordained minister is the sacramental bond that ties the liturgical action to what the apostles said and did and, through them, to the words and actions of Christ, the source and foundation of the sacraments."[81]

---

76. John Murray, *Select Lectures in Systematic Theology*, vol. 2 of *Collected Writings of John Murray* (Edinburgh: Banner of Truth, 1977), 366–67.
77. CCC, 247–55.
78. CCC, 249.
79. CCC, 252.
80. CCC, 256.
81. CCC, 257.

Rome maintains there are seven sacraments: baptism, confirmation, the Eucharist, penance, the anointing of the sick, holy orders, and matrimony. It claims all of these were instituted by Christ; Scripture, the apostolic tradition, and the consensus of the fathers all point to Christ as their author. However, we reply, while each has biblical warrant, they do not all qualify as sacraments, as seals of the covenant of grace instituted by Christ in the days of his flesh with specific promises of grace attached. For instance, matrimony is a creation ordinance, not related to the covenant.

For Rome, the sacraments efficaciously convey God's grace *ex opere operato* (by their being performed). They contain the grace they signify because Christ is at work. However, this is not automatic or by any intrinsic power but "by virtue of the saving work of Christ, accomplished once for all." It follows that the efficacy of the sacraments depends not on "the righteousness of either the celebrant or the recipient, but [on] the power of God."[82] "Nevertheless, the fruits of the sacraments also depend on the disposition of the one who receives them."[83] This ought to be noted carefully, for Protestant polemic frequently looks to create division and distinction where none exists. There is a difference here between Rome and the Reformed, but it is not what is often supposed. Both agree that the efficacy of the sacraments derives from the power of God, the risen Christ working in them by the Spirit, and that the status of the celebrant and recipients does not determine the validity of the sacraments, since they belong to Christ. The difference lies in the respective weight given to faith in the recipient and the corresponding extent to which the Spirit conveys grace.

Nevertheless, Rome confuses the sign with the reality. In the Eucharist, the bread and wine undergo a change of substance (what a thing is in itself) and become the body and blood of Christ, while retaining the accidents (what is not intrinsic to a thing) of bread and wine.[84] This appears to Protestants to short-circuit the need for faith on the part of the recipient; while the CCC recognizes that they are to be "celebrated worthily in faith," yet they "confer the grace that they signify."[85]

---

82. CCC, 258.
83. CCC, 259.
84. CCC, 304–5, 309–11.
85. CCC, 258.

Rome places the sacraments in an exceedingly broad context. The CCC states that through them we are enabled to share in the worship in heaven. Pointing to the scenes in Revelation, where participating in the worship of God are the heavenly powers, all creation (the four living beings), the servants of old and new covenants (the twenty-four elders), the new people of God (the one hundred and forty-four thousand), the martyrs, the mother of God (the woman), the bride of the Lamb, and a great multitude that no one could number, the CCC continues, "It is in this eternal liturgy that the Spirit and the Church enable us to participate whenever we celebrate the mystery of salvation in the sacraments."[86] At root, we live in a sacramental universe. This is a point shared by the Orthodox and lost by Protestantism, with devastating consequences, for in many sections of evangelicalism worship is close to entertainment, or a place for emotional manipulation.

Orthodoxy. The sacraments have an intensely personal character in Orthodoxy. In the liturgy the priest mentions the Christian name of the recipient as he administers the sacraments. In the Eucharist he says, "The servant of God [name] partakes of the holy, precious Body and Blood of Our Lord," while at the anointing of the sick he says, "O Father, heal Thy servant [name] from his sickness both of body and soul."[87]

A common misconception of Orthodoxy by the West is that it is saturated by mysticism. Certainly, its theology is strongly mystical, but as George Every noted: "The popular religion of Eastern Europe is liturgical and ritualistic, but not wholly otherworldly. A religion that continues to propagate new forms for cursing caterpillars and for removing dead rats from the bottoms of wells can hardly be dismissed as pure mysticism."[88]

The Orthodox hold views similar to Rome's on the sacraments but, unlike Rome, make no attempt to explain them in philosophical terms, accenting instead their character as mysteries. There is no fixed number of sacraments. Many hold there to be seven—baptism, chrismation (the equivalent of confirmation in the West), the Eucharist, repentance or confession (penance in the West), holy orders, holy matrimony, and the anointing of the sick. Not until the seventeenth century, when the impact

86. CCC, 260–61.
87. Timothy Ware, *The Orthodox Church* (London: Penguin, 1969), 283.
88. George Every, *The Byzantine Patriarchate 451–1204* (London: SPCK, 1947), 198.

of the West was at its height, did seven gain wide acceptance. However, unlike Rome, there is no absolute dogmatic significance to the number seven. It is more a convenience for teaching, popular because of its supposed mystical value. Even for those who accept seven, baptism and the Eucharist are set apart as "pre-eminent among the mysteries." Gregory Palamas thought there were only two sacraments, baptism and the Eucharist: "On these two our whole salvation is rooted."[89]

The sacraments are called mysteries, Ware indicates, following Chrysostom, "because what we believe is not the same as what we see, but we believe one thing and see another." As Ware puts it:

> This double character, at once outward and inward, is the distinctive feature of a sacrament. . . . At baptism the Christian undergoes an outward washing in water, and he is at the same time cleansed inwardly from his sins; at the Eucharist he receives what appears from the visible point of view to be bread and wine, but in reality he eats the Body and Blood of Christ.

In the sacraments Christ takes material things and makes them a vehicle for the Spirit. So the sacraments look backward to the incarnation, when Christ took material flesh, and they look forward to and anticipate the *apocatastasis* and the final redemption of matter at the last day.[90]

Lutheranism. Lutheranism considers only baptism and the Lord's Supper as sacraments of the new covenant. It avoids the identification of sign and reality typical of Rome but still connects them closely in an objective manner, such that "the unworthy and unbelieving receive the true body and blood of Christ" in the Lord's Supper.[91] The sacramental grace of God is invariably efficacious unless resisted by the recipient. This is parallel with its view on the inherent power of the Word preached. Since infants are incapable of resisting the power of God in the sacraments, it follows that baptism is a necessary means of grace. In the case of infants, baptism is necessary for salvation.[92]

---

89. Ware, *Orthodox Church*, 281–83; John Meyendorff, *Byzantine Theology: Historical Trends and Doctrinal Themes* (New York: Fordham University Press, 1979), 191.

90. Ware, *Orthodox Church*, 281.

91. The Formula of Concord (1576), art. 7, in Schaff, *Creeds*, 3:140; *The Saxon Visitation Articles* (1592), 1:6, in Schaff, *Creeds*, 3:182.

92. Augsburg Confession (1530), 9; Formula of Concord (1576), 7; Saxon Visitation Articles (1592), 1, 3; in Schaff, *Creeds*, 3:13, 139–46, 181–84.

Anabaptism and contemporary evangelicalism. The Anabaptists effectively were antisacramental. Baptism and the Lord's Supper were for them merely "ordinances" that Jesus commanded but which were, at most, symbolic and neither exhibited nor conveyed grace. Much, but by no means all, of the evangelical world today follows this line.[93] Private Bible study, small group activity, and one-to-one discipleship and counseling are as important and valuable as any public, corporate church activity, it is thought, whether in theory or practice. Even many Presbyterians take this view.[94] The default position is that baptism and the Supper convey to the faithful nothing that cannot be obtained elsewhere but exist mainly for the benefit of the participants, as badges of their profession of faith. Indeed, modern evangelicals are keener to deny that there is any grace transmitted than to affirm it.[95] Iain Murray propounds an Independent ecclesiology with a decidedly Zwinglian attitude toward the sacraments.[96] In his massive 1,225 page, two-volume biography of Martyn Lloyd-Jones, he fails to mention whether and when Lloyd-Jones was baptized.[97] Others classified as Reformed theologians strongly reject the position of Calvin and are effectively Zwinglian.[98]

Reformed. There is a difference between the followers of Zwingli and the followers of Calvin, along with the bulk of the Reformed confessions. Zwingli considered the sacraments to be merely symbolic, emblems or memorials, visible signs of a person's profession of faith. He thought baptism was like the flag of Swiss cantons, identifying the soldiers as belonging to the army of their particular canton. Baptism identifies its recipients as belonging to Christ. Zwingli was strongly influenced by Neoplatonism,

---

93. This is nowhere more evident than in the 1677/1689 confession of the Particular Baptists, one of the most thorough confessions and widely accepted today, who sought to demonstrate their affinity with the Westminster Assembly by adopting the great majority of the WCF as their own. Chapters 27–29 refer to "ordinances" and refuse to use the word *sacrament*. Moreover, there is nothing on the efficacy of the sacraments. *A Faith to Confess: The Baptist Confession of 1689 rewritten in Modern English* (Leeds: Carey, 1975), 61–64.

94. Letham and Macleod, "Evangelicalism."

95. In the United Kingdom, a typical example is the doctrinal statement of the Fellowship of Independent Evangelical Churches, which states, among other things, "Baptism and the Lord's Supper have been given to the churches by Christ as visible signs of the gospel. Baptism is a symbol of union with Christ and entry into his Church but does not impart spiritual life. The Lord's Supper is a commemoration of Christ's sacrifice offered once for all and involves no change in the bread and wine. All its blessings are received by faith." https://fiec.org.uk/about-us/beliefs. Accessed 4 October 2016.

96. Iain H. Murray, *Evangelicalism Divided* (Edinburgh: Banner of Truth, 2000).

97. Iain H. Murray, *David Martyn Lloyd-Jones: The First Forty Years 1899–1939* (Edinburgh: Banner of Truth, 1982); Murray, *David Martyn Lloyd-Jones: The Fight of Faith 1939–1981* (Edinburgh: Banner of Truth, 1990).

98. William Cunningham, *Historical Theology* (Edinburgh, 1870).

which held that matter was on a lower level than spirit. Hence, he found it difficult or impossible to conceive how material elements could be the means of conveying spiritual blessing.[99] He maintained that "no external thing can make us pure or righteous."[100] As Stephens says:

> A number of factors combine to make Zwingli deny that the sacraments give faith or the Spirit. Fundamental among them is the understanding of the sovereignty of God and the freedom of the Spirit, together with his view of faith, but there is also the Neoplatonist element in his view of man which denies that outward things can reach and affect the soul.[101]

Conversely, Bucer, Calvin, and Vermigli held that God conveys grace in connection with material elements, but they maintained the need for faith on the part of recipients.[102]

For the Reformed churches there are three sacraments, only two of which belong to the new covenant.[103] In these the intended grace is efficacious by the power of the Holy Spirit through faith. Sacramental efficacy is not automatic; faith is required in those who receive them. However, they are more than symbolic. Brian Gerrish distinguished between *symbolic memorialism*, characteristic of Zwingli; *symbolic parallelism*, where grace is given as the elements are consumed, which is evident in Bullinger and Bucer; and *symbolic instrumentalism*, in which the sacrament is the means by which grace is given, seen in Calvin.[104]

The classic Reformed confessions regard the sacraments as means of grace, conveying blessing to faithful recipients. Their efficacy resides not in the sacramental elements or in the sacramental action, nor in the character or intention of the one who administers them, but in Christ's blessing and the working of the Spirit in the beneficiaries. They are means of grace only to those who fulfill the conditions of the covenant of which they are signs and seals.[105]

---

99. W. P. Stephens, *The Theology of Huldrych Zwingli* (Oxford: Clarendon, 1986), 86–107, 180–93.

100. In *Of Baptism* (1525), in G. W. Bromiley, *Zwingli and Bullinger* (London: SCM, 1953), 130.

101. Stephens, *Zwingli*, 192.

102. Robert Letham, "Baptism in the Writings of the Reformers," *SBET* 7 (1989): 21–44.

103. There are, of course, three current sacraments: baptism, the Lord's Supper, and the rainbow.

104. B. A. Gerrish, *Grace and Gratitude: The Eucharistic Theology of John Calvin* (Minneapolis: Fortress, 1993), 166–68.

105. WCF, 27–29; W. G. T. Shedd, *Dogmatic Theology* (Grand Rapids, MI: Zondervan, 1971), 3:502.

The Church of England holds to two sacraments which are "cer-taine sure witnesses and effectuall signes of grace and Gods good wyll towardes us, by the which he doth worke invisiblie in us, and doth not only quicken, but also strengthen and confirme our fayth in hym."[106] This is a Reformed statement from the Thirty-Nine Articles in line with the classic Reformed consensus. In practice, the Church of England cur-rently includes a wide range of theological identities extending as far as Anglo-Catholicism.

22.4.3   The Necessity of the Sacraments

In considering the necessity of the sacraments, we must distinguish be-tween necessity of precept and necessity of means. In the former sense, the sacraments are necessary because Christ commanded them to be ob-served. But in the latter, they are not absolutely necessary for individual salvation, since a person can be saved without them, such as the dying thief or others converted on their deathbeds.

Some argue that the sacraments convey nothing we do not receive through the Word. This may be so, since it is Christ whom we receive in both cases. But such thinking has often led to their practical neglect. Instead, as Robert Bruce remarked, in the Lord's Supper we "get Christ better."[107] Or else, why did Christ require their constant use? If we can be saved without them and there is nothing in them we cannot get else-where, what's the big deal? Is there here a form of gnostic dualism that despises the physical and material and is hesitant to accept that material objects can be the means of spiritual grace? While the sacraments are not absolutely necessary for salvation, neither is any other element entrusted to the church by Christ, including the Bible, the ministry of the Word, and prayer. Some can be saved without hearing the gospel preached (WCF, 10.3). Some, like the Philippian jailor, can be saved without having read the Bible; vast numbers before the printing press was invented were in this category. Yet ordinarily it is necessary to hear the Word preached (Rom. 10:14–17). The sacraments are necessary to salvation inasmuch as they are the means Christ has appointed for our entrance into and growth in grace.

How may we determine the validity or irregularity of the sacraments? Protestants have shied away from dogmatism since they recognize that

---

106. Schaff, *Creeds*, 3:502.
107. Bruce, *Mystery*, 84–85.

the efficacy of the sacraments depends on the blessing of Christ through the Holy Spirit. But this is exactly what Rome says! If we are to be faithful to Christ's intention, the elements must be as Christ instituted them, there must be the giving and receiving of the elements as Christ commanded, and the intention must be to do what Christ required, as expressed in the reading of the Word of God that records their institution. These things are necessary for the sacrament to be valid.

Since Christ has appointed order in his church, officers for ruling and teaching, it is a violation of good order for the sacraments to be administered by someone not called to those offices. The sacraments are defined by the Word and are to be administered in connection with the Word preached. Therefore, the one administering them should have been ordained to the ministry of the Word. When administered otherwise, they are irregular. While irregularity does not entail invalidity, neither does the validity of the sacrament justify irregular administration.

Further Reading
Calvin, John. *Institutes of the Christian Religion*. Bk. 4.

Study Questions
1. Look through the index of any hymnal or worship songbook, and note the proportions of items that are set in the singular as opposed to the plural. This is not wrong; many of the Psalms are in the singular too, although these are often by David in his representative capacity. Consider how far the individualism of the Renaissance and the Enlightenment has affected us.

2. Why is the preaching of the Word of God important? Do other proposed methods of communication bear comparison?

3. Explain the comparative neglect of the sacraments in evangelicalism.

23

The Beginning of the
Christian Life (1)

Effectual Calling and Regeneration

In the creation, God calls all people to seek and recognize him. That people do not seek the living and true God is due to their own sin. In the gospel, God calls people to find him in Jesus Christ, his Son, and so partake of his promises. It is by another call, the effectual call, that sinners are enabled to attain a saving knowledge of Christ. In this, the Holy Spirit brings about the whole process of transition from unbelief to faith. While it can be considered from a number of angles, regeneration, as the initial stage of transformation, is also likened to a resurrection and a new creation. It is a mysterious, inward work of the Spirit, in conjunction with the Word of God and baptism, since individual salvation is found in the context of the church and its ministry. Regeneration, union with Christ, and baptism are all connected in the New Testament. Baptism and regeneration both occur at the point at which a person can first be called a Christian; both are theologically related to union with Christ in his death and resurrection. The connection with baptism is not causal, or temporal, but theological.

✣

The elements of the *ordo salutis* are all aspects of union with Christ. While, of necessity, I discuss them sequentially, they occur simultaneously. Moreover, they are associated with the preaching of the Word and the sacraments, as we considered in the previous chapter.

23.1 Calling

Paul cites calling first in Romans 8:29–30, following predestination and foreordination. Calling refers to the totality of God's action in bringing us out of unbelief to faith.

23.1.1 The Universal Call

God's revelation in creation is indiscriminate, calling all people to respond. Psalm 19:1 states that "the heavens declare the glory of God." This revelation of God's glory in the world around us declares his nature and calls for a response on our part (vv. 1–6). The psalm continues by reflecting on the wonders of God's law and its impact on the human heart (vv. 7–12). In Romans 1:20, Paul remarks that what is known about God in creation leaves people without excuse. The εἰς + infinitive introduces a result clause; God's revealing himself places a responsibility on people to obey him but provides no power to change their ungodly nature, with the result that it renders them inexcusable. People do not respond, because they are rebels against God. This universal call is inescapable but not redemptive. It is insufficient for salvation but sufficient for its purpose. This prompts us to consider what Calvin terms the *special call*, God's calling us to salvation.

23.1.2 The Gospel Call

The offer of the gospel to sinners shares some features with the universal call. The universal call is universal and, by definition, indiscriminate; the gospel call is indiscriminate and aspirationally universal. However, whereas the universal call concerns God as Creator, the gospel call concerns God as Redeemer.

The gospel call and common grace. The gospel call flows from God's blessing on humanity after the flood (Gen. 9:1). In blessing Noah's three sons, God includes the whole race as it descended from them. Jesus echoes this in the Sermon on the Mount, where he refers to God making the rain fall on the just and unjust indiscriminately (Matt. 5:45). The Noachic covenant entails the preservation of the race, the reaffirmation of creation, and an extension of its blessings by providing additional food supplies and restricting violent behavior. From this, particularly in Dutch theology, developed the idea of common grace, by which the widespread blessings of order, prosperity, artistic and musical and literary gifts, sporting prowess, and technological advance are given by God without regard to people's redemptive status. In the context of sin and depravity, one might wonder why and how humanity could continue, let alone thrive. Common grace was the answer suggested by Kuyper and Bavinck,[1] although its roots lie in the earlier Reformed tradition.

The term *common grace* does not appear at the Westminster Assembly. Charles Hodge discusses it in his *Systematic Theology* after the gospel call.[2] Others, such as Herman Hoeksema, have rejected the idea. If some are the objects of reprobation and wrath, how can they also be the objects of grace? Is not what is apparently grace in reality judgment? Is not grace always particular, not general? Does not the idea of common grace minimize the extent of human depravity?[3] The Westminster documents talk only of the nonelect possibly having "some common operations of the Spirit" (WCF, 10.4); this could suggest the idea but no more. Certainly, the WLC, in speaking of grace being offered to the nonelect, refers to grace in Christ in the covenant of grace (WLC, 68). However, it is anachronistic to ask a seventeenth-century Assembly to address the questions of two centuries later.

Two comments are in order. First, the idea of common grace is a *theologoumenon* (theological opinion) and does not have confessional status. Second, Hoeksema has a dominant doctrine of election that controls the historical outworking of redemption in such a way as to eliminate the idea of grace being operative indiscriminately. Does this tend to undermine the historical dimension? Is it wrong to consider the many blessings of human life as grace, since they come to humanity, which by sin has forfeited all claims to God's benefits? Whether we think of health, material well-being, or artistic and cultural life, all are products of the good and wise God, who in his rich bounty has lavished them upon those who have not the slightest concern to know, love, or obey him. In this sense, the preaching of the gospel is the greatest gift of all, since it brings an offer, invitation, and command to believe in Christ and

---

1. Abraham Kuyper, *Common Grace: God's Gifts for a Fallen World*, trans. Nelson D. Kloosterman and Ed. M. Van der Mass, vol. 1 (Bellingham, WA: Lexham, 2016), the first of three volumes published in Dutch as *De Gemeene Gratie* (Amsterdam: Höveker & Wormser, 1902); Bavinck, *RD* 2:329–34; Herman Bavinck, "Common Grace," *CTJ* 24 (1989): 35–65.

2. Charles Hodge, *Systematic Theology* (Grand Rapids, MI: Eerdmans, 1977), 2:654–75.

3. Throughout his *Reformed Dogmatics*, Herman Hoeksema strenuously opposes the idea, which has no confessional status. See, among comments elsewhere, Hoeksema, *Reformed Dogmatics* (Grand Rapids, MI: Reformed Free Publishing Association, 1966), 205, 207, 236–37, 470–78.

receive the supreme blessing of everlasting life. Moreover, it is to be offered indiscriminately, with no prior qualifications other than that one be a member of the rebellious human race.[4]

Elements of the gospel call. What is the gospel? What is said when the gospel is preached? Reformed theologians have customarily distinguished three broad aspects.

Announcement of the plan of salvation. At root is instruction concerning what God has done to save his people from their sin. There is an objective element; the gospel has content. Converts are baptized in the name of the Trinity; that entails teaching about God. This content centers on creation, God, the status of humans, the person and work of Christ, and his death and resurrection. Today we need to give special attention to who God is, to creation and providence—distinguishing carefully between Creator and creature due to the prevalence of New Age monism—and even more basically, the existence and nature of truth itself in a postmodern world, for which objective truth does not exist. Nevertheless, the heart of the gospel relates to Christ; all roads must eventually lead there. This is clear from the sermons to Jewish and Gentile audiences in Acts. Paul's comment in 1 Timothy 1:15 is crucial: "Christ Jesus came into the world to save sinners." God has revealed good news; this central point is the gospel strictly speaking, and all other elements relate to it the way the rim and spokes of a bicycle wheel are connected to the hub.

Announcement of the promise of redemption. This is not a promise made to all people unconditionally. God promises redemption (the forgiveness of sins, the gift of the Holy Spirit, eternal life, the righteousness of Christ) to all who believe and trust in Jesus Christ. It is a promise made to believers (Gal. 3:22). Behind this promise is the faithfulness of God. He keeps his promises, and his Word is reliable. It demands that something be known about the character of God.

Invitation to believe. This distinguishes preaching from teaching. Teaching is designed to impart information, to encourage thought from new perspectives and from an informed mind. However, preaching is

---

4. John Murray and Ned B. Stonehouse, "The Free Offer of the Gospel," *Minutes of the Fifteenth General Assembly of the Orthodox Presbyterian Church* (1948): app., 51–63; John Murray, *The Claims of Truth*, vol. 1 of *Collected Writings of John Murray* (Edinburgh: Banner of Truth, 1976), 59–85.

designed to change people's lives—now, without delay. To that end, information and intellectual perspectives are necessary but not sufficient. There is an overlap between teaching and preaching, but they are clearly distinct.

In Matthew 11:28, Jesus, after thanking God for his sovereignty in granting knowledge of himself, turns to those around him, urging them to come to him and find rest. First, there is an objective element, contained in the word "me" and all it entails. His teaching throughout his ministry on who he is and his relation to the Father is summed up in this one word. Then he makes a promise—"I will give you rest"—followed by an exhortation—"Come to me . . . take my yoke."

In Acts 2:22–36, Peter unfolds God's plan of salvation, centering on the life, ministry, death, and resurrection of Jesus. Then he issues an exhortation—"Repent and be baptized, every one of you"—with urgency, for thousands were baptized that very day. He also conveys a promise—"you will receive the gift of the Holy Spirit" (v. 38).

There are a number of pertinent points. First, there is no difference in gospel preaching directed toward the elect versus the nonelect. Peter in Acts 2:21 addresses his hearers indiscriminately. Knowledge of who are the elect is exclusive to God. The secret counsel of God cannot be made a rule of faith and practice (Deut. 29:29). Second, the gospel call does not presuppose any inherent ability of hearers to accept the message in faith. The command to repent and believe no more assumes human ability to repent than does the first commandment. This is in contrast to semi-Pelagianism, which assumes that the unregenerate can take the first small step, God then providing the rest. Third, it follows that the gospel call does not of itself overcome people's sinful inability to believe. A special work of the Spirit is needed, accompanying the preaching, without which the appeal will fall on deaf ears. Fourth, nevertheless the gospel is the power of God for salvation, since it comes from God, centers on Christ, and is the means the Spirit uses to effect it.

The authority of the gospel call. In the previous chapter we saw how preaching by those lawfully called is the word of Christ. As the single most widely adopted Reformed confession, the Second Helvetic Confession (1562), put it with celebrated clarity, "The preaching of the Word of God is the Word of God [*Praedicatio verbi Dei est verbum Dei*]" (1.4, marginal reference). And again, "Therefore when even today the

Word of God is proclaimed in the churches by duly called preachers, we believe that the Word of God is proclaimed [*credimus ipsum Dei verbum annunciari*] and accepted by the faithful."[5]

These confessional commitments are based on a number of texts in Scripture. In Romans 10:14 ("How are they to believe in him of whom they have never heard?") the case rests on whether Paul uses an objective or subjective genitive. Many, including Murray and Cranfield, argue that he means that Christ is speaking through the preacher. Murray writes:

> A striking feature of this clause is that Christ is represented as being heard in the gospel when proclaimed by the sent messenger. The implication is that Christ speaks in the gospel proclamation. . . . The dignity of the messengers . . . is derived from the fact that they are the Lord's spokesmen.[6]

So too Cranfield:

> The use of οὖ indicates that in the second or third questions, the thought is of their hearing Christ speaking in the message of the preachers. (To explain οὖ οὐκ ἤκουσαν as meaning "about whom they have not heard" is not really feasible; for the use of ἀκούειν with the simple genitive of the person meaning "to hear about (someone)" would be very unusual.)[7]

Many others agree.[8]

Even more striking is Paul's comment in Ephesians 2:17: "He [Christ] came and preached peace to you who were far off and peace to those who were near." To what preaching does he refer? There is no record of Jesus having visited Ephesus, let alone preached there, whether pre- or post-resurrection. Paul himself took the gospel to the Gentiles, and to Ephesus. He refers to his own preaching at Ephesus; in Paul's preaching, Christ himself was heard. But can this be restricted to the ministry of Paul or the apostles? Certainly, there is an apostolic framework here (v. 20), but the church is to grow on this apostolic foundation (v. 21).

---

5. Philip Schaff, *The Creeds of Christendom* (Grand Rapids, MI: Baker, 1966), 3:237–38, 832.

6. John Murray, *The Epistle to the Romans* (Grand Rapids, MI: Eerdmans, 1965).

7. C. E. B. Cranfield, *A Critical and Exegetical Commentary on the Epistle to the Romans*, The International Critical Commentary (Edinburgh: T&T Clark, 1975), 2:534.

8. William Sanday and Arthur C. Headlam, *A Critical and Exegetical Commentary on the Epistle to the Romans*, The International Critical Commentary (Edinburgh: T&T Clark, 1905), 296; Leon Morris, *The Epistle to the Romans* (Grand Rapids. MI: Eerdmans, 1988), 389–90; James D. G. Dunn, *Romans 9–16*, Word Biblical Commentary 38B (Dallas: Word, 1988), 620.

Additionally, the presence of Christ is related to the preaching of peace (v. 17), the *content* of preaching rather than the identity of the preacher. We recall that Jesus promised his continual presence in the church's on-going ministry (Matt. 28:19–20). When the gospel of peace through the cross of Christ is preached, Christ himself addresses the hearers.

Other passages in the Gospels support this argument. In Luke 10:1–16, Jesus appoints the seventy-two as his special representatives and equates their message with his own, their persons with his, their words with his. If they were accepted or rejected, then ipso facto both he and the Father would be accepted or rejected. The issue is not the intrinsic quality of the preaching—it is that they were directly commissioned by Jesus. This cannot be restricted to the seventy-two, as if they were the only ones commissioned by Christ. This is akin to the words of the Talmud, which speaks of one sent as the legal representative of another (a שליח),[9] as being the same as the one who sent him.[10] So Paul writes of himself and all true preachers as "ambassadors for Christ" (2 Cor. 5:20), possessing in the discharge of their office the same authority as Christ himself.

In John 5:25, Jesus talks of a resurrection, in this case not a physical but a spiritual one, for he describes it as already present ("and is now"), whereas he talks of the physical resurrection in verses 28–29 as future. This already-present, spiritual resurrection comes through hearing the word of Christ and believing (v. 24), or hearing the voice of the Son of God (v. 25). This, the miracle of regeneration, occurs not only during Jesus's earthly ministry but afterward as well, wherever the gospel is preached. Thus, true preaching is equated with "the voice of the Son of God."

The work of the Holy Spirit. In Matthew 11:25–27, Jesus refers to revelation by the Father. The verb ἀποκαλύπτω, "reveal," is used, in contrast to κρύπτω, "conceal."[11] The Father reveals, as does the Son. They reveal one another. This revealing is a unique and sovereign matter. The result is knowledge (ἐπιγινώσκω).[12] In Matthew 16:17 the same word is used for the revelatory activity of the Father. Peter could not

9. *shaliyakh.*
10. Karl Heinrich Rengstorf, "ἀπόστολος," in *TDNT*, 1:419–22.
11. *apokalyptō, kryptō.*
12. *epiginōskō.*

arrive at a true recognition of Jesus's identity by his own processes; this is beyond human capabilities.

In John 6:44–45, Jesus states that no one comes to him unless the Father draws him. Teaching is involved. The Father calls by way of instruction, so that the truth is received both intellectually and practically. So far, the Spirit has not been mentioned. However, in John 16:13–15 he is in the foreground, in connection with his teaching the apostles what Jesus had hitherto not taught them due to their inability to understand. Yet the leading and teaching of the Spirit cannot be separated from the work of the Father and the Son. What was earlier attributed to the Father is now, after Pentecost, ascribed to the Spirit. Thus, in 1 John 2:20, 27, John writes of an anointing that believers have received, which is from "the Holy One" and "teaches you." The reference is to the Spirit, either the gift or the person. Since the phrase "the Holy One" is used of Christ in John 6:69, implied here is that the Spirit is the Spirit of Christ. The result of the Spirit's coming is that the believers "know all things" (1 John 2:20, my trans.), reminiscent of the statement in John that he would lead the apostles into all truth. Thus, they do not need others to teach them, since they are taught of God. The context—opposition to a form of proto-gnosticism?—points not to a denial of the need for human ministry but to John's countering an autocratic teaching hierarchy, heterodox on the person of Christ. The "all things" taught by the Spirit is obviously not literal—the Spirit did not teach the early church the general and special theories of relativity—but refers to those things relating to Christ and salvation. A further consequence of the Spirit's ministry is that believers confess the truth (2:23), especially concerning the Father and the Son. Moreover, the Spirit's teaching is permanent, not transient, and is associated with mutual indwelling, since he abides or remains in us, and thus we have confidence when Christ returns (v. 28).

Paul says similar things. In 1 Corinthians 2:4–15 he discusses the character of his preaching. It was not eloquent or dependent on the classical *trivium*—grammar, logic, and rhetoric. Instead, he depended utterly on the Holy Spirit. He preached the Word of the Spirit in dependence on its author (1 Cor. 2:2). This is inaccessible to the natural man, who cannot receive it. In 1 Corinthians 12:3, Paul expresses the same idea; our confession of faith in Jesus Christ comes exclusively from the Spirit's work. Thus, Paul's preaching centers on Christ, not himself; its effectiveness comes from God. In 2 Corinthians 4:4–7, he compares it to the work of creation. The verb λάμπω[13] denotes inward illumination in the heart and is attributable to God shining with light akin to the original creation light. In Genesis, there was utter darkness, with the Spirit of God moving across the face of the waters. Then God said, "Let there be light," and there was light. The Spirit's illuminating work as the gospel is preached is a new creation—in contrast with the work of the god of this world, who causes blindness. Preaching must therefore be in the power of the Spirit, for the enemy is greater than human. Again, in 1 Thessalonians 1:5–6, 2:13 the gospel is said to be proclaimed with power. The Word is self-authenticating, the Spirit certifying it.

The Spirit's ministry here is described as revelation, teaching, leading, disclosure, enlightenment, and power. The Father and the Son reveal what they know; this cannot come from flesh and blood. The Son bears witness to the Father and to himself, while the promised Holy Spirit was to continue this witness (John 16:13–15). The Spirit does more than accompany Paul's preaching—Paul depends on the Spirit at every point. The result of his ministry is enlightenment, learning, knowledge. This is not purely intellectual, although there is and must be an intellectual component. It encompasses entering into the truth, coming to the Father, and confessing Christ. The Spirit bears witness and teaches, and our experience follows. Moreover, the effects are permanent.

The Spirit does not convey truth additional to what is in Scripture. He convinces us of what is already in Scripture and enables us to receive Christ, of whom the whole of Scripture—which he has authored—testifies. Scripture does not need anything extra. The problem is our own spiritual blindness.

23.1.3 Effectual Call

Because of sin, no one can respond unaided to the universal call of creation; besides, it provides no remedy for sin. Furthermore, no one can respond unaided to the gospel call either. The will is bound (John 8:34; Rom. 6:13; 7:13–14). By nature, people are dead in sin (Eph. 2:1) and so cannot see the kingdom of God (John 3:3); they cannot understand the

---

13. *lampō.*

things of the Spirit of God (1 Cor. 2:14) and so cannot be subject to the law of God (Rom. 8:7). In summary, fallen humanity cannot do good in the sight of God (Rom. 3:18; 15:5; 2 Cor. 3:5). A positive response to the call to fellowship with Christ is from the human standpoint impossible. How, then, do people believe? The answer is in terms of effectual calling (Matt. 19:26).

Biblical calling is efficacious. Murray points out that wherever the New Testament speaks of effectual calling, it is a summons that secures our response.[14] The Spirit produces faith in us. The connection between this and the gospel call is evident in Matthew 22:14; the gospel call is more comprehensive than election. "Many are called, but few are chosen"; such calling refers to the gospel call.

Arminianism claims that calling in the New Testament generally refers to the call of the gospel. It understands Romans 8:29–30 this way, seeing foreordination as God's foreknowledge of our faith. However, in this passage, "those whom he called" cannot be a larger group than those covered by the following terms, those who are justified and glorified. Again, in Romans 1:6 the called of Jesus Christ are distinguished from the rest of the Gentiles; in 1 Corinthians 1:13–26 the called are distinct from the Jews and the Greeks; while in 1 Corinthians 1:26–27, 2 Peter 1:10, and Revelation 7:14 calling and election are inseparably associated. Clearly, effectual calling occurs to a narrower group than those who receive the gospel call, to which many do not respond.

Biblical background. In the Old Testament, Abraham was called by God to leave Ur, "called to go out to a place that he was to receive as an inheritance" (Heb. 11:8). This found its fulfillment in the new covenant (Heb. 9:15; 1 Pet. 1:4; 3:9). Calling is ultimately to this eternal inheritance (1 Tim. 6:12; Heb. 9:15; 1 Pet. 5:10; Rev. 19:9), but it also carries with it present blessing (2 Pet. 1:3), everything relating to life and godliness here and now (1 Thess. 2:12; 2 Thess. 2:14; 1 Pet. 2:9). It is also calling to service, linked closely with sanctification (Gal. 5:13; Col. 3:15; 1 Pet. 1:15; 2:21).

The nature of effectual calling. As Murray demonstrates, since calling is the work of the Holy Spirit, it is effectual and immutable (Rom.

---

14. John Murray, *Redemption Accomplished and Applied* (London: Banner of Truth, 1961), 88–94.

11:29); is high, holy, and heavenly; and has as its goal fellowship with God's Son, union with Christ.[15] Here is the answer to the question of how people respond to the gospel. Calling itself cannot be understood in terms of our faith, although it includes our response of repentance and faith in order to reach its goal. The Spirit, in calling, unites us to Christ by awakening faith in us. He does this by regenerating us.

According to Murray, God is the author (1 Cor. 1:9; 2 Tim. 1:8–9), but specifically the Father calls us; the evidence is "copious and conclusive," he thinks.[16] Conversely, Hodge argued that the Holy Spirit is the agent.[17] However, strictly, the Father calls us by the Spirit; calling is the work of the Spirit, although the author is the Father (John 14:26; 15:26; 16:7).

23.2   Regeneration

There are a number of ways in which regeneration is understood in both the Bible and theology.[18] Broadly, it refers to the entirety of salvation as personal transformation. More strictly and commonly, it is used for the initial stages of transformation, to the commencement of the work of the Holy Spirit within.

23.2.1   Regeneration as the Equivalent of Salvation

The broader use of the word *regeneration* indicates that salvation consists not only in freedom from the guilt and the penalty of sin but also freedom from sin itself and all its consequences. Warfield, stressing the goal of our salvation, states that "we cannot and ought not to think of our salvation as anything less than our own perfected and completed sinlessness and holiness."[19] He asserts that a truncation of the ethical side of salvation is an assault upon God.[20] Viewed this way, regeneration is close to the Eastern view of *theōsis*, which is effectively the Protestant doctrine of regeneration narrowly considered, plus sanctification, plus glorification, considered together as one. In this sense, regeneration both includes and follows the initial act of saving faith.

---

15. Murray, *Redemption*, 88–94.
16. Murray, *Redemption*, 89–90.
17. Hodge, *Systematic Theology*, 2:639–41, 675–77.
18. Bavinck, *RD*, 4:33–95.
19. B. B. Warfield, "On the Biblical Notion of 'Renewal,'" in *Biblical and Theological Studies*, ed. Samuel G. Craig (Philadelphia: Presbyterian and Reformed, 1952), 374.
20. Warfield, "Renewal," 355ff.

The Reformers objected not only to the Roman Catholic doctrine of justification but also to Rome's view of sanctification, since it implied that it is something we do ourselves. Since the penalty of sin is death, the destruction of death also entails the destruction of sin and, with it, the process and event of sanctification.

Paul speaks frequently of salvation as resurrection, renewal, and a new creation, each of which is an effective synonym for regeneration in this broad sense. He uses ἀνανεόω (renew), τὸν καινὸν ἄνθρωπον (the new man), and κτίζω (create) (Eph. 4:23–24);[21] τὸν νέον τὸν ἀνακαινούμενον (the new man, being renewed) (Col. 3:10);[22] and κτίσις (creation)[23] in parallel with renewal and combined with καινός (2 Cor. 5:17; Gal. 6:15).[24] The new creation is patterned on the old (2 Cor. 4:6), emphasizing the sovereign initiative of God. It is a new creation (2 Cor. 5:17).

In Titus 3:5, Paul says that God saved us "by the washing of regeneration [παλιγγενεσία][25] and renewal of the Holy Spirit" in contrast to works, associating regeneration and renewal with a thoroughgoing transformation. The only other occasion in the New Testament where παλιγγενεσία is used is Matthew 19:28, referring to the consummation of all things at the end of the age, cosmic in scope.

In John 3, Jesus states that being born again, or born from above, includes entering the kingdom of God. This is the work of the Spirit, beyond the ability of the flesh (John 3:5). The incident involving the rich young man (ruler) is analogous, since again Jesus insists that a radical change is needed to enter eternal life, one accomplished only by God and beyond human capacities (Matt. 19:16–22). The incident occurs just before the reference to παλιγγενεσία (Matt. 19:28). What God does to us, not what we do, secures entrance. The result is a radically new state of affairs, permanent and eternal, encompassing the entirety of the new creation.

Behind this lie the passages in Ezekiel with which Nicodemus, as a member of the Sanhedrin, should have been familiar—Ezekiel 11:19–20, 36:25–28, and 37:1ff. In Ezekiel 11 regeneration is seen as a new heart and a new spirit, but in verses 18–20 the emphasis is on the fruit of the

21 *ananeoō, ton kainon anthrōpon, ktizō.*
22 *ton neon ton anakainoumenon.*
23. *ktisis.*
24. *kainos.*
25. *palingenesia.*

divine transformation, walking in Yahweh's statutes. A radical transformation will have taken place.

In summary, New Testament usage indicates that *regeneration* can span a very broad spectrum. However, from the seventeenth century the term began to be restricted to the start of the process. Francis Turretin, whose theology was to a great measure taken over by Hodge, used the terms *conversio habitualis* (habitual conversion), the infusion of the new heart, and *conversio actualis* (actual conversion), distinguishing between the hidden work of the Spirit and our response.[26] On the other hand, over a century earlier, Calvin made the distinction between *illumination*, which he reserved for the start of the process of transformation, regarded in a mainly noetic sense—although he sometimes called this regeneration—and *regeneration*, which he used in the broader sense, the latter following faith.[27] Unless otherwise indicated, I will reserve the term for the initial stage.

23.2.2   Regeneration as Personal Transformation

Regeneration is closely connected with repentance and faith but it is distinct. It refers to what God does in us, not to what we do. It takes place within, whereas faith and repentance are outwardly oriented. It is not restricted to mental activities, although they are part of it. It is not to be equated with the Spirit's powerful accompaniment of the preached Word. It is the creative work of the Spirit renewing the whole person.

The focus of regeneration is the heart, which the Bible regards as comprising the totality of our nature. However, it extends to life in all its expressions, body and mind—hence its connection with the resurrection and the renewal of the cosmos. It contemplates the total renewal included in the total redemption of the human race. It is the beginning of that vast process. It is also as total as our depravity. Depravity affects the entire person; so does redemption and regeneration—its beginning—in-

---

26. Francis Turretin, *Institutes of Elenctic Theology*, trans. George Musgrave Giger, ed. James T. Dennison Jr. (Phillipsburg, NJ: P&R, 1992), 2:517–631; see esp. 551.

27. On John 1:13, see John Calvin, *Calvin's Commentaries: The Gospel according to St. John 1–10*, trans. T. H. L. Parker (Grand Rapids, MI: Eerdmans, 1961), 19; Calvin, *In evangelium secundum Johannem commentarius pars prior*, Ioannis Calvini opera exegetica (Geneva: Droz, 1997), 28–29: "Videtur tamen Evangelista praepostere regenerationem fide facere priorem, quum potius effectus sit fidei, ideoque posterior." Again, "we obtain regeneration by Christ's death and resurrection only if we are sanctified by the Spirit and imbued with a new and spiritual nature." John Calvin, *Institutes*, 4.15.6. On illumination, see Calvin, *Institutes*, 1.9.1–3, 2.2.20–21, 3.2.33–35, 3.24.2–3.

clude every facet of our being. Total regeneration mirrors total depravity; we are not sinlessly perfect yet, just as total depravity does not imply we were as bad as could be.

Regeneration is an act of God in which we play no part whatsoever. We had no role to play in creation. We cannot raise the dead. Therefore, we cannot make ourselves alive; regeneration precedes our response of faith and repentance.

23.2.3 *Regeneration as the Initial Stage of Personal Transformation*

James 1:18; 1 Peter 1:23. The verbs ἀποκυέω in James 1:18[28] and ἀναγεννάω in 1 Peter 1:23[29] are distinctive; neither is used by Paul or John. Do these refer to the broad or narrow senses of regeneration? This question is suggested by the mention of the Word's instrumentality in our lives. One would expect reference to the Spirit if this were intended of the start of Christian experience, while the Word is normally used of subsequent progress in sanctification. Warfield believes that it is "tolerably clear" that in contrast to the broad sense of regeneration, both passages are "of narrower connotation." Both Peter and James look back to the origins of the readers' Christian life. However, how can the Word be said to be instrumental? Warfield describes regeneration as an "act of God. . . . mediated by nothing," which "pushes itself into man's consciousness by the mediation of the word."[30] Is this a contradiction?

Here the Aristotelian distinction between efficient and instrumental causality is helpful. The efficient cause, the effective originator of regeneration, is the Spirit. In this his work is unmediated. However, the instrumental cause is the Word. The Spirit uses his Word so that the regenerated person immediately believes the content of the gospel call, revealed in the Word. Regeneration cannot be isolated from what precedes and what follows. It does not take place in abstraction from the Word. As Paul taught, "faith comes from hearing, and hearing through the word of Christ" (Rom. 10:17). Again, an invariable consequence is repentance and faith; God regenerates in order that we may believe and repent. We believe in Christ, the Son of God; faith is not empty, devoid of content. As a corollary of this, regeneration cannot be abstracted from

---

28. *apokueō.*
29. *anagennaō.*
30. Warfield, "Renewal."

the other elements of the *ordo salutis*. It is always integral to effectual calling and always produces faith and repentance.

John 3:1–8. In John 3:3 ἄνωθεν[31] means "again," although it can also mean "from above." Of more significance is γεννάω.[32] The verb has two meanings—"bear" and "beget," which distinguish the actions of the mother and the father in the reproduction of a child. It is not clear which is meant here—Nicodemus's reference to the mother is relevant—nor is it absolutely necessary to know. The same metaphor is used by John with begetting in mind (1 John 3:9). The person begotten or born is passive; regeneration occurs quite apart from any action on our part. As in John 1:12–13 ("not of bloods, nor of the will of the flesh, nor of the will of a man," my trans.), a new life comes into being. The focus is on the initiation of the new life, which enters into the kingdom of God.

In John3:3, Jesus says that without this new life, one cannot apprehend the kingdom of God, and in verse 5, one cannot enter it. Seeing and apprehending the kingdom of God, the individual enters into it. John equates the kingdom of God with eternal life. Kingdom activity for John is life, gradually unfolding and enlarged until its eschatological fulfillment.

In verse 5, the meaning of ἐξ ὕδατος καὶ πνεύματος[33] has been debated through the centuries. Are water and the Spirit to be distinguished or identified? Verse 8 speaks simply of ἐκ τοῦ πνεύματος and does not mention water. Nevertheless, in Matthew 3:11, John the Baptist is said to have baptized with water, whereas the coming One will baptize with the Holy Spirit. John 7:38–39 mentions the Holy Spirit in terms of "rivers of living water." In 1 Corinthians 12:13, drinking the Spirit is related to being baptized by one Spirit. All these bring the two together.

The idea that water refers to baptism in John 3:5 is historically the majority position. Rome regards baptism as the indispensable means of regeneration, working *ex opere operato*. In Lutheranism, baptism is the mediate cause of regeneration, the Holy Spirit the efficient cause. Unlike Rome, Lutheranism does not regard baptism as both the immediate and efficient cause, but baptism brings regeneration unless the Spirit is resisted, and it is invariably efficacious with infants, since infants cannot

---

31. *anōthen.*
32. *gennaō.*
33. *ex hydatos kai pneumatos.*

resist the Spirit. Thus, baptism is often considered the outward sign of regeneration.

Murray differs from this line of thought. He argues that baptism is not mentioned in John 3, and so, unless compelling reasons exist to see it in verse 5, we should not infer it. Moreover, baptism was not yet instituted, so Nicodemus would not have understood what Jesus meant if that was his point. He would have thought of purification and thus taken Jesus to mean that to enter the kingdom of God, it would be necessary first to purify himself, the exact opposite of what Jesus intended.[34] Again, Murray argues, the characteristic idea of baptism is as an outward sign not of regeneration but of union with Christ, which is out of place in this context.[35] Thus Murray seeks the meaning of ὕδατος elsewhere, in its Old Testament reference to purification, with which Nicodemus would have been familiar (Ex. 29:4; 30:18–21; Lev. 11:32; 15:5ff.; Deut. 23:11; Ezek. 16:4, 9; 36:25; cf. Eph. 5:26; Heb. 10:22). Regeneration has a negative side to it, Murray argues, that of purification. The positive side is indicated by πνεύματος, meaning the Holy Spirit (John 3:5–6). Since "born . . . of God" occurs at 1:13, as well as in the letters of John, the whole work is due to the Spirit, and we are simply passive. Purification and renewal are thus the two elements of regeneration in John 3, the same as in Ezekiel 36:25–26 and Titus 3:5.[36]

However, can baptism be excluded? John has already mentioned the baptism of John the Baptist (John 1:25–34)! The next chapter recounts Jesus's own disciples baptizing (John 4:1–2). Jesus refers to many things in advance of when they happen, including his death and resurrection, the existence and discipline of the church, the future destruction of the temple, his return, and the final judgment, while John 6 has a probable anticipatory account of the Eucharist. Moreover, σάρξ is used in 3:6 in contrast to πνεῦμα; the idea is that human nature is unable to transcend its sinful condition. The strong language of 3:7 points to the only transition possible as that of the new birth. This language of dramatic crisis is appropriate to a reference to baptism.[37] Finally, Jesus compares the work of the Spirit to the wind. The wind is mysterious, powerful, and

---

34. Murray, *Redemption*, 97–98.
35. John Murray, *Select Lectures in Systematic Theology*, vol. 2 of *Collected Writings of John Murray* (Edinburgh: Banner of Truth, 1977), 181, in direct opposition to WCF, 28.1.
36. Murray, *Writings*, 2:182–86.
37. Compare Paul's association of baptism with resurrection and new life (Rom. 6:1–11).

irresistible, but its results are observable. Thus, not only does regeneration bring about tangible results (faith and repentance), but as a mysterious inward work, it has an outward counterpart too (baptism).

John 1:12–13. "Not of bloods" (my trans.): why does John use the plural? The point is that regeneration does not depend on heredity, in contrast to Jewish dependence on family and tribal lines. "Nor of the will of the flesh nor of the will of man" rules out the human will as making us the children of God—not so much the will of *fallen* humanity but the will of humanity as such. This is underlined by the use not of ἄνθρωπος,[38] "man" generically, but of ἀνήρ,[39] thus the will of a human male, humanity in its most aggressive aspect. Instead, entrance into the kingdom of God is "of God" alone.

1 John 2:29; 3:9; 4:7; 5:1, 4, 18. John indicates an invariable connection between regeneration and its fruit. Regeneration cannot be isolated from the process it starts. Murray correctly opposes any idea that regeneration is separate from its effects.[40] Yet it has a logical and causal priority. This is explicit in 1 John 3:9, where John says that the regenerate one cannot continue sinning habitually. This implies a similar relationship in the other passages. Kuyper appears to have thought a person could be regenerated at one point and converted at some later date.[41] However, these passages imply, as Murray argued, that the fruit follows immediately, ruling out a temporal delay, except in the case of an infant. The absence of fruit implies no regeneration.

Ezekiel 36:25–27. The focus here is the initial cleansing and changing of the heart. The notion of obedience, realized simultaneously, is also present and inseparable.

2 Corinthians 5:14–17. We are united with Christ in his death and resurrection; in him we all die and all live. As Christ's death marked the end of his time in incarnate lowliness κατὰ σάρκα (according to the flesh),[42] his resurrection being the beginning of his glorified humanity ac-

---

38. *anthrōpos.*
39. *anēr.*
40. Murray, *Redemption,* 103–4.
41. Abraham Kuyper, *The Work of the Holy Spirit,* trans. Henri De Vries (Grand Rapids, MI: Eerdmans, 1975), 293–353.
42. *kata sarka.*

cording to the Spirit, so those united to him have died and now are raised to newness of life. So we do not consider Christ according to the flesh anymore, nor view anyone or anything from that perspective. "Therefore, if anyone is in Christ, he is a new creation" (v. 17). New creation, resurrection, regeneration—these related terms attest the newness and permanence of the reality.

23.2.4 Regeneration, Union with Christ, and Baptism

We noted the unbreakable connection between regeneration and union with Christ. We are united with Christ in his resurrection. Resurrection marked his entry into a new aspect of humanity, no longer in an environment dominated by the fall, no longer subject to the weakness and decay of that world, but instead under the direction and domination of the Holy Spirit. For us, regeneration is in principle the same as sharing in his resurrection. This is clear in 1 Peter 1:3: "According to his great mercy, he has caused us to be born again to a living hope through the resurrection of Jesus Christ from the dead." Born again through the resurrection of Jesus Christ—Peter's comment is grounded on what Paul had said, for example, in Romans 6.

Romans 6 also brings before us the connection between regeneration, union with Christ in his resurrection, and baptism. The point of transition from death to life here is baptism, something clearly visible and external, marking the point where we are identified with Christ. In denying that we should continue in sin so that grace might abound, Paul argues that we were baptized and, as such, united to Christ. Baptism places on us the responsibility to live for Christ and to turn from sin (Rom. 6:1–14; 1 Cor. 10:1–13). In baptism, we were united to Christ in his death and resurrection. Therefore, we have died and risen to new life. The old man is dead, and we are now new creatures. It will not do to separate in analytic and dualist fashion water baptism from Spirit baptism; the two go together.[43] Baptism with water is one of what Tony Lane describes as "the four spiritual doors" that are the focus of the early apostolic preaching.[44]

Protestantism has increasingly downplayed the sacraments. Many are afraid to mention baptism, since it would appear too close to the

---

43. D. Martyn Lloyd-Jones, *Romans: An Exposition of Chapter 6: The New Man* (London: Banner of Truth, 1972).

44. Anthony N. S. Lane, *Exploring Christian Doctrine* (London: SPCK, 2013), 175–84. The phrase was first proposed by David Pawson.

doctrine of Rome that baptism is the instrumental cause of justification. Others are opposed to baptismal regeneration, the idea that baptism is a cause of regeneration or that baptism should be regarded *as* regeneration.[45]

These questions should be clarified carefully. First, we are not regenerate *because* we have been baptized. A connection in which baptism were made the efficient cause of regeneration would undermine the grace of God and place the initiation of the *ordo salutis* within our own, or the church's, power. Regeneration is a sovereign action of the Spirit over which we have no control. Baptism cannot be considered the efficient cause of regeneration.

Second, nor when we are baptized does regeneration follow *automatically*. There is no invariable *temporal* sequence between the two—first baptism, then regeneration—or the idea that regeneration occurs at the moment of baptism. Here again such a connection is on a purely human level. Causality may have gone, but temporality replaces it; some creaturely connection is substituted for the sovereignty of the Spirit. In the New Testament, this temporal indifference is evident insofar as, for converts from paganism, or those like John the Baptist (who was sanctified from his mother's womb), baptism would follow regeneration. Conversely, with many infants, what may occur first is baptism, then at a later date profession of faith, regeneration probably following baptism. Since regeneration occurs secretly, we cannot know definitely what the temporal connection with baptism is in any particular instance and thus in all particular instances.

Third, instead, the connection is *theological*, to be understood in the following way. Both regeneration and baptism mark the start of the Christian life, on different levels. Regeneration begins the process in an ineffable and secret way; baptism begins the process visibly. We do not baptize because a person is regenerate, for we can never be sure about that; nor can we hold that a person is regenerate because he or she has been baptized, for reasons outlined above. Nor can we maintain that a person becomes regenerate at the moment of baptism, for again that is a matter beyond our competence. Nevertheless, on the theological level baptism and regeneration are intimately connected as the entry points to the Christian life, so that we can point, like Paul, to baptism as evidence

---

45. Lloyd-Jones, *Romans 6*, 30–37.

of belonging to Christ and thus of regeneration, with all its ensuing consequences, including responsibility to live for Christ and to turn from sin.

Fourth, in the sacraments God's action is primary. In regeneration, the Holy Spirit is the efficient cause, the Word is the instrumental cause, and baptism the accompanying cause.[46]

As the WCF states, baptism signifies, seals, and exhibits union with Christ in—among other things—regeneration, this being conferred by the Holy Spirit to the elect in God's own time (WCF, 28.1, 6). Again, the connection is not causal, automatic, or temporal but theological. If anyone is in doubt, recall the New Testament connection between baptism and the remission of sins (Acts 2:38; 22:16; Titus 3:5).

Regeneration, resurrection, and new creation are all New Testament metaphors for the start of the Christian life. Their respective meanings overlap; they are close to synonymous. Baptism is inseparably related to these. Baptism is connected to participating in the resurrection of Christ (Rom. 6:1ff.; 1 Pet. 3:19–21). Regeneration is also connected to participating in the resurrection of Christ (1 Pet. 1:3). Participation in the resurrection of Christ is a new creation (2 Cor. 5:17), entailing justification (Rom. 4:25) and sanctification (Rom. 6:1–11). In light of this connection, baptism is to be administered at the point a person is to be regarded as a Christian, whether on profession of faith, in the case of an unbaptized convert, or at birth, in the case of a child of a believing parent or parents. For this reason, it is part of the gospel call (Acts 2:38; 22:16).[47]

23.2.5 *Regeneration and Gospel Proclamation*

Regeneration is not central to the gospel message, strictly speaking. The preacher does not urge the congregation to become regenerate but calls people to faith in Christ. Regeneration is a secret work of the Spirit. Jesus stressed it to Nicodemus since he was a leading teacher of Israel, a member of the governing body, the Sanhedrin, and a sincere enquirer into Jesus's claims. He should have known the Old Testament teaching on the sovereignty of the work of the Spirit of God, which ruled out of court the idea that he could enter the kingdom of God under his own steam or

---

46. The efficient cause is what brings about the effect, the instrumental cause is the means through which this is effected, and the accompanying cause is the attendant circumstance associated with it.

47. Lane, *Christian Doctrine*, 175–84.

by virtue of his privileged status. Moreover, Nicodemus regarded Jesus as merely a great teacher, sent by God but nothing more (John 3:1–2). There are occasions when this sort of warning is needed.

In the gospel, people are asked to do something they cannot do from an ethical and Godward standpoint. But inability does not limit responsibility. The demand for faith is made in the name and in the power of the Spirit; the sovereignty of the Spirit in regeneration is the link between the demand and the response. The priority of regeneration does not provide any excuse for denying the urgency of gospel preaching or for rationalizing human unbelief.

Neither does the gospel consist in a call to prepare for regeneration or to seek it. Preparationism, the idea that there is something people can do by placing themselves in the way of the Holy Spirit by attending the ministry of the Word, is rejected by WCF, 9.3: "A natural man, being altogether averse from that good, and dead in sin, is not able, by his own strength, to convert himself, *or to prepare himself thereunto*" (italics mine). Once I heard a man tell his children they must not pray but instead ask God to regenerate them. The irony was that the proposed request was nevertheless a prayer! The need for regeneration, when preached, should not be to lead people to look inward but to drive them out of themselves to Christ.

Does one preach to a congregation as regenerate or unregenerate? Neither. We preach to a congregation as sinners in need of Christ, and as covenant members who have vast privileges and great responsibilities. The covenant of grace is one of blessing, but there is also the shadow side of judgment. None of us will outgrow this here on earth. The covenant, not the hidden work of God, gives us the perspective for preaching.

Further Reading
WCF, 28

Study Questions
1. Consider the relationship between effectual calling and regeneration.

2. In what distinct ways can we speak of regeneration?

3. Distinguish the close connection between baptism, regeneration, and cleansing from sin from the Roman Catholic doctrine of baptismal regeneration.

24

The Beginning of the Christian Life (2)

Justification

Saving faith and repentance are both necessary for salvation. They are works of God. Faith is knowledge, assent, and trust in Jesus Christ alone, while repentance involves turning from sin. They are inseparable. Justification entails a right standing with God, in which he declares us righteous, forgiving our sins and imputing or reckoning to us the righteousness of Jesus Christ. It is only by faith, since faith looks exclusively to Christ for salvation; faith contributes nothing but merely receives from God. Consequently, nothing in us contributes to justification. Nevertheless, good works, produced by the Holy Spirit, always follow our justification, in that God's grace, in vindicating us legally, also transforms us. Justification is no legal fiction; in our union with Christ, his righteousness is now ours. We are constituted righteous. The doctrine became an issue only at the Reformation. In this context, in the New Testament baptism is associated with cleansing from sin and reception of the Holy Spirit, in union with Christ in his death and resurrection. Since Christ rose for our justification, it is appropriate to consider how these gifts are given by God in baptism in God's own time to those to whom they belong. This chapter considers the theology of baptism and who should be baptized.

In connection with justification we will need to consider the nature of faith and its relationship to repentance, together with the question of why justification is only by faith. We must bear in mind that saving faith results from regeneration, which we discussed in the previous chapter. It is a gift of God and cannot be manufactured autonomously (John 6:44–45, 64–65; Eph. 2:8–9), although as creatures of God we are all responsible to repent and believe.

24.1   Saving Faith and Repentance

24.1.1   Saving Faith: Terminology

The word πίστις[1] means "trustworthiness," and in the passive sense can be translated by "faithfulness" (Gal. 5:22). It is most commonly used for the faith, reliance, or trust that we exercise—the *fides qua*—but it is also employed for the faith that is believed ("the faith")—the *fides quae*.

God's revelation calls for, and demands, a response (Acts 2:21; 16:30–31; Heb. 11:9). Faith in the biblical sense is to be contrasted with opinion. Opinion is a belief based on relatively insubstantial evidence. God does not expect us to be credulous, and our faith does not rest on flimsy foundations. We are never asked to believe where there are no reasons for it (John 20:24–31; Acts 1:1–3; 1 Pet. 3:15). The primary reason is the testimony of Scripture—there is no more infallible proof than the Word of God (2 Pet. 1:17–21). Contrary to a common misconception that faith is not assent to propositions but instead a heart relationship to Christ, there is an essential intellectual element to faith.

24.1.2   The Object of Saving Faith

Faith in the Word of God. Faith is directed to the words of Scripture, since these are the words of God. In John 2:22 faith is in the word Jesus spoke, which is on the same level as "the Scripture." Jesus says in John 5:45–47 that if the Jews had believed Moses's writings, they would have believed him; they cannot believe him if they disbelieve the Scriptures. Paul, in his own defense, claimed to believe all the writings of the Law and the Prophets (Acts 24:14–15; 26:4–7, 22–23; 28:17–20, 23). Jesus promised the apostles the Holy Spirit, who was to guide them into all

---

1. *pistis.*

truth (John 16:13). The disciples at Berea compared Paul's words to the rest of Scripture (Acts 17:11).

There is no dichotomy between faith in the Bible and faith in Christ, contrary to the claims of neoorthodox critics, who have argued that Scholasticism wormed its way into Protestant theology after the Reformation.[2] According to Jesus, if the Jews had believed the Old Testament, they would have believed him (John 5:39). It is vital to understand Jesus's relationship to the apostles. In Acts 1:8 he commissioned them to testify about him. Consequently, to receive the apostles was to receive Christ. The author of Hebrews identifies the divine witness to the Son with the Bible (Heb. 2:3–4). These, then, are not two separate faiths but one and the same (WCF, 14.2).

The Holy Spirit is the original author of Scripture, who spoke through men of his appointing (2 Tim. 3:16; 2 Pet. 1:20–21). The Spirit was sent from the Father by the ascended Christ. Thus, the Spirit's ministry is integrally connected with the ministry of Christ, the works of the Trinity being inseparable. The Bible, which the Spirit inspired, is part of Christ's ministry. Faith in the Bible and faith in Christ are fully compatible.

Faith is in God, especially his promises, and thus in Jesus Christ. Faith is of course directed to God. The first direct reference to faith is in Genesis 15:6: "[Abraham] believed the LORD, and he counted it to him as righteousness." The verb אמן (*amn*) is associated with firmness, security. God's covenant with Abraham contained promises, which seemed far from realization. Notwithstanding, Abraham was confident, for he knew who had given him the promises. His faith was buttressed by his trust in the character of God.

In the New Testament, Hebrews 11:6 refers to faith as believing that God is, and that he rewards those who trust him. The chapter has a pervasive bias toward the future fulfillment of God's promises. We believe since we know he is faithful. Verse 1 sets the stage, and the examples that follow simply underline the point.

Consequently, in faith we believe what God tells us, in anticipation of its future fulfillment. In particular, faith refers to the gospel message addressed to sinners. Whereas some seek to downplay mention of sin so

2. Jack B. Rogers, *Scripture in the Westminster Confession* (Grand Rapids, MI: Eerdmans, 1967); Jack B. Rogers and Donald K. McKim, *The Authority and Interpretation of the Bible: An Historical Approach* (San Francisco: Harper & Row, 1979).

as to avoid negativity, the Bible is emphatic. All have sinned; all need a Savior.

Notwithstanding, while conviction of sin of some sort is needed, it is not a qualification to believe in Christ. All sinners, all people, are commanded to believe—*now*—with no prior qualifications. Thus, preeminently, saving faith is directed to Christ, the one Savior of sinners (1 Tim. 1:15ff.). This is overwhelmingly clear in the Gospels and letters of the New Testament and follows the pervasive focus on the promise(s) of God's covenant back to the Abrahamic covenant (Gen. 12:1–3; 17:1–8), and even to the *protevangelium* (Gen. 3:15).

24.1.3   The Elements of Saving Faith

*Knowledge (*notitia*).* Saving faith, directed to the Word of God and its promises, and centrally to Jesus Christ, entails a certain amount of knowledge. The Christian faith entails propositions about God, the world, humanity and its predicament, Christ, and salvation. Intelligent understanding is essential. We cannot have faith in Jesus Christ if we do not know who he is. Paul makes this clear in Romans 10:9–10. Where propositional revelation is denied, we are left with blind trust.

However, while knowledge is necessary to saving faith, it is not of itself sufficient. Even the devils believe (James 2:19). Revelation is propositional, but it is more than that, just as human beings are more than information processors. We were made in the image of God for partnership with him. We are persons. Saving faith is *more* than an enrichment of knowledge, but it *is* knowledge. Evangelism must include teaching the content of the Christian faith. Jesus's parting instructions to the apostles require this (Matt. 28:18–20).

Even the dying thief had knowledge when he pleaded with Jesus to remember him in his kingdom (Luke 23:32–43). He knew that he was guilty, deserving to die, and that Jesus was innocent. He was aware that Jesus had taught about the kingdom of God and, moreover, recognized that Jesus himself was the King. He believed that the dying Jesus, condemned as a criminal, would rise from the dead, enter his kingdom, and receive sinners such as he. He trusted Jesus to receive him in his guilt and helplessness.

*Assent (*assensus*).* This involves agreement with the gospel and all its particulars. It entails conviction not only that the gospel is true but also that it applies to me personally (practical assent), in both its diagnosis of my sinful condition and its prescription for its remedy, the one Savior from sin, Jesus Christ. It is built upon knowledge, but it is distinguished from mere belief.

Trust (fiducia). The Latin corresponds to the New Testament use of πιστεύω.[3] The verb is used in a number of ways in accordance with the preposition that follows, and the context. With πιστεύω + dative, the idea is of faith in or upon something or someone, a more personal focus, faith resting upon Christ or God. With the accusative, whether πιστεύω + εἰς + accusative or πιστεύω + ἐπί + accusative, there is the notion of direction toward, resting on an object. WCF, 14.3, speaks of saving faith receiving and resting upon Christ alone for salvation. There is a commitment to the truth, above all to him who is the truth. This is the most common meaning of saving faith in the New Testament, distinguishing it from false faith and connecting it to other aspects of the Christian life; that is why, in Hebrews, faith and obedience are virtual synonyms. There is a connection, then, between cognition, conviction, and confidence.[4]

The interrelatedness of these elements. All three of these elements are present together in some degree or other. There is no chronological sequence. Some will have more intellectual faith, others more emotional, but to some extent all the elements will be present. Again, since saving faith is a gift of God and points outside ourselves to its object, Christ, it is a distinguishing mark of the grace of God, highlighting that salvation is a work of God.

The relationship between saving faith and assurance of salvation. I will examine this question in greater detail later, but for now we may note a difference of emphasis within Reformed theology. Rome denied the possibility of infallible assurance in this life. A conjectural assurance, based on good works, was all that was possible. Hence, assurance could not be part of faith. The Council of Trent anathematized any who claimed that certainty of ultimate salvation was possible in this life, outside special revelation or the pronouncement

3. *pisteuō*.
4. Robert W. A. Letham, "The Relationship between Saving Faith and Assurance of Salvation" (ThM thesis, Westminster Theological Seminary, 1976).

of the church.[5] Saving faith was essentially implicit faith in church pronouncements. Calvin and others, in contrast, held that saving faith entails assurance of salvation.[6] Later, however, many denied that assurance was of the essence of saving faith, although they recognized there to be an element of assurance present. The WCF has often been taken in this way.

24.1.4 Repentance: Biblical Terminology

The noun μετάνοια and the cognate verb μετανοέω[7] are the most common terms for repent(ance) (e.g., Matt. 3:2; 4:17; Acts 3:19; 20:21; Heb. 6:1). They denote a change of mind and will. This includes internal sorrow, but it requires more, a turning away from sin, the cause of the grief or sorrow. The popular idea that repentance is feeling sorry for your sins is inadequate. While sorrow is a necessary part of repentance, present in different ways and differing degrees from person to person, it is only part of the picture.

In Acts 26:18, Paul sees the goal of his apostolic commission as turning the Gentiles from darkness to light. Here the verb is ἐπιστρέφω (turn).[8] In Acts 26:20, μετανοέω, ἐπιστρέφω, and μετάνοια are all present. A substantive form, ἐπιστροφή, is used in Acts 15:3 in the sense of converting or turning around. In 1 Thessalonians 1:9 both ideas occur, a change of mind and also turning from sin to God. The two together, used interchangeably, denote the radical process of repentance, even though they might superficially appear to refer to differing aspects.

In addition, there is μεταμέλομαι[9] (Matt. 21:32), also used of Judas (Matt. 27:3), which refers not necessarily to actions of genuine repentance but rather to an emotional feeling of remorse that may or may not issue in repentance.

In the Old Testament the two prominent terms are שוב, "turn or change one's course of life," prominent in the prophets and frequently used for repentance from sin and turning toward God, and נחם, where the idea of grief is prominent and where God is most often the subject who repents.[10]

5. Canons 13 and 16 on justification; see Philip Schaff, *The Creeds of Christendom* (Grand Rapids, MI: Baker, 1966), 2:103.
6. Calvin, *Institutes*, 3.2.7.
7. *metanoia, metanoeō.*
8. *epistrephō.*
9. *metamelomai.*
10. *shuv, nakham.*

24.1.5   *The Meaning of* Repentance

Sorrow or remorse for sin. Though not the heart of repentance, remorse is still indispensable (Jer. 31:19; Joel 2:12–13; 2 Cor. 7:10). It is the same in both the Old Testament and the New, for both share a concern for godly sorrow that leads to a turning from sin. In Psalm 51:3–4, David confesses that his sin is contrary not only to God's law but also to his very nature. Therefore, this sorrow leads to an abandonment of the practice of and the love for sin.

Forsaking sin (Ezek. 18:30–31; 2 Cor. 7:11; 1 Thess. 1:9). Turning from sin to the living God in obedience is of the essence of repentance. The Christian tradition has held that hatred of sin is an essential element in genuine repentance. Since the gospel call is a call to turn from sin to Christ, it requires of us both faith and repentance. The two go together. Acts 20:21 and 26:17–18 bring the two into conjunction. Repentance entails turning from sin; faith is directed to Christ. They are two sides of the same coin. It is impossible to be an unrepentant believer, just as there cannot be a repentant unbeliever.

24.1.6   *The Necessity of Repentance*

Repentance is in no way meritorious, any more than is faith. The connection between baptism, repentance, and remission of sins in both John the Baptist and Christian baptism is prominent (Luke 3:3; Acts 2:38; 5:31). Superficially it might appear that remission of sins is a direct consequence of repentance and so the latter is the meritorious cause of the former. But the context shows that this is not so and that forgiveness does not depend on some action by the one forgiven, but rather results from the pure grace of God (Isa. 43:25; Jer. 31:18; Acts 5:31; 11:18). Repentance is owed to God quite apart from considerations of pardon. Sinners ought to turn from sin because sin is against God. That God forgives penitent sinners is due to his grace. Pardon is the annulment of the judicial sentence of condemnation and happens because Christ has borne the condemnation for us. Faith is abandonment of oneself and trust in Christ alone; repentance is the abandonment of sin and a turning to Christ alone for salvation.

Repentance is therefore indispensable for salvation. It cannot be isolated from faith. There is no salvation apart from faith in Jesus Christ (John 3:18), nor is there salvation apart from repentance. There is no forgiveness without repentance. Therefore, repentance is continuous and lifelong; we always need to turn from sin, just as we always have to believe.

Therefore, repentance must be preached. It should also be confessed. The confession of sins has always been an integral part of the liturgy of the historic church. Its absence in many evangelical churches is a serious concern. The prophets constantly harped on the theme. John the Baptist came with a message of repentance. Jesus began by preaching repentance. This must not be confused with preparationism, which argues that we wait for the law to do its work and only then preach repentance and the gospel promises. The law and the gospel are never isolated in Scripture, as if there needs to be some temporal separation between the preaching of the law and the preaching of the gospel.

Repentance and faith are interdependent. If we compare Acts 11:21 ("a great number who believed turned to the Lord") with Acts 20:21 ("testifying . . . of repentance toward God and of faith in our Lord Jesus Christ"), faith is prominent in the former passage, whereas repentance is prior in the latter. It might seem that priority belongs to conviction of sin, and so to repentance, which then leads to faith. In support, the fullness of law was revealed before the fullness of grace (John 1:17), and the gospel call in the Old Testament was normally couched in terms of repentance, whereas in the New Testament it is usually in terms of faith. Yet such reasoning is casuistical. The law and the prophets addressed a community already called by God's grace, and Paul stresses in Galatians 3 that the promise came before the law. In reality, the two go together. However, faith is preeminently suited to portray the grace of God in Christ, for its very nature entails abandonment of reliance on everything we ourselves do and are, so we are said to be justified by faith, not by repentance.

Union with Christ is vital to faith and repentance. Jesus fulfilled the law on our behalf. His life of faithful obedience entailed a perfect human faith, exercised, as all his actions, on our behalf and in our place. In this sense, Paul can say we are justified by the faithfulness of Christ (Gal. 2:16). Since we are united with Christ in all he has done, his perfect obedience and faithfulness, with all it entails, is ours. If a penniless young woman were to marry a billionaire, all his wealth would become hers. In union with Christ, our faith is complete, even though in ourselves it is weak and defective.

My father, dying just short of his ninety-first birthday after seventy-five years as a believer, deeply bemoaned the weakness of his faith at a crucial point in his life. I assured him that this was of no account, for our salvation resides in Christ, not in the strength of our faith. As he lapsed into his final unconsciousness, to die the next day, he repeatedly affirmed, "Our salvation is in Christ." His last words were to repeat the Book of Common Prayer's powerful expression "in sure and certain hope of the resurrection to eternal life."

24.2   Justification

The following is a brief summary of justification, the elements of which we will go on to explore. Justification refers to our legal standing with God. It is the obverse of the condemnation we were under due to sin. Justification is a forensic act; to justify means to declare righteous. The ground of justification is the righteousness of Christ imputed, or reckoned to us, *not* the righteousness of Christ imparted or infused, which is the doctrine of Rome. In this, following Augustine, Rome conflated justification and sanctification, viewing justification as involving the whole Christian life, justification being by "faith working through love" (Gal. 5:6).

Justification is only by faith. When a person believes in the sense I have described, he or she is thereby justified on the grounds of Christ and his righteousness, whatever his or her past state may have been. However, while justification is only by faith, since it depends on the work of Christ, it is a constitutive act. Those declared righteous are truly righteous (Rom. 5:19). This is not a legal fiction, since by union with Christ, his righteousness is ours too. Among the questions I will address are why justification is through faith alone, and, since repentance and good works are inseparable from saving faith, why do they have no part to play in it?

24.2.1   *The History of Debate*

Before Augustine, there was very little discussion of justification.[11] T. F. Torrance concluded that the apostolic fathers had no doctrine of grace worth speaking of.[12] However, Thomas Oden has produced a range

---

11. Oliver P. Rafferty, "Catholic Views of Justification," in *Justification: Five Views*, ed. James K. Beilby and Paul Rhodes Eddy (London: SPCK, 2012), 269.

12. Thomas F. Torrance, *The Doctrine of Grace in the Apostolic Fathers* (Edinburgh: Oliver & Boyd, 1946).

of extracts to claim that "the ancient fathers," covering the period to Charlemagne (741–814), were aware of the Pauline teaching;[13] yet the extracts stop short of establishing that there was a coherent articulated doctrine. Notwithstanding, Origen's commentary on Romans appears to teach justification by faith only.[14] Until Augustine broke with the tradition in 396 during his dispute with the Pelagian Julian of Eclanum, predestination was generally seen as based on God's foreknowledge, protecting free will, with humans taking the first step—not conducive soil for the doctrine to sprout.

Augustine. There is no entry on justification in the 952-page encyclopedia *Augustine through the Ages;*[15] it was not a matter of controversy in his time. However, that is not to say that Augustine thought it unimportant. He believed that "the salvation and justification of those predestined thereto, that is, of those whom he foreknoweth, shall continue forever," and that it is a work "which I might, without hesitation, call greater than the heavens and the earth"[16] In the background was Augustine's conviction that fallen humanity lacks the ability to do other than evil, having inherited original sin from Adam, with its concomitant guilt. Humans cannot make a free choice for good apart from God's grace.[17] While justification is a reward for merit, that merit is obtained by Christ.

God, in predestination, loved Jacob and rejected Esau. Salvation and justification depend on this sovereign choice of God, involving a fixed number of the elect that cannot be altered.[18] Thus faith is a gift of God.[19] God's grace precedes human actions and enables them. "In beginning he works in us that we may have the will, and in perfecting works with us when we have the will," and "he operates, therefore, without us, in order that we may will; but when we will, and so will that we may act, he co-operates with us. We can, however, ourselves do nothing to effect good works of piety without him either working that we may will, or co-working when we will."[20] Again:

---

13. Thomas C. Oden, *The Justification Reader* (Grand Rapids, MI: Eerdmans, 2002), 15–159.
14. Paul Rhodes Eddy, "Justification in Historical Perspective," in Beilby and Eddy, *Justification*, 17–19.
15. Allan D. Fitzgerald, ed., *Augustine through the Ages: An Encyclopedia* (Grand Rapids, MI: Eerdmans, 1999).
16. Augustine, *On John* 72.3 (NPNF¹, 7:330–31).
17. Rafferty, "Catholic Views," 269.
18. Augustine, *Predestination of the Saints* 10–11, 16 (NPNF¹, 5:503–4, 506).
19. Augustine, *Grace and Free Will* 7.17 (NPNF¹, 5:450–51).
20. Augustine, *Grace and Free Will* 17.33 (NPNF¹, 5:458).

In this matter, no doubt, we do ourselves, too, work; but we are fellow-workers with him who does the work, because his mercy anticipates us. He anticipates us, however, that we may be healed; but then he will also follow us, that being healed we may grow healthy and strong. He anticipates us that we may be called; he will follow us that we may be glorified. He anticipates us that we may lead godly lives; he will follow us that we may always live with him, because without him we can do nothing.[21]

In *The Spirit and the Letter*, discussing Romans 2:13, Augustine considered that the verb *iustificare* means "to make righteous." In this he followed the Latin translation rather than the Greek original. It had portentous consequences. "For what else does the phrase 'being justified' signify than 'being made righteous,' by him, of course, who justifies the ungodly man, that he may become a godly one instead?"[22] This shaped his understanding of justification. Against the background of fallen humans' bondage to sin, justification involves God granting the ability to do good. God operates to initiate justification, giving a will that desires to do good, and then cooperates with that will to effect good works and so bring justification to its goal.[23] It is both an act and a process of grace.

Faith without love is of no value. So, for Augustine justification embraces the entire Christian life; no proposal existed at the time to restrict it to the beginning. This would be of momentous significance for the future. "Man's personal union with the Godhead, which forms the basis of his justification, is brought about by love, and not by faith."[24] Augustine regarded justification as transformative. A justified person was made righteous; this righteousness was by grace but was also inherent, so that the justified one was really righteous.

Consequently, justification was closely connected with deification.[25] Recent scholarship has drawn attention to the latter theme in Augustine. In sermon 192 he echoes Athanasius and refers to *theōsis* in his commentary on the Psalms, considering it to be an act of God's grace by adoption, not generation, for he considered it the exact equivalent

---

21. Augustine, *Nature and Grace* 31.35 (NPNF[1], 5:133).
22. Augustine, *The Spirit and the Letter* 26.45 (NPNF[1], 5:102).
23. Alister E. McGrath, *Iustitia Dei: A History of the Christian Doctrine of Justification: The Beginnings to the Reformation* (Cambridge: Cambridge University Press, 1986), 1:27.
24. McGrath, *Iustitia Dei*, 1:30.
25. Augustine, *De Trinitate* 14.15 (NPNF[1], 3:191–2).

to adoption as sons.[26] In his sermon on Psalm 82 (81 in the original), Augustine expounds these ideas. We were born to mortality, we endure infirmity, and we look for divinity, for God wishes not only to give us life but also to deify us (*Gerimus mortalitatem, toleramus infirmitatem, exspectamus divinitatem. Vult enim Deus non solum vivificare, sed etiam deificare nos*). God made man, God was made man, and God will make us men gods. The Son of God was made the Son of Man that the sons of men might be made sons of God (*Filius Dei factus est filius hominis, ut filios hominum faceret filios Dei*). This does not mean that we undergo a change of substance, for it is a change appropriate to creatures in contrast to the Creator.[27] The "gods" in this psalm are gods not by nature but by adoption and grace. There is only one true God, who is eternal and who deifies. We worship God who makes us gods.[28]

Augustine denied that any merit attached to works done before justification, or after justification, considered in themselves apart from the grace of God. When works are viewed as the fruit of God's grace, "it is his own gifts that God crowns, not your merits. . . . If, then, your good merits are God's gifts, God does not crown your merits as your merits, but as his own gifts."[29]

James Buchanan argued that Augustine held to a doctrine at one with the forensic doctrine of Protestantism. Buchanan, not referring to textual sources, missed the point that Augustine understood justification to include the whole Christian life. He recognized that Augustine used the term *justification* in this wider sense, but he argued, on the basis of Augustine's theology of sin and grace, that he saw clearly the distinction between justification and sanctification.[30]

Undoubtedly Augustine's doctrine of sin, predestination, and grace would and should lead logically to a forensic justification grounded on the righteousness of Christ. Ellingsen draws attention to passages in Augustine's writings, in the *Enchiridion* and *De Spiritu et littera*, where he

---

26. Gerald Bonner, "Deification, Divinization," in Fitzgerald, *Augustine through the Ages*, 265–66; Bonner, "Augustine's Concept of Deification," *JTS* 37 (1986): 369–86; Bonner, "Deificare," in *Augustinus-Lexicon*, ed. C. Mayer (Basel: Schwabe, 1986), 1:265–67; David Meconi, "St. Augustine's Early Theory of Participation," *AugStud* 27 (1996): 81–98; Serge Lancel, *Saint Augustine*, trans. Antonia Nevill (London: SCM, 2002), 132, 151.

27. F. Dolbeau, "Nouveaux sermons de Saint Augustin pour la conversion des païens et des Donatistes," *RÉAug* 39, no. 1 (1993): 97.

28. Dolbeau, "Nouveaux sermons," 98.

29. Augustine, *Grace and Free Will* 6.15 (NPNF[1], 5:450).

30. James Buchanan, *The Doctrine of Justification: An Outline of Its History in the Church and of Its Exposition from Scripture* (1867; repr., Grand Rapids, MI: Baker, 1977), 88–91.

views justification as grounded on the extrinsic righteousness of Christ, but Ellingsen acknowledges that there are many passages to the contrary, and that even Oberman is forced to agree that Augustine's view of righteousness differs from Luther's.[31] Much debate has surrounded this question.[32] Certainly, evidence can be found in Augustine for a doctrine of justification akin to the later Reformation one. However, he was also prepared to think of it as encompassing the whole Christian life and did not see that this posed a major problem.[33] This is not entirely surprising, since justification was not a topic of controversy at the time; in such circumstances there can be apparently contradictory sounds from the same individual.[34]

Later, in the early Middle Ages, justification was treated in relation to the sacraments, especially penance. Unclear, often contradictory statements were common, but in general, with no real distinction between justification and sanctification, there was a growing stress on the grace of God imparted or infused.[35] This was facilitated by Jerome's Vulgate translation of *iustificare*, which effectively meant "to make righteous."

Aquinas. For Thomas, justification is "a rightness of order in people's disposition . . . when what is highest in people is subject to God and the lower powers of their souls are subject to what is highest in them, their reason."[36] It takes place in union with Christ, merited by Christ by his obedience.[37] He identifies it with salvation, for, commenting on Ephesians 2:8, he says, "To be saved is the same as to be justified,"[38] while grace is justification from sin.[39]

There are four factors in justification, Aquinas maintains. First is infusion of grace, second comes remission of guilt, third is a movement of the free will toward God, which is faith, and finally a movement of the free will against sin, which is contrition.[40] He reiterates this when

31. Mark Ellingsen, "Augustinian Origins of the Reformation Reconsidered," *SJT* 64 (2011): 13–28.
32. Eddy, "Historical Perspective," 19–21.
33. McGrath, *Iustitia Dei*, 1:47.
34. There are references to justification by faith as early as Irenaeus, *Against Heresies* 4.13 (*ANF*, 1:477). However, they are very sparse.
35. See the discussion in Rafferty, "Catholic Views," 271–78.
36. Aquinas, *ST* 1a2ae.113.1.
37. Aquinas, *ST* 3a.46.3, 3a.47.2.
38. St. Thomas Aquinas, *Commentary on Saint Paul's Epistle to the Ephesians*, trans. Matthew L. Lamb (Albany, NY: Magi, 1966), 95.
39. Aquinas, *Ephesians*, 44.
40. Aquinas, *ST* 1a2ae.113.6.

commenting on John 4:46–54.[41] These four occur simultaneously in one event, the origin and cause being the infusion of grace by God.[42] God's action comes first, in the infusion of grace. Both divine and human work together, but the priority is God's action.[43] The ultimate goal is the remission of sins.[44] This involves the nonimputation of sin.[45] It is a greater thing for God to justify the ungodly than to create the universe.[46] There is no hint that Aquinas holds to the imputation of Christ's righteousness.[47]

Following this, Aquinas maintains that faith is a gift of God.[48] However, it must be informed or expressed by love,[49] as in Augustine.[50] Aquinas states, "In justification of souls, two things occur together, namely, the remission of guilt and the newness of life through grace."[51] So justification is inclusive of all other aspects of the Christian life, including deification.[52] Aquinas has no substantive difference from Augustine.

Biel. Gabriel Biel (1420–1495) was a significant voice in the period before the Reformation. His theology had a profound influence on Luther before his evangelical breakthrough. He maintained that God had supreme authority (*potentia absoluta*), no human action being able to obligate him. However, according to the late medieval idea of covenant (*pactum*), God decides freely according to his ordained power (*potentia ordinata*) to produce the effects of justification in the life of the Christian. This happens when a person does what is in himself or herself (*facere quod in se est*) by making an initial response to God's prevenient grace.[53] The problem for Luther is that he could never be sure that he had done what was needed. Following this, the medieval view of justification envisioned a real change in the sinner, a process, cooperation with

---

41. St. Thomas Aquinas, *Commentary on the Gospel of St. John*, trans. James A. Weisheipl and Fabian R. Larcher (Albany, NY: Magi, 1980), 272–78.
42. Aquinas, *ST* 1a2ae.113.7.
43. Aquinas, *ST* 1a2ae.113.3.
44. Aquinas, *ST* 1a2ae.113.8.
45. Aquinas, *ST* 1a2ae.113.2.
46. Aquinas, *ST* 1a2ae.113.9.
47. See also the discussion in Bruce L. McCormack, "What's at Stake in the Current Debates over Justification?," in *Justification: What's at Stake in the Current Debates*, ed. Mark Husbands and Daniel J. Treier (Leicester: Apollos, 2004), 85–90.
48. Aquinas, *Ephesians*, 95–96; Aquinas, *John*, 360; St. Thomas Aquinas, *Commentary on Saint Paul's Epistle to the Galatians*, trans. Fabian R. Larcher (Albany, NY: Magi, 1966), 76.
49. Aquinas, *Galatians*, 83, 133, 156.
50. McGrath, *Iustitia Dei*, 1:29–30.
51. Aquinas, *ST* 3a.56.2.4.
52. Aquinas, *John*, 77–82.
53. Heiko Augustinus Oberman, *The Harvest of Medieval Theology: Gabriel Biel and Late Medieval Nominalism* (Grand Rapids, MI: Eerdmans, 1967).

divine grace, with actual intrinsic righteousness, from the fact that the righteousness of Christ was infused.

R. Scott Clark sums up the situation before the Reformation:

> It is impossible to understand the development of Luther's Protestant doctrine of justification without some grasp of the views he came to reject. For our purposes, it is essential that one understand that there was a broad consensus in medieval theology that one is ordinarily justified because and to the degree that one is intrinsically sanctified, whether as a necessity because of the divine nature (as in realism) or as a consequence of an apparently arbitrary divine will (as in voluntarism), whether from a strongly predestinarían standpoint (e.g., Bradwardine) or a Pelagianizing approach (e.g., Ockham). Justification was a process begun at baptism and ordinarily concluded only at the judgment. This process was described in different ways with differing degrees of emphasis on the nature and role of human cooperation, but, in virtually every pre-Reformation scheme, God is said to have taken the initiative (*gratia praeveniens*) to infuse within the sinner divine grace. By all accounts, the sinner was obligated to cooperate with that grace toward final justification. In the medieval schemes, grace begins as alien to the sinner but, for righteousness to result, it cannot remain alien but it must become proper. Peter Lombard (c. 1100–1160) represents the consensus through the twelfth century: the ground of justification was proper, intrinsic righteousness, which is the product of created grace and cooperation with that grace.[54]

As a corollary, it was impossible to attain assurance of salvation under such a system, since one's definitive standing before God was in suspense lifelong. Moreover, to claim such assurance was, in the eyes of Rome, to undermine the doctrine of salvation.

The Reformation. McGrath identifies three distinctive features that Protestants held in common, despite the differences that existed between them.[55] These are repeated and expanded by Lane with some pithy comments.[56] First, justification is forensic, involving a declaration by God as in a law court. It is an important part of salvation but does not cover

---

54. R. Scott Clark, "*Iustitia Imputata Christi*: Alien or Proper to Luther's Doctrine of Justification?," *CTQ* 70 (2006): 269–310.

55. McGrath, *Iustitia Dei*, 2:2.

56. Anthony N. S. Lane, *Justification by Faith in Catholic-Protestant Dialogue: An Evangelical Assessment* (London: T&T Clark, 2002), 17–19.

the whole of our relationship to God; if anything, adoption is of greater significance. Second, justification is clearly and pervasively distinguished from regeneration and sanctification. It refers to our legal standing, whereas the latter relate to our condition. As Lane comments, "Justification is about God's attitude to me changing; sanctification is about God changing me. . . . Justification is about Christ dying for my sins on the cross; sanctification is about Christ at work within me by the Holy Spirit changing my life."[57] Third, justification is in Christ and involves an alien righteousness. Lane explains, "For the Reformers we are accepted because of the work of Christ on the cross; for Trent it is because of the work of the Spirit in our hearts."[58]

Luther. There have been differences on the precise nature of Luther's doctrine. McGrath argues that Luther did not have a forensic doctrine of justification but remained with Augustine in seeing it as both an event and a healing process, although he held to alien righteousness, the righteousness of Christ, whom we grasp by faith.[59] McGrath claims that it was Melanchthon who introduced the forensic doctrine, although

> it is clear that his [Luther's] anthropological presuppositions dictate that justifying righteousness be conceived extrinsically, thus laying the foundations for the Melanchthonian doctrine of the imputation of the righteousness of Christ to the believer. The origins of the concept of "imputed righteousness," so characteristic of Protestant theologies of justification after the year 1530, may therefore be considered to lie with Luther.[60]

Althaus noted that Luther used *iustificare* and *iustificatio* in both senses throughout his life, for God's declaration of a sinner as righteous and also for the whole event of being made righteous.[61] Luther's tumultuous existential experiences perhaps account for his occasionally conflicting comments.

Clark, in contrast, argues that from 1513 to 1521, Luther came gradually to reject progressive justification in favor of a forensic

---

57. Lane, *Justification by Faith*, 18.
58. Lane, *Justification by Faith*, 25.
59. Alister E. McGrath, "Forerunners of the Reformation: A Critical Examination of the Evidence for Precursors of the Reformation Doctrines of Justification," *HTR* 75 (1982): 219–42, esp. 225–26; McGrath, *Iustitia Dei*, 2:10–20, 23–25.
60. McGrath, *Iustitia Dei*, 2:14.
61. Paul Althaus, *The Theology of Martin Luther*, trans. Robert C. Schultz (Philadelphia: Fortress, 1966), 226.

model.[62] Luther, he believes, moved to Augustinianism around 1513–1514 through his "Lectures on the Psalms" but did not discover an extrinsic, forensic justification. That came later, in 1518–1519 in the "Lectures on Galatians."[63] In the 1535 "Lectures on Galatians" he distinguished between active righteousness (what Christ achieved) and passive righteousness (our reception by faith in Christ), faith no longer a virtue but simply an instrument.[64] Clark concludes:

> I see no compelling reason to treat Luther's doctrine of union and his doctrine of justification as if they were mutually exclusive. Both doctrines were important to Luther's Protestant development, but they were logically distinct. . . . We are justified by virtue of our legal union with Christ, who accomplished active righteousness *pro nobis*, and, for Luther, the justified life is lived in vital union with Christ and is inconceivable apart from that union. That is not the same thing as saying, however, that sinners are justified by virtue of a theotic union with Christ. Even if it is discovered definitively that Luther did conceive of some sort of theotic union between Christ and the believer, it is clear that it never entered his doctrine of justification. For Luther, union with Christ is a consequence of the forensic, definitive act of justification.[65]

The so-called Finnish school of Luther interpretation has argued that Luther included *theōsis* as an integral part of justification. This originated with Tuomo Mannermaa's claim that, for Luther, Christ is not merely the object of faith but also its subject. Christ is present in the faith itself. He is the form of faith.[66] Moreover, God gives himself to us in his Word. "Faith means justification precisely on the basis of Christ's person being present in it as a favor and gift. *In ipsa fide Christus adest*: in faith itself Christ is present, and so the whole of salvation."[67] Here Mannermaa takes occasional comments by Luther as if they were worked out systematically and developed to the status of constituent

62. Clark, "*Iustitia*," 287–88.

63. Clark, "*Iustitia*," 292; see "Lectures on Galatians," 1519, in *LW*, 27:217–21, 241.

64. Clark, "*Iustitia*," 294–96; Mark A. Seifrid, "Paul, Luther, and Justification in Gal 2:15–21," *WTJ* 65 (2003): 215–30, esp. 223–27.

65. Clark, "*Iustitia*," 309–10.

66. Tuomo Mannermaa, "Justification and Theosis in Lutheran-Orthodox Perspective," in *Union with Christ: The New Finnish Interpretation of Luther*, ed. Carl E. Braaten and Robert W. Jenson (Grand Rapids, MI: Eerdmans, 1998), 25–41.

67. Tuomo Mannermaa, "Why Is Luther So Fascinating? Modern Finnish Luther Research," in Braaten and Jenson, *Union with Christ*, 14–15.

elements of his thought. That Luther on occasions sought to relate the forensic and transformational elements of salvation is hardly surprising. However, to elevate sporadic comments to the level of centrality, taken out of context, is at best misleading.[68] This is even more so when the source is the young Luther rather than his mature thought.[69] Ozment argued persuasively that Luther, after 1518, showed little interest in the speculations of the German mystics in union with God.[70]

Clark's comments are accurate. As early as his "Lectures on Romans" in 1515–1516, it is possible to detect in Luther a recognition of righteousness as received by imputation.[71] By the 1535 "Lectures on Galatians," he wrote that "the true way of being justified is not that you begin 'to do what lies within you,'"[72] since "a man cannot do anything but sin."[73] Rather, "faith grasps and embraces Christ," and "when he has been grasped by faith, we have righteousness and life."[74] Therefore, "the doctrine of justification is this, that we are pronounced righteous . . . solely by faith in Christ, and without works."[75] So we are justified "solely through his accounting mercy."[76] Luther explains why only faith is related to justification. "Faith alone lays hold of the promise, believes God . . . accepts what he offers. . . . Love, hope, patience are concerned with other matters. . . . They do not lay hold of the promise; they carry out the commands."[77] Consequently, one should "attribute righteousness to mercy alone, to the promise concerning Christ alone."[78] "We know that faith is never alone but brings with it love . . . but what is characteristic of faith alone should not be attributed to other virtues."[79] Luther has

---

68. For further discussion of these themes in the Finnish school, see Robert W. Jenson, "Response to Mark Seifrid, Paul Metzger, and Carl Trueman on Finnish Luther Research," *WTJ* 65 (2003): 245–50; Paul Louis Metzger, "Mystical Union with Christ: An Alternative to Blood Transfusions and Legal Fictions," *WTJ* 65 (2003): 201–13; Mark A. Seifrid, "Paul, Luther, and Justification in Gal 2:15–21," *WTJ* 65 (2003): 215–30; Carl R. Trueman, "Is the Finnish Line a New Beginning? A Critical Assessment of the Reading of Luther Offered by the Helsinki Circle," *WTJ* 65 (2003): 231–44.
69. Lowell C. Green, "Faith, Righteousness, and Justification: New Light on Their Development under Luther and Melanchthon," *SCJ* 4, no. 1 (1973): 65–86.
70. Stephen Ozment, *The Age of Reform 1250–1550* (New Haven, CT: Yale University Press, 1980), 240–41.
71. In *LW*, 25:256.
72. In *LW*, 26:173.
73. In *LW*, 26:174.
74. In *LW*, 26:177.
75. In *LW*, 26:223. See the "Lectures on Genesis 15–20," in *LW*, 3:20–21, where he says that faith is imputed for righteousness.
76. "Lectures on Genesis 15–20," in *LW*, 3:22.
77. "Lectures on Genesis 15–20," in *LW*, 3:24.
78. "Lectures on Genesis 15–20," in *LW*, 3:25.
79. "Lectures on Genesis 15–20," in *LW*, 3:25.

a direct, robust understanding of justification but without the nuances and distinctions that emerge later.

Calvin. In contrast to Luther, Calvin has a clearly articulated forensic doctrine.

> He is said to be justified in God's sight who is both reckoned righteous in God's judgment and has been accepted on account of his righteousness. . . . Now he is justified who is reckoned in the condition not of a sinner, but of a righteous man; and for that reason, he stands firm before God's judgment seat while all sinners fall.[80]

> Justified by faith is he who, excluded from the righteousness of works, grasps the righteousness of Christ through faith, and clothed in it, appears in God's sight not as a sinner but as a righteous man. Therefore, we explain justification simply as the acceptance with which God receives us into his favor as righteous men. And we say that it consists in the remission of sins and the imputation of Christ's righteousness.[81]

Calvin maintains that justification is by Christ alone.[82] It exists in union with Christ and flows from it; this for Calvin is entirely compatible with the imputation of Christ's righteousness. "As long as Christ remains outside of us, and we are separated from him, all that he has suffered and done for the salvation of the human race remains useless and of no value to us. Therefore, to share with us what he has received from the Father, he had to become ours and to dwell within us." Again, "All that he possesses is nothing to us until we grow into one body with him." We obtain this by faith. It is through the secret energy of the Spirit that we come to enjoy Christ and all his benefits. "The Holy Spirit is the bond by which Christ effectually unites us to himself."[83] Again, in an important passage, Calvin writes, "We do not . . . contemplate him outside ourselves from afar in order that his righteousness may be imputed to us but because we put on Christ and are engrafted into his body—in short, because he deigns to make us one with him."[84]

As Lane comments, faith is the instrument of justification "not because of what faith merits or *achieves* but because of what it *receives*."[85]

---

80. Calvin, *Institutes*, 3.11.2, 11.
81. Calvin, *Institutes*, 3.11.2.
82. Calvin, *Institutes*, 3.11.4.
83. Calvin, *Institutes*, 3.1.1.
84. Calvin, *Institutes*, 3.11.10.
85. Lane, *Justification by Faith*, 26.

"By faith alone" does not imply that faith is ever alone. Lane prefers "only by faith," as this highlights the instrumental role of faith without the negative impression that faith may be divorced from good works. For Calvin, we are justified *by* faith alone but not *with* faith alone, since the faith that justifies, saving faith, is not dead faith and is never devoid of works and love.[86] The crucial point is that faith justifies because it receives Christ. Love is certainly greater than faith, because it is more fruitful, but it is not appropriate to justification, in which we rely exclusively on Christ.[87]

In line with this, faith implies certainty and is often used to express confidence.[88] It is grounded on the Father's generosity: "Here, indeed, is the chief hinge on which faith turns: that we do not regard the promises of mercy that God offers as true only outside ourselves, but not at all in us; rather that we make them ours by inwardly embracing them."[89] While Calvin identifies saving faith as assurance of the Father's goodwill, he recognizes it is always tinged with doubt but denies that we ever depart from this assurance.[90] The key is Christ, "for we await salvation from him not because he appears to us afar off, but because he makes us, ingrafted into his body, participants not only in all his benefits but also in himself." So "we ought not to separate Christ from ourselves or ourselves from him," since "Christ is not outside us but dwells within us. Not only does he cleave to us by an indivisible bond of fellowship, but with a wonderful communion, day by day, he grows more and more into one body with us, until he becomes completely one with us."[91]

It follows that justification is an integral aspect of union with Christ, flowing from it, together with, although distinct from, sanctification.[92] Citing 1 Corinthians 1:30, Calvin states: "Christ justifies no one whom he does not at the same time sanctify. These benefits are joined together by an everlasting and indissoluble bond. . . . We are justified not without works yet not through works."[93] As Lane remarks, "For Calvin justifica-

---

86. Lane, *Justification by Faith*, 27.

87. Calvin, *Institutes*, 3.11.20, 3.18.8; John Calvin, *Calvin's Commentaries: The First Epistle of Paul the Apostle to the Corinthians*, trans. John W. Fraser (Grand Rapids, MI: Eerdmans, 1960), 276, 283–84.

88. Calvin, *Institutes*, 3.2.7, 15.

89. Calvin, *Institutes*, 3.2.16.

90. Calvin, *Institutes*, 3.2.17.

91. Calvin, *Institutes*, 3.2.24.

92. Calvin, *Institutes*, 3.11.6, 10.

93. Calvin, *Institutes*, 3.16.1.

tion and sanctification both follow inevitably from union with Christ. It should be noted that Calvin, unlike some of his interpreters, does not speak of justification as the cause of sanctification, nor of the latter as the fruit or the consequence of the former. Both are the fruit and consequence of union with Christ."[94]

Good works follow justification but are not its instrumental cause. We are justified not by works but not without works.[95] God accepts our works in Christ. Believers' works are justified, for "by faith alone not only we ourselves but our works as well are justified,"[96] since they are done in Christ and in faith. They are not sinlessly perfect, but God overlooks their blemishes and accepts them in Christ. Calvin was echoing Ephesians 2:10 and Revelation 14:13.[97] God leads us to our ultimate salvation by a path of good works; sequence rather than cause is meant.[98] Nevertheless, justification is through faith, not works. Why? "Because by faith we grasp Christ's righteousness."[99] Indeed, the justified are still sinners;[100] while sin no longer reigns over us, it still dwells in us.[101]

Rome

The Council of Trent. In keeping with the long-standing teaching of the Roman church, and in response to what it considered the Protestant doctrine to be, Trent maintained that "justification is not only the remission of sins, but also the sanctification and renewal of the interior man."[102] The meaning of the justification of the ungodly is

> not only remission of sins but also the sanctification and renewal of the inner man through *susceptio* of grace and gifts, from whence from being unjust one is made just and from enmity a friend, and "an heir according to the hope of eternal life" (*quae non est sola peccatorum remissio, sed et sanctificatio et renovatio interioris hominis*

---

94. Lane, *Justification by Faith*, 25.
95. Calvin, *Institutes*, 3.16.1; Lane, *Justification by Faith*, 28.
96. Calvin, *Institutes*, 3.17.10.
97. Cf. Calvin, *Institutes*, 3.15.3f., 3.17.3–10.
98. Calvin, *Institutes*, 3.14.21.
99. Calvin, *Institutes*, 3.16.1.
100. Calvin, *Institutes*, 3.3.10.
101. Calvin, *Institutes*, 3.3.11. This is contrary to Marcus Johnson, "Luther and Calvin on Union with Christ," *Fides et Historia* 39, no. 2 (2007): 59–77, who argues that in Calvin union with Christ in its transformative sense is the basis of justification, together with imputation. For the classic Reformed confessions on justification, see the Heidelberg Catechism, 59–64, in Schaff, *Creeds*, 3:326–28; WCF, 11; the Thirty-Nine Articles of the Church of England, 11, in Schaff, *Creeds*, 3:494.
102. *DS*, 1528.

*per voluntariam susceptionem gratiae et donorum, unde homo ex
iniusto fit iustus et ex inimico amicus, ut sit "heres secundum spem
vitae aeternae").*[103]

In short, justification is the sanctification and renewal of the inner man,
and entails being made just. Here again, as Lane remarks, lies the crux of
the difference with the Reformers over justification: "For the Reformers
we are accepted because of the work of Christ on the cross; for Trent it
is because of the work of the Spirit in our hearts."[104]

Moreover, according to Trent, while the final cause is the glory of God
and Christ, and the efficient cause is the mercy of God, the meritorious
cause being Christ, the instrumental cause is baptism, which is the indispensable sacrament of faith. Moreover, the formal cause is the righteousness of God, *non qua ipse iustus est, sed qua nos iustus facit* (not that by
which he himself is just, but that by which he makes us just), so that we
are renewed in the spirit of our mind and are truly just (*vere iusti*).[105] The
merits of Christ are infused, and so the righteousness in view is inherent
(*per Spiritum Sanctum caritas Dei diffunditur in cordibus eorum, qui
iustificantur, atque ipsis inhaeret*). Faith, hope, and love are all infused.[106]

Rafferty, citing Trent, points to the instrumental cause, baptism, "the
sacrament of faith, without which no one can be justified."[107] Formally,
Trent avoided the philosophical language of the medievals and was more
biblical in approach. However, materially, it opposed the idea of twofold righteousness—that in addition to the righteousness associated with
good works it is necessary to call on the mercy of God—since it saw
inherent, infused righteousness as sufficient on the day of judgment.
Accordingly, Trent proceeded to anathematize those who taught that
justification is only by faith and that faith is devoid of love, and those
who claimed infallible certainty of final salvation. It opposed what it
mistakenly thought Protestants taught, and did so mainly from writings
before 1526, believing that such teaching would undermine good works.

In reality, justification was not significant to Rome's theology, nor is
it today. Trent's decree on justification was a necessary riposte to the Lutherans but not germane to Rome's own soteriology. As Lane observes:

---

103. *DS*, 1528.
104. Lane, *Justification by Faith*, 25.
105. *DS*, 1529.
106. *DS*, 1530.
107. Rafferty, "Catholic Views," 280.

Reading it can give one a false impression of the importance of the doctrine within Roman Catholicism. The decree was needed and the doctrine received the attention that it did because of the Protestant challenge. But for the inner life of the Catholic Church the doctrine was not very important. . . . At the heart of the Christian life in Catholicism is not justification but the sacramental system.[108]

Nor, Lane continues, is the decree to be equated with Catholic doctrine. "Trent is what the Roman Catholic Church chose to say at that time in response to what it then understood the Reformers to be saying." To understand what Rome is now saying in response to what it understands Protestants to believe, we need to attend to recent documents.[109] However, for many Roman Catholics, Trent is still the authoritative voice.

The Catechism of the Catholic Church. It is noteworthy in the *Catechism* that in all major particulars there is very little substantive difference from Trent. There is a biblical presentation, the grace of God in Christ is accentuated, and justification by faith is recognized. However, the main focus is still the righteousness of Christ *infused*.[110] Justification cleanses us from our sins and communicates the righteousness of God through faith in Jesus Christ.[111] It is merited by the passion of Christ and conforms us to the righteousness of God, "who makes us inwardly just by the power of his mercy."[112] It establishes a cooperation between God's grace and human freedom.[113] The old synergism of grace and human free will is evident, as is justification as inward transformation. So, while justification derives from the grace of God,[114] it is a participation in the life of God;[115] it is still transformative. It is supernatural[116] and the source of sanctification and deification.[117]

Recent ecumenical discussions. Noteworthy among these are the discussions between Rome and the Lutheran World Ministries in 1983 and then the Joint Declaration on the Doctrine of Justification between

---

108. Lane, *Justification by Faith*, 84.
109. Lane, *Justification by Faith*, 85.
110. CCC, 1989–91.
111. CCC, 1991.
112. CCC, 1992.
113. CCC, 1993.
114. CCC, 1996.
115. CCC, 1997.
116. CCC, 1998.
117. CCC, 1999.

Rome and the Lutheran World Federation brokered in 1999.[118] Lane is positive to a point. He thinks Rome has moved and made some concessions, although not removing the main stumbling blocks that go back to the Reformation. Horton is more negative, thinking that the Lutherans made the main movement and that the classic Lutheran teaching is hardly to be seen.[119] The balance, to my mind, is closer to Horton's assessment than to Lane's. The difference between Rome and Protestantism remains. The crux in practice is that if, as Rome holds, justification embraces the entire Christian life, there can be no assurance of salvation. Rome recognizes this. Its doctrine of justification obscures and erodes the gospel.

The Westminster Confession of Faith. In the mid-seventeenth century there were twin threats to the Reformed doctrine. The antinomians, whom the Assembly considered the main danger at the time, held to justification from eternity. In the Assembly's debates, the divines in effect looked over their shoulders at the rising antinomian sentiment in London.[120] At the other end of the spectrum was Richard Baxter, who veered to neonomianism, holding that sincere obedience to the moral law is one of the conditions of the new covenant. Most of Baxter's work was written after the Assembly.[121] Mike Christ argues that Walter Marshall's important book on the doctrine of sanctification, published later in 1692, was forged against these twin threats.[122]

Consequently, the Assembly framed its statements carefully. Elsewhere I have written of its teaching:

> [It] is the result of the work of God's grace to his elect by which he powerfully and graciously draws them to Christ by the Holy Spirit. As such, justification is freely given, a work of his grace. Here, in [WCF] 11.1, is a refutation of both the Roman Catholic and Arminian doctrines. Justification does not involve the infusion

118. Lane, *Justification by Faith*, 87–221.

119. Michael Horton, "Traditional Reformed View," in Beilby and Eddy, *Justification*, 90.

120. John Eaton, *The Honey-combe of Free Justification by Christ Alone* (London: Robert Lancaster, 1642) [Wing E115]; Tobias Crisp, *Christ Alone Exalted* (London: Richard Bishop, 1643) [Wing, 2d ed., 1994; C6955]; John Saltmarsh, *Free Grace or, the Flowings of Christs Blood Freely to Sinners* (London: Giles Calvert, 1645) [Wing, 2d.ed., S484].

121. Richard Baxter, *Aphorismes of Justification, with Their Explication Annexed* (Hague: Abraham Brown, 1655), 96–102, 213–19.

122. Timothy Michael Christ, *A New Creation in Christ: A Historical-Theological Investigation into Walter Marshall's Theology of Sanctification in Union with Christ in the Context of the Seventeenth-Century Antinomian and Neonomian Controversy* (PhD diss., University of Chester, 2016).

of righteousness. Instead it consists in the remission of sins and the accounting righteous of the persons justified. This is accomplished by imputing to them the obedience and satisfaction of Christ. Thus, justification is forensic, by the imputation or accounting of Christ's righteousness, not renovative by the impartation or infusion of grace, as Rome taught. On the other hand, contrary to Arminian teaching, faith itself is not imputed, neither is any other evangelical obedience involved. This would simply be another form of the Roman Catholic doctrine, for justification would then be related to something present in the one believing, albeit the consequence of grace. This the Confession strenuously opposes since it does not depend on "anything wrought in them, or done by them." It is based on Christ alone. For their part, the justified simply receive and rest on Christ and his righteousness by faith. This faith itself is the gift of God. Faith is appropriate to justification, since it is described in WCF 14.2 as "accepting, receiving, and resting upon Christ alone for justification, sanctification, and eternal life, by virtue of the covenant of grace." Faith looks to Christ alone; it does not contemplate the works of grace or the self. It answers from the human side the exclusively gracious, objective, and forensic nature of justification in Christ and his righteousness alone.[123]

Again, its repudiation of antinomianism is evident, as I remark:

God eternally decreed to justify all the elect, and in human history Christ died for the sins of all the elect and rose from the dead for them ([WCF] 11.4). The insistent theme of the antinomians was that the crucial center of gravity of justification was the eternal decree and the historical accomplishment of Christ. To counter this position, which the divines saw would undermine the doctrine of sanctification, the section goes on to assert that the elect are not *actually* justified until the Holy Spirit applies Christ to them through faith. This means that our receiving Christ in our own life-history is the Archimedean point of justification, not the decree of God in eternity. However, the sovereign decree of God is asserted and the application of salvation to the elect maintained. The Confession will have nothing to do with antinomianism; neither will it make concessions to Arminianism.[124]

---

123. Robert Letham, *The Westminster Assembly: Reading Its Theology in Historical Context* (Phillipsburg, NJ: P&R, 2009), 269–70.
124. Letham, *Westminster Assembly*, 272.

Barth and T. F. Torrance. Moving ahead to recent times, for Torrance, "justification means justification by Christ alone."[125] This entails the imputation of the active and passive obedience of Christ, the imputation of Christ's righteousness. For Barth, there could not be the true church without justification.[126] For both, the importance of justification stems from their commitment to the centrality of Jesus Christ. Molnar argues that justification shapes every area of theology for both men.[127]

24.2.2   Biblical Teaching

Justification refers to our legal standing before God. Judicial categories relate to the question of guilt. These are far from popular today. Over the past few decades theologians have distanced themselves from the idea that God has any connection with law. Yet they have done so at the cost of discounting both the Old and New Testaments. The existence of objective moral guilt is the occasion for the plan of salvation, which is concerned with, among other things, the removal of such guilt by Christ. Murray writes that justification refers to God's declaring that we are not guilty but upright before his law.[128] Adam was just before God before the fall through the keeping of God's law, having been created upright. After the fall, the great question is how do humans become just, having lost their righteous standing? This is the question of justification.

Justification is a forensic act. The basic meaning of *justify* is "declare righteous." It has in view a definitive judgment. It does not mean "make righteous," which would produce a change of character. Justification is declaratory rather than transformative. The latter, strictly speaking, is sanctification, not justification. Rome's doctrine was influenced by the Latin *iustificare*, from the Vulgate translation. Murray points out that the language of justification is used in contexts where the idea "make just" could not possibly apply.[129] He cites Luke 7:29, which has the sense of justifying God, while Deuteronomy 25:1–3 describes a courtroom situation where the judge declares the innocent just and condemns the

---

125. Thomas F. Torrance, *Theology in Reconstruction* (Grand Rapids, MI: Eerdmans, 1965), 161.

126. Barth, CD, IV/1:523.

127. Paul D. Molnar, "The Importance of the Doctrine of Justification in the Theology of Thomas F. Torrance and of Karl Barth," *SJT* 70 (2017): 198–226, here 207.

128. John Murray, *Redemption Accomplished and Applied* (London: Banner of Truth, 1961), 119.

129. Murray, *Redemption*, 119–20.

guilty.[130] Murray also indicates that it contrasts to condemnation in Deuteronomy 25:1–3, 1 Kings 8:32, Proverbs 17:15, and Romans 5:16 and 8:33–34. As these passages refer to a *declaration* of condemnation and not to *making* someone wicked, so acquittal or justification refers to a declaration, not a transformation. Moreover, correlative expressions imply judgment (Ps. 143:2; Rom. 3:19–20; 8:33). The forensic force of the terms for justification is stressed by the synonymous expression "to impute righteousness" or "to reckon righteous" (Rom. 4:3, 5–6, 11; 2 Cor. 5:19–21).[131]

D. A. Carson, commenting on Romans 4, states, "One must conclude that in these passages, 'to justify' is a forensic term; it cannot mean 'to make (personally and ethically) righteous.'"[132] On 2 Corinthians 5:21 he writes that the nonimputation of our sins to ourselves on the ground that God made Christ to be sin for us means that it is natural to take, as parallel, Christ's righteousness as imputed to us.[133] He adds, "So why should a scholar who accepts that Paul teaches that our sins are imputed to Christ, even though no text explicitly says so, find it so strange that many Christians have held that Paul teaches that Christ's righteousness is imputed to us, even though no text explicitly says so?"[134]

Justification is grounded forensically both before and after the fall. Adam was a just man at creation due to his own moral standing, whereas after the fall we are justified due to the righteousness of Christ. In both cases legal standing is in view. However, if we follow Athanasius's teaching on creation *in Christ*, which we considered in chapter 9, the righteousness Adam possessed before the fall cannot be abstracted from Christ. Moreover, justification is more than acquittal from guilt; it entails receiving the righteousness of Christ.

In justification we are constituted righteous. Since justification is soteric, it is not only forensic and declaratory but also constitutive. The ungodly one is declared righteous and thus given a new status. What was once true of the justified person is now false. The Old Testament

---

130. John Murray, *Writings*, 2:204. The entire chapter is a dense analysis of the biblical terminology, 202–22.

131. Murray, *Select Lectures in Systematic Theology*, vol. 2 of *Collected Writings of John Murray* (Edinburgh: Banner of Truth, 1977), 204–5.

132. D. A. Carson, "The Vindication of Imputation: On Fields of Discourse and Semantic Fields," in Husbands and Treier, *Justification: What's at Stake*, 62.

133. Carson, "Vindication of Imputation," 69.

134. Carson, "Vindication of Imputation," 78.

declared it an abomination for a judge to acquit the guilty (Ex. 23:6–7; Deut. 27:19; Prov. 17:15, 26). Thus, the one declared righteous is truly righteous, or else an abomination would exist. The righteous person is not intrinsically righteous but is so because of the righteousness of Jesus Christ. Declared righteous with the imputed righteousness of Christ, one is simultaneously truly righteous. It is not a legal fiction, a "just as if," a pretense. Justification brings about the status of "righteous" without falling into the error of Rome of "making righteous." Underlying this is union with Christ; all that is Christ's is now ours. Again, it is akin to a poor woman marrying a billionaire; all his wealth is now hers due to the relation she now has to him.

On union with Christ and its relationship to justification in the New Testament, Carson writes:

> In short, although the "union with Christ" theme has often been abused, rightly handled it is a comprehensive and complex way of portraying the various ways we are identified with Christ and he with us. In its connections with justification, "union with Christ" terminology, especially when it is tied to the great redemptive event, suggests that although justification cannot be reduced to imputation, justification in Paul's thought cannot long be maintained without it.[135]

This is evident in Romans 5:19, where Paul uses καθίστημι, "constitute."[136] That this is an act of God's free grace is clear from the context, which speaks of the "free gift" of righteousness (vv. 16–17). This righteousness does not reside in something within us, even if by God's grace. Rather, it is from without, from the obedience of the second Adam. There is a contrast in this section between the connections of *sin*—condemnation, death from Adam—and of *righteousness*—justification, life from Jesus Christ, the second Adam.

This is the direct corollary of the imputation of righteousness. In Romans 4:3, 9, Paul writes of Abraham being reckoned righteous (λογίζομαι), no works being imputed. Imputation can exist without a constitutive act, as with Abraham. But, with the work of Christ and all that his obedience entails, the imputation of his righteousness simultaneously establishes as righteous those to whom his righteousness is

---

135. Carson, "Vindication of Imputation," 77.
136. *kathistēmi.*

reckoned. This is due to his perfect obedience. Thus, in Romans 3:24, justification is a gift, unearned and unmerited, while in 5:16, Paul uses δικαίωμα,[137] "righteousness," for the result of the imputation and concurrent constitution.

The basis of justification. Here the conflict with Rome comes into view. We saw that Rome holds that we are justified on the ground of the righteousness of Christ infused into us. The Council of Trent spoke of the infusion of merit driving out sin; sin can no longer be held against us since it has been driven out. However, for sins committed after baptism, fresh infusions of sacramental grace are required. Thus, there is no ordinary possibility of assurance of salvation. For all its protestations of upholding the grace of God, in reality Rome cannot but undermine it by making something in us the ground of justification rather than the perfect, finished work of Christ.

The New Testament is strong in attacking any reliance on works we may do or have done (Rom. 3:20; 4:2; 10:3–4; Gal. 2:16; 3:11; 5:4; Phil. 3:9; Titus 3:5).[138] It draws a clear antithesis between the righteousness of Christ and our own righteousness. Faith and works are in contrast in this context since faith looks to Christ, not to anything in or done by us. Certainly, the New Testament acknowledges that keeping God's law leads to justification (Rom. 2:13; 7:10; 10:5), but only Christ has done this. He obeyed the Father both in what he did and in what he suffered. Therefore, since he alone is inherently righteous, in order for us to be saved by the righteous God, Christ's righteousness must be reckoned to us and become ours. There is no other way.

Thus, positively speaking, the ground of justification is the righteousness of God in Jesus Christ. This, in relation to us, is an alien righteousness, from outside ourselves, and therefore by grace (Rom. 3:24–26; 5:15–21). It is in Christ (Acts 13:39; Rom. 8:1; Gal. 2:17; Eph. 1:7), effective through union with Christ, that all he is and has done for us becomes ours. This righteousness proceeds from his redemptive work on the cross. It is the righteousness of God (Rom. 1:17; 3:21–22; 10:3–4;

---

137. *dikaiōma.*
138. According to D. A. Carson, Jewish exegesis read Gen. 15:6 in the light of Genesis 22 to refer to Abraham being faithful. Paul in Romans is distancing himself from this pattern. Carson, "Vindication of Imputation," 56. On Rom. 4:4–5, Carson comments that Abraham in Gen. 15:6 simply believed God's promise; he didn't do anything to earn the righteousness attributed to him. Detached from Genesis 22, Abraham's faith can hardly be called a work in any sense, he concludes (59).

2 Cor. 5:21; Phil. 3:9). Not only does God provide it and accept it, but he also accomplishes it in the incarnate Christ. Paul sets it against human righteousness in part, at least, to show that it is something we have not attained or ever could attain. At the same time, it *is* a human righteousness, since it was worked out in the incarnate Christ; without his human obedience, we could never be saved. But it belongs to Jesus Christ, the Word become flesh, according to both natures, since to separate the divine and human would lead us into Nestorianism.

Second Corinthians 5:21 is vital. Christ was made sin for us although he was utterly righteous. He identified himself with us to the ultimate degree. In turn, we are righteous in him. This carries us beyond the idea of being beneficiaries of his righteousness to being identified with him. Imputation leads to constitution and so to identification. However, there are strong checks. The vocabulary of justification is pervasively forensic, not mystical. Imputed righteousness, not infused, is the key. Whatever the wonders entailed by the many modulations in justification, the tonic major is the gratuitous work of Christ on our behalf, his righteousness freely imputed. To that we must always return.

Faith and justification. Justification presupposes faith. Key is Genesis 15:6, which lies at the background of Galatians 2:16. When God justifies the ungodly (Rom. 4:5), it is the ungodly who believe. We believe in Jesus with the result that we are justified.

Vitally, faith is not the ground of justification. We are not justified because we believe. Faith does not achieve justification; Jesus Christ is its sole ground. In Romans 4 the stress is on its gratuitous nature. Paul's appeal to Genesis 15:6 establishes that justification is entirely by grace and therefore through faith. Faith is simply the vehicle by which we receive Christ. Justification is therefore *per fidem* (through faith), not *propter fidem* (because of faith). In Romans 10:9–10, the connection between faith and justification is analogous to that between confession and salvation. We are saved not on the grounds of our confession but through our confession.

In short, faith is the instrument for our appropriation of the righteousness of Christ. Faith is the *instrumental cause*, not—as Rome teaches—the sole *formal cause* (an infused grace, formed by love). Thus, faith is not only appropriate to justification, since we abandon ourselves to Christ, but also necessary (Rom. 4:23–24; 11:6), so that the promise would be by grace, not of works.

Justification and good works. Works of unbelievers cannot earn justification. On this, from different angles, Augustine, Aquinas, and Calvin agreed. Augustine attributed it to unbelievers' lack of love, Calvin to their lack of faith, and Aquinas to their inability to perform supernatural good.[139] However, good works became a central bone of contention at the Reformation. Having conflated justification and sanctification, Rome accused Protestants of undermining sound moral living by the teaching of justification by faith alone. This was why Calvin dealt with sanctification before justification in the 1559 *Institutes*. Paul deals with a similar objection in Romans 6. His teaching on justification supports the Reformers in their later conflict, for he considered it necessary to rebut accusations of precisely the same kind.

It is impossible to separate faith from good works. We saw that faith and repentance are two sides of the same coin, occurring simultaneously. Moreover, good works are the fruit of faith, following from the presence of the Holy Spirit. This connection is clear in Ephesians 2:8–10. There Paul says we are saved by grace through faith, not by works (vv. 8–9), yet this is precisely *for* good works (v. 10). In light of this connection, some have argued that good works, together with faith, are the instrument of justification. For this it is claimed that there is only one reference to God justifying the ungodly, while the Old Testament speaks repeatedly of his justifying the righteous. Moreover, since justification entails faith, while faith is inseparable from repentance, and since repentance is a good work, therefore good works are, together with faith, said to be the instrumental cause of justification.

This is hardly distinguishable from the position of Rome. The whole point is that justification is by Christ. In one sense, we *are* justified by works—Christ's works. From another angle, we are justified by faith—Christ's faith (or better faithfulness) again exercised for us, in our place and on our behalf. Galatians 2:16 and other places may well support this. Whatever the case, we are justified entirely on the basis of what Christ has done. Therefore, it is by grace, not works. Faith is "the alone instrument" of justification because it relies exclusively on Christ. While

---

139. Lane, *Justification by Faith*, 30–31.

good works, to be good, must be done in faith, nevertheless they are done by us and are the fruit of faith. To bring them into the equation here is to confuse and undermine the gratuitous nature of justification. Justification and sanctification are not separate—here Rome is correct. But neither are they merged—here Rome is wrong.

Justification and forgiveness. It is clear that justification includes the forgiveness of sins. However, it is more—it is reception of the imputed righteousness of Christ and constitution as righteous (WCF, 11.1).

Justification does not merely mean "just as if I had never sinned"; that is a half-truth. In fact, modern English usage has also eroded the meaning of forgiveness. At stake are three intertwined elements. First, the penalty of sin is death and all it entails, including condemnation. Christ has removed the penalty by his death and resurrection (Rom. 4:25). "There is therefore now no condemnation for those who are in Christ Jesus" (Rom. 8:1). Second, behind the penalty is the guilt incurred by sin, owing to our actual sins and the sin of Adam. By his atonement, Christ has deleted entirely the guilt we incurred by bearing it himself. Third, this guilt rests on the existence of sin which, as a juridical factor, has been buried in the depths of the sea (Mic. 7:19).

When someone asks for our forgiveness, we often have a real tussle to follow through, particularly if the offense is serious. As C. S. Lewis pointed out, echoing Christ, we may have to forgive our brother seventy times seven for the same offense.[140] In practice, forgiveness (in a legal sense) now usually refers to *consequences* resulting from an offense rather than the offense itself. Other words have similar limitations. The term *pardon* in contemporary law relates to the termination, in whole or in part, of a sentence, actual or putative. President Gerald Ford pardoned ex-president Richard Nixon for his alleged crimes in the Watergate scandal, even though he had not been charged, let alone convicted. Pardon presupposes the continued existence of guilt and thus of criminal activity that creates that guilt. It is the eradication of a sentence, not the removal of a crime or its resulting guilt. The same situation surrounds the word *remission*. Normally, in law remission refers to the curtailment of a penalty and implies the continued existence of guilt and thus the reality of an objective offense.

---

140. C. S. Lewis, *Reflections on the Psalms* (London: Geoffrey Bles, 1958), 24–25.

One word that sums up better what is meant in biblical terms is the word *absolution*. It includes all that the other terms state but also refers to the removal of guilt (*absolvere*). Unfortunately, many evangelicals fear this word, supposing it to be redolent of Roman Catholicism. Too bad. The pronouncement of the absolution of sins was a standard part of classic Reformed liturgies.

Crucial biblical passages point to the stupendous reality that in the sight of God the sins of the justified are utterly removed, as if they had never been. Not only is the penalty of sin remitted, the guilt of sin absolved, but sin itself has been definitively removed (Ps. 103:11–12, from the ritual of the Day of Atonement, Lev. 16:5–10, 15–22; also Isa. 44:21–22; Mic. 7:18–19). The pastoral implications are immense.[141]

24.2.3 Two Questions

James and justification by works. The connection between justification only by faith and James's teaching that we are justified by works has been debated at length (James 2:14–26). James discusses the works of faith, whereas Paul opposes the works of the law; the one deals with good works, the fruit of faith, and the other with the exclusion of our human action in the justifying verdict of God. That James writes of something different than Paul is seen in James's reference to Abraham offering Isaac in Genesis 22, whereas Paul refers to Abraham's faith in Genesis 15. Abraham's action was the fruit of Abraham's faith; James undermines the idea that faith can be devoid of works.

Alexander Stewart refers to comments by Schreiner and Caneday that "for many evangelicals, salvation is punctiform. . . . They conceive of salvation as a point, not a continuum that includes beginning, process and consummation."[142] Many miss the fact that salvation is not only past but also present and future, that this life is integral to salvation, and that good works, while not meriting salvation, are the way God brings us to it. This is James's point, viewing as he does salvation as incomplete until the last day. This is what, in common with Protestant theology, Turretin

---

141. This monumental forgiveness in justification does not obviate the need to seek forgiveness for sins on a daily basis (1 John 1:7–9; WCF, 11.1, 4).

142. Alexander Stewart, "James, Soteriology, and Synergism," *TynBul* 61 (2010): 293–310.

stated when he denied that works are included in justification but affirmed that they are essential to salvation.[143]

The "New Perspective on Paul." The "new perspective on Paul" (NPP) was a term coined by N. T. Wright in his Tyndale Lecture in 1978: "I want now to contribute to it by offering a new way of looking at Paul which provides, I believe, not only an advance in the debate between [Krister] Stendahl and [Ernst] Käsemann but also a new perspective on other related Pauline problems."[144] The phrase was given its settled form by James Dunn in 1982. It is something of a misnomer since it is used for a variety of different, although related, proposals about Paul. Moreover, it is no longer new.

Dunn lists four aspects that, amidst the differences, are held in common by its various advocates. First, the NPP arises from a new perspective on Judaism. Second, Paul's Gentile mission is the context for his teaching on justification. Third, the NPP's focus is on why justification is by faith in Christ and not by works of the law. Fourth, the whole gospel of Paul must be taken into account.[145]

Dunn's first aspect is important. He remarks, "It turns out that what actually unites advocates of the new perspective is not so much a single 'perspective' on Paul (here significant diversity emerges), but rather a broadly shared perspective on first-century Judaism."[146] Behind this was an influential article by Stendahl, raising questions over the way Paul had been interpreted in the Western church.[147] It argued that the Reformers and subsequent scholarship were governed by individualistic, introspective presuppositions alien to the world of the first century. This argument

---

143. Francis Turretin, *Institutes of Elenctic Theology*, trans. George Musgrave Giger, ed. James T. Dennison Jr. (Phillipsburg, NJ: P&R, 1992), 2:702–5. The New Testament consistently stresses the necessity of works, not for initial justification but for final salvation, such as in Matt. 25:31–46; Rom. 2:6–10; Gal. 5:19–21; 6:7–8; Eph. 5:5–10; Phil. 2:12–13; Heb. 12:14; 2 Pet. 1:10–11; 1 John 3:1–10; Rev. 2:10–11. The distinction between justification and salvation is important to grasp. Russell Shedd notes: "the claim that justification can be genuine without the confirmation of sanctification is a dangerous deception." Shedd, "Justification and Personal Christian Living," in *Right with God: Justification in the Bible and the World*, ed. D. A. Carson (Carlisle: Paternoster, 1992), 176. See also Richard Bauckham, *James: Wisdom of James, Disciple of Jesus the Sage* (London: Routledge, 1999): 165.

144. N. T. Wright, "The Paul of History and the Apostle of Faith: The Tyndale New Testament Lecture, 1978," *TynBul* 29 (1978): 65.

145. James D. G. Dunn, "New Perspective View," in Beilby and Eddy, *Justification*, 177.

146. Paul Rhodes Eddy and James K. Beilby, "Justification in Contemporary Debate," in Beilby and Eddy, *Justification*, 57.

147. Krister Stendahl, "The Apostle Paul and the Introspective Conscience of the West," *HTR* 56 (1963): 199–215.

was not entirely new with Stendahl, but his article crystallized ideas germinated over several decades.

E. P. Sanders[148] brought about a revolution in Pauline studies, "a new perspective on ancient Judaism."[149] He argued, contrary to what he took to be a common belief, that there was no recognizable group in first-century Judaism that attempted to earn justification on the basis of their own works. Rather the overall consensus was that membership of God's covenant was due to the grace of God. Once one was a member of the covenant, obedience was necessary to remain within it.[150] Sanders's research was facilitated by the discovery of the Dead Sea Scrolls. He argued that the Jews had a positive understanding of the law, seeing it as a blessing. He called this "covenantal nomism." Consequently, interpretations of Paul that posited his opposing a theology of justification by works were considered misplaced. The issue was that Paul's opponents did not accept that Jesus is the Messiah.

According to Dunn, Paul's discussion in Romans related mainly to the law as a boundary marker of the covenant in Jewish eyes, particularly aspects such as circumcision and the Sabbath. Since Paul raises the question of justification in Romans and Galatians but not elsewhere, Dunn argues that it has to be seen in those contexts that relate to the Gentile mission. The admission of the Gentiles to the covenant was a huge surprise that took repetitive visions and firsthand experience of the descent of the Spirit for Peter to acknowledge. It was uniformly accepted that Gentile proselytes were to be welcomed into the commonwealth of Israel. Following this, some Jewish members of the churches in Galatia and Rome insisted that Gentile converts adhere to the full Jewish law, especially "boundary markers" such as circumcision, the Sabbath, and the laws of clean and unclean. Paul rejected this outright and states that the Gentiles were in the right by faith in Christ and were not to observe the distinctively Jewish customs. The expression in Paul's writings "the works of the law" is a general phrase "which refers to the principle of keeping the law in all its requirements," whereas "'the truth of the gospel' that Paul insisted on in both situations (Gal. 2:5, 14) was that the gospel is free to all who believe without taking on any further obligation, as a gospel requirement, and

---

148. E. P. Sanders, *Paul and Palestinian Judaism: A Comparison of Patterns of Religion* (Philadelphia: Fortress, 1977).
149. Eddy and Beilby, "Contemporary Debate," 57.
150. Sanders, *Paul*, 75, 420, 482, 484, 543, 552.

'work of the law' that implied that the gospel was not free to Gentiles as Gentiles."[151] Dunn insists that his position is compatible with classic Protestant teaching and that he has not been out to oppose it.[152] The focus on the corporate, covenantal context is welcome.

The movement, such as it was, came to the attention of evangelicalism largely through the work of N. T. Wright. Wright's claims relate closely to justification. He argues that justification is not about soteriology so much as ecclesiology. It points not to how a person enters the favor of God and his covenant but rather to who is a member of the covenant, not to one's initial entry but to his or her continuing status. Moreover, justification has no bearing on righteousness or justice.

A major methodological feature of the movement is its reliance on the literature of Second Temple Judaism as a grid with which to interpret Paul. This, it is argued, rather than the Old Testament, provides the lens that clarifies his thought. Consequently, in considering what Paul says on justification, it is necessary to examine rabbinical and other Jewish texts. This approach assumes that the New Testament documents are simply a limited example of a wide range of historical evidence. Of course, any historical document—biblical ones included—needs to be seen in its historical context. However, to assume that the canonical Scriptures are on the same level as the writings of this or that intertestamental Jew, whether a leading rabbi or an exponent of a radical sect, is to reject the church's historic recognition of the biblical canon.

Moreover, it also ignores the evidence of the New Testament texts themselves. All the New Testament writers cite the canonical Old Testament Scriptures repeatedly, with the prefixed signs ὅτι, γέγραπται, or λέγει. There are a handful of explicit noncanonical citations. Paul quotes the Greek poets Aratus (Acts 17:28), Epimenides (Acts 17:28; Titus 1:12), and Menander (1 Cor. 15:32–33), while Jude refers to the apocryphal book of Enoch (Jude 14–15). Why should the New Testament be interpreted in the light of texts it largely ignores?

Holland writes, in relation to Second Temple Judaism:

> To suggest that these communities and their documents are the key to understanding the teaching of the apostles would be seriously off target. Many of these groups were openly opposed to the early church and its

---

151. Dunn, "New Perspective View," 194.
152. Dunn, "New Perspective View."

message of Jesus; can they really be reliable witnesses of the apostles' teaching? . . . When the apostles, who claimed to speak for Christ, taught the fledgling congregations, would they integrate the teachings of other religious groups into their writings . . . the writings of groups they had denounced as heretics and enemies of the gospel of Christ? . . . Of course, such a suggestion assumes that they knew of the writings' existence in the first place—and the evidence for this is far from established.[153]

Behind all this is the immensely variegated nature of Second Temple Judaism. According to Charlesworth and Evans, there were "many divergent groups."[154] The designation Second Temple Judaism itself is about as useful as *twentieth-century Americanism.* Get two or three Americans together from various times within the previous century, and there will doubtless be at least four or five opinions! So it is with intertestamental Judaism. The New Testament itself witnesses to a wide range of groups, while others, such as the Essenes, do not even get a mention. Furthermore, the identity and origin of much, if not most, of this literature is unknown. Charlesworth points to the discovery of the Dead Sea Scrolls leading to the abandonment of R. H. Charles's claim of a "normative Judaism" shaped by the ruling orthodoxy in Jerusalem. He writes, "Because of the variegated, even contradictory nature of the ideas contained in post-exilic Judaism, it is obvious that Judaism was not monolithically structured or shaped by a central and all-powerful 'orthodoxy.'" Indeed, "we cannot identify with certainty any author of a pseudepigraphon as being a Pharisee or an Essene, or a member of another sect."[155] It would seem difficult to construct an accurate and coherent new perspective on Judaism in the wake of such diversity, let alone command attention sufficient to sustain a rewriting of the doctrine of justification.

24.3 Baptism[156]

For a number of reasons, it is appropriate to bring baptism into the equation at this point. The New Testament presents baptism as one

153. Tom Holland, *Tom Wright and the Search for Truth* (London: Apiary, 2017), 171–72.
154. James H. Charlesworth and Craig A. Evans, eds. *The Pseudepigrapha and Early Biblical Interpretation* (Sheffield: Sheffield Academic, 1993), 40.
155. James H. Charlesworth, ed., *The Old Testament Pseudepigrapha* (New York: Doubleday, 1983), 2:xxix. See also the 2015 printing (Peabody, MA: Hendrickson). I thank Tom Holland for directing me to the work of Charlesworth.
156. This is a greatly condensed version of my book *A Christian's Pocket Guide to Baptism* (Fearn: Christian Focus, 2012).

of the points of entry into salvation, together with repentance, faith, and the reception of the Holy Spirit; these all feature in the evangelistic sermons in Acts. Throughout the New Testament Epistles there are allusions to baptism in this connection. Moreover, Rome makes baptism the instrumental cause of justification; while this has had unfortunate consequences, it alerts us to the need to provide some coherent answer. We saw in the previous chapter the close connections between regeneration, union with Christ, and baptism, connections often missed in evangelical and much recent Reformed thought. The Western world has been prone to thinking in analytical categories, breaking realities down into component parts, with distinctions to the forefront rather than connections. There is a need to repair this imbalance in our present context. I referred to this in the introduction.

24.3.1   The Necessity of Baptism

Baptism is essential to the church's ministry. Jesus instituted it and required it as primary (Matt. 28:18–20). The way the church is to make the nations disciples is first by baptizing them. This occurred at Pentecost only a few days later (Acts 2:37–41). There, Peter linked baptism to the gift of the Spirit and cleansing from sin (1 Pet. 3:21). Paul also connects baptism with cleansing from sin (Acts 22:16) and elsewhere mentions baptism in the same breath as membership of the body of Christ and the gift of the Spirit (1 Cor. 12:13). It is the entry point into the church and so marks, in its way, the entrance to salvation.

24.3.2   Baptism Involves Washing with Water

In baptism, water is used. The verb βαπτίζω has the main meaning of "dip," but it can also mean "sprinkle." However, there is another verb, ῥαντίζω,[157] that means "sprinkle," so the choice of βαπτίζω may intentionally denote dipping or immersion. The Greek church, which knows a thing or two about its own language, has always practiced immersion.[158] As for Rome, the *Catechism of the Catholic Church* states that "baptism is performed in the most expressive way by triple immersion in the baptismal water. However, from ancient times it has also been able to be

---

157. *hrantizō.*
158. Timothy Ware, *The Orthodox Church* (London: Penguin, 1969), 283–84.

conferred by pouring the water three times over the candidate's head."[159] The 1552 *Boke of Common Prayer and Administracion of the Sacramentes, and Other Rites and Ceremonies in the Churche of England* specified that "the Priest shal take the childe in his handes, and . . . shal dippe it in the water, so it be discretely and warely done." However, "yf the child be weke, it shall suffyce to power water upon it."[160] After an extensive debate, the Westminster Assembly agreed, by a narrow margin, on the lawfulness of dipping, while holding that sprinkling or pouring was the most appropriate mode.[161] Almost all credobaptists practice immersion, but the practice is much older than their churches. Indeed, in the early stages of the Reformation, the Reformers were inclined to favor immersion.[162] However, apart from the Orthodox and many credobaptists, there is general agreement that the mode of baptism is not the most important thing and that baptism can be administered by sprinkling, pouring, or immersion. In terms of its visual and symbolic character, each of these portrays a particular aspect, whether cleansing from sin or union with Christ in death and resurrection.

24.3.3 The Baptism of Christ

All this is grounded in the baptism of Christ. Jesus's baptism at the hands of John the Baptist was a precursor of his death on the cross to fulfill all righteousness (Matt. 3:13–17). Later he spoke of his impending baptism, referring to the cross (Luke 12:50). Jesus's death was a once-for-all event. It secured our salvation. Thus, his baptism was unrepeatable, unique. Indeed, the unusual word βάπτισμα is used for it.

So, in baptism the Spirit baptizes us into union with Christ in his death and resurrection (Rom. 6:1ff.; 1 Cor. 12:13; Col. 2:12–13), giving us to share in the one βάπτισμα of Christ for sins upon the cross.[163] A

---

159. CCC, 1240.

160. Church of England, *The First and Second Prayer Books of Edward VI* (London: Dent, 1968), 398.

161. Letham, *Westminster Assembly*, 339–43. Three votes were taken: 25–24 in support of immersion as a valid mode, then 25–24 against it, and finally 25–24 in favor. Evidently, there was a floating voter.

162. Robert Letham, "Baptism in the Writings of the Reformers," *SBET* 7 (1989): 21–44; Hughes Oliphant Old, *The Shaping of the Reformed Baptismal Rite in the Sixteenth Century* (Grand Rapids, MI: Eerdmans, 1992), 264–82; Joseph C. McLelland, *The Visible Words of God: An Exposition of the Sacramental Theology of Peter Martyr Vermigli 1500–62* (Edinburgh: Oliver and Boyd, 1957), 140; Martin Bucer, *In epistolam D. Pauli ad Romanos* (1536; repr., Basel, 1562), 321; Calvin, *Institutes*, 4.15.19; Pietro Martire Vermigli, *In epistolam S. Pauli apostoli ad Romanos commentarii doctissimi* (Basel: Petrum Pernam, 1558), 199.

163. Thomas F. Torrance, *Theology in Reconciliation* (Grand Rapids, MI: Eerdmans, 1975), 82–105.

corollary is that baptism is into the triune name (Matt. 28:19). Baptism belongs to the holy Trinity. This makes Trinitarian baptism (whether administered by Protestant, Roman Catholic, or Orthodox) Christian baptism. It rules out of court rites administered by sects such as the Jehovah's Witnesses.

24.3.4 Baptism and Biblical Interpretation

Our reading of Scripture is often governed by unconscious principles that influence what we can see. Moreover, many things in the Bible are hard to understand (2 Pet. 3:16). We cannot appreciate either the Old Testament or the New aright in isolation. Jesus's own method of biblical interpretation was to see all parts of Scripture—the Old Testament as we now have it—as referring ultimately to himself (Luke 24:25–27, 44–47). To grasp the meaning of the New Testament, we must have a hold of the Old Testament. With baptism, we need a canonical perspective, taking into view the whole Bible. Baptism is a covenant sign of the New Testament, but its meaning and significance cannot be established from the New Testament alone. It must be understood in connection with the history and fulfillment of the covenant with which it is connected.

24.3.5 The Meaning of Baptism

Baptism and cleansing from sin. Baptism is a washing. Water cleanses. Since the sacraments are signs appropriately related to the reality they signify, baptism is the washing away of sin. Ananias told Paul to "rise and be baptized and wash away your sins, calling on his name" (Acts 22:16), an allusion to baptism in the name of the Father, the Son, and the Holy Spirit. "Calling upon the name of the Lord" is often used for an act of worship.

Paul refers to baptism as washing. Christ cleanses the church by the washing of water with the Word (Eph. 5:26), the ministry of the Word and the sacrament being the means by which the church is purified and cleansed. He refers to the kindness of God in saving us "by the washing of regeneration and renewal of the Holy Spirit" (Titus 3:5), understood through the ages as referring to the Spirit working in and through our baptism.[164] Baptism is the washing common to all the church and would

---

164. "*Washing (loutron)* is almost certainly a reference to water baptism. All the early church fathers took it this way." John Stott, *The Message of 1 Timothy and Titus: The Life of the Local Church* (Leicester: Inter-Varsity Press, 1996), 204. In footnote 20, Stott points to 1 Cor. 6:11 and Eph. 5:26 in support. See also Calvin's comment: "I have no doubt that there is at least an allu-

readily have been understood to be in view.[165] In 1 Corinthians 6:11, Paul addresses those who became Christian from a dissolute background, laden with a range of major sins. He says, "But you were washed, you were sanctified, you were justified in the name of the Lord Jesus Christ and by the Spirit of our God." Paul was accustomed to using the word *theos* (God) for the Father. From this it follows that he refers to a washing in the name of the Trinity, with all three persons indivisibly active. The Corinthians were washed in the name of the Lord Jesus and in the Spirit of our Father—the baptismal reference is clear-cut. This cleansing he connects with their being transferred from the kingdom of darkness to the body of Christ—sanctification in its primary, spatial meaning—and their being declared righteous in union with Christ. We have echoes of this in Jesus's own comments to Nicodemus stressing the necessity for him to be born "of water and the Spirit" in order to enter the kingdom of God (John 3:5). Baptism is the entry point, the place at which a decisive transfer occurs from sin to faith, from being in Adam to being in Christ, for it is the moment when discipleship begins, in accordance with Jesus's last words to his apostles.

Baptism and reception of the Holy Spirit. From the connection between baptism and cleansing it follows that a relationship exists between baptism and our receiving the Holy Spirit, for the Spirit grants us faith and repentance, and so brings about our cleansing from sin through the atoning death of Christ. Indeed, this connection is explicit in the New Testament. At Pentecost, Peter announced that his hearers must repent and be baptized "for the forgiveness of your sins," adding, "and you will receive the gift of the Holy Spirit" (Acts 2:37–39)—repentance and baptism, on the one hand; forgiveness of sins and the Holy Spirit, on the other.

Some might balk at the inclusion of baptism in this command. However, the material and spiritual, while distinct realms, are inseparable. God conveys his grace through material means. Evidently baptism is more than a mere symbol of something detached from it. There is a certain instrumentality to it. Peter points beyond human action to divine

---

sion here to baptism and, I have no objection to the explanation of the whole passage in terms of baptism." Calvin, *Second Corinthians*, 382. I am indebted to the Rev. Todd Matocha for directing me to these references.

165. Titus 3:5 was one of the most frequently cited texts in the Westminster Assembly's extensive debates on baptism.

grace. Our faith and repentance cannot secure or earn our salvation or gain us the gift of the Spirit, and neither can baptism. These are the means through which the grace of God operates, much like Naaman dipping in the despised river Jordan for cleansing (2 Kings 5:1–14). Behind this is the baptism of Jesus, which foreshadowed his greater baptism on the cross (Matt. 3:13–15; Luke 12:49–50). Immediately, as Jesus came out of the water, heaven was "opened," the Spirit descended and rested on him in the form of a dove, and the voice of the Father publicly declared him to be his beloved Son. The connection between baptism and the Spirit could hardly be clearer.

No consistent temporal pattern emerges between baptism and the reception of the Spirit. In Acts, Peter implies that the gift of the Spirit will follow repentance and baptism. Paul's filling with the Spirit and his baptism take place at the same time, through Ananias's laying on of hands (Acts 9:17–18). With Cornelius and his guests, the Spirit descends on them while they listen to Peter's message, whereupon Peter commands them to be baptized (Acts 10:34–48). While there is no fixed temporal order, the Spirit baptizes *us all* into the one body of Christ; the Spirit, baptism, and union with Christ are all parts of a complex of connections, whether viewed in redemptive-historical terms as a once-for-all happening or in its outworking (1 Cor. 12:13).

Baptism, union with Christ, and salvation. First Peter 3:21 states that "baptism . . . saves you." This statement has been used to justify the idea that the sacraments work grace by the fact of their being performed, so that baptism is necessary for salvation. It has also been evaded as uncomfortable or explained as pure symbolism. Neither alternative is satisfactory. What does the context tell us about Peter's intention?

Peter is writing to churches enduring persecution (1 Pet. 3:14–17). He compares their situation with Noah's isolation while building the ark, implicitly condemning his contemporaries and no doubt receiving ridicule and abuse (v. 20). Above all, Peter points his readers to Christ, who suffered "the righteous for the unrighteous" (v. 18). In both cases, Noah and Christ were vindicated—Noah by the ark, in which he was rescued from the flood, Christ in his resurrection. In verses 19–21, Peter makes a parenthetical digression. His chain of thought, broken off at the end of verse 18, is not resumed until verse 22; it runs like this: "[Christ was] put to death in the flesh but made alive in the Spirit [in his resurrection] . . . who has gone into heaven and is at the right hand of God." This was Christ's triumphant vindication by the Father; it is intended to buttress the faith of the struggling churches. The digression in verses 19–21—one of the most difficult passages in the Bible—refers to Christ's actions in his resurrection when he was "made alive in the Spirit"; he proclaimed condemnation to the fallen angels, particularly those that worked behind the scenes in Noah's time. Noah was saved through the ark, Peter says, whereas Peter's readers are saved through baptism. In both instances God graciously saves, but he saves through means. In the case of baptism, Peter makes clear that "baptism . . . now saves you . . . through the resurrection of Jesus Christ."[166]

In short, God's salvation for his church is achieved by Christ in his resurrection. Peter's view of union with Christ is remarkably close to Paul's. He has already stated that we have been "born again to a living hope through the resurrection of Jesus Christ" (1 Pet. 1:3). Christ was raised from the dead; we share in that resurrection, as a rebirth. We do so since we are united to him. He was brought into new, transcendent life, and in union with him, so were we. Consequently, Peter affirms that we share in the vindication of Christ, in his resurrection. Christ's death and resurrection are his baptism,[167] which saves us by virtue of our union with him, our being incorporated into Christ. To that great reality baptism itself is inseparably fused. The connection with water is obvious in 3:19–21; the ark saved Noah, and he was vindicated in the waters, as the persecuted churches to which Peter wrote are saved by the resurrection of Christ in and through baptismal waters. As with the relationship between the tree of life and eternal life in Genesis and Revelation, the sign and reality are distinct but inseparable, the sign appropriate to the reality to which it points and with which it is connected.

Baptism admits the person baptized into the visible church. It is the first thing to be done in discipling the nations (Matt. 28:19–20). However, it is more; it is also a sign and seal of the covenant of grace. It is a

---

166. See Bo Reicke, *The Disobedient Spirits and Christian Baptism* (Copenhagen: Acta Seminaii Neotestamentici Upsaliensis, 1946); William J. Dalton, SJ, *Christ's Proclamation to the Spirits: A Study of 1 Peter 3:18–4:6* (Rome: Editrice Pontificio Instituto Biblico, 1989); J. N. D. Kelly, *A Commentary on the Epistles of Peter and Jude* (London: Adam & Charles Black, 1969), 150–64; Wayne Grudem, *The First Epistle of Peter: An Introduction and Commentary* (Leicester: Inter-Varsity Press, 1988), 203–39.

167. Luke 12:49–50.

sign because it is a sacrament and so points to a reality. It seals because it is a mark of ownership, for Christ has taken the one baptized as his own. Baptism marks the one baptized as owned by the Trinity, in whose name the sacrament is administered. This corresponds with circumcision in the Abrahamic covenant—a seal of the righteousness Abraham had through faith (Rom. 4:11). The covenant of grace, of which baptism is a sign and seal, consists of engrafting into Christ. The one baptized is a member of Christ and of his body, the church. Therefore, baptism both signifies and seals the covenant blessings of regeneration, remission of sins, and belonging to God through Jesus Christ to live in newness of life (WCF, 28.1).[168] It is more than admission to the visible church—certainly more than a symbolic representation.

The efficacy of baptism. What is the precise connection between the sacrament and the reality, between baptism and cleansing? Is it purely symbolic? Certainly, the sacraments are full of symbolism. Yet there is an efficacy that goes beyond this. Besides, an exclusively symbolic interpretation tends to rest on a dualistic view of the relationship of spirit to matter.

Is the grace signified in baptism, the reality itself, to be regarded as *parallel* to its outward manifestation? Does it mean that as we are washed with the baptismal waters, so also in parallel the Holy Spirit grants us grace, faith, and repentance? This has been called "symbolic parallelism." Or is what is signified actually *effected* by the Spirit? Does the Spirit bring this to pass by baptism? This is sometimes called "symbolic instrumentalism."[169]

Rome holds that baptism, as the other sacraments, is effective by the fact of its being performed. When a baby is born, the baby must be baptized at once in case he or she were suddenly to die. This rests upon Rome's belief that baptism is necessary for salvation, for "the Church does not know of any means other than Baptism that assures entry into eternal beatitude."[170] Hence, Rome makes provision, in an emergency, for baptism by midwives or laypersons.[171] Lutheranism also has a highly

---

168. See *A Faith to Confess: The Baptist Confession of Faith of 1689*, 29.1.
169. Brian Gerrish uses this terminology in his discussion of Calvin's view of the Lord's Supper. Gerrish, *Grace and Gratitude: The Eucharistic Theology of John Calvin* (Minneapolis: Fortress, 1993). He concludes that Calvin holds to the latter position.
170. CCC, 285–86; but see 1257, 1261.
171. CCC, 284–85.

objective view of baptism. The sacrament conveys grace efficaciously unless it is resisted.[172]

Much modern evangelicalism operates at the other extreme. It has a purely symbolic view. Baptism is effectively a visual aid. Immersion portrays union with Christ in his death and resurrection. Those who practice baptism by sprinkling see it as portraying cleansing from sin. However, union with Christ and cleansing from sin are hardly mutually exclusive. Many view baptism as an act of human obedience, a testimony to grace already received. However, in each of these common evangelical positions, the connection between baptismal sign and the reality is largely incidental.

The description of baptism in the New Testament is alien to many evangelicals today, who view material actions and the conveyance of spiritual grace as separate. This separation is at odds with the New Testament's strong connection between baptism and salvation, and with the theology of union with Christ underlying it. As Tony Lane says, "In the New Testament salvation, union with Christ, forgiveness, washing, regeneration and receiving the Holy Spirit are all attributed to baptism."[173] He continues, "This may not accord with the view of the majority of Evangelicals today but they should take up their complaint with the apostles."[174]

Grace is exhibited. Augustine described the sacraments as "a kind of visible word of God."[175] Baptism as a sign graphically portrays union with Christ, by immersion in water, demonstrating our union with Christ in death, burial, and resurrection (Rom. 6:1ff.),[176] and by sprinkling, pointing to cleansing from sin (Acts 22:16).[177] God's grace is visibly evident. Paul regards as of first importance that "Christ died for our sins in accordance with the Scriptures, that he was buried, that he was raised on the third day in accordance with the Scriptures" (1 Cor. 15:3–4). This primary point in the gospel is dramatically exhibited in baptism

---

172. The Saxon Visitation Articles, 3.2–5, in Schaff, *Creeds*, 3:183–84.
173. Lane, *Justification by Faith*, 187.
174. Lane, *Justification by Faith*, 186.
175. Augustine, *John* 80.3 (NPNF[1], 7:344).
176. As in the Book of Common Prayer of the Church of England, where the baby is to be dipped, and in the Greek Orthodox Church, which has practiced trine immersion throughout its history. The Westminster Assembly voted to affirm that immersion was a valid form of baptism, although not required; see Letham, *Westminster Assembly*, 339–43.
177. WCF, 28.3.

into Christ. The Westminster divines, in using the verb "exhibit" to speak of the efficacy of baptism, stressed something stronger than today's meaning; "exhibit" was then closer to "confer," denoting that what was displayed was actually given and bestowed to the one to whom it was exhibited.[178]

Grace is conferred through baptism by the Holy Spirit. We saw that the sacraments are primarily signs for God, who works to confirm his promises and to grant grace. We noted how he keeps his appointments. That this pattern is present with baptism can be seen in the strong language the New Testament uses with it. As with the tree of life, the rainbow, circumcision, and the Passover, baptism signifies, seals, and exhibits the grace of God, while the Holy Spirit powerfully confers that grace of union with Christ.

This does not mean that God's grace in baptism is given automatically. In contrast to Rome, this grace is received through faith. For Rome, "from the moment that a sacrament is celebrated in accordance with the intention of the Church, the power of Christ and his Spirit acts in and through it."[179] Therefore, "in case of necessity, any person, even someone not baptized, can baptize, if he has the required intention." This arises since "baptism is necessary for salvation."[180] In the case of infants who die unbaptized, "the Church can only entrust them to the mercy of God," for we can only hope. "All the more urgent is the Church's call not to prevent little children coming to Christ through the gift of holy Baptism."[181] In contrast, the Reformed hold that the Holy Spirit is sovereign and is not tied to the act of baptism. We are not made members of Christ, nor regenerated, *because* we have been baptized. Grace is not given to a baptized person on the grounds of baptism, but, rather, it is due to the electing grace of God in Christ. Thus, grace is given in baptism "to those to whom it belongs."[182] Not all who are baptized will be saved. Saving faith is necessary. At Pentecost, Peter, alongside his requirement of baptism, proclaimed the demand for repentance.

Notwithstanding, the grace of union with Christ—signified, sealed, and exhibited in baptism—is conferred by the Holy Spirit. This is due to

---

178. Letham, *Westminster Assembly*, 332–33, 346–47.
179. CCC, 1128.
180. CCC, 1256–57.
181. CCC, 1261.
182. WCF, 28.6.

the Spirit alone, yet it occurs not independently of baptism but rather in and through it. Once again, baptism, as a sacrament, primarily points to what God does. He keeps his appointments, using the means he has chosen for his purposes. The sign and the reality are fully appropriate and compatible.[183]

This grace of regeneration and union with Christ is received through faith. At a time known only to God, he regenerates a person. This, the New Testament asserts, is connected to the preaching of the Word (Rom. 10:14–17; James 1:18; 1 Pet. 1:23); it is not tied to the Word, but neither is it separated from it. It happens *with* the Word preached. However, regeneration is also connected to baptism. Regeneration may be at the instant of baptism, possibly many years afterward, or earlier, even from the womb, as with John the Baptist. When an adult convert is baptized, one assumes that regeneration has already occurred, since baptism is on profession of faith. There is a connection between baptism and regeneration. It is not automatic, temporal, or logical, but *theological.*

Both baptism and regeneration occur at the moment our Christian life begins. Baptism was administered in the New Testament immediately after an adult professed faith. There was no delay. Again, it is the first step in the process of discipling the nations (Matt. 28:18–20). Furthermore, regeneration is a resurrection (1 Pet. 1:3). We have been "born [or begotten] again . . . through the resurrection of Jesus Christ from the dead," united to Christ in his resurrection as we were in his death and burial. This union takes effect as we share in Christ's resurrection in our regeneration. Paul refers to our being united with Christ in his resurrection, and thus renewed to newness of life (Rom. 6:1ff.). In Ephesians the resurrection motif is again present, when Paul affirms we have been made alive together with Christ. The allied concept of a new creation is present in 2 Corinthians 5:17. This epochal moment is marked by baptism. Since baptism is into union with Christ in his death and resurrection, and since we are regenerated in union with Christ's resurrection, our baptism and regeneration are inseparably connected theologically.[184]

---

183. God's covenant contains promised blessings but also warnings to those who do not believe or who live in disobedience. Baptism, as a sacrament of the new covenant, also conveys a curse as well as blessing. This is clear in 1 Corinthians 10:1ff. However, while unbelief and its consequences occur, they are not germane to the purpose of the sacrament but are incidental to it.

184. The Reformed confessions are clear on the connection between baptism and regeneration. They consistently oppose the Roman Catholic doctrine of *ex opere operato* but are equally severe on those who would reduce baptism to a mere symbol. See the Tetrapolitan Confession (1530); the First Helvetic Confession (1536); the French Confession (1559), 34–38; the Heidelberg Catechism

Divergent interpretations. Following Karl Barth, some New Testament scholars, such as James Dunn and Gordon Fee, have made a sharp separation between what they call "Spirit-baptism" and "water-baptism."[185] By this distinction, passages historically understood to refer to baptism are instead said to describe the work of the Spirit in regeneration or in baptizing the corporate body of Christ. This line of thought is mistaken. Apart from its divergence from the consensus of expositors throughout church history, there is a damaging theological weakness. The theory implies a nature-grace dualism, a radical separation of the material and the spiritual, with far-reaching ontological implications. The wedge it drives between the material and the spiritual results in something akin to Gnosticism. Furthermore, it also posits a dichotomy between the individual and the corporate, whereas—as I have argued—the two stand together throughout the Bible. Again, the claim stems from analytic thinking, by which constituent elements are considered separately and in isolation rather than from synthetic thought, which sees the connections and thinks them together.

The material and the spiritual, baptism and union with Christ. The two elements, the material and the spiritual, are admirably tied together by Paul in 1 Corinthians 12:13. In the face of a culture that despised the body and all things material—hence the questions over the resurrection (1 Cor. 15:1–58)—Paul stresses the material means God uses to dispense his grace. To a church riven by factions (1 Cor. 1:10–17) he makes the point that *they all* were baptized into *one body* by the *one Spirit*—whether Jew or Greek, slave or free—and were given *one Spirit* to drink. The obvious reference is to the baptism *all* would have seen and experienced—the baptism to which Paul refers in 1:13–17, where, denying that they were baptized into the name of Paul, he implies that they were all baptized into the name of the Trinity (Matt. 28:19), or the Lord Jesus Christ (Acts 2:38; 22:16). This same baptism is probably in view in 1 Corinthians 6:11, where Paul refers to their being "washed . . . in the

---

(1563), QQ. 69–73; the Belgic Confession (1561), 33–34; the Scots Confession (1560), 21; the Thirty-Nine Articles of the Church of England (1563, 1571), art. 25–27; the Second Helvetic Confession (1566), 30. See also the landmark work the Leiden Synopsis (1625), Johannes Polyander et al., *Synopsis purioris theologiae, disputationibus quinquaginta duabus comprehensa* (Leiden: Ex officina Elzeverianus (1625), 644–54.

185. Anthony R. Cross, "Baptism in the Theology of John Calvin and Karl Barth," in *Calvin, Barth and Reformed Theology*, ed. Neil B. MacDonald and Carl Trueman (Eugene, OR: Wipf & Stock, 2008), 80.

name of the Lord Jesus Christ and by the Spirit of our God." In 10:1ff. he comments on baptism into Moses in the cloud and the sea, urging the Corinthians to be on guard against temptation; they all were baptized, but so were all the Israelites who nonetheless sinned. The evidence is overwhelming that the Corinthians would have understood that they all had been baptized into the one body of Christ, and that this was done by the Holy Spirit. The Spirit, the water, and the blood go together. The Baptist theologian G. R. Beasley-Murray affirmed that here "we meet an explicit declaration that baptism leads into the Church" with the result of "the incorporation of the baptized through the Spirit into the Body of Christ."[186] As Paul wrote to Titus, it was due to "the washing of regeneration and renewal of the Holy Spirit" (Titus 3:5). Beasley-Murray agrees here that "no statement of the New Testament, not even John 3:5, more unambiguously represents the power of baptism to lie in the operation of the Holy Spirit."[187] In summary, Paul argues that we are the body of Christ, and each is a member of it, through the work of the Spirit. This the Spirit effects in and through baptism and all that it signifies. Moreover, we are thenceforth given the Spirit to drink (1 Cor. 12:13)—a possible allusion to the Eucharist.[188]

I have remarked that the general view of evangelicals today differs greatly from that of their Protestant forebears. The classic confessions of the Reformed church all speak of the Spirit conveying grace in connection with baptism, while strenuously opposing the Roman Catholic doctrine. Today it is common to read denials that the sacraments convey grace in any form. This would meet the uninhibited opposition of a man like John Knox, who "utterly damned" the vanity of those who thought the sacraments were only symbols.[189] How has this change occurred? One major reason is a fear of association with Rome, probably spurred in Britain by the Oxford Movement of the nineteenth century. Thereafter, British evangelicalism tended to run in the opposite direction. In the USA, at the same time, a large influx of immigrants from Catholic

186. G. R. Beasley-Murray, *Baptism in the New Testament* (Exeter: Paternoster, 1972), 167, 170.
187. Beasley-Murray, *Baptism*, 215.
188. See T. F. Torrance's chapter, "The One Baptism Common to Christ and His Church," originally a lecture delivered to the Académie Internationale des Sciences Religieuses, in Torrance, *Theology in Reconciliation*, 82–105. In a masterly way, Torrance brings together the complex relationship between Christ's baptism at the Jordan, the cross, the Spirit's baptizing of us into Christ, and the sacrament.
189. Schaff, *Creeds*, 3:467–70.

countries aroused similar anxieties, even provoking riots. Out of fear, the baby has been thrown out with the bath water.

24.3.6   Who Is to Be Baptized?

Baptism is to be administered when a person can be called Christian. Since baptism is mentioned first in Jesus's program for the discipling of the nations (Matt. 28:18–20), it is paradigmatic for the church and its mission. Baptism is the sacrament of initiation into the new covenant, administered in the new covenant name of the holy Trinity.[190] From this, the church has acknowledged that baptism in the name of the Trinity is valid from whatever source, since the sacrament belongs not to any particular church but to the Trinity.

The apostles made no delay in baptizing, even at the risk that a person might fall away from the faith afterward. The tragic possibility of apostasy always exists; the most meticulous teaching or the presence of the apostles was not of itself sufficient to prevent it. This proved true in the case of Simon in Acts 8:9–24. Many heretics appeared in New Testament times; some of the community to which Hebrews was addressed had publicly repudiated Christ (Heb. 6:1–8; 10:26–31).

Baptism is always to be administered in connection with faith. According to Calvin, faith is "the principal work of the Spirit."[191] In faith "we receive and rest on Christ alone for salvation."[192] Moreover, faith is necessary at all stages of the Christian life, since "we walk by faith, not by sight" (2 Cor. 5:7). The Spirit unites us to Christ through faith. It follows that baptism as the sign of union with Christ is administered in connection with saving faith. It marks the entrance into the church of all who are baptized, inextricably connected to saving faith.

Baptism is to be administered for converts on profession of faith. Since baptism is to be administered at the point at which a person can be considered to be Christian, in the New Testament this was on profession of faith for converts from paganism and for adult Jews. In any mission context this is the norm. Many such instances are recorded in

---

190. Robert Letham, *The Holy Trinity: In Scripture, History, Theology, and Worship* (Phillipsburg, NJ: P&R, 2004), 59–60, for a discussion of the new covenant name of God.

191. Calvin, *Institutes*, 3.1.4.

192. WCF, 14.1–2; *A Faith to Confess*, 14:1–2.

Acts. Some were of Jews, in view of the transition to the new covenant, others being pagans.

At Pentecost, Peter, addressing a Jewish audience, calls for repentance and baptism at once for the remission of sins and reception of the Spirit (Acts 2:37–39). When the Roman centurion Cornelius and his friends receive the Spirit while Peter preaches, he orders them to be baptized on the spot (Acts 10:44–48). On Paul's travels, Lydia and the jailor at Philippi are both baptized, together with their households, as they profess faith (Acts 16:14–15, 30–34).

In all cases, baptism was given without delay. The apostles were prepared to take risks. Baptism followed faith instantly. Some may argue that the apostles had special insight and therefore could do this without fear. This proposal is untenable, as the cases of Simon and the heretics who challenged the apostles demonstrate.

What of the infant offspring of believers? Credobaptists restrict baptism to those who make a profession of faith on their own behalf. Covenantal paedobaptists argue that the infant children of believers are also to be baptized and, as in the case of converts, at the point at which they can be considered Christian, as soon as possible after birth. This is due to the covenant promises of God, which include the offspring of covenant members. Behind this is the continuity of the Old and New Testaments, the unity of the covenant of grace, and the continuance of the household as a basis of covenantal administration in the New Testament.[193] I discussed various positions on membership of the covenant of grace in chapter 15.

What is the basis for exclusive credobaptism? There are a number of hermeneutical assumptions:

1. One is a stress on elements of discontinuity between Old Testament and New Testament. Because of this, evidence tends to be drawn from the New Testament rather than the whole Bible.
2. Another is focusing on the individual. Thus, individuals must decide for themselves whether to be baptized.
3. The basic paradigm that faith precedes baptism.

Following these hermeneutical commitments, a number of specific arguments are developed:

---

193. In what follows, I will give more space to the paedobaptist argument since the de facto position of most evangelicals is exclusive credobaptism.

1. There is no record in the New Testament of the baptism of an infant. Therefore, infants and children below a certain age are not to be baptized.
2. The stress in the New Testament is "believe and be baptized."
3. Baptism requires faith. Infants cannot believe. Therefore, infants should not be baptized.
4. The church is a spiritual body, not a hereditary one. The qualification for membership is not fleshly birth but the new birth.
5. Infant baptism has evil effects. It forestalls the voluntary obedience of the child. It induces reverence for a mere rite. It creates an unregenerate church membership.
6. Against the covenant argument of paedobaptists, some contend that the children of Abraham are those who share his faith (Gal. 3:26–29).

What is the basis for paedobaptism? Paedobaptists approach the question from differing perspectives. One group has the sacralist idea that all people in a given territory are to be regarded as Christian and therefore should receive baptism. This arose in feudal times and was maintained later for essentially historical and pragmatic reasons. It rests on realist assumptions, specifically the ontological priority of the nation. We will concern ourselves with a different line of reasoning. Here the practice is derived from covenant history recorded in the Bible.

Paedobaptists also make a number of hermeneutical assumptions:

1. Amid elements of discontinuity, there is a basic harmony and continuity between Old Testament and New.
2. In the Bible, the individual fits into a corporate context; people are seen in relation to their ancestors, tribe, and offspring. In Joshua 7:11 the sin of one man is the sin of all Israel, and all Israel suffers as a consequence. In the New Testament the paralytic is healed through the faith of those who brought him (Matt. 9:1–8); the Philippian jailor's household rejoices and receives baptism as a result of his faith (Acts 16:34; the NIV exegetes this out); the sick person is healed through the prayer of faith of the elders (James 5:14–15); while the condition of any one member of a body has immediate impact on all others (1 Cor. 12:26).
3. A "Calvinist" order sees grace as prior to faith. God's grace in baptism precedes our response.

From this follow specific arguments.

1. Male infants received the covenant sign in the Old Testament; thus, in keeping with the greater and wider blessing in the new covenant, both male and female infants are to receive the covenant sign in the New Testament. This is based on covenant membership embracing the household, including the infant offspring of believers, inasmuch as infants in Old Testament Israel were covenant members. From this comes the connection between circumcision and baptism drawn by Paul, proposed by Zwingli, developed by Bullinger, and brought to full maturity by Bucer, Calvin, and Vermigli.[194] If infants were debarred from the covenant sign in the New Testament after receiving it in the Old Testament, Pentecost would have been the greatest occasion of mass excommunication in history. Furthermore, there is greater grace in the New Testament than in the Old.

2. Since baptism signifies union with Christ in his death and resurrection, it is grounded in God's grace rather than our response—that is, on what God has done in Christ. God's grace comes first. Baptism relates primarily to God's grace rather than our faith. Consequently, the promise of the Abrahamic covenant is fulfilled in Acts 2:39 ("the promise is for you and for your children"). God has a covenant claim on the children of believers (1 Cor. 7:14, even where only one parent believes). Both faith and baptism unite us to Christ (for faith, Eph. 3:17; for baptism, Rom. 6:3–4; Gal. 3:27; Col. 2:12); both receive the righteousness of Christ (for faith, Gal. 3:6–11; for baptism, Col. 2:12–15); both receive the Holy Spirit (for faith, Gal. 3:14; for baptism, Acts 2:38); both save (for faith, Acts 16:31; for baptism, 1 Pet. 3:21). For paedobaptism, faith and baptism are the inside and outside of the same reality—salvation. Grace gives rise to both, the temporal sequence being indeterminate.

3. While there is no record in the New Testament of an infant receiving baptism, neither is there a record in the New Testament of a child born in a Christian home having his or her baptism postponed until adulthood. The credobaptist argument is cancelled out.

4. Corporate solidarity is an essential feature of biblical revelation. The household is primary in the administration of God's covenant. The records of household baptisms (Acts 16 for Lydia and the Philippian jailor; 1 Cor. 1:13–16 and 16:15 for Stephanas) indicate that the household continues as the unit of covenantal administration in the New

---

194. Letham, "Baptism," 21–44.

Testament. In recounting his visit to Cornelius, the effective start of the Gentile mission, Peter announces that the angel declared to Cornelius that the gospel was directed to him *and all his household*. This council, setting the foundation for the future ministry of the church, determined that the message of salvation is for individuals *and the household to which they belong*, not to individuals in isolation (Acts 11:14). This is in continuity with Joshua's call for faithfulness to God's covenant and his declaration that he *and his house* would follow the Lord (Josh. 24:15). If this were otherwise, Paul's Judaizing opponents would have pounced on this matter; but such a question was never on their minds. Therefore, there is no need for a specific account of an infant receiving baptism. Since the household is the primary unit, whenever an infant happened to be present in the household, he or she would receive baptism, *without it being a noteworthy event*. If infants were excluded, these repeated and unrestricted references to households would be out of place.

5. The New Testament relationship between faith and baptism is not first faith and second baptism but first baptism and second faith. In the major contexts where baptism is considered, the relationship is not between baptism and the faith that precedes but between baptism and the faith that follows (Rom. 6:1ff.; 1 Cor. 10:1–13).[195]

6. Children are addressed in the New Testament not with a command to repent but in terms of their covenantal responsibilities. In both Ephesians and Colossians, where each letter was addressed to the whole church, Paul turns to particular groups (husbands and wives, masters and slaves, parents and children), treating them as Christians and explaining their covenantal responsibilities. Children are considered "in the Lord," while their responsibilities are reinforced by the covenantal obligation and promise of the Decalogue (Eph. 6:1–3), demonstrating their covenant membership, together with all its privileges and responsibilities.

Further Reading

Beasley-Murray, G. R. *Baptism in the New Testament*. Exeter: Paternoster, 1972.

Beilby, James K., and Paul Rhodes Eddy, eds. *Justification: Five Views*. London: SPCK, 2012.

---

195. See Oscar Cullmann, *Early Christian Worship*, trans. A. Stewart Todd and James B. Torrance (London: SCM, 1953), 86–87.

Lane, Anthony N. S. *Justification by Faith in Catholic-Protestant Dialogue: An Evangelical Assessment*. London: T&T Clark, 2002.

Torrance, Thomas F. "The One Baptism Common to Christ and His Church." In *Theology in Reconciliation*, 82–105. Grand Rapids, MI: Eerdmans, 1975.

Study Questions

1. Explain the neglect of the doctrine of justification in the first fifteen hundred years of the church.

2. What were, and are, the main features distinguishing the Protestant view from the Roman Catholic view of justification?

3. Why is justification only by faith? Why is baptism not the instrumental cause of justification?

4. How do forms of dualism affect a person's understanding of baptism?

5. Consider how the New Testament addresses the efficacy of baptism.

25

The Progress of the Christian Life (1)

Assurance, Adoption, and Sanctification

Assurance of salvation came into prominence in the Reformation. Rome held that it was not possible, beyond a purely conjectural assurance. There were differences among Reformed theologians about whether assurance was a necessary element of saving faith or it was subsequent to faith. In one sense, it is an outflow of adoption. Adoption is distinct from regeneration and justification. Little has been written on it, but it is in many ways the crowning gift of redemption. Both adoption and assurance are inextricably linked with sanctification, which is at root a spatial concept, signifying that we now belong to God. Sanctification is a work of the Holy Spirit, from one angle a definitive breach with sin, but more commonly understood as a lifelong and gradual process of dying to sin and progressively living to God. Its criterion is the law of God; the means for its progress are the Word, the sacraments, and prayer; and its goal is eschatological conformity to the glorified Christ. This process is undergirded by the faithfulness and promises of God, by whom we are preserved in faith in the midst of many and various obstacles and difficulties.

25.1   Assurance of Salvation

25.1.1   The Meaning of Assurance

Assurance of salvation is a conviction, *properly founded*, that one is in the state of grace and will attain everlasting salvation. Romans 8:28–39 is a classic passage to this effect. The foundation is the truth of the gospel, from God's foreordination to the death, resurrection, ascension, and enthronement of Christ. The logic of the passage demonstrates an integral connection between assurance and perseverance. Because God preserves his elect in faith to the end, it is possible, by the Holy Spirit, to have a conviction that we will attain to eternal life. First John is all about assurance (1 John 5:13). "We know" occurs fifty-five times. John explains that we know we belong to Christ by our belief in the truth (1 John 2:19ff.; 4:1ff.), by the indwelling of the Holy Spirit (1 John 3:21), and by the love we have for the brothers (1 John 3–4).

25.1.2 Historical Debates

Rome denied the possibility of assurance in this life. The Council of Trent stated, "No one . . . so long as he is in this mortal life, ought so far to presume . . . as to determine for certain that he is assuredly in the number of the predestinate . . . for except by special revelation, it cannot be known whom God hath chosen unto himself."[1] Chapter 13 of the decree on justification declared that no one could promise himself with certainty that he would persevere in faith; a conjectural probability was the best one could hope for. The canons of Trent anathematized those who taught that a certain or infallible assurance of remission of sins, justification, election, and perseverance was possible in this life.[2] At root, this denial was the product of a synergistic soteriology, humans cooperating with God's grace, for people could never attain assurance in reliance on their own contribution and on a sacramental system that placed a high reliance on penance.

In Reformed theology, debate has surrounded the connection between assurance and saving faith. Calvin defines saving faith as "a firm and certain knowledge of God's benevolence toward us, founded upon the truth of the freely given promise in Christ, both revealed to our minds and sealed upon our hearts through the Holy Spirit."[3] The Heidelberg Catechism (1), answering the question "What is your only comfort in life and in death?" says, "that I am not my own but belong, in body and soul, in life and in death, to my faithful Savior Jesus Christ."[4] Both imply

---

1. Philip Schaff, *The Creeds of Christendom* (Grand Rapids, MI: Baker, 1966), 2:103.
2. Schaff, *Creeds*, 2:113–14.
3. Calvin, *Institutes*, 3.2.7.
4. For an older translation, see Schaff, *Creeds*, 3:307–8.

that certainty of salvation is an integral ingredient of saving faith and thus normative for the Christian life.

However, much of Puritanism tended to teach that assurance is not of the essence of faith or at least that many may lack it. William Perkins held it to be "a fruite of faith," belonging only to those who are of "ripe years in Christ."[5] Yet, in *A Reformed Catholike*, written in opposition to Rome, he affirmed that "true faith is both an unfallible assurance, and a particular assurance of the remission of sins, and of life everlasting."[6] That this latter comment was not typical is evident in pastoral works such as *A Declaration of Certaine Spiritual Desertions*[7] and A *Case of Conscience*.[8] William Ames termed assurance a "reflex act" resulting from self-examination,[9] "an act flowing from faith,"[10] and thus he too considered infallible certainty of salvation possible.[11] Thomas Goodwin pointed to the logical absurdity of supposing assurance was present in justifying faith. He argued that assurance presupposed God's verdict in justification, which, in turn, required the prior act of faith. Therefore, justifying faith could not have assurance as a constituent element, since it would then have an object both antecedent and consequent to itself.[12] Assurance, he wrote, is a reflex act, by which one observes the presence of faith, whereas justifying faith is a direct act with Christ as its object.[13] These differences led many to posit a chasm between Calvin and the Calvinists.[14]

However, the matter is not quite as simple as that. There were always two broad understandings of the relationship between saving faith and assurance in Reformed theology of the sixteenth and early seven-

---

5. William Perkins, *The Workes of That Famous and Worthy Minister of Christ in the Universitie of Cambridge, Mr. William Perkins* (Cambridge: John Legatt, 1612), 1:125.

6. Perkins, *Workes* (1612), 1:564.

7. Perkins, *Workes* (1612), 1:415–20.

8. Perkins, *Workes* (1612), 1:421.

9. William Ames, *An Analyticall Exposition of Both the Epistles of the Apostle Peter* (London: John Rothwell, 1641), 165.

10. *William Ames: The Marrow of Theology*, trans. John L. Eusden (1629; repr., Boston: Pilgrim, 1968), 82.

11. William Ames, *Conscience, with the Power and Cases Thereof* (London: John Rothwell, 1643), bk. 4, p. 6.

12. Thomas Goodwin, *The Works of Thomas Goodwin* (Edinburgh: James Nichol, 1864), 8:212–13.

13. Goodwin, *Works*, 8:338–39.

14. Basil Hall, "Calvin against the Calvinists," in *John Calvin*, ed. Gervase E. Duffield (Abingdon: Sutton Courtenay, 1966), 19–37; R. T. Kendall, *Calvin and English Calvinism to 1649* (Oxford: Oxford University Press, 1979); Alan C. Clifford, *Atonement and Justification: English Evangelical Theology 1640–1790: An Evaluation* (Oxford: Clarendon, 1990).

teenth centuries.[15] Furthermore, the differences were not as far-reaching as might at first appear. The WCF does not go so far as to separate the two, even though they are treated in noncontiguous chapters. "This infallible assurance doth not so belong to the essence of faith, but that a true believer may wait long, and conflict with many difficulties, before he be partaker of it" (WCF, 18.3).

In WLC, 81, the distinction is more explicit: "Assurance of grace and salvation not being of the essence of faith. . . ." Whereas the previous question asserted that believers can be infallibly assured that they are in the estate of grace and will persevere in it, question 81 is unrelieved in its gloom. Not only may true believers wait long to obtain assurance, but once it is obtained, they "may have it weakened and intermitted." Yet the Holy Spirit "keeps them from sinking into utter despair." This seems light-years from the New Testament. It is true that Calvin implies that a true believer may suffer the absence of assurance on occasion.[16] However, this is more of an exception and a concession. A crucial axiom is that the object of faith governs its nature; faith and assurance should be shaped by Christ, the reality and finality of his work for us, and our union with him.

Another important factor is that a definition of faith may not represent the practical experience of individuals. Even if assurance of salvation is considered a part of saving faith, as in Calvin, it may not always be experienced. If our faith is low, so will our assurance be; weak faith will mean weak assurance. Personality disturbances, illness, and traumatic events may for a time eclipse it. Mercifully, this does not imperil our salvation. We believe in Christ, not in our own experience. But we are exhorted to make our salvation more certain (2 Pet. 1:10; 1 John 5:13).

Assurance of salvation must be carefully distinguished from assurance concerning the gospel. This is the difference between the *fides quae*, "the faith," the truth of the gospel, and the *fides qua*, the faith we ourselves exercise and our conviction that we will ultimately be saved.

---

15. Robert Letham, "Faith and Assurance in Early Calvinism: A Model of Continuity and Diversity," in *Later Calvinism: International Perspectives*, ed. W. Fred Graham (Kirksville, MO: Sixteenth Century Journal Publishers, 1994), 355–84; Letham, "Faith and Assurance in Reformed Theology: Zwingli to the Synod of Dort," 2 vols. (PhD diss., University of Aberdeen, 1979).

16. Calvin, *Institutes*, 3.2.4, 17, 20, 4.1.7.

25.1.3   *The Privilege and Duty of Assurance*

Assurance is not presumption. It is inextricably linked with holiness, and this connection must never be forgotten (Rom. 8:12–17; 1 Pet. 1:13–16; 1 John 3:21–24). It is incongruous and wrong to expect assurance of salvation if we have willfully plunged into sin. One Puritan, I cannot recall which, remarked that God promises forgiveness when we repent, but he does not promise repentance when we sin. Without holiness, no one will see the Lord (Heb. 12:14). The possibility of assurance impels us to the responsibility of obedience.

In this, allowance should be made for differences of individual temperaments. Some are naturally morose and introspective, others suffer from depression, while serious illness or even a bad cold can cloud our mental horizons. Adverse circumstances can throw us off course emotionally. We are living in a fallen world and have not yet attained to glory; it is hardly surprising if we find ourselves in a disturbed or doubtful state. The remedy is to focus on God's promises, and on Christ, their personal embodiment.

25.1.4   *The Foundation of Assurance*

Assurance is grounded in the grace of God in salvation and in his faithfulness. He never acts out of character (James 1:17). He is free to be himself. He cannot lie (Heb. 6:18) or deny himself (2 Tim. 2:13). The fulfillment of redemption in Christ is therefore certain. What God has promised, he performs. Consequently, assurance is grounded on the truth and reliability of God's promise "I will be your God, and you shall be my people." The New Testament stresses that saving faith is directed to the promise, in Christ, which expresses the will of God to bring us into covenantal union. In the gospel, God gives himself to us in covenantal grace.

Moreover, faith is trust in God. It is a confident expectation that the promise of salvation applies to us personally.[17] Paul, in Romans 8:23–25, equates faith with hope—hope indicating not wishful thinking but expectation of future blessing. The definition of faith in Hebrews 11:1 is couched in the same terms, with examples all looking for the future fulfillment of God's promise (Heb. 11:13–16).

---

17. Herman Bavinck, *Our Reasonable Faith*, trans. Henry Zylstra (Grand Rapids, MI: Baker, 1977), 431–33; Abraham Kuyper, *The Work of the Holy Spirit*, trans. Henri De Vries (Grand Rapids, MI: Eerdmans, 1975), 400.

The sovereignty of God's grace destroys all objections. His invincible and irrevocable will is that of a loving and self-sacrificing Father (Rom. 8:32). The chain of salvation in Romans 8:29–30 presses the matter forcefully. The doctrine of perseverance is the key, for theologies that undermine perseverance can have no doctrine of assurance of future salvation; this is true both for Rome and for classic Arminianism. In the latter case, the Remonstrants left the question of perseverance undecided. Because they did not espouse a clear doctrine of perseverance, they could not have a doctrine of assurance of final salvation. However, the Synod of Dort affirmed what the Remonstrants could not. If there is no certainty that God will preserve his elect in faith to the end of their lives, the possibility exists that we will fall from grace and perish.

Furthermore, salvation is a radical break with the world of sin and death. Without question, for John the church and the world are clearly distinct as the children of light and the children of darkness. This distinction is a present, continuous reality (1 John 2:19–27; 3:1–15, 19–24; 5:1–5, 13, 18–19).

Finally, the testimony of the Holy Spirit clinches the matter. He is a seal (2 Cor. 1:20–21; Eph.1:13–14), denoting ownership. He is the guarantee of our future inheritance, an earnest or deposit securing the full payment at a later date.[18] Here lies the difference with Rome. Rome allows assurance based on good works, but this amounts to no more than a conjectural probability. The Reformers stressed the infallibility of assurance, since the testimony of the Spirit is infallible. This is no mystical experience unchecked by any objective criterion. His testimony is based on the promise of salvation revealed in his Word. It is rooted in Scripture, the ministry of the Word, and the sacraments. A correct and scriptural theology is essential for assurance. Moreover, the Spirit brings experience of the world to come, the eschatological dimension. Thus, Donald Macleod could write that "to lack assurance is not humility. It is not spirituality. It is a violation of the Scriptural

---

18. Thomas Goodwin argued that this is a postconversion experience of overwhelming power; *Works*, 1:233–48. He based this on a wooden translation of the aorist participle ἀκούσαντες in Eph. 1:13 as "after you believed." John Owen corrected him in *The Works of John Owen*, ed. William H. Goold, 23 vols. (1850–1855; repr., London: Banner of Truth, 1965–1968), 4:399–406. I am grateful to J. I. Packer for pointing this out to me in correspondence in 1974. It is a participle of attendant circumstance. Goodwin's proposal has been influential among those who teach "second blessing" theologies.

pattern of Christian experience."[19] As Calvin put it, "If Pighius asks how I know I am elect, I answer that Christ is more than a thousand testimonies to me."[20]

Our assurance is confirmed, in a subordinate and secondary manner, by our good works. Augustine stated that "grace is pointed at by the law, in order that the law may be fulfilled by grace."[21] This includes self-examination (2 Cor. 13:5; 2 Pet. 1:10), with the caveat that if self-examination leads us away from Christ to introspection, it is false. It should direct us to Christ, not away from him.[22] This obedience is directly related to the testimony of the Spirit (Rom. 8:15–16). Paul contrasts the Spirit of adoption with a putative "spirit of slavery." The Holy Spirit provides a joint witness with our spirit that we belong to God, as he enables us to put to death the deeds of the flesh.

25.2   Adoption

25.2.1   *Terminology*

Paul uses υἱοθεσία in Romans 8:15 and Galatians 4:5.[23] There has been much debate as to whether this word should be translated "adoption" or "sonship." John uses υἱός[24] and τέκνον,[25] as Paul does; these have no reference to adoption as such but refer to our status as sons.[26] There is an important distinction between adoption, the process by which we enter into this privilege, and sonship, our resulting and continuous status. Adoption is by grace, a process contrary to our natural condition, whereas sonship is the legally grounded filial status and privilege we possess forever.

It is amazing how little has been written on the topic of adoption in Christ. Trumper notes only a handful of creeds that even address it, and of those, two are express derivatives of the WCF—the Savoy Declaration (1658) of the Congregationalists and the Baptist Confession of Faith (1677, 1689). Even here it is surprising how little the chapters state. Ac-

---

19. Donald Macleod, "Christian Assurance 1," *The Banner of Truth*, October 1974, 17–18.

20. John Calvin, *Concerning the Eternal Predestination of God*, trans. J. K. S. Reid (repr., London: James Clarke, 1961), 130.

21. Augustine, *On the Grace of God and Original Sin* 1.10.9 (NPNF¹, 5:221).

22. Problems with assurance in some conservative Reformed denominations are largely due to an inordinate stress on self-examination.

23. *huiothesia.*

24. *huios.*

25. *teknon.*

26. Adoption relates to all who are in Christ, male and female. Here the use of "sons," rather than "sons and daughters," simply highlights the central point that our relationship to God by adoption and grace is identical to the natural relation Christ the Son has to the Father.

cording to Trumper, "One is not only staggered by the lack of attention adoption has received, but also by the silence about this inattention! As a matter of fact adoption has rarely been thoroughly considered as a doctrine in its own right."[27]

25.2.2   Adoption and Justification

Adoption and justification are distinct benefits of Christ. Adoption refers to entry into the family of God and the reception of the responsibilities that this entails. While adoption has obvious legal connections (and thus similarities with justification), it is a filial relation as well as a judicial one. In justification Jesus becomes our righteousness, with God as our Judge, whereas in adoption God becomes our Father and we are given the status of sons.[28]

25.2.3   Adoption and Regeneration

It might be thought that the use of τέκνον, "child," and its cognate verb τίκτω,[29] "bear children," would point to regeneration as making us sons of God. However, adoption puts us into a different sphere than natural begetting or bearing. Adoption assumes no prior relationship; the adopted son is not a natural son. Conversely, the metaphors for begetting and conceiving entail a natural relationship between the begetter or conceiver and the child. The metaphors are different. This distinction, found in John (who uses terms related to natural birth) and Paul (where adoption is explicit), is not straightforward.[30]

Moreover, regeneration is appropriated to the Holy Spirit, whereas the Father adopts. Although the key texts for adoption bring the Spirit into immediate connection (Rom. 8:15–16; Gal. 4:5), the context is expressly Trinitarian. Additionally, there are legal ramifications to adoption that are not present in regeneration. Although inseparable, they represent different aspects of salvation.

John 1:12–13 illustrates this point. There is a sequence; first comes regeneration, being "born . . . of God," then faith or receiving him (the

---

27. Tim Trumper, "The Metaphorical Import of Adoption: A Plea for Realisation: I: The Adoption Metaphor in Biblical Usage," *SBET* 14 (1996): 131.

28. This distinction is sometimes blurred. See Chad B. Van Dixhoorn, "The Sonship Program for Revival: A Summary and Critique," *WTJ* 61 (1999): 227–46. John Murray, *Select Lectures in Systematic Theology*, vol. 2 of *Collected Writings of John Murray* (Edinburgh: Banner of Truth, 1977), 228.

29. *tiktō*.

30. Trumper, "Adoption I," 135–40.

true light), believing in his name, and, as a direct consequence, adoption as children of God, τέκνα θεοῦ. This is simultaneous, a logical sequence, not a temporal one. Murray argues for the following sequence—regeneration, reception of Christ, bestowal of authority, and adoption. He sees a similar order in 1 John 3:1–3: the Father is the agent and grants the privilege; the calling highlights the dignity of the status; and the marvel of the Father's love indicates the status is "the apex and epitome of grace." It is a present possession as well as a future attainment, the status ensuring that in the future we will be conformed to the image of the Father. In short, by regeneration we become members of God's kingdom, while by adoption we are made members of God's family.[31]

Trumper contends that adoption completes what is begun but left somewhat hanging in the metaphor of redemption. In redemption we are delivered from bondage (to sin, to the devil, to the law, to the pagan gods) by the payment of a price—the blood of Christ. Of itself, however, the idea of redemption does not disclose what we are delivered to. The main contexts relating to adoption suggest the completion of redemption (Rom. 8:23; Gal. 4:4–6).[32]

25.2.4 Israel, the Church, and Adoption

Paul unfolds this connection in Galatians 3. He compares Israel to a child in his minority, under the protection of a *pedagogos* (v. 24), a slave entrusted with the care and upbringing of the son before adulthood. The law was the *pedagogos*, and Israel was in a state of immaturity. Now that Christ has come and the Spirit is given, the people of God have emerged from their childhood and have arrived at the maturity of adult sons (Gal. 4:1ff.).

At the same time, there is another, allied, background at the start of chapter 4. Israel was delivered from slavery in Egypt under Moses and brought into the promised inheritance. The church is now delivered from slavery to the law by Christ, a second Moses, and given the inheritance of sons.

Furthermore, the Gentiles have been delivered from bondage to the elementary forces of the world—the pagan deities (4:8). Both divine interventions (the exodus, and its fulfillment) came at the appointed

---

31. Murray, *Writings*, 2:228–29.
32. Tim Trumper, "The Metaphorical Import of Adoption: A Plea for Realisation: II: The Adoption Metaphor in Theological Usage," *SBET* 15 (1997): 98–115.

time. Trumper unfolds this effectively, building on earlier work by J. M. Scott.[33] Trumper concludes: "The completion and perfection of Christ's work exhibits the unbreakable connection between redemption and adoption. . . . Redemption is not an end in itself, but finds its completion in a relationship with the Father."[34]

25.2.5   Adoption and the Holy Spirit

The Holy Spirit witnesses to our status (Rom. 8:15–16; Gal. 4:6). Two elements are present, according to Murray. First, there is the creation and cultivation within us of the affection and confidence appropriate to our status; and, second, there is the conjoint witness of the Holy Spirit to our status. No approach to God has the intimacy, confidence, and love comparable to that expressed in the phrase "Abba, Father," both Jew and Gentile saying the same thing, in Aramaic and Greek.[35] Murray connects adoption with predestination (Eph. 1:5), arguing that in our consciousness of sonship, we attain assurance of our predestination. "The confidence implicit in the address, 'Abba, Father' is one that draws to itself the assurance of predestinating love and these mutually support and encourage one another."[36]

In one sense, all people are the children of God. Paul cites the Greek poet Aratus, who wrote that we are all God's offspring, without challenging the claim but instead reasserting it (Acts 17:28–29). However, the overwhelming focus of the Bible is that the sons of God are those with faith in Jesus Christ. John stresses that being the children of God is an astonishing demonstration of the Father's love and is the result of union with Christ (1 John 3:1–2).[37]

25.3   Sanctification

25.3.1   The Meaning of the Term

I have emphasized that despite its common association with ethics, at root sanctification is a spatial category; it refers to the fact that believers

---

33. J. M. Scott, *Adoption as the Sons of God: An Exegetical Investigation into the Background of* Huiothesia *in the Pauline Corpus*, Wissenschaftliche Untersuchungen zum Neuen Testament (Tübingen: Mohr, 1992).

34. Trumper, "Adoption II," 112–13.

35. *Abba* (Aramaic) and *pater* (Greek) both mean "father." Note James Barr, "Abba Isn't Daddy," *JTS* 39 (1988): 28–47.

36. Murray, *Writings*, 2:230.

37. For further reflection on adoption, see Tim J. R. Trumper, "A Fresh Exposition of Adoption: II: Some Implications," *SBET* 23 (2005): 194–215.

belong to God and have been transferred from the kingdom of darkness to the kingdom of God's Son. It is rooted in the Old Testament distinction between the holy and the common, the clean and the unclean. As such, sanctification means we belong to God—we are not our own, we have been bought with a price (1 Cor. 3:16–17, with respect to the church; 6:19–20, in relation to its members). The ethical dimension follows from this.

In John 17:16–19 we read that Jesus sanctifies (consecrates, sets apart) himself. He also prays (requests) to the Father that they (those the Father had given him out of the world) be sanctified (consecrated, set apart) in truth. Jesus's sanctification is in order to the second—note the ἵνα purpose clause. The setting apart of the elect, his people, is on the basis of, and flows from, his own setting apart or consecration. It is in the truth—which throughout John's Gospel is seen to be fulfilled and embodied in Jesus Christ (John 1:14–17; 4:21–24; 14:1–6). Hence, it is in union with Christ, in Christ's own sanctification, that his people are set apart and sanctified. Thus, sanctification is in Christ. Christ is himself the place of sanctification for his people. Implied too is the Trinity; the Father sets apart his Son by the Holy Spirit.[38]

25.3.2 Sanctification Is a Work of God

Paul writes of us having been predestined to sanctification by the Father (Eph. 1:4–5). Elsewhere he speaks of it being the will of God (1 Thess. 4:3), and of our receiving the Holy Spirit for that purpose (John 17:17, 19; Eph. 5:25, 27; 1 Thess. 4:7–8; 5:23; Titus 2:14; Heb. 13:12). Specifically, sanctification is appropriated to the Spirit (Rom. 8:13–14; 2 Thess. 2:13; 1 Pet. 1:1–2). He indwells the people of God. Scripture is silent as to how the Spirit operates, for this is beyond our understanding, as Jesus points out in John 3. Notwithstanding, sanctification requires our fullest effort as well. It is not a case of sitting back and letting the Holy Spirit take over, for the Spirit works through our own responsible engagement. Here Romans 8:12ff. is important to grasp. We are obliged to put to death the deeds of the flesh. However, it is by the Spirit that this is done. Again, in Philippians 2:11–12, Paul writes that we are to work out our salvation; but it is God who puts this desire in us and brings it to effect.

---

38. Recall Basil's comment that the Holy Spirit is the place of the saints and so the place of true worship. Basil, *De Spiritu Sancto* 26.62.

Similarly, Paul can say that the grace of God was evident in his life, since he worked harder than anyone else (1 Cor. 15:10).

25.3.3 Sanctification Begins with a Break with Sin

Sanctification requires breaking with sin. This is implied in 1 Corinthians 1:30, where justification is inseparable from sanctification. Hebrews 13:12 may point to this too. Although in Hebrews sanctification normally refers to the whole of salvation, the implication here is that Jesus's suffering outside the camp set his people apart from that which had rejected him and thus had become common and unholy. However, Romans 6 is perhaps the clearest text on this separation.[39] Murray approaches the subject via calling. He argues that calling from death to life entails a definitive breach with sin. Since sanctification and regeneration are both accomplished by the Holy Spirit, they bring about a definitive break from the love and power of sin. Murray views 1 John 3:9 and 5:18 in that light. At the same time, the reality of sin in the life of the believer is acknowledged in 1 John 1:8–2:1. So while this is a definitive breach, it is not an absolute one. Nor is the breach the result of a process or attained by human effort. It is brought about by the power of the Spirit once for all. It involves a breach with all sin, not simply known sin. There is "some decisive action that occurs at the inception of the Christian life." It is "a once-for-all definitive and irreversible breach with the realm in which sin reigns in and unto death."[40]

The antitheses that occur right through Romans 6 serve to underline this reality. Peter has the same basic position (1 Pet. 2:24; 4:1–2). And John is very clear (1 John 3:6–9) in a letter written explicitly against notions of sinless perfection (1 John 1:7–2:1). Murray, pointing to Romans 6:7, argues that when we are united to Christ in his death and resurrection, there is a juridical action that establishes this clear breach with the realm of sin. This is not justification, where we are delivered from the guilt of sin, but sanctification, deliverance from the power of sin. In effect, he means that "he who died is quit of sin."[41] The context talks of the reigning power of sin in the ungodly. Sin and the law are lords, reigning over those in their thrall. Behind sin are the power of Satan and

---

39. John Murray, "Definitive Sanctification," *CTJ* 2 (1967): 5–21; Murray, *Writings*, 2:277–84.
40. Murray, *Writings*, 2:278.
41. Murray, *Writings*, 2:288.

the principalities and powers. Jesus dealt with the destruction of Satan's power in terms of judgment (John 12:31). Thus, we have been released from the power of sin definitively in Christ's resurrection, but this deliverance is effected in our own life histories.[42]

How does this differ, if at all, from regeneration? A distinction is difficult, since the two occur simultaneously. Regeneration in its narrow sense is the beginning of progressive sanctification; in its more rarely discussed wider sense, to which I referred in chapter 23, regeneration and progressive sanctification are effectively the same. This beginning of sanctification has connections with justification, because justification destroys the penalty due us for our sin, part of which is the corrupt nature we inherit from Adam. Thus, our justification accomplishes in principle our sanctification.

25.3.4   *The Progress of Sanctification*

Justification and sanctification are inseparable, yet distinct. Tony Lane compares them to two legs of a pair of trousers.[43] Justification removes the guilt and condemnation of the sinner and thus is a forensic act. Sanctification overcomes the pollution due to sin and thus is a series of acts. Justification is the same for all—there are no degrees—while sanctification in this progressive sense is not the same for all. Justification affects our legal status, while sanctification affects our moral condition. With justification, righteousness is imputed to us, whereas in sanctification righteousness is imparted or infused. Justification gives us a just basis for the right to eternal life, while sanctification prepares us for eternal life by conforming us to the image of Christ. However, the two are inseparable, for both are given in union with Christ (1 Cor. 1:30). Sanctification is important in connection with assurance (1 John 3:22).

Debate has arisen over whether justification is the cause of sanctification. Michael Horton argues for the priority of justification in the *ordo salutis*, going so far as to say that justification causes sanctification.[44]

---

42. See the exchange between J. V. Fesko, "Sanctification and Union with Christ: A Reformed Perspective," *EQ* 82 (2010): 197–214, and Ralph Cunnington, "Definitive Sanctification: A Response to John Fesko," *EQ* 84 (2012): 234–52.

43. Anthony N. S. Lane, *Justification by Faith in Catholic-Protestant Dialogue* (London: T&T Clark, 2002), 18.

44. Michael S. Horton, *Covenant and Salvation: Union with Christ* (Louisville: Westminster John Knox, 2007), 189–205; Horton, *The Christian Faith: A Systematic Theology for Pilgrims on the Way* (Grand Rapids, MI: Zondervan, 2011), 594n11.

There is warrant for a certain priority, in that status can be held to undergird condition. We are not justified on the basis of our being transformed, but our transformation is grounded on our status as righteous. Others see both justification and sanctification as aspects of union with Christ, given simultaneously and symmetrically.[45] Both sides use Calvin in support, the latter with more substance, to my mind. Paul Helm, commenting on this discussion, points to the varieties of causality in Aristotelianism. In this sense, justification can be said to be the necessary condition for sanctification but not the efficient cause.[46]

To my mind, the efficient cause—the agent that effects an outcome—in both justification and sanctification is God. It is hard to see how a status can of itself effect a condition distinct from itself. A material cause—of what is justification and sanctification composed?—does not make sense in this context. It is reasonable to conclude, with Helm, that justification should be regarded as the necessary condition for sanctification but not its efficient cause. Both are given by God in union with Christ, inseparably but distinct.

Sanctification is a process of death and resurrection. It is true that union with Christ in his death and resurrection has already happened, definitively so (Rom. 6:6). The old man has been crucified; we have died to sin and are no more under its dominion. Yet there are "remnants of corruption" (WCF, 13.2). A lifelong process remains. We are to put to death the remaining sinful inclinations, motivated by a hatred of sin (Rom. 8:12–17; Col. 3:3–5) and by a love for God. The corresponding quickening engenders a sensitivity to any departure from the law of God, the standard of righteousness God has provided. In this sense, sanctification entails sharing in the death and resurrection of Christ on an ongoing basis, just as in the definitive outset (2 Cor. 4:7–12). It is a lifelong process, often slow and painful but nonetheless real. Yes, you *are* being sanctified, whatever your wife, husband, children, or friends may say.

25.3.5 *The Criterion for Sanctification*

In Romans 6:17, Paul says that those united to Christ are conformed to the law of God in their heart. The law defines what is pleasing to

---

45. Mark A. Garcia, *Life in Christ: Union with Christ and Twofold Grace in Calvin's Theology* (Milton Keynes: Paternoster, 2008), 146.

46. Paul Helm, "Does Justification Cause Sanctification?," Helm's Deep (blog), June 1, 2011, http://paulhelmsdeep.blogspot.com/2011/06/does-justiification-cause.html.

God and what is not. It is a charter for Christian liberty, since God's requirements trump human regulations where these conflict. Sanctification includes deliverance from sin; since sin is defined by God in his law, it and its entailments function as the rule of life for Christians. The law points to the fact that ultimately complete conformity to Christ is in view (Matt. 5:48; cf. Eph. 4:24; Col. 3:10). In no way does this collide with love, for love is the fulfillment of the law, and the law is the expression of love (Matt. 22:34–40; James 2:8; 1 John 2:4–6; 3:23; 4:20–5:3).

25.3.6   *The Means of Sanctification*

The same means that bring us into the covenant keep us there (WSC, 88). There are no extraordinary sanctifying devices. The Spirit sanctifies us through the ministry of the Word, the sacraments, and prayer, since each provides access to Christ. Discipline also sanctifies, whether judicial discipline of the immoral (1 Cor. 5:5) or the positive discipline of fellowship (Heb. 10:24–25). Thus, sanctification is both a privilege and a duty. Since it is a work of the holy Trinity, it is our privilege (Ps. 119:165; Ezek. 36:27; Rom. 7:1–25), the Spirit enabling us to keep God's laws. But it is also a duty (2 Cor. 7:1; Phil. 2:12).

The multiservice cafeteria style of much popular American Christianity, the idea of a church with a wide range of programs catering for every taste, militates against our use of the ordinary means of growth in grace. It is neither necessarily nor intrinsically wrong to have ministries of various kinds. However, the issue is that God has provided the means of sanctification, all the tools we need to fit us to serve him during this life and to enter his eternal kingdom thereafter. These are the ministry of the Word, the sacraments, and prayer. What else do churches need in order to serve Christ? They may well require a barrage of services and programs in order to be successful and growing corporate entities. However, that is something completely different—meeting felt needs with felt solutions. What the church and its members really need are the faithful ministry of the Word, the right use of the sacraments, and prayer, with love as the outflow. These are the tools God has given.

We have considered the preaching of the Word. In the next chapter, we will focus on the Lord's Supper and prayer as instrumental means of sanctification.

25.3.7 *The Goal of Sanctification*

Since the law of God is the standard for sanctification, and the law represents the mind of God as it relates to human life, ultimately the pattern of sanctification cannot be anything less than God's own nature (Matt. 5:48). This reflects the requirement in the Old Testament that Israel be holy as Yahweh is holy (Lev. 11:44; 19:2; 20:7), repeated in the New Testament (1 Pet. 1:16), and points to our being renewed in the image of God (Rom. 8:29; Gal. 2:20).

Sin continues to indwell believers throughout this life. Some biblical statements, viewed superficially, might seem to suggest that sin is already abolished. Allusions to definitive sanctification (1 John 3:9) come to mind. Some passages describe people as righteous or perfect (Gen. 6:9; Job 1:1; Pss. 18:20–24; 26). The efficacy of the atonement might suggest it, inasmuch as Jesus dealt not only with the penalty and the guilt of sin but also with sin itself. Together, these factors all point to sin as an anomaly, an abnormality, corrected and overcome by Christ.

However, these do not contradict the reality of continuing sin. The persons described as perfect or righteous all have sins recorded in the Bible. Experience also presents a counterargument: perfection is complete conformity to the law of God; my experience is that I do not live in complete conformity to the law of God; the conclusion follows that I am not perfect.[47] The conflict in the believer between the flesh and the Spirit is very clear in the New Testament (Rom. 7:14–25; Gal. 5:16–26; Phil. 3:8–16; 1 Pet. 2:11).

On Romans 7 the majority verdict in Reformed interpretation is that, from verse 14, Paul refers to the believer. The change of tense in verse 14, together with the reference to delighting in the law of God in the inner man (v. 22), has been seen as crucial. In contrast, Arminian scholars have generally taken Paul to refer to unbelievers. Ridderbos (not an Arminian) adopted this view. However, the thrust of Paul's argument is redemptive-historical, referring not to individuals as such but rather to how union with Christ, expounded in chapter 6, affects our relationship to the law. Thus, he is talking the language of two *aeons*. Set free from the law, we are now married to Christ. That does not set the law aside, since it is

---

47. There is a story of a preacher who asked his congregation for any to stand who led a sinlessly perfect life. A man stood up. "Oh, you are perfect, are you?" was the preacher's challenge. "No," the man replied. "I'm standing on behalf of my wife's first husband!"

holy and good; indeed, it discloses what is sin and what is good, and so in the end will always, rightly used, direct us back to Christ (7:25ff.). However, one's position on the continuance of sin in the Christian life does not stand or fall on a reading of this difficult chapter.

Instead, the continuance of sin is confirmed by Galatians 5:16–26. Here two contrasting principles are set forth. If you live according to the flesh, you cannot enter the kingdom of God. But, Paul says, you have crucified the flesh. Nevertheless, it retains power and poses a danger. The raw force of this passage cannot be blunted. There is a real conflict, a life-and-death struggle. But the result is victory over the flesh by the power of the Spirit.

Again, in Philippians 3:8–16 progress is won through conflict. Perfection here is maturity, not sinless perfection. We press on through obstacles to the final goal. Death is the final negative transformation of sanctification, resurrection the final positive element. The goal of sanctification is achieved at the resurrection.

Perfectionism denies this. One prominent form was seen with Charles Finney, who followed Pelagius in teaching that sin is voluntary transgression of known law.[48] Thus, he held that conscious knowledge was necessary for acts to be sinful. However, the law does not legislate against known sin only but forbids everything not in conformity to it, whether known by us or not. In the Old Testament, sins of ignorance also required sacrificial offerings (Lev. 4:1–35). Indeed, the law functions to make sin known and to expose it, where previously it was hidden and unknown. The law of God reveals God's perfections. It is not adjusted to us; we are to be adjusted to it. Other forms of perfectionism have an overrealized eschatology, in which the present age is relativized; such may have been a problem Paul addressed in the Corinthian church.

Biblical evidence for the progressive and presently incomplete nature of sanctification is seen in comments such as Hebrews 12:1–3. The context from Hebrews 10:39 refers to the righteous in the Old Testament. A goal is still held out before them (Heb. 11:39–40). They are not made perfect apart from us. The process of sanctification is still occurring. Philippians 3:8–16 presents the same message, as does 1 John 1:6–2:2. Since our salvation will not be complete apart from the resurrection of

---

48. Charles G. Finney, *Lectures on Systematic Theology* (London: William Tegg, 1851). See Benjamin B. Warfield, *Perfectionism*, ed. Samuel G. Craig (Philadelphia: Presbyterian and Reformed, 1958), 166–215, esp. 187–89.

the body, we will not be perfected until then, although from the time of death we will no longer be able to sin.

25.3.8 Erroneous Views of Sanctification

Two crucial safeguards against faulty views of sanctification are Philippians 2:13, which states that we are to work out our salvation, since God is at work in us, and Romans 8:13–14, where Paul insists that we by the Spirit put to death the deeds of the body. It is God's work, but our responsibility.

Pelagianism held that fallen humans retain the ability to respond in faith to the gospel apart from God's grace. This view feeds into a mentality of trying harder. Be more dedicated. A common phrase in times past was that so and so was "a keen Christian." Pelagius was concerned about the moral standards in Rome. His teachings were based on a low view of sin, not taking into account its debilitating effects and our dire need for grace. Though his views were declared heresy at the Council of Carthage in 418, this mind-set still lures us into assuming that our own effort accomplishes God's purposes—as if by our sheer dedication we can advance. This ignores the fact that it is God who works in us, that the Spirit is the efficient cause of our killing the sinful inclinations that remain.

The Keswick doctrine of sanctification was developed in England by the Keswick Convention, which started in 1875. Its distinctive message related to the higher Christian life. Most Christians, it held, are leading substandard lives as defeated Christians. The convention program followed a set format. At first the message of defeat was preached, together with its proclaimed resolution to reckon ourselves dead to sin, based on Romans 6. This was considered the secret to the victorious Christian life. The conference attendees were led through this procedure and finally, at the end of the week, were encouraged to offer themselves for missionary service. This was the view of sanctification held by the convention until recently. Effectively, the message was "let go and let God," encouraging pietism, quietism, and mysticism. It was dealt a death blow by J. I. Packer in his first published work.[49] As Packer indicated, the Higher Life teaching has a kinship with Pelagianism, with a weak view of sin, a high view of human ability, and a correspondingly impoverished view of

---

49. James I. Packer, "'Keswick' and the Reformed Doctrine of Sanctification," *EQ* 27 (1955): 153–67.

grace. Much depends on the human "reckoning" of oneself dead to sin. Once done, the change was from defeat to volunteering for missionary service in the space of four days. What applies to Keswick is also relevant to other forms of perfectionism, or doctrines of sanctification that create a spiritual elite.

In some fundamentalist circles in the United States it has been common to distinguish between having Christ as one's Savior and having him as Lord. This assumes that it is possible to have faith in Christ but not submit to the lordship of Christ. This betrays a heretical Christology as well as soteriology. Without obedience and good works, it is not possible to be saved (Matt. 7:15–27; Heb. 12:14).

25.4   Perseverance[50]

25.4.1   The Meaning of the Term

The perseverance of the saints is grounded on the truth and reliability of the God's promise of salvation. The phrase "the perseverance of the saints" is important, for often the doctrine that true believers will continue in faith until the end and thus surely be saved is called "the eternal security of the believer." Perseverance is a much better description since it highlights the necessity of sanctification and the struggle entailed in it.

The word *perseverance* conjures up the idea of struggle against a variety of obstacles, "through many dangers, toils, and snares."[51] A host of enemies are ranged against us. There is the world, with its insidious attractions and subtle temptations. Closer to home, we battle against the flesh; even if we were to withdraw into the desert like the Egyptian monks and thus avoid the lure of the surrounding culture, we would carry with us the remaining bias toward sin. Lurking in the background, too, is the devil and the hosts of wickedness against which our warfare is waged (Eph. 6:10–18). From general suffering—the lot of all in a fallen world—to overt persecution for being a follower of Christ, together with temptations to sin, we face a legion of obstacles. Is it a surprise that Peter writes that "the righteous is scarcely saved" (1 Pet. 4:18)?

---

50. This section, through the end of the chapter, is based on the concluding section of R. W. A. Letham, "The Relationship between Saving Faith and Assurance of Salvation" (ThM thesis, Westminster Theological Seminary, 1976). Much of this was included in Robert Letham, "Perseverance and the Promises of God," *Testamentum Imperium* 1 (2005–2007): 1–10. See http://www.precious heart.net/ti/2007/index.htm Accessed 4 March 2019. This is an open access site with a very extensive series of articles on the subject.

51. From the hymn "Amazing Grace," by John Newton (1779).

The phrase "the perseverance of the saints" points to our need for God's help, for we "by God's power are being guarded through faith" (1 Pet. 1:5). We are in dire need of the help the Holy Spirit alone can give. This is a far cry from talk of security, which conjures up images of carefree reclining in comfortable, plush, padded chairs, safe and secure from all alarms, hermetically and unrealistically sealed from contact with the nasty realities of spiritual battle.

The phrase also draws attention to the essential factor of sanctification. Those who persevere are *the saints*, those who belong to Christ and are in the process of becoming conformed to his image. There is struggle; the Spirit's help is urgently needed. But this help is forthcoming, for the struggle is marked by progress, slow and erratic as it may be, but nonetheless heading in the right direction, to eventual conformity to Jesus Christ. Conversely, the phrase "the eternal security of the believer" makes the issue one of simply believing. While the saints are believers, this detaches faith from sanctification. We are talking here simply of definitions; those who use this phrase hardly intend to belittle this urgent task. The point is that the form of words does not do justice to an utterly essential element of salvation, "the holiness without which no one will see the Lord" (Heb. 12:14), and so the phrase implies a certain complacency.

What exactly is the perseverance of the saints? The doctrine means that all whom the Father has chosen to salvation in Christ will certainly be brought to saving faith, be maintained in faith by the Holy Spirit until the very end of their days, and so inherit eternal life. It entails, in the words of the Lambeth Articles (1595), that "a true, living, and justifying faith, and the Spirit of God justifying [sanctifying], is not extinguished, falleth not away; it vanisheth not away in the elect, either finally or totally."[52]

25.4.2 The Foundation of Perseverance

This fortifying and robust doctrine is founded on the indestructible pillars of the faithfulness of God, the truth of his promises, and the sovereignty of his grace.

The faithfulness of God. The uniform testimony of Scripture is that God does not act contrary to his own character. This is not because of

---

52. Schaff, *Creeds*, 3:523–24 See also *The Canons of the Synod of Dort, rejectio errorum circa doctrinam de perseverentia sanctorum.* Schaff, *Creeds*, 3:575.

any external constraint, of which there can be none, but because he is always true to himself; this is his freedom. Hence, he cannot change in himself (James 1:17). If he could, he might move from one degree of perfection to another and consequently at some point be less than perfect. Again, he cannot die, since he is "the living God" (Heb. 10:31). Nor can he deny himself (2 Tim. 2:13) or lie (Heb. 6:18). These characteristics affirm his freedom to be himself.

Hence, the covenant and our entire salvation rest upon the faithfulness of God. Since he is faithful and true, all he has done for sinful humanity in redemption is certain to be fulfilled. Because redemption is God's work, so is it free from the arbitrary and capricious uncertainty of human actions. That is why Abraham's faith rested on Yahweh and why he was satisfied to wander throughout his life estranged from the tangible possession of the promised covenant land. Since salvation is nothing short of the complete fruition of covenant fellowship with God in union with Christ, it is a progressive and eventually consummated awareness of the faithfulness of God realized in union with him.

The truth of God's promises. The truth of the central promise of God's covenant, "I will be your God, and you shall be my people," follows from the faithfulness of God himself. This—along with all the promises God makes in Christ—entails two things. First, it is true in contrast to false. It also means that it genuinely represents the attitude of God toward those to whom it is made.

Naturally, any idea of the falsity of the covenant promise is ruled out on the grounds of God's character. However, questions have arisen over the sincerity of God's intention when the gospel promise is made indiscriminately. How, it is asked, can God sincerely desire to grant salvation to any to whom the promise is made when many of those who hear it may be destined for everlasting destruction (2 Thess. 1:9)? Some, accepting these realities, believe that the gospel offer is to be restricted to those who are inwardly convicted of sin, since it would seem that God cannot and does not sincerely offer forgiveness and eternal life to those from whom he has decreed to withhold it and who will in fact never believe. This sounds very logical, but its Achilles' heel is the New Testament requirement that the gospel be proclaimed indiscriminately, as well as the apostolic example of preaching to as wide a circle as possible. Besides, we ourselves cannot know for sure who is under conviction of sin at any one point (Deut. 29:29).

There is another problem with restricting the gospel offer. That would make God's inscrutable decree of election the basis for our actions. On the one hand, the Bible clearly teaches that God chose his people to salvation "before the foundation of the world" (Eph. 1:4). On the other hand, we are also warned that the secret things belong to God; what is revealed belongs to us and prescribes what we may do (Deut. 29:29). If eternal election is made the basis for our actions, we are close to dehistoricizing salvation. What happens here and now in human history is then emptied of significance.

The sovereignty of God's grace. Paul frequently rests assurance of salvation on effectual calling. The ineffable decree of election is made known in its historical and temporal dimensions by God's gracious power displayed in the renewal of those who were dead in sin (Rom. 8:29–30). Salvation in its consummated form is inevitable for those who have been called by his invincible grace. This is not because of a rigidly deterministic fatalism, a matter of logical necessity that reduces us to robots, but because of the irrevocable will of the faithful God (Rom. 11:29). We must be clear that God's will is not that of an arbitrary despot but that of a loving and self-sacrificing Father who did not spare his own Son, not for good people but for outright sinners and rebels (Rom. 5:8; 8:32). The electing decree of God bursts into the milieu of history at the point of calling and justification, and thus provides the basis for the unbreakable "golden chain" of salvation in Romans 8:29–30. From first to last, salvation is an exercise of God's grace to elect sinners and so is lifted out of the realm of the merely possible. God's grace is given to us and maintained in us by the Spirit, who does not leave things half done but brings to perfection those works he has begun (Phil. 1:6).

As a corollary, assurance of salvation has only ever flourished where the sovereignty of grace has been clearly attested. The key to assurance is perseverance. A denial of the perseverance of the saints removes the confidence that we will possess the eternal inheritance the Father has promised in Christ to those who love him. If there is any chance that one may fall from grace and perish eternally, there can be no certainty that we will eventually be saved. Any such assurance we have is despite this theology rather than because of it. All remains in the balance until the end, like a game of soccer that swings dramatically one way and then the other until the final whistle. That is why the Articles of Remonstrance

(1610), produced by the followers of Arminius, adopting an equivocal position on perseverance, removed the possibility of assurance of ultimate salvation, and why, in response, the Synod of Dort (1618–1619) so strongly affirmed that the elect are given the grace to persevere and so are also able to obtain the certainty, by the Holy Spirit, of their preservation.[53] That is also why the theology of Rome denies the possibility of infallible certainty of ultimate salvation, apart from special revelation or the pronouncement of the church. Similarly, the Wesleyan movement has denied perseverance and so can lay claim only to assurance of the present possession of salvation, not to salvation in the ultimate sense, for no one can be sure that he or she will not fall from grace totally or finally.[54]

The focus of God's promises is in Christ. All that God intends and has effected for our salvation is in his Son and by his Spirit. In Christ all the promises of God find their clinching affirmation (2 Cor. 1:20).[55] In many places in Scripture, especially in the New Testament, God promises to preserve his elect people for salvation in and through his Son, Jesus Christ. Jesus speaks of the Father's determination to give a people to the Son. Each and every one of these will believe in him and will be raised from the dead at the last day (John 6:37–40). He distinguishes between his sheep, who believe him and follow him, and those who are not his sheep, who do not believe in him. He knows his sheep and calls them by name. He gives them eternal life. They shall never perish, and no one can snatch them out of his hand. Moreover, the Father will not allow this danger to occur either, and no one can snatch them out of the Father's hand (John 10:1–30, esp. vv. 28–30). In his great prayer to the Father, Jesus refers to the fact that none of those were lost whom the Father had given him (John 17:1–26). Paul declares that those called to salvation in Christ by the Spirit are justified by faith and glorified; so certain is this that Paul represents it as a definitive act, done and dusted. Elsewhere he writes of Christ's purpose to save, sanctify, and beautify his church as a bride in union with him (1 Cor. 1:8–9; Eph. 5:25–27; 1 Thess. 5:23–24). We could go on.

In contrast, Hebrews appears to counteract this in warning strenuously of the imminent danger of apostasy (Heb. 3:7–4:10; 6:1–8;

---

53. Schaff, *Creeds*, 3:548–49, 571–74.
54. Mark A. Noll, "John Wesley and the Doctrine of Assurance," *BSac* 132 (1975): 161–77.
55. Robert Letham, *The Work of Christ* (Leicester: Inter-Varsity Press, 1993), 39–53.

10:26–39; 12:25–29). Some Hebrew Christians may have idealized the wilderness generation of Israel, which, turning back from the Promised Land, perished in the desert. Many of their own number had repudiated Christ in some public way. The author's point is that, while the generation that experienced the exodus tasted the Word of God and saw his power, they did not believe his promises. Theirs was a superficial acquaintance with the saving work of Yahweh; it stopped short of saving faith (Ps. 106:12–15; Heb. 4:1–2, 6). The tenses in Hebrews 6:4–8 all suggest a punctiliar experience of God's works and a definitive repudiation of his promises. So too, those who identified with the Christian church but later reverted to some form of Judaism made a once-for-all repudiation of Christ. As John wrote of a heretical group that abandoned the church through a rejection of basic Christian teaching: "They went out from us, but they were not of us; for if they had been of us, they would have continued with us. But they went out, that it might become plain that they all are not of us" (1 John 2:19).

Paul, in Ephesians 1:3–14, unfolds the great drama of salvation from election before creation (v. 4), to redemption by the Son through the cross (v. 7), to the gift of the Spirit as the guarantor of the inheritance we shall receive at the end of history (vv. 13–14). This plan of salvation has a Trinitarian pattern: the Father has chosen and foreordained us (vv. 3–5), the Son has redeemed us and will head up all things (vv. 7–10), and the Spirit is the earnest of the full inheritance (vv. 13–14).[56] However, throughout this one huge sentence that makes up verses 3–14—"the most monstrous sentence conglomeration that I have encountered in Greek," said the early twentieth-century German scholar E. Norden[57]—there is a recurring phrase, "in him" or "in Christ," denoting that every aspect of salvation is in union with Christ. This is the central theme of the whole gamut of salvation from eternity through time to its ultimate consummation.[58]

In this context, Paul's frequent theme of Christ as the second Adam is significant.[59] Christ recapitulated Adam, taking our place and obeying God, where Adam had disobeyed. Precisely as the *incarnate* Son, one with us, Jesus offered himself to the Father. Consequently, we are

56. Robert Letham, *The Holy Trinity: In Scripture, History, Theology, and Worship* (Phillipsburg, NJ: P&R, 2004), 75–78.
57. E. Norden, *Agnostos Theos* (Leipzig: Teubner, 1913), 253n1.
58. Letham, *The Work of Christ*, 80–81, 86.
59. Philip Edgcumbe Hughes, *The True Image: The Origin and Destiny of Man in Christ* (Grand Rapids, MI: Eerdmans, 1989).

accepted in him and in him have access to the Father continually, by the Holy Spirit (Eph. 2:18).

In terms of Christ's mediation, he endured suffering throughout his life and ministry, reaching a pinnacle around the time of the cross. In the words of the Heidelberg Catechism, 37, "All the time he lived on earth, but especially at the end of his life, he bore, in body and soul, the wrath of God against the sin of the whole human race."[60] He was tempted in all points like we are, yet without sin (Heb. 4:14–15). He faced abandonment and betrayal by his friends, murderous hostility from the ruling authorities, the fierce onslaughts of Satan, and—on the cross—abandonment by the Father. Was this all in vain? On the third day he rose again from the dead, ascended into heaven, and sits on the right hand of God the Father almighty, from where he will come to judge the living and the dead. Why all this struggle and anguish?

In *The Lord of the Rings*, Frodo and Sam carry the ring through an endless succession of hideous adventures, death threatening at every turn. Eventually, exhausted and traumatized, they reach their goal; the ring is consigned, in remarkable circumstances, to destruction in the Cracks of Doom; and the evil empire of Mordor crumbles. Yet the two hobbits escape by the skin of their teeth; as the world around them quakes to its foundations and erupts in a consuming fireball, they are plucked from certain death and flown to safety by the eagles. But why? Why, my late uncle asked, why could not the eagles have flown them there in the first place and so relieved them of the desperate dangers?

Why, then, did Jesus Christ have to suffer so to bring us home to safety? The answer is the justice and righteousness of God, with whom, as the eternal Son of God, he was fully and completely one. There was no other way, since God is just and true to himself. There was no other way than by taking into union our nature and in our nature repairing the damage done by the first man. There was no way other than by uniting us to himself through the Holy Spirit and thus restoring us to God—even more, introducing us to something the first Adam never knew: union and communion with the holy Trinity in Christ.

Hence, the question of perseverance needs to be redrawn. While it refers to us and the question of our continuing in faith to the end of our life in this world and so to the ensuing completion of our salvation at Christ's

---

60. Schaff, *Creeds*, 3:319.

return, it is preeminently a question relating to Christ. Transcending the issue of our perseverance is the question of whether the Father will actually give to his Son his church, which he has purposed to do from all eternity. Will the Father fail to provide his Son with his bride? Remember Jesus's comment that an earthly father—being evil—knows how to give good gifts to his son (Matt. 7:7–11). In turn, will the Spirit fail to bring to the Son those whom the Father has given him? At the end of the day, will the Triune God be disappointed, frustrated, unable to implement his eternal plan? Will his purposes fail? The answer is obvious: he will no more be thwarted than he was in bringing the universe into being, or in bringing into effect the incarnation of his Son!

If from the side of God, the issue is clear-cut, then we must affirm from the human angle that God's ultimate purpose will not fail. Since there is to be no breakdown of the plans of the holy Trinity, from our side all true believers will persevere in faith to the end, whatever the obstacles may be. This is rooted in the purpose and promises of God, which come to expression in Jesus Christ. It is seen in the cross, where the living triune God goes to the utmost extremity to deliver us. It is heard in the cry of dereliction Jesus utters (Matt. 27:46), citing Psalm 22 and thus including in its ambit its triumphant conclusion. It is demonstrated in the empty tomb and in Jesus's ascension to the right hand of the Father, where he bears our humanity, his hands now uplifted in priestly benediction (Luke 24:50–51).

Thanks be to God!

Further Reading

Beeke, Joel R. *Knowing and Growing in Assurance of Faith*. Fearn: Christian Focus, 2017.

Collier, Jay T. *Debating Perseverance: The Augustinian Heritage in Post-Reformation England*. Oxford: Oxford University Press, 2018.

Garner, David B. *Sons in the Son: The Riches and Reach of Adoption in Christ*. Phillipsburg, NJ: P&R, 2017.

Owen, John. "Of the Mortification of Sin in Believers." In *The Works of John Owen*. Vol. 6, *Temptation and Sin*, edited by William H. Goold, 1–86. Reprint, Edinburgh: Banner of Truth, 1966.

Trumper, Timothy J. R. "The Metaphorical Import of Adoption: A Plea for Realisation: I: The Adoption Metaphor in Biblical Usage." *SBET* 14 (1996): 129–45.

Trumper, Timothy J. R. "The Metaphorical Import of Adoption: A Plea for Realisation: II: The Adoption Metaphor in Theological Usage." *SBET* 15 (1997): 98–115.

Study Questions

1. What are the grounds for assurance of salvation? Is it an integral component of saving faith?

2. What is adoption? How significant is the continuing status of sonship? Why has it been neglected over the years?

3. Discuss the question of perseverance from the perspective of the Father's gift of an inheritance to the Son (John 6:37–40).

26

The Progress of the
Christian Life (2)

The Lord's Supper and *Theōsis*

The Lord's Supper is one of the principal means God uses to develop our communion with Christ and to conform us to his image. It is a memorial of Christ and his work, whereby the gospel is proclaimed in visual form, but it is also communion, in which the faithful are enabled by the Holy Spirit to feed on Christ. The Supper is efficacious by the Holy Spirit through faith and is joined to and dependent upon the Word as it is read and proclaimed. This process is termed *theōsis*, by which we are made partakers of the divine nature (2 Pet. 1:4). This does not mean a blurring of the Creator-creature distinction, but it does mean that we progressively are made like Christ so that when he returns in glory, we shall be like him.

26.1 The Lord's Supper[1]

In the Reformation and its immediate aftermath, the Lord's Supper was the single most discussed topic. Martyrs were burned at the stake for their denial of the Roman dogma of transubstantiation. Intramural

---

1. The section on the Lord's Supper is a greatly condensed version of material in my book *The Lord's Supper: Eternal Word in Broken Bread* (Phillipsburg, NJ: P&R, 2001).

Protestant polemics attempted to explain the manner of Christ's presence in the sacrament. Yet, under the impact of post-Enlightenment individualism, evangelicalism relegated the Supper to an optional extra. The eighteenth-century revivals led to a Christian being understood as someone who could claim a personal experience of conversion, with the work of the Spirit on the individual paramount and church and sacraments often seen as divisive.

26.1.1 Biblical Foundations

Jesus instituted the Lord's Supper on the night he was betrayed (Matt. 26:20–30; Mark 14:17–26; Luke 22:14–23). Paul records the word of institution (1 Cor. 11:23ff.). Often the Last Supper is thought to be a Passover meal, but this is not entirely straightforward. Certainly, Jesus was crucified on the Passover; his death is clearly connected with it (1 Cor. 5:7). However, John records that the Supper occurred the night before. While Jesus was on trial, after the Supper, it was the time for preparation for the next day's Passover meal (John 18:28). There was a clear connection between these events and the Passover, but the point of contact was the cross.[2] The clearest connection with the Old Testament is with the covenant meal eaten by Moses and Aaron, Nadab and Abihu, and the seventy elders of Israel on the top of Mount Sinai (Ex. 24:1–11). Moses took half of the blood of the burnt offerings and fellowship offerings and sprinkled it on the altar (the rest he put in bowls), read the book of the Covenant to the people, and then sprinkled the remaining blood on the people, saying, "Behold the blood of the covenant" (Ex. 24:8). The leaders of Israel then climbed the mountain, saw the God of Israel, and ate and drank. This was a fellowship meal with the God of Israel. Jesus's words of institution clearly reflect this scene when he says, "This is my blood of the new covenant."[3]

New Testament terminology. The New Testament terms express different dimensions of meaning. The Supper is called the breaking of bread

---

2. Many scholars in Britain and Europe reject the idea that this was a Passover meal. See R. T. France, "Chronological Aspects of 'Gospel Harmony,'" *VE* 16 (1986): 50–54; C. K. Barrett, *The Gospel according to St John: An Introduction with Commentary and Notes on the Greek Text*, 2nd ed. (London: SPCK, 1978), 48–50; Joachim Jeremias, *The Eucharistic Words of Jesus* (London: SCM, 1966), 44–62. But see, in contrast, D. A. Carson, *The Gospel according to St John* (Leicester: Inter-Varsity Press, 1991), 455–57.

3. See Wayne A. Grudem, *Systematic Theology* (Grand Rapids, MI: Zondervan, 1994), 988–89.

(Acts 2:42; 20:7) and the Lord's Table (1 Cor. 10:21), a rite belonging to Christ, which he instituted, and at which he resides. It is the Lord's Supper (1 Cor. 11:20). Paul mentions communion in the body and blood of Christ (1 Cor. 10:16–17), *koinōnia* meaning "fellowship," "participation in," or "communion." A fifth term occurs in the institution of the Supper (Matt. 26:26–27; Mark 14:22–23; Luke 22:17–19; 1 Cor. 11:23–24). Jesus "took bread, gave thanks, [and] broke it." The verb εὐχαριστέω[4] means "give thanks" and gave rise to the liturgical term *Eucharist*. It is a thanksgiving.

What happens in the Eucharist

It is a memorial. Jesus's words "do this in remembrance of me" are popularly understood to mean an act of memory on our part. In covenantal terms, it is more like the memorial stones Israel set up to record the mighty acts of Yahweh (Gen. 28:18–22; Josh. 4:1–24).

It is a proclamation of the gospel (1 Cor. 11:26). Augustine described this vividly in calling the sacraments "a kind of visible word of God."[5] Whereas preaching brings the gospel to our ears, the sacraments portray it before our eyes. As we see a loaf of bread torn to pieces, the wine poured into a cup, so Christ's body was given and his blood outpoured that we might receive life.

It is communion with Christ. Paul calls the Eucharist "communion" or "participation" in the body and blood of the Lord (1 Cor. 10:16–17), relating to our union with Christ and its cultivation by the Holy Spirit as we eat and drink the material elements.

Does John 6:47–58 have any bearing on the Eucharist? Debate has surrounded whether John's description of Christ as the Bread of Life and our feeding on him refers to the sacrament. Many reject this connection. Two factors appear to support this reluctance. First, Jesus spoke these words before he gave instructions about the Eucharist. Would his words make sense if he intended to refer to the Supper? Second, some would say that to interpret this passage as sacramental leads us to view his statement about eating his flesh and drinking his blood as tantamount to cannibalism.

Against the first objection are many instances where Jesus mentions events before they happen. He referred to his death and resurrection, the

---

4. *eucharisteō.*
5. Augustine, *On John* 80.3 (*PL*, 35:1840, *NPNF*[1], 7:344).

gift of the Spirit, the persecution of the church, the destruction of the temple, church discipline, and the church itself long before those things came to be (Matt. 16:21–28; 24:1–36; John 16:1–4; cf. Matt. 16:13–20; 18:15–20; Mark 13:1–31; Luke 21:5–33). Why could he not have done the same with the Supper? Furthermore, the preceding narrative of the feeding of the five thousand has language similar to the Synoptic Gospels' description of the institution of the sacrament (Matt. 26:26–27; Mark 14:22–23; Luke 22:19; John 6:11). There is sufficient evidence there for at least an allusion to the Supper. Early Christian art often associated the Eucharist with that miracle.[6] Furthermore, the following section portrays apostasy by many disciples in the light of the "hard saying" of the discourse (John 6:60–71), while Jesus refers to Judas's defection. This recalls the events when Judas, having received the bread, stalked out to betray Jesus.

Furthermore, Jesus's language of eating his flesh and drinking his blood is best seen in the light of the Eucharist. The early church was later accused of cannibalism and incest, since they spoke of eating Christ's flesh and drinking his blood in the love feasts among brothers and sisters.[7] In the Patristic era this passage was normally understood to refer to the Eucharist. Interestingly, many scholars who dispute such a reference nevertheless recognize that what Jesus teaches here finds its fullest expression there.[8]

The context. Having fed the five thousand, Jesus reflects on the miraculous feeding of the Israelites by Yahweh in the desert, claiming to fulfill this event. Jesus is the Bread of Life, given by the Father to sustain his people through their earthly pilgrimage (John 6:25–40). He has come to feed and nourish us. Furthermore, this nourishment is eternal (vv. 37–40). All those the Father has given Jesus will come to him, believing in

---

6. Raymond E. Brown, *The Gospel according to John (I-XII)*, The Anchor Bible (Garden City, NY: Doubleday, 1966), 246f.; C. F. D. Moule, "A Note on Didache ix.4," *JTS* 6 (1955): 240–43.

7. J. Stevenson, ed., *A New Eusebius: Documents Illustrative of the History of the Church to AD 337*, rev. W. H. C. Frend (London: SPCK, 1987), 36, 66, citing Eusebius, *Ecclesiastical History*, and Athenagoras, *Legatio pro Christianis*.

8. George R. Beasley-Murray, *John*, Word Biblical Commentary 36 (Waco, TX: Word, 1987), 94–95; Carson, *St John*, 288–98. On the other hand, Raymond E. Brown argues that the Eucharist is a secondary theme. Brown, *John*, 282–83, 291–92. Barnabas Lindars claims that the sacraments are presupposed by John. Lindars, *The Gospel of John*, The New Century Bible Commentary (Grand Rapids, MI: Eerdmans, 1972), 59. Rudolph Schnackenberg points out that recent work on John has demonstrated that the words of institution lie behind the discourse. Schnackenburg, *The Gospel according to St John*, vol. 1, *Introduction and Commentary on Chapters 1–4*, trans. Kevin Smyth (Tunbridge Wells, Kent: Burns & Oates, 1968), 55.

him (v. 37). They will not be cast out but will be preserved in faith, be given eternal life, and ultimately be raised from the dead.

Jesus, the Bread of Life, is received through faith (vv. 41–47). The Jews grumble at these claims, much as Israel in the desert had done. Jesus met with unbelief and consternation. He stresses that faith is a gift of God (vv. 44–47) through which the Father draws us. He alone can break down this hostility. Jesus the Bread of Life is received through faith, the result of the Father's gift.

Jesus, the Bread of Life, is eaten and drunk in the Lord's Supper (vv. 48–58). Jesus adds that the bread he gives is his flesh given for the life of the world, referring to his death. The bread Jesus provides for our nourishment is himself offered on the cross, a full human fleshly reality. A figurative understanding of the cross is heretical. Newbigin remarks that σάρξ[9] here, instead of σῶμα[10] as in the Synoptics, "shifts the content of what it means to receive Jesus away from a purely mental and spiritual hearing and believing, in the direction of a physical chewing and swallowing."[11]

This was scandalous! "How can this man give us his flesh to eat?" the Jews asked each other (v. 52). The shock and revulsion were clear! To drink blood was forbidden by the law and, before that, by the legislation given after the flood (Gen. 9:4). Animal blood was to be drained before the meat could be eaten (Lev. 3:17; Deut. 12:23). Still less was human blood acceptable.

Nevertheless, Jesus did not moderate his language or explain it as figurative. Rather, he intensified it. He did not back off or correct any possible misunderstanding. Instead, he boldly underlined his assertion. The crowd understood him only too well; their reaction was rational. Jesus insisted that the eating and drinking were very physical! From John 6:54 there is a remarkable change of verb. Hitherto John used φαγεῖν,[12] from ἐσθίω,[13] which means simply "eat." Now he has switched to τρώγω,[14] a crude word meaning "chew, gnaw or bite audibly."[15] He uses this verb exclusively throughout the rest of the passage. In choosing

---

9. *sarx.*
10. *sōma,* "body."
11. Lesslie Newbigin, *The Light Has Come: An Exposition of the Fourth Gospel* (Grand Rapids, MI: Eerdmans, 1982), 84–85.
12. *phagein.*
13. *esthiō.*
14. *trōgō.*
15. Cf. Brown, *John,* 282–83, 291–92.

it he highlights the physical process of chewing and swallowing and the audible accompaniments that go with it. This is so in verses 54, 56, and 57. Far from appeasing his opponents, he challenges them head-on. This is clear by their ultimate reaction; these words are recognized as "a hard saying," an unbearable one (vv. 60–66). Many abandon discipleship. Even the Twelve waver.

Obviously, Jesus does not advocate cannibalism. But neither can his language be emptied of its raw force. If he had wanted to offset the Jewish hostility, he had every opportunity to do so. If we view the narrative as connected with the Eucharist, there is a solution. By talking of our eating his flesh and drinking his blood, Jesus shows exactly *how* he, the Bread of Life, feeds and nourishes us to everlasting life. Christ is to us the Bread of Life as we feed on him, eating his flesh and drinking his blood in the Supper. This means two inseparable things, like two sides of the same coin. Believing, on the one hand; eating and drinking, on the other—*both* go together, and *both* are necessary and indispensable.

First, *we feed on Christ, the Bread of Life, through faith*. The Eucharist is not magic, automatically conveying God's grace. As the wilderness generation fell short, and Jesus's opponents did not believe, so without faith we cannot eat the true bread and receive eternal life. Moreover, *Christ is the Bread of Life in his Supper*. Jesus does not teach magic, but neither does he purvey an idealized, spiritual salvation divorced from the flesh. Eating and drinking go together with faith. The Supper is central to the gospel. The Supper without faith profits us nothing; faith without the Supper is barren. In the Lord's Supper through faith, given by the Spirit, we eat Christ's flesh and drink his blood and so are nourished to everlasting life.

What are the consequences of eating Christ's flesh and drinking his blood in the Lord's Supper through faith? First, *we are granted union and communion with Christ by the Holy Spirit* (v. 56). As we eat, food becomes one with us. It enters our system, and we digest it and so produce energy that enables us to live an active life. So when we eat and drink Christ, he enters our system, indwelling us, and we remain in him. We grow into union. There is mutual indwelling—he in us his church, we in him. This is a great mystery.

Second, *we are introduced into the living fellowship of the triune God* (v. 57). The living Father sent the Son. The Father has life in himself. He sent the Son in the incarnation, when the word became flesh and lived among us (John 1:14). In turn, he gave the Son to have life in himself (John 5:26), so that the Son lives because of the Father. Thus, the Son receives life from the Father. There is an inviolable order in the indivisible Trinity. Furthermore, we receive life from the Son as we chew him in the Eucharist. Has this ever been better expressed than by Calvin?

> Accordingly, he shows that in his humanity there also dwells fullness of life, so that whoever has partaken of his flesh and blood may at the same time enjoy participation in life.
>
> We can explain the nature of this by a familiar example. Water is sometimes drunk from a spring, sometimes drawn, sometimes led by channels to water the fields, yet it does not flow forth from itself for so many uses, but from the very source, which by unceasing flow supplies and serves it. In like manner, the flesh of Christ is like a rich and inexhaustible fountain that pours into us the life springing forth from the Godhead into itself. Now who does not see that communion of Christ's flesh and blood is necessary for all who aspire to heavenly life?[16]

Third, *we receive eternal life* (John 6:47–51, 53–54, 58). Christ gave his flesh for the life of the world. He has eternal life, since he *is* eternal life. At the last day, we shall be raised from the dead, since we are united with him who is the life. This life is poured into us by the Spirit as, in faith, we feed on Christ in the Lord's Supper. It is a pledge to the faithful that we will share in the resurrection at the last day.

26.1.2 The Lord's Supper in Church History

The question remains, how is this so? The following have been the principal attempts to understand how we feed on Christ.

Transubstantiation. The view that the bread and wine undergo a change of substance and become the body and blood of Christ[17] surfaced as early as the second century,[18] developed over the years in the Latin church, and eventually became dogma at the Fourth Lateran Council in

---

16. Calvin, *Institutes*, 4.17.9.
17. The Council of Trent, *DS*, 1642; *CCC*, 297–311.
18. Justin Martyr, *Apology* 1.66 (*ANF*, 1:185). But this passage is ambiguous and has been claimed by Protestants as well.

1215.[19] In the East, transubstantiation also held sway, but Orthodoxy does not try to *explain* what happens, instead highlighting the aspect of mystery.

In the West, Aristotelian philosophy was used to explain how the bread and wine can be changed into the body and blood of Christ, when it is obvious to our eyes that they are still the same as they ever were. The Aristotelian distinction between *substance* and *accidents* was the means to resolving this conundrum. The substance of a thing is what that thing really is intrinsically. Accidents refer to incidental features, relating not to a thing's inner nature but to what it may appear to be, or to something adventitious that could be withdrawn without altering that thing's substance.[20] Hence, when the priest consecrates the elements, the bread and wine are held to change into the body and blood of Christ according to substance (*trans* = "change," *substantia* = "of substance"), according to what they are, while they remain bread and wine *per accidens*, in terms of appearances. This is not magic but a sacramental mystery.

This development is readily intelligible if Jesus's teaching in John 6 is sacramental. The most obvious potential misunderstanding would be to view his words in a corporeal sense. This simplification took root at the popular level, fostered by a growing idea that the ministers of the church were priests, priests offer sacrifices, and so the priests of the church presented the Eucharist as a sacrifice of the body and blood of Christ. As early as the third century, both Origen (185–254) and Cyprian (200–258) talked of the Supper as a "eucharistic sacrifice."[21]

Rome's position on the relationship between nature and grace also helped this development. Since, according to Rome, grace perfects nature, natural gifts and gifts from the Spirit are virtually identical. The material and the spiritual are so closely identified that in practice they merge. From this, it was held that the bread and wine were the body and

---

19. That it was not universal in the Western church until later is evident in the work of the ninth-century monk Ratramn (d. 868), in his *De corpore et sanguine Domini*. He stresses that the elements remain unchanged (xii–xiii), that John 6 is not to be taken corporally (xxix, xxxiii), that the sovereign power of the Holy Spirit is necessary (xxvi–xxxi), and that Christ is eaten spiritually, not physically (lix–lxii). As bread and wine nourish and intoxicate human beings, so the Word of God, who is the living bread, revives the minds of believers (xl). See *Ratramnus, De corpore et sanguine Domini: Texte original et notice bibliographique* (Amsterdam: North-Holland, 1974).

20. Richard A. Muller, *Dictionary of Latin and Greek Theological Terms Drawn Principally from Protestant Scholastic Theology* (Grand Rapids, MI: Baker, 1985), 18–19, 290–91.

21. Cyprian, *Epistola 63*; Johannes Quasten, *The Ante-Nicene Literature after Irenaeus*, vol. 2 of *Patrology* (Westminster, MD: Christian Classics, 1992), 85–87.

blood of Christ, spiritual grace conveyed more or less automatically by physical means. It is hard to see how this view could put in such an early appearance if the New Testament intended us to think of the Eucharist in purely figurative terms.[22]

Transubstantiation was opposed by the Reformers. Abandonment of the Mass was the single most decisive event marking the Reformation in its various centers. Why was that departure so significant?

First, transubstantiation confuses the sign with the reality. Rome stressed the connection at the expense of the distinction, compressing the spiritual and the physical, nature and grace.

Second, a number of consequences flow from the teaching. If the bread is now the actual body of Christ, it follows that the faithful must worship it. It is elevated for all to see and adore. It follows that any of the sacramental elements left over afterward must not be thrown away. One cannot drop the body of Christ into a garbage can or allow the blood of Christ to spill on the floor. Hence, the bread is reserved and must be preserved or consumed at a later date in another sacramental observation, while the wine is drunk immediately.

Third, and crucially, the doctrine of transubstantiation undermines the need for faith in the recipients. If the body and blood of Christ are consumed corporeally, then all who ingest them receive the grace conveyed *ex opere operato* (by the action performed). When the sacrament is objectified, the onus on the receivers to examine themselves and come to the Table with penitent and believing hearts is inevitably weakened.[23] Yet Jesus, in John 6, connects the eating and the drinking with believing. The two go together. Moreover, Paul stresses that self-examination is essential in the Supper (1 Cor. 11:23ff.). That Rome teaches the need for self-examination is despite its doctrine, not because of it.[24]

Consubstantiation. The Lutheran doctrine is that Christ's body and blood are corporeally or substantially present alongside the bread and wine.[25] For Luther and Lutheranism, the Supper also involves the

---

22. John Williamson Nevin, *The Mystical Presence: A Vindication of the Reformed or Calvinistic Doctrine of the Holy Eucharist* (1846; repr., Eugene, OR: Wipf & Stock, 2000), passim.

23. This is despite the qualifications made by CCC, 259, where it states that "the fruits of the sacraments also depend on the disposition of the one who receives them."

24. CCC, 313.

25. The Formula of Concord, art. 7: ". . . truly and substantially present, and are distributed with the bread and wine, and are taken with the mouth by all those who use this sacrament, be

substantial presence of the body and blood of Christ. However, Luther vehemently rejected transubstantiation. For him, the bread and wine remain bread and wine. They undergo no change of substance. Nevertheless, he understood Jesus's words "This is my body" literally. At the Colloquy of Marburg (1529), when he, Zwingli, Bucer, and others met to try to reach agreement in their conflict with Rome, he repeatedly scrawled on the table, *hoc est corpus meum*, underlining *est*.[26] Since the bread itself could not be the body, Luther concluded that Christ was physically present "in, with, and under" the elements. How could this be?

The solution was sought in the Christological innovation I discussed in chapter 18. Luther argued that there was a transference of divine attributes to the human nature of the incarnate Christ. Thus, among others, the attribute of ubiquity was communicated to Christ's human nature. From this, the risen Christ could be present everywhere not only according to his deity but according to his humanity also. He could be present in his body and blood simultaneously wherever the sacrament was celebrated. His body and blood could then be distributed and taken with the mouth.[27]

This explanation had no clear precedent in Christian thought. Its ingeniousness was its Achilles' heel. If divine attributes such as omnipresence were communicated to Christ's human nature, how could that human nature still be human? Is not an indispensable aspect of humanity the property of being in one place at one time? How could a body be omnipresent and still human? We saw earlier that Luther and Chemnitz argued for three forms of presence in attempting to offset this criticism. In seeking to maintain a corporeal presence of Christ in the Lord's Supper while rejecting transubstantiation, Luther may have bitten off more than he could chew.

The theory is also susceptible to the same objection as transubstantiation, insofar as for Lutheranism, all who receive the elements receive the body and blood of Christ, the sacrament being efficacious unless resisted. The need for faith in the receiver is eroded.

---

they worthy or unworthy, good or bad, believers or unbelievers." Philip Schaff, *The Creeds of Christendom* (Grand Rapids, MI: Baker, 1966), 3:135.

26. B. J. Kidd, *Documents Illustrative of the Continental Reformation* (1911; repr., Oxford: Clarendon, 1967), 247–54.

27. Formula of Concord, 7:1–11, 8:11–12, in Schaff, *Creeds*, 3:137–40. See the discussion of the *communicatio idiomatum* in chap. 18.

The doctrine of the real absence: the Eucharist as a memorial only. At the other end of the spectrum is the idea that the Lord's Supper is purely symbolic, consisting solely of a memorial of Christ's death. This is the position ascribed to Huldrych Zwingli, although he may have retreated from it before his premature death. However, it is now the most widespread view in evangelical circles. It is reinforced by an anxiety not to be identified with Rome.

Exponents of this idea deny that there is anything more in the Supper than the recipients' mental reflections. The Supper is not a channel of grace, for in no sense is Christ present corporeally, since his body is in heaven. There are clear biblical foundations for what this position affirms. The words of Jesus "Do this in remembrance of me" unmistakably teach that the Eucharist is a memorial. However, the memorial is akin to the memorials of the mighty acts of God recorded in the Old Testament (Gen. 28:18–22; Josh. 4:1–24).

Objections mainly relate to what the position denies. It is ironic, since Christ is present everywhere as the Son of God, that the stress is on his absence! Moreover, the purely symbolic idea supposes that John 6 is nonsacramental. This creates a difficulty surrounding Jesus's very realistic language. Can advocates of a purely symbolic interpretation do justice to this?

There is also a broader philosophical and theological problem. Zwingli was strongly influenced by Neoplatonism, with its dichotomy between the physical and the spiritual realms. Matter was regarded as on a lower plane than spirit. Zwingli had difficulty seeing how God's spiritual grace could be channeled through physical means. How could Christ be present in a sacrament in which bread and wine were used?[28] This is a continuing problem for the interpretation. It rests on a radical separation between sign and reality. If Rome confuses the two, the real absence separates them. If Rome virtually identifies natural and spiritual gifts, this position sets them apart. It fails to consider a number of crucial theological matters. God created all things, physical as well as spiritual. All things are his; he can use whatever he has made as a vehicle to communicate his goodness to us. In turn, in the incarnation the eternal Son assumed human nature, body and soul, into permanent

---

28. See W. P. Stephens, *The Theology of Huldrych Zwingli* (Oxford: Clarendon, 1986), 194–259. For Zwingli on baptism, see Robert Letham, "Baptism in the Writings of the Reformers," *SBET* 7 (1989): 21–44.

union. The physical has been created by God and, in Christ, taken into union with him. Moreover, our salvation is not complete until our bodies are raised. Consistently throughout the Bible, the physical and the spiritual go together. To separate them in the way this view does is to rend asunder what God has united. Calvin remarked that "to deny the true communion of Jesus Christ to be offered us in the Supper is to rend this holy sacrament frivolous and useless."[29]

The memorialist interpretation has been fostered by the rise of individualism in the West. Descartes, seeking to establish the existence of God and the self from a position of radical systemic doubt, took his starting point from the phrase "I think, therefore I am." Consequently, the existence of the thinking individual became the axiomatic basis of Western thought and culture. Its effect on the church and Christian thought has been immense. The evangelical movement of the eighteenth century focused on individual personal salvation at the expense of the corporate.[30] The Supper was relegated to a private, individual matter. The doctrine of the real absence of Christ fails to do justice to the nature of the sacrament on exegetical, philosophical, and theological grounds.

The doctrine of the real spiritual presence. In the classic Reformed view of the Eucharist, we are united with Christ by the Holy Spirit.[31] The Reformed join the advocates of memorialism in rejecting a corporeal presence of Christ. For Christ to be human entails his being restricted physically to one place at one time; he cannot be ubiquitous according to his humanity without ceasing to be human. Indeed, if he could, we could never be saved, since we need a human Christ to save us, a second Adam to undo the damage caused by the first.[32]

Notwithstanding, this viewpoint differs markedly from memorialism in claiming that Christ is indeed present in his Supper. More is involved than a remembrance on the part of the participants. Christ gives himself to be eaten and drunk in faith. This eating and drinking is not corporeal but is nonetheless real and true, and is joined to the corporeal consump-

29. John Calvin, *Short Treatise on the Holy Supper of Our Lord and Only Saviour Jesus Christ*, in *Calvin: Theological Treatises*, ed. J. K. S. Reid (Philadelphia: Westminster, 1954), 166.
30. Robert Letham, *The Work of Christ* (Leicester: Inter-Varsity Press, 1993), 211–20; Robert Letham and Donald Macleod, "Is Evangelicalism Christian?," *EQ* 67 (1995): 3–33.
31. WCF, 29.7; Scots Confession, 21; Belgic Confession, 35; French Confession, 36; Schaff, *Creeds*, 3:467–70, 428–31, 380.
32. Letham, *The Work of Christ*, 105–24.

tion of bread and wine. In the Supper, Christ does not come down to us in his body and blood. Instead, we are lifted up to him by the Holy Spirit. Christ, being the eternal Son of God, is omnipresent. Moreover, he has permanently united to himself the human nature assumed in the incarnation. In that sense, the person of Christ is present with us as we eat and drink. Yet on earth the Son of God was not restricted or confined to the humanity he assumed but simultaneously filled all things, directing the universe even as he walked the dusty roads of Palestine.[33] Now at the right hand of God, he fills and directs the universe (Col. 1:15–20), indivisibly united to his assumed humanity, while in terms of that same humanity he is limited and in one place. Yet that humanity is never separate or apart from the Son of God with whom and in whom it is one undivided person. Thus, in the sacrament the Spirit unites the faithful to the person of Christ as they eat and drink the signs, the physical elements of bread and wine. There is an inseparable conjunction of sign and reality. As truly as we eat the bread and drink the wine so we feed on Christ by faith.

Hence, there is a real, objective communion in the Lord's Supper, while the condition of the recipients is neither incidental nor superfluous. We feed on Christ through faith, as he taught. Faith does not exist apart from the Supper, but neither does the Supper apart from faith, for faith is indispensable. Just as we need a mouth to receive bread and wine, so we need faith to receive Christ. As Robert Bruce put it, "As soon as you receive the bread in your mouth (if you are a faithful man or woman) you receive the body of Christ in your soul, and that by faith." Bruce underlines that what we receive is first and foremost not the benefits of Christ, nor the graces that flow out of Christ, but Christ himself.[34] The recipients are therefore to be believing and receptive. The physical and the spiritual are not merged (as in transubstantiation), nor are they separated (as in memorialism). Instead, they are distinct but inseparable. The physical can be the channel of grace, since God created all things, Christ assumed our human flesh, and our bodies will be raised like his at the last day.

---

33. Calvin, *Institutes*, 2.13.4. For a fuller discussion of this point, see Edward David Willis, *Calvin's Catholic Christology: The Function of the So-Called Extra Calvinisticum in Calvin's Theology* (Leiden: Brill, 1966).

34. Robert Bruce, *The Mystery of the Lord's Supper: Sermons on the Sacrament Preached in the Kirk of Edinburgh in A.D. 1589*, ed. and trans. Thomas F. Torrance (London: James Clarke, 1958), 44–46.

26.1.3   Word and Sacrament

We encountered earlier the close relation between the Word of God and the sacraments. The two go together, but the Word has priority in both its written and its preached form. This is so for two reasons. First, the Bible is the speech of God, breathed out by God (2 Tim. 3:16), the product of the Holy Spirit sweeping the human authors along in a mighty current so that their own human discourse was, at the same time, the speech of God (2 Pet. 1:20–21). Behind this is the ministry of the ascended Christ, who received the promised Spirit from the Father.[35] Again, the preaching of the Word of God "by ministers of the gospel lawfully called"[36] is to be received as the Word of God himself (Rom. 1:14–15; Eph. 2:17).[37] A living, dynamic connection exists between the eternal Word, the written Word (Scripture), and preaching.[38] Thus, the reading and preaching of Holy Scripture shares, by the grace of God, in the priority of God's address to us in the gospel. Second, the Word creates the sacraments. This is true on a number of levels: (1) The incarnate Word, Jesus Christ, appointed both baptism and the Eucharist and so has full authority over them. (2) Jesus did this by his spoken word, recorded in the Bible; the written Word defines them for us. (3) As signs they point beyond themselves to the reality. This connection and significance requires explanation, or the sacrament is reduced to a bare ritual. Therefore, the Word must always go with sacrament, and since the Word has priority, the sacraments must always be administered by a minister of the Word properly ordained. Ordination sets a man apart to minister the Word of God. As the church ordains, so too does the Holy Spirit (Acts 13:1–7). Without the preaching of the Word by one lawfully called, there is no sacrament.[39]

26.1.4   The Lord's Supper and Union with Christ

We will consider the relationship of the Lord's Supper and union with Christ later in this chapter.

---

35. The Letham, *The Work of Christ*, 91–102.
36. *The Second Helvetic Confession*, 1:4, in Schaff, *Creeds*, 3:237–38, 831–33.
37. The Letham, *The Work of Christ*, 99.
38. Barth, *CD*, I/1.
39. Bruce, *Mystery*, 107–13.

26.1.5 The Lord's Supper and Practical Matters

Paedocommunion.[40] Recently, a growing number have advocated paedocommunion—giving communion to infants and very young children who have not made a public profession of faith. Two factors have encouraged this. One is a new interest in Eastern Orthodoxy, for the East has always practiced paedocommunion.[41] A second factor flows from covenant theology. Some argue that since the whole family participated in the Passover and does so in baptism, why should the Supper be different?

However, paedocommunion fits best with positions other than those of the Reformed confessions. The first fit is with transubstantiation. If the bread becomes the body of Christ, it follows that whoever eats the bread receives Christ's body. Therefore, to deny the bread to infants is to deny them grace. The other fit is memorialism. If the Supper is simply a figurative remembrance and not a means of grace, and so not a means of judgment to the unbelieving (1 Cor. 11:27–32), it hardly matters who receives it, since no adverse consequences are likely.

In contrast, the Reformed stress that the Lord's Supper requires faith, repentance, and self-examination.[42] If the means of grace can become a means of judgment, discipline, and even of damnation, it is essential that participants be qualified as penitent sinners.[43] So two qualifications are required for receiving the Supper. First is baptism, the sacrament of initiation. Second is profession of faith, for this is essential to feed on Christ, the Bread of Life. Because the Eucharist is a sacrament of the church, not a matter of private or individual choice, this faith must be tested by the officers of the church to detect, as far as possible, its credibility.

Frequency. The New Testament does not prescribe how often the Supper should be held. The church is at liberty on this. We know that the primitive church took the Supper frequently, for it was a constant feature of church life. The disciples devoted themselves to "the breaking of bread." This is in an ecclesiastical context, linked with the apostles'

---

40. The elements in the Eucharist are bread (ἄρτος, *artos*, the word used in the New Testament, referred to an everyday, leavened loaf) and wine (Jesus changed the water into wine; the temperance movement changed the wine into grape juice).

41. Timothy Ware, *The Orthodox Church* (London: Penguin, 1969), 295.

42. "The Lord's Supper is to be administered often . . . and that only to such as are of years and ability to examine themselves." WLC, 177.

43. Bruce, *Mystery*, 47, 49, 67.

teaching, their fellowship, the prayers, and the temple (Acts 2:42–47). The church at Troas met each week expressly "to break bread" (Acts 20:7). At Corinth, the regular purpose of church gatherings was to observe the Lord's Supper (1 Cor. 11:18ff.). Yet, while the example of the early church is a guide, it cannot bind us, any more than their disposal of personal property requires us to do likewise.

The Reformers and their successors called for frequent communion. The Scottish Reformation had a different hue than later developments. The Supper was to be held frequently, "commonly . . . once a month or so oft as the Congregation shall think expedient."[44] In 1561, when Knox ministered to his congregation in Edinburgh, he once held communion daily for a week.[45]

As for Calvin, his *Short Treatise on the Holy Supper* (1540) states:

> If we have careful regard to the end for which our Lord intended it, we should realise that the use of it ought to be more frequent than many make it. . . . Therefore the custom ought to be well established, in all churches, of celebrating the Supper as frequently as the capacity of the people will allow. . . . Though we have no express command defining the time and the day, it should be enough for us to know that the intention of our Lord is that we use it often; otherwise we shall not know well the benefits which it offers us.[46]

In his *Articles concerning the Organization of the Church and of Worship in Geneva* (1541), proposed to the Council of Ministers of Geneva, Calvin says, "It would be well to require that the Communion of the Holy Supper of Jesus Christ be held every Sunday at least as a rule."[47] He was overruled by the Little Council and the Council of Two Hundred.[48]

---

44. J. H. S. Burleigh, *A Church History of Scotland* (London: Oxford University Press, 1960), 163.

45. Richard L. Greaves, *Theology and Revolution in the Scottish Reformation* (Grand Rapids, MI: Christian University Press, 1980), 107. Greaves points out that Knox's preference for frequent communion is akin to Luther's and Calvin's and the English Reformers'. See also Norman Sykes, *The Crisis of the Reformation* (London: Centenary, 1946), 55, 68, 91–92.

46. Reid, *Calvin: Theological Treatises*, 153; John Calvin, *Tracts and Letters, Part 2*, ed. and trans. Henry Beveridge, vol. 2 of *Selected Works of John Calvin* (1849; repr., Grand Rapids, MI: Baker, 1983), 179–80.

47. John Calvin, *Articles concerning the Organization of the Church and Worship at Geneva Proposed by Ministers at the Council January 16, 1537*, in Reid, *Calvin: Theological Treatises*, 49. See also *Calvin, Institutes*, 4.17.43: "The Supper could have been administered most becomingly if it were set before the church very often, and at least once a week."

48. Wulfert De Greef, *The Writings of John Calvin: An Introductory Guide*, trans. Lyle D. Bierma (Grand Rapids, MI: Baker, 1993), 144–45; Ronald Wallace, *Calvin's Doctrine of the Word and Sacrament* (Edinburgh: Oliver and Boyd, 1953), 253.

In England, Thomas Cranmer, the great reforming archbishop of Canterbury, in his liturgy, insisted on frequent, at least weekly, communion.[49]

While Presbyterianism became known for infrequent communion, the Westminster Assembly took a different line. "The Directory for the Publick Worship of God" specified that the Lord's Supper be held often: "but how often, may be considered and determined by the ministers, and other church-governors of each congregation, as they shall find most convenient for the comfort and edification of the people committed to their charge."[50] Scottish Presbyterians moved to infrequent communion by historical accident rather than design. After the Restoration in 1660, Charles II attempted to enforce the Royal Supremacy over the kirk. Many dissented. Persecuted congregations were often forced to meet in secret, as ministers were in short supply. Communion could be held only every so often, when a minister happened to be in the area. By the time religious liberty was granted in 1688, infrequent communion had become part of the tradition.

The degree to which the church desires communion is a reliable gauge of how eagerly it wants Christ. The key word is "often." The question to ask is, how far do we desire communion with Christ? As Robert Bruce put it so vividly, "If Christ is not both eaten and digested, he can do us no good, but this digestion cannot exist where there is not a greedy appetite to receive him."[51]

26.1.6 The Lord's Supper and the Future

When initiating the Supper, Jesus said, "I will not eat it until it is fulfilled in the kingdom of God. . . . I will not drink again of the fruit of the vine until the kingdom of God comes" (Luke 22:16, 18). He looked forward to the time of fulfillment, the eschatological feast to which Isaiah alluded (Isa. 25:1–8). There, the relationship between Christ and his church will be consummated. The central covenant promise, "I will be your God, and you shall be my people," will come to its ultimate fruition. No longer will we "see through a glass darkly," for we shall see face-to-face. The communion the church enjoys with Christ will be unimpeded by sin.

---

49. James C. Spalding, *The Reformation of the Ecclesiastical Laws of England, 1552*, Sixteenth Century Essays and Studies 19 (Kirksville, MO: Sixteenth Century Journal Publishers, 1992), 120, 122.

50. "The Directory for the Publick Worship of God," in *The Confession of Faith, the Larger and Shorter Catechisms with the Scripture Proofs at Large, Together with The Sum of Saving Knowledge* (Applecross, Ross-shire: Publications Committee of the Free Presbyterian Church of Scotland, 1970), 384.

51. Bruce, *Mystery*, 45.

However, we have a foretaste of that great banquet already. Christ promises to have supper with us here and now (Rev. 3:20). The author of Hebrews indicates that the church already has one foot in heaven. Warning against the danger of Hebrew believers reverting to some form of Judaism by venerating the past, especially the wilderness generation led by Moses, he says that New Testament worship is, in essence, communion with the triune God in fellowship with the entire church and joined with the whole angelic throng.

> You have come to Mount Zion, and to the city of the living God, the heavenly Jerusalem, and to innumerable angels in festal gathering, and to the assembly of the firstborn who are enrolled in heaven, and to God, the judge of all, and to the spirits of the righteous made perfect, and to Jesus, the mediator of a new covenant, and to the sprinkled blood that speaks a better word than the blood of Abel. (Heb. 12:22–24)

The church's worship is therefore communion with the risen Christ, in company with the angels and the church in heaven. Revelation 4 and 5 present a picture of this scene. While we are engrossed in our everyday affairs, we are simultaneously lifted up to heaven by the Spirit to participate in the cosmic adoration in heaven, with other creatures joining in to add their voices. This comes to focus in the Eucharist. Preceded by the preached Word—into which angels long to look (1 Pet. 1:12)—the Supper draws us into ever-closer union with Christ. The Lord's Supper and the Lamb's Supper are two sides of the same reality, since the Lamb is the Lord. "Therefore with angels and archangels and with all the company of heaven, we proclaim your great and glorious name, forever praising you and saying Holy, holy, holy Lord, God of power and might. Heaven and earth are full of your glory. Hosanna in the highest."[52]

26.2   Theōsis[53]

26.2.1   Union with Christ and Theōsis

Union with Christ from regeneration to glorification has been understood differently in the Eastern and Western churches. As in some plant

---

52. "The Order for Holy Communion: Also Called the Eucharist and the Lord's Supper: Rite A," in *Services from the Alternative Service Book, 1980: Authorized for Use in the Church of England in Conjunction with the Book of Common Prayer* (Cambridge: Cambridge University Press, 1980), 139.

53. I have fuller expositions of this theme in my books *The Holy Trinity: In Scripture, History, Theology, and Worship* (Phillipsburg, NJ: P&R, 2004) and *Union with Christ: In Scripture, History, and Theology* (Phillipsburg, NJ: P&R, 2011).

forms, cross-fertilization can be a way to growth and advancement. Recent years have seen an increased interest in the Eastern church. This has been due to the growing exposure of Orthodoxy in the Western world and to a stream of conversions from Protestantism, largely of those disenchanted by the triviality of much evangelicalism.[54] Central to the Orthodox view of salvation is the doctrine of *theōsis*. Whereas Protestantism in general, and the Reformed churches in particular, have focused on the atonement and justification, the Eastern preoccupation from its earliest days has been on transformation by the Holy Spirit. In the second century, Irenaeus pointed the way, while Athanasius made his celebrated statement concerning the incarnation of Christ, "He became man that we might become God."[55]

This sounds alarming to Protestants. Reformed commentators have often considered *theōsis* to entail the pagan notion of apotheosis, humanity being elevated to divine status; such an idea blurs the Creator-creature distinction, foundational to biblical revelation. It has been seen by Harnack and Barth as man becoming God ontologically. Such would negate the church's Christology in its repudiation of Eutychianism's swamping of the humanity.[56] However, these fears are misinformed. Gavrilyuk writes, "Apparently, polemical resourcefulness at times frees theologians from the unrewarding responsibility to check the historical evidence."[57] *Theōsis* did not, nor does it, imply that humans become uncreated, divine beings. Yet there are grounds for Reformed misgivings, especially in the version associated with Gregory Palamas, in which, overall, there are significant elements at odds with Protestant theology, particularly in the synergistic view of the relationship between divine and human action.[58] Indeed, Gavrilyuk suggests that a full-scale retrieval of *theōsis* will lead to the unraveling of Protestant soteriology.[59] This could occur only if Protestantism opted for synergism. Notwithstanding, in the earlier work of the Alexandrians Athanasius and Cyril, *theōsis* encompasses under

54. Robert Letham, *Through Western Eyes: Eastern Orthodoxy: A Reformed Perspective* (Fearn: Mentor, 2007).

55. Athanasius, *On the Incarnation* 54 (*PG*, 25:192; *NPNF*, 4:65).

56. See chap. 17 for Eutychianism; also Adolf von Harnack, *History of Dogma*, trans. James Millar (London: Williams & Norgate, 1897), 2:318; Barth, *CD*, IV/2:81–82, I/2:19–20.

57. Paul L. Gavrilyuk, "The Retrieval of Deification: How a Once-Despised Archaism Became an Ecumenical Desideratum," *MTheol* 25 (2009): 647.

58. See Gavrilyuk, "Retrieval"; Gannon Murphy, "Reformed Theōsis?," *Theology Today* 65 (2008): 191–212.

59. Gavrilyuk, "Retrieval," 657.

one umbrella what in Reformed theology is understood to occur in the entire movement of God's grace in transforming us into his image in Christ: regeneration, sanctification, and glorification combined. On this, neither Athanasius nor Cyril has set the agenda for the East.

26.2.2   The Doctrine of Theōsis in Athanasius and Cyril of Alexandria

According to Fairbairn, there were two main branches in Eastern Christian thought. The first, in Origen and Gregory of Nyssa, is close to apotheosis. In this line of thought, a generic human nature was created by God and is now divinized. Salvation entails being absorbed into God, individuals losing their identity as they are merged into this deified humanity. However, another approach was adopted at Alexandria by Athanasius and Cyril. With these two, humans remain humans while deified; they do not lose their humanity. *Theōsis* does not mean becoming God ontologically. Nor is it merely communion with God's attributes (or energies, in the terms of Gregory Palamas). Rather, it is union and communion with the *persons* of the Trinity. This is achieved in our sharing, by grace, the relation to the Father that the Son has by nature, so retaining both personal and human identity.[60] It is with this second line of thought that I shall interact, as it provides some insights and clarifications that are helpful for our understanding of what union with Christ does and does not entail.

First, what does Athanasius actually mean when he says, "He [Christ] became man, that we might become God."[61] Russell writes that Athanasius means "either to emphasize the glorious destiny originally intended for the human race, or to explain that the biblical references to 'gods' do not encroach upon the uniqueness of the Word made flesh."[62] This follows from the uniqueness of the incarnation. Underlying this reality is Christ's assumption of human nature into personal union. The Son made us sons of the Father and deified humanity by becoming man himself.[63] By becoming incarnate and receiving a human body, he deified that nature, uniting in himself human nature with the nature of God.

---

60. Donald Fairbairn, "Patristic Soteriology: Three Trajectories," *JETS* 50 (2007): 298–310.
61. Athanasius, *Incarnation* 54 (NPNF², 4:65; PG, 25:192).
62. Norman Russell, *The Doctrine of Deification in the Greek Patristic Tradition* (Oxford: Oxford University Press, 2004), 168.
63. Athanasius, *Orations against the Arians* 1.38–39 (PG, 26:92–93; NPNF², 4:329).

The *theōsis* of the humanity of Christ by the Son in the incarnation is primary. Since from his conception the human nature was taken into personal union by the Son, the assumed humanity was made capable of such union. The Logos received a human body so that, having renewed it as its Creator, he might deify it in himself and thus bring us all into the kingdom of heaven in his likeness. He united the nature of the Godhead with the nature of humanity so that our salvation and deification might be made sure. Christ's humanity, body and soul, was given the grace of being capable of everlasting personal union with the eternal Son of God.[64]

The *theōsis* of Christ's humanity is the foundation of our own. Athanasius does not mean that Christ's human nature ceased to be human. This could hardly be the case. Being the staunchest defender of Christ's deity, Athanasius never means that the Son ceased to be God in becoming man. Therefore, when he states that we might become God, he cannot mean that we cease to be human, nor that Christ's humanity was not real humanity. He means that all things receive the characteristics of that in which they participate. Hence, by participating in the Holy Spirit we become holy; by participating in the Logos, we are able to contemplate the Father.[65] This, we could add, follows the principle that a person becomes increasingly like the object that commands his or her worship. Idolaters become like their worthless idols (Ps. 115:4–8; Rom. 1:22ff.); so in worshiping the holy Trinity we become like Christ and eventually will be exactly like him according to our humanity (2 Cor. 3:18; 1 John 3:1–2). Athanasius continues from this to maintain that in this way we are participants in Christ and God.[66]

Athanasius's main term for expressing this is μέτοχοι (partakers).[67] What does he mean? He clearly distinguishes our *theōsis* from Christ himself, who, he characteristically says, is "from the being of the Father" (ἐκ τῆς οὐσίας τοῦ Πατρός). Russell indicates that Athanasius normally couples μέτοχοι with an explanatory synonym so as to avoid possible misunderstanding. "Adoption, renewal, salvation, sanctification, grace, transcendence, illumination, and vivification are all

---

64. Athanasius, *Against the Arians* 3.23, 33–34 (PG, 26:369, 373, 393–97; NPNF², 4:406, 411–13).
65. Athanasius, *Serapion* 1.23–24 (PG, 26:584–89).
66. Athanasius, *Serapion* 1.24 (PG, 26:584c).
67. *metochoi.*

presented as equivalents to deification. Although the concept itself is not controversial, Athanasius may well be intending to exclude any possibility of misunderstanding."[68] For him, the notion of *theōsis* is expanded, moving the emphasis away from immortality and incorruption to the exaltation of human nature through participation in the life of God. "Deification is certainly liberation from death and corruption, but it is also adoption as sons, the renewal of our nature by participation in the divine nature, a sharing in the bond of love of the Father and the Son, and finally entry into the kingdom of heaven in the likeness of Christ."[69]

With Cyril, there is a development beyond Athanasius. For Cyril, we have a closer relationship to the whole Trinity, since he stresses strongly the indivisibility of the three in the one identical being of God.[70] Commenting on John 14:23, he states that the Holy Spirit is able to make us participants in the divine nature, since the Father, the Son, and the Spirit are one.[71] *Participation* is the key term for Cyril, in keeping with the frequency of his references to 2 Peter 1:4, "partakers of the divine nature."[72] The Son is God by nature; we are children of God by participation.[73] Cyril approaches the matter theologically rather than mystically; we share in the life of Christ because Christ is "in us" and we are "in Christ."[74] Cyril's Christology stresses the unity of Christ. The eternal Word or Son is the subject of all Christ's actions. The humanity, which is complete, body and soul, is the humanity of the Word. Therefore, everything Jesus did was done by the eternal Son of God; Christ as the divine Son is the agent of redemption.[75] His work of salvation is effected through the Spirit, initiating a dynamic relationship between us and God *through* the Spirit *in* Christ *with* the Father.[76] The incarnate Christ unites within himself the human and divine; he is united to God the Father, since he is God by nature; and he is united to humans, since he is truly

---

68. Russell, *Deification*, 176–77.
69. Russell, *Deification*, 178.
70. Russell, *Deification*, 191–92.
71. Cyril, *Expositio sive commentarius in Ioannes Evangelium*, on John 14:23 (PG, 74:291).
72. Russell, *Deification*, 192–94.
73. Cyril, *In Ioannes Evangelium*, lib. 11 (PG, 74:541d).
74. Russell, *Deification*, 197.
75. Russell, *Deification*, 198–99; Thomas G. Weinandy, "Cyril and the Mystery of the Incarnation," in *The Theology of St. Cyril of Alexandria*, ed. Weinandy (London: T&T Clark, 2003), 23–54.
76. Russell, *Deification*, 200–201; Cyril, *Dialogue on the Most Holy Trinity* 639e–640e (PG, 75:1089).

human.[77] From our side, we are not united hypostatically, but we are being transformed in the Eucharist. The Eucharist is filled with the energy of Christ, and so, when we participate in it, we are being changed, recovering the image and likeness of God.[78]

Russell sums up the Alexandrian teaching on *theōsis*:

> The Alexandrians used the metaphor of deification to indicate the glorious destiny awaiting human nature in accordance with the divine plan of salvation. The fundamental "moment" is the deification by the Logos of the representative human nature he received at the Incarnation. This has implications for individual human beings. The believer can participate in the deified flesh of Christ—the Lord's exalted humanity—through baptism, the Eucharist, and the moral life. Such participation leads to deification, not as a private mystical experience but as a transformation effected within the ecclesial body.[79]

Even in the strand of Eastern teaching exemplified by Maximus the Confessor, Russell concludes that Maximus

> is anxious to exclude both a Eutychian fusion of the divine and the human and an Origenistic ascent of the pure intellect to an undifferentiated assimilation to Christ. Deified human beings become god in the same measure that God became man, but although penetrated by divine energy they retain their created human status.[80]

26.2.3 Biblical Support for Theōsis

In support of *theōsis* is the compatibility between God and humanity, exemplified in the incarnation, Pentecost and the indwelling of the Holy Spirit, and the transformation of believers into the image of Christ. A number of passages shine light on the theme. In 2 Peter 1:3–4, Peter says,

> His divine power has granted to us all things that pertain to life and godliness, through the knowledge of him who called us to his own glory and excellence, by which he has granted to us his precious and very great promises, so that through them you may become partakers of the divine nature.

77. Russell, *Deification*, 201.
78. Russell, *Deification*, 202–3.
79. Russell, *Deification*, 204.
80. Russell, *Deification*, 193–94.

Through his precious and very great promises we become sharers of the divine nature (θείας κοινωνοὶ φύσεως). This is the goal of our calling by God; he has called us "to his own glory." Our destiny as Christians is to share the glory of God. It recalls Paul's comment that "all have sinned and fall short of the glory of God" (Rom. 3:23). Our proper place is to share God's glory; by sin we fell short and failed to participate in his glory; but in and through Christ we are brought to the glory of God as our ultimate destiny. Glory is what belongs distinctively and peculiarly to God. We are called to partake in a creaturely way of what God is. This is more than mere fellowship—intimate interaction but with no participation in the nature of the One with whom we interact. It goes far beyond external relations. It stops short of sharing in the being of God. There is an actual participation in the divine nature.[81] We shall explore this further shortly.

John records Jesus's words, that the Spirit, in coming at Pentecost, "will remain with you and shall be in you"; in the presence of the Spirit, Jesus himself was to be present (John 14:16–17). Jesus then declares regarding those who love him and keep his word, "My Father will love him, and we will come to him and make our home with him" (John 14:23). Μονή means "a place where one may remain or dwell,"[82] conveying the idea of permanence.[83] The coming of the Spirit is the coming of the Trinity; the Father, the Son, and the Spirit take up residence with those who love Jesus. This residence is permanent; the three remain with the faithful. It is the greatest possible intimacy; the three indwell the one who loves Jesus. The faithful thus have a relation with the Trinity far closer than with other humans. This again goes beyond fellowship to communion (or participation) and is strictly an unbreakable union.

Further, in 1 John 3:1–2, John writes: "See what kind of love the Father has given to us, that we should be called children of God; and so we are. . . . Beloved, we are God's children now, and what we will be has not

---

81. James Starr asks whether Peter relapses into Hellenistic dualism at this point. No, Starr concludes—he follows a Pauline and early Christian view of the world. Corruption is not the result of matter but of sin. If deification is equality with God or absorption into the divine essence, Peter does not teach it. If, however, it is participation in and enjoyment of certain divine attributes, in part now and fully at Christ's return, the answer is yes, Peter does teach it. James Starr, "Does 2 Peter 1:4 Speak of Deification?," in *Partakers of the Divine Nature: The History and Development of Deification in the Christian Traditions,* ed. Michael J. Christensen and Jeffery A. Wittung (Grand Rapids, MI: Baker Academic, 2007), 81–92.

82. LN, 1:732.

83. LS, 2:1143.

yet appeared; but we know that when he appears we shall be like him, because we shall see him as he is." The Father's love is such that we now share the relation to him that his Son has. We are now the children of God in Christ. Moreover, at his return, we will be transformed so as to be like Christ the Son. We shall see him in his glory. In union with him, we shall share his glory.

Paul describes the Christian life as lived "in Christ" from beginning to end. We considered this earlier in Ephesians 1, where the whole panorama of salvation from election to our future inheritance is in union with Christ. Paul writes of believers being transformed from one degree of glory to another by the Spirit of the Lord (2 Cor. 3:18). This surpasses the experience of Moses, whose face glowed after communing with Yahweh at Mount Sinai (2 Cor. 3:7–11).[84]

Beyond this evidence, the whole tenor of Scripture points to it. God created us in Christ, the image of the invisible God. Following our sin, and the Son's redemptive work, we are being remade in the image of Christ. The Trinity created us with a capacity to live *in him*, as creatures in and with our Creator. The incarnation proves it. Were it not for that created compatibility, Jesus Christ—God and man—could not be one person, for the difference between Creator and creature would be so great that the incarnation would not be possible.

There are two decisive moments in this great and overwhelming sweep of God's purpose for us. First, in the incarnation the Son takes into personal union a single human nature, while, second, the Spirit comes at Pentecost and indwells or pervades myriads of human persons. There are clear differences here that reflect the differences between the persons of the Trinity. The Son unites a *single* human *nature*, while with the Spirit *countless* human *persons* are involved. With the Son there is a *personal union*, whereas the Spirit *pervades* or *indwells* us.

The Spirit, at Jesus's baptism, rested on him and led him in his subsequent faith, obedience, and ministry. In Christ, we are united with the Spirit who rests on him. The idea of indwelling denotes permanence, for he comes to remain in us forever. However, the word *indwell* could connote a certain incompleteness, as when a liquid is poured into a bucket,

---

84. Finlan says it depends on what one means by *theōsis* as to whether Paul taught it. It cannot be separated from the sacrificial interchange associated with the death of Christ. He speaks of transformation, both progressive and eschatological, into the image of Christ. Stephen Finlan, "Can We Speak of Theosis in Paul?," in Christensen and Wittung, *Partakers*, 68–80.

leaving the bucket itself unaffected, the liquid merely filling the empty space. Pervasion, on the other hand, complements the image of indwelling by suggesting thorough saturation. Again, this does not diminish our humanity. Keep in mind that Jesus is fully and perfectly human, the most truly *human* man, and he is the Christ, the Anointed One, on whom the Spirit rests, directing him throughout the course of his life and ministry. So pervasion by the Holy Spirit *establishes* our humanity.[85] He makes us what we ought to be. He frees us from the grip of a sinful, fallen nature and renews us to be like Christ. This is what it is to be human.[86] Staniloae comments admirably in affirming that only the holy Trinity assures our existence as persons.[87]

Nicholas Cabasilas (1322–?) explains that as Christ flows into us and is blended with us, so he changes us and turns us to himself.[88] Panayiotis Nellas comments, "The essence of the spiritual life is represented clearly by St. Paul's statement, 'It is no longer I who live, but Christ who lives in me' (Gal. 2:20), provided that we take this statement in a literal sense." In fact, "the true nature of man consists in his being like God, or more precisely in his being like Christ and centered on Him."[89] In this, humanity's nature assumes the form of the deified humanity of Christ. This takes place not through the destruction of human characteristics but through their transformation.[90]

This is not pantheism; the incarnation did not entail that. It is not union with the essence of God. Nor is it some form of mixture of divine and human, as advocated by some Eastern religions, like ingredients in an ontological soup. Rather, our humanity is not merely preserved but enhanced. As Christ's humanity was not absorbed in the incarnation but retained its distinct integrity, so the Christian remains human, becoming the place where God dwells, not by nature but by grace. Even our bodies are temples of the Holy Spirit (1 Cor. 6:19).

85. This pervasion is somewhat akin to marriage, where the two become one flesh. Marriage unites a man and a woman, but it does not diminish either one or eliminate their proper characteristics.
86. Incidentally, this is why naturalistic evolution is incompatible with the Christian faith, for man is made to be in union with God—in Christ and permeated by the Holy Spirit. This, not a particular exegesis of a single word in Genesis 1, utterly demarcates Christianity from evolutionism.
87. Dumitru Staniloae, *The Experience of God: Orthodox Dogmatic Theology*, vol. 1, *Revelation and Knowledge of the Triune God*, trans. Iona Ionita (Brookline, MA: Holy Cross Orthodox Press, 1994), 276, 248.
88. Nicholas Cabasilas, *Life in Christ*, ed. Margaret Lisney (London: Janus, 1995), 44.
89. Panayiotis Nellas, *Deification in Christ: Orthodox Perspectives on the Nature of the Human Person*, trans. Norman Russell (Crestwood, NY: St Vladimir's Seminary Press, 1987), 120.
90. Nellas, *Deification in Christ*, 122–23.

Cabasilas thinks that union with Christ "is closer than any other union which man can possibly imagine and does not lend itself to any exact comparisons." This is why, he says, Scripture does not confine itself to one illustration but provides a wide range of examples: for example, a house and its occupants, wedlock, limbs and the head. Indeed, all these metaphors together can barely form an accurate picture. For example, the limbs as members of Christ's church are joined more firmly to him than to their own bodies, for the martyrs laid down their heads and limbs with exultation and could not be separated from Christ even so far as to be out of earshot of his voice. In short, this union is closer than what joins a man to himself.[91] Again, the children of God are closer to Christ than to their own parents. Separated from our parents, we survive; separated from Christ, we would die.[92]

This is a microcosm of the redemption of the whole created order. Christ, in his incarnation, took into union a centrally important part of this order. At the parousia the whole creation will be transformed and suffused with the glory of God (Rom. 8:18–23). Central to this is the redemption of the church and its own transformation. It can no more conflict with justification than can sanctification and glorification, for it comes from the sheer grace of God as a priceless gift.[93]

26.2.4 *The Western Church and* Theōsis

Following Harnack, it has been assumed that *theōsis* was an exclusively Eastern emphasis, alien to the Western church, which focused more on the atonement and justification. Recent scholarship has undermined this thesis. While East and West have had different understandings of the process of salvation, this comparison can be overdrawn. Though something like *theōsis* has by no means featured prominently in Western soteriology, there are still clear echoes to be heard. Gerald Bonner has drawn attention to the theme in Augustine, who in sermon 192 echoes Athanasius and refers to *theōsis* in his commentary on the Psalms, considering it an act of God's grace, by adoption not generation, for it is the exact equivalent,

---

91. Cabasilas, *Life in Christ*, 5–6.
92. Cabasilas, *Life in Christ*, 48–49.
93. For further reading on deification, see A. N. Williams, *The Ground of Union: Deification in Aquinas and Palamas* (New York: Oxford University Press, 1999); Carl Mosser, "The Greatest Possible Blessing: Calvin and Deification," *SJT* 55 (2002): 36–57; Emil Bartos, *Deification in Eastern Orthodox Theology: An Evaluation and Critique of the Theology of Dumitru Staniloae* (Carlisle: Paternoster, 1999).

in Augustine's mind, to adoption.[94] In his sermon on Psalm 82 (81 in the original, following the accepted structure of the Psalms at the time), Augustine expounds these ideas. We were born to mortality, we endure infirmity, we look for divinity, for God wishes not only to give us life but also to deify us (*Gerimus mortalitatem, toleramus infirmitatem, exspectamus divinitatem. Vult enim deus non solum vivificare, sed etiam deificare nos*). God made man, God was made man, and God will make us men gods. The Son of God was made the Son of Man that the sons of men might be made sons of God (*Filius dei factus est filius hominis, ut filios hominum faceret filios dei*). We do not undergo a change of substance, Augustine insists, for it is of a different order, appropriate to creatures in contrast to the Creator.[95] The "gods" in Psalm 82 are gods not by nature but by adoption and grace. There is only one true God, who is eternal, and who deifies. We worship God who makes us gods.[96]

Anna Williams maintains that the theme is present in Aquinas and compares his thought to his Eastern near-contemporary Gregory Palamas. Thomas and Gregory agree that salvation consists in becoming participants in the divine nature but also on the factors that surround it. They both stringently maintain the Creator-creature distinction, which cannot be breached. Humans are not changed into something other than what they are. Moreover, *theōsis* is—by definition—a gift from God; only he can enable us to share his nature. It is an act of grace, unearned and undeserved.[97] In short, Williams concludes, "the West has no grounds for rejecting deification, not only because it can be found in Aquinas but also because it figures extensively in the patristic corpus and derives ultimately from scripture."[98] She continues, "East and West may thus be said to make different uses of the idea of theosis, but this study indicates that at least until the Middle Ages, one cannot characterize the differences between East and West as deriving from two wholly divergent conceptions of either divinization or sanctification."[99] Williams's claims have come under criticism from Gösta Hallonstein, who points to a lack

---

94. Gerald Bonner, "Deification, Divinization," in *Augustine through the Ages: An Encyclopedia*, ed. Allan D. Fitzgerald, OSA (Grand Rapids, MI: Eerdmans, 1999), 265–66.

95. François Dolbeau, "Nouveaux sermons de Saint Augustin pour la conversion des païens et des Donatistes," *RÉAug* 39 (1993): 97.

96. Dolbeau, "Nouveaux Sermons," 98.

97. For Aquinas and Palamas, see Williams, *The Ground of Union*, 34–101 and 129–37 respectively.

98. Williams, *The Ground of Union*, 174.

99. Williams, *The Ground of Union*, 174.

of clarity over what exactly Williams means by deification, and also for her equating the *theme* of deification in Aquinas with the Eastern *doctrine* of deification in Palamas.[100]

Hallonstein's distinction between a theme and a doctrine is significant when it comes to the claims of the Finnish school of Luther interpretation that Luther's doctrine of justification by faith included *theōsis* as an integral part. This interpretation originated with Tuomo Mannermaa's claim that for Luther, Christ is not merely the object of faith but also its subject. Christ is present in the faith itself. He is the form of faith.[101] We considered this in chapter 24. Here occasional comments by Luther are taken as if they were worked out systematically and developed to the status of constituent elements of his thought. There is little doubt that while *theōsis* can be found in key Western figures, it is a dominating soteriological category in the East.

26.2.5 Excursus: Reformed Theology on Union with Christ and Transformation

Reformed theology has generally used the term *union with Christ* to refer to both the forensic and transformational elements of salvation. It is more Christocentric than Eastern pneumatocentrism.[102] However, since Christ and the Holy Spirit work indivisibly and are, together with the Father, one being from eternity, it seems to me that we should hold the work of Christ and the Spirit together in unbroken union. This is also eminently biblical, since the gift of the Spirit was from the ascended and glorified Christ (John 7:37–39; 14:16–23; 16:7–11; Acts 2:33–36), the work of the Spirit is to testify of Christ (John 16:8–15), and the glorified Christ and the Holy Spirit are in the closest possible union in the thought of Paul (2 Cor. 3:17–18).[103]

John Calvin. Calvin sees union with Christ to entail transformation into the image of Christ and profound communion with his humanity in the sacrament. He expresses this throughout his career, boldly before 1550 but in more qualified form later.

---

100. Gösta Hallonstein, "Theosis in Recent Research: A Renewal of Interest and a Need for Clarity," in Christensen and Wittung, *Partakers*, 281–93.

101. Tuomo Mannermaa, "Justification and Theosis in Lutheran-Orthodox Perspective," in *Union with Christ: The New Finnish Interpretation of Luther*, ed. Carl E. Braaten and Robert W. Jenson (Grand Rapids, MI: Eerdmans, 1998), 25–41.

102. Letham, *Through Western Eyes*, 243–65.

103. Vos argues that the phrases "in the Spirit" and "in Christ," where the latter is not used forensically, are equivalent in meaning in Paul's soteriology. Geerhardus Vos, *The Pauline Eschatology* (Grand Rapids, MI: Eerdmans, 1972), 166.

In his Romans commentary (1539), he talks of Christ pouring his power into us, with the result that we share in his risen life, as we depart from our nature into his (*in eius naturam ex nostra demigramus*).[104] Paul compares this union to a tree receiving sap from the root. In spiritual engrafting, not only do we derive the life that flows from Christ, but we also pass from our nature into his (*sed in eius naturam ex nostra demigramus*).[105] Calvin here suggests that union with Christ entails a change in our nature as Christ pours his life into us by the Spirit.

In his *Short Treatise* (1540), Calvin takes this further, concluding that "in receiving the sacrament in faith . . . we are truly made partakers of the real substance of the body and blood of Jesus Christ," and that "the Spirit of God is the bond of participation."[106] He reiterates this in 1546, in his commentary on 1 Corinthians.[107] Christ offers to us not only the benefit of his death and resurrection but also the same body in which he died and rose (*sed corpus ipsum, in quo passus est ac resurrexit*). That body is really (*realiter*) and truly (*vere*) given to us in the Supper, so that it may be health-giving food for our souls. Calvin thus draws to his clinching conclusion: "I mean that our souls are fed by the substance of his body, so that we are truly [*ut vere unum efficiamur cum eo*] made one with him; or, what amounts to the same thing, that a life-giving power from the flesh of Christ is poured into us through the medium of the Spirit, even though it is at a great distance from us, and is not mixed with us [*nec misceatur nobiscum*].[108] Hence, for Calvin union is particularly expressed in the Supper. Here we are fed with the body and blood of Christ. This is not corporeal, since Christ has ascended to the right hand of God, and his body is far from us spatially. However, the Spirit unites things separated by distance, however great. In so doing, he enables us to feed on the glorified humanity of Christ.

In his Ephesians commentary (1548), where Paul compares the marriage relationship to that between Christ and the church, Calvin claims again that in union with us, Christ communicates his substance to us.

---

104. Calvin, *CO*, 49:107; Calvin, *Commentarius in epistolam Pauli ad Romanos*, in *CO2* (1999), 121.

105. Calvin, *Ad Romanos*, 121.

106. In Reid, *Calvin: Theological Treatises*, 166. In the Genevan Catechism (1545) he states that in the Lord's Supper we are made partakers of Christ's substance (*je ne doubte par qu'il ne nous face participans de sa propre substance, pour nous unir avec soy en une vie*).

107. John Calvin, *Calvin's Commentaries: The First Epistle of Paul the Apostle to the Corinthians*, trans. John W. Fraser (Grand Rapids, MI: Eerdmans, 1960), 130.

108. Calvin, *First Corinthians*, 246; Calvin, *CO*, 49:487.

We grow into one body by the communication of his substance. So, he argues, in the Supper Christ offers his body to be enjoyed by us and to nourish us to eternal life.[109] Commenting on Ephesians 5:3, he states that in a sense Christ pours himself into us (*se quodammodo in nos transfundit*).[110] Note that Christ does this "in a sense"—*quodammodo*. Calvin is using metaphorical language, expressing in intelligible terms what transcends explanation. So he acknowledges that this "is a great mystery . . . no language can do it justice . . . whatever is supernatural is clearly beyond the grasp of our minds."[111]

After 1550, he seems to distance himself from the idea that Christ's substance is transmitted to us. Perhaps this reflects the need to seek accord with other Reformed centers that may not have shared his views, in the wake of the Augsburg Interim that reached an accommodation between Catholic and Lutheran jurisdictions and isolated the Reformed. However, this does not diminish his recognition that this is a transcendent mystery.

The note of qualification surfaces in 1551 in Calvin's comments on 2 Peter 1:4. Peter wrote that God has given us his promises so that we might "become partakers of the divine nature." Calvin recognizes the superlative nature of this gift, especially seeing the depths to which we had sunk in sin: "The excellence of the promises arises from the fact that they make us partakers of the divine nature, than which nothing more outstanding could be imagined."[112] Accordingly, "it is the purpose of the gospel to make us sooner or later like God; indeed, it is, so to speak, a kind of deification" (*Notemus ergo hunc esse Evangelii finem, ut aliquando conformes Deo reddamur; id vero est quasi deificari, ut ita loquamur*). He goes on to say that "nature" here means not essence but kind; we participate not in the being of God but in his attributes, his qualities, for his nature refers to what he is like rather than who he is.[113]

Garcia is wrong to rule out deification in Calvin—*quasi deificari* points in that direction.[114] Yet, the *quasi* indicates an ambivalence.

109. Calvin, CO, 16:272; Calvin, *Calvin's Commentaries: The Epistles of Paul to the Galatians, Ephesians, Philippians, and Colossians*, trans. T. H. L. Parker (Grand Rapids, MI: Eerdmans, 1965), 208–9.

110. Calvin, *Epistles of Paul*, 209; Calvin, CO, 16:273.

111. Calvin, CO, 16:273; Calvin, *Epistles of Paul*, 209–10.

112. John Calvin, *Calvin's Commentaries: The Epistle of Paul the Apostle to the Hebrews and the First and Second Epistles of St. Peter*, trans. William B. Johnston (Grand Rapids, MI: Eerdmans, 1963), 330; Calvin, *Commentarii in epistolas canonicas*, in CO2 (1996), 327–28.

113. Calvin, *Hebrews*, 330.

114. Garcia assumes that the Eastern position entailed a merging of divine and human, a participation in the essence of God. There is a lack of primary sources from the Greek tradition. In fact,

Calvin's comments like those above are, by this time of his writing, accompanied by "so to speak" (*ut ita loquor*), "in a certain way" (*quodammodo*), and the like. It is possible, of course, that Calvin may not have been entirely aware of the doctrine of deification in the Greek Patristic tradition himself. His use of Patristic sources might suggest that.[115]

A new reticence is evident in his commentary on John (1553). Union with Christ transcends our capacities and is known only in faith, as the Holy Spirit pours into us the life of Christ. Calvin refers to "the secret efficacy of the Spirit."[116] In commenting on John 17:21, he seems to contradict what he said in his Ephesians commentary, denying that Christ transfuses his substance into us. Instead, we receive his life, communicated to us by the Holy Spirit.[117]

In the final Latin edition of the *Institutes* in 1559, Calvin stresses the connection between the work of Christ and the Spirit. It is through "the secret energy of the Spirit, by which we come to enjoy Christ and all his benefits," for "the Holy Spirit is the bond by which Christ effectively joins us to himself."[118] As a result "Christ is not outside us but dwells within us. Not only does he cleave to us by an indivisible bond of fellowship, but with a wonderful communion, day by day, he grows more and more into one body with us, until he becomes completely one with us."[119] Therefore, in the sacraments the benefits are conferred by Christ through the Holy Spirit, who makes us participators in Christ.[120] This is applied to us more clearly through the sacred Supper, in which his life passes into us and is made ours (*ut vita sua in nos transeat*), just as when bread taken as food imparts vigor to the body.[121]

Earlier we saw how Calvin explains this.[122] This is effected by the Holy Spirit, who in the Supper "truly unites things separated by

---

his exposition of Calvin's views is very close to the position of Athanasius and Cyril. See Mark A. Garcia, *Life in Christ: Union with Christ and Twofold Grace in Calvin's Theology* (Milton Keynes: Paternoster, 2008), 257–58.

115. Anthony N. S. Lane, *John Calvin: Student of the Church Fathers* (Grand Rapids, MI: Baker, 1999), 67–86, 170–75, 232–34.

116. *Calvin's Commentaries: The Gospel according to St. John 11–21 and the First Epistle of John*, trans. T. H. L. Parker (Grand Rapids, MI: Eerdmans, 1959), 84; Calvin, *In evangelium secundum Johannem commentarius pars altera*, Ioannis Calvini opera exegetica (Geneva: Droz, 1998), 150.

117. Calvin, *John 11–21*, 148; Calvin, *Johannem pars altera*, 223.

118. Calvin, *Institutes*, 3.1.1.

119. Calvin, *Institutes*, 3.2.24.

120. Calvin, *Institutes*, 4.14.16.

121. Calvin, *Institutes*, 4.17.5.

122. Calvin, *Institutes*, 4.17.9.

distance."[123] The Spirit of Christ "is like a channel through which all that Christ himself is and has is conveyed to us." "On this account, Scripture, in speaking of our participation with Christ, relates its whole power to the Spirit."[124] Ultimately, Calvin's most frequent imagery is that the *life* of Christ—the risen and ascended Christ—is given to nourish us. At the root of this is that Christ has become one with us in the incarnation, and consequently his flesh receives the life of the Godhead poured into it. From this we receive life in union with him. Together with his concern for the integrity of the humanity of Christ, this leads him to couch his language on themes like deification with *quasi* (a kind of), *ut ita loquor* (so to speak), or *quodammodo* (in a certain manner), thereby opposing the Lutheran view of the *communicatio idiomatum*.[125]

Amandus Polanus (1561–1610). We now turn to a significant theologian from the late sixteenth and early seventeenth centuries. Polanus was more a consolidator of Reformed doctrine than an innovator and, for that reason, is representative of how Reformed theology stood at that time.[126]

In his *Partitiones theologicae* (1586), Polanus stresses the elevation of the humanity assumed by Christ in the incarnation. It is exalted to the highest and ineffable dignity, above all angels and humans, to personal union with the Logos. Moreover, the Holy Spirit gave the fullness of gifts possible for a human nature to have, not only in number but in excellence, as Head of the church and Judge of the world.[127] Like Calvin, Polanus connects our union with Christ with the sacraments. Christ, in communion with us, gives eternal life. In biblical terms, communion is a joining, a

---

123. Calvin, *Institutes*, 4.17.10.

124. Calvin, *Institutes*, 4.17.12.

125. Carl Mosser has argued that Calvin teaches a doctrine of deification. Mosser, "Calvin and Deification." He was strongly opposed by Jonathan Slater but from assumptions that are akin to Nestorianism. Jonathan Slater, "Salvation as Participation in the Humanity of the Mediator in Calvin's *Institutes of the Christian Religion*: A Reply to Carl Mosser," *SJT* 58 (2005): 39–58. Slater believes that Calvin treats the humanity of Christ as effectively autonomous; this precludes any idea of deification. Slater's interpretation of Calvin is suspect. His citations of Calvin are limited to the *Institutes*. Moreover, his Calvin is quasi-Nestorian, and it appears that Slater shares these thoughts himself. Objections to *theōsis* stem largely from a correct stress on the Creator-creature distinction at the expense of their compatibility. This tendency yields a Nestorian Christology, in which deity and humanity are kept separate.

126. See Robert Letham, "Amandus Polanus: A Neglected Theologian?," *SCJ* 21 (1990): 463–76. Richard Muller calls Polanus "a theologian of considerable stature." Richard A. Muller, *Christ and the Decree: Christology and Predestination in Reformed Theology from Calvin to Perkins* (Grand Rapids, MI: Baker, 1986), 130. And "the most compendious systematic theologian of the early orthodox period" of Reformed Scholasticism. Muller, *After Calvin: Studies in the Development of a Theological Tradition* (Oxford: Oxford University Press, 2003), 148.

127. Amandus Polanus, *Partitiones theologiae*, 2nd ed. (Basel, 1590), 59–60.

union, a coalescence, engrafting in Christ, eating his flesh and drinking his blood in the Supper, joining in one body under one Head, cleansing with the blood of Christ, vivification, being raised from the dead and placed in heaven as one with Christ.[128] Communion with Christ embraces justification, regeneration, and adoption.[129] However, in discussing the Supper, Polanus focuses on our participation in the benefits of the covenant of grace—reconciliation, justification, regeneration—so that, effectively, we feed on justification rather than Christ himself.[130] Nevertheless, in his *Syntagma theologiae Christianae* (1609), a more extensive work, Polanus goes much further. He writes of a union in which Christ and we are really and truly joined and remain so forever (*Communio ipsiusmet Christi, est unio ipsius nobiscum, qua nos sibi vere & realiter copulavit ut ipse in nobis & nos in ipso maneamus in sempiternam*).[131]

This has a threefold form: first, in nature, in the incarnation; second, in grace, in the elect; and third, after this life, when we are present with the Lord.[132] The first occurs through the assumption of our nature in the unity of Christ's person. The second is through Christ's assumption of our persons, not in one person with him but in grace, he as the Head, we the members of his body, of his flesh and bones. So, as Peter says, we partake of his divine nature.[133] The third form is the assumption of our nature with him in eternal glory. There is a progression from one form to the next, from nature to grace to glory.[134]

Polanus then discusses *what* our union with Christ is. It is true, real (*vere ac realis*), and indissoluble.[135] Polanus goes further than Calvin. This union, he says, *is essential.* We exist in our earthly bodies but with the divine nature of Christ dwelling in us. According to his humanity he is in heaven, but the same Holy Spirit unites us no less than the members of our bodies are joined. Consequently, this union consists in the communication not only of gifts but also of the substance of Christ. The union is substantial, actual, and corporeal, while its manner is spiritual. However, it is substantial and corporeal in terms of the subjects united,

---

128. Polanus, *Partitiones*, 82–83.
129. Polanus, *Partitiones*, 84–85.
130. Polanus, *Partitiones*, 127.
131. Amandus Polanus, *Syntagma theologiae Christianae* (Geneva: Petri Auberti, 1612), 2:330b.
132. Polanus, *Syntagma*, 2:330e.
133. Polanus, *Syntagma*, 2:330e–f.
134. Polanus, *Syntagma*, 2:330g.
135. Polanus, *Syntagma*, 2:331g–h.

since true substance and nature—his body and our nature—are related as we are joined to the substance and natures of Christ and so to his body.[136]

Polanus explains how we are united to Christ according to both natures. Citing 2 Peter 1:4, he says that Christ dwells in us according to his divine nature and conforms us to him (*ipse sua Deitate reipsa in nobis habitat & nos sibi conformes redit*).[137] We also commune with Christ according to his humanity. We participate according to nature—our nature is conformed to Christ by the Holy Spirit. We also participate in the Holy Spirit, who joins us to the Lord.[138]

The Holy Spirit unites us to Christ in the sacraments.[139] The sacramental union is spiritual, with a conjunction between the sign and the thing signified. The bread and wine we see with bodily eyes: the body and blood we see with the eyes of the soul, thus by faith.[140] The body of Christ is absent *in loco* but most present to us by our union with him, through the Spirit of Christ who dwells in him and in us.[141] Consequently, we are united to Christ through the Spirit and through faith.[142] Therefore the bread and wine are signs not only signifying but also *exhibiting* (*unde panis & vinum non tantum significativa signa sunt, sed etiam exhibitiva*). Therefore, Christ exhibits his body and blood and so gives the Holy Spirit to his disciples. Christ's body and blood are therefore present sacramentally and spiritually.[143]

26.2.6   *Nine Theses on* Theōsis

1. *The transformation that is part of union with Christ and called* theōsis, *comes to expression in, and is cultivated by, the Word and sacraments.* John 6 portrays the reality of union with Christ in a sacramental context. Those who have eternal life eat and drink Christ's flesh and blood. This is done by the Holy Spirit (John 6:63). John 6 teaches the extent and closeness of the union Christ has with his people.

Robert Bruce argued that there is nothing in the Lord's Supper that is not available in the Word, but in the Supper we "get a better hold of

---

136. Polanus, *Syntagma*, 2:332b–c.
137. Polanus, *Syntagma*, 2:332e.
138. Polanus, *Syntagma*, 2:332e–f.
139. Polanus, *Syntagma*, 2:434a–b.
140. Polanus, *Syntagma*, 2:445c–d.
141. Polanus, *Syntagma*, 2:445e.
142. Polanus, *Syntagma*, 2:455h.
143. Polanus, *Syntagma*, 2:456d.

Christ."[144] As Augustine described it, the Supper is "a kind of visible word of God."[145] It is the point of union covenantally and personally between Christ and his people.

2. *This is the most real union we can have.* As Cabasilas expressed it, union with Christ "is closer than any other union which man can possibly imagine and does not lend itself to any exact comparisons." This is why, he says, Scripture does not confine itself to one illustration but provides a wide range of examples.[146] As surely as we eat the bread and drink the wine, so Christ enters our souls.[147] As WCF, 29.7, says, the faithful receive and feed on Christ in the Lord's Supper really and truly. Jesus said, "My flesh is true meat and my blood is true drink" (John 6:51–58, my trans. of v. 55). In Paul's words, in union with Christ we are "made to drink of one Spirit" (1 Cor. 12:13). In the words of Bernard of Clairvaux,

> We taste thee, O thou living bread,
> and long to feast upon thee still;
> we drink of thee, the fountain-head,
> and thirst our souls from thee to fill.[148]

3. *This is not a union of essence. We do not cease to be human or get merged into God like ingredients in an ontological soup. This is not apotheosis.* The Eastern doctrine of deification had at its root a determined preservation of the distinction between Creator and creature. It opposed any suggestion that we partake of the divine essence, since we have to do with the energies of God. Calvin—and Polanus too—may have overstepped in talking of a union of substance. However, their intention was correct; to stress the reality, extent, and far-reaching effect of this union.

---

144. Bruce, *Mystery*, 64.
145. Augustine, *John* 80.3 (*PL*, 35:1840; *NPNF*[1], 7:344).
146. Cabasilas, *Life in Christ*, 5–6.
147. In the words of Robert Bruce:

I call them signs because they have the Body and Blood of Christ conjoined with them. Indeed, so truly is the Body of Christ conjoined with the bread, and the Blood of Christ conjoined with the wine, that as soon as you receive the bread in your mouth (if you are a faithful man or woman) you receive the Body of Christ in your soul, and that by faith. And as soon as you receive the wine in your mouth, you receive the Blood of Christ in your soul, and that by faith. It is chiefly because of this function that they are instruments to deliver and exhibit the things that they signify . . . [for] the Sacrament exhibits and delivers the thing that it signifies to the soul and heart, as soon as the sign is delivered to the mouth. (Bruce, *Mystery*, 44)

148. Bernard of Clairvaux, "Jesus, Thou Joy of Loving Hearts" (ca. 1150).

4. *Neither do we lose our personal identities in some universal, ge-neric humanity.* In the indivisible union of three hypostases in the one being of God, the eternal distinction of each *hypostasis* is preserved. The union of the Son of God with the humanity in the incarnation preserves the reality and integrity of the assumed humanity. Christ's union with the church maintains the humanity of the church. The Spirit's indwelling enhances rather than diminishes our humanity. With *theōsis*, we remain who we are; indeed, we become what God has intended we should be.

5. *In the Lord's Supper we are lifted up by the Holy Spirit to feed on Christ in the Spirit.* This is real and true, for it is communion with the Son in the Holy Spirit and thus entails personal access to the Father. We are given to share in the life of the Trinity. Since the Spirit is God, he joins things separated by distance, as Calvin said, uniting those that are spatially far apart.[149] The Spirit and the Son are indivisible with the Father in the unity of the holy Trinity. Moreover, the Spirit's distinctive work is to glorify Christ and lead his people to him through the faith he gives them. Paul regards the Spirit as so close to the risen Christ that he can call him "the Spirit of the Lord" and "the Lord who is the Spirit" (2 Cor. 3:17–18).

6. *We are not hypostatically united to the Son.* There is only one hypostatic union—in the incarnate Christ—which remains forever. The indwelling of the Trinity through the Holy Spirit (John 14:23) is differ-ent. Whereas in the incarnation the Son has indissolubly united himself to a human nature in one person, the Spirit indwells countless human persons. He thus enhances our humanity to be what God eternally in-tended it to be. In this, Jesus Christ is the archetype and exemplar; as man, he was led by the Holy Spirit at all times. He is the author, pioneer, and perfecter of our salvation in his incarnate life and work, sharing our faith, our very nature of flesh and blood, our temptations, our suffer-ings, our death and burial (Heb. 2:5–18), besides our resurrection (Rom. 8:10–11; 1 Cor. 15:35–37).

7. *It is union with Christ, with his person.* This goes beyond the indwelling of the Spirit in the church and its members, as explained by Jesus in John 14 and expanded by Paul in Romans 8. It is grounded in his incarnation; he is forever man and so one with us according to

---

149. *Inter alia*, Calvin, *Institutes*, 4.17.10.

his human nature. In this case, the Holy Spirit unites us to Christ in a spiritual union. Yet, in this union, we all retain our distinctive identities.

The result is that we have more than fellowship with Christ. Fellowship takes place between separate persons by means of presence, recognition, conversation, shared interests, and the like. Adam had fellowship with God before the fall. Redemption has not restored us to that. The incarnation has happened; the Son of God is forever human. The outpouring and indwelling of the Spirit has occurred and endures; the Spirit of God has taken up permanent residence in and with those who love Christ, and in so doing the holy Trinity now lives in us.

This goes beyond communion. It entails union. It is more than participation in the communicable attributes of God. It is not to be restricted to union with righteousness, goodness, holiness, or truth, neither is it union with the benefits of Christ, as if it were union with the doctrine of sanctification. It is union with *Christ*. Moreover, the humanity of Christ was not simply united to some of God's attributes; if it were, we would be left with an extreme form of Nestorianism.

8. *It is effected and developed by the Holy Spirit through faith*, in and through the means of grace: the ministry of the Word, the sacraments, and prayer (WSC, 88). It is churchly, not individualistic. It is not a private experience. It occurs in the humdrum use of the means God has appointed, not in superficially exciting or dramatic experiences.

It is not automatic; it is through faith. We are responsible to cultivate our union with Christ. Participation in the means of grace is essential, for there God has undertaken to meet with us. It is not a process under our control; it is initiated and developed by the Spirit. It is supernatural; it transcends our capacity to explain. However, we expect the Spirit to work through the means he has appointed.

9. *It eventually will lead to our being "like [Christ]"* (Rom. 8:29–30; 2 Cor. 3:18; 1 John 3:1–2), for "it is the intention of the gospel to make us sooner or later like God."[150] For the present we are "partakers of the divine nature" (2 Pet. 1:4). However, when he appears at his parousia, we shall see him as he is, in his glorified humanity, and we shall be finally and climactically transformed to be like him, our present lowly bodies changed to be like his glorious body (Phil. 3:20–21).

---

150. John Calvin, *Calvin's Commentaries: The Epistle of Paul the Apostle to the Hebrews and the First and Second Epistles of St. Peter*, trans. William B. Johnston (Grand Rapids, MI: Eerdmans, 1963), 330; CO2, 20:328.

Further Reading

Calvin, John. "A Short Treatise on the Holy Supper of Our Lord and Only Saviour Jesus Christ." In *Calvin: Theological Treatises*, edited by J. K. S. Reid, 140–66. Philadelphia: Westminster, 1954.

Letham, Robert. *The Lord's Supper: Eternal Word in Broken Bread*. Phillipsburg, NJ: P&R, 2001.

Letham, Robert. *Union with Christ: In Scripture, History, and Theology*. Phillipsburg, NJ: P&R, 2011.

Russell, Norman. *The Doctrine of Deification in the Greek Patristic Tradition*. Oxford: Oxford University Press, 2004.

Study Questions

1. Consider the nature of the Lord's Supper as communion with Christ and feeding on Christ. What difference might this make versus seeing the Supper merely as a symbol?

2. How frequently should the Lord's Supper be held?

3. We are in the process of being transformed, ultimately to be like the glorified Christ when he returns. Orthodox iconography portrays the saints with solid golden halos to indicate that this process is occurring. What difference do you suppose it might make if we were to view fellow believers in this way?

27

The Church and Its Offices

There is but one holy, catholic, and apostolic church, attributes of the church rooted in Scripture, as in Ephesians 2. All four aspects are vital to maintain. The church can be understood to be the sum total of the elect, or can be identified in terms of its visible manifestation. Various doctrines of the church have been developed. Rome has a hierarchical structure, with the pope and magisterium in the highest authority. Orthodoxy differs, not having a monolithic hierarchy but having various autonomous and autocephalous sees, more akin to the Anglican communion, where no one bishop has greater authority than any other. The Church of England has adopted a conciliar model, with its general synod composed of houses of bishops, clergy, and laity. Presbyterian and Reformed denominations are governed by both ministers and elders, in courts that have increased powers in accordance with their geographical scope. Independent or Congregationalist churches use synods in a purely advisory manner; many independent congregations are not formally linked to any others. Overall, the Bible and Reformed theology give precedence to the one church, from which particular expressions emerge.

27.1   The Marks of the Church

What exactly is the church? The *Catechism of the Catholic Church*, citing *Lumen Gentium*, states that for Rome,

> the sole Church of Christ [is that] which our Saviour, after his Resurrection, entrusted to Peter's pastoral care. . . . This Church, consti-

tuted and organized as a society in the present world, subsists in the Catholic Church, which is governed by the successor of Peter and by the bishops in communion with him.[1]

As for churches not in communion with Rome, "Christ's Spirit uses [them] . . . as means of salvation," since their power "derives from the fullness of grace and truth that Christ has entrusted to the Catholic Church."[2] So the church subsists in the Catholic Church, governed by the bishop of Rome. Other churches derive whatever validity they have from the grace Christ has entrusted to Rome.

Calvin held that there are two marks of the church: "The Word of God purely preached and heard" and "the sacraments administered according to Christ's institution." If these are present in a church, "it deserves without doubt to be held and considered a church."[3] A church with these marks is not to be abandoned.[4] The Scots Confession (1560) adds discipline, "as Goddis Worde prescribes,"[5] with which the Belgic Confession agrees, adding that if these marks are present, "no man has a right to separate himself."[6] The WCF does not mention discipline. Is fellowship a mark of the church? Acts 2:42 includes it as one of the four characteristics of the post-Pentecostal church, but this could be seen as an aspect of discipline, in a nurturing rather than a judicial sense (Heb. 3:12–14).

Writing before Vatican II and strongly criticizing Rome, Barth affirmed that Scripture has authority in and over the church, owing to its connection with revelation. Scripture rules out any autonomous authority for the church. Yet it also establishes its subordinate authority in its hearing and receiving the Word. Barth considers the canon, the fathers, and confessions; all these are indirect, relative, and formal authorities, in principle reformable, although hasty and frivolous changes are to be avoided.[7]

Some claim there are nine marks of a healthy church.[8] However, the question here is what are the inalienable and essential marks of the church.

---

1. CCC, 816.
2. CCC, 819.
3. Calvin, *Institutes*, 4.1.9.
4. Calvin, *Institutes*, 4.1.10–22.
5. Philip Schaff, *The Creeds of Christendom* (Grand Rapids, MI: Baker, 1966), 3:462.
6. Schaff, *Creeds*, 3:419–20.
7. Barth, CD, I/2:538–660.
8. See https://9marks.org/about/, accessed 17 February 2017. Noticeably absent from these marks of a healthy church are the sacraments.

27.2   The Attributes of the Church

One, holy, catholic, and apostolic. "We believe in one holy, catholic and apostolic Church" runs the Niceno-Constantinopolitan Creed. That this was no new proposal but one rooted in the Bible is evident in Ephesians 2:11–22. There Paul states that the church is *one* body in Christ, composed of Jew and Gentile. It is *holy*, belonging to God as his holy temple, indwelt by the Spirit, and exists in the Lord, the risen Son. It is *catholic*, found throughout the world, and *apostolic*, grounded on the apostles and prophets.[9] These features are given to the church by Christ, objective realities that encompass the whole church throughout the world, past, present, and future.

Unity. Because Christ is one, the Trinity is one, and the Spirit is one, so is the church. This is unity consistent with diversity (1 Cor. 12:4–31; Eph. 4:1–16). Christ gave unity to his church, as part of his work of reconciliation (Eph. 2:14–18), breaking down the barrier between Jew and Gentile. Above all, Jesus prays for the visible manifestation of this unity in the world (John 17:20–23). It is not an optional extra.[10]

Holiness. The church belongs to God. It is the church of the living God (1 Tim. 3:15), the household of God (Eph. 2:19), a holy temple in the Lord (Eph. 2:21), a dwelling place for God in the Spirit (Eph. 2:22). Christ gave himself for the church to nourish and cherish it (Eph. 5:25–27).

Apostolicity. The church is founded on the apostles and prophets. The apostolic teaching is the bedrock of the church (Acts 2:42), based as it was on the Old Testament Scriptures; the Law, the Prophets, and the Writings. The apostles were commissioned by Jesus to be witnesses of his resurrection, to teach with his authority.

Catholicity. The church is international, found throughout the world. No longer confined to Israel, it extends to all nations (Matt. 28:18–20). Paul stresses this as a key element of the gospel, especially in Ephesians 2, but it also underlies Galatians, Romans, and the rest of his corpus. John's vision in Revelation 7:9–17 expresses it vividly. This is a warning against identifying national interests with the gospel.

These four attributes need to be held together. Liberal theology focused on unity and catholicity at the expense of apostolicity. The ecu-

---

9. Robert Letham, "Catholicity Global and Historical: Constantinople, Westminster, and the Church in the Twenty-First Century," *WTJ* 72 (2010): 43–57.

10. I have written on this theme in *Through Western Eyes: Eastern Orthodoxy: A Reformed Perspective* (Fearn: Mentor, 2007), 291–96.

menical movement of the last century followed suit. A reverse problem is to highlight apostolicity and holiness at the expense of catholicity and unity; this is the hallmark of sects. Failure to pursue Christ's prayer for unity is as serious a departure as liberalism. The pursuit of ecumenical orthodoxy is a sine qua non, to be sought at the expense of neither doctrinal commitments nor a recognition of common ground.[11] Churches may degenerate so as to be no churches of Christ through departure from the gospel; the same may tragically be true through isolation.

Heresy differs from error. Error is a divergence from the teaching of Scripture on this or that. Heresy is something that would falsify the Christian faith; it strikes right at the heart of the gospel.

27.3 The Visible and the Invisible Church

The *visible church* is the church here in this world, as an organism and an institution. It has order and offices, administers the sacraments, preaches and teaches the Word, exercises discipline, proclaims the gospel, and disciples the nations. It has many problems, some severe, but Paul describes imperfect churches as churches (1 Cor. 1:2). In the book of Revelation, Christ addresses seven in a close geographical area, each distinct (Rev. 2:1–3:22). The most successful come in for the most searching criticism and warning. Commended are the ones that are either weak or about to face intense persecution. This is the reverse of Americanism, which supposes that bigger is better and that fast growth is the norm, with outward success serving as the hallmark of health. Christ's evaluation is not necessarily ours.

The *invisible church* consists of the entire company of the elect in all ages (Rev. 7:4–17). It is invisible not because its members are spirits or are never active in this world but because it consists not only of believers alive now but also of those who have died, those yet to profess faith, and those yet to be born. Moreover, its membership is known only to God.

The relationship between the visible and invisible church. Conceptions of the relationship between the church visible and the church invisible vary.

Perfectionism. One view aims to secure an identity here and now between the visible and invisible church. The church is thereby defined as

---

11. Letham, "Catholicity."

a community of disciples; all others are rejected. Credobaptist churches of whatever stripe come into this category. Membership is based on regeneration, a hidden work of the Spirit of which, it is claimed, we can assess the signs. The Evangelical Awakening fueled this development. Testimonies of dramatic conversion experiences were required to establish that an individual had the accepted features of a regenerate person.

State churches. At the other end of the spectrum, state churches regard everyone in a territory as a Christian by baptism. In this sense, 59 percent of the population of the United Kingdom in the 2011 census (down from 72 percent in 2001) was counted as Christian by self-identification. Such a situation is common in Orthodox countries, where church and nation are often indistinguishable. It is a problem occasioned by the success of the gospel in transforming a country, but with a subsequent decline in vitality.

Augustine. The church and the elect are two contiguous and overlapping circles, according to Augustine. Not all the elect are in the church; some have not yet believed. Not all in the church are elect; some may fall away. The visible church is not and cannot be an exact replica of the invisible church, unlike the claim of the Donatists in Augustine's day and the Anabaptists at the time of the Reformation. The Reformed churches were in line with Augustine. Yet many within Reformed churches today take a more Anabaptist or perfectionist line.

Is Rome a true church or not? Rome retains some of the marks of the church. The Reformers accepted its baptism. Most Reformed denominations accept Roman Catholic baptism since it is Trinitarian; baptism belongs to God, not to a denomination. Consequently, Rome retains something of the truth. Indeed, as J. Gresham Machen remarked, the Reformed are far closer to Rome than to Protestant liberalism; Rome has a defective view of the gospel, placing church authority on a par with Scripture, but liberalism is another religion entirely.[12] There is a wide area of common ground and common doctrine; the heritage of the Latin church belongs as much to Protestantism. The answer to the question of whether Rome is a true church must be equivocal. Something similar

---

12. "How great is the common heritage which unites the Roman Catholic Church . . . to devout Protestants today! . . . The Church of Rome may represent a perversion of the Christian religion; but naturalistic liberalism is not Christianity at all." J. Gresham Machen, *Christianity and Liberalism* (London: Victory, 1923), 52.

applies to Orthodoxy. There are many ways in which the Reformed are closer to the Orthodox than to Rome; the East has fewer dogmas to divide, and no pope. Yet there are huge differences too, and in other ways the Reformed are closer to Rome, sharing the common Latin Christian heritage. Can we lump Rome and Orthodoxy together? No.[13]

27.4   The Members of the Visible Church

For Rome, those who are born anew, of water and the Spirit, by baptism and faith are in the church. This particularly applies to those in communion with the bishop of Rome, but it also includes people in church bodies not in communion with the bishop of Rome but who preserve the intention of Catholic baptism.[14] All are called to this catholic unity of the people of God, and to it in different ways are ordered the Catholic faithful, others who believe in Christ, and finally all mankind, called by God's grace to salvation.[15] This last category includes Jews, Muslims (who acknowledge the Creator, hold the faith of Abraham, and adore the one merciful God).[16] So, on the one hand, Rome has a naive view of Islam. On the other hand, outside the church there is no salvation.[17] These poles are held together by saying that those who *refuse* to enter the church cannot be saved; others, however, through no fault of their own, do not know Christ and his church but nevertheless are part of this Catholic unity.[18]

For Orthodoxy, the deciding factor is being in communion with the Orthodox Church. Since it practices paedocommunion, this includes all who have been baptized in the Orthodox Church.

Credobaptist churches require a personal profession of faith, usually identified with baptism. The church is composed of believers only; it is usually a postadolescent church from which children are excluded. Some such churches require an account of spiritual experience, and for them, regeneration is the condition of church membership, a practice dating back to John Owen, although he was not himself a Baptist.[19]

---

13. See Letham, *Through Western Eyes*.
14. CCC, 838.
15. CCC, 836.
16. CCC, 836, 841.
17. CCC, 846.
18. CCC, 847–48.
19. John Owen, *The True Nature of a Gospel Church*, in *The Works of John Owen*, ed. William H. Goold, 23 vols. (1850–1855; repr., London: Banner of Truth, 1965–1968), 16:11–20.

Reformed churches hold that the members of the church are all those who profess the true religion, together with their children (WCF, 25.2). This supposes professing Christians have been baptized. Converts are baptized on profession of faith, while birth to a believing parent makes a person a member of the church. A child does not become a church member by being baptized; a child is baptized being a member of the church already by virtue of God's covenant. However, there is a certain tension evident in the Westminster Assembly's "Directory for the Publick Worship of God." On the one hand, "children, by baptism, are solemnly received into the bosom of the visible church," and in the same paragraph, "they are Christians, and federally holy before baptism, and therefore are they baptized."[20]

27.5   Major Doctrines of the Church

27.5.1   Rome[21]

Christ and the church. According to *Lumen Gentium*, cited in the *CCC*, the "light of Christ . . . shines out visibly from the church." The church is like the moon, reflecting the light of the sun, having no other light than Christ.[22] We do not believe *in* the church, "so as not to confuse God with his works."[23] The church, in Christ, is like a sacrament, a sign and instrument of communion with God and of unity among all people. It is therefore the sacrament of the unity of the human race. In the church this unity has already begun. Like a sacrament, the church is Christ's instrument for the salvation of all.[24]

The church is centered in Rome under the leadership of Peter and his successors. Hence, in *Lumen Gentium*:

> The sole church of Christ is that which our Saviour, after his resurrection, entrusted to Peter's pastoral care, commissioning him and the other apostles to extend and rule it. . . . This church, constituted and organized as a society in the present world, subsists in the Catholic

---

20. *The Confession of Faith, the Larger and Shorter Catechisms with the Scriptural Proofs at Large, Together with The Sum of Saving Knowledge* (Applecross, Ross-shire: Publications Committee of the Free Church of Scotland, 1970), 383.

21. For a critical evaluation of Rome's ecclesiology, see Kenneth J. Collins and Jerry L. Walls, *Roman but Not Catholic: What Remains at Stake 500 Years after the Reformation* (Grand Rapids, MI: Baker Academic, 2017), 84–111.

22. *LG*, 1; *CCC*, 748.

23. *CCC*, 750.

24. *LG*, 1, 9; *CCC*, 775–76.

Church, which is governed by the successor of Peter and by the bishops in communion with him.[25]

Vatican II's decree on ecumenism states:

> For it is through Christ's Catholic Church alone . . . that the fullness of the means of salvation can be obtained. It was to the apostolic college alone, of which Peter is the head, that we believe that our Lord entrusted all the blessings of the New Covenant, in order to establish on earth the one Body of Christ into which all those should be fully incorporated who belong in any way to the People of God.[26]

What about other churches that have broken away from Rome? The CCC recognizes that in the rifts at the Reformation, both sides were to some extent to blame. However, those born into those communities cannot be charged with the sin of the separation.

> The Catholic Church accepts them with respect and affection as brothers. . . . All those who have been justified by faith in baptism are incorporated into Christ. They have a right to be called Christians and with good reason are accepted as brothers in the Lord by the children of the Catholic Church.[27]

Many evidences of truth are acknowledged to be found outside the visible Catholic Church—the written Word of God and the life of grace, faith, hope, and love.[28] Thus, Christ uses other churches as means of salvation. However, this stems from "the fullness of grace and truth that Christ has entrusted to the Catholic Church."[29] Therefore, any validity attaching to the churches of the Reformation is derived from the fullness of grace and truth that Christ has given to the church of Rome!

Hierarchical structure. The preeminence of Rome emerged gradually. The church was prominent from the start due to Rome's position in the empire. Both Peter and Paul were martyred there in the 60s, so they are seen as forever present, presiding in the church.

---

25. *LG*, 8.2; *CCC*, 816.
26. *UR*, 3.5; *CCC*, 816.
27. *UR*, 3.1; *CCC*, 817–18.
28. *LG*, 15; *UR*, 3.2; *CCC*, 819.
29. *CCC*, 819.

Rome bases its claims to authority on biblical exegesis. In Matthew 16:18 Jesus's announcement that he will build his church on Peter is taken to refer to Peter personally and his successors as bishops of Rome. This argument has three premises: First, Jesus singles out Peter from the other apostles. However, it is probable that Peter represents the apostles as a whole, as Cyprian argued, or the foundation is Peter's confession of faith, as the Orthodox maintain.[30] The argument that Jesus, in Matthew 16, refers to the person of Peter was first proposed by popes in the early third century and gained traction in the fourth and fifth centuries.[31] Additionally, texts held to grant Peter a future pastoral role over the whole church (Luke 22:32; John 21:15–17) are used in support.[32] Second, it is assumed that Peter became bishop of Rome, for which there is no credible historical evidence; nor does the New Testament hint at it. Third, depending on the validity of both preceding premises, Jesus implies that all subsequent bishops of Rome are included in the authority granted to Peter. This is at best an inference built on highly contestable foundations. These texts do not provide sufficient grounds for Rome's claim for Peter, still less an ongoing succession.

At first Rome claimed only a pastoral role over other churches. However, by the fourth century it began to issue canons granting the right of appeal from bishops in western Europe and set itself up as a court of appeal from churches in Africa and the East. By the time of Leo the Great (440–461), the primacy of Rome was effectively complete. However, Leo intervened only to defend the gospel and never thought he had authority over other churches. Later, Gregory the Great (590–604) saw the primacy of Rome as one of help and counsel. The Greeks, for their part, accorded Rome a primacy of honor, not of universal jurisdiction.

The extension of papal powers was based on documents later shown to be forgeries. *The Donation of Constantine* claimed that the emperor Constantine had acknowledged Pope Sylvester's right to rule the western empire after he had cured Constantine of leprosy. During the Renaissance, Lorenzo Valla established that the document dated from the eighth century. *The Pseudo-Isidorian Decretals* were mid-ninth-century

---

30. Olivier Clément, *You Are Peter: An Orthodox Theologian's Reflection on the Exercise of Papal Primacy* (New York: New City, 2003), 25–27.
31. See Clément, *You Are Peter*, for a simple but accurate description of the growth of papal power and claims.
32. CCC, 551–53.

forgeries, frequently used to undergird the claims of Gregory VII (1073–1084), whose reforms enormously enlarged papal power.

In the fourteenth and fifteenth centuries came a reaction against papal supremacy, the papacy was forced through civil unrest to leave Rome and base itself in Avignon (1309–1377), rival Popes were elected (1377–1413), and this chaos led to the rise of the Conciliar Movement, with general councils holding power and bishops in the vanguard. The Council of Constance (1415) decreed that the council held, directly from Christ, the power before which all others—emperors and popes—must bow. The Council of Basel (1431–1449) made the pope its agent. While the movement overreached itself and fizzled out, there has been continued tension between papal power and the conciliar tendency ever since.

This tension was seen in 1870, when Vatican I acknowledged that the pope speaking *ex cathedra* was infallible; Clément cites the comment that the pope needed a council to pronounce infallibly that he never needed it![33] Thereafter, the tension is seen in two different metaphors for the church: *the body of Christ*, entailing a head, the pope, and *the people of God*, pointing to collegiality. With Vatican II the latter was prominent, but with Pope John Paul II the pendulum swung back toward the papacy and the magisterium.

The papacy claims jurisdiction over the entire Christian church: hence *Roman* Catholicism. This claim flows from the apostolicity of the church. Assuming the succession noted above, the office transmitted to Peter alone was also transmitted to his successors, while the office the other apostles received of shepherding the church was thought to be exercised uninterruptedly by the bishops. Thus, the bishops have by divine appointment taken the place of the apostles, and whoever listens to them listens to Christ.[34]

Consequently, the bishop of Rome "is the perpetual and visible source and foundation of the unity both of the bishops and of the whole company of the faithful—he has full, supreme and universal power over the whole church, a power which he can always exercise unhindered."[35] The college of bishops has no authority unless it is united with the Roman pontiff. When this is so, this college has "supreme and full authority

---

33. Clément, *You Are Peter*, 65.
34. CCC, 860–62.
35. *LG*, 22–23; CCC, 880–82.

over the universal Church," a power that can only be exercised with the agreement of the Roman pontiff.[36] The individual bishops are the visible source and foundation of unity in their own particular churches. But as members of the episcopal college, each bishop shares in the concern for all the churches.[37]

Bishops, with priests as coworkers, have as their first task to preach the gospel to all.[38] The magisterium's task is to preserve God's people from deviations, keeping the true faith without error. "To fulfill this service, Christ endowed the Church's shepherds with the charism of infallibility in matters of faith and morals."[39] The exercise of this charism takes many forms. The pope is said to enjoy this infallibility in virtue of his office when, as supreme pastor and teacher of all the faithful, he proclaims by a definitive act a doctrine pertaining to faith and morals. This infallibility is also present in the body of bishops when, together with Peter's successor, they exercise the supreme magisterium.[40]

While to Protestants this sounds over the top, it is nonetheless the case that any preacher can make an infallible pronouncement from the pulpit. Central truths of the gospel, declarations on the deity of Christ, and the like come into this category. However, these are based on the infallibility of doctrine and do not reside in the holder of office. This is the fissure highlighted by the Reformation—supreme authority resides in Holy Scripture, not in an amalgam of Scripture and tradition.

27.5.2   Orthodoxy

The East has never had a hierarchical structure. It has been close to the doctrine of the church expounded by Cyprian, who wrote that all bishops sit *in solidum* on the chair of Peter. He saw the passage in Matthew 16 as referring to all bishops.[41] This means that each province is theoretically equal. There is no one center of power.

Moreover, the legal emphasis of the West, resulting from the position of Rome and Roman law, is absent. The ecumenical councils, based in the East, did not impose authoritative verdicts on the whole church, since they were conscious of simply confessing the faith. They recognized the

---

36. *LG*, 22; *CCC*, 883–84.
37. *LG*, 23; *CCC*, 886.
38. *LG*, 25; *CCC*, 818.
39. *CCC*, 890.
40. *LG*, 25; *CCC*, 891–92.
41. Cyprian, *On the Unity of the Catholic Church* 4–6 (*ANF*, 5:422–23).

truth, and the people received it, the validity of the decisions mirroring their recognition.

In keeping with this, the Eastern church has a parity of bishops. No one bishop has greater authority than any other. While the most prominent dioceses are accorded a higher respect, they are *primus inter pares*, no more. Thus, each main Orthodox communion is autocephalous; no other jurisdiction can claim authority over it. This was evidenced in the widespread rejection of the agreements brokered with Rome by the bishops at Lyons (1274) and Florence (1439), which were unacceptable to the populace. Other jurisdictions are autonomous; while they are self-governing, their primate must be appointed or approved by the church that granted it autonomy.[42] The main problems Orthodoxy has faced stem from the connection of the church to the nation. The restriction of communion to those of the host nation—phyletism—was declared heresy by the Council of Constantinople in 1872.

27.5.3 Anglicanism

Anglicanism has some hierarchical elements, but these are combined with conciliar features, particularly recently. In the Church of England, the monarch is the supreme governor of the church. There is thus a close connection between church and state that does not exist in other branches of Anglicanism. In fact, Clifford Longley has argued that since, constitutionally, the monarch exercises his or her power in Parliament, and Parliament's power is based in the House of Commons, which is elected by universal adult suffrage, therefore each adult person living in England is the governor of the Church of England![43] The monarch appoints all senior clergy, on recommendation of the prime minister. In turn, the prime minister acts on the advice of ecclesiastical committees (on which both church and state are represented) but retains the final power to select from a short list, usually of two. There are thus inevitable temptations to pick candidates who are going to be the least threat politically and thus avoid having to cry out, "Who shall rid me of this turbulent priest?"[44]

---

42. This commonly held distinction is increasingly challenged; the earliest churches were autocephalous and did not need approval to become such. See John H. Erickson, "Autocephaly and Autonomy," *SVTQ* 60 (2016): 91–110.

43. In *The Times* (London) in 1987 or 1988, I cannot remember the precise date. At the time, Longley was the religious affairs correspondent.

44. A saying popularly attributed, possibly erroneously, to Henry II (1133–1189) in reference to Thomas à Becket, archbishop of Canterbury.

At the top of the totem pole are archbishops and bishops, each of whom presides over a province or diocese respectively. Archbishops have additional powers of jurisdiction as an appellate court and in ecclesiastical appointments. However, the archbishop of Canterbury has no authority outside his diocese. Major decisions are taken in general synod, which covers the whole country and comprises three houses—of bishops, clergy, and laity. A majority is usually necessary in each house for major action to be taken. This is a quasi-Presbyterian system grafted onto a hierarchical one.

The various provinces of the worldwide Anglican communion are autonomous. The archbishops of each province meet every ten years in the Lambeth Conference. Anglican practice is based on the "Lambeth Quadrilateral," espoused at the conference in 1888, consisting of Scripture, the early creeds, the sacraments of baptism and the Lord's Supper, and the historic episcopate. The doctrine of the Church of England is stated in the Thirty-Nine Articles of Religion (1563, 1571), a Reformed document, but one largely ignored.

Excursus: The rise of the episcopate. The classic discussion of the rise of the episcopate is provided by J. B. Lightfoot.[45] The following is a digest of his argument. Under the direction of the apostles, Lightfoot wrote, it was necessary to appoint special officers for the conduct of worship. As the New Testament progresses, there is a growing stress on the permanent ministry, as the apostles passed from the scene. In the New Testament, the *episkopos* (ἐπίσκοπος) is synonymous with the *presbyteros* (πρεσβύτερος), presiding over a congregation. But before the middle of the second century, each church had three orders of ministers: bishops, presbyters, and deacons—"on this point there cannot reasonably be two opinions."[46] Bishop and presbyter had become separate offices.

First came the diaconate (Acts 6), chosen by popular election and ordained by the apostles, an entirely new office with no Jewish background, dedicated to "serving at tables." However, largely due to their personal character, deacons assumed a wider role, becoming effectively ministers of the Word.

---

45. J. B. Lightfoot, "The Christian Ministry," in *Saint Paul's Epistle to the Philippians: A Revised Text, with Introductions, Notes, and Dissertations* (London: Macmillan, 1881), 181–269.
46. Lightfoot, "Christian Ministry," 186.

For the *presbyterate*, we have no details of its origin, since elders already existed in the Jewish synagogue. It emerged, probably at Jerusalem, after the dispersion of the apostles that resulted from the persecution subsequent to the martyrdom of Stephen. The presbyters at Jerusalem were together with the apostles at the Council of Jerusalem (Acts 15). Paul appointed presbyters in every church (Acts 14:23).

The *episkopos* and presbyter were originally one and the same.[47] *Episkopos* was applied to the Gentile churches as a synonym for *presbyter* (Acts 20:28; Phil. 1:1; 1 Tim. 3:1–2; Titus 1:7; 1 Pet. 2:25; 5:2). In the next generation, the title was used in a letter written by the Greek church of Rome to the Greek church of Corinth (1 Clement). Later, when the *episkopos* was a higher office, the word was still used for the elder.

The presbyters were both rulers and instructors of the congregation (Acts 20:28; Eph. 4:11; 1 Pet. 5:2; cf. 1 Pet. 2:25). Government was their main task, but teaching became increasingly prominent over time. Thus, Paul insisted on the faculty of teaching as a qualification; while it was incidental to the office (1 Tim. 5:17), there is no ground for thinking that teaching and ruling belonged to separate members of the presbyterial college.

At the close of the apostolic age traces of the episcopate as a separate office were few and indistinct. The apostles did not hold a local office; they itinerated. The episcopate probably developed out of the presbyterate: "not out of the apostolic office by localization but out of the presbyterial by elevation."[48] The title came to be used of the chief among them. At Jerusalem, James was effectively a bishop in the later sense. He took precedence even over Peter and John where the affairs of the Jewish church were considered (Acts 15:13ff.; 21:18; Gal. 2:9).

Two stages are evident in the emergence of the episcopate in the Gentile churches. First, the apostles superintended the churches under their care, in person or by letter (1 Cor. 5:3ff.). Then, as the apostolic visits became less frequent, a trustworthy disciple was delegated to stay in the area and supervise. In the Pastoral Epistles, this is true of Timothy in Ephesus, and of Titus in Crete. It appears their role was to be temporary (1 Tim. 1:3; 3:14–15; 2 Tim. 4:9, 21; Titus 1:5; 3:12).

---

47. Lightfoot, "Christian Ministry," 193.
48. Lightfoot, "Christian Ministry," 196.

There is no further development evident in the apostolic writings. There is no trace of a bishop around AD 70. But "early in the second century the episcopal office was firmly and widely established. Thus during the last three decades of the first century, and consequently during the lifetime of the latest surviving apostle, this change must have been brought about."[49] Possibly the deaths of James, Peter, and Paul in quick succession, plus the end of the Jerusalem church owing to the Jewish War and its aftermath, required new organization?[50] A leading member of the presbyterate would tend to emerge, with teaching or administrative skill, so as to become *primus inter pares*. By whom was this organization brought about? Lightfoot says, "This great work must be ascribed to the last surviving apostle. St. John especially . . . for Asia Minor was the centre from which the new movement spread." Hence, "the silence of history clearly proclaims the fact which the voice of history but faintly suggests."[51] By this course, Lightfoot argues that the episcopal office has apostolic approval, emerging out of the presbyterate with the sanction of the last surviving apostle. He distinguishes the episcopal office as it emerged from the monarchical episcopate in its later development. His discussion is compatible with the Presbyterian position.

27.5.4 Independency

The term *Independency* covers Congregationalists, Baptists, and miscellaneous others. Each local church is self-governing (there is no dispute here with the Reformed) and autonomous (here there is), with no outside body having any governmental rights over the local congregation. Independency emerged in the late sixteenth century and gained force in the seventeenth. There were several Independents at the Westminster Assembly. These accepted the need for synods on a wider basis. Their charter document was the Savoy Declaration (1658). The real fulcrum of authority was the local congregation, which granted advisory, consultative functions to the synods.[52] However, in much contemporary

49. Lightfoot, "Christian Ministry," 201.
50. Lightfoot, "Christian Ministry," 201.
51. Lightfoot, "Christian Ministry," 202.
52. The Savoy Declaration, "Of the Institution of Churches, and the Order Appointed in Them by Jesus Christ," 3, 6, 8, 9, 22, 25, 26; in Schaff, *Creeds*, 3:724–29. Particular churches are alone entrusted with the means of grace and authority (6): the members of particular churches are visible saints (8); synods have no power to exercise discipline, for this is seated in

evangelicalism, Independency means complete freedom from any form of joint jurisdiction.

Two factors helped it arise. First, the system was more secure from persecution. Presbyterianism emerged in England in the 1570s and 1580s but was soon suppressed, although never entirely eliminated.[53] Once presbytery minutes were discovered, its member congregations were known. Conversely, Independent congregations could be uncovered only one at a time. The process of persecution and elimination took longer, and by the time it had advanced, the movement had gained a momentum of its own. Second, late medieval nominalism, which gave priority to the particular over the universal, provided the philosophical and cultural milieu for Independency, with the priority of the individual.

John Owen was a leading exponent of Congregationalism. Eventually, the Congregationalist version of Independency placed power within the congregation with the people themselves rather than the ministers. Here there was a significant difference from Rome, Orthodoxy, and Anglicanism, where power lies either in whole or in part with the clergy, and from Presbyterianism, where it is shared by ministers and elders, but congregational integrity is preserved locally.

27.5.5 Presbyterian and Reformed

Reformed churches are synodical and conciliar. They are *synodical*, since church government is exercised at levels wider and higher than the local church. Presbyteries or synods comprise all the churches within a given region, General Assemblies cover a national area, while international bodies exist for advice and coordination. They are *conciliar*, for no one person or office has supremacy. Church courts are composed of representatives of both ruling offices, which have equal power.

Differences exist over the extent of the powers of regional and national synods and assemblies. In Presbyterianism, higher powers are given to jurisdictions covering a wider geographical location. On the other hand, a few Continental churches allow these bodies wider scope

congregations (22); synods are advisory bodies having no jurisdiction over particular churches (26).

53. Polly Ha, "English Presbyterianism c. 1590–1640" (PhD diss., Cambridge University, 2006).

but not higher power, as local congregations retain greater autonomy. In this they are close to the model of seventeenth-century Independents.

A classic statement of the historical basis of Presbyterian government is that of T. M. Lindsay.[54] Lindsay argues from the Pastoral Epistles that "pastor" and "overseer" describe the kind of work done, and "elder" the title of the office.

> All this shows us that during the last decades of the first century each Christian congregation had for its office-bearers a body of deacons and a body of elders—whether separated into two colleges or forming one must remain unknown—and that the elders took the "oversight" while the deacons performed the "subordinate services."[55]

The ruling body was a senate without a president. This organization "has no resemblance to any modern ecclesiastical organization, and yet contains within it the roots of all whether Congregational, Presbyterian . . . or Episcopal."[56] Proofs for the identity of the offices of elder and bishop in the first century can be found in Scripture (Acts 20:17; 1 Tim. 3:1–7; 1 Pet. 5:1–2; cf. 1 Tim. 5:17–19; Titus 1:5–7). The word *episkopos* "is not, during the first century, the technical term for an office-bearer; it is rather the word which describes what the office-bearer, i.e. the elder, does."[57]

In the second century, the prophetic ministry passed away, its functions appropriated by the permanent officers of the local churches. Every church supplemented its organization by placing one man at the head of the college of elders.[58]

> The ministry of each congregation or local church instead of being, as it had been, two-fold—of elders and deacons—became three-fold—of pastor or bishop, elders and deacons. This was the introduction of what is called the three-fold ministry. It is commonly called the beginning of episcopacy; but that idea is based on the erroneous conception that a three-fold ministry and episcopacy are identical.[59]

---

54. T. M. Lindsay, *The Church and the Ministry in the Early Centuries* (London: Hodder & Stoughton, 1903).
55. Lindsay, *Church and Ministry*, 154.
56. Lindsay, *Church and Ministry*, 155.
57. Lindsay, *Church and Ministry*, 165.
58. Lindsay, *Church and Ministry*, 169.
59. Lindsay, *Church and Ministry*, 170.

Lindsay notes that the Presbyterian or conciliar system is as much a threefold ministry as episcopacy.

Classic Reformed polity. Geneva, as witnessed by Calvin,[60] had four permanent offices: pastors, teachers, elders , and deacons (see fig. 1). This is evident in the *Ecclesiastical Ordinances* (1561), section 2.[61] In France, there were three offices, according to the *Ecclesiastical Discipline* (1559): ministers, elders, and deacons.[62] Scotland, in *The Book of Discipline* (John Knox, 1560), was the same,[63] but *The Second Book of Discipline* (Andrew Melville, 1581) had four offices (see fig. 2).[64] The *Church Order of the Synod of Dort* (1619) prescribed four offices too— ministers, professors of theology, elders, and deacons—with two-year terms for elders and deacons.[65] The Westminster Assembly's "Form of Presbyterial Church-Government" (1647) also listed four kinds of ordinary and perpetual officers: pastors, teachers, other church governors, and deacons (see fig. 3).[66]

Figure 1   Church offices according to John Calvin

Pastors	Doctors/ Teachers	Elders	Deacons
teach doctrine	teach doctrine	exercise discipline	administer funds to hospitalers
preach	preach		care for sick and poor widows
administer sacraments	administer sacraments		

Figure 2   Church offices according to the Church of Scotland, The Second Book of Discipline (1581)

Ministers/Preachers	Elders	Deacons
doctrine	discipline	distribution

60. Calvin, *Institutes*, 4.3.4–9.
61. David W. Hall and Joseph H. Hall, eds., *Paradigms in Polity: Classic Readings in Reformed and Presbyterian Church Government* (Grand Rapids, MI: Eerdmans, 1994), 140–48.
62. Hall and Hall, *Paradigms*, 134–39.
63. Hall and Hall, *Paradigms*, 219–25.
64. Hall and Hall, *Paradigms*, 233–47.
65. Hall and Hall, *Paradigms*, 175–79.
66. *The Confession of Faith*, 398–403.

Figure 3   Church offices according to the Westminster Assembly (1643–1648), "The Form of Presbyterial Church-Government"

Pastors	Teachers	Elders	Deacons
pray with/for flock	also minister	govern	take care of the poor
preach	teach doctrine	(serve as "other church governors") do not preach or administer sacraments	distribute to needs of the poor
publicly read Scripture			
administer sacraments			
catechize (part of preaching)			
bless the people from God			
exercise ruling power			

Recent innovations. A recent innovation in some Presbyterian circles is the idea that there are only two offices. This entered via incipient Congregationalism in sixteenth-century France through Jean Morély. The Reformed church reacted vehemently against the claim.[67] As can be seen, Calvin and the Westminster Assembly had four offices. Pastor and teacher were in many respects connected, but there is no evidence that pastor and teacher were ever connected with elder.

One fairly recent defense of pastors and elders holding the same office was presented by George W. Knight III.[68] Within the office of elder, Knight held, there is a distinction between teaching and ruling. The teaching function may be present in a heightened way with some, but not all, elders. His case is based on the New Testament alone, on 1 Timothy 3 and Titus 1, read as speaking of one office with two distinct aspects. For Knight, *presbyteros* and *episkopos* refer to the same group, evident in a

---

67. See Robert M. Kingdon, *Geneva and the Consolidation of the French Protestant Movement 1564–1572: A Contribution to the History of Congregationalism, Presbyterianism, and Calvinist Resistance Theory* (Geneva: Droz, 1967); Tadataka Maruyama, *The Ecclesiology of Theodore Beza: The Reform of the True Church* (Geneva: Droz, 1978).

68. George W. Knight III, "Two Offices (Elders/Bishops and Deacons) and Two Orders of Elders (Preaching/Teaching Elders and Ruling Elders): A New Testament Study," *Presbyterion* 11 (Spring 1985): 1–12.

number of passages (Acts 20:17, 28; 1 Tim. 3:1ff.; 5:17; Titus 1:5, 7). Elders and bishops are synonyms, *presbyteros* describing their seniority, *episkopos* their responsibilities. Peter uses *presbyteros* as a wide-ranging term to cover all ruling, including himself as a presbyter (1 Pet. 5:1), while the apostles and elders act together in Acts 15. The elders as a group lay on hands (1 Tim. 4:14), a group that includes Paul the apostle (2 Tim. 1:6), while those who impose hands on Paul in Acts 13 are prophets and teachers. The officers at Ephesus are called elders or bishops (Acts 20:17, 28; 1 Tim. 3:1; 5:17) but also evangelists, pastors, and teachers (Eph. 4:11). Thus evangelists, pastors, and teachers are also elders.

Late in Paul's career, when church government was settled, the apostle mentioned only elders and deacons (1 Timothy 3). The plurality of elders in each church precludes the possibility that these passages refer to today's ministers. Knight held that the New Testament speaks with one voice. One group has oversight, is called bishops or elders, and includes teaching and ruling functions. Within this group there are two orders, preaching/teaching elders and ruling elders (1 Tim. 5:17). All elders are to be able to teach (1 Tim. 3:2; Titus 1:9ff.), but some are called by God to give their lives to this calling and deserve to be remunerated for it. This is described as the ministry of preaching the Word (2 Tim. 4:1–7).

Knight was answered by Robert S. Rayburn.[69] Rayburn argued strongly for the classic Reformed position of three offices, classic if one excludes the four-office pattern of Calvin, Westminster, and others. Rayburn pointed out that the two-office position has support exclusively from the New Testament. He countered that we need to see the Old Testament background to the polity of the New Testament church. Behind it is the Old Testament distinction between the priest and the elder. His argument continues as follows.

"Elder" is an Old Testament term and is introduced without explanation in Acts 11:30, suggesting that the office is based on Old Testament precedent. In the Old Testament the elder was a representative figure, drawn from across the nation, speaking on behalf of the people. His function was rule and judgment. There is no evidence that the teaching of the law was ever given to the elders.

---

69. Robert S. Rayburn, "Ministers, Elders, and Deacons," *Presbyterion* 12 (Fall 1986): 105–14. This was reissued in a revised form in Mark R. Brown, ed., *Order in the Offices: Essays Defining the Roles of Church Officers* (Duncansville, PA: Classic Presbyterian Government Resources, 1993), 219–33.

There was another distinct Old Testament office for teaching, the Levitical office, and within it the priesthood (Deut. 33:9–10), Rayburn continues. The priests and Levites shared with the elders the task of ruling and judging (Deut. 17:8–13; 21:5; 1 Chron. 23:3–4), but this was adjunct to their primary calling as superintendents of Israel's worship. They were from the tribe of Levi and were not representatives of the whole people. This distinction still existed in first-century Israel (Matt. 21:23; 26:3; Acts 6:12). The functions of these offices were carried over into the New Testament church without comment and were not abrogated.

Apostles and elders are clearly distinguished in Acts 15:2, 4. While "elder" is used in a generic sense in the New Testament, apostle and elder were different. An apostle was by definition a ruler, but an elder was not an apostle. Moreover, Paul distinguishes between gifts of teaching and of ruling (Rom. 12:4–8; 1 Cor. 12:1–31).

In Ephesians 4, Paul discusses various aspects of the ministry of the Word. In view is not rule but preparing God's people for works of service. Pastor-teachers share rule with elders, but as an adjunct to their proper ministry. Elders do not share the office of the Word; to them chiefly the Lord entrusts the responsibility of rule. Therefore, the specifications in 1 Timothy 3 and Titus 1 apply to the *episkopos*, the minister of the Word, who is called to teach. The warrant for the elder is found in 1 Corinthians 12:28 and Romans 12:7–8, where both Calvin and the Westminster Assembly locate it.[70] Moreover, the emergence in the early second century of episcopacy is far easier to explain if the church was already accustomed to ministers in distinction from elders.[71]

To my mind, Rayburn is on sounder ground than Knight with a more canonical grasp of the question. The Reformed in the sixteenth and seventeenth centuries did everything in their power to fight the threat of incipient Congregationalism, which they determined would have the effect of weakening the ministry of the Word.[72]

27.6   The Priority of the One Church

A late medieval debate over universals has had profound consequences on Western culture ever since. Realists held to the existence of universals.

---

70. Edmund P. Clowney, *The Church* (Downers Grove, IL: InterVarsity Press, 1995), 211–12; "The Form of Presbyteriall Church-Government," in *The Confession of Faith*, 402.

71. See Alan D. Strange, "Do the Minister and the Elder Hold the Same Office?," *Ordained Servant Online*, December 2013, www.opc.org/os.html?article_id=393&cur_iss=Y.

72. Kingdon, *Geneva and the Consolidation of the French Protestant Movement*.

Is there such a thing as whiteness, or does whiteness exist exclusively in particular white objects—a white wall, a white flower, white paint, and so forth? For them, whiteness had a real existence, white objects being instantiations of its real existence. In contrast, nominalists argued that universals had no real existence; only particular white objects had reality.

In practice, nominalism has come to dominate Western society, with its rampant individualism, in contrast to traditional societies, where the family, clan, and tribe have priority. In theology and ecclesiology, nominalism is evident in ecclesial models where the ontological priority of the individual is axiomatic. It impacts the question of whether the individual, particular congregation is foundational or, instead, the one holy, catholic, apostolic church.

The church derives from the ascended Christ by the Holy Spirit, from Pentecost and beyond. The process is from the one to the many; particular congregations are instantiations of the one church. There is *one* holy, catholic, and apostolic church. At Rome, Paul addressed at least three different congregations but only one church (Rom. 16:1ff.).[73] Collective decisions by the apostles and elders were binding on the individual congregations (Acts 11:1–18; 15:1–31). It seems that in systems of church polity where each congregation is not merely self-governing but autonomous, separate to itself, the teaching of the historic church can only be accepted on an advisory and provisional basis, and thus the unity of the church is impaired.

27.7 The Ordination of Women to Teaching and Ruling Offices

The practice of ordaining women to teaching and ruling offices gained ground in the late twentieth century, reflecting changes in Western society. It has become standard in many Protestant denominations, apart from some conservative evangelical and Reformed churches. All believers are called to ministry, all have been given gifts for ministry, and all should use those gifts. At the end of Romans, where Paul sends greetings to his fellow workers, he names ten women among the twenty-six names. With women admitted to virtually every other type of work, to bar them from the pastoral ministry can seem, at best, anachronistic.

---

73. Bavinck, *RD*, 4:280, 300–301, 373, 436; James Eglinton, *Trinity and Organism: Towards a New Reading of Herman Bavinck's Organic Motif* (London: Bloomsbury, 2012), 200–201.

However, the arbiter is Scripture. In 1 Timothy 2:8–3:7, Paul insists that the office of overseer is restricted to certain qualified men; it is not for men as opposed to women but for some men who meet the qualifications as opposed to all other men, women, and children. If we correctly ignore the chapter divisions, interpolated by later editors, it is apparent that Paul is discussing the *episkopos*. Preeminent are ethical and spiritual qualities, but also involved is the ability to teach the gospel. In contrast, women are to remain silent and not to usurp this authority. A woman is not to teach an adult male (ἀνήρ). Why? Paul grounds the case in the order of creation. Adam was formed first, the woman afterward (1 Tim. 2:12–15). This requirement is a standard that overrides differences of culture and times. The only alternative is to claim either that Paul was bound by his own historical and cultural setting or that he was plain wrong. In either case readers set themselves over the apostle and the Word of God. The Christian faith is a matter of discipleship, of submission to Christ and his apostles. Christ judges culture; culture has no mandate to sit in judgment on the Word of Christ.

That does not mean that women are debarred from teaching. Indeed, Priscilla was prominent, in conjunction with Aquila, her husband, not as an individual but as part of the solidaric household unit. Older women are to teach younger women (Titus 2:3–5), something from which Titus and, by extrapolation, men in general were excluded.[74] To women is entrusted the vital task of childbirth and the nurture of children, integral to the covenant of grace but derided by much of today's Western culture (1 Tim. 2:15). For Christians to belittle this great privilege is to assault God's covenant, which is advanced along household lines. The instruction of the very young in the rudiments of the faith, when their minds are open, uncluttered, and receptive, is vital for the good of the church and the future of the gospel. Probably most teaching in the church is conducted by women. The office of *episkopos* is the exception; it is tragic that so many branches of the church have abandoned the Word of God and capitulated to the spirit of the age.[75] In so doing, they quench their own prophetic voice, for this demands a countercultural edge.

---

74. Sadly, too many ministers have made shipwreck of their ministry and faith by neglecting this matter.

75. The literature on this is vast. I do not have space here to do other than point to the main issue.

Further Reading

Bannerman, James. *The Church of Christ*. Edinburgh: Banner of Truth, 2015.

Clowney, Edmund P. *The Church*. Downers Grove, IL: InterVarsity Press, 1995.

Study Questions

1. Sometimes the doctrine of the church is said to be "nonessential." Is this a valid suggestion?

2. Why is the oneness of the church the premise for Reformed ecclesiology, rather than multiplicity? Does the New Testament lend support for this unity as foundational?

3. Consider how the holiness and apostolicity of the church can be pursued while we seek to maintain its unity and catholicity.

PART 8

THE ULTIMATE
PURPOSES OF GOD

We look for the resurrection of the dead, and the life of the world to come.

Niceno-Constantinopolitan Creed (381)

O merciful God, the Father of our Lord Jesus Christ, who is the resurrection and the life, in whom whoever believes shall live, though he die; and whoever lives, and believes in him, shall not die eternally; who also has taught us, by his holy Apostle Saint Paul, not to be sorry, as men without hope, for those that sleep in him; we meekly beseech you, O Father, to raise us from the death of sin to the life of righteousness, that, when we shall depart this life, we may rest in him ... and that, at the general Resurrection in the last day, we may be found acceptable in your sight; and receive that blessing, which your well-beloved Son shall then pronounce to all that love and fear you, saying, Come, ye blessed children of my Father, receive the kingdom prepared for you from the beginning of the world; Grant this, we beseech you, O merciful Father, through Jesus Christ, our Mediator and Redeemer. Amen.

Collect at the Burial of the Dead, Book of Common Prayer (1662)

28

The Future

Eschatology refers to the last things. The whole Bible has an orientation to the future and God's fulfillment of all his promises. While futurism regards the majority of eschatological references in Scripture as relating to the time immediately before the parousia, and realized eschatology holds that most have been fulfilled already, inaugurated eschatology seeks to preserve a tension between past fulfillment and future, complete realization. Personal eschatology includes death and the intermediate state before the resurrection. Erroneous views of this condition include purgatory and soul sleep. Often overlooked is the New Testament teaching about the destruction of the temple and the end of the sacrificial system; the Olivet Discourse is occasioned by Jesus's prediction of the end of the Mosaic covenant. The future prospects for the church and the gospel are quite different than what is frequently taught. This chapter focuses on clear didactic passages in the New Testament and seeks to understand the place of Israel in that light.

✠

28.1 Inaugurated Eschatology

The word "eschatology" derives from ἔσχατος,[1] meaning last or last things. Traditionally eschatology was concerned with events at the end of the age; the parousia, the resurrection, the last judgment, and heaven and hell. However, with developed historical awareness arising in the

---

1. *eschatos.*

nineteenth century, the whole of redemptive history was recognized as having an eschatological orientation. An impetus in this direction came from conservative circles, spearheaded by the work of Geerhardus Vos,[2] in whose wake have followed scholars such as Herman Ridderbos and Richard B. Gaffin Jr.[3] Renewed interest in eschatology has resulted from severe atrocities such as the Holocaust and Hiroshima, poverty and oppression, and ecological concerns.[4]

28.1.1   *Promise and Fulfillment*

The Bible's promise-and-fulfillment orientation is seen from the early chapters of Genesis. Adam had the prospect of everlasting life on condition of continued obedience. Following his sin came the promise of deliverance by the offspring of the woman, ultimately to be fulfilled by Christ (Gen. 3:15; cf. John 12:31–32; Rom. 16:20). Adam and Eve were made *in* the image of God (Gen. 1:26–27), pointing us to Christ, who *is* the image of the invisible God (2 Cor. 4:4–6; Col. 1:15; Heb. 1:3), who will renew the creation (Eph. 1:10).

In turn, the successive covenants in the Old Testament anticipate an eventual fulfillment in the undisclosed future. The Abrahamic covenant promised the offspring in whom the world would be blessed (Gen. 12:1–3), reaching its expression in Christ (Gal. 3:16). The ritual of the Mosaic covenant's sacrificial system was fulfilled by Christ (Heb. 7:1–10:18). The expectation of the new covenant (Jer. 31:31–34; Ezek. 36:22–38) is realized in Christ's blood and the consequent sending of the Holy Spirit (Joel 2:28–32).

In the New Testament, with all its stress on Christ's fulfilling the Old Testament and its promises, this eschatological orientation remains and pervades. In Ephesians 1:3–14, Paul constantly stresses purpose. Election is in order to our being holy and blameless (v. 4); foreordination is in order to sonship through Jesus Christ (vv. 5–6). God's grand purpose in

---

2. Geerhardus Vos, *Biblical Theology: Old and New Testaments* (Grand Rapids, MI: Eerdmans, 1948); Vos, *The Pauline Eschatology* (Grand Rapids, MI: Eerdmans, 1972).

3. Herman Ridderbos, *Paul: An Outline of His Theology* (Grand Rapids, MI: Eerdmans, 1975); Richard B. Gaffin Jr., *The Centrality of the Resurrection: A Study in Paul's Soteriology* (Grand Rapids, MI: Baker, 1978).

4. To instance just one prominent author among very many, Jürgen Moltmann, *The Crucified God: The Cross of Christ as the Foundation and Criticism of Christian Theology* (Minneapolis: Fortress, 1993); Moltmann, *On Human Dignity: Political Theology and Ethics* (Minneapolis: Fortress, 1984); Moltmann, *God in Creation: A New Theology of Creation and the Spirit of God* (San Francisco: HarperSanFrancisco, 1991).

Christ relates to "a plan for the fullness of time" (v. 10), whereby Christ will unite and rule the redeemed cosmos. We, in turn, are foreordained to be to the praise of God's glory (vv. 11–12). The promised Spirit is the earnest of our inheritance (vv. 13–14). Each element is drawn to the future, as by a magnet.

The tension between the "already" and the "not yet." There are patently elements that have been fulfilled and others that await their realization in the future. Various theories have been proposed to account for these strands.

Futurism, which is associated with premillennialism, considers the bulk of eschatological references to be fulfilled immediately preceding and surrounding the parousia. Some, especially dispensationalists, hold that many of these events relate to the nation of Israel. Questions need to be asked of this theory. While the New Testament has plenty of references to the parousia and related events, if its overall eschatological teaching were confined to that, how would it have relevance to the situations of those to whom the documents were originally addressed?

Preterism, or *realized eschatology*, takes a diametrically opposite position. Some, like C. H. Dodd, believe that "the Age to come has come," so that "all that the prophets means by the Day of the Lord is realized." While the focus is on realization, it is not to the exclusion of events occurring afterward.[5] More radical forms of preterism have been expressed by Milton Terry and J. Stuart Russell.[6] Radical preterism claims that New Testament references to the future, including the parousia, resurrection, and last judgment, were all realized in the destruction of the temple and Jerusalem in AD 70—hence preterism, from *praeter* (already). I will discuss this later. The theory is not found in any early Christian creed and teeters into heresy over creation and the reality of the resurrection body.

However, preterist interpretations of this or that biblical passage are a different matter. Each biblical book was addressed to a certain community living at the time. It is in harmony with the whole of Scripture to conclude that the major concerns of each were directly related to the circumstances of those who were addressed. Whatever the future

---

5. C. H. Dodd, *The Apostolic Preaching and Its Developments* (London: Hodder & Stoughton, 1944), 85–87.

6. Milton S. Terry, *Biblical Hermeneutics: A Treatise on the Interpretation of the Old and New Testaments* (repr., Grand Rapids, MI: Zondervan, n.d.); J. Stuart Russell, *The Parousia: The New Testament Doctrine of Our Lord's Second Coming* (Grand Rapids, MI: Baker, 1999).

implications, the present concerns were paramount, and recognizing them is a necessary check on speculation.

Inaugurated eschatology considers some events to have already taken place and others to lie in the indefinite future. It is the mainstream position, summed up in the phrase "already and not yet." It regards the Old Testament perspective of promise to be realized in Jesus, the offspring of the woman, the seed promised in the Abrahamic covenant, the archetypal sacrifice, the Davidic King, the anointed Messiah, the inaugurator of the new covenant, the One who sends the Spirit. In short, Old Testament eschatology has become a present reality in Jesus. Since his resurrection and ascension, we are living in the last days. So, according to Jesus, the kingdom of God has already come (Matt. 12:28; 13:1–46; Mark 1:15; Luke 7:22–23; 11:20). For Paul, the death and resurrection of Christ are decisive (Gal. 1:4; Eph. 1:13–14; Col. 1:13), and so the focus is on elements that are already present.

However, the full consummation of the kingdom is in the future, and so we pray "your kingdom come" (Matt. 6:10; 8:11–12; Luke 6:20–21). Jesus depicts the kingdom as growing (Matt. 13:1–52), an event to be fully realized at the end of the world (Matt. 25:31–46).

Between the resurrection and the parousia, the church has the task of making the nations obedient disciples (Matt. 28:18–20; 1 Cor. 15:20–26; 2 Cor. 10:1–5), thus subjecting all things to Christ (Ps. 110:1–4; 1 Cor. 15:20–27; 2 Cor. 10:3–6; Eph. 1:21–23). The present age and the world to come overlap (Heb. 2:5–9); Vos stresses that in Paul the future thrusts itself into the present, the Spirit being "the circumambient atmosphere" in which we live and move.[7] Suffering and expectation, mission and social action go together:

> They suffer with their Lord below,
> they reign with him above.[8]

We share Christ's sufferings and we will share Christ's glory (Acts 14:22; Rom. 8:17; 2 Cor. 4:17; Heb. 12:2; 1 Pet. 4:13).

The future consummation is the basis for the exhortation to live for Christ in the present (Rom. 13:11–14; 1 Cor. 15:58; 1 Thess. 5:1–11). It calls for patient endurance. Thiselton remarks, "There can be no doubt

---

7. Vos, *The Pauline Eschatology*, 163.
8. From the hymn "The Head That Once Was Crowned with Thorns," by Thomas Kelly (1820).

that the central teaching of Jesus looks to a decisive moment of vindication and sovereign intervention of God in the future."[9] The Eucharist presents this vividly: a memorial of the momentous past, a proclamation of and communion with the ascended Christ in the present, and an eschatological relation to the consummate marriage supper of the Lamb.

28.1.2 What Is the Kingdom of God?

God's reign and rule. In the British constitution, the Queen is a constitutional monarch, as the Crown's powers are exercised in and by Parliament. I believe it was Thomas Macaulay who first wrote that "the Queen reigns but does not rule." She exercises neither executive nor legislative functions. She merely has, as Bagehot described, "the right to be consulted, the right to encourage, the right to warn."[10] The kingdom of God is very different. God reigns and he also rules. He is not a constitutional ruler, limited by imposed constraints of law and convention so as to operate within bounds. His province is not, as Bagehot put it, the dignified or ceremonial part of the kingdom rather than the efficient part, for he rules over the entire universe. The only limitations he has are those that flow from his own character and his sovereign determinations.

The kingdom of heaven and the kingdom of God. Dispensationalists distinguish between the kingdom of heaven and the kingdom of God, assigning to them different realities. However, the terms are used interchangeably in the New Testament. Matthew prefers the former expression, possibly because he wrote for a predominantly Jewish readership for whom the name of God was sacred and not to be used lightly.

When does Christ's kingdom begin? Jesus, we saw, proclaimed that the kingdom was at hand, near, about to arrive (Mark 1:15). It is inaugurated following his resurrection. Resurrected, he announces, "All authority in heaven and on earth has been given to me" (Matt. 28:18), indicating a definite investiture. Paul's treatment of the resurrection supports this (1 Cor. 15:20–27; Eph. 1:15–22; Phil. 2:9–11). Paul's attention is on the exaltation of Christ; we do not find the Gospels' expression

9. Anthony C. Thiselton, *The Last Things: A New Approach* (London: SPCK, 2012), 100.
10. Walter Bagehot, *The English Constitution: With an Introduction by R. H. S. Crossman* (1867; repr., London: Collins, 1963), 111.

"kingdom of God" or "kingdom of heaven" anymore. This is because Jesus Christ is exalted as King, and the kingdom of God is embodied in the Son.

It is both a heavenly reign, since Christ is in heaven ruling by the Holy Spirit, and an earthly reign, finding expression in the world, since the creation belongs to Christ. All authority in heaven and earth belongs to him. No realm is outside his jurisdiction, no second kingdom autonomously apart from his kingship. He is "the ruler of kings on earth" (Rev. 1:5). The whole world is answerable to him. There is one kingdom with distinct expressions in the church and in the world. Thus, political rulers are "servant[s] of God" (Rom. 13:4), answerable for their actions.

28.1.3 Genesis 1–2 and Eschatology

John Fesko argues that the early chapters of Genesis are eschatological. In this he is in agreement with Geerhardus Vos.[11] Fesko is critical of popular interpretive models of these chapters. Evolutionary theory has dominated discussion of Genesis among conservatives and diverted attention from its central message. Hodge and Warfield, Fesko argues, gave too much ground to the new theories, while young-earth creationists have adopted a literal hermeneutic characteristic of dispensationalism. Fesko contends that it is as wrong-headed to look to Genesis for a detailed scientific description of the origin of the earth as it is to look to Romans. The literary genre of Genesis is not that of a science manual. It is written from the perspective of an ancient Middle Eastern agriculturalist, using the language of everyday observation.[12] We might add that to impose modern questions on an ancient text savors of anachronism.

Fesko asks how the creation of man in the image of God is to be understood in the light of a canonical view of Scripture? He points to its fulfillment by Christ, as I have done above. Because of the connection of Adam with Christ, Fesko questions whether Adam was merely an agriculturalist. Instead, his task in relation to God was as a priest-king, the garden effectively a temple, and Adam given the task of extending the garden to cover the earth, exercising dominion over it as God's vicegerent. Moreover, the covenant God established with him foreshadowed the covenant fulfilled

---

11. John V. Fesko, *Last Things First: Unlocking Genesis 1–3 with the Christ of Eschatology* (Fearn: Mentor, 2007); Vos, *Biblical Theology*, 38–55.

12. Fesko, *Last Things*, 14–23.

by the second Adam. The ultimate goal God planned for the race was to share his eternal Sabbath rest, signified by the seventh day.[13]

Fesko's argument aligns with the principle that what is last in execution is first in intention. As mentioned earlier, if we intend to build a house, the first thing to determine is the kind of house we want. How large will it be, and how many rooms should it have? What about the yard—what shrubs, flowers, and trees should be there? Only after thinking about the end product will we hire an architect to produce the detailed plans, followed by various contractors to construct the house and landscape its surrounds, starting with the foundations, then the superstructure, and eventually the arrangements inside and out.

If Fesko's case is sound, it follows that eschatology pervades the Bible and the history of redemption. At each point, including our current location, the pointers are to the future and to the consummation of redemption. Even then, the final eternal state is likely not to be static but to be an everlasting dynamic progression in the knowledge of God and service for him and in partnership with him. It will no longer be redemptive, but it will be a full-scale eschatological flourishing beyond the bounds of our imagination (1 Cor. 2:9).

28.2 Future Dimensions

I will attempt to follow the basic hermeneutical principle of using the clearer didactic passages to interpret the more obscure and figurative ones (WCF, 1.9).

28.2.1 The Personal Level

Death and the intermediate state. According to Thiselton, in the Old Testament "the worst feature of death was possible separation from God, after a life of communion with him."[14] Death was seen as a descent into *sheol* (*hades* in the LXX), where the dead existed as a shade of who they were. Later, in Isaiah 26:17–19 and 38:10–18, and by the time of the New Testament, *hades* was restricted to a place of punishment for the wicked, evident in the case of the rich man in Luke 16.[15] Since Jesus won victory

---

13. Fesko, *Last Things*, 183–203.
14. Thiselton, *Last Things*, 3.
15. Thiselton, *Last Things*, 4.

on the cross, death has lost its sting, although, insofar as the effects of sin still remain, death is not without sorrow.[16]

Human death is the result and the reward of sin (Gen. 2:15–17; Rom. 5:12ff.; 6:23). Sin is a choice for death as opposed to life, of which God is the author. Adam was created in a communion of life with God his Creator but chose to go his separate way. Consequently, death was operative from the moment of his fateful choice. It was evident in his damaged relationship with Eve, and also in their descendants, in murder, conflict, and warfare (Genesis 3–5). Alienation from God, and the life he alone gives, led to the dissolution of the human being and the cessation of embodied, physical life. The question before us is how this affects those united to Christ. I will examine four contexts where this is discussed.

Philippians 1:21–24. Paul, in prison, awaiting trial and its uncertain outcome, faces a quandary. What is his preferred outcome? To remain alive and continue his ministry would bring benefit to the church, in line with his exhortation in Philippians 2:1–5 to look to the interests of others. This was his wish. However, if he were to be sentenced to death, the outcome would be beneficial for him. This is because he would be "with Christ, which is very far better" (1:23, my trans.). It would consist of heightened communion with Christ; he would be in close personal proximity to Christ, taking up residence with him; his union with Christ would be expressed in new ways that would surpass his present condition. Perhaps Paul's experience when the glorified Christ encountered him on the road to Damascus gave him a foretaste of that heightened communion and so whetted his appetite that he had a strong "desire [ἐπιθυμία][17] . . . to depart and be with Christ." However, love trumps personal advantage.[18]

1 Thessalonians 4:13–18. Paul writes of highly charged questions surrounding the death of believers. It is natural for us to mourn the loss of loved ones. Death is an intrusion into God's creation, a cruel dissolution of our humanity, often preceded by a grim process of decay or a terrible

---

16. Thiselton, *Last Things*, 5.
17. *epithymia.*
18. Once a Christian woman who had suffered some brain damage at birth asked me, since it was to the advantage of believers to die and be with Christ, whether it might not be best to commit suicide to that end. The answer, in part, is that Christians have the fruit of the Spirit and therefore act in love for, and ministry to, others; and so the thought of personal gain must be subordinate to the imperative of love. This is to say nothing of the built-in creational bias toward the preservation of life, especially one's own, the sin of suicide, and the primary reality that God is the living God and our relationship with him is one in which we receive, preserve, and nurture the life he gives.

accident. It is an unknown; we have never experienced it and do not know what lies in store. It hangs over us like a threat. Mourning is not a sign of a lack of faith; it is a demonstration of our humanity. Jesus wept at the grave of Lazarus, bristling with anger at death and all it entailed. Jesus was sinless and exercised perfect faith. He wept then, and later was overcome with grief in Gethsemane, because he was human.

However, Christians are not to mourn like the rest of the world, who have no hope. For the unbelieving world, the outlook is hopeless; a grim outlook can be evaded only by placing a taboo over the subject or by treating it flippantly. Christian mourning is very different; it is marked by hope. Hope for Paul is not wishful thinking or uncertainty, but it is related to futurity. We expect God's promises to be fulfilled—but at some time in the future. We look for the resurrection of the dead and the life of the world to come. Christians mourn, but with joyful anticipation for the ultimate consummation of salvation in Jesus Christ.

Paul provides good reasons why this is so. First, "we believe that Jesus died" (v. 14). Who *is* Jesus? He is the eternal Son of God, one with the Father in the indivisible Trinity. In our nature, he submitted to human death and traveled on the path from death through the tunnel of burial. Human death is an experience now known to God himself. Furthermore, we believe that Jesus died *and rose again*. Death was not the end. Jesus conquered it. The Father raised him from the dead by the Holy Spirit (Rom. 8:10–11). There is *a past triumph*. We can grieve with hope, knowing that Christ has experienced death and has triumphed over it.

We also have confident expectation because there is *present protection*. One of the greatest affirmations in Scripture is here, where Paul describes believers who have died as "dead in Christ." Union with Christ in his burial is a triumphant assertion of victory over sin and death. All the hatred of the devil and the process of death and decay cannot separate us from the union Christ has established. "Death's mightiest powers have done their worst"[19] and are a spent force. The putrefying corpse is lowered into the grave, there to rot, but still in unbreakable union with Christ. Death cannot curtail it.

Moreover, when Christ returns, the dead in Christ will be at no disadvantage compared with those still alive, for they will rise first, and Christ will bring them *with him*. Entailed is that, while in the state of

---

19. From the Latin hymn "The Strife Is O'er, the Battle Done," trans. Francis Pott (1861).

death, they are with Christ. While the wicked "are kept in their graves as in their prisons," believers "rest in their graves as in their beds" (WLC, 86). We will be protected by Christ. When he returns, all who have died in him are in no way disadvantaged but come with him, raised from the dead and glorified.

Finally, there will be *a future reunion*. "We will always be with the Lord" (1 Thess. 4:17). In that glorified state, union with Christ will be brought to its consummation, for "we shall be like him," fully conformed to his glorified image into the endless vistas of eternity (1 John 3:1–2).

Revelation 6:9–11. In this vision accorded to John, the souls of the martyrs are conscious of the passing of time, aware of their surroundings, and able to communicate "with a loud voice" in their own sphere. They have an awareness of the delay of the parousia and the consummation, and long for its fulfillment and the execution of justice, when things are set right.

2 Corinthians 5:1–10. The resurrection engendered much debate in the Corinthian church. The Greeks in general had an aversion to the material, finding bodily resurrection inexplicable. Paul had explained what the resurrection is (1 Cor. 15:1–58). (We will consider this later.) Here Paul contrasts our present weak condition with the future fulfillment of all God's promises. In 2 Corinthians 5:1–5 he contrasts our present earthly body—fragile and temporary—with our future resurrection body, which is from God, not limited by the present created order, and eternal, permanent. This is his major expectation; the resurrection of the dead. Note the verbs στενάζω and ἐπιποθέω,[20] which convey powerful emotional force—we groan, strongly desiring this resurrection body. We are pressed down by these forces.

Between now and then is the intermediate state (vv. 6–9). Here the verbs lack the visceral power associated with our expectation of the resurrection. "We are always of good courage" (θαρροῦντες,[21] v. 6). This is not Paul's number one hope; it is something to be accepted. The reason for this is that there are pluses and minuses associated with our condition after death. On the one hand, we will be absent from the body (vv. 8–9). Since we are embodied creatures, the disruption of death will be experienced keenly. We will be restricted. We will not function properly as

20. *stenazō, epipotheō.*
21. *tharrountes.*

humans. We are not just embodied souls.[22] Notwithstanding, there will be compensating factors; we will be present with the Lord (v. 8). We will take up residence with Christ. This is the language of immigration and emigration, but it is not Paul's main desire, for his anticipation of the resurrection body surpasses this. From one perspective we will suffer loss, but yet, in an enfeebled and broken condition, we will be given access to heightened communion with the glorified Christ, an experience beyond our current calculations. However, Paul looks ahead to the time when both aspects—embodiment, imperishable and enhanced, and fully realized union and communion with the glorified Christ—will be present in unalloyed splendor. Then there will be no minuses.

As Thiselton remarks, resurrection is more than "the resumption and extension of a spoiled life." Citing Moltmann, he suggests that it is the chance to become the person God intended us to be.[23] There is a vast contrast between believers in Christ and others. Thiselton continues, "Those who mourn see only the preresurrection, this-worldly, side of death. From the perspective of faith, one believes that death has a postresurrection side also."[24] Life remains provisional until the whole work of God is complete in the resurrection.[25] However, by faith we can have a provisory but reasonable understanding.[26] By this Thiselton appears to mean that we do not yet see or possess the ultimate embodied fulfillment. "Disbelief in life after death makes life meaningless; belief in life after death invites a working and provisional meaning, which is grounded in God's promise and human trust; postresurrection experience will bring access to a full and definitive meaning of all things."[27]

Erroneous ideas about the intermediate state
The Greek idea of the immortality of the soul. Stemming from Greek thought is the idea that the soul inherently possesses immortality. This

---

22. On the metaphysics of the intermediate state, see e.g., John W. Cooper, *Body, Soul, and Life Everlasting* (Grand Rapids, MI: Eerdmans, 2000); and for a critical assessment in the light of Christological orthodoxy, James T. Turner Jr., "On Two Reasons Christian Theologians Should Reject the Intermediate State," *JRT* 11 (2017): 121–39. Turner argues that dualist accounts of the human constitution locate the substance of humanity in the soul and so render the incarnation untenable. My argument is that humans are a duality-in-unity, that death disrupts and renders inoperative the human being, while retaining some element of consciousness, so that our hope is the resurrection of the body.
23. Thiselton, *Last Things*, 9.
24. Thiselton, *Last Things*, 9.
25. Thiselton, *Last Things*, 10.
26. Thiselton, *Last Things*, 11.
27. Thiselton, *Last Things*, 15.

notion went in tandem with a belief that the soul is eternal. As Moltmann comments:

> The doctrine of the immortality of the soul is not a doctrine about a life after death; it teaches that the human being possesses a divine identity which is beyond birth and death. What cannot die when the body dies, was not born when the body was born either, and has never lived in the life of the body.[28]

He reflects that, on that basis, "because death means the liberation of the soul from the mortal body, death is the feast day of the soul."[29]

Nothing could be further removed from the biblical teaching about what it is to be human. The Greek idea renders the incarnation redundant since, if embodiment is less than properly human, the Son would not have needed to take human flesh, and the human organism born by Mary would not be intrinsic to the substance of being human.[30] Moreover, humans are created and have a beginning, being psychosomatic, a duality-in-unity. Immortality is a gift of God, contingent, not an intrinsic human possession. Moreover, it applies to the body as well as the soul. I will discuss conditional immortality and annihilationism in chapter 30.

Purgatory. Rome's doctrine of purgatory is expressed in the *CCC*, "All who die in God's grace and friendship, but still imperfectly purified, are indeed assured of their eternal salvation; but after death they undergo purification, so as to achieve the holiness necessary to enter the joy of heaven."[31] This refers to "the final purification of the elect, which is entirely different from the punishment of the damned." It is "a cleansing fire"[32] and is based on the practice of prayer for the dead, seen in 2 Maccabees 12:46.[33] Contrary to Venema, there is within Catholicism no express dogmatic commitment to the proportion of believers who will undergo these purifying processes.[34]

Rome bases its dogma of purgatory partly on the tradition of the church, stemming from the days of Origen but only reaching official

---

28. Jürgen Moltmann, *The Coming of God: Christian Eschatology*, trans. Margaret Kohl (Minneapolis: Fortress, 1996), 59.
29. Moltmann, *The Coming of God*, 60.
30. See Turner, "Two Reasons."
31. CCC, 1030.
32. CCC, 1031.
33. CCC, 1032.
34. Cornelis P. Venema, *The Promise of the Future* (Edinburgh: Banner of Truth, 2000), 64–68.

status in the thirteenth century, together with texts such as 2 Maccabees 12:43–45, Matthew 12:31–32, 1 Corinthians 3:10–15, and 1 Peter 1:7.

> [Judas] also took up a collection, man by man, to the amount of two thousand drachmas of silver, and sent it to Jerusalem to provide for a sin offering. In doing this he acted very well and honourably, taking account of the resurrection. For if he were not expecting that those who had fallen would rise again, it would have been superfluous and foolish to pray for the dead. But if he was looking to the splendid reward that is laid up for those who fall asleep in godliness, it was a holy and pious thought. Therefore he made atonement for the dead, that they might be delivered from their sin. (2 Macc. 12:43–45)

Second Maccabees is apocryphal, according to the Protestant canon. The passage refers to sacrifice on behalf of the dead but includes those who, in the eyes of the Roman church, have committed *mortal* sins. This, as Venema points out, does not qualify under the doctrine of purgatory, which is said to purify from *venial* sin.[35] However, the passage establishes that in the second century BC, pious Jews believed in conscious existence after death, as well as the resurrection of the dead.

In 1 Corinthians 3:10–15, Paul writes of rewards or losses that accrue to ministers of the gospel for the faithfulness of their ministries. The focus is on the final judgment. It is the works, not the persons, that will be tested by fire and either be burned up or else be shown to be genuine. First Peter 1:7 refers to the trial by fire of believers undergoing persecution (cf. 1 Pet. 4:13), an experience in the present life, not one after death. As for Matthew 12:31–32, Jesus refers there to the sin against the Holy Spirit that will not be forgiven, either in this age or in the age to come. Jesus's stress is on the dire nature of this sin, but the text undermines the argument for purgatory, since it includes the age after the parousia, beyond the reach of purgatory.

However, the most crucial weakness of the dogma is theological. If there were sins for which a postmortem purification were needed, the finality and sufficiency of the work of Christ would be eroded.[36]

---

35. Venema, *Promise*, 69–70.

36. While some Orthodox writers have argued for a doctrine similar to that of Rome, these are purely the views of the authors; the only official church dogmas on the afterlife are found in the Nicene Creed, as noted by Paul Ladouceur, "Orthodox Theologies of the Afterlife," *SVTQ* 62 (2018): 51–72.

Psychopannychia (soul sleep). Many Anabaptists propounded the idea that there is no conscious existence after death, no conscious moment between death and the judgment.[37] In sleep one is unaware of the passage of time, so after death there will be no experience of any intervening interval, but it will feel as though one is passing straight to the judgment. Calvin's first theological treatise was written against this notion. The biblical passages referenced above refute it, as does the tradition of the Christian church. In this, Rome and the Orthodox Church are at one with Protestants.

The doctrine of soul sleep is founded on the idea that to posit continued conscious postmortem existence is to belittle the body. Rather, the death of the body signals the decisive interruption of all consciousness. Besides, it is argued, the Bible refers to the dead as sleeping.

However, where the Bible refers to believers sleeping after death, it uses a common euphemism. The WLC, 86, uses similar language in contrasting the postmortem condition of believers with that of the wicked. Whereas the latter are "kept in their graves as in their prisons," believers "rest in their graves as in their beds." Yet, the resting does not countenance their being in a state of unconsciousness.

T. F. Torrance, on the basis of the relationship between time and eternity, suggests that existentially there will seem for us to be no interval between death and the final judgment. This is due to eternity being supratemporal, enveloping time.[38] Thiselton points to what has been considered a logical paradox about the preferred state of being with Christ and yet an indefinite delay, and points to a resolution in a distinction between an observer, for whom there appears to be a delay, and a participant, who is conscious that being with Christ is the next thing. For this, Thiselton thinks that the believer or participant "will know nothing of the intermediate state," for "his or her 'sleep' cannot be interrupted."[39] It seems that the claims of neither Torrance nor Thiselton are entirely in harmony with the classic teaching. As for me, I am in no rush to find out whether this is so; besides, once I do find out, I will be unable to inform you. It is more than sufficient to know that we will be "with Christ."

---

37. George Huntston Williams, *The Radical Reformation* (Philadelphia: Westminster, 1975), 104–6, 580–92.
38. Thomas F. Torrance, *Space, Time, and Resurrection* (Grand Rapids, MI: Eerdmans, 1976), 102; Paul D. Molnar, *Thomas F. Torrance: Theologian of the Trinity* (Farnham: Ashgate, 2009).
39. Thiselton, *Last Things*, 79.

28.2.2   Israel and the Mosaic Covenant

Matthew 24–25. For this significant discourse of Jesus's, the parallel passage in Luke 21 is important. There Jesus answers a question about the imminent destruction of the temple.

Possible interpretations. The most common interpretations of Matthew 24–25 are as follows: (1) Verses 1–35 were fulfilled in AD 70, whereas 24:36–25:46 refers to the parousia.[40] (2) All is to be fulfilled at the parousia. (3) There was a fulfillment at AD 70 and another at the parousia, moving from one to the other throughout the passage, although without unanimity about exactly where these transitions occur. (4) The passage refers to the entire period from the resurrection to the end.[41]

The questions. The context was Jesus's departure from the temple, whereupon the disciples remarked about the temple buildings. The departure was significant, since Jesus would not return; it was more than a merely physical departure. Matthew recorded steadily increasing antagonism from the religious establishment toward Jesus. In chapter 23 this reached a climax as Jesus denounced his antagonists for their wicked unbelief. The time had arrived for the judgment of God, for the covenant sanctions to hang like the sword of Damocles over the nation. Jesus replied to the disciples that the temple would be overthrown. Not one stone would be left (24:2). His departure demonstrated that judgment was imminent. This exchange is mirrored in Luke 21:5–6, where the disciples' comments focus explicitly on the beauty of the temple buildings, but Jesus's answer is effectively the same. The temple was the focal point of Yahweh's covenant relationship with Israel; its destruction signaled the overthrow of all they held dear and the inauguration of the new covenant. This set the scene for what would follow.

The disciples raised questions (Matt. 24:3): "When will these things be, and what will be the sign of your coming [parousia] and of the end of the age?" These appear to have been two distinct questions. However, in the minds of the disciples, it is likely that they were one. It would be unthinkable that the end of the age was something separable from the overthrow of the temple, the place where Yahweh and his people met in covenant relationship, with the priesthood and the sacrifices. From their

40. R. T. France, *The Gospel according to Matthew: An Introduction and Commentary* (Leicester: Inter-Varsity Press, 1985), 333–36.

41. W. D. Davies Jr. and Dale C. Allison, *A Critical and Exegetical Commentary on the Gospel according to Saint Matthew* (Edinburgh: T&T Clark, 1988), 3:328–33, provide a thorough survey.

angle, Jesus was speaking about the day of the Lord, the end and fulfillment of the covenant. Jesus's answer was not what they had expected.

Jesus warned against premature conclusions that might arise from dramatic events around them (24:5–14). There might be enticing voices purporting to know that the end was near, that the temple's days were done, that the existing order was about to be overthrown. Some would claim to be the Messiah (v. 5). There would be wars and crises (v. 6), natural disasters and recurrent famines (v. 7). Persecution was to break out, and some would be martyred (vv. 9–13). The gospel was to be preached "throughout the whole world" (v. 14); only then would the end come. Natural disasters, political upheavals, and persecution were not signs of the imminence of the temple's overthrow. They were all features of life in a fallen world, marked by social disorder, typified by disruption and conflict.

Instead, a range of distinct signs would immediately precede the event. Jesus mentioned "the abomination of desolation spoken of by the prophet Daniel, standing in the holy place" (v. 15). In Luke the reference is to "Jerusalem surrounded by armies [infantry or foot-soldiers]" (Luke 21:20), pointing to the Roman armies besieging the city in the Jewish revolt. In Matthew, the reference points to the blasphemous action of Titus Vespasian in entering the temple and proclaiming his divine status. Daniel's vision looks down the centuries to a similar action in 165 BC when Antiochus Epiphanes IV, following a siege and a time of intense persecution of the Jews, who were led by the Maccabees, offered a sow on the temple altar, an event strikingly similar to the one mentioned here.

In the face of this very public sign Jesus instructed his followers to escape for their lives (Matt. 24:17–22). This would be an unparalleled time of suffering, for "there will be great tribulation, such as has not been from the beginning of the world." Over one million perished in the siege of AD 70, with cannibalism common. In view of the downfall of Jerusalem and the destruction of the temple, it seemed that all for which Israel had hoped for so long was in ruins. The calamity was colossal. It demonstrated publicly that the Mosaic covenant had ended, its sanctions enforced.

During this time, false hopes would be rife. Many would claim special revelation, signs and wonders would be on display, and reports of the arrival of the Messiah would alarm many. None of these portents were to be accepted by Jesus's disciples (vv. 23–26) for the parousia of the Son of Man was to be of a very different order, universally evident, raising no doubts or questions (v. 27). In the case of the temple and Jerusalem, the eagles would be surrounding the carcass, the armies ready in predatory mode to gorge themselves on the decadent Jewish state and corrupt temple establishment (v. 28).

The apocalyptic language that follows is reminiscent of Isaiah 13:10ff., where the prophet foretold the downfall of Babylon (Matt. 24:29). There a mighty world power was brought to its knees; here the nation God had taken for his own and nurtured was to be struck down— political convulsions both, portrayed in vivid Technicolor. Something like this is portrayed in verse 30, with the sequel in verse 31, where God sends his messengers to gather his elect throughout the world. This suggests the Gentiles being gathered into the kingdom of heaven, in keeping with the overall thrust of Matthew (1:1; 8:11–12; 28:19–20), rooting the apocalyptic language and the remarkable signs in the events of AD 70, the Son of Man coming in judgment on Israel.

This conclusion is reinforced by the parable of the fig tree, which follows in Matthew 24:32–34. It points to the preceding signs as immediate precursors of the end, of the Son of Man acting in judgment. Jesus reinforces the point by affirming that "this generation will not pass away until all these things take place." The clearest meaning of this comment is that the temple will be destroyed within the lifetime of the generation hearing Jesus's words. The parallel passage in Luke 21 is effectively identical to Matthew 24:1–35 and explicitly addresses the question of the overthrow of the temple. Moreover, Matthew has focused on the increased tension between Jesus and the establishment, with Jesus launching a barrage of condemnation on the unbelief and hypocrisy of the scribes and Pharisees. They were to bear the accumulated wrath of God from previous times (Matt. 23:35). The clincher is that "all these things will come upon this generation" (Matt. 23:36). The evidence points overwhelmingly to the current generation being called to account.[42]

In the sections following, from verse 36, very different circumstances prevail. Until now there has been a great deal of detail, with many signs

---

42. The Scofield Reference Bible, the manual of dispensationalism, considered γενεά to refer to "race, kind, family, stock, breed (so all lexicons)." However, this is one meaning only; it also means "the sum total of those born at the same time, expanded to include all those living at a given time." BAG, 153. The context determines its meaning here.

preceding the event in view. From verse 36 there is no forewarning of the event Jesus has in mind. In each case it happens suddenly and unexpectedly. Whereas the temple is to be destroyed following the abomination of desolation and the portents in heaven, "the *parousia* of the Son of Man" (v. 37) is foreshadowed by nothing at all. The comparison with the days of Noah (vv. 37–41) and the parables of the householder (vv. 42–44), the wise servant (vv. 45–51), the wise and foolish virgins (25:1–13), and the talents (25:14–30) all stress that "you do not know on what day your Lord is coming" (Matt. 24:42). The conclusion is that Jesus is talking about two different happenings—Jerusalem and its defeat in 24:1–35, and his parousia from 24:36–25:46. The disciples may have thought the overthrow of the temple would mark the end of the age but, in reality, these are two distinct events separated by indefinite time.

The passage highlights the importance of the events of AD 70. It removes the idea of the "great tribulation" (v. 21), from the realm of events that are still to happen before the return of Christ. The dominance of claims of a period of unspeakable persecution in the future has engendered a pessimistic outlook on the ministry of the church, implying that things will go from bad to worse. If this were to be the case, I suggest it could not be based on the Olivet Discourse.

Hebrews. Hebrews has a number of references to the impending end of the Mosaic covenant and its sacrificial system. Implied in this is the end of the temple as well; if the sacrifices are made obsolete, so is the place where they are offered. The letter to the Hebrews represents the Old Testament priests as standing, evidently still going about their business, requiring the letter to have been written shortly before AD 70 (Heb. 9:1–10; 10:1–14).

Israel is on the verge of judgment, having received the Word of God and decisively rejected it, and is near to being cursed (Heb. 6:4–8). Their idealization of the wilderness generation is a lesson in futility, as the bodies of those people fell in the desert (Heb. 3:12–19). The Old Testament Aaronic priesthood has been set aside, superseded by Christ (Heb. 7:1–28). Its God-given purpose has been met. The old covenant is growing old and close to disappearing (Heb. 8:13). Christ has done away with the Old Testament sacrifices (Heb. 10:9). Any reversion to that covenant is irreparable apostasy from Christ (Heb. 2:1–4; 6:4–8; 10:19–39; 12:19–29). From this perspective, it seems necessary that the temple and the sacrificial ritual be permanently ended. That raises the question of whether Israel still has a place in God's redemptive purposes and, if so, how? We will consider this shortly.

28.2.3 The Church and the Progress of the Gospel

Paul on events preceding the parousia (2 Thess. 2:1ff.). Paul warns his readers against letters claiming that the day of the Lord, the parousia, is at hand. Some in the church, thinking Christ was about to return, had stopped working in order to prepare for his appearance (2 Thess. 2:1ff.; 3:6ff.). This, Paul says, is unacceptable behavior based on an untenable hypothesis.

Rather, the return of Christ will not happen until two events have taken place. There is "the apostasy" (my trans.), and "the man of lawlessness is revealed, the son of destruction, who opposes and exalts himself against every . . . object of worship, so that he takes his seat in the temple of God, proclaiming himself to be God" (2 Thess. 2:3–4).

Understandings of Paul's teaching. Premillennialists claim that Paul is referring to events immediately before the parousia. Dispensationalists think the church will be removed from the earth in the rapture, its preservative influence thus taken away, and the Holy Spirit, who indwells the church, no longer present to the world (vv. 6–8). In tandem with this, the claim is that the church will slide into apostasy beforehand. In turn, the man of lawlessness, or the Antichrist, will be made known, who will unleash persecution on the church, or on Israel if the church is no longer there. He will proclaim himself to be God in the temple, rebuilt by the Jews in the kingdom period after the rapture of the church. Historical premillennialists make no speculations about Israel or the rapture but follow the same line of thought in relation to the apostasy, persecution, and the man of lawlessness.

Conversely, Warfield argued that for this passage to be relevant to the Thessalonian church, it must relate to events that were to happen in the first century. Paul intended to refer to the apostasy of the Jews, their persistent and obstinate refusal to accept their Messiah, and to the succession of Roman emperors who proclaimed themselves to be divine and then launched savage persecution of the church, invading Israel, destroying the temple and Jerusalem. Warfield pointed to Titus Vespasian as epitomizing the principle of lawlessness and bringing the prophecy to its climax when he entered the temple and proclaimed himself to be God in AD 70.[43] This seems to me to be far more plausible.

To what extent can we access Paul's teaching here? Often missed is that Paul expects his readers to know what he is saying. He had taught them previously in person: "Do you not remember that when I was still with you I told you these things?" (2 Thess. 2:5). For us, the problem is that we were not there to hear what he had to say, and so we lack the resources to make a definite conclusion. We cannot make dogmatic statements on subjects for which we have no firsthand knowledge. This warns us against using a passage like this as a basis for clear doctrinal pronouncements. Whatever Paul meant, if we are to glean anything from it, we need to see it in terms of what he mentions elsewhere.

Perhaps the most relevant passage where Paul discusses events preceding the parousia is 1 Thessalonians 5:1ff., written following his brief visit when he planted the church and gave the teaching to which he refers in 2 Thessalonians 2. There he states that the coming of the Lord will be sudden and unexpected, "like a thief in the night" (1 Thess. 5:2). That rules out the view that the events in 2 Thessalonians 2 are *immediate* precursors of the return of Christ. Whatever they are, they do not happen then. Indeed, 2 Thessalonians 2 gives us no grounds to conclude anything about the situation before Christ returns. For reasons such as this, Venema's comment that this chapter, together with Matthew 24 and Daniel 9, marks out "the period of history immediately prior to the close of the age" is not to be accepted without much reservation.[44] The idea of a calamitous time just before the parousia should be regarded with skepticism.

The New Testament on the prospects for the church's task

Matthew 28:18–20. Jesus's last mandate to his apostles has in prospect the whole of the time from then until the consummation of the age. His command is that the church is to make the nations disciples. This is to be done first by baptism and then by teaching them to obey everything he commanded them. Discipleship entails baptism, being taught, and obeying. The obedience envisaged is comprehensive. The nations are to be made not merely converts but also disciples. Their discipleship is to

---

43. B. B. Warfield, "The Prophecies of St. Paul," in *Biblical and Theological Studies*, ed. Samuel G. Craig (Philadelphia: Presbyterian and Reformed, 1952), 463–502.
44. Venema, *Promise*, 156, 163–64, 175–78.

be thorough; they are to be taught not only all that Jesus commanded but also that they are to obey all he commanded.

We cannot restrict this to anything less than a scenario in which the nations of the world have been brought into obedient discipleship to Christ. If this sounds like a remote possibility, a pipe dream, Jesus assures the apostles, "I will be with you all the days until the consummation of the age" (v. 20, my trans.). That this is no pious platitude without impact on what happens is clear from his introductory report, "All authority in heaven and on earth has been given to me" (v. 18). He has been installed at the right hand of the Father as our Savior and given comprehensive, plenipotentiary authority over the universe for this very purpose, that the church should disciple the nations and bring them into full obedience. This passage envisages nothing less.

1 Corinthians 15:20–26. Christ's resurrection is the firstfruits of the resurrection of all who belong to him (1 Cor. 15:23). This took place sometime around AD 30; ours will occur at his parousia. We will note in chapter 29 that these are part of the same reality, behaving identically. Between these two stupendous events is the time in which we now live, when the church proclaims the gospel to the far corners of the earth. Paul describes Christ at this time as reigning. Alluding to Psalm 110:1, he says, "He must reign until he has put all his enemies under his feet" (1 Cor. 15:25). Christ is reigning now. It is not merely that he *is* reigning but that he *must* reign. It is the eternal plan of God that as our incarnate Savior and Mediator, he has been given all authority. His reign is from his resurrection to ours. During this time, he progressively subdues his enemies, bringing them under his feet as a mighty conqueror. "The last enemy to be rendered inoperative is death" (1 Cor. 15:26, my trans.). As the context indicates, death is ultimately banished when we are resurrected at his return. Therefore, the intervening period is a progressive triumph over all his enemies, leaving death on its own, to be eradicated at the parousia. Prior to that, all other enemies will have been vanquished.

While Christ's great triumphal procession is in progress, evil will also increase (2 Tim. 3:13), aided by scientific and technological advances that extend its reach and further its systematic implementation. This should keep us from triumphalism. Sin and suffering continue until Christ returns. Persecution intensifies. Evil will grow and become more fearsome still. But we have been given the weapons to overcome it;

these are intellectual in scope, consisting of reasoning, dethroning arguments, and leading every thought captive (2 Cor. 10:3–6), just as Paul
persuaded, reasoned with, and convinced others (Acts 17:3; 18:4, 19;
19:8–10).

*The mystery of Israel's unbelief and the promise of the future: Does
Israel have a future in God's purposes? (Romans 9–11).* Given the divisions between Jew and Gentile in the church at Rome, the question of the
continuing place of Israel was very pertinent. It is a leitmotif throughout
the letter (Rom. 1:14–17; 2:6–5:21; 7:1–8:11; 9:1–11:36; 14:1–15:33).
After unfolding the wonders of the gospel, which is for the Jew first,
Paul poses the nagging issue, where does this leave the Old Testament
people of God?

Paul expresses his deep anguish for his compatriots because they
have seemingly shut their minds to Christ. He has deep sorrow over their
current state and their potential future. Their unbelief has come in the
wake of huge privileges: "To them belong the adoption, the glory, the
covenants, the giving of the law, the worship, and the promises." Beyond
these great benefits were "the patriarchs" and "Christ" (Rom. 9:1–5).

Does his compatriots' unbelief mean the Word of God has failed
(9:6–13)? No, Paul says, for throughout Israel's history some were elect
and others not, some believed and others disobeyed. God made his covenant with Isaac, not Ishmael, with Jacob rather than Esau. So the present
circumstances are not new. God's purpose in election was worked out in
the midst of these distinctions.

Is God thereby unjust in choosing the one and rejecting the other
(9:14–18)? Again, Paul refutes the charge. God is sovereign and has a
perfect right to do what he chooses. Even the bitter persecution under
Pharaoh was part of his electing plan. Pharaoh served God's purpose,
unwittingly and unintentionally occasioning the display of his grace and
power.

If this is so, and all depends on God's sovereign purpose, how can
humans be judged (9:19–29)? This is a question we have no right to ask.
God created us and has absolute authority to do as he wills with those
he has made. In the end, he will display his glory in showing mercy to
those whose natural inclination was to rebel. Meanwhile Israel has persisted in unbelief and God has been merciful to the Gentiles (9:30–33).
Israel has missed the point that salvation is by grace, received through

faith in Jesus. Instead, they have placed their hopes in the law and their own privileges.

Paul reiterates his deep concerns for his fellow Israelites (Rom. 10:1–13). They were zealous for God but in the wrong way, trying to establish their own righteousness rather than receiving the righteousness of Christ (vv. 1–4). They missed the focus of the Old Testament, of Moses particularly, which is now realized in Christ, and that this message is the same for everyone, Gentiles and Jews.

How can this situation be reversed (10:14–17)? If salvation is through faith in Christ, then they need to hear the gospel, and someone must be sent to them to proclaim it. Indeed, in the words of the gospel preacher, Christ himself is heard (10:14). Nevertheless, Paul's compatriots have heard, in the witness of creation (10:18) and especially through covenant revelation via Moses and the prophets (10:19–20). The problem is, and was, that they did not receive it in faith (10:21).

Does this mean that God has cast Israel off, rejecting them due to their ongoing recalcitrance (Rom. 11:1–6)? Emphatically not. Paul himself is a Jew. As in Elijah's day, there is still a faithful remnant. However, this remnant exists by grace; it is not sustained by its own obedience. This is the crux of the problem. The situation is that the elect have received grace and salvation, but the rest remain hardened in unbelief, just as in the times of David, Elijah, and Isaiah (Rom. 11:7–10).

Therefore, given that God has not rejected Israel, has Israel put itself beyond recovery (Rom. 11:11–24)? Again, Paul dismisses the idea emphatically, for several reasons. First, Israel's unbelief is the occasion of worldwide blessing, in fulfillment of the Abrahamic covenant. Second, as a corollary, Israel will become jealous of the Gentiles, which may provoke them to turn from unbelief (vv. 11–14). Third, God's covenant was established first with Israel; so they have a prior claim as the firstfruits (vv. 15–16), as the natural, cultivated olive tree in comparison with a wild olive (vv. 17–22). It would be entirely appropriate for Israel to be received back, since the covenant was originally made with Abraham and his offspring. Moreover, God is able to do this; if he has grafted in the Gentiles, who were outside his original covenantal commitment, it is a lesser thing to grant his mercy to its first recipients (vv. 23–24). Israel has not stumbled irretrievably. There is still hope, a hope with real substance to it.

Thus far throughout these chapters Paul has been discussing his compatriots, the Jews of his day. The nation is in view, not any spiritual counterpart. It is the nation that does not believe, that has a zeal for God but has rejected Christ. Unless there is clear evidence otherwise, it is reasonable to suppose that further reference to Israel be read the same way.

At this point Paul reveals a mystery (Rom. 11:25–26). A mystery is something once hidden that is now revealed, a matter that would not be known otherwise.[45] Of what does this mystery consist? It is that a partial hardening has happened to Israel, which Paul has discussed in the preceding section. This hardening in unbelief is coterminous with the fullness of the Gentiles coming in. While Israel has largely rejected Christ, the Gentiles are receiving him. This dual reality can only be preliminary to the disclosure, since it was clearly evident at the time and did not require special revelation to make it known. The mystery relates to what immediately follows.

There Paul states, "And in this way all Israel will be saved" (v. 26). This statement has, broadly, two main lines of interpretation. One regards Paul to have switched his meaning, now referring not to Israel the nation, as he has done hitherto, but to "the spiritual Israel," the elect from all nations, the church. In turn οὕτως[46] is translated "in this way." Paul is understood to say that the current situation with Israel will continue until the end of the age, and in this way all the spiritual Israel will be saved.

There are three large problems with this. The first relates to the sudden and far-reaching change of meaning of "Israel." This runs against the grain of the discussion of the previous three chapters and the underlying Jew-Gentile dynamic of the letter. The second is that the proposed meaning is hardly a mystery that is now revealed. It was common knowledge to all that the elect will be saved. Third, Paul would have spent three chapters describing Israel's plight, holding out hope for its future, only to end by saying that the current state of affairs for Israel will continue unchanged. The section would end in anticlimax, hardly the basis for the extended outburst of praise, wonder, and acclamation that follows.

In contrast, the more reasonable interpretation is that Paul reveals something new, that a time will come when the current state of affairs

---

45. C. E. B. Cranfield, *A Critical and Exegetical Commentary on the Epistle to the Romans*, The International Critical Commentary (Edinburgh: T&T Clark, 1975), 2:573.
46. *houtōs.*

will be reversed, the Jewish people grafted back into the covenant by God's grace through faith in Christ, the gospel being first for the Jew. Hence, the expressions of virtual ecstasy that follow (Rom. 11:33–36). From this Paul concludes that a transformation will occur akin to "life from the dead" (11:12–15). While this could refer to the resurrection, the fact that elsewhere no signs immediately precede the parousia suggest that he contemplates a quantum galvanization of the church. His comments in 11:28–32 would reinforce this impression, holding out the prospect of a worldwide eruption of church growth following a large-scale conversion of the Jewish people. If this is so, it suggests that prayer for the effective reception of the gospel by the Jewish people worldwide is something close to the heart of God and should be made a priority.

Further Reading

Commentaries on Matthew 24 and Romans 9–11.

Cooper, John W. *Body, Soul, and Life Everlasting*. Grand Rapids, MI: Eerdmans, 2000.

Thiselton, Anthony C. *The Last Things: A New Approach*. London: SPCK, 2012.

Warfield, Benjamin B. "Are They Few That Be Saved?" and "The Prophecies of St. Paul." In *Biblical and Theological Studies*, edited by Samuel G. Craig, 334–50, 463–502. Philadelphia: Presbyterian and Reformed, 1952.

Study Questions

1. Read passages like Ephesians 1–2 carefully and note how constantly Paul points to the future purpose of God.

2. How would you argue for continued conscious existence after death as a biblical theme?

3. Consider the place of Israel in God's purposes on the basis of clear didactic passages in the New Testament.

4. What are the prospects for the gospel in future years before Christ's return?

29

The Parousia and the Resurrection

This chapter analyzes various millennial theories. There follows extensive
exegesis of key passages such as Revelation 20, taking various contextual
and literary features into consideration. The New Testament teaching on
the parousia is outlined, together with discussion of its connections with
the resurrection and the judgment. The chapter ends with exegesis of Paul's
teaching on the resurrection in 1 Corinthians 15.

✠

29.1 Principal Millennial Theories

I will keep to concise summaries of the main millennial perspectives,
since the ground has been covered many times, and evaluations of each
are plentiful.

29.1.1 Premillennialism

The historic premillennial position, allowing for variations by its disparate exponents, is distinguished by the following features. The parousia
will be preceded by the evangelization of the world, the conversion of
Israel, and a period of intense persecution known as the great tribulation. At this time, a figure known as the man of sin or the Antichrist
will be revealed. At the parousia the dead saints will be resurrected and,
together with the living saints, transformed; the Antichrist overthrown;
and the nation of Israel restored to its former territory. There will follow

a reign of Christ on earth for a period of one thousand years. This will be a time of worldwide blessing in which large numbers of the Gentiles will believe. However, at the end of this thousand-year millennium, the wicked will be resurrected and the final judgment will take place.

Notable advocates of premillennialism have included Joseph Meade, J. A. Bengel, Frederic Godet, Henry Alford, C. J. Ellicott, Theodore Zahn, and R. C. Trench. In the early church there was a strand of premillennialism—*chiliasm*, as it was termed, after the Greek *chilia*, "a thousand." The *Epistle of Barnabas* held that the earth would last for seven thousand years, based on the creation week and the statement in 2 Peter 3 that with the Lord a thousand years is as one day. Four thousand years preceded the coming of Christ; the church age was to last for two thousand years; this would be followed by the thousand years foretold in Revelation 20.[1]

This idea rests on a literalist hermeneutic, from which Revelation 20:1–6 is understood to refer to a literal one-thousand-year reign of Christ. (In my exegesis, I will consider other interpretations of this passage.) There are significant theological problems with this position. It posits the glorified Christ and the glorified saints coexisting with masses of humanity governed and directed by a fallen and corrupt nature. This is evident by the interpretative methodology requiring the chapter to teach a full-scale rebellion toward the end of the millennium (vv. 7–10). Again, while not so vivid as in dispensationalism, there is a dualism between the church and Israel that runs counter to the New Testament teaching, exemplified by Romans 9–11. While a premillennial view was generally claimed to be the consensus position of the early church, the evidence does not support such an argument.[2]

29.1.2 Dispensational Premillennialism

A more complex form of premillennialism emerged in the nineteenth century through the Irish Anglican turned leader of the early Plymouth Brethren, J. N. Darby. His ingenious claims were popularized by the American evangelist D. L. Moody and later by the Scofield Reference Bible. Institutions such as Moody Bible Institute and Dallas Theological

---

1. *Epistle of Barnabas* 15 (ANF, 1:146).
2. Charles E. Hill, Regnum Caelorum: *Patterns of Millennial Thought in Early Christianity*, 2nd ed. (Grand Rapids, MI: Eerdmans, 2001).

Seminary ensured that it became the standard among American fundamentalists and evangelical Baptists. It also spread beyond North America.

Allowing for variations, dispensationalism contended that the history
of the world is divisible into seven or eight epochs or dispensations, God
dealing differently with humanity in each. These cover the dispensation
of innocency (from the creation of man until the fall), conscience (from
the fall until the flood), human government (from the Noachic covenant
until Abraham), promise (from the Abrahamic covenant until the giving
of the law at Sinai), law (from Moses until Christ), grace (from the resurrection of Christ until the great apostasy and the rapture of the church),
and the kingdom (the millennial reign of Christ on earth). There follow
the new heavens and the new earth.[3]

Each of these dispensations ends in failure. Adam sinned; the world
of Noah's day was destroyed; Abraham's descendants became slaves in
a foreign land; Israel disobeyed the law and refused the Messiah; the
church was seen by Darby to be "in ruins"; Israel is to be persecuted
almost to death in the tribulation; and the millennium will end with a
rebellion. God's purposes in each case fail; he tries new plans and methods each time but without success.

One of the premises underlying the schematism is a radical division
between Israel and the church. Not only are they distinct, but God's
methods with them are diametrically opposed. Indeed, the church is an
afterthought, an interlude contingent on Israel's refusal to accept Jesus
as its King. Because of this, God turns to the Gentiles to offer a spiritual
salvation based on grace apart from law. When the church is in ruins
and is raptured from the earth, God again offers the kingdom to Israel
in the great tribulation. The millennium represents God's rule over Israel
centered in Jerusalem.

This is contrary to the New Testament's insistence that "through
him [Christ] we both [Jew and Gentile] have access in one Spirit to the
Father" (Eph. 2:18). A sharp distinction between Israel and the church
relegates the church of Christ, which he bought with his own blood, to
a secondary place with God's purposes centered on the land and people
of Israel. It departs from the ancient ecumenical creeds confessed by the
church in all ages, which declare, "We believe in one holy, catholic and
apostolic Church," and from the teaching of Paul that for Israel to re-

---

3. *Scofield Reference Bible* (n.p., n.d. [ca. 1917]), first pages with publication details missing.

ceive the blessings of God's grace, it must believe in Christ and join with the Gentiles in the church, for there is no other hope.

So intricate is the dispensational proposal, so entrenched is the Israel-church dualism, that there are pluralities of the same realities. Christ returns twice: in a secret rapture for his saints before the tribulation, and with his saints to end the tribulation. There are multiple resurrections: dead saints are raised in the secret rapture, the wicked are raised for judgment when Christ returns with his saints, and—presumably—those who die in the millennium are also to be raised at the end. There is also a series of judgments: the judgment seat of Christ before which the saints are to be judged, the judgment of angels, the judgment of the nations when Christ returns the second time, and the final judgment of the great white throne depicted in Revelation.

The same objections prevail as with historic premillennialism. However, in dispensationalism, there are many additional problems. The millennial restoration of the Old Testament theocracy complete with temple, sacrifices, and the reappearance of Israel's old enemies on the world stage are all features absent from the New Testament. Indeed, the letter to the Hebrews condemns as apostasy any reversion to the old order.

This millennial view is associated with constant speculation about whether leading political figures are the Antichrist or man of sin, of whether this or that world situation is the immediate forerunner of the rapture. I encountered an example of this—sad if it were not so amusing—when, in a hotel room in Florida, I briefly switched on the television and saw a world-famous preacher and media tycoon declare that the United States was to be annihilated in a nuclear war. How could he say that? He discovered that there is no reference to the United States in the Bible. If the US were to be in existence in "the end times," he figured, it would surely be mentioned! Consequently, it must have been wiped off the face of the earth beforehand! He concluded that it was to be obliterated, a nuclear war the likeliest cause.

The theory misses the point that the New Testament presents the parousia, the resurrection, and the judgment as one embracive reality and as temporally convergent. Thus, the parousia and the resurrection are indivisibly connected (1 Cor. 15:20–23; 1 Thess. 4:13–18), as are the parousia and the judgment (2 Thess. 1:6ff.). I will develop this point below.

In common with historic premillennialism, dispensationalism encounters the same problems with the supposed coexistence of the glorified Christ and sinful humanity in the millennium. This fails to account
for the glory that is Christ's and will be his elect peoples' (1 John 3:1–2),
the glory of God that cannot abide iniquity and will inexorably burn up
the forces of corruption.

Fundamentally, dispensationalism is governed by two premises, both
of which are faulty. The first is a pessimism about the purposes of God
in this world. However, our sovereign God never fails, and he does not
intend that his church should fail, for the Holy Spirit animates it, and
the risen Christ is with it all the days until the consummation of the age.
The gates of hell cannot prevail against it (Matt. 16:17–18). The second
premise is a dependence on a literal hermeneutic deployed on a handful of the more obscure biblical passages, which include Revelation 20,
2 Thessalonians 2, and Daniel 9. This method flouts a basic principle
of biblical interpretation, which is to understand the more difficult passages in the light of clearer ones (WCF, 1.9). We are first to consider the
clearer, didactic passages and only then to turn to the more difficult ones,
at the same time taking into consideration the context and the literary
genre of each.

29.1.3 Preterism

From the extreme far side of the spectrum, in recent years there has been
a cult revival of sorts in some circles in the US of the claim that the parousia, the resurrection, and the judgment have happened already (Latin,
praeter, "already") in the events of AD 70. The idea was connected with
the Congregational minister J. Stuart Russell and with Milton Terry.[4]
Their claim was that all prophetic elements in the New Testament were
realized at that time. Though certain echoes of this teaching appear in
the legitimate realized eschatology that has sometimes been advocated
in scholarly works, this is realized eschatology with a vengeance. The
destruction of the temple and the downfall of Jerusalem were momentous events, signaling publicly the end of the Mosaic covenant, and the
implementation of its covenantal sanctions. I have argued that these

---

4. Milton S. Terry, *Biblical Hermeneutics: A Treatise on the Interpretation of the Old and New
Testaments* (repr., Grand Rapids, MI: Zondervan, n.d.); J. Stuart Russell, *The Parousia: The New
Testament Doctrine of Our Lord's Second Coming* (Grand Rapids, MI: Baker, 1999).

events are by no means overlooked in the New Testament. However, preterism as an eschatological position raises acute questions. It has no official position, as its exponents vary in their expositions, but there are definite features in common.

The New Testament gives not the slightest hint that the final events were to occur shortly. There is plenty of evidence against the common notion that the apostles expected Christ to return within their lifetimes. Peter knew he was to be martyred (John 21:15–19; 2 Pet. 1:12–15). Paul, writing at the end of his life (around AD 65), instructed Timothy on safeguarding the future ministry of the church, saying, "The things you have heard from me among many witnesses commit to faithful people who will be able to teach others also" (2 Tim. 2:2, my trans.). He envisaged here what John Stott called an apostolic succession of doctrine passing down from one generation to another.[5] Paul conveyed no inkling of any thought that within four or five years of writing, all living believers would be raptured; that would have left unanswered questions about who would be present to carry on the preaching of the gospel. Moreover, there is no historical evidence to support the argument. If the church had suddenly been cut off by rapture, to resume by whatever means at a later date, it would obviously be known to its contemporaries; these things don't happen every day. Preterism also ignores the uniform testimony of the church's creeds and confessions that the parousia is an event in the future that we await with eager expectation.

Besides these historical and biblical deficits, preterism raises more acute theological problems. If the resurrection has already taken place, what happens to the bodies of believers who have lived after AD 70? If they pass immediately into glory and are given a resurrection body, their earthly bodies will continue to lie in the grave, a collection of decaying bones. This is the replacement of the body, not its resurrection. Since our present bodies are what we are, it cannot be we who are then present in the eschatological kingdom; or if it is, we are effectively defined in our present state by our souls alone, which is a form of ontological dualism that borders on docetism.

From this, questions arise about creation. If the final kingdom is already present, out of our sight and beyond our present ken, the current

5. John R. W. Stott, *Guard the Gospel: The Message of 2 Timothy* (Downers Grove IL: InterVarsity Press. 1973), 51–52.

order of creation has no purpose. It will continue as it is, and, whatever its future, the heavenly kingdom will be something quite different. This is contrary to the consistent witness of the Bible, which affirms the goodness of creation and the gracious purpose of God toward it. In both these matters, the body and creation, we are faced by more than a deviant eschatology; it is heresy.

29.1.4   *Postmillennialism and Amillennialism*

In contrast to premillennialism is postmillennialism, which argues that Christ will return after the millennium. Here we enter rather slippery territory. Historically, postmillennial advocates have expected that there will be a period during which the gospel will take root to the extent that the world would be effectively Christianized. When Christ returns, it will be to a world ready and waiting to receive him.

However, postmillennialism has taken other forms. Many believe that the reference to one thousand years in Revelation 20 signifies the entire period between the ascension of Christ and his parousia, seen from the angle of the saints living and reigning with Christ. From this, Christ's return will be after (*post*) this figurative thousand years. In this they are at one with most amillennialists. In fact, amillennialism was commonly termed *postmillennialism*, since it held that the parousia comes after the time Christ reigns as depicted in Revelation.

I find it hard to distinguish the two in a way that does justice to the concerns of both. There are three basic positions. First, there is the idea that a privileged period exists within the time between the ascension and the parousia, in which the world will largely be Christianized. Christ will return some time after or toward the end of this golden age. The expectation is for the gospel to triumph more or less universally in the future before the parousia. Second, at the other end of the scale are the convinced amillennialists who—perhaps influenced by the pessimism of premillennialism—teach that evil will grow worse and worse, the church will have a hard time, and eventually there will be a large-scale persecution, after which Christ will return. Here there is no period before or after the parousia corresponding to any visible millennium on earth. Third, between these poles are those who believe that the reference to the thousand years in Revelation 20 is to the whole period between the ascension and the parousia, during which the bulk of the world will become Christian.

Christ will return after the metaphorical thousand years. However, within the ongoing history of the world, between ascension and parousia, there is no specially privileged time distinct from any other time, no golden age as such, but the whole period is one in which the church preaches and witnesses, the world persecutes but Christ reigns. Some might call this "postmillennialism"; others, "optimistic amillennialism." There is a continuum, clearly distinguished from all premillennialism.

The reason for the distance from premillennialism is that each of these other perspectives rejects the idea of a literal period of one thousand years after the parousia in which Christ will set up an earthly reign. Further, there is no significant space between the parousia, the resurrection, and the judgment, for, in the words of the Apostles' Creed, "he will come to judge the living and the dead." In what follows, while trying to do justice to the other claims, I will argue for the third of these aspects in the amillennial–postmillennial continuum, since I consider this to reflect most accurately the combined perspectives of the New Testament writers.

29.2   Revelation 20

Since Revelation 20 is the cornerstone of premillennial interpretations, I will address it now before moving on to consider the parousia itself.

Premillennialists argue that there are two resurrections. The first resurrection consists of the martyrs, who live and reign with Christ for one thousand years (v. 4), while the rest of the dead do not come to life until the thousand years are completed (v. 5). Those who participate in the first resurrection are blessed by God, and the second death has no power over them (v. 6). Later, the sum total of the dead are judged (vv. 11–15). From this it is unclear whether the entire church reigns with Christ in the millennium or only the martyrs do. Moreover, it is "the souls" of those who were beheaded that live and reign. While they participate in a resurrection, it is unclear whether that takes a physical form. Those who interpret the passage in terms of metaphor and imagery tend to consider this a spiritual reign.

29.2.1   Main Interpretative Questions

To whom was Revelation addressed? The seven churches in Asia Minor (Rev. 1:4).

When was it written? There are two major possibilities. The first proposal is that it was composed before AD 70, relating immediately to the imminent end of the Jewish state, the destruction of the temple, and the end of the old covenant. If so, we might ask, why was it addressed to the seven churches of Asia Minor, and why was their situation highlighted in the letters in chapters 2 and 3? Further, most historical clues suggest a later date.

The other possibility, the clear majority view, is that it originated after AD 70 and around the time of the onset of persecution under the Emperor Domitian (81–96). In favor are the focus on Rome (chap. 17), the combination of political and religious forces arrayed against the church (chap. 13), and the known cult of emperor worship that was being imposed on the trade guilds, requiring believers to face a stark choice between submitting to the requirement of emperor worship and faithfulness to Christ. Moreover, a regular feature of New Testament books is that they are addressed to their recipients. The book of Revelation would make no sense if the context in Asia Minor were ignored.

What situation did the addressees face? I have already referred to the context above.

What is the literary genre? A combination of elements are present. There are letters directed to churches (chaps. 2–3). There is a series of visions. Much of the language is symbolic.[6] The book is saturated in Old Testament imagery and allusions. Almost every sentence, virtually every clause, is set against the background of the Old Testament. For this reason, much of the book consists of figurative language and is not to be taken in a literal way. Instead, it is to be understood primarily as fulfillment of the Old Testament. There are elements of predictive prophecy.

29.2.2   Differing Interpretations

Futurist. The main focus, according to this line of thought, is on the events surrounding the parousia and the judgment. In dispensationalist interpretation, the nation of Israel is also in view. Clearly, the parousia and judgment are prominent. However, clearly there are immediate communications to first-century churches. It is far from obvious how

---

6. G. K. Beale, *The Book of Revelation: A Commentary on the Greek Text* (Grand Rapids, MI: Eerdmans, 1999), 50–69.

the main focus of a book addressed to churches in the first century can primarily refer to events in the far-distant future.

Idealist. According to this paradigm, Revelation displays broad principles operative across church history. The supremacy of Christ, the inevitability of persecution, the ultimate deliverance of the church, and the call to faithful discipleship are the most prominent themes. However, if the immediate context of the seven churches and the reality of the parousia and future judgment were relegated in favor of overall principles, the basic message of the book would be lost, and the door opened to speculation.

Historicist. This interpretation claims that the book unfolds the future history of the church from the resurrection of Christ to the parousia. The seven letters to the churches represent addresses to various stages in the church's history. This view was promoted by the Scofield Reference Bible and fits nicely with the programmatic framework of history adopted by dispensationalism. However, a number of insuperable problems surround this claim. It is purely speculative; there is no outside evidence that the book was intended to be read this way. In this reading, the church of Laodicea represents the final stage of the church before the return of Christ; it is seen as lukewarm and impotent. Many down through the ages have seen the church of their time in this way. This model entails sweeping categorizations of lengthy periods of the church, each highly contestable. Moreover, the scheme is based on two problematic premises. The first is that the present time, from the late nineteenth century on, is the final period of the church, the parousia being immediately imminent. The second and more damning, is that the scheme is based on church history in Western Europe and North America. The growth of the church in other parts of the world is ignored, as if it did not exist; yet it constitutes the vast majority of the church today.

Preterist. The preterist interpretation—to be distinguished from preterism as an eschatological position—assumes that the book, written to the seven churches in Asia Minor toward the end of the first century, is devoted largely to matters of direct import to those churches. This makes sense when the foci of the other New Testament books are taken into consideration. The interpretation does not rule out that a focus on the seven churches also embraces principles operative throughout church history, nor does it ignore the obvious point that, particularly in the latter part of the book, the parousia and judgment are brought into view. To my mind, with these caveats, this approach makes the most sense.

29.2.3 Matters to Be Decided

The binding of Satan. Elsewhere, John records Jesus as attesting that his death and resurrection were the occasion for the overthrow of "the ruler of this world" (John 12:31–33). Paul reaffirms this, writing that at the cross Christ despoiled the principalities and powers (Col. 2:14–15). Peter writes that, in his resurrection, Christ proclaimed judgment on the fallen angels—"the spirits in prison"—that formerly disobeyed in the days of Noah (1 Pet. 3:19). The author of Hebrews considers the death of Christ to have released his people from bondage to the devil (Heb. 2:14). All these passages relate to the overthrow of Satan in the death and resurrection of Christ. Can any alternative compete with this? Indeed, earlier in Revelation there is the declaration from the Spirit that those who die in the Lord *from now on* are blessed, for they rest from their hard, chafing labors (Rev. 14:13), the turning point clearly being the resurrection of Christ, when he burst from his prison and released the captives.

The point of the imprisonment of the devil in Revelation 20 is that he might no longer deceive the nations. This coincides with the time when the kingdom of God is opened to the nations, in contrast to the preceding period when God permitted them to continue in their ignorance. Now the gospel is preached throughout the world, and the nations are to be made disciples. Satan is confined on a leash and cannot hinder this great work, for the risen, ascended, and glorified Christ is with his church to the end of the age for this purpose (Matt. 28:18–20). This would have been a message of great encouragement to the struggling churches of Asia Minor as they faced the imminent persecuting might of the Roman Empire.

The first resurrection. Central to Revelation 20:1–6, the section on the "thousand years" (v. 6), is the identity of "the first resurrection" (v. 5).[7] How does John understand the resurrection, and what most

---

7. On this, see Philip Edgcumbe Hughes, *The Book of Revelation: A Commentary* (Leicester: Inter-Varsity Press, 1990), 212–16.

probably expresses his understanding? The likeliest candidate must be the resurrection of Jesus Christ; could any other resurrection warrant precedence? It is not only first in time but also first in significance as the basis for the general resurrection and eternal life. It is the climactic event of the cosmos!

This suggestion is reinforced by the crucial role the resurrection of Christ has already played in the book of Revelation. Jesus is called "the firstborn of the dead" (Rev. 1:5). He appears to John, declaring, "I am the first and the last, and the living one. I died, and behold I am alive forevermore" (Rev. 1:17–18). He dictates letters to the seven churches (Rev. 2:1–3:20). To the church at Smyrna he repeats the statement he made to John (Rev. 2:8), with the promise that the one who overcomes will not be harmed by the second death (Rev. 2:11), a theme present in chapter 20. The Lamb is seen standing "as though it had been slain," opening the seals that govern world history (Rev. 5:6). This connects with Paul's reference to Christ's resurrection as "the firstfruits" (1 Cor. 15:20–23).

The burden of evidence suggests that John considers the first resurrection to be the resurrection of Christ. From this it follows that the section from verse 4 to verse 6 of Revelation 20 refers to the martyred saints sharing in the reign of Christ, who has conquered death. Underlying this is the reality of union with Christ. United with him in a martyr's death, they share in his resurrection. While suffering in this world, they are nevertheless reigning with him.

The second death. This clearly refers to hell and everlasting judgment.[8]

Thousand years. If this reading is correct, it means that the thousand years mentioned in Revelation 20 is a reference to the time between the resurrection of Christ and his parousia. Numerology is prominent in Revelation, and one thousand is generally held to refer to completion.[9] It points to the completeness of the reign of Christ. The martyrs are prominent, for death could not conquer them. While the church struggles

---

8. Beale, *Revelation*, 1005–8.
9. Thus the 144,000 in Rev. 7:4–8 represent the twelve tribes of Israel multiplied by the twelve apostles of the Lamb multiplied by one thousand, signifying the completed church from both the Old Testament and the New. In what follows in verses 9–17 we see a multitude that no one can number from every nation under heaven, presenting the church from another visual and conceptual angle.

in this world, the reality behind the scenes is that it shares with Christ in his reign over the nations. Those who share in the resurrection of Christ, the churches of Asia Minor and the whole church universal, live and reign with him for a perfect and complete period. In the words of the hymn by Thomas Kelly,

> They suffer with their Lord below,
> they reign with him above.[10]

The second death cannot touch them (v. 6). It is a priestly kingdom, fulfilling the purpose of God in relation to Israel in the Old Testament.

What the passage may say about the thousand-year reign of Christ. The passage teaches that Christ reigns now, with his church. Whereas the world around us is in rebellion against God, the reality is that all things promote the ultimate glory of God and the good of Christ's church. The passage does not refer to a future thousand-year reign of Christ on earth, still less one based in Jerusalem and Israel. No important doctrine is ever based on a single passage of Scripture isolated from the wider context of the rule of faith. If we begin with the clearer passages of the New Testament, we end up with a far different conclusion than if we focus on the more obscure ones. And we are disabused of crippling notions of pessimism. We may well be persecuted, sometimes to death (Rev. 12:11), but the ultimate and most basic datum is that we are united to Christ, who is at the right hand of the Father as the Lamb who governs the history of the world, and so we reign with him.

29.3   Biblical Teaching on the Parousia

29.3.1   *New Testament Words for the Parousia*

The most common word for the return of Christ is παρουσία,[11] the state of being present. The word was used for the coming of an emperor. In the New Testament, it refers to the public and victorious coming of Christ. In 1 Thessalonians 4:13–18, Paul sees this as important for the confidence of the church in view of concerns over the state of those who have died. Paul is aware that a declining belief in the parousia will weaken the church. Earlier in the same letter, he anticipates the time when the Thes-

---

10. From the hymn "The Head That Once Was Crowned with Thorns" (1820).
11. *parousia.*

salonian church will be his glory and joy, at Christ's parousia, implying that this will occur at the judgment (1 Thess. 2:19–20). This is the goal toward which we are heading and for which the God of peace will keep us (1 Thess. 5:23). Writing to the Corinthians, Paul states that the resurrection of believers will occur at Christ's parousia (1 Cor. 15:23). Matthew records Jesus as saying that no one knows when this will happen and so it will take everyone by surprise (Matt. 24:37, 39). This calls for patience, James says (James 5:7), while John urges his readers to remain in Christ so as to avoid being ashamed at his parousia (1 John 2:28).

Ἐπιφάνεια,[12] or "appearing," denotes a public appearance, a visible reality, not a secret (1 Tim. 6:14). In 2 Timothy 1:10, Paul uses the term for the first coming of Christ, the appearing of our Savior, Jesus Christ, who revealed God's grace given us in eternity. It was a making known of what was previously hidden. In the future ἐπιφάνεια, when the Lord Jesus appears again, he will destroy the lawless one by the breath of his mouth (2 Thess. 2:8); this will be a public spectacle connected with Jesus's kingdom and with his judgment of the living and the dead (2 Tim. 4:1). When he appears, we shall see him as he is, in his undiluted glory (1 John 3:2).

The third major term, ἀποκάλυψις,[13] means "revelation" or "full disclosure," again a self-evidently public event, open to human perception (2 Cor. 12:7; Gal. 1:12; 2:2). Here there is greater focus on judgment (2 Thess. 1:7).

Each term indicates that there is no secret about the parousia. It will not be done in a corner, out of sight of all but a select group. Like a crater after a bomb explosion, there will be no need for corroboration. That this is a future event is demonstrable by its universally public nature and its description as occurring at "the end of the age" (Matt. 13:39–40; 24:3; 28:20; 1 Cor. 15:24).

Did Paul think this great event would occur in his lifetime? His phrase "we . . . who are left" (1 Thess. 4:15) has led many to suppose he did, at least at this early stage in his ministry. Most modern commentators think so, but the fathers thought not, and Thiselton agrees with the older view.[14] The question at Thessalonica was whether the departed would be at a disadvantage when Christ returned; it did not concern Paul's expectations of timing, if indeed he had any. In this case, he puts all believers

---

12. *epiphaneia.*
13. *apokalypsis.*
14. Anthony C. Thiselton, *The Last Things: A New Approach* (London: SPCK, 2012), 95–98.

on the same footing, himself included. Paul was open to the future, not knowing when he would die or when the parousia would occur. He writes in a concessive manner. His concern was pastoral, not predictive.

In Hebrews, the author refers to the return of Christ in the context of the once-for-all nature of his ministry, death, and ascension (Heb. 9:24–28).[15] Christ, having gone into heaven, has disappeared from view, as did the high priest in entering the Most Holy Place on the Day of Atonement; but like the high priest, he will reappear to consummate the salvation. The public and self-evident nature of this reappearance is prominent; we await him and he will be seen. The reappearance is as certain as death, and it is a prelude to the judgment. As Thiselton remarks, the focus in Hebrews is on the heavenly fulfillment in the future.[16]

We can summarize these findings by saying that the parousia will be universally evident—"every eye will see him" (Rev. 1:7)—as well as sudden and unexpected, with no immediately preceding signs. It will catch many unawares and so calls for constant vigilance on the part of the faithful (Matt. 24:36ff.; 1 Thess. 5:1ff.; 2 Pet. 3:10ff.). It will be a self-evident demonstration of the glory of Christ and his conquest of the devil. This is nowhere clearer than in 1 Thessalonians 4:13–18. Here, as in Revelation 1:7, Christ will come "with the clouds." We noted earlier that the clouds are frequently associated in Scripture with the glory of God—at Mount Sinai, at the transfiguration, and at the ascension. As such, when Christ returns, it will be an unveiling, a full disclosure of the glory he has with the Father from eternity and into which he entered as our incarnate Mediator, his assumed humanity suffused and permeated with the glory of God. On those occasions when Paul and John were encountered by the glorified Christ, even accommodated to their limited capacities, the life was virtually knocked out of them. However, when he returns, we shall be like him. How then can the unregenerate stand with this open and overwhelming manifestation of the glory of Christ? It will be impossible for them to survive or coexist in an earthly kingdom in that environment.

Moreover, at that time it will be a public exhibition of the overthrow of Satan and his hostile minions. The air was considered the domain of evil spirits; hence the description of the devil as "the prince of the power of the air" (Eph. 2:2). It is in this context that the parousia will occur.

15. Thiselton, *Last Things*, 104.
16. Thiselton, *Last Things*, 105.

When Paul says we will be caught up in the clouds to meet Christ in the air, he is not reporting on changes in the laws of physics but stating that we will share his glory in a public demonstration of the overthrow of the forces of evil. It will be universally self-evident that Christ has triumphed over the powers of darkness, which for a time have operated on a leash, unwittingly fulfilling God's eternal purposes, but now demonstrably and definitively overthrown. This triumphant, self-attesting revelation of the cosmic supremacy of Christ is the central and inescapable message.

No wonder Thiselton can say, "In spite of those who underestimate the central importance of the Return of Christ in the New Testament, the concept remains central from the earliest New Testament writings to the latest,"[17] while Venema can remark that it is "the great centrepiece of biblical hope and expectation for the future."[18] It underlines the point that in the light of present world conditions and the dire descent of Western culture, "things are not what they seem: the Beast seems to be victorious, but in fact God is sovereign."[19]

29.3.2 The Connections of the Parousia

In the New Testament, the parousia is connected to the resurrection and the final judgment. These three events are one synchronous, complex, coherent reality, not separated by any significant time or space.

The New Testament connects the parousia and the resurrection of the dead. In 1 Corinthians 15:20–58, referring to the resurrection of believers, Paul states explicitly that this will occur "at his [Christ's] coming" (1 Cor. 15:23). Again, in 1 Thessalonians 4:13–18, in relation to those alive at Christ's coming, the dead in Christ are not at a disadvantage, for they are still in Christ and will rise first. Those who are alive will not need to be resurrected, but, together with the dead in Christ, they will be transformed. This will occur at the self-same time as the parousia. Again, in Philippians 3:20–21 the appearing of Christ from heaven will be the occasion when we are transformed bodily. Our present lowly body will undergo a change (μετασχηματίσει)[20] so as to be conformed to the body of the glorified Christ. Furthermore, in 1 John 2:28–3:2 the appearing or

---

17. Thiselton, *Last Things*, 89.
18. Cornelis P. Venema, *The Promise of the Future* (Edinburgh: Banner of Truth, 2000), 79.
19. Thiselton, *Last Things*, 108.
20. *metaschēmatisei*.

parousia of Christ is the time when we will become like him in his glory: "When he appears we shall be like him, because we shall see him as he is."

The parousia is the occasion for the final judgment. Jesus refers to his coming as the Son of Man in his kingdom as the occasion for the judgment of the nations, the one set of people entering eternal life and the other destined for eternal punishment (Matt. 25:31–46). Paul makes this explicit in 2 Thessalonians 1:5–10. God's judgment is inflicted on the ungodly who have persecuted the church. It is a "righteous judgment" (v. 5), repaying the wicked equitably for what they have done (v. 6). They have not obeyed the gospel and so will not receive its blessings but rather be eternally and catastrophically excluded (vv. 8–9).[21] At the same time, the faithful will be given "relief" (v. 7), which is reminiscent of God's eternal rest on the seventh day (Gen. 2:1–3), which Jesus offers to all who are weary and come to him (Matt. 11:28–30). This rest entails glorification (2 Thess. 1:10). The judgment includes blessing and cursing, in harmony with all the covenantal administrations of redemptive history. This single, two-sided, and ultimate judgment occurs "when the Lord Jesus is revealed from heaven with his mighty angels" (v. 7), "when he comes on that day to be glorified in his saints" (v. 10).

Peter also associates the coming of Christ with a cosmic judgment ushering in a new heaven and a new earth in which righteousness is inherent (2 Pet. 3:1–13). This connection is echoed in the Apostles' Creed: "From there he [Christ] will come to judge the living and the dead." This is a terrible prospect for those who do not believe in him. When the church cries, "Come, Lord Jesus!" (Rev. 22:20; cf. 1 Cor. 16:22; 2 Pet. 3:11–13), it is praying for judgment (Rev. 6:9–11).

The resurrection and the judgment are also integrally connected. This is evident even in the Old Testament, where Daniel foresees a general resurrection, some to everlasting life, others to everlasting contempt (Dan. 12:1–2). This is reiterated by Jesus (Matt. 25:31–46; John 5:29) and affirmed in Revelation (Rev. 20:11–15).

Hence, the parousia is immediately related to the resurrection and also to the final judgment. There is no significant interval between these events; the New Testament writers see them as happening together. The

---

21. We will explore what this may mean in the next chapter.

idea of a period of one thousand years during which Christ will reign over an earthly kingdom, thereby separating the parousia and the resurrection from the final judgment, has no basis in Scripture.

This complex of events demonstrates the weakness of human efforts to bring in some form of utopia; that was debarred from the moment of the fall, when God prohibited Adam and Eve from returning to the garden, guarding the way back with cherubim and a flaming sword (Gen. 3:24). The future is a work of God in his utter sovereignty. All future events are in his charge and care (Rom. 8:37–39).

The main focus in the New Testament is the demand for vigilance, obedience, and a life of service for Christ. Speculation is firmly discouraged (Matt. 24:36–37; Acts 1:7). Throughout we are urged to live for Christ now, since the future is in God's hands and outside our purview. That the parousia is to happen at a time God has fixed, to which we are not privy, calls for us to be about his business at all times.

Our ignorance and need for preparedness are stressed in the Belgic Confession, 37 and the WCF, 33.3. It is a prominent motif in the Gospels (Matt. 25:13; Mark 13:32; Luke 12:39–40), and in Paul (1 Thess. 5:1–2). Peter makes it an emphatic requirement, especially in the face of unbelieving mockery (2 Pet. 3:1–13). Jesus announces that the exact timing of his parousia was hidden from him in his incarnate state (Matt. 24:36); this places an even greater onus on us to be ready (Matt. 24:37–51; 25:1–13). It is not for us to know, and no signs that precede it give us a hint as to when it is going to happen; it will catch the entire world unawares (Acts 1:7). Paul's oral teaching to the newly planted Thessalonian church—in which he disclosed aspects of preceding events, however near or remote to the parousia they might be—is something to which we are not privy and about which we cannot make any authoritative pronouncement (2 Thess. 2:5). The key throughout is to live for Christ and so be prepared (Matt. 24:36ff.; 2 Pet. 3:10–13).

Underlining this point is that *the apostles were clearly aware that a series of events were to occur beforehand*, each of which was a stimulus to work and to long-term planning. The gospel was to be taken to Jerusalem and Judea, then to Samaria, the Gentiles, and the ends of the earth (Acts 1:8). There was a long-term agenda of missionary outreach stretching ahead into the far-distant future. Jesus informed Peter of the nature of the apostle's death (John 21:15–19); evidently the parousia would not happen at least until Peter had died. Later, Paul envisaged a succession of preachers who would pass on the gospel to the succeeding generations (2 Tim. 2:2). He wrote of the eventual large-scale conversion of the Jewish people. There was also the thorny question of "the rebellion" and the revelation of the man of sin (2 Thess. 2:1–12); even if this happened in the first century, it still demonstrated that events lay ahead that were to occur first. The great parting statement of the risen Christ pointed to the nations of the world becoming disciples and obeying all his commands (Matt. 28:19–20). Indeed, with the Lord one day is as a thousand years; already while Peter was still alive, skeptics were remarking on the apparent delay of the parousia (2 Pet. 1:1–13).

Yet, precisely because a lengthy vista of work by the church was in view, stretching into the indefinite future, from another perspective the New Testament writers present the parousia as an imminent existential reality. "Lord, come" was one of the earliest Christian confessions (1 Cor. 16:22); "Come, Lord Jesus!" is the last call of the church (Rev. 22:20).[22] In historical reality, in the unfolding of time, it is in the unknown future; in terms of personal awareness and present urgency, it is on our immediate horizon.

29.4   The Resurrection of the Dead (1 Corinthians 15)

Christ's resurrection and ours are one reality (1 Cor. 15:12–19). Paul argues that the church is united to Christ and so participates in his resurrection. The apostle argues from one to the other and back again. Deny Christ's resurrection, and there can be no general resurrection. Deny the general resurrection, and Christ could never have been raised. The two are inseparable. This results from union with Christ. Christ took our humanity into union with himself, lived and died in our flesh, and in our flesh rose from the dead. Since we are united to him, Paul writes that we died with him and are resurrected with him (Rom. 6:1–9). He was raised to life sometime around AD 30; we will be raised in the indefinite future. Here there is analogy with the Einstein-Podolsky-Rosen theory. First postulated by Einstein and his research associates in 1935, and later developed by John Bell in 1964, the theory referred to a case

---

22. See Venema, *Promise*, 96–106, for discussion of the claim that the New Testament writers changed their minds about the imminence of the *parousia* and so were mistaken to believe initially that it would happen in their own lifetime.

where two quantum systems interact in such a way as to link both their spatial co-ordinates in a certain direction and also their linear momenta (in the same direction) even when the systems are widely separated in space. As a result of this "entanglement," determining either position or momentum for one system would fix (respectively) the position or the momentum of the other.[23]

This proposes identical behavior separated by indefinite space. With the resurrection, the one reality—separated by indefinite time—also behaves identically in both aspects.[24]

Christ is the firstfruits of the full harvest (1 Cor. 15:20). The firstfruits precede the full harvest. However, the firstfruits are identical to the rest. The firstfruits of the peach harvest are peaches! So Christ's resurrection has a temporal priority, and it also represents the guarantee of the full harvest at his return, for it is the same kind as the rest.[25]

Christ and Adam, death and resurrection (1 Cor. 15:21–22). The whole race was in solidarity with Adam in his sin. When he sinned, all sinned. The penalty of death that he received applied to all humanity, since they were in union with him. Consequently, the world came under the curse of the Adamic covenant. However, Christ, as the second or last Adam, conquered death in our flesh, bringing life and immortality. He experienced death but vanquished it. In union with him, we are raised to new life and at his return will participate in the resurrection of the body.

The "order" (1 Cor. 15:23). This order means "that which has been arranged."[26] First is Christ's resurrection; then all united to him will be resurrected at his parousia, in the indefinite future.

---

23. Arthur Fine, "The Einstein-Podolsky-Rosen Argument in Quantum Theory," *The Stanford Encyclopedia of Philosophy*, ed. Edward N. Zalta (Winter 2017), https://plato.stanford.edu/archives/win2017/entries/qt-epr/>.

24. See Sang Hoon Lee, "Toward an Understanding of the Eschatological Presence of the Risen Jesus with Robert Jenson," *SJT* 71 (2018): 85–101, for interaction with retrocausality in physics and preincarnate appearances of the risen Jesus, in passing commenting on the EPR theory.

25. Anthony C. Thiselton, *The First Epistle to the Corinthians: A Commentary on the Greek Text* (Grand Rapids, MI: Eerdmans, 2000), 1223–24; Joseph A. Fitzmyer, SJ, *First Corinthians: A New Translation with Introduction and Commentary*, The Anchor Yale Bible (New Haven, CT: Yale University Press, 2008), 569; Gordon D. Fee, *The First Epistle to the Corinthians* (Grand Rapids, MI: Eerdmans, 1987), 748–49.

26. Thiselton, *First Corinthians*, 1229; Archibald Robertson, *A Critical and Exegetical Commentary on the First Epistle of St Paul to the Corinthians* (Edinburgh: T&T Clark, 1999), 354.

Christ's reign (1 Cor. 15:24–27). When this occurs, two things will have happened. First, Christ will hand over the kingdom to God the Father. This does not imply that he and the Father are two different beings. Nor does it suggest that the Son is less than the Father, subordinate to the Father's rule. It simply marks the completion of his mediatorial task, the work for which the Father sent him. Second, Christ will render all hostile powers inoperative and will subject all his enemies to his rule, fulfilling Psalm 110:1. This is necessary (δεῖ γὰρ αὐτὸν βασιλεύειν), integral to God's eternal purpose. It is not postponed to the distant future or to a limited period. It is already happening but will reach its consummation at Christ's return, when every knee will bow and every tongue confess that Jesus Christ is Lord, to the glory of God the Father.

The last enemy to be destroyed, or rendered inoperative, is death (1 Cor. 15:26). This will be at Christ's return, when the dead are raised. Here the resurrection of the wicked is not in view. Paul puts the verb κα-ταργεῖται in the present indicative; death is already being destroyed, the final blow to be administered when Christ appears in glory. The process of annihilation of death began at Christ's resurrection and is completed at his parousia. The verb is a prophetic present, linking Christ's resurrection and ours.

The nature of the resurrection body (1 Cor. 15:35–49). It was thought in some branches of Jewish apocalyptic literature that in the resurrection the body would be an assemblage of particles of the rotting corpse, configured as before, so as not to differ from the present body.[27] That seems to be the reason for Paul's outburst, "You foolish person!" in verse 36.[28]

The resurrection body is not identical to our present body (15:35–38). Paul uses an agricultural model. He has already offered the analogy of harvests, and he now resumes this theme. The sequence is the process of sowing and reaping. A seed is sown, dies, and comes to life transformed (vv. 36–37). In an analogous way, the resurrection is a transformation to a different level of existence. Yet there is also continuity and identity. The transformation takes place through death, while new life follows. "What you sow is not the body that is to be," for "what you sow does not come to life unless it dies." A seed or kernel ends up as grain. In the case of the resurrection, the present body undergoes death,

---

27. Robertson, *First Corinthians*, 368.
28. Fitzmyer, *First Corinthians*, 587–88.

and life emerges in a different form. The resurrection body is a gift from God. "God gives [δίδωσιν] it a body as he has chosen" (v. 38). Paul later writes of it as "from heaven" (2 Cor. 5:1). God sovereignly determines the nature of the resurrection body. There is order and variety. It is beyond our knowledge, since it is in God's hands. Yet, because of the unity between Christ's resurrection and ours, it follows that ours will be shaped by his. Christ was recognized as a human being, engaged in conversation, ate food, cooked breakfast, and was mistaken for other people, but after the initial shock his disciples realized that it was he. Therefore, while we will experience a transformation, there is to be a recognizable continuity between our present and our resurrection bodies. As Thiselton remarks, "The manifestation of Christ's raised body occurred *within the conditions of this world.* We still cannot have a *comprehensive* view of this 'body,' which is *more than* 'physical' but *not less than* 'physical.'"[29]

There is a wide diversity of bodies (15:39–41). Paul reinforces the difference between the two bodies. A radical transformation will occur. The raised body will not be identical to the one that rots in the grave. The diverse range of creatures is proof. Humans, animals, birds, and fish all differ. The sun, moon, and stars differ from earthly beings; there is a vast variety among themselves.

There will be discontinuity between the Adamic body and the resurrection body (15:42–44). Paul lists four pairs of contrasts: perishable versus imperishable, humiliation versus splendor, weakness versus power, and natural versus spiritual. These highlight the dramatic transformation we will share in Christ's resurrection.

Our present body is perishable. Before the fall, Adam's body was potentially perishable. This potentiality became actual for Adam and us all upon his violation of the covenant of life by his choice of death. So each person's present body decays, its powers decline, it weakens, and it eventually dies. It is weak, limited, and vulnerable. It is a natural (ψυχικόν)[30] body, designed at its best for the mundane and fallen realm.

In contrast, the resurrection body is invulnerable. It achieves the ultimate purpose God has designed for humans. It is not static; it is the dynamic, flourishing fullness of life, "an ever-increasing condition."[31] It

---

29. Thiselton, *Last Things*, 90.
30. *psychikon.*
31. Thiselton, *Last Things*, 121.

is glorious; glory (δόξα)[32] signifies what belongs to God. We will partake of the divine nature. Glorification is the goal of the Christian life and consists of sharing the glory Christ has with the Father (John 17:24; 2 Pet. 1:4). It will be powerful in contrast to our present weakness; all decay, disease, and frustration will have gone. Above all, it will be a spiritual body (σῶμα πνευματικόν) in contrast to a natural one (σῶμα ψυχικόν). It is designed for the eternal state, in which we will have immeasurably greater work. Paul does not mean it will be a spirit in contrast to a material body; that would destroy his entire argument, since the change would not be resurrection but metamorphosis. He means that the resurrection body will be under the sway of the Holy Spirit.[33] When Paul uses πνεῦμα (spirit), he means the Holy Spirit, unless the context demands otherwise. Christ's resurrection body was inseparably directed by the Holy Spirit, so much so that Paul virtually equates Christ and the Spirit (2 Cor. 3:17). It will be a body no less physical, but it will be more than physical, constituted by the Spirit. It will be "able to do all that we seek to do,"[34] enhanced above and beyond its present limitations. It will be a body for the new creation, the realm of the Holy Spirit, which includes the physical. Thiselton refers to the senses of other creatures here and now that far exceed our own as suggestive of the enhanced abilities we will have then.[35]

Adam and the risen Christ (15:45–49). Paul sharpens the contrast in terms of the two heads of the two teams that make up the human race. Adam was made a living being, his body correspondingly provisional, having a life that could potentially be lost in death. In contrast, the risen Christ, the last Adam, is "life-giving spirit." He is the author and giver of life. Adam received life. The risen Christ gives life and is the source of life, for he is life. So the resurrection is not a return to this present life. It is a quantum leap beyond our current imagination, a new creation (2 Cor. 5:17). We have brief previews in the resurrection appearances of Christ and in his revelation to Paul and John from glory.

There is a proper order to this progression. First comes the natural order, from the dust of the ground, weak and vulnerable, subject to

---

32. *doxa.*

33. Herman Ridderbos, *Paul: An Outline of His Theology* (Grand Rapids, MI: Eerdmans, 1975), 540–48; Richard B. Gaffin Jr., *The Centrality of the Resurrection: A Study in Paul's Soteriology* (Grand Rapids, MI: Baker, 1978), 78–92.

34. Thiselton, *Last Things*, 121.

35. Thiselton, *Last Things*, 210–13.

mortality. Then we will be like the last Adam, the second man, the man from heaven, raised by the Holy Spirit to power and dominion. We have borne the image of the earthly Adam. Then we will be like Christ in glory.

Transformation and resurrection (1 Cor. 15:50–58). Resurrection and transformation are the same event, both instantaneous: "in a moment, in the twinkling of an eye" (v. 52). The last trumpet indicates a sudden and dramatic event, for the trumpet sound in the Old Testament was a manifestation of God, public and loud (Ex. 19:16; 1 Chron. 16:6; Ps. 47:5; Joel 2:1; Zech. 9:14). Yet there is clear continuity. "This perishable body" becomes imperishable; "this mortal body" is clothed with immortality. Otherwise, we would not be the ones who are saved. Paul says the same in Romans 8:11, writing of the Father raising "your mortal bodies." Paul is speaking of a recognizable identity in a different form. This is not the type of transformation that changes a caterpillar into a butterfly, for that is an immanent process that constantly occurs in the natural course of events. Moreover, the butterfly is unrecognizable from the caterpillar. In the resurrection the transformation includes recognition. The result is that we will be beyond the possibility of death, even as Christ is (Rom. 6:9). As Augustine put it in his *Sermons for the Feast of Ascension*, "Is he who was able to make you when you did not exist not able to make over what you once were?"[36]

Resurrection is not the mere resuscitation of a corpse, returning to the same state as before. It is far greater in kind. So "we look for the resurrection of the body and the life of the world to come." No wonder the early church prayed standing and facing the east, the direction from which Christ was to return, in eager anticipation.

Further Reading

Beale, G. K. *The Book of Revelation: A Commentary on the Greek Text.* Grand Rapids, MI: Eerdmans, 1999.

Hill, Charles E. Regnum Caelorum: *Patterns of Millennial Thought in Early Christianity.* 2nd ed. Cambridge: Cambridge University Press, 2001.

Thiselton, Anthony C. *The First Epistle to the Corinthians: A Commentary on the Greek Text.* Grand Rapids, MI: Eerdmans, 2000.

36. Cited by Thiselton, *First Corinthians*, 1297n195.

Thiselton, Anthony C. *The Last Things: A New Approach*. London: SPCK, 2012.

Venema, Cornelis. *The Promise of the Future*. Edinburgh: Banner of Truth, 2000.

Study Questions

1. How would you summarize the biblical teaching on the nature of the millennium described in Revelation 20?

2. What signs precede the parousia?

3. What are some elements of continuity and discontinuity in the resurrection of the body?

30

The Judgment and Hell

Judgment will be according to works and therefore just, not arbitrary or capricious. This implies that the verdict will fit the degree of sin and responsibility, since God always does what is right. This chapter examines universalism, pluralism, and inclusivism, with particular reference to developments in the Roman church and evangelicalism. The fate of the unevangelized is a matter for much debate recently. Historically, the church has maintained that the Bible teaches everlasting conscious punishment for those who do not believe in Jesus Christ. There is an extensive discussion of objections arising from exegetical and theological angles. It is claimed that hell is incompatible with the justice of God, the love of God, and the victory of God. Beyond this, it is common to contend that after the judgment the impenitent will be annihilated, largely due to considerations relating to the character of God. What biblical and historical reasons are there in defense of the historic position of the church? At the same time, the way hell has sometimes been portrayed casts question marks over its advocates' view of God. Within the orthodox position there is need for careful and responsible thought.

Heaven, hell, death, and judgement are the traditional Four Last Things of Christian Theology, but . . . twentieth-century theologians have, for the most part, been embarrassed at saying much about any of them. In this they stand in sharp contrast to the majority of nineteenth-century divines.[1]

---

1. Geoffrey Rowell, *Hell and the Victorians* (Oxford: Clarendon, 1974), 1.

30.1   The Final Judgment

John Perry comments: "I know of no Christian moral theory under which the traditional Augustinian view of hell can plausibly be seen as good or just. In the long run, this means that we either need better moral theories or better conceptions of hell."[2] Comments such as this are typical of the consensus of contemporary opinion. This view resonates with many Christians today. Is the final judgment something to hold believers in terror? Many preachers have used it to that end, threatening congregations with the specter of all their sins being paraded before the moral universe, a prospect to cower the most hardy soul. That this is seriously wrong can be deduced from the point we noted in the previous chapter, that when we appear before the judgment seat of Christ, we will already be glorified. We will be resurrected, transformed to be like the glorified Christ (1 John 3:1–2). Indeed, in Christ we will participate in judging the world and the angels (1 Cor. 6:1–3). There is a great need to orient our thinking to the wider biblical and theological context.

30.1.1   General Considerations

We saw that in the New Testament, the final judgment is connected with the parousia and the resurrection, and that there is only one judgment. The justice and holiness of God are crucial for understanding the biblical teaching on judgment. That God always does what is just and right is axiomatic. Whatever his judgment will be is appropriate to the case. This entails that the wrongs and injustices of this life will be put right. Job saw that this would not happen in the present but that God will deal with sin and injustice eschatologically. Further, God's wrath against sin will also be in accord with his justice; it will not be out of proportion, neither capricious nor uncontrolled, but exactly what is in harmony with his righteous and holy nature. After all, his wrath is his settled and holy antagonism to sin, which is rebellion against his wise and gracious purposes and is a choice for death rather than life.[3]

30.1.2   Christ the Judge

The New Testament presents Christ as the Judge, a function belonging only to one who is God. The Father has committed judgment into his

---

2. John Perry, "Putting Hell First: Cruelty, Historicism, and the Missing Moral Theory of Damnation," *SJT* 69 (2016): 3.

3. R. V. G. Tasker, *The Biblical Doctrine of the Wrath of God* (London: Tyndale Press, 1951).

hands (John 5:27–30). He is the Son of Man, who judges the nations (Matt. 25:31–46). We will all appear before his judgment seat (2 Cor. 5:10), for he alone has the right and authority to exercise rule and issue God's judgments in the world (Rev. 5:1–14). This is an aspect of his kingly office.

30.1.3   The Basis for Judgment

Judgment will be on the basis of works. Since God is just, it is clear that judgment will be appropriate to each person's actions (Gen. 18:22–25; 2 Cor. 5:10; Rev. 20:11–13). It will be on the basis of his or her life as a whole; Paul's use of a constative aorist in 2 Corinthians 5:10 plus a neuter object, despite a masculine noun governing it, indicates it is a holistic judgment, relating to the whole of life, rather than individual actions in isolation.[4]

C. F. D. Moule argues for the presence of the theme of judgment in the sacraments. In baptism we are united to Christ in his death and resurrection, which entails, among other things, acceptance of God's verdict of guilty on account of sin, with its result of subjection to death. Moule indicates the connection between the Lord's Supper and the judgment in 1 Corinthians 11:28–32.[5]

Justification itself, being a forensic declaration, has judgment as its theme (Rom. 2:12–13, 16; 3:24; 4:5; 8:1; 1 Cor. 1:8; Gal. 5:5).[6] It is an effective judgment by God that secures its own performance. Using speech-act theory, Thiselton indicates that while an assertion or propositional content makes the words fit the world, promises and requests—illocutions—make the world fit the words.[7] In this sense, justification is a verdictive act—it effects what it pronounces. Thiselton borrows Austin's analogy: when an umpire gives a batsman out in cricket, the batsman is out by virtue of the umpire's official position.[8] Consequently, God looks

---

4. Philip Edgcumbe Hughes, *Paul's Second Epistle to the Corinthians: The English Text, with Introduction, Exposition and Notes* (London: Marshall, Morgan & Scott, 1961), 179–83; Victor Paul Furnish, *II Corinthians*, The Anchor Bible (New York: Doubleday, 1984), 275–77.

5. C. F. D. Moule, "The Judgement Theme in the Sacraments," in *The Background of the New Testament and Its Eschatology: Studies in Honour of C. H. Dodd*, ed. W. D. Davies and D. Daube (Cambridge: Cambridge University Press, 1964), 465–70, cited in Anthony C. Thiselton, *The Last Things: A New Approach* (London: SPCK, 2012), 175.

6. Thiselton, *Last Things*, 176.

7. Thiselton, *Last Things*, 177; John R. Searle, *Expression and Meaning: Studies in the Theory of Speech-Acts* (Cambridge: Cambridge University Press, 1979), 3.

8. Thiselton, *Last Things*, 178; J. L. Austin, *How to Do Things with Words: The William James Lectures Delivered in Harvard University in 1955* (Oxford: Oxford University Press, 1976), 153.

on Christians as sinners within the realm of law but as righteous in terms of Christology and eschatology.[9]

Judgment of unbelievers. Some ask, is it fair for God to judge those who have never heard the gospel? The presence of sin means there can be no excuse (Gen. 3:1ff.; Rom. 1:18–20; 3:9–20; 5:12–21). The wonder is not that sinners are judged but that anyone is delivered.

The consequences of sin. Since sin is rejection of God, who is the living God, death results.

Degrees of knowledge and of sin, of rewards and punishments. In the Gospels, Jesus indicates that some are punished more severely than others (Matt. 11:20–24; Luke 12:35–48). The justice of God suggests that this is so, since judgment is according to works and there are obvious differences of evil; Hitler and Pol Pot have clearly engaged in more extensively sinful actions than the nice neighbor next door. All are sinners and under the wrath of God, but not all have sinned in the same ways or to the same degree. Abraham asks, "Shall not the Judge of all the earth do what is just?" (Gen. 18:23–25). A one-size-fits-all judgment is inherently unjust. Aristotle thought that to treat unequals equally is as unequal as to treat equals unequally.[10]

God's verdict will not be known until the final judgment. Only God can make a definitive judgment about a person (1 Cor. 4:1–5).[11] The parables of reversal indicate that the current situation has an inherent ambiguity, the final verdict coming at the judgment; the parables of the wheat and tares (Matt. 13:24–30) and the drag net (Matt. 13:47–48) illustrate this.[12]

---

9. Anthony C. Thiselton, *The Two Horizons: New Testament Hermeneutics and Philosophical Description with Special Reference to Heidegger, Bultmann, Gadamer, and Wittgenstein* (Grand Rapids, MI: Eerdmans, 1980), 407–27.

10. Aristotle, *Politics* 3.16.2, in *The Politics of Aristotle*, ed. and trans. Ernest Barker (London: Oxford University Press, 1958), 145. Commenting on Aristotle's *Ethics* 5.c.6.4, on pp. 363–64, Barker says that according to Aristotle,

distributive justice which gives unequal awards to unequal degrees of merit, *in exact proportion to the inequality of degrees*, is still connected with equality or fairness, because the proportion of the award to merit is kept unswervingly equal. . . . Men *may* be arithmetically equal, if each has the same merit as others, and accordingly receives the same award as others; but normally men will be proportionately equal, in the sense that, while they are of unequal merit, each still gets an award which is proportionate to his merit, and all are therefore equally treated in virtue of receiving an award proportionate to their merits. (italics original)

11. Thiselton, *Last Things*, 165.

12. Joachim Jeremias, *The Parables of Jesus*, trans. S. H. Hooke (London: SCM, 1954), 153–57.

30.2 Purported Pathways to Salvation

30.2.1 Oblivion

Some say there is only oblivion after we die, but this is hardly a pathway to salvation! It is a typical notion of the future according to atheism, for which nothing awaits us after death. It is neither a biblical nor a Christian position. As Moltmann writes, it is a charter for mass murderers and terrorists, for if nothing awaits us when we die, they will never have to appear before the judgment of God to give an account for their enormities.[13] In short, there will be no judgment, no setting right of wrongs. On this theory, the universe is harsh, bleak, and amoral. There can be no objective basis for morality, no way to distinguish between the greatest saint and Adolf Hitler.

30.2.2 Universal Salvation

Some claim that all people will be saved. Schleiermacher dissented from the claim that those who die out of fellowship with Christ will endure eternal misery, for "the figurative sayings of Christ . . . [will] be found insufficient to support any such conclusion. . . . Still less can the idea of eternal damnation itself bear close scrutiny."[14] The quickened consciences of the redeemed could hardly fail to have intense sympathy for those in misery and will instill a bitter feeling when we regard the disparity.[15] So he held to universal salvation; God will save all people.[16] And they all lived happily ever after.

Varieties of universalism. We should distinguish between those who affirm universal salvation and those, like Barth and T. F. Torrance, who deny its necessity, oppose its assertion as heresy, but hope for its possibility. Barth's theology leads to a prima facie conclusion by many critics that he holds to universal salvation. Since the whole of creation and salvation is comprised in God's determination to be God in Christ, election, incarnation, and atonement embrace all people, with the apparent conclusion that all will be saved. Yet Barth strongly resisted this conclusion, prompting the claim of incoherence.[17] Hunsinger sums up in saying of

---

13. Jürgen Moltmann, *The Coming of God: Christian Eschatology*, trans. Margaret Kohl (Minneapolis: Fortress, 1996), 109.

14. Friedrich Schleiermacher, *The Christian Faith*, ed. H. R. Mackintosh and J. S. Stewart (1830; repr., Edinburgh: T&T Clark, 1999), 720.

15. Schleiermacher, *The Christian Faith*, 721–22.

16. See Moltmann, *The Coming of God*, 248.

17. Oliver D. Crisp, "On Barth's Denial of Universalism," *Them* 29 (2003): 18–29.

Barth that "although universal salvation cannot be deduced as a necessity, it cannot be excluded as a possibility."[18] Colwell considers there to be no such problem, since Barth's doctrine of election is dynamic, not static, its primal nature being authentically temporal.[19]

Torrance opposes both definite atonement and universal salvation on the grounds that they are rationalistic attempts to expound a mystery, examples of what he calls "the Latin heresy." Both doctrines place limits over the freedom of God.[20] Molnar points to Torrance's Christocentric doctrine of election as obviating any attempt at a rationalistic and deterministic soteriology.[21] These two poles are both attempts to explain the work of Christ in detachment from his person.[22] Hence, Torrance writes that it is possible for some to go to hell.[23] So, while there remains the *possibility* of universal salvation, in Torrance's estimation, any claim that it is the case threatens the gospel.[24] Indeed, earlier Torrance condemned universalism as "a heresy for faith and a menace to the gospel."[25]

Moltmann, in *The Coming of God*, adopts universalism, while weighing the case for other proposals.

> The Christian doctrine about the restoration of all things denies neither damnation nor hell. On the contrary: it assumes that in his suffering and dying Christ suffered the total and true hell of God-forsakenness for the reconciliation of the world, and experienced for us the true and total damnation for sin. . . . It is Christ's descent into hell that is the ground for the confidence that nothing will be lost but that everything will be brought back again and gathered into the eternal kingdom of God.[26]

---

18. George Hunsinger, "Hellfire and Damnation: Four Ancient and Modern Views," *SJT* 51 (1998): 429.

19. John Colwell, "The Contemporaneity of the Divine Decision: Reflections on Barth's Denial of 'Universalism,'" in *Universalism and the Doctrine of Hell: Papers Presented at the Fourth Edinburgh Conference in Christian Dogmatics, 1991*, ed. Nigel M. de S. Cameron (Carlisle: Paternoster, 1992), 139–60.

20. Paul D. Molnar, "Thomas F. Torrance and the Problem of Universalism," *SJT* 68 (2015): 164–86.

21. Molnar, "Torrance and Universalism," 173–74. Molnar has a lecture online in which he presents a resolution of this conundrum in Torrance. However, that it takes such a brilliant mind and highly complex argument one hour to come to this conclusion only serves to demonstrate its difficulty.

22. Molnar, "Torrance and Universalism," 184.

23. Thomas F. Torrance, *Atonement: The Person and Work of Christ*, ed. Robert T. Walker (Milton Keynes: Paternoster, 2009), 156–58; Torrance, *The School of Faith: The Catechisms of the Reformed Church* (London: James Clarke, 1959), cxv–cxvii.

24. Molnar, "Torrance and Universalism," 186.

25. T. F. Torrance, "Universalism or Election?," *SJT* 2 (1949): 310.

26. Moltmann, *The Coming of God*, 251.

So hell is a reality, but ultimately all will be saved.

> It is a source of endlessly consoling joy to know, not just that the
> murderers will finally fail to triumph over their victims, but that they
> cannot in eternity even remain the murderers of their victims. The
> eschatological doctrine about the restoration of all things has these
> two sides: God's *judgment*, which puts things to rights, and *God's*
> *kingdom*, which awakens to new life.[27]

In his later book *Sun of Righteousness, Arise!* Moltmann explicitly advocates universalism to the point that hell will be eradicated.[28]

Trevor Hart[29] distinguishes between pluralistic universalism, exemplified by John Hick,[30] and the Christian universalism of J. A. T.
Robinson.[31] Pluralistic universalism has, at best, a very weak view
of sin and makes the cross superfluous. It denies the exclusivity of
Christ. Christian universalism, in contrast, Hart contends, is based on
a Christian paradigm and the work of Christ. In the face of the commonly posed conundrum of how an omnipotent and loving God could
simultaneously allow people to reject him, raising the question of either
a defeat of his omnipotence or a failure of his love, Robinson concludes
that God would have failed if any were lost.[32] Robinson recognizes
the human possibility of hell but thinks people will choose life. Hart
argues, debatably, that Robinson does not minimize the severity of sin
or the depth and efficacy of the atonement, for it is this that constrains
people to believe. Robinson believes in the reality of hell but thinks
it will be vacant.[33] The weakness lies in his assumption that God is
omnipotent love, in the sense of "the non-negotiable absolute around
which all else revolves"; without this, Robinson's case fails.[34] Hart
suggests that the failure is due to Robinson's idea that God's universal
love is omnipotent and always achieves his purpose. Robinson's logic

27. Moltmann, *The Coming of God*, 255.
28. Jürgen Moltmann, *Sun of Righteousness, Arise! God's Future for Humanity and the Earth*, trans. Margaret Kohl (London: SCM, 2010), 142.
29. Trevor Hart, "Universalism: Two Distinct Types," in Cameron, *Universalism and the Doctrine of Hell*, 1–34.
30. John Hick, *Evil and the God of Love: God and the Universe of Faiths* (London: Macmillan, 1966); John Hick, *God Has Many Names: Britain's New Religious Pluralism* (London: Macmillan, 1980).
31. J. A. T. Robinson, *In the End, God* (London: James Clarke, 1950).
32. Hart, "Universalism," 18–19.
33. Hart, "Universalism," 22.
34. Hart, "Universalism," 29.

874   *The Ultimate Purposes of God*

secures universalism at the expense of the personal freedom and the relational nature of humans and God.[35]

The history of Christian universalism. Thiselton supports the common idea that Origen held to universal salvation, including that of the devil. He cites passages in Origen's *De principiis*.[36] However, in none of these passages can the claim be established. In *De principiis* 3.5.6 and 3.6.6, Origen simply reflects the biblical language without comment (1 Cor. 15:27–28; Eph. 1:10), while in 2.3.7 he does not address the question at all. Crouzel remarks:

> It will be seen how extremely delicate and qualified a reply must be given to the question of the universality of the *apocatastasis* in Origen. It cannot be said that he held this view, or that he firmly professed it, for if there are texts pointing firmly in that direction, too many others exist on the other side, showing other aspects which must form part of the answer. At most it can be said that he hoped for it, in a period when the rule of faith was not fixed as it would be later on.[37]

To be fair, Thiselton refers to Frederick W. Norris as rejecting this idea in Origen.[38]

Thiselton also cites Gregory of Nyssa, in his *Great Catechism*, 24 and 25.[39] But in neither of these passages does Gregory address the idea. In section 24 he refers to humanity as such being brought from a state of death, while in section 25 he writes of human nature being rescued from death and transformed in the divine. He writes of humanity as a whole, not of the salvation of each and every individual. Other statements in *The Making of Man* and in *The Great Catechism* are equally to be understood that way.[40]

Bearing in mind my previous comments, Moltmann has an extensive and even-handed discussion of the question in *The Coming of God*. He

---

35. Hart, "Universalism," 31.
35. Hart, "Universalism," 31.
36. Origen, *On First Principles* 2.3.7, 3.5.6, 3.6.6 (*ANF*, 4:275, 343, 347–48, cited in Anthony C. Thiselton, *Systematic Theology* (London: SPCK, 2015), 387.
37. Henri Crouzel, *Origen*, trans. A. S. Worrall (Edinburgh: T&T Clark, 1989), 265.
38. Thiselton, *Systematic Theology*, 388. See the nuanced paper by Frederick W. Norris, "Universal Salvation in Origen and Maximus," in Cameron, *Universalism and the Doctrine of Hell*, 35–72.
39. In *NPNF²*, 5:494–95, cited in Thiselton, *Systematic Theology*, 388; Thiselton, *Last Things*, 147.
40. Gregory of Nyssa, *The Making of Man* 17.2 (*NPNF²*, 5:407); Gregory, *Catechism* 8, 40 (*NPNF²*, 5:483, 508).

considers the respective merits and weaknesses, as he sees them, of universalism and particularism, coming down on the side of universalism.[41] He agrees that Barth thrust universalism onto the theological agenda, where he was strongly opposed by Brunner, who insisted on the biblical teaching of double outcomes. Paul Althaus took a mediating position, attempting to hold on to the idea and the fear of being eternally lost, together with the hope of universal salvation. Gerhard Ebeling sided with Brunner.[42]

In his consideration of the biblical and theological arguments, Moltmann presents something of a caricature of particularism. He asks, "Why did God create human beings if he is going to damn most of them in the end, and will only redeem the least part of them? Can God hate what he has created without hating himself?"[43] Moltmann assumes that particularism requires that the majority will go to hell. This may not be the case if one's interpretation of the New Testament passages on the future is anything like those of Warfield and Hodge, which we will consider shortly.

Rome, having moved to inclusivism at Vatican II, advanced further toward universalism with the papal encyclical *Redemptor Hominis*, issued by John Paul II in 1979, which declared that "every man without exception has been redeemed by Christ."[44]

Against the assertion or expectation of universal salvation are set the following damning considerations: the reality and gravity of sin, clear biblical pronouncements that not all will be saved, and the urgency of gospel proclamation in the New Testament. Hart comments on universalism, "It is quite unnecessary for a person to know about or to believe in Jesus Christ in order to be saved, but, strictly speaking, quite unnecessary also for Christ to have lived or died. The significance of the Christ event is utterly relativized."[45]

A modified form of universal salvation, that all will be saved except for those who explicitly reject Christ as offered in the gospel, encounters serious problems. I remember a conversation I had with a Norwegian girl when I was on a mission team touring the Loire Valley in 1970. The

---

41. Moltmann, *The Coming of God*, 240–55.
42. Moltmann, *The Coming of God*, 239.
43. Moltmann, *The Coming of God*, 239.
44. *Redemptor Hominis*, 14, cited by Hart, "Universalism," 9.
45. Hart, "Universalism," 13.

girl thought that all who did not hear the gospel would be saved, but they would be condemned if they heard it and rejected it. I retorted to the effect that, if this were so, gospel preaching would be immoral. It would be better not to preach, since if any person rejects Christ when he is presented, that person is liable for hell, whereas the person who has not heard the gospel would be saved. According to this notion, gospel proclamation, not sin, is the instrumental cause of a person's damnation.

Pannenberg allows that "we certainly cannot rule out the possibility of the eternal damnation of some. . . . But this possibility is not a constitutive part of the thought of divine judgment in terms of the purifying fire of 1 Cor. 3:10–15."[46] Quite, since in that passage Paul is referring not to the wicked or unbelievers or those who have never heard of Christ but to Christian preachers and the evaluation of their work. I will discuss this passage in the final chapter.[47]

30.2.3   Pluralism

Pluralism is the belief that all religions, or at least many, lead to God, and so their sincere adherents will be saved. John Hick became a foremost exponent of this idea, following years of work on interfaith bodies.[48] It is based on the unity of the race and the universal love of God. At root, this is a denial of the uniqueness of Christ and so places itself outside the parameters of the Christian faith. It also supposes the identity of the various objects of worship.

30.2.4   Inclusivism

Inclusivists maintain that many of those who have not heard the gospel will be saved. They do so from a variety of different commitments.

Christian inclusivism. Since the middle of the last century, Rome has moved to an explicitly inclusivist position. Karl Rahner, in a lecture in 1961, introduced the phrase "anonymous Christians." He wrote that "the others who oppose [the Church] are merely those who have not yet recognized what they nevertheless really already are (or can be) even

---

46. Wolfhart Pannenberg, *Systematic Theology*, trans. Geoffrey W. Bromiley, 3 vols. (Grand Rapids, MI: Eerdmans, 1991–1998), 3:620.
47. For recent universalist proposals, see Gregory MacDonald, *All Shall Be Well: Explorations in Universalism and Christian Theology from Origen to Moltmann* (Eugene, OR: Cascade, 2011).
48. Hick, *Evil*; Hick, *Many Names*.

when, on the surface of existence, they are in opposition; they are already anonymous Christians." Indeed, "the Christian cannot renounce this 'presumption'" of anonymous Christianity. It should engender tolerance to all religions.[49] While avoiding universalism this is clearly inclusivist.

At Vatican II, *Nostra Aetate* asserted that Hinduism, Buddhism, and other religions "often reflect a ray of that truth which enlightens all men," although only through Christ do people find "the fullness of religious life."[50] This suggests a version of fulfillment theology, in which other religions are held to prepare for Christ in an analogous way to Israel in the Old Testament. This idea, popular in missiological circles, ignores the uniqueness of God's covenant with Israel. Throughout the Old Testament there was both contrast and conflict with other religions.[51] Daniel Strange, in agreement with Abraham Kuyper, argues that other religions retain elements of God's original revelation in creation but are trajectories of departure, whereas Israel received additional special revelation expressly designed to lead to Christ.[52]

Furthermore, *Lumen Gentium* added that such religions are pre-Christian, not non-Christian. "Nor is God Himself far distant from those . . . who seek the unknown God," because God is their Creator. God wills all to be saved if they seek him with a sincere heart and try to do his will. If so, they "can attain to everlasting salvation."[53] The CCC adds, "The plan of salvation also includes those who acknowledge the Creator, in the first place amongst whom are the Muslims; these profess to hold the faith of Abraham, and together with us they adore the one, merciful God, mankind's judge on the last day."[54] This bond is due to common origin from God, and a common destiny to God.[55] Thus,

> the church recognizes in other religions that search . . . for the God who is unknown and yet near since he gives life and breath and all things, and wants all men to be saved. Thus, the Church considers

49. Karl Rahner, *Theological Investigations*, vol. 5, *Later Writings*, trans. Karl-H. Kruger (London: Darton, Longman & Todd, 1966), 134.

50. *Nostra Aetate*, 2, in Walter M. Abbott, *The Documents of Vatican II* (New York: Guild, 1966), 662.

51. See Adam Sparks, *One of a Kind: The Relationship between Old and New Covenants as the Hermeneutical Key for Christian Theology of Religions* (Eugene, OR: Pickwick, 2010).

52. See Daniel Strange, *"For Their Rock Is Not as Our Rock": An Evangelical Theology of Religion* (Nottingham: Inter-Varsity Press, 2014).

53. *LG*, 16; Abbott, *Documents*, 35.

54. *CCC*, 841.

55. *CCC*, 842.

all goodness and truth found in these religions as "a preparation for the Gospel, and given by him who enlightens all men that they may at length have life."[56]

In this view, the ancient claim that apart from the church there is no salvation is not aimed at people such as this, who through no fault of their own do not know Christ and his church.[57]

Pannenberg opposes "an unfair particularism in the idea that for all of us salvation depends on our fellowship with Jesus Christ."[58] Many have not been reached by the preaching of the gospel, he argues, and so this cannot be the universal criterion for salvation or exclusion, since the New Testament teaching on the love of God embraces all people. What counts is whether "individual conduct actually agrees with the will of God that Jesus proclaimed."[59] Pannenberg maintains that for those who believe in Christ now, there will be the purifying fire Paul mentions in 1 Corinthians 3. This is a form of purgatory, only postponed from the postmortem state until, during, or after the last judgment.[60]

Evangelical inclusivism. Some self-styled evangelicals argue that those who have never heard the gospel but have framed their lives in accordance with what they know of God from general revelation may be saved in virtue of the work of Christ. Clark Pinnock[61] and John Sanders[62] are examples. Daniel Strange defines the distinction between this group and evangelicals in general as surrounding whether salvation is universally accessible through general revelation apart from knowledge of Christ or whether it is to be found exclusively through special revelation, by the proclamation of Christ.[63]

Pinnock advocates universal accessibility via the cosmic scope of the Holy Spirit in creation; because the Spirit is omnipresent in creation,

---

56. CCC, 843; LG, 16.

57. CCC, 847. But note the increasing challenges to Vatican II. Stephen Morgan, "Cracks in the Edifice: Recent Challenges to the Received History of Vatican II," *DRev* 133 (January 2015): 66–85.

58. Pannenberg, *Systematic Theology*, 3:615.

59. Pannenberg, *Systematic Theology*, 3:615.

60. See Pannenberg's discussion of the relationship of his claim to the development of the dogma of purgatory. Pannenberg, *Systematic Theology*, 3:617–19.

61. Clark H. Pinnock, *A Wideness in God's Mercy: The Finality of Jesus Christ in a World of Religions* (Grand Rapids, MI: Zondervan, 1992).

62. John Sanders, *No Other Name: An Investigation into the Destiny of the Unevangelized* (Grand Rapids, MI: Eerdmans, 1992).

63. Daniel Strange, *The Possibility of Salvation among the Unevangelised: An Analysis of Inclusivism in Recent Evangelical Theology* (Carlisle: Paternoster, 2002), 36.

God is present to everyone. Pinnock sees the Spirit's grace in creation as linked with saving grace.[64]

Sanders describes what he regards as a tension between two essential biblical axioms: God's will for all to be saved and salvation only being found in Christ.[65] On the basis of the traditional view, he deems it hard to see how God is serious about loving the world, since salvation is not offered to all.[66] Moreover, there is confusion, Sanders thinks, between Christ being the only way of salvation and knowing that this is so.[67]

Rejecting universalism as well as what he terms "restrictivism," Sanders contends that the possibility of encountering Christ at death, held by some Roman Catholics, is speculative and unsustainable. In effect, universal evangelization at death empties the present life of meaning.[68] The idea of middle knowledge, that God will save those who would have believed if they had heard the gospel—itself the subject of controversy—Sanders rejects on the grounds that it is a form of modified restrictivism.[69] Sanders discusses the possibility of postmortem evangelization, based mainly on an interpretation of 1 Peter 3:18–4:6.[70] This is perhaps the most difficult passage in the New Testament, with no one proposed interpretation entirely free from problems. However, the likeliest scenario is that 3:19–21 is a parenthetical description of Jesus's activity in his resurrection in proclaiming judgment on fallen angels.[71] It hardly provides grounds for an idea that could be said to undermine the urgency of gospel proclamation as seen in the New Testament.

Sanders prefers the "wider hope," the belief that people can be saved through Christ, there being no other way, but without having heard the gospel.[72] In its favor, he argues, is a distinction between Christians, who have conscious faith in Christ, and believers, who simply believe in God insofar as they may be aware of him. Various Gentiles in the Old Testament are proposed as examples, along with Old Testament Israelite believers themselves and Cornelius, who was a God-fearer but had not

---

64. Strange, *Salvation*, 86–100.
65. Sanders, *No Other Name*, 25.
66. Sanders, *No Other Name*, 60.
67. Sanders, *No Other Name*, 62.
68. Sanders, *No Other Name*, 172–73.
69. Sanders, *No Other Name*, 173–75.
70. Sanders, *No Other Name*, 177–214.
71. Robert Letham, *The Work of Christ* (Leicester: Inter-Varsity Press, 1993), 150–51, and sources cited there.
72. Sanders, *No Other Name*, 215–80.

known of Christ.[73] However, when these are viewed in relation to the covenant of grace, with continuity between Old and New Testaments, the point is not knowledge of Jesus as such so much as a connection with, and an identification with, the covenant Yahweh established with his people. The point Sanders and the missiologists he cites miss is what Adam Sparks highlights: the uniqueness of Israel in distinction from the nations, precluding the latter's religions being preparations for Christ.[74] As Strange comments, "Old Testament believers confessed Christ as Christ was revealed to them in their place in the redemptive-historical index."[75] Moreover, Cornelius had identified himself with the synagogue, with the covenant, as Rahab had chosen the people of Yahweh. The absence of the covenant is most striking when Sanders considers the fate of children dying in infancy. He mentions four main views on the question of their salvation but does not mention the promise of the covenant of grace to believers and their children.[76]

Inclusivists also argue that general revelation has saving power, since its source is God.[77] This ignores Paul's sermons (Acts 14:8–18; 17:22–31) where he speaks of the "times of ignorance" when the Gentiles were without the revelation of Christ. It also undermines the necessity of Scripture.

Sanders says, "Wider-hope theories all affirm that God makes salvation universally accessible," but they disagree on three points: "(1) that a person must have explicit knowledge of Jesus Christ in order to be saved, (2) that it is necessary to learn about the work of Christ from human agents, and (3) that our final destiny is settled at death."[78]

Strange makes an obvious but vital point, that "there is no biblical evidence to suggest that anyone has been saved apart from God's special revelation."[79] Moreover, he identifies a fatal Christological error in Pinnock's idea of universal accessibility to salvation. What this does is relegate Christ from finality.[80] Pinnock states that "uniqueness and finality belong to God. If they belong to Jesus, they belong to him only derivatively."[81] This must apply to all forms of inclusivism. If knowledge

---

73. Sanders, *No Other Name*, 224–32.
74. Sparks, *One of a Kind*.
75. Strange, *Salvation*, 197.
76. Sanders, *No Other Name*, 288.
77. Sanders, *No Other Name*, 233–36.
78. Sanders, *No Other Name*, 225ff.
79. Strange, *Salvation*, 197.
80. Strange, *Salvation*, 200.
81. Pinnock, *Wideness*, 53.

of Christ is not necessary to salvation, Christ is not the final and decisive Word of God.

The WLC, 60, is emphatic that "they who, never having heard the gospel, know not Christ, and believe not in him, cannot be saved, be they never so diligent to frame their lives according to the light of nature, or the laws of that religion which they profess." In this the WLC follows the Thirty-Nine Articles, 18, which states:

> They also are to be had accursed that presume to say, that every man shall be saved by the law or sect which he professeth, so that he be diligent to frame his life according to that law, and the light of nature. For Holy Scripture doth set out unto us only the Name of Jesus Christ, whereby men must be saved.

Strange comments that "in Reformed theology, the pressure to resolve universality and particularity is not as acute as it is . . . in Pinnock's theology because the universality axiom is not a presupposition of that paradigm."[82]

Romans 2:14–15 is often cited in support of the idea of pagans doing what pleases God. However, the context points to Paul referring to Gentile Christians, not pagans. It is believing Gentiles who demonstrate the obedience of faith and so shame the Jewish unbelievers and the strongly nationalistic Judaizers.

30.2.5 Exclusivism

Exclusivists maintain that only those with faith in Jesus Christ will be saved. This asserts the urgency of preaching the gospel. Baptists stress that salvation is only by conscious faith in Jesus Christ, since for them the individual is primary.

Not all exclusivists maintain that conscious faith in Jesus Christ is an indispensable necessity in each and every case. Indeed, a reticence to insist on conscious faith in Scripture has been shared by orthodox Christians throughout history. W. G. T. Shedd suggests that people may be saved without hearing of Christ. He writes of "such of the pagan world as God pleases to regenerate without the written word."[83] He refers to the Second Helvetic Confession, 1.7 in its expression of ignorance as to

82. Strange, *Salvation*, 285.
83. W. G. T. Shedd, *The Dogmatic Theology* (Grand Rapids, MI: Zondervan, 1971), 1:436.

whether God regenerates apart from the external ministry of the Word, recognizing that it is within his power to do so.[84] He cites Calvin, *Institutes*, 4.16.19, discussing the salvation of infants who die.[85] This begs the question, since even in these instances, salvation is in and with the Word insofar as it can never be at odds with the message of the gospel. The regenerate will always bear the fruit of the Spirit, according to the level of their age and maturity, and will believe when Christ is presented to them. In this way, regeneration cannot be independent of the Word, even though the preached Word may not be present at the precise time that regeneration occurs. Shedd concludes that whether any of the heathen are saved outside of Christian missions depends on whether they have been regenerated by Christ through the Spirit.[86]

The WCF, 10.3, affirms that elect infants dying in infancy will be saved, as will other elect persons who are constitutionally unable to hear or understand the Word. In these cases also, conscious faith in Christ is not necessary for salvation. Here the key is election; all the elect will be saved, whether or not they have heard the gospel. It could be argued against this that it undermines the case against Christian inclusivism, since that can also affirm that all the elect will be saved.[87] However, the Westminster divines understood their statement in the context of the covenant of grace, which places the infant offspring of a believing parent within the covenant and so receptive of the mercies of God. A strong balancing assertion comes in WCF, 10.4, supported by WLC, 60, that the nonelect, and those not professing the Christian religion cannot be saved. Besides this, Shedd's case rests on speculation. Nevertheless, we cannot ourselves pronounce on the eternal destiny of particular individuals; this is in the hands of God.

30.2.6 Calvinistic Exclusivist Eschatological Universalism

Charles Hodge famously remarked that "we have reason to believe . . . that the number of the finally lost in comparison with the whole number of the saved will be very inconsiderable."[88] Warfield held that "nothing less than the world will be saved" by Christ, the world as an organic

---

84. Shedd, *Dogmatic Theology*, 1:437.
85. Shedd, *Dogmatic Theology*, 1:438.
86. Shedd, *Dogmatic Theology*, 1:440.
87. I am grateful to Tony Lane for pointing this out.
88. Charles Hodge, *Systematic Theology* (Grand Rapids, MI: Eerdmans, 1977), 3:879–80.

whole. Indeed, "the number of the saved shall in the end not be small but large," and will far outnumber the lost.[89]

In a sermon "God's Immeasurable Love," Warfield strongly opposed the idea that the elect are a small remnant of the world, since they *are* the world. In this light, he wrote:

> Through all the years one increasing purpose runs, one *increasing* purpose: the kingdoms of the earth become ever more and more the kingdom of our God and his Christ. The process may be slow; the progress may appear to our impatient eyes to lag. But it is God who is building: and under his hands the structure rises as steadily as it does slowly, and in due time the capstone shall be set into its place, and to our astonished eyes shall be revealed nothing less than a saved world.[90]

In "The Prophecies of St. Paul," he describes the time from the advent to the parousia as "a period of advancing conquest," Christ "progressively overcoming evil, throughout this period."[91] Furthermore, Romans 11 "promises the universal Christianization of the world,—at least the nominal conversion of all the Gentiles and the real salvation of all the Jews . . . the widest practicable extension of Christianity."[92] We should hope, pray, and work to that end.

30.3 Hell

30.3.1 *Hell as a Place of Everlasting Conscious Punishment*

Tertullian cites the language of 2 Thessalonians 1 about everlasting destruction and stresses punishment.[93] Chrysostom, preaching on the same passage, comments:

> If they that have not obeyed the gospel suffer vengeance, what will they not suffer who besides their disobedience also afflict you? And see his intelligence; he says not here those who afflict you, but those "who obey not." So that although not on your account, yet on his own, it is necessary to punish them.[94]

---

89. B. B. Warfield, "Are They Few That Be Saved?," in *Biblical and Theological Studies*, ed. Samuel G. Craig (Philadelphia: Presbyterian and Reformed, 1952), 349.
90. B. B. Warfield, "God's Immeasurable Love," in *Biblical and Theological Studies*, 518–19.
91. B. B. Warfield, "The Prophecies of St. Paul," In *Biblical and Theological Studies*, 485.
92. Warfield, "Prophecies," 486.
93. Tertullian, *Against Marcion* 5.16 (ANF, 3:463).
94. Chrysostom, *Homilies on 2 Thessalonians* 2 (NPNF[1], 13:382–83).

In the next homily he adds: "But that it is not temporary, hear Paul now saying, concerning those who know not God, and who do not believe in the gospel, that 'they shall suffer punishment, even eternal destruction.' How then is that temporary which is everlasting? 'From the face of the Lord,' he says."[95] Augustine argues that punishment is correlative with eternal life.[96] He adds that to say, "Life eternal shall be endless, punishment eternal shall come to an end, is the height of absurdity."[97]

Later, the Fourth Lateran Council (1215) affirmed the "perpetual punishment with the devil."[98] Aquinas, in considering the disparity between the infinite nature of the offense of sin, by virtue of the infinitude of God, and the finite creature, concludes that "punishment cannot be infinite in intensity, because the creature is incapable of an infinite quality, it must needs be infinite at least in duration." This allows for gradations of punishment in accordance with the relative gravity of sins so that "the measure of punishment corresponds to the measure of fault."[99]

Calvin, addressing a similar set of factors, states that "no description can deal adequately with the gravity of God's vengeance against the wicked." Consequently,

> we ought especially to fix our thoughts upon this: how wretched it is to be cut off from all fellowship with God. And not that only but so to feel his sovereign power against you that you cannot escape being pressed by it. . . . It would be more bearable to go down into any bottomless depths and chasms than to stand for a moment in these terrors. What and how great is this, to be eternally and unceasingly besieged by him?[100]

Commenting on 2 Thessalonians 1:9, he writes that Paul "explains the nature of the punishment . . . it is eternal punishment and death which has no end. The perpetual duration of this death is proved from the fact that its opposite is the glory of Christ. This is eternal and has no end. Hence the violent nature of that death will never cease."[101]

---

95. Chrysostom, *Homilies on 2 Thessalonians* 3 (NPNF¹, 13:384).
96. Augustine, *City of God* 21.17–24 (NPNF¹, 2:466–72).
97. Augustine, *City of God* 21.23 (NPNF¹, 2:469).
98. *DS*, 801.
99. Aquinas, *ST* 3Suppl.99.1.
100. Calvin, *Institutes*, 3.25.12.
101. John Calvin, *Calvin's Commentaries: The Epistles of Paul the Apostle to the Romans and to the Thessalonians*, trans. Ross MacKenzie (Grand Rapids, MI: Eerdmans, 1973), 392.

Rome agrees, although there is now an element of equivocation.[102] So does Orthodoxy. As Ware puts it, "Hell exists as well as heaven." To argue that this is inconsistent with the love of God "is to display a sad and perilous confusion of thought."[103] God has given us free will, and so it is possible to reject God. "Since free will exists, hell exists for hell is nothing else than the rejection of God. If we deny hell, we deny free will."[104] "Christ at his second coming will come as *judge*."[105] "Hell is not so much a place where God imprisons man, as a place where man . . . chooses to imprison himself."[106] A classic defense of the doctrine was written by W. G. T. Shedd.[107]

30.3.2 Exegetical Objections to Hell as a Place of Endless Punishment

John Stott holds that in the New Testament destruction (ἀπόλλυμι, ὄλεθρος)[108] means extinction of being, not everlasting conscious punishment.[109] He argues for the literal sense of the words; to destroy means to destroy, and the property of fire is that it destroys. So, "if to kill is to deprive the body of life, hell would seem to be . . . an extinction of being."[110] Indeed, "it would seem strange . . . if people who are said to suffer destruction are in fact not destroyed."[111] The image of fire signifies destruction.[112] Therefore annihilation is in view. Stott has other, theological, arguments for his position, but these are the main exegetical ones. David Powys writes along similar lines. The language means destruction with no hint of duration, let alone eternity.[113]

Thiselton notes that Paul never speaks of hell, only of death and destruction. Even in 2 Thessalonians 1 it is destruction, "eternal" denoting its quality rather than its duration.[114] He agrees that it is a more serious

102. CCC, 633, 1034–37; cf. 1058.
103. Timothy Ware, *The Orthodox Church* (London: Penguin, 1969), 265.
104. Ware, *Orthodox Church*, 266.
105. Ware, *Orthodox Church*, 266.
106. Ware, *Orthodox Church*, 266.
107. W. G. T. Shedd, *The Doctrine of Endless Punishment* (1885; repr., Edinburgh: Banner of Truth, 1990).
108. *apollymi, olethros.*
109. David L. Edwards and John Stott, *Essentials: A Liberal-Evangelical Dialogue* (London: Hodder & Stoughton, 1988), 314–15.
110. Edwards and Stott, *Essentials*, 315.
111. Edwards and Stott, *Essentials*, 316.
112. Edwards and Stott, *Essentials*, 316.
113. David J. Powys, *"Hell": A Hard Look at a Hard Question* (Carlisle: Paternoster, 1998), 284, 310.
114. Thiselton, *Last Things*, 154.

situation than merely cessation of existence, he refers to those who say it means endlessness, and he notes the language of Revelation 14:9–11, 20:10, 21:8, and Daniel 12:2.[115]

Nevertheless, extinction is not the meaning of ἀπόλλυμι in 2 Peter 3:6, since the world was not annihilated by the flood. Moreover, fire not only destroys; it also purifies (1 Cor. 3:11–15; 1 Pet. 1:6–7). Packer argues that the verb ἀπόλλυμι, "destroy," means "wreck," rendering inoperative rather than extinguishing, just as to be excluded or "away from the presence" entails existence (2 Thess. 1:9), since it is only those who exist who can be excluded.[116]

Matthew 25:31–46. Stott argues against punishment in verse 46 being everlasting. Jesus simply contrasts eternal life and its opposite as starkly as possible.[117] "Eternal" denotes quality rather than quantity or duration.

However, the contrast in the verdicts relating to the sheep and the goats is in itself stark. The sheep are told to come and enter the kingdom prepared for them from the foundation of the world, whereas the goats are summarily dismissed, "Depart from me" (vv. 34, 41). The word κόλασις means "punishment" here,[118] as it can only mean elsewhere (Acts 4:21). Consequently, the outcomes in Matthew 25:46 are equally contrary. If "eternal life" denotes duration, one assumes that "eternal punishment" does too. Stott's argument creates greater problems than it can solve. As for the punishment, Davies and Allison observe that "there is no trace of its being remedial."[119] Rather, "Matthew, by coupling αἰώνιος[120] with 'fire' (18:8; 25:41; cf. 25:46), seems to show agreement with those who believed the damned would suffer for ever. . . . The wicked will be ever dying, never dead."[121] Hill, however, suggests that "the word *eternal* . . . means 'that which is characteristic of the Age to come'; the emphasis on temporal lastingness is secondary."[122] That may be so, but duration would still be present, since that is entailed in the age to come.

---

115. Thiselton, *Last Things*, 155.
116. James I. Packer, "The Problem of Eternal Punishment" (Leon Morris Lecture for the Evangelical Alliance, Melbourne, Australia, August 21, 1990); Packer, "Evangelical Annihilationism in Review," http://www.the-highway.com/annihilationism_Packer.html, accessed February 26, 2016.
117. Edwards and Stott, *Essentials*, 317.
118. *kolasis*; BAG; LN.
119. W. D. Davies Jr. and Dale C. Allison, *A Critical and Exegetical Commentary on the Gospel according to Saint Matthew* (Edinburgh: T&T Clark, 1988), 3:431.
120. *aiōnios*.
121. Davies and Allison, *Matthew*, 1:515.
122. David Hill, *The Gospel of Matthew* (London: Marshall, Morgan & Scott, 1972), 331.

On the other hand, France considers that the word itself does not settle the issue. He does not see αἰώνιος as having identical meaning in both clauses.[123]

New Testament imagery of death, destruction, fire, and darkness. While this is something about which we do not want to venture beyond the biblical imagery, I will cautiously suggest the following, not treading too close to the precipice. It was Erasmus who wrote that if one were to speak with undue confidence about hell, it would imply that one lived there.[124] Moreover, "it is a fearful thing to fall into the hands of the living God" (Heb. 10:31). The biblical images require continued conscious existence. That they are not to be taken literally is clear from Matthew 24:51, where the evil servant is sliced in two and then sent to the place where there is weeping and gnashing of teeth.

Outer darkness signifies isolation, both from God and from other people. Darkness itself denotes distress, particularly in relation to judgment (Zeph. 1:14–18); this is heightened by the isolation. It is contrary to the purpose for which we were made. At creation Adam and Eve were made in the image of God, in relation to each other and to God himself. They were also put in relation to the created order, with the command to cultivate the garden and to extend its boundaries to cover the entire earth. Darkness was the first obstacle to human living to be eliminated in the creation account.

Exclusion is evident in the parables of Matthew 24–25.[125] These entail isolation from God (see Matt. 7:22–23; 25:12, 41; Rom. 9:3; 2 Thess. 1:9). As noted above, Packer demonstrates that exclusion is not extinction, for only those who exist can be excluded.[126]

Weeping and gnashing of teeth denotes extreme anguish and sorrow, deep and lasting regret, the consequence of remorse at failure to live in relation to God and thus to fellow humans and to the environment. Deprivation of God, who is love, means a context devoid of love.

123. R. T. France, *The Gospel according to Matthew: An Introduction and Commentary* (Leicester: Inter-Varsity Press, 1985), 358.

124. "[The theologians] are happy too while they're depicting everything in hell down to the last detail, as if they'd spent several years there!" Desiderius Erasmus, *Praise of Folly*, trans. Betty Radice, rev. A. H. T. Levi (London: Penguin, 1991), 93–94. Thanks to Tony Lane for referring me to this comment by Erasmus.

125. Kendall S. Harmon, "The Case against Conditionalism," in Cameron, *Universalism and the Doctrine of Hell*, 193–224.

126. It could also be argued that annihilation is the most emphatic form of exclusion.

Fire is existence in pain, which may or may not be physical. It implies a person's continual conscious realization that the purpose God had for humanity is not fulfilled in him or her. It also connotes the infliction of the just and holy wrath of God, his settled antagonism toward sin and the sinner. Instead of fire's purifying force, evident elsewhere in the New Testament (1 Pet. 1:6–7; 4:12–13), this is a judicial infliction reflecting the extent to which the person's works are worthy of the just retribution of God.

Destruction refers to being wrecked or rendered inoperative rather than being annihilated. I have noted that the penalty is proportionate to the offense. Some will, in effect, be beaten with few stripes, others with many. The punishment will be just and appropriate. It will entail setting things right. There will be no regrets on the part of the church. Rather, the book of Revelation depicts rejoicing over the final vindication of the glorious justice of God (Rev. 11:17–18; 12:7–12; 14:13; 15:2–8; 16:4–7; 18:19–20; 19:1–8). Relationships here and now will be changed; marriage is for the present. Further, based on the doctrine of divine simplicity, God's punitive justice will be good, right, holy, kind, and loving.

30.3.3 Theological Objections to Hell as a Place of Endless Punishment

The immortality of the soul is a Greek idea and is foreign to the Bible. The Greeks held that the soul is eternal, without beginning, intrinsically immortal. Behind this view lay a radical dualism between body and soul, material and spiritual. The Bible is different. The soul, being created, had a beginning and is not inherently immortal but contingently immortal, since immortality is God's gift. On this there is agreement. However, this contingency feeds the idea of conditional immortality, which in turn underlies objections to hell as everlasting. But the contingent nature of human existence, including the soul, does not of itself settle the question of the duration of punishment one way or another.

Everlasting punishment is incompatible with the justice of God. Stott condemns a casual attitude toward the lost and the judgment:[127] "Emotionally, I find the concept [of everlasting punishment] intolerable and do not understand how people can live with it without either cauterising

---

127. Edwards and Stott, *Essentials*, 313.

their feelings or cracking under the strain."[128] But, he recognizes, the question is, what does the Word of God say? As I have noted, he considers it to use the language of destruction and therefore annihilation. Effectively, this means the same penalty for all those who are condemned.

It is hard to see how a one-size-fits-all penalty could be just. Is there not a moral contrast between Hitler or Pol Pot and, say, the kindly neighbor across the street? Will not the Judge of all the earth do right? Judgment is according to works. The fact that God judges according to the case (Rev. 20:12–13; 22:12), since he is just, points to gradations of punishment appropriate to the persons concerned and leaves no lingering question of injustice. Annihilation eradicates this distinction. We saw that Aquinas considered there to be a gradation of punishments in accordance with the gravity of offenses. Since finite beings cannot endure an infinite intensity of punishment for offenses infinite in nature, the infinitude is expressed in duration.[129]

If the historic church doctrine of hell were not true, Moltmann's verdict would apply. Annihilation following immediately on death would be good news for mass murderers, as they would not need to come face-to-face with God to account for their crimes. Annihilation after the judgment is redolent of brutal military dictatorships where the regime's opponents have simply "disappeared."[130]

Although it is not the whole story, it is true that no one will go to hell against his or her will. A life spent ignoring God leads to an eternity excluded from fellowship and communion with God. As Pannenberg puts it, "The judgment is simply that sinners are left to the consequences of their own deeds."[131] However, Pannenberg thinks that in the last judgment those reconciled with God will undergo the fires of purification (1 Cor. 3:12–13), a case of purgatory postponed. Moving beyond Pannenberg, the reason this is not the whole story is that the judgment entails a judicial action by God, a consequent recompense, together with a removal of those forces in the present world that restrain sin. It is not *merely* a ratification of past choices. WCF, 3.7, states that "the rest of mankind" are ordained "*to dishonour and wrath* for their sin" (italics mine).

---

128. Edwards and Stott, *Essentials*, 314.
129. Aquinas, *ST* 3Suppl.99.1.
130. Moltmann, *The Coming of God*, 109.
131. Pannenberg, *Systematic Theology*, 3:611.

Moltmann argues that the purpose of the judgment is not exact ret-ribution but putting things right.[132] However, his notion of "putting things right" entails just retribution for the perpetrators of horrendous evils, enabling those who have ignored God to persist forever in that condition, and respecting the freedom of those who despise him. If these people were to be saved, he argues, would it not be an infringement of their will, a coercive contradiction of their free choices, a breach of their human rights?

Everlasting punishment is incompatible with the love of God. This-elton, for his part, says that love is a permanent quality in God, whereas wrath is a temporal one.[133] While there are eight Hebrew words for wrath or anger in the Old Testament, used over three hundred times, mostly but not always for the wrath of God, the Greek New Testament has only two words—ὀργή and θυμός[134]—employed in around forty occurrences.[135] Thiselton appears to imply that in the end love triumphs over wrath, which in the wider context, of course, is so. Perhaps the extra use of words for the wrath of God in the Old Testament is ex-plained by the Old Testament being much larger, ancient Israel more rebellious, lexical stock, and literary style.

Hughes thinks that it is contrary to the revealed character of God to punish people forever.[136] However, as I have remarked, does an equal sentence for all unbelievers manifest the justice of God? If there were to be no differentiation between Hitler, Stalin, and Pol Pot, on the one hand, and your kind friend who cares for the needy, on the other, how would things have been set right? Moreover, the argument requires knowledge of the nature of the punishment. Too often the vivid portrayals of medi-eval art influence our thinking.

But while the focus of the faith is on deliverance, there is also a subsidiary theme to the effect that God's justice will be exacted on the impenitent and unjust. While we look with keenest anticipation for the resurrection of the dead and the life of the world to come, and we do not confess hell, that is quite different from saying it is not a reality. It

---

132. Moltmann, *Sun of Righteousness*, 130–48.
133. Thiselton, *Last Things*, 159.
134. *orgē, thymos.*
135. Thiselton, *Last Things*, 159–60.
136. Philip Edgcumbe Hughes, *The True Image: The Origin and Destiny of Man in Christ* (Grand Rapids, MI: Eerdmans, 1989), 402–7.

is not as important as heaven and glorification, but it is a reality, and to preach it is a litmus test of the faithfulness of the church. Moreover, whenever we pray, "Come, Lord Jesus!" we are praying for judgment on the wicked, for the everlasting overthrow of the beast and the false prophet, and for the imminence of the lake of fire and brimstone. Thiselton is on better lines when he warns that "those who imagine that the coming and work of Christ mean a sudden cessation of wrath are out of tune with a gradually 'realized' eschatology."[137]

Perry considers hell to have four characteristics: it is penal, consists of conscious torment, is unending, and is predestined and so not merely a matter of human choice. The last element misses the point made in the WCF that the reprobate are condemned for their sins and that hell demonstrates God's justice. Those who suffer do so in just confirmation of their wishes, as expressed throughout the course of their lives.[138] Perry cites Brendan Cassidy, who reflects that since there is not much in the Bible depicting hell, medieval artists were free to let their imaginations run riot without fear of violating any dogmatic pronouncement by the church.[139] There is a good point to this. It would be salutary if some preachers exercised caution in their descriptions of a reality one assumes they wish to avoid. Again, Erasmus's comment is pertinent, that those who know what will happen in hell are acting as though they have spent some time there already.

Everlasting punishment is incompatible with the victory of God; it is dualistic. Thiselton asks, "How can we conceive of God eternally sustaining both the life of believers in fellowship with him, and also that of a group who are in every other sense 'separate' from him."[140] He refers to Berdyaev's argument that if there were no hell, human freedom would be eroded under a compulsion to be installed in heaven.[141] Ultimately Thiselton takes a reserved agnostic position, not happy with eternal punishment, nor with universalism, nor entirely with annihilationism in its various forms. He thinks that there is less revealed on the subject

137. Thiselton, *Last Things*, 164.
138. Perry, "Putting Hell First," 5.
139. Perry, "Putting Hell First," 7n17.
140. Thiselton, *Last Things*, 149.
141. Nicholas Berdyaev, *The Destiny of Man* (London: Bles, 1937), 267, cited in Thiselton, *Last Things*, 150.

than is often thought.[142] This is a valuable warning; believers in Christ do not want to know too much about hell, for our expectation is to be with Christ in heaven.

God's grace is more powerful than human sin. Moltmann, who says in his introduction to *The Coming of God* that he is not defending any particular position but rather is engaged in a journey of curiosity and exploration, attempts to present both sides of the picture at each turn. Here he proposes the argument that the existence of hell could be seen as detracting from the triumph of God's grace. What speaks against a double outcome of judgment—hell as well as heaven—is that God "says no to the sin because he says yes to the sinner," for he kills in order to bring life and is angry simply for the moment (1 Sam. 2:6; Ps. 30:5). In this, "the historical particularism of the divine election and rejection must serve the universalism of salvation."[143]

On the other hand, Moltmann agrees that what speaks against universalism is the question of human freedom and human rights. God desires to save people through faith, "not by overpowering them but by convincing them." He respects human freedom.[144] However, by presenting both sides in an even-handed way at this point, Moltmann is expressly noncommittal, except for his underlying universalism.

30.4   Conditional Immortality

Immortality is inherent only to God (1 Tim. 1:17; 6:16). Conditional immortality asserts that, in human terms, immortality is a gift of God on condition of faith in Christ. Consequently, nonbelievers will at some point be annihilated. They have opted for death instead of life with the living God. The idea of conditional immortality underlies theories of annihilation, but the two are to be distinguished. Conditional immortality is the basis on which annihilationism is founded. Thiselton rightly points out that nowhere in the New Testament is resurrection attributed to any intrinsic human capacity.[145]

There is much in the Bible that appears to commend conditional immortality. After Adam sinned, he and Eve were prohibited by God from

---

142. Thiselton, *Last Things*, 157–59.
143. Moltmann, *The Coming of God*, 243.
144. Moltmann, *The Coming of God*, 244.
145. Thiselton, *Last Things*, 155.

returning to the garden, in case they should eat from the tree of life and live forever (Gen. 3:22). Implied is that if they had remained in a state of righteousness, they would have had access to the tree. The parallel between the first and second Adams supports this; Christ, following his obedience, was raised from the dead, never again to die (Rom. 6:9–10). As a corollary, excluded from the garden, fallen humans are thereby prevented from living forever.

Moreover, we saw how the biblical teaching on humanity cannot be equated with the Platonic doctrine of the immortality of the soul, since we are creatures and had a beginning, our bodily existence being integral to who we are.[146] However, this in itself does not preclude the possibility that we shall live forever as humans, regardless of our redemptive state.

Perhaps the main evidence against conditional immortality *in its futurist aspect* consists of the statements concerning the final judgment as never ending (Matt. 25:46; 2 Thess. 1:9; Rev. 20:7–10). In this, it is not necessary to deny that God is the exclusive possessor of immortality. He is intrinsically immortal; he cannot die because of who he is, the living God, life itself. Any immortality we possess is a gift he confers. We are not intrinsically immortal; on that, there is agreement with those who hold to conditional immortality. The question is whether, in creating us, God has graciously conferred on every human being some capacity to live forever, not as an inherent property but as a sovereign gift. *Contingent immortality* is the term I prefer; God has conferred immortality upon humans, but it is not an inherent, intrinsic property. This differs from conditional immortality in that it is not conditional on faith.

Thiselton correctly points to the confusion over terms by those who support eternal punishment. Frequently, advocates of annihilationism are lumped together with supporters of conditional immortality, and the only two alternatives are held to be eternal conscious punishment and extinction at the moment of death. Thiselton correctly rejects this false dilemma.[147]

According to Thiselton, conditional immortality was first broached by Irenaeus (*Against Heresies* 3.19.1, 4.39).[148] This is stretching the point. In 4.39 Irenaeus refers to unbelievers as "involved in darkness." God has preserved "habitations" for believers and unbelievers respectively—for the latter, "darkness suitable to persons who oppose the light," "an

---

146. Pannenberg, *Systematic Theology*, 3:571–73.
147. Thiselton, *Last Things*, 155.
148. Thiselton, *Systematic Theology*, 387.

appropriate punishment," "a place worthy of their flight," "a habitation in accordance with their feeling." They will be subject to "the just judgement of God . . . punishment . . . [will] dwell in darkness . . . destitute of light . . . inhabiting eternal darkness."[149] This does not look like extinction. In 3.19.1 there may be grounds for drawing the conclusions Thiselton does, for there Irenaeus allows no other means to attain to incorruption and immortality than being "united to incorruption and immortality." Even then, he considers the impenitent to "remain in mortal flesh, debtors to death," implying that this is an ongoing experience.[150]

The idea of conditional immortality emerged strongly following the Enlightenment and rose to prominence in nineteenth-century England. Its incursion into evangelicalism was first mooted tentatively by T. R. Birks, a prominent evangelical Anglican, vicar in Cambridge, and professor of theology at the university. While superficially holding to traditional views on hell, Birks harbored some idiosyncratic ideas of his own. He distinguished between "the elect church," "the mystic bride of Christ," and a vast multitude of redeemed people over whom Christ will reign, to which there is no limit, presumably on the basis of a literal reading of Revelation 7. He said, "The number of the elect church may be far less than of the souls that are condemned in the judgment, but the number of the saved . . . may be vastly greater, and continually increase, world without end."[151] In turn, the resurrection of the wicked to judgment is part of the redeeming work of Christ. Based on the atonement, by being resurrected they share victory over death with the redeemed. Birks made a distinction between the federal aspect of humans and their personal aspect.[152] He posited a corresponding difference eschatologically. Personal character will remain, but there will be a federal recovery of all people. Once death and hell are cast into the lake of fire, the souls of the lost will glorify God amidst penal judgment. To glorify God in shame and punishment will entail infinite loss, but in contrast to the reign of death, now ended, it will be an infinite gain. So, while the penal sentence is irreversible, the love of God assures that it will not be an eternity of unmitigated misery, for due to the simplicity of God, his judgment is merciful as well as righteous, and Christ is "the

149. *ANF*, 1:523.
150. *ANF*, 1:448.
151. Thomas Rawson Birks, *The Difficulties of Belief, in Connection with the Creation and the Fall, Redemption and Judgment*, 2nd ed., enlarged (London: Macmillan, 1876), 215–16.
152. Birks, *Difficulties of Belief*, 229–34.

saviour of all, especially those that believe."[153] While opposing universal salvation, and especially annihilationism, Birks nevertheless mitigated the doctrine of eternal punishment by positing a multilayered eschaton, with gradations. This represented a marked softening of the classic doctrine.

30.5   Annihilationism

Annihilationism is the belief that the impenitent, after they are resurrected—either before or, far more likely, after the judgment—will all be exterminated. Major advocates have been L. E. Froom[154] and Edward Fudge.[155] Annihilationism has been favored by many evangelical Anglicans. J. W. Wenham suggested in 1974 that it was to be preferred, but that the traditional view was not to be surrendered lightly, and that further study was required.[156] He was followed by John Stott[157] and P. E. Hughes, among others.[158] Wenham, Stott, and Hughes did not, however, deny the reality of judgment, the fearsomeness of God's wrath, or the everlasting effect of judgment on the impenitent. Their espousal of conditional immortality led them to annihilationism, not universalism. Nor, as Anglicans, were they infringing the Thirty-Nine Articles, which are silent on the matter, as are all confessions except the Belgic Confession, 31, and the WCF, 33.

At the root of this development was Basil Atkinson, senior librarian at Cambridge University and advisor and counselor to generations of evangelical students at Cambridge. Atkinson was a strong advocate of annihilationism.[159] Opposition to this trend, now widespread in evangelicalism and pervasive beyond, has been voiced by J. I. Packer,[160] Paul Helm,[161] and Eryl Davies.[162] In a later paper, Wenham is critical of Packer and Helm for failing to address conditionalists' arguments in favor of

---

153. Birks, *Difficulties of Belief*, 235–37.
154. Le Roy Edwin Froom, *The Conditionalist Faith of Our Fathers* (Washington, DC: Review and Herald, 1966).
155. Edward Fudge, *The Fire That Consumes* (Houston: Providential, 1982).
156. John W. Wenham, *The Goodness of God* (London: Inter-Varsity Press, 1974), 34–41.
157. Edwards and Stott, *Essentials*, 314–15.
158. Hughes, *The True Image*, 398–407.
159. In his privately printed manuscript "Life and Immortality" (1968), 101, cited in Packer, "Evangelical Annihilationism in Review."
160. Packer, "Evangelical Annihilationism." See also Packer, "The Problem of Eternal Punishment."
161. Paul Helm, *The Last Things: Death, Judgment, Heaven, Hell* (Edinburgh: Banner of Truth, 1989).
162. Eryl Davies, *An Angry God: The Biblical Doctrine of Wrath, Final Judgment, and Hell* (Bridgend: Evangelical Press of Wales, 1991).

annihilationism.[163] He analyzes all places in the New Testament where the fate of unbelievers is mentioned and argues that the evidence points overwhelmingly to their being annihilated.

Moltmann cautions:

> The *annihilationists* think that unbelievers do not go to hell eternally but are simply destroyed and fall into an eternal nothingness; but this too does not seem to me compatible with the coming omnipotence of God and his faithfulness to what he has created. For the lost to "disappear" conforms to the terrible experiences with the murder squads in military dictatorships, but it does not accord with God.[164]

As for what Moltmann terms "the evangelical idea" that the impenitent will not be raised from the dead but simply be extinguished on death, he comments, "I do not find this very helpful either, because it excludes God's judgment. Mass murderers might possibly welcome this solution because they would then not have to answer before God's judgment for what they had done."[165]

A problem we have inherited is the grotesque imagery from medieval art. Hell was portrayed as a frightening nightmare where torture prevails forever, with God portrayed as a sadist. Brendan Cassidy indicates that

> in representing hell, unlike, say, the Nativity or the Crucifixion where the iconography was controlled by canonical texts and the requirements of sacred decorum, artists were allowed an unprecedented degree of latitude. There are numerous examples of writers, artists, and their patrons populating imagined hells with their opponents and critics.[166]

This was commonplace; Protestants did the same with Catholics.[167] It was taken to an extreme by Jonathan Edwards in his sermon "Sinners in the Hands of an Angry God," depicting God as a sadistic torturer, holding souls by a thread over an abyss of fire, like a cat playing with a mouse. The intent was clearly to press home the urgency of faith and repentance, but the imagery looms larger.

---

163. John W. Wenham, "The Case for Conditionalism," in Cameron, *Universalism and the Doctrine of Hell*, 161–91.

164. Moltmann, *The Coming of God*, 109.

165. Moltmann, *The Coming of God*, 109.

166. Brendan Cassidy, "Laughing with Giotto at Sinners in Hell," *Viator: Medieval and Renaissance Studies* 35 (2004): 356.

167. See Craig Harbison, *The Last Judgment in Sixteenth-Century Northern Europe: A Study of the Relation between Art and the Reformation* (New York: Garland, 1976).

God is a great deal more angry with great numbers that are now on earth; yea, doubtless with many that are now in this congregation . . . than he is with many of those who are now in the flames of hell. . . . The wrath of God burns against them, their damnation does not slumber; the pit is prepared, the fire is made ready, the furnace is now hot, ready to receive them; the flames do now rage and glow.[168]

The God that holds you over the pit of hell, much as one holds a spider, or some loathsome insect, over the fire, abhors you, and is dreadfully provoked: his wrath towards you burns like fire; he looks upon you as worthy of nothing else, but to be cast into the fire; . . . you are ten thousand times more abominable in his eyes, than the most hateful venomous serpent is in ours. . . . And yet, it is nothing but his hand that holds you from falling into the fire every moment.[169]

Both conditionalism and annihilationism are relatively recent proposals, in the wider context of church history. Against this is the tradition of the church—Catholic, Orthodox, and Protestant—in the light of which we should pause before abandoning its teaching. It may be that it is wrong, but there need to be good and overwhelming reasons to show that this consensus has been misplaced. Indeed, there is more than enough evidence that this is also the teaching of the Bible. Moreover, the supposed moral problem of God punishing sinners forever must be seen in the context of the counterproposal that presents him as a dictator who arranges that his opponents "disappear."

30.6 In Perspective

Heaven and hell, election and reprobation, are asymmetrical. They equally depend on the will of God, but the biblical and confessional focus is on election and heaven. The great ecumenical councils confess and express our readiness for the resurrection but do not include hell. As Calvin has it in his Genevan Catechism (1545), in response to the question of why the Apostles' Creed mentions eternal life and not hell, "nothing is held by faith except what contributes to the consolation of the souls of the pious. . . . Therefore it is not added what fate may await the impious whom we know to be outcasts from the Kingdom of God."[170]

---

168. Jonathan Edwards, *Sermons*, vol. 2 of *Select Works of Jonathan Edwards* (1839; repr., London: Banner of Truth, 1959), 185.

169. Edwards, *Select Works*, 2:191.

170. In *Calvin: Theological Treatises*, ed. J. K. S. Reid (Philadelphia: Westminster, 1954), 104; "Quoniam nihil hic, nisi quod ad consolationem piarum mentium faciat, habetur." Calvin, *OS*, 2:92.

Still, hell is a reality. It must be preached. It is a litmus test of the church's faithfulness. There are grounds for linking the health and vitality of the church with the extent to which this is believed and taught. Yet the imbalance remains. We look for the resurrection of the dead and the life everlasting; we do not look for or confess hell. It is not an explicit part of the church's confession. We do not look for everlasting punishment. We are responsible to warn, in the most serious and responsible manner, but it is not something about which we want to know a lot.

Further Reading

Cameron, Nigel M. de S., ed. *Universalism and the Doctrine of Hell.* Carlisle, UK: Paternoster, 1992.

Moltmann, Jürgen. *The Coming of God: Christian Eschatology.* Translated by Margaret Kohl. Minneapolis: Fortress, 1996.

Strange, Daniel. *The Possibility of Salvation among the Unevangelized: An Analysis of Inclusivism in Recent Evangelical Theology.* Carlisle, UK: Paternoster, 2002.

Tasker, R. V. G. *The Biblical Doctrine of the Wrath of God.* London: Tyndale Press, 1951.

Thiselton, Anthony C. *The Last Things: A New Approach.* London: SPCK, 2012.

Venema, Cornelis. *The Promise of the Future.* Edinburgh: Banner of Truth, 2000.

Study Questions

1. How does Jesus's teaching on those beaten with many or with few lashes relate to the judgment of unbelievers? Will judgment be on a one-size-fits-all basis?

2. How is the Bible's doctrine of hell compatible with its portrayal of the character of God? How should this affect our own presentation of hell? Why has the church been comparatively silent on hell in recent generations?

3. Why is the teaching of annihilationism inherently unjust?

4. How would you answer the question of the fate of those who have never heard the gospel? Should we have a greater zeal to spread the gospel, and, if so, why?

31

The Life of the World to Come

Heaven is a state in which we will be glorified like Christ, living transformed in a different realm, although, as embodied, on the present earth. It appears that rewards will be given, on the basis of grace, although we do not know of what they will consist; there will be rewards for faithful ministers of the gospel, according to 1 Corinthians 3. Sin and suffering will be abolished, and we will be conformed to Christ, living in an ever-increasingly enhanced manner compared with the present, with the task of participating in the government of the renewed cosmos under the headship of Christ. Above all else, including our own renewed humanity, we will enjoy unfettered union and communion with Christ, which will surpass everything we now know.

31.1   Biblical Teaching

There is a distinction between heaven as God's dwelling place and heaven as an eternal state. God is omnipresent, transcending and pervading the created order. He fills all things and transcends them. *Heaven*, in one sense, means "God's place" in contrast to ours. When Christ ascended, he went from our location to "God's place."[1] Heaven is in relation to the infinite and transcendent triune God, a dimension beyond our current capacity (1 Cor. 2:9).

---

1. Thomas F. Torrance, *Space, Time and Resurrection* (Grand Rapids, MI: Eerdmans, 1976), 123–42.

In terms of time, heaven is eternal as God is eternal. Space precludes our entering into the debate on the relation of God to time and eternity.[2] Suffice it to say that when we think of heaven from our perspective, we can only think of endless time. Classically, the church has taught that God's eternity is timeless and that he created time. We are creatures of time and space but are given to share in some measure in God's eternity; the incarnation proves that, since Christ's human nature was taken into an unbreakable union.

In both senses, heaven is for us our entering into a new dimension, one that immeasurably outstrips our present domain. However, since it is seen primarily in relation to God, it is to be understood as a realm or sphere, the members of Christ being glorified, with enhanced relation to God. In this sense, it includes the renewed earth, the proper location of our embodied existence. The resurrection of the body should ensure that we do not understand it in a docetic, spiritual, nonmaterial sense.

31.2   Will There Be Rewards?

31.2.1   *Biblical Support for Rewards*

There is strong support in the New Testament for God-given rewards. Jesus mentions these in the Sermon on the Mount (Matt. 5:3–12; 6:3–6). He speaks of the rewards for a prophet, a righteous person, and one who gives a cup of cold water to another disciple (Matt. 10:41–42). Each person will receive recompense for what he has done (Matt. 16:27), including those who have made sacrifices for his sake (Matt. 19:29). Paul writes that we will receive back from the Lord for the good we have done (Eph. 6:8), including the crown of righteousness that he will award to all who love his appearing (2 Tim. 4:8). A full reward awaits the faithful, John says (2 John 8). The final judgment includes God's rewarding his saints (Rev. 11:18). Indeed, the good works of those who die in the Lord follow them after death as they enter the blessed rest of eternity with Christ (Rev. 14:13).

On what basis will rewards be given? All agree that it will be by grace. The parable of the unprofitable servant highlights this (Luke 17:7–10), as does the wider context of the gospel. But there is a nuance to it. In most

---

2. Richard Sorabji, *Time, Creation and the Continuum: Theories in Antiquity and the Early Middle Ages* (Ithaca, NY: Cornell University Press, 1983); Paul Helm, *Eternal God: A Study of God without Time*, 2nd. ed. (New York: Oxford University Press, 2011); R. T. Mullins, *The End of the Timeless God* (Oxford: Oxford University Press, 2016).

passages rewards are connected with works. Judgment itself is to be on the basis of works. That does not mean it is contrary to grace, for all such rewards are at root entirely gracious. We do not earn a reward; the giving is more like a parent's rewarding a child for a first effort at writing.[3]

Lane comments on the difference between extrinsic and intrinsic rewards. A parent may offer a reward for practicing the piano (an extrinsic reward), while the intrinsic reward is learning to play the instrument. This is useful in demonstrating that we readily respond to the possibility of rewards—although in some cases a child might not wish to do so!—and that rewards can be good and valuable as a secondary motivation after love for God and one's neighbor.[4]

What are the rewards in view? We don't know. Perhaps the best clue is in the parable of the talents. In view of the eschatological goal in which Christ rules the new creation in union with his church, a reward may be connected with responsibilities in that task. Since the age to come is defined as being "with the Lord" (1 Thess. 4:17), the reward may lie in closer union and communion with Christ. Either way, it will not cause friction within the redeemed community. Sin will have been eradicated, while the supreme and overwhelming reality will be glorification, in which we will be like the glorified Christ (1 John 3:2). In view of that, none of the members of Christ's body will be lacking.

31.2.2 Two Key Pauline Passages

Two key passages in which rewards are taught are in Paul's Corinthian correspondence.

1 Corinthians 3:8–15. Who and what are in view in 1 Corinthians 3? The Corinthian church is divided into factions, each claiming allegiance to its favorite leader (vv. 1–4). Paul diagnoses this as spiritual immaturity. It is a failure to recognize that preachers are simply human, instruments in the hands of God. Paul planted, Apollos watered, God gave the increase (v. 5–8). Neither Paul nor Apollos, nor Peter, was competent to effect this. The Spirit used their preaching as an instrument and occasion for the church's birth and flourishing. The context refers to Christian preachers and ministers, not to each and every member of the church.

---

3. Anthony N. S. Lane, *Exploring Christian Doctrine* (London: SPCK, 2013), 220.
4. Lane, *Christian Doctrine*, 220.

Paul refers to the foundation of the church, Jesus Christ (v. 11). He has built on that foundation, as will others who follow (vv. 10, 12). These builders may use good materials, such as "gold, silver, precious stones," or inferior, producing shoddy work, akin to "wood, hay, straw" (v. 12). The reality of their respective work will not be known until "the Day," the future day of judgment (v. 13). It will be revealed by fire, which purges away the dross to leave the pure metal. Then the value of the work of each will be revealed. Those whose work stands the test of fire, emerging pure and intact, will receive a reward (v. 14). The nature of the reward is unspecified; elsewhere Paul expects that he will receive a crown of righteousness (2 Tim. 4:7–8), but again we do not know what that is. Conversely, some will "suffer loss," their work burned up, shown to be dross, constructed with inadequate tools or in an unsatisfactory manner (v. 15). They themselves will be saved; the fiery test does not affect their salvation, although that will be by the skin of their teeth, "as by fire." Paul is discussing the judgment of the worth of the work of preachers, not making a blanket statement related to all believers. However, there is an unspecified reward in view.

2 Corinthians 5:10. This statement does apply to all Christians. We all await with deep intensity our heavenly body (2 Cor. 5:1–5). We are courageous in facing death, knowing that while we will be absent from the body, we will simultaneously be "at home with the Lord" (vv. 6–9). In view of this, "we must all appear before the judgment seat of Christ" (v. 10). I referred to this passage in chapter 28.

On what basis does this judgment consist? Paul states that "each one [will] receive what is due for what he has done in the body, whether good or evil." Preachers have rubbed their congregations' consciences raw by insisting that every one of our sins, known and unknown, will be paraded in front of the watching cosmos, to our shame and mortification. As noted earlier, the language of the text will not sustain this notion. First, the verb ἔπραξεν[5] is an aorist and has constative force. It refers to what happens as a whole, as a punctiliar dot rather than a continuous line or series of dots. It means that the judgment will deal with our whole life, rather than every individual thought, word, or deed in isolation. Beyond this, while the subject, ἕκαστος[6] (each one), is masculine singular,

---

5. *epraxen.*
6. *hekastos.*

the object and associated adjectives are neuter, supporting the thought that judgment will be on the basis of general character.[7]

We recall that when the judgment takes place, believers will already have been glorified, being like the glorified Christ. We look with the keenest anticipation for the resurrection; we do not cower in dread. The idea that Paul teaches an everlasting hierarchy in heaven is far from the meaning of the text. Certainly, it places on us the onus to live for Christ here and now; Paul pursues this theme in the following section (vv. 11–14), where he says that "the love of Christ constrains us" (v. 14, my trans.), that is, leaves us with no alternative.

31.3 Aspects of the World to Come

31.3.1 *Absence of Sin and Suffering*

We are called to rest from hard, chafing burdens. This is reflective of God's rest (Gen. 2:1–3), which the Bible represents as never ending (Heb. 4:9) and into which Jesus invites us (Matt. 11:28–30). Jesus's invitation is to an exchange of burdens in which we lay down the heavy and intolerable demands of religious rulers and the searing problems due to sin, and instead take the yoke of discipleship. Since a yoke is shared by a number of oxen, its burden is easy to bear; moreover, Jesus is gentle and lowly of heart.

In Revelation 14:13 the comparison between labor and rest relates to death and resurrection. Those who die in the Lord are blessed from then on, because of the resurrection of Christ. They rest from their labors, the hard drudgery of struggle in a fallen world that is hostile to the faith and antagonistic to Christ. They are truly blessed since the presence of sin and sufferings associated with decay and death are now over.

Sin is committed in the body, whether the sin is bodily or mental, since our embodied existence is the effective vehicle for sin. Death removes the possibility of sinning. At a stroke, we are removed from the sphere in which sinful actions are possible. We will no longer be in a fallen world. The transformation in the resurrection removes us from all vestiges of the curse due to sin. Death's disruption of our existence will be triumphantly overcome.

---

7. Philip Edgcumbe Hughes, *Paul's Second Epistle to the Corinthians: The English Text, with Introduction, Exposition and Notes* (London: Marshall, Morgan & Scott, 1961), 181–82; Victor Paul Furnish, *II Corinthians*, The Anchor Bible (New York: Doubleday, 1984), 276.

31.3.2   *Enhancement and Glorification*

Earlier we considered *theōsis* and how we will be changed to be like the glorified Christ, partakers of the divine nature as fulfilled humans (John 14:16–24; Rom. 8:29; 2 Cor.3:18; 2 Pet. 1:4; 1 John 3:1–2). This at last will reach its eternal apex.

Even now we know that our experience of the world is limited. Thiselton points to the dimensions of this present world that are outside our experience.[8] Animals have ranges of perception that are beyond us—the hearing of dogs, the flight of bats, the navigation of birds that migrate for thousands of miles by using the earth's magnetic field and a variety of other means that scientists have only recently begun to understand.[9]

The nature of Christ's resurrection, insofar as it is revealed in the New Testament, indicates that human powers will be greatly enhanced. He passed through closed doors (Luke 24:36; John 20:19, 26) and knew of Thomas's questions even though he was not physically present at the time the disciple voiced them (John 20:24–29). Since our resurrection shares the characteristics of Christ's, there will be dimensions of human activity that transcend our present experience (1 Cor. 2:7–10). Furthermore, we will be like Christ in glory, transformed, partakers of the divine nature. What this will be we do not know now (1 John 3:2), but "we look for the resurrection of the dead and the life of the world to come."

> I know not, O I know not,
> what joys await us there;
> what radiancy of glory,
> what bliss beyond compare.[10]

31.3.3   *The Renewal of the Cosmos*

Will the new earth mentioned by Peter (2 Pet. 3:13) be the same earth or a different one? Some think it will be entirely new, coming after the present earth is destroyed by fire. This implies that the present world is destined to end, that it has no inherent and lasting value. It seems to me that this is to deny the intrinsic goodness of creation, to posit a dualism

---

8. Anthony C. Thiselton, *The Last Things: A New Approach* (London: SPCK, 2012), 212.
9. See Frederick C. Lincoln, *Migration of Birds*, rev. Steven R. Peterson and John L. Zimmerman (n.p.: U.S. Fish and Wildlife Service, 1998), https://www.csu.edu/cerc/researchreports/documents/MigrationofBirdsCircular.pdf., accessed March 18, 2019.
10. From the twelfth-century hymn "Jerusalem the Golden," by Bernard of Cluny, trans. John M. Neale (1858).

that will undermine the gospel. It is also a highly contestable reading of the passage. The first world, of Noah's day, was destroyed by water; but this did not mean it was wiped out or replaced (2 Pet. 3:5–7). In turn, the destruction by fire described by Peter entails not the end of the present world but rather its renewal. Fire has purifying qualities. Indeed, Peter refers to fire in this way in 1 Peter 1:7–8. Moreover, the fire stored up for the heavens and the earth is for the judgment and destruction—the wrecking—of the ungodly, not the annihilation of the cosmos.[11] Much of the language of the passage is apocalyptic, which is figurative, not literal.

Whatever the eventual reality, the argument for a literal destruction of the cosmos and its replacement by a new one cannot be sustained from a reading of this passage or any other. Rather, the "all things" that will be headed up by Christ (Eph. 1:10) will consist of the very things he created. The universe is currently groaning in agony, like a woman in labor, since it has been subjected to futility on account of sin. Its expectation is the redemption of the church, the manifestation of the children of God. At that time, it will itself experience liberation, entering into the unimaginable outburst of glory that will accompany the return of Christ (Rom. 8:18–23). It is hard to reconcile the liberation of the cosmos with destruction. Rather, its future is dynamic. From our present perspective, unimaginable vistas will open up before us.

31.3.4 *Administering the Renewed Cosmos in Christ*

The author of Hebrews, countering a belief that angels (perhaps led by the archangel Michael) were to be in charge of the messianic kingdom, asserts that this task has been entrusted to the Son (Heb. 2:5–9). He or she[12] cites Psalm 8, which poetically reflects on God's entrusting to humanity the government of the earth. In Hebrews 2:9 the focus shifts from humanity in general, with its failure to subdue the world for God's glory, to Jesus in particular. He has brought human government over the cosmos to expression. He was made a little lower than the angels in the incarnation. He has been crowned with glory and honor following his sufferings and death. It is to him that "the world to come" (v. 5) has been committed. It is to him as the pioneer of our salvation that this is true. This passage

---

11. See Cornelis P. Venema, *The Promise of the Future* (Edinburgh: Banner of Truth, 2000), 465–69.

12. Some think this could have been written by Priscilla—the anonymity might suggest the possibility. The use of a masculine singular pronoun by the author might undermine the suggestion.

dovetails with the author's emphasis on the ascension, Christ entering the presence of the Father as the forerunner on our behalf.

Christ will govern the new creation as man. Of course, the universe was created by the triune God. The indivisible Trinity, the Father, the Son, and the Holy Spirit, govern it. It was God's plan from eternity that the renewal of creation be undertaken in partnership with the redeemed humanity in union with, and under the headship of, Jesus Christ, the Son incarnate (Eph. 1:10). We are united to him in his resurrection and glorification. We will judge the world and angels under his leadership (1 Cor. 6:3). The creation mandate of Genesis 1:26–28 is realized in union with Christ. When Paul writes of Christ handing over the kingdom to the Father (1 Cor. 15:28), he is referring to his mediatorial work, now brought to completion at his parousia. Christ is, of course, indivisibly one with the Father and the Spirit from eternity and in the eternal economy reigns and rules supreme.

31.3.5   *Everlasting Union and Communion with Christ*

Paul brings to its goal the reassurance he gives the Thessalonian church in the face of the deaths of their members by saying that after the resurrection "we will always be with the Lord" (1 Thess. 4:17). This is the crowning blessing, the reward par excellence. "We look for the resurrection of the dead and the life of the world to come," we say when we recite the Niceno-Constantinopolitan Creed. That is the origin of standing in prayer facing the east, for that was the direction of Jerusalem for the Greek-speaking church. Doing so signaled expectancy for the parousia, for the appearance of Christ to claim his church and consummate salvation. Standing indicated readiness—all other things laid aside—being primed for a great journey and transformation, anticipating the arrival of the Lord from heaven.

Even more than everlasting life, viewed in itself, more than the unimaginable quantum leap in experience and responsibility in the renewed cosmos, the supreme blessing of heaven is to be with Christ, not for a time, with a future ending casting a shadow over each moment, but forever. We will be reunited with all other believers, purged from sin, delivered from sufferings, equipped to live and work and unendingly flourish; but the supreme feature will be that we will be together with the glorified Lord.

Thomas Aquinas's reply to an auditory vision he reported as happening at the communion service in the Priory Chapel at Naples sums it up. He heard Christ say to him, "You have written well of me, Thomas. What do you desire as a reward for your labours?" Thomas replied, "Lord, only yourself."[13]

Come, Lord Jesus.

Further Reading

(none)

Study Question

Here language falls short. This is an occasion for awe, worship, thanksgiving, and prayer.

---

13. Aidan Nichols, OP, "St. Thomas Aquinas on the Passion of Christ: A Reading of *Summa Theologiae* IIIa, q.46," *SJT* 43 (1990): 447–59.

Appendix 1

Main Interpretations of Genesis 1

The biblical doctrine of creation is found throughout both the Old and New Testaments and is not confined to the first chapters of Genesis. We recall that each passage of Scripture is to be understood in the light of the whole. Notwithstanding, the descriptions in early Genesis are crucial.

Hermeneutical Considerations

Genesis 1 is a limited account of creation. There is no mention of the creation of angels. The focus is entirely on the immediate context of humanity, on the visible material world, the earth. The rest of the cosmos is only incidental insofar as it relates to the earth.

Moreover, the text is in the language of everyday observation common to all peoples. It was edited in the world of livestock farmers in the ancient Near East. Modern Western concerns must not be imposed on an ancient text, assumptions about which Moses and the original readers knew nothing. Much popular comment on the chapter is anachronistic. Scientific writing as we know it began only in the seventeenth century; it has no bearing on the text of Genesis.

The genre is prose narrative. The persistent use of the *waw* consecutive plus the imperfect is the normal pattern in narrative accounts in the Old Testament; it is neither poetry nor myth. It has a commonality with other Old Testament reportage. Nevertheless, there are two important caveats. First, there are a number of unexpected words—*greater light* and *lesser light*, *expanse* or *firmament*, and so on.[1] The language is not what the reader would expect. Second, there are two clearly poetic elements. The first is the repeated refrain "And there was evening and there was morning, the [first, second, etc.] day." The second and more important poetic element is the parallelism in verse 27:

> So God created man in his own image,
>   in the image of God he created him;
>   male and female he created them.

This, standing in bold relief, highlights prominently the chief purpose of the section, the creation of humanity in the image of God. All is preparation for that great event.

Furthermore, note the overall picture painted by the chapter. The world was created empty, dark, shapeless, and wet (v. 2), unfit for human habitation. Thereafter, God progressively brings about conditions suitable for Adam to live, creating light, forming dry land, shaping and distinguishing the earth, and populating it.[2] God is the primary actor and subject—note the number of times "God" appears in the text.

The seventh day is also a major emphasis. The designation "the seventh day" is repeated threefold within the description of its events, contrary to the other six days. The first five ordinals lack the definite article, the sixth has the article, but the seventh day has the article three times. Moreover, there is no refrain for the seventh day; Scripture elsewhere attests its continuation into eternity (Matt. 11:28–30; Hebrews 3–4; Rev. 14:13). The weight of the passage consequently falls here.

While Genesis 1 is in the language of historical reporting, it is not the same as historical writing. No eyewitnesses were present, nor were there contemporary validated documents. The chapter is revelation; God revealed what would otherwise not be known.

The Twenty-Four-Hour-Day Theory

The theory that creation occurred in six periods of twenty-four hours each, corresponding to solar days, is widely held. Genesis 1 is interpreted literally, the language regarded as that of normal historical observation.

---

1. C. John Collins, *Genesis 1–4: A Linguistic, Literary, and Theological Commentary* (Phillipsburg, NJ: P&R, 2006), 43–44.
2. Gerhard von Rad, *Genesis: A Commentary*, rev. ed. (Philadelphia: Westminster, 1961), 49–63.

The Appeal of the Theory

The interpretation appears to fit the plainest meaning of the language.[3] It is argued that the fourth commandment (Ex. 20:8–11) is based on the assumption that the creation week is a regular workweek. The twenty-four-hour-day theory is clearly a major exegetical possibility. Moreover, the consistent use of the normal Hebrew narrative form presents the passage as a whole, apart from Genesis 1:27 and the refrains, as narrative.

Objections

Several objections to the theory can be identified. First, the word *yom* is used in four different ways in the context: (1) It is repeated at the end of the refrains, relating to the first through sixth days. (2) It means daylight in contrast to darkness (Gen. 1:3–5). (3) It refers to the seventh day (Gen. 2:1–3). This day lacks the refrain that appears at the end of the preceding six days; Hebrews represents the seventh day as still in effect and thus as eternity (Heb. 4:6–10). Murray argues that it comprises the entirety of history after the completion of creation.[4] God's rest is the destiny to which we are invited through Christ. Jesus claims to give this rest (Matt. 11:28–30), thus identifying himself with Yahweh. (4) In Genesis 2:4 *yom* refers to the whole process of creation—"in the day that the LORD God made the earth and the heavens." Consequently, the claim that *yom must* refer to a period of twenty-four hours is weakened and should be decided on other grounds.

Second, the first three days occur before the creation of the sun and moon (Gen. 1:3–13, 14–19). Therefore, the text excludes the possibility that these days are to be understood in relation to the sun, and so they cannot be solar days. This has been recognized since the third century.[5] An existent cannot be defined in relation to a nonexistent, nor can an entity be dependent on a later entity.[6]

---

3. Barth, CD, III/1:99–228, esp. 125, where he says, "According to Gen. 1:5, God has made and given us a day which is not of a thousand years' duration but of twenty-four hours."

4. John Murray, *Principles of Conduct: Aspects of Biblical Ethics* (London: Tyndale Press, 1954), 30–31.

5. Origen, *On First Principles* 4.1.8 (ANF, 4:356).

6. See Aristotle, *Metaphysics* 5.11, in *The Complete Works of Aristotle*, rev. Oxford trans., ed. Jonathan Barnes, vol. 2 (Princeton: Princeton University Press, 1995), 1609; Kit Fine, "Ontological Dependence," *Proceedings of the Aristotelian Society* 95 (1995): 270; cited in Justin J. Daeley, "It Could Not Have Been Otherwise: An Articulation and Defense of Divine Source Compatibilism" (PhD diss., Middlesex University, 2017), 78; Daeley, *Why God Must Do What Is Best: A Philosophical Investigation of Theistic Optimalism* (New York: Bloomsbury Academic, forthcoming).

Third, as a counter to the argument that anything other than the twenty-four-hour-day theory undermines the truth of the creation account, it can be said that an account does not have to be set forth in chronological sequence to be a valid prose narrative. Either Genesis 1 or Genesis 2 comes into this category. If Genesis 1 is taken to be chronologically sequential, the order of creation conflicts with the order in chapter 2. In chapter 1 the order is vegetation (day 3), land animals (day 6), and human male and human female together (day 6). Chapter 2 presents the order as human male, vegetation, land animals, and human female. The most natural construction on this basis—and the twenty-four-hour-day theory asks us to see the passage in this way—is that at least one of these chapters is ordered topically rather than sequentially. A topical arrangement does not of itself undermine historical accuracy; it merely presents the details differently. We have topical arrangements in the Gospels.[7] When I wrote a history of my congregation in Delaware on its centenary in 1996, I began not with its origin but with the pivotal events of the Presbyterian crisis of 1932–1936 and then reverted to earlier days; it was no less historical for that.

Fourth, if with Murray we suppose that God's seventh day represents the entire history of the world subsequent to creation, the argument that the fourth commandment equates the creation days and our week is seriously undermined. Murray distinguishes between the transcendental realm of God's days, of his *opera ad extra*, and our workweek.[8] There is a connection by analogy but not by identity.

Fifth, the argument proceeds on the basis of univocal predication in relation to God's days and ours. This runs counter to language relating to God and eternity being neither *equivocal* (having no connection, breeding agnosticism) nor *univocal* (with an identity between God's knowledge and ours) but *analogical*. This principle was close to the heart of Cornelius Van Til's theology and apologetics.

Sixth, the purpose of the chapter lies elsewhere. We noted the parallelism in Genesis 1:27 with reference to the creation of humanity. This

---

7. Luke is structured by Jesus's ministry in Galilee (chaps. 4–9), his journey to Jerusalem (chaps. 9–19), and his final ministry in Jerusalem (chaps. 20–24), whereas in John, Jesus constantly goes to and from Jerusalem. "Report of the Committee to Study the Views of Creation" (submitted to the seventy-first general assembly of the Orthodox Presbyterian Church, 2004), lines 2473–82, http://opc.org/GA/CreationReport.pdf, accessed December 8, 2016 (hereafter, OPC Report). For a comprehensive and even-handed discussion on this and every aspect of the question, this report is invaluable.
8. Murray, *Principles*, 30–32.

is conjoined with the unique self-deliberation of God when he said, "Let us make man in our image" (Gen. 1:26). The author highlights this point for all to see, setting it off in relief. The creation of man *in* the image of God is the central theme, ultimately pointing to the incarnation of the Son, who *is* the image of God. I argued earlier that all that precedes leads to this.

Seventh, as in the case of any other passage in the Bible, meaning must be sought in connection with the whole of Scripture. Here a dose of caution is needed, as administered by God to Job:

> Where were you when I laid the foundation of the earth?
>> Tell me, if you have understanding.
> Who determined its measurements—surely you know!
>> Or who stretched the line upon it?
> On what were its bases sunk,
>> or who laid its cornerstone,
> when the morning stars sang together
>> and all the sons of God shouted for joy? . . .
>
> Have you commanded the morning since your days began,
>> and caused the dawn to know its place. . . .
>
> Have you entered into the springs of the sea,
>> or walked in the recesses of the deep? . . .
>
> Where is the way to the dwelling of light,
>> and where is the place of darkness,
> that you may take it to its territory
>> and that you may discern the paths to its home?
> You know, for you were born then,
>> and the number of your days is great! (Job 38:4–7, 12, 16, 19–21)

Eighth, if the twenty-four-hour-day theory were correct, it would require a virtual rewriting of human knowledge about the cosmos. From the findings of geology to the speed of light, much would need revision or abandonment. Of course, in the final analysis the Bible as the Word of God trumps all else. However, what is at stake is more the *interpretation* of the Bible in relation to the interpretation of scientific information. We have to balance the respective contributions of general and special revelation. Scientific theories require empirical support and are subject to modification as the evidence requires. By the same token, exegetical theories are also provisional, or else we would elevate our own interpretation to the status of the Word of God. Those who oppose the method by which ancient rocks are dated normally avail themselves of the benefits of modern science when their health is at stake, despite the fact that "it is the same physics that is used to build the machine that screens for breast cancer at a hospital as is used to date a piece of ancient rock from Greenland."[9] Moreover, when oil companies need to drill, they turn to geologists.[10]

Ninth, while advocates of the theory contend that it is *the* traditional view of the chapter, they are wrong. We shall see that Augustine's idea of instantaneous creation held the ground for centuries. Moreover, the world is vastly different than it was in past centuries, so that "present-day adherence to a literal creation week implies a stance towards geology, biology, and science generally that ancient interpreters could not have imagined, still less chosen. . . . In that sense, present-day literalism is a new phenomenon."[11]

Finally, we saw that the account is not history as practiced by historians. No eyewitnesses were present to see these events, nor is there any contemporary documentary evidence. The account is revelation given by God to Moses in a form indicating its historicity but in language decidedly unusual. Collins has pointed out that repeatedly Genesis 1 refers to this or that entity with words not customarily used. He calls the unit "exalted prose narrative."[12] And as noted above, the ordinals of the first five days surprisingly lack the definite article, while the sixth and seventh days have the article. In turn, the phrase "the seventh day" is mentioned three times within the account of the day's events (Gen. 2:2–3), with the article each time, unlike the rest of the narrative. Both

---

9. Denis Alexander and Robert S. White, *Beyond Belief: Science, Faith and Ethical Challenges* (Oxford: Lion Hudson, 2004), 94.

10. "Orthodox geologists have a remarkably successful record of predicting what, on the basis of normal geological theory, is likely to lie a mile below the surface at any given spot. In other words, conventional geology *works*. On the other hand, 'Flood geology' can give no useful guidance at all to oil companies or mineral prospectors. Thus, the experimental facts prove that it is the orthodox geologists, and not the 'Flood geologists,' who are on the right lines." Alan Hayward, *Creation and Evolution: The Facts and Fallacies* (London: SPCK, 1985), 204 (italics original).

11. Andrew J. Brown, *The Days of Creation: A History of Christian Interpretation of Genesis 1:1–2:3* (Blandford Forum: Deo Publishing, 2014), 296.

12. As two examples among many, the phrase "evening and morning" is very unusual; the sun and moon are denoted by "the greater light" and "the lesser light"; see Collins, *Genesis 1–4*, 43–44.

these features imply that the narrative is weighted toward its conclusion, the eschatological fulfillment in Christ, who is the image of God whom Adam prefigures.

In the words of the Orthodox Presbyterian Church's "Report of the Committee to Study the Views of Creation":

> How can one hold that the creation week concluded but the seventh day continues on? The answer to these questions is suggested by the strange use of the definite article prefixed to the ordinals in the creational day codas. The ordinals of days one through five have no definite articles and days six and seven have them. It should be understood that the normal Hebrew idiom requires a definite article on the adjective modifying a noun if the adjective-noun unit is definite (the nth day), but days one through five say "an nth day" in Hebrew. That this is not simply a stylistic peculiarity is established by the introduction of the definite article in the coda of days six and seven. This strange phenomenon sets these two days apart from their fellows. So, the question is, why are the last two days of the week set apart as different? Or, in other words, how are they different than all the other days? If one wanted to mark both of them as the end of a sequence and say that they are concluding days logically (so to say), while presenting the seventh day as a day that is open-ended temporally (but as truly a "day"), this is the way such a goal might be accomplished in Hebrew. Hence, the sixth day is marked as the end of days one through six, and the seventh day is marked as the end of days one through seven. At the same time, the seventh day is called a real day (a period of time in created history) but an open-ended day.[13]

Furthermore, the first day has the progression *darkness, light, darkness*, which entails that it cannot be a solar twenty-four-hour day.

Augustine: Instantaneous Creation[14]

In his *In Genesim ad litteram* (410–415)[15] and later in a section of *De civitate Dei* (417–418), Augustine argues that God created the universe instantaneously.

---

13. OPC Report, lines 1489–1503.
14. The next few paragraphs build on a portion of my article "The Space of Six Days: The Days of Creation from Origen to the Westminster Assembly," *WTJ* 61 (1999): 149–74.
15. This was the second of two works Augustine wrote on Genesis, the first being abandoned, unfinished and retracted. The two are not to be confused.

In *De civitate Dei* he stresses that it is extraordinarily difficult for us to grasp the meaning of Genesis 1. It teaches that God created the world and that it is not eternal.[16] God also created time.[17] As for the days of creation, "it is extremely difficult, or perhaps impossible for us to conceive, and how much more to say!"[18] "Our ordinary days have no evening but by the setting . . . of the sun; but the first three days of all were passed without sun, since it is reported to have been made on the fourth day."[19] As for the light, "it is beyond the reach of our senses; neither can we understand how it was, and yet must unhesitatingly believe it." It either was some material light or signified the holy city. The text never mentions night, only morning and evening. The knowledge of the creature is, in comparison with knowledge of the Creator, mere twilight, while, when the creature returns to the praise and love of the Creator, morning returns. When it does so in the knowledge of itself, that is the first day; when in the knowledge of the firmament or sky, that is the second day, and so on.

The creation days are therefore stages in the creature's knowledge of creation, either in itself or in praise and love of God. Their duration is beyond our knowledge. There is no mention in Genesis of the creation of angels. However, God rested on the seventh day, and before the creation of heaven and earth he seems to have made nothing. Elsewhere, Scripture describes the angels as made by God; therefore they were made at some point during the six days. Job 38:7 says they were made before the stars, and so before the fourth day. They could not have been created on the third or second days, so consequently they were made on the first day. Indubitably, then, they are the "light" called "day," whose unity Scripture recognizes by calling that day "one day."[20] Augustine determines that the second and subsequent days are not different from the "one day"; rather, the same "one day" is repeated so as to complete the number six or seven. The angels were created as sharers of the eternal light, the only-begotten Son of God, so that they might become light and be called day.

These themes Augustine developed at greater length in his earlier work *In Genesim ad litteram*.[21] Augustine was influenced by number the-

---

16. Augustine, *City of God* 11.4 (*PL*, 41:319–20). For an English translation, see NPNF[1], 2:206–7.

17. Augustine, *City of God* 11.5 (*PL*, 41:320–21; NPNF[1], 2:207–8).

18. Augustine, *City of God* 11.6 (*PL*, 41:321–22; NPNF[1], 2:208).

19. Augustine, *City of God* 11.7 (*PL*, 41:322–23; NPNF[1], 2:208–9).

20. Augustine, *City of God* 11.9 (*PL*, 41:323–25; NPNF[1], 2:209–10).

21. *PL*, 34:246–486. For an English translation, see Augustine, *St. Augustine: The Literal Meaning of Genesis*, trans. John Hammond Taylor, 2 vols., Ancient Christian Writers 41–42 (New York: Paulist, 1982); hereafter, *LMG*.

ory as expounded by Nicomachus of Gerasa. Augustine was fascinated that God arranged creation into six days, six being a perfect number, the sum of its parts, and the smallest of such numbers. It has three parts, which, when added together, make six. God, therefore, accomplished the works of his creation in a perfect number of days. Even more intriguing is that creation is ordered like the number six, which rises in three steps from the three parts. On the first day, light was created. On the two following days, the universe was created in its higher and lower parts. On the remaining three days the remainder of the universe was created. This supports the words of Scripture "You have ordered all things in measure, number, and weight."[22] The number six is not perfect because God creates in six days, but rather God created in six days because the number six is perfect![23] After six days, God rested from creating new things and now governs what he made.[24]

Augustine considers the nature of the six days. The seven days of our experience follow sequentially. However, those first six days occurred

> in a form unfamiliar to us as intrinsic principles within things created. Hence evening and morning, like light and darkness, that is, day and night, did not produce the changes that they do for us with the motion of the sun. This we are clearly forced to admit with regard to the first three days, which are recorded and numbered before the creation of the heavenly bodies.[25]

God finished the works of creation at the conclusion of the sixth day, so it is not clear when he created the seventh day, for on that day he rested from all that he had made. In fact, he did not create it. But how could he have rested on a day he did not create? Augustine finds the solution in God having created only one day, which recurred seven times. So it was unnecessary for God to create the seventh day, for it was the seventh recurrence of the one day he had created.[26] How God seven times made present the light he had made on the first day is beyond our experience. It relates to the spiritual dimension

---

22. *PL*, 34:295–97; *LMG*, 1:103–5.
23. "Sed senarius Deum sex diebus perfecisse opera sua, quia senarius numerus perfectus est." *PL*, 34:301; *LMG*, 1:112.
24. *PL*, 34:303–5; *LMG*, 1:116–18.
25. *PL*, 34:308–9; *LMG*, 1:124–25.
26. *PL*, 34:310–11, 321–22; *LMG*, 1:127–28, 146–48.

of creation. Morning and evening are the knowledge of the angels, knowing the creation in itself (evening) and in the light of the Word of God (morning).[27]

So all creation was finished by the sixfold recurrence of the day whose evening and morning consists in angelic knowledge. The angels knew the things created in God, in whom they were made, and in themselves as they were actually made. Thus, the day God made recurs not by a material passage of time but by spiritual knowledge.

> Thus, in all the days of creation there is one day, and it is not to be taken in the sense of our day, which we reckon by the course of the sun; but it must have another meaning, applicable to the three days mentioned before the creation of the heavenly bodies. This special meaning of "day" must not be maintained just for the first three days, with the understanding that after the third day we take the word "day" in its ordinary sense. But we must keep the same meaning even to the sixth and seventh days. Hence, "day" and "night," which God divided, must be interpreted quite differently from the familiar "day" and "night," which God decreed the lights that he created in the firmament should divide. . . . For it was by the latter act that he created our day, creating the sun whose presence makes the day. But that other day which he originally made had already repeated itself three times when, at its fourth occurrence, these lights of the firmament were created.[28]

These days "are beyond the experience and knowledge of us mortal earthbound men." Moreover, if we want to understand this, "we ought not to rush forward with an ill-considered opinion, as if no other reasonable and plausible interpretation could be offered." Our terrestrial days indeed recall the days of creation "but without in any way being really similar to them."[29] Augustine denies that this is a figurative or allegorical interpretation. Material light is not literally "light," and the light to which Genesis refers is only metaphorical. This latter light is more excellent and truer than the material light we know. Yet Augustine does not advance his interpretation dogmatically.[30]

---

27. *PL*, 34:311–13; *LMG*, 1:128–32.
28. *PL*, 34:314; *LMG*, 1:134.
29. ". . . in hac nostra mortalitate terrena experiri ac sentiri non possumus"; "non debemus temerarium praecipitare sententiam, tanquam de his aliud sentiri congruentius probabiliuque non possit."; ". . . ut non eos illis similes." *PL*, 34:314, 322; *LMG*, 1:135, 148.
30. *PL*, 34:314–15; *LMG*, 1:135–36.

In reflecting on the ability of the angelic mind to grasp things simultaneously, he asks whether all things were made simultaneously or were created at different times and on different days. He favors the first alternative, for if creation took place over a process of time, plants and vegetation would have required many days to germinate beneath the ground and could not have sprung forth in one day. Moreover, while Scripture says God created in six days, it is also written that he created all things together (Ecclus. 18:1). He created all things simultaneously and also created this one day, repeated six more times. These six days are listed in order so as to teach those who cannot understand simultaneous creation, God accommodating himself to weaker intellects, presenting creation as if it were a process.[31] Augustine refers to the rising of the sun to show that our vision crosses the distance between us and the sun instantly, while passing through the intervening space in an orderly progression.[32] Thus, the days of creation teach not a temporal succession but a causal connection.[33]

Popularity of the Interpretation

Augustine's view became the majority opinion for roughly a millennium. Anselm, writing in *Cur Deus homo?* in 1098, considered the most obvious meaning of the Genesis days to be sequential but also recognized the possibility of instantaneous creation.[34] In discussing whether the total of the elect will exceed the number of the fallen angels, he says, "This is possible, even if man was not created at the same time as the angels, and it seems necessary *if they were created together—as the majority think.*"[35] Augustine's exegesis is supported by the majority nearly seven hundred years after he advanced it.

Later, Aquinas argued that it cannot be proved philosophically whether or not the world had a beginning. God could have created either way. That it had a beginning is an article of faith, because of what the Bible says.[36] Yet "it is manifest that creation is instantaneous."[37] However, he

---

31. *PL*, 34:317–18, 322–23; *LMG*, 1:141–42, 149.
32. *PL*, 34:319–20; *LMG*, 1:143–45.
33. *PL*, 34:325–26; *LMG*, 1:154.
34. Eugene R. Fairweather, *A Scholastic Miscellany: Anselm to Ockham* (New York: Macmillan, 1970), 127.
35. Fairweather, *A Scholastic Miscellany*, 128 (my italics).
36. Aquinas, *ST* 1a.46.
37. Aquinas, *ST* 1a.63.5.

discusses other interpretations besides Augustine's.[38] Elsewhere Aquinas distinguishes between those aspects of the doctrine of creation that are crucial to the faith and those on which differences of opinion may exist:

> What pertains to faith is distinguished in two ways, For some are as such of the substance of faith, such that God is three and one, and the like, about which no one may licitly think otherwise. . . . Other things are only incidental to faith insofar as they are treated in Scripture. . . . On such matters even the saints disagree, explaining Scripture in different ways. Thus with respect to the beginning of the world something pertains to the substance of faith, namely that the world began to be by creation, and all the saints agree on this.
>
> But how and in what order this was done pertains to faith only incidentally insofar as it is treated in scripture, the truth of which the saints save in the different explanations they offer. For Augustine holds that at the very beginning of creation there were some things specifically distinct in their proper nature, such as the elements, celestial bodies, and spiritual substances, but others existed in seminal notions alone, such as animals, plants, and men, all of which were produced in their proper nature in that work that God governs after it was constituted in the work of the six days. . . . With respect to the distinction of things we ought to attend to the order of nature and doctrine, not to the order of time.
>
> As to nature . . . things which are naturally prior are mentioned first. . . . But in the order of teaching, as is evident in those teaching geometry, although the parts of the figure make up the figure without any order of time, still the geometer teaches the constitution as coming to be by the extension of line from line. . . . So too Moses, instructing an uncultivated people on the creation of the world, divides into parts what was done simultaneously.
>
> Ambrose, however, and other saints hold the order of time is saved in the distinction of things. This is the more common opinion and superficially seems more consonant with the text, but the first is more reasonable and better protects Sacred Scripture from the derision of infidels, which Augustine teaches in his literal interpreta-

---

38. Aquinas, *ST* 1a.68.1–69.1. Thus, in *ST* 1a.68.1: "If, however, we take these days to denote merely sequence in the natural order, as Augustine holds (*Gen. ad lit*. iv. 22, 24), and not succession in time . . ." In *ST* 1a.68.2 Thomas discusses a range of interpretations of each of the days. In *ST* 1a.69.1 he points out that Augustine holds that there is no temporal order in the works described in Genesis 1, but an order of origin and nature, while, according to others, there is a temporal order. Thomas's argument develops by comparing Augustine's interpretation with the more literal one of Basil and Ambrose without casting pejorative aspersions upon either.

tion of Genesis is especially to be considered . . . and this opinion is more pleasing to me. However, the arguments sustaining both will be responded to.[39]

Weaknesses of Augustine's Interpretation

Augustine's theory is speculative. There is nothing on angels in Genesis 1, apart from the elusive comment that "in the beginning, God created the heavens." It is better to follow Calvin's advice in this whole matter— where God leaves off teaching, we remain silent. The interpretation may also indicate a negative view toward time, as Gunton has suggested.[40]

The Restitution (Gap) Theory

According to Bavinck the restitution theory originated with the Remonstrants.[41] It was revived in 1856 by Thomas Chalmers,[42] advanced by G. H. Pember,[43] and popularized by the Scofield Reference Bible.[44] In its revived form, the theory was largely a response to evolutionary ideas and to scientific arguments that the earth was many millions of years old. It proposed that Genesis 1:1 refers to creation. Since the creation and fall of the angels are not considered in Genesis 1, the theory argued that these untold events occurred between verse 1 and verse 2—"the earth was without form and void, and darkness was over the face of the deep"—which was seen as the judgment of God on the fallen angels. Vast geological ages could be fit in the gap between verses 1 and 2. At a stroke, the findings of nineteenth-century science could be accommodated, and the biblical doctrine of creation preserved. What follows from verse 3 refers to the restitution of the earth following the judgment on the fallen angels.

Linguistic Objections

The Achilles' heel of the theory is that verse 2 requires a passive tense, the *niphal*, so as to read, "The earth became formless and void." In fact,

39. Aquinas, "The Work of the Six Days of Creation," in *Commentary on Peter Lombard*, sentences 2.2, d.12, in *Thomas Aquinas: Selected Writings*, ed. Ralph McInerny (London: Penguin, 1998), 91–92.
40. Colin Gunton, *The Triune Creator* (Grand Rapids, MI: Eerdmans, 1998), 80–96.
41. Herman Bavinck, *In the Beginning: Foundations of Creation Theology*, ed. John Bolt, trans. John Vriend (Grand Rapids, MI: Baker, 1999), 114–18.
42. OPC Report, lines 473–75.
43. G. H. Pember, *Earth's Earliest Ages: And Their Connection with Modern Spiritualism and Theology*, 14th ed. (1876; repr., London: Pickering & Inglis, n.d.).
44. *Scofield Reference Bible* (n.p., n.d. [ca. 1917]), 3n3.

the text has the *qal*, an active tense, and so correctly reads, "The earth was formless and void." The theory fails exegetically. Moreover, it is an attempt to do two things, neither of which is tenable. It was devised to accommodate contemporary science, ignoring that Genesis was written millennia beforehand. Moreover, in addressing the history of the angels, it claimed to know more than God revealed.

The Day-Age Theory

Another attempt to harmonize Genesis with scientific theories holds that the six days are creative periods parallel to geological ages. The theory emerged in the eighteenth century under the impetus of believing geologists and was advanced in the 1830s in Scotland by Hugh Miller.[45] Charles Hodge, A. A. Hodge, and J. Gresham Machen held to this position.[46]

Its Main Problems

As with the restitution theory, the premise on which the day-age theory is built—relating the days of creation to geological ages—is suspect, and the attempt to achieve its goal failed. Moreover, significant exegetical issues arose. Adherence to this interpretation has declined in recent decades.[47]

The Synthesis Theory

Given the failure of the day-age theory, a synthesis theory attempted to combine the twenty-four-hour-day theory with long geological ages intervening. The six days are bursts of God's creative activity punctuating lengthy ages in the earth's history, between which the vast cosmic process unfolds.

Its Weaknesses

The weaknesses of this theory are identical to those of the day-age theory; its self-conscious adaptation to scientific developments fails. Moreover, it rests on speculation.

---

45. Bavinck, *In the Beginning*, 114–18.
46. Charles Hodge, *Systematic Theology* (Grand Rapids, MI: Eerdmans, 1977), 1:570–71; J. Gresham Machen, *The Christian View of Man* (New York: Macmillan, 1937), 115.
47. For a fuller discussion, see the OPC Report, lines 1619–834.

Days of Unspecified Length

Another theory holds that Genesis 1 is a sequential, historical account of creation but that there is insufficient evidence to determine the length of the creation days. While God could certainly either have created in six twenty-four-hour days or have created instantaneously if he had determined to do so, the text—so it is claimed—does not provide us with this information. Among the exponents of this position are W. H. Green, B. B. Warfield, Herman Bavinck, and Edward J. Young.[48]

Young considered the days to be of indeterminate lengths and the age of the universe to be unknown. He concluded that "the length of the days is not stated. What is important is that each of the days is a period of time which may legitimately be denominated *yom* ('day')." Additionally, he believed that "the first three days were not solar days such as we now have, inasmuch as the sun, moon, and stars had not yet been made."[49] In his "Uncle Joe" letters, written in 1946 as from an uncle to a nephew about to go to college, he writes:

> As we have seen before, the Bible does not say how old the earth is. The fossils also, despite claims to the contrary, do not tell how old the earth is, nor do they declare how long man has existed upon the earth, nor do they show that, the earth existed for millions of years before man appeared upon it. Such claims cannot be proved. Since, therefore, history shows that civilization has existed for but a few thousand years, is it not wiser to conclude that, as far as we know, man has not been upon the earth for more than a few thousand years? How long the earth existed before man appeared upon it, we do not know. It may have existed for millions of years; it may not. The Bible does not say. The days which existed before the creation of man may very possibly represent long periods of time. In fact, I am inclined to think that they do represent such long periods.[50]

Shortly before he died in 1968, Young stated in a lecture, subsequently published, "One matter that Christians like to talk about is the length of these days. It is not too profitable to do so, for the simple reason that God has not revealed sufficient for us to say very much about it."[51]

---

48. OPC Report, lines 1171–213.
49. Edward J. Young, *Studies in Genesis One* (Nutley, NJ: Presbyterian and Reformed, 1975), 104.
50. Edward J. Young, *Presbyterian Guardian*, May 10, 1946, 139.
51. Edward J. Young, *In the Beginning* (Carlisle, PA: Banner of Truth, 1976), 43.

The Framework Theory

The framework theory posits six revelatory scenes in parallel. It is commonly thought to have emerged in the twentieth century, propounded by A. Noordtzij, N. H. Ridderbos, Meredith Kline, and others.[52] However, there are clear antecedents in the thirteenth century, with Robert Grosseteste (writing 1230–1235)[53] and Thomas Aquinas.[54] I will consider the older interpretation first.

Grosseteste and Aquinas both argue that the Genesis 1 account is to be understood in terms of creation (v. 1), distinction (days 1–3), and adornment (days 4–6). Grosseteste, within this paradigm, adopts a pluralistic interpretation, a masterly synthesis of the major alternative views that were canvassed in previous exegesis.[55]

Aquinas, in his *Summa theologia*, considers Genesis 1 to convey a threefold division. First is *the work of creation* (v. 1); in this the heaven and the earth were produced, but without form. The first three days concern *the work of distinction*, in which the parts of creation are distinguished from one another—the heavens (day 1), water (day 2), and the earth (day 3). Heaven and earth are perfected as God gives them form or grants the intrinsic order and beauty due them. The final three days are devoted to *the work of adornment*, in which various entities are made to inhabit the distinguished parts of heaven and earth. On day 4 lights are created to adorn the heavens. On day 5 birds and fish are made to beautify the intermediate element. On day 6 animals are brought forth to live on the earth.[56]

The first part, then, is distinguished on the first day and adorned on the fourth, the middle part distinguished on the middle day and adorned on the fifth, and the third part distinguished on the third day and adorned on the sixth.[57]

---

52. A. Noordtzij, *Gods Woord en der Eeuwen Getuigenis: Het Oude Testament in het Licht der Oostersche Opgravingen* (Kampen, 1924), cited by Young, *Genesis One*, 44; N. H. Ridderbos, *Is There a Conflict between Genesis 1 and Natural Science?* (Grand Rapids, MI: Eerdmans, 1957); Meredith G. Kline. "Because It Had Not Rained," *WTJ* 20 (1958): 146–57; Henri Blocher, *In the Beginning: The Opening Chapters of Genesis* (Downers Grove IL: InterVarsity Press, 1984).

53. Robert Grosseteste, *On the Six Days of Creation: Translation of the Hexaëmeron*, trans. C. F. J. Martin, Auctores Britannici Medii Aevi (Oxford: Oxford University Press for the British Academy, 1996).

54. Aquinas, *ST* 1a.66–74.

55. Grosseteste, *Six Days of Creation*. See Letham, "The Space of Six Days"; Brown, *Days of Creation*, 82–85.

56. Aquinas, *ST* 1a.70.1.

57. Aquinas, *ST* 1a.74.1.

Aquinas, like Grosseteste, finds no incompatibility with Augustine's position,[58] for the works of creation and adornment might take place within a day, while the creation itself could be simultaneous. On whether the days were one day repeated seven times, as Augustine taught but others denied, arguing that there were seven distinct days, Aquinas holds that the difference is more apparent than real, but he appears to support an order and sequence.[59] God created all things together (Ecclus. 18:1), with distinction and adornment following.[60] Both Grosseteste and Aquinas allow for a sequential presentation but do not *demand* that it be applied strictly.

In the modern development of the framework theory, day 1 is paralleled by day 4, day 2 by day 5, and day 3 by day 6. The first triad consists of particular spheres of creation (light on day 1, sky and seas on day 2, dry land and vegetation on day 3), while days 4–6 refer to the created rulers of those spheres (sun and moon, fish and birds, land animals and humans respectively).

Temporal recapitulation exists between the two triads, similar to what is found in Genesis 2. There the man is placed in the garden in verse 8, only to be placed in the garden again in verse 15. The simplest solution is that the reference to the garden in verse 8a is developed in verses 9–14, while verse 8b is developed beginning in verse 15. Narrative does not require chronologically sequential presentation. However, the overall thrust of the modern framework theory is that the account as a whole is primarily figurative. It may not do justice to the narrative.

This theory must not be dismissed as an overt attempt to adapt the Bible to modern science, for it takes seriously the text of Genesis and the structure of the passage. Indeed, since this is the controlling element, criticism of the theory should proceed on that basis. In this case, its weakness is that the proposed parallel arrangement is not watertight. On its own basis, a chronological sequence is present. Day 4 must follow day 1, day 5 must follow day 2, and day 6 must follow day 3. Moreover, days 4–6 must follow days 1–3. Furthermore, the sun, moon, and stars are created on day 5 but placed in the firmament, which is made on day 2. The fish are created on day 5 but the seas were not formed until day 3. Again, man rules not merely the dry land of day 3 but the whole earth.

---

58. Aquinas, *ST* 1a.70.1, 1a.74.1.
59. Aquinas, *ST* 1a.74.2.
60. Grosseteste, *Six Days of Creation*, 82–85 (II:5).

The Analogical Theory

W. G. T. Shedd, Herman Bavinck, Jack Collins, and W. Robert Godfrey[61] advocate versions of the analogical theory. This theory claims that the length of days is not specified. It argues that the creation account is analogous to God's activity, on the principle of analogy—established from the Patristic period—that is basic to human knowledge of God. Our days reflect God's workdays, not vice versa. In support, the language of the passage is highly unusual, indicating that the creation week is quite *unlike* our week.[62] The account is held to be broadly consecutive, but Genesis 1:1–2 describes an indeterminate period before the creation week, the length of which is irrelevant. In the creation week itself, God's workweek is the pattern and basis for our own workweek.

The theory is compatible with several of the previous positions, although not tied to any one of them. To quote again the Orthodox Presbyterian Church's "Report of the Committee to Study the Views of Creation":

> As suggested earlier, the Analogical Day view claims that the literary structure of Genesis 1 provides a stylized narrative similar to the one found in Judges 2:11–23. Likewise, Luke structures his gospel around a threefold geographical pattern: Jesus' ministry in Galilee (chh. 4–9), the road to Jerusalem (chh. 9–19) and his ministry in Jerusalem (chh. 19–24), while John has Jesus constantly going back and forth to Jerusalem. If we only had one gospel we might not notice the importance of the literary structure. But the literary structure of the gospels does not eliminate the historical character of Jesus' life and ministry any more than the literary structure of Genesis 1 eliminates the historical character of the creative acts of God. The days of Genesis 1 happened in space and time. They refer to the six periods of God's creative work. The Analogical view rejects the idea of instantaneous creation, and affirms with Bavinck that God "resumed and renewed" his labor six times.[63]

Murray argues that the seventh day represents God's eternal rest and so provides an analogical contrast between the days of God's work,

---

61. W. G. T. Shedd, *Dogmatic Theology* (Grand Rapids, MI: Zondervan, 1971), 1:474–77; Bavinck, *In the Beginning*, 120–26; W. Robert Godfrey, *God's Pattern for Creation: A Covenantal Reading of Genesis 1* (Phillipsburg, NJ: P&R, 2003); Collins, *Genesis 1–4*, 124–25.

62. Collins, *Genesis 1–4*, 43–44.

63. OPC Report, lines 2473–81. See also Bavinck, *In the Beginning*, 126.

which are transcendental, and our workweek.[64] He refers the seventh day to the entire history of the universe subsequent to the completion of creation.[65] Murray throughout contrasts "the sphere of God's action" with "*our* weekly cycle" (Murray's italics). Thus, the seventh day in Genesis 2:2 is "unquestionably the seventh day in sequence with the six days of creative activity, the seventh day in the sphere of God's action, not the seventh day in *our* weekly cycle. In the realm of God's activity in creating the heavens and the earth there were six days of creative action and one day of rest." Murray draws his conclusions: "There is the strongest presumption in favour of the interpretation that this seventh day is not one that terminated at a certain point in history, but that the whole period of time subsequent to the end of the sixth day is the sabbath rest alluded to in Genesis 2:2." Consequently, "it is in accord with this emphasis to regard the seventh day of rest as comprising all of history that is not comprised in the six days. The considerations supporting this view may be regarded as conclusive."[66] On Exodus 20:8–11, Murray agrees that God's Sabbath rest is the reason given for our Sabbath rest. But here again he stresses a difference between our weekly cycle and God's sphere of operation: "In the transcendent realm of God's *opera ad extra*, on the grand plan of his creative action" he rested on the seventh day.[67]

Athanasius: Creation in Christ

Athanasius based his comments about creation on the biblical teaching regarding the involvement of the Son. Weinandy remarks that this discloses "a unique and multifaceted relationship between 'the Word' and creation."[68] Athanasius points to the Father having created through the Word, so that the Word sustains an unbreakable relationship to the creation, the Father governing everything through the Word. The Word "is an unchanging image of his own Father," ordering all things and holding them together. The Father guides and settles creation by his own Word, who is himself God, so that by the governing and ordering action of the Word, creation may continue securely: "It shares [partakes] in the Word who is truly from the Father, and [the creation] is helped by

---

64. Murray, *Principles*, 30.
65. Murray, *Principles*, 30–31.
66. Murray, *Principles*, 30.
67. Murray, *Principles*, 32.
68. Thomas G. Weinandy, *Athanasius: A Theological Introduction* (Aldershot: Ashgate, 2007), 22.

him to exist."[69] The Word is present in all things and extends his power everywhere, "continuing and enclosing them in himself."[70]

Athanasius's interpretation of Genesis 1 is directed by this foundational theme. In a classic passage at the start of *De incarnatione*, he writes:

> We will begin, then, with the creation of the world and with God its Maker, for the first fact that you must grasp is this: *the renewal of creation has been wrought by the self-same Word who made it in the beginning.* There is thus no inconsistency between creation and salvation; for the one Father has employed the same agent for both works, effecting the salvation of the world through the same Word who made it at first.[71]

In this the Father made human beings after his own image, "giving them a portion even of the power of his own Word; so that [they have] as it were a kind of reflexion of the Word . . . being made rational."[72] Hence, the Son, as the original agent in creation and in redemption, "conjoins protology and soteriology and, ultimately, eschatology."[73] Leithart observes that, for Athanasius, "the creation is 'enfolded' in the Father-Son relation, the common object of their delight . . . because the world bears the imprint of the Son."[74] So the Son is "the pattern and 'archetype' of creation. There is a logic, a rationality, to the creation, and that rationality is the work of the Word and the impress of the Word on the creation. The Father loves the world because it is made in the image of his image, the Son."[75] Athanasius has a literal view of the days of creation,[76] but his main emphasis is that all parts of creation are limited—the sun only shines during the day—but all find their unity in Christ.[77] Indeed, the Son is like a king who imprints his name on every building in a new city.[78] This is why the creation reveals the Son, for the Son is its Creator.

---

69. Athanasius, *Contra Gentes* 41 (NPNF[2], 4:26; PG, 25:81, 84; my trans.).
70. Athanasius, *Contra Gentes* 42 (NPNF[2], 4:26; PG, 25:84; my trans.).
71. Athanasius, *On the Incarnation* 1.4, in Athanasius, *On the Incarnation: The Treatise De Incarnatione Verbi Dei*, trans. Sister Penelope Lawson (New York: Macmillan, 1946), 4 (italics original to the translation) (cf. NPNF[2], 4:36).
72. Athanasius, *Incarnation* 3.3 (NPNF[2], 4:37).
73. Weinandy, *Athanasius*, 28.
74. Peter J. Leithart, *Athanasius* (Grand Rapids, MI: Baker Academic, 2011), 91.
75. Leithart, *Athanasius*, 92.
76. Athanasius, *Against the Arians* 2.19 (NPNF[2], 4:358).
77. Athanasius, *Against the Arians* 2.28 (NPNF[2], 4:362). See Leithart, *Athanasius*, 95.
78. Athanasius, *Against the Arians* 2.79 (NPNF[2], 4:391).

Summary

Expositions like those of Athanasius place disputes over the meaning of words in their proper context. Much contemporary discussion in conservative circles misses the wood for the trees. Genesis 1, and behind it the creation itself, is a "theatre of God's glory" made and fashioned by the Trinity, with Christ its Mediator. Genesis 1 has been debated more than any other passage of literature. We need to cultivate an attitude of humility before the sheer mystery of creation. Job 38 should point us in that direction.

We have no need to accept current scientific theories uncritically, prone as they are to revision at some future point. The closer the commitment to current paradigms, the greater the danger when they are jettisoned or relativized. Notwithstanding, we need to be cautious about our exegetical theories when the evidence may not be as clear cut as we might suppose, and weaknesses are present in all of them. Here we face the great danger of identifying our own understanding with the truth of God. Scientific theories are at root provisional, liable to be improved or abandoned by further evidence; so it is with biblical exegesis. As the WCF puts it, "All things in Scripture are not alike plain in themselves" (WCF, 1.7). This does not mean we cannot ever have certainty; rather, it indicates the need for humility. Sometimes the observations of science can help inform our biblical exegesis; we learn about gravity from empirical observation and scientific theory, not from the letters of Paul. However, science itself is shaped by the presuppositions of its practitioners. The Christian doctrine of creation ex nihilo had a profound effect on science; it is hard to imagine how further developments can long continue in a world in which objective truth claims are ruled invalid. In short, as Calvin put it, "when God makes an end of teaching, we should make an end of trying to be wise."[79]

The Debates at the Westminster Assembly

The Westminster Assembly minutes do not record any debate on the creation days. This was despite the divines' awareness of the variegated history of interpretation.[80] These were men who cited the fathers and medievals widely. This absence of interest was despite the scientific ferment caused by

---

79. Calvin, *Institutes*, 3.21.3.
80. See Letham, "The Space of Six Days."

Copernicus. Indeed, the Assembly members, and the English Puritans in general, showed surprisingly little interest in creation or in Genesis 1. They published few commentaries on Genesis or dedicated works on creation.[81]

Here it is important to understand the nature of confessions and the Assembly's own position on them, which was highly traditional. Many matters were held to be true but not thought to be matters to put in a confession of faith. Thus, a proposal that the WCF should refer to the Sabbath as "consisting of twenty-four hours" was rejected; the Assembly had this possibility for the creation days at its disposal but did not use it.[82] Moreover, not all that went into the confession and catechisms was thought to be equally significant or to be considered binding on the ministry. Its task, among other things, was to unify the church in the three kingdoms, not to divide it. Precision in the exegesis of particular biblical passages was never a matter for a confession, then or before; this was not even up for discussion.[83]

Carl Trueman, referring to the impact of recent historiography on our understanding of classic Reformed theology and its confessions, notes:

> It highlights how important the consensus nature of confessions was in the sixteenth and seventeenth centuries. The process of producing confessions was complex and not uniform. Some were written by individuals and later adopted by churches (for example, the Belgic Confession); others were in origin committee productions always intended as ecclesiastical documents. What the new approach has done is demonstrate that, with the confessional Reformed world, there was always a certain amount of legitimate diversity on many topics. Thus, matters such as the distinction between infra- and supralapsarianism are not matters on which the confessions take hard and fast positions; and even where they have distinct preferences, historically these were not issues of ecclesiastical division.[84]

Furthermore, no other major Reformed confession of the sixteenth and seventeenth centuries comments on the days of creation. Since the di-

---

81. Robert Letham, *The Westminster Assembly: Reading Its Theology in Historical Context* (Phillipsburg, NJ: P&R, 2009), 190–92.

82. OPC Report, lines 2639–52. I understand that this section of the report was the work of Alan Strange.

83. Chad Van Dixhoorn, "Reforming the Reformation: Theological Debate at the Westminster Assembly 1643–1652," 7 vols. (PhD diss., Cambridge University, 2004); Letham, *Westminster Assembly*, 47–119; John V. Fesko, *The Theology of the Westminster Standards: Historical Context and Theological Insights* (Wheaton, IL: Crossway, 2014), passim.

84. Carl Trueman, "The Revised Historiography of Reformed Orthodoxy: A Few Practical Implications," *Ordained Servant Online*, October 2012, http://www.opc.org/os.html?article_id=325.

vines were anxious to be in alignment with the Continental Reformed churches, this is decisive in interpreting its statements.[85]

In appraising past confessional statements, it is vital to appreciate their historical contexts. A simple, straightforward reading may easily be misjudged. An important insight of Quentin Skinner is that we need to know what the authors were *doing*, what effect they expected to achieve.[86] In this light, many scholars consider the comment in the WCF that creation took place "within the space of six days" to be a refutation of Augustine. There are two clear precedents for the phrase "within the space of six days," by Calvin and by William Ames; both explicitly refute Augustine.[87]

The report on creation written for the Orthodox Presbyterian Church makes the following comment:

> The Westminster Standards were written, as were all of the Reformation confessions, as consensus documents, and the Divines often expressed themselves in language that could be understood in different legitimate senses. In his groundbreaking study of Reformed scholasticism, historian Richard Muller emphasizes that confessions have a two-fold function: they establish both unity in the faith and diversity in the faith. Confessions are not designed to solve all theological disputes; instead, they are intentionally crafted to leave some questions unanswered. Rightly understood, Confessions encourage theological creativity by establishing the conditions under which exegetical and theological investigation can take place. With respect to the phrase, "in the space of six days," even if one grants that the Divines meant ordinary days by that expression, it does not necessarily follow that they intended to restrict the meaning of that phrase in that way. And even if they intended such a restriction, they did not indicate such an intention explicitly in the language that they used.[88]

The Slippery Slope Fallacy

A popular argument in some circles says that not maintaining the twenty-four-hour-day theory will result in doctrinal decline. This argument is

---

85. Letham, *Westminster Assembly*, 84–98.
86. Quentin Skinner, "Meaning and Understanding in the History of Ideas," in *Visions of Politics*, vol. 1, *On Method* (Cambridge: Cambridge University Press, 2002), 57–89.
87. Calvin, *Genesis*, in Calvin, CO, 23:18; William Ames, *The Marrow of Theology* (Franeker, 1633), sec. 28.
88. OPC Report, lines 185–95. I understand that this section of the report was written by John Muether and Alan Strange.

untenable. Many who take this line regard Hodge, Warfield, and the Princetonians as weak on the matter. Yet these were the staunchest opponents of theological liberalism. In the 1920s it was J. Gresham Machen—who refused to become embroiled in the Scopes trial on behalf of the conservative side in opposition to evolution, and who personally favored the day-age theory—who was the champion of orthodoxy against liberalism.[89] He and others like him imposed no commitment to a particular interpretation of Genesis 1, since they were confessional, and the confession was always held to permit liberty of biblical exegesis within the bounds of its theological parameters. Machen and the then faculty of Westminster Theological Seminary, who made no such commitments, were the bulwark against classic liberalism in the United States. On the other hand, adherence to the twenty-four-hour-day theory is no guarantee of orthodoxy. One of the staunchest exponents of the theory was John Biddle, the foremost early English Socinian.[90]

The exegesis of Genesis 1 is far from cut and dried. No proposal on the chapter is free from problems. It is true that some interpretations have been devised expressly with a view to seeking an accommodation with Darwinian evolution or with geology. However, the twenty-four-hour-day theory, while having a pedigree throughout the history of the church, was by no means the only one in the field.

---

89. Machen, *Christian View of Man*, 131. H. L. Mencken, an acerbic skeptic and the leading journalist of the time, wrote that Machen was to William Jennings Bryan as the Matterhorn is to a wart.

90. John Biddle, *A Twofold Catechism* (London: J. Cottrel for Ri. Moore, 1654), 22.

Appendix 2

Historic Creeds

Ecumenical Creeds

Ecumenical creeds are statements that came from what the Greek and Eastern churches regard as the seven ecumenical councils. These councils were ecumenical in the sense that, while they were overwhelmingly composed of bishops from the East, they received approval from Rome as well, and thus had the support of the whole undivided church.

The Creed of Nicaea (AD 325)

One of the few items of which we have clear evidence from the Council of Nicaea is the creed directed against the teaching of Arius. This is not what is today known as the Nicene Creed (abbreviated above as C), which is the product of the Council of Constantinople of 381, although that is clearly based on the Creed of Nicaea (abbreviated above as N). This earlier creed is as follows:

> We believe in one God, the Father Almighty, maker of all things visible and invisible:
>
> And in one Lord Jesus Christ, the Son of God, begotten from the Father, only-begotten, that is, from the substance (*ousia*) of the Father, God from God, Light from Light, true God from true God, begotten not made, of one substance with the Father, through whom all things came into being, things in heaven and things on earth; who because of us men and because of our salvation came down

and became incarnate, becoming man, suffered and rose again on the third day, ascended to the heavens, will come to judge the living and the dead:

And in the Holy Spirit.

But as for those who say, "there was when he was not," and "Before being born he was not," and that he came into existence out of nothing, or who assert that the Son of God is of a different *hypostasis* or *ousia*, or is subject to alteration or change—these the Catholic and Apostolic Church anathematizes.[1]

The Niceno-Constantinopolitan Creed (the Nicene Creed) (AD 381)

The Nicene Creed is the creed produced by the Council of Constantinople, which resolved the fourth-century Trinitarian crisis. The first substantiated evidence of its existence is from the record of proceedings of the Council of Chalcedon (AD 451), where it was said to represent the confession of the fathers who gathered at Constantinople. However, there is good reason to accept this at face value.[2]

We believe in one God the Father Almighty, maker of heaven and earth and of all things visible and invisible;

And in one Lord Jesus Christ the Son of God, the Only-begotten, begotten by his Father before all ages, Light from Light, true God from true God, begotten not made, consubstantial with the Father, through whom all things came into existence, who for us men and for our salvation came down from the heavens and became incarnate by the Holy Spirit and the Virgin Mary and became a man, and was crucified for us under Pontius Pilate and suffered and was buried and rose again on the third day in accordance with the Scriptures and ascended into the heavens and is seated at the right hand of the Father and will come again with glory to judge the living and the dead, and there will be no end to his kingdom;

And in the Holy Spirit, the Lord and life-giver, who proceeds from the Father, who is worshipped and glorified together with the Father and the Son, who spoke by the prophets;

And in one holy, catholic and apostolic Church;

---

1. Following the Dossetti text, in N. D. Kelly, *Early Christian Creeds* (London: Longman, 1972), 215–16.

2. Kelly, *Creeds*, 305–12; Robert Letham, *The Holy Trinity: In Scripture, History, Theology, and Worship* (Phillipsburg, NJ: P&R, 2004), 168–72.

We confess one baptism for the forgiveness of sins;
We wait for the resurrection of the dead and the life of the coming age. Amen.[3]

The Definition of Chalcedon (AD 451)

In composing the Definition, which excluded the teaching of Eutyches
as well as Nestorius, the bishops at the Council of Chalcedon (AD 451)
drew on Cyril's *Second Letter to Nestorius*, Cyril's *Letter to the Antiochenes*, Flavian's *Confession*, and Leo's *Tome*. According to Pelikan,
Leo's *Tome* was the single most decisive contributor, even though there
were more quotations from Cyril.[4] The Definition clearly distinguishes
between person and nature.

> Therefore, following the holy Fathers, we all with one accord teach
> men to acknowledge one and the same Son, our Lord Jesus Christ,
> at once complete in Godhead and complete in manhood, truly God
> and truly man, consisting also of a reasonable soul and body; of one
> substance with the Father as regards his Godhead, and at the same
> time of one substance with us as regards his manhood; like us in all
> respects, apart from sin; as regards his Godhead, begotten of the Fa-
> ther before the ages, but yet as regards his manhood begotten, for us
> and for our salvation, of Mary the Virgin, the God-bearer; one and
> the same Christ, Son, Lord, Only-begotten, recognized in two na-
> tures, without confusion, without change, without division, without
> separation; the distinction of natures being in no way annulled by the
> union, but rather the characteristics of each nature being preserved
> and coming together to form one person and subsistence, not as
> parted or separated into two persons, but one and the same Son and
> only-begotten God, the Word, Lord Jesus Christ; even as the prophets
> from earliest times spoke of him, and our Lord Jesus Christ himself
> taught us, and the creed of the Fathers has handed down to us.

Constantinople II (AD 553)

The Second Council of Constantinople maintained that the Son took
into hypostatic union a human nature, such that it became the human

---

3. Translation by R. P. C. Hanson, *The Search for the Christian Doctrine of God: The Arian
Controversy 318–381* (Edinburgh: T&T Clark, 1988), 815–16, from the Greek text printed by
G. L. Dossetti, *Il Symbolo di Nicea e di Costantinopoli* (Rome: Herder, 1967), 244ff.
4. R. V. Sellers, *The Council of Chalcedon: A Historical and Doctrinal Survey* (London: SPCK,
1953), 209–10.

body and soul of the Son. From this, all actions of the incarnate One are predicated of the Son, one of the Trinity, according to the flesh.

> If anyone shall not confess that the Word of God has two nativities, the one from all eternity of the Father, without time and without body; the other in these last days, coming down from heaven and being made flesh of the holy and glorious Mary, Mother of God and always a virgin, and born of her: let him be anathema. (*capitulum* 2)

> If anyone shall not acknowledge as the holy Fathers teach, that the union of God the Word is made with the flesh animated by a reasonable and living soul, and that such union is made synthetically and hypostatically, and that therefore there is only one Person, to wit: our Lord Jesus Christ, one of the holy Trinity: let him be anathema. (*capitulum* 4)

> If anyone does not confess that our Lord Jesus Christ who was crucified in the flesh is true God and the Lord of Glory and one of the Holy Trinity: let him be anathema. (*capitulum* 10)[5]

Constantinople III (AD 680–681)

Here follows the statement of the Third Council of Constantinople refuting the monothelites, who asserted that Christ has one will. Instead, the council declares that, since will is a characteristic of a nature, he has both a divine and a human will, or else he could not be properly or fully human, and we could not be saved.

> We . . . declare that in him are two natural wills and two natural operations indivisibly, inconvertibly, inseparably, inconfusedly, according to the teaching of the holy Fathers. And these two natural wills are not contrary the one to the other (God forbid!) as the impious heretics assert, but his human will follows and that not as resisting and reluctant, but rather as subject to his divine and omnipotent will. . . . For as his flesh is called and is the flesh of God the Word, so also the natural will of his flesh is called and is the proper will of God the Word, as he himself says: "I came down from heaven, not that I might do mine own will but the will of the Father which sent me!" where he calls his own will the will of his flesh, inasmuch as his flesh

---

5. Henry R. Percival, *The Seven Ecumenical Councils of the Undivided Church: Their Canons and Dogmatic Decrees*, A Select Library of Nicene and Post-Nicene Fathers of the Christian Church: Second Series (repr., Edinburgh: T&T Clark, 1997), 313–14.

was also his own. For as his most holy and immaculate animated flesh was not destroyed because it was deified but continued in its own state and nature . . . so also his human will, although deified, was not suppressed, but was rather preserved according to the saying of Gregory Theologus: "His will [i.e., the Savior's] is not contrary to God but altogether deified."

We glorify two natural operations indivisibly, immutably, inconfusedly, inseparably, in the same our Lord Jesus Christ our true God, that is to say a divine operation and a human operation, according to the divine preacher Leo, who most distinctly asserts as follows: "For each form does in communion with the other what properly pertains to it, the Word, namely, doing that which pertains to the Word, and the flesh that which pertains to the flesh."

For we will not admit one natural operation in God and in the creature, as we will not exalt into the divine essence what is created, nor will we bring down the divine nature to the place suited to the creature. . . . Preserving therefore the inconfusedness and indivisibility, we make briefly this whole confession, believing our Lord Jesus Christ to be one of the Trinity and after the incarnation our true God, we say that his two natures shone forth in his one subsistence in which he hath both performed the miracles and endured the sufferings through the whole of his economic conversation, and that not in appearance only but in very deed, and this by reason of the difference of nature which must be recognized in the same Person, for although joined together yet each nature wills and does the things proper to it and that indivisibly and inconfusedly. Wherefore we confess two wills and two operations, concurring most fitly in him for the salvation of the human race.[6]

Latin Creeds

The Latin creeds are accepted only in the Western church. Yet this does not mean that they are rejected by the East.

The Apostles' Creed

An early Latin baptismal creed, the Apostles' Creed probably originated in the second century in the church of Rome. It has gained universal approval in the Western church but is not in use in the East.

---

6. Percival, *Seven Ecumenical Councils*, 345–46.

I believe in God the Father Almighty, creator of heaven and earth;

And in Jesus Christ, his only Son, our Lord, who was conceived by the Holy Spirit, born from the virgin Mary, suffered under Pontius Pilate, was crucified, dead and buried, descended to hell, on the third day rose again from the dead, ascended to heaven, sits at the right hand of God the Father Almighty, thence he will come to judge the living and the dead.

I believe in the Holy Spirit, the holy catholic church, the communion of saints, the remission of sins, the resurrection of the flesh, and eternal life. Amen.[7]

---

7. Textus Receptus, printed in Kelly, *Creeds*, 369.

Glossary

allegory. A pattern of exegesis that uses the literal meaning of a passage as a springboard for determining a spiritual meaning, which may bear little recognizable connection to the text.

androcentrism. A pattern of thought and practice centered upon the primacy of men as opposed to women.

anhypostasia. The dogma that the human nature of Christ has no personal existence of its own, apart from the union into which it was assumed in the incarnation. This means the Son of God took into union not a human being (which would entail two separate personal entities) but a human nature.

anthropocentrism. A pattern of thought and practice centered upon the primacy or experience of humans as opposed to God.

anthropomorphism. A statement or figure of speech relating to God that is expressed in human properties.

apocatastasis. The idea that there will be a universal deliverance for the whole of the human race in the eschaton.

Apollinarianism. The idea of Apollinaris, who taught that the eternal Logos took the place of the human soul in the incarnate Christ. This teaching was condemned at Constantinople I (AD 381), since it entailed a less than fully human Christ, threatening the gospel; if Christ had not been fully human, he would not have been able to save us.

apophatic. Involving the dominant idea in the Eastern church that we know God primarily through mystical contemplation rather than through positive propositions or intellectual activity. Indeed, we are to empty our minds of logical and intellectual categories and, in ignorance, engage in prayer.

appropriations. The doctrine that, since God is one, all three persons act together in all God's works, yet each work is particularly attributable (appropriated) to one person. Only the Son became incarnate, and only the Holy Spirit came at Pentecost. This does not deny that the other two persons were also involved in these acts.

archē. The Father as the source of the hypostatic relations of the Son and the Holy Spirit within the indivisible Trinity.

Arians. Advocates of ideas similar to those of Arius (ca. 276–337), who taught that the Son was a creature who came into being and was the agent through whom the world was made but who was neither coeternal with the Father nor of the same being.

attributes. Particular characteristics of God, such as holiness, sovereignty, justice, goodness, mercy, and love.

being. Something that *is*, an existent.

cataphatic. In Orthodox theology a cataphatic approach is contrasted to apophatic theology, which is based on negations. Instead, cataphatic theology consists of positive affirmations. According to Dionysius the Areopagite, a cataphatic approach leads us to some knowledge of God but is an imperfect way. The perfect way, the only way that is fitting in regard to God, who is in his very nature unknowable, is the apophatic method—which leads us finally to total ignorance.

Christological. Relating to the person of Christ.

common person. Someone who is head and representative of a large corporate body of persons.

communicatio idiomatum. The concept that, in the hypostatic union, wherein Christ took a human nature into personal union, attributes of both natures are predicable of the person of Christ. From this, reference can be made to Christ acting in one nature in terms relating to the other (e.g., "they crucified the Lord of glory").

concupiscence. A disordered desire that is not necessarily sinful but may be the source of sin.

consubstantiality. The dogma that the Son and the Holy Spirit are of the same substance or being as the Father. This means all three persons are fully God, and the whole God.

cosmological. Relating to the cosmos.

credo ut intelligam. "I believe in order to understand": an expression from Anselm, with roots in Augustine, that identifies understanding as flowing from faith rather than vice versa.

culpa. Guilt.

deification. According to the Eastern church, the goal of salvation is to be made like God. This the Holy Spirit effects in us. It involves no blurring of the Creator-creature distinction but rather focuses on the union and communion we are given by God in which, as Peter says, we are made partakers of the divine nature (2 Pet. 1:4). *See also theōsis.*

docetism. The early heresy that Christ's humanity was apparent and not real. The term is a derivative of the Greek verb *dokein*, "seem" or "appear." This view is heretical, since, if Christ were not fully human, we could not be saved; only a perfect, sinless human can atone for the sins of humanity.

Donatism. A movement in North Africa during the fourth to sixth centuries, taking its name from a bishop called Donatus, which abandoned the church on the grounds of its moral laxity in restoring bishops who had lapsed under persecution.

donum superadditum. Gifts of righteousness and holiness granted to Adam at creation on top of his natural gifts of reason.

double predestination. The belief not only that God elects certain persons to salvation but also that in his decree of reprobation he either passes the rest by or positively decrees them to damnation.

doxology. An ascription of praise, normally to God.

dyothelitism. The doctrine that there are two wills in the incarnate Christ. This supposes that will is a property of natures rather than of persons. It in no way implies that these wills are in conflict.

economic Trinity. The Trinity as revealed in creation and salvation, acting in our world, in human history.

efficient cause. An agent that brings about a motion or change in a series of effects.

energies. God's powers at work in the creation. According to Gregory Palamas, the essence of God is unknowable. Instead, we have to do with God's energies.

enhypostasia. The dogma promulgated at the Second Council of Constantinople (553) that the eternal Son is the person of the incarnate Christ, a human nature conceived by the Holy Spirit in the womb of the Virgin Mary being taken into union. Behind this lies the biblical teaching that humanity is made in the image of God and is thus ontologically compatible with God on a creaturely level. Thus, the Son of God provides the personhood for the assumed human nature.

eschatological. Relating to the last things, from the Greek word *eschatos* (ἔσχατος, "last").

essence of God. What God *is*, his being (from the Latin *esse*, "to be").

eternal sin. In Roman Catholic theology, the blasphemy against the Holy Spirit, a deliberate refusal to accept God's mercy by repenting.

Eunomius. A fourth-century heretic who, like Arius, believed that the Son was created and so was not of the same being as the Father.

Eutychianism. The view of Eutyches that so stressed the unity of Christ's person that his humanity was swamped by his deity. This threatened salvation, for if Christ were not fully human, we could not be saved. Eutyches was condemned as a heretic at the Council of Chalcedon (AD 451).

extra-Calvinisticum. The belief of the Reformed church, in agreement with the Catholic tradition, that the Son exists beyond the bounds of the human nature assumed into union in the incarnation. The term was coined by the Lutherans, who claimed that the assumed humanity received divine attributes, including omnipresence, by virtue of the hypostatic union.

fides quaerens intellectum. An expression dating from Anselm meaning that, as an inherent property, faith exhibits a desire to understand its object.

filioque. A disputed phrase added to the Niceno-Constantinopolitan Creed (AD 381). The creed had stated that the Holy Spirit proceeds "from the Father." Later the Western church added "and the Son" (*filioque*), which has been the source of ongoing controversy and division ever since.

generation (eternal). The unique property of the Son in relation to the Father. Since God is eternal, the relation between the Father and the Son is eternal. This is not to be understood on the basis of human generation or begetting, since God is spiritual. It is beyond our capacity to understand.

gynocentrism. A pattern of thought and practice based on the primacy of women as opposed to men.

gnomic will. The human will as it makes choices based on desire after a process of deliberation.

Gnosticism. Various systems of belief of syncretistic religious and philosophical natures during the time of the early church that were generally pantheistic or panenthiestic, viewing the universe as an emanation from a supreme monad, and tending to regard the material as inferior.

hermeneutic. A principle of interpretation that governs how texts or realities are to be understood.

hypostasis. A Greek word meaning "something with a concrete existence." In terms of the Trinity, it came to mean "person." Thus, by the end of the fourth-century controversy, it referred to what is distinct in God, the way he is three, while *ousia* was reserved for the one being of God.

homoousios. "Of the same being," meaning that the Son and the Spirit are of the same identical being as the Father.

homoiousios. "Of similar or like being," a term used by many who were afraid the Creed of Nicaea identified the Father and the Son. Many of these *homoiousians* gave their support to the settlement of the Trinitarian controversy in 381.

immanent Trinity. The Trinity in itself, or the three persons as they relate to one another without regard to creation. *See* ontological Trinity.

in concreto. With reference to a concrete existent rather than to an abstraction.

instrumental cause. The means or tool used to bring about an effect.

kenosis. The self-emptying of Christ (Phil. 2:7), interpreted by some as his divestiture of certain divine attributes in becoming man, and by the tradition as his taking the form of a servant and seeking the interests of others.

kyriocentric/kyriarchal. Having to do with a pattern of belief and practice that assumes a patriarchal and hierarchical ordering of human relationships.

liturgy. The order of worship in a church service, usually in the form of written prayers, responses, and ascriptions of praise to God.

Macedonians. The putative followers of Macedonius, bishop of Constantinople from 342 until his deposition in 360, who denied the deity of the Holy Spirit. Macedonius himself may not have shared these views.

Manicheans. These held to an extreme form of ontological dualism, maintaining that there are two coequal realities, good and evil.

Marcellus (of Ancyra). A bishop who held that God is one *hypostasis* in one *ousia*. This appeared to be little different from modalism, in which the three are names only. The flesh of Christ will be discarded permanently at the end of his reign (1 Cor. 15:28). In rebuttal, the Niceno-Constantinopolitan Creed, propounded at Constantinople I (AD 381), states that Christ's kingdom "shall have no end."

material cause. The basis of a motion or change on which the efficient cause works.

modalism. The blurring or erasing of the real, eternal, and irreducible distinctions between the three persons of the Trinity. This danger can arise when the unity of God, or the identity in being of the three, is overstressed at the expense of the personal distinctions. It can also surface where there is a pervasive stress on salvation history, so as to eliminate any reference to eternal realities. When that happens, God's revelation in human history as the Father, the Son, and the Holy Spirit is no longer held to reveal who he is eternally in himself.

monarchy (monarchianism). Sole rule, the rule of one. It refers to the unity of God, his oneness (see Deut. 6:4). Sometimes this term is used of the Father, leaving the door open to subordination of the Son and the Spirit. It may be better to reserve the term ἀρχή (*archē*) for the Father as the source.

monism. Reduction of reality to one principle.

monophysitism. The view of the Monophysites stressing "the one incarnate nature of God the Word," which thus threatened the integrity of Christ's human nature.

monotheism. Belief that there is only one God or Supreme Being.

monotheletism. The idea, rejected by the church, that in the incarnate Christ there was only one will. The reason for its rejection was that will was regarded as a predicate of nature. If there were only one will, the human nature of Christ would be threatened.

mortal sin. In Roman Catholic theology, this is a sin that destroys charity in the heart by a grave violation of God's law, undertaken with full knowledge and consent. It involves turning away from God by preferring an inferior good. A new initiative of God is required in conversion and reconciliation to overcome it.

nature of God. What God is *like*—for example, love, just, holy, omnipotent. These particular aspects of his nature are termed attributes. In the fourth century the nature of God was sometimes used as a synonym for God's essence or being.

natura. Nature. The word can be used for creation, or for an existent, or for the particular type of existent. In relation to God, it is used to explain what God is like. In Christology, it is used for deity and human nature.

naturalism. The idea that everything arises from natural causes and that the supernatural is ruled out.

necessary existence. A perfection of the self-existent God, whereby there is no possibility that he cannot be. This contrasts with all other entities, which he brought into existence freely, which depend on him for their continuance, and which might not have existed and might not exist in the future, depending on his will.

Neoplatonism. A movement in the third and fourth centuries that built on and adapted certain aspects of Platonic philosophy together with elements from other sources, including Christianity. This influenced to varying degrees Clement of Alexandria, Origen, and the pre-Christian Augustine. How far Augustine extricated himself from the impact of Neoplatonism is a continued subject of debate.

Nestorianism. The view of Nestorius, who stressed the reality of Christ's humanity while undermining the unity of his person. In this excessive focus on the two natures of Christ, it appeared that his deity and humanity were separate, side by side, with no union between them, and thus there was no incarnation. Nestorius was condemned as a heretic at the Council of Ephesus (AD 431).

nominalism. A prominent late medieval philosophical movement that denied the reality of universals and held that reality exists only in particular, individual entities. Hence, the idea of whiteness has no existence in reality, for that is a property only of particular white objects.

ontological. Relating to being, that which is.

ontological Trinity. The Trinity in itself, or the three persons as they relate to one another without regard to creation. *See* immanent Trinity.

order (τάξις). The relations between the three persons of the Trinity. The Father begets the Son and sends the Holy Spirit in or through the Son. These relations are never reversed.

ordo salutis. The order of salvation, or the way we are brought to salvation by the Holy Spirit and kept there. It encompasses effectual calling, regeneration, faith and repentance, justification, adoption, sanctification, perseverance, and glorification, all of which are received in union with Christ.

ousia. Being (that which is). Since there is only one God, he has only one *ousia.* Thus the word refers to the one being of God. However, before the Trinitarian crisis of the fourth century was resolved, this word had a range of meanings, and so there was much confusion.

Palamite. A body of thought and practice in the Eastern church looking to Gregory Palamas as its source.

parousia. Coming, particularly in reference to the second coming of Jesus Christ.

peccatum alienum. A sin committed by someone else. The phrase is usually in reference to the sin of Adam.

peccatum proprium. A sin committed by oneself.

Pelagianism. The idea taught by Pelagius in the early fifth century that fallen humans could of themselves respond to the gospel, without the help of divine grace. This was rejected as heresy at the Council of Carthage in AD 418.

perichorēsis. The mutual indwelling of the three persons of the Trinity in the one being of God.

persons. The Father, the Son, and the Holy Spirit. There has been much debate about whether *person* is an appropriate or adequate term for the three, in view of its modern usage, which entails separate individuals. However, no proposed alternatives have succeeded in establishing themselves, for they invariably yield a less-than-personal view of God.

physis. A Greek word meaning "nature."

pneumatomachii. The "fighters against the Spirit," who, while accepting the deity of the Son, did not hold that the Holy Spirit is God. Their rise to prominence in the fourth century occasioned the Council of Constantinople (381), which resolved the Trinitarian crisis and declared this view heretical.

poena. Punishment.

privatio. A privation, deprivation, or absence of good. Sin, according to Latin theology from the time of Augustine, arose not from some previously existent entity but from a deficiency in the human agent.

processions. The eternal begetting of the Son and the eternal procession of the Holy Spirit. These are matched by the *missions*, the historical sending of the Son and the Spirit.

procession (eternal). The eternal relation of the Holy Spirit to the Father (and to the Son, under Western eyes).

properties. A term used in reference to individual persons of the Trinity to designate, for example, paternity, filiation, active spiration, passive spiration, and innascibility.

prosopological. A method of biblical interpretation in which the human author is enabled to access intra-Trinitarian discourse relating to Christological events in human history that were to occur in the future, or events that occurred in prehistory. *See prosōpon.*

prosōpon (προσώπον). A Greek word meaning "face" and used in the ancient world as an attempt to describe human beings, with the connotation of a mask worn by an actor. As Trinitarian and Christological doctrine developed, *hypostasis* came into use to refer to the human person, and *prosōpon* fell by the wayside.

realism. A philosophical movement holding that universals are real existents. Hence, not only do particular white objects exist, but also the idea of whiteness is real too. This is in contrast to nominalism, which denies the existence of universals.

reatus. Liability, frequently used in *reatus poenae*, liability to punishment on account of sin.

relations. A term used to speak of the relationships between the Father and the Son, the Son and the Father, the Father/Son and the Holy Spirit, the Holy Spirit and the Father/Son. These are considered differently in the Eastern church than in the West. The relations between the three persons differ in that the Father begets the Son and spirates the Spirit, but he neither is begotten nor proceeds; the Son is begotten and (according to the West) shares with the Father in the spiration or sending of the Spirit, but he does not proceed; the Spirit proceeds from the Father and (or through) the Son, but he does not beget, nor is he begotten. These relations are irreversible.

Sabellianism. The view of the third-century heretic Sabellius, who taught that the Father, the Son, and the Holy Spirit were merely three ways in which the one God revealed himself.

sarx. Flesh. This can refer to the human body, to fallen human nature, or to human weakness, as in the case of Christ's state of humiliation.

semi-Pelagianism. The belief that God gives his grace to sinners contingent on their taking the first step, on their doing their best. It is characteristic of the nominalist theology encountered by the early Luther, and of Arminianism.

sensus divinitatis. The innate knowledge, possessed by humans, that there is a Supreme Being to whom allegiance is due.

social Trinity. An understanding of the Trinity that sees the three persons as a community, interacting with one another. Its basic premise is the priority of the three persons over the one being (essence), contrary to the pro-Nicene settlement.

sophia. Wisdom. This is a theme developed by Russian Orthodox theology in the last two centuries. It has had an appeal for feminist theologians, on the irrelevant basis that in Greek, *sophia* is a feminine noun.

soteriology. The doctrine of salvation (from the Greek *sōtēr*, "savior").

spiration. The defining characteristic of the Holy Spirit, who proceeds from (or is breathed out by) the Father. The West insists that the Spirit also proceeds from the Son (thus the *filioque* clause).

subordinationism. A teaching that the Son and the Holy Spirit are of lesser being or status than the Father.

substance. In reference to the triune God, the "stuff" that is God. The Father, the Son, and the Spirit all participate fully and absolutely in the one identical substance. The essence of God is what God *is* (from the Latin *esse*, "to be").

teleological. Relating to the end, to the ultimate purpose of God.

theōsis. The process by which the Holy Spirit conforms us to the image of Christ, leading to eschatological likeness to the divine nature.

theotokos **(God-bearer).** The term that describes the Virgin Mary as the one who gave birth to the Son of God incarnate. It also entails his personal identity with the eternal Son. This term Nestorius and his followers rejected, preferring *Christotokos* (Christ-bearer). In so doing, they jeopardized the unity of Christ's person.

transubstantiation. The claim that in the Lord's Supper, the bread and wine undergo a change of substance and become the actual physical body and blood of Christ. In the Roman Catholic Church this is explained by Aristotelian philosophical categories (the *substance*—what the thing is—is changed, while the *accidents*—what is adventitious to the thing, what the thing appears to be—remain the same). However, in the Eastern Church there has been no attempt to explain what happens, for the Eucharist is regarded as a mystery.

tritheism. The belief that there are three gods, not one. An exaggerated stress on the three persons can, it is claimed, lead to a belief in tritheism.

typological. Having to do with the correspondence between an entity, event, or person in the Old Testament (the type) and a corresponding entity, event, or person in the New Testament (the antitype). Typology generally focuses on the person and work of Christ as realizing the meaning of the original type.

unbegotten/begotten. Contrasting properties of the Father and the Son. The property of the Son is that he is begotten by the Father from eternity. The Father is unbegotten. Begetting is qualitatively different from begetting in creation, refers to the eternal relations of the Father and the Son, distinguishes the Son from the creatures, and is beyond our capacity to understand.

venial sin. In Roman Catholic theology, a sin that—unlike mortal sin—allows charity to subsist even though it offends and wounds it. A venial sin is disobedience to the moral law but without full knowledge or complete consent. It does not break the covenant with God and is humanly reparable.

Bibliography

Abbott, Roger Philip. *Sit on Our Hands, or Stand on Our Feet? Exploring a Practical Theology of Major Incident Response for the Evangelical Catholic Christian Community in the U.K.* Eugene, OR: Wipf & Stock, 2013.

Abbott, Walter M. *The Documents of Vatican II.* New York: Guild, 1966.

"Agreed Statement on the Holy Trinity between the Orthodox Church and the World Alliance of Reformed Churches." *Touchstone* 5, no. 1 (1992): 22–23.

Alexander, Denis, and Robert S. White. *Beyond Belief: Science, Faith and Ethical Challenges.* Oxford: Lion Hudson, 2004.

Allison, Greg R. *Historical Theology: An Introduction to Christian Doctrine.* Grand Rapids, MI: Zondervan, 2011.

Althaus, Paul. *The Theology of Martin Luther.* Translated by Robert C. Schultz. Philadelphia: Fortress, 1966.

Ames, William. *An Analyticall Exposition of Both the Epistles of the Apostle Peter.* London: John Rothwell, 1641.

Ames, William. *Conscience, with the Power and Cases Thereof.* London: John Rothwell, 1643.

Ames, William. *The Marrow of Theology.* 1629. In *The Marrow of Theology: William Ames, 1576–1633.* Translated and Edited by John L. Eusden. Boston: Pilgrim, 1968.

Amyraut, Moïse. *Brief traité de la prédestination et des ses principales dépendances.* Saumur, 1634.

Anatolios, Khaled. *Retrieving Nicaea: The Development and Meaning of Trinitarian Doctrine.* Grand Rapids, MI: Baker Academic, 2011.

Anatolios, Khaled. "Yes and No: Reflections on Lewis Ayres: Nicaea and Its Legacy." *HTR* 100 (2007): 153–58.

Aquinas, Thomas. *Commentary on Saint Paul's Epistle to the Ephesians.* Translated by Matthew L. Lamb. Albany, NY: Magi, 1966.

Aquinas, Thomas. *Commentary on Saint Paul's Epistle to the Galatians*. Translated by Fabian R. Larcher. Albany, NY: Magi, 1966.

Aquinas, Thomas. *Commentary on the Gospel of St. John*. Translated by James A. Weisheipl and Fabian R. Larcher. Albany, NY: Magi, 1980.

Aristotle. *Metaphysics*. Everyman Library. Translated by John Warrington. London: J. M. Dent, 1955.

Aristotle. *The Politics of Aristotle*. Edited and Translated by Ernest Barker. London: Oxford University Press, 1958.

[Arminius, James.] *The Works of James Arminius*. Translated by James Nichols and William Nichols. London, 1825–1828. Reprint, Grand Rapids, MI: Baker, 1996.

Arnold, C. E. "Ephesians." In *Dictionary of Paul and His Letters*, edited by Gerald F. Hawthorne, 238–49. Downers Grove IL: InterVarsity Press, 1993.

Athanasius. *On the Incarnation*. Translated by John Behr. Yonkers, NY: St Vladimir's Seminary Press, 2011.

Athanasius. *On the Incarnation: The Treatise De Incarnatione Verbi Dei*. Translated by Sister Penelope Lawson. New York: Macmillan, 1946.

Augustine. *St. Augustine: The Literal Meaning of Genesis*. Translated by John Hammond Taylor. 2 vols. New York: Paulist, 1982.

Augustine. *The Works of Saint Augustine: A Translation for the 21st Century: The Trinity*. Translated by Edmund Hill, OP. Edited by John E. Rotelle. Hyde Park, NY: New City, 1991.

Aulén, Gustaf. *Christus Victor: An Historical Study of the Three Main Types of the Idea of Atonement*. 1931. Reprint, New York: Macmillan, 1969.

Austin, J. L. *How to Do Things with Words: The William James Lectures Delivered in Harvard University in 1955*. Oxford: Oxford University Press, 1976.

Ayres, Lewis. *Augustine and the Trinity*. Cambridge: Cambridge University Press, 2010.

Ayres, Lewis. *Nicaea and Its Legacy: An Approach to Fourth-Century Trinitarian Theology*. Oxford: Oxford University Press, 2004.

Ayres, Lewis. "Nicaea and Its Legacy: An Introduction." *HTR* 100 (2007): 141–44.

Ayres, Lewis. "A Response to Critics of Nicaea and Its Legacy, *HTR* 100 (2007): 159–71.

Bagehot, Walter. *The English Constitution: With an Introduction by R. H. S. Crossman*. 1867. Reprint, London: Collins, 1963.

Baglow, Christopher T. "Sacred Scripture and Sacred Doctrine in Saint Thomas Aquinas." In *Aquinas on Doctrine: A Critical Introduction*, edited by Thomas G. Weinandy, Daniel A. Keating, and John P. Yocum, 1–25. London: T&T Clark, 2004.

Baillie, D. M. *God Was in Christ: An Essay on Incarnation and Atonement.* New York: Charles Scribner's Sons, 1948.

[Balcanqual, Walter.] *Letters of Walter Balcanqual from the Synod of Dort to the R. Honourable Sir D. Carlton, L. Embassador.* London, 1659.

Ball, John. *A Treatise of the Covenant of Grace.* London: Simeon Ash, 1645.

Balthasar, Hans Urs von. *Theo-Drama: Theological Dramatic Theory.* Translated by Graham Harrison. San Francisco: Ignatius, 1994.

Bangs, Carl. *Arminius: A Study in the Dutch Reformation.* Nashville: Abington, 1971.

Bannerman, James *The Church of Christ.* Edinburgh: T&T Clark, 1868.

Bannerman, James. *Inspiration: The Infallible Truth and Divine Authority of the Holy Scriptures.* Edinburgh: T&T Clark, 1865.

Barnes, Michel René. "De Régnon Reconsidered." *AugStud* 26 (1995): 51–79.

Barnes, Michel René. "Rereading Augustine on the Trinity." In *The Trinity: An Interdisciplinary Symposium on the Trinity,* edited by Stephen T. Davis, Daniel Kendall, and Gerald O'Collins, 145–76. Oxford: Oxford University Press, 1999.

Barr, James. "Abba Isn't Daddy." *JTS* 39 (1988): 28–47.

Barr, Stephen M. "Anthropic Coincidences." *First Things,* June–July 2001. https://www.firstthings.com/article/2001/06/anthropic-coincidences. Accessed July 1, 2014.

Barraclough, Geoffrey. *The Medieval Papacy.* London: Thames and Hudson, 1968.

Barrett, C. K. *The Gospel according to St John: An Introduction with Commentary and Notes on the Greek Text.* 2nd ed. London: SPCK, 1978.

Barrett, Matthew M. *God's Word Alone: The Authority of Scripture.* Grand Rapids, MI: Zondervan, 2016.

Barrett, Matthew, ed. *Reformation Theology: A Systematic Summary.* Wheaton, IL: Crossway, 2017.

Barth, Karl. *Church Dogmatics,* trans. Geoffrey W. Bromiley. 14 vols. Edinburgh: T&T Clark, 1956–1977.

Barth, Karl. *Fides Quaerens Intellectum: Anselm's Proof of the Existence of God in the Context of His Theological Scheme.* Pittsburgh: Pickwick, 1975.

Barth, Karl. *The Theology of the Reformed Confessions: 1923.* Translated by Darrell L. Guder and Judith J. Guder. Louisville: Westminster John Knox, 2002.

Barth, Markus. *Ephesians: Translation and Commentary on Chapters 4–6*. The Anchor Bible. New York: Doubleday, 1974.

Bartos, Emil. *Deification in Eastern Orthodox Theology: An Evaluation and Critique of the Theology of Dumitru Staniloae*. Carlisle: Paternoster, 1999.

Baschera, Luca. "Total Depravity? The Consequences of Original Sin in John Calvin and Later Reformed Theology." In Calvinus Clarissimus Theologus: *Papers of the Tenth International Congress on Calvin Research*, edited by Herman J. Selderhuis, 37–59. Göttingen: Vandenhoeck & Ruprecht, 2012.

Bates, Matthew W. *The Birth of the Trinity: Jesus, God, and Spirit in New Testament and Early Christian Interpretations of the Old Testament*. Oxford: Oxford University Press, 2015.

Bauckham, Richard. *James: Wisdom of James, Disciple of Jesus the Sage*. London: Routledge, 1999.

Bauckham, Richard. *Jesus and the Eyewitnesses: The Gospels as Eyewitness Testimony*. 2nd ed. Grand Rapids, MI: Eerdmans, 2017.

Bauckham, Richard. *Jesus and the God of Israel: God Crucified and Other Studies in the New Testament's Christology of Divine Identity*. Milton Keynes: Paternoster, 2008.

Bauckham, Richard. "The Sonship of the Historical Jesus in Christology." *SJT* 31 (1978): 245–60.

Bauer, D. R. "Son of God." In *Dictionary of Jesus and the Gospels*, edited by Joel B. Green, 769–75. Downers Grove, IL: InterVarsity Press, 1992.

Bavinck, Herman. "Common Grace." *CTJ* 24 (1989): 35–65.

Bavinck, Herman. *The Doctrine of God*. Translated by William Hendriksen. Reprint, Edinburgh: Banner of Truth, 1977.

Bavinck, Herman. *In the Beginning: Foundations of Creation Theology*. Edited by John Bolt. Translated by John Vriend. Grand Rapids, MI: Baker, 1999.

Bavinck, Herman. *Our Reasonable Faith*. Translated by Henry Zylstra. Grand Rapids, MI: Baker, 1977.

Bavinck, Herman. *Reformed Dogmatics*. 4 vols. Edited by John Bolt. Translated by John Vriend. Grand Rapids, MI: Baker, 2003–2008.

Baxter, Richard. *Aphorismes of Justification, with Their Explication Annexed*. Hague: Abraham Brown, 1655.

Beach, J. Mark. *Christ and the Covenant: Francis Turretin's Federal Theology as a Defense of the Doctrine of Grace*. Göttingen: Vandenhoeck & Ruprecht, 2007.

Beach, J. Mark. "A Tale of Two Kingdoms: Some Critics of the Lutheran Doctrine of Two Kingdoms." *MAJT* 25 (2014): 35–73.

Beale, G. K. *The Book of Revelation: A Commentary on the Greek Text.* Grand Rapids, MI: Eerdmans, 1999.

Beasley-Murray, G. R. *Baptism in the New Testament.* Exeter: Paternoster, 1972.

Beasley-Murray, G. R. *John.* Word Biblical Commentary 36. Waco, TX: Word, 1987.

Beckwith, Roger. "The Calvinist Doctrine of the Trinity." *Churchman* 115 (2001): 308–16.

Beckwith, Roger. *The Old Testament Canon of the New Testament Church and Its Background in Early Judaism.* Grand Rapids, MI: Eerdmans, 1985.

Beeke, Joel R. *Knowing and Growing in Assurance of Faith.* Fearn: Christian Focus, 2017.

Beeley, Christopher A. *Gregory of Nazianzus on the Trinity and the Knowledge of God: In Your Light We Shall See Light.* Oxford: Oxford University Press, 2008.

Beeley, Christopher A. *The Unity of Christ: Continuity and Conflict in Patristic Tradition.* New Haven, CT: Yale University Press, 2012.

Behr, John. "Final Reflections." *HTR* 100 (2007): 173–75.

Behr, John. "Response to Ayres: the Legacies of Nicaea, East and West." *HTR* 100 (2007): 145–52.

Bellarmine, Robert. *An Ample Declaration of the Christian Doctrine.* Translated by Richard Hadock. Roan: n.p., 1604.

Berdyaev, Nicholas. *The Destiny of Man.* London: Bles, 1937.

Berkhof, Louis. *Systematic Theology.* London: Banner of Truth, 1958.

Berkouwer, G. C. *Man: The Image of God.* Translated by Dirk W. Jellema. Grand Rapids, MI: Eerdmans, 1962.

Berkouwer, G. C. *Sin.* Grand Rapids, MI: Eerdmans, 1971.

Berns, Roy S. *Billmeyer and Saltzman's Principles of Color Technology.* 3rd ed. New York: John Wiley & Sons, 2000.

Bethune-Baker, J. F. *An Introduction to the Early History of Christian Doctrine to the Time of the Council of Chalcedon.* 6th ed. London: Methuen, 1938.

Betz, Otto. *What Do We Know about Jesus?* London: SCM, 1968.

Beilby, James K., and Paul Rhodes Eddy, eds. *Justification: Five Views.* London: SPCK, 2012.

Biddle, John. *A Twofold Catechism: The One Simply Called a Scripture Catechism; the Other a Brief Scripture-Catechism for Children.* London: J. Cottrel for Ri. Moore, 1654.

Billings, J. Todd. *Union with Christ: Reframing Theology and Ministry for the Church.* Grand Rapids, MI: Baker, 2011.

Birks, Thomas Rawson. *The Difficulties of Belief, in Connection with the Creation and the Fall, Redemption and Judgment.* 2nd ed., enlarged. London: Macmillan, 1876.

Black, Antony. "The Conciliar Movement." In *The Cambridge History of Medieval Political Thought c. 350–c. 1450*, edited by J. H. Burns, 573–87. Cambridge: Cambridge University Press, 1988.

Blocher, Henri. *In the Beginning: The Opening Chapters of Genesis.* Downers Grove IL: InterVarsity Press, 1984.

Bobrinskoy, Boris. *The Mystery of the Trinity: Trinitarian Experience and Vision in the Biblical and Patristic Tradition.* Translated by Anthony P. Gythiel. Crestwood, NY: St Vladimir's Seminary Press, 1999.

Bock, Darrell L., ed. *Three Views on the Millennium and Beyond.* Grand Rapids, MI: Zondervan, 1999.

Bonner, Gerald. "Augustine's Concept of Deification." *JTS* 37 (1986): 369–86.

Bonner, Gerald. "Deificare." In *Augustinus-Lexicon.* Vol. 1, edited by C. Mayer, 265–67. Basel: Schwabe, 1986.

Bonner, Gerald. "Deification, Divinization." In *Augustine through the Ages: An Encyclopedia*, edited by Allan D. Fitzgerald, OSA, 265–66. Grand Rapids, MI: Eerdmans, 1999.

Braaten, Carl E., and Robert W. Jenson. *Union with Christ: The New Finnish Interpretation of Luther.* Grand Rapids, MI: Eerdmans, 1998.

Bradshaw, Paul. *The Search for the Origins of Christian Worship.* New York: Oxford University Press, 1992.

Bratt, James D., ed. *Abraham Kuyper: A Centennial Reader.* Grand Rapids, MI: Eerdmans, 1988.

Braine, David. *The Reality of Time and the Existence of God: The Project of Proving God's Existence.* Oxford: Clarendon, 1988.

Bray, Gerald. "The 'Filioque' Clause in History and Theology." *TynBul* 34 (1983): 91–144.

Bray, Gerald. *The Doctrine of God.* Leicester: Inter-Varsity Press, 1993.

Bray, Gerald. *The Personal God.* Carlisle: Paternoster, 1998.

Bromiley, Geoffrey W. *An Introduction to the Theology of Karl Barth.* Grand Rapids, MI: Eerdmans, 1979.

Bromiley, Geoffrey W. *Zwingli and Bullinger.* London: SCM, 1953.

Brooke, Z. N. "Lay Investiture and Its Relation to the Conflict of Empire and Papacy." *Proceedings of the British Academy* 25 (1939): 217–47.

Brown, Andrew J. *The Days of Creation: A History of Christian Interpretation of Genesis 1:1–2:3.* Blandford Forum: Deo Publishing, 2014.

Brown, Raymond E. *The Gospel according to John (I–XII).* The Anchor Bible. Garden City, NY: Doubleday, 1966.

Bruce, A. B. *The Humiliation of Christ*. Edinburgh: T&T Clark, 1905.

Bruce, F. F. *The Gospel of John*. Grand Rapids, MI: Eerdmans, 1984.

Bruce, Robert. *The Mystery of the Lord's Supper: Sermons on the Sacrament Preached in the Kirk of Edinburgh in A.D. 1589*. Edited and Translated by Thomas F. Torrance. London: James Clarke, 1958.

Bucanus, Guilielmus. *Institutiones theologicae seu locorum communium Christianae religionis*. [Geneva]: Ioannes & Isaias LePreux, 1604.

Bucanus, William. *Institutions of Christian Religion, Framed out of Gods Word, and the Writings of the Best Divines*. London: George Snowdon and Leonell Snowdon, 1606.

Bucer, Martin. *In epistolam D. Pauli ad Ephesios*. Basel, 1561.

Bucer, Martin. *In epistolam D. Pauli ad Romanos*. 1536. Reprint, Basel, 1562.

Bucer, Martin. *Metaphrasis et enarrationes in perpetuae epistolarum D. Pauli apostoli: Tomus primus*. Strassburg, 1536.

Buchanan, James. *The Doctrine of Justification: An Outline of Its History in the Church and of Its Exposition from Scripture*. 1867. Reprint, Grand Rapids, MI: Baker, 1977.

Bulgakov, Sergei. *Le Paraclet*. Translated by Constantin Andronikof. Paris: Aubier, 1946.

Bulgakov, Sergei. *The Wisdom of God: A Brief Summary of Sophiology*. London: Williams and Norgate, 1937.

Bullinger, Heinrich. *Antiquissima fides et vera religio*. Zürich, 1534.

Bullinger, Heinrich. *The Decades of Henry Bullinger*. Edited by Thomas Harding. Translated by H. I——. Cambridge: Cambridge University Press, 1850.

Bullinger, Heinrich. *De testamento seu foedere Dei unico et aeterno brevis expositio*. Zürich, 1534.

Bultmann, Rudolph. "προγινώσκω, πρόγνωσις." In *Theological Dictionary of the New Testament*. Edited by Gerhard Kittel and Gerhard Friedrich. Translated by Geoffrey W. Bromiley. Vol. 1, 715–16. Grand Rapids, MI: Eerdmans, 1964.

Burleigh, J. H. S. *A Church History of Scotland*. London: Oxford University Press, 1960.

Burrell, David B. "Act of Creation with Its Theological Consequences." In *Aquinas on Doctrine: A Critical Introduction*, edited by Thomas G. Weinandy, Daniel A. Keating, and John P. Yocum, 27–44. London: T&T Clark, 2004.

Cabasilas, Nicholas. *Life in Christ*. Edited by Margaret Lisney. London: Janus, 1995.

Calvin, John. *Articles concerning the Organization of the Church and Worship at Geneva Proposed by Ministers at the Council January 16, 1537.* In *Calvin: Theological Treatises*, edited by J. K. S. Reid, 140–66. Philadelphia: Westminster, 1954.

Calvin, John. *Calvin's Commentaries: The Epistle of Paul the Apostle to the Hebrews and the First and Second Epistles of St. Peter.* Translated by William B. Johnston. Grand Rapids, MI: Eerdmans, 1963.

Calvin, John. *Calvin's Commentaries: The Epistles of Paul the Apostle to the Romans and to the Thessalonians.* Translated by Ross MacKenzie. Grand Rapids, MI: Eerdmans, 1973.

Calvin, John. *Calvin's Commentaries: The Epistles of Paul to the Galatians, Ephesians, Philippians, and Colossians.* Translated by T. H. L. Parker. Grand Rapids, MI: Eerdmans, 1965.

Calvin, John. *Calvin's Commentaries: The First Epistle of Paul the Apostle to the Corinthians.* Translated by John W. Fraser. Grand Rapids, MI: Eerdmans, 1960.

Calvin, John. *Calvin's Commentaries: The Gospel according to St. John 1–10.* Translated by T. H. L. Parker. Grand Rapids, MI: Eerdmans, 1961.

Calvin, John. *Calvin's Commentaries: The Gospel according to St. John 11–21 and the First Epistle of John.* Translated by T. H. L. Parker. Grand Rapids, MI: Eerdmans, 1959.

Calvin, John. *Calvin's Commentaries: The Second Epistle of Paul the Apostle to the Corinthians and the Epistles to Timothy, Titus, and Philemon.* Translated by T. Smail. Grand Rapids, MI: Eerdmans, 1964.

Calvin, John. *Commentaries on the First Book of Moses Called Genesis.* Translated by John King. Grand Rapids, MI: Eerdmans, 1979.

Calvin, John. *Commentarii in epistolas canonicas.* Ioannis Calvini opera exegetica. Geneva: Droz, 2009.

Calvin, John. *Commentarii in Pauli epistolas ad Galatas, ad Ephesios, ad Philippenses, ad Colossenses.* Ioannis Calvini opera exegetica. Geneva: Droz, 1992.

Calvin, John. *Commentarii in priorem epistolam Pauli ad Corinthios.* Strassburg: Wendelium Ribelium, 1546.

Calvin, John. *Commentarius in epistolam Pauli ad Romanos.* Ioannis Calvini opera omnia. Geneva: Droz, 1999.

Calvin, John. *Commentarius in epistolam ad Hebraeos.* Ioannis Calvini opera exegetica. Geneva: Droz, 1996.

Calvin, John. *Concerning the Eternal Predestination of God.* Translated by J. K. S. Reid. Reprint, London: James Clarke, 1961.

Calvin, John. *In evangelium secundum Johannem commentarius pars altera.* Ioannis Calvini opera exegetica. Geneva: Droz, 1998.

Calvin, John. *In evangelium secundum Johannem commentarius pars prior.* Ioannis Calvini opera exegetica. Geneva: Droz, 1997.

Calvin, John. *Institutes of the Christian Religion.* Edited by John T. McNeill. Translated by Ford Lewis Battles. Philadelphia: Westminster, 1960.

Calvin, John. *Joannis Calvini opera selecta.* Edited by Peter Barth and Wilhelm Niesel. 5 vols. Munich: Kaiser, 1926–1952.

Calvin, John. *Short Treatise on the Holy Supper of Our Lord and Only Saviour Jesus Christ.* In *Calvin: Theological Treatises,* edited by J. K. S. Reid, 140–66. Philadelphia: Westminster, 1954.

Calvin, John. *Tracts and Letters, Part 2.* Edited and Translated by Henry Beveridge. Vol. 2 of *Selected Works of John Calvin.* 1849. Reprint, Grand Rapids, MI: Baker, 1983.

Cameron, John. *The Threefold Covenant of God with Man.* London, 1645.

Cameron, Nigel M. de S. *Universalism and the Doctrine of Hell: Papers Presented at the Fourth Edinburgh Conference in Christian Dogmatics, 1991.* Carlisle: Paternoster, 1992.

Campbell, Iain D. "Re-Visiting the Covenant of Redemption." In *The People's Theologian: Writings in Honour of Donald Macleod,* edited by Iain D. Campbell and Malcolm MacLean, 173–94. Fearn: Mentor, 2011.

Campbell, John McLeod. *The Nature of the Atonement and Its Relation to Remission of Sins and Eternal Life.* 1856. Reprint, London: James Clarke, 1959.

Capes, D. B. "Pre-Existence." In *Dictionary of the Later New Testament and Its Development,* edited by Ralph P. Martin and Peter H. Davids, 955–61. Downers Grove, IL: InterVarsity Press, 1997.

Carlyle, R. W., and A. J. Carlyle, *A History of Medieval Political Theory in the West.* 6 vols. Edinburgh, 1892–1936.

Carrick, John. *The Imperative of Preaching: A Theology of Sacred Rhetoric.* Edinburgh: Banner of Truth, 2002.

Carson, D. A. *Exegetical Fallacies.* Grand Rapids, MI: Baker, 1984.

Carson, D. A. *The Gospel according to St John.* Leicester: Inter-Varsity Press, 1991.

Carson, D. A. "The Vindication of Imputation: On Fields of Discourse and Semantic Fields." In *Justification: What's at Stake in the Current Debates,* edited by Mark Husbands, 46–78. Leicester: Apollos, 2004.

Cassidy, Brendan. "Laughing with Giotto at Sinners in Hell." *Viator: Medieval and Renaissance Studies* 35 (2004): 355–73.

Catechism of the Catholic Church. London: Geoffrey Chapman, 1994.

Charlesworth, James H. *The Old Testament Pseudepigrapha*. 2 vols. New York: Doubleday, 1983.

Charlesworth, James H., and Craig A. Evans, eds. *The Pseudepigrapha and Early Biblical Interpretation*. Journal for the Study of the Pseudepigrapha, Supplement Series 14. Sheffield: Sheffield Academic, 1993.

Chemnitz, Martin. *The Two Natures in Christ*. Translated by J. A. O. Preus. 1578. Reprint, St. Louis: Concordia, 1971.

Childs, Brevard. "Speech-Act Theory and Biblical Interpretation." *SJT* 58 (2005): 375–92.

Christ, Carol P. "Why Women Need the Goddess: Phenomenological, Psychological, and Political Reflections." In *Womanspirit Rising: A Feminist Reader in Religion*, edited by Carol P. Christ and Judith Plaskow, 273–87. San Francisco: Harper & Row, 1979.

Christ, Timothy Michael. *A New Creation in Christ: A Historical-Theological Investigation into Walter Marshall's Theology of Sanctification in Union with Christ in the Context of the Seventeenth-Century Antinomian and Neonomian Controversy*. PhD diss., University of Chester, 2016.

Chul Won Suh. *The Creation-Mediatorship of Jesus Christ*. Amsterdam: Rodopi, 1982.

Church of England. *The First and Second Prayer Books of Edward VI*. London: Dent, 1968.

Church of England. "The Order for Holy Communion: Also Called the Eucharist and the Lord's Supper: Rite A." In *Services from the Alternative Service Book, 1980: Authorized for Use in the Church of England in Conjunction with the Book of Common Prayer*. Cambridge: Cambridge University Press, 1980.

Clark, John C. *The Incarnation of God: The Mystery of the Gospel as the Foundation of Evangelical Theology*. Wheaton, IL: Crossway, 2015.

Clark, R. Scott. "*Iustitia Imputata Christi*: Alien or Proper to Luther's Doctrine of Justification?" *CTQ* 70 (2006): 269–310.

Clément, Olivier. *You Are Peter: An Orthodox Theologian's Reflection on the Exercise of Papal Primacy*. New York: New City, 2003.

Clifford, Alan C. *Atonement and Justification: English Evangelical Theology 1640–1790: An Evaluation*. Oxford: Clarendon, 1990.

Clowney, Edmund P. *The Church*. Downers Grove, IL: InterVarsity Press, 1995.

Coakley, Sarah. "Introduction: Disputed Questions in Patristic Trinitarianism." *HTR* 100 (2007): 125–38.

Coakley, Sarah. "What Does Chalcedon Solve and What Does It Not? Some Reflections on the Status and Meaning of the Chalcedonian Definition." In *The Incarnation*, edited by Stephen T. Davis, Daniel Kendall, and Gerald O'Collins, 143–63. Oxford: Oxford University Press, 2002.

Collier, Jay T. *Debating Perseverance: The Augustinian Heritage in Post-Reformation England.* Oxford: Oxford University Press, 2018.

Collins, C. John. *Genesis 1–4: A Linguistic, Literary, and Theological Commentary.* Phillipsburg, NJ: P&R, 2006.

Collins, Kenneth J., and Jerry L. Walls. *Roman but Not Catholic: What Remains at Stake 500 Years after the Reformation.* Grand Rapids, MI: Baker Academic, 2017.

Collins, Sheila. "Reflections on the Meaning of Herstory." In *Womanspirit Rising: A Feminist Reader in Religion*, edited by Carol P. Christ and Judith Plaskow, 68–73. San Francisco: Harper & Row, 1979.

Colwell, John. "The Contemporaneity of the Divine Decision: Reflections on Barth's Denial of 'Universalism.'" In *Universalism and the Doctrine of Hell: Papers Presented at the Fourth Edinburgh Conference in Christian Dogmatics, 1991*, edited by Nigel M. de S. Cameron, 139–60. Carlisle: Paternoster, 1992.

The Confession of Faith, the Larger and Shorter Catechisms with the Scripture Proofs at Large, Together with the Sum of Saving Knowledge. Applecross: Publications Committee of the Free Presbyterian Church of Scotland, 1970.

Cooper, John W. *Body, Soul, and Life Everlasting.* Grand Rapids, MI: Eerdmans, 2000.

Craig, William Lane. *Divine Foreknowledge and Human Freedom: The Coherence of Theism: Omniscience.* Leiden: Brill, 1991.

Craig, William Lane. "The Incarnation." In *Philosophical Foundations for a Christian Worldview*, by J. P. Moreland and William Lane Craig, 599–611. Downers Grove, IL: InterVarsity Press, 2003.

Cranfield, C. E. B. *A Critical and Exegetical Commentary on the Epistle to the Romans.* 2 vols. The International Critical Commentary. Edinburgh: T&T Clark, 1975.

Crick, Francis. *The Astonishing Hypothesis: The Scientific Search for the Soul.* New York: Simon & Schuster, 1994.

Crisp, Oliver D. "Desiderata for Models of the Hypostatic Union." In *Christology Ancient and Modern: Explorations in Constructive Dogmatics*, edited by Oliver D. Crisp and Fred Sanders, 19–41. Grand Rapids, MI: Zondervan, 2013.

Crisp, Oliver D. *Divinity and Humanity: The Incarnation Reconsidered.* Cambridge: Cambridge University Press, 2007.

Crisp, Oliver D. "The Election of Jesus Christ." *JRT* 2 (2008): 131–50.

Crisp, Oliver D. *God Incarnate: Explorations in Christology.* London: T&T Clark, 2009.

Crisp, Oliver D. "On Barth's Denial of Universalism." *Them* 29 (2003): 18–29.

Crisp, Oliver D. "On the Orthodoxy of Jonathan Edwards." *SJT* 67 (2014): 304–22.

Crisp, Oliver D. "Penal Non-Substitution." *JTS* 59 (2008): 140–68.

Crisp, Oliver D. *The Word Enfleshed: Exploring the Person and Work of Christ.* Grand Rapids, MI: Baker Academic, 2016.

Crisp, Tobias. *Christ Alone Exalted.* London: Richard Bishop, 1643.

Cross, Anthony R. "Baptism in the Theology of John Calvin and Karl Barth." In *Calvin, Barth and Reformed Theology*, edited by Neil B. MacDonald and Carl Trueman, 57–87. Eugene, OR: Wipf & Stock, 2008.

Cross, Richard. "Duns Scotus on God's Essence and Attributes: Metaphysics, Semantics, and the Greek Patristic Tradition." *RTPM* 83 (2016): 353–83.

Crouzel, Henri. *Origen.* Translated by A. S. Worrall. Edinburgh: T&T Clark, 1989.

Cullmann, Oscar. *Early Christian Worship.* Translated by A. Stewart Todd and James B. Torrance. London: SCM, 1953.

Cunningham, William. *Historical Theology.* Edinburgh, 1870.

Cunningham, William. *Theological Lectures.* London: James Nisbet, 1878.

Cunnington, Ralph. "Definitive Sanctification: A Response to John Fesko." *EQ* 84 (2012): 234–52.

Cyril of Alexandria. *On the Unity of Christ.* Translated by John Anthony McGuckin. Crestwood, NY: St Vladimir's Seminary Press, 1995.

Cyril of Alexandria. *Thesaurus on the Holy and Consubstantial Trinity.*

Dabney, Robert L. *Lectures in Systematic Theology.* 1878. Reprint, Grand Rapids, MI: Zondervan, 1972.

Daeley, Justin J. "It Could Not Have Been Otherwise: An Articulation and Defense of Divine Source Compatibilism." PhD diss., Middlesex University, 2017.

Daeley, Justin J. *Why God Must Do What Is Best: A Philosophical Investigation of Theistic Optimalism.* New York: Bloomsbury Academic, forthcoming.

Dahms, John V. "The Generation of the Son." *JETS* 32 (1989): 493–501.

Dahms, John V. "The Johannine Use of Monogenēs Reconsidered." *NTS* 29 (1983): 222–32.

Dahms, John V. "The Subordination of the Son." *JETS* 37 (1994): 351–64.

Dalton, William J., SJ. *Christ's Proclamation to the Spirits: A Study of 1 Peter 3:18–4:6.* Rome: Editrice Pontificio Instituto Biblico, 1989.

Daly, Mary. "Why Speak about God?" In *Womanspirit Rising: A Feminist Reader in Religion*, edited by Carol P. Christ and Judith Plaskow, 210–18. San Francisco: Harper & Row, 1979.

Davenant, John. *Dissertationes duae.* Cambridge: ex officinia Rogeri Danielis, 1650.

Davies, Brian. *Anselm of Canterbury: The Major Works.* Oxford: Oxford University Press, 1998.

Davies, Brian. *Thomas Aquinas's* Summa contra Gentiles*: A Guide and Commentary.* Oxford: Oxford University Press, 2016.

Davies, Brian. *Thomas Aquinas's* Summa Theologiae*: A Guide and Commentary.* Oxford: Oxford University Press, 2014.

Davies, Brian. *The Thought of Thomas Aquinas.* Oxford: Clarendon, 1992.

Davies, Eryl. *An Angry God: The Biblical Doctrine of Wrath, Final Judgment, and Hell.* Bridgend: Evangelical Press of Wales, 1991.

Davies, W. D., Jr., and Dale C. Allison. *A Critical and Exegetical Commentary on the Gospel according to Saint Matthew.* 3 vols. Edinburgh: T&T Clark, 1988.

Davis, Leo Donald. *The First Seven Ecumenical Councils (325–787).* Collegeville, MN: Liturgical, 1990.

Dawkins, Richard. *The God Delusion.* London: Black Swan, 2007.

De Greef, Wulfert. *The Writings of John Calvin: An Introductory Guide.* Translated by Lyle D. Bierma. Grand Rapids, MI: Baker, 1993.

Delitzsch, Franz. *A System of Biblical Psychology.* 2nd ed. Translated by Robert Ernest Wallis. 1899. Reprint, Grand Rapids, MI: Baker, 1977.

DelCogliano, Mark, Andrew Radde-Gallwitz, and Lewis Ayres, trans. *Works on the Spirit: Athanasius and Didymus.* Yonkers, NY: St Vladimir's Seminary Press, 2011.

De Lubac, Henri, SJ. *Medieval Exegesis.* 3 vols. Translated by Mark Sebanc. 1959. Reprint, Grand Rapids, MI: Eerdmans, 1998–2009.

de Margerie, Bertrand, SJ. *The Christian Trinity in History.* Translated by Edmund J. Fortman, SJ. Petersham. MA: St. Bede's, 1982.

de Margerie, Bertrand, SJ. *An Introduction to the History of Exegesis.* 3 vols. Petersham, MA: Bede, 1991–1995.

Dempsey, Michael T., ed. *Trinity and Election in Contemporary Theology.* Grand Rapids, MI: Eerdmans, 2011.

Dempster, Stephen. "A Member of the Family or a Stranger? A Review Article of Jeffrey J. Niehaus, *Ancient Near Eastern Themes in Biblical Theology.*" *Them* 35 (2010): 228–37.

Dennison, James, Jr., Scott F. Sanborn, and Benjamin W. Swinburnson. "Merit or 'Entitlement' in Reformed Covenant Theology: A Review." *Kerux* 24, no. 3 (2009): 3–152.

de Régnon, Theodore. *Études de théologie positive sur la Sainté Trinité.* Paris: Retaux, 1898.

DeWeese, Garrett J. "One Person, Two Natures: Two Metaphysical Models of the Incarnation." In *Jesus in Trinitarian Perspective: An Introductory Christology*, edited by Fred Sanders and Klaus Issler, 114–53. Nashville: B&H Academic, 2007.

de Witt, John R. *Jus Divinum: The Westminster Assembly and the Divine Right of Church Government.* Kampen: Kok, 1969.

Di Berardino, Angelo, ed. *Encyclopedia of the Early Church.* Translated by Adrian Walford, 2 vols. New York: Oxford University Press, 1992.

Di Berardino, Angelo, ed. *Patrology: The Eastern Fathers from the Council of Chalcedon (451) to John of Damascus (†750).* Translated by Adrian Walford. Cambridge: James Clarke, 2008.

Dodd, C. H. *The Apostolic Preaching and Its Developments.* London: Hodder & Stoughton, 1944.

Dodd, C. H. "*Hilaskesthai*, Its Cognates, Derivatives, and Synonyms in the Septuagint." *JTS* 32 (1931): 352–60.

Dodd, C. H. *The Interpretation of the Fourth Gospel.* Cambridge: Cambridge University Press, 1953.

Dolbeau, François. "Nouveaux sermons de Saint Augustin pour la conversion des païens et des Donatistes." *RÉAug* 39 (1993): 57–108.

Dolezal, James E. *All That Is in God: Evangelical Theology and the Challenge of Classical Christian Theism.* Grand Rapids, MI: Reformation Heritage, 2017.

Dolezal, James E. *God without Parts: Divine Simplicity and the Metaphysics of God's Absoluteness.* Eugene, OR: Pickwick, 2011.

Dowey, Edward A., Jr. *The Knowledge of God in Calvin's Theology.* Grand Rapids, MI: Eerdmans, 1994.

Drecoll, Volker Henning. "Lewis Ayres, Augustine and the Trinity." *SJT* 66 (2013): 88–98.

Drewery, Benjamin. *Origen and the Doctrine of Grace.* London: Epworth, 1960.

Driver, S. R. *The Book of Genesis: With Introduction and Notes.* London: Methuen, 1926.

Duncan, J. Ligon, III, ed. *The Westminster Confession into the 21st Century*. 3 vols. Fearn: Mentor, 2003–2009.

Dunn, James D. G. *Christology in the Making: A New Testament Inquiry into the Origins of the Doctrine of the Incarnation*. Philadelphia: Westminster, 1980. Second edition, London: SCM, 1989.

Dunn, James D. G. "The New Perspective on Paul." In *Jesus, Paul and the Law: Studies in Mark and Galatians*, 183–214. Louisville: Westminster John Knox, 1990.

Dunn, James D. G. "New Perspective View." In *Justification: Five Views*, edited by James K. Beilby and Paul Rhodes Eddy, 176–218. London: SPCK, 2012.

Dunn, James D. G. *The Parting of the Ways between Christianity and Judaism and Their Significance for the Character of Christianity*. Philadelphia: Trinity Press International, 1991.

Dunn, James D. G. *Romans 1–8*. Word Biblical Commentary 38A. Dallas: Word, 1988.

Dunn, James D. G. *Romans 9–16*. Word Biblical Commentary 38B. Dallas: Word, 1988.

Dupont, Anthony. "Original Sin in Tertullian and Cyprian: Conceptual Presence and Pre-Augustinian Content." *RÉAug* 63 (2017): 1–29.

Eaton, John. *The Honey-combe of Free Justification by Christ Alone*. London: Robert Lancaster, 1642.

Eddy, Paul Rhodes. "Justification in Historical Perspective." In *Justification: Five Views*, edited by James K. Beilby and Paul Rhodes Eddy, 176–218. London: SPCK, 2012.

Eddy, Paul Rhodes, and James K. Beilby. "Justification in Contemporary Debate." In *Justification: Five Views*, edited by James K. Beilby and Paul Rhodes Eddy, 53–82. London: SPCK, 2012.

Edwards, David L., and John Stott. *Essentials: A Liberal-Evangelical Dialogue*. London: Hodder & Stoughton, 1988.

Edwards, Jonathan. *Sermons*. Vol. 2 of *Select Works of Jonathan Edwards*. 1839. Reprint, London: Banner of Truth, 1959.

Edwards, Jonathan. *The Works of Jonathan Edwards*. Edited by Perry Miller, John E. Smith, and Harry S. Stout. 26 vols. New Haven, CT: Yale University Press, 1957–2008.

Eglinton, James. *Trinity and Organism: Towards a New Reading of Herman Bavinck's Organic Motif*. London: Bloomsbury, 2012.

Elders, Leo. *The Philosophical Theology of St. Thomas Aquinas*. Leiden: Brill, 1990.

Ella, George M. "Where Luther Puts Olyott Right." *Biographia Evangelica.* http://www.evangelica.de/articles/where-luther-puts-olyott-right/. Accessed December 21, 2012.

Ella, George M. "Where Olyott Got It Wrong." *Biographia Evangelica.* http://www.evangelica.de/articles/where-olyott-got-it-wrong/. Accessed December 21, 2012.

Ellicott, Charles John. *A Bible Commentary for English Readers.* London: Cassell, 1897.

Ellingsen, Mark. "Augustinian Origins of the Reformation Reconsidered." *SJT* 64 (2011): 13–28.

Emery, Gilles. *The Trinity: An Introduction to Catholic Doctrine of the Triune God.* Translated by Matthew Levering. Washington, DC: Catholic University of America Press, 2011.

Emery, Gilles, and Matthew Levering, eds. *The Oxford Handbook of the Trinity.* Oxford: Oxford University Press, 2011.

Enns, Peter. *Inspiration and Incarnation: Evangelicals and the Problem of the Old Testament.* Grand Rapids, MI: Baker, 2005.

Ensor, Peter. "Justin Martyr and Penal Substitutionary Atonement." *EQ* 83 (2011): 217–32.

Erasmus, Desiderius. *Praise of Folly.* Translated by Betty Radice. Revised by A. H. T. Levi. London: Penguin, 1991.

Erickson, John H. "Autocephaly and Autonomy." *SVTQ* 60 (2016): 91–110.

Evans, G. R. *Anselm.* London: Geoffrey Chapman, 1989.

Evans, Ivor H. *Brewer's Dictionary of Phrase and Fable.* London: Cassell, 1981.

Evans, William B. *Imputation and Impartation: Union with Christ in American Reformed Theology.* Eugene, OR: Wipf & Stock, 2008.

Every, George. *The Byzantine Patriarchate 451–1204.* London: SPCK, 1947.

Fairweather, Eugene R., ed. *A Scholastic Miscellany: Anselm to Ockham.* New York: Macmillan, 1970.

Farrow, Douglas. *Ascension and Ecclesia: On the Significance of the Doctrine of the Ascension for Ecclesiology and Cosmology.* Edinburgh: T&T Clark, 1999.

Featley, Daniel. *The Dippers Dipt, or the Anabaptists Duck'd and Plung'd over Head and Eares, at a Disputation in Southwark.* London: Nicholas Bourne and Richard Royston, 1645.

Fairbairn, Donald. *Grace and Christology in the Early Church.* Oxford: Oxford University Press, 2003.

Fairbairn, Donald. "The One Person Who Is Jesus Christ: The Patristic Perspective." In *Jesus in Trinitarian Perspective: An Introductory Christol-*

ogy, edited by Fred Sanders and Klaus Issler, 80–113. Nashville: B&H Academic, 2007.

Fairbairn, Donald. "Patristic Exegesis and Theology: The Cart and the Horse." *WTJ* 69 (2007): 1–19.

Fairbairn, Donald. "Patristic Soteriology: Three Trajectories." *JETS 50* (2007): 298–310.

Fee, Gordon D. *The First Epistle to the Corinthians*. Grand Rapids, MI: Eerdmans, 1987.

Fee, Gordon D. *Paul's Letter to the Philippians*. Grand Rapids, MI: Eerdmans, 1995.

Fenner, Dudley. *Sacra theologia, sive veritas quae secundum pietatem*. Geneva, 1585.

Ferguson, Sinclair B., David F. Wright, and J. I. Packer, eds. *New Dictionary of Theology*. Leicester: Inter-Varsity Press, 1988.

Ferrar, W. J., ed. and trans. *The Proof of the Gospel*. Eugene, OR: Wipf & Stock, 2001.

Ferry, Brenton C. "Cross-Examining Moses' Defense: An Answer to Ramsey's Critique of Kline and Karlberg." *WTJ* 67 (2005): 163–68.

Fesko, John V. *Death in Adam, Life in Christ: The Doctrine of Imputation*. Fearn: Mentor, 2016.

Fesko, John V. *Diversity within the Reformed Tradition: Supra- and Infralapsarianism in Calvin, Dort, and Westminster*. Greenville, SC: Reformed Academic Press, 2003.

Fesko, John V. *Last Things First: Unlocking Genesis 1–3 with the Christ of Eschatology*. Fearn: Mentor, 2007.

Fesko, John V. "Sanctification and Union with Christ: A Reformed Perspective." *EQ* 82 (2010): 197–214.

Fesko, John V. *The Theology of the Westminster Standards: Historical Context and Theological Insights*. Wheaton, IL: Crossway, 2014.

Fesko, John V. *The Trinity and the Covenant of Redemption*. Fearn: Mentor, 2016.

Fesko, John V. "The Westminster Confession and Lapsarianism: Calvin and the Divines." In *The Westminster Confession into the 21st Century*, edited by J. Ligon Duncan III, 2:477–525. Fearn: Mentor, 2005.

Fiddes, P. *Past Event and Present Salvation*. London: Darton, Longman & Todd, 1989.

Figgis, J. N. *Studies of Political Thought from Gerson to Grotius, 1414–1625: Seven Studies*. 2nd ed. Cambridge: Cambridge University Press, 1916.

Fine, Arthur. "The Einstein-Podolsky-Rosen Argument in Quantum Theory." *The Stanford Encyclopedia of Philosophy*, edited by Edward N.

Zalta (Winter 2017). https://plato.stanford.edu/archives/win2017/entries /qt-epr/>.

Finlan, Stephen. "Can We Speak of Theosis in Paul?" In *Partakers of the Divine Nature: The History and Development of Deification in the Christian Traditions*, edited by Michael J. Christensen and Jeffery A. Wittung, 68–80. Grand Rapids, MI: Baker Academic, 2007.

Finney, Charles G. *Lectures on Systematic Theology*. London: William Tegg, 1851.

Fiorenza, Elisabeth Schüssler. *Changing Horizons: Explorations in Feminist Interpretation*. Minneapolis: Fortress, 2013.

Fiorenza, Elisabeth Schüssler. *In Memory of Her: A Feminist Theological Reconstruction of Christian Origins*. New York: Crossroad, 1983.

Fiorenza, Elisabeth Schüssler. *Jesus: Miriam's Child, Sophia's Prophet: Critical Issues in Feminist Christology*. 2nd ed. London: Bloomsbury, 2015.

Fiorenza, Elisabeth Schüssler. "Toward a Feminist Biblical Hermeneutics: Biblical Interpretation and Liberation Theology." In *A Guide to Contemporary Hermeneutics*, edited by Donald K. McKim, 358–82. Grand Rapids, MI: Eerdmans, 1986.

Fitzgerald, Allan D. *Augustine through the Ages: An Encyclopedia*. Grand Rapids, MI: Eerdmans, 1999.

Fitzmyer, Joseph A., SJ. *First Corinthians: A New Translation with Introduction and Commentary*. The Anchor Yale Bible. New Haven, CT: Yale University Press, 2008.

Fitzmyer, Joseph A., SJ. *The Gospel according to Luke (I-IX)*. The Anchor Bible. New York: Doubleday, 1970.

Flavel, John. *The Mystery of Providence*. 1678. Reprint, London: Banner of Truth, 1963.

Flood, Derek. "Substitutionary Atonement and the Church Fathers: A Reply to the Authors of *Pierced for Our Transgressions*." *EQ* 82 (2010): 142–59.

Florovsky, Georges. *The Eastern Fathers of the Fourth Century*. Vol. 7 of *The Collected Works of Father Georges Florovsky*. Edited by Richard S. Haugh. Vaduz: Büchervertriebsanstalt, 1987.

Florovsky, Georges. "St. Athanasius' Concept of Creation." In *Aspects of Church History*. Vol. 4 of *The Collected Works of Georges Florovsky*. Edited by Richard S. Haugh, 39–62. Vaduz: Büchervertriebsanstalt, 1987.

Frame, John M. *The Doctrine of God*. Phillipsburg, NJ: P&R, 2002.

Frame, John M. *Systematic Theology*. Phillipsburg, NJ: P&R, 2013.

France, R. T. "Chronological Aspects of 'Gospel Harmony.'" *VE* 16 (1986): 50–54.

France, R. T. *The Gospel according to Matthew: An Introduction and Commentary*. Leicester: Inter-Varsity Press, 1985.

Frend, W. H. C. *The Rise of the Monophysite Movement*. Cambridge: Cambridge University Press, 1972.

Froom, Le Roy Edwin. *The Conditionalist Faith of Our Fathers*. Washington, DC: Review and Herald, 1966.

Fudge, Edward. *The Fire That Consumes*. Houston: Providential, 1982.

Furnish, Victor Paul. *II Corinthians*. The Anchor Bible. New York: Doubleday, 1984.

Gaffin, Richard B., Jr. *By Faith, Not by Sight: Paul and the Order of Salvation*. Milton Keynes: Paternoster, 2006.

Gaffin, Richard B., Jr. *The Centrality of the Resurrection: A Study in Paul's Soteriology*. Grand Rapids, MI: Baker, 1978.

Gallaher, Brandon. *Freedom and Necessity in Modern Trinitarian Theology*. Oxford: Oxford University Press, 2016.

Gamble, Richard C. *The Whole Counsel of God*. Vol. 2, *The Full Revelation of God*. Phillipsburg, NJ: P&R, 2018.

Garcia, Mark A. "Imputation and the Christology of Union with Christ: Calvin, Osiander, and the Contemporary Quest for a Reformed Model." *WTJ* 68 (2006): 219–51.

Garcia, Mark A. *Life in Christ: Union with Christ and Twofold Grace in Calvin's Theology*. Milton Keynes: Paternoster, 2008.

Garner, David B. *Sons in the Son: The Riches and Reach of Adoption in Christ*. Phillipsburg, NJ: P&R, 2017.

Gaunilo of Marmoutiers. *Pro insipiente (On Behalf of the Fool)*.

Gavrilyuk, Paul. "Creation in Early Christian Polemical Literature: Irenaeus against the Gnostics and Athanasius against the Arians." *MTheol* 29, no. 2 (2013): 22–32.

Gavrilyuk, Paul. "The Reception of Dionysius in Twentieth-Century Eastern Orthodoxy." *MTheol* 24 (2008): 707–23.

Gavrilyuk, Paul. "The Retrieval of Deification: How a Once-Despised Archaism Became an Ecumenical Desideratum." *MTheol* 25 (2009): 647–59.

Gerrish, B. A. *Grace and Gratitude: The Eucharistic Theology of John Calvin*. Minneapolis: Fortress, 1993.

Gibson, David, and Jonathan Gibson, eds. *From Heaven He Came and Sought Her: Definite Atonement in Historical, Biblical, Theological, and Pastoral Perspective*. Wheaton, IL: Crossway, 2013.

Giles, Kevin. *The Eternal Generation of the Son: Maintaining Orthodoxy in Trinitarian Theology*. Downers Grove, IL: IVP Academic, 2012.

Giles, Kevin. "The Father as the *Mia Archē*, the One Originating Source of the Son and the Spirit, and the Trinity as the *Monarchia*, the One Undivided Sovereign Ruler." *Colloquium* 46, no. 2 (2014): 175–92.

Giles, Kevin. *The Trinity and Subordinationism*. Downers Grove, IL: InterVarsity Press, 2002.

Gillespie, George. *A Treatise of Miscellany Questions*. Edinburgh: Gedeon Lithgow for George Swintoun, 1649.

Glare, P. G. W. *Oxford Latin Dictionary*. Oxford: Oxford University Press, 1996.

Godfrey, W. Robert. *God's Pattern for Creation: A Covenantal Reading of Genesis 1*. Phillipsburg, NJ: P&R, 2003.

Godfrey, W. Robert. "Tensions within International Calvinism: The Debate on the Atonement at the Synod of Dort." PhD diss., Stanford University, 1974.

Gomarus, Franciscus. "Oratio de Foedere Dei." In *Opera Theologica Omnia*. Amsterdam, 1664.

Goodwin, Thomas. *Christ Our Mediator*. 1692. Reprint, Grand Rapids, MI: Sovereign Grace Publishers, 1971.

Goodwin, Thomas. *An Exposition of Ephesians Chapter 1 to 2:10*. N.p.: Sovereign Grace Book Club, 1958.

Goodwin, Thomas. *The Works of Thomas Goodwin*. Edinburgh: James Nichol, 1864.

Gough, J. W. *The Social Contract: A Critical Study of Its Development*. 2nd ed. Oxford: Clarendon, 1957.

Grayston, Kenneth. *The Johannine Epistles*. The New Century Bible Commentary. Grand Rapids, MI: Eerdmans, 1984.

Greaves, Richard L. *Theology and Revolution in the Scottish Reformation*. Grand Rapids, MI: Christian University Press, 1980.

Green, Bradley G. *Colin Gunton and the Failure of Augustine: The Theology of Colin Gunton in the Light of Augustine*. Eugene, OR: Pickwick, 2011.

Green, Joel B. *The Gospel of Luke*. Grand Rapids, MI: Eerdmans, 1997.

Green, Lowell C. "Faith, Righteousness, and Justification: New Light on Their Development under Luther and Melanchthon." *SCJ* 4, no. 1 (1973): 65–86.

Gregg, Robert C. *Early Arianism—a Way of Salvation*. Philadelphia: Fortress, 1981.

Grider, J. K. "Arminianism." In *Evangelical Dictionary of Theology*, edited by Walter A. Elwell, 79–81. Basingstoke: Marshall Pickering, 1985.

Grillmeier, Aloys, SJ. *Christ in Christian Tradition*. Vol. 1, *From the Apostolic Age to Chalcedon (451)*. 2nd ed. Translated by John Bowden. Atlanta: John Knox, 1975.

Grillmeier, Aloys, SJ. *Christ in Christian Tradition.* Vol. 2, *From the Council of Chalcedon (451) to Gregory the Great (590–604).* Pt. 2, *The Church of Constantinople in the Sixth Century.* Translated by Theresia Hainthaler and John Cawte. London: Mowbray, 1995.

Grosseteste, Robert. *On the Six Days of Creation: Translation of the Hexaëmeron.* Translated by C. F. J. Martin. Auctores Britannici Medii Aevi. Oxford: Oxford University Press, 1996.

Grotius, Hugo. *Opera omnia theologica.* London: Moses Pitt, 1679.

Grudem, Wayne A. *The First Epistle of Peter: An Introduction and Commentary.* Leicester: Inter-Varsity Press, 1988.

Grudem, Wayne A. *The Gift of Prophecy in the New Testament and Today.* Westchester, IL: Crossway, 1988.

Grudem, Wayne A. *Systematic Theology.* Grand Rapids, MI: Zondervan, 1994.

Gunton, Colin. *The Actuality of Atonement.* Edinburgh: T&T Clark, 1988.

Gunton, Colin. "Augustine, the Trinity, and the Theological Crisis of the West." *SJT* 43 (1990): 33–58.

Gunton, Colin. *The Triune Creator.* Grand Rapids, MI: Eerdmans, 1998.

Gunton, Colin. "Two Dogmas Revisited: Edward Irving's Christology." *SJT* 41 (1988): 359–76.

Guthrie, Donald. *New Testament Theology.* Leicester: Inter-Varsity Press, 1981.

Ha, Polly. "English Presbyterianism c. 1590–1640." PhD diss. Cambridge University, 2006.

Habets, Myk, ed. *Ecumenical Perspectives on the Filioque for the Twenty-First Century.* London: Bloomsbury, 2014.

Hales, John. *Letters from the Synod of Dort to Sir Dudley Carlton, the English Embassador at the Hague.* Glasgow, 1765.

Hall, Basil. "Calvin against the Calvinists." In *John Calvin,* edited by Gervase E. Duffield, 19–37. Abingdon: Sutton Courtenay, 1966.

Hall, David W., and Joseph H. Hall, eds. *Paradigms in Polity: Classic Readings in Reformed and Presbyterian Church Government.* Grand Rapids, MI: Eerdmans, 1994.

Hallonstein, Gösta. "Theosis in Recent Research: A Renewal of Interest and a Need for Clarity." In *Partakers of the Divine Nature: The History and Development of Deification in the Christian Traditions,* edited by Michael J. Christensen and Jeffery A. Wittung, 281–93. Grand Rapids, MI: Baker Academic, 2007.

Hampson, Daphne. *Theology and Feminism.* Oxford: Basil Blackwell, 1990.

Hanson, R. P. C. *Allegory and Event: A Study of the Sources and Significance of Origen's Interpretation of Scripture.* 1959. Reprint, Louisville: Westminster John Knox, 2002.

Hanson, R. P. C. *The Search for the Christian Doctrine of God: The Arian Controversy 318–381.* Edinburgh: T&T Clark, 1988.

Harbison, Craig. *The Last Judgment in Sixteenth-Century Northern Europe: A Study of the Relation between Art and the Reformation.* New York: Garland, 1976.

Hardy, Edward Roche. *Christology of the Later Fathers.* Philadelphia: Westminster, 1954.

Harnack, Adolf von. *History of Dogma.* Translated by James Millar. London: Williams & Norgate, 1897.

Harnack, Adolf von. *Das wesen des Christentums: Sechzehn Vorlesungen vor Studierenden aller Facultäten im Wintersemester 1899/1900 an der Universität Berlin gerhalten.* Leipzig: Hinrichs, 1901.

Harris, Mark. "When Jesus Lost His Soul: Fourth-Century Christology and Modern Neuroscience." *SJT* 70 (2017): 74–92.

Harrison, F. H. W. "The Nottinghamshire Baptists: Polity." *BQ* 25 (1974): 212–31.

Harrison, Verna E. F. "The Relationship between Apophatic and Kataphatic Theology." *PrEccl* 6 (1995): 318–32.

Hart, D. G. *John Williamson Nevin: High-Church Calvinist.* Phillipsburg, NJ: P&R, 2005.

Hart, D. G. *A Secular Faith: Why Christianity Favors the Separation of Church and State.* Chicago: Ivan R. Dee, 2006.

Hart, Trevor. "Universalism: Two Distinct Types." In *Universalism and the Doctrine of Hell: Papers Presented at the Fourth Edinburgh Conference in Christian Dogmatics, 1991.* Edited by Nigel M. de S. Cameron, 1–34. Carlisle: Paternoster, 1992.

Hasker, William, David Basinger, and Eef Dekker. *Middle Knowledge: Theory and Application.* Frankfurt am Main: Peter Lang, 2000.

Haugh, Richard S. *Photius and the Carolingians: The Trinitarian Controversy.* Belmont, MA: Norland, 1975.

Hawking, Stephen W. *A Brief History of Time: From the Big Bang to Black Holes.* New York: Bantam, 1988.

Hays, Richard B. *Echoes of Scripture in the Gospels.* Waco, TX: Baylor University Press, 2016.

Hayward, Alan. *Creation and Evolution: The Facts and Fallacies.* London: SPCK, 1985.

Heans, Simon. "Original Sin or Original Sinfulness? A Comment." *Heythrop Journal* 54 (2013): 55–69.

Heeren, Fred. "Home Alone in the Universe?" *First Things*, March 2002. https://www.firstthings.com/article/2002/03/home-alone-in-the-universe-36. Accessed July 1, 2014.

Heidegger, Joh. Heinrici. *Corpus theologiae Christianae*. Zurich: Joh. Henrici Bodmeri, 1700.

Helm, Paul. "Does Justification Cause Sanctification?" Helm's Deep (blog), June 1, 2011. http://paulhelmsdeep.blogspot.com/2011/06/does-justiification-cause.html.

Helm, Paul. *Eternal God: A Study of God without Time*. 2nd ed. New York: Oxford University Press, 2011.

Helm, Paul. *John Calvin's Ideas*. Oxford: Oxford University Press, 2004.

Helm, Paul. *The Last Things: Death, Judgment, Heaven, Hell*. Edinburgh: Banner of Truth, 1989.

Helm, Paul. "The Logic of Limited Atonement." *SBET* 3 (1985): 50.

Helm, Paul. *The Providence of God*. Leicester: Inter-Varsity Press, 1993.

Hendel, Ronald S., William W. Hallo, and Kenneth A. Kitchen. "The Kitchen Debate." *Biblical Archaeology Review* 31, no. 4 (2005): 48–53.

Hennessy, Kristin. "An Answer to De Régnon's Critics: Why We Should Not Speak of 'His' Paradigm." *HTR* 100 (2007): 179–97.

Hick, John. *Evil and the God of Love: God and the Universe of Faiths*. London: Macmillan, 1966.

Hick, John. *God Has Many Names: Britain's New Religious Pluralism*. London: Macmillan, 1980.

Hill, Charles E. Regnum Caelorum: *Patterns of Millennial Thought in Early Christianity*. 2nd ed. Grand Rapids, MI: Eerdmans, 2001.

Hill, David. *The Gospel of Matthew*. London: Marshall, Morgan & Scott, 1972.

Hillerbrand, Hans J., ed. *The Oxford Encyclopedia of the Reformation*. 4 vols. New York: Oxford University Press, 1996.

Hodge, A. A. "Inspiration." *Presbyterian Review* 2 (April 1881): 225–60.

Hodge, A. A. *Outlines of Theology*. Grand Rapids, MI: Eerdmans, 1972.

Hodge, Charles. *A Commentary on the Epistle to the Ephesians*. London: Banner of Truth, 1964.

Hodge, Charles. *A Commentary on the Second Epistle to the Corinthians*. London: Banner of Truth, 1959.

Hodge, Charles. *Systematic Theology*. 3 vols. Grand Rapids, MI: Eerdmans, 1977.

Hoeksema, Herman. *Reformed Dogmatics*. Grand Rapids, MI: Reformed Free Publishing Association, 1966.

Hoffmeier, James K. *Ancient Israel in Sinai: The Evidence for the Authenticity of the Wilderness Tradition.* New York: Oxford University Press, 2011.

Hogg, David S. *Anselm of Canterbury: The Beauty of Theology.* Aldershot: Ashgate, 2004.

Holland, Tom. *Contours of Pauline Theology: A Radical New Survey of the Influences on Paul's Biblical Writings.* Fearn: Mentor, 2004.

Holland, Tom. *Tom Wright and the Search for Truth.* London: Apiary, 2017.

Holmes, Stephen R. *The Holy Trinity: Understanding God's Life.* Milton Keynes: Paternoster, 2012.

Hoogland, Marvin P. *Calvin's Perspective on the Exaltation of Christ in Comparison with the Post-Reformation Doctrine of the Two States.* Kampen: Kok, 1966.

Hoover, Roy W. "The Harpagmos Enigma: A Philological Solution." *HTR* 64 (1971): 95–119.

Horton, Michael. *The Christian Faith: A Systematic Theology for Pilgrims on the Way.* Grand Rapids, MI: Zondervan, 2011.

Horton, Michael. *Covenant and Salvation: Union with Christ.* Louisville: Westminster John Knox, 2007.

Horton, Michael. "Traditional Reformed View." In *Justification: Five Views*, edited by James K. Beilby and Paul Rhodes Eddy, 83–130. London: SPCK, 2012.

Hughes, Philip Edgcumbe. *The Book of Revelation: A Commentary.* Leicester: Inter-Varsity Press, 1990).

Hughes, Philip Edgcumbe. "The Christology of Hebrews." *SwJT* 28 (1985): 19–27.

Hughes, Philip Edgcumbe. *A Commentary on the Epistle to the Hebrews.* Grand Rapids, MI: Eerdmans, 1977.

Hughes, Philip Edgcumbe. *Paul's Second Epistle to the Corinthians: The English Text, with Introduction, Exposition and Notes.* London: Marshall, Morgan & Scott, 1961.

Hughes, Philip Edgcumbe. *The True Image: The Origin and Destiny of Man in Christ.* Grand Rapids, MI: Eerdmans, 1989.

Hunsinger, George. "Election and the Trinity: Twenty-Five Theses on the Theology of Karl Barth." *MTheol* 24 (2008): 179–98.

Hunsinger, George. "Hellfire and Damnation: Four Ancient and Modern Views." *SJT* 51 (1998): 406–34.

Hurtado, Larry W. "Christology." In *Dictionary of the Later New Testament and Its Development*, edited by Ralph P. Martin and Peter H. Davids, 170–84. Downers Grove, IL: InterVarsity Press, 1997.

Hurtado, Larry W. "Lord." In *Dictionary of Paul and His Letters*, edited by Gerald F. Hawthorne, 560–69. Downers Grove, IL: InterVarsity Press, 1993.

Hurtado, Larry W. *Lord Jesus Christ: Devotion to Jesus in Earliest Christianity.* Grand Rapids, MI: Eerdmans, 2005.

Hurtado, Larry W. *One God, One Lord: Early Christian Devotion and Ancient Jewish Monotheism.* 3rd ed. London: T&T Clark, 2015.

Hurtado, Larry W. "Pre-Existence." In *Dictionary of Paul and His Letters*, edited by Gerald F. Hawthorne, 743–46. Downers Grove, IL: InterVarsity Press, 1993.

Hurtado, Larry W. "Son of God." In *Dictionary of Paul and His Letters*, edited by Gerald F. Hawthorne, 900–906. Downers Grove, IL: InterVarsity Press, 1993.

Hussey, M. Edmund. "The Palamite Trinitarian Models." *SVTQ* 16 (1972): 83–89.

Hutchinson, George P. *The Problem of Original Sin in American Presbyterian Theology.* Nutley, NJ: Presbyterian and Reformed, 1972.

Irving, Edward. *Collected Writings.* London: Alexander Strahan, 1864–1865.

Jeffery, Steve, Michael Ovey, and Andrew Sach. *Pierced for Our Transgressions: Recovering the Glory of Penal Substitution.* Wheaton, IL: Crossway, 2007.

Jenson, Robert W. "Once More the *Logos Asarkos*." *IJST* 13 (2011): 130–33.

Jenson, Robert W. "Response to Mark Seifrid, Paul Metzger, and Carl Trueman on Finnish Luther Research." *WTJ* 65 (2003): 245–50.

Jeremias, Joachim. *The Eucharistic Words of Jesus.* London: SCM, 1966.

Jeremias, Joachim. *The Parables of Jesus.* Translated by S. H. Hooke. London: SCM, 1954.

Jersak, Brad, and Michael Hardin, eds. *Stricken by God? Nonviolent Identification and the Victory of Christ.* Grand Rapids, MI: Eerdmans, 2007.

Jewett, Paul K. *Election and Predestination.* Grand Rapids, MI: Eerdmans, 1986.

John of Damascus. *Three Treatises on the Divine Images.* Translated by Andrew Louth. Crestwood, NY: St Vladimir's Seminary Press, 2003.

Johnson, Elizabeth. *Jesus-Sophia: Ramifications for Contemporary Theology: Mary Ward Lecture, 1999.* Cambridge: Margaret Beaufort Institute for Theology, 1999.

Johnson, Elizabeth. *She Who Is.* New York: Crossroad, 1996.

Johnson, Marcus. "Luther and Calvin on Union with Christ." *Fides et Historia* 39, no. 2 (2007): 59–77.

Joly, Robert. *Le vocabulaire Chrétien de l'amour est-il original? Filein et agapan dans le Grec antique.* Bruxelles: Presses Universitaires de Bruxelles, 1968.

Jones, Peter R. "The Apostle Paul: Second Moses to the New Covenant Community." In *God's Inerrant Word,* edited by John Warwick Montgomery, 219–41. Minneapolis: Bethany Fellowship, 1974.

Jordan, Mark. *Rewritten Theology: Aquinas after His Readers.* Oxford: Blackwell, 2006.

Junius, Franciscus. *Opera theologica.* Geneva, 1613.

Kannengiesser, Charles. *Arius and Athanasius: Two Alexandrian Theologians.* Aldershot, Hampshire: Variorum, 1991.

Kant, Immanuel. *Immanuel Kant's Critique of Pure Reason.* 2nd impression with corrections. Translated by Norman Kemp Smith. 1933. Reprint, London: Macmillan, 1970.

Kapic, Kelly. "The Son's Assumption of a Human Nature: A Call for Clarity." *IJST* 3 (2001): 154–66.

Karlberg, Mark W. "Recovering the Mosaic Covenant as Law and Gospel: J. Mark Beach, John H. Sailhammer, and Jason C. Meyer as Representative Expositors." *EQ* 83 (2011): 233–50.

Karlberg, Mark W. "The Search for an Evangelical Consensus on Paul and the Law." *JETS* 40 (1997): 563–79.

Käsemann, Ernst. *Commentary on Romans.* Translated by Geoffrey W. Bromiley. Grand Rapids, MI: Eerdmans, 1980.

Keating, James F., and Thomas White. *Divine Impassibility and the Mystery of Human Suffering.* Grand Rapids, MI: Eerdmans, 2009.

Kelly, Douglas F. *Systematic Theology.* Vol. 2, *Grounded in Holy Scripture and Understood in the Light of the Church: The Beauty of Christ: A Trinitarian Vision.* Fearn: Mentor, 2014.

Kelly, J. N. D. *A Commentary on the Epistles of Peter and Jude.* London: Adam & Charles Black, 1969.

Kelly, J. N. D. *Early Christian Doctrines.* London: Adam & Charles Black, 1968.

Kelly, J. N. D. *Golden Mouth: The Story of John Chrysostom—Ascetic, Preacher, Bishop.* Grand Rapids, MI: Baker, 1995.

Kelly, J. N. D. "The Nicene Creed: A Turning Point." *SJT* 36 (1983): 29–39.

Kendall, R. T. *Calvin and English Calvinism to 1649.* Oxford: Oxford University Press, 1979.

Kenney, Anthony. *The Five Ways: St. Thomas Aquinas; Proofs for God's Existence.* London: Routledge, 2008.

Kern, Fritz. *Kingship and Law in the Middle Ages.* Oxford: Basil Blackwell, 1939.

Kerr, Fergus. "Theology in Philosophy: Revisiting the Five Ways." *International Journal for Philosophy of Religion* 50, no. 1/3 (2001): 115–30.

Kettler, Christian D. *The Vicarious Humanity of Christ and the Reality of Salvation.* Lanham, MD: University Press of America, 1991.

Kidd, B. J. *Documents Illustrative of the Continental Reformation.* 1911. Reprint, Oxford: Clarendon, 1967.

Kim, Seyoon. *The Origin of Paul's Gospel.* Grand Rapids, MI: Eerdmans, 1982.

Kim, Seyoon. *Paul and the New Perspective: Second Thoughts on the Origin of Paul's Gospel.* Grand Rapids, MI: Eerdmans, 2002.

Kingdon, Robert M. *Geneva and the Consolidation of the French Protestant Movement 1564–1572: A Contribution to the History of Congregationalism, Presbyterianism, and Calvinist Resistance Theory.* Geneva: Droz, 1967.

Kitchen, Kenneth A. *On the Reliability of the Old Testament.* Grand Rapids, MI: Eerdmans, 2003.

Kitchen, Kenneth A., and Paul J. N. Lawrence, *Treaty, Law and Covenant in the Ancient Near East.* Weisbaden: Harrassowitz, 2012.

Kline, Meredith G. "Because It Had Not Rained." *WTJ* 20 (1958): 146–57.

Kline, Meredith G. *By Oath Consigned: A Reinterpretation of the Covenantal Signs of Circumcision and Baptism.* Grand Rapids, MI: Eerdmans, 1968.

Kline, Meredith G. "Covenant Theology under Attack." *NH,* February 1994, 1–4.

Kline, Meredith G. *The Structure of Biblical Authority.* Grand Rapids, MI: Eerdmans, 1972.

Knight, George W., III. "Two Offices (Elders/Bishops and Deacons) and Two Orders of Elders (Preaching/Teaching Elders and Ruling Elders): A New Testament Study." *Presbyterion* 11 (Spring 1985): 1–12.

Kodama. Takeshi. "The Unity and Catholicity of the Church: A Comparison of Calvin and the Westminster Assembly." PhD diss., University of Wales, Trinity Saint David, 2011.

Kraus, Hans-Joachim. "Calvin's Exegetical Principles." *Interpretation* 31 (1977): 8–18.

Kreeft, Peter. *A Summa of the Summa: The Essential Philosophical Passages of St. Thomas Aquinas'* Summa Theologica *Edited and Explained for Beginners.* San Francisco: Ignatius, 1990.

Kruger, Michael J. *The Question of Canon: Challenging the Status Quo in the New Testament Debate.* Nottingham: Apollos, 2013.

Kuyper, Abraham. *Common Grace: God's Gifts for a Fallen World.* Vol. 1. Translated by Nelson D. Kloosterman and Ed M. van der Mass. Bellingham, WA: Lexham, 2016.

Kuyper, Abraham. *The Work of the Holy Spirit.* Translated by Henri De Vries. Grand Rapids, MI: Eerdmans, 1975.

Lacoste, Jean-Yves. *Encyclopedia of Christian Theology.* Abingdon: Routledge, 2005.

Ladouceur, Paul. "Evolution and Genesis 2–3: The Decline and Fall of Adam and Eve." *SVTQ* 57 (2013): 135–76.

Ladouceur, Paul. "Orthodox Critiques of the Agreed Statements between the Orthodox and Oriental Orthodox Churches." *SVTQ* 60 (2016): 333–68.

Ladouceur, Paul. "Orthodox Theologies of the Afterlife." *SVTQ* 62 (2018): 51–72.

Lagrange, M.-J. *Evangile selon Saint Jean.* Paris: Gabalda, 1948.

Lampe, G. W. H., ed. *A Patristic Greek Lexicon.* Oxford: Clarendon, 1961.

Lancel, Serge. *Saint Augustine.* Translated by Antonia Nevill. London: SCM, 2002.

Landis, Robert W. *The Doctrine of Original Sin Received and Taught by the Churches of the Reformation Stated and Defended, and the Error of Dr. Hodge in Claiming That This Doctrine Recognizes the Gratuitous Imputation of Sin, Pointed Out and Refuted.* Richmond, VA: Whittet & Sheperson, 1884.

Lane, Anthony N. S. *Exploring Christian Doctrine.* London: SPCK, 2013.

Lane, Anthony N. S. "Is the Truth Out There? Creatures, Cosmos and New Creation." *EQ* 84 (2012): 291–306; 85 (2013): 3–18.

Lane, Anthony N. S. *John Calvin: Student of the Church Fathers.* Grand Rapids, MI: Baker, 1999.

Lane, Anthony N. S. *Justification by Faith in Catholic-Protestant Dialogue: An Evangelical Assessment.* London: T&T Clark, 2002.

Lane, Anthony N. S. "Scripture, Tradition and Church: An Historical Survey." *VE* 9 (1975): 37–55.

Lattier, Daniel J. "The Orthodox Rejection of Doctrinal Development." *PrEccl* 20 (2011): 389–410.

Lebreton, Jules. *History of the Dogma of the Trinity: From Its Origins to the Council of Nicaea.* 8th ed. Translated by Algar Thorold. London: Burns Oates and Washbourne, 1939.

Lee, Sang Hoon. "Toward an Understanding of the Eschatological Presence of the Risen Jesus with Robert Jenson." *SJT* 71 (2018): 85–101.

Lee, Seung Goo. "The Relationship between the Ontological Trinity and the Economic Trinity." *JRT* 3 (2009): 90–107.

Leith, John H. *Assembly at Westminster: Reformed Theology in the Making.* Richmond, VA: John Knox, 1973.

Leith, John H. "Calvin's Doctrine of the Proclamation of the Word and Its Significance for Us Today." In *John Calvin and the Church: A Prism of Reform*, edited by Timothy George, 206–29. Louisville: Westminster John Knox, 1990.

Leithart, Peter J. *Athanasius.* Grand Rapids, MI: Baker Academic, 2011.

Lennox, John C. *God's Undertaker: Has Science Buried God?* Oxford: Lion, 2007.

Letham, Robert. "Amandus Polanus: A Neglected Theologian?" *SCJ* 21 (1990): 463–76.

Letham, Robert. "The Authority of Preaching." *Baptist Reformation Review* 3, no. 4 (1974): 21–29.

Letham, Robert. "Baptism in the Writings of the Reformers." *SBET* 7 (1989): 21–44.

Letham, Robert. "Catholicity Global and Historical: Constantinople, Westminster, and the Church in the Twenty-First Century." *WTJ* 72 (2010): 43–57.

Letham, Robert. *A Christian's Pocket Guide to Baptism.* Fearn: Christian Focus, 2012.

Letham, Robert. "The Doctrine of Eternal Generation in the Church Fathers." In *One God in Three Persons: Unity of Essence, Distinction of Persons, Implications for Life*, edited by Bruce A. Ware and John Starke, 109–25. Wheaton, IL: Crossway, 2015.

Letham, Robert. "Faith and Assurance in Early Calvinism: A Model of Continuity and Diversity." In *Later Calvinism: International Perspectives*, edited by W. Fred Graham, 355–84. Kirksville, MO: Sixteenth Century Journal Publishers, 1994.

Letham, Robert. "Faith and Assurance in Reformed Theology: Zwingli to the Synod of Dort." 2 vols. PhD diss., University of Aberdeen, 1979.

Letham, Robert. "The *Foedus Operum*: Some Factors Accounting for Its Development." *SCJ* 14 (1983): 63–76.

Letham, Robert. "The Hermeneutics of Feminism." *Them* 17 (1992): 4–7.

Letham, Robert. *The Holy Trinity: In Scripture, History, Theology, and Worship.* Phillipsburg, NJ: P&R, 2004.

Letham, Robert. "'In the Space of Six Days': The Days of Creation from Origen to the Westminster Assembly." *WTJ* 61 (1999): 149–74.

Letham, Robert. *The Lord's Supper: Eternal Word in Broken Bread.* Phillipsburg, NJ: P&R, 2001.

Letham, Robert. *The Message of the Person of Christ: The Word Made Flesh.* Nottingham: Inter-Varsity Press, 2013.

Letham, Robert. "'Not a Covenant of Works in Disguise' (Herman Bavinck): The Place of the Mosaic Covenant in Redemptive History." *MAJT* 24 (2013): 143–77.

Letham, Robert. "Old and New, East and West, and a Missing Horse." In *The Holy Trinity Revisited: Essays in Response to Stephen R. Holmes*, edited by T. A. Noble and Jason S. Sexton, 27–41. Milton Keynes: Paternoster, 2015.

Letham, Robert. "The Person of Christ." In *Reformation Theology: A Systematic Summary*, edited by Matthew Barrett, 313–45. Wheaton, IL: Crossway, 2017.

Letham, Robert. "The Relationship between Saving Faith and Assurance of Salvation." ThM thesis, Westminster Theological Seminary, 1976.

Letham, Robert. *Through Western Eyes: Eastern Orthodoxy: A Reformed Perspective*. Fearn: Mentor, 2007.

Letham, Robert. "The Trinity between East and West." *JRT* 3 (2009): 42–56.

Letham, Robert. "The Triune God, Incarnation, and Definite Atonement." In *From Heaven He Came and Sought Her: Definite Atonement in Historical, Biblical, Theological, and Pastoral Perspective*, edited by David Gibson and Jonathan Gibson, 437–60. Wheaton, IL: Crossway, 2013.

Letham, Robert. *Union with Christ: In Scripture, History, and Theology*. Phillipsburg, NJ: P&R, 2011.

Letham, Robert. "The Westminster Assembly and the Communion of Saints." In *Learning from the Past: Essays in Reception, Catholicity, and Dialogue in Honour of Anthony N. S. Lane*, edited by Jon Balserak and Richard Snoddy, 131–45. London: T&T Clark, 2015.

Letham, Robert. *The Westminster Assembly: Reading Its Theology in Historical Context*. Phillipsburg, NJ: P&R, 2009.

Letham, Robert. *The Work of Christ*. Leicester: Inter-Varsity Press, 1993.

Letham, Robert, and Donald Macleod. "Is Evangelicalism Christian?" *EQ* 67 (1995): 3–33.

Lewis, Bernard. *What Went Wrong? Western Impact and Middle Eastern Response*. New York: Oxford University Press, 2002.

Lewis, C. S. *Mere Christianity*. San Francisco: Harper, 1960.

Lewis, C. S. *Reflections on the Psalms*. London: Geoffrey Bles, 1958.

Lightfoot, J. B. *Saint Paul's Epistle to the Philippians: A Revised Text with Introduction, Notes, and Dissertations*. London: Macmillan, 1881.

Lillback, Peter A. *The Binding of God: Calvin's Role in the Development of Covenant Theology*. Grand Rapids, MI: Baker Academic, 2001.

Lindars, Barnabas. *The Gospel of John*. The New Century Bible Commentary. Grand Rapids, MI: Eerdmans, 1972.

Lindsay, T. M. *The Church and the Ministry in the Early Centuries*. London: Hodder & Stoughton, 1903.

Lloyd-Jones, D. Martyn. *Preaching and Preachers*. Grand Rapids, MI: Zondervan, 1971.

Lloyd-Jones, D. Martyn. *Romans: An Exposition of Chapter 6: The New Man*. London: Banner of Truth, 1972.

Loder, James E., and W. Jim Neidhardt. *The Knight's Move: The Relational Logic of the Spirit in Theology and Science*. Colorado Springs: Helmers & Howard, 1992.

Lombard, Christopher. "Problems concerning the Term *Person* in Karl Barth's *Church Dogmatics* (I/1) and Karl Rahner's *The Trinity*." MTh thesis, Middlesex University, 2014.

Lombard, Peter. *The Sentences*, Bk. 3, *On the Incarnation of the Word*. Toronto: Pontifical Institute of Medieval Studies, 2008.

López-Farjeat, Luis Xavier. "Avicenna's Influence on Aquinas' Early Doctrine of Creation." *RTPM* 79 (2012): 305–37.

Louth, Andrew. *John Damascene: Tradition and Originality in Byzantine Theology*. Oxford: Oxford University Press, 2002.

Louth, Andrew. *Modern Orthodox Thinkers: From the Philokalia to the Present*. London: SPCK, 2015.

Lossky, Vladimir. *The Mystical Theology of the Eastern Church*. London: James Clarke, 1957.

Luther, Martin. "Confession Concerning Christ's Supper." In *Luther's Works*. American Edition. Edited by Jaroslav Pelikan. Vol. 37, *Word and Sacrament III*. Translated by Robert H. Fischer. Reprint, Philadelphia: Fortress, 1961.

Luther, Martin. *Luther's Works*. American Edition. Edited by Jaroslav Pelikan. 55 vols. St. Louis: Concordia; Philadelphia: Fortress, 1955–1974.

Luther, Martin. "That These Words of Christ, 'This Is My Body,' etc., Still Stand Firm against the Fanatics." In *Luther's Works*. American Edition. Edited by Jaroslav Pelikan. Vol. 37, *Word and Sacrament III*. Translated by Robert H. Fischer. Reprint, Philadelphia: Fortress, 1961.

Macaskill, Grant. *Union with Christ in the New Testament*. Oxford: Oxford University Press, 2013.

Machen, J. Gresham. *Christianity and Liberalism*. London: Victory, 1923.

Machen, J. Gresham. *The Christian View of Man*. New York: Macmillan, 1937.

Mackintosh, H. R. *The Doctrine of the Person of Jesus Christ*. Edinburgh: T&T Clark, 1912.

Macleod, Donald. "Christian Assurance 1." *The Banner of Truth*, October 1974.

Macleod, Donald. *The Person of Christ*. Leicester: Inter-Varsity Press, 1998.

Madeume, Hans. "'The Most Vulnerable Part of the Whole Christian Account': Original Sin and Modern Science." In *Adam, the Fall, and Original Sin: Theological, Biblical, and Scientific Perspectives*, edited by Hans Madeume and Michael Reeves, 225–49. Grand Rapids, MI: Baker Academic, 2014.

Madeume, Hans, and Michael Reeves, eds. *Adam, the Fall, and Original Sin: Theological, Biblical, and Scientific Perspectives*. Grand Rapids, MI: Baker Academic, 2014.

Madeume, Hans, and Michael Reeves. "Threads in a Seamless Garment: Original Sin in Systematic Theology." In *Adam, the Fall, and Original Sin: Theological, Biblical, and Scientific Perspectives*, edited by Hans Madeume and Michael Reeves, 209–24. Grand Rapids, MI: Baker Academic, 2014.

Mannermaa, Tuomo. "Justification and Theosis in Lutheran-Orthodox Perspective." In *Union with Christ: The New Finnish Interpretation of Luther*, edited by Carl E. Braaten and Robert W. Jenson, 25–41. Grand Rapids, MI: Eerdmans, 1998.

Mannermaa, Tuomo. "Why Is Luther So Fascinating? Modern Finnish Luther Research." In *Union with Christ: The New Finnish Interpretation of Luther*, edited by Carl E. Braaten and Robert W. Jenson, 1–20. Grand Rapids, MI: Eerdmans, 1998.

Marshall, I. Howard. *The Gospel of Luke: A Commentary on the Greek Text*. The New International Greek Testament Commentary. Exeter: Paternoster, 1978.

Martens, Peter W. *Origen and Scripture: The Contours of the Exegetical Life*. Oxford: Oxford University Press, 2012.

Martin, Hugh. *The Atonement: In Its Relations to the Covenant, the Priesthood, the Intercession of Our Lord*. Edinburgh: Lyon and Gemmell, 1877.

Martin, Ralph P. *Carmen Christi: Philippians ii.5–11 in Recent Interpretation and in the Setting of Early Christian Worship*. Grand Rapids, MI: Eerdmans, 1983.

Martin, Ralph P. *Philippians*. The New Century Bible Commentary. Grand Rapids, MI: Eerdmans, 1980.

Maruyama, Tadataka. *The Ecclesiology of Theodore Beza: The Reform of the True Church*. Geneva: Droz, 1978.

Mascall, E. L. *Christ, the Christian and the Church*. London: Longmans, Green and Co., 1946.

Maximus the Confessor. *On the Cosmic Mystery of Jesus Christ: Selected Writings from St. Maximus the Confessor*. Translated by Paul M. Blowers and Robert Louis Wilken. Crestwood, NY: St Vladimir's Seminary Press, 2003.

McCormack, Bruce L. "Divine Impassibility or Simply Divine Constancy: Implications of Barth's Later Christology for Debates over Impassibility." In *Divine Impassibility and the Mystery of Human Suffering*, edited by James F. Keating and Thomas Joseph White, 150–86. Grand Rapids, MI: Eerdmans, 2009.

McCormack, Bruce L. *For Us and Our Salvation: Incarnation and Atonement in the Reformed Tradition*. Studies in Reformed Theology and History. Princeton, NJ: Princeton Theological Seminary, 1993.

McCormack, Bruce L. "Grace and Being: The Role of God's Gracious Election in Karl Barth's Theological Ontology." In *The Cambridge Companion to Karl Barth*, edited by John Webster, 92–110. Cambridge: Cambridge University Press, 2000.

McCormack, Bruce L. *Karl Barth's Critically Realistic Dialectical Theology: Its Genesis and Development 1909–1936*. Oxford: Clarendon, 1995.

McCormack, Bruce L. "What's at Stake in the Current Debates over Justification?" In *Justification: What's at Stake in the Current Debates*, edited by Mark Husbands and Daniel J. Treier, 81–117. Leicester: Apollos, 2004.

McCready, Douglas. *He Came Down from Heaven: The Pre-Existence of Christ and the Christian Faith*. Downers Grove, IL: InterVarsity Press, 2005.

McGiffert, Michael C. "From Moses to Adam: The Making of the Covenant of Works." *SCJ* 19 (1988): 131–55.

McGinnis, Andrew M. *The Son of God beyond the Flesh: A Historical and Theological Study of the Extra-Calvinisticum*. Edinburgh: T&T Clark, 2014.

McGowan, Andrew T. B. *The Divine Spiration of Scripture: Challenging Evangelical Perspectives*. Downers Grove, IL: InterVarsity Press, 2007.

McGrath, Alister. "Forerunners of the Reformation: A Critical Examination of the Evidence for Precursors of the Reformation Doctrines of Justification." *HTR* 75 (1982): 219–42.

McGrath, Alister. *Iustitia Dei: A History of the Christian Doctrine of Justification: The Beginnings to the Reformation*. 2 vols. Cambridge: Cambridge University Press, 1986.

McGrath, Alister. "The Moral Theory of the Atonement: An Historical and Theological Critique." *SJT* 38 (1985): 205–20.

McGrath, Alister. *Reformation Thought: An Introduction*. 2nd ed. Oxford: Blackwell, 1993.

McGuckin, J. A. *Saint Cyril of Alexandria and the Christological Controversy.* Crestwood, NY: St Vladimir's Seminary Press, 2010.

McGuckin, J. A. "On the Mystical Theology of the Eastern Church." *SVTQ* 58 (2014): 373–99.

McIlhenny, Ryan C., ed. *Kingdoms Apart: Engaging the Two Kingdoms Perspective.* Phillipsburg, NJ: P&R, 2012.

McInerny, Ralph, ed. *Thomas Aquinas: Selected Writings.* London: Penguin, 1998.

McKim, Donald K. *Ramism in William Perkins' Theology.* New York: Peter Lang, 1987.

McKinley, John E. *Tempted for Us: Theological Models and the Practical Relevance of Christ's Impeccability and Temptation.* Milton Keynes: Paternoster, 2009.

McLelland, Joseph C. *The Visible Words of God: An Exposition of the Sacramental Theology of Peter Martyr Vermigli 1500–62.* Edinburgh: Oliver and Boyd, 1957.

Meconi, David. "St. Augustine's Early Theory of Participation." *AugStud* 27 (1996): 81–98.

Melling, David J. "Adam and Eve." In *The Blackwell Dictionary of Eastern Christianity*, edited by Ken Parry and David J. Melling, 4–6. Oxford: Blackwell, 2001.

Mendenhall, G. F. *Law and Covenant in Israel and the Ancient Near East.* Philadelphia: Biblical Colloquium, 1955.

Metzger, B. M. "The Punctuation of Rom. 9:5." In *Christ and Spirit in the New Testament: Studies in Honour of C. F. D. Moule*, edited by Barnabas Lindars and Stephen S. Smalley, 95–112. Cambridge: Cambridge University Press, 1973.

Metzger, Paul Louis. "Mystical Union with Christ: An Alternative to Blood Transfusions and Legal Fictions." *WTJ* 65 (2003): 201–13.

Meyendorff, John. *Byzantine Theology: Historical Trends and Doctrinal Themes.* New York: Fordham University Press, 1979.

Meyendorff, John. *Christ in Eastern Christian Thought.* Crestwood, NY: St Vladimir's Seminary Press, 1975.

Migne, Jacques-Paul, et al., eds. *Patrologiae cursus completes: Series Graeca.* 162 vols. Paris, 1857–1866.

Migne, Jacques-Paul, et al., eds. *Patrologiae cursus completes: Series Latina.* 217 vols. Paris, 1844–1864.

Mitchell, Alex F. *Minutes of the Sessions of the Westminster Assembly of Divines (November 1644 to March 1649): From Transcripts of the Originals Procured by a Committee of the General Assembly of the*

Church of Scotland. Edinburgh and London: William Blackwood and Sons, 1874.

Molnar, Paul D. *Divine Freedom and the Doctrine of the Immanent Trinity: In Dialogue with Karl Barth and Contemporary Theology*. London: T&T Clark, 2002.

Molnar, Paul D. *Faith, Freedom and the Spirit: The Economic Trinity in Barth, Torrance and Contemporary Theology*. Downers Grove, IL: IVP Academic, 2015.

Molnar, Paul D. "The Importance of the Doctrine of Justification in the Theology of Thomas F. Torrance and of Karl Barth." *SJT* 70 (2017): 198–226.

Molnar, Paul D. "Thomas F. Torrance and the Problem of Universalism." *SJT* 68 (2015): 164–86.

Molnar, Paul D. *Thomas F. Torrance: Theologian of the Trinity*. Farnham: Ashgate, 2009.

Moltmann, Jürgen. *The Coming of God: Christian Eschatology*. Translated by Margaret Kohl. Minneapolis: Fortress, 1996.

Moltmann, Jürgen. *God in Creation: A New Theology of Creation and the Spirit of God*. San Francisco: HarperSanFrancisco, 1991.

Moltmann, Jürgen. *Sun of Righteousness, Arise! God's Future for Humanity and the Earth*. Translated by Margaret Kohl. London: SCM, 2010.

Moltmann, Jürgen. "Theological Proposals towards the Resolution of the Filioque Controversy." In *Spirit of God, Spirit of Christ: Ecumenical Reflections on the Filioque Controversy*, edited by Lukas Vischer, 164–73. London: SPCK, 1981.

Moltmann, Jürgen. *The Trinity and the Kingdom: The Doctrine of God*. London: SCM, 1991.

Moody, Dale. "God's Only Son: The Translation of John 3:16 in the Revised Standard Version." *JBL* 72 (1953): 213–19.

Moore, Jonathan D. *English Hypothetical Universalism: John Preston and the Softening of Reformed Theology*. Grand Rapids, MI: Eerdmans, 2007.

Morales, Xavier. "Basile de Césarée est-il l'introducteur du concept de relation en théologie trinitaire?" *RÉAug* 63 (2017): 141–80.

Morgan, Stephen. "Cracks in the Edifice: Recent Challenges to the Received History of Vatican II." *DRev* 133 (2015): 66–85.

Morris, Edward D. *Theology of the Westminster Symbols: A Commentary Historical, Doctrinal, Practical on the Confession of Faith and Catechisms, and the Related Formularies of Presbyterian Churches*. Columbus, OH: n.p., 1900.

Morris, Leon. *The Apostolic Preaching of the Cross.* London: Tyndale Press, 1955.

Morris, Leon. *The Cross in the New Testament.* Exeter: Paternoster, 1967.

Morris, Leon. *The Epistle to the Romans.* Grand Rapids. MI: Eerdmans, 1988.

Morris, Leon. *The Gospel according to John: The English Text with Introduction, Exposition and Notes.* London: Marshall, Morgan & Scott, 1971.

Morris, Leon. *Luke: An Introduction and Commentary.* Leicester: Inter-Varsity Press, 1997.

Morris, Thomas V. "The Metaphysics of God Incarnate." In *Oxford Readings in Philosophical Theology.* Vol. 1, *Trinity, Incarnation, and Atonement,* edited by Michael Rea, 211–24. Oxford: Oxford University Press, 2009.

Mosser, Carl. "The Greatest Possible Blessing: Calvin and Deification." *SJT* 55 (2002): 36–57.

Moule, C. F. D. *The Birth of the New Testament.* New York: Harper & Row, 1962.

Moule, C. F. D. "A Note on Didache ix.4." *JTS* 6 (1955): 240–43.

Moulton, James Hope. *A Grammar of New Testament Greek.* Vol. 1, *Prolegomena.* 3rd ed. Edinburgh: T&T Clark, 1908.

Muller, Richard A. *After Calvin: Studies in the Development of a Theological Tradition.* Oxford: Oxford University Press, 2003.

Muller, Richard A. *Christ and the Decree: Christology and Predestination in Reformed Theology from Calvin to Perkins.* Grand Rapids, MI: Baker, 1986.

Muller, Richard A. *Dictionary of Latin and Greek Theological Terms Drawn Principally from Protestant Scholastic Theology.* Grand Rapids, MI: Baker, 1985.

Muller, Richard A. "Divine Covenants, Absolute and Conditional: John Cameron and the Early Orthodox Development of Reformed Covenant Theology." *MAJT* 17 (2006): 11–56.

Muller, Richard A. *Divine Will and Human Choice: Freedom, Contingency, and Necessity in Early Modern Reformed Thought.* Grand Rapids, MI: Baker Academic, 2017.

Muller, Richard A. "The Placement of Predestination in Reformed Theology: Issue or Non-Issue?" *CTJ* 40 (2005): 184–210.

Muller, Richard A. *Post-Reformation Reformed Dogmatics: The Rise and Development of Reformed Orthodoxy, ca. 1520 to ca. 1725.* 2nd ed. 4 vols. Grand Rapids, MI: Baker, 1993.

Muller, Richard A. "Toward the *Pactum Salutis*: Locating the Origins of a Concept." *MAJT* 18 (2007): 11–65.

Muller, Richard A. *The Unaccommodated Calvin: Studies in the Foundation of a Theological Tradition.* New York: Oxford University Press, 2000.

Mullins, R. T. *The End of the Timeless God.* Oxford: Oxford University Press, 2016.

Murphy, Gannon. "Reformed Theosis?" *Theology Today* 65 (2008): 191–212.

Murray, Iain H. *David Martyn Lloyd-Jones: The Fight of Faith, 1939–1981.* Edinburgh: Banner of Truth, 1990.

Murray, Iain H. *David Martyn Lloyd-Jones: The First Forty Years, 1899–1939.* Edinburgh: Banner of Truth, 1982.

Murray, Iain H. *Evangelicalism Divided.* Edinburgh: Banner of Truth, 2000.

Murray, John. *The Claims of Truth.* Vol. 1 of *Collected Writings of John Murray.* Edinburgh: Banner of Truth, 1976.

Murray, John. *The Covenant of Grace.* London: Tyndale Press, 1954.

Murray, John. "Definitive Sanctification." *CTJ* 2 (1967): 5–21.

Murray, John. *The Epistle to the Romans.* Grand Rapids, MI: Eerdmans, 1965.

Murray, John. *The Imputation of Adam's Sin.* Grand Rapids, MI: Eerdmans, 1959.

Murray, John. *Principles of Conduct: Aspects of Biblical Ethics.* London: Tyndale Press, 1954.

Murray, John. *Redemption Accomplished and Applied.* London: Banner of Truth, 1961.

Murray, John. *Select Lectures in Systematic Theology.* Vol. 2 of *Collected Writings of John Murray.* Edinburgh: Banner of Truth, 1977.

Murray, John, and Ned B. Stonehouse. "The Free Offer of the Gospel." In *Minutes of the Fifteenth General Assembly of the Orthodox Presbyterian Church*, append., 1–63 (n.p., 1948).

Murray, Robert. "Revelation (*Dei Verbum*)." In *Modern Catholicism: Vatican II and After*, edited by Adrian Hastings, 74–83. London: SPCK, 1991.

Musculus, Wolfgang. *In epistolam D. apostoli Pauli ad Romanos, commentarii.* Basel: Sebastian Henric Petri, 1555.

Musculus, Wolfgang. *Loci communes theologiae sacrae.* Basel: Sebastian Henric Petri, n.d.

Nee, Watchman. *The Release of the Spirit.* Bombay: Gospel Literature Service, 1965.

Needham, Nick. "The Filioque Clause: East or West?" *SBET* 15 (1997): 142–62.

Nellas, Panayiotis. *Deification in Christ: Orthodox Perspectives on the Nature of the Human Person.* Translated by Norman Russell. Crestwood, NY: St Vladimir's Seminary Press, 1987.

Nevin, John Williamson. *The Mystical Presence: A Vindication of the Reformed or Calvinistic Doctrine of the Holy Eucharist.* 1846. Reprint, Eugene, OR: Wipf & Stock, 2000.

Newbigin, Lesslie. *The Light Has Come: An Exposition of the Fourth Gospel.* Grand Rapids, MI: Eerdmans, 1982.

Newman, John Henry. *An Essay on the Development of Christian Doctrine.* Notre Dame, IN: University of Notre Dame Press, 1989.

Newman, John Henry. *Parochial and Plain Sermons.* London: Longman, Green, 1901.

Nichols, Aidan, OP. "St. Thomas Aquinas on the Passion of Christ: A Reading of *Summa Theologiae* IIIa, q.46." *SJT* 43 (1990): 447–59.

Nicholson, Ernest. "Review of Noel Weeks, *Admonition and Curse: The Ancient Near Eastern Treaty/Covenant Form as a Problem in Inter-Cultural Relationships. JTS* 57 (2006): 608–10.

Nicole, Roger. "C. H. Dodd and the Doctrine of Propitiation." *WTJ* 17 (1955): 117–57.

Nikodimos of the Holy Mountain, St., and St. Makarios of Corinth. *The Philokalia.* Translated by Kallistos Ware, G. E. H. Palmer, and Philip Sherrard. London: Faber & Faber, 1983.

Noble, T. A. "Paradox in Gregory Nazianzen's Doctrine of the Trinity." *StPatr* 27 (1993): 94–99.

Noll, Mark. "John Wesley and the Doctrine of Assurance." *BSac* 132 (1975): 161–77.

Noll, Mark. *The Princeton Theology 1812–1921: Scripture, Science, and Theological Method from Archibald Alexander to Benjamin Breckinridge Warfield.* Phillipsburg, NJ: Presbyterian and Reformed, 1983.

Nolland, John. *Luke 1–9:20.* Word Biblical Commentary 35A. Dallas: Word, 1989.

Norris, Frederick W. "Universal Salvation in Origen and Maximus." In *Universalism and the Doctrine of Hell: Papers Presented at the Fourth Edinburgh Conference in Christian Dogmatics, 1991,* edited by Nigel M. de S. Cameron, 35–72. Carlisle: Paternoster, 1992.

Norris, Richard A., Jr. *The Christological Controversy.* Philadelphia: Fortress, 1980.

Oberdorfer, Bernd. *Filioque: Geschichte und Theologie eines ökumenischen Problems*. Göttingen: Vandenhoeck & Ruprecht, 2001.

Oberman, Heiko Augustinus. *The Dawn of the Reformation: Essays in Late Medieval and Early Reformation Thought*. Grand Rapids, MI: Eerdmans, 1992.

Oberman, Heiko Augustinus. *The Harvest of Medieval Theology: Gabriel Biel and Late Medieval Nominalism*. Grand Rapids, MI: Eerdmans, 1967.

O'Collins, Gerald, SJ. *The Tripersonal God: Understanding and Interpreting the Trinity*. London: Geoffrey Chapman, 1999.

Oden, Thomas C. *The Justification Reader*. Grand Rapids, MI: Eerdmans, 2002.

Oden, Thomas C. *The Word of Life*. Vol. 2 of *Systematic Theology*. New York: Harper & Row, 1989.

O'Donnell, Laurence R., III. "Not Subtle Enough: An Assessment of Modern Scholarship on Herman Bavinck's Reformulation of the *Pactum Salutis* contra 'Scholastic Subtlety.'" *MAJT* 22 (2011): 89–106.

O'Keefe, John J., and R. R. Reno. *Sanctified Vision: An Introduction to Early Christian Interpretation of the Bible*. Baltimore: Johns Hopkins University Press, 2005.

Old, Hughes Oliphant. *The Reading and Preaching of the Scriptures in the Worship of the Christian Church*. Vol. 1, *The Biblical Period*. Grand Rapids, MI: Eerdmans, 1998.

Old, Hughes Oliphant. *The Reading and Preaching of the Scriptures in the Worship of the Christian Church*. Vol. 2, *The Patristic Age*. Grand Rapids, MI: Eerdmans, 1998.

Old, Hughes Oliphant. *The Reading and Preaching of the Scriptures in the Worship of the Christian Church*. Vol. 3, *The Medieval Church*. Grand Rapids, MI: Eerdmans, 1999.

Old, Hughes Oliphant. *The Shaping of the Reformed Baptismal Rite in the Sixteenth Century*. Grand Rapids, MI: Eerdmans, 1992.

Olevian, Caspar. *De substantia foederis gratuiti inter Deum et electos*. Geneva, 1585.

Olevian, Caspar. *In epistolam D. Pauli apostoli ad Romanos notae*. Geneva: Eustathium Vignon, 1584.

Olyott, Stuart. "Some Personal Thoughts on Ministerial Training." *The Evangelical Magazine* 48, no. 1 (2009), 16–17.

Olyott, Stuart. "Where Luther Got It Wrong—and Why We Need to Know About It." *The Banner of Truth*, December 2009, 27.

O'Neill, J. C. "How Early Is the Doctrine of *Creatio ex Nihilo*?" *JTS* 53 (2002): 449–65.

Ong, Walter J. *Ramus, Method, and the Decay of Dialogue.* Cambridge, MA: Harvard University Press, 1958.

Oord, Thomas Jay. *The Uncontrolling Love of God: An Open and Relational Account of Providence.* Downers Grove, IL: IVP Academic, 2015.

Oppy, Graham. *Ontological Arguments and Belief in God.* Cambridge: Cambridge University Press, 1995.

Origen. *The Commentary of Origen on S. John's Gospel: The Text Revised with a Critical Introduction and Indices.* Edited by A. E. Brooke. Cambridge: Cambridge University Press, 1896.

Origen. *Homilies on Numbers.* Translated by Thomas P. Scheck. Edited by Christopher A. Hall. Ancient Christian Texts. Downers Grove, IL: IVP Academic, 2009.

Origen. *Origène. Philocalie, 1–20 sur les Écritures: Introduction, texte, traduction et notes par Marguerite Harl.* Sources Chrêtiennes 302. Paris: Les Éditions du Cerf, 1983.

Origen. *The Philocalia of Origen: A Compilation of Selected Passages from Origen's Works Made by St. Gregory of Nazianzus and St. Basil of Caesarea.* Translated by G. Lewis. Edinburgh: T&T Clark, 1911.

Orr, James. *The Progress of Dogma: Being the Elliot Lectures, Delivered at the Western Theological Seminary, Allegheny, Penna., USA.* Grand Rapids, MI: Eerdmans, 1901.

Orthodox Presbyterian Church. "Report of the Committee to Study the Views of Creation." Submitted to the seventy-first general assembly of the Orthodox Presbyterian Church, 2004. http://opc.org/GA/Creation Report.pdf.

Owen, John. "Salus Electorum, Sanguis Jesu; or The Death of Death in the Death of Christ: A Treatise of the Redemption and Reconciliation That Is in the Blood of Christ." In *The Works of John Owen.* Vol. 10, edited by William H. Goold, 140–421. Reprint, London: Banner of Truth, 1967.

Owen, John. "The True Nature of a Gospel Church." In *The Works of John Owen.* Vol. 16, edited by William H. Goold, 11–20. Reprint, London: Banner of Truth, 1968.

Owen, John. *The Works of John Owen.* Edited by William H. Goold. 23 vols. 1850–1855. Reprint, London: Banner of Truth, 1965–1968.

Ozment, Stephen. *The Age of Reform 1250–1550.* New Haven, CT: Yale University Press, 1980.

Packer, James I. "Evangelical Annihilationism in Review." http://www.the-highway.com/annihilationism_Packer.html. Accessed February 26, 2016.

Packer, James I. *"Fundamentalism" and the Word of God: Some Evangelical Principles*. London: Inter-Varsity Press, 1958.

Packer, James I. "Hermeneutics and Biblical Authority." *Them* 1 (1975): 3–12.

Packer, James I. "'Keswick' and the Reformed Doctrine of Sanctification." *EQ* 27 (1955): 153–67.

Packer, James I. "The Problem of Eternal Punishment." The Leon Morris Lecture for the Evangelical Alliance, Melbourne, Australia, August 21, 1990.

Pannenberg, Wolfhart. *Jesus—God and Man*. Translated by Lewis L. Wilkins and Duane A. Priebe. Philadelphia: Westminster, 1968.

Pannenberg, Wolfhart. *Systematic Theology*. Translated by Geoffrey W. Bromiley. 3 vols. Grand Rapids, MI: Eerdmans, 1991–1998.

Papanikolaou, Aristotle. "Is John Zizioulas an Existentialist in Disguise? Response to Lucian Turcescu." *MTheol* 20 (2004): 601–7.

Parry, Ken, and David J. Melling, eds. *The Blackwell Dictionary of Eastern Christianity*. Oxford: Blackwell, 2001.

Pelikan, Jaroslav. *The Christian Tradition*. Vol. 1, *The Emergence of the Catholic Tradition (100–600)*. Chicago: University of Chicago Press, 1971.

Pelikan, Jaroslav. *The Christian Tradition*. Vol. 2, *The Spirit of Eastern Christendom*. Chicago: University of Chicago Press, 1974.

Pelikan, Jaroslav. *The Melody of Theology: A Philosophical Dictionary*. Cambridge, MA: Harvard University Press, 1988.

Pelikan, Jaroslav. *The Vindication of Tradition*. New Haven, CT: Yale University Press, 1984.

Pember. G. H. *Earth's Earliest Ages: And Their Connection with Modern Spiritualism and Theology*. 14th ed. 1876. Reprint, London: Pickering & Inglis, n.d.

Percival, Henry R. *The Seven Ecumenical Councils of the Undivided Church: Their Canons and Dogmatic Decrees*. A Select Library of Nicene and Post-Nicene Fathers of the Christian Church: Second Series. Reprint, Edinburgh: T&T Clark, 1997.

Perkins, William. *Armilla aurea*. Latin edition. 1590. The first English edition of *A Golden Chaine* appeared in 1600.

Perkins, William. *A Cloud of Faithfull Witnesses, Leading to the Heavenly Canaan*. 2nd ed. London: Humfrey Lownes for Leo. Greene, 1607.

Perkins, William. *De praedestinationis modi et ordine: et de amplitudine gratiae divinae Christiana & perspicua disceptatio*. Cambridge, 1598.

Perkins, William. *Workes*. London: John Legatt, 1631. Pagination differs from the 1608 edition.

[Perkins, William.] *The Workes of That Famous and Worthie Minister of Christ, in the Universitie of Cambridge, Mr. W. Perkins.* [Cambridge]: Iohn Legate, 1608.

Perry, John. "Putting Hell First: Cruelty, Historicism, and the Missing Moral Theory of Damnation." *SJT* 69 (2016): 1–19.

Photios, Saint. *On the Mystagogy of the Holy Spirit.* N.p.: Studion, 1983.

Pinnock, Clark H. *A Wideness in God's Mercy: The Finality of Jesus Christ in a World of Religions.* Grand Rapids, MI: Zondervan, 1992.

Pinnock, Clark H., Richard Rice, John Sanders, William Hasker, and David Basinger. *The Openness of God: A Biblical Challenge to the Traditional Understanding of God.* Downers Grove, IL: InterVarsity Press, 1994.

Piscator, Johannes. *Aphorismi doctrinae Christianae.* 1590. Reprint, Oxford, 1630.

Piscator, Johannes. *De iustificatione hominis coram Deo.* Leiden: Andreas Clouquius, 1609.

Piscator, Johannes. *Epistolarum Pauli ad Romanos, Corinthios, Galatas Ephesios, Philippenses, Colossenses, Thessalonicenses.* London: George Bishop, 1590.

Plantinga, Alvin. *Where the Conflict Really Lies: Science, Religion, and Naturalism.* Oxford: Oxford University Press, 2011.

Polanus, Amandus. *Partitiones theologiae.* 2nd ed. Basel, 1590.

Polanus, Amandus. *Syntagma theologiae Christianae.* Basel, 1609.

Polanus, Amandus. *Syntagma theologiae Christianae.* Geneva: Petri Auberti, 1612.

Polanyi, Michael. *Personal Knowledge: Towards a Post-Critical Philosophy.* Chicago: University of Chicago Press, 1958.

Polanyi, Michael. *The Tacit Dimension.* Chicago: University of Chicago Press, 1958.

Polyander, Johannes, Andreas Rivetus, Antonius Walaeus, and Anthonius Thysius. *Synopsis purioris theologiae, disputationibus quinquaginta duabus comprehensa.* Leiden: Ex officina Elzeverianus, 1625.

Powell, Anthony. *Books Do Furnish a Room.* In *A Dance to the Music of Time: Fourth Movement.* 1971. Reprint, Chicago: University of Chicago Press, 1995.

Powys, David J. *"Hell": A Hard Look at a Hard Question.* Carlisle: Paternoster, 1998.

Poythress, Vern S. "Adam versus Claims from Genetics." *WTJ* 75 (2013): 65–82.

Poythress, Vern S. "Canon and Speech Act: Limitations in Speech-Act Theory, with Implications for a Putative Theory of Canonical Speech Acts." *WTJ* 70 (2008): 337–54.

Poythress, Vern S. "Reforming Ontology and Logic in the Light of the Trinity: An Application of Van Til's Idea of Analogy." *WTJ* 57 (1995): 187–219.

Prestige, G. L. *Fathers and Heretics*. London: SPCK, 1940.

Price, Richard. "The Second Council of Constantinople (553) and the Malleable Past." In *Chalcedon in Context: Church Councils 400–700*, edited by Richard Price and Mary Whitby, 117–32. Liverpool: Liverpool University Press, 2009.

Quasten, Johannes. *Patrology*. 4 vols. Westminster, MD: Christian Classics, 1992.

Rafferty, Oliver P. "Catholic Views of Justification." In *Justification: Five Views*, edited by James K. Beilby and Paul Rhodes Eddy, 265–81. London: SPCK, 2012.

Rahner, Karl. *Theological Investigations*. Vol. 5, *Later Writings*. Translated by Karl-H. Kruger. London: Darton, Longman & Todd, 1966.

Rahner, Karl. *The Trinity*. Translated by Joseph Donceel. New York: Crossroad, 1997.

Raitt, Jill. *The Colloquy of Montbéliard: Religion and Politics in the Sixteenth Century*. New York: Oxford University Press, 1993.

Ramsey, D. Patrick. "In Defense of Moses: A Confessional Critique of Kline and Karlberg." *WTJ* 66 (2004): 373–400.

[Ratramn.] *Ratramnus, De corpore et sanguine Domini: Texte original et notice bibliographique*. Amsterdam, North-Holland, 1974.

Rayburn, Robert S. "Ministers, Elders, and Deacons." *Presbyterion* 12 (Fall 1986): 105–14.

Reicke, Bo. *The Disobedient Spirits and Christian Baptism*. Copenhagen: Acta Seminaii Neotestamentici Upsaliensis, 1946.

Reid, J. K. S., ed. *Calvin: Theological Treatises*. Philadelphia: Westminster, 1954.

Relton, Herbert M. *A Study in Christology: The Problem of the Relation of the Two Natures in the Person of Christ*. London: SPCK, 1917.

Rengstorf, Karl Heinrich. "ἀπόστολος." In *Theological Dictionary of the New Testament*. Edited by Gerhard Kittel and Gerhard Friedrich. Translated by Geoffrey W. Bromiley. Vol. 1, 419–22. Grand Rapids, MI: Eerdmans, 1963.

Reventlow, Henning Graf. *The Authority of the Bible and the Rise of the Modern World*. Philadelphia: Fortress, 1984.

Reymond, Robert L. *A New Systematic Theology of the Christian Faith*. New York: Nelson, 1998.

Reynolds, Gregory Edward. *The Word Is Worth a Thousand Pictures: A Resource for Preaching in the Twenty-First Century*. Eugene, OR: Wipf & Stock, 2001.

Ridderbos, Herman. *Paul: An Outline of His Theology*. Grand Rapids, MI: Eerdmans, 1975.

Ridderbos, N. H. *Is There a Conflict between Genesis 1 and Natural Science?* Grand Rapids, MI: Eerdmans, 1957.

Rist, John M. "Basil's 'Neoplatonism': Its Background and Nature." In *Basil of Caesarea: Christian, Humanist, Ascetic: A Sixteen-Hundredth Anniversary Symposium*, edited by Paul Jonathan Fedwick. Vol. 1, 137–220. Toronto: Pontifical Institute of Medieval Studies, 1981.

Robertson, Archibald. *A Critical and Exegetical Commentary on the First Epistle of St Paul to the Corinthians*. Edinburgh: T&T Clark, 1999.

Robinson, H. Wheeler. *The Christian Doctrine of Man*. 3rd ed. Edinburgh: T&T Clark, 1926.

Robinson, J. A. T. *In the End, God*. London: James Clarke, 1950.

Rogers, Jack B. *Scripture in the Westminster Confession*. Grand Rapids, MI: Eerdmans, 1967.

Rogers, Jack B., and Donald K. McKim. *The Authority and Interpretation of the Bible: An Historical Approach*. San Francisco: Harper & Row, 1979.

Rollock, Robert. *In epistolam S. Pauli apostoli ad Romanos*. Geneva: Franc. LePreux, 1596.

Rollock, Robert. *Quaestiones et responsiones aliquot de foedere Dei, deque sacramento quod foederis Dei sigillum est*. Edinburgh: Henricus Charteris, 1596.

Rollock, Robert. *Tractatus de vocatione efficaci*. Edinburgh: Robert Waldegrave, 1597.

Rollock, Robert. *A Treatise of God's Effectual Calling*. Translated by Henry Holland. London: Felix Kyngston, 1603.

Ross, Philip. *From the Finger of God: The Biblical and Theological Basis for the Threefold Division of the Law*. Fearn: Mentor, 2010.

Rowell, Geoffrey. *Hell and the Victorians*. Oxford: Clarendon, 1974.

Ruether, Rosemary Radford. *Sexism and God-Talk: Toward a Feminist Theology*. Boston: Beacon, 1983.

Ruether, Rosemary Radford. *Womanguides: Readings Toward a Feminist Theology*. Boston: Beacon, 1986.

Runia, Klaas. "Preaching, Theology Of." In *New Dictionary of Theology*, edited by Sinclair B. Ferguson, David F. Wright, and J. I. Packer, 527–28. Leicester: Inter-Varsity Press, 1988.

Russell, J. Stuart. *The Parousia: The New Testament Doctrine of Our Lord's Second Coming*. Grand Rapids, MI: Baker, 1999.

Russell, Letty. *Feminist Interpretation of the Bible.* Philadelphia: Westminster, 1985.

Russell, Norman. *Cyril of Alexandria.* London: Routledge, 2000.

Russell, Norman. *The Doctrine of Deification in the Greek Patristic Tradition.* Oxford: Oxford University Press, 2004.

Sanday, William, and Arthur C. Headlam. *A Critical and Exegetical Commentary on the Epistle to the Romans.* The International Critical Commentary. Edinburgh: T&T Clark, 1905.

Sanders, E. P. *Paul and Palestinian Judaism: A Comparison of Patterns of Religion.* Philadelphia: Fortress, 1977.

Sanders, Fred. "Introduction to Christology: Chalcedonian Categories for the Gospel Narrative." In *Jesus in Trinitarian Perspective: An Introductory Christology,* by Fred Sanders and Klaus Issler, 1–41. Nashville: B&H Academic, 2007.

Sanders, John. *The God Who Risks: A Theology of Divine Providence.* Downers Grove, IL: IVP Academic, 2007.

Sanders, John. *No Other Name: An Investigation into the Destiny of the Unevangelized.* Grand Rapids, MI: Eerdmans, 1992.

Saltmarsh, John. *Free Grace or, the Flowings of Christs Blood Freely to Sinners.* London: Giles Calvert, 1645.

Schaff, Philip. *The Creeds of Christendom.* Grand Rapids, MI: Baker, 1966.

Schendel, Joshua. "'That Justice Might Not Be Infringed Upon': The Judgment of God in the Passion of Christ in Irenaeus of Lyons." *SJT* 71 (2018): 212–25.

Schleiermacher, Friedrich. *The Christian Faith.* Edited by H. R. Mackintosh and J. S. Stewart. 1830. Reprint, Edinburgh: T&T Clark, 1999.

Schlesinger, Eugene R. "Trinity, Incarnation and Time: A Restatement of the Doctrine of God in Conversation with Robert Jenson." *SJT* 69 (2016): 189–203.

Schnackenburg, Rudolf. *The Gospel according to St John,* Vol. 1, *Introduction and Commentary on Chapters 1–4.* Translated by Kevin Smyth. Tunbridge Wells, Kent: Burns & Oates, 1968.

Schumacher, Lydia. "The Lost Legacy of Anselm's Argument: Re-Thinking the Purpose of Proofs for the Existence of God." *MTheol* 27 (2011): 87–101.

Scofield Reference Bible. N.p.: n.d. (ca. 1917).

Scott, J. M. *Adoption as the Sons of God: An Exegetical Investigation into the Background of Huiothesia in the Pauline Corpus.* Wissenschaftliche Untersuchungen zum Neuen Testament. Tübingen: Mohr, 1992.

Searle, John R. *Expression and Meaning: Studies in the Theory of Speech-Acts*. Cambridge: Cambridge University Press, 1979.

Seifrid, Mark A. "Paul, Luther, and Justification in Gal 2:15–21." *WTJ* 65 (2003): 215–30.

Sellers, R. V. *The Council of Chalcedon: A Historical and Doctrinal Survey*. London: SPCK, 1953.

Shedd, Russell. "Justification and Personal Christian Living." In *Right with God: Justification in the Bible and the World*, edited by D. A. Carson, 163–177. Carlisle: Paternoster, 1992.

Shedd, W. G. T. *The Doctrine of Endless Punishment*. 1885. Reprint, Edinburgh: Banner of Truth, 1990.

Shedd, W. G. T. *Dogmatic Theology*. 3 vols. Grand Rapids, MI: Zondervan, 1971.

Siecienski, A. Edward. *The Filioque: History of a Doctrinal Controversy*. New York: Oxford University Press, 2010.

Simonetti, Manlio. *Biblical Interpretation in the Early Church: An Historical Introduction to Patristic Exegesis*. Translated by John A. Hughes. Edinburgh: T&T Clark, 1994.

Skinner, Quentin. "Meaning and Understanding in the History of Ideas." In *Visions of Politics*, Vol. 1, *On Method*, 57–89. Cambridge: Cambridge University Press, 2002.

Slater, Jonathan. "Salvation as Participation in the Humanity of the Mediator in Calvin's *Institutes of the Christian Religion*: A Reply to Carl Mosser." *SJT* 58 (2005): 39–58.

Slotemaker, John Thomas. ""Fuisse in Forma Hominis" Belongs to Christ Alone': John Calvin's Trinitarian Hermeneutics in His Lectures on Ezekiel." *SJT* 68 (2015): 421–36.

Sorabji, Richard. *Time, Creation and the Continuum: Theories in Antiquity and the Early Middle Ages*. Ithaca, NY: Cornell University Press, 1983.

Spalding, James C. *The Reformation of the Ecclesiastical Laws of England, 1552*. Sixteenth Century Essays and Studies 19. Kirksville, MO: Sixteenth Century Journal Publishers, 1992.

Span, John. "John Calvin's View of 'the Turks' and of Finding Truth in Non-Biblical Texts." *Hapshin Theological Review* 4 (December 2015): 187–228.

Sparks, Adam. *One of a Kind: The Relationship between Old and New Covenants as the Hermeneutical Key for Christian Theology of Religions*. Eugene, OR: Pickwick, 2010.

Stanglin, Keith G. "The Rise and Fall of Biblical Perspicuity: Remonstrants and the Transition Towards Modern Exegesis." *CH* 83 (2014): 38–59.

Staniloae, Dumitru. *The Experience of God: Orthodox Dogmatic Theology.* Vol. 1, *Revelation and Knowledge of the Triune God.* Translated by Iona Ionita. Brookline, MA: Holy Cross Orthodox Press, 1994.

Staniloae, Dumitru. "The Procession of the Holy Spirit from the Father and His Relation to the Son, as the Basis for Our Deification and Adoption." In *Spirit of God, Spirit of Christ: Ecumenical Reflections on the Filioque Controversy,* edited by Lukas Vischer, 174–86. London: SPCK, 1981.

Starr, James. "Does 2 Peter 1:4 Speak of Deification?" In *Partakers of the Divine Nature: The History and Development of Deification in the Christian Traditions,* edited by Michael J. Christensen and Jeffery A. Wittung, 81–92. Grand Rapids, MI: Baker Academic, 2007.

Stendahl, Krister. "The Apostle Paul and the Introspective Conscience of the West." *HTR* 56 (1963): 199–215.

Stephens, W. P. *The Theology of Huldrych Zwingli.* Oxford: Clarendon, 1986.

Stevenson, J., ed. *A New Eusebius: Documents Illustrative of the History of the Church to AD 337.* Revised by W. H. C. Frend. London: SPCK, 1987.

Stewart, Alexander. "James, Soteriology, and Synergism." *TynBul* 61 (2010): 293–310.

Stibbs, A. M. *The Meaning of the Word "Blood" in Scripture.* London: Tyndale Press, 1948.

Stone, William. "Adam and Modern Science." In *Adam, the Fall, and Original Sin: Theological, Biblical, and Scientific Perspectives,* edited by Hans Madeume and Michael Reeves, 53–81. Grand Rapids, MI: Baker Academic, 2014.

Stott, John. *The Cross of Christ.* Leicester: Inter-Varsity Press, 1986.

Stott, John. *The Epistles of John: An Introduction and Commentary.* London: Tyndale Press, 1964.

Stott, John. *Guard the Gospel: The Message of 2 Timothy.* Downers Grove, IL: InterVarsity Press, 1973.

Stott, John. *The Message of 1 Timothy and Titus: The Life of the Local Church.* Leicester: Inter-Varsity Press, 1996.

Strange, Alan D. "Comments on the Centrality of Preaching in the Westminster Standards." *MAJT* 10 (1999): 185–238.

Strange, Alan D. "Do the Minister and the Elder Hold the Same Office?" *Ordained Servant Online,* December 2013. www.opc.org/os.html?article _id=393&cur_iss=Y.

Strange, Daniel. *"For Their Rock Is Not as Our Rock": An Evangelical Theology of Religion.* Nottingham: Inter-Varsity Press, 2014.

Strange, Daniel. *The Possibility of Salvation among the Unevangelised: An Analysis of Inclusivism in Recent Evangelical Theology*. Carlisle: Paternoster, 2002.

Strehle, Stephen. "The Extent of the Atonement and the Synod of Dort." *WTJ* 51 (1989): 1–23.

Studer, Basil. *The Grace of Christ and the Grace of God in Augustine of Hippo: Christocentrism or Theocentrism?* Collegeville, MN: Liturgical, 1997.

Studer, Basil. *Trinity and Incarnation: The Faith of the Early Church*. Translated by Matthias Westerhoff. Edited by Andrew Louth. Collegeville, MN: Liturgical, 1993.

Stylianopoulos, Theodore. *The New Testament: An Orthodox Perspective*, Vol.1, *Scripture, Tradition, Hermeneutics*. Brookline, MA: Holy Cross Orthodox Press, 1997.

Stylianopoulos, Theodore, ed. *Spirit of Truth: Ecumenical Perspectives on the Holy Spirit*. Brookline, MA: Holy Cross Orthodox Press, 1986.

Suh, Chul Won. *The Creation-Mediatorship of Jesus Christ*. Amsterdam: Rodopi, 1982.

"The Sum of Saving Knowledge." In *The Confession of Faith, the Larger and Shorter Catechisms with the Scriptural Proofs at Large, Together with The Sum of Saving Knowledge*, 321–26. Applecross, Ross-shire: Publications Committee of the Free Church of Scotland, 1970.

Sumner, Darren O. "Fallenness and Anhypostasia: A Way Forward in the Debate Over Christ's Humanity." *SJT* 67 (2014): 195–212.

Swete, H. B. *The Holy Spirit in the Ancient Church: A Study of Christian Teaching in the Age of the Fathers*. Reprint, Eugene, OR: Wipf & Stock. 1912.

Swinburne, Richard. *Is There a God?* Oxford: Oxford University Press, 1995.

Sykes, Norman. *The Crisis of the Reformation*. London: Centenary, 1946.

Tanner, Kathryn. "Beyond the East/West Divide." In *Ecumenical Perspectives on the* Filioque *for the Twenty-First Century*, edited by Myk Habets, 198–210. London: Bloomsbury, 2014.

Tasker, R. V. G. *The Biblical Doctrine of the Wrath of God*. London: Tyndale Press, 1951.

Taylor, R. O. P. "Was Abelard an Exemplarist?" *Theology* 31 (1935): 207–13.

Tellenach, Gerd. *Church, State and Christian Society at the Time of the Investiture Contest*. Oxford: Basil Blackwell, 1940.

Terry, Milton S. *Biblical Hermeneutics: A Treatise on the Interpretation of the Old and New Testaments*. Reprint, Grand Rapids, MI: Zondervan, n.d.

Theobald, M. *Die Fleischwerdung des Logos*. Münster: Aschendorf, 1988.

Thiselton, Anthony C. *The First Epistle to the Corinthians: A Commentary on the Greek Text*. Grand Rapids, MI: Eerdmans, 2000.

Thiselton, Anthony C. *Interpreting God and the Post-Modern Self: On Meaning, Manipulation and Promise*. Edinburgh: T&T Clark, 1995.

Thiselton, Anthony C. *The Last Things: A New Approach*. London: SPCK, 2012.

Thiselton, Anthony C. *New Horizons in Hermeneutics*. Grand Rapids, MI: Zondervan, 1992.

Thiselton, Anthony C. *Systematic Theology*. London: SPCK, 2015.

Thiselton, Anthony C. *The Two Horizons: New Testament Hermeneutics and Philosophical Description with Special Reference to Heidegger, Bultmann, Gadamer, and Wittgenstein*. Grand Rapids, MI: Eerdmans, 1980.

Thistlethwaite, Susan Brooks. "Every Two Minutes: Battered Women and Feminist Interpretation." In *Feminist Biblical Interpretation*, edited by Letty M. Russell, 96–108. Philadelphia: Westminster, 1985.

Thornwell, James Henley. *The Collected Writings of James Henley Thornwell*. 4 vols. 1875. Reprint, Edinburgh: Banner of Truth, 1974.

Toon, Peter. *Our Triune God: A Biblical Portrayal of the Trinity*. Wheaton, IL: BridgePoint, 1996.

Torrance, James B. "The Concept of Federal Theology—Was Calvin a Federal Theologian?" In *Calvinus Sacrae Scripturae professor: Die Referate des Congres International des Recherches Calviniennes*, edited by Wilhelm H. Neuser, 15–40. Grand Rapids, MI: Eerdmans, 1994.

Torrance, James B. "Covenant or Contract? A Study of the Background of Worship in Seventeenth-Century Scotland." *SJT* 23 (1970): 51–76.

Torrance, James B. "The Incarnation and Limited Atonement." *EQ* 55 (1983): 82–94.

Torrance, Thomas F. *Atonement: The Person and Work of Christ*. Edited by Robert T. Walker. Milton Keynes: Paternoster, 2009.

Torrance, Thomas F. "The Christian Apprehension of God the Father." In *Speaking the Christian God: The Holy Trinity and the Challenge of Feminism*, edited by Alvin F. Kimel Jr., 120–43. Grand Rapids, MI: Eerdmans, 1992.

Torrance, Thomas F. *The Christian Doctrine of God: One Being, Three Persons*. 2nd ed. Edinburgh: T&T Clark, 2016.

Torrance, Thomas F. *The Doctrine of Grace in the Apostolic Fathers*. Edinburgh: Oliver & Boyd, 1946.

Torrance, Thomas F. *Incarnation: The Person and Life of Christ*. Milton Keynes: Paternoster, 2008.

Torrance, Thomas F. *The Mediation of Christ*. Grand Rapids, MI: Eerdmans, 1983.

Torrance, Thomas F. *Reality and Evangelical Theology*. Philadelphia: Westminster, 1983.

Torrance, Thomas F. *The School of Faith: The Catechisms of the Reformed Church*. London: James Clarke, 1959.

Torrance, Thomas F. *Scottish Theology: From John Knox to John McLeod Campbell*. Edinburgh: T&T Clark, 1996.

Torrance, Thomas F. *Space, Time and Resurrection*. Grand Rapids, MI: Eerdmans, 1976.

Torrance, Thomas F. *Theological Dialogue between Orthodox and Reformed Churches*. Vol. 2. Edinburgh: Scottish Academic Press, 1993.

Torrance, Thomas F. *Theology in Reconciliation*. Grand Rapids, MI: Eerdmans, 1975.

Torrance, Thomas F. *Theology in Reconstruction*. Grand Rapids, MI: Eerdmans, 1965.

Torrance, Thomas F. *Transformation and Convergence in the Frame of Knowledge: Explorations in the Interrelations of Scientific and Theological Enterprise*. Grand Rapids, MI: Eerdmans, 1984.

Torrance, Thomas F. *Trinitarian Perspectives: Toward Doctrinal Agreement*. Edinburgh: T&T Clark, 1994.

Torrance, Thomas F. "Universalism or Election?" *SJT* 2 (1949): 310–18.

Trueman, Carl R. "Is the Finnish Line a New Beginning? A Critical Assessment of the Reading of Luther Offered by the Helsinki Circle." *WTJ* 65 (2003): 231–44.

Trueman, Carl R. *John Owen: Reformed Catholic, Renaissance Man*. Aldershot: Ashgate, 2007.

Trueman, Carl R. "The Revised Historiography of Reformed Orthodoxy: A Few Practical Implications." *Ordained Servant Online*, October 2012. http://www.opc.org/os.html?article_id=325.

Trumper, Tim J. R. "Covenant Theology and Constructive Calvinism." *WTJ* 64 (2002): 387–404.

Trumper, Tim J. R. "A Fresh Exposition of Adoption: II. Some Implications." *SBET* 23 (2005): 194–215.

Trumper, Tim J. R. "The Metaphorical Import of Adoption: A Plea for Realisation: I: The Adoption Metaphor in Biblical Usage." *SBET* 14 (1996): 129–45.

Trumper, Tim J. R. "The Metaphorical Import of Adoption: A Plea for Realisation: II: The Adoption Metaphor in Theological Usage." *SBET* 15 (1997): 98–115.

Tuckney, Anthony. *Praelectiones theologicae, nec non determinationes quaestionum variarum insignium in Scholis Academicis Cantabrigiensibus habitae; quibus accedunt exercitia pro gradibus capassendis.* Amsterdam: Ex officina Stephani Smart, impensis Jonathanis Robinsonii, & Georgii Wells, Bibliopolarum Londinensium, 1679.

Turner, James T., Jr. "On Two Reasons Christian Theologians Should Reject the Intermediate State." *JRT* 11 (2017): 121–39.

Turretin, Francis. *Institutes of Elenctic Theology.* Translated by George Musgrave Giger. Edited by James T. Dennison Jr. 3 vols. Phillipsburg, NJ: P&R, 1992–1997.

Twombly, Charles C. *Perichoresis and Personhood: God, Christ, and Salvation in John of Damascus.* Eugene, OR: Pickwick, 2015.

Ursinus, Zacharias. "*Summa Theologia.*" In *Opera Theologia.* Heidelberg, 1612.

Ussher, James. *A Body of Divinitie, or The Summe and Substance of Christian Religion.* London, 1645.

Vaggione, Richard Paul. *Eunomius of Cyzicus and the Nicene Revolution.* Oxford: Oxford University Press, 2000.

Van Caenegem, R. "Government, Law and Society." In *The Cambridge History of Medieval Political Thought c. 350–c. 1450,* edited by J. H. Burns, 174–210. Cambridge: Cambridge University Press, 1988.

Van Dixhoorn, Chad. "Reforming the Reformation: Theological Debate at the Westminster Assembly 1643–1652." 7 vols. PhD diss., Cambridge University, 2004.

Van Dixhoorn, Chad. "Reforming the Reformation, Vol. 2: Introduction to Appendixes: Note on the Membership of the Westminster Assembly: Table of Contents for John Lightfoot's Journal and the Minutes of the Westminster Assembly; Appendix A: 'A Briefe Journal of Passages in the Assembly of Divines' by John Lightfoot." PhD diss., Cambridge University, 2004.

Van Dixhoorn, Chad. "Reforming the Reformation, Vol. 6: Minutes of the Westminster Assembly; Folio 293v– ; 18 November 1644–14 April 1648." PhD diss., Cambridge University, 2004.

Van Dixhoorn, Chad. "The Sonship Program for Revival: A Summary and Critique." *WTJ* 61 (1999): 227–46.

Van Driel, Edwin Chr. "Karl Barth on the Eternal Existence of Jesus Christ." *SJT* 60 (2007): 45–61.

VanDrunen, David. *A Biblical Case for Natural Law.* Grand Rapids, MI: Acton Institute, 2006.

VanDrunen, David. "Israel's Recapitulation of Adam's Probation under the Law of Moses." *WTJ* 73 (2011): 303–24.

VanDrunen, David. *Living in God's Two Kingdoms*. Wheaton, IL: Crossway, 2010.

VanDrunen, David. *Natural Law and the Two Kingdoms: A Study in the Development of Reformed Social Thought*. Grand Rapids, MI: Eerdmans, 2009.

VanDrunen, David. "Natural Law and the Works Principle under Adam and Moses." In *The Law Is Not of Faith: Essays on Works and Grace in the Mosaic Covenant*, edited by Bryan D. Estelle, J. V. Fesko, and David VanDrunen, 283–314. Phillipsburg, NJ: P&R, 2009.

Vanhoozer, Kevin J. "God's Mighty Speech-Acts: The Doctrine of Scripture Today." In *A Pathway into the Holy Scripture*, edited by Philip E. Satterthwaite and David F. Wright, 143–81. Grand Rapids, MI: Eerdmans, 1994.

Vanhoozer, Kevin J. *Is There Meaning in This Text? The Bible, the Reader, and the Morality of Literary Knowledge*. Leicester: Apollos, 1998.

Van Til, Cornelius. *An Introduction to Systematic Theology*. Nutley, NJ: Presbyterian and Reformed, 1974.

Venema, Cornelis P. *Chosen in Christ: Revisiting the Contours of Predestination*. Fearn: Mentor, 2019.

Venema, Cornelis P. *Christ and Covenant Theology: Essays on Election, Republication, and the Covenants*. Phillipsburg, NJ: P&R, 2017.

Venema, Cornelis P. "Christ's Kingship in All of Life: Butchers, Bakers, and Candlestick Makers in the Service of Christ." *MAJT* 25 (2014): 7–33.

Venema, Cornelis P. "Covenant and Election in the Theology of Herman Bavinck." *MAJT* 19 (2008): 69–115.

Venema, Cornelis P. "The Mosaic Covenant: A 'Republication' of the Covenant of Works?" *MAJT* 21 (2010): 35–101.

Venema, Cornelis P. "One Kingdom or Two? An Evaluation of the 'Two Kingdoms' Doctrine as an Alternative to Neo-Calvinism." *MAJT* 23 (2012): 77–129.

Venema, Cornelis P. *The Promise of the Future*. Edinburgh: Banner of Truth, 2000.

Vermigli, Pietro Martire. *The Common Places of the Most Famous and Renowned Doctor Peter Martyr, Divided into Foure Principall Parts*. Translated by Anthonie Marten. London: Henrie Denham, Thomas Chard, William Broome, and Andrew Maunsell, 1583.

Vermigli, Pietro Martire. *In epistolam S. Pauli apostoli ad Romanos commentarii doctissimi*. Basel: Petrum Pernam, 1558.

Vischer, Lukas, ed. *Spirit of God, Spirit of Christ: Ecumenical Reflections on the Filioque Controversy*. London: SPCK, 1981.

von Rad, Gerhard. *Genesis: A Commentary*. Rev. ed. Philadelphia: Westminster, 1961.

von Wachter, Daniel. "Has Modernity Shown All Arguments for the Existence of God to Be Wrong?" *JRT* 10 (2016): 257–61.

Vos, Geerhardus. *Biblical Theology: Old and New Testaments*. Grand Rapids, MI: Eerdmans, 1948.

Vos, Geerhardus. *The Pauline Eschatology*. Grand Rapids, MI: Eerdmans, 1972.

Wainwright, Arthur. *The Trinity in the New Testament*. London: SPCK, 1963.

Wallace, Ronald. *Calvin's Doctrine of the Word and Sacrament*. Edinburgh: Oliver and Boyd, 1953.

Wallace-Hadrill, D. S. *Christian Antioch: A Study of Early Christian Thought in the East*. Cambridge: Cambridge University Press, 1982.

Ward, Timothy. *Word and Supplement: Speech Acts, Biblical Texts, and the Sufficiency of Scripture*. Oxford: Oxford University Press, 2002.

Ward, Timothy. *Words of Life: Scripture as the Living and Active Word of God*. Nottingham: Inter-Varsity Press, 2009.

Ware, Timothy. *The Orthodox Church*. London: Penguin, 1969.

Warfield, Benjamin B. "Are They Few That Be Saved?" In *Biblical and Theological Studies*, edited by Samuel G. Craig, 334–50. Philadelphia: Presbyterian and Reformed, 1952.

Warfield, Benjamin B. "The Biblical Doctrine of the Trinity." In *Biblical and Theological Studies*, edited by Samuel G. Craig, 22–59. Philadelphia: Presbyterian and Reformed, 1952.

Warfield, Benjamin B. "The Biblical Idea of Inspiration." In *The Inspiration and Authority of the Bible*, edited by Samuel G. Craig, 131–66. Philadelphia: Presbyterian and Reformed, 1970.

Warfield, Benjamin B. "Calvin's Doctrine of the Knowledge of God." In *Calvin and Augustine*, 29–132. Philadelphia: Presbyterian and Reformed, 1974.

Warfield, Benjamin B. "Calvin's Doctrine of the Trinity." In *Calvin and Augustine*, 189–284. Philadelphia: Presbyterian and Reformed, 1974.

Warfield, Benjamin B. "The Church Doctrine of Inspiration." *BSac* 51 (1894): 614–40.

Warfield, Benjamin B. "God's Immeasurable Love." In *Biblical and Theological Studies*, edited by Samuel G. Craig, 505–22. Philadelphia: Presbyterian and Reformed, 1952.

Warfield, Benjamin B. "Inspiration." In *The International Standard Bible Encyclopedia*, edited by James Orr, 1473–83. Chicago: Howard-Severance, 1915.

Warfield, Benjamin B. *The Inspiration and Authority of the Bible*. Edited by Samuel G. Craig. Philadelphia: Presbyterian and Reformed, 1970.

Warfield, Benjamin B. "On the Biblical Notion of 'Renewal.'" In *Biblical and Theological Studies*, edited by Samuel G. Craig, 351–74. Philadelphia: Presbyterian and Reformed, 1952.

Warfield, Benjamin B. *Perfectionism*. Edited by Samuel G. Craig. Philadelphia: Presbyterian and Reformed, 1958.

Warfield, Benjamin B. *The Person and Work of Christ*. Philadelphia: Presbyterian and Reformed, 1970.

Warfield, Benjamin B. *The Plan of Salvation*. Rev. ed. Grand Rapids, MI: Eerdmans, 1973.

Warfield, Benjamin B. "The Prophecies of St. Paul." In *Biblical and Theological Studies*, edited by Samuel G. Craig, 463–502. Philadelphia: Presbyterian and Reformed, 1952.

Warfield, Benjamin B. "The Spirit of God in the Old Testament." In *Biblical and Theological Studies*, edited by Samuel G. Craig, 127–56. Philadelphia: Presbyterian and Reformed, 1952.

Warfield, Benjamin B. *The Westminster Assembly and Its Work*. New York: Oxford University Press, 1934.

Watson, Francis. *Text, Church and World: Biblical Interpretation in Theological Perspective*. Edinburgh: T&T Clark, 1994.

Weaver, Denny. "The Nonviolent Atonement: Human Violence, Discipleship, and God." In *Stricken by God? Nonviolent Identification and the Victory of Christ*, edited by Brad Jersak and Michael Hardin, 316–55. Grand Rapids, MI: Eerdmans, 2007.

Weber, Max. *The Protestant Ethic and the Spirit of Capitalism*. New York: Charles Scribner's Sons, 1958.

Webster, John. *Holy Scripture: A Dogmatic Sketch*. Cambridge: Cambridge University Press, 2003.

Weeks, Noel. *Admonition and Curse: The Ancient Near Eastern Treaty / Covenant Form as a Problem in Inter-Cultural Relationships*. London: T&T Clark, 2004.

Weinandy, Thomas G. *Athanasius: A Theological Introduction*. Aldershot: Ashgate, 2007.

Weinandy, Thomas G. "Cyril and the Mystery of the Incarnation." In *The Theology of St. Cyril of Alexandria: A Critical Appreciation*, edited by Thomas G. Weinandy, 23–54. London: T&T Clark, 2003.

Weinandy, Thomas G. *Does God Change? The Word's Becoming in the Incarnation*. Still River, MA: St. Bede's, 1985.

Weinandy, Thomas G. *Does God Suffer?* Edinburgh: T&T Clark, 2000.

Weinandy, Thomas G. "The Eternal Son." In *The Oxford Handbook of the Trinity*, edited by Gilles Emery and Matthew Levering, 387–99. Oxford: Oxford University Press, 2011.

Weinandy, Thomas G. "The *Filioque*: Beyond Athanasius and Thomas Aquinas: An Ecumenical Proposal." In *Ecumenical Perspectives on the* Filioque *for the Twenty-First Century*, edited by Myk Habets, 185–97. London: Bloomsbury, 2014.

Weinandy, Thomas G. "The Marvel of the Incarnation." *Aquinas on Doctrine: A Critical Introduction*. Edited by Thomas G. Weinandy, Daniel A. Keating, and John P. Yocum. London: T&T Clark, 2004.

Weinandy, Thomas G., ed. *The Theology of St. Cyril of Alexandria: A Critical Appreciation*. London: T&T Clark, 2003.

Weinandy, Thomas G., Daniel A. Keating, John P. Yocum. *Aquinas on Doctrine: A Critical Introduction*. London: T&T Clark, 2004.

Weingart, R. E. *The Logic of Divine Love: A Critical Analysis of the Soteriology of Peter Abelard*. Oxford: Clarendon, 1970.

Weir, David A. *The Origins of Federal Theology in Sixteenth-Century Reformation Thought*. Oxford: Clarendon, 1990.

Wendebourg, D. "From the Cappadocian Fathers to Gregory Palamas: The Defeat of Trinitarian Theology." *StPatr* 17 (1982): 194–98.

Wenham, Gordon J. *Genesis 1–15*. Word Biblical Commentary 1. Waco, TX: Word, 1987.

Wenham, John W. "The Case for Conditionalism." In *Universalism and the Doctrine of Hell: Papers Presented at the Fourth Edinburgh Conference in Christian Dogmatics, 1991*, edited by Nigel M. de S. Cameron, 161–91. Carlisle: Paternoster, 1992.

Wenham, John W. *The Goodness of God*. London: Inter-Varsity Press, 1974.

Wesche, Kenneth Paul. *On the Person of Christ: The Christology of Emperor Justinian*. Crestwood, NY: St Vladimir's Seminary Press, 1991.

Westcott, Brooke Foss. *The Gospel according to St. John: The Greek Text with Introduction and Notes*. London: John Murray, 1908.

Westerholm, Stephen, and Martin Westerholm. *Reading Sacred Scripture: Voices from the History of Biblical Interpretation*. Grand Rapids, MI: Eerdmans, 2016.

Whitney, J. P. *Hildebrandine Essays*. Cambridge: Cambridge University Press, 1932.

Widdicombe, Peter. *The Fatherhood of God from Origen to Athanasius*. Oxford: Clarendon, 1994.

Wilkins, Jeremy D. "'The Image of His Highest Love': The Trinitarian Analogy in Gregory Palamas's Capita 150." *SVTQ* 47 (2003): 383–412.

Williams, A. N. "Does 'God' Exist?" *SJT* 58 (2005): 468–84.

Williams, A. N. *The Ground of Union: Deification in Aquinas and Palamas*. New York: Oxford University Press, 1999.

Williams, Frederick. *St. Gregory of Nazianzus: On God and Christ*. Crestwood, NY: St Vladimir's Seminary Press, 2002.

Williams, Garry J. "Penal Substitution: A Response to Recent Criticisms." *JETS* 50 (2007): 71–86.

Williams, Garry J. "Penal Substitutionary Atonement in the Church Fathers." *EQ* 83 (2011): 195–216.

Williams, George Huntston. *The Radical Reformation*. Philadelphia: Westminster, 1975.

Williams, Jarvis J. *Maccabean Martyr Traditions in Paul's Theology of Atonement: Did Martyr Theology Shape Paul's Conception of Jesus's Death?* Eugene, OR: Wipf & Stock, 2010.

Williams, Rowan. *Arius: Heresy and Tradition*. London: Darton, Longman, & Todd, 1987.

Williams, Scott M. "Henry of Ghent on Real Relations and the Trinity: The Case for Numerical Sameness without Identity." *RTPM* 79 (2012): 109–48.

Willis, Edward David. *Calvin's Catholic Christology: The Function of the So-Called Extra Calvinisticum in Calvin's Theology*. Leiden: Brill, 1966.

Wind, John. "The Keys of the Two Kingdoms: Covenantal Framework as the Fundamental Divide between VanDrunen and His Critics." *WTJ* 77 (2015): 15–33.

Winter, Robert. *The Beethoven Quartet Companion*. Berkeley: University of California Press, 1994.

Witherington, B., III. "Lord." In *Dictionary of the Later New Testament and Its Development*, edited by Ralph P. Martin and Peter H. Davids, 667–78. Downers Grove, IL: InterVarsity Press, 1997.

Woodine, George E., ed. *Bracton de legibus et consuetudinibus Angliae*. 4 vols. 1255–1268. New Haven, CT: Yale, 1922.

Wolterstorff, Nicholas. *Divine Discourse: Philosophical Reflections on the Claim That God Speaks*. Cambridge: Cambridge University Press, 1995.

Wright, David F. "Calvin's Accommodating God." In Calvinus Sincerioris Religionis Vindex: *Calvin as the Protector of the Purer Religion*. Sixteenth Century Essays and Studies 36, edited by Wilhelm H. Neuser and Brian G. Armstrong, 3–19. Kirksville, MO: Sixteenth Century Journal Publishers, 1997.

Wright, N. T. *The Epistles of Paul to the Colossians and to Philemon*. Leicester: Inter-Varsity Press, 1986.

Wright, N. T. "Harpagmos and the Meaning of Philippians ii.5–11." *JTS* 37 (1986): 321–52.

Wright, N. T. "The Paul of History and the Apostle of Faith: The Tyndale New Testament Lecture, 1978." *TynBul* 29 (1978): 61–88.

Young, Edward J. *Genesis 3: A Devotional and Exegetical Study.* London: Banner of Truth, 1966.

Young, Edward J. *In the Beginning.* Carlisle, PA: Banner of Truth, 1976.

Young, Edward J. *Studies in Genesis One.* Nutley, NJ: Presbyterian and Reformed, 1975.

Zanchius, Hieronymous. *Operum theologicorum omnium.* Amsterdam: Stephanus Gamonentus, 1613.

Zanchius, Jerome. *Omnium operum theologicorum.* Geneva: Samuel Crispin, 1619.

Zwingli, Ulrich. *Commentary on True and False Religion.* Edited by Samuel Macaulay Jackson. 1929. Reprint, Durham, NC: Labyrinth, 1981.

Name Index

Adam
  covenant headship of, 531–32
  in covenant with God, 349, 356–62
  created in image of God, 152, 358, 625
  fall of, 367–69
  as federal representative, 376–77, 378–79, 387
  formation of, 320–21
  as head of human race, 315, 316
  as head of tribe of humans, 318
  as historical person, 302, 315
  importance for Christology, 319
  as priest-king, 822
  as propagator of the race, 382
  as public person, 390, 552
  sin of, 359, 366, 375–76, 696
  as type of Christ, 375
  union with, 377–78, 861
Alexander, Denis, 302
Alford, Henry, 843
Allison, Dale C., 886
Althaus, Paul, 684, 875
Ambrose, 381, 411, 562, 564
Ames, William, 726, 931
Amyraut, Moïse, 416, 427, 428, 571–72
Andraeus, Jacob, 571
Anselm
  on days of Genesis, 919
  on impeccability of Christ, 525
  on incarnation, 147, 473, 474
  proof for existence of God, 42, 43–48, 49, 51
  on satisfaction, 564–66
  on Trinity, 151

Apollinaris, 492, 528
Aquinas. *See* Thomas Aquinas
Aristotle, 47, 48, 306, 344, 371, 870
Arius, 99–100
Arminius, Jacob, 175, 405, 407, 416, 420, 424–27, 431, 570
  on assurance, 426
  on foreknowledge, 613
  on perseverance, 426
Athanasius, 102, 107, 118
  on atonement, 142
  on canon, 186
  on creation, 272–73, 277, 278, 363–64, 419–20, 695, 927–29
  on grace, 355
  on humanity of Christ, 540
  on image of God, 334–35
  on incarnation, 147, 475, 476, 519
  on interpretation, 248
  on mutual indwelling, 108
  opposition to Eunomius, 101
  on rule of Christ, 587
  on satisfaction, 564
  on *theōsis*, 679, 769, 770–72
  on Trinitarian relations, 139–40
Athenagoras I, Patriarch, 133
Atkinson, Basil, 895
Augustine, 51, 57
  on biblical interpretation, 254, 257–60
  on church, 794
  continuity with Cappadocians, 131
  on creation, 273–74, 316
  on creation of soul, 346–47
  on deification, 679–80
  denounced as modalist, 132

Subject Index

Scripture Index